R.K. Hanson

Foundations of Computing

JOIN US ON THE INTERNET VIA WWW, GOPHER, FTP OR EMAIL:

WWW:	http://www.itcpmedia.com
GOPHER:	gopher.thomson.com
FTP:	ftp.thomson.com
EMAIL:	findit@kiosk.thomson.com

A service of I(T)P ®

Foundations of Computing

Jozef Gruska

INTERNATIONAL THOMSON COMPUTER PRESS

I(T)P® An International Thomson Publishing Company

London • Bonn • Boston • Johannesburg • Madrid • Melbourne • Mexico City • New York • Paris
Singapore • Tokyo • Toronto • Albany, NY • Belmont, CA • Cincinnati, OH • Detroit, MI

Copyright © 1997 International Thomson Computer Press

I(T)P® A division of International Thomson Publishing Inc.
The ITP logo is a trademark under license.

Printed in the United States of America.

For more information, contact:

International Thomson Computer Press
20 Park Plaza
13th Floor
Boston, MA 02116
USA

International Thomson Publishing Europe
Berkshire House
168-173 High Holborn
London WC1V 7AA
England

Thomas Nelson Australia
102 Dodds Street
South Melbourne, 3205
Victoria
Australia

Nelson Canada
1120 Birchmount Road
Scarborough, Ontario
Canada M1K 5G4

International Thomson Publishing Southern Africa
Bldg. 19, Constantia Park
239 Old Pretoria Road, P.O. Box 2459
Halfway House
1685 South Africa

International Thomson Publishing GmbH
Königswinterer Straße 418
53227 Bonn
Germany

International Thomson Publishing Asia
221 Henderson Road #05-10
Henderson Building
Singapore 0315

International Thomson Publishing Japan
Hirakawacho Kyowa Building, 3F
2-2-1 Hirakawacho
Chiyoda-ku, 102 Tokyo
Japan

International Thomson Editores
Campos Eliseos 385, Piso 7
Col. Polenco
11560 Mexico D.F. Mexico

International Thomson Publishing France
Tours Maine-Montparnasse
22 avenue du Maine
75755 Paris Cedex 15
France

All rights reserved. No part of this work covered by the copyright hereon may be reproduced or used in any form or by any means – graphic, electronic, or mechanical, including photocopying, recording, taping or information storage and retrieval systems – without the written permission of the Publisher.

Products and services that are referred to in this book may be either trademarks and/or registered trademarks of their respective owners. The Publisher(s) and Author(s) make no claim to these trademarks.

While every precaution has been taken in the preparation of this book, the Publisher and the Author assume no responsibility for errors or omissions, or for damages resulting from the use of information contained herein. In no event shall the Publisher and the Author be liable for any loss of profit or any other commercial damage, including but not limited to special, incidental, consequential, or other damages.

Library of Congress Cataloging-in-Publication Data
A catalog record for this book is available from the Library of Congress

ISBN: 1-85032-243-0

Publisher/Vice President: Jim DeWolf, ITCP/Boston
Projects Director: Vivienne Toye, ITCP/Boston
Marketing Manager: Christine Nagle, ITCP/Boston
Manufacturing Manager: Sandra Sabathy Carr, ITCP/Boston

Production: Hodgson Williams Associates, Tunbridge Wells and Cambridge, UK

Contents

Preface

One who is serious all day will never have a good time, while one who is frivolous all day will never establish a household.

Ptahhotpe, 24th century BC

Science is a discipline in which even a fool of this generation should be able to go beyond the point reached by a genius of the last.

Scientific folklore, 20th century AD

It may sound surprising that in computing, a field which develops so fast that the future often becomes the past without having been the present, there is nothing more stable and worthwhile learning than its foundations.

It may sound less surprising that in a field with such a revolutionary methodological impact on all sciences and technologies, and on almost all our intellectual endeavours, the importance of the foundations of computing goes far beyond the subject itself. It should be of interest both to those seeking to understand the laws and essence of the information processing world and to those wishing to have a firm grounding for their lifelong reeducation process – something which everybody in computing has to expect.

This book presents the automata-algorithm-complexity part of foundations of computing in a new way, and from several points of view, in order to meet the current requirements of learning and teaching.

First, the book takes a broader and more coherent view of theory and its foundations in the various subject areas. It presents not only the basics of automata, grammars, formal languages, universal computers, computability and computational complexity, but also of parallelism, randomization, communications, cryptography, interactive protocols, communication complexity and theoretical computer/communication architecture.

Second, the book presents foundations of computing as rich in deep, important and exciting results that help to clarify the problems, laws, and potentials in computing and to cope with its complexity.

Third, the book tries to find a new balance between the formal rigorousness needed to present basic concepts and results, and the informal motivations, illustrations and interpretations needed to grasp their merit.

Fourth, the book aims to offer a systematic, complex and up-to-date presentation of the main basic concepts, models, methods and results, as well as to indicate new trends and results whose detailed demonstration would require special lectures. To this end, basic concepts, models, methods and results are presented and illustrated in detail, whilst other deep/new results with difficult or rather obsure proofs are just stated, explained, interpreted and commented upon.

The topics covered are very broad and each chapter could be expanded into a separate book.

The aim of this textbook is to concentrate only on subjects that are central to the field; on concepts, methods and models that are simple enough to present; and on results that are either deep, important, useful, surprising, interesting, or have several of these properties.

This book presents those elements of the foundations of computing that should be known by anyone who wishes to be a computing expert or to enter areas with a deeper use of computing and its methodologies. For this reason the book covers only what everybody graduating in computing or in related area should know from theory. The book is oriented towards those for whom theory is only, or mainly, a tool. For those more interested in particular areas of theory, the book could be a good starting point for their way through unlimited and exciting theory adventures. Detailed bibliography references and historical/bibliographical notes should help those wishing to go more deeply into a subject or to find proofs and a more detailed treatment of particular subjects.

The main aim of the book is to serve as a textbook. However, because of its broad view of the field and up-to-date presentation of the concepts, methods and results of foundations, it also serves as a reference tool. Detailed historical and bibliographical comments at the end of each chapter, an extensive bibliography and a detailed index also help to serve this aim.

The book is a significantly extended version of the lecture notes for a one-semester, four hours a week, course held at the University of Hamburg.

The interested and/or ambitious reader should find it reasonably easy to follow. Formal presentation is concise, and basic concepts, models, methods and results are illustrated in a fairly straightforward way. Much attention is given to examples, exercises, motivations, interpretations and explanation of connections between various approaches, as well as to the impact of theory results both inside and outside computing. The book tries to demonstrate that the basic concepts, models, methods and results, products of many past geniuses, are actually very simple, with deep implications and important applications. It also demonstrates that foundations of computing is an intellectually rich and practical body of knowledge. The book also illustrates the ways in which theoretical concepts are often modified in order to obtain those which are directly applicable. More difficult sections are marked by asterisks.

The large number of examples/algorithms/protocols (277), figures/tables (214) and exercises aims to assist in the understanding of the presented concepts, models, methods, and results. Many of the exercises (574) are included as an inherent part of the text. They are mostly (very) easy or reasonably difficult and should help the reader to get an immediate feedback while extending knowledge and skill. The more difficult exercises are marked by one or two asterisks, to encourage ambitious readers without discouraging others. The remaining exercises (641) are placed at the end of chapters. Some are of the same character as those in the text, only slightly different or additional ones. Others extend the subject dealt with in the main text. The more difficult ones are again marked by asterisks.

This book is suported by an on-line supplement that will be regularly updated. This includes a new chapter 'Frontiers', that highlights recent models and modes of computing. Readers are also encouraged to contribute further examples, solutions and comments.

These additional materials can be found at the following web sites:

`//www.itcpmedia.com`

`//www.savba.sk/sav/mu/foundations.html`

Acknowledgement

This book was inspired by the author's three-year stay at the University of Hamburg within the Konrad Zuse Program, and the challenge to develop and practice there a new approach to teaching foundations of computing. Many thanks go to all those who made the stay possible, enjoyable and fruitful, especially to Rüdiger Valk, Manfred Kudlek and other members of the theory group. The help and supportive environment provided by a number of people in several other places was also essential. I would like to record my explicit appreciation of some of them: to Jacques Mazoyer and his group at LIP, École Normale Supérieure de Lyon; to Günter Harring and his group at University of Wien; to Rudolf Freund, Alexander Leitsch and their colleagues at the Technical University in Wien; and to Roland Vollmar and Thomas Worsch at the University of Karlsruhe, without whose help the book would not have been finished.

My thanks also go to colleagues at the Computing Centre of the Slovak Academy of Sciences for their technical backing and understanding. Support by a grant from Slovak Literary Foundation is also appreciated.

I am also pleased to record my obligations and gratitude to the staff of International Thomson Coputer Press, in particular to Sam Whittaker and Vivienne Toye, and to John Hodgson from HWA for their effort, patience and understanding with this edition.

I should also like to thank those who read the manuscript or parts at different stages of its development and made their comments, suggestions, corrections (or pictures): Ulrich Becker, Wilfried Brauer, Christian Calude, Patrick Cegielski, Anton Černý, Karel Čulik, Josep Díaz, Bruno Durand, Hennig Fernau, Rudolf Freund, Margret Freund-Breuer, Ivan Friš, Damas Gruska, Irene Guessarian, Annegret Habel, Dirk Hauschildt, Juraj Hromkovič, Mathias Jantzen, Bernd Kirsig, Ralf Klasing, Martin Kochol, Pascal Korain, Ivan Korec, Jana Košecká, Mojmír Křetínsky, Hans-Jörg Kreowski, Marco Ladermann, Bruno Martin, Jacques Mazoyer, Karol Nemoga, Michael Nölle, Richard Ostertag, Dana Pardubská, Dominico Parente, Milan Paštéka, Holger Petersen, Peter Rajčáni, Vladimír Sekerka, Wolfgang Slany, Ladislav Stacho, Mark-Oliver Stehr, Róbert Szelepcsényi, Laura Tougny, Luca Trevisan, Juraj Vaczulik, Róbert Vittek, Roland Vollmar, Jozef Vyskoč, Jie Wang and Juraj Wiedermann.

The help of Martin Stanek, Thomas Worsch, Ivana Černá and Manfred Kudlek is especially appreciated.

To my father

for his integrity, vision and optimism.

To my wife

for her continuous devotion, support and patience.

To my children

with best wishes for their future

1 Fundamentals

INTRODUCTION

Foundations of computing is a subject that makes an extensive and increasing use of a variety of basic concepts (both old and new), methods and results to analyse computational problems and systems. It also seeks to formulate, explore and harness laws and limitations of information processing. This chapter systematically introduces a number of concepts, techniques and results needed for quantitative analysis in computing and for making use of randomization to increase efficiency, to extend feasibility and the concept of evidence, and to secure communications. All concepts introduced are important far beyond the foundations of computing. They are also needed for dealing with efficiency within and outside computing.

Simplicity and elegance are the common denominators of many old and deep concepts, methods and results introduced in this chapter. They are the products of some of the best minds in science in their search for laws and structure. Surprisingly enough, some of the newest results presented in this book, starting with this chapter, demonstrate that randomness can also lead to simple, elegant and powerful methods.

LEARNING OBJECTIVES

The aim of the chapter is to demonstrate

1. methods to solve recurrences arising in the analysis of computing systems;
2. a powerful concept of generating functions with a variety of applications;
3. main asymptotic notations and techniques to use and to manipulate them;
4. basic concepts of number theory, especially those related to primes and congruences;
5. methods to solve various congruences;
6. problems of computing discrete square roots and logarithms that play an important role in randomized computations and secure communications;
7. basics of discrete probability;
8. modern approaches to randomness and pseudo-random generators.
9. aims, methods, problems and pitfalls of the asymptotic analysis of algorithms and algorithmic problems.

The firm, the enduring, the simple and the modest are near to virtue.

Confucius (551–479 BC)

Efficiency and inherent complexity play a key role in computing, and are also of growing importance outside computing. They provide both practically important quantitative evaluations and benchmarks, as well as theoretically deep insights into the nature of computing and communication. Their importance grows with the maturing of the discipline and also with advances in performance of computing and communication systems. The main concepts, tools, methods and results of complexity analysis belong to the most basic body of knowledge and techniques in computing. They are natural subjects with which to begin a textbook on foundations of computing because of their importance throughout. Their simplicity and elegance provide a basis from which to present, demonstrate and use the richness and power of the concepts and methods of foundations of computing.

Three important approaches to complexity issues in design and performance analysis of computing systems are considered in this chapter: recursion, (asymptotic) estimations and randomization.

The complex systems that we are able to design, describe or understand are often recursive by nature or intent. Their complexity analysis leads naturally to recurrences which is why we start this chapter with methods of solving recurrences.

In the analysis of complex computational systems we are generally unable to determine exactly the resources needed: for example, the exact number of computer operations needed to solve a problem. Fortunately, it is not often that we need to do so. Simple asymptotic estimations, providing robust results that are not dependent on a particular computer, are in most cases not only satisfactory, but often much more useful. Methods of handling, in a simple but precise way, asymptotic characterizations of functions are of key importance for analysing computing systems and are treated in detail in this chapter.

The discovery that randomness is an important resource for managing complexity is one of the most important results of foundations of computing in recent years. It has been known for some time that the analysis of algorithms with respect to a random distribution of input data may provide more realistic results. The main current use of randomness is in randomized algorithms, communication protocols, designs, proofs, etc. Coin-tossing techniques are used surprisingly well in the management of complexity. Elements of probability theory and of randomness are included in this introductory chapter and will be used throughout the book. These very modern uses of randomness to provide security, often based on old, basic concepts, methods and results of number theory, will also be introduced in this chapter.

1.1 Examples

Quantitative analysis of computational resources (time, storage, processors, programs, communication, randomness, interactions, knowledge) or of the size of computing systems (circuits, networks, automata, grammars, computers, algorithms or protocols) is of great importance. It can provide invaluable information as to how good a particular system is, and also deep insights into the nature of the underlying computational and communication problems.

Large and/or complex computing systems are often designed or described recursively. Their quantitative analysis leads naturally to recurrences. A **recurrence** is a system of equations or inequalities that describes a function in terms of its values for smaller inputs.

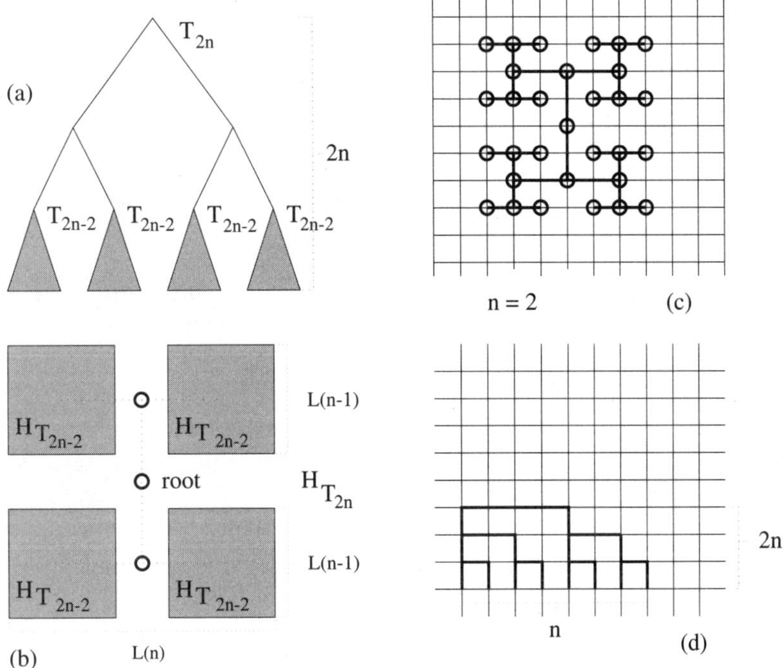

Figure 1.1 *H*-layout of complete binary trees

Example 1.1.1 (*H*-layout of binary trees) *A layout of a graph G into a two-dimensional grid is a mapping of different nodes of G into different nodes of the grid and edges (u,v) of G into nonoverlapping paths, along the grid lines, between the images of nodes u and v in the grid.*

The so-called H-layout $H_{T_{2n}}$ of a complete binary tree T_{2n} of depth $2n$, $n \geq 0$ (see Figure 1.1a for T_{2n} and its subtrees T_{2n-2}), is described recursively in Figure 1.1c.

A more detailed treatment of such layouts will be found in Section 10.6. Here it is of importance only that for length $L(n)$ of the side of the layout $H_{T_{2n}}$ we get the recurrence

$$L(n) = \begin{cases} 2, & \text{if } n = 1; \\ 2L(n-1)+2, & \text{if } n > 1. \end{cases}$$

As we shall see later, $L(n) = 2^{n+1} - 2$. A complete binary tree of depth $2n$ has $2^{2n+1} - 1$ nodes. The total area $A(m)$ of the H-layout of a complete binary tree with m nodes is therefore proportional to the number of nodes of the tree.[1] Observe that in the 'natural layout of the binary tree', shown in Figure 1.1d, the area of the smallest rectangle that contains the layout is proportional to $m \log m$. To express this concisely, we will use the notation $A(m) = \Theta(m)$ in the first case and $A(m) = \Theta(m \lg m)$ in the second case. The notation $f(n) = \Theta(g(n))$ – which means that '$f(n)$ grows proportionally to $g(n)$'[2] – is discussed in detail and formally in Section 1.5.

[1]The task of designing layouts of various graphs on a two-dimensional grid, with as small an area as possible, is of importance for VLSI designs. For more on layouts see Section 10.6.

[2]Or, more exactly, that there are constants $c_1, c_2 > 0$ such that $c_1|g(n)| \leq f(n) \leq c_2|g(n)|$ for all but finitely many n.

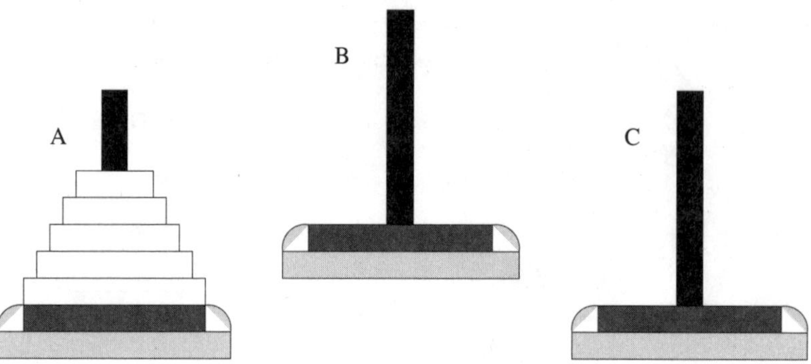

Figure 1.2 Towers of Hanoi

Algorithmic problems often have a recursive solution, even if their usual formulation does not indicate that.

Example 1.1.2 (Towers of Hanoi problem) *Suppose we are given three rods A, B, C, and n rings piled in descending order of magnitude on A while the other rods are empty – see Figure 1.2 for $n = 5$. The task is to move rings from A to B, perhaps using C in the process, in such a way that in one step only one ring is moved, and at no instant is a ring placed atop a smaller one.*

There is a simple recursive algorithm for solving the problem.

Algorithm 1.1.3 (Towers of Hanoi – a recursive algorithm)

1. Move $n-1$ top rings from A to C.
2. Move the largest ring from A to B.
3. Move all $n-1$ rings from C to B.

The correctness of this algorithm is obvious. It is also clear that the number $T(n)$ of ring moves satisfies the equations

$$T(n) = \begin{cases} 1, & \text{if} \quad n = 1; \\ 2T(n-1)+1, & \text{if} \quad n > 1. \end{cases} \tag{1.1}$$

In spite of the simplicity of the algorithm, it is natural to ask whether there exists a faster one that entails fewer ring moves. It is a simple task to show that such an algorithm does not exist. Denote by $T_{min}(n)$ the minimal number of moves needed to perform the task. Clearly, $T_{min}(n) \geq 2T_{min}(n-1)+1$, because in order to remove all rings from rod A to rod B, we have first to move the top $n-1$ of them to C, then the largest one to B, and finally the remaining ones to B. This implies that our solution is the best possible.

Algorithm 1.1.3 is very simple. However, it is not so easy to perform it 'by hand', because of the need to keep track of many levels of recursion. The second, 'iterative' algorithm presented below is from this point of view much simpler. (Try to apply both algorithms for $n = 4$.)

Algorithm 1.1.4 (Towers of Hanoi – an iterative algorithm)

Do the following alternating steps, starting with step 1, until all the rings are properly transferred:

1. Move the smallest top ring in clockwise order ($A \rightarrow B \rightarrow C \rightarrow A$) if the number of rings is odd, and in anti-clockwise order if the number of rings is even.

2. Make the only possible move that does not involve the smallest top ring.

In spite of the simplicity of Algorithm 1.1.4, it is far from obvious that it is correct. It is also far from obvious how to determine the number of ring moves involved until one shows, which can be done by induction, that both algorithms perform exactly the same sequences of moves.

Now consider the following modification of the Towers of Hanoi problem. The goal is the same, but it is not allowed to move rings from A onto B or from B onto A. It is easy to show that in this case too there is a simple recursive algorithm for solving the problem; for its number $T'(n)$ of ring moves we have $T'(1) = 2$ and

$$T'(n) = 3T'(n-1) + 2, \quad \text{for} \quad n > 1. \tag{1.2}$$

There is a modern myth which tells how Brahma, after creating the world, designed 3 rods made of diamond with 64 golden rings on one of them in a Tibetan monastery. He ordered the monks to transfer the rings following the rules described above. According to the myth, the world would come to an end when the monks finished their task.[3]

Exercise 1.1.5 *Use both algorithms for the Towers of Hanoi problem to solve the cases (a) $n = 3$; (b) $n = 5$; (c)* $n = 6$.*

Exercise 1.1.6**(Parallel version of the Towers of Hanoi problem) Assume that in each step more than one ring can be moved, but with the following restriction: in each step from each rod at most one ring is removed, and to each rod at most one ring is added. Determine the recurrence for the minimal number $T_p(n)$ of parallel moves needed to solve the parallel version of the Towers of Hanoi problem. (Hint: determine $T_p(1)$, $T_p(2)$ and $T_p(3)$, and express $T_p(n)$ using $T_p(n-2)$.)*

The two previous examples are not singular. Complexity analysis leads to recurrences whenever algorithms or systems are designed using one of the most powerful design methods – **divide-and-conquer**.

Example 1.1.7 *We can often easily and efficiently solve an algorithmic problem P of size $n = c^i$, where c, i are integers, using the following recursive method, where b_1, b_2 and d are constants (see Figure 1.3):*

1. *Decompose P, in time $b_1 n$, into subproblems of the same type and size $\frac{n}{c}$.*
2. *Solve all subproblems recursively, using the same method.*
3. *Compose, in time $b_2 n$, the solution of P from solutions of all its a subproblems.*

For the time complexity $T(n)$ of the resulting algorithm we have the recurrence:

$$T(n) = \begin{cases} d, & \text{if } n = 1; \\ aT(\frac{n}{c}) + b_1 n + b_2 n, & \text{if } n > 1. \end{cases}$$

[3]Such a prophecy is not unreasonable. Since $T(n) = 2^n - 1$, as will soon be seen, it would take more than 500,000 years to finish the task if the monks moved one ring per second.

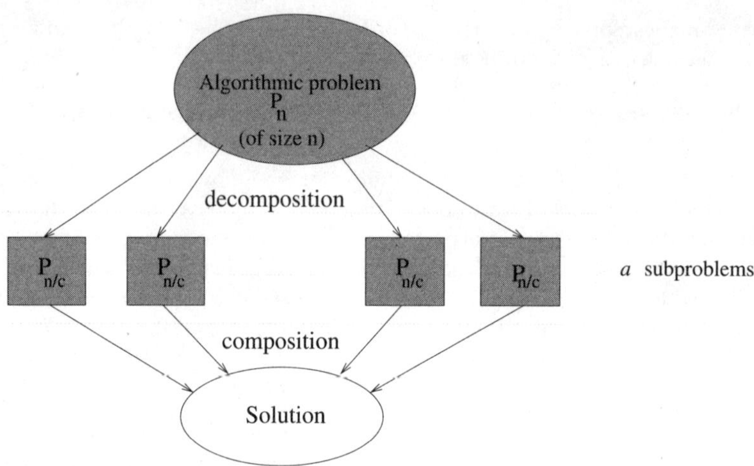

Figure 1.3 Divide-and-conquer method

As an illustration, we present the well-known recursive algorithm for sorting a sequence of $n = 2^k$ numbers.

Algorithm 1.1.8 (MERGESORT)

1. Divide the sequence in the middle, into two sub-sequences.
2. Sort recursively both sub-sequences.
3. Merge both already sorted subsequences.

If arrays are used to represent sequences, steps (1) and (3) can be performed in a time proportional to n.

Remark 1.1.9 Note that we have derived the recurrence (1.3) without knowing the nature of the problem P or the computational model to be used. The only information we have used is that both decomposition and composition can be performed in a time proportional to the size of the problem.

Exercise 1.1.10 *Suppose that n circles are drawn in a plane in such a way that no three circles meet in a point and each pair of circles intersects in exactly two points. Determine the recurrence for the number of distinct regions of the plane created by such n circles.*

An analysis of the computational complexity of algorithms often depends quite significantly on the underlying model of computation. Exact analysis is often impossible, either because of the complexity of the algorithm or because of the computational model (device) that is used. Fortunately, exact analysis is not only unnecessary most of the time, it is often superfluous. So-called asymptotic estimations not only provide more insights, they are also to a large degree independent of the particular computing model/device used.

Example 1.1.11 (Matrix multiplication) *Multiplication of two matrices* $A = \{a_{ij}\}_{i,j=1}^{n}$, $B = \{b_{ij}\}_{i,j=1}^{n}$, *of degree n, with the resulting matrix* $C = AB = \{c_{ij}\}_{i,j=1}^{n}$, *using the well-known relation*

$$c_{ij} = \sum_{k=1}^{n} a_{ik}b_{kj}, \tag{1.4}$$

requires $T(n) = 2n^3 - n^2$ *arithmetical operations to perform.*

It is again simpler and for the most part sufficiently informative, to say that $T(n) = \Theta(n^3)$ than to write exactly $T(n) = 2n^3 - n^2$. If a program for computing c_{ij} using the formula (4.3.3) is written in a natural way in a high-level programming language and is implemented on a normal sequential computer, then exact analysis of the number of computer instructions, or the time $T(n)$ needed is almost impossible, because it depends on the available compiler, operating system, computer and so on. Nevertheless, the basic claim $T(n) = \Theta(n^3)$ remains valid provided we assume that each arithmetical operation takes one unit of time.

Remark 1.1.12 If, on the other hand, parallel computations are allowed, quite different results concerning the number of steps needed to multiply two matrices are obtained. Using n^3 processors, all multiplications in equation (4.3.3) can be performed in one parallel step. Since any sum of n numbers $x_1 + \ldots + x_n$ can be computed with $\frac{n}{2}$ processors using the **recursive doubling technique**[4] in $\lceil \log_2 n \rceil$ steps, in order to compute all c_{ij} in (4.3.3) by the above method, we need $\Theta(n^3)$ processors and $\Theta(\log n)$ parallel steps.

Example 1.1.13 (Exponentiation) *Let* $b_{k-1} \ldots b_0$ *be the binary representation of an integer n with* b_0 *as the least significant bit and* $b_{k-1} = 1$. *Exponentiation* $e = a^n$ *can be performed in* $k = \lceil \log_2(n+1) \rceil$ *steps using the following so-called* **repeated squaring method** *based on the equalities*

$$e = a^{\sum_{i=0}^{k-1} b_i 2^i} = \prod_{i=0}^{k-1} a^{b_i 2^i} = \prod_{i=0}^{k-1} (a^{2^i})^{b_i}.$$

Algorithm 1.1.14 (Exponentiation)

```
begin e ← 1; p ← a;
      for i ← 0 to k − 1
          do if b_i = 1 then e ← e · p;
             p ← p · p
          od
end
```

Exercise 1.1.15 *Determine exactly the number of multiplications which Algorithm 1.1.14 performs.*

Remark 1.1.16 The term 'recurrence' is sometimes used to denote only the equation in which the inductive definition is made. This terminology is often used explicitly in cases where the specific value of the initial conditions is not important.

[4] For example, to get $x_1 + \ldots + x_8$, we compute in the first step $z_1 = x_1 + x_2, z_2 = x_3 + x_4, z_3 = x_5 + x_6, z_4 = x_7 + x_8$; in the second step $z_5 = z_1 + z_2, z_6 = z_3 + z_4$; and in the last step $z_7 = z_5 + z_6$.

1.2 Solution of Recurrences – Basic Methods

Several basic methods for solving recurrences are presented in this chapter. It is not always easy to decide which one to try first. However, it is good practice to start by computing some of the values of the unknown function for several small arguments. It often helps

1. to guess the solution;
2. to verify a solution-to-be.

Example 1.2.1 *For small values of n, the unknown functions $T(n)$ and $T'(n)$ from the recurrences (1.1) and (1.2) have the following values:*

n	1	2	3	4	5	6	7	8	9	10
$T(n)$	1	3	7	15	31	63	127	255	511	1,023
$T'(n)$	2	8	26	80	242	728	2,186	6,560	19,682	59,049

From this table we can easily guess that $T(n) = 2^n - 1$ and $T'(n) = 3^n - 1$. Such guesses have then to be verified, for example, by induction, as we shall do later for $T(n)$ and $T'(n)$.

Example 1.2.2 *The recurrence*

$$Q_n = \begin{cases} \alpha, & \text{if } n = 0; \\ \beta, & \text{if } n = 1; \\ \frac{\alpha\beta + \beta^2 - \beta Q_{n-1}}{Q_{n-2}}, & \text{if } n > 1; \end{cases}$$

where $\alpha, \beta > 0$, looks quite complicated. However, it is easy to determine that $Q_2 = \beta, Q_3 = \alpha, Q_4 = \beta$. Hence

$$Q_n = \begin{cases} \alpha, & \text{if } n = 3k \text{ for some } k; \\ \beta, & \text{otherwise.} \end{cases}$$

1.2.1 Substitution Method

Once we have guessed the solution of a recurrence, induction is often a good way of verifying the correctness of the guess.

Example 1.2.3 (Towers of Hanoi problem) *We show by induction that our guess $T(n) = 2^n - 1$ is correct. Since $T(1) = 2^1 - 1 = 1$, the initial case $n = 1$ is verified. From the inductive assumption $T(n) = 2^n - 1$ and the recurrence (1.1), we get, for $n > 1$,*

$$T(n+1) = 2T(n) + 1 = 2(2^n - 1) + 1 = 2^{n+1} - 1.$$

This completes the induction step.

Similarly, we can show that $T'(n) = 3^n - 1$ is the correct solution of the modified Towers of Hanoi problem, and $L(n) = 2^{n+1} - 2$ is the length of the side of the H-layout in Example 1.1.1. The inductive step in the last case is $L(n+1) = 2L(n) + 2 = 2(2^{n+1} - 2) + 2 = 2^{n+2} - 2$.

1.2.2 Iteration Method

Using an **iteration (unrolling)** of a recurrence, we can often reduce the recurrence to a summation, which may be easier to compute or estimate.

Example 1.2.4 *For the recurrence (1.2) of the modified Towers of Hanoi problem we get by an unrolling*

$$\begin{aligned} T'(n) &= 3T'(n-1)+2 = 3(3T'(n-2)+2)+2 = 9T'(n-2)+6+2 \\ &= 9(3T'(n-3)+2)+6+2 = 3^3T'(n-3)+2\times 3^2+2\times 3+2 \\ &\vdots \\ &= \sum_{i=0}^{n-1} 3^i \times 2 = 2\sum_{i=0}^{n-1} 3^i = 2\frac{3^n-1}{3-1} = 3^n - 1. \end{aligned}$$

Example 1.2.5 *For the recurrence* $T(1) = g(1)$ *and* $T(n) = T(n-1)+g(n)$, *for* $n > 1$, *the unrolling yields*

$$T(n) = \sum_{i=1}^{n} g(i).$$

Example 1.2.6 *By an unrolling of the recurrence*

$$T(n) = \begin{cases} b, & \text{if } n = 1; \\ aT(\frac{n}{c}) + bn, & \text{if } n = c^i > 1; \end{cases}$$

obtained by an analysis of divide-and-conquer algorithms, we get

$$\begin{aligned} T(n) &= aT\left(\frac{n}{c}\right)+bn = a\left(aT\left(\frac{n}{c^2}\right)+b\frac{n}{c}\right)+bn = a^2T\left(\frac{n}{c^2}\right)+bn\frac{a}{c}+bn \\ &= a^2\left(aT\left(\frac{n}{c^3}\right)+b\frac{n}{c^2}\right)+bn\frac{a}{c}+bn = a^3T\left(\frac{n}{c^3}\right)+bn\frac{a^2}{c^2}+bn\frac{a}{c}+bn \\ &\vdots \\ &= bn\sum_{j=0}^{\log_c n}\left(\frac{a}{c}\right)^j. \end{aligned}$$

Therefore,

- *Case 1,* $a < c$: $T(n) = \Theta(n)$, *because the sum* $\sum_{i=0}^{\infty}\left(\frac{a}{c}\right)^i$ *converges.*
- *Case 2,* $a = c$: $T(n) = \Theta(n \log n)$.
- *Case 3,* $a > c$: $T(n) = \Theta(n^{\log_c a})$.

Indeed, in Case 3 we get

$$\begin{aligned} T(n) &= bn\sum_{i=0}^{\log_c n}\left(\frac{a}{c}\right)^i = bn\frac{\left(\frac{a}{c}\right)^{\log_c n+1}-1}{\frac{a}{c}-1} \\ &\approx bn\left(\frac{a}{c}\right)^{\log_c n} \\ &= bn\frac{a^{\log_c n}}{n} = ba^{\log_c n} = bn^{\log_c a}, \end{aligned}$$

using the identity $a^{\log_c n} = n^{\log_c a}$.

Observe that the time complexity of a divide-and-conquer algorithm depends only on the ratio $\frac{a}{c}$, and neither on the problem being solved nor the computing model (device) being used, provided that the decomposition and composition require only linear time.

Exercise 1.2.7 *Solve the recurrences obtained by doing Exercises 1.1.6 and 1.1.10.*

Exercise 1.2.8 *Solve the following recurrence using the iteration method:*

$$T(n) = 3T(\frac{n}{4}) + n, \text{for } n = 4^k > 1.$$

Exercise 1.2.9 *Determine* g_n, n *a power of 2, defined by the recurrence*

$$g_1 = 3 \text{ and } g_n = (2^{\frac{n}{2}} + 1)g_{\frac{n}{2}} \text{ for } n \geq 2.$$

Exercise 1.2.10 *Express* $T(n)$ *in terms of the function* g *for the recurrence* $T(1) = a$, $T(n) = 2^p T(n / 2) + n^p g(n)$, *where* p *is an integer,* $n = 2^k$, $k > 0$ *and* a *is a constant.*

1.2.3 Reduction to Algebraic Equations

A large class of recurrences, the **homogeneous linear recurrences**, can be solved by a reduction to algebraic equations. Before presenting the general method, we will demonstrate its basic idea on an example.

Example 1.2.11 (Fibonacci numbers) *Leonardo Fibonacci*[5] *introduced in 1202 a sequence of numbers defined by the recurrence*

$$F_0 = 0, \quad F_1 = 1 \qquad \text{(the initial conditions);} \qquad (1.5)$$

$$F_n = F_{n-1} + F_{n-2}, \quad \text{if} \quad n > 1 \qquad \text{(the inductive equation).} \qquad (1.6)$$

Fibonacci numbers form one of the most interesting sequences of natural numbers:

$$0, 1, 1, 2, 3, 5, 8, 13, 21, 34, 55, 89, 144, 233, 377, 610, \ldots$$

Exercise 1.2.12 *Explore the beauty of Fibonacci numbers: (a) find all* n *such that* $F_n = n$ *and all* n *such that* $F_n = n^2$; *(b) determine* $\sum_{i=0}^{k} F_i$; *(c) show that* $F_{n+1}F_{n-1} - F_n^2 = (-1)^n$ *for all* n; *(d) show that* $F_{2n+1} = F_n^2 + F_{n+1}^2$ *for all* n; *(e) compute* $F_{16}, \ldots, F_{49}$ ($F_{50} = 12{,}586{,}269{,}025$).

[5] Leonardo of Pisa (1170–1250), known also as Fibonacci, was perhaps the most influential mathematician of the medieval Christian world. Educated in Africa, by a Muslim teacher, he was famous for his possession of the mathematical knowledge of both his own and the preceding generations. In his celebrated and influential classic *Liber Abachi* (which appeared in print only in the nineteenth century) he introduced to the Latin world the Arabic positional system and Hindu methods of calculation with fractions, square roots, cube roots, etc. The following problem from the *Liber Abachi* led to Fibonacci numbers: *How many pairs of rabbits will be produced in a year, beginning with a single pair, if in every month each pair bears a new pair which becomes productive from the second month on.*

It is natural to ask whether, given an integer n, we can determine F_n without computing F_i for all $i < n$. More precisely, can we find an explicit formula for F_n?

Let us first try to find a solution of the inductive equation (1.6) in the form $F_n = r^n$, where r is, so far, an unknown constant. Suppose r^n is a solution of (1.6), then

$$r^n = r^{n-1} + r^{n-2}$$

has to hold for all $n > 1$, and therefore either $r = 0$, which is an uninteresting case, or $r^2 = r + 1$. The last equation has two roots:

$$r_1 = \frac{1+\sqrt{5}}{2}, \qquad r_2 = \frac{1-\sqrt{5}}{2}.$$

Unfortunately, neither of the functions r_1^n, r_2^n satisfies the initial conditions in (1.5). We are therefore not ready yet. Fortunately, however, each linear combination $\lambda r_1^n + \mu r_2^n$ satisfies the inductive equation (1.6). Therefore, if λ, μ are chosen in such a way that the initial conditions (1.5) are also met, that is, if

$$\lambda r_1^0 + \mu r_2^0 = F_0 = 0, \qquad \lambda r_1^1 + \mu r_2^1 = F_1 = 1, \tag{1.7}$$

then $F_n = \lambda r_1^n + \mu r_2^n$ is the solution of recurrences (1.5) and (1.6). From (1.7) we get

$$\lambda = -\mu = \frac{1}{\sqrt{5}},$$

and thus

$$F_n = \frac{1}{\sqrt{5}}\left(\left(\frac{1+\sqrt{5}}{2}\right)^n - \left(\frac{1-\sqrt{5}}{2}\right)^n\right).$$

Since $\lim_{n\to\infty}\left(\frac{1-\sqrt{5}}{2}\right)^n = 0$, we also get a simpler, approximate expression for F_n of the form

$$F_n \approx \frac{1}{\sqrt{5}}\left(\frac{1+\sqrt{5}}{2}\right)^n, \qquad \text{for } n \to \infty.$$

□

The method used in the previous example will now be generalized. Let us consider a **homogeneous linear recurrence**: that is, a recurrence where the value of the unknown function is expressed as a linear combination of a fixed number of its values for smaller arguments:

$$u_n = a_1 u_{n-1} + a_2 u_{n-2} + \cdots + a_k u_{n-k} \quad \text{if } n \geq k, \qquad \text{(the inductive equation)} \tag{1.8}$$

$$u_i = b_i, \quad \text{if } 0 \leq i < k \qquad \text{(the initial conditions)} \tag{1.9}$$

where $a_1, \ldots, a_k$ and $b_0, \ldots, b_{k-1}$ are constants, and let

$$P(r) = r^k - \sum_{j=1}^{k} a_j r^{k-j} \tag{1.10}$$

be the **characteristic polynomial** of the inductive equation (1.8) and $P(r) = 0$ its **characteristic equation**. The roots of the polynomial (1.10) are called **characteristic roots** of the inductive equation (1.8). The following theorem says that we can always find a solution of a homogeneous linear recurrence when the roots of its characteristic polynomial are known.

Theorem 1.2.13 *(1) If the characteristic equation $P(r) = 0$ has k different roots $r_1, \ldots r_k$, then the recurrence (1.8) with the initial conditions (1.9) has the solution*

$$u_n = \sum_{j=1}^{k} \lambda_j r_j^n, \tag{1.11}$$

where λ_j are solutions of the system of linear equations

$$b_i = \sum_{j=1}^{k} \lambda_j r_j^i, \quad 0 \leq i < k. \tag{1.12}$$

(2) If the characteristic equation $P(r) = 0$ has p different roots, $r_1, \ldots, r_p$, $p < k$, and the root r_j, $1 \leq j \leq p$, has the multiplicity $m_j \geq 1$, then $r_j^n, nr_j^n, n^2 r_j^n, \ldots, n^{m_j-1} r_j^n$, are also solutions of the inductive equation (1.8), and there is a solution of (1.8) satisfying the initial conditions (1.9) of the form $u_n = \sum_{j=1}^{p} P_j(n) r_j^n$, where each $P_j(n)$ is a polynomial of degree $m_j - 1$, the coefficient of which can be obtained as the unique solution of the system of linear equations $b_i = \sum_{j=1}^{p} P_j(i) r_j^i$, $1 \leq i \leq k$.

Proof: (1) Since the inductive equation (1.8) is satisfied by $u_n = r_j^n$ for $1 \leq j \leq k$, it is satisfied also by an arbitrary linear combination $\sum_{j=1}^{k} a_j r_j^n$. To prove the first part of the theorem, it is therefore sufficient to show that the system of linear equations (1.12) has a unique solution. This is the case when the determinant of the matrix of the system does not equal zero. But this is a well-known result from linear algebra, because the corresponding (Vandermond) matrix and determinant have the form

$$det \begin{vmatrix} 1 & 1 & \ldots & 1 \\ r_1 & r_2 & \ldots & r_k \\ \vdots & \vdots & & \vdots \\ r_1^{k-1} & r_2^{k-1} & \ldots & r_k^{k-1} \end{vmatrix} = \prod_{j>i} (r_i - r_j) \neq 0.$$

(2) A detailed proof of the second part of the theorem is quite technical; we present here only its basic idea.

We have first to show that if r_j is a root of the equation $P(r) = 0$ of multiplicity $m_j > 1$, then all functions $u_n = r_j^n$, $u_n = nr_j^n$, $u_n = n^2 r_j^n, \ldots, u_n = n^{m_j-1} r_j^n$ satisfy the inductive equation (1.8). To prove this, we can use the well-known fact from calculus, that if r_j is a root of multiplicity $m_j > 1$ of the equation $P(r) = 0$, then r_j is also a root of the equations $P^{(j)}(r) = 0$, $1 \leq j < m_j$, where $P^{(j)}(r)$ is the jth derivative of $P(r)$.

Let us consider the polynomial

$$Q(r) = r \cdot (r^{n-k} P(r))' = r \cdot [(n-k) r^{n-k-1} P(r) + r^{n-k} P'(r)].$$

Since $P(r_j) = P'(r_j) = 0$, we have $Q(r_j) = 0$. However,

$$\begin{aligned} Q(r) &= r[r^n - a_1 r^{n-1} - \cdots - a_k r^{n-k}]' \\ &= nr^n - a_1(n-1)r^{n-1} - \cdots - a_{k-1}(n-k+1)r^{n-k+1} - a_k(n-k)r^{n-k}, \end{aligned}$$

and since $Q(r_j) = 0$, we have that $u_n = nr_j^n$ is the solution of the inductive equation (1.8).

In a similar way we can show by induction that all $u_n = n^s r_j^n$, $1 < s < m_j$, are solutions of (1.8) by considering the following sequence of polynomials: $Q_1(r) = Q(r)$, $Q_2(r) = rQ_1'(r), \ldots, Q_s(r) = rQ_{s-1}'(r)$.

It then remains to show that the matrix of the system of linear equations $b_i = \sum_{j=1}^{p} P_j(i) r_j^i$, $1 \leq i \leq k$, is nonsingular. This is a (nontrivial) exercise in linear algebra. □

Example 1.2.14 *The recurrence*

$$\begin{aligned} u_n &= 3u_{n-1} - 2u_{n-2}, \; n > 2; \\ u_0 &= 0, \; u_1 = 1, \end{aligned}$$

has the characteristic equation $r^2 = 3r - 2$ *with two roots:* $r_1 = 2, r_2 = 1$. *Hence* $u_n = \lambda_1 2^n + \lambda_2$, *where* $\lambda_1 = 1$ *and* $\lambda_2 = -1$ *are solutions of the system of equations* $0 = \lambda_1 2^0 + \lambda_2 1^0$ *and* $1 = \lambda_1 2^1 + \lambda_2 1^1$.

Example 1.2.15 *The recurrence*

$$\begin{aligned} u_n &= 5u_{n-1} - 8u_{n-2} + 4u_{n-3}, \; n \geq 3, \\ u_0 &= 0, \; u_1 = -1, \; u_2 = 2, \end{aligned}$$

has the characteristic equation $r^3 = 5r^2 - 8r + 4$, *which has one simple root,* $r_1 = 1$, *and one root of multiplicity 2,* $r_2 = 2$. *The recurrence therefore has the solution* $u_n = a + (b + cn)2^n$, *where* a, b, c *satisfy the equations*

$$0 = a + (b + c \cdot 0)2^0, \quad -1 = a + (b + c \cdot 1)2^1, \quad 2 = a + (b + c \cdot 2)2^2.$$

Example 1.2.16 *(a) The recurrence* $u_0 = 3, u_1 = 5$ *and* $u_n = u_{n-1} - u_{n-2}$, *for* $n > 2$, *has two roots,* $x_1 = \frac{1+i\sqrt{3}}{2}$ *and* $x_2 = \frac{1-i\sqrt{3}}{2}$, *and the solution* $u_n = (\frac{3}{2} - \frac{7}{6}i\sqrt{3})x_1^n + (\frac{3}{2} + \frac{7}{6}i\sqrt{3})x_2^n$. *(Verify that all* u_n *are integers!)*

(b) For the recurrence $u_0 = 0, u_1 = 1$ *and* $u_n = 2u_{n-1} - 2u_{n-2}$, *for* $n \geq 2$, *the characteristic equation has two roots,* $x_1 = (1+i)$ *and* $x_2 = (1-i)$, *and we get*

$$u_n = \frac{1}{2}i((1-i)^n - (1+i)^n) = 2^{\frac{n}{2}} \sin(\frac{n\pi}{4}),$$

using a well-known identity from calculus.

Exercise 1.2.17 *Solve the recurrences (a)* $u_0 = 6$, $u_1 = 8$, $u_n = 4u_{n-1} - 4u_{n-2}$, $n \geq 2$; *(b)* $u_0 = 1, u_1 = 0$, $u_n = 5u_{n-1} - 6u_{n-2}$, $n \geq 2$; *(c)* $u_0 = 4$, $u_1 = 10$, $u_n = 6u_{n-1} - 8u_{n-2}$, $n \geq 2$.

Exercise 1.2.18 *Solve the recurrences (a)* $u_0 = 0$, $u_1 = 1$, $u_2 = 1$, $u_n = 2u_{n-2} + u_{n-3}$, $n \geq 3$; *(b)* $u_0 = 7$, $u_1 = -4$, $u_2 = 8$, $u_n = 2u_{n-1} + 5u_{n-2} - 6u_{n-3}$, $n \geq 3$; *(c)* $u_0 = 1$, $u_1 = 2$, $u_2 = 3$, $u_n = 6u_{n-1} - 11u_{n-2} + 6u_{n-3}$, $n \geq 3$.

Exercise 1.2.19* *Using some substitutions of variables, transform the following recurrences to the cases dealt with in this section, and in this way solve the recurrences (a)* $u_1 = 1$, $u_n = u_{n-1} - u_n u_{n-1}$, $n \geq 2$; *(b)* $u_1 = 0$, $u_n = n(u_{n/2})^2$, *n is a power of 2; (c)* $u_0 = 1$, $u_1 = 2$, $u_n = \sqrt{u_{n-1}u_{n-2}}$, $n \geq 2$.

Finally, we present an interesting open problem due to Lothar Collatz (1930), a class of recurrences that look linear, but whose solution is not known.

For any positive integer i we define the so-called $(3x+1)$-recurrence by (a Collatz process) $u_0^{(i)} = i$, and for $n > 0$,

$$u_{n+1}^{(i)} = \begin{cases} \frac{u_n^{(i)}}{2}, & \text{if } u_n^{(i)} \text{ is even;} \\ 3u_n^{(i)} + 1, & \text{if } u_n^{(i)} \text{ is odd.} \end{cases}$$

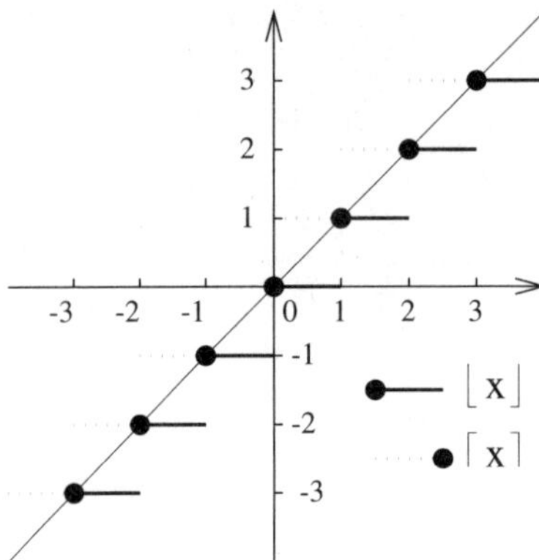

Figure 1.4 Ceiling and floor functions

It has been verified that for any $i < 2^{40}$ there exists an integer n_i such that $u_{n_i}^{(i)} = 1$ (and therefore $u_{n_i+1}^{(i)} = 4, u_{n_i+2}^{(i)} = 2, u_{n_i+3}^{(i)} = 1, \ldots$). However, it has been an open problem since the early 1950s – the so-called Collatz problem – whether this is true for all i.

Exercise 1.2.20 *Denote by $\sigma(n)$ the smallest i such that $u_n^{(i)} < n$. Determine (a) $\sigma(26), \sigma(27), \sigma(28)$; (b)* $\sigma(2^{50}-1), \sigma(2^{50}+1), \sigma(2^{500}-1), \sigma(2^{500}+1)$.*

1.3 Special Functions

There are several simple functions that are often used in the design and analysis of computing systems. In this section we deal with some of them: ceiling and floor functions for real-to-integer conversions, logarithms and binomial functions.

Despite their apparent simplicity, these functions have various interesting properties and also, as discussed later, surprising computational power in the case of ceiling and floor functions.

1.3.1 Ceiling and Floor Functions

Integers play an important role in computing and communications. The same is true of two basic reals-to-integers conversion functions.

Floor:	$\lfloor x \rfloor$ – the largest integer $\leq x$
Ceiling:	$\lceil x \rceil$ – the smallest integer $\geq x$

For example,

$$\lfloor 3.14 \rfloor = 3 = \lfloor 3.75 \rfloor, \qquad \lfloor -3.14 \rfloor = -4 = \lfloor -3.75 \rfloor;$$
$$\lceil 3.14 \rceil = 4 = \lceil 3.75 \rceil, \qquad \lceil -3.14 \rceil = -3 = \lceil -3.75 \rceil.$$

The following basic properties of the floor and ceiling functions are easy to verify:

$$\lfloor x+n \rfloor = \lfloor x \rfloor + n \text{ and } \lceil x+n \rceil = \lceil x \rceil + n, \quad \text{if } n \text{ is an integer;}$$
$$\lfloor x \rfloor = x \Leftrightarrow x \text{ is an integer } \Leftrightarrow \lceil x \rceil = x;$$
$$x-1 < \lfloor x \rfloor \le x \le \lceil x \rceil < x+1, \quad \text{for any } x;$$
$$\lfloor -x \rfloor = -\lceil x \rceil \text{ and } \lceil -x \rceil = -\lfloor x \rfloor, \quad \text{for any } x;$$
$$\lfloor x \rfloor \le \left\lceil \frac{x}{2} \right\rceil + \left\lfloor \frac{x}{2} \right\rfloor \le \lceil x \rceil;$$
$$\left\lceil \frac{x}{2} \right\rceil = \left\lfloor \frac{x+1}{2} \right\rfloor, \quad \text{for any } x;$$
$$\lceil x \rceil - \lfloor x \rfloor = \begin{cases} 0, & \text{if } x \text{ is an integer;} \\ 1, & \text{otherwise.} \end{cases}$$

In spite of the simplicity of ceiling and floor functions, expressions that involve more occurrences of these functions are usually not easy to handle. It is therefore natural to ask when we can remove some of these functions from formulas without affecting their values. The case $\lfloor \lceil x \rceil \rfloor$ is trivial. It is less obvious that we can also do this in such expressions as $\lfloor \sqrt{\lfloor x \rfloor} \rfloor$ and $\lceil \log \lceil x \rceil \rceil$. This follows from the following general result.

Lemma 1.3.1 *Let $f(x)$ be a continuous, strictly monotonically increasing function such that if $f(x)$ is an integer, then so is x. Then*

$$\lfloor f(\lfloor x \rfloor) \rfloor = \lfloor f(x) \rfloor \quad \textit{and} \quad \lceil f(\lceil x \rceil) \rceil = \lceil f(x) \rceil.$$

Proof: We show the result for the floor function. The proof for the ceiling function is similar. If $\lfloor x \rfloor = x$, then there is nothing to prove. Therefore, let $\lfloor x \rfloor < x$. Then $f(\lfloor x \rfloor) < f(x)$, since f is increasing. Thus $\lfloor f(\lfloor x \rfloor) \rfloor \le \lfloor f(x) \rfloor$. If $\lfloor f(\lfloor x \rfloor) \rfloor < \lfloor f(x) \rfloor$, there must exist a number y such that $\lfloor x \rfloor < y \le x, f(y) = \lfloor f(x) \rfloor$, because f is continuous. This means that $f(y)$ is an integer and, because of the special property of f, y must be too. This is a contradiction – there is no integer between $\lfloor x \rfloor$ and x. Hence $\lfloor f(\lfloor x \rfloor) \rfloor = \lfloor f(x) \rfloor$.
□

Exercise 1.3.2 *Draw graphs of the functions (a) $f(x) = \lfloor 2x \rfloor$; (b) $f(x) = \lfloor x/2 \rfloor$; (c) $f(x) = \lfloor x^2 \rfloor$.*

Exercise 1.3.3 *Show that (a) $\lfloor 2x \rfloor = \lfloor x \rfloor + \lfloor x + \frac{1}{2} \rfloor$, for any real x; (b) $\lceil n/k \rceil = \lfloor (n-1)/k \rfloor + 1$ for any integers $n, k \in \mathbf{N}^+$; (c) $\lfloor \sqrt{2n(n+1)} \rfloor = \lfloor \sqrt{2}(n+\frac{1}{2}) \rfloor$ for any $n \in \mathbf{N}$.*

Ceiling and floor functions often occur in recurrences obtained from an analysis of divide-and-conquer algorithms. For example, for the number of comparisons of the MERGESORT we get

$$T(1) = 0, \tag{1.13}$$
$$T(n) = n-1+T(\lfloor n/2 \rfloor)+T(\lceil n/2 \rceil), \tag{1.14}$$

because the most balanced partition of a sequence of n elements is into sequences of $\lfloor \frac{n}{2} \rfloor$ and $\lceil \frac{n}{2} \rceil$ elements. We deal with this type of recurrences in Section 1.6.2.

The following two identities indicate that sums of floors, and also of ceilings, that look complicated have simple solutions. For integers m, n and k we have

$$\sum_{k=0}^{m-1} \left\lfloor \frac{n+k}{m} \right\rfloor = n;$$

$$\sum_{k=0}^{n-1} \lfloor \sqrt{k} \rfloor = na - \frac{1}{3}a^3 - \frac{1}{2}a^2 - \frac{1}{6}a, \text{ where } a = \lfloor \sqrt{n} \rfloor.$$

1.3.2 Logarithms

The logarithmic function $\log_a x$, $a > 1$, is continuous and monotonically increasing for $x \geq 1$. If a is an integer, then $\log_a x$ acquires integer values only at integer points. By Lemma 1.3.1 we therefore get $\lceil \log_a \lceil x \rceil \rceil = \lceil \log_a x \rceil$ and $\lfloor \log_a \lfloor x \rfloor \rfloor = \lfloor \log_a x \rfloor$ for $x \geq 1$. Logarithmic functions with the bases $2, e$ and 10 are used so often that a special notation has been developed for them:

$$\begin{aligned} \lg n &= \log_2 n && \{\text{binary logarithm}\}; \\ \ln n &= \log_e n && \{\text{natural logarithm}\}; \\ \log n &= \log_{10} n && \{\text{decimal logarithm}\}. \end{aligned}$$

Since $\log_a b = \frac{\log_c b}{\log_c a}$, we have the following relations between the main logarithms:

$$\lg x \approx 1.4426952 \ln x \approx 3.3219286 \log x.$$

There are various interpretations of binary logarithms worth noticing: $\lceil \lg(n+1) \rceil$ is the number of bits in the binary representation of the integer n; $\lceil \lg n \rceil$ is the minimal depth of the binary tree with n leaves and also the minimal number of parallel steps to compute $x_1 \circ x_2 \circ \cdots \circ x_n$, where $\circ$ is an associative binary operation.

Since $\ln x = \ln 2 + \ln \frac{x}{2}$, of special importance are properties of the function $\ln(x+1)$ for $|x| < 1$. Two of them, derived by calculus, are

$$\ln(x+1) = x - \frac{x^2}{2} + \frac{x^3}{3} - \frac{x^4}{4} + \frac{x^5}{5} - \cdots, \quad \text{for } |x| < 1;$$

$$\frac{x}{1+x} \leq \ln(1+x) \leq x.$$

In the analysis of computations we often encounter powers and compositions of logarithmic functions. The following notation has been developed for them:

$$\begin{aligned} \lg^k n &= (\lg n)^k, \quad \text{where } k \text{ is an integer}; \\ \lg \lg n &= \lg(\lg n); \\ \lg \lg \lg n &= \lg(\lg(\lg n)); \\ \lg^{(k)} n &= \underbrace{\lg \lg \ldots \lg}_{k \text{ times}} n, \quad \text{if } \lg^{(k-1)} n > 0. \end{aligned}$$

Another, related function that also occurs often in complexity analysis is the **iterated logarithm**:

$$\lg^* n = \min\{i \geq 0 \mid \lg^{(i)} n \leq 1\}.$$

This function grows so slowly that its value is at most 5 for all 'feasible' arguments. Indeed,

$$\lg^* 2 = 1, \qquad \lg^* 4 = 2, \qquad \lg^* 16 = 3;$$
$$\lg^* 65536 = 4, \qquad \lg^*(2^{65536}) = 5.$$

(Observe that 2^{65536} is much greater than most of the current estimates for the number of atoms in the universe.) However, the functions $\lg\lg n$ and $\lg\lg\lg n$ also grow very slowly. Indeed,

$$\lg\lg 2^{65536} = 16, \ \lg\lg\lg 2^{65536} = 4.$$

This shows that doubly logarithmic and iterated logarithmic functions, which often occur in the analysis of algorithms, actually contribute to the overall complexity, as an additive or multiplicative factor, by only a small amount.

The inverse of the natural logarithmic function is e^x ($exp(x)$ is another notation that is sometimes more convenient).

1.3.3 Binomial Functions – Coefficients

The binomial function, or binomial coefficient which is the more common terminology, $\binom{r}{k}$ is defined for an arbitrary real r and an integer k as follows:

$$\binom{r}{k} = \begin{cases} \frac{r(r-1)\cdots(r-k+1)}{k(k-1)\cdots 1}, & k > 0; \\ 1, & k = 0; \\ 0, & k < 0. \end{cases} \tag{1.15}$$

Observe that if $r > k > 0$ are integers, then $\binom{r}{k}$ is the number of possibilities for choosing k elements from r elements.

There are various reasons why binomial coefficients often occur in discrete computations. One of them is the identity

Binomial theorem: $(x+y)^n = \sum_{0 \le k \le n} \binom{n}{k} x^k y^{n-k}$.

Another reason, of immediate importance to us, is that binomial coefficients often occur as coefficients of generating functions – a useful tool for solving recurrences, as we shall see in the next section.

Some important identities for binomial coefficients are listed below. They can easily be proved using the basic definition. Acquaintance with them may help one find simple solutions for quite complicated expressions and sums.

$$\binom{n}{k} = \frac{n!}{k!(n-k)!}, \quad n \ge k \ge 0 \qquad\qquad \binom{n}{k} = \binom{n}{n-k}, \quad n \ge 0,$$

$$\binom{r}{k} = \frac{r}{k}\binom{r-1}{k-1}, \quad k \ne 0 \qquad\qquad \binom{r}{k} = \frac{r}{r-k}\binom{r-1}{k}, \quad r \ne k,$$

$$\binom{r}{k} = \binom{r-1}{k} + \binom{r-1}{k-1}, \quad (*) \qquad\qquad \binom{r}{m}\binom{m}{k} = \binom{r}{k}\binom{r-k}{m-k} \quad (*)$$

Exercise 1.3.4 *Prove the identities listed above using the basic definition of* $\binom{n}{k}$.

Example 1.3.5 *If $n \geq r \geq 0$ are integers, then we can use the first identity in $(*)$ to compute the following sum:*

$$\sum_{0 \leq k \leq n} \binom{r+k}{k} = \binom{r}{0} + \binom{r+1}{1} + \binom{r+2}{2} + \cdots + \binom{r+n}{n} = \binom{r+n+1}{n}. \tag{1.16}$$

Indeed, it holds that

$$\begin{array}{l} \binom{r}{0} = \binom{r+1}{0} \\ \quad + \binom{r+1}{1} \underbrace{=}_{by(*)} \binom{r+2}{1} \\ \qquad + \binom{r+2}{2} \underbrace{=}_{by(*)} \binom{r+3}{2} \\ \qquad\quad + \binom{r+3}{3} \underbrace{=}_{by(*)} \binom{r+4}{3} \\ \qquad\qquad + \cdots \underbrace{=}_{by(*)} \binom{r+n+1}{n}, \end{array}$$

and using this idea we can easily prove (1.16) by induction.

Example 1.3.6 *Let $n \geq m \geq 0$ be integers. Compute*

$$\sum_{k=0}^{m} \frac{\binom{m}{k}}{\binom{n}{k}}.$$

Using the second identity in $(*)$ we get

$$\sum_{k=0}^{m} \frac{\binom{m}{k}}{\binom{n}{k}} = \sum_{k=0}^{m} \frac{\binom{n-k}{m-k}}{\binom{n}{m}} = \frac{1}{\binom{n}{m}} \sum_{k=0}^{m} \binom{n-k}{m-k}.$$

To solve the problem, we need to compute the last sum. If we replace k in that sum by $m-k$ and then use the result of the previous example, we get

$$\sum_{k=0}^{m} \binom{n-k}{m-k} = \sum_{k=0}^{m} \binom{n-(m-k)}{m-(m-k)} \tag{1.17}$$

$$= \sum_{k=0}^{m} \binom{n-m+k}{k} = \binom{n+1}{m}. \tag{1.18}$$

The overall result is therefore $\frac{n+1}{n-m+1}$.

Exercise 1.3.7* *Show the following identities for all natural numbers a, b and $n > 1$:* *(a)* $\binom{a+b}{n} = \sum_{k=0}^{\min(n,a)} \binom{a}{k}\binom{b}{n-k}$; *(b)* $\binom{2n}{n} = \sum_{k=0}^{n} \binom{n}{k}^2$; *(c)* $\binom{3n}{n} = \sum_{k=0}^{n} \sum_{i=0}^{n-k} \binom{n}{k}\binom{n}{i}\binom{n}{i+k}$.

Exercise 1.3.8* *Show that* $\sum_{k=0}^{n} \binom{n}{k}\binom{n-k}{m-k} = 2^m \binom{n}{m}$.

1.4 Solution of Recurrences – Generating Function Method

The concept of **generating functions** is fundamental, and represents an important methodology with numerous applications. In this chapter we describe and illustrate two of them. The first one is used to solve recurrences.

The essence of the power of generating functions, as a methodology, is that they allow us to reduce complex manipulations with infinite objects (sequences) to easy operations with finite objects, for example, with rational functions. This often allows us to solve quite complicated problems in a surprisingly simple way.

1.4.1 Generating Functions

With any infinite sequence $\langle a_0, a_1, a_2, \ldots \rangle$ of numbers we associate the following generating function – **formal power series**:

$$A(z) = a_0 + a_1 z + a_2 z^2 + \cdots = \sum_{k \geq 0} a_k z^k = \sum a_k z^k, \tag{1.19}$$

where the use of the symbol z for a variable indicates that it can deal with complex numbers (even in cases where we are interested only in natural numbers). The word 'formal' highlights the fact that the role of powers z^n in (1.19) is mostly that of position holders for elements a_n. (The question of convergences is not important here, and will be discussed later.) With regard to coefficients, it is sometimes convenient to assume that $a_k = 0$ for $k < 0$ and to use the notation $\sum a_k z^k$ (see (1.19)), with k running through all integers. Observe too that some a_k in (1.19) may be equal to zero. Therefore, finite sequences can also be represented by generating functions. For the coefficient of z^n in a generating function $A(z)$ we use the notation

$$[z^n]A(z) = a_n. \tag{1.20}$$

The main reason why generating functions are so important is that as functions of complex variables they may have simple, closed-form expressions that represent a whole (infinite or finite) sequence, as the following example illustrates.

Example 1.4.1 (1) $(1+z)^r$ *is the generating function for the sequence* $\langle \binom{r}{0}, \binom{r}{1}, \binom{r}{2}, \binom{r}{3}, \ldots \rangle$. *By the binomial theorem and the fact that* $\binom{r}{k} = 0$ *for* $k > r$, *we get*

$$(1+z)^r = \sum_{k \geq 0} \binom{r}{k} z^k.$$

(2) $\frac{1}{1-z}$ *is the generating function for the power series* $\sum_{n \geq 0} z^n$, *because*

$$(1-z)\Big(\sum_{n \geq 0} z^n\Big) = 1. \tag{1.21}$$

Such basic operations as addition, subtraction, multiplication, inversion of a function (if $a_0 \neq 0$), special division by z^n, derivation, and integration can be performed on generating functions 'component-wise'. Table 1.1, in which

$$F(z) = \sum_n f_n z^n \quad \text{and} \quad G(z) = \sum_n g_n z^n,$$

$$
\begin{aligned}
\alpha F(z)+\beta G(z) &= \sum_n (\alpha f_n+\beta g_n)\, z^n \\
F(z)G(z) &= \sum_n \left(\sum_{k=0}^{n} f_k g_{n-k}\right) z^n \\
\tfrac{1}{1-z}G(z) &= \sum_n \left(\sum_{k=0}^{n} g_k\right) z^n \quad \{\text{summation rule}\} \\
F^{-1}(z) &= \sum_{n\ge 0} b_n z^n, \text{ where } b_0 = f_0^{-1}, \\
& \qquad b_n = -f_0^{-1}\sum_{k=1}^{n} f_k b_{n-k} \\
z^m G(z) &= \sum_n g_{n-m} z^n \qquad m \ge 0 \\
\tfrac{G(z)-g_0-g_1 z-\cdots-g_{m-1}z^{m-1}}{z^m} &= \sum_{n\ge 0} g_{n+m} z^n \\
G'(z) &= \sum_n (n+1) g_{n+1} z^n \\
zG'(z) &= \sum_n n g_n z^n \\
\int_0^z G(t)dt &= \sum_{n\ge 1} \tfrac{1}{n} g_{n-1} z^n
\end{aligned}
$$

Table 1.1 Operations on generating functions and the corresponding sequences

summarizes some basic operations on generating functions and on the corresponding formal power series. These identities can be derived in a straightforward way. Some examples follow

Linear combination:

$$\alpha F(z)+\beta G(z) = \alpha \sum_n f_n z^n + \beta \sum_n g_n z^n = \sum_n (\alpha f_n + \beta g_n) z^n.$$

Multiplication by z^m ($m \ge 0$):

$$z^m G(z) = \sum_n g_n z^{n+m} = \sum_n g_{n-m} z^n.$$

Derivation:

$$G'(z) = g_1 + 2g_2 z + 3g_3 z^2 + \cdots = \sum_n (n+1) g_{n+1} z^n;$$

therefore $G'(z)$ is the generating function for the sequence $\langle (n+1)g_{n+1}\rangle = \langle g_1, 2g_2, \ldots\rangle$, and $zG'(z)$ for the sequence $\langle ng_n \rangle = \langle 0, g_1, 2g_2, \ldots \rangle$.

For **multiplication** we get

$$
\begin{aligned}
F(z)G(z) &= (f_0+f_1 z+f_2 z^2+\cdots)(g_0+g_1 z+g_2 z^2+\cdots) \\
&= f_0 g_0 + (f_0 g_1 + f_1 g_0)z + (f_0 g_2 + f_1 g_1 + f_2 g_0)z^2 + \cdots,
\end{aligned}
$$

and therefore

$$[z^n]F(z)G(z) = (f_0g_n + f_1g_{n-1} + \cdots + f_ng_0) = \sum_{k=0}^{n} f_kg_{n-k}.$$

The product $F(z)G(z)$, where $[z^n]A(n)B(n) = \sum_{k=0}^{n} f_kg_{n-k}$, is called the **discrete convolution** of $F(z)$ and $G(z)$.

The **summation rule** in Table 1.1 is a special case of multiplication with $F(z) = \frac{1}{1-z}$.

Remark 1.4.2 In the case of generating functions we often do not care about convergence of the corresponding power series. It is therefore natural to ask whether our manipulations with infinite sums, as for example in (1.21), are correct. There are two reasons not to worry. First, one can show formally that all the operations mentioned above are correct. The second reason is quite different. It is often not very important whether all the operations we perform on generating functions are correct. Why? Because once we get some results using these operations we can use other methods, for example, induction, to show their correctness.

Let us illustrate this approach with an example:

Example 1.4.3 *The functions* $(1+z)^r$ *and* $(1+z)^s$ *are generating functions for sequences* $\left\langle \binom{r}{0}, \binom{r}{1}, \binom{r}{2}, \ldots \right\rangle$ *and* $\left\langle \binom{s}{0}, \binom{s}{1}, \binom{s}{2}, \ldots \right\rangle$. *Because* $(1+z)^r(1+z)^s = (1+z)^{r+s}$, *we have*

$$[z^n](1+z)^r(1+z)^s = \sum_{k=0}^{n} \binom{r}{k}\binom{s}{n-k} = \binom{r+s}{n} = [z^n](1+z)^{r+s}.$$

In a similar way we can show, using the identity $(1-z)^r(1+z)^r = \left(1-z^2\right)^r$, that

$$\sum_{k=0}^{n} \binom{r}{k}\binom{r}{n-k}(-1)^k = (-1)^{\frac{n}{2}}\binom{r}{\frac{n}{2}}, \quad \text{if } n \text{ is even.}$$

In this way we have easily obtained two far from obvious identities for sums of binomial coefficients. Their correctness can now be verified by induction.

Generating functions for some important sequences are listed in Table 1.2. Some of the results in the table follow in a straightforward way from the rules in Table 1.1. The generating function for the sequence $\langle 1,2,3,\ldots \rangle$ can be obtained using the summation rule with $G(z) = \frac{1}{1-z}$. Since the sequence $\langle 1,2,3,\ldots \rangle$ also has the form $\langle 1,2,\binom{3}{2},\binom{4}{3},\binom{5}{4},\ldots \rangle$, we get, using the summation rule and the identity in Example 1.3.5, that $\frac{1}{(1-z)^3}$ is the generating function for the sequence $\langle 1,3,\binom{4}{2},\binom{5}{3},\binom{6}{4},\ldots \rangle$. By induction we can then show, again using the summation rule and the identity in Example 1.3.5, that, for an arbitrary integer c, $\frac{1}{(1-z)^c}$ is the generating function for the sequence $\langle 1,c,\binom{c+1}{2},\binom{c+2}{3},\ldots \rangle$. Generating functions for the last three sequences in Table 1.2 are well known from calculus.

sequence	generating function	closed form
$\langle 1,1,1,\ldots\rangle$	$\sum_{n\geq 0} z^n$	$\frac{1}{1-z}$
$\langle 1,-1,1,-1,\ldots\rangle$	$\sum_{n\geq 0}(-1)^n z^n$	$\frac{1}{1+z}$
$\langle \underbrace{1,0,0,\ldots}_{m},\underbrace{1,0,0,\ldots}_{m},1\ldots\rangle$	$\sum_{n\geq 0}[m\setminus n]z^n$	$\frac{1}{1-z^m}$
$\langle 1,2,3,4,\ldots\rangle$	$\sum_{n\geq 0}(n+1)z^n$	$\frac{1}{(1-z)^2}$
$\langle 1,c,\binom{c}{2},\binom{c}{3},\ldots\rangle$	$\sum_{n\geq 0}\binom{c}{n}z^n$	$(1+z)^c$
$\langle 1,c,\binom{c+1}{2},\binom{c+2}{3},\ldots\rangle$	$\sum_{n\geq 0}\binom{c+n-1}{n}z^n$	$\frac{1}{(1-z)^c}$
$\langle 0,1,\frac{1}{2},\frac{1}{3},\frac{1}{4},\ldots\rangle$	$\sum_{n\geq 1}\frac{1}{n}z^n$	$\ln\frac{1}{1-z}$
$\langle 0,1,-\frac{1}{2},\frac{1}{3},-\frac{1}{4},\ldots\rangle$	$\sum_{n\geq 1}\frac{(-1)^{n+1}}{n}z^n$	$\ln(1+z)$
$\langle 1,1,\frac{1}{2!},\frac{1}{3!},\ldots\rangle$	$\sum_{n\geq 0}\frac{1}{n!}z^n$	e^z

Table 1.2 Generating functions for some sequences and their closed forms

Exercise 1.4.4 *Find a closed form of the generating function for the sequences*

$$(a)\ a_n = 3^n + 5^n + n, n \geq 1;\ (b)\ \langle 0,2,0,\frac{2}{3},0,\frac{2}{5},0,\frac{2}{7},\ldots\rangle.$$

Exercise 1.4.5* *Find a generating function* $F(z)$ *such that* $[z^n]F(z) = \sum_{i=0}\binom{n}{i}\binom{n}{n-2i}$*, for* $n \geq 1$.

Exercise 1.4.6 *Use generating functions to show that* $\sum_{i=0}^{n}\binom{n}{i}^2 = \binom{2n}{n}$.

1.4.2 Solution of Recurrences

The following general method can often be useful in finding a closed form for elements of a sequence $\langle g_n\rangle$ defined through a recurrence

Step 1 Form a single equation in which g_n is expressed in terms of other elements of the sequence. It is important that this equation holds for any n; also for those n for which g_n is defined by the initial values, and also for $n < 0$ (assuming $g_n = 0$).

Step 2 Multiply both sides of the resulting equation by z^n, and sum over all n. This gives on the left-hand side $G(z) = \sum g_n z^n$ – the generating function for $\langle g_n\rangle$. Arrange the right-hand side in such a way that an expression in terms of $G(z)$ is obtained.

Step 3 Solve the equation to get a closed form for $G(z)$.

Step 4 Expand $G(z)$ into a power series. The coefficient of z^n is a closed form for g_n.

Examples

In the following three examples we show how to perform the first three steps of the above method. Later we present a method for performing Step 4 – usually the most difficult one. This will then be applied to finish the examples.

In the examples, and also in the rest of the book, we use the following mapping of the truth values of predicates $P(n)$ onto integers:

$$[P(n)] = \begin{cases} 1, & \text{if } P(n) \text{ is true;} \\ 0, & \text{if } P(n) \text{ is false.} \end{cases}$$

Example 1.4.7 *Let us apply the above method to the recurrences (1.5) and (1.6) for Fibonacci numbers with the initial conditions* $f_0 = 0,\ f_1 = 1$ *and the inductive equation*

$$f_n = f_{n-1} + f_{n-2},\ n > 1.$$

Step 1 The single equation capturing both the inductive step and the initial conditions has the form

$$f_n = f_{n-1} + f_{n-2} + [n = 1].$$

(Observe – and this is important – that the equation is valid also for $n \leq 1$, because $f_n = 0$ for $n < 0$.)
Step 2 Multiplication by z^n and a summation produce

$$\begin{aligned} F(z) = \sum_n f_n z^n &= \sum_n (f_{n-1} + f_{n-2} + [n = 1])\, z^n \\ &= \sum_n f_{n-1} z^n + \sum_n f_{n-2} z^n + \sum_n [n = 1] z^n \\ &= zF(z) + z^2 F(z) + z. \end{aligned}$$

Step 3 From the previous equation we get

$$F(z) = \frac{z}{1 - z - z^2}.$$

Example 1.4.8 *Solve the recurrence*

$$g_n = \begin{cases} 1, & \textit{if } n = 0; \\ 2, & \textit{if } n = 1; \\ 2g_{n-1} + 3g_{n-2} + (-1)^n, & \textit{if } n > 1. \end{cases}$$

Step 1 A single equation for g_n has the form

$$g_n = 2g_{n-1} + 3g_{n-2} + (-1)^n [n \geq 0] + [n = 1].$$

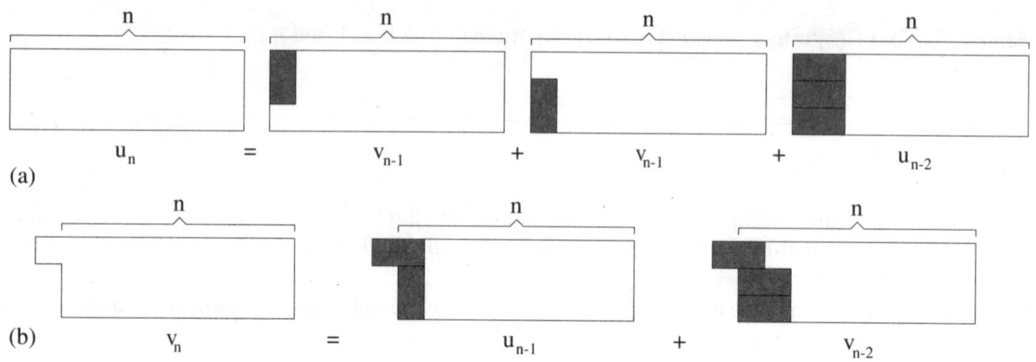

Figure 1.5 Recurrences for tiling by dominoes

Step 2 Multiplication by z^n and summation give

$$\begin{aligned} G(z) = \sum_n g_n z^n &= \sum_n (2g_{n-1} + 3g_{n-2} + (-1)^n[n \geq 0] + [n = 1])\, z^n \\ &= \sum_n 2g_{n-1}z^n + 3\sum_n g_{n-2}z^n + \sum_{n\geq 0}(-1)^n z^n + \sum_{n=1}^{1} z^n \\ &= 2zG(z) + 3z^2G(z) + \frac{1}{1+z} + z. \end{aligned}$$

Step 3 Solving the last equation for $G(z)$, we get

$$G(z) = \frac{z^2+z+1}{(1+z)^2(1-3z)}.$$

As illustrated by the following example, the generating function method can also be used to solve recurrences with two unknown functions. In addition, it shows that such recurrences can arise in a natural way, even in a case where the task is to determine only one unknown function.

Example 1.4.9 (Domino problem) *Determine the number u_n of ways of covering a $3 \times n$ rectangle with identical dominoes of size 1×2.*

Clearly $u_n = 0$ for $n = 1, 3$ and $u_2 = 3$. To deal with the general case, let us introduce a new variable, v_n, to denote the number of ways we can cover a $3 \times n$ with-a-corner-rectangle (see Figure 1.5b) with such dominoes. For the case $n = 0$ we have exactly one possibility: to use no domino. We therefore get the recurrences

$$\begin{aligned} &u_0 = 1, \quad u_1 = 0; && v_0 = 0, \quad v_1 = 1; \\ &u_n = 2v_{n-1} + u_{n-2}; && v_n = u_{n-1} + v_{n-2}, \qquad n \geq 2. \end{aligned}$$

Let us now perform Steps 1–3 of the above method.

Step 1 $u_n = 2v_{n-1} + u_{n-2} + [n = 0], \qquad v_n = u_{n-1} + v_{n-2}.$

Step 2 $U(z) = 2zV(z) + z^2U(z) + 1, \qquad V(z) = zU(z) + z^2V(z).$

Step 3 The solution of this system of two equations with two unknown functions has the form

$$U(z) = \frac{1-z^2}{1-4z^2+z^4}, \qquad V(z) = \frac{z}{1-4z^2+z^4}.$$

A general method of performing step 4

In the last three examples, the task in Step 4 is to determine the coefficients $[z^n]R(z)$ of a rational function $R(z) = P(z)\,/\,Q(z)$. This can be done using the following general method.

If the degree of the polynomial $P(z)$ is greater than or equal to the degree of $Q(z)$, then by dividing $P(z)$ by $Q(z)$ we can express $R(z)$ in the form $T(z) + S(z)$, where $T(z)$ is a polynomial and $S(z) = P_1(z)\,/\,Q(z)$ is a rational function with the degree of $P_1(z)$ smaller than that of $Q(z)$. Since $[z^n]R(z) = [z^n]T(z) + [z^n]S(z)$, the task has been reduced to that of finding $[z^n]S(z)$.

From the sixth row of Table 1.2 we find that

$$\frac{a}{(1-\rho z)^{m+1}} = \sum_{n\geq 0} \binom{m+n}{n} a\rho^n z^n,$$

and therefore we can easily find the coefficient $[z^n]S(z)$ in the case where $S(z)$ has the form

$$\sum_{i=1}^{m} \frac{a_i}{(1-\rho_i z)^{m_i-1}} \tag{1.22}$$

for some constants a_i, ρ_i and $m_i, 1 \leq i \leq m$. This implies that in order to develop a methodology for performing Step 4 of the above method, it is sufficient to show that $S(z)$ can always be transformed into either the above form or a similar one.

In order to transform $Q(z) = q_0 + q_1z + \cdots q_mz^m$ into the form $Q(z) = q_0(1-\rho_1z)(1-\rho_2z)\ldots(1-\rho_mz)$, we need to determine the roots $\frac{1}{\rho_1}, \ldots, \frac{1}{\rho_m}$ of $Q(z)$. Once these roots have been found, one of the following theorems can be used to perform Step 4.

Theorem 1.4.10 *If* $S(z) = \frac{P_1(z)}{Q(z)}$, *where* $Q(z) = q_0(1-\rho_1z)\ldots(1-\rho_mz)$, *the numbers* $\rho_1, \ldots, \rho_m$ *are distinct, and the degree of* $P_1(z)$ *is smaller than that of* $Q(z)$, *then*

$$[z^n]S(z) = a_1{\rho_1}^n + \cdots + a_l{\rho_m}^n,$$

where

$$a_k = \frac{-\rho_k P_1(\frac{1}{\rho_k})}{Q'(\frac{1}{\rho_k})}.$$

Proof: It is a fact well known from calculus that if all ρ_i are different, there exists a decomposition

$$S(z) = \frac{a_1}{(1-\rho_1z)} + \cdots + \frac{a_l}{(1-\rho_lz)},$$

where $a_1, \ldots, a_l$ are constants, and thus

$$[z^n]S(z) = a_1\rho_1^n + \cdots + a_l\rho_l^n.$$

Therefore, for $i = 1, \ldots, l$,

$$a_i = \lim_{z \to 1/\rho_i} (1 - \rho_i z) R(z),$$

and using l'Hospital's rule we obtain

$$a_i = \frac{-\rho_i P_1(\frac{1}{\rho_i})}{Q'(\frac{1}{\rho_i})},$$

where Q' is the derivative of the polynomial Q. □

The second theorem concerns the case of multiple roots of the denominator. For the proof, which is more technical, see the bibliographical references.

Theorem 1.4.11 *Let $R(z) = \frac{P(z)}{Q(z)}$, where $Q(z) = q_0(1 - \rho_1 z)^{d_1} \ldots (1 - \rho_l z)^{d_l}$, ρ_i are distinct, and the degree of $P(z)$ is smaller than that of $Q(z)$; then*

$$[z^n]R(z) = f_1(n)\rho_1^n + \cdots f_l(n)\rho_l^n, \quad n \geq 0,$$

where each $f_i(n)$ is a polynomial of degree $d_i - 1$, the main coefficient of which is

$$a_i = \frac{(-\rho_i)^{d_i} P(\frac{1}{\rho_i}) d_i}{Q^{(d_i)}(\frac{1}{\rho_i})},$$

where $Q^{(d_i)}$ is the i-th derivative of Q.

To apply Theorems 1.4.10 and 1.4.11 to a rational function $\frac{P(z)}{Q(z)}$ with $Q(z) = q_0 + q_1 z + \cdots + q_m z^m$, we must express $Q(z)$ in the form $Q(z) = q_0(1 - \rho_1 z)^{d_1} \ldots (1 - \rho_m z)^{d_m}$. The numbers $\frac{1}{\rho_i}$ are clearly roots of $Q(z)$. Applying the transformation $y = \frac{1}{z}$ and then replacing y by z, we get that ρ_i are roots of the 'reflected' polynomial

$$Q^R(z) = q_m + q_{m-1}z + \cdots + q_0 z^m,$$

and this polynomial is sometimes easier to handle.

Examples – continuation

Let us now apply Theorems 1.4.10 and 1.4.11 to finish Examples 1.4.7, 1.4.8 and 1.4.9. In Example 1.4.7 it remains to determine

$$[z^n]\frac{z}{1 - z - z^2}.$$

The reflected polynomial $z^2 - z - 1$ has two roots:

$$\phi_1 = \phi = \frac{1 + \sqrt{5}}{2}, \; \phi_2 = \bar{\phi} = \frac{1 - \sqrt{5}}{2}.$$

Theorem 1.4.10 therefore yields

$$F_n = [z^n]\frac{z}{1 - z - z^2} = a_1\phi^n + a_2\bar{\phi}^n,$$

where $a_1 = \frac{1}{\sqrt{5}}, a_2 = -\frac{1}{\sqrt{5}}$.

To finish Example 1.4.8 we have to determine

$$g_n = [z^n]\frac{1+z+z^2}{(1-3z)(1+z)^2}.$$

The denominator already has the required form. Since one root has multiplicity 2, we need to use Theorem 1.4.11. Calculations yield

$$g_n = (\frac{1}{4}n+c)(-1)^n + \frac{13}{16}3^n.$$

The constant $c = \frac{3}{16}$ can be determined using the equation $1 = g_0 = c + \frac{13}{16}$. Finally, in Example 1.4.9, it remains to determine

$$[z^n]U(z) = [z^n]\frac{1-z^2}{1-4z^2+z^4} \quad \text{and} \quad [z^n]V(z) = [z^n]\frac{z}{1-4z^2+z^4}. \tag{1.23}$$

In order to apply our method directly, we would need to find the roots of a polynomial of degree 4. But this, and also the whole task, can be simplified by realizing that all powers in (1.23) are even. Indeed, if we define

$$W(z) = \frac{1}{1-4z+z^2},$$

then

$$U(z) = (1-z^2)W(z^2), \text{ and } V(z) = zW(z^2).$$

Therefore

$$\begin{array}{rclcl} U_{2n+1} & = & [z^{2n+1}]U(z) & = & 0, \\ V_{2n} & = & [z^{2n}]V(z) & = & 0, \end{array} \qquad \begin{array}{rcl} U_{2n} & = & W_n - W_{n-1}; \\ V_{2n+1} & = & W_n; \end{array}$$

where

$$W_n = [z^n]\frac{1}{1-4z-z^2},$$

which is easier to determine.

Exercise 1.4.12 *Use the generating function method to solve the recurrences in Exercises 1.2.17 and 1.2.18.*

Exercise 1.4.13 *Use the generating function method to solve the recurrences*
(a) $u_0 = 0$, $u_1 = 1$, $u_n = u - n - 1 + u_{n-2} + (-1)^n$, $n \geq 2$;
(b) $g_n = 0$, *if* $n < 0$, $g_0 = 1$ *and* $g_n = g_{n-1} + 2g_{n-2} + \ldots + ng_0$ *for* $n > 0$.

Exercise 1.4.14 *Use the generating function method to solve the system of recurrences* $a_0 = 1$, $b_0 = 0$; $a_n = 5a_{n-1} + 12b_{n-1}$, $b_n = 2a_{n-1} + 5b_{n-1}$, $n \geq 1$.

Remark 1.4.15 In all previous methods for solving recurrences it has been assumed that all components – constants and functions – are fully determined. However, this is not always the case in practice. In general, only some estimations of them are available. In Section 1.6.2 we show how to deal with such cases. But before doing so, we switch to a detailed treatment of asymptotic estimations.

1.5 Asymptotics

Asymptotic estimations allow one to produce often surprisingly simple, deep, powerful, useful and technology independent analysis of the performance or size of computing systems. They have contributed much to the rapid development of a deep, practically relevant theory of computing.

In the asymptotic analysis of a function $T(n)$ (from integers to reals) or $A(x)$ (from reals to reals), the task is to find an **estimation in limit** of $T(n)$ for $n \to \infty$ or $A(x)$ for $x \to a$, where a is a real. The aim is to determine as good an estimation as possible, or at least good lower and upper bounds for it.

The key underlying problem is how to compare 'in a limit' the growth of two functions. The main approaches to this problem, and the relations between them, will now be discussed. An especially important role is played here by the $\mathcal{O}$-, Ω- and Θ-notations and we shall discuss in detail ways of handling them.

Because of the special importance and peculiarities of asymptotic estimations, a discussion of their merits seems appropriate.

There is a quite widespread illusion that in science and technology exact solutions, analyses and so on are required and to be aimed for. Estimations are often seen as substitutes, when exactness is not available or achievable. However, this does not apply to the analysis of computing systems. Simple, good estimations are what are really needed. There are several reasons for this.

Feasibility. Exact analyses are often not possible, even for apparently simple systems. There are often too many factors of enormous complexity involved. For example, to make a really detailed time analysis of even a simple program one would need to study complicated compilers, operating systems, computers and, in the case of multi-user systems, the patterns of their interactions.

Usefulness. An exact analysis could be many pages long and therefore all but incomprehensible. Moreover, as the results of asymptotic analysis indicate, most of it would be of negligible importance. In addition, what we really need are results of analysis of computing systems that are independent of the particular computer and, in general, of the underlying hardware and software technology. What we require are estimations that are some kind of **invariants** of computing technologies. Various constant factors that reflect these technologies are not of prime interest. Finally, what is most often needed is not knowledge of the performance of particular systems for particular data, but knowledge about the growth of the performance of systems as a function of the growth of the size of their input data. Again, factors with negligible growth and constant factors are not of prime importance for asymptotic analysis, even though they may be of great importance for applications.

Example 1.5.1 *How much time is needed to multiply two n-digit integers (by a person or by a computer) when a classical school algorithm is used?*

The exact analysis may be quite complicated. It also depends on many factors: which of many variants of the algorithm is used (see the one in Figure 1.6), who executes it, how it is programmed, and the computer on which it is run. However, all these cases have one thing in common: k^2 times more time is needed to multiply k times larger integers. We can therefore say, simply and in full generality, that the time taken to multiply two integers by a school algorithm is $\Theta(n^2)$. Note that this result holds no matter what kind of positional number system is used to represent integers: binary, ternary, decimal and so on.

It is also important to realize that simple, well-understood estimations are of great importance even when exact solutions are available. Some examples follow.

Example 1.5.2 *In the analysis of algorithms one often encounters so-called* **harmonic numbers:**

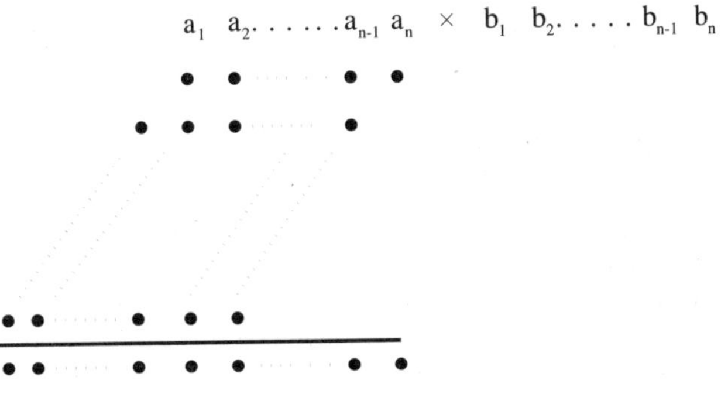

a1 a2. . . . . . an-1 an × b1 b2. . . . . bn-1 bn

Figure 1.6 Integer multiplication

$$H_n = 1 + \frac{1}{2} + \frac{1}{3} + \cdots + \frac{1}{n} = \sum_{i=1}^{n} \frac{1}{i}. \tag{1.24}$$

Using definition (1.24) we can determine H_n exactly for any given integer n. This, however, is not always enough. Mostly what we need to know is how big H_n is in general, as a function of n, not for a particular n. Unfortunately, no closed form for H_n is known. Therefore, good approximations are much needed. For example,

$$\ln n < H_n < \ln n + 1, \qquad \text{for } n > 1.$$

This is often good enough, although sometimes a better approximation is required. For example,

$$H_n = \ln n + 0.5772156649 + \frac{1}{2n} - \frac{1}{12n^2} + \Theta(n^{-4}).$$

Example 1.5.3 *The factorial $n! = 1 \cdot 2 \cdot \ldots \cdot n$ is another function of importance for the analysis of algorithms. The fact that we can determine $n!$ exactly is not always good enough for complexity analysis. The following approximation, due to James Stirling (1692–1770),*

$$n! = \sqrt{2\pi n}\left(\frac{n}{e}\right)^n \left(1 + \Theta\left(\frac{1}{n}\right)\right)$$

may be much more useful. For example, this approximation yields

$$\lg n! = \Theta(n \log n).$$

1.5.1 An Asymptotic Hierarchy

An important formalization of the intuitive idea that one function grows essentially faster than another function is captured by the relation $\prec$ defined by

$$f(n) \prec g(n) \Leftrightarrow \lim_{n \to \infty} \frac{f(n)}{g(n)} = 0.$$

Basic properties of this relation can be summarized as follows:

$$f(n) \prec g(n), g(n) \prec h(n) \quad \Rightarrow \quad f(n) \prec h(n) \qquad \text{(transitivity);} \qquad (1.25)$$

$$f(n) \prec g(n) \quad \Leftrightarrow \quad \frac{1}{g(n)} \prec \frac{1}{f(n)} \qquad \text{(for } f, g \text{ never equal zero);} \qquad (1.26)$$

$$1 \prec f(n) \prec g(n) \quad \Rightarrow \quad c^{|f(n)|} \prec c^{|g(n)|} \qquad \text{(if } c > 1 \text{ is a constant);} \qquad (1.27)$$

$$n^{\alpha} \prec n^{\beta} \quad \Leftrightarrow \quad \alpha < \beta, \qquad \text{(if } \alpha, \beta \text{ are positive reals).} \qquad (1.28)$$

These properties, as well as the following hierarchy (with $0 < \varepsilon < 1 < c$), can be derived from the basic definition of the relation $\prec$ using elementary methods of calculus.

$$1 \prec \lg^{\star} n \prec \lg\lg n \prec \lg n \prec n^{\varepsilon} \prec n^{c} \prec n^{\lg n} \prec c^{n} \prec n^{n} \prec c^{c^{n}}. \qquad (1.29)$$

These results remain valid when lg is replaced by ln or log.

Example 1.5.4 *Where in this hierarchy does the function $2^{\sqrt[m]{\lg n}}$, $m > 1$, lie? Clearly, $\lg\lg n \prec \sqrt[m]{\lg n} \prec \varepsilon \lg n$, for any $\varepsilon > 0$, and therefore, by (1.27), $2^{\lg\lg n} \prec 2^{\sqrt[m]{\lg n}} \prec 2^{\varepsilon \lg n}$. Since $2^{\lg\lg n} = \lg n$ and $2^{\varepsilon \lg n} = n^{\varepsilon}$, we get*

$$\lg n \prec 2^{\sqrt[m]{\log n}} \prec n^{\varepsilon}.$$

Exercise 1.5.5 *Which of the functions grows faster: (a) $n^{(\ln n)}$ or $(\ln n)^{n}$; (b) $(\ln n)!$ or $n^{\ln n \ln\ln n}$?*

In a similar way, we can formalize the intuitive idea that two functions $f(n)$ and $g(n)$ have the same rate of growth, as follows:

$$f(n) \sim g(n) \Leftrightarrow \lim_{n \to \infty} \frac{f(n)}{g(n)} = 1. \qquad (1.30)$$

It would be nice if we could say that for any two functions $f(n)$ and $g(n)$ one of the relations $f(n) \prec g(n)$, $f(n) \sim g(n)$, or $g(n) \prec f(n)$ holds. This, however, is not the case. For example, for the pairs $f(n) = n$, $g(n) = 2n$ and $f(n) = 1$, $g(n) = \sin n$ none of these relations holds. The relation $\sim$ is simply too strong.

There is another formalization of the intuitive idea that two functions have the same rate of growth:

$$f(n) \asymp g(n) \quad \Leftrightarrow \quad |f(n)| \le c|g(n)| \quad \text{and} \quad |g(n)| \le c|f(n)| \qquad (1.31)$$

for a constant c and every large enough n. This has the pleasing and important property that for any two of the **logarithmico-exponential functions** $f(n)$ and $g(n)$, exactly one of the relations $f(n) \prec g(n)$, $f(n) \asymp g(n)$ or $g(n) \prec f(n)$ holds.

The family of logarithmico-exponential functions contains practically all the functions one encounters in asymptotic analysis. It has been introduced by G. H. Hardy (1910) and it can be defined as the smallest family, $\mathcal{L}$, of functions satisfying the following properties:

1. Functions $f(n) = n$ and $f(n) = c$ (a constant) are in $\mathcal{L}$.

2. If $f(n), g(n)$ are in $\mathcal{L}$, then so are functions $f(n)+g(n), f(n)-g(n), f(n)\cdot g(n), e^{f(n)}, \lfloor f(n) \rfloor$ $g(n)/f(n)$ and $\log f(n)$ – if $f(n) > 0$ for almost all n.

Asymptotic relations such as $\prec$ and the ones to be defined later, which capture 'in limit' our intuition about the growth of functions, require us to stretch our imagination, and to **THINK BIG**. For example, if $f(n) \prec g(n)$, then this means that eventually, for all $n \geq n_0$ for some $n_0, f(n) < g(n)$. However, such an n_0 can be very large! For example,

$$\log n \prec n^{0.0001},$$

but the smallest n_0 such that $\log n < n^{0.0001}$ for all $n \geq n_0$ is between 10^{10^3} and 10^{10^4}.

In general, asymptotic analysis results are more relevant the larger the arguments we have. This implies that the practical importance of asymptotic analysis results increases with the growth of the performance of computers and of the size of the problems that need to be solved.

1.5.2 $\mathcal{O}$-, Θ- and Ω-notations

The main concepts of asymptotic analysis: 'to grow as fast as', 'to grow not faster than' and 'to grow at least as fast as' seem to be captured best by the following $\mathcal{O}$-(big oh), Θ-(big theta) and Ω-(big omega) notations, with a function $g(n)$ as argument.

$$\begin{aligned}
\mathcal{O}(g(n)) &= \{f(n) \mid \exists c : |f(n)| \leq c|g(n)|\}. \\
\Theta(g(n)) &= \{f(n) \mid \exists c_1, c_2 : c_1|g(n)| \leq |f(n)| \leq c_2|g(n)|\}. \\
\Omega(g(n)) &= \{f(n) \mid \exists c > 0 : c|g(n)| \leq |f(n)|\}.
\end{aligned}$$

$\mathcal{O}$-notation was introduced in 1892 by the German mathematician P. H. Bachmann (1837–1920). It became more widely known through the work of another German mathematician, Edmund Landau (1877–1938) and came to be known as Landau notation. However, it was actually D. E. Knuth who introduced the Ω- and Θ-notation and popularized these notations.

$\Theta(g(n)), \mathcal{O}(g(n))$ and $\Omega(g(n))$ are sets of functions. However,

$$\begin{array}{lcccccccccc}
\text{instead of} & f(n) & \in & \Theta(g(n)), & f(n) & \in & \mathcal{O}(g(n)), & f(n) & \in & \Omega(g(n)), \\
\text{we usually write} & f(n) & = & \Theta(g(n)), & f(n) & = & \mathcal{O}(g(n)), & f(n) & = & \Omega(g(n)).
\end{array}$$

There are two reasons for using this notation with the 'equals' sign. The first is tradition. $\mathcal{O}$-notation with the equals sign is well established in mathematics, especially in number theory. Moreover, we often read '=' as 'is'. For example, we read $H_n = \Theta(\lg n)$ as 'H_n is a big theta of $\lg n$'. The second reason is that in asymptotic calculations, as will be illustrated later, we often need to use this notation in the middle of an expression. Our intuition is better satisfied if we interpret the equals sign as signifying equality rather than inclusion, as discussed later.

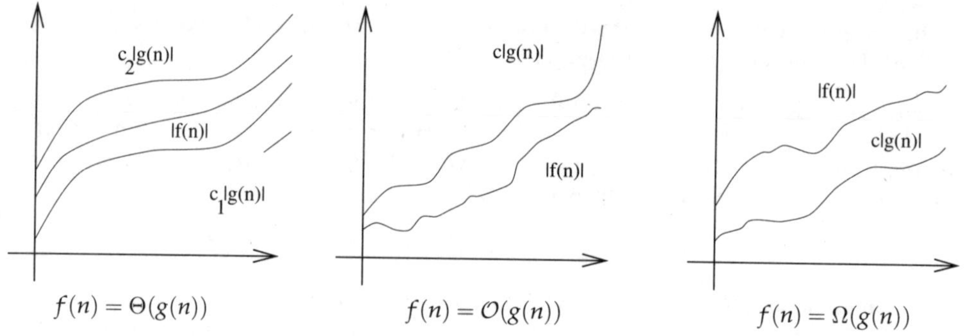

Figure 1.7 Asymptotic relation between functions

Relations between functions $f(n)$ and $g(n)$ such that $f(n) = \Theta(g(n))$, or $f(n) = \Omega(g(n))$ or $f(n) = \mathcal{O}(g(n))$ are illustrated in Figure 1.7.

Transitivity is one of the basic properties of $\mathcal{O}$-, Θ- and Ω-notation. For example,

$$f(n) = \mathcal{O}(g(n)) \text{ and } g(n) = \mathcal{O}(h(n)) \Rightarrow f(n) = \mathcal{O}(h(n)).$$

$\mathcal{O}$-, Θ- and Ω-notations are also used with various restrictions on the variables. For example, the notation

$$f(n) = \Theta(g(n)) \qquad \text{for } n \to \infty \tag{1.32}$$

means that there are $c_1, c_2 > 0$ and n_0 such that $c_1|g(n)| \leq |f(n)| \leq c_2|g(n)|$ for $n \geq n_0$.

Note that the notation $\Theta(f(n))$, and also $\mathcal{O}$- and Ω-notations are very often used as in (1.32), without writing $n \to \infty$ explicitly.

Example 1.5.6 *In order to show that $(n+1)^2 = \Theta(n^2)$, we look for $c_1, c_2 > 0$ such that*

$$c_1n^2 \leq |n^2 + 2n + 1| \leq c_2n^2, \quad \textit{for } n > 0,$$

or, after dividing by n^2, $c_1 \leq 1 + \frac{2}{n} + \frac{1}{n^2} \leq c_2$. This inequality is satisfied, for example, with $c_1 = 1$ and $c_2 = 4$.

Example 1.5.7 *To show that $\frac{n^2-1}{n+1} = \Theta(n)$, for $n \to \infty$, we need constants $c_1, c_2 > 0$ such that*

$$c_1n \leq \left|\frac{n^2-1}{n+1}\right| \leq c_2n, \quad \textit{for} \quad n \geq n_0.$$

For $n > 1$, this is equivalent to finding c_1, c_2 such that $c_1n \leq |n-1| \leq c_2n$, or, equivalently,

$$c_1 \leq |1 - \frac{1}{n}| \leq c_2.$$

This inequality is satisfied for $n > 1$ with $c_1 = \frac{1}{2}$ and $c_2 = 1$.

Example 1.5.8 *Since*

$$\sum_{i=1}^{n} i^k \leq \sum_{i=1}^{n} n^k,$$

we get

$$\sum_{i=1}^{n} i^k = \mathcal{O}(n^{k+1}).$$

Example 1.5.9 *To prove that* $4n^3 \neq \mathcal{O}(n^2)$ *for* $n \to \infty$, *let us assume that there are* c_1 *and* n_0 *such that* $4n^3 \leq c_1 n^2$, *for* $n \geq n_0$. *This would imply* $n \leq c_1 / 4$ *for all* $n \geq n_0$ *– a contradiction.*

The Θ-, $\mathcal{O}$- and Ω-notations are also used for functions with variables over reals and for convergence to a real. For example, the notation

$$f(x) = \mathcal{O}(g(x)) \qquad \text{for } x \to 0$$

means that there are constants $c, \varepsilon > 0$ such that

$$|f(x)| \leq c|g(x)| \qquad \text{for } 0 < |x| \leq \varepsilon.$$

Example 1.5.10 $x^2 = \mathcal{O}(x)$ *for* $x \to 0$.

Exercise 1.5.11 *Show that (a)* $\lfloor x \rfloor \lceil x \rceil = \Theta(x^2)$; *(b)* $(x^2+1) / (x+1) = \Theta(x)$.

Exercise 1.5.12 *Give as good as possible an* $\mathcal{O}$*-estimation for the following functions:*
(a) $(n! + 3^n)(n^2 + \log(n^3+1))$; *(b)* $(2^n + n^2)(n^3 + 5^n)$; *(c)* $n^{2^n} + n^{n^2}$.

The $\mathcal{O}$-notation has its peculiarities, which we shall now discuss in more detail. Expressions of the type $f(n) = \mathcal{O}(g(n))$, for example,

$$\frac{1}{2}n^3 - 2n^2 + 3n - 4 = \mathcal{O}(n^3),$$

should be seen as **one-way-equalities**, and should never be written with the sides reversed. Thus, we should not write $\mathcal{O}(n^3) = \frac{1}{2}n^3 - 2n^2 + 3n - 4$. This could lead to incorrect conclusions. For example, from $n = \mathcal{O}(n^3)$ and $\mathcal{O}(n^3) = n^2$ one might be inclined to conclude that $n = \mathcal{O}(n^3) = n^2$. This does not mean that $\mathcal{O}$-notation cannot be used on the left-hand side of an equation. It has only to be dealt with properly and interpreted consistently as a set of functions. One can also write $\mathcal{O}(g_1(n)) + \mathcal{O}(g_2(n))$ or $\mathcal{O}(g_1(n)) \cdot \mathcal{O}(g_2(n))$, and so on, with the usual interpretation of operations on sets. For example,

$$\mathcal{O}(g_1(n)) + \mathcal{O}(g_2(n)) = \{h(n) \,|\, h(n) = h_1(n) + h_2(n), h_1(n) = \mathcal{O}(g_1(n)), h_2(n) = \mathcal{O}(g_2(n))\}.$$

We can therefore write

$$2n + \mathcal{O}(n^2) + \mathcal{O}(n^3) = \mathcal{O}(n^3),$$

which actually means that $2n + \mathcal{O}(n^2) + \mathcal{O}(n^3) \subseteq \mathcal{O}(n^3)$.

If the $\mathcal{O}$-notation is used in some environment, it actually represents a set of functions over all variables that are 'free' in that environment. Let us illustrate this by the use of $\mathcal{O}$-notation within a sum. This often happens in the analysis of algorithms. We show the identity

$$\sum_{k=0}^{n} \left(2k^2 + \mathcal{O}(k)\right) = \frac{2}{3}n^3 + \mathcal{O}(n^2).$$

The expression $2k^2 + \mathcal{O}(k)$ represents, in this context, a set of functions of the form $2k^2 + f(k,n)$, for which there is a constant c such that $f(n,k) \leq ck$, for $0 \leq k \leq n$. Therefore

$$\sum_{k=0}^{n} 2k^2 + f(k,n) \leq 2\sum_{k=0}^{n} k^2 + c\sum_{k=0}^{n} k = 2(\frac{n^3}{3} + \frac{n^2}{2} + \frac{n}{6}) + c\frac{n^2}{2} + c\frac{n}{2} \quad (1.33)$$

$$= \frac{2}{3}n^3 + (1 + \frac{c}{2})n^2 + (\frac{1}{3} + \frac{c}{2})n \quad (1.34)$$

$$\leq \frac{2}{3}n^3 + c_1 n^2, \text{ for } c_1 = c + 2. \quad (1.35)$$

In complexity analysis it often happens that estimations depend on more than one parameter. For example, the complexity of a graph algorithm may depend on the number of nodes and also on the number of edges. To deal with such cases, the $\mathcal{O}$-, Θ- and Ω-notations are generalized in a natural way. For example,

$$\mathcal{O}(f(m,n)) = \{g(m,n) \mid \exists c, n_0 : |f(m,n)| \leq c|g(m,n)|, \text{ for all } n \geq n_0, m \geq n_0\}.$$

Notation $\mathcal{O}$ is sometimes used also to relate functions $f, g : \Gamma \to \mathbf{N}$, where Γ is an arbitrary infinite set. $f(x) = \mathcal{O}(g(x))$ then means that there exists a constant c such that $f(x) \leq cg(x)$ for almost all $x \in \Gamma$.

Exercise 1.5.13 *Show that (a)* $n^a = \mathcal{O}(n^b)$ *if* $0 \leq a \leq b$; *(b)* $a^n = \mathcal{O}(b^n)$ *if* $1 \leq a \leq b$; *(c)* $n^a = \mathcal{O}(b^n)$, *for any* $a > 0, b > 1$.

Exercise 1.5.14 *Show that (a)* $n!$ *is not* $\mathcal{O}(2^n)$; *(b)* n^n *is not* $\mathcal{O}(n!)$.

Exercise 1.5.15 *Show that* $f(n) = \mathcal{O}(n^k)$ *for some* k *if and only if* $f(n) \leq kn^k$ *for some* $k > 0$.

Remark 1.5.16 One of the main uses of Θ-, Ω- and $\mathcal{O}$-notations is in the computational analysis of algorithms. For example, in the case of the running time $T(n)$ of an algorithm the notation $T(n) = \Theta(f(n))$ means that $f(n)$ is an asymptotically tight bound; notation $T(n) = \Omega(f(n))$ means that $f(n)$ is an asymptotic lower bound; and, finally, notation $T(n) = \mathcal{O}(f(n))$ means that $f(n)$ is an asymptotic upper bound.

1.5.3 Relations between Asymptotic Notations

The following relations between $\mathcal{O}$-, Θ- and Ω-notations follow directly from the basic definition:

$$f(n) = \mathcal{O}(g(n)) \Leftrightarrow g(n) = \Omega(f(n)),$$
$$f(n) = \Theta(g(n)) \Leftrightarrow f(n) = \mathcal{O}(g(n)) \text{ and } f(n) = \Omega(g(n)).$$

In addition,

$$f(n) = \Theta(g(n)) \Leftrightarrow f(n) \asymp g(n).$$

The following 'little oh' notation,

$$f(n) = o(g(n)) \Leftrightarrow |f(n)| \leq \varepsilon|g(n)| \text{ for all } \varepsilon > 0, n > n_0(\varepsilon),$$

and its inverse notation 'little omega',

$$f(n) = \omega(g(n)) \Leftrightarrow g(n) = o(f(n)),$$

are also sometimes used. Between the 'little oh' and $\asymp$ notation, there is the relation

$$f(n) \asymp g(n) \Leftrightarrow f(n) = g(n) + o(g(n)).$$

Exercise 1.5.17 *Show that (a) $x^3 = o(x^4)$; (b) $x \lg x = o(x^2)$; (c) $x = o(x^{1+\varepsilon})$ if $\varepsilon > 0$; (d) $x^2 = o(2^x)$.*

Given two functions $f(n)$ and $g(n)$, it may not be obvious which of the asymptotic relations holds between them. The following theorem contains a useful sufficient condition for determining that.

Theorem 1.5.18 *If $f(n), g(n) > 0$ for all $n > 0$, then*

1. $\lim_{n\to\infty} \frac{f(n)}{g(n)} = a \neq 0 \quad \Rightarrow \quad f(n) = \Theta(g(n))$;

2. $\lim_{n\to\infty} \frac{f(n)}{g(n)} = 0 \quad \Rightarrow \quad f(n) = \mathcal{O}(g(n)), f(n) = o(g(n))$ *but not* $f(n) = \Theta(g(n))$;

3. $\lim_{n\to\infty} \frac{f(n)}{g(n)} = \infty \quad \Rightarrow \quad g(n) = \mathcal{O}(f(n))$ *and not* $g(n) = \Theta(f(n))$.

Proof: Let $\lim_{n\to\infty} \frac{f(n)}{g(n)} = a \neq 0$. Then there are $\varepsilon \geq 0$ and an integer n_0 such that for all $n > n_0$

$$\left| \frac{f(n)}{g(n)} - a \right| \leq \varepsilon.$$

This implies $(a-\varepsilon)g(n) \leq f(n) \leq (a+\varepsilon)g(n)$. Therefore $f(n) = \Theta(g(n))$. Proofs of (2) and (3) are left as exercises.

Example 1.5.19 *For $a, b > 1$, $\lim_{n\to\infty} \frac{(\log n)^a}{n^b} = 0$, and therefore $(\log n)^a = \mathcal{O}(n^b)$.*

Exercise 1.5.20 *Fill out the following table with a cross whenever the pair of functions in that row is in the relation $A = \psi(B)$, where ψ is the symbol shown by the column head. In the table we use integer constants $k, c \geq 1$ and $\varepsilon > 0$.*

A	B	$\mathcal{O}$	o	Ω	ω	Θ
$\ln^k n$	n^ε					
n^k	c^n					
$n \lg n$	$n^{\cos n}$					
2^n	$3^{\frac{3}{2}}$					
$n^{\log m}$	$m^{\log n}$					
$\lg n!$	$\lg n^n$					

1.5.4 Manipulations with $\mathcal{O}$-notation

There are several simple rules regarding how to manipulate $\mathcal{O}$-expressions, which follow easily from the basic definition.

$$
\begin{aligned}
n^m &= \mathcal{O}(n^{m'}) \quad \text{if } m \le m'; && (1.36)\\
f(n) &= \mathcal{O}(f(n)); && (1.37)\\
c\mathcal{O}(f(n)) &= \mathcal{O}(cf(n)) = \mathcal{O}(f(n)); && (1.38)\\
\mathcal{O}(\mathcal{O}(f(n))) &= \mathcal{O}(f(n)); && (1.39)\\
\mathcal{O}(f(n)) + \mathcal{O}(g(n)) &= \mathcal{O}(\max\{|f(n)|, |g(n)|\}); && (1.40)\\
\mathcal{O}(f(n))\mathcal{O}(g(n)) &= \mathcal{O}(f(n)g(n)); && (1.41)\\
\mathcal{O}(f(n)g(n)) &= f(n)\mathcal{O}(g(n)). && (1.42)
\end{aligned}
$$

For example, from (1.36), (1.38) and (1.40) we get for a fixed m

$$\sum_{i=0}^{m} a_i n^{m-i} = \sum_{i=0}^{m} \mathcal{O}(n^m) = \mathcal{O}(mn^m) = \mathcal{O}(n^m).$$

The rule (1.40) is often used in the analysis of algorithms to get the overall $\mathcal{O}$-estimation for the time complexity of an algorithm from estimations of the complexity of its parts.

Manipulations with power series aimed at getting better and better estimations also play an important role in complexity analysis. For example, if the power series

$$S(z) = \sum_{n \ge 0} a_n z^n$$

converges absolutely for a complex number z_0, then $S(z) = \mathcal{O}(1)$ for all $|z| \le |z_0|$, because

$$|S(z)| \le \sum_{n \ge 0} |a_n||z|^n \le \sum_{n \ge 0} |a_n||z_0|^n = c < \infty$$

for a constant c. This implies that we can truncate the power series after each term and estimate the remainder with $\mathcal{O}$ as follows:

$$
\begin{aligned}
S(z) &= a_0 + \mathcal{O}(z);\\
S(z) &= a_0 + a_1 z + \mathcal{O}(z^2);\\
&\vdots\\
S(z) &= \textstyle\sum_{i=0}^{k} a_i z^i + \mathcal{O}(z^{k+1}).
\end{aligned}
$$

The following power series are of special interest in asymptotic analysis:

$$
\begin{aligned}
e^z &= 1 + z + \frac{z^2}{2!} + \frac{z^3}{3!} + \frac{z^4}{4!} + \mathcal{O}(z^5); && (1.43)\\
\ln(1+z) &= z - \frac{z^2}{2} + \frac{z^3}{3} - \frac{z^4}{4} + \mathcal{O}(z^5). && (1.44)
\end{aligned}
$$

With the truncation method one can use these power series to show the correctness of the following rules:

$$
\begin{aligned}
\ln(1 + \mathcal{O}(f(n))) &= \mathcal{O}(f(n)) && \text{if } f(n) \prec 1; && (1.45)\\
e^{\mathcal{O}(f(n))} &= 1 + \mathcal{O}(f(n)) && \text{if } f(n) = \mathcal{O}(1); && (1.46)\\
(1 + \mathcal{O}(f(n)))^{\mathcal{O}(g(n))} &= 1 + \mathcal{O}(f(n)g(n)) && \text{if } f(n) \prec 1, f(n)g(n) = \mathcal{O}(1). && (1.47)
\end{aligned}
$$

$f(n) = \mathcal{O}(g(n))$	$\Leftrightarrow$	$\exists c \in \mathbf{N} \overset{\infty}{\underset{n}{\forall}} f(n) \leq cg(n)$
$f(n) = \Omega(g(n))$	$\Leftrightarrow$	$g(n) = \mathcal{O}(f(n))$
	$\Leftrightarrow$	$\exists c \in \mathbf{N} \overset{\infty}{\underset{n}{\forall}} f(n) \geq \frac{1}{c}g(n)$
$f(n) = o(g(n))$	$\Leftrightarrow$	$\forall c \in \mathbf{N} \overset{\infty}{\underset{n}{\forall}} f(n) \leq \frac{1}{c}g(n)$
$f(n) = \omega(g(n))$	$\Leftrightarrow$	$g(n) = o(f(n))$
	$\Leftrightarrow$	$\forall c \in \mathbf{N} \overset{\infty}{\underset{n}{\forall}} f(n) \geq cg(n)$
$f(n) = \Theta(g(n))$	$\Leftrightarrow$	$f(n) = \mathcal{O}(g(n))$ and $f(n) = \Omega(g(n))$

Table 1.3 Summary of asymptotic notations

Proof of (1.45): Since $f(n) \prec 1$, whenever $g(n) \in \mathcal{O}(f(n))$, there are constants C, c such that $|g(n)| \leq c|f(n)| \leq C < 1$ for $n \geq n_0$. Hence

$$\ln(1+g(n)) = g(n)\left(1 - \frac{1}{2}g(n) + \frac{1}{3}g^2(n) - \cdots\right) \tag{1.48}$$

$$\leq g(n)\left(1 + \frac{1}{2}C + \frac{1}{3}C^2 + \cdots\right) \leq (\frac{1}{1-C})g(n) = \mathcal{O}(f(n)); \tag{1.49}$$

and therefore $\ln(1 + \mathcal{O}(f(n))) = \mathcal{O}(f(n))$. In a similar way we can prove (1.46). It also holds that

$$\begin{aligned}(1+\mathcal{O}(f(n)))^{\mathcal{O}(g(n))} &= e^{\mathcal{O}(g(n))\ln(1+\mathcal{O}(f(n)))} &= e^{\mathcal{O}(g(n))\mathcal{O}(f(n))} \\ &= e^{\mathcal{O}(f(n)g(n))} &= 1 + \mathcal{O}(f(n)g(n)).\end{aligned}$$

□

Exercise 1.5.21 *Determine $\mathcal{O}(f(n))$ for (a) $f(n) = (1+n^2)^{\frac{1}{n^3}}$; (b) $f(n) = e^{\frac{1}{\sqrt{n}}}$.*

1.5.5 Asymptotic Notation – Summary

In Table 1.3 we present simpler definitions for the $\mathcal{O}$-, Θ- and Ω-notations which are often used and are mostly sufficient. We also summarize definitions for the o- and ω-notations. The notation $\overset{\infty}{\underset{n}{\forall}}$ used in the table means 'for almost all n'; $f(n)$ and $g(n)$ are nonnegative functions from integers to integers.

In the following we say that an algorithm is a **polynomial time algorithm** if it runs in time $\mathcal{O}(n^k)$ for some constant k on a typical sequential computer. Such an algorithm will also be called **feasible,** or even efficient. An algorithmic problem is called **feasible** or **tractable** if it can be solved by an algorithm running in polynomial time. Otherwise it is called **unfeasible** or **intractable**. This will be discussed more in Section 1.10, and especially in Chapters 4 and 5.

1.6 Asymptotics and Recurrences

Two basic problems concerning the use of asymptotics in solving recurrences and ways of solving them will now be considered. First, we show a method that uses asymptotics to find solutions of recurrences. Second, we show how to solve recurrences some terms of which are known only asymptotically. This is the case we find most frequently in practice when attempting to analyse the efficiency of complex recursive systems.

1.6.1 Bootstrapping

This is a quite general method for finding better and better approximations for terms of sequences defined by recurrences. The basic idea is simple. One first guesses an approximation (after computing some of the first values), then substitutes this approximation in the recurrence to obtain a better approximation. The process terminates when it does not seem to provide an improvement any more.

Example 1.6.1 *Find, for $n \to \infty$, an approximation of the coefficients g_n of the generating function*

$$G(z) = exp(\sum_{k=1}^{\infty} \frac{z^k}{k^2}) = \sum_{n=0}^{\infty} g_n z^n. \tag{1.50}$$

Differentiation of $G(z)$, with respect to z, yields

$$G'(z) = \sum_{n=0}^{\infty} n g_n z^{n-1} = \left(\sum_{k=1}^{\infty} \frac{z^{k-1}}{k} \right) G(z);$$

if we compare the coefficients of z^{n-1} on both sides of the equation, we get

$$n g_n = \sum_{k=0}^{n-1} \frac{g_k}{n-k}. \tag{1.51}$$

It is easy to see from (1.50) that $g_0 = 1$, and from (1.51) that $g_1 = 1$. By induction, we can then prove that $0 < g_n \leq 1$ for all n. We can therefore start with the approximation $g_n = \mathcal{O}(1)$. From (1.51) we get

$$n g_n = \sum_{k=0}^{n-1} \frac{\mathcal{O}(1)}{n-k} = \left(\sum_{k=0}^{n-1} \frac{1}{n-k} \right) \mathcal{O}(1) = H_n \mathcal{O}(1) = \mathcal{O}(\log n),$$

so we have the second approximation:

$$g_n = \mathcal{O}\left(\frac{\log n}{n} \right) \qquad \text{for } n > 1.$$

After the next step of bootstrapping,

$$\begin{aligned} ng_n &= \frac{1}{n}+\sum_{0<k<n}\frac{\mathcal{O}((\log k)/k)}{n-k} &&= \frac{1}{n}+\sum_{0<k<n}\frac{\mathcal{O}(\log n)}{k(n-k)} \\ &= \frac{1}{n}+\sum_{0<k<n}\left(\frac{1}{k}+\frac{1}{n-k}\right)\frac{\mathcal{O}(\log n)}{n} &&= \frac{1}{n}+\frac{2}{n}H_{n-1}\mathcal{O}(\log n) \\ &= \frac{1}{n}\mathcal{O}(\log n)\mathcal{O}(\log n) &&= \frac{1}{n}\mathcal{O}(\log n)^2, \end{aligned}$$

we get the third approximation:

$$g_n = \mathcal{O}\left(\frac{\log n}{n}\right)^2.$$

We could continue with bootstrapping, but the next step does not lead to an improvement.

Exercise 1.6.2 *Use bootstrapping to solve the recurrence* $u_0 = 1$, $u_n = n + u_{n-1}$, $n \geq 1$.

1.6.2 Analysis of Divide-and-conquer Algorithms

We now present a general method for solving recurrences arising from analysis of algorithms and systems that are designed using the divide-and-conquer method. They are recurrences

$$T(n) = aT(\frac{n}{c}) + f(n), \tag{1.52}$$

where for $f(n)$ only an asymptotic estimation is known. The following theorem shows how to determine $T(n)$ for most of the cases.

Theorem 1.6.3 *Let* $T(n) = aT(\frac{n}{c}) + f(n)$ *for all sufficiently large n and constants* $a \geq 1$, $c > 1$. *Let* $\frac{n}{c}$ *mean here either* $\lfloor \frac{n}{c} \rfloor$ *or* $\lceil \frac{n}{c} \rceil$. *Then*

1. *If* $f(n) = \mathcal{O}(n^{(\log_c a)-\varepsilon})$, $\varepsilon > 0$, *then* $T(n) = \Theta(n^{\log_c a})$;
2. *If* $f(n) = \Theta(n^{\log_c a})$, *then* $T(n) = \Theta(n^{\log_c a}\log n)$;
3. *If* $f(n) = \Omega(n^{(\log_c a)+\varepsilon})$, $\varepsilon > 0$, $af(\frac{n}{c}) \leq bf(n)$ *for almost all n and some* $b > 1$, *then* $T(n) = \Theta(f(n))$.

The proof of this 'master theorem' for asymptotic analysis is very technical, and can be found in Cormen, Leiserson and Rivest (1990), pages 62–72. We present here only some remarks concerning the theorem and its applications.

1. It is important to see that one does not have to know $f(n)$ exactly in order to be able to determine $T(n)$ asymptotically exactly. For more complex systems an exact determination of $f(n)$ is practically impossible anyway.

2. From the asymptotic point of view, $T(n)$ equals the maximum of $\Theta(f(n))$ and $\Theta(n^{\log_c a})$, unless both terms are equal. In this case $T(n) = \Theta(n^{\log_c a}\log n)$.

3. In order to apply Case 1, it is necessary that $f(n)$ be not only asymptotically smaller than $n^{\log_c a}$; but smaller by a polynomial factor – this is captured by the '$-\varepsilon$' in the exponent. Similarly, in Case 3, $f(n)$ must be larger by a polynomial factor, captured by '$+\varepsilon$' in the exponent.

4. Note that the theorem does not deal with all possible cases of $f(n)$.

Example 1.6.4 *Consider the recurrence* $T(n) = T(\frac{2n}{3}) + 1$. *We have* $a = 1, c = \frac{3}{2}, n^{\log_c a} = n^0 = 1$. *Therefore Case 2 applies, and yields* $T(n) = \Theta(\log n)$.

Example 1.6.5 *Consider the recurrence* $T(n) = 3T(\frac{n}{4}) + n\log n$. *We have* $a = 3$, $c = 4$, $n^{\log_c a} = \mathcal{O}(n^{0.793})$, *and therefore* $f(n) = \Omega(n^{\log_4 3+\varepsilon})$ *for* $\varepsilon = 0.2$. *Moreover,* $af(\frac{n}{c}) = 3\frac{n}{4}\log(\frac{n}{4}) \leq \frac{3}{4}n\log n$. *Therefore, Case 3 of the theorem applies, and* $T(n) = \Theta(n\log n)$.

Example 1.6.6 (Integer multiplication) *Consider the following divide-and-conquer algorithm for an integer multiplication. Let x and y be two n-bit integers, where n is even. Then* $x = x_1 2^{\frac{n}{2}} + x_2$, $y = y_1 2^{\frac{n}{2}} + y_2$ *where* x_1, x_2, y_1, y_2 *are* $\frac{n}{2}$*-bit integers. Then*

$$xy = x_1y_1 2^n + (x_1y_2 + x_2y_1)2^{\frac{n}{2}} + x_2y_2.$$

This seems to mean that in order to compute $x \cdot y$ *one needs to perform four multiplications of* $\frac{n}{2}$*-bit integers, two additions and two shifts. There is, however, another method for computing* x_1y_1, $x_1y_2 + x_2y_1$ *and* x_2y_2. *We first compute* x_1y_1, x_2y_2, *which requires three multiplications, and then*

$$z_1 = (x_1 + x_2)(y_1 + y_2) = x_1y_1 + x_1y_2 + x_2y_1 + x_2y_2,$$

which requires the third multiplication. Finally, we compute $z_1 - x_1y_1 - x_2y_2 = x_1y_2 + x_2y_1$, *which requires only two subtractions.*

This means that the problem of multiplication of two n-bit integers can be reduced to the problem of three multiplications of $\frac{n}{2}$-bit integers and some additions, subtractions and shifts – which requires an amount of time proportional to n. The method can easily be adjusted for the case where n is odd. Since in this algorithm $a = 3$, $c = 2$, we have Case 1 of Theorem 1.6.3. The algorithm therefore requires time $\Theta(n^{\log \frac{3}{2}}) = \Theta(n^{1.73})$.

Example 1.6.7 (MERGESORT) *Concerning the analysis of the number of comparisons of MERGESORT, Theorem 1.6.3 yields, on the basis of the recurrence (1.14),* $T(n) = \Theta(n\lg n)$.

Exercise 1.6.8 *Find asymptotic solutions for the following recurrences: (a)* $T(n) = 7T(\frac{n}{3}) + n^2$; *(b)* $T(n) = 7T(\frac{n}{2}) + n^2$; *(c)* $T(n) = 2T(\frac{n}{4}) + \sqrt{n}$.

1.7 Primes and Congruences

Primes and congruences induced by the modulo operation on integers have been playing an important role for more than two thousand years in perhaps the oldest mature science – number theory. Nowadays they are the key concepts and tools in many theoretically advanced and also practically important areas of computing, especially randomized computations, secure communications, and the analysis of algorithms.

We start with an introduction and analysis of perhaps the oldest algorithm that still plays an important role in modern computing and its foundations.

1.7.1 Euclid's Algorithm

If n, m are integers, then the **quotient of** n **divided by** m is $\lfloor n / m \rfloor$. For the **remainder** the notation '$n \bmod m$' is used – m is called the **modulus**. This motivation lies in the background of the following definition, in which n and m are arbitrary integers:

$$n \bmod m = \begin{cases} n - m\lfloor n / m \rfloor, & \text{for } m \neq 0; \\ 0, & \text{otherwise.} \end{cases}$$

For example,

$$\begin{array}{ll} 7 \bmod 5 = 2, & 7 \bmod -5 = -3; \\ -7 \bmod 5 = 3, & -7 \bmod -5 = -2. \end{array}$$

The basic concepts of divisibility are closely related. We say that an integer m divides an integer n (notation $m \backslash n$) if n / m is an integer; that is:

$$m \backslash n \Leftrightarrow (n \bmod m = 0). \tag{1.53}$$

A similar relation is 'n is a multiple of m'. Related concepts are those of the **greatest common divisor** of integers m and n – $\gcd(m,n)$ – and the **least common multiple** of m and n – $\mathrm{lcm}(m,n)$ – which are defined thus for $m+n>0$, $m \geq 0$, $n \geq 0$:

$$\gcd(m,n) = \max\{k \,|\, k \backslash m \text{ and } k \backslash n\}; \tag{1.54}$$

$$\mathrm{lcm}(m,n) = \min\{k \,|\, k > 0, m \backslash k \text{ and } n \backslash k\}. \tag{1.55}$$

To compute $\gcd(m,n)$, $0 \leq m < n$, we can use the following, more than 2,300-year-old algorithm, a recurrence.

Algorithm 1.7.1 (Euclid's algorithm) For $0 \leq m < n$,

$$\begin{aligned} \gcd(0,n) &= n; \\ \gcd(m,n) &= \gcd(n \bmod m, m), \quad \text{for } m > 0. \end{aligned}$$

For example, $\gcd(27,36) = \gcd(9,27) = \gcd(0,9) = 9$; $\gcd(214,352) = \gcd(138,214) = \gcd(76,138) = \gcd(62,76) = \gcd(14,62) = \gcd(6,14) = \gcd(2,6) = \gcd(0,3) = 3$.

Euclid's algorithm can also be used to compute, given $m \leq n$, integers n' and m' such that

$$m'm + n'n = \gcd(m,n),$$

and this is one of its most important applications. Indeed, if $m = 0$, then $m' = 0$ and $n' = 1$ will do. Otherwise, take $r = n \bmod m$, and compute recursively r'', m'' such that $r''r + m''m = \gcd(r,m)$. Since $r = n - \lfloor n / m \rfloor m$ and $\gcd(r,m) = \gcd(m,n)$, we get

$$r''(n - \lfloor n / m \rfloor m) + m''m = \gcd(m,n) = (m'' - r''\lfloor n / m \rfloor)m + r''n.$$

If Euclid's algorithm is used, given m, n, to determine $\gcd(m,n)$ and also integers m' and n' such that $m'm + n'n = \gcd(m,n)$, we speak of the **extended Euclid's algorithm**

Example 1.7.2 *For* $m = 57, n = 237$ *we have* $\gcd(57,237) = \gcd(9,57) = \gcd(3,9) = 3$. *Thus*

$$\begin{aligned} 237 &= 4 \cdot 57 + 9, \\ 57 &= 6 \cdot 9 + 3, \end{aligned}$$

and therefore

$$3 = 57 - 6 \cdot 9 = 57 - 6 \cdot (237 - 4 \cdot 57) = 25 \cdot 57 - 6 \cdot 237.$$

If $\gcd(m,n) = 1$, we say that the numbers n and m are **relatively prime** – notation $n \perp m$. The above result therefore implies that if m,n are relatively prime, then we can find, using Euclid's algorithm, an integer denoted by $m^{-1} \bmod n$, called the **multiplicative inverse** of m modulo n, such that

$$m(m^{-1} \bmod n) \equiv 1 \pmod{n}$$

Exercise 1.7.3 *Compute a,b such that $ax + by = \gcd(x,y)$ for the following pairs x,y: (a) $(34,51)$; (b) $(315,53)$; (c) $(17,71)$.*

Exercise 1.7.4 *Compute (a) $17^{-1} \bmod 13$; (b) $7^{-1} \bmod 19$; (c) $37^{-1} \bmod 97$.*

Analysis of Euclid's algorithm

Let us now turn to the complexity analysis of Euclid's algorithm. In spite of the fact that we have presented a variety of methods for complexity analysis, they are far from covering all cases. Complexity analysis of many algorithms requires a specific approach. Euclid's algorithm is one of them.

The basic recurrence has the form, for $0 < m \leq n$,

$$\gcd(m,n) = \gcd(n \bmod m, m).$$

This means that after the first recursive step the new arguments are (n_1, m), with $n_1 = n \bmod m$, and after the second step the arguments are (m_1, n_1), with $m_1 = m \bmod n_1$. Since $a \bmod b < \frac{a}{2}$ for any $0 < b < a$ (see Exercise 49 at the end of the chapter), we have $m_1 \leq \frac{m}{2}, n_1 \leq \frac{n}{2}$. This means that after two recursion steps of Euclid's algorithm both arguments have at most half their original value. Hence $T(n) = \mathcal{O}(\lg n)$ for the number of steps of Euclid's algorithm if n is the largest argument.

This analysis was made more precise by E. Lucas (1884) and Lamé (1884) in what was perhaps the first deep analysis of algorithms.

It is easy to see that if F_n is the nth Fibonacci number, then after the first recursive step with arguments (F_n, F_{n-1}) we get arguments (F_{n-1}, F_{n-2}). This implies that for arguments (F_n, F_{n-1}) Euclid's algorithm performs $n-2$ recursive steps.

Even deeper relations between Euclid's algorithm and Fibonacci numbers were established. They are summarized in the following theorem. The first part of the theorem is easy to prove, by induction using the fact that if $m \geq F_{k+1}, n \bmod m \geq F_k$, then $n \geq m + (n \bmod m) \geq F_{k+1} + F_k = F_{k+2}$. The second part of theorem follows from the first part.

Theorem 1.7.5 *(1) If $n > m \geq 0$ and the application of Euclid's algorithm to arguments n,m results in k recursive steps, then $n \geq F_{k+2}, m \geq F_{k+1}$.*

(2) If $n > m \geq 0, m < F_{k+1}$, then application of Euclid's algorithm to the arguments n,m requires fewer than k recursive steps.

Remark 1.7.6 It is natural to ask whether Euclid's algorithm is the fastest way to compute the greatest common divisor. This problem was open till 1989, and is discussed in more detail in Section 4.2.4.

1.7.2 Primes

A positive integer $p > 1$ is called **prime** if it has just two divisors, 1 and p; otherwise it is called **composite**. The first 25 primes are as follows:

$$2,3,5,7,11,13,17,19,23,29,31,37,41,43,47,53,59,61,67,71,73,79,83,89,97.$$

Primes play a central role among integers and also in computing. This will be demonstrated especially in the chapter on cryptography. The following, easily demonstrable theorem is the first reason for this.

Theorem 1.7.7 (Fundamental theorem of arithmetic) *Each integer n has a unique prime decomposition of the form $n = \prod_{i=1}^{k} p_i^{e_i}$, where $p_i < p_{i+1}, i = 1, \ldots, k-1$, are primes and e_i are integers.*

There exist infinitely many primes. This can easily be deduced from the observation that if we take primes $p_1, \ldots, p_k$, none of them divides $p_1 \cdot p_2 \cdot \ldots \cdot p_k + 1$. There are even infinitely many primes of special forms. For example,

Theorem 1.7.8 *There exist infinitely many primes of the form $4k+3$.*

Proof: Suppose there exist only finitely many primes $p_1, p_2, \ldots, p_s$ of the form $4k+3$, that is, $p_i \bmod 4 = 3, 1 \leq i \leq s$. Then take $N = 4 \cdot p_1 \cdot p_2 \cdot \ldots \cdot p_s - 1$. Clearly, $N \bmod 4 = 3$. Since $N > p_i, 1 \leq i \leq s$, N cannot be a prime of the form $4k+3$, and cannot be divided by a prime of such a form. Moreover, since N is odd, N is also not divisible by a number of the type $4k+2$ or $4k$. Hence N must be a product of primes of the type $4k+1$. However, this too is impossible. Indeed, $(4k+1)(4l+1) = 4(kl+k+l)+1$; for any integers k, l, therefore any product of primes of the form $4k+1$ is again a number of such a form – but N is of the form $4k+3$. In this way we have ruled out all possibilities for N, and therefore our assumption, that the number of primes of the form $4k+3$ is finite, must be wrong. □

The discovery of as large primes as possible is an old problem. All primes up to 10^7 had already been computed by 1909. The largest discovered prime at the time this book went to press, due to D. Slowinski and Gage in 1996: using computer Cray T94 is $2^{1257787} - 1$ and has 378,632 digits.[6]

Another important question is how many primes there are among the first n positive integers; for this number the notation $\pi(n)$ is used. The basic estimation $\pi(n) = \Theta(\frac{n}{\ln n})$ was guessed already by Gauss[7] at the age of 15. Better estimations are

$$\frac{n}{\ln n} < \pi(n) \leq \frac{5}{4}\frac{n}{\ln n} \qquad \text{for } n \geq 114$$

[6]Finding as large primes as possible is an old problem, and still a great challenge for both scientists and technology. The first recorded method is the 'sieve method' of Eratosthenes of Cyrene (284–202 BC). Fibonacci (C. 1200) improved the method by observing that sieving can be stopped when the square root of the number to be tested is reached. This was the fastest general method up to 1974, when R. S. Lehman showed that primality testing of an integer n can be done in $\mathcal{O}(n^{\frac{1}{3}})$ time.

The previous 'world records' were $2^{859433} - 1$ (1994) and $2^{756,839} - 1$ (1992), both due to D. Slowinski. The largest prime from the pre-computer era was $2^{127} - 1$ (1876). This record lasted for 76 years. Next world records were from 1952: $2^{521} - 1, 2^{607} - 1, 2^{1,279} - 1, 2^{2,203} - 1, 2^{2,281} - 1$. All the known very large primes have the form $2^p - 1$, where p is a prime; they are called 'Mersenne primes'. It is certainly a challenge to find new, very large Mersenne primes, especially because all numbers smaller than $2^{350,000}$ and also in the range $2^{430,000} - 2^{520,000}$ have already been checked for primality, and it is not known whether there are infinitely many Mersenne primes.

[7]Karl Friedrich Gauss (1752–1833), German mathematician, physicist and astronomer considered to be the greatest mathematician of his time, made fundamental contributions in algebra, number theory, complex variables, differential geometry, approximation theory, calculation of orbits of planets and comets, electro- and geomagnetism. Gauss developed foundations for the absolute metric system, and with W. Weber invented the electrical telegraph.

and

$$\pi(n) = \frac{n}{\ln n} + \frac{n}{(\ln n)^2} + \frac{2!n}{(\ln n)^3} + \frac{3!n}{(\ln n)^4} + \frac{4!n}{(\ln n)^5} + \Theta\left(\frac{n}{(\ln n)^6}\right). \tag{1.56}$$

Additional information about the distribution of primes is given in the following theorem in which ϕ is the **Euler phi function.** $\phi(n)$ is the number of positive integers smaller than n that are relatively prime to n – for example, $\phi(p) = p-1$ and $\phi(pq) = (p-1)(q-1)$ if p, q are primes.

Theorem 1.7.9 (Prime number theorem)[8] *If* $\gcd(b,c) = 1$, *then for the number* $\pi_{b,c}(n)$ *of primes of the form* $bk+c$ *we have*

$$\pi_{b,c}(n) \sim \frac{1}{\phi(b)} \frac{n}{\ln n}.$$

The following table shows how good the estimation $\pi(n) = n / \ln n$ is.

n	10^4	10^7	10^{10}
$\pi(n)$	1,229	664,579	455,052,511
$n / \ln n$	1,089	621,118	434,782,650
$\pi(n) / (n / \ln n)$	1.128	1.070	1.046

The largest computed value of $\pi(x)$ is $\pi(10^{18}) = 24{,}739{,}954{,}287{,}740{,}860$, by Deliglise and Rivat in 1994.

We deal with the problem of how to determine whether a given integer is a prime in Section 5.6.2 and with the problem of finding large primes in Section 8.3.4. The importance of primes in cryptography is due to the fact that we can find large primes efficiently, but are not able to factorize large products of primes efficiently. Moreover, some important computations can be done in polynomial time if an argument is prime, but seem to be unfeasible if the argument is an arbitrary integer.

Exercise 1.7.10 *Show that if* n *is composite, then so is* $2^n - 1$.

Exercise 1.7.11** *Show that there exist infinitely many primes of the type* $6k+5$.

1.7.3 Congruence Arithmetic

The modulo operation and the corresponding congruence relation

$$a \equiv b \pmod{m} \Leftrightarrow a \bmod m = b \bmod m \tag{1.57}$$

defined for arbitrary integers a, b and $m > 0$, play an important role in producing (pseudo-)randomness and in randomized computations and communications. We read '$a \equiv b \pmod{m}$' as 'a **is congruent to** b **modulo** m'. From (1.57) we also get that $a \equiv b \pmod{m}$ if and only if $a - b$ is a multiple of m. This congruence defines an equivalence relation on $\mathbf{Z}$, and its equivalence classes are called **residue classes modulo** n. $\mathbf{Z}_n$ is used to denote the set of all such residue classes, and $\mathbf{Z}_n^*$ its subset, consisting of those classes elements of which are relatively prime to n.

[8]The term 'prime number theorem' is also used for the Gauss estimation for $\pi(n)$ or for the estimation (1.56).

The following properties of congruence can be verified using the definition (1.57):

$$a \equiv b \text{ and } c \equiv d \pmod{m} \;\Rightarrow\; a+c \equiv b+d \pmod{m}; \tag{1.58}$$

$$a \equiv b \text{ and } c \equiv d \pmod{m} \;\Rightarrow\; a-c \equiv b-d \pmod{m}; \tag{1.59}$$

$$a \equiv b \text{ and } c \equiv d \pmod{m} \;\Rightarrow\; ac \equiv bd \pmod{m}; \tag{1.60}$$

$$ad \equiv bd \pmod{m} \;\Leftrightarrow\; a \equiv b \pmod{m} \text{ for } d \perp m; \tag{1.61}$$

$$ad \equiv bd \pmod{md} \;\Leftrightarrow\; a \equiv b \pmod{m} \text{ for } d \neq 0; \tag{1.62}$$

$$a \equiv b \pmod{mn} \;\Leftrightarrow\; a \equiv b \pmod{m} \text{ and } a \equiv b \pmod{n} \text{if } m \perp n. \tag{1.63}$$

The property (1.63) can be used to simplify the computation of congruences as follows. If $\prod_{i=1}^{k} p_i^{e_i}$ is the prime decomposition of m, then

$$a \equiv b \pmod{m} \Leftrightarrow a \equiv b \pmod{p_i^{e_i}} \text{ for } 1 \leq i \leq k. \tag{1.64}$$

Congruences modulo powers of primes are therefore building blocks for all congruences modulo integers.

Exercise 1.7.12 *Show that* $((a \bmod n)(b \bmod n) \bmod n) = ab \bmod n$ *for any integers a, b, n.*

Exercise 1.7.13 *Show that* $2^{xy^2} \bmod (2^{xy} - x) = x^y$.

One of the main uses of the modulo operation in randomization is related to the fact that solving 'nonlinear' congruence equations is in general a computationally intractable task.

By contrast, the linear congruence equations

$$cx \equiv d \,(\text{mod } m)$$

are easy to deal with. Indeed, we have the following theorem.

Theorem 1.7.14 *A linear congruence* $cx \equiv d\,(\text{mod } m)$ *has a solution if and only if d is a multiple of* $\gcd(c,m)$. *In this case, the equation has exactly* $k = \gcd(c,m)$ *distinct integer solutions*

$$x_0\frac{d}{k}, x_0\frac{d}{k} + \frac{m}{k}, \ldots, x_0\frac{d}{k} + (k-1)\frac{m}{k},$$

in the interval $(0,m)$, *where* x_0 *is the unique integer solution of the equation* $cx + ym = \gcd(c,m)$ – *which can be found using Euclid's algorithm.*

The proof is easy once we realize that the problem in solving the equation $cx \equiv d\,(\text{mod } m)$ is equivalent to the one in finding integer solutions to the equation $cx + ym = d$.

Another useful fact is that if $cx \equiv d\,(\text{mod } m)$, then $c(x+m) \equiv d\,(\text{mod } m)$.

Example 1.7.15 *For the congruence* $27x \equiv 1\,(\text{mod } 47)$ *we have* $\gcd(27,47) = 1$ *and* $7 \cdot 27 - 4 \cdot 47 = 1$. *Hence* $x = 7$ *is the unique solution.*

Example 1.7.16 *For the congruence* $51x \equiv 9\,(\text{mod } 69)$ *we have* $\gcd(51,69) = 3$ *and* $-4 \cdot 51 + 3 \cdot 69 = 3$. *Hence* $x = -12, 11, 34$, *or, expressed using only positive integers,*

$$x = 11, 34, 57.$$

Exercise 1.7.17 *Solve the linear congruence equations (a)* $4x \equiv 5 \pmod 9$; *(b)* $2x \equiv 17 \pmod{19}$.

There is an old method for solving special systems of linear congruences. The following result, easy to verify, has been attributed to Sun Tsŭ of China, around AD 350.

Theorem 1.7.18 (Chinese remainder theorem) *Let* $m_1, \ldots, m_t$ *be integers,* $m_i \perp m_j$ *for* $i \neq j$*, and* $a_1, \ldots, a_t$ *be integers with* $0 < a_i < m_i$*. Then the system of congruences*

$$x \equiv a_i \pmod{m_i} \quad \textit{for } i = 1, \ldots, t$$

possesses the solution (which is straightforward to verify)

$$x = \sum_{i=1}^{t} a_i M_i N_i, \tag{1.65}$$

where $M = \prod_{i=1}^{t} m_i, M_i = M / m_i$ *and* $N_i = M_i^{-1} \bmod m_i, 1 \leq i \leq t$*. Moreover, the solution (1.65) is unique up to the congruence modulo M; that is,* $z \equiv x \pmod M$ *for any other solution z.*

The Chinese remainder theorem has numerous applications. One of them is the following modular representation of integers.

Let $m_1, \ldots, m_n$ be pairwise relatively prime and M their product. It follows from Theorem 1.7.18 that each integer $0 \leq x < M$ is uniquely represented by the n-tuple

$$(x \bmod m_1, \ldots, x \bmod m_n).$$

For example, if $m_1 = 2, m_2 = 3, m_3 = 5$, then $(1,0,2)$ represents 27. Such a modular representation of integers may look artificial. However, it has its advantages, because it allows parallel, component-wise execution of basic arithmetic operations.

Exercise 1.7.19 *(a) Find modular representations of integers* $7, 13, 20, 6$ *and* 91 *with respect to the integers* $m_1 = 2, m_2 = 5, m_3 = 11, m_4 = 19$*; (b) Show that if* $(x_1, \ldots, x_n)$ *is a modular representation of an integer x and* $(y_1, \ldots, y_n)$ *of an integer y, both with respect to pairwise primes* $(m_1, \ldots, m_n)$*, and* $\circ$ *is one of the operations addition, subtraction or multiplication, then*

$$((x_1 \circ y_1) \bmod m_1, \ldots, (x_n \circ y_n) \bmod m_n)$$

represents the number $x \circ y$ *– provided this number is smaller than m.*

In cryptographical applications one often needs to compute **modular exponentiation** $a^b \bmod n$, where a, b and n can be very large; n may have between 512 and 1024 bits, and a also has about that number of bits. Moreover, b can easily have several hundred bits. In such a case a^b would have more than 10^{30} bits. To compute such numbers would appear to be difficult. Fortunately, congruences have various properties that allow one to simplify computation of modular exponentiations substantially. For example,

$$a^2 \equiv (a \bmod n)^2 \pmod n$$

for any a and b. This allows, together with the exponentiation Algorithm 1.1.14, computation of $a^b \bmod n$ in such a way that one never has to work with numbers that have more than twice as many bits as numbers a, b, n. For example,

$$a^8 \bmod n \equiv (((a \bmod n)^2 \bmod n)^2 \bmod n)^2 \pmod n.$$

Efficient modular exponentiation is also at the heart of efficient primality testing, as shown in Section 5.6.2. To simplify modular exponentiation, one can also use the following theorem and its subsequent generalization. Both these results also play an important role in cryptography.

Theorem 1.7.20 (Fermat's[9] little theorem, 1640) *If p is a prime, $a \in \mathbf{N}$, then*

$$a^p \equiv a \pmod p, \tag{1.66}$$

and if a is not divisible by p, then

$$a^{p-1} \equiv 1 \pmod p. \tag{1.67}$$

Proof: It is true for $a = 1$. Assuming that it is true for a, then by induction $(a+1)^p \equiv a^p + 1 \equiv a + 1 \pmod p$, because $\binom{p}{k} \equiv 0 \pmod p$ for $0 < k < p$. So Theorem 1.7.20 holds for all $a \in \mathbf{N}$. □

A more general version of this theorem, which needs a quite different proof, the so-called **Euler totient theorem**, has the form

$$n^{\phi(m)} \equiv 1 \pmod m \text{ if } n \perp m, \tag{1.68}$$

where ϕ is Euler's phi function defined on page 44.

Example 1.7.21 *In order to compute $3^{1000} \bmod 19$ we can use the fact that by Fermat's little theorem, $3^{18} \equiv 1 \bmod 19$. Since $1000 = 18 \cdot 55 + 10$, we get*

$$3^{1000} = 3^{18 \cdot 55 + 10} = (3^{18})^{55}(3^5)^2 \equiv (3^5 \bmod 19)^2 \equiv (15)^2 \equiv 225 \equiv 16 \pmod{19}.$$

Exercise 1.7.22 *Compute (a) $2^{340} \bmod 11$; (b) $3^{100} \bmod 79$; (c) $5^{10000} \bmod 13$.*

Exercise 1.7.23 *Show that $\sum_{i=1}^{p-1} i^{p-1} \equiv -1 \pmod p$.*

1.8 Discrete Square Roots and Logarithms*

In this section we deal with two interesting and computationally intriguing problems of great importance, especially for modern cryptography.

---

[9]Pierre de Fermat, a French lawyer, who did mathematics, poetry and Greek philosophy as a hobby. At his time one of the most famous mathematicians in Europe – in spite of the fact that he never published a scientific paper. His results were distributed by mail. Fermat is considered as a founder of modern number theory and probability theory.

1.8.1 Discrete Square Roots

The problem of solving quadratic congruence equations

$$x^2 \equiv a \pmod{m}$$

or, in other words, computing 'discrete' square roots modulo m, is intriguing and of importance for various applications.

For an integer m denote

$$\begin{aligned}\mathbf{Z}_m &= \{0,1,\ldots,m-1\},\\ \mathbf{Z}_m^* &= \{a \mid a \in \mathbf{Z}_m, \gcd(a,m)=1\},\end{aligned}$$

and let their elements denote the corresponding residue classes. Observe that $\mathbf{Z}_n^*$ has $\phi(n)$ elements.

Example 1.8.1 $\mathbf{Z}_{10}^* = \{1,3,7,9\}$, $\mathbf{Z}_{11}^* = \{1,2,3,4,5,6,7,8,9,10\}$.

An integer $x \in \mathbf{Z}_m^*$ is called a **quadratic residue modulo** m if $x \equiv y^2 \pmod{m}$ for some $y \in \mathbf{Z}_m^*$; otherwise x is called a **quadratic nonresidue modulo** m. Notation:

QR_m - the set of all quadratic residues modulo m,
QNR_m - the set of all quadratic nonresidues modulo m.

Exercise 1.8.2 *Show that if p is prime, then each quadratic residue modulo p has exactly two distinct square roots.*

Exercise 1.8.3* *Explain why exactly half of the integers* $1,\ldots,p-1$ *are quadratic residues modulo p.*

Exercise 1.8.4* *Find all square roots of* 64 *modulo* 105.

To deal with quadratic residues, it is useful to use the following notation, defined for any integer m and $x \in \mathbf{Z}_m^*$:

$$(x|m) = \begin{cases} 1 & \text{if } x \in QR_m \quad \text{and } m \text{ is a prime;}\\ -1 & \text{if } x \in QNR_m \quad \text{and } m \text{ is a prime;}\\ \prod_{i=1}^{n}(x|p_i) & \text{if } m = \prod_{i=1}^{n} p_i, x \perp m \text{ and } p_i \text{ are primes.}\end{cases}$$

$(x|m)$ is called the **Legendre symbol** if m is prime and the **Legendre-Jacobi**[10] **symbol** if m is composite. It is easy to determine whether $x \in \mathbf{Z}_m^*$ is a quadratic residue modulo m if m is a prime – one need only compute $(x|m)$. This can be done in $\mathcal{O}(\lg m)$ time using the following identities.

Theorem 1.8.5 *Let* $x, y \in \mathbf{Z}_m^*$.

1. $x^{(p-1)/2} \equiv (x|p) \pmod{p}$ *for any prime* $p > 2$ *and* $x \in Z_p^*$.[11]
2. *If* $x \equiv y \pmod{m}$, *then* $(x|m) = (y|m)$.

[10] Adrien Marie Legendre (1752–1833), a French mathematician; Carl Gustav Jacobi (1804–51), a German mathematician.

[11] This claim is also called Euler's criterion.

3. $(x|m) \cdot (y|m) = (x \cdot y|m)$.
4. $(-1|m) = (-1)^{(m-1)/2}$ *if m is odd.*
5. $(2|m) = (-1)^{(m^2-1)/8}$ *if m is odd.*
6. *If* $m \perp n$ *and* m, n *are odd, then* $(n|m)(m|n) = (-1)^{(m-1)(n-1)/4}$.[12]

Example 1.8.6

$$\begin{aligned} (28|97) &= (2|97) \cdot (2|97) \cdot (7|97) = (7|97) \\ &= (97|7) \cdot (-1)^{(97-1)(7-1)/4} = (6|7) \\ &= (2|7) \cdot (3|7) = (-1)^6 (3|7) = (7|3) \cdot (-1)^3 \\ &= -(1|3) = -1. \end{aligned}$$

Exercise 1.8.7 *Compute (a)* $(32|57)$*; (b)* $(132|37)$*; (c)* $(47,53)$*; (d)* $(3|p)$*, where p is prime.*

It is straightforward to see from Euler's criterion in Theorem 1.8.5 that if p is a prime of the form $4k+3$ and $x \in QR_p$, then $\pm\, x^{(p+1)/4} \bmod p$ are two square roots of x modulo p. For such a p and x one can therefore efficiently compute square roots. By contrast, no efficient deterministic algorithm for computing square roots is known when p is a prime of the form $4k+1$. However, we show now that even in this case there is an efficient randomized algorithm for the job.

Informally, an algorithm is called random if its behaviour is determined not only by the input but also by the values produced by a random number generator – for example, if in a computation step a number is randomly chosen (or produced by a random number generator). Informally again, an algorithm is called a polynomial time algorithm if it can be realized on a typical sequential computer in such a way that the time of computation grows polynomially with respect to the size of the input data.

The concepts of 'a randomized algorithm' and a 'polynomial time' algorithm are among the most basic investigated in foundations of computing. As we shall see later, one of the main outcomes is that these two concepts are very robust and practically independent of the choice of computer model or a source of randomness. This also justifies us in starting to use them now on the basis of the above informal description. A formal description provided later will be necessary once we try to show the properties of these concepts or even the nonexistence of such algorithms for some problems.

Theorem 1.8.8 (Adleman–Manders–Miller's theorem) *There exists a randomized polynomial time algorithm to compute the square root of a modulo p, where* $a \in QR_p$*, and p is a prime.*

Proof: Let us consider a decomposition $p-1 = 2^e P$, where P is odd. Choose randomly[13] $b \in QNR_p$, and let us define the sequence $a_1, a_2, \ldots$ of elements from QR_p and of integers $e \geq k_1 > k_2 > \ldots > k_i > \ldots$ inductively as follows:

- $a_1 = a$;

[12]This assertion, due to F. L. Gauss, is known as the law of quadratic reciprocity. It plays an important role in number theory, and at least 152 different proofs of this 'law' are known to Gesternhaber (1963).

[13]This means that one chooses randomly $b \in \mathbf{Z}_p$ and verifies whether $b \in QR_p$. If not, one chooses another b until a $b \in QNR_p$ is found. Thanks to Exercise 1.8.3, this can be done efficiently with high probability.

- $k_i =$ the smallest $k \geq 0$ such that $a_i^{2^k p} \equiv 1 \pmod p$ for $i \geq 1$;
- $a_i = a_{i-1} b^{2^{e-k_{i-1}}} \bmod p$ for $i > 1$.

We show now that $k_i < k_{i-1}$ for all $i > 1$. In doing so, we make use of the minimality of k_i and the fact that $b^{2^{e-1}p} = b^{(p-1)/2} \equiv (b|p) \equiv -1 \pmod p$ by (6) of Theorem 1.8.5. Since

$$a_i^{2^{k_{i-1}-1}p} \equiv (a_{i-1} b^{2^{e-k_{i-1}}})^{2^{k_{i-1}-1}p} \equiv a_{i-1}^{2^{k_{i-1}-1}p} b^{2^{e-1}p} \equiv (-1)(-1) \equiv 1 \pmod p,$$

k_i must be smaller than k_{i-1}. Therefore, there has to exist an $n < e$ such that $k_n = 0$. For such an n we have $a_n^{p+1} \equiv a_n \bmod p$, which implies that $a_n^{(p+1)/2}$ is a square root of a_n.

Let us now define, by the reverse induction, the sequence $r_n, r_{n-1}, \ldots, r_1$ as follows:

- $r_n = a^{(P+1)/2} \bmod p$,
- $r_i = r_{i+1}(b^{2^{e-k_i-1}})^{-1} \bmod p$ for $i < n$.

It is easy to verify that $a_i = r_i^2 \bmod p$, and therefore $a = r_1^2 \bmod p$.

Clearly, $n < \lg p$, and therefore the algorithm requires polynomial time of length p and a – plus time to choose randomly a b such that $(b|p) = -1$. □

There is an algorithm to compute square roots that is conceptually much simpler. However, it requires work with congruences on polynomials and application of Euclid's algorithm to find the greatest common divisor of two polynomials, which can be done in a quite natural way. In other words, a little bit more sophisticated mathematics has to be used.

Suppose that a is a quadratic residue in $\mathbf{Z}_p^*$ and we want to find its square roots. Observe first that the problem of finding an x such that $x^2 \equiv a \pmod p$ is equivalent to the problem, for an arbitrary $c \in \mathbf{Z}_p^*$, of finding an x such that $(x-c)^2 \equiv a \pmod p$ – in order to solve the original problem, only a shift of roots is required. Suppose now that $(x-c)^2 - a \equiv (x-r)(x-s) \pmod p$. In such a case $rs \equiv c^2 - a \pmod p$ and, by (2) in Theorem 1.8.5, $((c^2-a)|p) = (r|p)(s|p)$. So if $((c^2-a)|p) = -1$, then either r or s is a quadratic residue. On the other hand, it follows from Euler's criterion in Theorem 1.8.5 that all quadratic residues in $\mathbf{Z}_p^*$ are roots of the polynomial $x^{(p-1)/2} - 1$. This implies that the greatest common divisor of the polynomials $(x-c)^2 - a$ and $x^{(p-1)/2} - 1$ is the first-degree polynomial whose root is that of $(x-c)^2 - a$, which is the quadratic residue. This leads to our second randomized algorithm.

Algorithm 1.8.9

- Choose randomly $c \in \mathbf{Z}_p^*$.
- If $((c^2-a)|p) = -1$, then compute $\gcd(x^{(p-1)/2} - 1, (x-c)^2 - a) = \alpha x - \beta$.
- Output $\pm(c + \alpha^{-1}\beta)$ as the square root of a modulo p.

The efficiency of the algorithm is based on the following fundamental result from number theory: if a is a quadratic residue from $\mathbf{Z}_p^*$ and c is chosen randomly from $\mathbf{Z}_p^*$, then with a probability larger than $\frac{1}{2}$ we have $((c^2-a)|p) = -1$.

Another important fact is that there is an effective way to compute square roots modulo n, even in the case where n is composite, if prime factors of n are known.

Theorem 1.8.10 *If $p,q > 2$ are distinct primes, then $x \in QR_{pq} \Leftrightarrow x \in QR_p \wedge x \in QR_q$. Moreover, there is a polynomial time algorithm which, given as inputs x,u,v,p,q such that $x \equiv u^2 \pmod{p}$, $x \equiv v^2 \pmod{q}$, computes w such that $x \equiv w^2 \pmod{pq}$.*

Proof: The first claim follows directly from (3) of Theorem 1.8.5. To prove the rest of the theorem, let us assume that x,u,v,p and q satisfy the hypothesis. Using Euclid's algorithm we can compute a,b such that $ap+bq=1$. If we now denote $c = bq = 1-ap$ and $d = ap = 1-bq$, then

$$c \equiv 0 \pmod{q}, \quad d \equiv 0 \pmod{p}, \quad c \equiv 1 \pmod{p}, \quad d \equiv 1 \pmod{q}. \tag{1.69}$$

This will now be used to show that for $w = cu + dv$ we have $x \equiv w^2 \pmod{pq}$. In order to do so, it is enough, due to the first part of the theorem, to prove that $x \equiv w^2 \pmod{p}$ and $x \equiv w^2 \pmod{q}$. We do this only for p; the other case can be treated similarly. By (1.69),

$$w^2 = (cu+dv)^2 = c^2u^2 + 2cduv + d^2v^2 \equiv u^2 \equiv x \pmod{p}.$$

□

On the other hand, no effective algorithm is known, given an integer n and an $a \in QR_n$, for computing a square root of a modulo n. As shown in the proof of Theorem 1.8.16, this problem is as difficult as the problem of factorization of integers – the problem of intractability on which many modern cryptographical techniques are based – see Chapters 8 and 9.

Before presenting the next theorem, let us look more deeply into the problem of finding square roots modulo a composite integer n.

Lemma 1.8.11 *Any quadratic residue $a \in QR_n$, $n = pq$, p and q are distinct odd primes, has four square roots modulo n.*

Proof: Let $a \in QR_n$ and $a \equiv a_1^2 \pmod{n}$. By the Chinese remainder theorem there are integers u,v such that

$$u \equiv a_1 \pmod{p}, \qquad v \equiv -a_1 \pmod{q};$$
$$u \equiv a_1 \pmod{q}, \qquad v \equiv -a_1 \pmod{p}.$$

Since p,q are odd, u,v,a_1 and $-a_1$ must be distinct. Moreover, $u^2 \equiv v^2 \equiv a_1^2 \pmod{pq}$, and therefore $u,v,a_1,-a_1$ are four distinct square roots of a. □

Remark 1.8.12 If an integer n has t different odd prime factors, then it has 2^t square roots.

Exercise 1.8.13* *Find all four solutions of the congruences: (a) $x^2 \equiv 25 \pmod{33}$; (b) $x^2 \equiv 11 \pmod{p}$.*

Exercise 1.8.14 *Determine in general the number of square roots modulo n for an $a \in QR_n$.*

Of special interest is the case where $n = pq$ and $p \equiv q \equiv 3 \pmod{4}$. Such integers are called **Blum integers**. In this case, by Theorem 1.8.5,

$$(-x|n) = (-x|p)(-x|q) = (x|p)(-1)^{(p-1)/2}(x|q)(-1)^{(q-1)/2} = (x|p)(x|q) = (x|n).$$

Moreover, the following theorem holds.

Theorem 1.8.15 *(1) If $x^2 \equiv y^2 \pmod{n}$ and $x, y, -x, -y$ are distinct modulo n, then $(x|n) = -(y|n)$.*
(2) If $n = pq$ is a Blum integer, then the mapping

$$x \to x^2 \bmod n$$

is a permutation of QR_n. In other words, each quadratic residue has a unique square root that is also a quadratic residue, and is called its **principal square root**.

Proof: (1) Since pq divides $(x^2 - y^2) = (x+y)(x-y)$ and $x, y, -x, -y$ are distinct modulo n, neither $x+y$ nor $x-y$ can be divided by both p and q. Without loss of generality, assume that p divides $(x-y)$ and q divides $(x+y)$; the other case can be dealt with similarly. Then $x \equiv y \pmod{p}, x \equiv -y \pmod{q}$, and therefore $(x|p) = (y|p), (x|q) = -(y|q)$. Thus $(x|n) = -(y|n)$.

(2) Let a be any quadratic residue modulo n. By Lemma 1.8.11, a has exactly four roots – say $x, -x, y, -y$. By (1) $(x|n) = -(y|n)$. Let x be a square root such that $(x|p) = 1$. Then either $(x|p) = (x|q) = 1$ or $(-x|p) = (-x|q) = 1$. Hence either x or $-x$ is a quadratic residue modulo n. □

For Blum integers two key algorithmic problems of modern cryptography are computationally equivalent with respect to the existence of a polynomial time randomized algorithm.

Theorem 1.8.16 (Rabin's theorem) *The following statements are equivalent:*

1. *There is a polynomial time randomized algorithm to factor Blum integers.*
2. *There is a polynomial time randomized algorithm to compute the principal square root for $x \in QR_n$ if n is a Blum integer.*

Proof: (1) Assume that a polynomial time randomized algorithm $\mathcal{A}$ for computing principal square roots modulo Blum integers is given. A Blum integer n can be factored as follows.

1. Choose a random y such that $(y|n) = -1$.
2. Compute $x \equiv y^2 \pmod{n}$.
3. Find, using $\mathcal{A}$, a $z \in QR_n$ such that $x \equiv z^2 \pmod{n}$.

We now show that $\gcd(y+z, n)$ is a prime factor of $n = pq$. Clearly, pq divides $(y-z)(y+z)$. Since $(-z|n) = (-1|n)(z|n) = (-1)^{\frac{p-1}{2}}(-1)^{\frac{q-1}{2}}(z|n) = 1$, we have $y \not\equiv -z \pmod{n}$, and therefore $\gcd(y+z, n)$ must be one of the prime factors of n.

(2) Assume that we can efficiently factor n to get p, q such that $n = pq$. We now show how to compute principal square roots modulo n. Let $x \in QR_n$.

- Using the Adleman–Manders–Miller algorithm, compute $u \in QR_p$ and $v \in QR_q$ such that $x \equiv u^2 \bmod p, x \equiv v^2 \pmod{q}$.
- Using Euclid's algorithm, compute a, b such that $ap + bq = 1$.
- Compute $c = bq, d = ap$.

We show now that $w = cu + dv$ is in QR_n and that it is a square root of x. Indeed, since $c \equiv 1 \pmod{p}$ and $d \equiv 1 \pmod{q}$, we have $w^2 \equiv u^2 \equiv x \pmod{p}, w^2 \equiv v^2 \equiv x \pmod{q}$, and by (1.63), $w^2 \equiv x \pmod{n}$. To show that $w \in QR_n$, we proceed as follows.

Since $c \equiv 0 \pmod{q}, d \equiv 0 \pmod{p}$, we get $(w|p) = (u|p) = 1, (w|q) = (v,q) = 1$, and therefore $(w|pq) = (w|p)(w|q) = 1$. □

1.8.2 Discrete Logarithm Problem

This is the problem of determining, given integers a, n, x, an integer m such that $a^m \equiv x \pmod{n}$, if such an m exists.

It may happen that there are two such m, for example, $m = 10$ and $m = 4$ for the equation $5^m \equiv 16 \pmod{21}$, or none, for example, for the equation $5^m \equiv 3 \pmod{21}$. An important case is when g is a **generator** or a **principal root** of $\mathbf{Z}_n^*$, that is, if

$$\mathbf{Z}_n^* = \{g^i \bmod n \,|\, 0 \leq i \leq \phi(n)\}.$$

In such a case, for any $x \in \mathbf{Z}_n^*$ there is a unique $m < \phi(n)$ such that $x \equiv g^m \pmod{n}$. Such an m is called the **discrete logarithm** or **index** of x with respect to n and g – in short, $index_{n,g}(x)$.

If $\mathbf{Z}_n^*$ has a principal root, then it is called cyclic. It was known already to F. L. Gauss that $\mathbf{Z}_n^*$ is cyclic if and only if n is one of the numbers $2, 4, p^i, 2p^i$, where $p > 2$ is a prime and i is a positive integer.

Example 1.8.17 *The table of indices, or discrete logarithms, for* $\mathbf{Z}_{13}^*$ *and the generator* 2,

x	1	2	3	4	5	6	7	8	9	10	11	12
m	0	1	4	2	9	5	11	3	8	10	7	6

No efficient deterministic algorithm is known that can compute, given a, n and x, the discrete logarithm m such that $a^m \equiv x \pmod{n}$. This fact plays an important role in cryptography and its applications, and also for (perfect) random number generators (see next section). An exception is the case in which p is a prime and factors of $p - 1$ are small, of the order $\mathcal{O}(\log p)$.[14]

Exercise 1.8.18 *Find all the principal roots in* $\mathbf{Z}_{11}^*$, *and compute all the discrete logarithms of elements in* $\mathbf{Z}_{11}^*$ *with respect to these principal roots.*

Exercise 1.8.19* *Let* g *be a principal root modulo the prime* $p > 2$. *Show that for all* $a, b \in \mathbf{Z}_p^*$
(a) $index_{p,g}(ab) \equiv index_{p,g}(a) + index_{p,g}(b) \pmod{n}$; *(b)* $index_{p,g}(a^n) \equiv n \cdot index_{p,g}(a) \pmod{p-1}$.

1.9 Probability and Randomness

In the design of algorithms, communication protocols or even networks, an increasingly important role is played by randomized methods, where random bits, or, less formally, coin-tossings, are used to make decisions. The same is true for randomized methods in the analysis of computing systems – both deterministic and randomized. Basic concepts and methods of discrete probability and randomness are therefore introduced in this section.

1.9.1 Discrete Probability

A **probability** (or **sample) space** is a set Ω (of all possible things that can happen), together with a **probability distribution** Pr, that maps each element of Ω onto a nonnegative real such that

$$\sum_{\omega \in \Omega} Pr(\omega) = 1.$$

[14] In the general case of a prime p the fastest algorithm, due to Adleman (1980), runs in time $\Theta(2^{\sqrt{\lg p \lg \lg p}})$. However, there is a polynomial time randomized algorithm for a (potential) quantum computer to compute the discrete logarithm due to Shor (1994).

A subset $E \subseteq \Omega$ is called an **event**; its probability is defined as $Pr(E) = \sum_{\omega \in E} Pr(\omega)$. Elements of Ω are called **elementary events**. If all elementary events have the same probability, we talk about a **uniform probability distribution**.

For example, let Ω_0 be the set of all possible outcomes of throwing simultaneously three dice. $|\Omega_0| = 216$, and if all the dice are perfect, then each elementary event has the probability $\frac{1}{216}$.

From the definition of a probability distribution, the following identities, in which A, B are events, follow easily:

$$Pr(\bar{A}) = 1 - Pr(A), \qquad Pr(A \cup B) = Pr(A) + Pr(B) - Pr(A \cap B).$$

Exercise 1.9.1 *Let $E_1, \ldots, E_n$ be events. Show:*
(a) **Bonferroni's inequality***: $Pr(E_1 \cap E_2 \cap \ldots \cap E_n) \geq Pr(E_1) + Pr(E_2) + \cdots + Pr(E_n) - (n-1)$;*
(b) **Bode's inequality***: $Pr(E_1 \cup E_2 \cup \ldots \cup E_n) \leq Pr(E_1) + \cdots + Pr(E_n)$.*

The **conditional probability** of an event A, given that another event B occurs, is defined by

$$Pr(A|B) = \frac{Pr(A \cap B)}{Pr(B)}. \tag{1.70}$$

This formalizes an intuitive idea of having a priori partial knowledge of the outcome of an experiment.

Comparing $Pr(A|B)$ and $Pr(B|A)$, expressed by (1.70), we get

Theorem 1.9.2 (Bayes' theorem)

$$Pr(A)Pr(B|A) = Pr(B)Pr(A|B).$$

Two events A, B are called **independent** if $Pr(A \cap B) = Pr(A) \cdot Pr(B)$.

Exercise 1.9.3 *What is the conditional probability that a randomly generated bit string of length four contains at least two consecutive 0's, assuming that the probabilities of 0 and 1 are equal and the first bit is 1?*

A **random variable** X is any function from a sample space Ω to reals. The function $F_X(x) = Pr(X = x)$ is called the **probability density function** of X.

For example, if $X(\omega)$ ($\omega \in \Omega_0$) is the sum of numbers on dices, then its probability density function has the form

X	3	4	5	6	7	8	9	...
$F_X(x)$	$\frac{1}{216}$	$\frac{3}{216}$	$\frac{6}{216}$	$\frac{10}{216}$	$\frac{12}{216}$	$\frac{21}{216}$	$\frac{25}{216}$	...

Two random variables X and Y over the same sample space Ω are called **independent** if for any $x, y \in \Omega$

$$Pr(X = x \text{ and } Y = y) = Pr(X = x)Pr(Y = y).$$

Exercise 1.9.4 (Schwartz' lemma)** *Let p be a polynomial with n variables that has degree at most k in each of its variables. Show that if p is not identically 0 and the values* α_i*, $i = 1,2,\ldots,n$, are chosen in the interval $[0, N-1]$ independently of each other according to the uniform distribution, then* $Pr(p(\alpha_1,\ldots,\alpha_n) = 0) \leq \frac{kn}{N}$. *(Use induction and the decomposition* $p = p_1x_1 + p_2x_1^2 + \ldots + p_tx_1^t$*, where* $p_1,\ldots,p_t$ *are polynomials of variables* $x_2,\ldots,x_n$*.)*

An intuitive concept of an average value of a random variable X on a probability space Ω is defined formally as the **mean** or **expected value**

$$EX = \sum_{\omega\in\Omega} X(\omega)Pr(\omega), \tag{1.71}$$

provided this potentially infinite sum exists.

If X, Y are random variables, then so are $X+Y, cX, X\cdot Y$, where c is a constant. Directly from (1.71) we easily get

$$E(X+Y) = EX+EY \tag{1.72}$$
$$E(cX) = cE(X) \tag{1.73}$$
$$E(X\cdot Y) = EX\cdot EY, \quad \text{if } X, Y \text{ are independent.} \tag{1.74}$$

Exercise 1.9.5 *A ship with a crew of 77 sailors sleeping in 77 cabins, one for each sailor, arrives at a port, and the sailors go out to have fun. Late at night they return and, being in a state of inebriation, they choose randomly a cabin to sleep in. What is the expected number of sailors sleeping in their own cabins? (Hint: consider random variables* X_i *the value of which is 1 if the i-th sailor sleeps in his own cabin and 0 otherwise. Compute* $E[\sum_{i=1}^{77} X_i]$*.)*

Other important attributes of a random variable X are its **variance** VX and **standard deviation** $\sigma X = \sqrt{VX}$, where

$$VX = E((X-EX)^2).$$

Since

$$E((X-EX)^2) = E(X^2 - 2X(EX) + (EX)^2) \tag{1.75}$$
$$= E(X^2) - 2(EX)(EX) + (EX)^2, \tag{1.76}$$

we get another formula for VX:

$$VX = E(X^2) - (EX)^2. \tag{1.77}$$

The variance captures the spread of values around the expected value. The standard deviation just scales down the variance, which otherwise may take very large values.

Example 1.9.6 *Let X, Y be two random variables on the sample space $\Omega = \{1,2,\ldots,10\}$, where all elementary events have the same probability, and $X(i) = i$, $Y(i) = i-1$, for $i \leq 5$; $Y(i) = i+1$, for $i > 5$. It is easy to check that* $EX = EY = 5.5, E(X^2) = \frac{1}{10}\sum_{i=1}^{10} i^2 = 38.5, E(Y^2) = 44.5$, *and therefore* $VX = 8.25, VY = 14.25$.

The probability density function of a random variable X whose values are natural numbers can be represented by the following **probability generating function**:

$$G_X(z) = \sum_{k\geq 0} Pr(X=k)z^k.$$

Since $\sum_{k\geq 0} Pr(X=k) = 1$, we get $G_X(1) = 1$. Probability generating functions often allow us to compute quite easily the mean and the variance. Indeed,

$$EX = \sum_{k\geq 0} kPr(X=k) = \sum_{k\geq 0} Pr(X=k)(k1^{k-1}) \quad (1.78)$$

$$= G'_X(1); \quad (1.79)$$

and since

$$E(X^2) = \sum_{k\geq 0} k^2 Pr(X=k) = \sum_{k\geq 0} Pr(X=k)(k(k-1)1^{k-2} + k1^{k-1}) \quad (1.80)$$

$$= G''_X(1) + G'_X(1), \quad (1.81)$$

we get from (1.77)

$$VX = G''_X(1) + G'_X(1) - G'_X(1)^2.$$

Two important distributions are connected with experiments called **Bernoulli trials**. The experiments have two possible outcomes: **success** with the probability p and **failure** with the probability $q = 1-p$. Coin-tossing is an example of a Bernoulli trial experiment.

Let the random variable X be the number of trials needed to obtain a success. Then X has values in the range **N**, and it clearly holds that $Pr(X=k) = q^{k-1}p$. The probability distribution X on **N** with $Pr_X(k) = q^{k-1}p$ is called the **geometric distribution**.

Exercise 1.9.7 *Show that for the geometric distribution*

$$EX = \frac{1}{p}, \qquad VX = \frac{q}{p^2}. \quad (1.82)$$

Let the random variable Y express the number of successes in n trials. Then Y has values in the range $\{0,1,2,\dots n\}$, and we have

$$Pr(Y=k) = \binom{n}{k} p^k q^{n-k}.$$

The probability distribution Y on the set $\{1,2,\dots,n\}$ with $Pr(Y=k) = \binom{n}{k} p^k q^{n-k}$ is called **the binomial distribution**.

Exercise 1.9.8 *Show that for the binomial distribution*

$$EY = np, \qquad VY = npq. \quad (1.83)$$

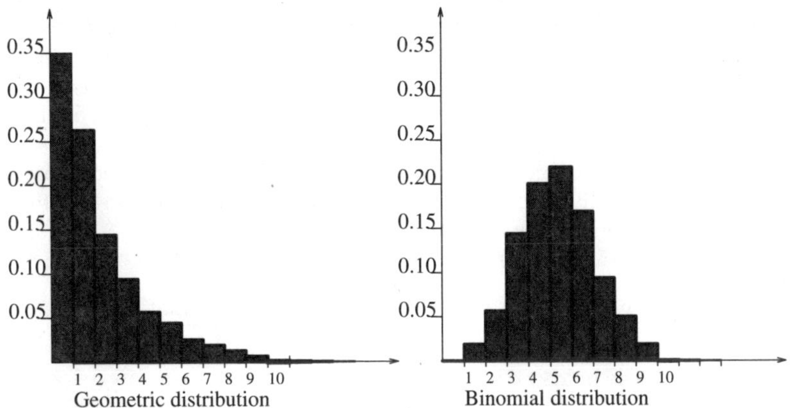

Figure 1.8 Geometric and binomial distributions

Geometric and binomial distributions are illustrated for $p = 0.35$ and $n = 14$ in Figure 1.8.

> **Exercise 1.9.9** (Balls and bins)* *Consider the process of randomly tossing balls into b bins in such a way that at each toss the probability that a tossed ball falls in any given bin is $\frac{1}{b}$. Answer the following questions about this process:*
>
> 1. *How many balls fall on average into a given bin at n tosses?*
> 2. *How many balls must one toss, on average, until a given bin contains a ball?*
> 3. *How many balls must one toss, on average, until every bin contains a ball?*

The following example illustrates a probabilistic average-case analysis of algorithms. By that we mean the following. For an algorithm $\mathcal{A}$ let $T_{\mathcal{A}}(x)$ denote the computation time of $\mathcal{A}$ for an input x, and let Pr_n be, for all integers n, a probability distribution on the set of all inputs of $\mathcal{A}$ of length n. By the average-case complexity $ET_{\mathcal{A}}(w)$ of $\mathcal{A}$, we then mean the function

$$ET_{\mathcal{A}}(n) = \sum_{|x|=n} Pr_n(x)T_{\mathcal{A}}(x).$$

Example 1.9.10 *Determine the average-time complexity of Algorithm 1.9.11 for the following problem: given an array* $X[1], X[2], \ldots, X[n]$ *of distinct elements, determine the maximal j such that*

$$X[j] = max\{X[i] \mid 1 \leq i \leq n\}.$$

Algorithm 1.9.11 (Finding the last maximum)

```
begin j ← n; m ← X[n];
      for k ← n − 1 downto 1 do if X[k] > m
                                then j ← k; m ← X[k]
end
```

The time complexity of this algorithm for a conventional sequential computer is $T(n) = k_1 n + k_2 A + k_3$, where k_1, k_2, k_3 are constants, and A equals the number of times the algorithm executes the statements $j \leftarrow k$; $m \leftarrow X[k]$. The term $k_1 n + k_2$ captures here $n-1$ decrement and comparison operations. The value of A clearly does not depend on the particular values in the array X, only on the relative order of the sequence $X[1], \ldots, X[n]$.

Let us now analyse the above algorithm for a special case that all elements of the array are distinct. If we also assume that all permutations of data in X have the same probability, then the average-time complexity of the above algorithm depends on the average value A_n of A.

Let p_{nk}, for $0 \leq k < n$, be the probability that $A = k$. Then

$$p_{nk} = \frac{\text{number of permutations of } n \text{ elements such that } A = k}{n!},$$

and the following fact clearly holds:

$$A_n = \sum_{k=0}^{n-1} k p_{nk}.$$

Our task now is to determine p_{nk}. Without loss of generality we can assume that data in the array form a permutation $x_1, \ldots, x_n$ of $\{1,2,\ldots,n\}$, and we need to determine the value of A for such a permutation. If $x_1 = n$, then the value of A is 1 higher than that for $x_2, \ldots, x_n$ – in this case $X[1] \geq m$ in the algorithm. If $x_1 \neq n$, then the value of A is the same as for $x_2, \ldots, x_n$ – in this case $X[1] < m$. Since the probability that $x_1 = n$ is $\frac{1}{n}$, and the probability that $x_1 \neq n$ is $\frac{n-1}{n}$, we get the following recurrence for p_{nk}:

$$p_{nk} = \frac{1}{n} p_{(n-1)(k-1)} + \frac{n-1}{n} p_{(n-1)k}, \tag{1.84}$$

with the initial conditions

$$p_{10} = 1,\ p_{1k} = 0, \ \text{ for } \ k > 0;\ p_{nk} = 0 \text{ for } k < 0 \text{ or } k \geq n.$$

In order to determine A_n, let us consider the generating function

$$G_n(z) = \sum_{k=0}^{n} p_{nk} z^k.$$

Clearly, $G_n(1) = 1$, and from (1.84) we get

$$G_n(z) = \frac{z}{n} G_{n-1}(z) + \frac{n-1}{n} G_{n-1}(z) = \frac{z+n-1}{n} G_{n-1}(z). \tag{1.85}$$

We know (see (1.79)) that $A_n = G_n'(1)$. For $G_n'(z)$ we get from (1.85)

$$G_n'(z) = \frac{1}{n} G_{n-1}(z) + \frac{z+n-1}{n} G_{n-1}'(z),$$

and therefore

$$G_n'(1) = \frac{1}{n} + G_{n-1}'(1).$$

Thus

$$A_n = \sum_{i=2}^{n} \frac{1}{i} = H_n - 1,$$

where H_n is the nth harmonic number. □

1.9.2 Bounds on Tails of Binomial Distributions*

It is especially the binomial distribution, expressing the probability of k successes during n Bernoulli trials (coin-tossings), that plays an important role in randomization in computing. For the analysis of randomized computing it is often important to know how large the **tails of binomial distributions** are – the regions of the distribution far from the mean.

Several bounds are known for tails. For the case of one random variable X with a probability of success p and of failure $q = 1-p$, the following basic bounds for $Pr(X \geq k)$ and for $Pr(X \leq l)$ can be derived by making careful estimations of binomial coefficients. The first two bounds are general, the last two are for tails far from the mean.

For any $0 \leq k, l \leq n$,

$$Pr(X \geq k) \leq \binom{n}{k} p^k, \qquad Pr(X \leq l) \leq \binom{n}{l} q^{n-l}; \tag{1.86}$$

and for $n > k > np > l > 0$,

$$Pr(X > k) < \binom{n}{k} \frac{n-k}{k-np} p^{k+1} q^{n-k}, \qquad Pr(X < l) < \binom{n}{l} \frac{kq}{np-k} p^k q^{n-k+1}. \tag{1.87}$$

The following bound is also often used.

Lemma 1.9.12 (Markov's inequality) *$Pr(X \geq kEX) \leq \frac{1}{k}$ for any random variable X acquiring nonnegative integer values and $k > 0$.*

Proof: The lemma follows from the following inequality:

$$E(X) = \sum_{i \in \mathbf{N}} iPr(X = i) = \sum_{i < kE(X)} iPr(X = i) + \sum_{i \geq kE(X)} iPr(X = i) \geq kE(X)Pr(X \geq kE(X)).$$

□

In order to motivate the next bound, which will play an important role later, especially in Chapter 9, let us assume that we have a biased coin-tossing, one side having the probability $\frac{1}{2} + \varepsilon$, the other side $\frac{1}{2} - \varepsilon$. But we do not know which is which. How do we find this out? The basic idea is simple. Toss the coin many times, and take the side that comes up most of the time as the one with probability $\frac{1}{2} + \varepsilon$. However, how many times does one have to toss the coin in order to make a correct guess with a high probability?

Lemma 1.9.13 (Chernoff's bound) *Suppose $X_1, \ldots, X_n$ are independent random variables that acquire values 1 and 0 with probabilities p and $1-p$, respectively, and consider their sum $X = \sum_{i=1}^{n} X_i$. Then for all $0 \leq \theta \leq 1$,*

$$Pr(X \geq (1+\theta)pn) \leq e^{-\frac{\theta^2}{3}pn}. \tag{*}$$

Proof: Since $Pr(X \geq (1+\varepsilon)pn) = Pr(e^{tX} \geq e^{t(1+\varepsilon)pn})$, for any $t \geq 0$ and $\varepsilon > 0$, Markov's inequality yields

$$Pr(X \geq (1+\varepsilon)pn) = e^{-t(1+\varepsilon)pn} e^{t(1+\varepsilon)pn} Pr(e^{tX} \geq e^{t(1+\varepsilon)pn}) \leq e^{-t(1+\varepsilon)pn} E(e^{tX}).$$

Since $X = \sum_{i=1}^{n} X_i$, and X_i are independent, we get, making use of the inequality $(1+a)^n \leq e^{an}$, which holds for any $a \in \mathbf{R}, n \in \mathbf{N}$,

$$E(e^{tX}) = (E(e^{tX_1}))^n = ((pe^t + (1-p))^n = (1 + p(e^t - 1))^n \leq e^{pn(e^t - 1)}.$$

Putting $t = \ln(1+\varepsilon)$ yields

$$Pr(X \geq (1+\varepsilon)pn) \leq (1+\varepsilon)^{-(1+\varepsilon)pn} e^{\varepsilon pn},$$

and therefore

$$Pr(X \geq (1+\varepsilon)pn) \leq \left(\frac{e^{\varepsilon}}{(1+\varepsilon)^{1+\varepsilon}}\right)^{pn} = \left(e^{\varepsilon-(1+\varepsilon)\ln(1+\varepsilon)}\right)^{pn}.$$

Since $\varepsilon - (1+\varepsilon)\ln(1+\varepsilon) = -\frac{1}{2}\varepsilon^2 + \frac{1}{3}\varepsilon^3 - \ldots \leq -\frac{1}{3}\varepsilon^2$ for $0 \leq \varepsilon \leq 1$, we get the inequality (∗). □

Exercise 1.9.14 *Show that (a)* $Pr(X \geq (1+\varepsilon)pn) \leq \left(\frac{e}{1+\varepsilon}\right)^{(1+\varepsilon)pn}$*; (b)* $Pr(X \geq r) \leq 2^{-r}$ *for* $r \geq 6pn$.

Exercise 1.9.15 *Show that* $Pr(X \leq (1-\varepsilon)pn) \leq e^{-\frac{\varepsilon^2}{2}pn} \leq \left(\frac{e^{\varepsilon}}{(1+\varepsilon)^{1+\varepsilon}}\right)^{pn}$*, if* $0 \leq \varepsilon \leq 1$.

In other words, Chernoff's bound says that a big difference from the expected value is unlikely.

1.9.3 Randomness and Pseudo-random Generators

A **random number generator** can be seen as a stochastic process RANDOM(a,b) which, each time it is activated, produces an integer between a and b, inclusive, with each such integer being equally likely, and with each new integer produced by the process RANDOM(a,b) being independent of the integers returned on previous calls of RANDOM(a,b). For example, RANDOM$(0,1)$ produces 0 or 1, both with probability $\frac{1}{2}$. One can imagine RANDOM(a,b) as rolling a perfect $(b-a+1)$-sided dice to obtain its output.

The basic problem is how to realize such a random number generator. There are quantum-mechanical processes that produce true randomness. Of course, they are not cheap. It is therefore natural to try to use deterministic algorithms that could produce long sequences of pseudo-random bits, given an input of a few really random bits. That would be sufficiently good for many applications.

Intuitively, the sequence of bits

$$0101010101010101010101010101010101010101010$$

is less random than the sequence

$$10010110001011110110001001111101000111010101010111;$$

but how does one formalize this intuition? A classical way of dealing with the problem is through **statistical tests** (e.g. the so-called χ^2-test, the Kolmogorov-Smirnov test) or empirical tests of frequency, uniformity, permutations, sub-sequences and so on.

An infinite sequence of bits $b = (b_1, b_2, \ldots)$ is said to be random with respect to a set S of (statistical and other) tests of randomness if b passes all tests in S. There are many tests available.

Some examples of tests: A random infinite sequence of bits must be **normal**. For each integer k it must hold that the frequency of occurrences of each particular subword of length k in the prefix of length n goes to the limit 2^{-k} for $n \to \infty$. The number of 1s minus the number of 0s in the prefix of length n must be positive for infinitely many n and also negative for infinitely many n.

The view of randomness in terms of **polynomial time indistinguishability**, as discussed below, seems to be better suited to computing. Still another approach to randomness is discussed in Section 6.5.

Deterministic algorithms that take as an input a short random sequence and produce a longer 'almost random' sequence of bits are called pseudo-random generators. They play, surprisingly, a fundamental role in the theory and practice of computing.

More formally, a **pseudo-random generator** is a deterministic polynomial time algorithm which expands short random sequences (called **seeds**) into longer bit sequences (each with a certain probability) such that the resulting probability distribution is in polynomial time indistinguishable from the uniform probability distribution.

More specifically, a pseudo-random generator, say G, expands an n-bit sequence into a longer, say n^k-bit sequence for some $k \in \mathbf{N}$, such that for every polynomial time algorithm with 0-1 output – called **test**, T – for any $\varepsilon > 0$ and for sufficiently large n,

$$|Pr(T(G(X_n)) = 1) - Pr(T(X_{n^k}) = 1)| \leq n^{-\varepsilon},$$

where X_m is a random variable obtaining as values strings of length m, with uniform probability distribution. One can say that a generator of pseudo-random numbers can fool any polynomial time algorithm T trying to check whether its outcomes are really random numbers. Observe too that what we can do with nonpolynomial time algorithms is not of interest to us, because they cannot finish their work in a reasonable time.

A classical proposal for a pseudo-random generator was the **linear congruential generator** of D. H. Lehmer (1948). One chooses four n-bit numbers m, a, b, X_0 and generates an n^3-bit sequence $X_1X_2 \ldots X_{n^2}$ of n-bit numbers by the iterative process

$$X_{i+1} = (aX_i + b) \bmod m.$$

The choice of parameters m, a, b and X_0 is crucial. Although the resulting sequence $X_0, X_1, X_2, \ldots$ is eventually periodic, it is desirable that the period be as large as possible. For example, for $a = b = 7$, $m = 10$ and $X_0 = 7$, we get $7, 6, 9, 0, 7, \ldots$.[15]

Exercise 1.9.16 *Show that for the linear congruential generator*
(a) $x_n \equiv a^n x_0 + (a^{n-1} + a^{n-2} + \cdots + a + 1)b \,(\mathrm{mod}\; m)$;
(b) if $\gcd(a, m) = 1$, *then* $(a-1) \setminus b \Rightarrow x_n = x_{\phi(m)+n}$.

It was shown that Lehmer's pseudo-random generator does not satisfy the strong requirements stated above. For example, there is a polynomial time algorithm (with respect to $\lg m$) such that, given a sufficiently long sequence $X_0, X_1, \ldots X_t$ produced by a linear congruential generator, the algorithm determines a, b and m used to produce this sequence. However, there are no proofs yet, although there is already strong evidence, that pseudo-random generators satisfying the strong requirements formulated above do exist.

The existing candidates depend on the fact that there are **intractable algorithmic problems** for which no polynomial time algorithms exist. For example, the existence of pseudo-random generators satisfying such strong requirements has been proved on the assumption that factorization of integers

[15] It has turned out that for 32-bit arithmetic an appropriate choice of parameters for a linear congruential generator is $m = 2^{31} - 1$, $b = 0$, $a = 7^5 = 16{,}807$.

is intractable. One such candidate is called the **Blum–Micali pseudo-random generator**, or **index generator**, and is based on the intractability of the discrete logarithm problem. It is defined as follows.

Let p be a prime such that $p-1$ has only small factors (smaller than $\lg p$), and let g be a principal root of Z_p^*. The Blum–Micali pseudo-random generator is based on the iteration

$$X_{i+1} = g^{X_i} \bmod p$$

producing the sequence of bits

$$b_1, b_2, b_3, \ldots,$$

where

$$b_i = \begin{cases} 1, & X_i \leq \frac{p-1}{2}; \\ 0, & \text{otherwise,} \end{cases}$$

satisfies the condition on polynomial time indistinguishability provided computation of the discrete logarithm is intractable.

Another example of a simple pseudo-random generator that satisfies the requirement of polynomial time indistinguishability on the assumption that factoring of integers is intractable is the so-called BBS pseudo-random generator. It is based on the iteration

$$x_{i+1} = x_i^2 \bmod n,$$

where $x_0 \in QR_n$ is randomly chosen and n is a Blum integer. It produces the pseudo-random sequence $b_0, b_1, b_2, \ldots$, where $b_i = x_i \bmod 2$. We discuss the design of pseudo-random generators in more detail in Chapter 8.

The fact that it is much cheaper for computers to produce pseudo-randomness than for quantum-mechanical processes to produce true randomness is not the only reason for using pseudo-random generators. We often need to repeat randomized computational processes for various reasons, including error checking. In that case, if our source of randomness is a real one, then the only way to use random bits again is to store them. Moreover, in many applications we actually do not need truly random bits. For example, in cryptography pseudo-random bits are quite sufficient.

Randomness has become a computational resource. The question of how much and what quality of randomness we really need for specific tasks is important to computing. The task of economizing the amount of randomness needed for particular applications is also important. The concept of randomness presented above for sequences can be transferred to other objects. For example, an integer is said to be random if its binary representation is a random string (sequence). To generate a random integer of n bits, therefore, means to generate an n-bit binary sequence.

A more general random generator can be used. For example, a process can be used that for any two real numbers, $a < b$, as parameters, returns a rational number x randomly, uniformly and independently, chosen from the interval $a \leq x \leq b$. Similarly, RANDOM(X) for a set X is expected to return an element chosen randomly, uniformly and independently from among the elements of X. Such random number generators can often be constructed using a RANDOM(0,1) generator as the basic source of randomness.

A theory of pseudo-randomness is being developed that is aimed at understanding the minimum amount of randomness which a randomized method of computation really needs.

1.9.4 Probabilistic Recurrences*

If the efficiency of recursive randomized algorithms or designs is analysed, a special type of recurrence, the so-called probabilistic recurrence, with random variables arises.

For example, consider a randomized algorithm $\mathcal{A}$ that generates, with an input x, in time $a(x)$, a subproblem of size $S(x)$, where $S(x)$ is a random variable with values in $[0,x]$ whose probability distribution depends on $\mathcal{A}$ – and then solves the subproblem recursively. The time complexity of the algorithm is described by the **(probabilistic) recurrence**

$$T(x) = a(x) + T(S(x)). \tag{1.88}$$

$T(x)$ is therefore a random variable whose distribution depends on the distribution of $S(x)$.

The performance of such a randomized algorithm can be characterized by various statements regarding the distribution of the random variable T: for example, by information on the tail of the distribution of T. We discuss two such bounds. They have a quite general character, and are easy to apply.

Consider again the recurrence (1.88), where $E(S(x)) \leq m(x)$ for a fixed function m such that $0 \leq m(x) \leq x$, and where a is a nondecreasing function. The recurrence

$$u(x) = a(x) + u(m(x)) \tag{1.89}$$

is regarded as the deterministic counterpart of the probabilistic recurrence (1.88).

Using the iteration method to solve recurrences, we get that whenever the recurrence (1.89) has a solution, then this solution has the form $u(x) = \sum_{i\geq 0} a(m^{(i)}(x))$, where $m^{(0)}(x) = x$ and $m^{(i+1)}(x) = m(m^{(i)}(x))$ for $i \geq 0$.

We are now in a position to formulate two bounds on tails of T.

Theorem 1.9.17 (Karp's bound) *If $m(x)$ and $a(x)$ are continuous functions such that $m(x)/x$ is nondecreasing and $a(x)$ is increasing on $\{x \mid a(x) > 0\}$, then for every $x \in \mathbf{R}^+$ and $w \in \mathbf{N}^+$,*

$$Pr[T(x) \geq u(x) + wa(x)] \leq \left(\frac{m(x)}{x}\right)^w,$$

where u is the solution of the deterministic recurrence (1.89), and T of the probabilistic recurrence (1.88).

The second bound is weaker but easier to apply.

Theorem 1.9.18 *If m, u and T are as in Theorem 1.9.17, then for any sufficiently large $k \in \mathbf{N}$,*

$$Pr[T(x) \geq ku(x)] \leq \left(\frac{m(x)}{x}\right)^{\frac{k}{2}-1}.$$

Proofs of both theorems are beyond the scope of this book, even though the proof of the second one is based on Markov's inequality and a variation of Chernoff's bound (see references).

Example 1.9.19 (Maximal clique of a graph) *A clique of a graph G is its subgraph, which is a complete graph – each two of its nodes are connected by an edge. There is no polynomial time algorithm known that will find a maximal clique in a graph. However, there is a very simple randomized algorithm for doing it. This is, surprisingly, the fastest known randomized algorithm for this problem.*

Algorithm 1.9.20 Start with the given graph G and an empty clique C, and repeat the following step until the set of nodes of the graph under consideration is empty.

- Choose randomly a node from the given graph, add it to the clique C, remove from the graph under consideration the chosen node and also all nodes that are not adjacent to it.

In order to analyse the algorithm, we need to consider its application to a random graph $G_{n,p}$ with n nodes in which each edge is presented with the probability p. At a certain step of the algorithm, when the set of vertices has size m, the expected number of vertices that do not get deleted is $p(m-1)$. Denote by $C(n)$ the size of the clique when the algorithm is applied to $G_{n,p}$ for any fixed p. Then

$$C(n) = 1 + C(S(n)),$$

where $E(S(n)) = p(n-1) \leq pn$. The corresponding deterministic recurrence is therefore

$$u(n) = 1 + u(pn).$$

Using the methods of Section 1.2 we get $u(n) = \lg n / \lg(1/p)$. An application of Theorem 1.9.18 gives, for sufficiently large k, the bound

$$Pr[C(n) > \frac{k \lg n}{\lg(1/p)}] \leq p^{\frac{k}{2}-1}.$$

Exercise 1.9.21* *If $C'(n)$ denotes the number of adjacency checks of the above randomized algorithm, then for $C'(n)$ we have the recurrence $C'(n) = n - 1 + C'(S(n))$. Find bounds for the tails of $C'(n)$.*

1.10 Asymptotic Complexity Analysis

A variety of concepts, methods and results of fundamental importance for complexity analysis was formally introduced and demonstrated in previous sections. Now we discuss informally global problems, paradigms, tools and methods, as well as pitfalls, of complexity investigations and interpretations. In doing so we have three main aims in mind:

1. to complement the presentation of the technical tools introduced so far with a global view of complexity analysis, its aims, problems, methods and merits;
2. to introduce informally concepts vital for complexity considerations that will be formally defined and investigated later in the book, but will be used before then starting in the next chapter;
3. to provide a rationale for the contents of the book and a summary of its main goals and topics.

1.10.1 Tasks of Complexity Analysis

The main goal of complexity analysis is to determine how good are, asymptotically, the best possible solutions of important problems in computing and communication: for example, problems of designing algorithms, automata, computers, networks or circuits to perform certain tasks, with respect to various computational or communication models and computational resources. In other words, we seek to determine the inherent complexity of computational or communication problems: for example, the minimum number of arithmetical operations needed to multiply two matrices of degree n.

It is of great practical and theoretical importance to establish the inherent complexity of computational problems . If it is known how good the best possible solution is, then a **benchmark** is established with which any specific solution can be compared. Moreover, it turns out that the study of the inherent complexity of computational, communication and design problems brings deep insights into the nature of computing.

There are two basic approaches to determining inherent complexity. The first is a direct one, where the inherent complexity of a specific problem is explicitly determined. For example, $\Theta(n \lg n)$ is the inherent complexity of sorting of n numbers with respect to the number of comparisons. The second is an indirect one, in which relations between the complexities of various problems are established. For example, it is shown that the complexity of one problem is not larger than that of another, or that two problems have asymptotically the same complexity. Another possibility is to show that a problem is feasible if and only if another one is too. For example, matrix multiplication has been shown to be of the same complexity with respect to the number of arithmetical operations as matrix inversion. Integer factorization was shown in Section 1.7 to be feasible if and only if computing square roots of modulo an arbitrary integer is so. Methods presented in this chapter are of importance for both these approaches. In order to develop the indirect approach, a deeper knowledge of the structure of complexity classes and reduction methods is needed. We will deal with this in Chapter 5.

There are two basic types of computational problems: those in which we have complete information about input and those in which we have only incomplete or contaminated information. Problems of the first type, for example, computational problems on graphs, are typical of computing with discrete objects, and they are of main interest in this book. Their solutions and asymptotic complexity analyses require us to use methods of discrete mathematics, as discussed in this chapter. Problems of the second type, for example, computing an integral of a function given by its values at certain points only, are typical of computing with continuous objects and their solutions. Asymptotic complexity analysis requires us to use deep methods of calculus. However, we do not deal with these problems in this book. They are of great importance for computing, but would require us to extend the scope of the book substantially.

There are also two basic types of computational and communication paradigms: determinism and randomization. Randomized algorithms are those that make random choices during their execution. Different methods are used for complexity analysis of deterministic and randomized systems. Deterministic algorithms are further divided into those providing exact and those providing approximate solutions. Complexity analysis of approximation algorithms requires special approaches and tools.

Randomization seems to be very powerful. For many problems we have fast randomized algorithms, but no fast deterministic ones. Computation of square roots modulo a prime is an example. On the other hand, we still lack proofs that polynomial time randomized computing is essentially more powerful than deterministic computing. This is dealt with in Chapter 5.

There are several basic types of randomized algorithms and communication protocols.

- **Las Vegas.** The results are always correct, but it may happen, with small probability, that no result is produced.
- **Monte Carlo.** Results of a certain type are always correct; others may be wrong, but the probability of this is small. We talk also of **one-sided Monte Carlo** algorithms. (For example, a Monte Carlo algorithm may test primality in such a way that if it says that a given integer is composite, then this is 100% true; however, if it says that it is a prime, this may be, with a small probability, wrong.)
- **BEP (Bounded error probability).** No output is 100% correct, but in any specific case the probability of error is small and bounded. We talk also of **two-sided Monte Carlo** algorithms.

The power and methods of randomization are discussed extensively in this book. Probabilistic finite automata are considered in Chapter 3; randomized computations on universal computers in Chapter 4; randomized complexity classes in Chapter 5; limitations of randomness in Chapter 6. An intensive use of randomness is found in cryptography (Chapter 8), interactive protocols (Chapter 9) and communications (Chapter 11). Randomization also plays an important role in futuristic approaches to computing. For example, quantum computing is in principle randomized.

It is natural to ask what makes randomization so powerful. One explanation is simple. It is sometimes preferable to choose, during a computation, a course of actions at random rather than spending time finding out which alternative is better or trying all of them. Such situations arise when the time needed to determine the optimal choice is large compared with the time saved on average by making the optimal choice.

1.10.2 Methods of Complexity Analysis

The complexity analysis of computational, communication and design problems and systems depends on several factors:

Inputs: the way inputs are presented and their size is measured;

Computer and communication models: models of sequential computers (Turing machines, RAM, a model of a conventional sequential computer), models of parallel computers (PRAM, a parallel version of RAM), automata, circuits, networks;

Computing and communication modes: deterministic, nondeterministic, randomized;

Complexity analysis modes: worst case, average case, expected case;

Computation resources: time, storage, programs, processors, communication, randomness.

All these problems are considered in this book. Various representations of integers, graphs and other objects are considered in Chapter 2; several types of automata in Chapters 3 and 7; models of universal computers in Chapter 4; networks in Chapter 10; circuits in Chapters 2, 4, 5 and 11; interactive protocols in Chapter 9, communication models in Chapter 11.

Computational analysis is performed with respect to the size of the input data as the main parameter. Since there are generally many inputs of the same size, two basic approaches are used to deal with this problem: determination of the so-called worst-case complexity and determination of the average-case complexity for inputs of a given size.

Worst-case complexity analysis is in general simpler. It is of main importance for critical real-time applications and has been very successful in providing insights into the nature of computing. The results of worst-case complexity analysis may be quite irrelevant for some applications, or at least questionable, for example, for cryptography. This is due to the fact that the worst case may be achieved only for pathologically 'bad' input data which do not normally, or often, occur, it may happen that these 'bad' data are actually 'nice' ones. For example, QUICKSORT performs at worst for already sorted inputs.

Average-case complexity analysis seems to be producing results that are more realistic for many applications. The difficulty here lies in the fact that one has to know the probability distribution of the input data, and this is rarely easily available. The usual assumption, namely that all data of a given size have the same probability, is often easy to deal with, but rarely realistic. Moreover, it can be shown that for an important probability distribution, the so-called *a priori* probability distribution (see Section 6.5.3) the average-case complexity actually equals the worst-case complexity. Finally, for some important algorithmic problems no good average-case analysis is known. For others there is

size of inputs / function	2^3	2^5	2^7	2^9	2^{11}
$\lg^* n$	2	2	2	3	3
$\lg n$	3	5	7	9	11
$8n$	2^6	2^8	2^{10}	2^{12}	2^{14}
$n \lg n$	$3 \cdot 2^3$	$5 \cdot 2^5$	$7 \cdot 2^7$	$9 \cdot 2^9$	11.2^{11}
n^2	2^6	2^{10}	2^{14}	2^{18}	2^{22}
2^n	2^8	2^{32}	2^{128}	2^{512}	$2^{2,048}$
$n!$	2^{15}	2^{118}	717	$2^{3,876}$	$2^{19,581}$
n^n	2^{24}	2^{160}	2^{896}	$2^{4,608}$	$2^{22,528}$

Table 1.4 Growth of some functions – results for $n!$ are shown as 2^x, where $2^x < n! \leq 2^{x+1}$

no big difference between the worst-case and the average-case results. For example, for HEAPSORT the worst-case and the average-case complexity are the same – $\Theta(n \lg n)$.

The aim is to get asymptotic analysis results in terms of Θ-notation. This is in general not easily achievable. The task is then to find the smallest possible upper bound and the largest possible lower bound. To get a better upper bound, a better system, for example, a faster algorithm, is needed. To improve a lower bound, a better proof technique is needed.

In the case of randomized algorithms we also speak of **expected-time** performance. This is the mean time for solving a problem for the same input. This is essentially different from the concept of the average-case complexity, which refers to deterministic algorithms and the average performance when all inputs are considered, each with a certain probability. It is therefore meaningful to speak about the average-case expected time and the worst-case expected time.

Asymptotic complexity analysis results are robust. In order to get them, one usually ignores the details of the algorithm and concentrates on its loop and data structures. This robustness is the strength, but also the weakness, of asymptotic analysis. In any case, it is this robustness, coupled with the fact that asymptotically better systems are mostly better in practice, that makes asymptotic complexity analysis so interesting and important.

1.10.3 Efficiency and Feasibility

Table 1.4 shows the time needed by algorithms of different complexities to solve problems with different sizes of inputs.[16] The table demonstrates that algorithms whose time complexity grows exponentially cannot be used to solve larger problems, no matter how fast are the computers which may be available.

Unfortunately, for too many practically important problems we know only algorithms with exponential time complexity. Three of them, the **travelling salesman problem**, the **graph isomorphism problem**, and **integer factorization**, will be discussed from several points of view in this book. For example, there is no computer foreseeable that could find the shortest route for a traveller who wants to visit 10,000 cities or to decompose a 1,000-bit-long composite integer. For many of these problems there is still a very large gap, exponential in fact, between the best-known upper bound (exponential) and the lower bound (sometimes even linear).

[16]Some numbers, according to Dyson (1979), that help us to get a more realistic feeling about how large some numbers in Table 1.4 are: time to the next ice age – 2^{28} sec.; the age of the universe – 2^{48}sec.; total lifetime of the universe (if the universe is closed) – 2^{61} sec.; time until all matter is liquid at zero temperature – 2^{240}sec.; number of atoms in the universe (black matter excluded) – 2^{265}; volume of the universe 2^{280} cm^3; time until all matter collapses into black holes – $10^{10^{76}}$ sec.

There are several ways of dealing with the fact that for some very important computational problems no polynomial time sequential algorithm is known with respect to worst-case complexity.

1. One method is to design (heuristic) algorithms that have exponential worst-case complexity but average-case polynomial complexity; or algorithms that have been experimentally verified to be fast on data occurring in real applications.

2. Another, in the case of optimization algorithms, is to develop, if possible, a fast, good approximation algorithm. This is an intriguing problem discussed in Chapter 5.

3. A third is to develop fast randomized algorithms, provided they exist. Computational hardness can often be traded off for randomness, which thus becomes a precious computational resource.

The development of an understanding as to when to consider an algorithmic problem or an algorithm as tractable (feasible) is one of the central tasks of foundations of computing. This is discussed intensively in Chapters 4, 5 and 9. There is a general consensus that a problem should be called tractable if it can be solved in polynomial time. However, views differ as to which computational modes to consider: deterministic, randomized, interactive. These may give rise to very substantial differences, as shown in Chapter 9.

It is now undoubtedly the case that consideration of sequential deterministic polynomial time computations as those representing feasible computations has been very successful with respect to the development of efficient computing systems. This has also brought deep insights into the nature of computing. However, this approach is not without serious problems. Why should one consider algorithms the time complexity of which is proportional to a very high-degree polynomial as feasible? For example, one can hardly consider as practical an algorithm the time complexity of which is n^{10000}. Fortunately, it has turned out that if there is a polynomial time algorithm for a reasonable problem that has a simple, understandable formulation, then the degree of such a polynomial is reasonably small.

A polynomial time algorithm is in general an acceptable solution to a problem. However, we consider as really fast only algorithms of complexity $\mathcal{O}(n)$ or $\mathcal{O}(n \lg n)$ in the case of sequential computing, and of complexity $\mathcal{O}(\lg n)$ or $\mathcal{O}(\lg^2 n)$ for parallel computing.

Algorithms for solving a problem may differ dramatically in their efficiency. This is clear for the case in which there is an exponential time algorithm and also a polynomial time algorithm for the same problem. It seems to be less obvious that even apparently very small time complexity differences between algorithms, for example, $\Theta(n^2)$ and $\Theta(n \lg n)$, can produce quite dramatic differences.

Assume, for example, that an $\Theta(n^2)$ algorithm A_1 has been cleverly programmed for a supercomputer with 10^8 operations per second, to run in time $T(n) = 2n^2$, and that another algorithm, A_2, for the same problem, with asymptotic complexity $\Theta(n \lg n)$, is badly programmed for a PC with 10^6 operations per second, to run in time $50n \log n$. For $n = 10^6$, A_1 needs 2,000 seconds, whereas A_2 needs only 100 seconds!

We see that even small asymptotic differences in time performance of algorithms may have a larger practical impact than the difference in performance between a personal computer and a supercomputer. Observe too that in the above example even supercomputers with a $\Theta(n^2)$ algorithm cannot beat a PC with a $\Theta(n \lg n)$ algorithm. Algorithms, networks, etc. should therefore be seen as important technologies, and progress in these technologies can be matched with that in hardware. Asymptotic complexity analysis, with its benchmarks and performance evaluation, is an important factor contributing to the fast development of such technology.

1.10.4 Complexity Classes and Complete Problems

One of the important tasks in foundations of computing is to develop an understanding of the power and structure of the main computational and communication complexity classes. What kinds of

constant	$\mathcal{O}(1)$
almost constant	$\mathcal{O}(\lg^* n)$
polylog	$\mathcal{O}(\lg^{\mathcal{O}(1)})$
subpolynomial	$n^{o(1)}$
polynomial	$n^{\mathcal{O}(1)}$
superpolynomial	$n^{polylog}$
subexponential	$2^{n^{o(1)}}$
exponential	$2^{n^{\mathcal{O}(1)}}$

Table 1.5 Main resource bounds

problems can be solved using a particular computing model and a specific amount of computational resources? Which relations hold between various complexity classes, and what kind of structure do these classes have?

Table 1.5 summarizes the main resource bounds used in complexity analysis, and the following list gives the main complexity classes.

NC Class of problems solvable by circuits of polynomial size and polylogarithmic depth; or, alternatively, the class of problems solvable by PRAM in polynomial time with polylog number of processors.

P Class of problems solvable in polynomial time by a sequential machine (RAM, Turing machine).[17]

NP Class of problems that have solutions verifiable in polynomial time on sequential computers.

PSPACE Class of problems solvable in polynomial space by a sequential computer or in polynomial time by a parallel computer or by an interactive protocol.

One of the main results in foundations of computing is that all the complexity classes listed above are very robust and to a large degree independent of the details of a specific computer model. The robustness of these concepts also justifies their use in this book even before they have been formally introduced.

Another robust and key concept is that of **complete problems** for a complexity class and a type of reduction. Informally, complete problems of a complexity class are the hardest problems of that class. All other problems in that class can be reduced to them using an 'easy' reduction. The **NP**-complete problems are of special importance. They are those problems in **NP** that any other problem in **NP** can be reduced to in polynomial time. Several thousands of (important) algorithmic problems have already been identified as **NP**-complete. For none of these problems is a polynomial time deterministic algorithm known; nor is there a proof that no such algorithm exists. Their importance lies especially in the fact that finding a polynomial time deterministic algorithm for one of them would provide polynomial time deterministic algorithms for all of them.

1.10.5 Pitfalls

Asymptotic complexity analysis has many pitfalls, and it is important to be aware of them. Let us discuss some of them.

[17] The distinguished role of polynomial time algorithms is underscored by the fact that some natural syntactical conditions can be imposed on algorithms that are equivalent to the requirement that they run in polynomial time. For example, an algorithm runs in polynomial time if and only if it can be programmed in Pascal without the constructs **goto**, **repeat** and **while** and with upper bounds in the size of input for **for** cycles.

1. As already stated, the real meaning of complexity analysis results given in terms of $\mathcal{O}$-, o-, Ω-, ω- and Θ-notation may depend very much on the way the inputs are presented, their size counted, the computing model used, the complexity measures considered, etc. These dependencies are not always clearly stated in papers and books.

   For example, it is usually stated that the time complexity of MERGESORT is $\mathcal{O}(n \lg n)$. This is true in the sense that there is a constant c such that for any n elements drawn from a totally ordered set, at most $cn \lg n$ comparisons are needed to produce a sorted sequence. This means that nothing else is counted except the number of comparisons; each comparison is considered to take one time unit. Other time-consuming operations, such as transportation of elements, are ignored, as well as the size of the elements.

2. Constant factors, which are for good reasons ignored by asymptotic complexity analysis, may sometimes be prohibitively large. Because of this, it may turn out that an algorithm with larger asymptotic complexity is more efficient for practical purposes.

3. Care is also needed in the interpretation of complexity results in cases where the complexity depends, apart from the size of the input, on particular input data. For example, for complexity $T(n)$ of INSERTSORT we get $T(n) = \Omega(n)$ and $T(n) = \mathcal{O}(n^2)$. Neither the lower bound nor the upper bound can be improved, because there are inputs requiring quadratic time and inputs for which linear time is enough. However, if the worst-case complexity is considered, then $T_w(n) = \Theta(n^2)$.

4. There is often a confusion between $\mathcal{O}$-notation and Θ- notation; $\mathcal{O}$-notation is often used where actually Θ-notation is more appropriate, because the indicated upper bound is asymptotically also a lower bound.

Moral: The analysis of even simple computing systems can be a challenge. Complexity analysis is an art, a science and an engineering task. A good rule of thumb for complexity analysis is therefore, as in life, to use common sense, exercise good taste, and listen to your conscience.

1.11 Exercises

1. Denote by u_n the number of binary strings of length n that do not contain two consecutive 0's. Construct a recurrence, and determine u_n for any n.

2. Find a recurrence relation, including the initial conditions, for the number of ways to climb n stairs if the person climbing can take one stair or two stairs at a time.

3. Find a recurrence relation, including the initial conditions, for the number of binary strings of length n containing a pair of consecutive 0s.

4. Find a recurrence for the number of bit strings of length n containing neither three consecutive 0s nor three consecutive 1s.

5. Express $T(n)$ from the recurrence

$$T(1) = a, \qquad T(n) = kT(n/2) + g(n),$$

   as a function of g – for example, by a reduction to the problem in Exercise 1.2.10.

6. Find a recurrence for the number of distinct binary trees with n nodes.

7. Solve the recurrence $u_1 = 1, u_n = au_{n/b} + d(n)$, where $d(n)$ is a multiplicative function and b is a constant; that is, $d(xy) = d(x)d(y)$ for any x,y, as a consequence and, $d(b^i) = (d(b))^i$ for any $i \in \mathbf{N}$.

8. Solve the recurrences with $u_1 = 1$ and for every $n > 1$: (a) $u_n = 4u_{n/2} + n$; (b) $u_n = 4u_{n/2} + n^2$; (c) $u_n = 4u_{n/2} + n^3$.

9. Solve the recurrence $u_0 = a, u_n = 3\sum_{k=0}^{n-1} u_k + 1$ for $n \geq 1$. (There is a very easy solution.)

10. Show the identities (a) $F_{n+1} = \sum_{k=0}^{n} \binom{n-k}{k}$; (b) $F_{2n} = \sum_{k=0}^{n} F_k$.

11. Show the following properties of Fibonacci numbers:
(a) $F_{n+m} = F_m F_{n+1} + F_{m+1} F_n$; (b) $F_{2n} = \sum_{k=1}^{n} F_{2k-1}$; (c) $\sum_{k=0}^{n} F_k^2 = F_n F_{n+1}$.

12. **Lucas numbers** satisfy the recurrence $L_0 = 2, L_1 = 1, L_n = L_{n-1} + L_{n-2}$. (a) Determine L_n. (b) Show that $L_{n+1} = F_n + F_{n+1}$. (c) Show that $\sum_{i=0}^{n} L_i^2 = L_n L_{n+1} + 2$.

13. Solve the recurrence $u_1 = a, u_{2n} = 2u_n + 3, u_{2n+1} = 2u_n + 8$ for $n > 1$.

14.* Show that for the recurrence

$$u_n = a_1 u_{n-1} + \cdots + a_k u_{n-k} + b^n p(n), \tag{1.90}$$

where $b, a_1, \ldots, a_k$ are constants and $p(n)$ is a polynomial of degree d, the corresponding characteristic equation has the form

$$(x^k - a_1 x^{k-1} - \cdots - a_{k-1}x - a_k)(x-b)^{d+1} = 0,$$

and that once this equation is solved we can find the solution of the recurrence (1.90) in a similar way as in the homogeneous case (when $p(n) = 0$).

15. Solve the recurrence (a) $u_1 = 1, u_n = u_{n-1} + 4^n$ for $n > 1$; (b) $u_1 = 1, u_n = 3u_{n-1} + n$, for $n > 1$.

16. Show that $\lceil \frac{n}{m} \rceil = \lfloor \frac{n+m-1}{m} \rfloor$ for each $m \in \mathbf{N}^+$ and $n \in \mathbf{N}$.

17. Show, for any integer n and reals $a, b > 0$, that (a) $\lceil \lceil n/a \rceil / b \rceil = \lceil n/ab \rceil$; (b) $\lfloor \lfloor n/a \rfloor / b \rfloor = \lfloor n/ab \rfloor$.

18. Let $f : R \to R$ be a monotonically increasing function such that $0 < f(x) < x$ for $x > 0$. Define $f^{(0)}(x) = x, f^{(i+1)}(x) = f(f^{(i)})(x)$ and, for a $c > 0, f_c^*(x) = \min\{i \geq 0, f^{(i)}(x) < c\}$. Determine $f_c^*(x)$ for (a) $f(x) = \frac{x}{2}, c = 1$; (b) $f(x) = \sqrt{x}, c = 1$.

19.** Show the inequalities (a) $n! > ((\frac{n}{2})!)^2$ if n is even; (b) $n! \geq (\frac{n+1}{2})!(\frac{n-1}{2})!$ if n is odd; (c) $(\frac{n}{3})^n < n! < (\frac{n}{2})^n$ for all $n \geq 6$.

20. Show the following identities, where n, k are integers and r is a real:
(a) $\binom{-r}{k} = (-1)^k \binom{r+k-1}{k}$; (b) $\sum_{k=0}^{m} (-1)^k \binom{n}{k} = (-1)^m \binom{n-1}{m}$; (c) $\sum_{k=0}^{n} (-1)k\binom{n}{k} = 0, n \geq 1$.

21.* Show the following identities: (a) $\binom{n}{r-1} = \binom{n+2}{r+1} - 2\binom{n+1}{r+1} + \binom{n}{r+1}$; (b) $\sum_{j=1}^{n} \binom{j}{2} = \binom{n+1}{3}$.

22.* Prove the following identities for binomial coefficients: (a) $\sum_{k=1}^{n} k\binom{n}{k} = n2^{n-1}$;
(b) $\sum_{k=1}^{n} k\binom{n}{k}^2 = n\binom{2n-1}{n-1}$.

23. Show the inequalities (a) $\binom{k}{l} \leq \left(\frac{k\cdot e}{l}\right)^l$; (b) $\binom{b}{r}\left(\frac{1}{n}\right)^r \leq \left(\frac{e}{r}\right)^r$, where e is the base of natural logarithms.

24. Find the generating function for the sequence $\langle F_{2i}\rangle_{i=0}^{\infty}$.

25.* Show, for example, by expressing the generating function for Fibonacci numbers properly, that

$$\sum_{k=0}^{n} F_k F_{n-k} = \frac{1}{5}(2nF_{n+1} - (n+1)F_n).$$

26. In how many ways can one tile a $2 \times n$ rectangle with 2×1 and 2×2 'dominoes'?

27. Use the concept of generating functions to solve the following problem: determine the number of ways one can pay n pounds with 10p, 20p and 50p coins.

28. Show (a) $\sqrt{4+\sqrt{3x}} = \Theta(x^{\frac{1}{4}})$; (b) $(1+\frac{2}{x})^x = \Theta(1)$.

29. Show (a) $x^2+3x \sim x^2$; (b) $\sin\frac{1}{x} \sim \frac{1}{x}$.

30. Find two functions $f(n)$ and $g(n)$ such that neither of the relations $f(n) = \mathcal{O}(g(n))$ or $g(n) = \mathcal{O}(f(n))$ holds.

31. Find an $\mathcal{O}$-estimation for $\sum_{j=1}^{n} j(j+1)(j+2)$.

32. Show that if $f(n) = a, f(n) = cf(n-1) + p(n)$ for $n > 1$, where $p(n)$ is a polynomial and c is a constant, then $f(n) = \Theta(n)$.

33. Show that $\sum_{i=1}^{n} i^k = \Theta(n^{k+1})$.

34. Which of the following statements is true: (a) $(n^2+2n+2)^3 \sim n^6$; (b) $n^3(\lg\lg n)^2 = o(n^3 \lg n)$; (c) $\sin x = \Omega(1)$; (d) $\sqrt{\lg n + 2} = \Omega(\lg\lg n)$?

35. Find a function f such that $f(x) = \mathcal{O}(x^{1+\varepsilon})$ is true for every $\varepsilon > 0$ but $f(x) = \mathcal{O}(x)$ is not true.

36.* Order the following functions according to their asymptotic growth; that is, find an ordering $f_1(n), \ldots, f_{35}(n)$ of the functions such that $f_{i+1}(n) = \Omega(f_i(n))$.

$\lg(\lg^* n)$	$2^{\lg^* n}$	F_n	$(\sqrt{2})^{\lg n}$	n^2
$n!$	$(\lg n)!(4/3)^n$	n^3	$2^{\lg^8 n}$	$e^{\lg n^3}$
$\lg^2 n$	$\lg(n!)$	2^{2^n}	$n^{1/\ln n}$	$\ln\ln n$
$\lg^* n$	$n \cdot 2^n$	$n^{\lg\lg n}$	$\ln n$	H_n
1	$\pi(n)$	$2^{\lg n}$	$(\ln n)^{\ln n}$	e^n
$8^{\lg n}$	$(n+1)!$	$\sqrt{\ln n}$	$\lg^*(\lg n)$	$\lg^* \lg^* n$
$2^{\sqrt{3}\lg n}$	n	2^n	$n\lg n$	$2^{2^{n+2}}$

37. Suppose that $f(x) = \mathcal{O}(g(x))$. Does this imply that (a) $2^{f(x)} = \mathcal{O}(2^{g(x)})$; (b) $\lg f(x) = \mathcal{O}(\lg g(x))$; (c) $f^k(x) = \mathcal{O}(g^k(x))$, for $k \in \mathbf{N}$?

38. Show that if $f_1(x) = o(g(x)), f_2(x) = o(g(x))$, then $f_1(x) + f_2(x) = o(g(x))$.

39. Show that (a) $\sin x = o(x)$; (b) $\frac{1}{x} = o(1)$; (c) $100\lg x = o(x^{0.3})$.

40. Show that (a) $\frac{1}{1+x^2} = \mathcal{O}(1)$; (b) $\frac{1}{1+x^2} = o(1)$.

41. Does $f(x) = o(g(x))$ imply that $2^{f(x)} = o(2^{g(x)})$?

42. Show that $f(x) = o(g(x)) \Rightarrow f(x) = \mathcal{O}(g(x))$, but not necessarily that $f(x) = \mathcal{O}(g(x)) \Rightarrow f(x) = o(g(x))$.

43. Show that if $f_1(x) = \mathcal{O}(g(x)), f_2(x) = o(g(x))$, then $f_1(x) + f_2(x) = \mathcal{O}(g(x))$.

44. Show that $o(g(n)) \cap \omega(g(n))$ is the empty set for any function $g(n)$.

45. What is wrong with the following deduction? Let $T(n) = 2T(\lfloor \frac{n}{2} \rfloor) + n$, $T(1) = 0$. We assume inductively that $T(\lfloor \frac{n}{2} \rfloor) = \mathcal{O}(\lfloor \frac{n}{2} \rfloor)$ and $T(\lfloor \frac{n}{2} \rfloor) \leq c\lfloor \frac{n}{2} \rfloor$. Then $T(n) \leq 2c\lfloor \frac{n}{2} \rfloor + n \leq (c+1)n = \mathcal{O}(n)$.

46. Solve the recurrences (a) $T(1) = a, T(n) = 2T(n/2) + n\lg n$; (b) $T(1) = a, T(n) = 7T(n/2) + \mathcal{O}(n^2)$.

47. Let $T(n) = 2T(\lfloor \sqrt{n} \rfloor) + \lg n$. Show (using the substitution $n = 2^m$), that $T(n) = \mathcal{O}(\lg n \lg \lg n)$.

48. Show that $u_n = \mathcal{O}(n!)$ if u_n is defined by recurrence $u_n = 1, u_n = nu_{n-1} + bn^2$. Can you find a better estimation for u_n?

49. Show that if $n > m$, then $n \bmod m < \frac{n}{2}$.

50. Show that $d \backslash n \Rightarrow F_d \backslash F_n$.

51. Compute the greatest common divisor for the following pairs of numbers: (a) $(325, 53)$; (b) $(2002, 2339)$; (c) $(3457, 4669)$; (d) $(143, 1326)$; (e) $(585, 3660)$.

52. Express the greatest common divisor of each of the following pairs of integers as a linear combination of these integers: (a) (117, 213); (b) (3454, 4666); (c) (21, 55); (d) (10001, 13422); (e) (10233, 33341).

53. Show, by induction, that the number of steps required to compute $\gcd(n, m), n > m$, is smaller than $\log_r n$, where $r = (1+\sqrt{5})/2$.

54. Find a prime n such that $2^n - 1$ is not a prime.

55. Show that the nth prime is smaller than $2^{2^{n+1}}$.

56. Show that an integer n is prime if and only if there exists an $0 < a < n$ such that $a^{n-1} \equiv 1 \bmod n$, and for each prime q dividing $n-1$ we have $a^{\frac{n-1}{q}} \not\equiv 1 \pmod{n}$.

57. (Wilson's prime number test) Show that $(p-1)! \equiv -1 \pmod{p}$ iff p is a prime.

58. An integer is called perfect if it equals the sum of its proper divisors. (For example, 6 and 28 are perfect integers.) (a) Find the first ten perfect numbers; (b) show that if $2^n - 1$ is prime, then $2^{n-1}(2^n - 1)$ is perfect.

59. Compute (a) $5^{11}3^{14} \bmod 26$; (b) $4^{80} \bmod 65$; (c) $3^{100} \bmod 79$; $3^{1000} \bmod 17$; (d) $5^{11}3^{14} \bmod 26$; (e) $4^{80} \bmod 65$; (f) $2^{34} \bmod 341$.

60. Show that if $a, b \in \mathbf{N}^+$, then (a) $(2^a - 1) \bmod (2^b - 1) = 2^{a \bmod b} - 1$; (b) $\gcd(2^a - 1, 2^b - 1) = 2^{\gcd(a,b)} - 1$.

61. Compute (a) $(\sum_{i=1}^{100} i!) \bmod 12$; (b) $(\sum_{i=1}^{90} i^5) \bmod 4$.

62. Solve the congruences (a) $32x \equiv 6 \pmod{70}$; (b) $7x \equiv 3 \pmod{24}$; (c) $32x \equiv 1 \pmod{45}$; (d) $14x \equiv 5 \pmod{54}$.

63. Determine the inverses (a) $4^{-1} \bmod 9$; (b) $7^{-1} \bmod 17$; (c) $21^{-1} \bmod 143$.

64. Show that if a is odd, then $a^{2^{n-2}} \equiv 1 \pmod{2^n}$ for each $n \geq 3$.

65. Let n be an integer, $x < 2^n$ a prime, $y < 2^n$ a composite number. Show, by using the Chinese remainder theorem, that there is an integer $p < 2n$ such that $x \not\equiv y \pmod{p}$.

66. Design a multiplication table for (a) $\mathbf{Z}_9^*$; (b) $\mathbf{Z}_{11}^*$.

67. Let $p > 2$ be a prime and g a principal root of $\mathbf{Z}_p^*$. Then, for any $x \in \mathbf{Z}_p^*$, show that $x \in QR_p \Leftrightarrow index_{p,g}(x)$ is even.

68. Show that if p is a prime, $e \in \mathbf{N}$, then the equation $x^2 \equiv 1 \pmod{p^e}$ has only two solutions: $x = 1$ and $x = -1$.

69. Show that if g is a generator of Z_n^*, then the equality $g^x \equiv g^y \pmod{n}$ holds iff $x \equiv y \pmod{\phi(n)}$.

70. Show, for any constant a, b and a random variable X, (a) $E(aX + b) = aEX + b$; (b) $V(aX + b) = a^2 VX$.

71. (Variance theorem) Show, for random variables X, Y and reals a, b, that (a) $V(aX + bY) = a^2 VX + b^2 VY + 2abE((X - EX)(Y - EY))$; (b) $V(X + Y) = VX + VY$.

72. Find the probability that a family of four children does not have a girl if the sexes of children are independent and if (a) the probability of a girl is 51%; (b) boys and girls are equally likely.

73. Find the following probabilities when n independent Bernoulli's trials are carried out with probability p of success: (a) the probability of no failure; (b) of at least one failure; (c) of at most one failure; (d) of at most two failures.

74. Determine the probability that exactly seven 0s are generated when 10 bits are generated and the probability that 0 is generated is 0.8, the probability that 1 is generated is 0.2, and bits are generated independently.

75. (Birthday paradox) Birthdays are important days. (a) Determine the probability that in a group of n persons there are at least two with the same birthday (assume that all 366 days are equally likely as birthdays). (b) How many people are needed to make the probability that two people have the same birthday greater than $1/2$?

76. There are many variants of Chernoff's bound. Show the correctness of the following one: if $X_1, \ldots, X_n$ are independent random variables and $Pr(X_i = 1) = p$ for all $1 \leq i \leq n$, then $Pr(\sum_{i=1}^{n} X_i \geq pn + a) \leq e^{\frac{-2a^2}{n}}$.

77. Show **Chebyshev's inequality**: if X is a random variable, then $Pr((X - EX) > \alpha) < \frac{VX}{\alpha^2}$ for all $\alpha > 0$.

78. Let $p(x_1, \ldots, p_n)$ be a polynomial with rational coefficients of degree d and not identically 0. Show that $p(\alpha) \neq 0$ for at least half of all vectors $\alpha \in \{-nd, \ldots, 0, \ldots, nd\}^n$.

79. Show for the linear congruential generator $x_{i+1} = (ax_i) \bmod m$ that if m is prime and a choice of a yields the maximum period (of $m-1$), then a^k also yields the maximum period, provided $k < m$ and $(m-1)$ is not divisible by k.

80. Suppose that $m, n \in \mathbf{N}^+$. What is the probability that a randomly chosen positive integer smaller than mn is not divisible by either m or n?

81. Show for the iteration $x_{i+1} = (ax_i + b) \bmod m, i \geq 0$ that if $a \perp m$, then x_0 repeats periodically in $x_1, x_2, \ldots$.

82. Show for the linear congruential generator and $X'_n = X_{n+1} - X_n$ that (a) $X'_n \equiv a^{n-1}X'_1 \pmod m$; (b) $X'_n = X'_{\phi(m)+n}$.

QUESTIONS

1. Is F_n larger than $\left(\frac{1+\sqrt{5}}{2}\right)^n$?
2. Is it true that $3^{n+2} = \mathcal{O}(3^n)$ and $3^{2n} = \mathcal{O}(3^n)$?
3. We know that $n! \prec n^n$. Which of the relations $n^n \prec (n!)^2$ and $(n!)^2 \prec n^n$ holds?
4. Are the functions $\lceil \lg n \rceil!$ and $\lceil \lg \lg n \rceil!$ polynomially bounded?
5. Is it true that $\Theta(f(n) + g(n)) = \Theta(\max\{f(n), g(n)\})$?
6. How many primes do we have of a given length n?
7. How do you interpret the equation $3n^3 + \Theta(n^2) = \Theta(n^3)$?
8. What properties do Blum integers have?
9. In which cases is it better to use a pseudo-random generator than a true random generator?
10. Why are constant factors in the analysis of algorithms not of importance and why are they of importance?

1.12 Historical and Bibliographical References

The history of basic concepts, methods and results used in the analysis of algorithms is deeply rooted in the history of mathematics. The most important contribution to their introduction and further development for computing was made by Donald E. Knuth, who received the Turing award in 1974. His monumental work and pioneering books: Knuth (1968); Knuth (1969); Knuth (1973); Greene and Knuth (1981); Graham, Knuth and Patashnik (1989) are also the main sources of detailed historical and bibliographical references. Moreover, the last of these, a textbook, is a masterpiece of a quality hardly matched in computing.

Concrete Mathematics by Graham, Knuth and Patashnik (1989) is not only the main textbook recommended for a more detailed and deeper treatment of the subject but has also influenced the choice of material and presentation in a large portion of this chapter. Additional books used and recommended are Kranakis (1986); Harel (1987); Brassard and Brattey (1988); Cormen, Leiserson and Rivest (1990); Aigner (1993); Arnold and Guessarian (1996). An extensive introduction to the analysis of algorithms is found in Sedgewick and Flayolet (1996), and for more advanced tools see the comprehensive book by Hofri (1995).

We deal in some detail with layouts of graphs and especially trees in Section 10.6. The Towers of Hanoi problem and its accompanying myth were introduced by Lucas (1894), according to Graham, Knuth and Patashnik (1989), where the problem and several of its modifications are analysed. Its generalization to four rods is considered by Gedeon (1992). Methods of solving recurrences are discussed by Bentley, Haken and Saxe (1978); Luecker (1980); Greene and Knuth (1981); Aho, Hopcroft and Ullman (1983); Purdom and Brown (1985); Brassard and Brattey (1988); Graham, Knuth and Patashnik (1989); Cormen, Leiserson and Rivest (1990); Aigner (1993); and Arnold and Guessarian (1996).

The generating function concept has been intensively used since L. Euler, 1741, and L. Laplace, 1812; its use in solving recurrences is elaborated by Graham, Knuth and Patashnik (1989). The domino problem and the bootstrapping method also come from there. A detailed proof of Theorem 1.4.11 can be found in Aigner (1993). A survey of the $3x+1$ problem is found in Lagarias (1985).

Names and notation for the ceiling and floor functions are due to Iverson (1960). Lemma 1.3.1 is due to Graham, Knuth and Patashnik (1989), where binomial coefficients are also discussed in detail.

The family $\mathcal{L}$ of logarithmico-exponential functions has been introduced by G. H. Hardy (1910) and it has been further explored in Hardy (1924). For example, it has been shown that every function in $\mathcal{L}$ is eventually monotonic and bounded from below by a function $\lg^{l} n$ for some l. (This implied that $\lg^{*} n$ is not in $\mathcal{L}$.)

The amazing story of primes and records of primes is nicely presented in a book by Ribenboim (1996) and in an expository paper by Zagier (1977). Estimations of $\pi(n)$ can be found in Rosser and Schoenfeld (1962). For computing of $\pi(x)$ see Lagarias, Miller and Odlyzko (1985). The prime number theorem is due to Dirichlet, Hadamard and de la Vallée Poussin; a proof can be found in Landau (1953).

Quadratic residues, computation of discrete square roots, discrete logarithms and their applications in pseudo-random generators and cryptography are well presented in Kranakis (1986). Section 1.7 profited much from it and the proof of Theorem 1.8.5 can also be found there. A polynomial time algorithm for computing square roots modulo a prime was first designed by Berlekamp (1970). An elegant Las Vegas algorithm for computing square roots modulo a prime is found in Karp (1991), and is credited to Lehmer (1951). A polynomial time algorithm for computing a discrete logarithm modulo a prime p such that $p-1$ has only small factors is due to Pohlig and Hellman (1978). Theorem 1.8.16 is, like many basic results in foundations of computing, due to Michael Rabin (1979), who received the Turing award in 1976. Gauss's characterizations of those n for which Z_N^* is cyclic can be found in Kranakis (1986). For a survey of algorithmic number theory see Adleman (1994).

There are many excellent books on probability, for example, Feller (1964) and Billingsley (1986). Exercise 1.9.5 follows Montwani and Raghavan (1995). Classical approaches to pseudo-random generators are treated exhaustively by Knuth (1969), and the complexity-based approaches are well presented in Kranakis (1986). The analysis of Algorithm 1.9.11 is due to Knuth (1968). For proofs of inequalities (1.86) and (1.87) see, for example, Cormen, Rivest and Leiserson (1990). For Chernoff's bound see Hagerup and Rüb (1989). The concept of polynomial time indistinguishability is due to Yao (1982) and Blum and Micali (1982). The BBS pseudo-random generator is due to Blum, Blum and Shub (1986); the Blum–Micali pseudo-random generator was introduced by Blum and Micali (1982). The result on the predictability of linear congruential generators is due to Plumstead (1982). Methods of solving probabilistic recurrences have been worked out by Richard M. Karp, winner of the Turing award for 1985, who has contributed significantly to the development of randomized computing. Theorem 1.9.17 is due to Karp (1991), and Theorem 1.9.18 to Chaudhuri and Dubhashi (1995).

D. Harel's *Algorithmics* (1987) is another masterpiece which provides not too formal but deep insights into computing, including complexity analysis. This is an excellent reference for additional insights regarding the aims, methods, results and merits of complexity analysis discussed in Section 1.10.

2 Foundations

INTRODUCTION

Foundations of computing are deeply rooted in mathematics, and fluency in basic mathematics is essential for computer science. In addition, computing itself has had a strong impact on mathematics. This chapter therefore has several aims. First, it summarizes the foundational concepts of mathematics needed in computing and sets up terminology and notational conventions, thus serving as a reference source. Second, it presents, illustrates and discusses new paradigms of computing brought into these foundational areas of mathematics that are of key importance for computing. In doing so, it introduces some basic problems, as well as basic methods for solving them. In this way the chapter provides a rationale and introduction to various topics of the book. Third, special concepts and methods that will be used later are introduced and illustrated.

LEARNING OBJECTIVES

The aim of the chapter is to demonstrate

1. basic concepts, terminology and notations concerning sets, relations, functions, graphs, languages and algebras;
2. new paradigms that computing has brought into the foundational areas of mathematics, which are of importance for science in general and computing science in particular;
3. basic methods of representation of objects, sets, relations and graphs;
4. several methods for visualizing words and languages and for representing pictures and images by words and languages;
5. methods to compute transitive closure of relations;
6. several classes of functions having a special importance for computing: Boolean functions, one-way functions, hash functions;
7. methods to deal with graph matching, colouring and traversal problems;
8. special classes of graphs, for example, Cayley graphs, planar graphs, bipartitie graphs;
9. very basic concepts concerning monoids, semigroups, groups, quasi-rings, rings, and fields.

If in other sciences we should arrive at certainty without doubt and truth without error, it behooves us to place the foundations of knowledge on mathematics.

Roger Bacon (c.1214–94) [1]

Basic mathematical structures, such as sets, relations, functions, graphs, algebras and formal languages, play an important role in the foundations of any mature science. This alone is sufficient reason to summarize basic concepts and results of these areas, as well as to fix terminology and notation, in an introductory chapter of a book on foundations of computing. However, the aim of this chapter goes further. Foundations of computing also bring into these key areas of modern science new deep paradigms, concepts, methods and problems that are of great importance for the whole of computing. The second aim of this chapter is to point out, motivate and illustrate these viewpoints, concepts, problems and methods, establishing basic rationales for many subjects with which the book deals. Complexity standpoints and asymptotic estimations play an irreplaceable role here, providing guidance and evaluations. For this reason the chapter follows rather than precedes that on the fundamentals of complexity analysis and randomness.

2.1 Sets

The simplest, and at the same time perhaps the richest and most complex, mathematical objects are sets. Their position and role in computing are similarly complex and rich. They are fundamental (discrete) structures on which other (discrete) structures are built. Many key problems in foundations of computing can be seen as problems concerning sets.

2.1.1 Basic Concepts

A **set** is a collection of distinguishable objects (elements). The **empty set** $\emptyset$ has no objects. If A is a set, then $x \in A$ ($x \notin A$) denotes that x is (is not) an object of A. Notation $A \subseteq B$ expresses that set A is a **subset** of set B, each object of A is in B. Notation $A \subset B$ (or $A \subsetneq B$) means that A is a **proper subset** of B. Sets A and B are **equal**, notation $A = B$, if $A \subseteq B$ and $B \subseteq A$. Two sets are said to be **disjoint** if no object is in both of them. If elements of a set $\mathcal{A}$ are sets, we use the term **family of sets** for $\mathcal{A}$. Notation $x \in_{\mathcal{D}} A$ is used to denote that x is an element of the set A randomly chosen with respect to the probability distribution $\mathcal{D}$. Notation $x \in_{\mathcal{U}} A$ is reserved for choosing an element of A with respect to the uniform distribution.

Exercise 2.1.1 *Find two sets A and B such that $A \in B$ and $A \subseteq B$.*

It is often assumed that all the sets we deal with are subsets of a **universal set** U. With each $A \subseteq U$ we can then associate a **characteristic function** (or a **membership predicate**) $f_A : U \to \{0,1\}$, defined by $f_A(x) = [x \in A]$.

[1] An English philosopher and natural scientist sometimes considered the first theoretician of the experimental sciences.

Binary operations on sets:

$$\begin{aligned}
\textbf{union } A \cup B &= \{x \,|\, x \in A \text{ or } x \in B\};\\
\textbf{intersection } A \cap B &= \{x \,|\, x \in A \text{ and } x \in B\};\\
\textbf{difference } A - B &= \{x \,|\, x \in A \text{ and } x \notin B\};\\
\textbf{symmetric difference } A = B \triangle C &= A - B \cup B - A;\\
\textbf{Cartesian product } A \times B &= \{(a,b) \,|\, a \in A, b \in B\}.
\end{aligned}$$

The concept of the Cartesian product can be generalized, in a natural way, to more than two sets. Since union and intersection are commutative and associative operations, we consider also

$$\begin{aligned}
\textbf{generalized union } & \bigcup_{i \in I} A_i = \{x \,|\, \exists i \in I, x \in A_i\};\\
\textbf{generalized intersection } & \bigcap_{i \in I} A_i = \{x \,|\, x \in A_i, \forall i \in I\};\\
\textbf{generalized Cartesian product } & \bigotimes_{i=1}^{n} A_i = \{x \,|\, x = (x_1, \ldots, x_n), x_i \in A_i\},
\end{aligned}$$

where $I \neq \emptyset$ is an index set. For the Cartesian product of a set A with itself we use the notation $A^i = \bigotimes_{j=1}^{i} A$.

Two special versions of union and difference operations are of interest in computing: **insertion** $A \cup \{x\}$ and **deletion** $A - \{x\}$, where A is a set and x an object. If the underlying set is clear from the context, a simpler notation INSERT(x) and DELETE(x) is often used.

Unary operations on sets:

$$\begin{aligned}
\textbf{complement } A^c &= U - A; \text{ another notation: } \overline{A};\\
\textbf{power set } 2^A &= \{B \,|\, B \subseteq A\};\\
\textbf{iterations } A^*(A^\omega)[A^{\omega\omega}] &= \text{a set of all finite (infinite) [bi-infinite] sequences of elements of } A.
\end{aligned}$$

Exercise 2.1.2 *Let A, B be sets. Do the following implications hold: (a) $A \cap B = \emptyset \Rightarrow 2^A \cap 2^B = \emptyset$; (b) $2^A = 2^B \Rightarrow A = B$?*

Exercise 2.1.3 *Which of the following relations hold: (a) $2^A \cap 2^B = 2^{A \cap B}$; (b) $2^A \cup 2^B = 2^{A \cup B}$?*

Partition of a set A is a family (finite or infinite) of mutually disjoint subsets $B_i, i \in I$, of A such that $A = \bigcup_{i \in I} B_i$. Notation $C = A \,\dot\cup\, B$ will be used to express the fact that the set C is partitioned into two disjoint subsets A and B.

Important number sets: $\emptyset$ (the empty set), **N** (nonnegative integers), $\mathbf{N}^+$ (positive integers), **Z** (all integers), **Q** (rational numbers), **R** (real numbers), $\mathbf{R}^+$ (positive real numbers), **C** (complex numbers), $\mathbf{Z}_n$ (the set of residue classes modulo n) and $\mathbf{Z}_n^*$ (those residue classes from $\mathbf{Z}_n$ that contain elements relatively prime to n). Moreover, if $n \in \mathbf{N}$, then $[n] = \{0, 1, \ldots, n-1\}$. In particular, $[2] = \{0, 1\}$.

The term **alphabet** will often be used to denote an arbitrary finite nonempty set A. In this case elements of A are called symbols, elements of A^* strings (or words), and elements of A^ω ω-strings. Subsets of A^* are called languages, and subsets of A^ω are ω-languages. Elements of the set $\mathbf{B} = \{0, 1\}$ will be interpreted, depending on the context, either as integers or (binary) symbols – bits – or Boolean (truth) values. Elements of the set $\mathbf{B}^*$ are often called **binary strings**, and elements of the set $\mathbf{B}^\omega$ are called **infinite binary strings**. The set **B** is also called the **binary alphabet**.

Exercise 2.1.4 *A* **multiset** *is a collection of elements in which an element can occur more than once. Let* $\{m_1.a_1,\ldots,m_k.a_k\}$ *denote the multiset in which the element* a_i *occurs* m_i *times. Define in a natural way operations of union, intersection and difference for multisets, and determine, for* $A=\{2.a,4.b,3.c\}$, $B=\{1.a,2.b,3.c\}$, $A\cup B, A\cap B$ *and* $A-B$.

Cardinality: $|A|$ denotes the cardinality of the set A. If A is finite, $|A|$ is the number of its elements. For infinite sets cardinality is defined indirectly. Two infinite sets A and B are said to have the same cardinality if there is a bijection between them. Sets that have the same cardinality as $\mathbf{N}$ are called **countable**. The set $\mathbf{R}$ is said to have cardinality of **continuum**.

Power set and iteration operations can increase cardinality by a large amount. If A is a finite set, then clearly

$$|2^A| = 2^{|A|}, \qquad |A^*| = |\mathbf{N}|, \qquad |A^\omega| = |\mathbf{R}|. \tag{2.1}$$

In addition, $|2^{\mathbf{N}}| = |\mathbf{R}|$.

Remark 2.1.5 The description of a set as a collection of objects, based on an intuitive notion of object, is due to G. Cantor (1895). The resulting set theory is called **naïve set theory,** and this is what we will use. The discovery by Russell[2] (1902) that this theory leads to **paradoxes**, or **logical inconsistencies**, at first caused a nightmare in mathematics. This was later resolved through the development of **axiomatic set theory**.

Russell's paradox: *Let S be the set that contains a set X if and only if X does not belong to itself – in other words, let* $S=\{x\,|\,x\notin x\}$. *Is* $S\in S$? *If yes, then necessarily* $S\notin S$; *if not, then necessarily* $S\in S$ *– a contradiction in both cases.*

The existence of paradoxes looks like a negative phenomenon. However, like many other negative results, as we shall see later, paradoxes play an important positive role in foundations of computing. For example, they have been used to show several important results concerning the limitations of computing and formalization. This will be discussed in detail in Chapter 6.

2.1.2 Representation of Objects by Words and Sets by Languages

By a representation of objects of a set A by objects of a set C, the term **encoding** is often used, a mapping $c: C\rightarrow A$ is understood, which maps uniquely objects of C into objects of A. $c(a)$ is then the object represented by the 'code' a.

It follows from (2.1) that the sets of binary strings and infinite binary strings have enough elements to encode uniquely objects of any set that in practice we need to deal with in computing. Not only that, for almost all sets we deal with there is a natural encoding of their elements by binary strings. Moreover, most of the basic problems in computing have a natural formulation in terms of sets (of strings). This is why in foundations of computing it is to a large degree sufficient to deal with sets of (binary) strings, called languages.

[2]Bertrand Arthur William Russell (1872–1970), an English philosopher, logician, mathematician and social reformer. His *Principles of Mathematics* and *Principia Mathematica* (with A. N. Whitehead) influenced modern logic. He wrote more than 68 books, was several times imprisoned for his articles and anti-military activities, and received the Nobel prize for literature.

Example 2.1.6 (Binary number representations) *There are several ways in which binary strings can be seen as representing integers. Each finite binary word $b = b_1 \dots b_n$ and each infinite binary word $c = c_1c_2\dots$ can be seen as representing an integer, notation $bin(b)$, and a real number in $[0,1]$, notation $bre(c)$, defined by*

$$\mathrm{bin}(b) = \sum_{i=1}^{n} b_i 2^{n-i}, \qquad \mathrm{bre}(c) = \sum_{i=1}^{\infty} c_i 2^{-i}. \tag{2.2}$$

Observe that the mapping $\mathrm{bre}: \mathbf{B}^\omega \to [0,1)$ is one to one if we restrict it to the set $\mathbf{B}^\omega - \mathbf{B}^*\{1\}^\omega$. If $x < 2^n$, $x, n \in \mathbf{N}$, then x can be uniquely represented by an n-bit string $b = b_1 \dots b_n$, notation $\mathrm{bin}_n^{-1}(x)$, such that $\mathrm{bin}(\mathrm{bin}_n^{-1}(x)) = x$. (Observe that $b_i = \lfloor \frac{x}{2^{n-i}} \rfloor \bmod 2$.) Notation $\mathrm{bin}^{-1}(n)$ will be used to denote the binary representation of n with the left-most bit equal to 1 if $n \neq 0$ and $\mathrm{bin}^{-1}(0) = 0$ otherwise.

Exercise 2.1.7 (Dyadic representation of integers) *If $w \in \{1,2\}^*$, then define $dya(\varepsilon) = 0$ and for $w = a_{n-1} \dots a_0, a_i \in \{1,2\}$, $dya(w) = \sum_{i=0}^{n-1} a_i 2^i$. (a) Show that each nonnegative integer has a unique dyadic representation; (b) show dyadic representations for the numbers 7,77,777,7777,777777; (c) design an algorithm to add two integers given by their dyadic representations.*

Exercise 2.1.8 (Fibonacci number representation) *(a)* Show that each nonnegative integer has a unique 'Fibonacci representation' $n = \sum_{i=1}^{k} F_{m_i}$, where $m_i \geq m_{i+1} + 2$ for $1 \leq i < k$, and either $n = 0$ or $m_k \geq 2$; (b) determine the Fibonacci number representations of integers $2^i, 1 \leq i \leq 10$.*

Example 2.1.9 (Universality of binary representations) *Let $A = \{a_1, \dots, a_n\}$ be a finite set, the alphabet, and $2^{m-1} \leq n < 2^m$ for some integer m. Each element of A can be uniquely encoded by a binary string of length m. This can in turn be used to encode each element of A^* and of A^ω by a finite or an infinite binary string – each symbol from A is simply replaced by its binary code. This simple encoding of strings from a finite alphabet by binary strings often allows us to deal, without loss of generality, only with sets of binary strings.*

Example 2.1.10 (Binary string representation of matrices) *Let $M = \{a_{ij}\}$ be an $n \times n$ matrix of nonnegative integers. M can be represented by the following word over the alphabet $\Sigma = \{0,1,\#\}$:*

$$bin^{-1}(a_{11})\#bin^{-1}(a_{12})\#\dots\#bin^{-1}(a_{1n})\#\#bin^{-1}(a_{21})\#\dots\#bin^{-1}(a_{2n})\#\#\dots\#\#bin^{-1}(a_{n1})\#\dots\#bin^{-1}(a_{nn}).$$

We can then use, for example, the encoding $0 \to 00$, $1 \to 11$ and $\# \to 01$, to get a completely binary encoding of M.

In special cases simpler encoding of matrices by binary strings is available. For example, an $n \times n$ symmetric Boolean matrix can be encoded by a binary string of length $n(n+1)/2$ by simply listing, one after another, all rows of the matrix above the main diagonal.

For each set there are infinitely many ways in which its objects can be encoded by strings over an alphabet. Which of them is best depends on the way that the set is to be dealt with.

There are also infinitely many ways in which strings and sets of strings can be interpreted. It may also happen, as the following example indicates, that very simple sets of strings can represent quite complex objects.

Example 2.1.11 *Each string $(a_1,b_1),\dots,(a_n,b_n)$ over the alphabet $A = \{(0,0),(0,1),(1,0)\}$ can be interpreted as a point in a plane with coordinates $(0.a_1 \dots a_n, 0.b_1 \dots b_n)$. On this interpretation A^* represents the set of points of the fractal structure called the Sierpiński triangle, shown in Figure 2.1a.*

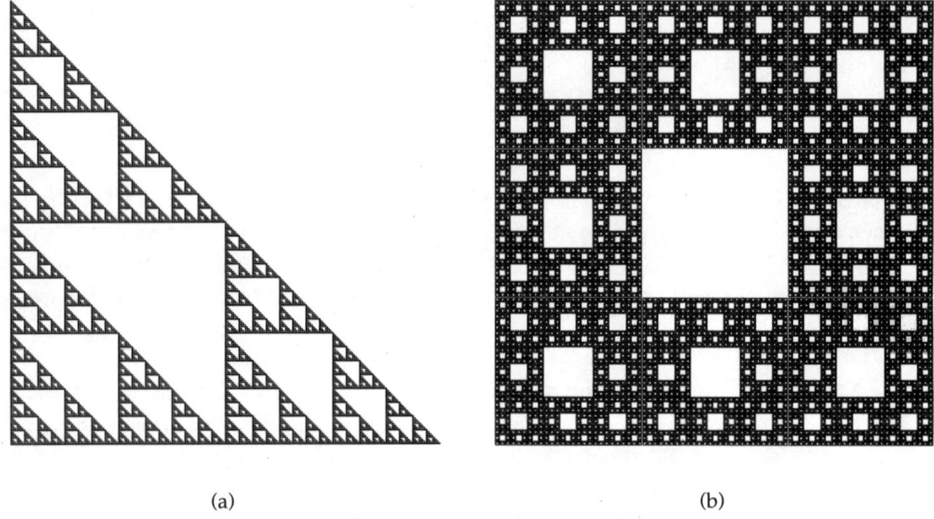

(a) (b)

Figure 2.1 Sierpiński triangle and Cantor carpet

Exercise 2.1.12 *Find a finite set A and an interpretation of strings over A such that A^* represents the fractal structure called the Cantor carpet, shown in Figure 2.1b.*

Exercise 2.1.13 *Find a nice, simple set description of the Sierpiński tetrahedron whose construction is shown in Figure 2.2.*

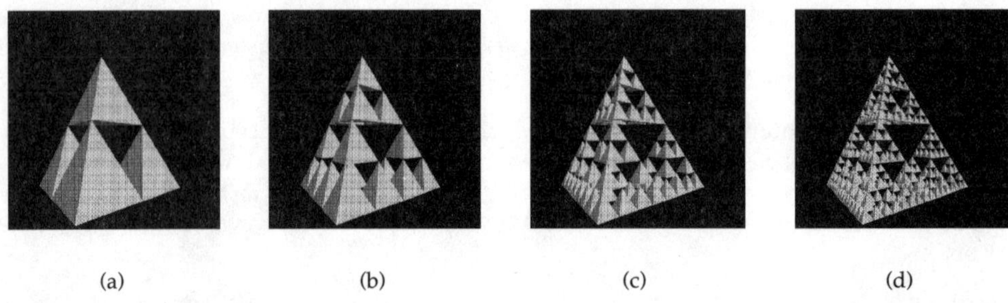

(a) (b) (c) (d)

Figure 2.2 A stepwise design of the Sierpiński tetrahedron

2.1.3 Specifications of Sets – Generators, Recognizers and Acceptors

Basic problems concerning set specifications (descriptions) can be summarized as follows.

1. How to specify a set in a simple and useful way. For example, it is certainly not obvious that the sets of points shown in Figure 2.1 have such a simple description.

2. How to determine, given a set description, which set it describes and which objects are in the specified set. For example, which natural numbers are in the set described by formula (2.3) on page 83? In particular, how do we find out, given a set specification and an object, whether this object is in the specified set?

3. How to specify important families of sets, for example, those that can be accepted by automata of a certain type.

4. How to determine which properties have sets specified using some particular specification language, for example, logical formulas of a certain type, programs, automata or grammars of a certain type.

5. How to determine which sets have specifications which allow one to find efficiently answers to various basic questions, for example, whether a given element is in the set, or whether the set is empty (infinite).

All these problems are among the most fundamental ones in computing, and we will deal with them intensively in this book. There are several basic ways to specify sets.

1. **Enumeration.** Enumerating elements of a finite set. For example,

$$\begin{aligned} P &= \{19,31,61,89,107,127,521,607,1279,2203,2281,3217,4253,4423,9689 \\ &\quad 9941,11213,19937,21701,23209,44497,86243,216091,756839,859433\} \end{aligned}$$

is the set of all primes p such that $2^p - 1$ was for the period 1589–1996 the largest known prime. Enumeration clearly does not work if the set is too big, and even if it is not, enumeration can be far from the most effective way of describing a set. For example, the set of the first 2^{65536} primes, which has such a short description, cannot be practically enumerated. On the other hand, enumeration is not to be forgotten as a way of describing sets because, as shown later, most finite sets are so random that there is no shorter way to describe them.

2. **Binary strings representation.** If the universal set U is finite and has n elements $u_1, \ldots, u_n$, then each subset $A \subseteq U$ can be uniquely represented by the binary word $b = b_1 \ldots b_n$, where $b_i = 1 \Leftrightarrow u_i \in A$. Note that with this representation of subsets of U it is possible to perform, in one parallel step, set union, intersection and subtraction! If U is countable, then any subset of U can be represented by an ω-string.

3. **Logical formulas.** A formal or informal logical formula can be used to describe a set by specifying properties of its objects. For example,

$$F = \{n \mid n \in N, n > 2, \exists \text{ integers } x,y,z > 0, x^n + y^n = z^n\} \tag{2.3}$$

used to be perhaps the most famous description of a set in mathematics.

4. **Generators.** A generator that produces all elements of a set A and no others can be seen as specifying the set A. There are many forms which a generator may take. It can be a deterministic automaton – see Figure 2.3a for a generator that generates a set of integers – or a randomized

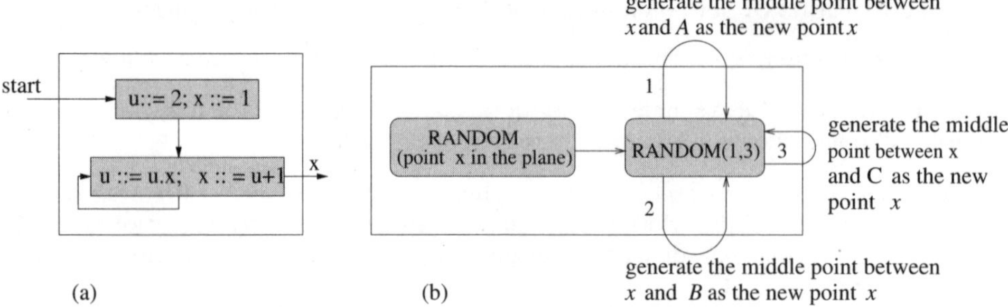

Figure 2.3 Deterministic and randomized generators

automaton – see Figure 2.3b for an automaton that can be seen as generating, given three points A, B and C of the plane forming nodes of an equilateral triangle, a Sierpiński triangle with nodes at points A, B and C – with the exception of few initial points.

A generator can also take the form of a so-called rewriting system. For example, with the (rewriting) rules

$$A \rightarrow aAb, \qquad A \rightarrow ab, \tag{2.4}$$

which are used as follows, the generator starts with the symbol A and in each generation step replaces A in the string generated in the last step, if there is an A there, by the string aAb or by the string ab. If the string obtained at the last step does not contain A, generation terminates. In this way the rewriting system specified in (2.4) generates the set of strings $\{a^n b^n \mid n \geq 1\}$.

Exercise 2.1.14 *Are all the integers generated by the generator in Figure 2.3a primes?*

Exercise 2.1.15 *Design rewriting systems generating (a) the set of strings* $\{a^n b^n a^m b^m \mid n, m \geq 1\}$; *(b) the set of all palindromes in the English alphabet (or in some other alphabet) – that is, those words that read the same from the left and the right.*

A generator can also be specified by some other processes: for instance, through a recurrence. The recurrence (1.6) in Section 1.2 can be seen as a process (generator) generating Fibonacci numbers.

Example 2.1.16 (Cantor set) *The sequence of sets (see Figure 2.4) defined by the recurrence*

$$\begin{array}{lcl} C_0 & = & \{x \mid 0 \leq x < 1\} = [0,1), \\ C_i, & & i > 0, \text{is obtained from } C_{i-1} \text{ by deleting, in each maximal subinterval } [a,b) \text{ of } C_{i-1}, \\ & & \text{its middle open subinterval } [a + \frac{1}{3}(b-a), a + \frac{2}{3}(b-a)), \end{array}$$

is decreasing, and its intersection $C = \bigcap_{i=0}^{\infty} C_i$ *is called the* **Cantor set**.[3] *(Note that the Cantor set can be seen as a diagonal of the Cantor carpet.)*

[3]Georg Cantor (1845–1918), a German mathematician of Russian origin, one of the founders of the modern set theory, introduced the set that is named after him in 1889 as an example of an exceptional (monster) set.

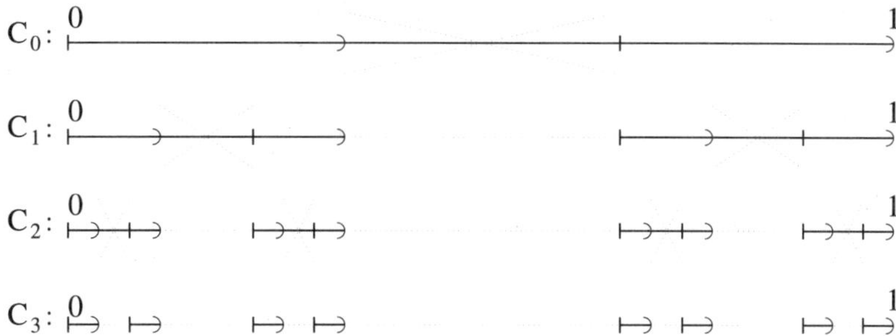

Figure 2.4 Cantor set

Exercise 2.1.17 *Determine the cardinality of (a) a set of points of the Sierpiński triangle; (b)* a set of numbers of the Cantor set.*

Example 2.1.18 *Consider the process that starts with the curve shown in Figure 2.5a and in each step of which all edges of the curve obtained at the last step are replaced by the curve of the type shown in Figure 2.5a, with each edge of length one-third the length of the former one. The resulting set contains the so-called* **Koch curves.** *See Figures 2.5b, c, d for the first three of them.*

Exercise 2.1.19 *Consider the same process as in Example 2.1.18 but starting with the equilateral triangle. The curves obtained are called* **Koch snowflakes**. *Generate a few of them. Another possibility is to start with a square. What do you get 'in the limit' in such a case?*

Example 2.1.20 *The process defined by the mapping*

$$p_c^1(z) = z^2 + c,$$

and, for $i > 1$,

$$p_c^i(z) = (p_c^{i-1})^2 + c,$$

where c is a complex number, defines the so-called **Mandelbrot set**

$$M = \{c \in \mathbf{C} \mid \lim_{n\to\infty} |p_c^n(0)| \text{ is not } \infty\},$$

where $p_c^n(0)$ is the result of the n-th iteration of the process with 0 as the initial value.

The resulting set of (very black) points is shown in Figure 2.6.

5. **Recognizers and acceptors.** A **deterministic recognizer** (see Figure 2.7a) for a subset S of a universal set U is an automaton $\mathcal{A}$ that stops for any input $x \in U$ and says 'yes' ('no') if and only if $x \in S$ ($x \notin S$). This way $\mathcal{A}$ describes, or defines, S. For example, Figure 2.8a shows a recognizer that has

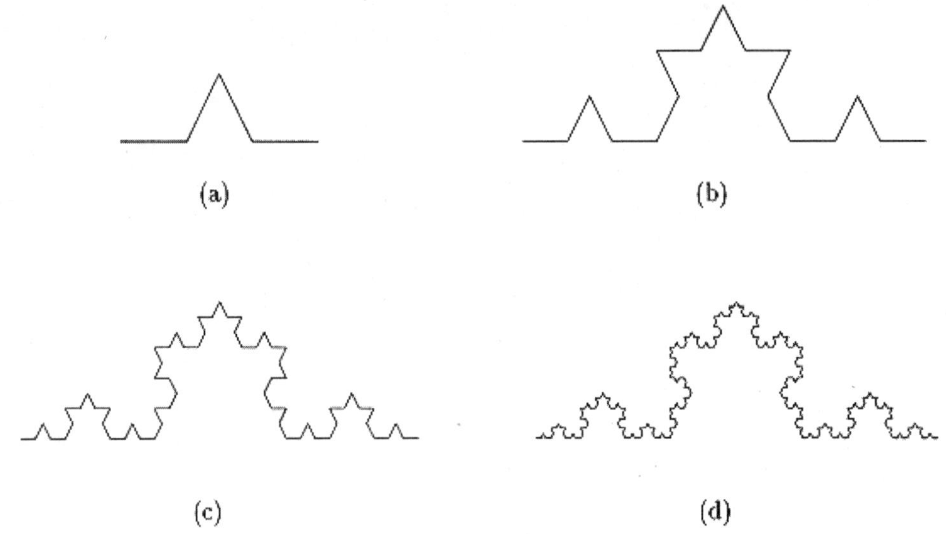

Figure 2.5 Koch curves

been used to find very large Mersenne primes. It realizes the Lucas–Lehmer test to decide whether a given prime p is in the set $\{p \,|\, 2^p - 1 \text{ is a prime}\}$.

A **Monte Carlo randomized recognizer** (see Figure 2.7b) for a set $S \subseteq U$ is an automaton that uses a random number generator to compute and that stops for any input $x \in U$ and says either 'no', then surely $x \notin S$, or 'maybe', which should mean that $x \in S$, except that error is possible, though the probability of error is less than $\frac{1}{2}$.

Is such a recognizer useful when we cannot be sure whether its outcome is correct? Can it be seen as a description of a set? It can because we can find out, with as high probability as we wish, whether a given input is in the set specified by the acceptor. Indeed, let us take the same input more times, say 100 times. If the answer is 'no' at least once we know that the input is not in the set specified by the acceptor. If we get the answer yes 100 times, then the probability that the input is not in the set is less than $\frac{1}{2^{100}}$, which is practically 0.

For example, Figure 2.8b shows a recognizer that recognizes whether two input numbers x and y are the same by first choosing randomly a prime p and then computing as in Figure 2.8b. (This may seem to be a very complicated way of comparing two numbers, but assume, for a moment, that x and y are given by very long strings, that their sources are far away from each other, and that sending x and y to the place where comparison is done is very costly. In Chapter 11 we shall see another situation in which this makes good sense. There it will be shown that if p is properly chosen, then in this way we get a really good Monte Carlo recognizer.)

An **acceptor** (see Figure 2.7c) for a set $S \subseteq U$ is an automaton that for an input $x \in U$ may stop, and it surely stops when $x \in S$ and reports 'yes' in such a case. If $x \notin S$, the acceptor may stop and report 'no', or it may not stop at all. This means that if the automaton 'keeps running', then one has no idea whether it will eventually stop and report something or not.

For example, let us imagine an automaton that for an input $x \in \mathbf{N}$ performs the Collatz process described on page 13 and stops when it gets 1 as the outcome. According to our current knowledge,

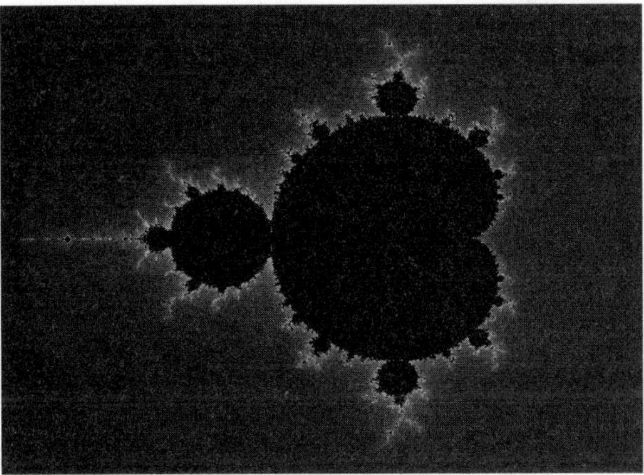

Figure 2.6 Mandelbrot set

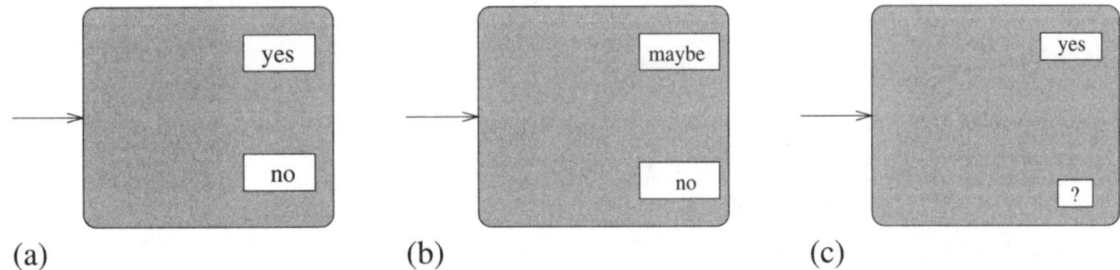

Figure 2.7 Automata: a recognizer, a Monte Carlo randomized recognizer and an acceptor

this is an acceptor that accepts the set of all integers for which the Collatz process stops.

Exercise 2.1.21 *Design a prime recognizer.*

Exercise 2.1.22* *Design an acceptor for the set* $\{n \mid \exists p > n, 2^p - 1 \text{ is a prime}\}$.

2.1.4 Decision and Search Problems

Computational problems can be roughly divided into two types. A **decision problem** for a set $S \subseteq U$ and an element $x \in U$ is the problem of deciding whether $x \in S$. A **search problem** for a relation $R \subseteq U \times U$ and an element $x \in U$ is the problem of finding a $y \in U$, if such exists, such that $(x,y) \in R$.

For example, the problem of deciding whether a given integer is a prime is a decision problem; that of finding a Mersenne prime that is larger than a given integer is a search problem.

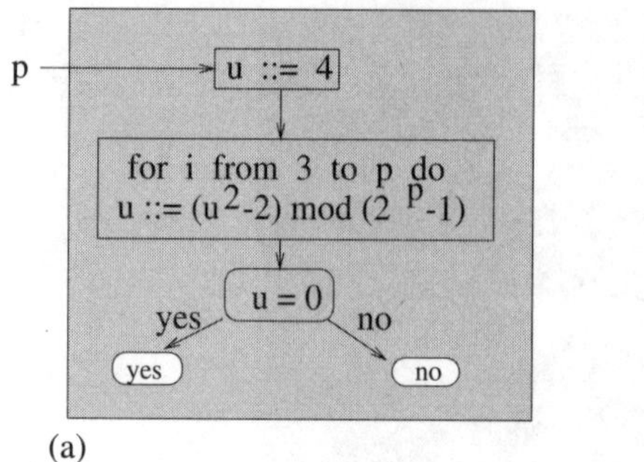

(a)

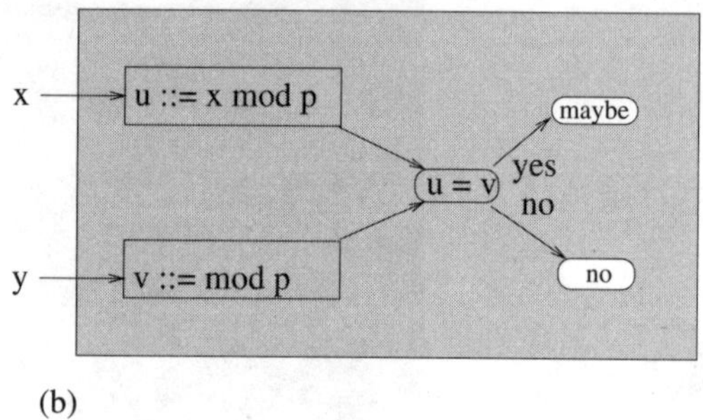

(b)

Figure 2.8 Deterministic and randomized recognizers

Exercise 2.1.23 *The famous Goldbach conjecture says that any even positive integer can be written as the sum of two primes. Design an automaton that for any integer n finds two primes p_n and p'_n, if they exist, such that $n = p_n + p'_n$.*

There are three basic decision problems concerning sets with which we deal repeatedly in this book. In all three cases at least one of the inputs is a description of a set.

Emptiness problem: Given a description of a set, does it describe the empty set?

Membership problem: Given a description of a set and an element a, is a in the set?

Equivalence problem: Given two descriptions of sets, do they describe the same set?

At first glance the emptiness problem does not seem to be a big deal. But actually it is and some of the most important problems in computing (and not only in computing) are of this type. For example, perhaps the most famous problem in mathematics for the last 200 years was that of finding out whether **Fermat's last theorem**[4] holds. This theorem claims that the set specified by formula (2.3) is empty. Moreover, the equivalence problem for two sets A and B can be reduced to the emptiness problem for the sets $A - B$ and $B - A$. It is clearly often of importance to find out whether two sets are equal. For example, currently the most important problem in foundations of computing, and perhaps also one of the most important problems in science in general, is that of determining whether **P** = **NP**.

The most interesting variants of decision and search problems occur when computational complexity questions start to be important. Is there a (feasible) [fast] algorithm for deciding, given a set description of a certain type, whether the specified set is empty? Or is there a (feasible) [fast] algorithm for deciding, given two descriptions of sets from a certain set of set descriptions, whether they describe the same set? And likewise for the set membership problem.

[4]Fermat wrote in the margin of the Latin translation of Diophantus's book *Arithmetica* that he had a truly marvellous demonstration of the statement. The proof was not found, and numerous attempts to prove it failed until June 1993. It is now believed by the experts that Andrew Wiles has proved Fermat's last theorem, but the proof (more than 200 pages) is too big to fit in this note.

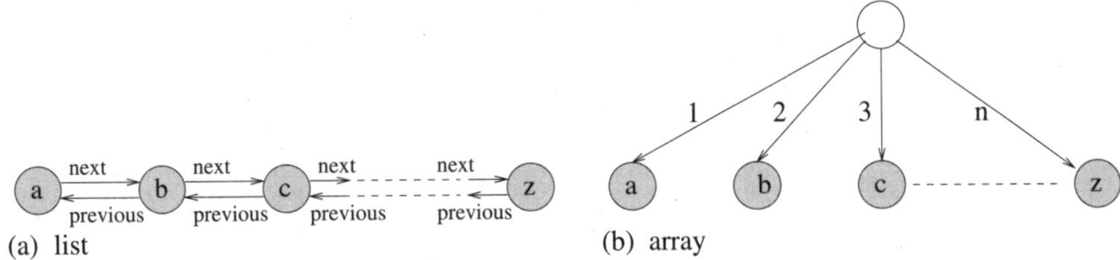

Figure 2.9 A list and an array as data structures

2.1.5 Data Structures and Data Types

In computing, any manipulation with a set, or with elements of a set, even a 'look from one element of a set to another', costs something. This is a new factor, not considered in classical set theory, that initiated the development of a new theory, practically important and theoretically interesting, of efficient representations of sets and multisets and efficient implementations of operations and predicates on them.

A general scheme for representing sets by graphs of a certain type, whose nodes are used 'to store' set elements and whose edges represent access paths to elements of the set and among these elements, is called a **data structure**. For example, two basic data structures for representing sets are **lists** and (sorted or unsorted) **linear arrays** (see Figure 2.9). We deal with various more sophisticated data structures for representing sets in Sections 2.4, 2.5, 4.3.24 and 10.1.

Observe too that the aim of some frequently used algorithms is only to change one representation of a set, or a multiset, into another one that is better in some sense. For example, sorting and merging algorithms are of this type.

There are many important set operations and predicates on sets. However, any particular algorithm uses only a few of them, though usually many times. The most basic operations are **INSERT, DELETE, MEMBER**. (**MEMBER**$(a, A) = [a \in A]$ – if the underlying set A is clear, we use the notation **MEMBER**(a).)

A set and a collection of set operations and predicates is called a **data type**. For example, a set with the predicate **MEMBER** and operations **INSERT, DELETE** forms a data type called **dictionary**. If a data type is defined in an implementation-independent way, we speak of an **abstract data type**.

One of the important tasks of computational set theory is to understand the complexity of implementations of frequently used data types and to develop the best possible implementations for them.

As an illustration, two simple sequential and one simple parallel implementation of the data type dictionary will be discussed. A third, with pseudo-random features, will be dealt with in Section 2.3.4.

Example 2.1.24 (Dictionary implementations) *In the following table the worst-case complexity of dictionary operations is shown for the cases where sorted or unsorted arrays are used to represent the set. (To simplify the discussion, we consider also* **MEMBER** *as an operation.) n denotes the number of elements of the underlying set. Observe that the linear time complexity of the operations* **INSERT** *and* **DELETE** *for the case in which a sorted array is used is due to the need to shift part of the array when performing insertion or deletion. In the unsorted case, linear time is needed to find out whether an element, to delete or to insert, is actually in the array.*

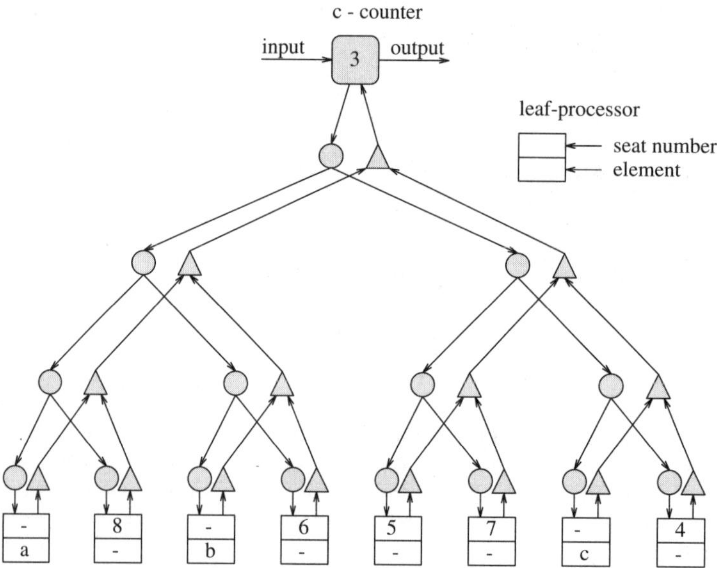

Figure 2.10 A binary tree implementation of dictionary data type

set representation	INSERT	DELETE	MEMBER
sorted array	$\Theta(n)$	$\Theta(n)$	$\Theta(\lg n)$
unsorted array	$\Theta(n)$	$\Theta(n)$	$\Theta(n)$

Using a complete binary tree representation for the underlying set, a $\Theta(\lg n)$ performance can be achieved for all three dictionary operations on a normal sequential computer.

We show now that by a simple parallel implementation of dictionary operations we can achieve not only $\Theta(\lg n)$ performance for all dictionary operations, but also only $\mathcal{O}(1)$ steps long **period** of computation.[5] This will now be shown on the assumption that the underlying set never has more than n elements, and that one never tries to add (delete) an element that is (is not) in the underlying set. For simplicity we assume that $n = 2^k$ for some k.

We use a complete binary tree network of processors with n leaf-processors (see Figure 2.10). Each leaf-processor can be seen as having a 'seat' that is either occupied, by an element of the to-be-represented set, or empty. At any moment all empty seats are numbered, by consecutive integers $1, 2, \ldots, k$ as their 'seat numbers', and the number k is stored in the counter of the root processor, which is both the input and the output processor. All other internal processors can be seen as consisting of two subprocessors. ○-processors are used to transmit information from the root processor to the leaf processors. △-processors process information obtained from their children, and send the results to their parent. Dictionary operations are implemented as follows:

MEMBER(a): The request is sent to all leaf-processors, and their responses are processed ('OR-ed') by △-processors until, in time $2\lg n$, the final answer is assembled by the root-processor.

[5]The period of a parallel computation is the time one must wait after an input starts to be processed until the processing of the next input can begin.

INSERT(a): The triple (i,a,k), indicating that the operation is insert, the element is a, and the content of the counter in the root processor is k, is transmitted from the root to all leaf-processors. Once this information leaves the root, the content of its counter is decreased by 1. Once the triple (i,a,k) reaches the leaves, a is stored 'on the seat' of the processor which has a free seat with k as the seat number.

DELETE(a): The content of the counter in the root processor is increased by 1, and the triple (d,a,k) is sent to all leaf-processors. The leaf-processor that contains a removes a, and labels its now free seat k.

Observe that the root processor can start each time tick to process a new operation. It initiates a flow of data from the root-processor to the leaf-processor and back. The key point is that at no time does a subprocessor of an internal node have to handle more than two flows of data. (Explain why.) Therefore, up to $2\lg n$ operations can be simultaneously processed by the system. Moreover, if handling of the root counter is done in the way described above, then all operations are implemented correctly.

Exercise 2.1.25* *The data type called* **priority queue** *has the predicate MEMBER(a) as well as the operations INSERT(a) and DELETEMIN – to delete the smallest element from the set of concern. Find an efficient implementation for this data type.*

2.2 Relations

The intuitive concept of a relationship between objects is captured by the mathematical concept of a relation. Its applications in computing are numerous. Relations are used to describe the structure of complex objects.

2.2.1 Basic Concepts

Let $S_1, \ldots, S_n$ be sets. Any subset $R \subseteq S_1 \times \cdots \times S_n$ is called an n-**ary relation** on $S_1, \times \ldots, \times S_n$. If $n = 2$, we speak of a **binary relation**.

The concept of an n-ary relation is needed in some areas of computing in its full generality, for example, in databases. Binary relations are, however, the basic ones.

For a binary relation $R \subseteq A \times B$, we define

$$\begin{aligned} \text{domain}(R) &= \{a \mid \exists b \in B, (a,b) \in R\}; \\ \text{range}(R) &= \{b \mid \exists a \in A, (a,b) \in R\}. \end{aligned}$$

Two basic unary operations on relations are

$$\begin{aligned} R^{-1} &= \{(b,a) \mid (a,b) \in R\}, && \text{the } \textbf{inverse relation} \text{ to } R; \\ R^c &= A \times B - R, && \text{the } \textbf{complement relation} \text{ to } R. \end{aligned}$$

Exercise 2.2.1 *Let R, R_1, R_2 be relations on a set A. Show that (a) $(R_1 \cup R_2)^{-1} = R_1^{-1} \cup R_2^{-1}$; (b) $(R^c)^{-1} = (R^{-1})^c$; (c) $R_1 \subseteq R_2 \Rightarrow R_1^{-1} \subseteq R_2^{-1}$.*

The most important binary operation on relations is the **composition** $R_1 \circ R_2$ – in short, R_1R_2, defined for the case that range$(R_1) \subseteq$ domain(R_2) by

$$R_1R_2 = \{(x,z) \mid \exists y \ (x,y) \in R_1, (y,z) \in R_2\}.$$

If $R \subseteq S \times S$ for a set S, then R is said to be a relation on S. The identity relation $I_S = \{(a,a) \mid a \in S\}$ is such a relation. (If S is clear from the context, we write the identity relation on S simply as I.) For a relation R on a set S we define its **powers** R^i, **transitive closure** R^+ and **transitive and reflexive closure** R^* by

$$R^0 = I, \ R^{i+1} = RR^i, \ i \geq 0;$$

$$R^+ = \bigcup_{i=1}^{\infty} R^i, \quad R^* = \bigcup_{i=0}^{\infty} R^i.$$

Basic properties of relations: A binary relation $R \subseteq S \times S$ is called

reflexive	if	$a \in S \Rightarrow (a,a) \in R$,
symmetric	if	$(a,b) \in R \Rightarrow (b,a) \in R$,
antisymmetric	if	$(a,b) \in R \Rightarrow (b,a) \notin R$,
weakly antisymmetric	if	$(a,b) \in R, a \neq b \Rightarrow (b,a) \notin R$,
transitive	if	$(a,b) \in R, (b,c) \in R \Rightarrow (a,c) \in R$,
a partial function	if	$(a,b) \in R, (a,c) \in R \Rightarrow b = c$.

Exercise 2.2.2 *Determine whether the relation R on the set of all integers is reflexive, symmetric, antisymmetric or transitive, where $(x,y) \in R$ if and only if (a) $x \neq y$; (b) $xy \geq 1$; (c) x is a multiple of y; (d) $x \geq y^2$.*

In addition, R is

an **equivalence**	if	R is reflexive, symmetric and transitive;
a **partial order**	if	R is reflexive, weakly antisymmetric and transitive;
a **total order (ordering)**	if	R is a partial order and, for every $a,b \in S$, either $(a,b) \in R$ or $(b,a) \in R$.

If R is an equivalence on S and $a \in S$, then the set $[a]_R = \{b \mid (a,b) \in R\}$ is called an **equivalence class** on S with respect to R. This definition yields the following lemma.

Lemma 2.2.3 *If R is an equivalence on a set S and $a,b \in S$, then the following statements are equivalent:*

$$(a)\ (a,b) \in R, \quad (b)\ [a]_R = [b]_R, \quad (c)\ [a]_R \cap [b]_R \neq \emptyset.$$

This implies that any equivalence R on a set S defines a partition on S such that two elements a,b of S are in the same set of the partition if and only if $(a,b) \in R$. Analogically, each partition of the set S defines an equivalence relation on S – two elements are equivalent if and only if they belong to the same set of the partition.

Example 2.2.4 *For any integer n, $R_n = \{(a,b) \mid a \equiv b (\text{mod } n)\}$ is an equivalence on* **N**. *This follows from the properties of the congruence relation shown in Section 1.7.*

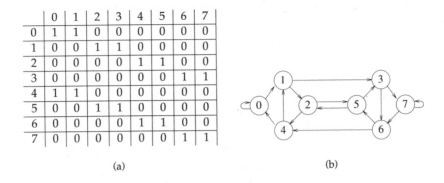

	0	1	2	3	4	5	6	7
0	1	1	0	0	0	0	0	0
1	0	0	1	1	0	0	0	0
2	0	0	0	0	1	1	0	0
3	0	0	0	0	0	0	1	1
4	1	1	0	0	0	0	0	0
5	0	0	1	1	0	0	0	0
6	0	0	0	0	1	1	0	0
7	0	0	0	0	0	0	1	1

(a)

(b)

Figure 2.11 A matrix and a graph representation of a binary relation

Exercise 2.2.5 *Which of the following relations on the set of all people is an equivalence: (a)* $\{(a,b)\,|\,a$ *and* b *have common parents*$\}$*; (b)* $\{(a,b)\,|\,a$ *and* b *share a common parent*$\}$*?*

Exercise 2.2.6 *Which of the following relations on the set of all functions from* **Z** *to* **Z** *is an equivalence: (a)* $\{(f,g)\,|\,f(0)=g(0)$ *or* $f(1)=g(1)\}$*; (b)* $\{(f,g)\,|\,f(0)=g(1)$ *and* $f(1)=g(0)\}$*?*

Two important types of total order are **lexicographical ordering** on a Cartesian product of sets and **strict ordering** on sets A^*, where A is an alphabet (endowed with a total order).

Let $(A_1,\preceq_1),(A_2,\preceq_2),\dots,(A_n,\preceq_n)$ be totally ordered sets. A lexicographical ordering $\preceq$ on the Cartesian product $A_1\times\dots\times A_n$ is defined as follows: $(a_1,\dots,a_n)\preceq(b_1,\dots,b_n)$ if and only if either $(a_1,\dots,a_n)=(b_1,\dots,b_n)$ or $a_i\preceq_i b_i$ for the smallest i such that $a_i\neq b_i$.

A strict ordering on a set A^*, induced by a total order $(A,\preceq)$, where A is an alphabet, is defined as follows. If a string s is shorter than a string u, then $s\preceq u$. If they have the same length, then $s\preceq u$ if and only if either they are the same or $s_i\preceq u_i$ for the smallest i such that the ith symbol of s, s_i, is different from the ith symbol, u_i, of u.

For example, for the alphabet $A=\{0,1,2\}$ with the total order $0\preceq 1\preceq 2$, we get the following strict ordering of strings on A^*:

$$\varepsilon,0,1,2,00,01,02,10,11,12,20,21,22,000,001,002,010,011,012,020,021,022,100,\dots.$$

There is a close relationship between relations and functions. To any relation $R\subseteq A\times B$ we can associate a function $f_R:A\times B\to\{0,1\}$ – the so-called characteristic function of R defined by $f(a,b)=1$ if and only if $(a,b)\in R$. Similarly, to any function $f:A\times B\to\{0,1\}$ we can associate the relation R_f such that $(a,b)\in R_f$ if and only if $f(a,b)=1$.

2.2.2 Representations of Relations

Two of the most important representations of binary relations are by **Boolean matrices** and **directed graphs.**

A binary relation $R\subseteq S\times S$, with $|S|=n$, can be represented by an $n\times n$ Boolean matrix M_R, the rows and columns of which are labelled by elements of S, such that there is 1 in the entry for a row a

and a column b if and only if $(a,b) \in R$. See, for example, the representation of the relation

$$R = \{(0,0),(0,1),(1,2),(1,3),(2,4),(2,5),(3,6),(3,7),(4,0),(4,1),(5,2),(5,3),(6,4),(6,5),(7,6),(7,7)\}$$

by the matrix in Figure 2.11a.

Similarly, any binary relation $R \subseteq S \times S$ can be represented by a directed graph $G_R = \langle V, E \rangle$, where $V = \text{domain}(R) \cup \text{range}(R)$ and $E = \{(a,b) \mid (a,b) \in R\}$ – see the representation of the relation in Figure 2.11a in Figure 2.11b.

There is clearly a one-to-one correspondence, up to the notation of elements, between binary relations, Boolean matrices and directed graphs. Moreover, one can easily, in low polynomial time with respect to the size of the relation, that is, $|\{(a,b) \mid aRb\}|$, transform one of these representations to another. On the other hand, n-ary relations for $n > 2$ are represented by **hypergraphs** (see Section 2.4).

Both representations of binary relations, Boolean matrices and directed graphs, have their advantages.

If $M_{R_i}, i = 1,2$, is a Boolean matrix representation of a relation R_i, then for the matrix representations of the union and the intersection of these relations we get

$$M_{R_1 \cup R_2} = M_{R_1} \vee M_{R_2}, \quad M_{R_1 \cap R_2} = M_{R_1} \wedge M_{R_2},$$

where $\vee$ and $\wedge$ are component-wise disjunction and conjunction operations on the elements of Boolean matrices.

On the other hand, if a binary relation $R \subseteq S \times S$ is represented by a directed graph G_R, then $(a,b) \in R^i$ if and only if there is a path of length at most i in G_R from node a to node b. Similarly, $(a,b) \in R^*$ if and only if there is a path in G_R from node a to node b. Using these facts, one can in principle easily construct from the graph G_R the graphs representing the relations $R^i, i > 1$, R^+ and R^*. Moreover, if $|S| = n$, then there is a path in G_R from a node a to a node b only if there is a path from a to b of length at most $n-1$. This implies that the relations R^+ and R^* can be expressed using finite unions as follows:

$$R^+ = \bigcup_{i=1}^{n} R^i, \quad R^* = \bigcup_{i=0}^{n} R^i.$$

Exercise 2.2.7 *Design a matrix and a graph representation of the relation*

$$R = \{(i, (2i) \bmod 16), (i, (2i+1) \bmod 16) \mid i \in [16]\}.$$

2.2.3 Transitive and Reflexive Closure

The concept of a process as a sequence of elementary steps is crucial for computing. An elementary step is often specified by a binary relation R on the set of so-called configurations of the process. $(a,b) \in R^*$ then means that one can get from a configuration a to a configuration b after a finite number of steps. This is one reason why computation of the transitive and reflexive closure of binary relations is of such importance in computing. In addition, it allows us to demonstrate several techniques for the design and analysis of algorithms.

If $R \subseteq S \times S$ is a relation, $|S| = n$, and M_R is the Boolean matrix representing R, then it clearly holds that

$$M_{R^*} = \bigvee_{i=0}^{n} M_R^i,$$

where $M_R^0 = I, M_R^{i+1} = M_R \vee M_R^i$, for $i > 0$. Therefore, in order to compute the transitive and reflexive closure of R, it is sufficient to compute the transitive and reflexive closure of the Boolean matrix M_R that is equal to $\bigvee_{i=0}^n M_R^i$. We present three methods for doing this. The most classical one is the so-called Warshall algorithm.

Let $M = \{a_{ij}\}, 1 \le i,j \le n, a_{ij} \in \{0,1\}$, be a Boolean matrix, and G_M the directed graph representing the relation defined by M, with nodes labelled by integers $1,2,\dots,n$. The following algorithm computes elements c_{ij} of the matrix $C = M^*$.

Algorithm 2.2.8 (Warshall's algorithm)

begin for $i \leftarrow 1$ **to** n **do** $c_{ii}^0 \leftarrow 1$;
  for $1 \le i,j \le n, i \ne j$ **do** $c_{ij}^0 \leftarrow a_{ij}$;
  for $k \leftarrow 1$ **to** n **do**
    for $1 \le i,j \le n$ **do** $c_{ij}^k \leftarrow c_{ij}^{k-1} \vee (c_{ik}^{k-1} \wedge c_{kj}^{k-1})$;
  for $1 \le i,j \le n$ **do** $c_{ij} \leftarrow c_{ij}^n$
end

In order to demonstrate the correctness of this algorithm, it is sufficient to show that

$c_{ij}^k = 1$ if and only if there is a path in the graph G_M from node i to node j that passes only through nodes of the set $\{1,2,\dots,k\}$,

which can easily be done by induction on k.

The time complexity of this algorithm is $\Theta(n^3)$. Indeed, for any $1 \le k \le n$, the algorithm performs n^2 times statements updating c_{ij}^k.

The second method for computing M^* is based on the equality

$$M^* = (I \vee M)^n,$$

which is easy to verify using the binomial theorem and the fact that $A \cup A = A$ for any set A.

Let $m(n) = \Omega(n^2)$ be the time complexity of the multiplication of Boolean matrices of degree n. Using the repeated squaring method (see Algorithm 1.1.14) we can compute $(I \cup M)^n$ with $\lg n$ Boolean matrix multiplications and at most the same number of Boolean matrix additions (each addition can be performed in $\Theta(n^2)$ time). The overall complexity is therefore $\mathcal{O}(m(n)\lg n)$. It has been shown that $m(n) = \mathcal{O}(n^{2.376})$ (see also page 245) if time is counted by the number of arithmetical operations needed, and $m(n) = \mathcal{O}(n^{2.376} \lg n \lg\lg n \lg\lg\lg n)$ if only bit operations are counted. Therefore the second algorithm is asymptotically faster than the first.

The third algorithm, asymptotically even better than the second, is based on the divide-and-conquer method.

Algorithm 2.2.9 (Divide-and-conquer algorithm for transitive closure)

1. Divide M into four submatrices A,B,C,D, as shown below, where A is a $\lfloor \frac{n}{2} \rfloor \times \lfloor \frac{n}{2} \rfloor$ matrix and D a $\lceil \frac{n}{2} \rceil \times \lceil \frac{n}{2} \rceil$ matrix.

$$M = \left[\begin{array}{c|c} A & B \\ \hline C & D \end{array}\right].$$

2. Recursively compute D^*.

3. Compute $F = A + BD^*C$.

4. Recursively compute F^*.

5. Set

$$M^* = \left[\begin{array}{c|c} F^* & F^*BD^* \\ \hline D^*CF^* & D^* + D^*CF^*BD^* \end{array} \right].$$

The correctness of this algorithm can be shown informally by the following argument. Let us assume that nodes of the graph G_M are partitioned into two sets N_A and N_D in such a way that A describes edges between nodes of N_A, B edges from nodes in N_A to nodes in N_D, C edges from nodes in N_D to nodes in N_A, and D edges between nodes of N_D. Then F^* clearly determines all paths from nodes in N_A to nodes in N_A in G_M. F^*BD^* determines all paths that start from a node in N_A and go to a node in N_D. Similarly, for other matrix expressions in the formula for M^* in item 5 of Algorithm 2.2.9.

For the complexity $T(n)$ of the algorithm we get the recurrence

$$T(n) = 2T(\frac{n}{2}) + cm(\frac{n}{2}) + d(\frac{n}{2})^2,$$

where c and d are constants. Since $m(n) = \Omega(n^2)$, we can assume that $m(n) \leq \frac{1}{4}m(2n)$. Therefore we can use Case 3 of Theorem 1.6.3 to get $T(n) = \Theta(m(n))$.

Similarly, we can show that if there is an algorithm to calculate M^* in time $T(n)$, then there is an algorithm to multiply two Boolean matrices of degree n in time $\mathcal{O}(T(3n))$. Indeed, if we put two Boolean matrices A and B of degree n in a proper way as parts of a $3n \times 3n$ Boolean matrix, we get

$$\begin{bmatrix} 0 & A & 0 \\ 0 & 0 & B \\ 0 & 0 & 0 \end{bmatrix}^* = \begin{bmatrix} I & A & AB \\ 0 & I & B \\ 0 & 0 & I \end{bmatrix}.$$

Exercise 2.2.10 *Compute* R^2, R^3, R^4, R^* *for* $R = \{(1,3),(2,4),(3,1),(3,5),(5,1),(5,2),(5,4),(2,6),(5,6),(6,3),(6,1)\}$.

Exercise 2.2.11 *Determine transitive closure for the following relations:* *(a)* $\{(1,2),(1,3),(1,4),(2,3),(2,4),(3,4)\}$; *(b)* $\{(a,b),(a,c),(a,e),(b,a),(b,c),(c,a),(d,c),(e,d)\}$; *(c)* $\{(1,5),(2,1),(3,4),(4,1),(5,2),(5,3)\}$.

Exercise 2.2.12 *Compute* a_n, b_n, c_n, d_n *defined by*

$$\begin{pmatrix} a_n & b_n \\ c_n & d_n \end{pmatrix} = \begin{pmatrix} 1 & 1 \\ 1 & 0 \end{pmatrix}^n$$

with the matrix multiplication being: (a) ordinary matrix multiplication; (b) Boolean matrix multiplication.

2.2.4 Posets

A set S together with a partial order relation R on S is called a **partially ordered set** or **poset**, and is denoted by (S,R). In the case of posets one usually uses notation aRb to denote that $(a,b) \in R$.

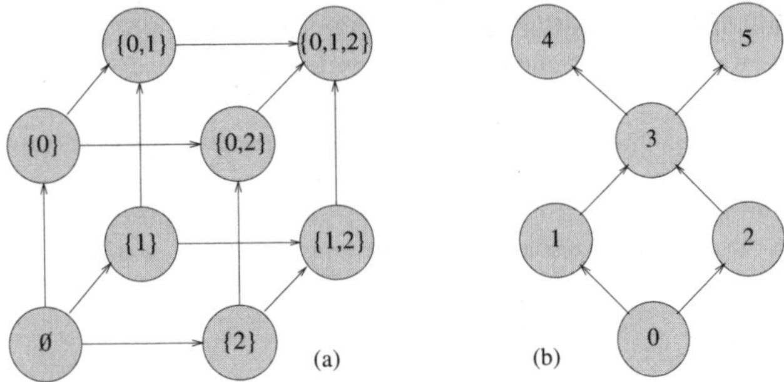

Figure 2.12 Hasse diagrams

Example 2.2.13 *If $\backslash$ denotes the divisibility relation among integers, then $(\mathbf{N}, \backslash)$ is a poset but not a totally ordered set. $(\mathbf{Z}, \leq), (\mathbf{Q}, \leq)$ and $(\mathbf{R}, \leq)$ are totally ordered sets with respect to the relation 'smaller than or equal to'. If A is any set, then $(2^A, \subseteq)$ is also a poset.*

Posets can be represented graphically more economically by so-called **Hasse diagrams**. These are based on the fact that if aRb and bRc in a poset (S, R), then certainly aRc, so this particular relationship does not have to be shown explicitly.

Let (S, R) be a poset. Denote $R_H \subseteq R$ the relation defined as follows: aR_Hb if and only if aRb and there is no $a \neq c \neq b$ such that aRc and cRb. In other words, R_H is the smallest subset of R such that $R_H^* = R$. The graph G_{R_H} is called the Hasse diagram for R.

For example, the Hasse diagram for the poset $(2^{\{0,1,2\}}, \subseteq)$ is shown in Figure 2.12a, and the Hasse diagram for the relation

$$R = \{(0,1),(0,2),(0,3),(0,4),(0,5),(1,3),(1,4),(1,5),(2,3),(2,4),(2,5),(3,4),(3,5)\}$$

in Figure 2.12b.[6]

The Hasse diagram for a relation R represented by a graph G_R can clearly be obtained from G_R by a process in which at each step one removes an edge the existence of which can be deduced from the transitivity or reflexivity of the relation of partial order, if there is such an edge; otherwise the process comes to a halt.

The economy and transparency of descriptions are the main advantages of Hasse diagrams.

Exercise 2.2.14 *Draw the Hasse diagram for the divisibility relation on the set* $\{1,2,3,6,12,24,36,48\}$.

Exercise 2.2.15** *Show that for every $n \in \mathbf{N}$ there is a relation which is represented by a graph with n edges, and that the Hasse diagram for this relation has $\lfloor\sqrt{n}\rfloor$ edges.*

2.3 Functions

The modern concept of a function, as a special type of relation, is an abstraction and a significant generalization of the old intuitive concept of a mapping provided by a computation. To develop a

[6] Observe that if a set A has n elements, then the Hasse diagram for the poset $(2^A, \subseteq)$ is actually the n-dimensional hypercube – a graph treated in detail in Section 10.1.

deeper understanding of which functions are computable (theoretically, practically, fast, or even very fast) is one of the main goals in foundations of computing. Some classes of functions play a special role in this – for example, Boolean functions.

Of increasing importance in computing are functions that exhibit randomized or chaotic behaviour with respect to the input–output relation they represent, and thereby help to utilize the power of randomization. These functions are actually not new; their potential for creating randomness has been recognized only recently, for example, one-way functions and hash functions.

2.3.1 Basic Concepts

Intuitively, a (total) **function** $f : A \to B$ assigns to any object from the set A an object from the set B. Formally, f is a relation on $A \times B$ such that to any $a \in A$ there is exactly one $b \in B$ such that $(a,b) \in f$. Instead of $(a,b) \in f$, we usually write $f(a) = b$, to emphasize the assignment. A is called the **domain** of f, B its **co-domain**, and the set $\{b \mid b \in B, \exists a \in A, f(a) = b\}$ is the **range** of f. If $f(a) = b$, then b is called the **image** of a, and a is a **pre-image** of b. If $A_0 \subset A$, then $f(A_0) = \{b \mid b = f(a), a \in A_0\}$. The set of all functions from A to B is denoted by B^A. The value of a function $f : A \to B$ for an $a \in A$ is denoted by $f(a)$ or $f(x)|_{x=a}$.

Exercise 2.3.1 *Show that if A and B are finite sets, then $|B^A| = |B|^{|A|}$.*

A partial function $f : A \to B$ is a mapping that assigns to some elements of A elements from B. The set $\{a \mid a \in A, f(a) \text{ is defined}\}$ is called the domain of f.

Example 2.3.2 *Observe that*

$$f = \{(a,b) \mid a,b \in \mathbf{N}, b = a \bmod 2\}$$

is a function, but the relation

$$g = \{(a,b) \mid a,b \in \mathbf{N}, b \equiv a \pmod 2\}$$

is not.

A function $f : A \to B$ is called

surjective (resp. a surjection),	if range$(f) = B$;
injective (resp. an injection),	if $f(a) = f(b) \Rightarrow a = b$;
bijective (resp. a bijection),	if f is surjective and injective.

A surjection is sometimes called a **mapping of** A **onto** B, an injection a **one-to-one mapping**, a bijection a **one-to-one correspondence** between A and B.

The **inverse** f^{-1} of a function f is the relation $f^{-1} = \{(b,a) \mid f(a) = b\}$. If f is an injection, then f^{-1} is also a (partial) function.

For example, observe that the inverse of the function $f : \mathbf{N}^+ \to \mathbf{Z}$ with $f(n) = (-1)^n \lfloor \frac{n}{2} \rfloor$ is a function, but the inverses of $g(n) = \lfloor \frac{n}{2} \rfloor$ and $h(n) = (-1)^{-n} \lfloor \frac{n}{3} \rfloor$ are not.

Two (partial) functions f_1 and f_2 are called **equal** if they have the same domain and co-domain and $f_1(a) = f_2(a)$ for all a in the domain. The **composition** $f_1 \circ f_2$ of functions $f_1 : A \to B$ and $f_2 : B \to C$ is a function from A to C defined by $f_1 \circ f_2(a) = f_2(f_1(a))$ for any $a \in A$.

Exercise 2.3.3 *(Pigeonhole principle) Show that if A and B are finite sets such that* $|A| > |B|$ *and* $f : A \to B$*, then* f *is not bijective.*

Exercise 2.3.4 *Let* $f : A \to B$ *be a function. Characterize properties '*f *is injective', '*f *is surjective' and '*f *is bijective' in terms of* $f^{-1}(\{y\})$*, where* $y \in B$*.*

Exercise 2.3.5 *Show that for a function* $f : A \to B$
(a) f *is injective if and only if* $\forall X \subseteq A, f^{-1}(f(X)) = X$*;*
(b) f *is surjective if and only if* $\forall Y \subseteq B, f(f^{-1}(Y)) = Y$*;*
(c) f *is bijective if and only if* $\forall X,Y \subset A, f(X \cap B) = f(X) \cap f(Y)$*.*

The **graph of a function** $f : X \to Y$ is the set $\{(x, f(x) \mid x \text{ is in the domain of } f\}$.

If $f : A \to A$ is a function, then any $x \in A$ such that $f(x) = x$ is called a **fixed point** of f. Any subset A_0 of A such that $f(A_0) = A_0$ is called an **invariant** of f. For example, the mapping $f(x) = x^3 - 6x^2 + 12x - 6$ has three fixed points: $1, 2, 3$.

Exercise 2.3.6** *Let nodes of the Sierpiński triangle (see Figure 2.1) be arbitrarily denoted as* $1, 2, 3$*, and for* $i = 1, 2, 3$ *the mapping* f_i *be defined on the plane as mapping any point* x *to the middle point of the line connecting* x *and the node* i *of the triangle. Show that for all these three mappings the set of points of the Sierpiński triangle is an invariant.*

Iterations $f^{(i)}, i \geq 0$, of a function $f : X \to X$ are defined by $f^{(0)}(x) = x$ and $f^{(i+1)}(x) = f(f^{(i)}(x))$ for $i > 0$.

A function $f : \{1, \ldots, n\} \to A$ is called a **finite sequence**, a function $f : \mathbf{N} \to A$ an **infinite sequence**, and a function $f : \mathbf{Z} \to A$ a **doubly infinite sequence**.

When the domain of a function is a Cartesian product, say $f : A_1 \times A_2 \times \ldots \times A_n \to B$, then the extra parentheses surrounding n arguments are usually omitted, and we write simply $f(a_1, \ldots, a_n)$ instead of $f((a_1, \ldots, a_n))$.

Two case studies in the remainder of this subsection will illustrate the basic concepts just summarized, and introduce important functions and notions that we will deal with later.

Case study 1 – permutations

A bijection $f : S \to S$ is often called a **permutation**. A permutation of a finite set S can be seen as an ordering of elements of S into a sequence with each element appearing exactly once. Examples of permutations of the set $\{1, 2, 3, 4\}$ are $(1, 2, 3, 4)$; $(2, 4, 3, 1)$; $(4, 3, 2, 1)$. If S is a finite set, then the number of its permutations is $|S|!$.

Since elements of any finite set can be numbered by consecutive integers, it is sufficient to consider only permutations on sets $\mathbf{N}_n = \{1, 2, \ldots, n\}, n \in \mathbf{N}^+$. A permutation π is then a bijection $\pi : \mathbf{N}_n \to \mathbf{N}_n$. Two basic notations are used for permutations:

enumeration of elements: $\pi = (a_1, \ldots, a_n)$ such that $\pi(i) = a_i, 1 \le i \le n$.
Example: $\pi = (3,4,1,5,2,6)$.

enumeration of cycles: $\pi = c_1 c_2 \ldots c_k, c_i = \langle b_0, \ldots, b_s \rangle, 1 \le i \le k$,
such that $\pi(b_j) = b_{(j+1) \bmod (s+1)}, 0 \le j \le s$.
Example: $\pi = \langle 1,3\rangle\langle 2,4,5\rangle\langle 6\rangle$; that is,
$\pi(1) = 3, \pi(3) = 1, \pi(2) = 4, \pi(4) = 5, \pi(5) = 2, \pi(6) = 6$.

Special permutations: **identity permutation,** $id = (1,2, \ldots, n)$; that is, $id(i) = i$ for $1 \le i \le n$; **transposition,** $\pi = [i_0, j_0]$, where $1 \le i_0, j_0 \le n$ (that is, $\pi(i_0) = j_0$, $\pi(j_0) = i_0$ and $\pi(i) = i$, otherwise). For example, $\pi = [2,4] = (1,4,3,2,5,6)$.

The **inverse permutation,** π^{-1}, to a permutation π is defined by $\pi^{-1}(i) = j \Leftrightarrow \pi(j) = i$. For example, if $\pi = (3,4,1,5,2,6)$, then $\pi^{-1} = (3,5,1,2,4,6)$.

Composition of permutations π_1 and π_2 is the permutation $\pi = \pi_1 \circ \pi_2$, where $\pi(i) = \pi_2(\pi_1(i))$, for $1 \le i \le n$. For example, $(3,5,1,2,6,4) \circ (2,6,1,3,4,5) = (1,4,2,6,5,3)$. Clearly, $\pi \circ \pi^{-1} = id$ for any permutation π.

Powers of permutations: $\pi^1 = \pi, \pi^{i+1} = \pi \circ \pi^i, i \ge 1$. For example,

$$(3,5,1,2,6,4)^2 = (1,6,3,5,4,2) \quad (3,5,1,2,6,4)^4 = (1,2,3,4,5,6).$$

An **inversion** of a permutation π on $\{1, \ldots, n\}$ is any pair $1 \le i < j \le n$ such that $\pi(j) < \pi(i)$.

As the following lemma indicates, powers of a permutation always lead to the identity permutation.

Lemma 2.3.7 *For any permutation π of a finite set there is an integer k (the so-called* **degree** *of π) such that $\pi^k = id$.*

Proof: Clearly, there are $i < j$ such that $\pi^i = \pi^j$. Then $id = \pi^i \circ \pi^{-i} = \pi^j \circ \pi^{-i} = \pi^{j-i}$. □

Exercise 2.3.8 *Determine the degree of the following permutations:*
(a) $(2,3,1,8,5,6,7,4)$; *(b)* $(8,7,6,5,4,3,2,1)$; *(c)* $(2,4,5,8,1,3,6,7)$.

Exercise 2.3.9* *Determine the number of permutations $\pi : \{1, \ldots, n\} \to \{1, \ldots, n\}$ such that $\pi(i) \ne i$ for all i.*

Case study 2 – cellular automata mappings

Informally, a one-dimensional cellular automaton $\mathcal{A}$ is a doubly infinite sequence of processors (see Figure 2.13)

$$\ldots, P_{-i}, P_{-i+1}, \ldots, P_{-1}, P_0, P_1, \ldots, P_{i-1}, P_i, \ldots,$$

and at each moment of the discrete time each processor is in one of the states of a finite set of states Q. Processors of $\mathcal{A}$ work in parallel in discrete time steps. At each moment of the discrete time each processor changes its state according to the local transition function, which takes as arguments its current state and the states of its k neighbours on the left and also its k neighbours on the right, for a fixed k.

Formally, a **one-dimensional cellular automaton** $\mathcal{A} = \langle Q, k, \delta \rangle$ is defined by a finite set Q of **states,** an integer $k \in \mathbf{N}$ – the size of the **neighbourhood** – and a **local transition function** $\delta : Q^{2k+1} \to Q$.

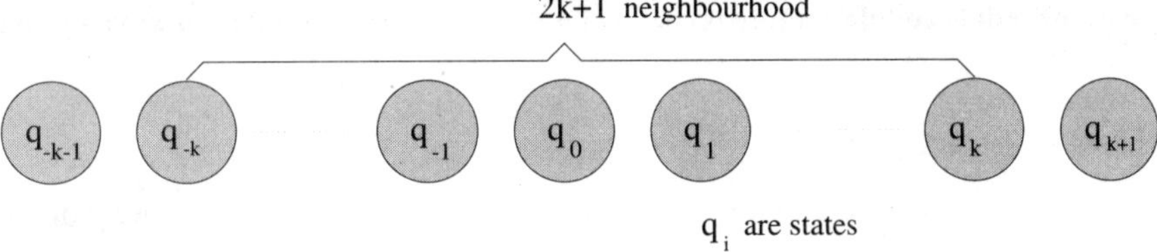

Figure 2.13 One-dimensional cellular automaton

A mapping $c : \mathbf{Z} \to Q$ is called a **configuration** of $\mathcal{A}$. The **global transition function** $G_{\mathcal{A}}$ maps the set $Q^{\mathbf{Z}}$ of all configurations of $\mathcal{A}$ into itself, and is defined by

$$G_{\mathcal{A}}(c) = c', \text{ where } c'(i) = \delta(c(i-k), c(i-k+1), \ldots, c(i+k-1), c(i+k)) \text{ for all } i \in \mathbf{Z}.$$

Moreover, a cellular automaton $\mathcal{A}$ is called **reversible** (or its global transition function is called reversible) if there is another cellular automaton $\mathcal{A}' = \langle Q, k', g' \rangle$ such that for any configuration $c \in Q^{\mathbf{Z}}$ we have $G_{\mathcal{A}'}(G_{\mathcal{A}}(c)) = c$.

Exercise 2.3.10* *Show that the following one-dimensional cellular automaton $\mathcal{A} = \langle \{0,1\}, 2, g \rangle$, is reversible, where the local transition function $g : \{0,1\}^5 \to \{0,1\}$ is defined as follows:*

$00000 \to 0$	$00100 \to 1$	$01000 \to 0$	$01100 \to 1$
$10000 \to 0$	$10100 \to 1$	$11000 \to 0$	$11100 \to 1$
$00001 \to 0$	$00101 \to 1$	$01001 \to 0$	$01101 \to 1$
$10001 \to 0$	$10101 \to 1$	$11001 \to 0$	$11101 \to 1$
$00010 \to 1$	$00110 \to 0$	$01010 \to 1$	$01110 \to 0$
$10010 \to 1$	$10110 \to 0$	$11010 \to 1$	$11110 \to 0$
$00011 \to 0$	$00111 \to 1$	$01011 \to 0$	$01111 \to 1$
$10011 \to 0$	$10111 \to 1$	$11011 \to 0$	$11111 \to 1$.

Cellular automata are an important model of parallel computing, and will be discussed in more detail in Section 4.5. We mention now only some basic problems concerning their global transition function.

The **Garden of Eden** problem is to determine, given a cellular automaton, whether its global transition function is surjective: in other words, whether there is a configuration that cannot be reached in a computational process. Problems concerning injectivity and bijectivity of the global transition function are also of importance. The following theorem holds, for example.

Theorem 2.3.11 *The following three assertions are equivalent for one-dimensional cellular automata:*

1. *The global transition function is injective.*
2. *The global transition function is bijective.*
3. *The global transition function is reversible.*

The problem of reversibility is of special interest. Cellular automata are being considered as a model of microscopic physics. Since the processes of microscopic physics are reversible, the existence of (universal) reversible cellular automata is crucial for considering cellular automata as a model of the physical world.

2.3.2 Boolean Functions

An n-input, m-output **Boolean function** is any function from $\{0,1\}^n$ to $\{0,1\}^m$. Let $\mathcal{B}_n^m$ denote the set of all such functions.

There are three reasons why Boolean functions play an important role in computing in general and in foundations of computing in particular.

1. Boolean functions are precisely the functions that computer circuitry implements directly. Boolean circuits and families of Boolean circuits (discussed in Section 4.3) form the very basic model of computers.

2. A very close relation between Boolean functions and truth functions of propositional logic, discussed later, allows one to see Boolean functions – formulas – and their identities as formalizing basic rules and laws of formal reasoning.

3. String-to-string functions, which represent so well the functions we deal with in computing, are well modelled by Boolean functions. For example, a function $f:\{0,1\}^* \rightarrow \{0,1\}$ is sometimes called Boolean, because f can be seen as an infinite sequence $\{f_i\}_{i=1}^{\infty}$ of Boolean functions, where $f_i \in \mathcal{B}_i^1$ and $f_i(x_1,\ldots,x_i) = f(x_1,\ldots,x_i)$. In this way we can identify the intuitive concept of a computational problem instance with a Boolean function from a set $\mathcal{B}_n^m$, and that of a computational problem with an infinite sequence of Boolean functions $\{f_i\}_{i=1}^{\infty}$, where $f_i \in \mathcal{B}_i^1$.

A Boolean function from $\mathcal{B}_n^m$ can be seen as a collection of m Boolean functions from $\mathcal{B}_n^1$. This is why, in discussing the basic concepts concerning Boolean functions, it is mostly sufficient to consider only Boolean functions from $\mathcal{B}_n^1$. So instead of $\mathcal{B}_n^1$ we mostly write $\mathcal{B}_n$.

Boolean functions look very simple. However, their space is very large. $\mathcal{B}_n$ has 2^{2^n} functions, and for $n = 6$ this gives the number 18,446, 744, 073, 709, 551, 616 – exactly one more than the number of moves needed to solve the 'original' Towers of Hanoi problem.

The most basic way of describing a Boolean function $f \in \mathcal{B}_n$ is to enumerate all 2^n possible n-tuples of arguments and assign to each of them the corresponding value of f. For example, the following table describes in this way the most commonly used Boolean functions of one and two variables.

		identity	negation	OR	AND	XOR	equiv.	NOR	NAND	implic.
x	y	x	$\bar{x}$	$x+y$	$x \cdot y$	$x \oplus y$	$x \equiv y$	$\overline{x+y}$	$\overline{x \cdot y}$	$\bar{x}+y$
0	0	0	1	0	0	0	1	1	1	1
0	1	0	1	1	0	1	0	0	1	1
1	0	1	0	1	0	1	0	0	1	0
1	1	1	0	1	1	0	1	0	0	1

For some of these functions several notations are used, depending on the context. For example, we can write $x \vee y$ or $x\, OR\, y$ instead of $x+y$ for **conjunction**; $x \wedge y$ or $x\, AND\, y$ instead of xy for **disjunction**, and $\neg x$ instead of $\bar{x}$.

A set Γ of Boolean functions is said to be a **base** if any Boolean function can be expressed as a composition of functions from Γ. From the fact that each Boolean function can be described by enumeration it follows that the set $\Gamma_0 = \{\neg, \vee, \wedge\}$ of Boolean functions forms a base.

Exercise 2.3.12 *Which of the following sets of Boolean functions forms a base: (a)* $\{OR, NOR\}$*; (b)* $\{\neg, NOR\}$*; (c)* $\{AND, NOR\}$*; (d)* $\{\bar{x} \wedge y, 0, 1\}$*?*

Exercise 2.3.13 *Use the NAND function to form the following functions: (a) NOT; (b) OR; (c) AND; (d) NOR.*

The so-called monotone Boolean functions play a special role. Let $\preceq_m$ be the so-called montone ordering on $\{0,1\}^n$ defined by $(x_1, \ldots, x_n) \preceq_m (y_1, \ldots, y_n)$ if and only if $\forall_{i=1}^n (x_i = 1 \Rightarrow y_i = 1)$. A Boolean function $f : \{0,1\}^n \rightarrow \{0,1\}$ is called **monotone** if

$$(x_1, \ldots, x_n) \preceq (y_1, \ldots, y_n) \Rightarrow f(x_1, \ldots, x_n) \preceq f(y_1, \ldots, y_n).$$

OR and AND are examples of monotone Boolean functions; XOR is not.

Boolean expressions, or formulas

Another way to describe Boolean functions, often much more concise, is to use Boolean formulas, or expressions. These can be defined over an arbitrary base. For example, Boolean expressions over the base Γ_0, described above, can be defined inductively by assuming that an infinite pool $V = \{x_1, x_2, \ldots\}$ of Boolean variables is available, as follows.

1. $0, 1, x_1, x_2, \ldots$ are Boolean expressions.
2. If E_1, E_2 are Boolean expressions, then so are $\neg E_1, (E_1 \vee E_2), (E_1 \wedge E_2)$.

An expression of the form x_i or $\neg x_i$ (or alternatively $\bar{x}_i$) is called a **literal**.

An inductive definition of Boolean expressions can be used to define, or to prove, various properties of Boolean expressions and Boolean functions. For example, the Boolean function $f(E)$ represented by a Boolean expression E can be defined as follows.

1. $f(E) = E$ if $E \in \{0,1\} \cup V$;
2. $f(\neg E) = \overline{f(E)}; f(E_1 \vee E_2) = f(E_1) \vee f(E_2); f(E_1 \wedge E_2) = f(E_1) \wedge f(E_2)$.

Two Boolean expressions E_1 and E_2 are said to be **equivalent**, notation $E_1 \equiv E_2$, if $f(E_1) = f(E_2)$; that is, if E_1 and E_2 are two different representations of the same Boolean function.

Exercise 2.3.14 *Show that each monotone Boolean function can be represented by a Boolean expression that uses only the functions* 0, 1, $x \vee y$, $x \wedge y$.

Disjunctive and conjunctive normal forms

Boolean expressions are a special case of expressions in Boolean algebras, and the most basic pairs of equivalent Boolean expressions can be obtained from column 1 of Table 2.1, which contains the laws of Boolean algebras. These equivalences, especially those representing idempotence, commutativity, associativity, distributivity and de Morgan's laws, can be used to simplify Boolean expressions. For example, parentheses can be removed in multiple conjunctions and disjunctions, as in $(x_3 \vee (x_2 \vee x_1)) \vee ((x_4 \vee x_5) \vee (x_6 \vee x_2))$. This allows us to use the notation

$$\bigwedge_{i=1}^{k} E_i = E_1 \wedge E_2 \wedge \ldots \wedge E_k, \qquad \bigvee_{i=1}^{k} E_i = E_1 \vee E_2 \vee \ldots \vee E_k.$$

In the case that E_i are literals, the expression $\bigwedge_{i=1}^{k} E_i$ is called a **minterm**, and the expression $\bigvee_{i=1}^{k} E_i$ a **clause**. Two closely related normal forms for Boolean expressions are

$$\bigvee_{i=1}^{n} \bigwedge_{j=1}^{m_i} L_{ij} \qquad \textbf{disjunctive normal form (DNF)} \tag{2.5}$$

$$\bigwedge_{i=1}^{n} \bigvee_{j=1}^{m_i} L_{ij} \qquad \textbf{conjunctive normal form (CNF)} \tag{2.6}$$

where L_{ij} are literals. For example,

$$(x_1 \vee \neg x_2 \vee x_3) \wedge (x_1 \vee x_2 \vee \neg x_3),$$
$$(x_1 \wedge \neg x_2 \wedge x_3) \vee (x_1 \wedge x_2 \wedge \neg x_3).$$

Theorem 2.3.15 *Every Boolean expression is equivalent to one in a conjunctive normal form and one in a disjunctive normal form.*

Proof: By induction on the structure of Boolean expressions E. The case $E \in \{0,1\} \cup V$ is trivial. Now let

$$E_1 = \bigwedge_{i=1}^{n_1} \bigvee_{j=1}^{r_{1,i}} L_{ij}^{(c1)}, \qquad E_1 = \bigvee_{k=1}^{m_1} \bigwedge_{l=1}^{s_{1,k}} L_{kl}^{(d1)},$$

$$E_2 = \bigwedge_{p=1}^{n_2} \bigvee_{q=1}^{r_{2,p}} L_{pq}^{(c2)}, \qquad E_2 = \bigvee_{u=1}^{m_2} \bigwedge_{v=1}^{s_{2,u}} L_{uv}^{(d2)},$$

be CNF and DNF for E_1 and E_2. Using de Morgan's laws, we get that

$$\neg E_1 = \bigvee_{i=1}^{n_1} \bigwedge_{j=1}^{r_{1,i}} \neg L_{ij}^{(c1)} \quad \text{and} \quad \neg E_1 = \bigwedge_{k=1}^{m_1} \bigvee_{l=1}^{s_{1,i}} \neg L_{kl}^{(d1)}$$

are DNF and CNF for $\neg E_1$, where the double negation law is used, if necessary, to make a literal out of $\neg L_x^{(y)}$. Similarly,

$$\bigwedge_{i=1}^{n_1} \bigvee_{j=1}^{r_{1,i}} L_{ij}^{(c1)} \wedge \bigwedge_{p=1}^{n_2} \bigvee_{q=1}^{r_{2,p}} L_{pq}^{(c2)} \quad \text{and} \quad \bigvee_{k=1}^{m_1} \bigwedge_{l=1}^{s_{1,k}} L_{kl}^{(d1)} \vee \bigvee_{u=1}^{m_2} \bigwedge_{v=1}^{s_{2,u}} L_{uv}^{(d2)}$$

are a CNF for $E_1 \wedge E_2$ and a DNF for $E_1 \vee E_2$. Finally,

$$\bigwedge_{i=1}^{n_1} \bigwedge_{p=1}^{n_2} (\bigvee_{j=1}^{r_{1,i}} L_{ij}^{(c1)} \vee \bigvee_{q=1}^{r_{2,k}} L_{pq}^{(c2)}) \quad \text{and} \quad \bigvee_{k=1}^{m_1} \bigvee_{u=1}^{m_2} (\bigwedge_{l=1}^{s_{1,k}} L_{kl}^{(d1)} \wedge \bigwedge_{u=1}^{s_{2,u}} L_{uv}^{(d2)}) \tag{2.7}$$

are a CNF for $E_1 \vee E_2$, and a DNF for $E_1 \wedge E_2$. □

The algorithm presented in Theorem 2.3.15 for the construction of a DNF or a CNF equivalent to a given Boolean expression is simple in principle. However, the size of the Boolean expression in step (2.7) can double with respect to that for E_1 and E_2. It can therefore happen that the resulting CNF or DNF for a Boolean expression E has a size exponential with respect to a size of E.

Exercise 2.3.16 *Design disjunctive normal forms for the functions (a)* $x \Rightarrow y$; *(b)* $(x+\bar{y}+z)(x+\bar{y}+\bar{z})(\bar{x}+y+z)(\bar{x}+\bar{y}+z)$.

Exercise 2.3.17 *Design conjunctive normal forms for the functions (a)* $x \Rightarrow y$; *(b)* $\bar{x}\bar{y}\bar{z}+\bar{x}\bar{y}z+x\bar{y}z+xyz$.

Satisfiability

Another important concept for Boolean expressions is that of **satisfiability**. The name is derived from a close relation between Boolean expressions and expressions of the propositional calculus.

A **(truth) assignment** T to a set S of Boolean variables is a mapping $T: S \rightarrow \{0,1\}$. If S_E is a set of variables occurring in a Boolean expression E, and $T: S_E \rightarrow \{0,1\}$ is an initial assignment, then we say that T satisfies E, notation $T \models E$, or that T does not satisfy E, notation $T \not\models E$, if the following holds (using the inductive definition):

1. $T \models 1, T \not\models 0$;
2. if $x \in V$, then $T \models x$ if and only if $T(x) = 1$;
3. $T \models \neg E$ if and only if $T \not\models E$;
4. $T \models (E_1 \vee E_2)$ if and only if either $T \models E_1$ or $T \models E_2$;
5. $T \models (E_1 \wedge E_2)$ if and only if $T \models E_1$ and $T \models E_2$.

Exercise 2.3.18 *Show that two Boolean expressions E_1 and E_2 are equivalent if and only if $T \models E_1 \Leftrightarrow T \models E_2$ for any assignment T on $S_{E_1 \vee E_2}$.*

The most basic way to show the equivalence of two Boolean expressions E_1 and E_2 is to determine, using the **truth table** with an enumeration of all initial assignments, step by step, the values of all subexpressions of E_1 and E_2. For example, in order to show that $x \wedge (y \vee z)$ and $x \wedge y \vee x \wedge z$ are equivalent Boolean expressions, we can proceed as follows.

xyz	$y \vee z$	$x \wedge (y \vee z)$	$x \wedge y$	$x \wedge z$	$x \wedge y \vee x \wedge z$
000	0	0	0	0	0
001	1	0	0	0	0
010	1	0	0	0	0
011	1	0	0	0	0
100	0	0	0	0	0
101	1	1	0	1	1
110	1	1	1	0	1
111	1	1	1	1	1

A Boolean expression E is said to be **satisfiable** if there is a truth assignment T_E such that $T_E \models E$, and it is called a **tautology** (or **valid**) if $T_E \models E$ for any truth assignment to variables of E.

There is another conceptually simple algorithm for constructing a DNF equivalent to a given Boolean expression E. For each truth assignment $T \models E$ one takes a minterm such that the literal corresponding to a variable x is x if $T(x) = 1$, and $\bar{x}$ otherwise. For a Boolean expression with n variables this gives a DNF of size $\mathcal{O}(n2^n)$.

The problem of finding out whether a given Boolean expression E is satisfiable is called the **satisfiability problem**. In spite of its simplicity, it plays an important role in complexity theory, and we deal with it in Chapter 5. The satisfiability problem is actually the first known **NP**-complete problem.

There is a close relation between Boolean formulas and formulas of propositional logic containing only negation, conjunction and disjunction. If 0 is interpreted as the truth value **false**, 1 as **true**, and the Boolean operations of negation, OR and AND as logical negation, conjunction and disjunction, then a Boolean formula can be regarded as a formula of the propositional calculus and vice versa.

Arithmetization of Boolean functions

Of importance also is a representation of Boolean functions by multilinear polynomials.

Definition 2.3.19 *A function $g: \mathbf{R}^n \to \mathbf{R}$ approximates a Boolean function $f: \{0,1\}^n \to \{0,1\}$, if $f(\alpha) = g(\alpha)$ for every $\alpha \in \{0,1\}^n$.*

It is easy to see that the basic Boolean functions have the following approximations by multilinear polynomials:

$$\textbf{true} \textit{ and } \textbf{false} \text{ are approximated by } 1 \text{ and } 0; \quad (2.8)$$
$$x \wedge y \text{ is approximated by } xy; \quad (2.9)$$
$$x \vee y \text{ is approximated by } 1-(1-x)(1-y); \quad (2.10)$$
$$\bar{y} \text{ is approximated by } 1-y. \quad (2.11)$$

If a given Boolean formula is first transformed into an equivalent disjunctive normal form, and the rules (2.8), (2.9), (2.10), (2.11) are then used, a multivariable polynomial approximating f can be obtained in a straightforward way. Using the identities $0^n = 0, 1^n = 1$ for any n, all powers x^n can then be replaced by x. In this way a multilinear polynomial approximating f is obtained. We have thereby shown the following theorem.

Theorem 2.3.20 *Any Boolean function can be approximated by a multilinear polynomial.*

Example 2.3.21 *The Boolean formula*

$$f(x,y,z) = (x \vee y \vee z) \wedge (x \vee \bar{y} \vee z)$$

can be transformed first into the polynomial

$$(x+y+z-xy-xz-yz+xyz)(1-y+xy+yz-xyz),$$

and then, after the multiplication and simplifications, the following polynomial approximation is obtained:

$$x+z-xz.$$

Exercise 2.3.22 *Construct multilinear polynomial approximations for the following functions: (a) $x \Rightarrow y$; (b) $x \equiv y$; (c) $(x \wedge y \vee z)(\bar{z} \vee zx)$; (d) XOR; (e) NOR.*

2.3.3 One-way Functions

Informally, a function, say $f : \mathbf{N} \to \mathbf{N}$, is called a **one-way function** if it is easily computable, in polynomial time, but a computation of its inverse is not feasible, meaning that it cannot be done in polynomial time.

This intuitively simple concept of a one-way function turns out to be deeply related to some of the main problems in the foundations of computing and also to important applications. It plays a central role in Chapters 8 and 9.

It is easy to give an informal example of a one-way function: write a message on a sheet of paper, cut the paper into thousands of pieces and mix them. This is easy to do, but the resulting message is practically unreadable.

There are several nonequivalent definitions of one-way functions. The reason is that for different purposes more or less strong requirements on 'one-wayness' are needed. We present now the definition of so-called strong one-wayness. Two other definitions are discussed in Chapter 5.

Definition 2.3.23 *A function $f : \{0,1\}^* \to \{0,1\}^*$ is called strongly one-way if the following conditions are satisfied:*

1. *f can be computed in polynomial time.*
2. *There are $c, \varepsilon > 0$ such that $|x|^{\varepsilon} \leq |f(x)| \leq |x|^{c}$. (Otherwise, any function that shrinks the input exponentially, for example, $f(n) = \lceil \lg n \rceil$, could be considered one-way.)*
3. *For every randomized polynomial time algorithm $\mathcal{A}$ and any constant $c > 0$, there exists an N_c such that for $n > N_c$*

$$Pr(\mathcal{A}(f(x)) \in f^{-1}(f(x))) < \frac{1}{n^c}.$$

(The probability space is that of all pairs $(x,r) \in S_n \times R_n$, where $S_n = \{0,1\}^n$ and R_n denote all possible sequences of coin-tossings of $\mathcal{A}$ on inputs of length n.)

Exercise 2.3.24 *Explain how it can happen that f and g are one-way functions but neither of the functions $f+g$ or $f \cdot g$ is one-way.*

Note that Definition 2.3.23 allows that a polynomial time randomized algorithm can invert f, but only for a negligibly small number of values. There are no proofs, only strong evidence, that one-way functions exist. Some candidates:

1. Modular exponentiation: $f(x) = a^x \bmod n$, where a is a generator of $\mathbf{Z}_n^*$;
2. Modular squaring: $f(x) = x^2 \bmod n$, where n is a Blum integer;
3. Prime number multiplication: $f(p,q) = pq$, where p,q are primes of almost the same length.

All these functions are easy to compute, but no one knows polynomial time deterministic algorithms for computing their inverses. As we saw in Section 1.7, in the case of modular squaring there is a proof (Theorem 1.8.16) that the computation of square roots is exactly as hard as factoring integers.

A proof that a one-way function exists (or not) would have a far-reaching impact on foundations of computing, as we shall see later. One-way functions also have numerous applications. They will be discussed especially in Chapters 8 and 9. We present now only one of them.

Example 2.3.25 (Passwords) *Passwords are an important vehicle for protecting unauthorized use of computers. After a to-be-authorized user has typed in a password, the computer must verify its correctness. However, it is unsafe to keep in a computer a password file with entries of user and his/her password. There are many ways in which an adversary can get in and misuse knowledge of the password. It is safer to use a one-way function f to compute f(password) each time a user tries to identify herself and to use a file with entries: (user, f(users's password)). Since f is one-way, even an adversary who could get this file would not be able to pretend that he is a user, because from f(password) he could not find out the password. (Unless he were to try all possibilities for passwords and for each one check the whole password–code table.)*

In spite of the simplicity of the informal definition of one-wayness, and the technicalities of the formal definition, an additional explanation seems to be in order to make clear what makes one-way functions so special. They actually exhibit such random or chaotic relations between pre-images and images that from knowledge of f and $f(x)$ there is no practically realizable way to find an x' such that $f(x') = f(x)$. This also implies that f may map values which are close to each other in some sense to images that are far apart, and vice versa.

2.3.4 Hash Functions

Another important family of functions that performs pseudo-random mappings is the so-called **hash functions**. Informally, an ideal hash function maps elements of a large finite set into elements of a smaller set in a maximally uniform and at the same time random way. Any element of the domain is equally likely to be mapped into any element of the co-domain.

More formally, let h map a set U (of objects) into a set A, and let $Pr(u)$ be the probability that u is picked up as the argument for h. The requirement of **simple uniform hashing** is that for any $a \in A$,

$$\sum_{\{u \mid h(u)=a\}} Pr(u) = \frac{1}{|A|}.$$

The main problem with this definition is that, in general, the probability distribution Pr is not known in applications. The tendency is to consider hash functions that perform reasonably well quite independently of the pattern in which the data occur.

Let us assume that $U = \{0,1, \ldots ,n\}$ for some integer n. (By a suitable coding we can usually work it that a set of codes, or keys, of objects under consideration is such a set.) The following list contains hash functions that have turned out to be useful:

$$h(u) = u \bmod m \quad \text{(division method)}; \tag{2.12}$$

$$h(u) = \lfloor m(au - \lfloor au \rfloor) \rfloor \quad \text{(multiplication method)}; \tag{2.13}$$

where $m \in \mathbf{N}$ and $a \in \mathbf{R}$.

The choice of a suitable hash function and of its parameters, m in (2.12), a in (2.13), depends on the application; they can also be chosen experimentally for a particular application. For example, it is usually good to choose for m a prime not close to a power of 2 in (2.12) and $a = (\sqrt{5} - 1) / 2 = 0.6180339$ in (2.13), by Knuth (1969).

Exercise 2.3.26 *Explain why one should not use as m a power of* 2 *or* 10 *if the division method is used for hashing.*

Exercise 2.3.27 *Show how to implement multiplication hashing efficiently on a microcomputer.*

Exercise 2.3.28 *Show, using hash functions, that the equality of two multisets with n elements can be checked in* $\mathcal{O}(n)$ *time with high probability.*

Hash functions play an increasingly important role in foundations of computing and also in various applications. However, it was for the dictionary problem (Example 2.1.24) that they were invented by Luhn (1953) and for which they first helped obtain a surprisingly efficient implementation.

Dictionary – a hash table implementation

Assume that any object o of a finite universe U has a unique integer key $key(o)$, and that the set of these keys $K = \{0,1 \ldots ,m-1\}$ has m elements. Assume also that we have at our disposal a table $T[0 : m-1]$ of size m. Any set $S \subseteq U$ can easily be stored in T by storing every element o in the array entry $T[key(o)]$ (see Figure 2.14a). This is called the 'direct-access representation' of the set S. With such a representation one clearly needs only $\mathcal{O}(1)$ time to perform any of the dictionary operations.

A more realistic case is when the size of U is much larger than the size m of T, but the dynamically changing set of the dictionary never has more than m elements and can be stored, in principle, in the table T. Can we also achieve in such a case a constant time performance for dictionary operations? Yes, but only on average, in the following way.

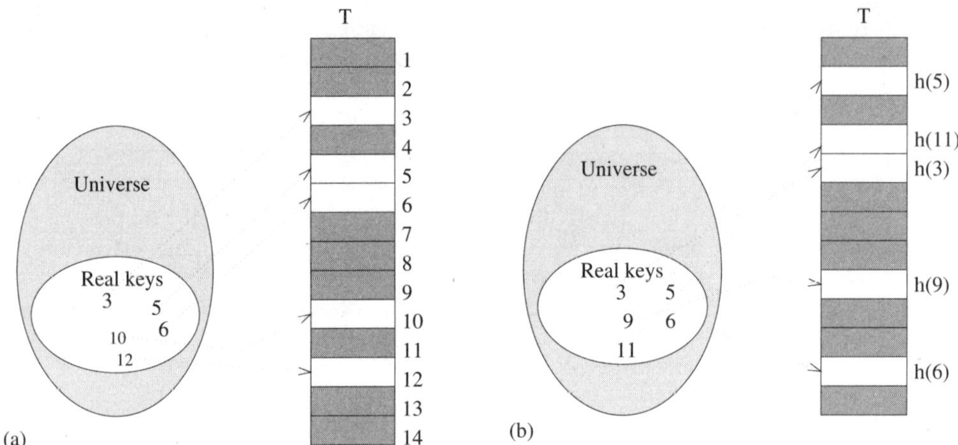

Figure 2.14 Direct-access and hash-table implementations of dictionaries

Let $h : U \to \{0, 1, \ldots, m\}$ be a hash function. The basic idea is to store an object o not in the table entry $T[key(o)]$ as before, but in $T[h(key(o))]$ (see Figure 2.14b). If h is a good hash function, then different elements from the dictionary set S are stored, with a large probability, in different entries of the table T. In such a case T is usually called the **hash table**. If this always happened, we could hope to get $\mathcal{O}(1)$ time performance for all dictionary operations.

Unfortunately, if the size of U is larger than that of T, it may happen, no matter how good an h is chosen, that $h(x) = h(y)$ for the keys of two elements to be stored in T. In such a case we speak of a **collision**.

On the assumption of **uniform hashing**, that is a uniform distribution of keys, there are simple methods for dealing with the collision problem that lead to $\mathcal{O}(1)$ time performance for all dictionary operations, where the constant is very small. For example, if the table entry $T[h(key(o))]$ is already occupied at the attempt to store o, then o is stored in the first empty entry among $T[h(key(o)) + 1], \ldots, T[m-1], T[0], \ldots, T[h(key(o)) - 1]$. Alternatively we can put all elements that hash to the same entry of the hash table in a list; this is the **chaining method**. The worst-case performance is, however, $\mathcal{O}(n)$, where n is the size of the dictionary set. It may happen that an adversary who knows h can supply storage requests such that all elements to be stored are mapped, by hashing, to the same entry of table T.

Exercise 2.3.29 *Show how to implement dictionary operations efficiently when a hash table and the chaining method for collisions are used to store the underlying set.*

Exercise 2.3.30 *Consider a hash table of size $m = 1{,}000$. Compute locations to which the keys 2^i, $1 \le i \le 9$, and 126, 127, 129, 130 are mapped if the multiplication method is used for hashing and $a = (\sqrt{5} - 1) / 2$.*

The way to avoid getting intentionally bad data is to choose the hash functions randomly, in the run time, from a carefully constructed family of hash functions. This approach is called **universal hashing**. In the case of dictionary implementations, it guarantees a good average performance, provided the set of hash functions to choose from has the following property of universality.

Definition 2.3.31 *A finite family $\mathcal{H}$ of hash functions mapping the universe U into the set $\{0,1,\ldots,m-1\}$ is called* **universal** *if*

$$\forall x,y \in U \quad |\{h \mid h \in \mathcal{H}, h(x) = h(y)\}| = \frac{|\mathcal{H}|}{m}.$$

In other words, if h is randomly chosen from $\mathcal{H}$, then the chance of a collision $h(x) = h(y)$ for $x \neq y$ is exactly $\frac{1}{m}$, which is also exactly the chance of a collision when two elements $h(x)$ and $h(y)$ are randomly picked from the set $\{0,\ldots,m-1\}$. The following result confirms that a universal family of hash functions leads to a good performance for a dictionary implementation.

Theorem 2.3.32 *If h is chosen randomly from a universal family $\mathcal{H}$ of hash functions mapping a set U to $\{0,\ldots,m-1\}$, with $|U| > m$, and h maps a set $S \subset U$, $|S| = n < m$, into $\{0,\ldots,m-1\}$, then the expected number of collisions involving an element of S is less than* 1.

Proof: For any two different elements x,y from U let X_{xy} be a random variable on $\mathcal{H}$ with value 1 if $h(x) = h(y)$, and 0 otherwise. By the definition of $\mathcal{H}$ the probability of a collision for $x \neq y$ is $\frac{1}{m}$; that is, $EX_{xy} = \frac{1}{m}$. Since E is additive (see (1.72)), we get for the average number of collisions involving x the estimation

$$EX_x = \sum_{y \in S} EX_{xy} = \frac{n}{m} < 1.$$

□

The result is fine, but does a universal family of hash functions actually exist? It does, and it can be constructed, for example, as follows.

Assume that m, the size of T, is a prime and that a binary representation of any $u \in U$ can be expressed as a sequence of $r+1$ binary strings $s_0 \ldots s_r$ such that $u_i = bin(s_i) < m$ for $0 \leq i \leq r$.

To each $(r+1)$-tuple $a = (a_0, a_1, \ldots, a_r)$ of elements from $\{0,\ldots,m-1\}$, let h_a be the function from U to $\{0,\ldots,m-1\}$ defined by

$$h_a(u) = \sum_{i=0}^{r} a_i u_i \bmod m, \tag{2.14}$$

and let

$$\mathcal{H} = \{h_a \mid a \in \{0,\ldots,m-1\}^{r+1}\} \tag{2.15}$$

Clearly $|\mathcal{H}| = m^{r+1}$, and we get the following theorem.

Theorem 2.3.33 *The family of functions $\mathcal{H} = \{h_a \mid a \in \{0,\ldots,m-1\}^{r+1}\}$, defined by the formula*

$$h_a(u) = \sum_{i=0}^{r} a_i u_i \bmod m,$$

is a universal family of functions.

Proof: If $x \neq y$ are from U, then there is an i such that $x_i \neq y_i$, where x_i, y_i are the ith substrings in the representation of x, y. Assume for simplicity that $i = 0$. (Other cases can be dealt with similarly.) For any fixed $a_1, \ldots, a_r$, there is exactly one a_0 such that

$$a_0(x_0 - y_0) \equiv \sum_{i=1}^{r} a_i(x_i - y_i) \pmod{m},$$

and therefore

$$h_a(x) = h_a(y).$$

Indeed, since m is prime and $|x_0 - y_0| < m$, then Euclid's algorithm can be used to compute an inverse of $(x_0 - y_0) \bmod m$, and a_0 does exist. Hence, each pair $x, y \in U$ collides exactly for m^r values of a, because they collide exactly once for each possible r-tuple from $\{0, \ldots, m-1\}$. Since there are m^{r+1} possibilities for a, they collide with probability $\frac{m^r}{m^{r+1}} = \frac{1}{m}$, and this proves the theorem. □

In some applications the above-mentioned requirement on the quality of elements in $\mathcal{H}$ can be relaxed, but the size of $\mathcal{H}$ may be an issue. (The fewer elements $\mathcal{H}$ has, the fewer random bits are needed to choose a hash function from $\mathcal{H}$.) In other applications hash functions may need to have stronger properties, for example, that they map elements that are 'close' to each other to elements 'far apart' from each other.

Exercise 2.3.34* *Let $\mathcal{H}$ be a family of hash functions mapping the universe of keys K into the set $[m]$. We say that $\mathcal{H}$ is k-universal if for every fixed sequence of k distinct keys $(x_1, \ldots, x_k)$ and for any h chosen randomly from $\mathcal{H}$, the sequence $(h(x_1), \ldots, h(x_k))$ is equally likely to be any of the m^k sequences of length k with elements from $[m]$. (a) Show that if $\mathcal{H}$ is 2-universal, then it is universal; (b) show that the family of functions defined by (2.14) is not 2- universal; (c) show that if the definition of the set $\mathcal{H}$ (2.15) is modified to consider functions $h_{a,b} = \sum_{i=0}^{k}(a_i u_i + b_i) \bmod m$, then $\mathcal{H}$ is 2-universal.*

Remark 2.3.35 Of great importance for applications are those hash functions that map any (binary) message up to a very large length n to a binary string of fixed (and small) length m, which then serves as the **authenticator (fingerprint)** of the original message. Such hash functions should have the following properties:

1. $h(x)$ should be easy to compute, but it should be unfeasible, given a y to find an x such that $h(x) = y$ (in other words, h should be a one-way hash function).
2. Given x, it should be unfeasible to find a y such that $h(x) = h(y)$, and it should also be unfeasible to find a pair (x, y) such that $h(x) = h(y)$.

A very simple idea, and still quite good even if it does not satisfy either of the above two conditions, is to partition a given binary message x into substrings $x_1, \ldots, x_k$ of length m and compute $h(x) = \bigoplus_{i=1}^{k} x_i$.

The practical importance of such hash functions for modern communications is so great that in 1993 the National Institute of Standards and Technology (NIST) in the United States developed a standard hash function (algorithm) called SHA (secure hash algorithm) that maps any binary string with up to 2^{64} bits to a 160-bit binary string.

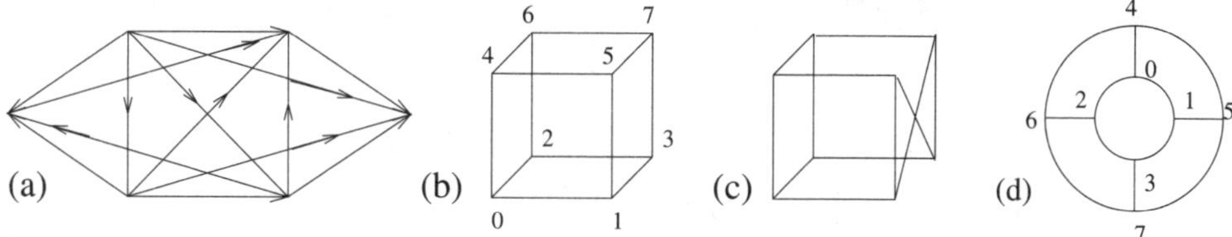

Figure 2.15 A directed graph and undirected graphs

2.4 Graphs

Graph concepts are of limitless use in all areas of computing: for example, in representing computational, communication and co-operational processes, automata, networks and circuits and in describing relationships between objects. Graph theory concepts, methods and results and graph algorithmic problems and algorithms play an important role in complexity theory and the design of efficient algorithms and computing systems in general.

2.4.1 Basic Concepts

A directed (undirected) **graph** $G = \langle V,E \rangle$ consists of a set V of **vertices**, also called **nodes**, and a set $E \subseteq V \times V$ of **arcs (edges)**. A graph is **finite** if V is; otherwise it is **infinite**. In a directed graph an arc (u,v) is depicted by an arrow from the node u to the node v (Figure 2.15a); in undirected graphs edges are depicted by simple lines connecting the corresponding vertices (Figure 2.15b, c). An edge (u,v) can be seen as consisting of two arcs: (u,v) and (v,u).

Incidences and degrees. If $e = (u,v)$ is an arc or an edge, then vertices u,v are **incident** with e, and e is an arc (edge) **from** u **to** v incident with both u and v. The vertex v is called **adjacent** to u, and u is also called the **neighbour** of v. Similarly, v is adjacent to u, and is also its neighbour. An arc (u,v) is an **ingoing** arc of the vertex v and an **outgoing** arc of the vertex u. The **degree** of a vertex v, notation *degree*(v), in an undirected graph is the number of edges incident with v. In a directed graph, the **in-degree** of a vertex v, *in-degree*(v), is the number of ingoing arcs of v; the **out-degree**, *out-degree*(v), is the number of outgoing arcs of v. Finally, the degree of v is the sum of its in-degree and out-degree. The degree of a graph G, *degree*(G), is the maximum of the degrees of its vertices. For example, the graphs in Figure 2.15a, b, c have degrees 5,3 and 3, respectively.

Walks, trails, paths and **cycles**. A **walk** p of length k from a vertex u, called the origin, to a vertex v, called the terminus, is a sequence of nodes $p = \langle u_0, u_1, \ldots, u_k \rangle$ such that $u_0 = u$, $u_k = v$ and $(u_i, u_{i+1}) \in E$ for $0 \leq i < k$. $u_0, \ldots, u_k$ are vertices on the walk p, or the vertices the walk p contains. Moreover, $(u_i, u_{i+1}), 0 \leq i < k$, are arcs (edges) on the walk p, or arcs (edges) p contains. If there is a walk from a vertex u to a vertex v, then we say that v is **reachable** from u and that u and v are **connected**. The *distance*(u,v) is the length of the shortest walk from u to v.

A walk is called a **trail** if it contains no arc (edge) twice, and a **path** if it contains no vertex twice.

A walk is closed if its origin and terminus coincide. A closed trail is called a **cycle**. A cycle is called a **simple cycle** if the only two identical nodes are its origin and terminus. For example, the graph in Figure 2.15b has simple cycles only, of length 4, 6 and 8. A cycle $(a,a), a \in V$, is called a **self-loop**, and a simple cycle of length 3 is called a **triangle**. For example, none of the graphs in Figure 2.15 has a triangle, but the graph in Figure 2.16a has 16 triangles. (Find them!)

A graph is called **acyclic** if it does not contain any cycle. A directed acyclic graph is also called a **dag**. For example, the graph in Figure 2.15a is acyclic.

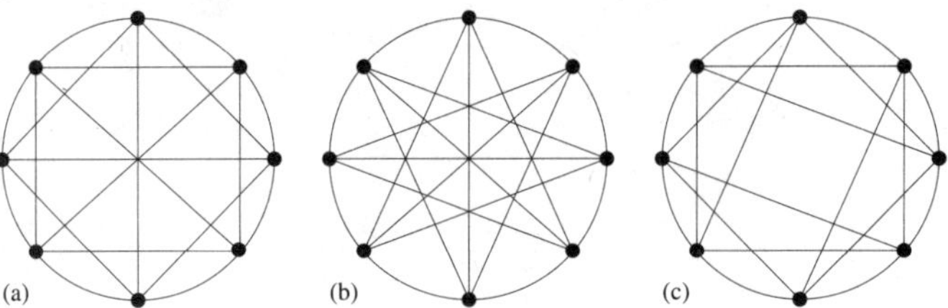

Figure 2.16 Graph isomorphism

Exercise 2.4.1 *(a) Determine the number of simple cycles of the graph in Figure 2.15c; (b) determine the number of triangles of the graph in Figure 2.16b.*

Exercise 2.4.2* *Show that in any group of at least two people there are always two with exactly the same number of friends inside the group.*

Connectivity. In an undirected graph the relation 'connected' is an equivalence relation on the set of vertices, and its equivalence classes are called **connected components**. An undirected graph is called **connected** if all pairs of its vertices are connected. A directed graph is called **strongly connected** if for any two vertices u, v there is a path from u to v. The equivalence classes on the set of vertices of a directed graph, with respect to the relation 'mutually connected', are called **strongly connected components.**

In various applications it is important 'how well connected' a given graph is. Intuitively, each successive graph in Figure 2.17 is more connected than the previous one. Indeed, the graph in Figure 2.17a can be disconnected by removing one edge, that in Figure 2.17b by removing one vertex. This is not the case for the graphs in Figure 2.17c, d.

There are two main quantitative measures of the connectivity of graphs. **Vertex-connectivity**, $v\text{-conn}(G)$, is the minimum number of vertices whose removal disconnects a graph G. **Edge-connectivity**, $e\text{-conn}(G)$, is the minimum number of edges whose removal disconnects G.

Exercise 2.4.3 *Show that* $v\text{-conn}(G) \leq e\text{-conn}(G) \leq degree(G)$ *for any graph G.*

Exercise 2.4.4** *Show that if* $e\text{-conn}(G) \geq 2$ *for a graph G, then any two vertices of G are connected by at least two edge-disjoint paths.*

If a graph represents a communications network, then the vertex-connectivity (edge-connectivity) becomes the smallest number of communication nodes (links) whose breakdown would jeopardize communication in the network.

Isomorphism. Two graphs, $G_1 = \langle V_1, E_1 \rangle$ and $G_2 = \langle V_2, E_2 \rangle$, are called **isomorphic** if there is a bijection (called **isomorphism** in this case) $\iota : V_1 \rightarrow V_2$ such that $(u,v) \in E_1 \Leftrightarrow (\iota(u), \iota(v)) \in E_2$. For example, the graphs in Figure 2.15b, d are isomorphic, and those in Figure 2.15b, c are not. Any isomorphism of a graph with itself is called an **automorphism**.

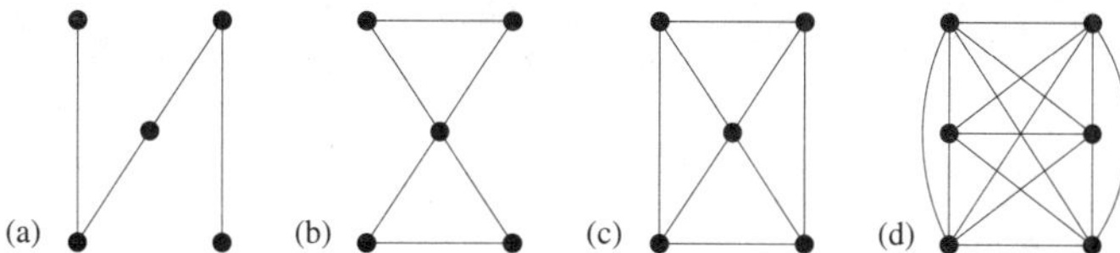

Figure 2.17 More and more connected graphs

To show that two graphs are isomorphic, one has to show an isomorphism between them. For example, the graphs in Figure 2.15b, d are isomorphic, and the corresponding isomorphism is given by the mapping that maps a node labelled by an i in one graph into the node labelled by the same label in the second graph. Two isomorphic graphs can be seen as identical; it is only their representations that may differ. To show that two graphs are not isomorphic is in general much harder.

Exercise 2.4.5 *Which pairs of graphs in Figure 2.16 are isomorphic, and why?*

Exercise 2.4.6 *Show that if two graphs are isomorphic, then there must exist a bijection between the sets of their vertices such that the corresponding nodes have the same degree and lie in the same number of cycles of any length.*

Regularity. Graphs encountered in both applications and theory can be very complex and large. In order to manage large graphs in a transparent and effective way, they must have some degree of regularity. There are several approaches to the problem of how to define regularity of graphs. Perhaps the simplest is to consider a graph as **regular** if all its vertices have the same degree; it is k-regular, $k \in \mathbf{N}$, if all vertices have degree k. A stronger concept, useful especially in the case of graphs modelling interconnection networks, is that of symmetry. A graph $G = \langle V, E \rangle$ is called **vertex-symmetric** if for every pair of vertices u, v there is an automorphism α of G such that $\alpha(u) = v$. Clearly, each vertex-symmetric graph is regular. As an example, the graph in Figure 2.15b is vertex-symmetric, whereas that in Figure 2.15c is not, even if it is regular. A graph G is called **arc-symmetric** if for every two arcs (u_1, v_1) and (u_2, v_2) there is an automorphism α of G such that $\alpha(u_1) = u_2$ and $\alpha(v_1) = v_2$. A graph G is called **edge-symmetric** if for every two edges (u_1, v_1) and (u_2, v_2) there is an automorphism α of G such that either $\alpha(u_1) = u_2$ and $\alpha(v_1) = v_2$ or $\alpha(u_1) = v_2$ and $\alpha(v_1) = u_2$.

An example of a graph that is vertex-symmetric but not edge-symmetric, the so-called cube-connected cycles, is shown in Figure 2.35b. The importance of these concepts lies in the fact that a vertex-symmetric graph can be seen as 'looking from each node (processor) the same' and an edge (arc)-symmetric graph as 'looking from each edge (arc) the same'.

Exercise 2.4.7 *Are the graphs in Figures 2.16 and 2.18 vertex-, arc- and edge-symmetric?*

Exercise 2.4.8* *Show that if G is a regular graph and degree$(G) \geq 3$, then v-conn$(G) = e$-conn(G).*

Exercise 2.4.9 *Find an example of a graph that is (a)* edge- and not vertex-symmetric; (b)* vertex- but not edge-symmetric; (c)** vertex- and edge- but not arc-symmetric.*

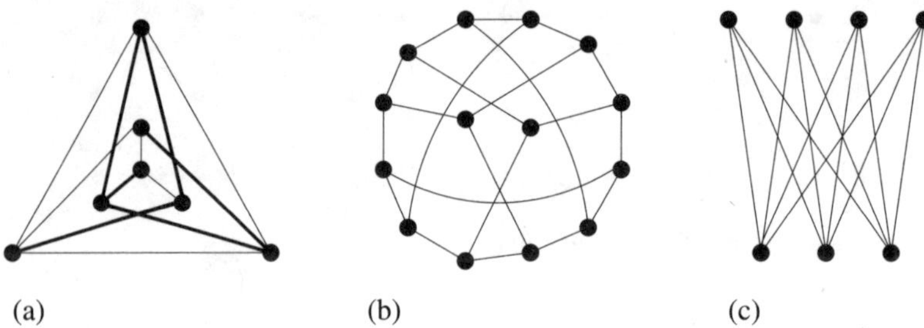

Figure 2.18 A spanning tree and bipartite graphs

Subgraphs. A graph $G_1 = \langle V', E' \rangle$ is a **subgraph** of the graph $G = \langle V, E \rangle$ if $V' \subseteq V$ and $E' \subset E$. We usually say also that a graph G' is a subgraph of a graph G if G' is isomorphic with a subgraph of G. For example, the graph in Figure 2.16c is a subgraph of the graph in Figure 2.16b – show it!

Several special types of graphs are used so often that they have special names.

Complete graphs of n nodes, notation K_n, are graphs with all nodes of degree $n-1$; see Figure 2.19 for K_5. Another name for complete graphs is **clique**.

Bipartite graphs. An undirected graph is called **bipartite** if its set of vertices can be partitioned into two subsets V_1, V_2 in such a way that each edge of G connects a vertex in V_1 and a vertex in V_2. The term **bipartition** is often used for such a partition. For example, the graphs in Figures 2.15b and 2.18b, c are bipartite, and those in Figures 2.15c, and 2.18a are not. A **complete bipartite graph** $K_{m,n}$ is a bipartite graph of $m+n$ nodes whose nodes can be partitioned into sets A and B with $|A| = m$, $|B| = n$, and two vertices are connected by an edge if and only if one is from A and another from B. Figure 2.18c shows $K_{4,3}$.

Exercise 2.4.10 *Show that the graphs in Figures 2.18b and 2.23d are bipartite.*

Exercise 2.4.11* *Show that a graph is bipartite if and only if it contains no cycle of odd length.*

Bipartite graphs may seem to be very simple. However, some of the most important and also the most complicated graphs we shall deal with are bipartite.

Trees. An undirected acyclic graph is called a **forest** (see Figure 2.27b), and if it is connected, a **tree**. We deal with trees in more detail in Section 2.4.36. A subgraph $T = \langle V, E' \rangle$ of an undirected graph $G = \langle V, E \rangle$ is called a **spanning tree** of G if T is a tree. The subgraph depicted by bold lines in Figure 2.18a is a spanning tree of the whole graph shown in Figure 2.18a. In general, if $G_1 = \langle V, E_1 \rangle$, $G_2 = \langle V, E_2 \rangle$, $E_1 \subseteq E_2$, then G_1 is called a **spanning subgraph** of G_1.

Exercise 2.4.12 *Design a spanning tree for the graph in Figure 2.18b. How many different spanning trees does this graph have?*

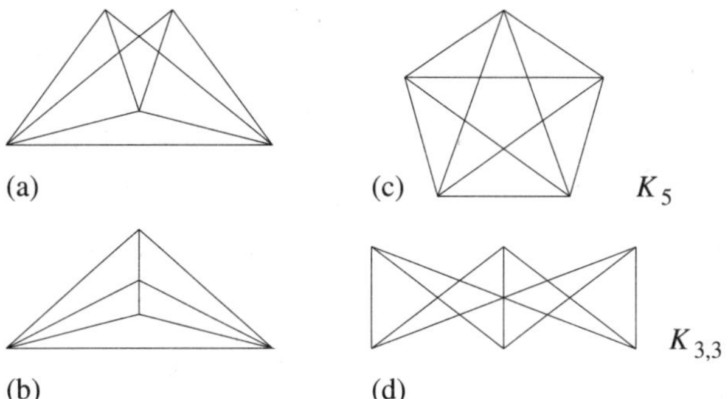

Figure 2.19 Planar and nonplanar graphs

Planar graphs. A graph is called **planar** if its vertices and edges can be drawn in a plane without any crossing of edges. Planarity is of importance in various applications: for example, in the design of electrical circuits. Figure 2.19a shows a graph that does not look planar but is (see the other drawing of it in Figure 2.19b).

There is a simple-to-state condition for a graph not being planar. To formulate this condition, we define a graph G' as a topological version of G if it is obtained from G by replacing each edge of G with an arbitrarily long, nonintersecting path.

Theorem 2.4.13 (Kuratowski's theorem) *A graph is nonplanar if and only if it contains a subgraph that is a topological version either of the graph K_5 in Figure 2.19c or $K_{3,3}$ in Figure 2.19d.*

Exercise 2.4.14 *Show that each graph G is spatial; that is, its nodes can be mapped into points of three-dimensional space in such a way that no straight-line edges connecting the corresponding nodes of G intersect either with other edges or with points representing nodes of G. (Hint: map the i-th node of G into the point (i, i^2, i^3).)*

Graph complexity measures. Numbers of vertices, $|V|$, and edges, $|E|$, are the main size measures of graphs $G = \langle V, E\rangle$. Clearly, $|E| \leq |V|^2$. Other graph characteristics of a special importance in computing are:

diameter	$\max\{distance\,(u,v) \mid u, v \in V\}$
bisection-width	the minimum number of edges one needs to remove from E to partition V into sets of $\lfloor \frac{\lvert V\rvert}{2} \rfloor$ and $\lceil \frac{\lvert V\rvert}{2} \rceil$ vertices.

For example, the graph in Figure 2.15b has diameter 3 and bisection-width 4, and the graph in Figure 2.15c has diameter 2 and bisection-width 4.

Exercise 2.4.15 *Determine the bisection-width of the graphs in Figures 2.16 and 2.18.*

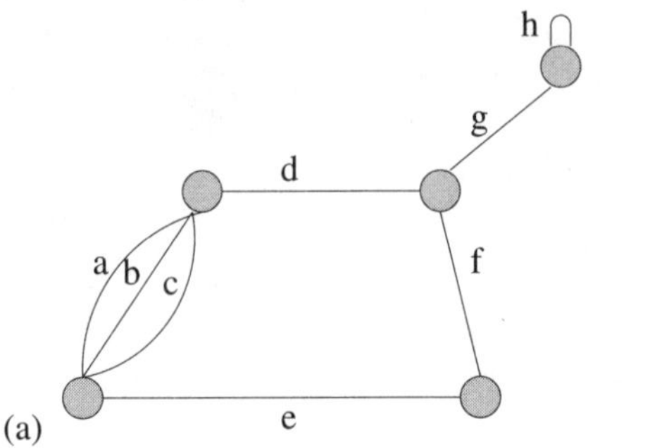

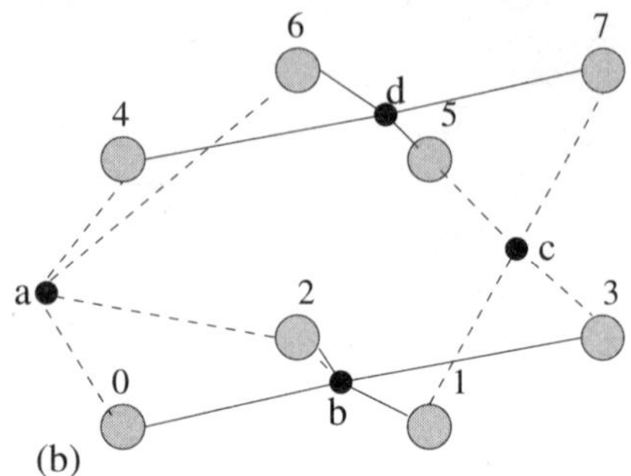

Figure 2.20 Multigraph and hypergraph

Diameter and bisection-width are of importance for graphs that model communication networks; the longer the diameter of a graph, the more time two processor nodes may need to communicate. The smaller the bisection-width, the narrower is the bottleneck through which node processors of two parts of the graph may need to communicate.

Multigraphs and **hypergraphs**. These are several natural generalizations of the concept of an (ordinary) graph, as introduced above. A **multigraph** is like a (directed or undirected) graph, but may have multiple arcs or edges between vertices (see Figure 2.20a). Formally, a multigraph can be modelled as $G = \langle V, E, L \rangle$, where V is a set of vertices, $E \subseteq V \times V \times L$, and L is a set of labels. An arc $(u, v, l) \in E$ is an arc from the vertex u to the vertex v labelled l. Labels are used to distinguish different arcs between the same vertices.

A walk in a multigraph G is any sequence $w = v_0 e_1 v_1 e_2 \ldots e_k v_k$ whose elements are alternatively nodes and arcs, and e_i is an arc from v_{i-1} to v_i. On this basis we define trails and paths for multigraphs. The concept of isomorphism is defined for multigraphs similarly to how it was defined for graphs.

Also, just as graphs model binary relations, so **hypergraphs** model n-ary relations for $n > 2$. An edge of a hypergraph is an n-tuple of nodes $(v_1, \ldots, v_n)$. An edge can therefore connect more than two vertices. In Figure 2.20b we have a hypergraph with eight nodes and four hyperedges, each with four nodes: $a = (0,2,4,6)$, $b = (0,1,2,3)$, $c = (1,3,5,7)$ and $d = (4,5,6,7)$.

2.4.2 Graph Representations and Graph Algorithms

There are four basic methods for providing explicit representations of graphs $G = \langle V, E \rangle$.

Adjacency lists: For each vertex u a list $L[u]$ of all vertices v such that $(u, v) \in E$ is given.

Adjacency matrices: A Boolean matrix of size $|V| \times |V|$, with rows and columns labelled by vertices of V, and with 1 as the entry for a row u and a column v if and only if $(u, v) \in E$. Actually, this is a Boolean matrix representation of the relation E.

Incidence matrices: A Boolean matrix of size $|V| \times |E|$ with rows labelled by vertices and columns by arcs of G and with 1 as the entry for a row u and a column e if and only if the vertex u is incident with the arc e.

Words: w_G is a binary word $u_1 \ldots u_{|V|}$, where u_i is the binary word of the ith row of the adjacency matrix for G. In the case of undirected graphs the adjacency matrix is symmetric, and therefore it is sufficient to take for u_i only the last $n - i + 1$ elements of the ith row of the adjacency matrix.

A graph $G = \langle V, E \rangle$ can be described by a list of size $\Theta(|E|)$, an adjacency matrix of size $\Theta(|V|^2)$, an incidence matrix of size $\Theta(|V||E|)$ and a word of size $\Theta(|V|^2)$. Lists are therefore in general the most economical way to describe graphs. Matrix representation is advantageous when direct access to its elements is needed.

Exercise 2.4.16 *Show that there are more economical representations than those mentioned above for the following graphs: (a) bipartite; (b) binary trees.*

None of the above methods can be used to describe infinite graphs, an infinite family of graphs or very large graphs. (This is a real problem, because in some applications it is necessary to work with graphs having more than 10^7 nodes.) In such cases other methods of describing graphs have to be used: specification of the set of nodes and edges by an (informal or formal) formula of logic, generation by generative, for example, rewriting, systems; and in applications a variety of hierarchical descriptions is used. Implicit methods for describing families of graphs are used, for example, in Sections 2.6 and 10.1.

Computational complexity of graph problems. It is often important to decide whether a graph is connected or planar, whether two graphs are isomorphic, or to design a spanning tree of a graph. In considering computational complexity of algorithmic problems on graphs, one of the above graph representation techniques is usually used and, unless explicitly specified otherwise, we assume that it is the adjacency matrix.

Two of the tasks mentioned above are computationally easy. Connectivity can be decided for graphs with n nodes in $\Theta(n)$ time on a sequential computer. A spanning tree can be constructed in $\mathcal{O}(n \lg n)$ time on a sequential computer. Surprisingly, there is an $\mathcal{O}(n)$ time algorithm for sequential computers for determining planarity of graphs.

Graph isomorphism, on the other hand, seems to be a very hard problem computationally, and (as we shall see in Section 5.6) it has a special position among algorithmic problems. No polynomial time algorithm is known for graph isomorphism, but there is no proof that none exists. It is also not known whether graph isomorphism is an **NP**-complete problem; it seems that it is not. Interestingly enough, if two graphs are isomorphic, there is a short proof of it – just presenting an isomorphism. On the other hand, no simple way is known in general of showing that two nonisomorphic graphs are really nonisomorphic. However, as discussed in Chapter 9, there is a polynomial time interactive randomized protocol to show graph nonisomorphism.

2.4.3 Matchings and Colourings

Two simple graph concepts with numerous applications are matching and colouring.

Definition 2.4.17 *If $G = \langle V, E \rangle$ is a graph, then any subset $M \subseteq E$ is called a* **matching** *in G if no two edges of M coincide. A matching M* **saturates** *a set of nodes $V_0 \subseteq V$ if every node of V_0 is incident with an edge of M. A matching M is called* **perfect** *if it saturates V.*

Figure 2.21a shows a graph and its perfect matching, and Figure 2.21b a graph that has no perfect matching.

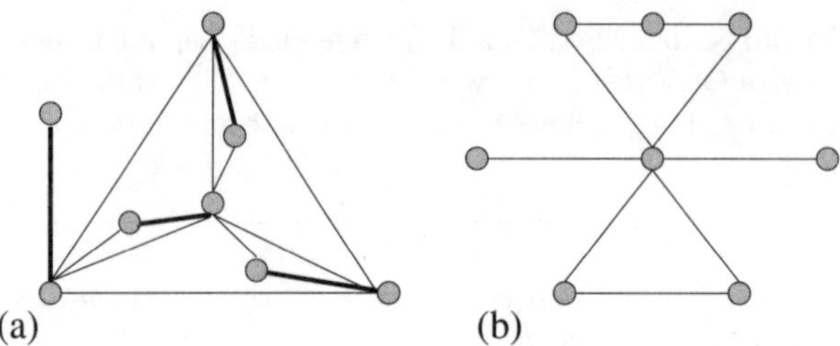

Figure 2.21 Graph matching

Exercise 2.4.18 *Show that a binary tree has at most one perfect matching.*

Exercise 2.4.19* *Two people play a game on a graph $G = \langle V, E\rangle, |V| > 2$, by alternately selecting distinct nodes to form a path. The last player able to select a node wins. Show that the first player has a winning strategy if and only if G has no perfect matching.*

Of special interest is the matching of bipartite graphs. The following theorem contains the key result, which says that if any subset of a set X of vertices of a bipartite graph 'expands' by edges of the graph, then there is a matching that saturates X.

Theorem 2.4.20 (Hall's theorem) *Let $G = \langle V, E\rangle$ be a bipartite graph with a bipartition (X, Y). G has a matching that saturates X if, for every $S \subseteq X$, $|A(S)| \geq |S|$, where $A(S) = \{y \mid y \in Y, \exists x \in S, (x,y) \in E\}$.*

As a corollary we get the following theorem.

Theorem 2.4.21 *If G is a regular bipartite graph, then G has a perfect matching.*

Proof: Let G be a k-regular bipartite graph with a bipartition (X, Y). Since G is k-regular, $k|X| = |E| = k|Y|$, and therefore $|X| = |Y|$. Now let $S \subseteq X$, and let E_1 be the set of edges incident with S, and E_2 the set of edges incident with $A(S)$. It follows from the definition of $A(S)$ that $E_1 \subseteq E_2$:

$$k|A(S)| = |E_2| \geq |E_1| = k|S|.$$

We therefore have $|A(S)| \geq |S|$. By Theorem 2.4.20 there is a matching M that saturates X, and since $|X| = |Y|$, M is a perfect matching. □

Theorem 2.4.21 is also called the marriage theorem, because it can be restated as follows: if every girl in a village knows exactly k boys, and every boy knows exactly k girls, then each girl can marry a boy she knows, and each boy can marry a girl he knows.

The following fundamental result is useful, especially for proving the nonexistence of perfect matchings.

Theorem 2.4.22 (Talle's theorem) *A graph has a perfect matching if and only if, for any k, if k vertices are deleted, there remain at most k connected components of odd size.*

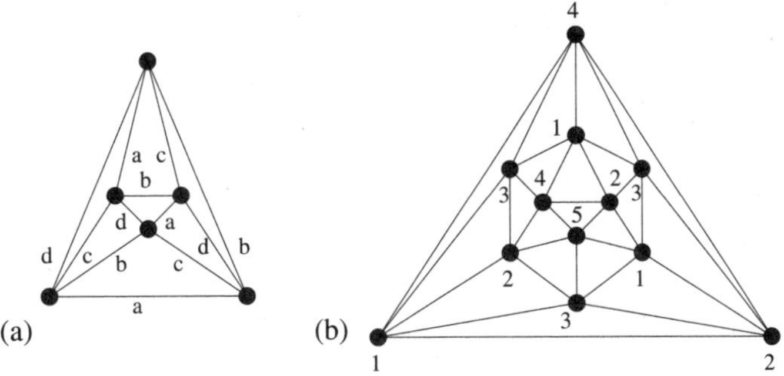

Figure 2.22 Edge and node colourings of graphs

Exercise 2.4.23** *Let* $G = \langle V, E\rangle$ *be a bipartite graph with bipartition of vertices into sets* $A = \{a_1, \ldots, a_n\}$, $B = \{b_1, \ldots, b_n\}$. *To each edge* (a_i, b_j) *assign a variable* x_{ij}. *Let* $M_G = \{m_{ij}\}$ *be an* $n \times n$ *matrix such that* $m_{ij} = x_{ij}$ *if* $(a_i, b_j) \in E$ *and* $m_{ij} = 0$ *otherwise. Show that G has a perfect matching if and only if* $\det(M)$ *is not identically* 0.

There are two types of graph colourings: edge and vertex colouring.

Definition 2.4.24 *An* **edge k-colouring** *of a graph* $G = \langle V, E\rangle$ *is an assignment of k elements (called colours) to edges of E in such a way that no two adjacent edges are assigned the same colour. The* **chromatic index** *of G,* $\chi'(G)$, *is the minimal number of colours with which one can colour edges of G. (See, for example, the edge colouring of the graph in Figure 2.22a.)*

Two important results concerning edge colouring that relate the degree of a graph and its chromatic index are now summarized.

Theorem 2.4.25 *(1) (***Vizing's theorem***) If G has no self-loops, then either* $\chi'(G) = degree(G)$ *or* $\chi'(G) = degree(G) + 1$.[7] *(2) If G is a bipartite graph, then* $\chi'(G) = degree(G)$.

Exercise 2.4.26 *Show that* $\chi'(G) = degree(G) + 1$ *for the Petersen graph shown in Figure 2.36.*

Exercise 2.4.27 *Show how to colour a bipartite graph* $K_{m,n}$ *with* $degree(K_{m,n})$ *colours.*

Exercise 2.4.28 *Show that if* M_1 *and* M_2 *are disjoint matchings of a graph G with* $|M_1| > |M_2|$, *then there are disjoint matchings* M_1' *and* M_2' *such that* $|M_1'| = |M_1| - 1$, $|M_2'| = |M_2| + 1$ *and* $M_1 \cup M_2 = M_1' \cup M_2'$.

As an application of Theorem 2.4.25 we get the following.

[7]Interestingly enough, deciding which of these two possibilities holds is an **NP**-complete problem even for 3-regular graphs (by Holyer (1981)).

Theorem 2.4.29 *If G is a bipartite graph and $p \geq degree(G)$, then there exist p disjoint matchings $M_1, \ldots, M_p$ of G such that*

$$E = \bigcup_{i=1}^{p} M_i,$$

and, for $1 \leq i \leq p$,

$$\left\lfloor \frac{|E|}{p} \right\rfloor \leq |M_i| \leq \left\lceil \frac{|E|}{p} \right\rceil.$$

Proof: Let G be a bipartite graph. By Theorem 2.4.25 the edges of G can be partitioned into $k = degree(G)$ disjoint matchings $M'_1, \ldots, M'_k$. Therefore, for any $p \geq k$ there exist p disjoint matchings (with $M'_i = \emptyset$ for $p > i \geq k$). Now we use the result of Exercise 2.4.28 to get a well-balanced matching. □

Finally, let us define a vertex colouring of graphs. A **vertex k-colouring** of a graph G is an assignment of k colours to vertices of G in such a way that no incident nodes are assigned the same colour. The **chromatic number,** $\chi(G)$, of G is the minimum k for which G is vertex k-colourable. See Figure 2.22b for a vertex 5- colouring of a graph (called an isocahedron).

One of the most famous problems in mathematics in this century was the so-called four-colour problem, formulated in 1852: Is every planar graph 4-colourable? [8] The problem was solved by K. Appel and W. Haken (1971), using ideas of B. Kempe. Their proof, made with the help of a computer, created a lot of controversy. They used a randomized approach to perform and check a large number of reductions. The written version takes more than 100 pages, and at that time it was expected that one would need 300 hours of computer time for proof checking.

2.4.4 Graph Traversals

Graphs are mathematical objects. In applications vertices represent processes, processors, gates, cities, plants, firms. Arcs or edges represent communication links, wires, roads. Numerous applications and graph algorithms require one to traverse graphs in some thorough and efficient way so that all vertices or edges are visited. There are several basic techniques for doing this. Two of them, perhaps the most ideal ones, are Euler[9] tours and Hamilton[10] paths and cycles.

A **Euler tour** of a graph G is a closed walk that traverses each edge of G exactly once. A graph is called **Eulerian** if it contains a Euler tour.

A path in a graph G that contains every node of G is called a **Hamilton path** of G; similarly, a Hamilton cycle is a simple cycle that contains every node of G. A graph is **Hamiltonian** if it contains a Hamilton cycle.

For example, the graph in Figure 2.23a is Eulerian but not Hamiltonian; the graph in Figure 2.23b is both Eulerian and Hamiltonian; the graph in Figure 2.23c, called a dodecahedron, is Hamiltonian but not Eulerian; and the graph in Figure 2.23d, called the Herschel graph, is neither Hamiltonian nor Eulerian.

[8] The problem was proposed by a student F. Guthree, who got the idea while colouring a map of counties in England. In 1879 B. Kempe published an erroneous proof that for ten years was believed to be correct.

[9] Leonhard Euler (1707–83), a German and Russian mathematician of Swiss origin, made important contributions to many areas of mathematics and was enormously productive. He published more than 700 books and papers and left so much unpublished material that it took 49 years to publish it. His collected works, to be published, should run to more than 95 volumes. Euler and his wife had 13 children.

[10] William Rowan Hamilton (1805–65), an Astronomer Royal of Ireland, perhaps the most famous Irish scientist of his era, made important contributions to abstract algebra, dynamics and optics.

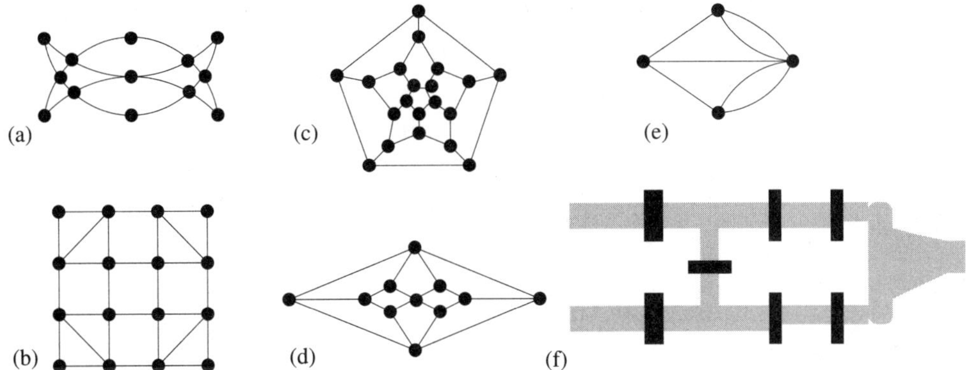

Figure 2.23 Euler tours and Hamilton cycles

Exercise 2.4.30 *Show that for every $n \geq 1$ there is a directed graph G_n with $2n+3$ nodes that has exactly 2^n Hamilton paths (and can therefore be seen as an encoding of all binary strings of length n).*

Graph theory is rich in properties that are easy to define and hard to verify and problems that are easy to state and hard to solve. For example, it is easy to see whether the graphs in Figure 2.23 do or do not have a Euler tour or a Hamilton cycle. The problem is whether this is easily decidable for an arbitrary graph. Euler tours cause no problem. It follows from the next theorem that one can verify in $\Theta(|E|)$ time whether a multigraph with the set E of edges is Eulerian.

Theorem 2.4.31 *A connected undirected multigraph is Eulerian if and only if each vertex has even degree. A connected directed multigraph is Eulerian if and only if in-degree(v) = out-degree(v) for any vertex v.*

Proof: Let $G = \langle V, E, L \rangle$ be an undirected multigraph. If a Euler cycle enters a node, it has to leave it unless the node is the starting node. From that the degree condition follows. Let us now assume that the degree condition is satisfied. This implies that there is a cycle in G. (Show why!) Then there is a maximal cycle that contains no edge twice. Take such a cycle C. If C contains all edges of G, we are done. If not, consider a multigraph G' with V as the set of nodes and exactly those edges of G that are not in C. Clearly, G' also satisfies the even-degree condition, and let C' be a maximal cycle in it with no edge twice. Since G is connected, C and C' must have a common vertex. This means that from C and C' we can create a larger cycle than C having no edge twice, which is a contradiction to the maximality of C. The case of directed graphs is handled similarly. □

Exercise 2.4.32 *Design an algorithm to construct a Euler tour for a graph (provided it exists), and apply it to design a Euler tour for the graph in Figure 2.23a.*

Theorem 2.4.31, due to Euler (1736), is considered as founding graph theory. Interestingly enough, the original motivation was an intellectual curiosity about whether there is such a tour for the graph

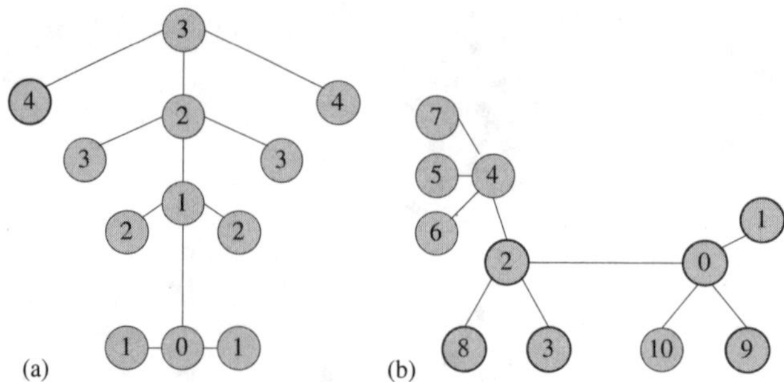

Figure 2.24 Breadth-first search and depth-first search

shown in Figure 2.23e. This graph models paths across seven bridges in Königsberg (Figure 2.23f) along which Euler liked to walk every day.

It may seem that the problem of Hamilton cycles is similar to that of Euler tours. For some classes of graphs it is known that they have Hamilton cycles (for example, hypercubes); for others that they do not (for example, bipartite graphs with an odd number of nodes). There is also an easy-to-describe exponential time algorithm to solve the problem – check all possibilities. The problem of deciding whether a graph has a Hamilton cycle or a Hamilton path is, however, **NP**-complete (see Section 5.4).

Exercise 2.4.33 *Design a Hamilton cycle for the graph in Figure 2.23c. (This is an abstraction of the original Hamilton puzzle called 'Round the World' that led to the concept of the Hamilton cycle – the puzzle was, of course, three-dimensional.)*

Another way to traverse a graph so that all nodes are visited is to move along the edges of a spanning tree of the graph. To construct a spanning tree for a graph G is easy. Start with S as the empty set. Check all edges of the graph, each once, and add the checked edge to S if and only if this does not make out of S a cyclic graph. (The order in which this is done does not matter.)

Two other general graph traversal methods, often useful in the design of efficient algorithms (they also design spanning trees), are the **breadth-first search** and the **depth-first search**. They allow one to search a graph and collect data about the graph in linear time.

Given a graph $G = \langle V, E \rangle$ and a source node u, the **breadth-first search** first 'marks' u as the node of distance 0 (from u), then visits all nodes reachable through an arc from u, and marks them as nodes of distance 1. Recursively, in the ith round, the breadth-first search visits all nodes marked by i and marks all nodes reachable from them by an arc, and not marked yet, by $i+1$. The process ends if in some round no unmarked nodes are found. See Figure 2.24a for an example of a breadth-first traversal of a graph. This way the breadth-first search also computes for each node its distance from the source node u.

A **depth-first search** also starts traversing a graph from a source node u and marks it as 'visited'. Each time it gets through an edge to a node that has not yet been marked, it marks this node as 'visited', and tries to move out of that node through an edge to a node not yet marked. If there is no such edge, it backtracks to the node it came from and tries again. The process ends if there is nothing else to try. See Figure 2.24b for an example of a depth-first traversal of a graph.

The graph traversal problem gets a new dimension when to each edge a nonnegative integer –

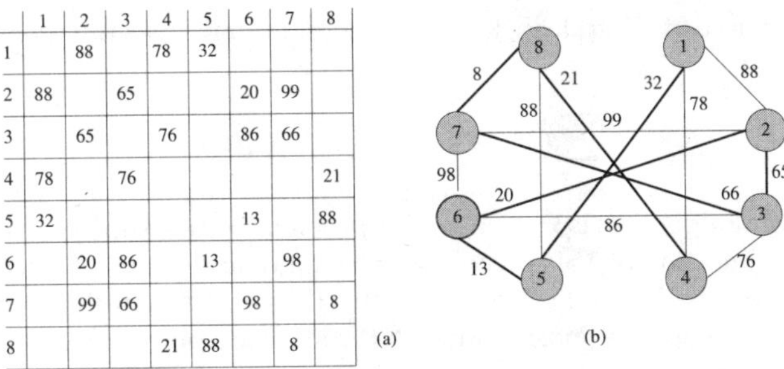

	1	2	3	4	5	6	7	8
1		88		78	32			
2	88		65			20	99	
3		65		76		86	66	
4	78		76					21
5	32					13		88
6		20	86		13		98	
7		99	66			98		8
8				21	88		8	

Figure 2.25 Minimal spanning tree

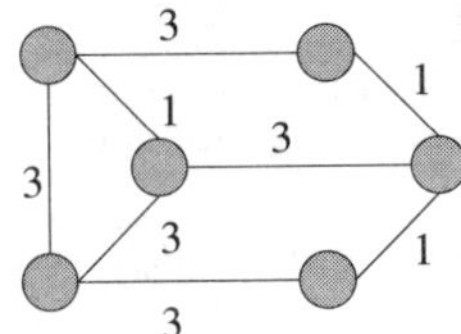

Figure 2.26 Minimal spanning tree

called its length – is associated (see Figure 2.25b). We then speak of a **distance graph**, and the task is to find the most economical (shortest) traversal of the distance graph.

The first idea is to use a **minimal spanning tree**. This is a spanning tree of the distance graph with minimal sum of the length of its edges.

There are several simple algorithms for designing a minimal spanning tree for a graph $G = \langle V, E\rangle$. Perhaps the best known are Prim's algorithm and Kruskal's algorithm. Both start with the empty set, say T, of edges, and both keep adding edges to T. **Kruskal's algorithm** takes care that edges in T always form a forest, **Prim's algorithm** that they form a tree. In one step both of them remove the shortest edge from E. Kruskal's algorithm inserts this edge in T if, after insertion, T still forms a forest. Prim's algorithm inserts the selected edge in T if, after insertion, T still forms a tree. Since dictionary operations can be implemented in $\mathcal{O}(\lg|V|)$ time, both algorithms can be implemented easily in $\mathcal{O}(|E|\lg|E|) = \mathcal{O}(|E|\lg|V|)$ time (Prim's algorithm even in $\mathcal{O}(|E| + |V|\lg|V|)$ time, which is a better result).

Exercise 2.4.34 *Find all the distinct minimal spanning trees of the graph in Figure 2.26.*

Exercise 2.4.35 *Use Kruskal's and Prim's algorithms to design a minimal spanning tree of the graph in Figure 2.26.*

A closely related graph traversal problem for distance graphs is a modification of the Hamilton cycle problem called the **travelling salesman problem** – TSP for short.

Given a complete graph $G = \langle V, V\times V\rangle$, $V = \{c_1, \ldots, c_n\}$ and a distance $d(c_i, c_j)$ for each pair of vertices (usually called cities in this case) c_i and c_j, the goal is to find a Hamilton path in G with the minimal sum of distances of all nodes – in other words, to find a permutation π on $\{1,\ldots,n\}$ that minimizes the quantity

$$\sum_{i=1}^{n-1} d(c_{\pi(i)},c_{\pi(i+1)}) + d(c_{\pi(n)},c_{\pi(1)}).$$

No polynomial time algorithm is known for this problem, but also no proof that such an algorithm does not exist. A modification of TSP, given a graph G and an integer k, to decide whether G has a travelling salesman cycle with total length smaller than k, is an **NP**-complete problem. The travelling salesman problem is perhaps the most studied **NP**-complete optimization problem, because of its importance in many applications (see Section 5.8).

2.4.5 Trees

Simple bipartite graphs very often used in computing are **trees**. As already mentioned (Section 2.4.1), a tree is an undirected, connected, acyclic graph. A set of trees is called a **forest**. See Figure 2.27 for a tree and a forest. The following theorem summarizes some of the basic properties of trees.

Theorem 2.4.36 *The following conditions are equivalent for a graph* $G = \langle V,E\rangle$*:*

1. *G is a tree.*
2. *Any two vertices in G are connected by a unique simple path.*
3. *G is connected, and $|E| = |V| - 1$.*
4. *G is acyclic, but adding any edge to E results in a graph with a cycle.*

Exercise 2.4.37 *Prove as many equivalences in Theorem 2.4.36 as you can.*

Exercise 2.4.38* *Determine (a) the number of binary trees with n nodes; (b) the number of labelled trees with n nodes.*

Special terminology has been developed for trees in computing. By a tree is usually meant a **rooted tree** – a tree where a special node is depicted as a **root**. All nodes on a path from the root to a node u, different from u, are called **ancestors** of u. If v is an ancestor of u, then u is a **descendant** of v. By the **subtree rooted in a node** x we understand the subtree containing x and all its descendants.

If (y,x) is the last edge on a path from the root to a node x, then y is **the parent** of x, and x a **child** of y. Two nodes with the same parent are called **siblings**. A node that has no child is called a **leaf**. All other nodes are called **internal**.

The number of children of a node is its **degree**, and its distance from the root is its **depth**. The **degree of a tree** is the maximal degree of its nodes, and the **depth of a tree** is the maximal depth of its leaves. (Note that this meaning of degree is different from that of graphs in general.)

A tree is an **ordered tree** if to each node, except the root, a natural number is associated in such a way that siblings always have different numbers. The number associated with a node shows which child of its parent that node is. (Observe that a node can have only one, for example, only the fifth child.)

The term **binary tree** is used in two different ways: first, as a tree in which any node has at most two children; second, as an ordered tree in which any node has at most two children and to all nodes numbers 1 or 2 are associated. (In such a case we can talk about the first or the second child, or about

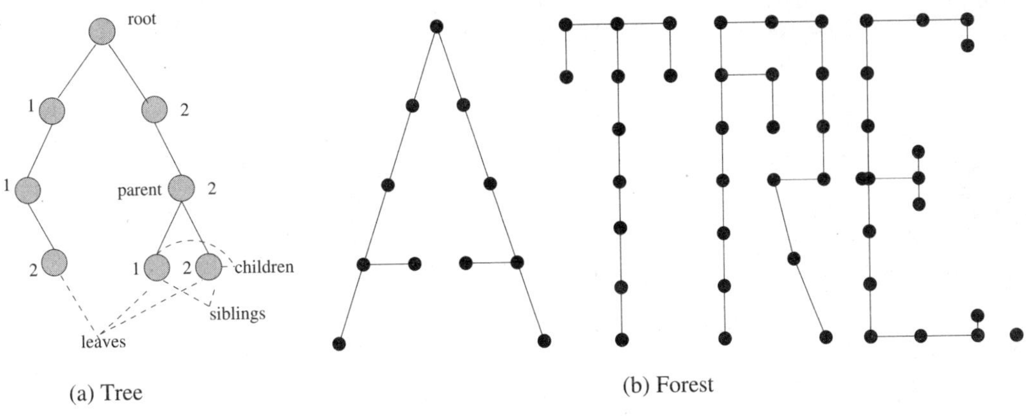

(a) Tree (b) Forest

Figure 2.27 A tree and a forest consisting of five trees

the left or the right child. Observe that in such a case a node can have only the left or only the right child.) A **complete (balanced) binary tree** is a tree or an ordered tree in which each node, except leaves, has two children. More generally, a k-nary balanced tree is a tree or an ordered tree all nodes of which, except leaves, have k children.

Basic **tree traversal algorithms** are described and illustrated in Figure 2.28 by the tree-labelling procedures, *pre-order* (Figure 2.28a), *post-order* (Figure 2.28b) and *in-order* (Figure 2.28c). All three procedures assume that there is a counter available that is initiated to 1 before the procedures are applied to the root, and that each time the procedure $Mark(u)$ is used, the current number of the counter is assigned to the node u, and the content of the counter is increased by 1. All three procedures can be seen also as providing a labelling of tree nodes.

Representation of binary trees. A binary tree with n nodes labelled by integers from 1 to n can be represented by three arrays, say $P[1:n], L[1:n], R[1:n]$. For each node i, the entry $P[i]$ contains the number of the parent of the node i, and entries $L[i]$ and $R[i]$ contain numbers of the left and the right child. With this tree representation any of the tree operations (a) go to the father; (b) go to the left son; (c) go to the right son, can be implemented in $\mathcal{O}(1)$ time. (Other, more economical, representations are possible if not all three tree operations are used.)

2.5 Languages

The concept of a (formal) language is one that is key to computing, and also one of the fundamental concepts of mathematics.

Formalization, as one of the essential tools of science, leads to representation of complex objects by words and languages. Modern information-processing and communication tools are also based on it. The understanding that complex objects, events and processes can be expressed by words and languages developed some time ago. Newer is the discovery that even simple languages can represent complex objects, if properly visualized.

2.5.1 Basic Concepts

An **alphabet** is an arbitrary (mostly finite) set of elements that is considered, in the given context, as having no internal structure.

pre-order(u)

begin
Mark(u);
pre-order(left son(u));
pre-order(right son(u));
end

post-order(u)

begin
post-order(left son(u));
post-order(right son(u));
Mark(u);
end

in-order(u)

begin
in-order(left son(u);
Mark(u);
in-order(right son(u);
end

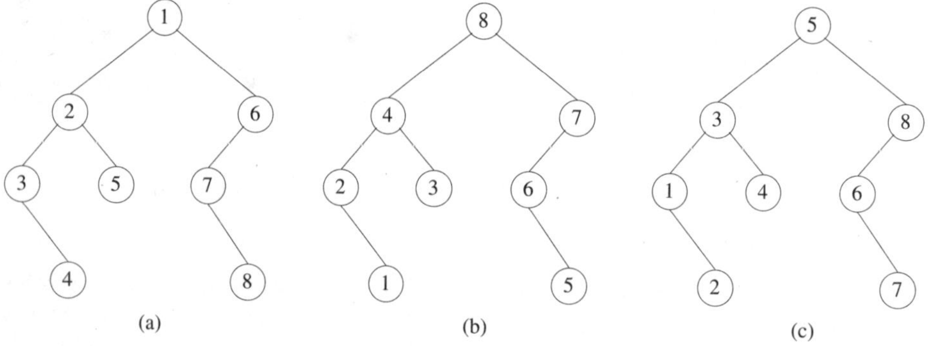

Figure 2.28 Tree traversal algorithms

Words. A **finite word (string)** w over an alphabet Σ is a finite sequence of elements from Σ, with $|w|$ denoting its length. ε is the empty word of length 0.

A finite word w over Σ of length n can also be viewed as a mapping $w : \{1, \ldots, n\} \rightarrow \Sigma$, with $w(i)$ as its ith symbol. In a similar way, an **infinite word** w over Σ (or an ω-word (ω-string)) can be seen as a mapping $w : \mathbf{N} \rightarrow \Sigma$, and a bi-infinite word w as a mapping $\mathbf{Z} \rightarrow \Sigma$. Analogically, one can also consider two-dimensional rectangular words. For example, $w : \{1, \ldots, n\} \times \{1, \ldots, m\} \rightarrow \Sigma$. Two-dimensional infinite words can be defined as mappings $w : \mathbf{N} \times \mathbf{N} \rightarrow \Sigma$ or $w : \mathbf{Z} \times \mathbf{Z} \rightarrow \Sigma$.

Σ^* denotes the set of all finite words over Σ, and Σ^+ the set of nonempty finite words over Σ. Σ^ω and $\Sigma^{\omega\omega}$ denote the sets of all infinite and doubly infinite words over Σ, respectively. $\Sigma^n (\Sigma^{\leq n})$ denotes the set of all strings over Σ of length n ($\leq n$).

Concatenation of a word u, of length n_1, and a word v, of length n_2, denoted by $u \cdot v$, or simply uv, is the word of length $n_1 + n_2$ such that $w(i) = u(i)$, for $1 \leq i \leq n_1$, and $w(i) = v(i - n_1)$, otherwise. Analogically, we define a concatenation of a word u from Σ^* and v from Σ^ω. **Powers** u^i for $u \in \Sigma^*$ and $i \in \mathbf{N}$ are defined by $u^0 = \varepsilon, u^{i+1} = uu^i$, for $i \geq 0$.

Subwords. If $w = xyz$ for some finite words x and y and a finite or ω-word z, then x is a **prefix** of w, y is a **subword** of w, and z is a **suffix** of w. If x is a prefix of w, we write $x \preceq w$, and if x is a **proper prefix** of w, that is, $x \neq w$ and $x \preceq w$, we write $x \prec w$. For a word w let $\mathit{Prefix}(w) = \{x \mid x \preceq w\}$.

The **reversal** of a word $w = a_1 \ldots a_n$, $a_i \in \Sigma$ is the word $w^R = a_n \ldots a_1$. A finite word w is a **palindrome** if $w = w^R$.[11]

Projections. For a word $w \in \Sigma^*$ and $S \subseteq \Sigma$, w_S is the word obtained from w by deleting all symbols

[11] Examples of palindromes in various languages (ignore spaces): RADAR, ABLE WAS I ERE I SAW ELBA, RELIEFPFEILER, SOCORRAM ME SUBI NO ONIBUS EM MARROCOS, SAIPPUAKAUPPIAS, ANANAS OLI ILO SANANA, REVOLTING IS ERROR RESIGN IT LOVER, ESOPE RESTE ICI ET SE REPOSE, EIN LEDER GURT TRUG REDEL NIE, SATOR AREPO TENET OPERA ROTAS, NI TALAR BRA LATIN, ARARA, KOBYLA MA MALY BOK, JELENOVI PIVO NELEJ .

not in S. $\#_S w$ denotes the number of occurrences of symbols from S in w. For example, for $w = a^3b^3c^3$, $w_{\{a,c\}} = a^3c^3$ and $\#_a w = 3$.

A **morphism** ϕ from an alphabet Σ_1 to an alphabet Σ_2 is a mapping $\phi : \Sigma_1 \rightarrow \Sigma_2^*$. ϕ is often considered as being extended to map Σ_1^* into Σ_2^* as follows: for a $w = a_1 \ldots a_n$, $a_i \in \Sigma_1, \phi(w) = \phi(a_1) \ldots \phi(a_n)$. ϕ can also be naturally extended to map two-dimensional words, ω-words and $\omega\omega$-words.

Infinite words can be defined, for example, through morphisms and recurrences. Some of them have been so intensively investigated that they have special names.

Example 2.5.1 (Thue ω-word)

$$THUE = abbabaabbaababbabaababbaabbabaab\ldots$$

is defined as $\lim_{i\to\infty} x_i$, *where*

$$x_0 = a, \qquad x_i = \phi(x_{i-1}), \textit{ for } i \geq 1,$$

and $\phi : \{a,b\} \rightarrow \{a,b\}^*$ *a morphism with*

$$\phi(a) = ab \quad \phi(b) = ba.$$

(Since $x_i \prec x_{i+1}$, *for all* $i \geq 0$, *we can define* $\lim_{i\to\infty} x_i$ *as the only* ω*-word such that all* x_i *are its prefixes.)*

Example 2.5.2 (Fibonacci ω-word)[12]

$$FIB = abaababaabaababaababa\ldots$$

is defined by the recurrence $y_0 = a, y_i = \rho(y_{i-1})$, *for* $i \geq 1$, *and the morphism* $\rho(a) = ab$, $\rho(b) = a$.

Languages. If Σ is an alphabet, then any subset $L \subseteq \Sigma^*$ is called a **language** over Σ. Any subset of Σ^ω is called an ω-language. Similarly, we define $\omega\omega$-languages.

Complement of a language L, notation L^c, is defined by $\Sigma^* - L$, where Σ is the smallest alphabet such that $L \subseteq \Sigma^*$.

Concatenation L_1L_2 of a language L_1 and a language or ω-language L_2 is defined by

$$L_1L_2 = \{uv \,|\, u \in L_1, v \in L_2\}.$$

If L is a language, then its **powers** $L^i, i \geq 0$, are defined by $L^0 = \{\varepsilon\}$, $L^{i+1} = LL^i$, for $i \geq 0$, and its iterations L^+, L^* and L^ω are defined by

$$L^+ = \bigcup_{i=1}^{\infty} L^i; \; L^* = \bigcup_{i=0}^{\infty} L^i,$$

and

$$L^\omega = \{u = u_1u_2u_3\ldots \,|\, u \text{ is an } \omega\text{-word and all } u_i \in L\}.$$

Shuffle operation on languages L_1 and L_2, notation shuffle (L_1, L_2), or $L_1 \diamond L_2$, is defined by $L_1 \diamond L_2 = \{x_1y_1x_2y_2\ldots x_ny_n \,|\, x_1\ldots x_n \in L_1, y_1\ldots y_n \in L_2\}$.

[12]The Fibonacci word has been intensively investigated, and has a variety of interesting properties; see Berstel (1985). For example, it has $n+1$ different subwords of length n for any integer n; if x is its subword, then so is x^R; there is an $x \neq \varepsilon$ such that x^3 is its subword, but there is no $x \neq \varepsilon$ such that x^4 is a subword of FIB.

Morphism and inverse morphism of languages. If $L \subseteq \Sigma^*$, $L_1 \subseteq \{\Sigma_1\}^*$ and $\phi : \Sigma \to \Sigma_1^*$ is a morphism, then $\phi(L) = \{\phi(w) \mid w \in L\}$ and $\phi^{-1}(L_1) = \{w \mid w \in \Sigma^*, \phi(w) \in L_1\}$.

Exercise 2.5.3 *Which of the following identities are valid for all languages L_1, L_2, L_3 and morphisms h: (a) $L_1(L_2 \cap L_3) = L_1L_2 \cap L_1L_3$; (b) $(L_1L_2)^*L_1 = L_1(L_2L_1)^*$; (c) $(L_1 \cup L_2)^* = L_2^*(L_1L_2^*)^*$; (d) $h(h(L_1)) = h(L_1)$; (e) $h(L_1L_2) = h(L_1)h(L_2)$; (f) $h(L_1^*) = h(L_1)^*$?*

A **substitution**, from an alphabet Σ to an alphabet Σ_1, is a mapping $\sigma : \Sigma \to 2^{\Sigma_1}$. It can be extended to map $\Sigma^* \to 2^{\Sigma_1^*}$ as follows.

$$\sigma(a_1 \ldots a_n) = \sigma(a_1) \ldots \sigma(a_n) \text{ if } a_1 \ldots a_n \in \Sigma^*, a_i \in \Sigma,$$

and for a language L

$$\sigma(L) = \bigcup_{w \in L} \sigma(w).$$

A **left quotient** of languages A, B is defined by

$$A^{-1}B = \{y \mid \exists x \in A, xy \in B\}.$$

For example, if $L = \{a^ib^i \mid i \geq 1\}$, then $\{a^2\}^{-1}L = \{a^ib^{i+2} \mid i \geq 0\}$.

Exercise 2.5.4 *Determine $A^{-1}B$ for the following pairs of languages: (a) $A = \{a^ib^i \mid i \geq 0\}$, $B = \{a^ib^j \mid j \geq i \geq 0\}$; (b) $A = \{ww \mid w \in \{0,1\}\}$, $B = \{ww^R \mid w \in \{0,1\}\}$.*

A **prefix closure** of a language L, $Prefix(L) = \{y \mid \exists z, yz \in L\} = \bigcup_{w \in L} Prefix(w)$. A language L is said to be a **prefix-closed language** if $Prefix(L) = L$. A language L is called **prefix-free** if $x \prec y$ for no two x, y in L; that is, no word in L is a proper prefix of another word in L.

Example 2.5.5 *If $L = \{a^ib^i \mid i \geq j \geq 0\}$, then $Prefix(L) = \{a^ib^j \mid i \geq j \geq 0\}$. The language L is prefix-free, and the language $Prefix(L)$ is prefix-closed.*

Exercise 2.5.6* *Let $L \subset \{0,1\}^*$ be a prefix-free language. Show that the following* **Kraft's inequality** *holds: $\sum_{w \in L} 2^{-|w|} \leq 1$.*

Families of languages. If $\mathcal{L}$ is a family of languages, then *co-*$\mathcal{L}$ is the family of languages whose complement belongs to $\mathcal{L}$; that is,

$$co\text{-}\mathcal{L} = \{L \mid L^c \in \mathcal{L}\} = \{L^c \mid L \in \mathcal{L}\}.$$

Example 2.5.7 *If $\mathcal{F}$ is the family of finite languages, then co-$\mathcal{F}$ is the family of 'co-finite languages' – that is, languages whose complements are finite.*

2.5.2 Languages, Decision Problems and Boolean Functions

As already discussed in Section 2.1, an intuitive concept of a computational problem can be formalized through a language decision problem, for an $L \subseteq \Sigma^*$, or a search problem, for an $R \subseteq \Sigma^* \times \Sigma^*$. Both can be further 'computerized': for languages and relations over the binary alphabet, through the concept of an infinite sequence of Boolean functions. For example, we can associate with a language $L \subseteq \{0,1\}^*$ the following sequence of Boolean functions $\{f_{L,i}\}_{i=1}^{\infty}$ defined by $f_{L,i}(x_1, \ldots, x_i) = 1$ if and only if $x_1 \ldots x_i \in L$, with each $f_{L,i}$ representing an instance of the given computational problem.

Example 2.5.8 *The graph isomorphism problem can be modelled by a language membership problem as follows. Let $L_{GI} \subseteq \{0,1\}^*$ be the set of all words w such that $w = xy$, where $x = w(G_1)$ and $y = w(G_2)$ for two isomorphic graphs. The problem of deciding whether two graphs G_1 and G_2 are isomorphic is then reduced to the problem of deciding whether $w(G_1)w(G_2) \in L_{GI}$.*

Example 2.5.9 *The Boolean matrix multiplication problem can be modelled by the language $L_{BMM} = \{w \mid w = w(M_1)w(M_2)w(M_3)$, where M_1, M_2, M_3 are Boolean matrices and $M_1 \cdot M_2 = M_3\}$. The problem of multiplying two Boolean matrices M_1 and M_2 of the same degree is then reduced to the problem of searching for a matrix M_3 such that $w(M_1)w(M_2)w(M_3) \in L_{BMM}$.*

Example 2.5.10 *The language $L = \{ww \mid w \in \{0,1\}^*\}$ is represented by the following family of Boolean functions $\mathcal{F} = \{f_L^n\}_{n=1}^{\infty}$, where*

$$f_L^n(x_1 \ldots x_n) = \begin{cases} \bigwedge_{i=1}^{n/2}(x_i \equiv x_{\frac{n}{2}+i}), & \text{if } n \text{ is even;} \\ 0, & \text{otherwise.} \end{cases}$$

In order to make the above idea really well defined, a fixed representation of objects of concern has first to be chosen, and also a fixed encoding of such a representation. Fortunately, as we shall see in Chapters 5 and 6, for investigation of such basic questions as 'which computations are (practically) feasible', most of the usual representations of objects we work with are 'equally good', and the same applies to encoding methods. For example, any of the following graph representations – lists, adjacency matrices, incidence matrices, and binary words – can easily, in low polynomial time, be converted into each other. Naturally, there are representations that are possible and sometimes even desirable which do not meet the condition of easy transferability to other usual representations. An important example of two 'exponentially' different representations is the case of integers. All representations in positional number systems can be considered as mutually transferable one to another. However, the representation of integers in the unary number system is essentially different because it is exponentially larger. As a result, as we shall see in Chapter 5, some algorithms that are exponential with respect to any positional representation of input integers become polynomial with respect to the size of unary representations of input integers.

Exercise 2.5.11 *Give a Boolean function representation for the following languages:*
(a) $L = \{www \mid w \in \{0,1\}^*\}$; (b) $L = \{w \mid w \in \{0,1\}^*, \#_1(w) = 3\}$;
(c) $L = \{w \mid w \in \{0,1\}^*, G(w)$ is a graph containing a triangle$\}$.

2.5.3 Interpretations of Words and Languages

Computational objects are not the only ones that have natural representations in terms of words and languages. There are also various general interpretations of words and languages that provide interesting objects.

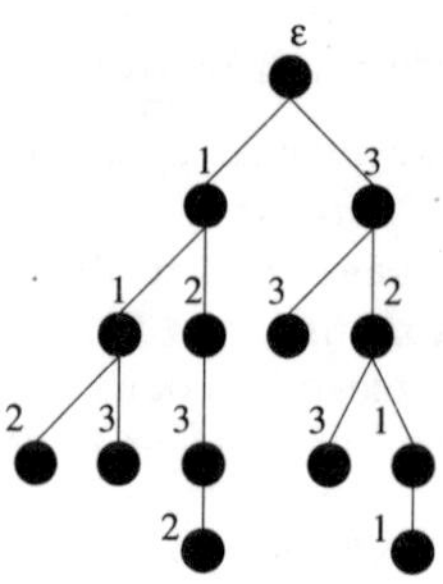

Figure 2.29 A tree representation of a language

Tree representations. Any rooted tree T, finite or infinite, of a finite degree, say k, can be represented by a language $L_T \subseteq \{1,\ldots,k\}^*$, using a node labelling, as follows (see Figure 2.29 for an illustration). The root is labelled ε, and the children of each node are labelled by distinct integers from the set $\{1,\ldots,k\}$. Let L_T be the set of words over the alphabet $\{1,\ldots,k\}$ that describe all possible paths in the tree T; for each path in the tree, starting in the root, the word consisting of labels of nodes on the path is taken into L_T. For example, for the tree in Figure 2.29 the language L_T contains the following words of length at most 2: $\varepsilon, 1, 3, 11, 12, 32, 33$.

Similarly, any language $L \subseteq \Sigma^*$ such that $Prefix(L) = L$ can be seen as a tree T_L. Each word of L is a node of T_L; ε is the root, and if $ua \in L, u \in L, a \in \Sigma$, then the vertex ua is a child of the vertex u. For example, the language $\{1,2,\ldots,k\}^*$ describes the infinite complete[13] k-nary tree.

The fact that prefix-closed languages represent ordered trees can be used to define various families of trees using language recurrences as shown below (see also Figure 2.30). Observe that in some cases we need to use the whole set of integers as the alphabet because there is no upper bound on the degree of trees in the family of trees that is being defined.

Balanced binary trees:	$BBT_0 = \{\varepsilon\}$, $BBT_i = \{\varepsilon\} \cup 0\,BBT_{i-1} \cup 1\,BBT_{i-1}, i \geq 1$;
Fibonacci trees:	$FT_0 = \{\varepsilon\}, FT_1 = \{\varepsilon\}$, $FT_i = \{\varepsilon\} \cup 0\,FT_{i-1} \cup 1\,FT_{i-2}, i > 1$;
Fibonacci heaps:	$FH_0 = \{\varepsilon\}, FH_1 = \{\varepsilon\} \cup \{0\}$, $FH_i = FH_{i-1} \cup (i-2)\,FH_{i-2}, i \geq 2$;
Binomial heaps:	$BH_0 = \{\varepsilon\}$, $BH_i = BH_{i-1} \cup (i-1)\,BH_{i-1}, i \geq 1$;
Doubly-logarithmic-depth trees:	$DLT_0 = \{\varepsilon, 0, 1\}$, $DLT_i = \{\varepsilon\} \cup 0\,DLT_{i-1} \cup \ldots \cup 2^{2^{i-1}-1}\,DLT_{i-1}$.

Similarly, any ω-language represents an infinite leafless tree.

Number representations. Any language $L \subseteq \{0,\ldots,k-1\}^*$ can be seen as representing a set of integers written in the k-nary positional system – the so-called radix notation. Similarly, any ω-language $L \subseteq \{0,\ldots,k-1\}^\omega$ can be interpreted as a set of reals in the interval $[0,1]$.

---

[13]The term 'balanced' is also used instead of 'complete'.

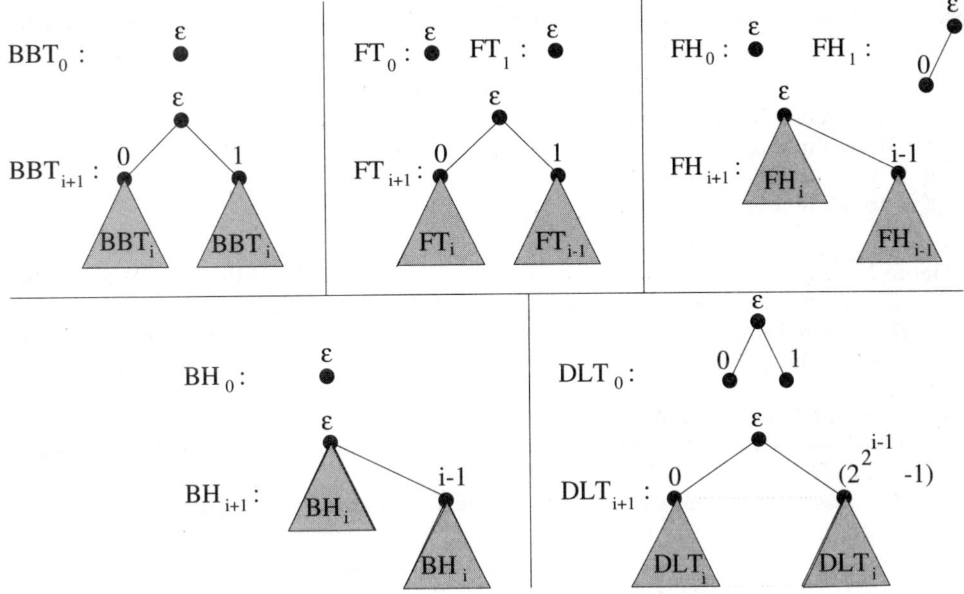

Figure 2.30 Recursively defined families of trees

Exercise 2.5.12* *Show that the language $\{0,2\}^\omega$ can be seen as representing the Cantor set defined in Example 2.1.2. (Since there is a trivial bijection between languages $\{0,1\}^\omega$ and $\{0,2\}^\omega$, and the first can be seen as representing all reals – in the binary system – in $[0,1)$, we get that the cardinality of the Cantor set is exactly $|\mathbf{R}|$.)*

Image representations. Surprisingly, simple words and languages can represent complex curves and images. This is again an example of how vizualisation brings a new dimension to investigations of formal objects. Basics of several such interpretations will now be discussed.

Chain code pictures. Any word over the alphabet $\{l,r,u,d\}$ can be seen as an algorithm for

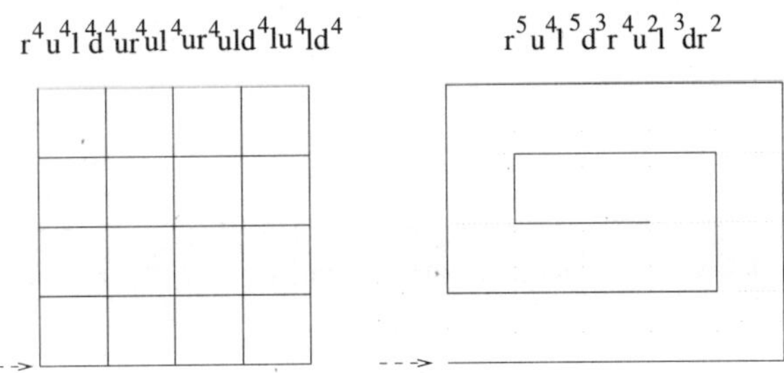

$r^4u^4l^4d^4ur^4ul^4ur^4uld^4lu^4ld^4$
$r^5u^4l^5d^3r^4u^2l^3dr^2$

Figure 2.31 Chain code pictures and their drawing algorithms

drawing a picture along the lines of the unit grid. A starting point in the grid is assumed, and symbols l, r, u, d are interpreted as follows:

l	draw a unit-line to the left,
r	draw a unit-line to the right,
u	draw a unit-line up,
d	draw a unit-line down.

Figure 2.31 shows two chain code pictures drawing algorithms (words) and the corresponding pictures (arrows point to the starting points). Naturally, each language $L \subseteq \{l,r,u,d\}^*$ represents a set of such pictures. For example, the language $\{r^n u^n l^n d^n \mid n \geq 1\}$ represents the infinite set of squares whose sides have integer lengths.

Turtle interpretation of words is a natural generalization of the idea of the chain code pictures. It is allowed to draw lines of various lengths, to turn through various angles, and to interrupt drawings. This is amplified by a special choice of sets of words which serve as drawing programs.

The basic idea of a turtle representation of words is the following. At the beginning of a drawing, and after each move, the 'turtle' is in a state (x, y, α), where (x, y) are coordinates of a point in the plane and α is an angle, called the **heading** – the direction the turtle is facing at that point. The picture that the turtle 'draws' is determined by the initial state (x_0, y_0, α_0) of the turtle, two parameters (d, the length, and δ, the angle), and by a **drawing algorithm** – a word over the alphabet $\{F, f, +, -\}$. Each symbol of such a word is taken as a statement with the following semantics:

F	draw a line of length d in the direction determined by the heading of the current state; that is, move from the current state (x, y, α) to the state $(x + d\cos\alpha, y + d\sin\alpha, \alpha)$, and draw a line between these two points;
f	make the same change of state as in the case of statement F, but draw no line – this allows one to interrupt a drawing;
+	turn left through the angle δ;
–	turn right through the angle δ.

Figure 2.32a shows a turtle interpretation of the string 'F-F-F-F' with $d = 1, \delta = 90$ and with the turtle initially facing up.

Interesting families of pictures can be obtained using turtle interpretations of strings obtained from some string w_0 by the iteration of a morphism ϕ using the scheme $w_i = \phi(w_{i-1}), i \geq 1$.

Example 2.5.13 *The interpretations of words w_1, w_2, w_3, for $w_0 = F - F - F - F$ and the morphism $\phi(F) = F - F + F + FF - F - F + F$, $\phi(-) = -$, and $\phi(+) = +$, are shown in Figure 2.32b, c, d. (The resulting curves are called Koch island figures.)*

Exercise 2.5.14 *Draw a turtle interpretation of w_2 for $w_0 = F + F + F + F$, $\phi(F) = F + f - FF + F + FF + Ff + FF - f + FF - F - FF - Ff - FFF$, $\phi(f) = ffffff$, $\phi(+) = +, \phi(-) = -$, and $d = 1$, $\delta = 90$.*

Turtle interpretations and various modifications of these interpretations will be discussed in more detail in Section 7.4.

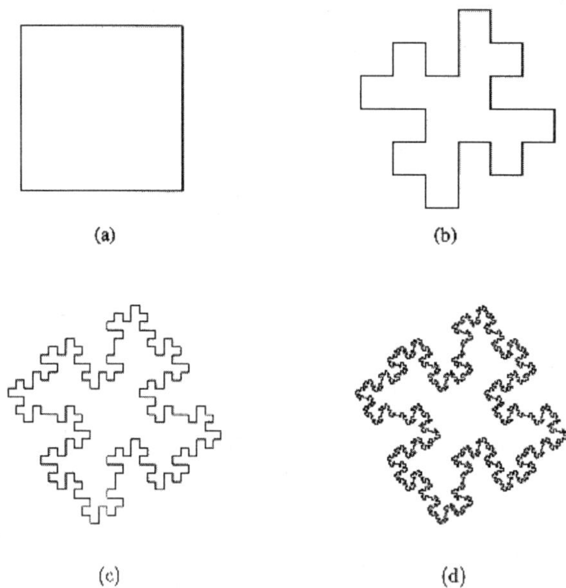

Figure 2.32 Koch island figures for n = 0, 1, 2, 3

Point representations. Let $A_k = \{(i,j) \mid 0 \leq i,j < k, i,j \in \mathbf{N}\}$ be an alphabet, where pairs (i,j) are taken as symbols. Any word

$$(x_1, y_1) \ldots (x_n, y_n)$$

over the alphabet A_k can be interpreted as the point of the square $[0,1) \times [0,1)$ with the coordinates

$$(0.x_1 \ldots x_n,\ 0.y_1 \ldots y_n),$$

where $0.x_1 \ldots x_n$ and $0.y_1 \ldots y_n$ are interpreted as fractions expressed in the k-nary positional system. Any language L over A_k represents, therefore, a set P_L of points in the square $[0,1) \times [0,1)$.

Example 2.5.15 *Points representation of languages* $\{(0,1),(1,0),(1,1)\}^*$ *and*

$$\{(0,0),(0,1),(0,2),(1,0),(1,1),(1,2),(2,0),(2,1),(2,2)\}^*,$$

with $k = 3$, *is shown in Figure 2.1. Figure 2.33a shows the image described by the language* $\{(0,1),(1,0)\}\{(0,0),(1,1)\}^2X^* \cup \{(0,0)(0,0),(1,1)(1,1)\}X^*$, *where* $X = \{(0,0),(0,1),(1,0),(1,1)\}$. *Figure 2.33b shows the image described by the language* $A^*(0,0)A^*(0,0)B^*$, *where* $A = \{(0,1),(1,0)\}$ *and* $B = A \cup \{(0,0),(1,1)\}$.

Let us now analyse the **image manipulation interpretations of basic language operations**. It is clear that union and intersection of languages yield union and intersection of images. More interesting are operations of concatenation, iteration and quotient.

Concatenation of two languages performs the **placement operation** on the corresponding images in the following sense. Let L_1, L_2 be languages over the alphabet A_k, for some k. Then the language

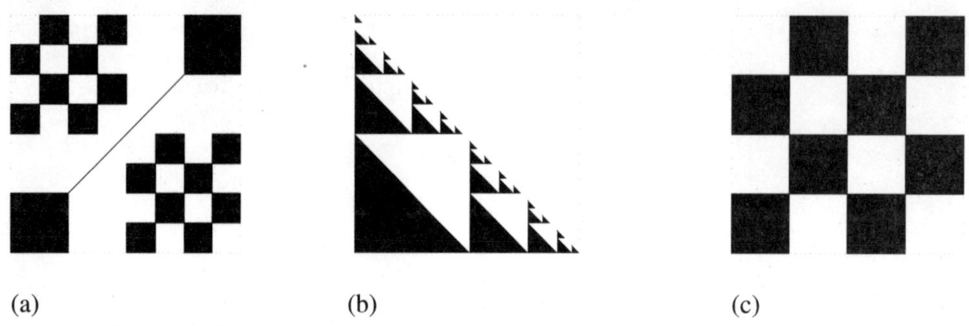

Figure 2.33 Fractal pictures

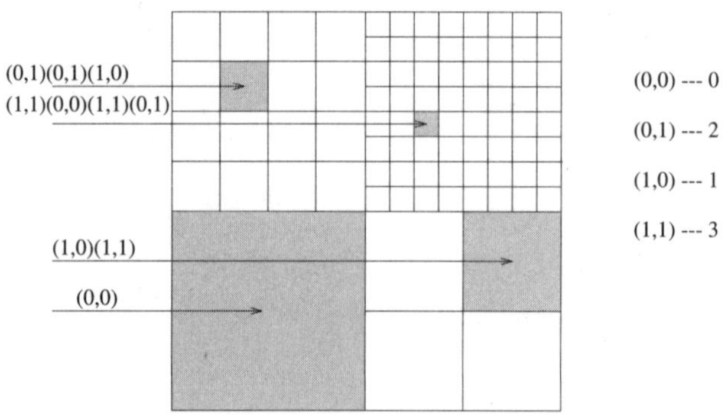

Figure 2.34 Pixel representation

$L = L_1L_2$ represents the image obtained by placing, appropriately scaled down (as described below), a copy of the image represented by the language L_2, at each point of the image represented by L_1. That is, if $(0.x_1 \ldots x_n, 0.y_1 \ldots y_n) \in P_{L_1}$, then a copy of P_{L_2}, scaled down by the factor $\frac{1}{k^n}$, is placed in the square of size $\frac{1}{k^n} \times \frac{1}{k^n}$ with its left-down corner located at the point $(0.x_1 \ldots x_n, 0.y_1 \ldots y_n)$.

For example, the language A_3^* represents the whole $[0,1) \times [0,1)$ square, and $\{(0,0),(0,2),(1,1),(2,0),(2,2)\}A_3^*$ represents the picture in Figure 2.33c.

The picture-manipulation meaning of the iteration is now clear. For example, the language $\{(0,0),(1,1)\}^*$ represents the diagonal of the unit square.

The left quotient operation represents **zooming** – an inverse of placement. The quotient $\{w\}^{-1}L$, where $w \in A_k^*, w = (x_1,y_1) \ldots (x_n,y_n)$ can be seen as picking up the subimage of P_L that is located in the square of size $\frac{1}{k^n} \times \frac{1}{k^n}$ with its left-down corner at the point $(0.x_1 \ldots x_n, 0.y_1 \ldots y_n)$, enlarging it k^n times and placing it in the quadrant $[0,1) \times [0,1)$. For example, $\{(0,1)\}^{-1}L$, for the language L representing the image in Figure 2.33a, describes the image shown in Figure 2.33c.

Exercise 2.5.16 *Draw the image obtained by the point representation of the expression* $(1,1)^*(0,0)I^*(1,0)T^*$, *where* $I = \{(0,0),(1,1)\}$ *and* $T = I \cup \{(0,1),(1,0)\}$.

Pixel representations. Words $w \in \{(0,0),(0,1),(1,0),(1,1)\}^*$ can also be seen as representing pixels of the unit square – subsquares of size $\frac{1}{2^{|w|}} \times \frac{1}{2^{|w|}}$ (see Figure 2.34). More exactly, a word $w = (a_1,b_1)\dots(a_n,b_n)$ represents a pixel of size $\frac{1}{2^n} \times \frac{1}{2^n}$ with the low left corner located at the point represented by w.

To simplify the notation, symbols 0,1,2,3 are often used in place of symbols (0,0), (1,0), (0,1), (1,1), respectively. For example, $\{00,03,10,13,20,23,30,33\}$ represents the image shown in Figure 2.33c.

Exercise 2.5.17 *Describe images having the following pixel representations: (a)* $\{0,1,2,3\}^*$*; (b)* $0\{0,1,2,3\}^*$*; (c)* $\{1,2\}^*0\{0,1,2,3\}^*$*; (d)* $0\{1,2\}^*0\{0,1,2,3\}^*$*; (e)* $\{1,2,3\}^*0\{1,2\}^*0\{0,1,2,3\}^*$.

2.5.4 Space of ω-languages*

ω-languages can be seen as formal counterparts of an intuitive concept of an (infinite) process. As such they play an important role in various areas of computing: for example, in the semantics of computational processes and in cellular automata.

The space of ω-languages is naturally more complex than that of languages. On the other hand, in order to deal with ω-languages, we can use powerful tools of mathematics. In this subsection we discuss the basic concepts of ω-languages from this point of view.

For any alphabet Σ with at least two symbols the set Σ^ω has the cardinality of the continuum, and it is a (compact) metric space with respect to the metric $d : \Sigma^\omega \times \Sigma^\omega \to \mathbf{R}$ defined, for $w_1, w_2 \in \Sigma^\omega$, by

$$d(w_1,w_2) = \begin{cases} 0, & \text{if } w_1 = w_2; \\ \frac{1}{2^i}, & \text{if } i \text{ is the smallest integer such that } w_1(i) \neq w_2(i). \end{cases}$$

With this metric at our disposal we can use methods and results of topology and functional analysis to deal with ω-languages. Surprisingly, the basic concepts of this approach can be expressed in terms of (ordinary) languages over Σ. To show this, we define for a language $L \subset \Sigma^*$

$$\overleftarrow{L} = L\Sigma^\omega; \tag{2.16}$$

$$\overrightarrow{L} = \{w \mid w \in \Sigma^\omega, \mathit{Prefix}(w) \cap L \text{ is infinite}\}; \tag{2.17}$$

$$\text{adherence}(L) = \overrightarrow{\mathit{Prefix}(L)}. \tag{2.18}$$

In the topology introduced by the metric d, a set S is open and closed simultaneously if and only if $S = \overleftarrow{L}$ for a finite language $L \subset \Sigma^*$; S is open if and only if $S = \overleftarrow{L}$ for a language $L \subset \Sigma^*$; and S is closed if and only if $S = \text{adherence}(L)$ for a language $L \subset \Sigma^\omega$. Finally, a set is a countable intersection of open sets if and only if $S = \overrightarrow{L}$ for a language $L \subset \Sigma^*$.

Example 2.5.18 *Let* $\Sigma = \{a,b\}$*. If* $L = \{a^ib^j \mid 0 \le i \le j\}$*, then* $\overleftarrow{L} = \{a,b\}^\omega$*,* $\overrightarrow{L} = a^*b^\omega$*, and adherence*$(L) = a^\omega \cup a^*b^\omega$.

Informally, $\overleftarrow{L}$ is the set of all ω-words having a prefix from L; $\overrightarrow{L}$ is the set of those ω-words that have infinitely many prefixes from L. Finally, *adherence*(L) is the set of those ω-words that have infinitely many prefixes that are prefixes of some words from L.

2.6 Algebras

An algebra $\mathcal{A} = \langle \Sigma, o_1, \ldots, o_n \rangle$ is a set Σ (the carrier of $\mathcal{A}$) and operations $o_1, \ldots, o_n$ defined on Σ and satisfying some axioms. Elements of the carrier are also considered as 0-ary operations. From a variety of important algebras, of special interest to us are monoids, groups, Boolean algebra and Kleene algebra.

2.6.1 Closures

Set extensions and closures. If $\circ$ is a binary operation and $\odot$ a unary operation on a set S, then we may **extend** these operations to apply to subsets of S in the following way:

$$\begin{aligned} A \circ B &= \{a \circ b \,|\, a \in A, b \in B\}, \\ \odot A &= \{\odot a \mid a \in A\}. \end{aligned}$$

A set $A \subseteq S$ is closed under the binary operation $\circ$ (the unary operation $\odot$) if $x, y \in A \Rightarrow x \circ y \in A$ $(x \in A \Rightarrow \odot a \in A)$.

Example 2.6.1 *For the operation + of addition and the operation $\surd$ of square root, on positive reals, we have, for the sets $A = \{x \,|\, 4 \leq x \leq 36\}$ and $B = \{x \,|\, 10 \leq x \leq 40\}$, $A + B = \{x \,|\, 14 \leq x \leq 76\}$, $\sqrt{A} = \{x \,|\, 2 \leq x \leq 6\}$.*

The **closure** of a set A under an operation is the least set that contains A, and it is closed under that operation.

2.6.2 Semigroups and Monoids

A **semigroup** $\mathcal{S} = \langle S, \cdot \rangle$ is a set S (a carrier of $\mathcal{S}$), with an associative operation '$\cdot$' (a semigroup multiplication). A **monoid** $\mathcal{M} = \langle S, \cdot, 1 \rangle$ is a semigroup $\langle S, \cdot \rangle$, with a **unit element** 1 such that $a \cdot 1 = 1 \cdot a = a$, for each $a \in S$. A semigroup (monoid) is called Abelian, or commutative, if its multiplication is such.

Example 2.6.2 *(1) $\langle \mathbf{N}, +, 0 \rangle, \langle \mathbf{Q}, +, 0 \rangle, \langle \mathbf{R}, +, 0 \rangle, \langle \mathbf{C}, +, 0 \rangle, \langle \mathbf{N}, \times, 1 \rangle, \langle \mathbf{Q}, \times, 1 \rangle, \langle \mathbf{R}, \times, 1 \rangle$ are commutative monoids.*

(2) If Σ is an alphabet, then $\langle \Sigma^*, \cdot, \varepsilon \rangle$ with '$\cdot$' as the concatenation, is a noncommutative monoid, also called a **free monoid**.

(3) For any fixed integer n, the set of all matrices of degree n, with elements from **Z**, *is a commutative monoid with respect to matrix addition and the null matrix and a noncommutative monoid with respect to matrix multiplication and the unit matrix.*

(4) $\langle \mathbf{N}^+, + \rangle$ is an example of a semigroup that is not a monoid.

If $\mathcal{M} = \langle S, \cdot, 1 \rangle$ is a monoid, then for any $A, B \subseteq S$ we define (multiplication) $A.B = \{a.b \,|\, a \in A, b \in B\}$. Similarly, we define $A^0, A^i, i \geq 1$, and A^*, A^+.

A **morphism** from a monoid $\mathcal{M}_1 = \langle S_1, \cdot_1, 1_1 \rangle$ to a monoid $\mathcal{M}_2 = \langle S_2, \cdot_2, 1_2 \rangle$ is a mapping $\mu : S_1 \rightarrow S_2$ such that $\mu(1_1) = 1_2$ and $\mu(u \cdot_1 v) = \mu(u) \cdot_2 \mu(v)$ for any $u, v \in S_1$.

A **congruence** over a monoid $\mathcal{M} = \langle S, \cdot, 1 \rangle$ is an equivalence relation, $\equiv$, on S which is compatible with the monoid operation, that is which satisfies the implication

$$u_1 \equiv v_1, u_2 \equiv v_2 \Rightarrow u_1 \cdot u_2 \equiv v_1 \cdot v_2.$$

Exercise 2.6.3 *Show that if* $\equiv$ *is a congruence over a monoid* $\mathcal{M} = \langle S, \cdot, 1\rangle$ *and for* $a \in S$ *we let* $[a]_\equiv$ *denote the equivalence class in which a is, then the set of all such equivalence classes forms a monoid, the so-called* **quotient monoid** $\mathcal{M}_\equiv$, *with the multiplication defined by* $[a]_\equiv \cdot [b]_\equiv = [a \cdot b]_\equiv$ *and the unit* $[1]_\equiv$.

Exercise 2.6.4 *Let* $L \subseteq \Sigma^*$ *be a language. Show that the relation* $\equiv_L$ *on* Σ^* *is defined by* $u \equiv_L v$ *if and only if* $\forall x, y \in \Sigma^*, xuy \in L \Leftrightarrow xvy \in L$ *is a congruence. (The corresponding quotient monoid is called the* **syntactical monoid** *of L.)*

Exercise 2.6.5 *Describe the syntactical monoids for the following languages L over the alphabet* $\{0,1\}$*: (a) the set of all words with no more than three consecutive 0's; (b)* $L = \{0^i 1^i \mid i \geq 0\}$.

2.6.3 Groups

A **group** $\mathcal{G} = \langle C, \cdot, ^{-1}, 1\rangle$ is a set C (the **carrier** of $\mathcal{G}$), with a binary operation '$\cdot$' (**multiplication**), a unary operation $^{-1}$ (**inverse**) and a **unit** $1 \in C$ such that $\langle C, \cdot, 1\rangle$ is a monoid, and for any $a \in C$

$$a \cdot a^{-1} = a^{-1} \cdot a = 1.$$

$\mathcal{G}$ is called **commutative**, or **Abelian**, if '$\cdot$' is such. Let $|\mathcal{G}|$ denote the cardinality of the carrier of $\mathcal{G}$.

Two elementary properties of groups are summarized in the following theorem.

Theorem 2.6.6 *If* $\mathcal{G} = \langle C, \cdot, ^{-1}, 1\rangle$ *is a group, then*

1. *For any* $a, b \in C$ *there is a unique x such that* $a \cdot x = b$*: namely,* $x = a^{-1} \cdot b$.
2. *For any* $a, b, c \in C$, $a \cdot c = b \cdot c \Rightarrow a = b$.

Example 2.6.7 *(1)* $\langle \mathbf{Z}, +, -, 0\rangle$ *and* $\langle \mathbf{Q} - \{0\}, \times, ^{-1}, 1\rangle$ *are commutative groups; '−' is here the unary operation of negation.*

(2) The set of all permutations of n elements is a group, for any integer n, with respect to the composition of permutations, inversion of permutations and the identical permutation.

Exercise 2.6.8 *Show that, for any integer n, the set* $\mathbf{Z}_n$ *of the residual classes with addition and negation (both modulo n) and with 0 is a commutative group. Similarly,* $\mathbf{Z}_n^*$ *is a commutative group with respect to multiplication and inversion (both modulo n) and with 1 as the unit.*

To the most basic concepts concerning groups belong those of subgroups, quotient groups and the isomorphism of groups.

Let $\mathcal{G} = \langle C, \cdot, ^{-1}, 1\rangle$ be a group. If C_1 is a subset of C that contains 1 and is closed under multiplication and inverse, then $\langle C_1, \cdot, ^{-1}, 1\rangle$ is called a **subgroup** of $\mathcal{G}$.

Two groups $\mathcal{G}_1 = \langle C_1, \cdot_1, ^{-1_1}, 1_1\rangle$ and $\mathcal{G}_2 = \langle C_2, \cdot_2, ^{-1_2}, 1_2\rangle$ are called **isomorphic** if there is a bijection $i : C_1 \rightarrow C_2$ such that $i(1_1) = 1_2, i(a^{-1_1}) = i(a)^{-1_2}, i(a \cdot_1 b) = i(a) \cdot_2 i(b)$ for any $a, b \in C$. An isomorphism of a group $\mathcal{G}$ with itself is called an **automorphism**.

Exercise 2.6.9* *If $\mathcal{H} = \langle S_1, \cdot, ^{-1}, 1\rangle$ is a subgroup of a group $\mathcal{G} = \langle S, \cdot, ^{-1}, 1\rangle$, then the sets aS_1, $a \in S$, are called* **cosets**. *Show that the family of cosets, together with the operation of multiplication, $(aS_1)\cdot(bS_1) = (ab)S_1$, inversion $(aS_1)^{-1} = a^{-1}S_1$, and the unit element S_1 is a group (the* **quotient group** *of $\mathcal{G}$ modulo $\mathcal{H}$, denoted $\mathcal{G}/\mathcal{H}$).*

Two basic results concerning the relations between the size of a group and its subgroups are summarized in the following theorem.

Theorem 2.6.10 *(1)(***Lagrange's**[14] **theorem***) If $\mathcal{H}$ is a subgroup of a group $\mathcal{G}$, then $|\mathcal{H}|$ is a divisor of $|\mathcal{G}|$.*

*(2) (***Cauchy's**[15] **theorem***) If a prime p is a divisor of $|\mathcal{G}|$ for a group $\mathcal{G}$, then $\mathcal{G}$ has a subgroup $\mathcal{H}$ with $|\mathcal{H}| = p$.*

Exercise 2.6.11 *Find all subgroups of the group of all permutations of (a) four elements; (b) five elements.*

Exercise 2.6.12* *Prove Lagrange's theorem.*

Exercise 2.6.13** *Let $\mathcal{G}$ be a finite Abelian group. (a) Show that all equations $x^2 = a$ have the same number of solutions in $\mathcal{G}$; (b) extend the previous result to equations of the form $x^n = a$.*

Example 2.6.14 (Randomized prime recognition) *It follows easily from Lagrange's theorem that if the following fast Monte Carlo algorithm, due to Solovay and Strassen (1977) and based on the fact that computation of Legendre-Jacobi symbols can be done fast, reports that a given number n is composite, then this is 100% true and if it reports that it is a prime then error is at most $\frac{1}{2}$.*

```
begin choose randomly an integer a ∈ {1, . . . , n};
      if gcd(a,n) ≠ 1 then return 'composite'
                       else if (a | n) ≢ a^((n-1)/2) (mod n)
                              then return 'composite';
return 'prime'
end
```

Indeed, if n is composite, then it is easy to see that all integers $a \in \mathbf{Z}_n^*$ such that $(a\,|\,n) \equiv a^{\frac{n-1}{2}} \pmod n$ form a proper subgroup of the group $\mathbf{Z}_n^*$. Most of the elements $a \in \mathbf{Z}_n^*$ are therefore such that $(a\,|\,n) \not\equiv a^{\frac{n-1}{2}} \pmod n$ and can 'witness' compositeness of N if n is composite.

Group theory is one of the richest mathematical theories. Proofs concerning a complete characterization of finite groups alone are estimated to cover about 15,000 pages. A variety of groups with very different carriers is important. However, occupying a special position are groups of permutations, so-called permutation groups.

[14]Joseph de Lagrange, a French mathematician (1736–1813).

[15]Augustin Cauchy (1789–1857), a French mathematician and one of the developers of calculus, who wrote more than 800 papers.

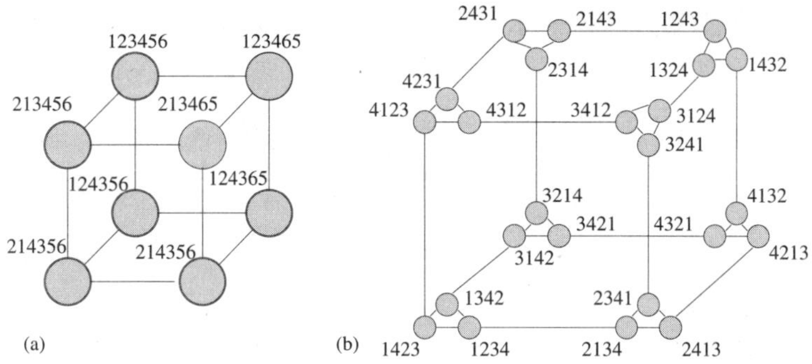

Figure 2.35 Cayley graphs

Theorem 2.6.15 (Cayley (1878)) *Any group is isomorphic with a permutation group.*

Proof: Let $\mathcal{G} = \langle C, \cdot, ^{-1}, 1\rangle$ be a group. The mapping $\mu : C \rightarrow C^C$, with $\mu(g) = \pi_g$, as the mapping defined by $\pi_g(x) = g \cdot x$, is such an isomorphism. This is easy to show. First, the mapping π_g is a permutation. Indeed, $\pi_g(x) = \pi_g(y)$ implies first that $g \cdot x = g \cdot y$ and therefore, by (2) of Theorem 2, that $x = y$. Moreover, μ assigns to a product of elements the product of the corresponding permutations. Indeed, $\mu(g.h) = \pi_{gh} = \pi_h \circ \pi_g$, because $\pi_h \circ \pi_g(x) = \pi_g(\pi_h(x)) = g \cdot h \cdot x = \pi_{gh}(x)$. Similarly, one can show that μ maps the inverse of an element to the inverse of the permutation assigned to that element and the unit of $\mathcal{G}$ to the identity permutation. □

Carriers of groups can be very large. It is therefore often of importance if a group can be described by a small set of its **generators**.

If $\mathcal{G} = \langle C, \cdot, ^{-1}, 1\rangle$ is a group, then a set $T \subseteq C$ is said to be a set of **generators** of $\mathcal{G}$ if any element of C can be obtained as a product of finitely many elements of T. If $1 \notin T$ and $g \in T \Rightarrow g^{-1} \in T$, then the set T of generators is called **symmetric**.

Example 2.6.16 *For any permutation g, $T = \{g, g^{-1}\}$ is a symmetric set of generators of the group $\{g^i \mid i \geq 0\}$.*

It has been known since 1878 that to any symmetric set of generators of a permutation group we can associate a graph, the **Cayley graph**, that is regular and has interesting properties. It has only recently been realized, however, that graphs of some of the most important communication networks for parallel computing are either Cayley graphs or closely related to them.

Definition 2.6.17 *A* **Cayley graph** *$G(\mathcal{G}, T)$, for a group $\mathcal{G} = \langle C, \cdot, ^{-1}, 1\rangle$ and its symmetric set T of generators, is defined by $G(\mathcal{G}, T) = \langle C, E\rangle$, where $E = \{(u, v) \mid \exists g \in T, ug = v\}$.*

Example 2.6.18 *Two Cayley graphs are shown in Figure 2.35. The first, called the three-dimensional hypercube, has eight vertices and is associated with a permutation group of eight permutations of six elements and three transpositions $\{[1,2], [3,4], [5,6]\}$ as generators. The graph in Figure 2.35b, the so-called three-dimensional cube-connected cycles, has 24 nodes and is the Cayley graph associated with the set of generators $\{[1,2], \langle 2,3,4\rangle, \langle 2,4,3\rangle\}$. It can be shown that this is by no means accidental. Hypercubes and cube-connected cycles of any dimension (see Section 10.1) are Cayley graphs.*

An important advantage of Cayley graphs is that their graph-theoretical characterizations allow one to show their various properties using purely group-theoretical means. For example,

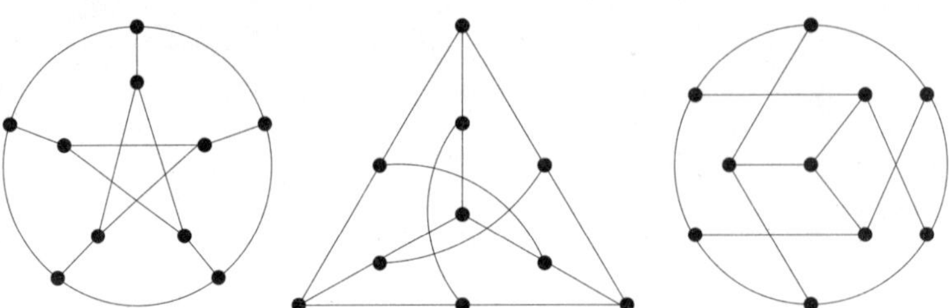

Figure 2.36 Petersen graph

Theorem 2.6.19 *Each Cayley graph is vertex-symmetric.*

Proof: Let $G = \langle V, E\rangle$ be a Cayley graph defined by a symmetric set T of generators. Let u, v be two distinct vertices of G: that is, two different elements of the group $\mathcal{G}(T)$ generated by T. The mapping $\phi(x) = vu^{-1}x$ clearly maps u into v, and, as is easy to verify, it is also an automorphism on $\mathcal{G}(T)$ such that $(u, v) \in E$ if and only if $(\phi(u), \phi(v)) \in E$. □

Exercise 2.6.20 *Show that all three graphs in Figure 2.36 are isomorphic.*

In a Cayley graph all vertices have the same degree, equal to the cardinality of the generator set. In the Petersen graph, shown in Figure 2.36, all vertices have the same degree. Yet, in spite of that, the Petersen graph is not a Cayley graph. This can be shown using Lagrange's and Cauchy's theorems.

Exercise 2.6.21* *A* **direct product of two graphs** $G_1 = \langle V_1, E_1\rangle$ *and* $G_2 = \langle V_2, E_2\rangle$ *is the graph* $G = \langle V_1 \times V_2, E\rangle$, *where* $((u_1, u_2), (v_1, v_2)) \in E$ *if and only if* $(u_1, v_1) \in E_1, (u_2, v_2) \in E_2$. *Show that the direct product of Cayley graphs is also a Cayley graph.*

2.6.4 Quasi-rings, Rings and Fields

In this section three algebras are introduced that are a natural generalization of those properties which basic number operations have. Their importance for computing lies in the fact that many algorithmic problems, originally stated for numbers, can naturally be generalized to be algorithmic problems on these more abstract algebras and then solved using a natural generalization of number algorithms.

Definition 2.6.22 *An algebra* $\mathcal{A} = \langle S, +, \cdot, 0, 1\rangle$ *is*

- **a quasi-ring** *if the following conditions are satisfied:*

  $\langle S, +, 0\rangle$ *is an Abelian monoid and* $\langle S, \cdot, 1\rangle$ *is a monoid;*

  $a \cdot 0 = 0 \cdot a = 0$, *for all* $a \in S$;

  the following distributive laws hold for all $a, b, c \in S$:

$$a \cdot (b + c) = (a \cdot b) + (a \cdot c) \quad \text{and} \quad (b + c) \cdot a = (b \cdot a) + (c \cdot a).$$

- **a ring** *if it is a quasi-ring and* $\langle S,+,0\rangle$ *is a group for a properly defined 'additive inverse'* $^{-1_a}$;
- **a field** *if it is a ring,* $\langle S,\cdot,1\rangle$ *is an Abelian monoid, and* $\langle S-\{0\},\cdot,1\rangle$ *is a group for a properly defined multiplicative inverse* $^{-1_m}$.

Example 2.6.23 $\langle\{0,1\},\vee,\wedge,0,1\rangle$ *is the* **Boolean quasi-ring**, *and* $\langle \mathbf{N},+,\cdot,0,1\rangle$ *with the integer operations of addition and multiplication is the* **integer quasi-ring**.

We can see rings as having defined an operation of subtraction (as an inverse of the operation $+$), and fields as having defined also an operation of division (as the inverse to the operation $\cdot$).

Example 2.6.24 $\langle \mathbf{Z},+,\cdot,0,1\rangle$ *is a ring and, in addition, for any integer n,* $\langle \mathbf{Z}_n,+_n,\cdot_n,0,1\rangle$ *is also a ring if* $+_n$ *and* $\cdot_n$ *are additions and multiplications modulo n. The set of all polynomials of one variable with real coefficients and the operations of addition and multiplication of polynomials also forms a ring.*

Exercise 2.6.25 *Show (a) that all matrices of a fixed degree over a quasi-ring also form a quasi-ring; (b) that all matrices of a fixed degree over a ring form a ring.*

Example 2.6.26 $\langle \mathbf{Q},+,\cdot,0,1\rangle$ *and* $\langle \mathbf{C},+,\cdot,0,1\rangle$ *are fields, and for any prime p,* $\langle \mathbf{Z}_p,+_p,\cdot_p,0,1\rangle$ *is a field – an example of a* **finite field**.

Exercise 2.6.27 *Show that if c is a rational number, then the set of all numbers of the form* $a+b\sqrt{c},\ a,b\in \mathbf{Q}$, *form a field (a* **quadratic field***) with respect to the operations of addition and multiplication of numbers.*

2.6.5 Boolean and Kleene Algebras

Two other algebras of importance for computing are Boolean algebras, due to G. Boole,[16] which have their origin in attempts to formalize the laws of thought (and have now found applications in computer circuits), and Kleene algebras, which are an abstraction from several algebras playing an important role in computing.

A **Boolean algebra** is any algebra of the form $\mathcal{B}=\langle S,+,\cdot,-,0,1\rangle$, where S is a set with two elements distinguished, 0 and 1, two binary operations, + (Boolean addition) and $\cdot$ (Boolean multiplication), and one unary operation $-$ (Boolean negation), satisfying the axioms listed in the first column of Table 2.1.

The set of all propositions with the two truth values **true** (1) and **false** (0), with disjunction (+), conjunction ($\cdot$) and negation (-), is the oldest example of a Boolean algebra. Set $\{0,1\}$ with Boolean addition, multiplication and negation is the smallest Boolean algebra. For any n the set of all Boolean functions with n variables forms a Boolean algebra with respect to Boolean addition, multiplication and negation of Boolean functions.

[16]George Boole (1815–64), an English mathematician and logician. His symbolic logic is central to the study of the foundations of mathematics and also of computing.

Boolean algebras	Axioms	Kleene algebras
$x+x=x$ $xx=x$	Idempotent laws	$x+x=x$
$x+0=x$ $x1=x$	Identity laws	$x+0=x$ $x1=x$
$x0=0$ $x+1=1$	Dominance laws	$x0=0$
$x+y=y+x$ $xy=yx$	Commutative laws	$x+y=y+x$ $xy=yx$
$x+(y+z)=(x+y)+z$ $x(yz)=(xy)z$	Associative laws	$x+(y+z)=(x+y)+z$ $x(yz)=(xy)z$
$x+yz=(x+y)(x+z)$ $x(y+z)=xy+xz$	Distributive laws	$(y+z)x=yx+zx$ $x(y+z)=xy+xz$
$\overline{(xy)}=\bar{x}+\bar{y}$ $\overline{(x+y)}=\bar{x}\bar{y}$	De Morgan's Laws	
$\bar{\bar{x}}=x$	Law of double negation	
	Iteration law	$ab^*c=\sup_{n\geq 0} ab^nc$

Table 2.1 Laws of Boolean and Kleene algebras

Exercise 2.6.28 *There are infinitely many Boolean algebras. Show, for example, that (a) $\langle 2^A, \cup, \cap, ^c, \emptyset, A\rangle$ is a Boolean algebra for any set A, where $C^c = A - C$ for any $C \subseteq A$ (this is the reason why set operations of union, intersection and negation are called Boolean operations); (b) the set $C = \{1,2,3,6\}$ with binary operations* gcd, lcm *and $x^{-1} = \frac{6}{x}$ is a Boolean algebra.*

A **Kleene algebra** is any algebra of the form $\mathcal{K} = \langle S, +, \cdot, ^*, 0, 1\rangle$, where S is a set containing two distinguished elements $0, 1$, two binary operation + (Kleene addition), $\cdot$ (Kleene multiplication), and one unary operation * (Kleene iteration) satisfying the axioms shown in the third column of Table 2.1.

The 'iteration law' axiom requires an explanation. In a Kleene algebra we can define that $a \leq b \Leftrightarrow a+b=b$. It then follows easily from the axioms that a relation such as $\leq$ is a partial order. For a set $A \subseteq S$ we define $\sup A$ to be an element y such that $x \leq y$ for all $x \in A$ (that is, y is an upper bound for A) and if $x \leq y'$ for all $x \in A$ and some y', then $y \leq y'$ (that is, y is the lowest upper bound). The iteration law axiom then says that $\sup\{ab^nc \mid n \geq 0\}$ exists and equals ab^*c.

Exercise 2.6.29 *Show that the set $\{0,1\}$ with Boolean operations + and . and with $a^* = 1$ for any $a \in \{0,1\}$ forms a Kleene algebra.*

Exercise 2.6.30* *Show that for any integer n the set of all Boolean matrices of degree n forms a Kleene algebra with respect to Boolean matrix addition, multiplication, iteration and the zero and unit matrices.*

Exercise 2.6.31** *Show that for any set S the family of all binary relations over S is a Kleene algebra with respect to addition, composition and iteration of relations, and with respect to the empty and identity relations.*

In all the previous examples it is in principle easy to verify that all axioms are satisfied. It is more difficult to show this for the Kleene algebra in the following example.

Example 2.6.32 *For any integer n and Kleene algebra $\mathcal{K}$, the set of all matrices of degree n with elements from the carrier of $\mathcal{K}$ forms a Kleene algebra with respect to the ordinary matrix addition and multiplication, with* 0 *as the zero matrix and* 1 *as the identity matrix and with the operation * defined recursively by the equation on page 96.*

Another example of a Kleene algebra, historically the first one and due to Kleene (1956), is introduced in the following chapter.

Moral: The foundations of any mature discipline of science are based on elementary but deep and useful ideas, concepts, models and results. A good rule of thumb for dealing with foundations in computing is therefore, as in life, to remember and behave according to the wisdom 'Wer das ABC recht kann, hat die schwerste Arbeit getan'.

2.7 Exercises

1. (a) Show that $|A \cup B \cup C| = |A| + |B| + |C| - |A \cap B| - |A \cap C| - |B \cap C| + |A \cap B \cap C|$;

   (b) generalize previous equality for the case of the union of n sets.

2. Let A, B be sets. Do the following implications hold: (a) $A \cap B = \emptyset \Rightarrow 2^A \cap 2^B = \emptyset$; (b) $2^A = 2^B \Rightarrow A = B$?

3. Form 2^A for the following sets: (a) $A = \{1\}$; (b) $A = \{1,2,3,4\}$; (c) $A = \{a,b,\{a,b\}\}$;

   (d) $A = \{\emptyset, a, b, \{a,b\}\}$.

4. Determine which of the following sets is the power set of a set: (a) $\emptyset$; (b) $\{\emptyset, \{a\}\}$; (c) $\{\emptyset, \{a\}, \{\emptyset, a\}\}$.

5. Show how you can simply describe the set of points of the **Menger sponge**. This is a subset of $\mathbf{R}^3$ constructed by the following infinite process. Begin with the unit cube of side 1. Divide it into 27 subcubes of identical size. Remove the middle one and also the middle one on each side – there remain 20 smaller cubes. Continue the process, and at each step do the same with all remaining subcubes.

6. A multiset with dictionary operations forms the data type called **bag**. How can one efficiently implement bags?

7. Let $R = \{(a,b) \mid a \text{ divides } b\}$ be the relation on the set of positive integers. Find $R^{-1}, \bar{R}$.

8. List 16 different relations on the set $\{0,1\}$, and determine which of them are (a) reflexive; (b) transitive; (c) symmetric; (d) antisymmetric.

9. How many relations on a set of n elements are (a) symmetric; (b) antisymmetric; (c) reflexive and symmetric?

10. Let R be a binary relation over some set A. Show that R is an equivalence if and only if the following conditions are satisfied: (i) $R = R^{-1}$; (ii) $RR \subseteq R$; (iii) $I_A \subseteq R$, where I_A is the identity relation on A.

11. Let $R = \{(1,3),(2,4),(3,1),(3,5),(5,1),\ (5,2),(5,4),(2,6),(5,6),(6,3),(6,1)\}$. Compute R^2, R^3, R^4, R^*.

12. Determine the transitive closure of the relations (a) $\{(1,2),(1,3),(1,4),(2,3),(2,4),\ (3,4)\}$; (b) $\{(a,b),(a,c),(a,e),\ (b,a),(b,c),(c,a),(d,c),(e,d)\}$; (c) $\{(1,5),(2,1),(3,4),\ (4,1),(5,2),(5,3)\}$.

13. Determine the transitive closure of the matrix

$$\begin{pmatrix} 0 & 1 & 0 & 0 \\ 0 & 0 & 1 & 0 \\ 0 & 0 & 0 & 1 \\ 0 & 0 & 1 & 0 \end{pmatrix}.$$

14. Which of the following relations on the set of all people or on the set of all functions from $\mathbf{Z}$ to $\mathbf{Z}$ are equivalences? (a) $\{(a,b) \mid a$ and b have common parents$\}$; (b) $\{(a,b) \mid a$ and b share common parents$\}$; (c) $\{(f,g) \mid f(0) = g(0)$ or $f(1) = g(1)\}$; (d) $\{(f,g) \mid f(0) = g(1)$ and $f(1) = g(0)\}$.

15. Modify Warshall's algorithm in such a way that it can be used to determine the shortest path between two nodes in edge-labelled graphs.

16. A total ordering $\leq$ is said to be compatible with the partial ordering R if $a \leq b$ whenever aRb. Construction of a total order compatible with a given partial order is called **topological sorting**. Design an algorithm to perform topological sorting.

17. Let $f(x) = ax + b$, $g(x) = cx + d$. Find conditions on a,b,c,d such that $f \circ g = g \circ f$.

18. Let a set A contain ten integers between 5 and 50. Show, for example using the pigeonhole principle, that there are two disjoint subsets B, C of A such that $\sum_{x\in A} x = \sum_{x\in B} x$.

19. Show that the mapping $f : \mathbf{N} \to \mathbf{N}^+ \times \mathbf{N}^+$ defined by $f(2^j(2k+1)) = (j,k)$ is a bijection.

20. Let $g_n : \mathbf{Z}_n^* \to \mathbf{Z}_n$ be the mapping defined by $g_n(i) = (i+1)^2 \bmod n$. Show that the mapping g_n is a bijection if and only if n is a prime.

21. Let the composition of two functions $f : A \to B$ and $g : B \to C$ be surjective. Does this mean that f is also surjective?

22. Let f_A be the characteristic function of the set A. Show that (a) $f_{A\cap B}(x) = f_A(x).f_B(x)$; (b) $f_{A\cup B}(x) = f_A(x) + f_B(x) - f_A(x)f_B(x)$; (c) $f_{\bar{A}}(x) = 1 - f_A(x)$.

23. Let B be an n-element multiset with k distinct elements $e_1, \ldots, e_k$, and let m_i denote the number of occurrences of the element e_i of B. Determine the number of distinct permutations of elements of B.

24. Show, using the truth table, the equivalence of the following Boolean formulas: (a) $p \vee (q \wedge r)$ and $(p \vee q) \wedge (p \vee r)$; (b) $(p \wedge g) \Rightarrow p$ and $p \Rightarrow (p \vee g)$.

25. Show the following implications using the truth table:

    (a) $[(p \Rightarrow q) \wedge (q \Rightarrow r)] \Rightarrow (p \Rightarrow r)$; (b) $[\bar{p} \wedge (p \vee q)] \Rightarrow q$.

26. Which of the following sets of Boolean functions forms a base: (a) $\{OR, NOR\}$; (b) $\{-, NOR\}$; (c) $\{AND, NOR\}$?

27. Use the NAND function to form the following functions: (a) NOT; (b) OR; (c) AND; (d) NOR.

28. Show the following properties of the operation NOR ($\oplus$): (a) $x \oplus y = x\bar{y} + \bar{x}y$; (b) $x \oplus x = 0, x \oplus 0 = x, x \oplus 1 = \bar{x}$; (c) $(x \oplus y) \oplus z = xz \oplus yz$; (d) $x + y = x \oplus y \oplus xy$.

29. Show that the Boolean functions NOR and AND do not form a base but that Boolean functions NOR, AND and 1 do form a base.

30. A Boolean function $f(x_1, \ldots, x_n)$ is said to depend essentially on an ith variable, x_i, if there are $a_1, \ldots, a_n \in \{0,1\}$ such that $f(a_1, \ldots, a_{i-1}, a_i, a_{i+1}, \ldots, a_n) \neq f(a_1, \ldots, a_{i-1}, \bar{a}_i, a_{i+1} \ldots a_n)$. For $1 \leq m \leq n$ determine the number of Boolean functions of n variables that depend essentially on at most m variables.

31. **(Post's theorem) Show that a set $\mathcal{B}$ of Boolean formulas forms a Boolean base if and only if the following conditions are satisfied: (1) $\exists f \in \mathcal{B} : f(0, \ldots, 0) = 1$; (2) $\exists f \in \mathcal{B} f(1, \ldots, 1) = 0$; (3) $\exists f \in \mathcal{B} : f$ is not monotone; (4) $\exists f \in \mathcal{B} : \exists x_1, \ldots, \exists x_n f(x_1, \ldots, x_n) \neq \bar{f}(\bar{x}_1, \ldots, \bar{x}_n)$; (5) $\exists f \in \mathcal{B} : f$ cannot be displayed as $x_{i_1} \oplus x_{i_2} \oplus \ldots x_{i_k} \oplus c$, where $c \in \{0,1\}$.

32. Given any family $\mathcal{H}$ of hash functions from A to B, where $|A| > |B|$, show that there exists $x, y \in A$ such that $|\{h \,|\, h(x) = h(y)\}| > \frac{|\mathcal{H}|}{|B|} - \frac{|\mathcal{H}|}{|A|}$.

33. For $a, b \in \mathbf{N}$, let $A = [a], B = [b]$ and $p \geq a$ be a prime. Let g map $\mathbf{Z}_p$ into B as closely as possible; that is, $|\{y \in \mathbf{Z}_p \,|\, g(y) = i\}| \leq \lceil \frac{p}{b} \rceil$ for all $i \in B$. Let $m, n \in \mathbf{Z}_p$, $m \neq 0$. We define $h_{m,n} : A \to \mathbf{Z}_p$ by $h_{m,n}(x) = (mx + n) \bmod p$. Show that the family $\mathcal{H} = \{f_{m,n} \,|\, m, n \in \mathbf{Z}_p, m \neq 0, f_{m,n}(x) = g(h_{m,n}(x))\}$ is universal.

34. Let $G = \langle V, E \rangle$ be a connected directed graph. For two vertices u, v define $u \equiv v$, if u and v lie in a simple cycle. Show that $\equiv$ is an equivalence relation on G. (The corresponding equivalence classes are called **biconnected components** of G.)

35. A complement of a graph $G = \langle V, E \rangle$ is the graph $\bar{G} = \langle V, V \times V - E \rangle$. Show that (a) if a graph G is self-complementary, that is, $G = \bar{G}$, then G has either $4m$ or $4m + 1$ vertices; (b) design all such graphs with at most eight vertices.

36. For a graph $G = \langle V, E \rangle$ and $S \subset V$ let G_{-S} be the graph obtained from G by removing the set S of vertices and edges incident with them. Show that G_{-S} has fewer connected components than $|S|$.

37. Determine which of the pairs of graphs shown in Figure 2.37 are isomorphic.

38. Show that if $v\text{-}conn(G) \geq 2$ for an undirected graph G, then any two vertices (or edges) of G lie in a common cycle.

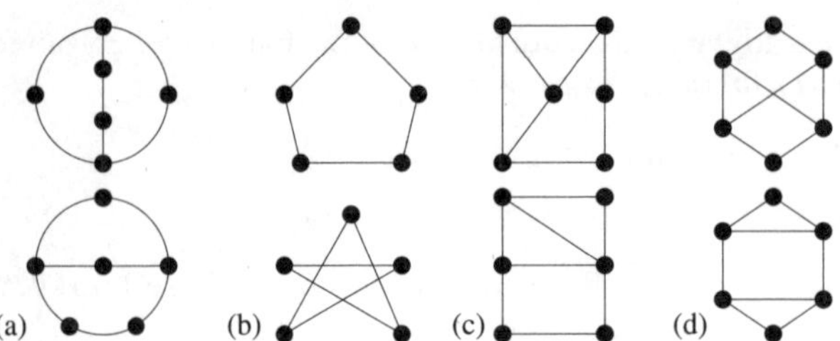

Figure 2.37 Isomorphism of graphs

39. Show that if a graph is not 2-vertex-connected, then it is not Hamiltonian.

40. Show that if a connected graph $G = \langle V, E \rangle$ has at least three vertices and each vertex has the degree at least $\frac{|V|}{2}$, then G is Hamiltonian.

41. The **closure** of a graph $G = \langle V, E \rangle$ is the graph obtained from G by recursively connecting pairs of nonadjacent vertices whose sum of degrees is at least $|V|$ until no such pair remains. (a) Show that the closure of each undirected graph is uniquely defined; (b) show that a graph is Hamiltonian if and only if its closure is Hamiltonian.

42. Knight's tour on an $n \times m$ chessboard is a sequence of legal moves by a knight starting at some square and visiting each square exactly once. Model the chessboard by a graph with one node per square of the board and with an edge between two nodes exactly when there is a legal move by a knight from one of the squares to another.

    (a) Show that a knight's tour exists if and only if there is a Hamilton path on the corresponding graph; (b) design the knight's tour for a 3×4 board.

43. If $G = \langle V, E \rangle$ is a planar graph, then each drawing of G such that no two edges intersect partitions the plane into a number of connected regions called **faces**; for example, the graph in Figure 2.19b partitions the plane into six regions. Show **Euler's formula**: If Φ is the number of faces of a planar graph $G = \langle V, E \rangle$, then $|V| - |E| + \Phi = 2$.

44.* Show that the Petersen graph, Figure 2.36, is not Hamiltonian.

45. Show that for each k there is a regular graph of degree k that has no perfect matching.

46. Show that it is impossible using 1×2 dominoes, to exactly cover an 8×8 square from which two opposite 1×1 corners have been removed.

47. For the following graph write down: (a) all depth-first traversals that start in the node h; (b) all breadth-first traversals that start in the node h.

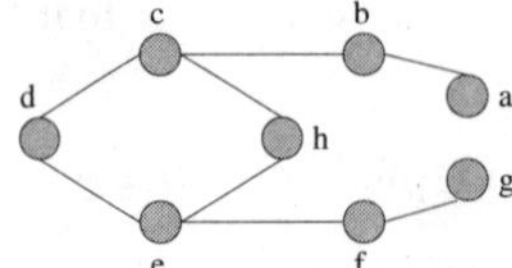

48. Design an algorithm to solve the following **personnel assignment problem**: n workers are available for n jobs, with each worker being qualified for one or more of the jobs. Can all these workers be assigned, one worker per job, to jobs for which they are qualified?

49. Show that the Petersen graph is 4-edge chromatic.

50. Let $G = \langle V, E\rangle$ be a graph. A subset $S \subseteq V$ is called an **independent set** of G if no two vertices of S are adjacent in G. An independent set is maximal if G has no independent set S' such that $|S| \leq |S'|$. A subset $S \subseteq V$ is called a **covering** of G if every edge of E is incident with at least one vertex of S. (a) Design a maximal independent set for the graphs in Figures 2.15b, c; 2.16a, b; 2.18b; (b) show that an $S \subseteq V$ is an independent set if and only if $V - S$ is a covering of G.

51. Show that the four-colour problem is equivalent to the problem of determining whether regions of each planar map can be coloured by four colours in such a way that no two neighbouring regions have the same colour.

52. Show that if u, v are words such that $uv = vu$, then there is a w such that $u = w^m$ and $v = w^n$ for some m, n.

53. Let Σ be an alphabet and $w \in \Sigma^*$. Show that $x = w^2$ is the unique solution of the equation $x^2 = wxw$.

54. Two words x and z in Σ^* are called **conjugates** if there exists $y \in \Sigma^*$ such that $xy = yz$. (a) Show that x and z are conjugates if and only if there exist $u, v \in \Sigma^*$ such that $x = uv$ and $z = vu$; (b) show that the conjugate relation is an equivalence on Σ^*; (c) show that if x is conjugate to y in Σ^*, then x is obtained from y by a circular permutation of symbols of y.

55. A word w is **primitive** if and only if it is not a nontrivial power of another word; that is, if $w = u^n$ implies $n = 1$. (a) Show that any word is a power of a unique primitive word; (b) show that if u and v are conjugate and u is primitive, then so is v; (c) show that if $uw = wv$ and $u \neq \varepsilon$, then there are unique primitive words u', v' and integers $p \geq 1, k \geq 0$ such that $u = (u'v')^p$, $v = (v'u')^p$, $w = (u'v')^k u'$.

56. Show the following language identities: (a) $(A \cup B)^* = A^*(BA^*)^*$; (b) $(A \cup B)^* = (A^*B)^*B^*$; (c) $(AB)^* = \{\varepsilon\} \cup A(BA)^*B$; (d) $A^* = (\{\varepsilon\} \cup A \cup A^2 \cup \ldots \cup A^{n-1})(A^n)^*$.

57. Let $\Sigma = \{0,1\}$ and $L = \Sigma^* - \Sigma^*\{00\}\Sigma^*$. Show that the language L satisfies the identities (a) $L = \{\varepsilon, 0\} \cup \{01, 1\}L$; (b) $L = \{\varepsilon, 0\} \cup L\{1, 10\}$; (c) $L = \bigcup_{k=0}^{\infty} L^k$.

58. Determine a language $L \subseteq \{a,b\}^*$ such that (a) $L = \{\varepsilon\} \cup \{ab\}L$; (b) $L = \{\varepsilon\} \cup L\{ab\}$.

59. Show that there is no language $L \subseteq \{0,1\}^*$ such that (a) $L \cup \{01\}L = \{\varepsilon\} \cup 0L$; (b) $L = \{\varepsilon\} \cup 0L \cup L1$.

60. Determine $L_1^{-1}L_2$ and $L_2^{-1}L_1$ if (a) $L_1 = \{a^ib^i \mid i \geq 0\}, L_2 = \{a^ib^j \mid 0 \leq i \leq j\}$; (b) $L_1 = \{ww \mid w \in \{0,1\}^*\}$, $L_2 = \{ww^R \mid w \in \{0,1\}^*\}$; (c) $L_1 = \{wcw \mid w \in \{0,1\}^*, c \notin \{0,1\}\}$, $L_2 = \{wcw^R \mid w \in \{0,1\}^*\}$.

61. Draw curves generated by the turtle interpretation of words w_0, w_1, w_2, w_3, where $w_0 = F - F - F - F$, $w_i = \phi(w_{i-1})$, $\phi(F) = F - F + F - F - F$, $\phi(-) = -$, $\phi(+) = +$, $d = 1$, $\alpha = 90$.

62. Determine $\overrightarrow{L}$, $\overleftarrow{L}$ and *adherence*(L) for the languages (a) $L = \{a^ib^j \mid j \geq i \geq 0\}$; (b) $L = \{ww \mid w \in \{0,1\}^*\}$; (c) $L = \{a^ib^j \mid i,j \geq 0\}$.

63. Show that (a) $shuffle(\{a\},\{b\}^*) = b^*ab^*$; (b) $shuffle(L_1,L_2 \cup L_3) = shuffle(L_1,L_2) \cup shuffle(L_1,L_3)$; (c) $shuffle(L_1,L_2) = shuffle(L_2,L_1)$.

64. Prove or disprove for any languages L, L_1 and L_2 and any homomorphism h that (a) $L \cdot shuffle(L_1,L_2) = shuffle(LL_1,L_2)$; (b) $h(shuffle(L_1,L_2)) = shuffle(h(L_1),h(L_2))$.

65. Solve the language equation $x = L_1 \cup L_2x$, where L_1, L_2 are languages and x is a language variable.

66. Determine the language L satisfying the identities (a) $L \cup abL = \{\varepsilon\} \cup aL$; (b) $L \cup baL = \{\varepsilon\} \cup aL \cup bL$.

67. For a language L let $L_n = \{x \mid x \in L, |x| = n\}$. The power series $g_L(z) = \sum_{n=0}^{\infty} |L_n| z^n$ is called the generating function of the language L. Show that $g(z) = \frac{12z}{1-2z^2}$ is the generating function for the language of palindromes over the two-letter alphabet.

68. Let $\mathcal{M} = \langle S, \cdot, 1 \rangle$ be a monoid, $A, B \subseteq S$. The **left quotient** of A and B, notation $A^{-1}B$, is defined by $A^{-1}B = \{c \mid c \in S, \exists a \in A, b \in B \text{ such that } c = a \cdot b\}$. Show that $(AB)^{-1}C = B^{-1}(A^{-1}C)$.

69. Let A be a finite set. Denote $Op_2(A)$ the set of all binary operations on A. For every $f, g \in Op_2(A)$, we define $h = f \circ g \Leftrightarrow (\forall x, y \in A)(h(x,y) = f(g(x,y), g(y,x)))$. Moreover, let $I_A(x,y) = x$. Show that $\langle Op_2(A), \circ, I_A \rangle$ is a monoid for any set A.

70. The **star graph** S_n on the set of all permutations of n elements is the Cayley graph with the set $\{[1,i] \mid 1 < i < n\}$ of transpositions as generators. Draw S_2, S_3, S_4, and determine the number of edges of S_n.

71. The **pancake graph** P_n on the set of all permutations of n elements is the Cayley graph with the set of generators $\{(i, i-1, \ldots, 1, i+1, \ldots, n) \mid 1 \leq i \leq n\}$. Draw P_2, P_3, P_4, and determine the number of edges of P_n.

72. A Cayley graph is called **strongly hierarchical** if it has a set of generators T such that for each ordering $g_1, \ldots, g_k$ of its generators and each $i > 1$ the generator g_i is not expressible using generators $g_1, \ldots, g_{i-1}$. Show that a strongly hierarchical Cayley graph is edge-symmetric.

73.* Show that the Petersen graph is not a Cayley graph.

74. Show that in a Boolean algebra $x = y$ if and only if $(x + \bar{y})(\bar{x} + y) = 1$.

75. Solve the following system of equations in a Boolean algebra: (a) $x + \bar{y} + x\bar{y} = x$, $xy = \bar{x} + y$; (b) $(x + \bar{y}) \cdot (\bar{x} + y) = x$; $x + y = x$.

QUESTIONS

1. What are the basic methods to specify sets, and what are the advantages of particular methods?

2. In which cases is $(2^A, \subsetneq)$ a totally ordered set?

3. Is the function $f(n) = \lfloor \lg n \rfloor$ one-way?

4. How many concepts of regularity of graphs do you know, and what are the relations between these concepts?

5. What is the relation between colouring the nodes of planar graphs and colouring maps?

6. Can one use depth-first search and breadth-first search methods to search infinite graphs?

7. How many solutions has a string equation $x^2 = wxw$ with unknown x?

8. Which languages L satisfy the equality $L \cup abL = \varepsilon \cup aL \cup bL^2$?

9. Can it happen that the same Cayley graph is generated by two different sets of generators? (If yes, give an example; if not, explain why.)

10. Which chain code pictures are generated by words of the following languages:
    (a) $\{ru^i rd^i \mid i \geq 1\}$; (b) $\{(ru)^i rur(dr)^i \mid i \geq 1\}$?

2.8 Historical and Bibliographical References

The basic mathematical concepts discussed in this chapter have been in the process of development for centuries, and are presented in many textbooks of various levels of sophistication. Some of those basic books with a greater orientation to computing are Rosen (1981) and Arnold and Guessarian (1996).

Georg Cantor (1845–1918), a German mathematician, and Ernst F. Zermelo (1871–1956), an Italian mathematician, are considered to be the main fathers of modern set theory, although discoveries of paradoxes led to a variety of additional approaches. The Sierpiński triangle, Koch curves, Mandelbrot sets and other fractal structures are treated in depth by Peitgen, Jürgens and Saupe (1992). Data structures are discussed in a variety of books: for example, Cormen, Leiserson and Rivest (1990), Gonnet (1984) and Mehlhorn (1984). The data type concept was introduced by several people: in its most abstract form by the ADJ group, see Guogen, Thatcher, Wagner and Wright (1977). The book by Ehrig and Mahr (1985) is currently perhaps the main reference on this topic. The binary tree implementation of dictionaries, described in Section 2.1, is due to Song (1981). Figure 2.2 is reproduced courtesy of Frank Drewers, and Figure 2.6 courtesy of Uwe Krüger and Heintz Wolf.

The two main algorithms for computing the transitive closure of a relation shown in Section 2.2 are due to Warshall (1962) and Kozen (1991).

The Garden of Eden problem and Theorem 2.3.11 are due to Moore (1962), Myhill (1963) and Richardson (1972). For a general treatment and survey of cellular automata mappings see Garzon (1995). Boolean functions are dealt with in almost every book on discrete mathematics. There are several definitions of one-way functions, the concept that forms the basis of modern cryptography. The one presented in Section 2.3.3 is from Goldreich (1989), in which an intensive analysis of related concepts is also presented. The idea of hashing appeared first in an internal report of IBM in 1953 by H. P. Luhn. Hashing is analysed in detail by Knuth (1973) and Gonnet (1984). The idea of universal hashing is due to Carter and Wegman (1979); see also Cormen, Leiserson and Rivest (1990) for a presentation of hashing and universal hashing.

Graph theory, initiated by Euler, has since then become a very intensively developed theory with many applications, and there are many books about it. A careful presentation of basic concepts and results much related to computing is, for example, Bondy and Murty (1976), in which one can also find proofs of Theorems 2.4.21 and 2.4.25. Several graphs, examples and exercises presented here are also from this book.

Salomaa's 'Formal languages' (1973) is still the main reference in formal language theory (see also Harrison (1978)). Chain code languages were introduced by Maurer, Rozenberg and Welzl (1982). Turtle interpretation of words, introduced by Prusinkiewicz, is discussed in detail by Prusinkiewicz and Lindenmayer (1990). The examples presented in Section 2.5.3 come from this book; the drawing programs were made by H. Fernau. The discussions of point and pixel representations of words are based on Culik and Dube (1993) and Culik and Kari (1993). Several of the exercises on languages are due to Eğecioğlu (1995).

MacLane and Birkhoff (1967) is a standard reference on modern algebra. Theorem 1 and the concept of the Cayley graph are due to Cayley (1878, 1889). Akers and Krishnamurthy (1986) started to explore properties of Cayley graphs from the interconnection network point of view.

Boolean algebras are dealt with in most books on discrete mathematics. An abstract concept of Kleene algebra is found in Kozen (1991).

3 Automata

INTRODUCTION

Finite state machines are the most basic model of machines, organisms and processes in technology, nature, society, the universe and philosophy, a model that captures the essence of finite systems and allows us to learn, demonstrate and utilize their power.

On a theoretical level, finite state machines represent the very basic model of automata to start with in designing, learning, analysing and demonstrating components, principles and power of real and idealized computers and also a variety of basic computation modes.

On a practical level, finite state machines approximate real machines, systems and processes closely enough. That is why the aim of applied research and development in computing is often to reduce idealized concepts and methods to those realizable by finite state machines.

Finite state automata are also a good model for demonstrating how finite devices working in discrete time can be used to process infinite or continuous objects.

LEARNING OBJECTIVES

The aim of the chapter is to demonstrate

1. the fundamental concept of finite state machine;
2. basic concepts, properties and algorithms concerning finite automata, their minimization and main decision problems;
3. basic concepts, properties and algorithms concerning regular expressions, regular languages and their closure properties;
4. finite transducers and their power and properties;
5. weighted finite automata and transducers and their use for image generation, transformation and compression;
6. how to use discrete finite automata to process infinite and continuous objects;
7. various modifications of finite automata: nondeterministic, probabilistic, two-way, multihead and linearly bounded automata and their power.

> The fact is, that civilization requires slaves. The Greeks were quite right there. Unless there are slaves to do the ugly, horrible, uninteresting work, culture and contemplation become almost impossible. Human slavery is wrong, insecure, and demoralizing. On mechanical slavery, on the slavery of the machine, the future of the world depends.
>
> *Oscar Wilde, 1895*

The concept of finite state devices is one of the most basic in modern science, technology and philosophy; one that in a strikingly simple way captures the essence of the most fundamental principle of how machines, nature and society work. The whole process of the development of a deterministic and mechanistic view of the world, initiated by R. Descartes whose thinking was revolutionary for its time, culminated in a very simple, powerful model of finite state machines, due to McCulloch and Pitts (1943), obtained from an observation of principles of neural activities.[1]

In this chapter we present, analyse and illustrate several models of automata, as well as some of their (also surprising) applications. The most basic model is that of a finite state machine, which is an abstraction of a real machine (and therefore of fixed size and finite memory machines), functioning in discrete time steps.

Finite state machines are building blocks, in a variety of ways, for other models of computing, generating and recognizing devices, both sequential and parallel, deterministic and randomized. This lies behind their fundamental role in the theory and practice of computing. Because of their simplicity, efficiency and well worked out theory, it is often a good practice to simplify sophisticated computational concepts and methods to such an extent that they can be realized by (co-operating) finite state machines.

Basic theoretical concepts and results concerning finite state machines are presented in the first part of this chapter. In the second part several applications are introduced, showing the surprising power and usefulness of the basic concepts concerning finite state machines: for example, for image generation, transformation and compression. Finally, various modifications of the basic model of finite state machines are considered. Some of them do not increase the power of finite state machines, but again show how robust the basic model is. Others turn out to be more powerful. This results in a variety of models filling the gap between finite state machines and universal computers discussed in the following chapter.

It will also be demonstrated that though such machines are finite and work in discrete steps, they can process, in a reasonable sense, infinite and continuous objects. For example, they can be seen as processing infinite words and computing (even very weird) continuous functions.

3.1 Finite State Devices

The finite state machine model of a device abstracts from the technology on which the device is based. Attention is paid only to a finite number of clearly distinguished **states** that the device can be in and

[1]Automata and automatization have for a long time been among the most exciting ideas for humankind, not only because they offer ways to get rid of dull work, but also because they offer means by which humankind can overcome their physical and intellectual limitations. The first large wave of fascination with automata came in the middle of the nineteenth century, when construction of sophisticated automata, imitating functions considered essential for living and/or intelligent creatures, flourished. The emerging automata industry, see the interesting account in Bailey (1982), played an important role in the history of modern technology. The second wave, apparently less mysterious but much more powerful, came with the advent of universal computers.

a finite number of clearly identified **events**, usually called **external inputs** or **signals**, that may cause the device to change its current state.

A simple finite state model of a digital watch is shown in Figure 3.1a. The model abstracts from what, how and by whom the watch is made, and shows only eight main states, depicted by boxes, the watch can be in, from the user's point of view ('update hours', 'display date', 'display time'), and transitions between the states caused by pushing one of four buttons a, b, c, d. Each transition is labelled by the button causing that transition. Having such a simple state transition model of a digital watch, it is easy to follow the sequence of states of the watch when the buttons are pushed in a given sequence. For example, by pushing buttons a, c, d, c, a, a, in this order, the watch gets, transition by transition, from the state 'display time' back to the same state.

The finite state model of a watch in Figure 3.1a models watch behaviour as a process that goes on and on (until the watch gets broken or the battery dies). Observe that this process has no other outputs beside the states themselves – various displays. Note also that in some states, for example, 'display watch', it is not specified for all buttons what happens if the button is pressed. (This can be utilized to make a more detailed model of a watch, with more states and actions, for example, to manipulate the stopwatch.) Note also that neither requirements nor restrictions are made on how often a button may be pressed and how much time a state transition takes.

There are many interesting questions one can ask/study about the model in Figure 3.1a. For example, given two states p and q, which sequence of buttons should one push in order to get from state p to state q?

Exercise 3.1.1 *Describe the five shortest sequences of buttons that make the watch in Figure 3.1a go from state p to state q if (a) $p =$ 'display alarm', $q =$ 'display hours'; (b) $p =$ 'display time', $q =$ 'display alarm'.*

Two other models of finite automata are depicted in Figures 3.1b, c. In both cases the states are depicted by circles, and transitions by arrows labelled by actions (external symbols or inputs) causing these transitions. These two finite state machines are more abstract. We do not describe what the states mean. Only transitions between states are depicted and states are partitioned into 'yes'- and 'no'-states. For these two models we can also ask the question: which sequences of inputs make the machine change from a given state p to a given state q; or a simpler question: which sequences of inputs make the machine go from the starting state to a 'yes'-state. For example, in the case of the model in Figure 3.1b, the sequences of letters 'the', 'thee', 'their' and 'then' have such a property; whereas the sequence 'tha' has not. In the case of the finite state model in Figure 3.1c a sequence of inputs makes the machine go from the initial state into the single 'yes'-state if and only if this sequence contains an even number of a's.

As we shall soon see, the questions as to which inputs make a finite state machine go from one state to another or to a 'yes'-state turn out to be, very important in relation to such an abstract model of finite state machines.

In our model of finite state machines we use a very general concept of a (global) state. A digital device is often composed of a large number of elementary devices, say n, such that each of them is always in one of the two binary states. Any combination of these elementary states forms the so-called 'global state'. The overall number of (global) states of the device is 2^n in such a case. However, in a simple finite state model of a device, very often only a few of the global states are used.

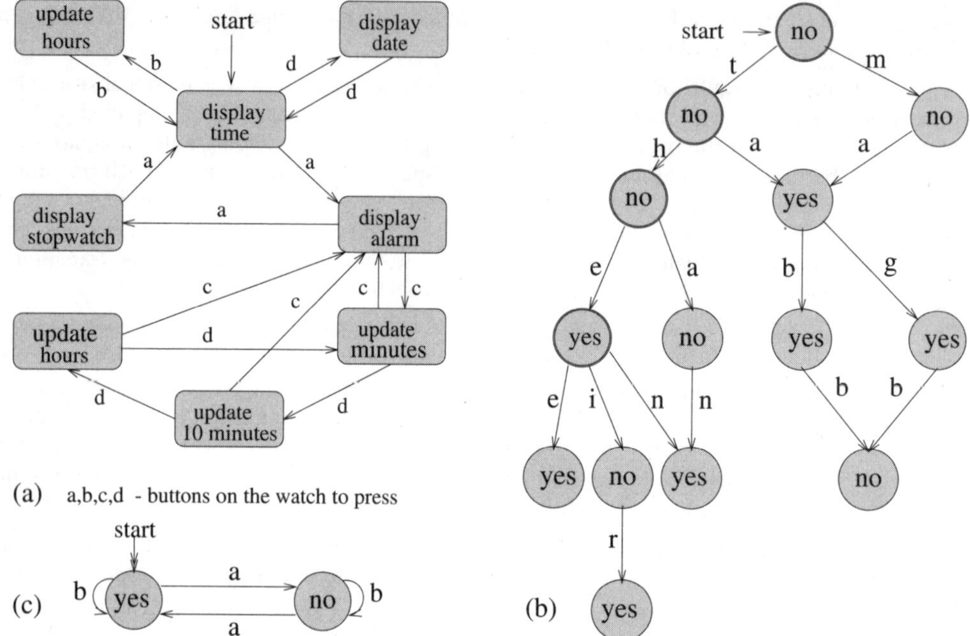

Figure 3.1 Finite state devices

Exercise 3.1.2 *Extend the finite state model of the watch in Figure 3.1 to incorporate other functions which a watch usually has.*

Exercise 3.1.3 *Express in a diagram possible states and transitions for a coffee vending machine that acts as follows. It takes 5, 10 and 20p coins, in any order, until the overall amount is at least 90p. At the moment this happens, the machine stops accepting coins, produces coffee and makes change. (Take into consideration only the money-checking activity of the machine.)*

Four basic types of finite state machines are recognizers, acceptors, transducers and generators (see Figure 3.2). A **recognizer** is a finite state machine $\mathcal{A}$ that always starts in the same initial state. Any input causes a state change (to a different or to the same state) and only a state change – no output is produced. States are partitioned into 'yes'-states (**terminal** states) and 'no'-states (**nonterminal** states). A sequence of inputs is said to be **recognized (rejected)** by $\mathcal{A}$ if and only if this sequence of inputs places the machine in a **terminal** state (a **nonterminal** state).

Example 3.1.4 *The finite state machine in Figure 3.3a recognizes an input sequence $(a_1,b_1)\ldots(a_{n-1},b_{n-1})(a_n,b_n)$, with (a_1,b_1) as the first symbol, if and only if there is a k, $1 \leq k \leq n$, such that $a_k = b_k = 1$. (Interestingly enough, this is precisely the case if $\binom{i+j}{i} \bmod 2 = 0$ for the integers $i = bin(a_na_{n-1}\ldots a_1)$ and $j = bin(b_nb_{n-1}\ldots b_1)$ – show that!)*

An **acceptor** is also a finite state machine that always starts in the same initial state. An input either

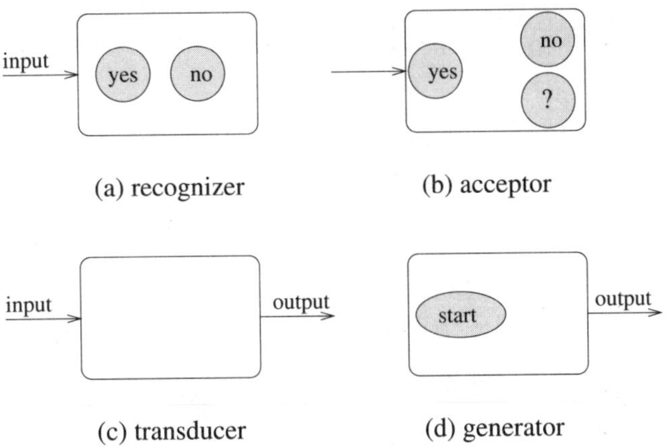

Figure 3.2 A recognizer, an acceptor, a transducer and a generator

causes a state transition or is not accepted at all, and again no output is produced. A sequence of inputs is said to be accepted if and only if it puts the automaton in a terminal state. (The other possibilities are that a sequence of inputs puts the automaton in a nonterminal state or that its processing is interrupted at some point, because the next transition is not defined.)

Example 3.1.5 *Figure 3.3d shows an acceptor that accepts exactly the words of the language* a^*cb^*.

A **transducer** acts as a recognizer, but for each input an output is produced.

Example 3.1.6 *The transducer shown in Figure 3.3b produces for each input word* $w = w_1cw_2c\ldots cw_{n-1}cw_n$, $w_i \in \{0,1\}^*$ *the output word* $w' = \phi(w_1)cw_2c\phi(w_3)c\ \ldots\ cw_{n-1}\phi(w_n)$ *if* n *is odd and* $w' = \phi(w_1)cw_2c\phi(w_3)c\ldots c\phi(w_{n-1})cw_n$ *if* n *is even, where* ϕ *is the morphism defined by* $\phi(c) = c$, $\phi(0) = 01$ *and* $\phi(1) = 10$. *In Figure 3.3b, in each pair 'i,o', used as a transition label, the first component denotes the input symbol, the second the output string.*

A **generator** has no input. It starts in an initial state, moves randomly, from state to state, and at each move an output is produced. For each state transition a probability is given that the transition takes place.

Example 3.1.7 *The generator depicted in Figure 3.3c has only one state, and all state changes have the same probability, namely* $1/3$. *It is easy to see that if a sequence of output symbols* $(x_1,y_1)\ldots(x_n,y_n)$ *is interpreted as a point of the unit square, with the coordinates* $(0.x_1\ldots x_n, 0.y_1\ldots y_n)$ *as in Section 2.1.2, then the generator produces the Sierpiński triangle shown in Figure 2.1.*

Is it not remarkable that a one-state generator can produce such a complex fractal structure? This is in no way an exception. As will be seen later, finite state generators can generate very complex images indeed.

3.2 Finite Automata

So far we have used the concepts of finite state recognizers and acceptors only intuitively. These concepts will now be formalized, generalized and analysed. The main new idea is the introduction of nondeterminism. In some states behaviour of the automaton does not have to be determined uniquely. We show that such a generalization is fully acceptable and, in addition, sometimes very useful.

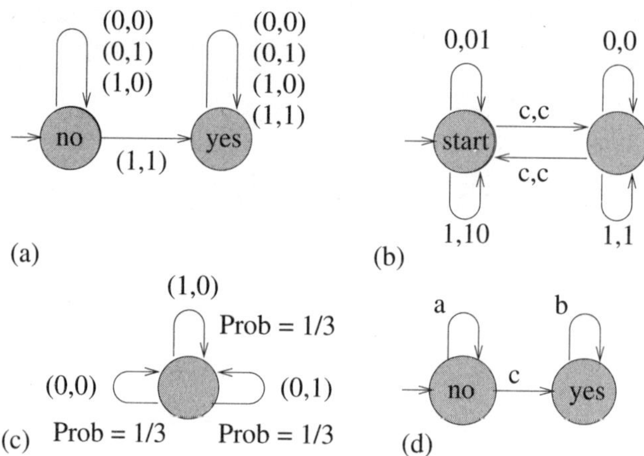

Figure 3.3 Examples of a recognizer, a transducer, a generator and an acceptor

3.2.1 Basic Concepts

Definition 3.2.1 *A* **(nondeterministic) finite automaton** $\mathcal{A}$ *(for short,* **NFA** *or* **FA***) over the (input)* **alphabet** Σ *is specified by a finite* **set of states** Q*, a distinct* **(initial) state** q_0*, a set* $Q_F \subseteq Q$ *of* **terminal (final) states** *and a* **transition relation** $\delta \subset Q \times \Sigma \times Q$*. Formally,* $\mathcal{A} = \langle \Sigma, Q, q_0, Q_F, \delta \rangle$*.*

If δ *is a function, that is* $\delta : Q \times \Sigma \to Q$*, we also use the notation* $\delta(q,a)$ *to specify the value of* δ *for arguments* q,a*.*

Informally, a computation of $\mathcal{A}$ for an input word w always starts in the initial state q_0 and continues by a sequence of **steps** (**moves** or **transitions**), one for each input symbol. In each step the automaton moves from its current state, say p, according to the next symbol of the input word, say a, into a state q such that $(p,a,q) \in \delta$ – if such a q exists. If there is a unique $q \in Q$ such that $(p,a,q) \in \delta$, then the transition from the state p by the input a is uniquely determined. We usually say that it is deterministic. If there are several q such that $(p,a,q) \in \delta$, then one of the possible transitions is chosen, and all of them are considered as being equally likely. If, for some state p and input a, there is no q such that $(p,a,q) \in \delta$, then we say that input a in state p leads to a termination of the computation. A computation ends after the last symbol of w is processed or a termination occurs. We can also say that a computation is performed in discrete time steps and the time instances are ordered $0,1,2,\ldots$ with 0 the time at which each computation starts.

For a formal definition of computation of a FA the concept of configuration is important. A **configuration** C of $\mathcal{A}$ is a pair $(p,w) \in Q \times \Sigma^*$. Informally, the automaton $\mathcal{A}$ is in the configuration (p,w), if it is in the state p and w is the part of the input word yet to be processed. A configuration (q_0,w) is called **initial**, and any configuration $(q,\varepsilon), q \in Q_F$ is called **final**.

A **computational step** of $\mathcal{A}$ is the relation

$$\vdash_{\mathcal{A}} \subseteq (Q \times \Sigma^*) \times (Q \times \Sigma^*)$$

between configurations defined for $p,q \in Q$, $a \in \Sigma$, $w \in \Sigma^*$ by

$$(p,aw) \vdash_{\mathcal{A}} (q,w) \;\Leftrightarrow\; (p,a,q) \in \delta.$$

Informally, $(p,aw) \vdash_{\mathcal{A}} (q,w)$ means that $\mathcal{A}$ moves from state p after input a to state q. A **computation** of $\mathcal{A}$ is the transitive and reflexive closure $\vdash_{\mathcal{A}}^*$ of the relation $\vdash_{\mathcal{A}}$ between configurations: that is, $C \vdash_{\mathcal{A}}^* C'$

$$\begin{array}{lllllll}\delta(q_0,0) & = & \{q_2\}, & \quad & \delta(q_0,2) & = & \{q_1,q_2\},\\ \delta(q_1,0) & = & \{q_3\}, & & \delta(q_1,1) & = & \{q_0\},\\ \delta(q_2,0) & = & \{q_0\}, & & \delta(q_2,2) & = & \{q_3,q_0\},\\ \delta(q_3,0) & = & \{q_1\}, & & \delta(q_3,1) & = & \{q_2\}.\end{array}$$

(a)

states	inputs		
	0	1	2
q_0	q_2	-	q_1,q_2
q_1	q_3	q_0	-
q_2	q_0	-	q_3,q_0
q_3	q_1	q_2	-

(b)

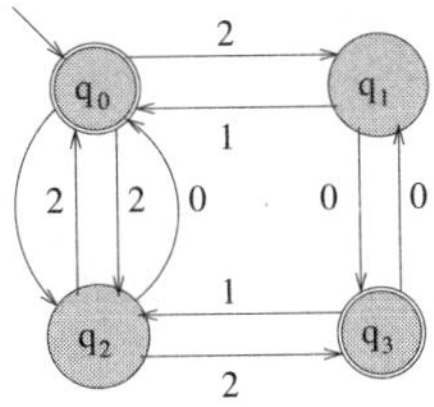

(c)

Figure 3.4 Finite automata representations

for configurations C and C' if and only if there is a sequence of configurations $C_1,\ldots,C_n$ such that $C=C_1$, $C_i \vdash_{\mathcal{A}} C_{i+1}$, for $1 \le i < n$, and $C_n = C'$.

Instead of $(p,w) \vdash_{\mathcal{A}}^* (q,\varepsilon)$, we usually use the notation $p \overset{*}{\underset{w}{\Longrightarrow}} q$. A state q is called reachable in $\mathcal{A}$ if there is an input word w such that $q_0 \overset{*}{\underset{w}{\Longrightarrow}} q$.

Exercise 3.2.2 *Let $\mathcal{A} = \langle \Sigma, Q, q_0, Q_F, \delta\rangle$ be a FA. Let us define a recurrence as follows: $A_0 = \{q_0\}$, $A_i = \{q' \mid (q,a,q') \in \delta$ for some $q \in A_{i-1}, a \in \Sigma\}$, for $i \ge 1$. Show that a state q is reachable in $\mathcal{A}$ if and only if $q \in A_j$ for some $j \le |Q|$. (This implies that it is easy to compute the set of all reachable states.)*

Three basic ways of representing finite automata are illustrated in Figure 3.4 on the automaton $\mathcal{A} = \langle \Sigma, Q, q_0, Q_F, \delta\rangle$, where $Q = \{q_0,q_1,q_2,q_3\}$, $\Sigma = \{0,1\}$, and $Q_F = \{q_0,q_3\}$: an **enumeration** of transitions (Figure 3.4a), a **transition matrix** (Figure 3.4b) with rows labelled by states and columns by input symbols, and a **state graph** or a **transition diagram** (Figure 3.4c) with states represented by circles, transitions by directed edges labelled by input symbols, the initial state by an ingoing arrow, and final states by double circles. For a finite automaton $\mathcal{A}$ let $G_{\mathcal{A}}$ denote its state graph. Observe that a state q is reachable in the automaton $\mathcal{A}$ if and only if the corresponding node is reachable in the graph $G_{\mathcal{A}}$ from its starting vertex.

To every finite automaton $\mathcal{A} = \langle \Sigma, Q, q_0, Q_F, \delta\rangle$ and every $q \in Q$, we associate the language $L(q)$ of those words that make $\mathcal{A}$ move from state q to a final state. More formally,

$$L(q) = \{w \in \Sigma^* \mid q \overset{*}{\underset{w}{\Longrightarrow}} p \in Q_F\}.$$

$L(\mathcal{A}) = L(q_0)$ is then the **language recognized** by $\mathcal{A}$. A language L is called a **regular language** if there is a finite automaton $\mathcal{A}$ such that $L = L(\mathcal{A})$. The **family of languages recognizable** by finite automata, or the **family of regular languages**, is denoted by

$$\mathcal{L}(FA) = \{L(\mathcal{A}) \mid \mathcal{A} \text{ is a finite automaton}\}.$$

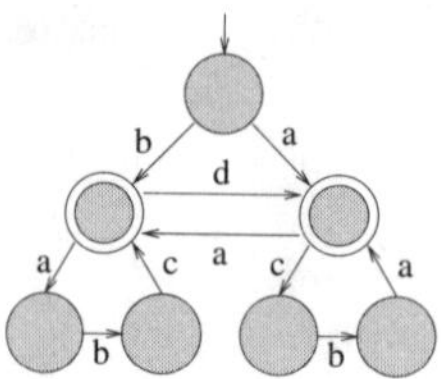

Figure 3.5 Finite automaton

Exercise 3.2.3 *Let* $L_n = \{uv \mid uv \in \{0,1\}^*, |u| = |v| = n, u \neq v\}$. *Design a FA accepting the language (a)* L_2*; (b)* L_3*; (c)* L_4.

Exercise 3.2.4 *Describe the language accepted by the FA depicted in Figure 3.5.*

Another way to define the language recognized by a finite automaton $\mathcal{A}$ is in terms of its state graph $G_{\mathcal{A}}$. A **path** in $G_{\mathcal{A}}$ is a sequence of triples $(p_1,a_1,p_2)(p_2,a_2,p_3)\ldots(p_n,a_n,p_{n+1})$ such that $(p_i,a_i,p_{i+1}) \in \delta$, for $1 \leq i \leq n$. The word $a_1 \ldots a_n$ is the label of such a path, p_1 its origin and p_{n+1} its terminus. A word $w \in \Sigma^*$ is recognizable by $\mathcal{A}$ if w is the label of a path with q_0 as its origin and a final state as its terminus. $L(\mathcal{A})$ is then the set of all words recognized by $\mathcal{A}$.

The language recognized by a finite automaton $\mathcal{A}$ can be seen as the computational process that $\mathcal{A}$ represents. This is why two finite automata $\mathcal{A}_1, \mathcal{A}_2$ are called **equivalent** if $L(\mathcal{A}_1) = L(\mathcal{A}_2)$; that is, if the corresponding languages (computational processes they represent) are equal.

Exercise 3.2.5 *A natural generalization is to consider finite automata* $\mathcal{A} = \langle \Sigma, Q, Q_I, Q_F, \sigma \rangle$ *with a set* Q_I *of initial states, where computation and recognition are defined similarly. Show that to each such finite automaton* $\mathcal{A}$ *we can easily construct an equivalent ordinary finite automaton.*

If two FA are equivalent, that is, if they are 'the same' insofar as the computational processes (languages) they represent are the same, they can nevertheless look very different, and can also have a different number of states. A stronger requirement for similarity is that they are **isomorphic** – they differ only in the way their states are denoted.

Definition 3.2.6 *Two FA* $\mathcal{A}_i = \langle \Sigma, Q_i, q_{0,i}, Q_{F,i}, \delta_i \rangle$, $i = 1,2$ *are isomorphic if there is a bijection* $\mu : Q_1 \to Q_2$ *such that* $\mu(q_{0,1}) = q_{0,2}$, $q \in Q_{F,1}$ *if and only if* $\mu(q) \in Q_{F,2}$, *and for any* $q, q' \in Q_1$, $a \in \Sigma$ *we have* $(q,a,q') \in \delta_1$ *if and only if* $(\mu(q), a, \mu(q')) \in \delta_2$.

Exercise 3.2.7 *Design a finite automaton that accepts those binary words that represent integers (with the most significant bit as the first) divisible by three.*

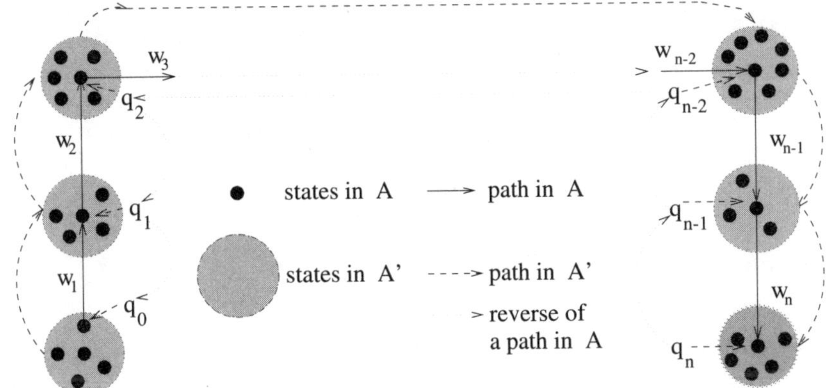

Figure 3.6 A path in a NFA and in an equivalent DFA obtained by the subset construction

3.2.2 Nondeterministic versus Deterministic Finite Automata

The formal definition of a FA (on page 158) allows it to have two properties that contradict our intuition: a state transition, for a given input, does not have to be unique and does not have to be defined. Our intuition seems to prefer that a FA is deterministic and complete in the following sense.

A finite automaton is a **deterministic finite automaton** if its transition relation is a partial function: that is, for each state $p \in Q$ and input $a \in \Sigma$ there is at most one $q \in Q$ such that $(p,a,q) \in \delta$. A finite automaton is called **complete** if for any $p \in Q, a \in \Sigma$ there is at least one q such that $(p,a,q) \in \delta$. In the following the notation DFA will be used for a deterministic and complete FA.

The following theorem shows that our definition of finite automata, which allows 'strange' nondeterminism, has not increased the recognition power of DFA.

Theorem 3.2.8 *To every finite automaton there is an equivalent deterministic and complete finite automaton.*

Proof: Given a FA $\mathcal{A} = \langle \Sigma, Q, q_0, Q_F, \delta \rangle$, an equivalent DFA $\mathcal{A}'$ can be constructed, by the **subset construction**, as

$$\mathcal{A}' = \langle \Sigma, 2^Q, \{q_0\}, \{B \,|\, B \in 2^Q, B \cap Q_F \neq \emptyset\}, \delta' \rangle,$$

where the new transition relation δ' is defined as follows:

$$(A, a, B) \in \delta' \text{ if and only if } B = \{q \,|\, \exists p \in A, (p,a,q) \in \delta\}.$$

The states of $\mathcal{A}'$ are therefore sets of the states of $\mathcal{A}$. There is a transition in $\mathcal{A}'$ from a state S, a set of states of $\mathcal{A}$, to another state S_1, again a set of states of $\mathcal{A}$, under an input a if and only if to each state in S_1 there is a transition in $\mathcal{A}$ from some state in S under the input a.

$\mathcal{A}$ is clearly deterministic and complete. To show that $\mathcal{A}$ and $\mathcal{A}'$ are equivalent, consider the state graphs $G_{\mathcal{A}}$ and $G_{\mathcal{A}'}$. For any path in $G_{\mathcal{A}}$, from the initial state to a final state, labelled by a word $w = w_1 \ldots w_s$, there is a unique path in $G_{\mathcal{A}'}$, labelled also by w, from the initial state to a final state (see Figure 3.6). The corresponding states of $\mathcal{A}'$, as the sets of states of $\mathcal{A}$, can be determined, step by step, using the transition function δ', from the initial state of $\mathcal{A}'$ and w. The state of $\mathcal{A}'$ reached by the path labelled by a prefix of w has to contain exactly the states of $\mathcal{A}$ reached, in $G_{\mathcal{A}}$, by the path labelled by

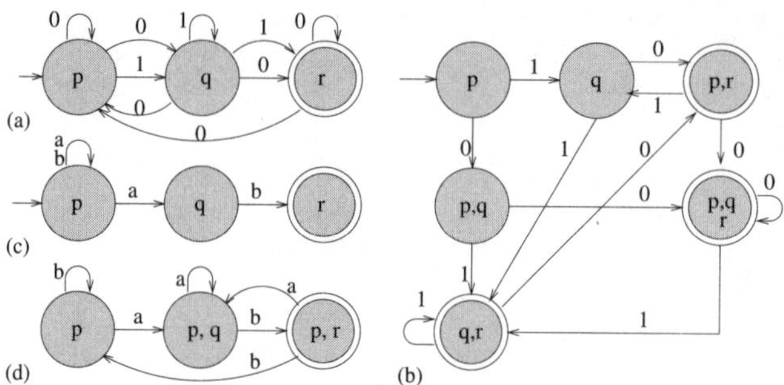

Figure 3.7 FA and equivalent DFA obtained by the subset construction

the same prefix of w. Similarly, to any path in $\mathcal{A}'$, from the initial to a final state, labelled by a word w, there is a path in $G_{\mathcal{A}}$ from the initial to a final state. The states on this path can be taken from the corresponding states of the path labelled by w in $G_{\mathcal{A}'}$ in such a way that they form a path in $G_{\mathcal{A}}$. To design it, one has to start in the last state (of $\mathcal{A}'$) of the path in $G_{\mathcal{A}'}$, to pick up a state q_n (terminal in $\mathcal{A}$), from this state of $\mathcal{A}'$ and go backwards to pick up states $q_{n-1}, q_{n-2}, \ldots, q_1$. This is possible, because whenever $A \underset{a}{\Longrightarrow} B$ in $\mathcal{A}'$, then for any $q' \in B$ there is a $q \in A$ such that $q \underset{a}{\Longrightarrow} q'$ in $\mathcal{A}$. □

Example 3.2.9 *Let $\mathcal{A} = \langle \Sigma, Q, q_0, Q_F, \delta \rangle$ be the nondeterministic finite automaton depicted in Figure 3.7a. The finite automaton obtained by the subset construction has the following transition function δ':*

$$\begin{array}{rclrcl}
\delta'(\emptyset,0) & = & \emptyset; & \delta'(\emptyset,1) & = & \emptyset; \\
\delta'(\{p\},0) & = & \{p,q\}; & \delta'(\{p\},1) & = & \{q\}; \\
\delta'(\{q\},0) & = & \{p,r\}; & \delta'(\{q\},1) & = & \{q,r\}; \\
\delta'(\{r\},0) & = & \{p,r\}; & \delta'(\{r\},1) & = & \emptyset; \\
\delta'(\{p,q\},0) & = & \{p,q,r\}; & \delta'(\{p,q\},1) & = & \{q,r\}; \\
\delta'(\{p,r\},0) & = & \{p,q,r\}; & \delta'(\{p,r\},1) & = & \{q\}; \\
\delta'(\{q,r\},0) & = & \{p,r\}; & \delta'(\{q,r\},1) & = & \{q,r\}; \\
\delta'(\{p,q,r\},0) & = & \{p,q,r\}; & \delta'(\{p,q,r\},1) & = & \{q,r\}.
\end{array}$$

The states $\{r\}$ and $\emptyset$ are not reachable from the initial state $\{p\}$; therefore they are not included in the state graph $G_{\mathcal{A}'}$ of $\mathcal{A}'$ in Figure 3.7b. The subset construction applied to the FA in Figure 3.7c provides the DFA shown in Figure 3.7d. Other states created by the subset construction are not reachable in this case.

Exercise 3.2.10 *Design a DFA equivalent to NFA in (a) Figure 3.8a; (b) Figure 3.8b.*

Since nondeterministic and incomplete FA conform less to our intuition of what a finite state machine is and, are not more powerful than DFA, it is natural to ask why they should be considered at all.

There are two reasons, both of which concern efficiency. The first concerns design efficiency. It is quite often easier, even significantly easier, to design a NFA accepting a given regular language than an equivalent DFA. For example, it is straightforward to design a NFA recognizing the language

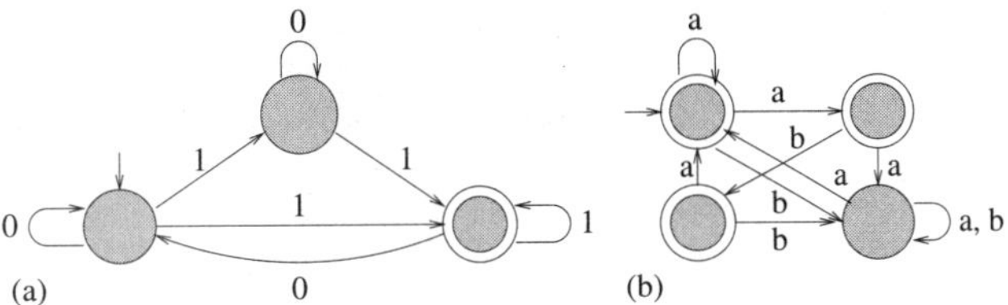

Figure 3.8 Examples of a NFA

$\{a,b\}^*a\{a,b\}^n$ (see Figure 3.9a for the general case and Figure 3.9b for $n = 2$). On the other hand, it is much more difficult to design a DFA for this language (see the one in Figure 3.9c for $n = 2$). The second reason concerns size efficiency, and this is even 'provably important'.

The number of states of a FA $\mathcal{A}$, in short $state(\mathcal{A})$, is its **state complexity**. In the case of the NFA in Figure 3.7c the subset construction does not provide a DFA with a larger number of states. On the other hand, the subset construction applied to the NFA in Figure 3.7a, has significantly increased the number of states. In general, the subset construction applied to a NFA with n states provides a DFA with 2^n states. This is the number of subsets of each set of n elements and indicates that the subset construction can produce exponentially more states. However, some of these states may not be reachable, as the example above shows. Moreover, it is not yet clear whether some other method could not provide a DFA with fewer states but still equivalent to the given NFA.

In order to express exactly how much more economical a NFA may be, compared with an equivalent DFA, the following economy function is introduced:

$$Economy^{\mathrm{DFA}}_{\mathrm{NFA}}(n) = \max\{\min\{state(\mathcal{B}) | \mathcal{B} \text{ is a DFA equivalent to } \mathcal{A}\} | \mathcal{A} \text{ is NFA}, state(\mathcal{A}) = n\}.$$

The following result shows that a DFA can be, provably, exponentially larger than an equivalent NFA.

Theorem 3.2.11 $Economy^{\mathrm{DFA}}_{\mathrm{NFA}}(n) = 2^n$.

Proof idea: The inequality $\mathrm{Economy}^{\mathrm{DFA}}_{\mathrm{NFA}}(n) \leq 2^n$ follows from the subset construction. In order to prove the opposite inequality, it is sufficient to show, which can be done, that the minimum DFA equivalent to the one shown in Figure 3.9d must have 2^n states. □

A simpler example, though not so perfect, of the exponential growth of states provided by the subset construction, is shown in Figure 3.9. The minimum DFA equivalent to the NFA shown in Figure 3.9a must have 2^{n-1} states. This is easy to see, because the automaton has to remember the last $n-1$ symbols. For $n = 2$ the equivalent DFA is shown in Figure 3.9c.

Corollary 3.2.12 *Nondeterminism of a NFA does not increase its computational power, but can essentially (exponentially) decrease the number of states (and thereby also increase the design efficiency).*

Exercise 3.2.13 *Design a DFA equivalent to the one in Figure 3.9d for (a) $n = 4$; (b) $n = 5$.*

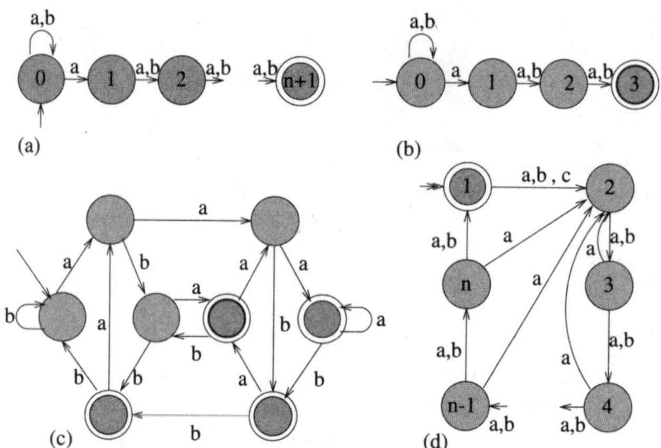

Figure 3.9 Examples showing that the subset construction can yield an exponential growth of states

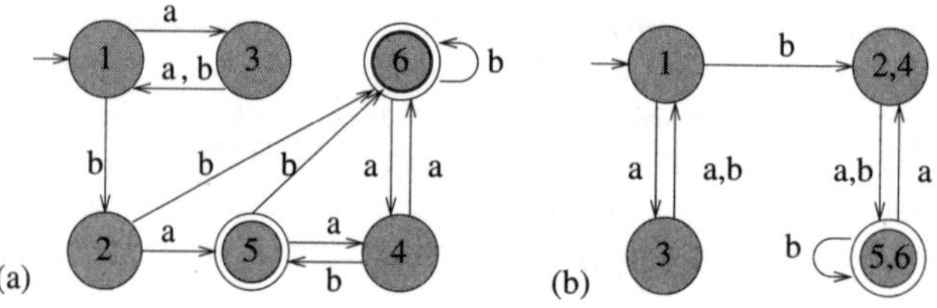

Figure 3.10 Two equivalent DFA

3.2.3 Minimization of Deterministic Finite Automata

Once we have the task of designing a DFA that recognizes a given regular language L, it is natural to try to find a 'minimal' DFA, with respect to the number of states, for L. Figure 3.10 shows that two equivalent DFA may have different numbers of states.

The following questions therefore arise naturally:

- How many different but equivalent minimal DFA can exist for a given FA?
- How can a minimal DFA equivalent to a given DFA be designed?
- How fast can one construct a minimal DFA?

In order to answer these questions, new concepts have to be introduced. Two states p, q of a FA $\mathcal{A}$ are called **equivalent**; in short $p \equiv_{\mathcal{A}} q$, if $L(p) = L(q)$ in $\mathcal{A}$. A FA $\mathcal{A}$ is called **reduced** if no two different states of $\mathcal{A}$ are equivalent. A DFA $\mathcal{A}$ is called **minimal** if there is no DFA equivalent to $\mathcal{A}$ and with fewer states.

We show two simple methods for minimizing finite automata. Both are based on the result, shown later, that if a DFA is reduced, then it is minimal.

1. **Minimization of DFA using the operations of reversal and subset construction.** The first method is based on two operations with finite automata. The operation of **reversal** assigns to a DFA $\mathcal{A} = \langle \Sigma, Q, q_0, Q_F, \delta \rangle$ the finite automaton $\rho(\mathcal{A}) = \langle \Sigma, Q, Q_F, \{q_0\}, \rho(\delta) \rangle$, that is, the initial and final

states are exchanged, and $q \in \rho(\delta)(q',a)$ if and only if $\delta(q,a) = q'$. The operation of **subset construction** assigns to any FA $\mathcal{A} = \langle \Sigma, Q, Q_I, Q_F, \delta \rangle$, with a set Q_I of initial states, a DFA $\pi(\mathcal{A})$ obtained from $\mathcal{A}$ by the subset construction (and containing only reachable states).

Theorem 3.2.14 *Let $\mathcal{A}$ be a finite automaton, then $\mathcal{A}' = \pi(\rho(\pi(\rho(\mathcal{A}))))$ is a reduced DFA equivalent to $\mathcal{A}$.*

Proof: Clearly $\mathcal{A}'$ is a DFA equivalent to $\mathcal{A}$. It is therefore sufficient to prove that $\pi(\rho(D))$ is reduced whenever $D = \langle \Sigma, Q', q'_0, Q'_F, \delta' \rangle$ is a FA and each of its states is reachable. Let $Q_1 \subseteq Q'$, $Q_2 \subseteq Q'$ be two equivalent states of $\pi(\rho(D))$. Since each state of D is reachable, for each $q_1 \in Q_1$ there is a $w \in \Sigma^*$ such that $q_1 = \delta'(q'_0, w)$. Thus $q'_0 \in \rho(\delta')(Q_1, w)$. As Q_1 and Q_2 are equivalent, we also have $q'_0 \in \rho(\delta')(Q_2, w)$, and therefore $q_2 = \delta'(q'_0, w)$ for some $q_2 \in Q_2$. Since δ' is a mapping, we get $q_1 = q_2$, and therefore $Q_1 \subseteq Q_2$. By symmetry, $Q_1 = Q_2$. □

Unfortunately, there is a DFA $\mathcal{A}$ with n states such that $\pi(\rho(\mathcal{A}))$ has 2^n states (see the one in Figure 3.9d). The time complexity of the above algorithm is therefore exponential in the worst case.

2. **Minimization of DFA through equivalence automata.** The second way of designing a reduced DFA $\mathcal{A}'$ equivalent to a given DFA $\mathcal{A}$ is also quite simple, and leads to a much more efficient algorithm. In the state graph $G_{\mathcal{A}}$ identify nodes corresponding to the equivalent states and then identify multiple edges with the same label between the same nodes. The resulting state graph is that of a reduced DFA. More formally,

Definition 3.2.15 *Let $\mathcal{A} = \langle \Sigma, Q, q_0, Q_F, \delta \rangle$ be a DFA. For any state $q \in Q$ let $[q]$ be the equivalence class on Q with respect to the relation $\equiv_{\mathcal{A}}$. The* **equivalence automaton** *$\mathcal{A}'$ for $\mathcal{A}$ is defined by*
$\mathcal{A}' = \langle \Sigma, Q', [q_0], Q'_F, \delta' \rangle$, where $Q' = \{[q] \mid q \in Q\}$, $Q'_F = \{[q] \mid q \in Q_F\}$, and $\delta' = \{([q_1], a, [q_2]) \mid (q'_1, a, q'_2) \in \delta$ for some $q'_1 \in [q_1], q'_2 \in [q_2]\}$.

Minimization of DFA is now based on the following result.

Theorem 3.2.16 *(1) The equivalence automaton $\mathcal{A}'$ of a DFA $\mathcal{A}$ is well defined, reduced and equivalent to $\mathcal{A}$.*
(2) $State(\mathcal{B}) \geq state(\mathcal{A}')$ for any DFA $\mathcal{B}$ equivalent to a DFA $\mathcal{A}$.
(3) Any minimal DFA $\mathcal{B}$ equivalent to a DFA $\mathcal{A}$ is isomorphic with $\mathcal{A}'$.

Proof: (1) If $q \equiv_{\mathcal{A}} q'$, then either both q and q' are in Q_F, or both are not in Q_F. Final states of $\mathcal{A}'$ are therefore well defined. Moreover, if $L(q) = L(q')$ for some $q, q' \in Q$, then for any $a \in \Sigma$, $L(\delta(q,a)) = L(\delta(q',a))$, and therefore all transitions of $\mathcal{A}'$ are well defined. If $w = w_1 \ldots w_n \in \Sigma^*$ and $q_i = \delta(q_0, w_1 \ldots w_i)$, then $[q_i] = \delta'([q_0], w_1 \ldots w_i)$. This implies that $L(\mathcal{A}) = L(\mathcal{A}')$. The condition of $\mathcal{A}'$ being reduced is trivially fulfilled due to the construction of $\mathcal{A}'$.

(2) It is sufficient to prove (2) assuming that all states of $\mathcal{B}$ are reachable from the initial state. Let $\mathcal{B} = \langle \Sigma, Q'', q''_0, Q''_F, \delta'' \rangle$ be a DFA equivalent to $\mathcal{A}$. Consider the mapping $g: Q'' \rightarrow Q'$ defined as follows: since all states of $\mathcal{B}$ are reachable, for any $q'' \in Q''$ there is a $w_{q''} \in \Sigma^*$ such that $\delta''(q''_0, w_{q''}) = q''$. Define now $g(q'') = \delta''([q_0], w_{q''})$. From the minimality of $\mathcal{A}'$ and its equivalence with $\mathcal{B}$, it follows that this mapping is well defined and surjective.

(3) In the case of minimality of $\mathcal{B}$ it is easy to verify that the mapping g defined in (2) is actually an isomorphism. □

Corollary 3.2.17 *If a DFA is reduced, then it is minimal.*

The task of constructing a minimal DFA equivalent to a given DFA $\mathcal{A}$ has therefore been reduced to that of determining which pairs of states of $\mathcal{A}$ are equivalent, or nonequivalent, which seems to be easier. This can be done as follows.

Let us call two states q, q' of $\mathcal{A}$

1. 0-**nonequivalent**, if one of them is a final state and the other is not;

2. i-**nonequivalent**, for $i > 0$, if they are either $(i-1)$-nonequivalent or there is an $a \in \Sigma$ such that $\delta(q,a)$ and $\delta(q',a)$ are $(i-1)$-nonequivalent.

Let A_i be the set of pairs of i-nonequivalent states, $i \geq 0$. Clearly, $A_i \subseteq A_{i+1}$, for all $i \geq 0$, and one can show that $A_n = A_{n+k}$ for any $k \geq 0$ if $n = \text{state}(\mathcal{A})$.

Two states q, q' are not equivalent if and only if there is a $w = w_1 \ldots w_m \in \Sigma^*$ such that $\delta(q,w) \in Q_F$ and $\delta(q',w) \notin Q_F$. This implies that states $\delta(q, w_1 \ldots w_{m-i})$ and $\delta(q', w_1 \ldots w_{m-i})$ are i-nonequivalent. Hence, if q and q' are not equivalent, they are n-nonequivalent.

The recurrent definition of the sets A_i actually specifies an $\mathcal{O}(n^2m)$ algorithm, $m = |\Sigma|$, to determine equivalent states, and thereby the minimal DFA.

Example 3.2.18 *The construction of i-nonequivalent states for the DFA in Figure 3.10a yields* $A_0 = \{(1,5),(1,6),(2,5),(2,6),(3,5),(3,6),(4,5),(4,6)\}$, $A_1 = A_0 \cup \{(1,2),(1,4),(2,3),(3,4)\}$, $A_2 = A_1 \cup \{(1,3)\}$, $A_3 = A_2$. *The resulting minimal DFA is depicted in Figure 3.10b.*

It can be shown, by using a more efficient algorithm to determine the equivalence, that one can construct the minimal DFA in sequential time $\mathcal{O}(mn \lg n)$, where m is the size of the alphabet and n is the number of states of the given DFA (see references).

Exercise 3.2.19 *Design the minimal DFA accepting the language (a) of all words over the alphabet* $\{a,b\}$ *that contain the subword 'abba' and end with the subword 'aaa'; (b) of all words over the alphabet* $\{0,1\}$ *that contain at least two occurrences of the subword '111';*
(c) $L = \{w \mid \#_a w \equiv \#_b w \pmod 3\} \subseteq \{a,b\}^*$.

3.2.4 Decision Problems

To decide whether two DFA, $\mathcal{A}_1$ and $\mathcal{A}_2$, are equivalent, it suffices to construct the minimal equivalent DFA $\mathcal{A}_1'$ to $\mathcal{A}_1$ and the minimal DFA $\mathcal{A}_2'$ to $\mathcal{A}_2$. $\mathcal{A}_1$ and $\mathcal{A}_2$ are then equivalent if and only if $\mathcal{A}_1'$ and $\mathcal{A}_2'$ are isomorphic. If $n = \max\{\mathit{state}(\mathcal{A}_1), \mathit{state}(\mathcal{A}_2)\}$ and m is the size of the alphabet, then minimization can be done in $\mathcal{O}(mn \lg n)$ sequential time, and the isomorphism can be checked in $\mathcal{O}(nm)$ sequential time.

One way to decide the equivalence of two NFA $\mathcal{A}_1$ and $\mathcal{A}_2$ is to design DFA equivalent to $\mathcal{A}_1$ and $\mathcal{A}_2$ and then minimize these DFA. If the resulting DFA are isomorphic, the original NFA are equivalent; otherwise not. However, this may take exponential time. It seems that there is no essentially better method, because the equivalence problem for NFA is a **PSPACE**-complete problem (see Section 5.11.2).

Two other basic decision problems for FA $\mathcal{A}$ are the **emptiness problem** – is $L(\mathcal{A})$ empty? – and the **finiteness problem** – is $L(\mathcal{A})$ finite? It follows from the next theorem that these two problems are decidable; one has only to check whether there is a $w \in L(\mathcal{A})$ such that $|w| < n$ in the first case and $n \leq |w| < 2n$ in the second case.

Theorem 3.2.20 *Let* $\mathcal{A} = \langle \Sigma, Q, q_0, Q_F, \delta \rangle$ *be a DFA and* $|Q| = n$.
(1) $L(\mathcal{A}) \neq \emptyset$ *if and only if there is a* $w \in L(\mathcal{A})$ *such that* $|w| \leq n$.
(2) $L(\mathcal{A})$ *is infinite if and only if there is a* $w \in L(\mathcal{A})$ *such that* $n < |w| < 2n$.

Theorem 3.2.20 is actually a corollary of the following basic result.

Lemma 3.2.21 (Pumping lemma for regular languages) *If $\mathcal{A}$ is a FA and there is a $w \in L(\mathcal{A})$, $|w| > n = state(\mathcal{A})$, then there are $x,y,z \in \Sigma^*$ such that $w = xyz$, $|xz| \le n, 0 < |y| \le n$, and $xy^iz \in L(\mathcal{A})$, for all $i \ge 0$.*

Proof: Let w be the shortest word in $L(\mathcal{A})$ with $|w| > n$ and $w = w_1 \ldots w_k, w_i \in \Sigma$. Consider the following sequence of states:

$$q_i = \delta(q_0, w_1 \ldots w_i), 0 \le i \le k.$$

Let us now take i_1 and i_2 such that $0 \le i_1 < i_2 \le k$, $q_{i_1} = q_{i_2}$, and $i_2 - i_1$ is as small as possible. Such i_1, i_2 must exist (pigeonhole principle), and clearly $i_2 - i_1 \le n$. Denote $x = w_1 \ldots w_{i_1}, y = w_{i_1+1} \ldots w_{i_2}$, $z = w_{i_2+1} \ldots w_k$. Then $\delta(q_0, xy^i) = q_{i_1} = q_{i_2}$ for all $i \ge 0$, and therefore also $xy^iz \in L(\mathcal{A})$. Because of the minimality of w we get $|xz| \le n$. □

Exercise 3.2.22 *Show the following modification of the pumping lemma for regular languages. Let L be a regular language. There exists an $N_L \in \mathbf{N}$ such that if for some strings x_1, x_2, x_3, $x_1x_2x_3 \in L$ and $|x_2| \ge N_L$, then there exist strings u, v and w such that $x_2 = uvw$, $v \neq \varepsilon$, $|uv| \le N_L$ and $x_1uv^iwx_3 \in L$ for all $i \ge 0$.*

Exercise 3.2.23 *Show, using one of the pumping lemmas for regular languages, that the language $\{wcw \mid w \in \{a,b\}^*\}$ is not regular.*

3.2.5 String Matching with Finite Automata

Finding all occurrences of a **pattern** in a text is a problem that arises in a large variety of applications, for example, in text editing, DNA sequence searching, and so on. This problem can be solved elegantly and efficiently using finite automata.

String matching problem. Given a string (called a **pattern**) $x \in \Sigma^*$, $|x| = m$, design an algorithm to determine, for an arbitrary $y \in \Sigma^*, y = y_1 \ldots y_n, y_j \in \Sigma$ for $1 \le j \le n$, all integers $1 \le i \le n$ such that x is a suffix of the string $y_1 \ldots y_i$.

A naïve string matching algorithm, which checks in m steps, for all $m \le i \le n$, whether x is a suffix of $y_1 \ldots y_i$, clearly requires $\mathcal{O}(mn)$ steps.

The problem can be reduced to that of designing, for a given x, a finite automaton $\mathcal{A}_x$ capable of deciding for a given word $y \in \Sigma^*$ whether $y \in \Sigma^*x$.

If $x = x_1 \ldots x_m, x_i \in \Sigma$, then the NFA $\mathcal{A}_x$ shown for an arbitrary x in Figure 3.11a and for $x = abaaaba$ in Figure 3.11b accepts Σ^*x. $\mathcal{A}_x$ has $m+1$ states that can be identified with the elements of the set P_x of prefixes of x – that is, with the set

$$P_x = \{\varepsilon, x_1, x_1x_2, \ldots, x_1x_2 \ldots x_m\}$$

or with the integers from 0 to m, with i standing for $x_1 \ldots x_i$.

It is easy to see that the DFA $\mathcal{A}'_x$, which can be obtained from $\mathcal{A}_x$ by the subset construction, has also only $m+1$ states. Indeed, those states of $\mathcal{A}'_x$ that are reachable from the initial state by a word y form exactly the set of those elements of P_x that are suffixes of y. This set is uniquely determined by the longest of its elements, say p, since the others are those suffixes of p that are in P_x. Hence, the states of $\mathcal{A}'$ can also be identified with integers from 0 to m. (See $\mathcal{A}'_x$ for $x = abaaaba$ in Figure 3.11d.)

Let $f_x : P_x \to P_x$ be the **failure function** that assigns to each $p \in P_x - \{\varepsilon\}$ the longest proper suffix of p that is in P_x. (For $x = abaaaba$ f_x is shown in Figure 3.11c, as a mapping from $\{0, \ldots, 7\}$ to $\{0, \ldots, 7\}$.)

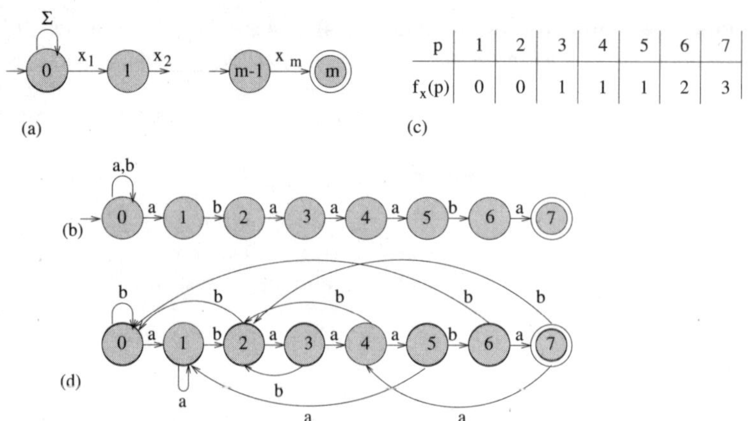

Figure 3.11 String matching automata and a failure function

Then the state of $\mathcal{A}'_x$ corresponding to the longest suffix p contains those states of $\mathcal{A}_x$ that correspond to the prefixes

$$p, f_x(p), f_x^2(p), \ldots, \varepsilon.$$

To compute f_x, for an $x \in \Sigma^*$, we can use the following recursive rule: $f_x(x_1) = \varepsilon$, and for all p, $pa \in P_x - \{\varepsilon\}$:

$$f_x(pa) = \begin{cases} f_x(p)a, & \text{if } f_x(p)a \in P_x; \\ f_x(f_x(p)a), & \text{otherwise.} \end{cases}$$

Once f_x is known, the transition function δ_x of $\mathcal{A}'$, for $p \in P_x$ and $a \in \Sigma$, has the following form:

$$\delta_x(p,a) = \begin{cases} pa, & \text{if } pa \in P_x; \\ \delta_x(f_x(p),a), & \text{otherwise.} \end{cases}$$

This means that we actually do not need to store δ. Indeed, we can simulate $\mathcal{A}'_x$ on any input word y by the following algorithm, one of the pearls of algorithm design, with the input x, f_x, y.

Algorithm 3.2.24 (Knuth–Morris–Pratt's string matching algorithm)

```
m ← |x|; n ← |y|, q ← 0;
for i ← 1 to n do while 0 < q < m and x_{q+1} ≠ y_i do q ← f_x(q) od;
        if q < m and x_{q+1} = y_i then q ← q+1;
        if q = m then print 'pattern found starting with (i − m)-th symbol';
                q ← f_x(q)
    od
```

$\mathcal{O}(m)$ steps are needed to compute f_x, and since q can get increased at most by 1 in an i- cycle, the overall time of Knuth–Morris–Pratt's algorithm is $\mathcal{O}(m+n)$. (Quite an improvement compared to $\mathcal{O}(mn)$ for the naïve algorithm.)

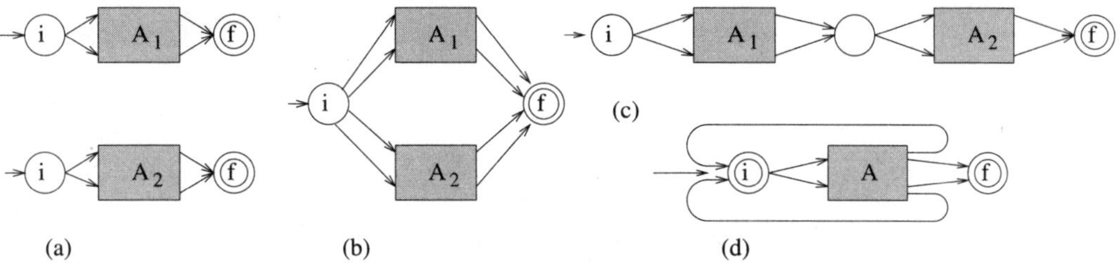

Figure 3.12 Closure of regular languages under union, concatenation and iteration

Exercise 3.2.25 *Compute the failure function for the patterns (a) aabaaabaaaab; (b) aabbaaabbb.*

Exercise 3.2.26 *Show in detail why the overall time complexity of Knuth–Morris–Pratt's algorithm is* $\mathcal{O}(m+n)$.

3.3 Regular Languages

Regular languages are one of the cornerstones of formal language theory, and they have many interesting and important properties.

3.3.1 Closure Properties

The family of regular languages is closed under all basic language operations. This fact can be utilized in a variety of ways, especially to simplify the design of FA recognizing given regular languages.

Theorem 3.3.1 *The family of regular languages is closed under the operations*

1. *union, concatenation, iteration, complementation and difference;*
2. *substitution, morphism and inverse morphism.*

Proof: To simplify the proof, we assume, in some parts of the proof, that the state graphs $G_{\mathcal{A}}$ of those FA we consider are in the normal form shown in Figure 3.12a: namely, there is no edge entering the input state i, and there is a single final state f with no outgoing edge. Given a FA $\mathcal{A} = \langle \Sigma, Q, q_0, Q_F, \delta \rangle$ accepting a regular language that does not contain the empty word, it is easy to construct an equivalent FA in the above normal form. Indeed, it is enough to add two new states, i – a new input state – and f – a new terminal state – and the following sets of state transitions:

- $\{(i,a,q) \mid (q_0,a,q) \in \delta\}$;
- $\{(p,a,f) \mid (p,a,q) \in \delta, q \in Q_F\}$;
- $\{(i,a,f) \mid (q_0,a,q) \in \delta, q \in Q_F\}$.

To simplify the proof of the theorem we assume, in addition, that languages we consider do not contain the empty word. The adjustments needed to prove the theorem in full generality are minor.

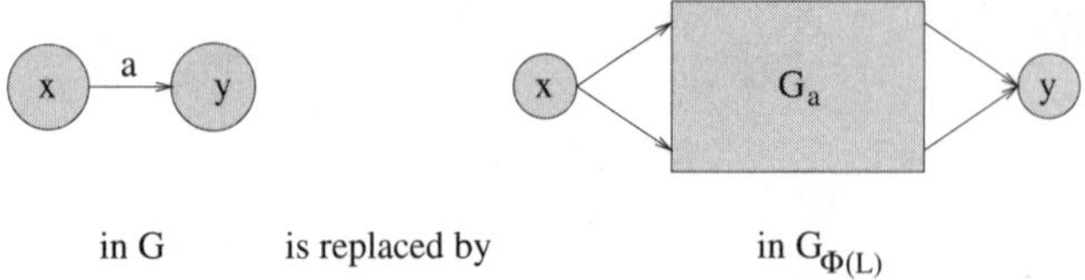

Figure 3.13 Closure of regular languages under substitution

For example, by taking the state i in Figure 3.12a as an additional terminal state, we add ε to the language.

Figures 3.12b, c, d show how to design a FA accepting the **union, concatenation** and **iteration** of regular languages provided that FA in the above normal form are given for these languages. (In the case of union, transitions from the new initial state lead exactly to those states to which transitions from the initial states of the two automata go. In the case of iteration, each transition to the final state is doubled, to go also to the initial state.)

Complementation. If $\mathcal{A}$ is a DFA over the alphabet Σ accepting a regular language L, then by exchanging final and nonfinal states in $\mathcal{A}$ we get a DFA accepting the complement of L – the language L^c. More formally, if $L = L(\mathcal{A})$, $\mathcal{A} = \langle \Sigma, Q, q_0, Q_F, \delta \rangle$, then $L^c = L(\mathcal{A}')$, where $\mathcal{A}' = \langle \Sigma, Q, q_0, Q - Q_F, \delta \rangle$.

Intersection. Let $L_1 = L(\mathcal{A}_1)$, $L_2 = L(\mathcal{A}_2)$, where $\mathcal{A}_1 = \langle \Sigma, Q_1, q_{1,0}, Q_{1,F}, \delta_1 \rangle$ and $\mathcal{A}_2 = \langle \Sigma, Q_2, q_{2,0}, Q_{2,F}, \delta_2 \rangle$ are DFA. The intersection $L_1 \cap L_2$ is clearly the language accepted by the DFA

$$\langle \Sigma, Q_1 \times Q_2, (q_{1,0}, q_{2,0}), Q_{1,F} \times Q_{2,F}, \delta \rangle,$$

where $\delta((p,q),a) = (\delta_1(p,a), \delta_2(q,a))$ for any $p \in Q_1$, $q \in Q_2$ and $a \in \Sigma$.

Difference. Since $L_1 - L_2 = L_1 \cap L_2^c$ the closure of regular languages under difference follows from their closure under complementation and intersection.

Substitution. Let $\phi : \Sigma \rightarrow 2^{\Sigma_1^*}$ be a substitution such that $\phi(a)$ is a regular language for each $a \in \Sigma$. Let L be a regular language over Σ, and $L = L(\mathcal{A})$, $\mathcal{A} = \langle \Sigma, Q, q_0, Q_F, \delta \rangle$. For each $a \in \Sigma$ let G_a be the state graph in the normal form for the language $\phi(a)$. To get the state graph for a FA accepting the language $\phi(L)$ from the state graph $G_{\mathcal{A}}$, it suffices to replace in $G_{\mathcal{A}}$ any edge labelled by an $a \in \Sigma$ by the state graph G_a in the way shown in Figure 3.13.

The closure of regular languages under **morphism** follows from the closure under substitution.

Inverse morphism. Let $\phi : \Sigma \rightarrow \Sigma_1^*$ be a morphism, $L \subset \Sigma_1^*$ a regular language, $L = L(\mathcal{A})$ for a FA $\mathcal{A}$. As defined in Section 2.5.1,

$$\phi^{-1}(L) = \{ w \in \Sigma^* \mid \phi(w) \in L \}.$$

Let $G_{\mathcal{A}} = \langle V, E \rangle$ be the state graph for $\mathcal{A}$. The state graph $G_{\phi^{-1}(L)}$ for a FA recognizing the language $\phi^{-1}(L)$ will have the same set of nodes (states) as $G_{\mathcal{A}}$ and the same set of final nodes (states). For any $a \in \Sigma$, $q \in V$ there will be an edge (p, a, q) in $G_{\phi^{-1}(L)}$ if and only if $p \overset{*}{\underset{\phi(a)}{\Longrightarrow}} q$ in $\mathcal{A}$. Clearly, w is a label of a path in $G_{\phi^{-1}(L)}$, from the initial to a final node, if and only if $\phi(w) \in L$. □

Using the results of Theorem 3.3.1 it is now easy to see that regular languages form a Kleene algebra. Actually, regular languages were the original motivation for the introduction and study of Kleene algebras.

Exercise 3.3.2 *Show that if $L \subseteq \Sigma^*$ is a regular language, then so are the languages (a) $L^R = \{w \mid w^R \in L\}$; (b) $\{u\}^{-1}L$, where $u \in \Sigma^*$.*

3.3.2 Regular Expressions

There are various formal systems that can be used to describe exactly regular languages. (That is, each language they describe is regular, and they can be used to describe any regular language.) The most important is that of **regular expressions.** They will now be defined inductively, together with their semantics (interpretation), a mapping that assigns a regular language to any regular expression.

Definition 3.3.3 *A regular expression E, over an alphabet Σ, is an expression formed using the following rules, and represents the language $L(E)$ defined as follows:*

1. *$\emptyset$ is a regular expression, and $L(\emptyset) = \emptyset$.*
2. *a is a regular expression for any $a \in \Sigma \cup \{\varepsilon\}$ and $L(a) = \{a\}$.*
3. *If E_1, E_2 are regular expressions, then so are*

$$(E_1 + E_2),\ (E_1 \cdot E_2),\ (E_1^*)$$

   and

$$L((E_1 + E_2)) = L(E_1) \cup L(E_2),\ L((E_1 \cdot E_2)) = L(E_1) \cdot L(E_2),\ L((E_1^*)) = L(E_1^*),$$

   respectively.

4. *There are no other regular expressions over Σ.*

Remark 3.3.4 Several conventions are used to simplify regular expressions. First, the following priority of operators is assumed: $*, \cdot, +$. Second, the operators of concatenation are usually omitted. This allows us to omit most of the parentheses. For example, a regular expression describing a word $w = a_1 \ldots a_n$ is usually written as $a_1a_2 \ldots a_n$ and not $(\ldots((a_1.a_2).a_3)\ldots a_n)$. Finally, the expression $\{w_1, \ldots, w_n\}$ is used to denote the finite language containing the words $w_1, \ldots, w_n$.

Example 3.3.5 $\{0,1\}^*$, $\{0,1\}^*000\{0,1\}^*$ *and* $\{a,b\}^*c\{a,b\}^*c\{a,b\}^*$ *are regular expressions.*

Regular expressions and finite automata

The following theorem, identifying languages accepted by finite automata and described by regular expressions, is one of the cornerstones of formal language and automata theory, as well as of their applications.

Theorem 3.3.6 (Kleene's theorem) *A language L is regular if and only if there is a regular expression E such that $L = L(E)$.*

Proof: It follows from Theorem 3.3.1 that each language described by a regular expression is regular. To finish the proof of the theorem, it is therefore sufficient to show how to design, given a DFA $\mathcal{A}$, a regular expression $E_{\mathcal{A}}$ such that $L(E_{\mathcal{A}}) = L(\mathcal{A})$. This is quite a straightforward task once a proper notation is introduced.

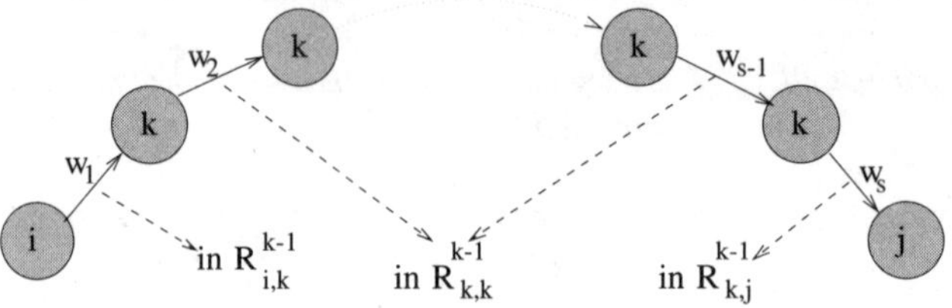

Figure 3.14 Decomposition of a computational path for a word $w \in R^k_{i,j}$, $w = w_1w_2 \ldots w_s$

Let $\mathcal{A} = \langle \Sigma, Q, q_0, Q_F, \delta \rangle$. Without loss of generality we assume that $Q = \{0, 1, \ldots, n\}$, $q_0 = 0$ and consider, for $0 \le i, j \le n$, $-1 \le k \le n$, the set R^k_{ij} defined by

$$R^k_{i,j} = \{w \in \Sigma^* \mid \delta(i,w) = j \text{ and } \delta(i,u) \le k \text{ for any proper prefix } u \text{ of } w\}.$$

In other words, the set $R^k_{i,j}$ contains those strings that make $\mathcal{A}$ go from state i to state j passing only through states in the set $\{0, 1, \ldots, k\}$. Clearly,

$$R^{-1}_{i,j} = \{a \mid \delta(i,a) = j\} \cup \{\varepsilon \mid \text{if } i = j\} \subseteq \Sigma \cup \{\varepsilon\},$$

and therefore there is a regular expression representing $R^{-1}_{i,j}$. Since

$$L(A) = \bigcup_{j \in Q_F} R^n_{0,j},$$

in order to prove the theorem, it suffices to show the validity of the recurrence (3.1) for any $R^k_{i,j}$:

$$R^k_{i,j} = \begin{cases} \emptyset, & \text{if } k = -1, i \neq j, \delta(i,a) \neq j; \\ \{a\}, & \text{if } k = -1, i \neq j, \delta(i,a) = j; \\ \{\varepsilon\}, & \text{if } k = -1, i = j, \delta(i,a) \neq j; \\ \{\varepsilon, a\}, & \text{if } k = -1, i = j, \delta(i,a) = j; \\ R^{k-1}_{i,j} \cup R^{k-1}_{i,k}(R^{k-1}_{k,k})^* R^{k-1}_{k,j}, & \text{if } k \ge 0. \end{cases} \tag{3.1}$$

Once this is done, it is straightforward to show by induction that for each language $R^k_{i,j}$ there is a regular expression representing it.

However, the validity of the recurrence (3.1) is actually easy to see. Any path in $G_{\mathcal{A}}$ from a state i to a state j that passes only through states $\{0, 1, \ldots, k\}$ can be decomposed into subpaths that may contain the state k only at the beginning or the end of the path (if the state k occurs on the path at all). See Figure 3.14 for the case that the state k occurs several times. These subpaths belong to one of the subsets $R^{k-1}_{i,k}$ or $R^{k-1}_{k,k}$ or $R^{k-1}_{k,j}$. □

Two regular expressions E_1 and E_2 are said to be equivalent if they describe the same language. Some of the most basic pairs of equivalent regular expressions are listed in the right-hand column of Table 2.1.

Exercise 3.3.7 *Determine which of the following equalities between regular languages are valid:*
(a)$(011 + (10)^*1 + 0)^* = 011(011 + (10)^*1 + 0)^*$;
(b) $((1+0)^*100(1+0)^*)^* = ((1+0)100(1+0)^*100)^*$.

Design of finite automata from regular expressions

One of the advantages of regular expressions is that they specify a regular language in a natural way in a linear form, by a string. Regular expressions are therefore very convenient as a specification language for regular languages, especially for processing on computers. An important practical problem is to design, given a regular expression E, a FA (or a DFA) that recognizes the language $L(E)$. An elegant way of doing this, by using the **derivatives of regular expressions**, will now be described. However, in order to do so, a proper notation has to be introduced.

For a regular expression E let $\rho(E)$ be a regular expression that is equal to ε if $\varepsilon \in L(E)$, and to $\emptyset$ otherwise. (That is, $\rho(E)F$ equals F if the empty word is in $L(E)$, and $\emptyset$ otherwise.) To compute $\rho(E)$ for a regular expression E, we can use the following inductive definition of ρ (where $a \in \Sigma$):

$$\begin{array}{lllllll} \rho(\emptyset) & = & \emptyset, & \rho(\varepsilon) & = & \varepsilon, & \rho(E+F) = \rho(E)+\rho(F), \\ \rho(a) & = & \emptyset, & \rho(E^*) & = & \varepsilon, & \rho(E\cdot F) = \rho(E)\cdot\rho(F). \end{array}$$

Definition 3.3.8 *The derivative of a regular expression E by a symbol a, notation $a^{-1}E$, is a regular expression defined recursively by $a^{-1}\emptyset = \emptyset$ and*

$$\begin{array}{lllllllll} a^{-1}\varepsilon & = & \emptyset, & a^{-1}b & = & \emptyset, \text{ if } a \neq b, & a^{-1}(E^*) & = & (a^{-1}E)\cdot E^*, \\ a^{-1}a & = & \varepsilon, & a^{-1}(E+F) & = & a^{-1}E + a^{-1}F, & a^{-1}(E\cdot F) & = & (a^{-1}E)F + \rho(E)a^{-1}F. \end{array}$$

The extension from the derivatives by symbols to derivatives by words is defined by $\varepsilon^{-1}E = E$ and $(wa)^{-1}E = a^{-1}(w^{-1}E)$.

It can be shown that with respect to any regular expression E the set Σ^* is partitioned into the equivalence classes with respect to the relation $w_1 \equiv w_2$ if $w_1^{-1}E = w_2^{-1}E$. $S_E = \{F \mid \exists w \in \Sigma^* : F = w^{-1}E\}$ has only finitely many equivalence classes with respect to the equivalence of regular expressions.

The following method can be used to design, given a regular expression E, a DFA $\mathcal{A}_E$ recognizing the language $L(E)$:

1. The state set of $\mathcal{A}_E$ is given by the set of equivalence classes with respect to the relation $\equiv$. We write w^{-1} for $[w]$.

2. For any state $[w]$ and any symbol $a \in \Sigma$ there will be a single transition from $w^{-1}E$: namely, that into the state $[wa]$.

3. The equivalence class for the whole expression E is the initial state. A state $w^{-1}E$ is final if and only if $\varepsilon \in L(w^{-1}E)$.

To illustrate the method, let us consider the regular expression $E = \{a,b\}^*a\{a,b\}\{a,b\}$. Using the notation $S = \{a,b\}$ we have $E = S^*aSS$. For derivatives we get:

$$\begin{array}{rclrcl} a^{-1}E & = & E+SS, & b^{-1}E & = & E, \\ (aa)^{-1}E & = & E+SS+S, & (ab)^{-1}E & = & E+S, \\ (aaa)^{-1}E & = & E+SS+S+\{\varepsilon\}, & (aab)^{-1}E & = & E+S+\{\varepsilon\}, \\ (aba)^{-1}E & = & E+SS+\{\varepsilon\}, & (abb)^{-1}E & = & E+\{\varepsilon\}. \end{array}$$

It is easy to verify that no two of these regular expressions are equivalent, and that further derivations do not provide new regular expressions. The resulting state graph is shown in Figure 3.15. Observe that it is the same state diagram as the one in Figure 3.9c, the state diagram obtained from the one in Figure 3.9b by the subset construction. The algorithm just presented for designing a DFA accepting the language described by a regular expression always provides the minimal DFA with this property.

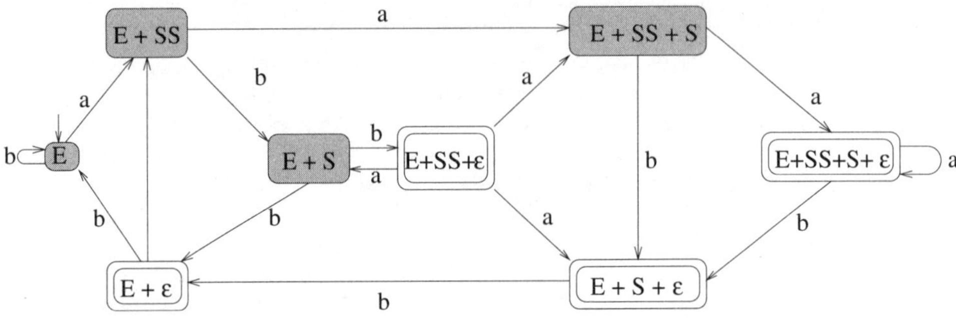

Figure 3.15 A DFA accepting the language represented by the regular expression $\{a,b\}^*a\{a,b\}\{a,b\}$ and designed using derivatives of regular expressions

Exercise 3.3.9 *Use the method of derivatives to design a DFA equivalent to the following regular expressions: (a)* $\{a,b\}^*aba\{a,b\}^*$*; (b)* $\{a,b\}^*\{ab,ba\}\{a,b\}^*$.

Exercise 3.3.10 *Show that the method of derivatives always creates the minimal DFA for a given language. (Hint: show that for each string* w*,* $w^{-1}E$ *is the state of the minimal DFA that is reached from the initial state by the input* w*.)*

On the other hand, using the ideas presented in the proof of Theorem 3.3.1, given a regular expression, one can design a NFA accepting the same language in linear time.

Exercise 3.3.11 *Design a NFA describing the same language as the following regular expressions: (a)* $\{\{a,b\}^*aaa\{a,b\}^*\}^*$*; (b)* $aaa\{ab,ba\}^* + aaa\{aa,bb\}^*$.

3.3.3 Decision Problems

Finite automata and regular expressions can be seen as two different specification tools for describing regular languages. But how different are they really? One way of understanding the difference is to compare the computational complexity of some main decision problems for DFA and regular expressions.

The membership problem. This is the problem of deciding whether, given a regular expression E, over an alphabet Σ, and a $w \in \Sigma^*$, $w \in L(E)$. This can be done in time $\mathcal{O}(|w||E|^2)$. Indeed, in time $\mathcal{O}(|E|)$ one can design a NFA $\mathcal{A}_E$ accepting the same language as E, and then, for each symbol of w in time $\mathcal{O}(|E|^2)$, calculate the potential states when simulating acceptance of w on $\mathcal{A}_E$.

Exercise 3.3.12 *Design in detail an algorithm that decides, given a NFA $\mathcal{A}$ and a word w, whether $w \in L(\mathcal{A})$.*

The emptiness problem and the **finiteness problem** are, on the other hand, very easy (here we assume that the symbol for the empty language is not used within the expression). They require time proportional to the length of regular expressions. Indeed, if E contains a symbol from Σ, then the language $L(E)$ is nonempty. Similarly, if E contains a symbol from Σ in the scope of an iteration operator, then the language is infinite, and only in such a case.

Exercise 3.3.13 *Show how to decide, given a FA $\mathcal{A}$ over the alphabet Σ, whether $L(\mathcal{A}) = \Sigma^*$.*

The equivalence problem for regular expressions is, as for NFA, **PSPACE**-complete.

In the rest of this section we discuss the equivalence problem for generalized regular expressions in order to illustrate how the computational complexity of a problem can be altered by a seemingly inessential change in the language used to describe input data. (We shall come to this problem again in Section 5.11.)

The idea of considering some generalized regular expressions is reasonable. We have seen in Section 3.3.1 that the family of regular languages is closed under a variety of operations. Therefore, in principle, we could enhance the language of regular expressions with all these operations: for example, with complementation and intersection, to be very modest. This would in no way increase the descriptional power of such expressions, if measured solely by the family of languages they describe.

Such generalizations of regular expressions look very natural. However, there are good reasons for not using them, unless there are special contra-indications. **Complementation and intersection have enormous descriptive power**. They can be used to describe succinctly various 'complex' regular languages. This in turn can make working with them enormously difficult. One can see this from the following surprising result concerning the equivalence problem for generalized regular expressions.

Theorem 3.3.14 *The following lower bound holds for the sequential time complexity $T(n)$ of any algorithm that can decide whether two generalized regular expressions with the operations of union, concatenation and complementation, of length n, are equivalent:*

$$T(n) = \Omega\left(2^{\left.2^{\cdot^{\cdot^{2^n}}}\right\}\log n \text{ times}}\right)$$

An even higher lower bound has been obtained for algorithms deciding the equivalence of regular expressions when the iteration operation is also allowed.

Why is this? There is a simple explanation. Using the operation of complementation, one can enormously shorten the description of some regular expressions. Since the time for deciding equivalence is measured with respect to the length of the input (and regular expressions with operations of negation can be very short), the resulting time can be very large indeed.

Example 3.3.15 *If Σ is an alphabet, $|\Sigma| \geq 2$, $x \neq y \in \Sigma^*$, then $\overline{\{x\}}$ and $\overline{(\Sigma^* x \Sigma^*)} \cap \overline{(\Sigma^* y \Sigma^*)}$ are simple examples of generalized regular expressions for which the corresponding regular expressions are much more complex.*

Exercise 3.3.16 *Give regular expressions that describe the same language as the following generalized regular expressions for* $\Sigma = \{a,b,c\}$: *(a)* $\overline{(\Sigma^* \cdot \{abc\} \cdot \Sigma^*)}$; *(b)* $\overline{(\Sigma^* \cdot \{aba\} \cdot \Sigma^*)} \cap \overline{(\Sigma^* \cdot \{bcb\} \cdot \Sigma^*)}$.

3.3.4 Other Characterizations of Regular Languages

In addition to FA and regular expressions, there are many other ways in which regular languages can be described and characterized. In this section we deal with three of them. The first concerns syntactical monoids (see Section 2.6.2).

Let $L \subseteq \Sigma^*$ be a language. The **context** of a string $w \in \Sigma^*$, with respect to L, is defined by

$$C_L(w) = \{(u,v) \mid uwv \in L\}.$$

The relation $\equiv_L$ on $\Sigma^* \times \Sigma^*$, defined by

$$x \equiv_L y \Longleftrightarrow C_L(x) = C_L(y),$$

is clearly an equivalence relation (the so-called **syntactical equivalence**). In addition, it is a congruence in the free monoid $(\Sigma^*, \cdot)$, because

$$x_1 \equiv_L y_1, x_2 \equiv_L y_2 \;\Rightarrow\; x_1x_2 \equiv_L y_1y_2.$$

This implies that the set of equivalence classes $[w]_L$, $w \in \Sigma^*$, with respect to the relation $\equiv_L$ and the operation $[w_1]_L \cdot [w_2]_L = [w_1w_2]_L$ forms a monoid, the **syntactical monoid** of L.

Theorem 3.3.17 (Myhill's theorem) *A language L is regular if and only if its syntactical monoid is finite.*

Proof: Let L be a regular language and $L = L(\mathcal{A})$ for a DFA $\mathcal{A} = \langle \Sigma, Q, q_0, Q_F, \delta \rangle$. For any $p \in Q$ let $l(p) = \{w \mid \delta(q_0, w) = p\}$. Moreover, for any $w \in \Sigma^*$ let $S_w = \{(p,q) \mid \delta(p,w) = q\}$. Clearly,

$$C_L(w) = \bigcup_{(p,q) \in S_w} l(p) \times L(q).$$

Since the number of different sets S_w is finite, so is the number of contexts $C_L(w)$; therefore the syntactical monoid of L is finite.

Now let us assume that the syntactical monoid $\mathcal{M}$ for a language $L \subseteq \Sigma^*$ is finite. We design a DFA recognizing L as follows. Elements of $\mathcal{M}$, that is the equivalence classes with respect to the relation $\equiv_L$, will be the states, with $[\varepsilon]_L$ the initial state. States of the form $[w]_L, w \in L$ will be the final states. For a state $[w]$ and a symbol $a \in \Sigma$ there will be a transition $([w]_L, a, [wa]_L)$. Clearly, the resulting DFA recognizes L. □

The second characterization is in terms of the **prefix equivalence** $\equiv_L^p$ defined for a language $L \in \Sigma^*$ by

$$w_1 \equiv_L^p w_2 \iff \forall u \in \Sigma^* (w_1 u \in L \Leftrightarrow w_2 u \in L).$$

Theorem 3.3.18 (Nerode's theorem) *A language L is regular if and only if its prefix equivalence has finitely many equivalence classes. If a language L is regular, then the number of its prefix equivalence classes equals the number of states of the minimal DFA for L.*

Proof: (1) If L is regular, then by Myhill's theorem the set of syntactical equivalence classes of L is finite. Since $u \equiv_L w \Rightarrow u \equiv_L^p w$, the set of prefix equivalence classes of L has to be finite also.

(2) Let the number of prefix equivalence classes $[w]_L^p$ be finite. These classes will be the states of a DFA $\mathcal{A}$ that will recognize L, and is defined as follows. $[\varepsilon]_L^p$ is the initial state and $\{[w]_L^p \mid w \in L\}$ are final states. The transition function δ is defined by $\delta([w]_L^p, a) = [wa]_L^p$. Since $w_1 \equiv_L^p w_2 \Rightarrow w_1 a \equiv_L^p w_2 a$ for all w_1, w_2 and a, δ is therefore well defined, and $\mathcal{A}$ clearly recognizes L.

The resulting DFA has to be minimal, because no two of its states are equivalent; this follows from the definition of prefix equivalence classes. □

Exercise 3.3.19 *Show that syntactical monoids of the following languages are infinite (and therefore these languages are not regular): (a)* $\{a^n b^n \mid n > 0\}$*; (b)* $\{a^i \mid i \text{ is prime}\}$.

Exercise 3.3.20 *Determine the syntax equivalence and prefix equivalence classes for the following languages: (a)* $\{a,b\}^* aa \{a,b\}^*$*; (b)* $\{a^i b^j \mid i,j \geq 1\}$.

Nerode's theorem can also be used to derive lower bounds on the number of states of DFA for certain regular languages.

Example 3.3.21 *Consider the language* $L_n = \{a,b\}^* a \{a,b\}^{n-1}$. *Let* x, y *be two different strings in* $\{a,b\}^n$, *and let them differ in the i-th left-most symbol. Clearly,* $xb^{i-1} \in L \Longleftrightarrow yb^{i-1} \notin L$, *because one of the strings* xb^{i-1} *and* yb^{i-1} *has a and the second b in the n-th position from the right. This implies that* L_n *has at least* 2^n *prefix equivalence classes, and therefore each DFA for* L_n *has to have at least* 2^n *states.*

Exercise 3.3.22 *Design an* $n+1$ *state NFA for the language* L_n *from Example 3.3.21 (and show in this way that for* L_n *there is an exponential difference between the minimal number of states of NFA and DFA recognizing* L_n*).*

Exercise 3.3.23 *Show that the minimal deterministic FA to accept the language* $L = \{w \mid \#_a w \bmod k = 0\} \subseteq \{a,b\}^*$ *has k states, and that no NFA with less than k states can recognize L.*

Example 3.3.24 (Recognition of regular languages in logarithmic time) *We show now how to use the syntactical monoid of a regular language L to design an infinite balanced-tree network of processors (see Figure 3.16) recognizing L in parallel logarithmic time.*

Since the number of syntactical equivalence classes of a regular language is finite, they can be represented by symbols of a finite alphabet. This will be used in the following design of a tree network of processors.

Each processor of the tree network has one external input. For a symbol $a \in \Sigma$ on its external input the processor produces as an output symbol representing the (syntactical equivalence) class $[a]_L$. For the input $\#$, a special marker, on its external input the processor produces as the output symbol representing the class $[\varepsilon]_L$.

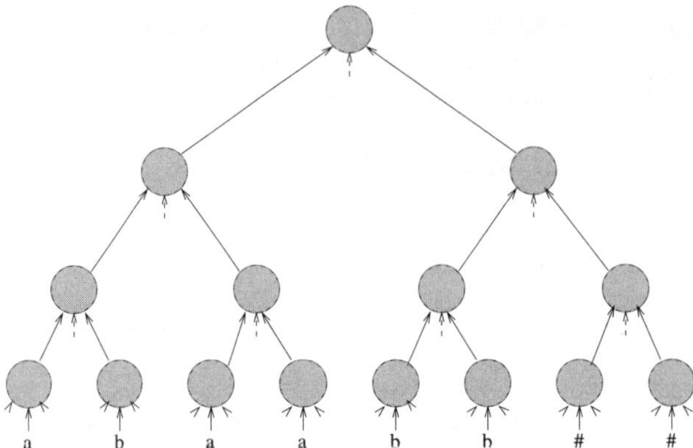

Figure 3.16 Tree automaton recognizing a regular language

The tree automaton works as follows. An input word $w = a_1 \ldots a_n \in \Sigma^*$ is given, one symbol per processor, to the external inputs of the left-most processors of the topmost level of processors that has at least $|w|$ processors. The remaining processors at that level receive, at their external inputs, the marker # (see Figure 3.16 for $n = 6$). All processors of the input level process their inputs simultaneously, and send their results to their parents. (Processors of all larger levels are 'cut off' in such a computation.) Processing in the network then goes on, synchronized, from one level to another, until the root processor is reached. All processors of these levels process only internal inputs; no external inputs are provided. An input word w is accepted if and only if at the end of this processing the root processor produces a symbol from the set $\{[w]_L \mid w \in L\}$.

It is clear that such a network of memory-less processors accepts the language L. It is a simple and fast network; it works in logarithmic time, and therefore much faster than a DFA. However, there is a price to pay for this. It can be shown that in some cases for a regular language accepted by a NFA with n states, the corresponding syntactical monoid may have up to n^n elements. The price to be paid for recognition of regular languages in logarithmic time by a binary tree network of processors can therefore be very high in terms of the size of the processors (they need to process a large class of inputs), and it can also be shown that in some cases there is no way to avoid paying such a price.

Exercise 3.3.25 *Design a tree automaton that recognizes the language (a) $\{a^{2^n} \mid n \geq 0\}$ (note that this language is not regular); (b) $\{w \mid w \in \{a\}^*\{b\}^*, |w| = 2^k, k \geq 1\}$.*

3.4 Finite Transducers

Deterministic finite automata are recognizers. However, they can also be seen as computing characteristic functions of regular languages – the output of a DFA $\mathcal{A}$ is 1 (0) for a given input w if $\mathcal{A}$ comes to a terminal (nonterminal) state on the input w. In this section several models of finite state machines computing other functions, or even relations, are considered.

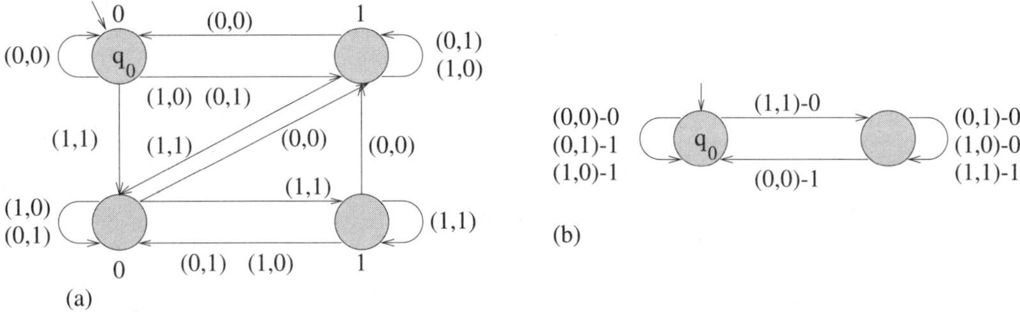

Figure 3.17 Moore and Mealy machines for serial addition

3.4.1 Mealy and Moore Machines

Two basic models of finite transducers, as models of finite state machines computing functions, are called the **Moore machine** and the **Mealy machine**. They formalize an intuitive idea of an input–output mapping realized by a finite state machine in two slightly different ways.

Definition 3.4.1 *In a* **Moore machine** $\mathcal{M} = \langle \Sigma, Q, q_0, \delta, \rho, \Delta \rangle$*, the symbols* Σ, Q, q_0 *and* δ *have the same meaning as for DFA,* Δ *is an* **output alphabet**, *and* $\rho : Q \to \Delta$ *an* **output function**.

For an input word $w = w_1 \dots w_n$, $w_i \in \Sigma$, $\rho(q_0)\rho(q_1)\dots\rho(q_n)$ is the corresponding output word, where $q_i = \delta(q_0, w_1 \dots w_i), 1 \le i \le n$. In a Moore machine the outputs are therefore 'produced by states'. Figure 3.17a shows a Moore machine for a serial addition of two binary numbers. (It is assumed that both numbers are represented by binary strings of the same length (leading zeros are appended if necessary), and for numbers $x_n \dots x_1, y_n \dots y_1$ the input is a sequence of pairs $(x_1,y_1), \dots, (x_n,y_n)$ in this order. Observe also that the output always starts with one 0 which is then followed by output bits of $bin^{-1}(bin(x_n, \dots, x_1) \times bin(y_n \dots y_1)$.

Definition 3.4.2 *In a* **Mealy machine** $\mathcal{M} = \langle \Sigma, Q, q_0, \delta, \rho, \Delta \rangle$, *symbols* $\Sigma, Q, q_o, \delta, \Delta$ *have the same meaning as in a Moore machine, and* $\rho : Q \times \Sigma \to \Delta$ *is an* **output function**.

For an input word $w = w_1 \dots w_n$, $w_i \in \Sigma$, $\rho(q_0, w_1) \dots \rho(q_{n-1}, w_n)$ is the corresponding output word, where $q_i = \delta(q_0, w_1 \dots w_i)$. Outputs are therefore produced by transitions. Figure 3.17b shows a Mealy machine for the serial addition of two binary numbers $x = x_1 \dots x_n, y = y_1 \dots y_n$, with inputs presented as above.

Let us now denote by $T_{\mathcal{M}}(w)$ the output produced by a Moore or a Mealy machine $\mathcal{M}$ for the input w. For a Moore machine $|T_{\mathcal{M}}(w)| = |w| + 1$ and for a Mealy machine $|T_{\mathcal{M}}(w)| = |w|$. A Moore machine can therefore never be fully equivalent to a Mealy machine. However, it is easy to see that for any Moore machine there is a Mealy machine (and vice versa) such that they are equivalent in the following slightly weaker sense.

Theorem 3.4.3 *For every Mealy machine* $\mathcal{M}$ *over an alphabet* Σ *there is a Moore machine* $\mathcal{M}'$ *over* Σ *(and vice versa) such that* $\rho(q_0)T_{\mathcal{M}}(w) = T_{\mathcal{M}'}(w)$, *for every input* $w \in \Sigma^*$, *where* ρ *is the output function of* $\mathcal{M}'$.

Exercise 3.4.4 *Design (a) a Moore machine (b) a Mealy machine, such that given an integer x in binary form, the machine produces* $\lfloor \frac{x}{3} \rfloor$.

Exercise 3.4.5* *Design (a) a Mealy machine (b) a Moore machine that transforms a Fibonacci representation of a number into its normal form.*

Exercise 3.4.6 *Design a Mealy machine* $\mathcal{M}$ *that realizes a 3-step delay. (That is,* $\mathcal{M}$ *outputs at time t its input at time* $t-3$*.)*

3.4.2 Finite State Transducers

The concept of a Mealy machine will now be generalized to that of a finite state transducer. One new idea is added: nondeterminism.

Definition 3.4.7 *A* **finite (state) transducer** *(FT for short)* $\mathcal{T}$ *is described by a finite set of* **states** Q*, a finite* **input alphabet** Σ*, a finite* **output alphabet** Δ*, the initial state* q_0 *and a finite* **transition relation** $\rho \subseteq Q \times \Sigma^* \times \Delta^* \times Q$*. For short,* $\mathcal{T} = \langle Q, \Sigma, \Delta, q_0, \rho \rangle$.

A FT $\mathcal{T}$ can also be represented by a graph, $G_{\mathcal{T}}$, with states from Q as vertices. There is an edge in $G_{\mathcal{T}}$ from a state p to a state q, labelled by (u,v), if and only if $(p,u,v,q) \in \rho$. Such an edge is interpreted as follows: the input u makes $\mathcal{T}$ transfer from state p to state q and produces v as the output.

Each finite transducer $\mathcal{T}$ defines a relation

$$\begin{aligned} R_{\mathcal{T}} &= \{(u,v) \mid \exists (q_0,u_0,v_0,q_1),(q_1,u_1,v_1,q_2),\ldots,(q_n,u_n,v_n,q_{n+1}), \\ &\quad \text{where } (q_i,u_i,v_i,q_{i+1}) \in \rho, \text{for } 0 \le i \le n, \text{ and } u = u_0 \ldots u_n, v = v_0 \ldots v_n\}. \end{aligned}$$

The relation $R_{\mathcal{T}}$ can also be seen as a mapping from subsets of Σ^* into subsets of Δ^* such that for $L \subseteq \Sigma^*$ $R_{\mathcal{T}}(L) = \{v \mid \exists u \in L, (u,v) \in R_{\mathcal{T}}\}$.

Perhaps the most important fact about finite transducers is that they map regular languages into regular languages.

Theorem 3.4.8 *Let* $\mathcal{T} = \langle Q, \Sigma, \Delta, q_0, \rho \rangle$ *be a finite transducer. If* $L \subseteq \Sigma^*$ *is a regular language, then so is* $R_{\mathcal{T}}(L)$.

Proof: Let $\Delta' = \Delta \cup \{\#\}$ be a new alphabet with $\#$ as a new symbol not in Δ. From the relation ρ we first design a finite subset $A_\rho \subset Q \times \Sigma^* \times \Delta'^* \times Q$ and then take A_ρ as a new alphabet. A_ρ is designed by a decomposition of productions of ρ. We start with A_ρ being empty, and for each production of ρ we add to A_ρ symbols defined according to the following rules:

1. If $(p,u,v,q) \in \rho$, $|u| \le 1$, then (p,u,v,q) is taken into A_ρ.

2. If $r = (p,u,v,q) \in \rho$, $|u| > 1$, $u = u_1 \ldots u_k$, $1 \le i \le k$, $u_i \in \Sigma$, then new symbols $t_1^r, \ldots, t_{k-1}^r$ are chosen, and all quadruples

$$(p,u_1,\#,t_1^r),(t_1^r,u_2,\#,t_2^r),\ldots,(t_{k-2}^r,u_{k-1},\#,t_{k-1}^r),(t_{k-1}^r,u_k,v,q)$$

are taken into A_ρ.

Now let Q_L be the subset of A_ρ^* consisting of strings of the form

$$(q_0,u_0,v_0,q_1)(q_1,u_1,v_1,q_2)\dots(q_s,u_s,v_s,q_{s+1}) \tag{3.2}$$

such that $v_s \neq \#$ and $u_0u_1\dots u_s \in L$. That is, Q_L consists of strings that describe a computation of $\mathcal{T}$ for an input $u = u_0u_1\dots u_s \in L$. Finally, let $\tau : A_\rho \mapsto \Delta'^*$ be the morphism defined by

$$\tau((p,u,v,q)) = \begin{cases} v, & \text{if } v \neq \#; \\ \varepsilon, & \text{otherwise.} \end{cases}$$

From the way $\mathcal{T}$ and Q_L are constructed it is readily seen that $\tau(Q_L) = R_{\mathcal{T}}(L)$.

It is also straightforward to see that if L is regular, then Q_L is regular too. Indeed, a FA $\mathcal{A}$ recognizing Q_L can be designed as follows. A FA recognizing L is used to check whether the second components of symbols of a given word w form a word in L. In parallel, a check is made on whether w represents a computation of $\mathcal{T}$ ending with a state in Q. To verify this, the automaton needs always to remember only one of the previous symbols of w; this can be done by a finite automaton.

As shown in Theorem 3.3.1, the family of regular languages is closed under morphisms. This implies that the language $R_{\mathcal{T}}(L)$ is regular. □

Mealy machines are a special case of finite transducers, as are the following generalizations of Mealy machines.

Definition 3.4.9 *In a* **generalized sequential machine** $\mathcal{M} = \langle Q,\Sigma,\Delta,q_0,\delta,\rho\rangle$, *symbols* Q,Σ,Δ *and* q_0 *have the same meaning as for finite transducers,* $\delta : Q\times\Sigma \rightarrow Q$ *is a transition mapping, and* $\rho : Q\times\Sigma\rightarrow\Delta^*$ *is an output mapping.*

Computation on a generalized sequential machine is defined exactly as for a Mealy machine. Let $f_{\mathcal{M}} : \Sigma^* \rightarrow \Delta^*$ be the function defined by $\mathcal{M}$. For $L \subseteq \Sigma^*$ and $L' \subseteq \Delta^*$ we therefore consider $f_{\mathcal{M}}(L)$ and define $f_{\mathcal{M}}^{-1}(L') = \{u \mid u \in \Sigma^*, f_{\mathcal{M}}(u) \in L'\}$.

It follows from Theorem 3.4.8 that if $\mathcal{M}$ is a generalized sequential machine with the input alphabet Σ and the output alphabet Δ and $L \subseteq \Sigma^*$ is a regular language, then so is $f_{\mathcal{M}}(L)$. We show now that a reverse claim also holds: if $L' \subseteq \Delta^*$ is a regular language, then so is $f_{\mathcal{M}}^{-1}(L')$.

Indeed, let $\mathcal{M} = \langle Q,\Sigma,\Delta,q_0,\delta,\rho\rangle$. Consider the finite transducer $\mathcal{T} = \langle Q,\Delta,\Sigma,q_0,\delta'\rangle$ with $\delta' = \{(p,u,v,q) \mid \delta(p,u) = q, \rho(p,u) = v\} \cup \{(p,\varepsilon,\varepsilon,q)\}$. Clearly, $f_{\mathcal{M}}^{-1}(L') = R_{\mathcal{T}}(L')$ and, by Theorem 3.4.8, $f_{\mathcal{M}}^{-1}(L')$ is regular. Hence

Theorem 3.4.10 *If* $\mathcal{M}$ *is a generalized sequential machine, then mappings* $f_{\mathcal{M}}$ *and* $f_{\mathcal{M}}^{-1}$ *both preserve regular languages.*

In Section 3.3 we have seen automata-independent characterizations of languages recognized by FA. There exists also a machine-independent characterization of mappings defined by generalized sequential machines.

Theorem 3.4.11 *For a mapping* $f : \Sigma^* \rightarrow \Delta^*$, *there exists a generalized sequential machine* $\mathcal{M}$ *such that* $f = f_{\mathcal{M}}$, *if and only if* f *satisfies the following conditions:*

1. f *preserves prefixes; that is, if* u *is a prefix of* v, *then* $f(u)$ *is a prefix of* $f(v)$.

2. f *has a bounded output; that is, there exists an integer* k *such that* $|f(wa)| - |f(w)| \leq k$ *for any* $w \in \Sigma^*, a \in \Sigma$.

3. $f(\varepsilon) = \varepsilon$.

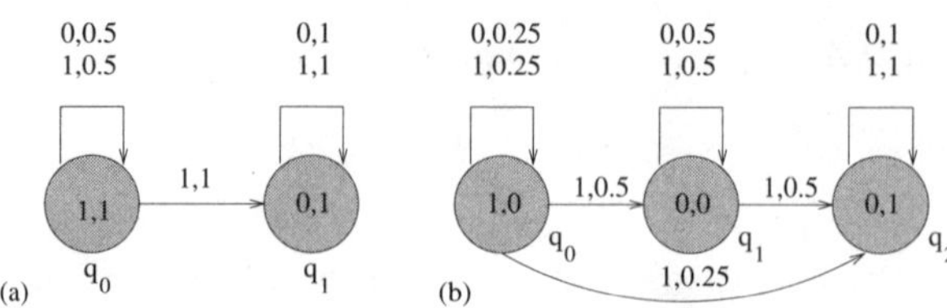

Figure 3.18 Two WFA computing functions on rationals and reals

4. *$f^{-1}(L)$ is a regular language if L is regular.*

Exercise 3.4.12 *Let f be the function defined by $f(a) = b, f(b) = a$ and $f(x) = x$ for $x \in \{a,b\}^* - \{a,b\}$. (a) Does f preserve regular languages? (b) Can f be realized by a generalized sequential machine?*

Exercise 3.4.13* *Show how to design, given a regular language R, a finite transducer $\mathcal{T}_R$ such that $\mathcal{T}_R(L) = L \diamond R$ (where $\diamond$ denotes the shuffle operation introduced in Section 2.5.1).*

3.5 Weighted Finite Automata and Transducers

A seemingly minor modification of the concepts of finite automata and transducers, an assignment of weights to transitions and states, results in finite state devices with unexpected computational power and importance for image processing. In addition, the weighted finite automata and the transducers introduced in this section illustrate a well-known experience that one often obtains powerful practical tools by slightly modifying and 'twisting' theoretical concepts.

3.5.1 Basic Concepts

The concept of a weighted finite automaton is both very simple and tricky at the same time. Let us therefore start with its informal interpretation for the case in which it is used to generate images. Each state p determines a function that assigns a greyness value to each pixel, represented by an input word w, and therefore it represents an image. This image is computed as follows: to each path starting in p and labelled by w a value (of greyness) is computed by multiplying the weights of all transitions along the path and, in addition, the so-called terminal weight of the final state of the path. These values are then added for all paths from p labelled by w. The initial weights of all nodes are then used to form a linear combination of these functions to get the final image-generating function. More formally,

Definition 3.5.1 *A* **weighted finite automaton** *(for short WFA) $\mathcal{A}$ is described by a finite set of* **input symbols** *Σ, a finite set of* **states** *Q, an* **initial distribution** *$i: Q \to \mathbf{R}$, and a* **terminal distribution** *$t: Q \to \mathbf{R}$ of states, as well as a* **weighted transition function** *$w: Q \times \Sigma \times Q \to \mathbf{R}$. In short, $\mathcal{A} = \langle \Sigma, Q, i, t, w \rangle$.*

To each WFA $\mathcal{A}$ we first associate the following distribution function $\delta_{\mathcal{A}}: Q \times \Sigma^* \to \mathbf{R}$:

$$\delta_{\mathcal{A}}(p,\varepsilon) = t(p); \qquad (3.3)$$

$$\delta_{\mathcal{A}}(p,au) = \sum_{q \in Q} w(p,a,q)\delta_{\mathcal{A}}(q,u) \text{ for each } p \in Q, a \in \Sigma, u \in \Sigma^*. \qquad (3.4)$$

A WFA $\mathcal{T}$ can be represented by a graph $G_{\mathcal{T}}$ (see Figures 3.18a, b) with states as vertices and transitions as edges. A vertex representing a state q is labelled by the pair $(i(q), t(q))$. If $w(p,a,q) = r$ is nonzero, then there is, in $G_{\mathcal{T}}$, a directed edge from p to q labelled by the pair (a, r).

A WFA $\mathcal{A}$ can now be seen as computing a function $f_{\mathcal{A}} : \Sigma^* \rightarrow \mathbf{R}$ defined by

$$f_{\mathcal{A}}(u) = \sum_{p \in Q} i(p)\delta_{\mathcal{A}}(p,u).$$

Informally, $\delta_{\mathcal{A}}(p,u)$ is the sum of all 'final weights' of all paths starting in p and labelled by u. The final weight of each path is obtained by multiplying the weights of all transitions on the path and also the final weight of the last node of the path. $f_{\mathcal{A}}(u)$ is then obtained by taking a linear combination of all $\delta_{\mathcal{A}}(p,u)$ defined by the initial distribution i.

Example 3.5.2 *For the WFA $\mathcal{A}_1$ in Figure 3.18a we get*

$$\delta_{\mathcal{A}_1}(q_0, 011) = 0.5 \cdot 0.5 \cdot 0.5 \cdot 1 + 0.5 \cdot 0.5 \cdot 1 \cdot 1 + 0.5 \cdot 1 \cdot 1 \cdot 1 = 0.875; \delta_{\mathcal{A}_1}(q_1, 011) = 1 \cdot 1 \cdot 1 \cdot 1 = 1,$$

and therefore $f_{\mathcal{A}_1}(011) = 1 \cdot 0.875 + 0 \cdot 1 = 0.875$. Similarly, $\delta_{\mathcal{A}_1}(q_0, 0101) = 0.625$ and $f_{\mathcal{A}_1}(0101) = 0.625$. For the WFA $\mathcal{A}_2$ in Figure 3.18b we get, for example,

$$\delta_{\mathcal{A}_2}(q_0, 0101) = 0.25 \cdot 0.5 \cdot 0.5 \cdot 1 \cdot 1 + 0.25 \cdot 0.25 \cdot 1 \cdot 1 \cdot 1 = 0.125,$$

and therefore also $f_{\mathcal{A}_2}(0101) = 0.125$.

Exercise 3.5.3 *Determine, for the WFA $\mathcal{A}_1$ in Figure 3.18a and for $\mathcal{A}_2$ in Figure 3.18b: (a) $\delta_{\mathcal{A}_1}(q_0, 10101), f_{\mathcal{A}_1}(10101)$; (b) $\delta_{\mathcal{A}_2}(q_0, 10101), f_{\mathcal{A}_1}(10101)$.*

Exercise 3.5.4 *Determine $f_{\mathcal{A}_3}(x)$ and $f_{\mathcal{A}_4}(x)$ for the WFA $\mathcal{A}_3$ and $\mathcal{A}_4$ obtained from $\mathcal{A}_1$ in Figure 3.18a by changing the initial and terminal distributions as follows: (a) $i(q_0) = 1$, $i(q_1) = 0$, $t(q_0) = 0$, and $t(q_1) = 1$; (b) $i(q_0) = i(q_1) = 1$, and $t(q_0) = t(q_1) = 1$.*

Exercise 3.5.5 *(a) Show that $f_{\mathcal{T}_1}(x) = 2bre(x) + 2^{-|x|}$ for the WFT $\mathcal{T}_1$ depicted in Figure 3.18. (b) determine functions computed by WFA obtained from the one in Figure 3.18a by considering several other initial and terminal distributions.*

If $\Sigma = \{0,1\}$ is the input alphabet of a WFA $\mathcal{A}$, then we can extend $f_{\mathcal{A}} : \Sigma^* \rightarrow \mathbf{R}$ to a (partial) **real function** $f_{\mathcal{A}}^{\omega} : [0,1] \rightarrow \mathbf{R}$ defined as follows: for $x \in [0,1]$ let $bre^{-1}(x) \in \Sigma^{\omega}$ be the unique binary representation of x (see page 81). Then

$$f_{\mathcal{A}}^{\omega}(x) = \lim_{n \rightarrow \infty} f_{\mathcal{A}}(Prefix_n(bre^{-1}(x))),$$

provided the limit exists; otherwise $f_{\mathcal{A}}^{\omega}(x)$ is undefined.

For the rest of this section, to simplify the presentation, a binary string $x_1 \ldots x_n$, $x_i \in \{0,1\}$ and an ω-string $y = y_1 y_2 \ldots$ over the alphabet $\{0,1\}$ will be interpreted, depending on the context, either as strings $x_1 \ldots x_n$ and $y_1 y_2 \ldots$ or as reals $0.x_1 \ldots x_n$ and $0.y_1 y_2 \ldots$. Instead of $bin(x)$ and $bre(y)$, we shall often write simply x or y and take them as strings or numbers.

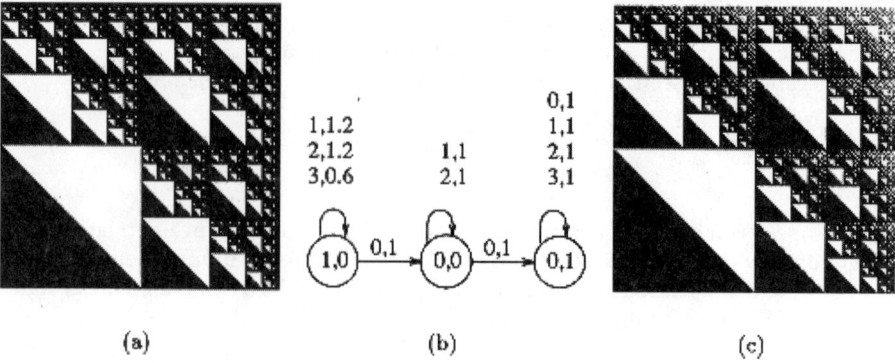

Figure 3.19 Generation of a fractal image

Exercise 3.5.6 *Show, for the WFA $\mathcal{A}_1$ in Figure 3.18a, that (a) if $x \in \Sigma^*$, then $f_{\mathcal{A}_1}(x0^n) = 2bre(x) + 2^{-(n+|x|)}$; (b) $f_{\mathcal{A}_1}(x) = 2bre(x)$.*

Exercise 3.5.7 *Show that $f_{\mathcal{A}}(x)^{\omega}(x) = x^2$ for the WFA $\mathcal{A}_2$ in Figure 3.18b.*

Exercise 3.5.8 *Determine $f^{\omega}_{\mathcal{A}_3}(x)$ for the WFA obtained from WFA $\mathcal{A}_2$ by taking other combinations of values for the initial and final distributions.*

Of special importance are WFA over the alphabet $P = \{0,1,2,3\}$. As shown in Section 2.5.3, a word over P can be seen as a pixel in the square $[0,1] \times [0,1]$. A function $f_{\mathcal{A}} : P^* \to \mathbf{R}$ is then considered as a multi-resolution image with $f_{\mathcal{A}}(u)$ being the greyness of the pixel specified by u. In order to have compatibility of different resolutions, it is usually required that $f_{\mathcal{A}}$ is **average-preserving**. That is, it holds that

$$f_{\mathcal{A}}(u) = \frac{1}{4}[f_{\mathcal{A}}(u0) + f_{\mathcal{A}}(u1) + f_{\mathcal{A}}(u2) + f_{\mathcal{A}}(u3)].$$

In other words, the greyness of a pixel is the average of the greynesses of its four main subpixels. (One can also say that images in different resolutions look similar if $f_{\mathcal{A}}$ is average-preserving – multi-resolution images contain only more details.)

It is easy to see that with the pixel representation of words over the alphabet P the language $L = \{1,2,3\}^*0\{1,2\}^*0\{0,1,2,3\}^*$ represents the image shown in Figure 3.19a (see also Exercise 2.5.17). At the same time L is the set of words w such that $f_{\mathcal{A}}(w) = 1$ for the WFA obtained from the one in Figure 3.19b by replacing all weights by 1. Now it is easy to see that the average-preserving WFA shown in Figure 3.19b generates the grey-scale image from Figure 3.19c.

The concept of a WFA will now be generalized to a **weighted finite transducer** (for short, WFT).

Definition 3.5.9 *In a WFT $\mathcal{T} = \langle \Sigma_1, \Sigma_2, Q, i, t, w \rangle$, Σ_1 and Σ_2 are input alphabets; Q, i and t have the same meaning as for a WFA; and $w : Q \times (\Sigma_1 \cup \{\varepsilon\}) \times (\Sigma_2 \cup \{\varepsilon\}) \times Q \to \mathbf{R}$ is a* **weighted transition function**.

We can associate to a WFT $\mathcal{T}$ the state graph $G_{\mathcal{T}}$, with Q being the set of nodes and with an edge from a node p to a node q with the label $(a_1, a_2 : r)$ if $w(p, a_1, a_2, q) = r$.

A WFT $\mathcal{T}$ specifies a **weighted relation** $R_{\mathcal{T}} : \Sigma_1^* \times \Sigma_2^* \to \mathbf{R}$ defined as follows. For $p,q \in Q$, $u \in \Sigma_1^*$ and $v \in \Sigma_2^*$, let $A_{p,q}(u,v)$ be the sum of the weights of all paths $(p_1,a_1,b_1,p_2)(p_1,a_2,b_2,p_2)\ldots(p_n,a_n,b_n,p_{n+1})$ from the state $p = p_1$ to the state $p_{n+1} = q$ that are labelled by $u = a_1 \ldots a_n$ and $v = b_1 \ldots b_n$. Moreover, we define

$$R_{\mathcal{T}}(u,v) = \sum_{p,q \in Q} i(p) A_{p,q}(u,v) t(q).$$

That is, only the paths from an initial to a final state are taken into account. In this way $R_{\mathcal{T}}$ relates some pairs (u,v), namely, those for which $R_{\mathcal{T}}(u,v) \neq 0$, and assigns some weight to the relational pair (u,v).

Observe that $A_{p,q}(u,v)$ does not have to be defined. Indeed, for some p, q, u and v, it can happen that $A_{p,q}(u,v)$ is infinite. This is due to the fact that if a transition is labelled by $(a_1, a_2 : r)$, then it may happen that either $a = \varepsilon$ or $a_2 = \varepsilon$ or $a_1 = a_2 = \varepsilon$. Therefore there may be infinitely many paths between p and q labelled by u and v. To overcome this problem, we restrict ourselves to those WFT which have the property that if the product of the weights of a cycle is nonzero, then either not all first labels or not all second labels on the edges of the path are ε.

The concept of a weighted relation may seem artificial. However, its application to functions has turned out to be a powerful tool. In image-processing applications, weighted relations represent an elegant and powerful way to transform images.

Definition 3.5.10 *Let $\rho : \Sigma_1^* \times \Sigma_2^* \to \mathbf{R}$ be a weighted relation and $f : \Sigma_1^* \to \mathbf{R}$ a function. An application of ρ on f, in short $g = \rho \circ f = \rho(f) : \Sigma_2^* \to \mathbf{R}$, is defined by*

$$g(v) = \sum_{u \in \Sigma_1^*} \rho(u,v) f(u),$$

for $v \in \Sigma_2^*$, if the sum, which can be infinite, converges; otherwise $g(u)$ is undefined. (The order of summation is given by a strict ordering on Σ_1^*.)

Informally, an application of ρ on f produces a new function g. The value of this function for an argument v is obtained by taking f-values of all $u \in \Sigma^*$ and multiplying each $f(u)$ by the weight of the paths that stand for the pair (u,v). This simply defined concept is very powerful. The concept itself, as well as its power, can best be illustrated by examples.

Exercise 3.5.11 *Describe the image transformation defined by the WFT shown in Figure 3.20a which produces, for example, the image shown in Figure 3.20c from the image depicted in Figure 3.20b.*

Example 3.5.12 (Derivation) *The WFT $\mathcal{T}_3$ in Figure 3.21a defines a weighted relation $R_{\mathcal{T}_3}$ such that for any function $f : \{0,1\}^* \to \mathbf{R}$, interpreted as a function on fractions, we get*

$$R_{\mathcal{T}_3} \circ f(x) = \frac{df(x)}{dx}$$

(and therefore $\mathcal{T}_3$ acts as a functional), in the following sense: for any fixed n and any function $f : \Sigma_1^n \to \mathbf{R}$, $R_{\mathcal{T}_3} \circ f(x) = \frac{f(x+h)-f(x)}{h}$, where $h = \frac{1}{2^n}$. (This means that if x is chosen to have n bits, then even the least

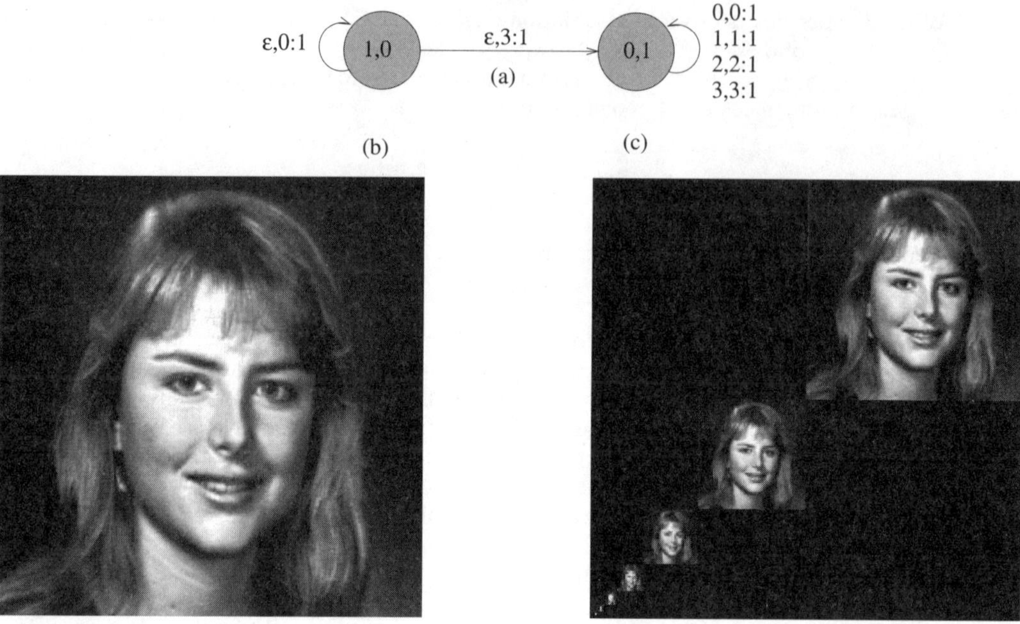

Figure 3.20 Image transformation

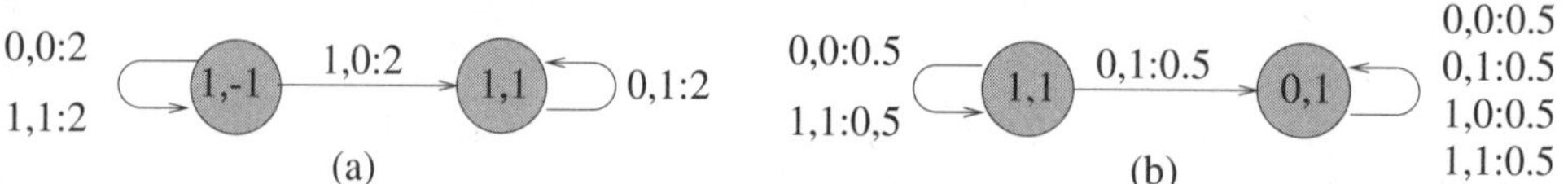

Figure 3.21 WFT for derivation and integration

significant 0, in a binary representation of x, matters.) Indeed, $R_{T_3}(x,y) \neq 0$, *for* $x,y \in \{0,1\}^*$ *if and only if either* $x = y$ *and then* $R_{T_3}(x,y) = -2^{|x|}$ *or* $x = x_1 10^k$, $y = x_1 01^k$, *for some k, and in such a case* $R_{T_3}(x,y) = 2^{|x|}$. *Hence* $R_{T_3} \circ f(x) = R_{T_3}(x,x)f(x) + R_{T_3}(x + \frac{1}{2^{|x|}}, x)f(x + \frac{1}{2^{|x|}}) = -2^{|x|}f(x) + 2^{|x|}f(x + \frac{1}{2^{|x|}})$. *Take now* $n = |x|$, $h = \frac{1}{2^n}$.

Example 3.5.13 (Integration) *The WFT* $\mathcal{T}_4$ *in Figure 3.21b determines a weighted relation* $R_{\mathcal{T}_4}$ *such that for any function* $f : \Sigma^* \to \mathbf{R}$

$$R_{\mathcal{T}_4} \circ f(x) = \int_0^x f(t)\,dt$$

in the following sense: $R_{\mathcal{T}_4} \circ f$ *computes* $h(f(0) + f(h) + f(2h) + \ldots + f(x))$ *(for any fixed resolution* $h = \frac{1}{2^k}$, *for some k, and all* $x \in \{0,1\}^k$*).*

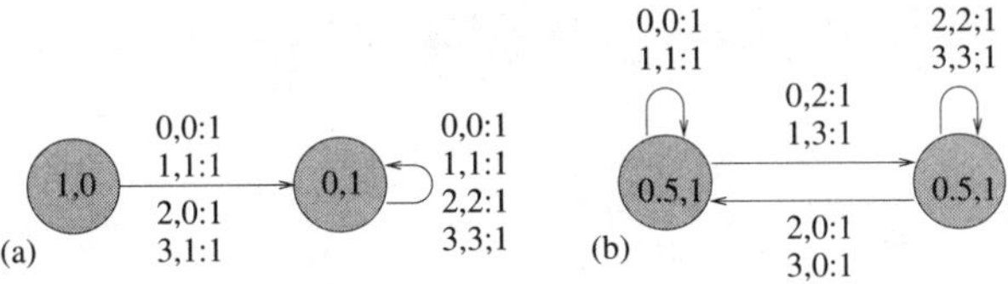

Figure 3.22 Two WFT

Exercise 3.5.14 *Explain in detail how the WFT in Figure 3.21b determines a functional for integration.*

Exercise 3.5.15* *Design a WFT for a partial derivation of functions of two variables with respect: (a) to the first variable; (b) to the second variable.*

The following theorem shows that the family of functions computed by WFA is closed under the weighted relations realized by WFT.

Theorem 3.5.16 *Let $\mathcal{A}_1 = \langle \Sigma_1, Q_1, i_1, t_1, w_1 \rangle$ be a WFA and $\mathcal{A}_2 = \langle \Sigma_2, Q_2, i_2, t_2, w_2 \rangle$ be an ε-loop free WFT. Then there exists a WFA $\mathcal{A}$ such that $f_{\mathcal{A}} = R_{\mathcal{A}_2} \circ f_{\mathcal{A}_1}$.*

This result actually means that to any WFA $\mathcal{A}$ over the alphabet $\{0,1\}$ two WFA $\mathcal{A}'$ and $\mathcal{A}''$ can be designed such that for any $x \in \Sigma^*, f_{\mathcal{A}'}(x) = \frac{df_{\mathcal{A}}(x)}{dx}$ and $f_{\mathcal{A}''}(x) = \int_0^x f_{\mathcal{A}}(x)dx$.

Exercise 3.5.17 *Construct a WFT to perform (a)* a rotation by 45 degrees clockwise; (b) a circular left shift by one pixel in two dimensions.*

Exercise 3.5.18 *Describe the image transformations realized by WFT in: (a) Figure 3.22a; (b) Figure 3.22b.*

Exercise 3.5.19* *Prove Theorem 3.5.16.*

3.5.2 Functions Computed by WFA

For a WFA $\mathcal{A}$ over the alphabet $\{0,1\}$, the real function $f_{\mathcal{A}}^{\omega} : [0,1] \to \mathbf{R}$ does not have to be total. However, it is always total for a special type of WFT introduced in Definition 3.5.20. As will be seen later, even such simple WFT have unexpected power.

Definition 3.5.20 *A WFA $\mathcal{A} = \langle \Sigma, Q, i, t, w \rangle$ is called a* **level weighted finite automaton** *(for short, LWFA) if*

1. *all weights are between 0 and 1;*
2. *the only cycles are self-loops;*

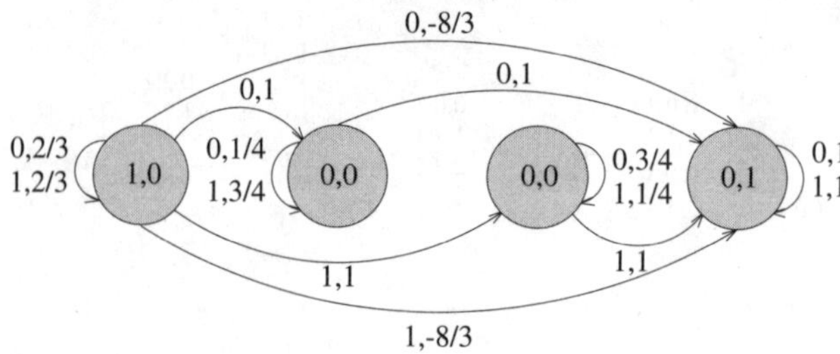

Figure 3.23 A LWFA that computes a function that is everywhere continuous and nowhere has a derivative

3. *if the weight of a self-loop is 1, then it must be a self-loop of a node that has no other outgoing edges than self-loops.*

For example, the WFA in Figure 3.18b is a LWFA; the one in Figure 3.18a is not. LWFA have unexpected properties summarized in the following theorem.

Theorem 3.5.21 *LWFA have the following properties:*

1. *It is decidable, given a LWFA, whether the real function it computes is continuous. It is also decidable, given two LWFA, whether the real functions they compute are identical.*
2. *Any polynomial of one variable with rational coefficients is computable by a LWFA. In addition, for any integer n there is a fixed, up to the initial distribution, LWFA $\mathcal{A}_n$ that can compute any polynomial of one variable and degree at most n. (To compute different polynomials, only different initial distributions are needed.)*
3. *If arbitrary negative weights are allowed, then there exists a simple LWFA (see Figure 3.23) computing a real function that is everywhere continuous and has no derivatives at any point of the interval $[0,1]$.*

Exercise 3.5.22* *Design a LWFA computing all polynomials of one variable of degree 3, and show how to fix the initial and terminal distributions to compute a particular polynomial of degree 3.*

3.5.3 Image Generation and Transformation by WFA and WFT

As already mentioned, an average-preserving mapping $f : P^* \to \mathbf{R}$ can be considered as a multi-resolution image. There is a simple way to ensure that a WFA on P defines an average-preserving mapping and thereby a multi-resolution image.

Definition 3.5.23 *A WFA $\mathcal{A} = \langle P, Q, i, t, w \rangle$ is average-preserving if for all $p \in Q$*

$$\sum_{a \in \Sigma, q \in Q} w(p,a,q)t(q) = 4t(p).$$

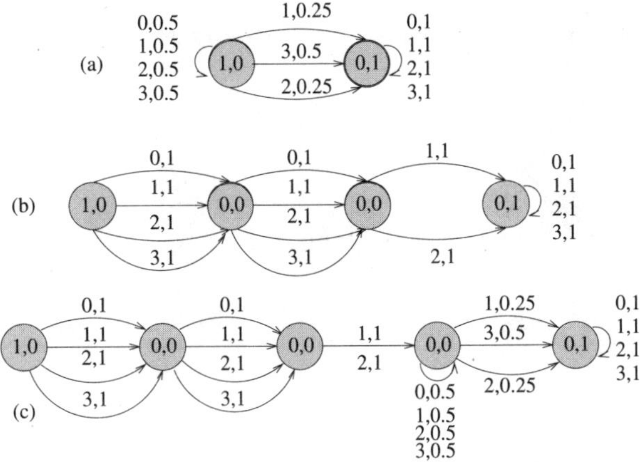

Figure 3.24 WFA generating two images and their concatenation

Indeed, we have

Theorem 3.5.24 *Let $\mathcal{A}$ be a WFA on P. If $\mathcal{A}$ is average-preserving, then so is $f_{\mathcal{A}}$.*

Proof: Let $u \in P^*, a \in P$. Since

$$f_{\mathcal{A}}(ua) = \sum_{q \in Q} \delta(q, ua) t(q) \tag{3.5}$$

$$= \sum_{p,q \in Q} \delta(p, u) w(p, a, q) t(q), \tag{3.6}$$

we have

$$\sum_{a \in P} f_{\mathcal{A}}(ua) = \sum_{p \in Q} \delta(p, u) \sum_{a \in P, q \in Q} w(p, a, q) t(q) \tag{3.7}$$

$$= \sum_{p \in Q} \delta(p, u) 4t(p) = 4f_{\mathcal{A}}(u). \tag{3.8}$$

□

The family of multi-resolution images generated by a WFA is closed under various operations such as addition, multiplication by constants, Cartesian product, concatenation, iteration, various affine transformations, zooming, rotating, derivation, integration, filtering and so on. Concatenation of WFA (see also Section 2.5.3) is defined as follows.

Definition 3.5.25 *Let $\mathcal{A}_1, \mathcal{A}_2$ be WFA over P and $f_{\mathcal{A}_1}, f_{\mathcal{A}_2}$ multi-resolution images defined by $\mathcal{A}_1$ and $\mathcal{A}_2$, respectively. Their concatenation $\mathcal{A}_1\mathcal{A}_2$ is defined as*

$$f_{\mathcal{A}_1\mathcal{A}_2}(u) = \sum_{u_1 u_2 = u} f_{\mathcal{A}_1}(u_1) f_{\mathcal{A}_2}(u_2).$$

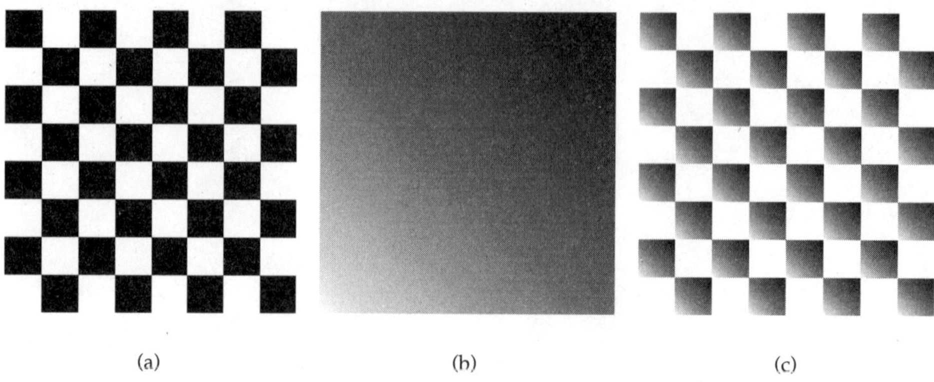

Figure 3.25 Concatenation of two images generated by WFA

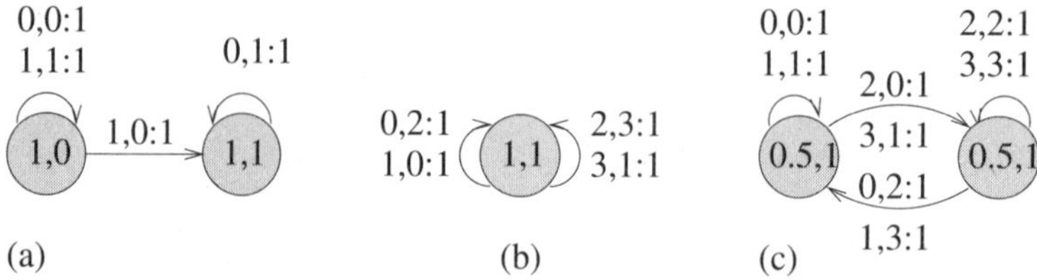

Figure 3.26 Image transformations defined by WFT: (a) circular shift left, (b) rotation, (c) vertical squeezing

Exercise 3.5.26 *(a) Show that the WFA in Figure 3.24b generates the chess board shown in Figure 3.25a; (b) that the WFA in Figure 3.24a generates the linear slope shown in Figure 3.25b; (c) that concatenation of the two images in Figures 3.24a, b (see the result in Figure 3.25c) generates the WFA in Figure 3.24c.*

Observe that several of the WFA we have considered, for example, the one in Figure 3.24b, are nondeterministic in the sense that if the weights are discarded, a nondeterministic FA is obtained. It can be shown that nondeterministic WFA generate more images than deterministic ones. For example, there is no deterministic WFA that generates the same linear slope as does the WFA in Figure 3.24a.

3.5.4 Image Compression

We have seen several examples of WFT generating images. From the application point of view, it is the inverse problem that is of special importance: given an image, how to design a WFT generating that image. Indeed, to store a multi-resolution image directly, a lot of memory is needed. A WFT generating the same image usually requires much less memory. There is a simple-to-formulate algorithm that can do image compression.

Algorithm 3.5.27 (Image compression) *Assume as input an image I given by a function $\phi : P^* \to \mathbf{R}$. (It can also be a digitalized photo.)*

1. *Assign the initial state q_0 to the image represented by the empty word, that is, to the whole image I, and define $i(q_0) = 1, t(q_0) = \phi(\varepsilon)$, the average greyness of the image I.*
2. *Recursively, for a state q assigned to a square specified by a string u, consider four subsquares specified by strings $u0, u1, u2, u3$. Denote the image in the square ua by I_{ua}. If this image is everywhere 0, then there will be no transition from the state q with the label a. If the image I_{ua} can be expressed as a linear combination of the images I_{v_i} corresponding to the states $p_1, \ldots, p_k$ – that is, $I_{ua} = \sum_{i=1}^{k} c_i I_{v_i}$ – add a new edge from q to each p_i with label a and with weight $w(q,a,p_i) = c_i (i = 1, \ldots, k)$. Otherwise, assign a new state r to the pixel ua and define $w(q,a,r) = 1, t(r) = \phi(I_{ua})$ – the average greyness of the image in the pixel ua.*
3. *Repeat step 3 for each new state, and stop if no new state is created.*

Since any real image has a finite resolution, the algorithm has to stop in practice. If this algorithm is applied to the picture shown in Figure 3.19a, we get a WFA like the one shown in Figure 3.19b but with all weights equal 1. Using the above 'theoretical algorithm' a compression of 5–10 times can be obtained. However, when a more elaborate 'recursive algorithm' is used, a larger compression, 50–60 times for grey-scale images and 100–150 times for colour images (and still providing pictures of good quality), has been obtained.

Of practical importance also are WFT. They can perform most of the basic image transformations, such as changing the contrast, shifts, shrinking, rotation, vertical squeezing, zooming, filters, mixing images, creating regular patterns of images and so on.

Exercise 3.5.28 *Show that the WFT in Figure 3.26a performs a circular shift left.*

Exercise 3.5.29 *Show that the WFT in Figure 3.26b performs a rotation by 90 degrees counterclockwise.*

Exercise 3.5.30 *Show that the WFT in Figure 3.26c performs vertical squeezing, defined as the sum of two affine transformations: $x_1 = \frac{x}{2}, y_1 = y$ and $x_2 = \frac{x+1}{2}, y_2 = y$ – making two copies of the original image and putting them next to each other in the unit square.*

3.6 Finite Automata on Infinite Words

A natural generalization of the concept of finite automata recognizing/accepting finite words and languages of finite words is that of finite automata recognizing ω-words and ω-languages. These concepts also have applications in many areas of computing. Many processes modelled by finite state devices (for instance, the watch in Section 3.1) are potentially infinite. Therefore it is most appropriate to see their inputs as ω-words. Two types of FA play the basic role here.

3.6.1 Büchi and Muller Automata

Definition 3.6.1 *A* **Büchi automaton** $\mathcal{A} = \langle \Sigma, Q, q_0, Q_F, \delta \rangle$ *is formally defined exactly like a FA, but it is used only to process ω-words, and acceptance is defined in a special way. An ω-word $w = w_0 w_1 w_2 \ldots \in \Sigma^\omega, w_i \in \Sigma$, is accepted by $\mathcal{A}$ if there is an infinite sequence of states $q_0, q_1, q_2, \ldots$ such that $(q_i, w_i, q_{i+1}) \in \delta$, for all $i \geq 0$,*

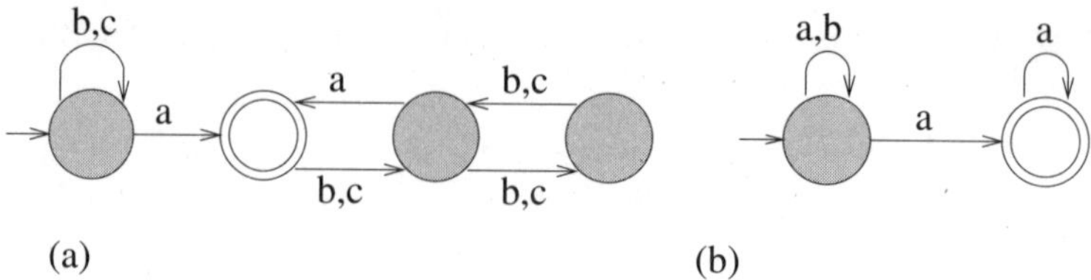

Figure 3.27 Büchi automata

and a state in Q_F occurs infinitely often in this sequence. Let $L^\omega(\mathcal{A})$ denote the set of all ω-words accepted by $\mathcal{A}$.

An ω-language L is called regular if there is a Büchi automaton accepting L.

Example 3.6.2 *Figure 3.27a shows a Büchi automaton accepting the ω-language over the alphabet $\{a,b,c\}$ consisting of ω-words that contain infinitely many a's and between any two occurrences of a there is an odd number of occurrences of b and c. Figure 3.27b shows a Büchi automaton recognizing the language $\{a,b\}^*a^\omega$.*

Exercise 3.6.3 *Construct a Büchi automaton accepting the language $L \subseteq \{a,b,c\}^*$ defined as follows: (a) $w \in L$ if and only if after any occurrence of the symbol a there is some occurrence of the symbol b in w; (b) $w \in L$ if and only if between any two occurrences of the symbol a there is a multiple of four occurrences of b's or c's.*

The following theorem summarizes those properties of ω-regular languages and Büchi automata that are similar to those of regular languages and FA. Except for the closure under complementation, they are easy to show.

Theorem 3.6.4 *(1) The family of regular ω-languages is closed under the operations of union, intersection and complementation.*

(2) An ω-language L is regular if and only if there are regular languages $A_1, \ldots, A_n$ and $B_1, \ldots, B_n$ such that $L = A_1B_1^\omega \cup \ldots \cup A_nB_n^\omega$.

(3) The emptiness and equivalence problems are decidable for Büchi automata.

Exercise 3.6.5 *Show that (a) if L is a regular language, then L^ω is a regular ω-language; (b) if L_1 and L_2 are regular ω-languages, then so are $L_1 \cup L_2$ and $L_1 \cap L_2$; (c)** the emptiness problem is decidable for Büchi automata.*

The result stated in point (2) of Theorem 3.6.4 shows how to define regular ω- expressions in such a way that they define exactly regular ω-languages.

One of the properties of FA not shared by Büchi automata concerns the power of nondeterminism. Nondeterministic Büchi automata are more powerful than deterministic ones. This follows easily from the fact that languages accepted by deterministic Büchi automata can be nicely characterized using regular languages. To show this is the task of the next exercise.

Exercise 3.6.6 *Show that an ω-language $L \subseteq \Sigma^\omega$ is accepted by a deterministic Büchi automaton if and only if*

$$L = \overrightarrow{W} = \{w \in \Sigma^\omega \mid Prefix_n(w) \in W, \text{ for infinitely many } n\},$$

for some regular language W.

Exercise 3.6.7* *Show that the language $\{a,b\}^\omega - \overrightarrow{(b^*a)^*}$ is accepted by a nondeterministic Büchi automaton but not by a deterministic Büchi automaton.*

There is, however, a modification of deterministic Büchi automata, with a different acceptance mode, the so-called **Muller automata**, that are deterministic and recognize all regular ω-languages.

Definition 3.6.8 *In a Muller automaton $\mathcal{A} = \langle \Sigma, Q, q_0, \mathcal{F}, \delta \rangle$, where Σ, Q, q_0 and δ have the same meaning as for DFA, but $\mathcal{F} \subseteq 2^Q$ is a family of sets of final states. $\mathcal{A}$ recognizes an ω-word $w = w_0w_1w_2\ldots$ if and only if the set of states that occur infinitely often in the sequence of states $\{q_i\}_{i=0}^\infty$, $q_i = \delta(q_0, w_0w_1w_2\ldots w_i)$, is an element of $\mathcal{F}$. (That is, the set of those states which the automaton $\mathcal{A}$ takes infinitely often when processing w is an element of $\mathcal{F}$.)*

Exercise 3.6.9* *Show the so-called McNaughton theorem: Muller automata accept exactly regular ω-languages.*

Exercise 3.6.10 *Show, for the regular ω-language $L = \{0,1\}^*\{0\}^\omega$ (that is, not a deterministic regular ω-language), that there are five non-isomorphic minimal (with respect to the number of states) Muller automata for L. (This indicates that the minimization problem has different features for Muller automata than it does for DFA.)*

3.6.2 Finite State Control of Reactive Systems*

In many areas of computing, for example, in operating systems, communication protocols, control systems, robotics and so on, the appropriate view of computation is that of a nonstop interaction between two agents or processes. They will be called **controller** and **disturber** or **plant** (see Figure 3..28). Each of them is supposed to be able to perform at each moment one of finitely many actions. Programs or automata representing such agents are called **reactive**; their actions are modelled by symbols from finite alphabets, and their continuous interactions are modelled by ω-words .

In this section we illustrate, as a case study, that (regular) ω-languages and ω-words constitute a proper framework for stating precisely and solving satisfactorily basic problems concerning such reactive systems. A detailed treatment of the subject and methods currently being worked out is beyond the scope of this book.

A **desirable interaction** of such agents can be specified through an ω-language $L \subseteq (\Sigma\Delta)^\omega$, where Σ and Δ are disjoint alphabets. An ω-word w from L has therefore the form $W = c_1d_1c_2d_2\ldots$, where

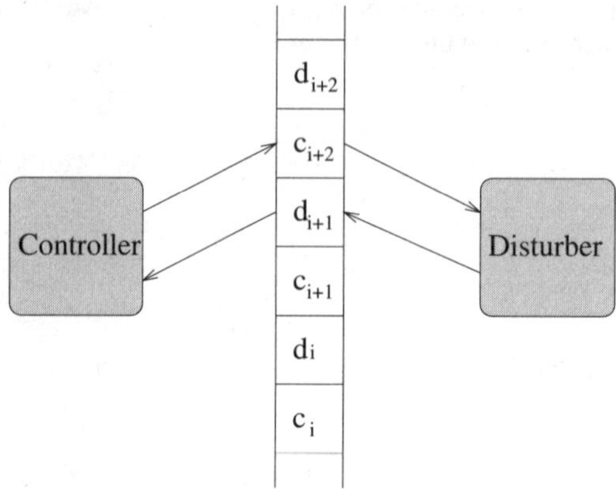

Figure 3.28 Controller and disturber

$c_i \in \Sigma$ ($d_i \in \Delta$). The symbol c_i (d_i) denotes the ith action that the controller (disturber) performs. The idea is that the controller tries to respond to the actions of the disturber in such a way that these actions make the disturber 'behave accordingly'.

Three basic problems arise when such a desirable behaviour is specified by an ω-language. The **verification problem** is to decide, given a controller, whether it is able to interact with the disturber in such a way that the resulting ω-word is in the given ω-language. The **solvability problem** is to decide, given an ω-language description, whether there exists a controller of a certain type capable of achieving an interaction with the disturber resulting always in an ω-word from the given ω-language. Finally, the **synthesis problem** is to design a controller from a given specification of an ω-language for the desired interaction with the disturber. Interestingly enough, all these problems are solvable if the ω-language specifying desirable behaviour of the controller–disturber interactions is a regular ω-language.

Problems of verification and synthesis for such reactive automata can be nicely formulated, like many problems in computing, in the framework of games – in this case in the framework of the **Gale–Stewart games** of two players, who are again called **controller** (C) and **disturber** (D). Their actions are modelled by symbols from alphabets Σ_C and Σ_D, respectively. Let $\Sigma = \Sigma_C \cup \Sigma_D$.

A **Gale–Stewart game** is specified by an ω-language $L \subseteq (\Sigma_C\Sigma_D)^\omega$. A **play** of the game is an ω-word $p \in \Sigma_C(\Sigma_D\Sigma_C)^\omega$. (An interpretation is that C starts an interaction by choosing a symbol from Σ_C, and then D and C keep choosing, in turn and indefinitely, symbols from their alphabets (depending, of course, on the interactions to that moment).) Player C **wins** the play p if $p \in L$, otherwise D wins. A **strategy** for C is a mapping $s_C : \Sigma_D^* \rightarrow \Sigma_C$ specifying a choice of a symbol from Σ_C (a move of C) for any finite sequence of choices of symbols by D – moves of D to that moment. Any such strategy determines a mapping $\bar{s}_C : \Sigma_D^\omega \rightarrow \Sigma_C^\omega$, defined by

$$\bar{s}_C(d_0d_1d_2\ldots) = c_0c_1c_2\ldots, \text{ where } c_i = s_C(d_0d_1\ldots d_{i-1}).$$

If D chooses an infinite sequence $\mu = d_0d_1\ldots$ of events (symbols) to act and C has a strategy s_C, then C chooses the infinite sequence $\gamma = \bar{s}_C(\mu)$ to create, together with D, the play $p_{\mu,\bar{s}_C} = c_0d_0c_1d_1\ldots$.

The main problem, the **uniform synthesis problem**, can now be described as follows. Given a specification language for a class $\mathcal{L}$ of ω-languages, design an algorithm, if it exists, such that, given any specification of an ω-language $L \in \mathcal{L}$, the algorithm designs a (winning) strategy s_C for C such that no matter what strategy D chooses, that is, no matter which sequence μ disturber D chooses, the play $p_{\mu,\bar{s}_C}$ will be in L.

In general the following theorem holds.

Theorem 3.6.11 (Büchi–Landweber's theorem) *Let Σ_C, Σ_D be finite alphabets. To any ω-regular language $L \subseteq \Sigma_C(\Sigma_D\Sigma_C)^\omega$ and any Muller automaton recognizing L, a Moore machine $\mathcal{A}_L$ with Σ_D as the input alphabet and Σ_C as the output alphabet can be constructed such that $\mathcal{A}_L$ provides the winning strategy for the controller with respect to the language L.*

The proof is quite involved. Moreover, this result has the drawback that the resulting Moore machine may have superexponentially more states than the Muller automaton defining the game. The problem of designing a winning strategy for various types of behaviours is being intensively investigated.

3.7 Limitations of Finite State Machines

Once a machine model has been designed and its advantages demonstrated, an additional important task is to determine its limitations.

In general it is not easy to show that a problem is not within the limits of a machine model. However, for finite state machines, especially finite automata, there are several simple and quite powerful methods for showing that a language is not regular. We illustrate some of them.

Example 3.7.1 (Proof of nonregularity of languages using Nerode's theorem) *For the language $L_1 = \{a^ib^i \mid i \geq 0\}$ it clearly holds that $a^i \not\equiv_{L_1} a^j$ if $i \neq j$. This implies that the syntactical monoid for the language L_1 is infinite. L_1 is therefore not recognizable by a FA.*

Example 3.7.2 (Proof of nonregularity of languages using the pumping lemma) *Let us assume that the language $L_2 = \{a^p \mid p \text{ prime}\}$ is regular. By the pumping lemma for regular languages, there exist integers $x, y, z, x+z \neq 0, y \neq 0$, such that all words $a^{x+iy+z}, i \geq 0$, are in L_2. However, this is impossible because, for example, $x+iy+z$ is not prime for $i = x+z$.*

Example 3.7.3 (Proof of nonregularity of languages using a descriptional finiteness argument) *Let us assume that the language $L_3 = \{a^icb^i \mid i \geq 1\}$ is regular and that $\mathcal{A}$ is a DFA recognizing L_3. Clearly, for any state q of $\mathcal{A}$, there is at most one $i \in \mathbf{N}$ such that $b^i \in L(q)$. If such an i exists, we say that q specifies that i. Since $a^icb^i \in L_3$ for each i, for any integer j there must exist a state q_j (the one reachable after the input a^jc) that specifies j. A contradiction, because there are only finitely many states in $\mathcal{A}$.*

Exercise 3.7.4 *Show that the following languages are not regular: $\{a^ib^{2i} \mid i \geq 0\}$; (b) $\{a^i \mid i$ is composite$\}$; (c) $\{a^i \mid i$ is a Fibonacci number$\}$; (d) $\{w \in \{0,1\}^* \mid w = w^R\}$.*

Example 3.7.5 *We now show that neither a Moore nor a Mealy machine can multiply two arbitrary binary integers given the corresponding pairs of bits as the input as in the case of binary adders in Figure 3.17. (To be consistent with the model in Figure 3.17, we assume that if the largest number has n bits, then the most significant pair of bits is followed by additional n pairs $(0,0)$ on the input.)*

If the numbers x and y to be multiplied are both equal to 2^{2m}, the $2m+1$-th input symbol will be $(1,1)$ and all others are $(0,0)$. After reading the $(1,1)$ symbol, the machine still has to perform $2m$ steps before producing *a 1 on the output. However, this is impossible, because during these 2m steps $\mathcal{M}$ has to get into a cycle. (It has only m states, and all inputs after the input symbol $(1,1)$ are the same – $(0,0)$.) This means that either $\mathcal{M}$ produces a 1 before the $(4m+1)$-th step or $\mathcal{M}$ never produces a 1. But this is a contradiction to the assumption that such a machine exists.*

Exercise 3.7.6 *Show that there is no finite state machine to compute the function (a) $f_1(n)$ = the n-th Fibonacci number; (b) $f(0^n1^m) = 1^{n \bmod m}$.*

Example 3.7.7 *It follows from Theorem 3.4.11 that no generalized sequential machine can compute the function $f:\{0,1\}^* \rightarrow \{0,1\}^*$ defined by $f(w) = w^R$. Indeed, the prefix condition from that theorem is not fulfilled.*

Example 3.7.8 *Let $L \subset \{0,1\}^\omega$ be a language of ω-words w for which there is an integer $k > 1$ such that w has a symbol 1 exactly in the positions k^n for all integers n. We claim that L is not a regular ω-language. Indeed, since the distances between two consecutive 1s are getting bigger and bigger, a finite automaton cannot check whether they are correct.*

Concerning weighted finite transducers it has been shown that they can compute neither exponential functions nor trigonometric functions.

3.8 From Finite Automata to Universal Computers

Several natural ideas for enhancing the power of finite automata will now be explored. Surprisingly, some of these ideas do not lead to an increase in the computational power of finite automata at all. Some of them, also surprisingly, lead to very large increases. All these models have one thing in common. The only memory they need to process an input is the memory needed to store the input. One of these models illustrates an important new mode of computation – probabilistic finite automata. The importance of others lies mainly in the fact that they can be used to represent, in an isolated form, various techniques for designing of Turing machines, discussed in the next chapter.

3.8.1 Transition Systems

A **transition system** $\mathcal{A} = \langle \Sigma, Q, q_0, Q_F, \delta \rangle$ is defined similarly to a finite automaton, except that the finite transition relation δ is a subset of $Q \times \Sigma^* \times Q$ and not of $Q \times \Sigma \times Q$ as for finite automata. In other words, in a transition system, a longer portion of an input word only can cause a single state transition. Computation and acceptance are defined for transition systems in the same way as for finite automata: namely, an input word w is accepted if there is a path from the initial state to a final state labelled by w.

Each finite automaton is a transition system. On the other hand, to each transition system $\mathcal{A}$ it is easy to design an equivalent FA which accepts the same language. To show this, we sketch a way to modify the state graph $G_{\mathcal{A}}$ of a transition system $\mathcal{A}$ in order to get a state graph of an equivalent FA.

1. Replace each transition (edge) $p \underset{w}{\Longrightarrow} q, w = w_1w_2\ldots w_k, w_i \in \Sigma, k > 1$ by k transitions $p \underset{w_1}{\Longrightarrow} p_1 \underset{w_2}{\Longrightarrow} p_2 \ldots p_{k-2} \underset{w_{k-1}}{\Longrightarrow} p_{k-1} \underset{w_k}{\Longrightarrow} q$, where $p_1,\ldots,p_{k-1}$ are newly created states (see the step from Figure 3.29a to 3.29b).

a	c	e	g	i	k	m	o	r	t	v
b	d	f	h	j	l	n	p	s	u	w

(a) one tape with two tracks

a	c	e	g	i	k	m	o	r	t	v
b	d	f	h	j	l	n	p	s	u	w

(b) one tape with one track

Figure 3.29 Derivation of a complete FA from a transition system

2. Remove ε-transitions. This is a slightly more involved task. One needs first to compute the transitive closure of the relation $\underset{\varepsilon}{\Longrightarrow}$ between states. Then for any triple of states p, q, q' and each $a \in \Sigma$ such that $p \overset{*}{\underset{\varepsilon}{\Longrightarrow}} q \underset{a}{\Longrightarrow} q'$, the transition $p \underset{a}{\Longrightarrow} q'$ is added. If, after such modifications, $q' \overset{*}{\underset{\varepsilon}{\Longrightarrow}} q$ for some $q' \in Q$ and $q \in Q_F$, add q' to the set of final states, and remove all ε-transitions and unreachable states (see the step from Figure 3.29b to 3.29c).
3. If we require the resulting automaton to be complete, we add a new 'sink state' to which all missing transitions are added and directed (see the step from Figure 3.29c to 3.29d). By this construction we have shown the following theorem.

Theorem 3.8.1 *The family of languages accepted by transition systems is exactly the family of regular languages.*

The main advantage of transition systems is that they may have much shorter descriptions and smaller numbers of states than any equivalent FA. Indeed, for any integer n a FA accepting the one-word language $\{a^n\}$ must have $n-1$ states, but there is a two-state transition system that can do it.

Exercise 3.8.2 *Design a transition system with as few states as possible that accepts those words over the alphabet $\{a, b, c\}$ that either begin or end with the string 'baac', or contain the substring 'abca'. Then use the above method to design an equivalent FA.*

Exercise 3.8.3 *Design a minimal, with respect to number of states, transition system accepting the language $L = (a^4b^3)^* \cup (a^4b^6)^*$. Then transform its state graph to get a state graph for a FA accepting the same language.*

3.8.2 Probabilistic Finite Automata

We have mentioned already the power of randomization. We now explore how much randomization can increase the power of finite automata.

Definition 3.8.4 *A* **probabilistic finite automaton** $\mathcal{P} = \langle \Sigma, Q, q_0, Q_F, \phi \rangle$ *has an* **input alphabet** Σ, *a* **set of states** Q, *the* **initial state** q_0, *a set of* **final states** Q_F *and a* **probability distribution mapping** ϕ *that assigns to each $a \in \Sigma$ a $|Q| \times |Q|$ matrix M_a of nonnegative reals with rows and columns of each M_a labelled by states and such that $\sum_{q \in Q} M_a(p, q) = 1$ for any $a \in \Sigma$ and $p \in Q$. Informally, $M_a(p, q)$ determines the probability that the automaton $\mathcal{P}$ goes, under the input a, from state p to state q; $M_a(p, q) = 0$ means that there is no transition from p to q under the input a.*

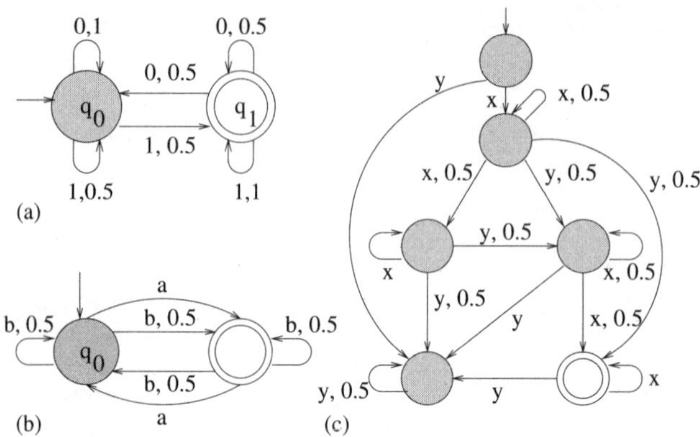

Figure 3.30 Probabilistic finite automata – missing probabilities are 1

If $w = w_1 \dots w_n$, $w_i \in \Sigma$, then the entry $M_w(p,q)$ of the matrix $M_w = M_{w_1} M_{w_2} \dots M_{w_n}$ is exactly the probability that $\mathcal{P}$ goes, under the input word w, from state p to state q. Finally, for a $w \in \Sigma^*$, we define

$$Pr_{\mathcal{P}}(w) = \sum_{q \in Q_F} M_w(q_0, q).$$

$Pr_{\mathcal{P}}(w)$ is the probability with which $\mathcal{P}$ recognizes w.

There are several ways to define acceptance by a probabilistic finite automaton. The most basic one is very obvious. It is called **acceptance with respect to a cut-point**. For a real number $0 \leq c < 1$ we define a language

$$L_c(\mathcal{P}) = \{u \mid Pr_{\mathcal{P}}(u) > c\}.$$

The language $L_c(\mathcal{P})$ is said to be the language recognized by $\mathcal{P}$ with respect to the **cut-point** c. (Informally, $L_c(\mathcal{P})$ is the set of input strings that can be accepted with a probability larger than c.)

Example 3.8.5 *Let $\Sigma = \{0,1\}$, $Q = \{q_0, q_1\}$, $Q_F = \{q_1\}$,*

$$M_0 = \begin{vmatrix} 1 & 0 \\ \frac{1}{2} & \frac{1}{2} \end{vmatrix}, \quad M_1 = \begin{vmatrix} \frac{1}{2} & \frac{1}{2} \\ 0 & 1 \end{vmatrix}.$$

Figure 3.30a shows the corresponding probabilistic finite automaton $\mathcal{P}_0$. Each edge is labelled by an input symbol and by the probability that the corresponding transition takes place. By induction it can easily be shown that for any $w = w_1 \dots w_n \in \Sigma^n$, the matrix $M_w = M_{w_1} M_{w_2} \dots M_{w_n}$ has in the right upper corner the number $0.w_n \dots w_1$, expressed in binary notation. (Show that!)

Exercise 3.8.6 *Determine, for all possible c, the language accepted by the probabilistic automaton in Figure 3.30b with respect to the cut-point c.*

Exercise 3.8.7 *Determine the language accepted by the probabilistic automaton in Figure 3.30c with respect to the cut-point 0.5. (Don't be surprised if you get a nonregular language.)*

First we show that with this general concept of acceptance with respect to a cut-point, the probabilistic finite automata are more powerful than ordinary FA.

Theorem 3.8.8 *For the probabilistic finite automaton $\mathcal{P}_0$ in Example 3.8.5 there exists a real $0 \leq c < 1$ such that the language $L_c(\mathcal{P}_0)$ is not regular.*

Proof: If $w = w_1 \dots w_n$, then (as already mentioned above) $Pr_{\mathcal{P}_0}(w) = 0.w_n \dots w_1$ (because q_1 is the single final state). This implies that if $0 \leq c_1 < c_2 < 1$ are arbitrary reals, then $L_{c_1}(\mathcal{P}_0) \subsetneq L_{c_2}(\mathcal{P}_0)$. The family of languages that $\mathcal{P}_0$ recognizes, with different cut-points, is therefore not countable. On the other hand, the set of regular expressions over Σ is countable, and so therefore is the set of regular languages over Σ. Hence there exists an $0 \leq c < 1$ such that $L_c(\mathcal{P}_0)$ is not a regular language. □

The situation is different, however, for acceptance with respect to **isolated cut-points**. A real $0 \leq c < 1$ is an isolated cut-point with respect to a probabilistic FA $\mathcal{P}$ if there is a $\delta > 0$ such that for all $w \in \Sigma^*$

$$|Pr_{\mathcal{P}}(w) - c| > \delta. \tag{3.9}$$

Theorem 3.8.9 *If $\mathcal{P} = \langle \Sigma, Q, q_0, Q_F, \phi \rangle$ is a probabilistic FA with c as an isolated cut-point, then the language $L_c(\mathcal{P})$ is regular.*

To prove the theorem we shall use the following combinatorial lemma.

Lemma 3.8.10 *Let P_n be the set of all n-dimensional random vectors, that is, $P_n = \{x = (x_1, \dots, x_n), x_i \geq 0, 1 \leq i \leq n$ – and $\sum_{i=1}^n x_i = 1\}$. Let, for an $\varepsilon > 0$, U_ε be such a subset of P_n that for any $x, y \in U_\varepsilon$, $x \neq y$ implies $\sum_{i=1}^n |x_i - y_i| \geq \varepsilon$. Then the set U_ε contains at most $(1 + \frac{2}{\varepsilon})^{n-1}$ vectors.*

Proof of the theorem: Assume that $Q = \{q_0, q_1, \dots, q_{n-1}\}$ and, for simplicity and without loss of generality, that $Q_F = \{q_{n-1}\}$. In this case the probability that $\mathcal{P}$ accepts some w is $Pr_{\mathcal{P}}(w) = M_w(q_0, q_{n-1})$, where M_w is an $n \times n$ matrix defined as on page 198.

Consider now the language $L = L_c(\mathcal{P})$, and assume that we have a set of k words $v_1, \dots, v_k$ such that no two of them are in the same prefix equivalence class with respect to the relation $\equiv_L^p$. This implies, by the definition of prefix equivalence, that for each pair $i \neq j, 1 \leq i, j \leq k$ there exists a word y_{ij} such that $v_i y_{ij} \in L$ and $v_j y_{ij} \notin L$ – or vice versa.

Now let $(s_1^i, \dots, s_n^i)$, $1 \leq i \leq k$, be the first row of the matrix M_{v_i}, and let $(r_1^{ij}, \dots, r_n^{ij})$ be the last column of the matrix $M_{y_{ij}}$. Since $M_{v_i y_{ij}} = M_{v_i} M_{y_{ij}}$ and q_{n-1} is the only accepting state, we get $Pr_{\mathcal{P}}(v_i y_{ij}) = s_1^i r_1^{ij} + \dots + s_n^i r_n^{ij}$ and $Pr_{\mathcal{P}}(v_j y^{ij}) = s_1^j r_1^{ij} + \dots + s_n^j r_n^{ij}$, and therefore

$$c < s_1^i r_1^{ij} + \dots + s_n^i r_n^{i,j} \quad \text{and} \quad s_1^j r_1^{ij} + \dots + s_n^j r_n^{ij} \leq c.$$

If we now use the inequality (3.9), we get

$$\sum_{l=1}^n (s_l^i - s_l^j) r_l^{ij} \geq 2\delta. \tag{3.10}$$

In addition, it holds that

$$\begin{aligned}
\sum_{l=1}^n (s_l^i - s_l^j) r_l^{ij} &\leq (\sum_{l=1}^n (s_l^i - s_l^j))^+ \max\{r_l^{ij} \,|\, 1 \leq l \leq k\} \\
&\quad + (\sum_{l=1}^n (s_l^i - s_l^j))^- \min\{r_l^{ij} \,|\, 1 \leq l \leq k\} \\
&= (\sum_{l=1}^n (s_l^i - s_l^j))^+ (\max\{r_l^{ij} \,|\, 1 \leq l \leq k\} - \min\{r_l^{ij} \,|\, 1 \leq l \leq k\}) \\
&\leq (\sum_{l=1}^n (s_l^i - s_l^j))^+ = \tfrac{1}{2} \sum_{l=1}^n |s_l^i - s_l^j|,
\end{aligned}$$

where $(\dots)^+$ denotes that only the positive numbers in the expression inside the parentheses are taken and, similarly, $(\dots)^-$ denotes taking only the negative numbers. In deriving these inequalities we have used essentially the fact that $|r_l^{ij}| \leq 1$ for all l, i, j.

A combination of the last inequality with the inequality 3.10 yields $\sum_{l=1}^{n} |s_l^i - s_l^j| \geq 4\delta$. An application of Lemma 3.8.10 then gives $k \leq \left(1 + \frac{1}{2\delta}\right)^{n-1}$. Now we can use Myhill's theorem to show that the language $L_c(\mathcal{P})$ must be regular. □

It has been shown that from the point of view of randomized computations, acceptance with respect to an isolated cut-point is very natural. Theorem 3.8.9 is therefore often seen as the main theorem showing the power of probabilistic finite automata. Unfortunately, it is still an open question whether it is decidable, given a probabilistic finite automaton $\mathcal{P}$ with rational probabilities of transitions and a rational λ, if λ is an isolated cut-point of $\mathcal{P}$.

Exercise 3.8.11* *A cut-point λ is weakly isolated for a probabilistic finite automaton $\mathcal{P}$ if $|Pr_{\mathcal{P}}(w) - \lambda| \geq \varepsilon$ or $Pr_{\mathcal{P}}(w) = \lambda$ for all $w \in \Sigma^*$ and some fixed ε. Prove that if λ is a weakly isolated cut-point for $\mathcal{P}$, then the language $L_\lambda(\mathcal{P})$ is regular.*

Exercise 3.8.12** *Two probabilistic finite automata $\mathcal{P}_1$ and $\mathcal{P}_2$ are called mutually isolated if $|Pr_{\mathcal{P}_1}(w) - Pr_{\mathcal{P}_2}(w)| \geq \varepsilon$ for all $w \in \Sigma^*$. Prove that if $\mathcal{P}_1$ and $\mathcal{P}_2$ are mutually isolated, then the language $L = \{w \mid Pr_{\mathcal{P}_1}(w) > Pr_{\mathcal{P}_2}(w)\}$ is regular.*

The concept of a probabilistic finite automaton is usually generalized. Instead of a fixed initial state an initial distribution of states is considered, that is, each state is an initial state of a given probability. In order to get the overall probability that a word is accepted, the probability of each path has to be multiplied by the probability that its starting state is initial. Languages accepted by such probabilistic finite automata with respect to a cut-point c are called c-stochastic. A language is called (finite state) **stochastic** if there is a probabilistic finite automaton $\mathcal{A}$ and a cut-point c such that $L = L_c(\mathcal{A})$.

Exercise 3.8.13 *Show that any regular language is c-stochastic for any cut-point $0 \leq c \leq 1$.*

Exercise 3.8.14 *Show that every 0-stochastic language is regular.*

Of special interest are probabilistic finite automata with uniform probability distributions of transitions – for each state q and each input symbol a all transitions from q under a have the same probability. Such probabilistic automata are formally defined exactly like nondeterministic automata; it is therefore natural to ask what is the difference between them. Actually, it is a very big one. Nondeterministic automata are very convenient to deal with, but are completely unrealistic models of computations. By contrast, probabilistic finite automata are very realistic models of computation.

Another way to regard probabilistic finite automata, often very useful for applications, is as defining a probability distribution on the set of inputs.

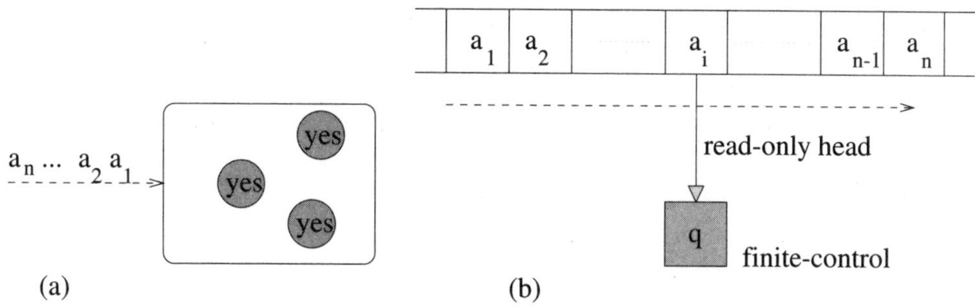

Figure 3.31 Two ways to see a FA

3.8.3 Two-way Finite Automata

In addition to the usual view of a FA as a finite state device (see Figure 3.31a) which processes an external input string symbol by a symbol, there is another view (see Figure 3.31b) that is the basis of several natural generalizations of FA.

As illustrated in Figure 3.31b, a (one-way) deterministic finite automaton $\mathcal{A} = \langle \Sigma, Q, q_0, Q_F, \delta \rangle$ can be seen as consisting of a **finite control** (determined by δ) that is always in one of the states in the set Q, a **bi-infinite tape** each cell of which may contain a symbol from Σ or a special blank symbol $\sqcup$ not in Σ, and a **read-only head** that always stays on a cell of the tape and can move only to the right, one cell per move (we refer to the two directions on the tape as left and right).

At the beginning of a computation the input word w is written, one symbol per cell, in $|w|$ consecutive cells, and the head is positioned on the cell with the first symbol of w. In each computational step $\mathcal{A}$ reads the symbol from the cell the head is on at that moment. Depending on the state of the finite control, $\mathcal{A}$ goes, according to the transition function of the finite control δ, to a new state q, and also moves its head to the next cell. If $\mathcal{A}$ reaches a final state at the moment when the head moves over the right end of the input word, then the input word is considered as accepted. In a similar way, nondeterministic finite automata can be defined.

With such a model of a finite automaton the question naturally arises as to whether a more powerful device could be obtained if the head were allowed to move also to the left. Let us explore this idea.

Definition 3.8.15 *A* **two-way finite automaton** $\mathcal{A} = \langle \Sigma, Q, q_0, Q_F, \delta \rangle$ *is defined similarly to an ordinary FA, except that the transition function has the form*

$$\delta : Q \times \Sigma \rightarrow Q \times \{\leftarrow, \downarrow, \rightarrow\}$$

and $\delta(p,a) = (q,d)$, *where* $d \in \{\leftarrow, \downarrow, \rightarrow\}$, *means that the automaton* $\mathcal{A}$ *in the state* p *moves, under the input* a, *to the state* q *and the head moves one cell in the direction* d – *that is, to the right if* $d = \rightarrow$, *to the left if* $d = \leftarrow$, *and does not move at all if* $d = \downarrow$. *The language* $L(\mathcal{A})$, *accepted by* $\mathcal{A}$, *is then defined as follows:*

$$L(\mathcal{A}) = \{w \in \Sigma^* |\ \mathcal{A} \text{ starting with the head on the first symbol of } w \text{ and in the state } q_0 \text{ moves, after a finite number of steps, over the right end of } w \text{ exactly when } \mathcal{A} \text{ comes to a final state}\}.$$

Nondeterministic two-way finite automata can be defined similarly.

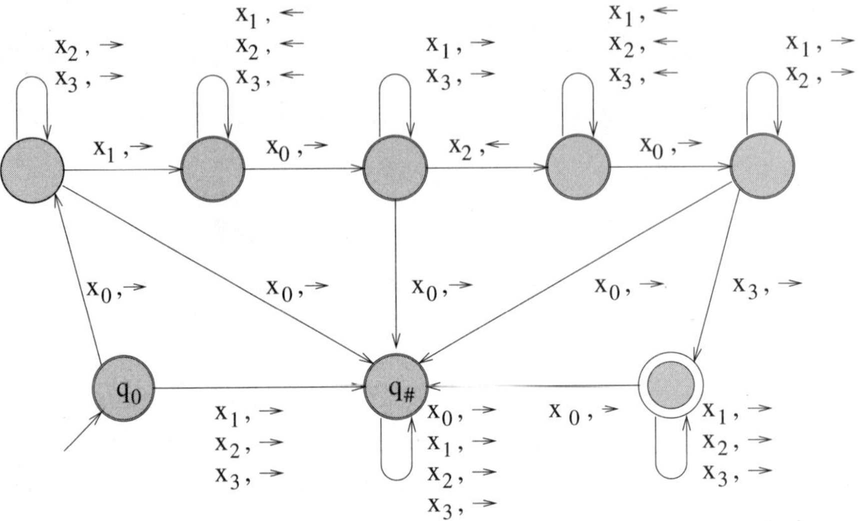

Figure 3.32 An example of a two-way finite automaton

Example 3.8.16 *The two-way finite automaton $\mathcal{A}_0$ in Figure 3.32 recognizes the language*

$$L = x_0(\Sigma - \{x_0\})^* \cap \Sigma^* x_1 \Sigma^* \cap \Sigma^* x_2 \Sigma^* \cap \Sigma^* x_3 \Sigma^*$$

of all words over the alphabet $\Sigma = \{x_0, x_1, x_2, x_3\}$ that begin with x_0, do not contain another occurrence of x_0 and contain all remaining symbols from Σ at least once. Indeed, $\mathcal{A}_0$ first verifies whether the first symbol really is x_0. If so, $\mathcal{A}_0$ starts a move to the right to search for an x_1. If found, $\mathcal{A}_0$ moves back to the left end and starts a search for an x_2. If found, $\mathcal{A}_0$ again moves to the left-most end and starts a search for an x_3. If x_0 is found twice, or the first symbol is not x_0, then $\mathcal{A}_0$ moves to the 'sink' state $q_\#$.

Two-way finite automata appear to be more powerful than FA. This, however, is misleading.

Theorem 3.8.17 *Nondeterministic two-way finite automata accept exactly the regular languages.*

Proof: We prove the lemma only for the deterministic case. For the nondeterministic case the idea of proof is the same but details are more technical.

The only way a prefix p of an input word w of a two-way FA $\mathcal{A} = \langle \Sigma, Q, q_0, Q_F, \delta \rangle$ can influence the behaviour of $\mathcal{A}$ when $\mathcal{A}$ is no longer reading p is through state transitions of $\mathcal{A}$ which p causes. Indeed, the external effect of p is completely determined by a function $T_p : Q \cup \{\#\} \rightarrow Q \cup \{\#\}$, that gives, for each state $q \in Q$ in which $\mathcal{A}$ re-enters p, the state $\mathcal{A}$ has when leaving p through its rightmost symbol for the next time, or the symbol $\#$ if $\mathcal{A}$ leaves p at its leftmost symbol or does not leave it at all. Moreover $T_p(\#)$ is the state in which $\mathcal{A}$ leaves for the first time the rightmost symbol of p when starting on the leftmost symbol in the starting state. The relation $w_1 \equiv w_2$ if and only if $T_{w_1} = T_{w_2}$ is finer than the prefix equivalence for $L(\mathcal{A})$. The number of functions T_w, $w \in \Sigma^*$, is finite (actually at most $(|Q|+1)^{|Q|+1}$). Therefore, by Nerode's Theorem, $L(\mathcal{A})$ is a regular language.

Because there are only finitely many of such functions possible for $\mathcal{A}$ and, in addition, from a table T_p, transitions of $\mathcal{A}$ and a tape symbol a of $\mathcal{A}$, one can construct table for T_{pa}, we can show that there exists a one-way FA $\mathcal{A}'$ that accepts the same language as $\mathcal{A}$. Indeed, $\mathcal{A}'$ will be such that after

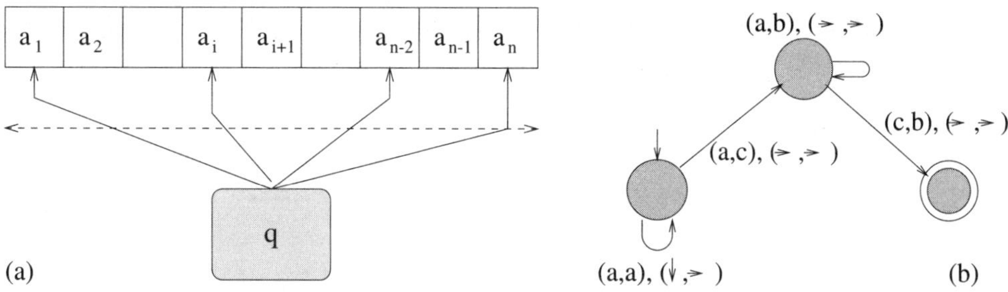

Figure 3.33 Multi-head finite automata

finishing reading p in a state (q, T_p), where q is the state $\mathcal{A}$ is after the first time $\mathcal{A}$ leaves p and T_p is the corresponding transition table for the prefix p. It is now obvious that given the transition function of $\mathcal{A}$ one can easily construct the transition function of $\mathcal{A}'$. If we now define that $\mathcal{A}'$ accepts an input w if and only if $\mathcal{A}'$, after reading w, comes into a state (q', T_w), where q' is a final state of $\mathcal{A}$, then $\mathcal{A}$ and $\mathcal{A}'$ accept the same language. □

Informally, the theorem actually says that **multiple readings do not help if writing is not allowed and the machine has only finite memory.**

On the other hand, a two-way finite automaton can be much smaller than an equivalent FA.

Example 3.8.18 *Let $\Sigma = \{a_0, a_1, \ldots, a_n\}$ and let L_0 be the set of all words over Σ that start with the symbol a_0, do not contain any other occurrence of a_0, and contain each of the remaining symbols from Σ at least once. Similarly, as in Example 3.8.16, a two-way finite automaton with $2n+2$ states can be constructed to accept L_0. On the other hand, it can be shown that any finite automaton recognizing L_0 must have at least 2^n states.*

One can show that even larger savings in description length can be achieved by using two-way finite automata compared with ordinary FA. It holds, for example, that

$$Economy^{DFA}_{2DFA}(n) = \Omega((n/5)^{n/5}).$$

where the economy function for replacing a DFA with an equivalent 2DFA is defined as on page 163.

Exercise 3.8.19 *Show, given an integer n, how to design a two-way finite automaton accepting the language*

$$L_n = \{10^{i_1}10^{i_2}1 \ldots 10^{i_n}2^k0^{i_k} \,|\, 1 \leq k \leq n, 1 \leq i_j \leq n, 1 \leq j \leq n\}.$$

3.8.4 Multi-head Finite Automata

Another natural idea for enhancing the power of finite automata is to admit a sort of parallelism by allowing the use of several read-only heads (see Figure 3.33a). Two types of multi-head finite automata are obvious: one-way, heads move in one direction only, two-way, heads can move in both directions.

Informally, a k-head two-way finite automaton (for short, k-2FA) has k heads, and at the beginning of any computation all heads stay on the cell with the first symbol of the input word. Each computation step is uniquely determined by the current state of the automaton and by the symbols the heads read. A step consists of a state change and moves of heads as specified by the transition function.

More formally, in a k-head two-way finite automaton $\mathcal{A} = \langle \Sigma, Q, q_0, Q_F, \delta \rangle$ the symbols Σ, Q, q_0, Q_F have the usual meaning, and

$$\delta : Q \times \underbrace{\Sigma \times \ldots \times \Sigma}_{k} \rightarrow Q \times \underbrace{\{\leftarrow, \downarrow, \rightarrow\} \times \ldots \times \{\leftarrow, \downarrow, \rightarrow\}}_{k},$$

where $\delta(p, b_1, \ldots, b_k) = (q, d_1, \ldots, d_k)$ means that if $\mathcal{A}$ is in state p and the ith head reads b_i, for $1 \leq i \leq k$, then $\mathcal{A}$ goes to state q and the jth head moves in the direction determined by d_i. Nondeterministic k-head two-way finite automata are defined similarly, as are one-way multi-head FA.

The language $L(\mathcal{A})$ is defined as the set of words w such that if $\mathcal{A}$ starts with all heads on the first symbol of w, then, after some number of steps, $\mathcal{A}$ moves to a final state exactly when one of the heads leaves the cells that are occupied by w, at the right end.

Example 3.8.20 *It is easy to see that the 2-head one-way finite automaton in Figure 3.33b recognizes the language $\{a^icb^i \mid i \geq 1\}$ that is not regular.*

Exercise 3.8.21 *(a) Design a 2-head FA that will accept the language $\{a^ib^ic^i \mid n \geq 1\}$; (b) design a 3-head FA that will accept the language $\{a^ib^{2i}c^{3i} \mid i \geq 1\}$.*

Once we know that even one-way 2-head finite automata are more powerful than 1-head finite automata, it is natural to ask whether any additional increase in the number of heads provides more power. To formulate the result, let us denote by $\mathcal{L}(k\text{-2DFA})$ ($\mathcal{L}(k\text{-2NFA})$) the family of languages accepted by deterministic (nondeterministic) two-way finite automata with k heads. In an analogical way we use notation $\mathcal{L}(k\text{-1DFA})$ and $\mathcal{L}(k\text{-1NFA})$.

Theorem 3.8.22 *For each $k \geq 1$ and $i = 1,2$, $\mathcal{L}(k\text{-}i\text{DFA}) \subsetneq \mathcal{L}((k+1)\text{-}i\text{DFA})$ and $\mathcal{L}(k\text{-}i\text{NFA}) \subsetneq \mathcal{L}((k+1)\text{-}i\text{NFA})$.*

The proofs are quite involved, and represent solutions of long-standing open problems. It follows from Theorem 3.8.22 that k-head finite automata, for $k = 1, 2, \ldots$, form an infinite hierarchy of more and more powerful machines!

How is this possible? It seems that k-head finite automata have again only finitely many states and use only a finite amount of memory. This impression, however, is misleading. The actual state of such a machine is determined not only by the state of its finite control but also by the positions of the heads. If an input word w has length n, then the overall number of global states (configurations) a k-head FA $\mathcal{A}$ can be in is $|Q|n^k$, where Q is the set of internal states of $\mathcal{A}$. The total number of global states of a k-head FA therefore grows polynomially with respect to the length of the input.

The following two closely related families of languages,

$$\bigcup_{k=1}^{\infty} \mathcal{L}(k\text{-2DFA}) \quad \text{and} \quad \bigcup_{k=1}^{\infty} \mathcal{L}(k\text{-2NFA}),$$

play an important role in complexity theory, and are the same as two families of languages defined with respect to space complexity, **L** and **NL**, introduced in Section 5.2.

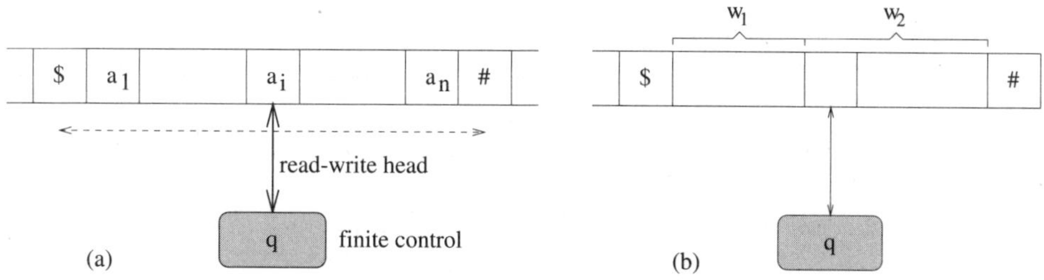

Figure 3.34 A linearly bounded automaton

3.8.5 Linearly Bounded Automata

Another natural generalization of finite automata are linearly bounded automata (LBA for short). The head of a LBA is not only allowed to move in both directions, it may also write (see Figure 3.34a). This is an essentially new and very powerful step in the generalization of the finite automata concept.

Since the head of a LBA can move in both directions and can also write, two markers, \$ and # are used to delimit the beginning and end of the tape section on which the input word is written. A LBA is allowed to move neither left from \$ nor right from #; nor is it allowed to write these markers on the tape or to erase them.

Formally, an LBA $\mathcal{A}$ is specified as $\mathcal{A} = \langle \Sigma, \Delta, Q, q_0, Q_F, \$, \#, \delta \rangle$, where Σ, Q, q_0, Q_F have the same meaning as for FA, and

- $\Delta \supseteq \Sigma$ is a **tape alphabet**;
- $\$, \# \in \Delta - \Sigma$ are special **markers**;
- $\delta \subseteq Q \times \Delta \times Q \times \Delta \times \{\leftarrow, \downarrow, \rightarrow\}$ is a **transition relation** satisfying the above-mentioned conditions (that is, if $(p,a,q,b,d) \in \delta$, then $b \notin \{\$, \#\}, a = \$ \Rightarrow d \neq \leftarrow, a = \# \Rightarrow d \neq \rightarrow), a = \$ \Rightarrow b = \$, a = \# \Rightarrow b = \#$.

A LBA $\mathcal{A}$ may perform a transition $(p,a,b,q,d) \in \delta$ when $\mathcal{A}$ is in the state p and the head reads a. In this case the finite control of $\mathcal{A}$ goes to state q, the head rewrites a by b and moves in the direction d. Of course, in general there may be more than one quintuple in δ starting with the same p and a; therefore a move of the head may be nondeterministic. If δ is a function of its first two arguments, then we have a **deterministic LBA** (**DLBA** for short).

To describe a **computation** on a LBA $\mathcal{A}$, the concept of **configuration** is again useful. This is a word of the form $w_1qw_2 \in \Delta^*Q\Delta^*$. A LBA $\mathcal{A}$ is in the configuration w_1qw_2 if q is its current state, w_1w_2 the contents of the tape, and the head is positioned on the first symbol of w_2 (see Figure 3.34b). A configuration is **initial** if it has the form q_0w, $w \in \Sigma^*$ (the input alphabet), and **final** if its state is final.

The concept of a configuration is very helpful in formally defining a computation on a LBA. In order to do this, we first introduce the concept of a computation step. A configuration C' is a **direct successor** of a configuration C; in short $C \vdash C'$, if C' is a configuration that can be obtained from C by performing a transition, a computation step. A configuration is called **terminating** if there is no configuration that would be its direct successor. (In a terminating computation the LBA 'halts'.) If $C \vdash^* C'$, then C' is called a **successor configuration** of C, or a configuration that can be **reached** from C. A **computation** of a LBA is a finite or infinite sequence of configurations that starts with the initial configuration, and, for any integer $i > 1$, the ith configuration is a direct successor of the $(i-1)$-th configuration. A **terminating computation** is a finite computation that ends with a terminating configuration.

The language accepted by a LBA $\mathcal{A}$ is defined as follows:

$$L(\mathcal{A}) = \{w \in \Sigma^* \mid \exists \text{ computation starting in } q_0 w \text{ and ending in a final configuration}\}.$$

To describe a LBA formally, its transition relation must be specified. To do this in detail may be tedious, but it is basically a straightforward task when a high-level algorithm describing its behaviour is given, as in the following example.

Example 3.8.23 *We describe the behaviour of a LBA which recognizes the language* $\{a^i b^i \mid i \geq 1\}$.

begin Check if the input word has the form $a^i b^j$ – if not, then reject;
  while there are at least one a and one b on the tape
    do erase one a and one b;
  if there is still a symbol a or b on the tape **then** reject **else** accept
end

Exercise 3.8.24 *Describe a LBA which accepts the language* $\{a^i b^i c^i \mid i \geq 1\}$.

The above examples show that DLBA can accept languages that are not regular; therefore DLBA are more powerful than finite automata. On the other hand, it is not known whether nondeterminism brings new power in the case of LBA.

Open problem 3.8.25 (LBA problem) *Are LBA more powerful as DLBA?*

This is one of the longest standing open problems in foundations of computing.

The next natural question to ask is how powerful are LBA compared with multi-head FA (because multi-head FA have been shown to be more powerful than finite automata). It is in a sense a question as to what provides more power: a possibility to write (and thereby to store immediate results and to make use of memory of a size proportional to the size of the input) or a possibility to use more heads (and thereby parallelism).

Let us denote by $\mathcal{L}(LBA)$ the family of languages accepted by LBA and by $\mathcal{L}(DLBA)$ the family of languages accepted by DLBA. For a reason that will be made clear in Chapter 7, languages from $\mathcal{L}(LBA)$ are called **context-sensitive**, and those from $\mathcal{L}(DLBA)$ are called **deterministic context-sensitive**.

Theorem 3.8.26 *The following relations hold between the families of languages accepted by multi-head finite automata and LBA:*

$$\bigcup_{k=1}^{\infty} \mathcal{L}(k\text{-2DFA}) \subsetneq \mathcal{L}(\text{DLBA}), \tag{3.11}$$

$$\bigcup_{k=1}^{\infty} \mathcal{L}(k\text{-2NFA}) \subsetneq \mathcal{L}(\text{NLBA}). \tag{3.12}$$

We show here only that each multihead 2DFA can be simulated by a DLBA. Simulation of a multihead 2NFA by a NLBA can be done similarly. The proof that there is a language accepted by a DLBA but not accepted by a multihead 2DFA, and likewise for the nondeterministic case, is beyond the scope of this book.

In order to simulate a k-head 2DFA $\mathcal{A}$ by a DLBA $\mathcal{B}$, we need:

(a) to represent a configuration of $\mathcal{A}$ by a configuration of $\mathcal{B}$;
(b) to simulate one transition of $\mathcal{A}$ by a computation on $\mathcal{B}$.

(a) **Representation of configurations.** A configuration of $\mathcal{A}$ is given by a state q, a tape content $w = w_1 \ldots w_n$ and the positions of the k heads. In order to represent this information in a configuration of $\mathcal{B}$, the jth symbol of w, that is, w_j, is represented at any moment of a computation by a $(k+2)$-tuple $(q, w_j, s_1, \ldots, s_k)$, where $s_i = 1$ if the ith head of $\mathcal{A}$ stays, in the given configuration of $\mathcal{A}$, on the ith cell, and $s_i = 0$, otherwise. Moreover, in order to create the representation of the initial configuration of $\mathcal{A}$, $\mathcal{B}$ replaces the symbol w_1 in the given input word w by $(q_0, w_1, 1, \ldots, 1)$ and all other $w_i, 1 < i \leq |w|$ by $(q_0, w_i, 0, \ldots, 0)$.

(b) **Simulation of one step of** $\mathcal{A}$. $\mathcal{B}$ reads the whole tape content, and remembers in its finite state control the state of $\mathcal{A}$ and the symbols read by heads in the corresponding configuration of $\mathcal{A}$. This information is enough for $\mathcal{B}$ to simulate a transition of $\mathcal{A}$. $\mathcal{B}$ need only make an additional pass through the tape in order to replace the old state of $\mathcal{A}$ by the new one and update the positions of all heads of $\mathcal{A}$. □

It can happen that a LBA gets into an infinite computation. Indeed, the head can get into a cycle, for example, one step right and one step left, without rewriting the tape. However, in spite of this the following theorem holds.

Theorem 3.8.27 *The membership problem for LBA is decidable.*

Proof: First an observation: the number of configurations of a LBA $\mathcal{A} = \langle \Sigma, \Delta, Q, q_0, Q_F, \$, \#, \delta \rangle$ that can be reached from an initial configuration q_0w is bounded by $c_w = |Q||\Delta|^{|w|}(|w|+2)$. ($\Delta^{|w|}$ is the number of possible contents of the tape of length $|w|$, $|w|+2$ is the number of cells the head can stand on, and $|Q|$ is the number of possible states.) This implies that if $\mathcal{A}$ is a DLBA, then it is sufficient to simulate c_w steps of $\mathcal{A}$ in order to find out whether there is a terminal configuration reachable from the initial configuration q_0w – that is, whether w is accepted by $\mathcal{A}$. Indeed, if $\mathcal{A}$ does not terminate in c_w steps, then it must be in an infinite loop. If $\mathcal{A}$ is not deterministic, then configurations reachable from the initial configuration q_0w form a configuration tree (see Figure 3.35), and in order to find out whether $w \in L(\mathcal{A})$, it is enough to check all configurations of this tree up to the depth c_w. □

The fact that a LBA may not halt is unfortunate. This makes it hard to design more complex LBA from simpler ones, for example, by using sequential composition of LBA. The following result is therefore of importance.

Theorem 3.8.28 *For each LBA there is an equivalent LBA that always terminates.*

To prove this theorem, we apply a new and often useful technique of dividing the tape into more tracks (see Figure 3.36), in this case into two. Informally, each cell of the tape is divided into an upper and a lower subcell. Each of these subcells can contain a symbol and the head can work on the tape in such a way as to read and write only to a subcell of one of the tracks. Formally, this is nothing other than using pairs $\frac{x}{y}$ of symbols as symbols of the tape alphabet, and at each writing changing either none or only one of them or both of them.

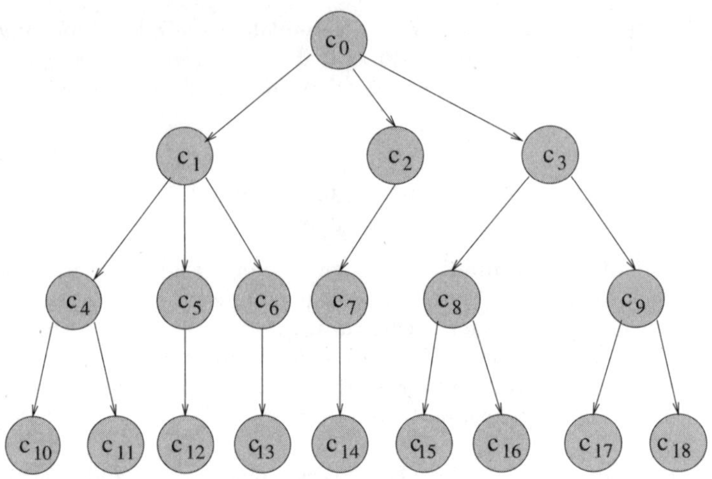

Figure 3.35 Configuration tree

	a	c	e	g	i	k	m	o	r	t	v	
	b	d	f	h	j	l	n	p	s	u	w	

(a) one tape with two tracks

	$\frac{a}{b}$	$\frac{c}{d}$	$\frac{e}{f}$	$\frac{g}{h}$	$\frac{i}{j}$	$\frac{k}{l}$	$\frac{m}{n}$	$\frac{o}{p}$	$\frac{r}{s}$	$\frac{t}{u}$	$\frac{v}{w}$	

(b) one tape with one track

Figure 3.36 A tape with two or one tracks

Proof: Given an LBA $\mathcal{A}$ with input alphabet Σ, we design from $\mathcal{A}$ another LBA $\mathcal{B}$ the tape of which consists of two tracks. At the beginning of a computation the input word w is seen as being written in the upper track. $\mathcal{B}$ first computes the number $c_w = |Q||\Delta|^{|w|}(|w|+2)$, the maximum number of possible configurations, and stores this number in the second track. (Such a computation is not a problem with LBA power.) Space is another issue. There is, however, enough space to write c_w on the second track, because $|Q||\Delta|^{|w|}(|w|+2) \leq (2|Q||\Delta|)^{|w|}$. Therefore it is enough to use a number system with a sufficiently large base, for example, $2|Q||\Delta|$, the size of which does not depend on the input word w. $\mathcal{B}$ then simulates the computation of $\mathcal{A}$ step by step. Whenever the simulation of a step of $\mathcal{A}$ is finished, $\mathcal{B}$ decreases the number on the second track by 1. If $\mathcal{A}$ accepts before the number on the second track is zero, then $\mathcal{B}$ accepts as well. If $\mathcal{B}$ decreases the number on the second track to zero, then $\mathcal{B}$ moves to a terminating, but not a final, state. Clearly, $\mathcal{B}$ accepts an input word w if and only if $\mathcal{A}$ does. □

The family of context-sensitive languages contains practically all formal languages one has to deal with in practice. It is a rich family, and one of its basic properties is stated in the following theorem.

Theorem 3.8.29 *Both families $\mathcal{L}(LBA)$ and $\mathcal{L}(DLBA)$ are closed under Boolean operations (union, intersection and complementation).*

Proof: Given two LBA (or DLBA) $\mathcal{A}_1, \mathcal{A}_2$ that always terminate, it is easy to design a LBA (or DLBA) that for a given input w simulates first the computation of $\mathcal{A}_1$ on w and then the computation of $\mathcal{A}_2$ on w, and accepts w if and only if both $\mathcal{A}_1$ and $\mathcal{A}_2$ accept w (in the case of intersection) or if at least one of them accepts it (in the case of union). This implies closure under union and intersection. To show closure under complementation is fairly easy for a DLBA $\mathcal{A} = \langle \Sigma, \Delta, Q, q_0, Q_F, \delta, \$, \#, \delta \rangle$, which always terminates. It is enough to take $Q - Q_F$ instead of Q_F as the set of the final states. The proof that the family $\mathcal{L}(LBA)$ is also closed under complementation is much more involved. □

Another natural idea for enhancing the power of finite automata is to allow the head to move everywhere on the tape and to do writing and reading everywhere, not only on cells occupied by the input word. This will be explored in the following chapter and, as we shall see, it leads to the most powerful concept of machines we have.

All the automata we have dealt with in this chapter can be seen as more or less restricted variants of the Turing machines discussed in the next chapter. All the techniques used to design automata in this chapter can be used also as techniques 'to program' Turing machines. This is also one of the reasons why we discussed such models as LBA in detail.

Moral: Automata, like people, can look very similar and be very different, and can look very different and be very similar. A good rule of thumb in dealing with automata is, as in life, to think twice and explore carefully before making a final judgement.

3.9 Exercises

1. Let $\mathcal{A}$ be the FA over the alphabet $\{a,b\}$ with the initial state 1, the final state 3, and the transition relation $\delta = \{(1,a,1),(1,b,1),(1,a,2),(2,b,3)\}$. Design an equivalent deterministic and complete FA.

2. Design state graphs for FA which accept the following languages: (a) $L = \{w \mid w \in \{a,b\}^*, aaa \text{ is not a subword of } w\}$; (b) $L = \{w \mid w \in \{a,b\}^*, w = xbv, |v| = 2\}$; (c) $L = \{w \mid w \in \{a,b\}^*, aaa$ is not a subword of of w and $w = xby, |y| = 2\}$.

3. Design a finite automaton to decide whether a given number n is divided by 3 for the cases: (a) n is given in binary, the most significant digit first; (b) n is given in binary, the least significant digit first; (c) n is given in decimal; (d)* n is given in Fibonacci number representation.

4. Show that if a language L_1 can be recognized by a DFA with n states and L_2 by a DFA with m states, then there is a DFA with $n2^m$ states that recognizes the language L_1L_2 (and in some cases no smaller DFA for L_1L_2 exists).

5.* Show that for any n-state DFA $\mathcal{A}$ there exists a DFA $\mathcal{A}'$ having at most $2^{n-1} + 2^{n-2}$ states and such that $L(\mathcal{A}') = (L(\mathcal{A}))^*$.

6. Show that a language $L \subseteq \{a\}^*$ over a one-symbol alphabet is regular if and only if there are two finite sets $M_1, M_2 \subset \{a\}^*$ and a $w \in \{a\}^*$ such that $L = M_1 \cup M_2\{w\}^*$.

7. Show that if R is a regular language, then so is the language $R_{half} = \{x \mid \exists y |x| = |y|, xy \in R\}$.

8. Show that the following languages are not regular: (a) $\{ww \mid w \in \{a,b\}^*\}$;

   (b) $\{a^ib^jc^j \mid i,j \geq 1\} \cup b^*c^*$; (c) $L = \{w \mid w \in \{a,b\}^*, w$ contains more a's than b's$\}$.

9. Which of the following languages is regular: (a) UNEQUAL=$\{a^nb^m \mid n,m \in \mathbf{N}, n \neq m\}$; (b) $\{a\}^*$UNEQUAL; (c) $\{b\}^*$UNEQUAL?

10. Show that the following languages are not regular: (a) $\{a^{2^n} \mid n \geq 1\}$; (b) $\{a^{n!} \mid n \geq 1\}$.

11. Let w be a string. How many states has the minimal DFA recognizing the set of all substrings of w?

12.* Let $L_n = \{x_1\#x_2\#\ldots x_m\#\#x \mid x_i \in \{a,b\}^n, x = x_j \text{ for some } 1 \le j \le m\}$. Show that each DFA accepting L_n must have 2^{2^n} states.

13. Let R_1 and R_2 be regular languages recognized by DFA $\mathcal{A}_1$ and $\mathcal{A}_2$ with r and s states, respectively. Show that the languages $R_1 \cup R_2$ and $R_1 \cap R_2$ can be recognized by DFA with rs states. (Hint: take the Cartesian product of the states of $\mathcal{A}_1$ and $\mathcal{A}_2$ as the new set of states.)

14. Find two languages L_1, L_2 such that neither of them is regular but their union and also their intersection are.

15. For two languages $K, L \subset \Sigma^*$ define the right quotient $K/L = \{u \in \Sigma^* \mid \exists v \in L, uv \in K\}$. Show that the family of regular languages is closed under the operation of right quotient.

16.* Let us assume that there exists a morphism ϕ from Σ^* to a finite monoid $\mathcal{M}$, and let for some $L \subseteq \Sigma^*, \phi^{-1}(\phi(L)) = L$. Prove that L is a regular language.

17.* Show that the regular language $\{10101\}^*$ can be expressed without the operation of iteration, using only the operations of union, concatenation, complementation and intersection.

18. Show that the family of regular languages is closed under the shuffle operation.

19. Show that if a tree automaton has the property that for the acceptance of an input word it does not matter which level of processors is used to start the computation with an input word w, provided the level has at least $|w|$ processors and the input is given to the left-most processor, one symbol per processor, then such a tree automaton always accepts a regular language.

20. Let $R \subset \Sigma^*$ be a regular language. Is the language $twist(R)$ defined by the following mapping: $TWIST : \Sigma^* \to \Sigma^*$; $TWIST(x) = x$ if $x \in \Sigma \cup \{\varepsilon\}$, $TWIST(awb) = abTWIST(w)$ if $a, b \in \Sigma$, regular?

21. Design a Moore or a Mealy machine with three states which for the input 00001000100010 produces as output 01010000101001.

22. Show that the family of relations defined by finite transducers is closed under composition.

23.* Let f be a bijection between Σ^* and Δ^* that preserves prefixes, lengths and regular sets. Show that f is realized by a generalized sequential machine.

24. Which image transformations realize the WFT in Figure 3.37?

25. Construct a WFT to perform (a)** a rotation by 90 degrees counterclockwise with linear slope; (b)* stretching defined by the mapping $(x,y) \to (x, \frac{3}{2}y)$.

26.** Show that the function computed by the LWFT depicted in Figure 3.38 is continuous if and only if the following two conditions are satisfied: (1) $\alpha + \beta = 1$, (2) $\delta(1-\alpha) = \gamma(1-\delta)$, $0 \le \alpha, \beta \le 1$, $0 \le \gamma, \delta$.

27.* Show that the polynomial x^n can be computed by a WFA with $n+1$ states $(q_n, \ldots, q_0)$ with the initial distribution $(1, 0, \ldots, 0)$, final distribution $(1, \ldots, 1)$ and the following transitions:

(1) $q_i \xrightarrow{j, 2^{-i}} q_i$ for $j = 0, 1, i = 0, 1, \ldots, n$; (2) $q_i \xrightarrow{1, 2^{-i}\binom{i}{t}} q_{i-t}$, for $i = 1, \ldots, n$ and $t = 1, \ldots, i$.

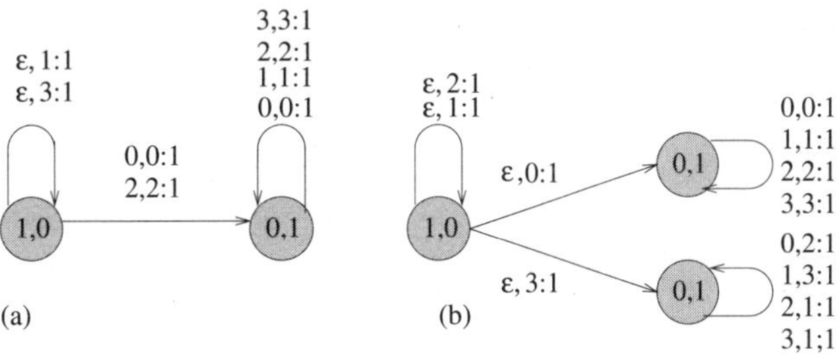

Figure 3.37 WFA

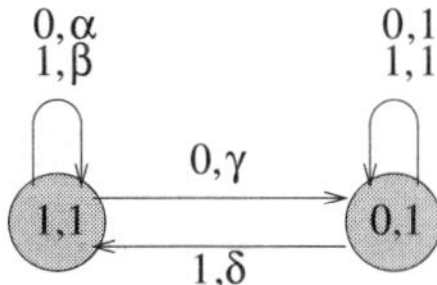

Figure 3.38 LWFT

28. Prove the second assertion of Theorem 3.6.4.

29. Show that the ω-language $\{a^n b^n c^\omega \mid n \geq 0\}$ is not regular.

30. Design Büchi automata that recognize the following ω-languages: (a) an ω-language consisting of ω-words over the alphabet $\{a,b,c\}$ with infinitely many a's and b's and such that there is an odd number of c's between any two symbols from $\{a,b\}$; (b) an ω-language consisting of all ω-words over $\{a,b,c\}$ with infinitely many a's and b's, but with never more than three c's in a row.

31. Determine whether the following ω-languages are regular: (a) $\{a^i b^i \mid i \geq 0\}^\omega$; (b) $\{a^i b^j \mid i,j \geq 0\}^\omega$; (c) $\{a^i b^j \mid 1 \leq i \leq j\}^\omega$.

32. Show that there is no finite state machine to compute the following functions $f : \mathbf{N} :\rightarrow \mathbf{N}$: (a) $f(n) = n^2$; (b) $f(n) = \lfloor \sqrt{n} \rfloor$.

33. Design a transition system with as few states as possible to recognize the languages (a) $\{a^{3i} b^{4j} \mid i,j \geq 1\}$; (b)* $L_n = \{a^i \mid 1 \leq i \leq n\}$.

34. Let $\mathcal{A} = \langle \Sigma, Q, Q_I, Q_F, \delta \rangle$ be a transition system with the alphabet $\Sigma = \{a,b,c\}$, states $Q = \{1,2,\ldots,7\}$, the initial states $Q_I = \{1,2\}$, the final states $Q_F = \{4,5\}$ and the transitions $\{(1,abc,5),(2,\varepsilon,4),\ (3,b,4),\ (4,a,6),\ (4,c,7),\ (6,c,5)\}$. Transform $\mathcal{A}$, step by step, into an equivalent transition system with the following properties: (a) only one initial state; (b) transitions only on symbols from $\Sigma \cup \{\varepsilon\}$; (c) transitions on all symbols from all states; (d) all states reachable from the initial state; (e) complete and deterministic FA.

35. Show that every stochastic language is c-stochastic for any $0 \leq c \leq 1$.

36.* Give an example of a probabilistic finite automaton which accepts a nonregular language with the cut-point $\frac{1}{3}$.

37. Design a multi-head FA that recognizes the languages (a) $\{a^ib^jc^id^j \mid i,j \geq 1\}$; (b) $\{ww^R \mid w \in \{0,1\}^*\}$.

38. Design LBA that recognize the languages (a) $\{a^i \mid i \text{ is a prime}\}$; (b) $\{ww^R \mid, w \in \{0,1\}^*\}$.

39. Which of the following string-to-string functions over the alphabet $\{0,1\}$ can be realized by a finite transducer: (a) $w \rightarrow w^R$; (b) $w_1 \ldots w_n \rightarrow w_1w_1w_2w_2 \ldots w_nw_n$; (c) $w_1 \ldots w_n \rightarrow w_1 \ldots w_nw_1 \ldots w_n$?

Questions

1. When does the subset construction yield the empty set of states as a new reachable state?
2. Are minimal nondeterministic finite automata always unique?
3. Is the set of regular languages closed under the shuffle operation?
4. Is the mapping $1^i \rightarrow 1^{F_i}$ realizable by a finite transducer?
5. What is the role of initial and terminal distributions for WFA?
6. How can one define WFA generating three-dimensional images?
7. Weighted finite automata and probabilistic finite automata are defined very similarly. What are the differences?
8. Does the power of two-way finite automata change if we assume that input is put between two end markers?
9. Are LBA with several heads on the tape more powerful than ordinary LBA?
10. What are natural ways to define finite automata on $\omega\omega$- words, and how can one define in a natural way the concept of regular $\omega\omega$- languages?

3.10 Historical and Bibliographical References

It is surprising that such a basic and elementary concept as that of finite state machine was discovered only in the middle of this century. The lecture of John von Neumann (1951) can be seen as the initiative to develop a mathematical theory of automata, though the concept of finite automata, as discussed in this chapter, is usually credited to McCulloch and Pitts (1943). Its modern formalization is due to Moore (1956) and Scott (1959). (Dana Scott received the Turing award in 1976.)

Finite automata are the subject of numerous books: for example, Salomaa (1969), Hopcroft and Ullman (1969), Brauer (1984) and Floyd and Beigel (1994). (John E. Hopcroft received the Turing award in 1986 for his contribution to data structures, Robert Floyd in 1978 for his contribution to program correctness.) A very comprehensive but also very special treatment of the subject is due to Eilenberg (1974). See also the survey by Perrin (1990).

Bar-Hillel and his collaborators, see Bar-Hillel (1964), were the first to deal with finite automata in more detail. The concept of NFA and Theorem 3.2.8 are due to Rabin and Scott (1959). The proof that there is a NFA with n states such that each equivalent DFA has 2^n states can be found in Trakhtenbrot and Barzdin (1973) and in Lupanov (1963). Minimization of finite automata and Theorem 3.2.16 are due to Huffman (1954) and Moore (1956). The first minimization algorithm, based on two operations, is from Brauer (1988) and credited to Brzozowski (1962). Asymptotically the fastest known minimization algorithm, in time $\mathcal{O}(mn \lg n)$, is due to Hopcroft (1971). The pumping lemma for regular language has emerged in the course of time; for two variants and detailed discussion see Floyd and Beigel (1994). For string-matching algorithms see Knuth, Morris and Pratt (1977).

The concepts of regular language and regular expression and Theorem 3.3.6 are due to Kleene (1956). The concept of derivatives of regular languages is due to Brzozowski (1964). Very high lower bounds for the inequivalence problem for generalized regular expressions are due to Stockmeyer and Meyer (1973). The characterization of regular languages in terms of syntactical congruences, Theorems 3.3.16 and 3.3.17 are due to Myhill (1957) and Nerode (1958). The recognition of regular languages in logarithmic time using syntactical monoids is due to Culik, Salomaa, and Wood (1984). The existence of regular languages for which each processor of the recognizing tree network of processors has to be huge is due to Gruska, Napoli and Parente (1994).

For two main models of finite state machines see Mealy (1955) and Moore (1956), and for their detailed analysis see Brauer (1984). The results concerning finite transducers and generalized sequential machines, Theorems 3.4.8–11 are due to Ginsburg and Rose (1963, 1966); see also Ginsburg (1966). (Moore and Mealy machines are also called Moore and Mealy automata and in such a case finite automata as defined in Section 3.1 are called Rabin-Scott automata.)

The concept of a weighted finite automaton and a weighted finite transducer are due to Culik and his collaborators: Culik and Kari (1993, 1994,1995); Culik and Friš (1995); Culik and Rajčáni (1996). See also Culik and Kari (1995) and Rajčáni (1995) for a survey. Section 3.4.2 and examples, exercises and images are derived from these and related papers. For a more practical 'recursive image compression algorithm' see Culik and Kari (1994). The idea of using finite automata to compute continuous functions is due to Culik and Karhumäki (1994). The existence of a function that is everywhere continuous, but nowhere has derivatives and is still computable by WFA is due to Derencourt, Karhumäki, Latteux and Terlutte (1994). An interesting and powerful generalization of WFT, the iterative WFT, has been introduced by Culik and Rajčáni (1995).

The idea of finite automata on infinite words is due to Büchi (1960) and McNaughton (1966). Together with the concept of finite automata on infinite trees, due to Rabin (1969), this created the foundations for areas of computing dealing with nonterminating processes. For Muller automata see Muller (1963). A detailed overview of computations on infinite objects is due to Gale and Stewart (1953) and Thomas (1990). For a presentation of problems and results concerning Gale–Stewart (1953) games see Thomas (1995).

The concept of a transition system and Theorem 3.8.1 are due to Myhill (1957). Probabilistic finite automata were introduced by Rabin (1963), Carlyle (1964) and Bucharaev (1964). Theorems 3.8.8 and 3.8.9 are due to Rabin (1963), and the proof of the second theorem presented here is due to Paz (1971). See also Salomaa (1969), Starke (1969) and Bucharaev (1995) for probabilistic finite automata.

Two-way finite automata were introduced early on by Rabin and Scott (1959), who also made a sketch of the proof of Theorem 3.8.17. A simpler proof is due to Shepherdson (1959); see also Hopcroft and Ullman (1969). Example 3.8.16 is due to Barnes (1971) and Brauer (1984). For results concerning the economy of description of regular languages with two-way FA see Meyer and Fischer (1971). Multi-head finite automata were introduced by Rosenberg (1966), and the existence of infinite hierarchies was shown by Yao and Rivest (1978) for the one-way case and Monien (1980) for two-way k-head finite automata.

Deterministic linearly bounded automata were introduced by Myhill (1960), nondeterministic ones by Kuroda (1964). The closure of DLBA under intersection and complementation was shown by Landweber (1963), and the closure of NLBA under complementation independently by Szelepcsényi (1987) and Immerman (1988).

4 Computers

INTRODUCTION

The discovery that there are universal computers, which in principle are very simple, is the basis of modern computing theory and practice. The aim of this chapter is to present and demonstrate the main models of universal computers, their properties, mutual relations and various deep conclusions one can draw from their existence and properties. Computer models help us not only to get insights into what computers can do and how, but also to discover tasks they cannot do.

The following computer models are considered in this chapter: several variants of Turing machines; several variants of random access machines, including parallel random access machines; families of Boolean circuits; and cellular automata. Each plays an important role in some theoretical and methodological considerations in computing. On the one hand, a large variety of these models demonstrates convincingly the robustness of the concept of universality in computing. On the other hand, different models allow us to deal in a transparent way with different modes and aspects of computing.

LEARNING OBJECTIVES

The aim of the chapter is to demonstrate

1. several basic models of universal computers, their properties and basic programming techniques for them;
2. basic time speed-up and space compression results;
3. methods of simulating the main models of universal computers on each other;
4. two classes of universal computers that correspond to inherently sequential and inherently parallel computers, respectively;
5. how to derive basic undecidability and unsolvability results;
6. the main theses of computing: Church's thesis, the sequential computation thesis and the parallel computation thesis.

> 'There's no use in trying', she said: 'one can't believe impossible things.'
> 'I daresay you haven't had much practice', said the Queen. 'When I was your age, I always did it for half-an-hour a day. Why, sometimes I've believed as many as six impossible things before breakfast.'
>
> *Lewis Carroll, Through the Looking-glass, 1872*

The discovery of universal computers is among the most important successes of twentieth-century science. It can be seen as a natural culmination of a centuries-long process of searching for principles and limitations of both mind and machines. Amplified by the enormous information-processing power of matter and advances in modern technology, the discovery of very simple universal computers resulted very soon in the most powerful tool of mind and humankind.

Several basic models of universal computers are introduced, demonstrated and analysed in this chapter. Mutual simulations of these models, on which we also concentrate, show a variety of methods for transforming programs for one universal computer to programs for another. They also show that there are actually two main classes of computer models: inherently sequential and inherently parallel.

Each model of a universal computer is essentially a universal programming language. However, these programming languages have control and data structures which are too simple to be useful in a practical application. However, their simplicity and elegance make them excellent tools for discovering the laws and limitations of computing, and allow us to use exact methods to demonstrate the correctness of our findings.

Models of sequential computers seem already to be quite satisfactorily developed. Some of them fully correspond to the needs of theory. Others model real computers sufficiently well and their theoretical analysis provides deep insights and useful forecasts. This does not seem to be the case yet in the area of parallel computing.

A clear tendency in computer development is to build larger and larger finite machines for larger and larger tasks. Though the detailed structure of bigger machines is usually different from that of smaller ones, there is some uniformity among computers of different size. Computer models therefore consist either of an infinite family of uniformly designed finite computers, or this uniformity has to be pushed to the limit and models infinite in size (of memory) have to be considered.

The concept of a universal computer demonstrates how little is sufficient to do everything one can do with algorithmic methods. It has turned out that the most important/fruitful way to study the power of various computer models and computational problems is to investigate the amount of computational resources needed to solve problems and to simulate one computer model on another. The main resources are time, storage, processors, programs, communication and randomness.

Time is the most natural resource, and is potentially unbounded for computers. It is therefore natural to consider as reasonable cases in which the amount of time needed to solve a problem grows with the size of the problem. Storage and processors, in the case of parallel computing, seem to be qualitatively different resources because their size is clearly bounded for any real computer. In spite of this, it has turned out to be very fruitful to consider for these resources that the amount grows with the size of the problem.

We deal in this chapter with time, storage and processors as resources, in Chapter 6 with (the size of) programs, and in Chapter 11 with communication.

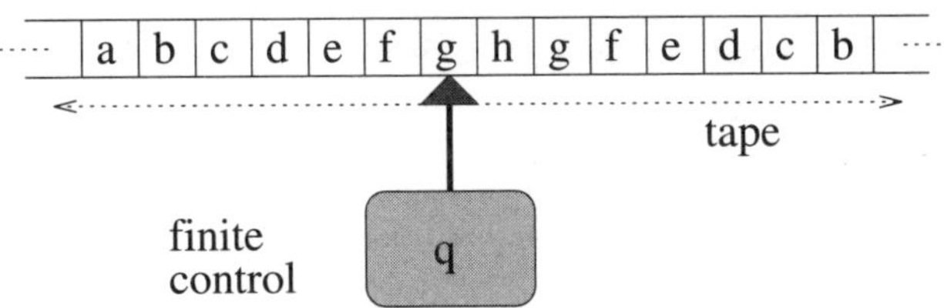

Figure 4.1 One-tape Turing machine

4.1 Turing Machines

The very first (infinite) model of a computer, was invented in 1936 by A. M. Turing,[1] one of the fathers of modern computer science and technology. It is called, in his honour, a **(one-tape) Turing machine**, for short, TM (see Figure 4.1). This model serves as a basis for several other basic computer and computational models and modes, on which complexity theory is developed, and some of the key concepts of modern science are built. The main reasons for the enormous importance of this model are its simplicity, elegance and flexibility and the fact that the basic step of Turing machines is indeed elementary, both from the operational and the communication point of view.

4.1.1 Basic Concepts

Informally, a one-tape TM is similar to the linearly bounded automaton discussed in Section 3.8, but without any restriction on the moves of the head. The head can also move, write and read outside the cells occupied by the input. This immediately implies that for Turing machines we can apply the basic concepts and also the programming techniques introduced for various generalizations of finite automata in Section 3.8.

Formally (see Figure 4.1), a (one-tape) TM $\mathcal{M}$ consists of a **bi-infinite tape** divided into an infinite number of cells in both directions, with one distinctive starting cell, or 0-th cell. Cells of the tape can contain any symbol from a finite **tape alphabet** Γ, or a symbol $\sqcup$ (that may also be in Γ), representing an empty cell; a **read–write head** positioned at any moment of the discrete time on a cell; a **finite control unit** that is always in one of the states: either of a finite **set** Q **of nonterminating states** (containing the initial state, say q_0) or one of the **terminal states** from the set $H = \{HALT, ACCEPT, REJECT\}$[2] and implementing a (partial) **transition function**

$$\delta : Q \times \Gamma \rightarrow (Q \cup H) \times \Gamma \times \{\leftarrow, \downarrow, \rightarrow\}.$$

Interpretation: $\delta(q,x) = (q',x',d)$ means that if $\mathcal{M}$ is in state q and the head reads x, then $\mathcal{M}$ enters the state q', stores x' in the cell the head is currently on, and the head moves in the direction d, to the right if $d = \rightarrow$, to the left if $d = \leftarrow$, and does not move at all if $d = \downarrow$. Formally, $\mathcal{M} = \langle \Gamma, Q, q_0, \delta \rangle$, but sometimes, if there is a need to consider explicitly a subset $\Sigma \subseteq \Gamma - \{\sqcup\}$ as the input alphabet, we consider a TM $\mathcal{M}$ of the form $\mathcal{M} = \langle \Sigma, \Gamma, Q, q_0, \delta \rangle$.

---

[1] Alan M. Turing (1912–54) was an English mathematician. He wrote fundamental papers on computability and artificial intelligence. During the Second World War Turing participated in the cryptographical project ULTRA in Bletchley Park and in the design of Colossus, the first powerful electronic computer. After the war he supervised the design and building of ACE, a large electronic digital computer at the National Physical Laboratory. His last and longest papers laid the foundation for mathematical biology.

[2] If conciseness is very important, we use notation *YES* and *NO* to denote states *ACCEPT* and *REJECT*, respectively.

A **computation** of a TM $\mathcal{M}$ can be defined formally using the concept of **configuration** of the form (q,w,w'), where $q \in Q \cup H$, and $w, w' \in \Gamma^*$. Each configuration contains a complete description of the current **'global' state** of the computation: the state q the machine is in, the content ww' of the tape and the position of the head – on the first symbol of w' (if $w' \neq \varepsilon$, or on the first cell after the last symbol of w). (We assume that only such tapes are used all but finitely many symbols of which are blanks $\sqcup$, and in writing down a configuration infinitely many left-most and right-most $\sqcup$'s are discarded.) If $\mathcal{M}$ moves in one step from a configuration C to a configuration C', we write $C \vdash_{\mathcal{M}} C'$. By writing $C \overset{m}{\underset{\mathcal{M}}{\vdash}} C'$, $(C \overset{*}{\underset{\mathcal{M}}{\vdash}} C')$, we denote that the configuration C yields in m steps (some finite number of steps) the configuration C'. Each configuration (q_0, ε, w), $w \in (\Gamma - \{\sqcup\})^*$ is called **initial**, and each configuration (q,w,w'), $q \in H$ is called **terminating**. A finite sequence of configurations $C_1, C_2, \ldots, C_m$ is called a **terminating computation** of $\mathcal{M}$, if C_1 is an initial configuration, C_m a terminating configuration and $C_i \vdash_{\mathcal{M}} C_{i+1}$ for $i \geq 1$. (There are two ways to interpret a terminating computation of a TM $\mathcal{M}$. The first is that $\mathcal{M}$ stops, and there is no next configuration – this will be called halting. The second is that $\mathcal{M}$ keeps staying in the same configuration – this will be called an idling termination.) An infinite sequence of configurations $C_1, C_2, \ldots$, such that $C_i \vdash_{\mathcal{M}} C_{i+1}$ for all $i \geq 1$, is called an **infinite computation**.

There are four types of computations of a TM $\mathcal{M}$ when $\mathcal{M}$ starts in an initial configuration (q_0, ε, x), with the first symbol of x in the cell of the tape the head is on. If $\mathcal{M}$ yields a terminating configuration with the state *ACCEPT* (*REJECT*) [*HALT*], then $\mathcal{M}$ is said to **accept** x (**reject** x) [terminate]. If the terminating configuration is (q,w,w'), then $\mathcal{M}$ is said to terminate with the output ww'; that is, $\mathcal{M}(x) = ww'$. Finally, if a computation of $\mathcal{M}$ does not terminate, then we say that $\mathcal{M}$ diverges on the input x; in short, $\mathcal{M}(x) = \nearrow$. If $\mathcal{M}$ does not diverge, we say that $\mathcal{M}$ converges; in short, $\mathcal{M}(x) = \searrow$.

4.1.2 Acceptance of Languages and Computation of Functions

Turing machines are a natural tool for studying language acceptance and decision problems, as well as computation of string-to-string functions. This can be easily extended, as we shall soon see, to computation of integer-to-integer functions. Since finite objects can be encoded by strings, this allows us to deal with a variety of decision and computational problems.

Definition 4.1.1 *(1) Let $\mathcal{M} = \langle \Sigma, \Gamma, Q, q_0, \delta \rangle$ be a TM with the input alphabet Σ. Then*

$$L(\mathcal{M}) = \{w \mid w \in \Sigma^*, \mathcal{M}(w) = ACCEPT\}$$

is the language, over Σ, **accepted** *by $\mathcal{M}$. In addition, if $\mathcal{M}$ terminates in one of the states ACCEPT or REJECT for any $x \in \Sigma^*$, then $L(\mathcal{M})$ is said to be the language* **decided (recognized)** *by $\mathcal{M}$.*

(2) A language $L \subseteq \Sigma^*$ is said to be **recursively enumerable**, *if there is a TM $\mathcal{M}$ that accepts $L = L(\mathcal{M})$, and is called* **recursive** *if there is a TM that decides (recognizes) L.*

The distinction between the concepts of recursivity and recursive enumerability of languages is, as we shall see, important and essential. For any recursive language $L \subseteq \Sigma^*$ there is a TM $\mathcal{M}$ that terminates for any input $x \in \Sigma^*$ and always says whether $x \in L$ or not – one only has 'to wait patiently'. For a recursively enumerable language $L \subseteq \Sigma^*$, it is guaranteed only that there is a TM $\mathcal{M}$ such that $\mathcal{M}$ stops and accepts for any $x \in L$. However, $\mathcal{M}$ may or may not stop for $x \notin L$, and one has no idea how long to wait in order to find out if $\mathcal{M}$ halts or does not halt.

Definition 4.1.2 *(1) A (partial) string-to-string function $f : \Sigma^* \to \Sigma^*$ is said to be (partially) computable by a TM $\mathcal{M} = \langle \Sigma, \Gamma, Q, q_0, \delta \rangle$, $\Sigma \subseteq \Gamma$, if $\mathcal{M}(x) = f(x)$ for any $x \in \Sigma^*$ from the domain of f and $\mathcal{M}(x) = \nearrow$, otherwise.*

state	$\sqcup$	0	1
q_0	$YES,\sqcup,\downarrow$	$r_0,\sqcup,\rightarrow$	$r_1,\sqcup,\rightarrow$
r_0	$YES,\sqcup,\downarrow$	$r_0',0,\rightarrow$	$r_0',1,\rightarrow$
r_1	$YES,\sqcup,\downarrow$	$r_1',0,\rightarrow$	$r_1',1,\rightarrow$
r_0'	$s_0,\sqcup,\leftarrow$	$r_0',0,\rightarrow$	$r_0',1,\rightarrow$
r_1'	$s_1,\sqcup,\leftarrow$	$r_1',0,\rightarrow$	$r_1',1,\rightarrow$
s_0	-	$l,\sqcup,\leftarrow$	$NO,\sqcup,\downarrow$
s_1	-	$NO,\sqcup,\downarrow$	$l,\sqcup,\leftarrow$
l	$q_0,\sqcup,\rightarrow$	$l,0,\leftarrow$	$l,1,\leftarrow$

(a)

q_0	1	q'	$\sqcup$	$\rightarrow$
q'	0	HALT	$\sqcup$	$\downarrow$
q'	1	q''	$\sqcup$	$\rightarrow$
q''	0	HALT	1	$\downarrow$
q''	1	q''	1	$\rightarrow$

(b)

Figure 4.2 Turing machines recognizing palindromes and computing $x+y$

(2) If there is a TM $\mathcal{M}$ that (partially) computes a function $f : \Sigma^* \rightarrow \Sigma^*$, then f is called **(partially) recursive**.

(3) A function $f : \mathbf{N}^t \rightarrow \mathbf{N}^s$ is called **(partially) recursive** *if there is a TM $\mathcal{M}$ such that $f(x_1, \ldots, x_t) = (y_1, \ldots, y_s)$, if and only if*

$$\mathcal{M}(1^{x_1+1}01^{x_2+1}0\ldots01^{x_t+1}) = 1^{y_1+1}0\ldots01^{y_s+1}.$$

Exercise 4.1.3 *A TM, as defined above, can perform in one step three actions: a state change, writing and a head move. Show that to each TM $\mathcal{M}$ we can design a TM $\mathcal{M}'$ which performs in each step at most two of these three elementary actions and (a) accepts the same language as $\mathcal{M}$; (b) computes the same function as $\mathcal{M}$.*

Exercise 4.1.4 *Explore the possibility that for each TM $\mathcal{M}$ we can construct another TM $\mathcal{M}'$ that behaves 'essentially as $\mathcal{M}$' and in each move performs only one of the three elementary actions.*

In the following examples we illustrate three basic ways of specifying a TM. They are similar to those used to describe finite automata: transition tables, enumeration of transition tuples and state graphs.

Example 4.1.5 *The TM $\mathcal{M}_1$ described by the transition table in Figure 4.2a decides whether an input $x \in \{0,1\}^*$ is a* **palindrome**. *Informally, starting in the initial state q_0, $\mathcal{M}_1$ reads the first symbol of the word on the tape, erases this symbol, enters one of the states r_0 or r_1, depending on the symbol read, and moves one cell to the right. If $\mathcal{M}_1$ now reads $\sqcup$, then $\mathcal{M}_1$ accepts. Otherwise $\mathcal{M}_1$ goes from the state r_0 (r_1) to the state r_0' (r_1') and moves to the right end of the input string. When coming to the first cell with $\sqcup$, $\mathcal{M}_1$ moves one symbol to the left and goes from the state r_0 (r_1) to the state s_0 (s_1). If $\mathcal{M}_1$ reads 0 (1) in the state s_0 (s_1), then $\mathcal{M}_1$ replaces the symbol being read by $\sqcup$, goes to the state l, and, being in the state l, $\mathcal{M}_1$ keeps moving left until a $\sqcup$ is reached. $\mathcal{M}_1$ then moves the head one cell to the right, goes to the state q_0, and repeats the procedure. If $\mathcal{M}_1$ reads 1(0) in the state s_0 (s_1), then $\mathcal{M}_1$ rejects. If $\mathcal{M}_1$ reads $\sqcup$ in the state q_0, then $\mathcal{M}_1$ accepts.*

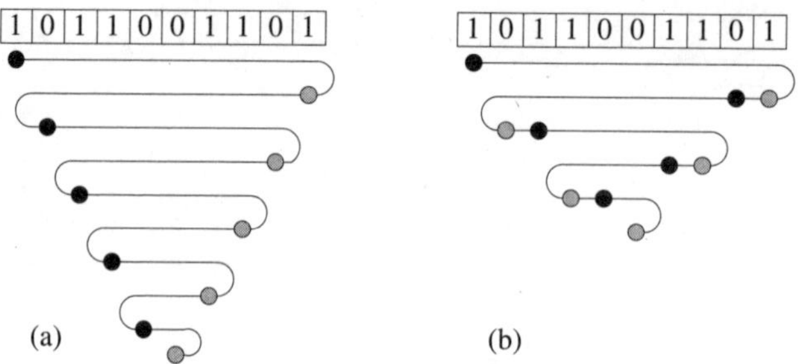

Figure 4.3 Movement of heads when recognizing palindromes

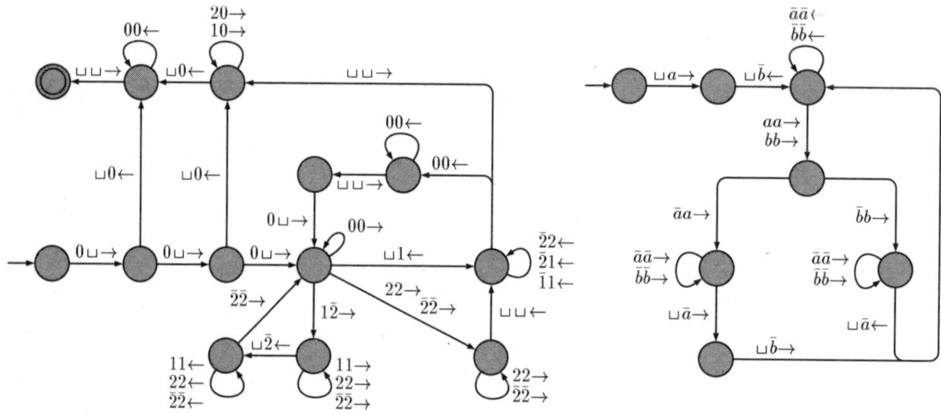

Figure 4.4 Turing machines computing Fibonacci numbers and generating Fibonacci ω-words

> **Exercise 4.1.6** *The head movement of the TM in Figure 4.2a is depicted in Figure 4.3a. Design another (faster) Turing machine with the head movement as shown in Figure 4.3b.*

Example 4.1.7 *TM $\mathcal{M}_2$, described by an enumeration of transitions in Figure 4.2b, computes the function $f(x,y) = x + y$. Indeed, $\mathcal{M}_2$ erases in the input $1^{x+1}01^{y+1}$ the first 1 and also the next 0, if $x = 0$. Otherwise, $\mathcal{M}_2$ erases also the second 1 in 1^{x+1} and moves to find the first 0. $\mathcal{M}_2$ replaces this 0 by 1 and halts.*

Example 4.1.8 *TM $\mathcal{M}_3$ depicted by the state diagram in Figure 4.4a produces for an input 0^{n+1} the output $0^{F_n'+1}$, where $F_0' = 0, F_1' = 1$ and $F_{n+1}' = F_n' + F_{n-1}'$, for $n > 1$.*

Example 4.1.9 *TM $\mathcal{M}_4$ in Figure 4.4b generates the Fibonacci ω-word (see Section 2.5) defined by $F(1) = ab, F(i) = h(F(i-1))$ for $i \geq 2$, where $h(a) = ab, h(b) = a$. (The verb 'generates' here means that $\mathcal{M}_4$, starting on the empty tape, keeps writing on its tape larger and larger words, and their prefixes from the alphabet $\{a,b\}$ form larger and larger prefixes of the Fibonacci ω-word.)*

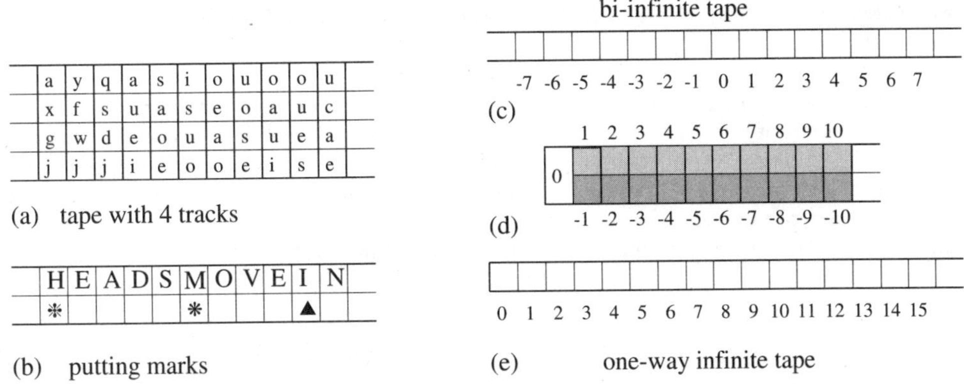

Figure 4.5 Tapes with tracks and a folding of a bi-infinite tape

Exercise 4.1.10 *Design a TM that multiplies two integers: that is, from the input* $1^{x+1}01^{y+1}$ *produces the output* 1^{xy+1}.

Exercise 4.1.11 *Design a TM that generates the Thue* ω*-word.*

Exercise 4.1.12 *Design a TM that recognizes whether a given integer is a prime.*

4.1.3 Programming Techniques, Simulations and Normal Forms

There are several basic techniques that are useful for the design of Turing machines. Dividing a tape into tracks and carrying symbols in the states are perhaps the two most basic ones. (We have actually already encountered them in Section 3.8.)

Dividing a tape into tracks. If Σ is a tape alphabet, then a division of a tape into k tracks (see Figure 4.5a for $k = 4$) actually corresponds to using the alphabet Σ^k instead of Σ. Informally, we can speak in such a case of 'changing a symbol of the ith track', but what this actually means is replacing a symbol from Σ^k by another which differs only in the ith component. One use of this technique is to leave markers on cells, as demonstrated in Figure 4.5b.

Carrying symbols in states. States can be used to 'carry symbols' or information about symbols from one part of a tape to another. Formally, this is done by creating 'compound states' (q,a), where q is an 'elementary' state, and a is a symbol to be carried out. (This technique has actually been used in Example 4.1.5.)

Example 4.1.13 *A TM with states* $\{q,q',(q,0),(q,1)\}$ *and transitions*

$$
\begin{array}{ll}
q,0,(q,0),\sqcup,\rightarrow, & q',j,q',i,\leftarrow, \\
q,1,(q,1),\sqcup,\rightarrow, & q',\sqcup,q,\sqcup,\rightarrow, \\
(q,i),j,(q,i),j,\rightarrow, & q,c,HALT,\sqcup,\downarrow, \\
(q,i),\sqcup,i,q',\leftarrow, &
\end{array}
$$

where i stands for any element from the set $\{0,1\}$ *and j stands for any element from the set* $\{0,1,c\}$*, transforms any input of the form ucw, where* $uw \in \{0,1\}^*$*, into the form wu.*

Simulation. One of the most important concepts for dealing with various models of computers is that of simulation of one machine $\mathcal{M}$ on another machine $\mathcal{M}'$. In the strong sense, this means that $\mathcal{M}'$ simulates steps of $\mathcal{M}$ in such a way that from a sequence of configurations representing a computation of $\mathcal{M}'$ one can easily obtain a sequence of configurations representing a computation of $\mathcal{M}$ for the same input. A very formal and fully general definition of this intuitive concept would be cumbersome. We shall therefore use this concept quite informally. In any particular case it will be clear what a simulation means. More restricted and more precise versions of simulation will be introduced later.

Turing machines with one-way infinite tapes. The 'normal form' of TM most often considered is that with one-way infinite tape (see Figure 4.5e). Such a TM can be seen as an ordinary Turing machine, the head of which never moves to the left from its starting position. It is easy to show that each TM $\mathcal{M}$ can be transformed into another TM $\mathcal{M}'$, with one-way infinite tape only, that simulates $\mathcal{M}$ in the same number of steps. The basic idea of such a construction is illustrated in Figure 4.5d: to fold the tape and then consider the folded tape as a two-track tape.

Exercise 4.1.14 *Show in detail how to transform any TM working on a bi-infinite tape into a TM working on a one-way infinite, two-track tape.*

Turing machines with end markers. To each TM $\mathcal{M} = \langle \Sigma, \Gamma, Q, q_0, \delta \rangle$ we can easily design a TM $\mathcal{M}' = \langle \Sigma, \Gamma \cup \{\#, \$\}, q_0, Q', \delta' \rangle$ which for an input $\#w\$$ with two end markers $\#$ and $\$$ behaves in a similar way to how $\mathcal{M}$ does on w. However, each time $\mathcal{M}'$ reaches an end marker and $\mathcal{M}$ at that moment would write or move outside the area between markers # and \$, $\mathcal{M}'$ first moves the marker accordingly, and then performs the step $\mathcal{M}$ would do.

Exercise 4.1.15 *Show that for each TM* $\mathcal{M}$ *we can design another TM* $\mathcal{M}'$ *that simulates* $\mathcal{M}$ *and in no state has the possibility of moving both right and left (that is, in no state does it have transitions of the type* $qaq'b \rightarrow$ *and also* $qcq''d \leftarrow$*).*

4.1.4 Church's Thesis

Alan Turing defined his machine model in order to formalize the intuitive concept of **effective procedure** or, as we call it today, **algorithm**.[3]

[3]The name for this intuitive concept of algorithm is derived from the Arab astronomer and mathematician Mohammed ibn Musa al-Khovârizmi (ninth century), considered to be the father of algebra. The term originated from the title *Al-jabr wa'l mugābalah* of one of his two books that played an important role in the history of mathematics and computing. In this particular book he provides algorithms for solving various linear and quadratic equations. His description of algorithms is entirely rhetorical, and deals always with particular equations. For example, the description of the procedure for solving the equation $x^2 + 10x = 39$ goes as follows: 'Take half the number of roots, that is, in this case five, then multiply this by itself and the result is five and twenty.

Intuitively, an effective procedure is a *set of rules which tells us, from step to step, precisely what to do*. For example, an effective procedure for computing a function f is a set of rules which tells us precisely what to do, from step to step, in order to obtain, from the input arguments of f, the resulting value of f after a finite number of steps.

The problem of finding an exact definition of an effective procedure becomes of crucial importance when one needs to show that there is no effective procedure for solving a given problem. It has actually never been a matter of major dispute whether a specific description is really an effective procedure. This is the main reason why the attempt to formalize such a very basic concept of science became urgent only at the beginning of this century.

The need for an exact definition of an effective procedure had already arisen in connection with the three famous problems of antiquity: **the squaring of the circle, the duplication of the cube** and **the trisection of the angle** using a straight edge and a compass only. However, these problems were very special and there was actually only intellectual curiosity behind them. The need to formulate an intuitive concept of effective procedure started to be of prime importance only at the beginning of this century, in connection with Hilbert's famous project of formalizing all our knowledge and his *Entscheidungsproblem*: given a reasonably powerful formal system, can we decide whether a given statement has a proof?

It is evident that a TM specifies an effective procedure, and that any function computable by a Turing machine is effectively computable in an intuitive sense. The concept of a TM is clearly a formalization of the intuitive concept of an effective procedure. However, since this is a very simple concept, it is natural to ask whether this formalization is not too narrow. In other words, are there algorithms or effective procedures that cannot be carried out by a Turing machine? Are there functions that are effectively computable, but not by a Turing machine?

One of the cornerstones not only of computing but also of modern science is the thesis which is usually called Church's thesis (or Church–Turing's thesis).[4]

Church's thesis Any process which could naturally be called an effective procedure can be realized by a Turing machine.

This thesis identifies a formal and an intuitive concept, and therefore cannot be proved formally. There is, however, such overwhelming evidence supporting the thesis that one can think of it as being a sort of natural law. The evidences supporting the thesis are of three types.

1. Many other formalizations of the concept of effective procedure have been developed, based on very different ideas. All of them have turned out to be provably equivalent: the μ-recursive functions of A. C. Kleene (1936); the λ-definable functions of A. Church (1941); the rewriting systems of E. L. Post (1936); the normal algorithms of A. A. Markov (1954) and several others.

2. The class of functions computed and the class of languages accepted or decided by Turing machines are very robust. Numerous modifications of the concept of Turing machines have no effect on these classes. Moreover, they are closed under all operations under which they should intuitively be closed.

3. No effective procedure is known that would not have its formal counterpart in terms of a Turing machine. There are no indications that there could exist an effective procedure that could not be programmed as a Turing machine.

Add this to nine and thirty, which gives sixty four; take the square root, or eight, and subtract from it half the number of roots, namely five, and there remains three. This is the root.'

[4] Alonzo Church (1903–94), an American logician.

Church's thesis can be and is often used as an essential tool in proofs. We shall also use it in that way in this book. Once something can be done by an effective procedure, we can assume that there is a Turing machine capable of doing it (after a proper encoding of the problem). This can always be replaced by a formal proof, though that can be a very tedious task. A formal construction of a TM resembles designing a program in an assembly code. Arguments based on Church's thesis resemble programming using a very high-level programming language.

Church's thesis is also an expression of the limitations of the concept of an effective procedure. It is therefore important to look at this thesis from the point of view of modern physics, and to ask whether there may be something beyond the Turing machine.

There is a significant physical principle underlying Church's thesis that can be formulated as follows: *Every finitely realizable physical system can be perfectly simulated by a model of a computing machine operating by finite means.*

Since classical physics is continuous and Turing machines are discrete, this principle is not obeyed by them. However, it is possible to develop a quantum generalization of Turing machines such that this machine and quantum physics are compatible with the principle.

One reason for assuming that there may be something beyond Turing machines lies in problems encountered when trying to understand the mind. There are serious views, though not shared by everybody, that the mind is more than a Turing machine and that current physical theories are insufficient to comprehend the mind; see Penrose (1990).

4.1.5 Universal Turing Machines

As an illustration of the power of Church's thesis, we establish the existence of a universal Turing machine – a specific Turing machine $\mathcal{M}_u$ that can simulate any other Turing machine, if properly encoded. The existence of universal computers is one of the cornerstones on which the power of modern computers and computing is based. An effective encoding and enumeration of Turing machines therefore plays an important role.

There are many ways in which a TM $\mathcal{M} = \langle \Gamma, Q, q_1, \delta \rangle$, where $\Gamma = \{a_1, a_2, \ldots, a_n\}$, $Q = \{q_1, \ldots, q_m\}$, $H = \{q_{m+1}, q_{m+2}, q_{m+3}\}$, can be encoded by a binary string. For example,

$$\text{a transition } \delta(q_i, a_j) = (q_k, a_l, d) \text{ can be encoded as } 0^i10^j10^k10^l10^{d'},$$

where $d' = 1$ if $d = \leftarrow$, $d' = 2$ if $d = \downarrow$, and $d' = 3$ if $d = \rightarrow$. The whole TM $\mathcal{M}$ can then be encoded by the string

$$\langle \mathcal{M} \rangle = 10^n110^m11\underbrace{0^{i_1}10^{j_1}10^{k_1}10^{l_1}10^{d'_1}}_{\text{first transition}}11\underbrace{\ldots\ldots\ldots\ldots}_{\text{other transitions}}111,$$

and a $w \in \Gamma^*$, $w = a_{i_1} \ldots a_{i_k}$ can be encoded by $\langle w \rangle = 0^{i_1}10^{i_2}1 \ldots 10^{i_k}$. These encodings will be used often.

Remark 4.1.16 The above encoding can be generalized to all Turing machines by assuming that tape symbols are from an infinite alphabet $\Gamma = \{a_1, a_2, a_3, \ldots\}$ and states from an infinite set $Q = \{q_1, q_2, q_3, \ldots\}$ with the first three states being three halting states.

Notice that the string '11' is used as a marker between two components and '111' as the suffix end marker. Observe also that such an encoding of TM has the **self-delimiting property**: no prefix of a code of a TM is a code of another TM.

With a fixed encoding of Turing machines, such as the one above, we can use a strict ordering of encodings of all Turing machines and enumerate all Turing machines as $\mathcal{M}_0, \mathcal{M}_1, \mathcal{M}_2, \ldots$. For the rest of the book the actual details of such encodings will not usually be of importance. The only requirement, clearly fulfilled by the above encoding, will be that there is an effective procedure for determining the ith Turing machine TM_i given i, and for determining i such that $TM_i = \mathcal{M}$, given $\mathcal{M}$. Any such enumeration of TM will be called a **Gödel** (or **effective**) **numbering** of Turing machines, and the number i such that $TM_i = \mathcal{M}$ will be called the **index** or **Gödel number** of $\mathcal{M}$ with respect to a chosen Gödel numbering. Sometimes it will be required that encodings have the self-delimiting property.

Let us now fix an integer k and denote, for any integer i, by f_i the partial recursive function of k integer variables computed by $\mathcal{M}_i$, as defined in Definition 4.1.2. The number i is then referred to as an index of f_i. Clearly, any partial recursive function has infinitely many indices.

We show now that for any k there is a single Turing machine $\mathcal{M}_u^k$ that is universal for computing all partial recursive functions of k variables in the following sense. If $\mathcal{M}_u^k$ gets on the input an index i and the values $x_1, \ldots, x_k$, then $\mathcal{M}_u^k$ computes $f_i(x_1, \ldots, x_k)$.

Theorem 4.1.17 (The existence of a k-universal Turing machine) *For every $k \geq 1$ there is an integer u_k such that for any $i \geq 1$ and all $x_1, \ldots, x_k, f_i(x_1, \ldots, x_k) = f_{u_k}(i, x_1, \ldots, x_k)$.*

Proof: Consider the following informal algorithm for computing a function of $k+1$ variables $i, x_1, \ldots, x_k$. Construct $\mathcal{M}_i$ and use it to compute with the arguments $x_1, \ldots, x_k$ as the inputs. If the computation halts, output the final result of computation. By Church's thesis, this algorithm can be carried out by a Turing machine $\mathcal{M}_u$, and this u is the index of the universal partial recursive function of $k+1$ variables for computing any partial recursive function of k variables. □

In Section 4.1.7 we discuss another variant of the above theorem, and show in more detail how to design a universal Turing machine capable of simulating efficiently any other Turing machine. Complete, detailed constructions of universal Turing machines can be found in the literature – for example, in Minsky (1967). It is interesting to see such a construction, though one does not learn from it much more than from the above proof based on Church's thesis.

Because of the enormous power of universal Turing machines one is inclined to expect that they must be quite complicated. Actually, just the opposite is true, and the search for **minimal universal Turing machines** has demonstrated that.

Intellectual curiosity is the main, but not the only, reason why the problem of finding minimal universal Turing machines is of interest. Extreme micro-applications, the search for principles and the power of genetic information processing, as well as the tendency to minimize size and maximize performance of computers, are additional reasons.

A nontrivial problem is what to choose as a complexity measure for Turing machines, with respect to which one should try to find a minimal universal TM. Number of states? Number of tape symbols? The following theorem indicates that this is not the way to go.

Theorem 4.1.18 *There is a universal Turing machine that has only two nonterminating states, and there is another universal Turing machine that uses only two tape symbols.*

Exercise 4.1.19* *Show that for any TM $\mathcal{M}$ there is another TM $\mathcal{M}'$ that uses only two states and computes the same integer-to-integer functions as $\mathcal{M}$.*

Exercise 4.1.20 *Show that no one-state Turing machine can be universal.*

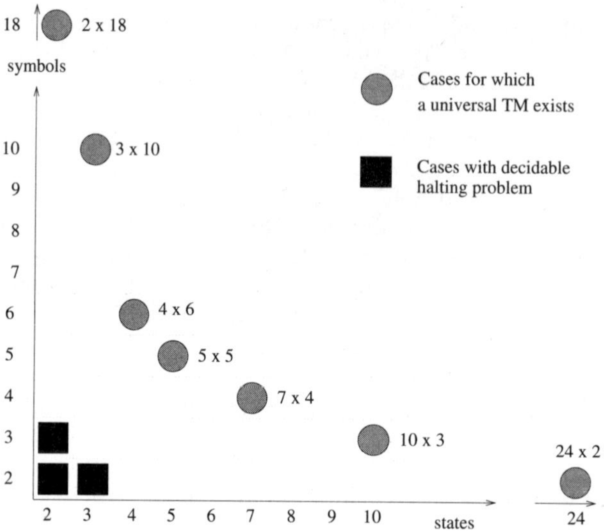

Figure 4.6 Minimal Turing machines

A better reflection of the intuitive concept of the **size** of Turing machines is their **product complexity**:

$$\text{number of states} \times \text{number of tape symbols},$$

or the total number of transitions. Concerning product complexity, the problem of finding a minimal universal Turing machine is still open, and currently the best upper and lower bounds are summarized in the following theorem.

Theorem 4.1.21 *There is a universal Turing machine with product complexity* 24 *(*4 *states and* 6 *symbols and* 22 *transitions), and there is no universal Turing machine with product complexity smaller than* 7.

Figure 4.6 shows, for different numbers of states (tape symbols), the current minimal number of tape symbols (states) needed to design a universal Turing machine. Figure 4.7 contains the transition tables of three universal Turing machines: one with 2 states and 18 symbols, one with 4 states and 6 symbols, and one with 24 states and 2 symbols. (To describe the movements of the heads, the symbols R instead of $\rightarrow$ and L instead of $\leftarrow$ are used.) The way Turing machines and inputs are encoded is the key point here, in which much of the complexity is hidden. (All these machines achieve universality by simulating a tag-system – see Section 7.1.)[5]

Remark 4.1.22 The existence of a **universal quantum computer** (universal quantum Turing machine) Q_u has also been shown. Such a universal quantum computer has the property that for each physical process $\mathcal{P}$ there is a program that makes Q_u perform that process. In particular, the universal quantum computer can, in principle, perform any physical experiments.

[5] In order to see the merit of these results, it is worth remembering that the first really powerful electronic computer ENIAC had 18,000 lamps, 70,000 capacitors, 60 tons weight and 30m length.

	0	1	2	3	4	5	6	7	8
q_0	$q_0 17L$	$q_0 4R$	$q_0 17L$	$q_0 0R$	$q_0 3L$	$q_0 7R$	$q_0 9R$	$q_0 5L$	$q_0 5R$
q_1	$q_1 2R$	$q_1 2R$	$q_1 1L$	$q_1 4R$	$q_1 0L$	$q_0 10R$	$q_1 7R$	$q_1 6L$	$q_1 9R$
	9	10	11	12	13	14	15	16	17
q_0	$q_0 8L$	$q_1 11L$	$q_1 8L$	$q_1 1L$	$q_0 14L$	$q_0 15L$	$q_1 16R$	–	$q_0 2R$
q_1	$q_1 6L$	$q_0 5R$	$q_1 9R$	$q_1 14R$	$q_1 14R$	$q_1 13L$	$q_1 17R$	$q_0 17L$	$q_1 12L$

UTM(2,18), Rogozhin (1995)

	q_0	q_1	q_2	q_3
0	$q_0 3L$	$q_1 4R$	$q_2 0R$	$q_3 4R$
1	$q_0 2R$	$q_2 2L$	$q_3 3R$	$q_1 5L$
2	$q_0 1L$	$q_1 3R$	$q_2 1R$	$q_3 3R$
3	$q_0 4R$	$q_1 2L$	–	–
4	$q_0 3L$	$q_1 0L$	$q_0 5R$	$q_1 5L$
5	$q_3 4R$	$q_1 1R$	$q_0 0R$	$q_3 1R$

UTM(4,6), Rogozhin (1982)

	q_0	q_1	q_2	q_3	q_4	q_5	q_6	q_7	q_8	q_9	q_{10}	q_{11}
0	$q_4 0R$	$q_0 1R$	$q_3 0L$	$q_{11} 1L$	$q_0 1R$	$q_6 0L$	$q_7 0L$	$q_6 0L$	$q_{18} 0R$	$q_3 1L$	$q_3 0L$	$q_{18} 0R$
1	$q_1 1R$	$q_2 1L$	$q_1 0L$	$q_8 0L$	$q_5 0L$	$q_6 1L$	$q_5 0L$	$q_1 1R$	$q_3 1L$	$q_{12} 0R$	–	$q_{13} 1L$
	q_{12}	q_{13}	q_{14}	q_{15}	q_{16}	q_{17}	q_{18}	q_{19}	q_{20}	q_{21}	q_{22}	q_{23}
0	$q_9 0R$	$q_{14} 0L$	$q_{15} 0R$	$q_{14} 0R$	$q_{15} 0R$	$q_{18} 0R$	$q_2 1L$	$q_{17} 1R$	$q_{21} 0R$	$q_9 1L$	$q_{20} 1R$	$q_{12} 0R$
1	$q_{23} 1R$	$q_{10} 1L$	$q_{16} 1R$	$q_9 1R$	$q_{20} 1R$	$q_{19} 1R$	$q_{17} 1R$	$q_{17} 0R$	$q_{22} 1R$	$q_{20} 1R$	$q_{20} 0R$	$q_2 0L$

UTM(24,2), Rogozhin (1982)

Figure 4.7 Transition tables of three small universal TM

4.1.6 Undecidable and Unsolvable Problems

A decision problem is called **undecidable** if there is no algorithm (Turing machine) for deciding it. A search problem is called **unsolvable** if there is no algorithm (Turing machine) for solving it.

We show first the undecidability of two basic problems concerning Turing machines. In doing this we assume that a Gödel numbering of Turing machines is fixed.

- The **self-applicability problem** is to decide, given an integer i, whether the ith Turing machine halts on the input i; that is, whether $TM_i(i) = \searrow$.
- The **halting problem** is to decide, given a Turing machine $\mathcal{M}$ and an input w, whether $\mathcal{M}$ halts on w; that is, whether $\mathcal{M}_w = \searrow$.

Theorem 4.1.23 *The self-applicability problem and the halting problem are undecidable for Turing machines.*

Proof: Let us define the function

$$f(n) = \begin{cases} \mathcal{M}_n(n) + 1, & \text{if } \mathcal{M}_n \text{ converges for the input } 1^n; \\ 0, & \text{otherwise.} \end{cases}$$

If either the self-applicability or the halting problem is decidable, then f is computable and, by Church's thesis, there is an m such that $f(n) = \mathcal{M}_m(n)$. In such a case $f(m) = \mathcal{M}_m(m) = \mathcal{M}_m(m) + 1$, a contradiction that implies that neither the self-applicability nor the halting problem is decidable.

□

Remark 4.1.24 The proof of Theorem 4.1.23 is based on the **diagonalization method**. First, an infinite matrix M is defined, the rows and columns of which are labelled by integers, and $M(i,x)$ is the value of the ith Turing machine for the input 1^{x+1}. The diagonal of the matrix $M(i,j)$ is then considered, and a function f is constructed such that $f(i) \neq M(i,i)$, for all i.

The unsolvability case, the existence of a well-defined but not computable function, will now be demonstrated by the **busy beaver function**, BB. $BB(n)$ is the maximal number of 1s that a Turing machine with n states and a two-symbol tape alphabet $\{\sqcup, 1\}$ can write on the tape when starting with the empty tape and terminating after a certain number of steps. Since the number of such TM is finite, $BB(n)$ is well defined, and $BB(n) \leq BB(n+1)$ for all n.

Theorem 4.1.25 *For any total recursive function f and any sufficiently large x, the inequality $f(x) < BB(x)$ holds. (As a consequence, the busy beaver function is not recursive.)*

Proof: Given any recursive function $f(x)$, let us consider the function

$$g(x) = max\{f(2x+2), f(2x+3)\}. \tag{4.1}$$

Clearly, the function g is total, and therefore by Church's thesis and Theorem 4.1.18 there is a Turing machine $\mathcal{M}_g$ with the tape alphabet $\{\sqcup, 1\}$ computing g. Let $\mathcal{M}_g$ have m states.

For each integer x we can easily construct a Turing machine $\mathcal{M}_x$ such that when $\mathcal{M}_x$ starts on the empty tape, it first writes 1^{x+1}, then moves to the left-most 1 and starts to work as $\mathcal{M}_g$. Clearly, $\mathcal{M}_x$ with this property can be designed so that it has $n = m + x + 2$ states and uses $\{\sqcup, 1\}$ as the tape alphabet. When started on the blank tape, $\mathcal{M}_x$ halts with precisely $g(x)$ symbols 1 on the tape. Thus,

$$g(x) < BB(m + x + 2),$$

and for $x = k \geq m$, we get $g(k) < BB(2k+2)$, and therefore

$$f(2k+2) < BB(2k+2), \qquad f(2k+3) < BB(2k+3).$$

Thus $f(x) < BB(x)$, for $x \geq m$. □

It is known that $BB(1) = 1, BB(2) = 4, BB(3) = 6, BB(4) = 13$, and Turing machines that achieve these maximal values are shown in Figures 4.8a, b, c, d, where 0 is written instead of the blank symbol. For larger n only the following lower bounds are currently known: $BB(5) \geq 4098, BB(6) \geq 136{,}612, BB(8) \geq 10^{44}, BB(12) \geq 6x_{164}^4$, where $x_0 = 4096$ and $x_i = x_{i-1}^{4096}$ for $i \geq 1$. TM in Figures 4.8b, c, d and e write the indicated number of 1s in 4, 11, 96 and 47,176,870 steps, respectively.

Exercise 4.1.26** *Verify that Marxen–Buntrock's TM really needs 47,176,870 steps to write 4098 1s.*

Exercise 4.1.27* *Get, by designing a TM, as good a lower bound for $BB(6)$ as you can.*

	A
0	1H
1	

(a)

	A	B
0	1BL	1AR
1	1BR	H

(b)

	A	B	C
0	1BR	1CR	1AL
1	1CL	1H	0BL

(c) Lin and Rado (1963)

	A	B	C	D
0	1BR	1AL	1H	1DL
1	OCR	1AR	1DR	OBL

(d) Weimann, Casper and Fenzl (1973)

	A	B	C	D	E
0	1BR	1CR	1DR	1AL	1H
1	1CL	1BR	0EL	1DL	0AL

(e) Marxen, Buntrock (1990)

Figure 4.8 Turing machines computing the busy beaver function for $n = 1,2,3,4,5$ ('H' stands for the halting state HALT)

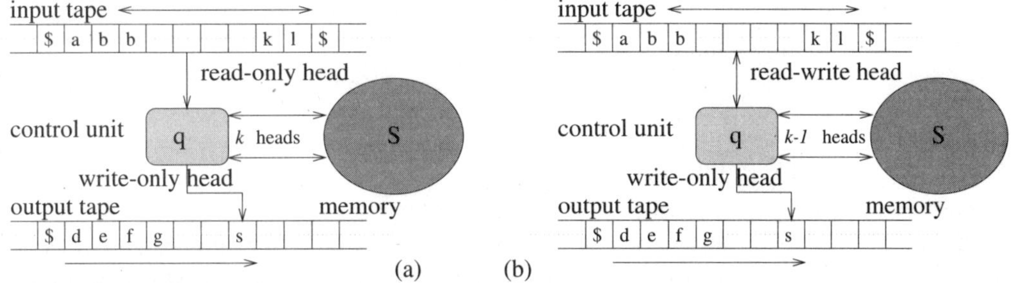

Figure 4.9 Off-line and on-line Turing machines

The existence of undecidable and unsolvable problems belongs to the main discoveries of science of this century, with various implications concerning the limitations of our knowledge. This will be discussed in more detail in Chapter 6, where insights into the structure of decidable and solvable problems, as well as several examples of undecidable and unsolvable problems, are discussed.

4.1.7 Multi-tape Turing Machines

There are many generalizations of one-tape Turing machines. Two main schemas of such generalizations are shown in Figure 4.9: **off-line Turing machines** (Figure 4.9a) and **on-line Turing machines** (Figure 4.9b). In both cases the Turing machine has an **input tape**, an **output tape** with a write-only head moving from left to right only, a **control unit** connected by heads with the input tape, the output tape and a 'memory' (or storage). The memory S has a potentially infinite number of cells. Each of them can contain a symbol of a finite alphabet. Cells of S are interconnected by some regular interconnection network (graph). A **configuration** of such a machine is determined by its state, the contents of the memory cells and the positions of the heads. A **step** is determined by the current state and by the symbols the heads read. A step results in a change of state, a replacement of symbols in the cells of the memory which the heads are on at that moment, and the moves of the heads to the neighbouring cells, along the interconnection structure of S.

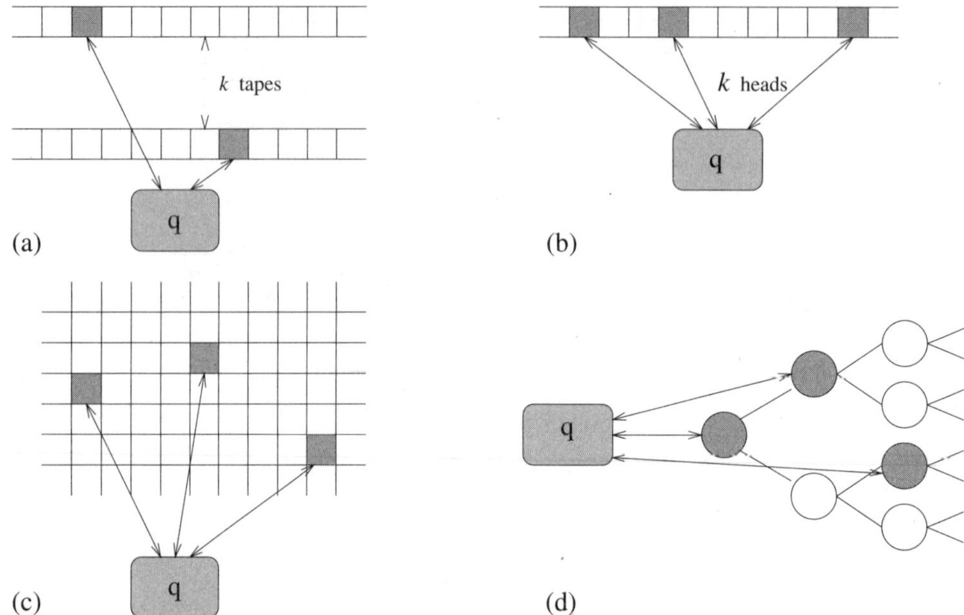

Figure 4.10 Four types of Turing machines

Four interconnection schemes for memory are illustrated in Figure 4.10: multi-tape Turing machines with one head on each tape (Figure 4.10a); a one-tape multi-head Turing machine (Figure 4.10b); a multi-head Turing machine with a two-dimensional tape (Figure 4.10c); and a Turing machine with a tree-structured memory (Figure 4.10d).

On-line and off-line versions differ only in the way in which the input tape is processed. In off-line Turing machines the input tape head is a read-only head that can move in both directions.[6] In on-line models, the input tape has a read–write head that can move in both directions. The main advantage of the off-line models of TM is that both input and output are completely separated from the memory.

Off-line Turing machines are of interest mostly when considering space complexity, as discussed later. We shall use on-line multi-tape Turing machines (MTM for short) as our basic model of Turing machines, unless it is specified explicitly that the off-line model is used. For that reason we define basic concepts for (on-line) MTM only. The extension to off-line MTM is straightforward.

Formally, a k-tape MTM $\mathcal{M} = \langle \Gamma, Q, q_0, \delta \rangle$ is specified by a **tape alphabet** Γ, a set of **states** Q, the **initial state** q_0 and a **transition function**

$$\delta : Q \times \Gamma^k \to (Q \cup H) \times \Gamma^k \times D^k,$$

where $D = \{\leftarrow, \downarrow, \rightarrow\}$ are the directions in which the heads can move.

The concepts of a **configuration**, a computation **step**, **yield** relations $\vdash_{\mathcal{M}}, \vdash^n_{\mathcal{M}}, \vdash^*_{\mathcal{M}}$ and a **computation** are defined as for one-tape TM. For example, a configuration is a $(2k+1)$-tuple of the form $(q, w_1, w_1', w_2, w_2', \ldots, w_k, w_k')$, where q is the current state and the ith tape contains the word $w_i w_i'$ with the head on the first symbol of w_i'. The **initial configuration** with an input word w has

[6] Sometimes it is assumed that the head on the input tape moves only to the right.

the form $(q_0, \varepsilon, w, \varepsilon, \ldots, \varepsilon)$. The contents of the output tape at termination is the overall output of an MTM.

Time and space bounds and complexity classes

It is straightforward to introduce basic concepts concerning time resources for computations on MTM. If an MTM $\mathcal{M}$ starts with a string w on its input tape and with all other tapes empty and yields in m steps a terminating configuration, then m is the time of the computation of $\mathcal{M}$ on w. Denote $Time_{\mathcal{M}}(n)$ the maximal number of steps of $\mathcal{M}$ for inputs of length n. $\mathcal{M}$ is said **to operate within the time bound** $f(n)$ for a function $f : \mathbf{N} \rightarrow \mathbf{N}$, or to be $f(n)$**-time bounded** if $\mathcal{M}$ terminates within $f(|w|)$ steps, for any input $w \in \Sigma^*$. If a language $L \subseteq \Sigma^*$ is decided by a $f(n)$-time bounded MTM, then we write $L \in Time(f(n))$. Thus, $Time(f(n))$ is the family of those languages that can be decided by a $f(n)$-time bounded MTM – a **time complexity class**. Observe also concerning the time requirements that there is no essential difference between on-line and off-line MTM. Sometimes we need to be more precise and therefore we use the notation $Time_k(f(n))$ to denote the family of languages accepted by k-tape MTM within the time bound $f(n)$.

Theorem 4.1.28 *For any on-line $f(n)$-time bounded k-tape MTM $\mathcal{M}$, $f(n) \geq n$, there is an off-line $\mathcal{O}(f(n))$-time bounded $(k+2)$-tape MTM $\mathcal{M}'$ that accepts the same language.*

Proof: $\mathcal{M}'$ first copies the input onto the second tape, moves the head on the second tape to the first symbol of the input word, then simulates $\mathcal{M}$ on $k+1$ tapes numbered $2, \ldots, k+2$. Finally, $\mathcal{M}'$ writes the output on its output tape. □

Before we define space bounds for MTM, let us consider two examples of MTM that recognize palindromes.

Example 4.1.29 *The MTM $\mathcal{M}$ in Figure 4.11 first copies the input w from the first tape to the second tape, then moves the head on the first tape to the left-most symbol, and, finally, moves both heads in opposite directions while comparing, symbol by symbol, the corresponding symbols of w and w^R until it either encounters a different pair of symbols or gets safely through. The time bound is clearly $\mathcal{O}(|w|)$, and $\mathcal{M}$ uses $|w|$ cells of the second tape.*

Example 4.1.30 *We sketch the behaviour of a 3-tape TM $\mathcal{M}$ that requires only $\mathcal{O}(\lg n)$ space on its noninput tapes to recognize whether an input string w of length n is a palindrome. The third tape will be used to store an integer $i \leq \frac{n}{2}$. This requires $\mathcal{O}(\lg n)$ space. To start with, $\mathcal{M}$ writes $\frac{n}{2}$ on the third tape and 1 on the second tape. For each i on the third tape $\mathcal{M}$ uses the counter on the second tape to find the i-th symbols from the left and the right in the input word. (To keep the counter requires $\mathcal{O}(\lg n)$ space.) $\mathcal{M}$ compares the two symbols found, and if they do not agree, then $\mathcal{M}$ rejects; otherwise $\mathcal{M}$ decreases i by 1, and the process continues until either $\mathcal{M}$ rejects, or i on the third tape reaches 1.*

Exercise 4.1.31 *Design an $\mathcal{O}(nk^2)$-time bounded 3-tape Turing machine that lexicographically orders strings $x_i \in \{a,b\}^k$, $1 \leq i \leq n$, given as an input string $x_1\#x_2\#\ldots\#x_n$.*

There are three basic ways of counting space for MTM. The first is to take the maximum overall configurations of a computation of the sum of the lengths of all strings on all tapes. The second is again to take the maximum overall configurations, but count for each configuration only the longest

$q_0, 0, \sqcup, q_0, 0, 0, \rightarrow, \rightarrow$	{Copying the content of the first
$q_0, 1, \sqcup, q_0, 1, 1, \rightarrow, \rightarrow$	tape onto the second tape.}
$q_0, \sqcup, \sqcup, q_l, \sqcup, \sqcup, \leftarrow, \leftarrow$	{Reaching the right end.}
$q_l, 0, x, q_l, 0, x, \leftarrow, \downarrow$	{Moving the first head to the left end.}
$q_l, 1, x, q_l, 1, x, \leftarrow, \downarrow$	{Moving the first head to the left end.}
$q_l, \sqcup, x, q_c, \sqcup, x, \rightarrow, \downarrow$	{Left end reached, start to move right.}
$q_c, 0, 0, q_c, \sqcup, \sqcup, \rightarrow, \leftarrow$	{Comparison of two symbols on two tapes.}
$q_c, 1, 1, q_c, \sqcup, \sqcup, \rightarrow, \leftarrow$	{Comparison of two symbols on two tapes.}
$q_c, 0, 1, REJECT, 0, 1, \downarrow, \downarrow$	{Corresponding symbols do not agree.}
$q_c, 1, 0, REJECT, 1, 0, \downarrow, \downarrow$	{Corresponding symbols do not agree.}
$q_c, \sqcup, \sqcup, ACCEPT, \sqcup, \sqcup, \downarrow, \downarrow$	{Hurrah, palindrome.}

Figure 4.11 A multi-tape Turing machine for palindrome recognition (x stands here for any symbol from $\{0,1\}$)

string on a tape. For a k-tape MTM these two ways of counting the space may differ only by a constant multiplicative factor (at most k). Therefore, we use the second one only. The third way is used only for off-line MTM. It is actually similar to the second except that the contents of the input and output tapes are not counted.

With the first two ways of counting, the space used during a computation for an input w is always at least $|w|$. The last approach allows us to obtain the sublinear space complexity for a computation. This is the case of the MTM in Example 4.1.30.

An MTM (or an off-line MTM) $\mathcal{M}$ is said to be $s(n)$-space bounded, where $s : \mathbf{N} \rightarrow \mathbf{N}$ is a function, if $\mathcal{M}$ uses at most $s(|w|)$ cells for any input w.

Suppose now that a language $L \subseteq \Sigma^*$ is decided by an MTM or an off-line MTM within the space bound $s(n)$. In such a case we say $L \in Space(s(n))$. $Space(s(n))$ is therefore a family of languages, a **space complexity class**.

Mutual simulations of Turing machines

Examples 4.1.29 and 4.1.30 indicate that by using more tapes we may speed up computations and sometimes also decrease the space needed. In general, it is of interest and importance to find out how powerful different machine models are with respect to time and space requirements. In order to deal with this problem, a general but quite weak concept of simulation of one machine on another is introduced

Definition 4.1.32 *A machine $\mathcal{M}$ simulates a machine $\mathcal{M}'$ for inputs from Σ^* if $\mathcal{M}'(x) = \mathcal{M}(x)$, for all $x \in \Sigma^*$.*

The following theorem shows that not much can be gained by using Turing machines with more heads, more tapes or more dimensional tapes.

Theorem 4.1.33 *Corresponding to any Turing machine $\mathcal{M}$ with several tapes or several heads or with a two-dimensional tape that operates within the time bound $t(n) \geq n$ and space bound $s(n)$, one can effectively construct a one-tape TM $\mathcal{M}'$ that simulates $\mathcal{M}$ and operates within the time bound $\mathcal{O}(t^2(n))$ and the space bound $\Theta(s(n))$.*

Proof: We carry out the proof only for MTM. In order to simplify the proof, we assume that the input is written always between two end markers. The other cases are left to the reader (see Exercises 4.1.34 and 4.1.35).

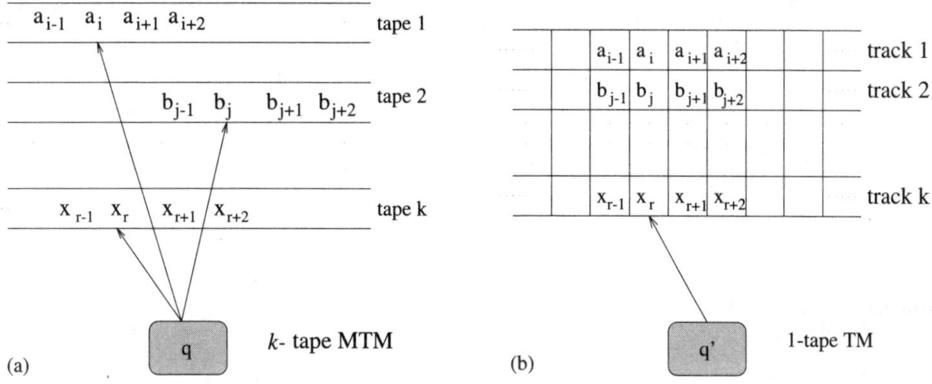

Figure 4.12 Simulation of a multi-tape TM by a one-tape TM

Let $\mathcal{M}$ be a k-tape MTM. We describe a one-tape TM $\mathcal{M}'$ that simulates $\mathcal{M}$. To each state q of $\mathcal{M}$ a state q' of $\mathcal{M}'$ will be associated in such a way that if $\mathcal{M}$ moves, in one step, from a state q_1 to a state q_2, then, in a number of steps proportional to $t(n)$, $\mathcal{M}'$ moves from the state q_1' to the state q_2'.

In order to simulate k tapes of $\mathcal{M}$, the only tape of $\mathcal{M}'$ is divided into k tracks, and the ith track is used to store the contents of the ith tape of $\mathcal{M}$. Each configuration C of $\mathcal{M}$ (see Figure 4.12a) is simulated by a configuration C' of $\mathcal{M}'$ (see Figure 4.12b), where all symbols simultaneously read by the heads of $\mathcal{M}$ in C are in one cell of the tape of $\mathcal{M}'$. This is the key point of the whole construction. Thus, $\mathcal{M}'$ can read in one step all the symbols that the k heads of $\mathcal{M}$ read. Therefore $\mathcal{M}'$ knows, by reading one cell, how to change the contents of its tape and state in such a way that it corresponds to the next configuration of $\mathcal{M}$. The main difficulty in doing this lies in the fact that some heads of $\mathcal{M}$ can move in one direction, others in the opposite direction, and some may not move at all. In order to implement all these changes and still have all heads of $\mathcal{M}$ on one cell of $\mathcal{M}'$, $\mathcal{M}'$ has to move some tracks to the left and some to the right. This is no problem because $\mathcal{M}'$ can store information about which track to shift and in which direction in its state. $\mathcal{M}'$ then moves to the right end of the occupied portion of the tape, and in one scan from the right to the left, $\mathcal{M}'$ can make all the necessary adjustments – to shift some tracks to the left, some to the right. After that, the head of $\mathcal{M}'$ moves to the cell that contains the contents of all the cells the heads of $\mathcal{M}$ will be on in the next configuration of $\mathcal{M}$. $\mathcal{M}'$ also moves to the new state. It is clear that in this way the space requirement of $\mathcal{M}'$ may be at most twice that for $\mathcal{M}'$. Concerning the time requirements, the fact that $\mathcal{M}$ makes at most $t(n)$ moves implies that the two ends of the occupied portion of the tape are never more than $n+t(n)$ cells apart. In order to simulate one step of $\mathcal{M}$, $\mathcal{M}'$ has to make at most $\mathcal{O}(t(n))$ moves: moving first to one end of the occupied tape, then to the other end, and, finally, to the cell the heads of $\mathcal{M}$ are on. The overall time complexity is therefore $\mathcal{O}(t^2(n))$. The space bound is clearly $\Theta(s(n))$. □

Exercise 4.1.34 *Show how to simulate, as fast as possible, a TM with a two-dimensional tape by a one-tape TM.*

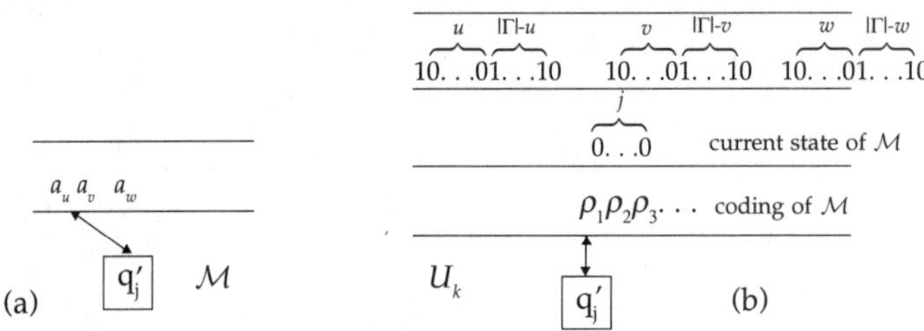

Figure 4.13 Universal Turing machine

Exercise 4.1.35 *Show how to simulate, as fast as possible, a multi-head one-tape TM by a one-head one-tape TM.*

Universal multi-tape Turing machines

We again show the existence of a universal TM, this time for the class of all k-tape MTM for a fixed k, and the proof will be constructive this time. The main new aim is to show that a universal Turing machine can simulate any Turing machine efficiently.

Theorem 4.1.36 *Let an integer k be fixed and also an alphabet $\Gamma \supseteq \{0,1\}$. Then there exists a universal k-tape MTM U_k with the following properties:*

1. *If $\langle\mathcal{M}\rangle$ is a self-delimiting Gödel encoding of a k-tape MTM $\mathcal{M}$ with the tape alphabet Γ, then on the input $\langle\mathcal{M}\rangle w$, $w \in \{0,1\}^*$, U_k simulates $\mathcal{M}$ on the input w.*
2. *The maximal number of steps U_k needed to simulate one step of $\mathcal{M}$ is bounded by $c_{U_k}|\langle\mathcal{M}\rangle|^{\alpha}$, where $\alpha = 2$ if $k = 1$, $\alpha = 1$ if $k \geq 2$, and c_{U_k} is a constant.*

Proof: Let $\Gamma = \{a_1, \ldots, a_m\}$. Given an input $\langle M\rangle w$, U_k first makes a copy of $\langle\mathcal{M}\rangle$ on the third track of its first tape (see Figure 4.13). During the simulation this string will always be positioned in such a way that at the beginning of a simulation of a step of $\mathcal{M}$ the head of U_k reads always the left-most symbol of $\langle\mathcal{M}\rangle$. The current state q_j of $\mathcal{M}$ will be stored as 0^j on the second track of the first tape of U_k, and again in such a way that U_k reads its left-most symbol whenever starting to simulate a step of $\mathcal{M}$. Strings on the tapes of $\mathcal{M}$ are stored in the first tracks of k-tapes of U_k. Each a_i is encoded by the string $10^i1^{|\Gamma|-i}0$. Thus, the encoding of any symbol of Γ takes exactly $|\Gamma|+2$ bits. Whenever U_k starts to simulate a step of $\mathcal{M}$, the heads of U_k read the first symbols of encodings of the corresponding symbols on the tapes of $\mathcal{M}$ at the beginning of that step of $\mathcal{M}$.

In order to simulate one step of $\mathcal{M}$, U_k reads and writes down, say on a special track of a tape, the current state of $\mathcal{M}$ and all the symbols the heads of $\mathcal{M}$ read in the corresponding configuration of $\mathcal{M}$. This pattern is then used to search through $\langle\mathcal{M}\rangle$ on the third track of its first tape, for the corresponding transition. This requires $\mathcal{O}(\langle\mathcal{M}\rangle)$ time. Once the transition is found, U_k replaces the old state of $\mathcal{M}$ by the new one, those symbols the heads of $\mathcal{M}$ would replace, and starts to realize all moves of heads of $\mathcal{M}$. Finally, U_k has to shift $\langle\mathcal{M}\rangle$ by at most $|\Gamma|+2$ cells, depending on the move of the head of $\mathcal{M}$, on the third track of its first tape. In order to simulate one step of $\mathcal{M}$, U_k has to make the number of steps proportional to $|\langle\mathcal{M}\rangle|$. In order to shift $\langle\mathcal{M}\rangle$, U_k needs time $c(|\Gamma|+2+|\langle\mathcal{M}\rangle|) \leq 2c|\langle\mathcal{M}\rangle|$, for a constant

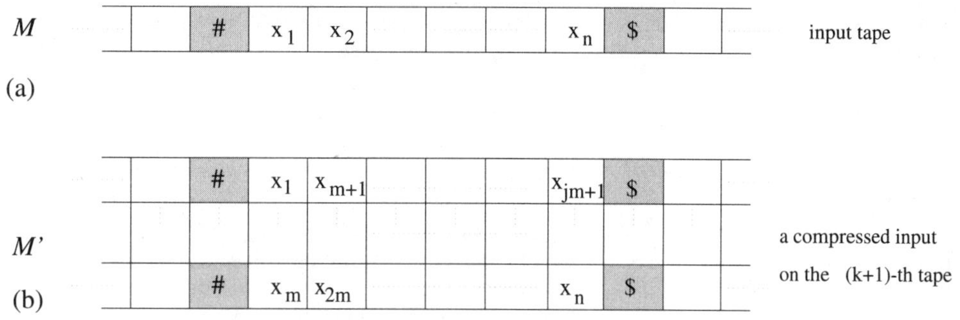

M | # | x_1 | x_2 | x_n | $ | input tape

(a)

| x_1 | x_{m+1} | x_{jm+1} | $

M'

| x_m | x_{2m} | x_n | $

(b)

a compressed input on the (k+1)-th tape

Figure 4.14 Linear speed-up of Turing machines

c, if $k > 1$, and therefore another tape is available for shifting $\langle\mathcal{M}\rangle$. The time is $c(|\Gamma|+2)|\langle\mathcal{M}\rangle| \leq |\langle\mathcal{M}\rangle|^2$, if $k = 1$. □

Exercise 4.1.37 *Show that one can design a single universal Turing machine $\mathcal{M}_u$ that can simulate any other MTM $\mathcal{M}$ (no matter how many tapes $\mathcal{M}$ has).*

Exercise 4.1.38 *Show how to simulate a one-tape k-head Turing machine by a k-tape Turing machine. Analyse the time complexity of the simulation. (It has been shown that a simulation of a k-head $t(n)$-time bounded Turing machine can be performed in time $\mathcal{O}(t(n))$.)*

The existence of universal computers that can simulate efficiently any other computer of the same type is the key result behind the enormous successes of computing based on classical physics. The existence of such an efficient universality is far from obvious. For example, the existence of a universal quantum Turing machine was shown already in 1985, but the fact that there is a universal quantum Turing machine that can simulate any other quantum Turing machine efficiently (that is, in polynomial time) was shown only in 1993.

4.1.8 Time Speed-up and Space Compression

In Chapter 1 we stated that multiplicative constants in the asymptotic time bounds for the computational complexity of algorithms are clearly of large practical importance but not of deep theoretical interest. One reason for this is that the hardware advances have been so rapid that algorithm designers could compete only by improving the rate of growth of algorithms. Two results of this section confirm that once MTM are taken as a computer model, then multiplicative constants are not of importance at all, either for time or space complexity. In other words, improvements in them can be compensated by so-called 'hardware improvements', such as by enlarging the tape alphabet.

Lemma 4.1.39 *If $L \in Time_k(f(n))$, then for any $\varepsilon > 0$, $L \in Time_{k+1}(n+\varepsilon(n+f(n))+5)$.*

Proof: Let $\mathcal{M}$ be an off-line k-tape MTM with time bound $f(n)$ and m be an integer (we show later how to choose m – the choice will depend on $\mathcal{M}$ and ε). We design a $(k+1)$-tape MTM $\mathcal{M}'_m$ that will simulate $\mathcal{M}$ as follows. $\mathcal{M}'_m$ starts its simulation by reading the input of $\mathcal{M}$, and, using the technique of storing symbols in the state, compresses each block of m input symbols into a single symbol (into an m-tuple of input symbols), and writes this symbol on its $(k+1)$-th tape (see Figure 4.14). This compression corresponds to using a tape with m tracks instead of a single-track input tape. (In case the length of the input is not a multiple of m, some $\sqcup$'s are added.) This process takes n steps, where n is the length of the input. $\mathcal{M}'_m$ then moves its head in $\lceil \frac{n}{m} \rceil$ steps to the left-most symbol on the $(k+1)$-th tape, and the simulation of $\mathcal{M}$ starts. During the simulation $\mathcal{M}'_m$ works with such m-tuples on all its tapes.

$\mathcal{M}'_m$ simulates $\mathcal{M}$ in such a way that m steps of $\mathcal{M}$ are simulated by four steps of $\mathcal{M}'_m$. At the beginning of each simulation of a sequence of m steps of $\mathcal{M}$, the machine $\mathcal{M}'_m$ reads an m-tuple of symbols on each tape. This includes not only information about symbols in the corresponding cells of $\mathcal{M}$, but also information on which of these symbols are the heads of $\mathcal{M}$ and in which state $\mathcal{M}$ is. Observe that in the next m moves $\mathcal{M}$ can visit only cells of that block and one of the neighbouring blocks of m symbols. By reading these two blocks on each tape, during two steps, $\mathcal{M}'_m$ gathers all the information needed to simulate m steps of $\mathcal{M}$. $\mathcal{M}'_m$ can then make the resulting changes in these two blocks in only two additional steps.

Time estimation: Choose $m = \lceil \frac{4}{\varepsilon} \rceil$. The number of steps $\mathcal{M}'_m$ has to perform is

$$\begin{aligned} n + \left\lceil \frac{n}{m} \right\rceil + 4 \left\lceil \frac{f(n)}{m} \right\rceil &\leq n + \lceil \varepsilon n \rceil + 4 \left\lceil \frac{\varepsilon f(n)}{4} \right\rceil \\ &\leq n + \varepsilon n + 1 + 4 \left(\frac{\varepsilon f(n)}{4} + 1 \right) \\ &\leq n + \varepsilon (n + f(n)) + 5. \end{aligned}$$

□

In the case of an on-line k-tape MTM, $k \geq 2$, any tape can be used to write down the compressed input, and therefore the $(k+1)$-th tape is superfluous. Observe that the trick which we have used, namely, a compression of m-tuples of symbols into one symbol of a bigger alphabet, corresponds actually to 'increasing the word length of the computer'. If $f(n) = cn$, then it follows from Lemma 4.1.39 that c can be compressed to be arbitrarily close to 1. In case $f(n) \succ n$, Lemma 4.1.39 says that the constant factor in the leading term can be arbitrarily small. To summarize:

Theorem 4.1.40 (Speed-up theorem) *For any integer $k \geq 2$ and a real $\varepsilon > 0$, $Time_k(f(n)) \subseteq Time_k(f_\varepsilon(n))$, where $f_\varepsilon(n) \leq \varepsilon f(n)$ for sufficiently large n, if $f(n) \succ n$, and $f_\varepsilon(n) \leq n + \varepsilon f(n)$ for sufficiently large n, otherwise.*

Theorem 4.1.40 justifies the use of asymptotic notation to express time complexity of MTM. In particular, if a language L is decided by some MTM in polynomial time, then $L \subseteq Time(n^k)$ for some k. From this it follows that the time complexity class

$$\mathbf{P} = \bigcup_{k=0}^{\infty} Time(n^k)$$

contains all languages that can be decided by MTM in polynomial time.

Exercise 4.1.41 *Show the following modification of the speed-up theorem: For every TM $\mathcal{M}$ and $\varepsilon > 0$, there is a TM $\mathcal{M}'$ over the same alphabet which recognizes the same language and for which $Time_{\mathcal{M}'}(n) \leq \varepsilon Time_{\mathcal{M}}(n) + n$. (Hint: instead of a compression requiring an enlargement of the alphabet, use more tapes.)*

Using the same compression technique as in the proof of Theorem 4.1.40, we can prove an analogous result for the space compression.

Theorem 4.1.42 (Linear space compression theorem) *For any function $s(n) > n$ and any real $\varepsilon > 0$ we have $Space(s(n)) = Space(\varepsilon s(n))$.*

Theorem 4.1.42 allows us to define

$$\mathbf{PSPACE} = \bigcup_{k=0}^{\infty} Space(n^k)$$

as the class of all languages that can be decided by MTM with a polynomial space bound.

4.2 Random Access Machines

Turing machines are an excellent computer model for studying fundamental problems of computing. However, the architecture of Turing machines has little in common with that of modern computers and their programming has little in common with programming of modern computers. The most essential clumsiness distinguishing a Turing machine from a real sequential computer is that its memory is not immediately accessible. In order to read a memory far away, all intermediate cells also have to be read. This difficulty is bridged by the **random access machine** model (RAM), introduced and analysed in this section, which has turned out to be a simple but adequate abstraction of sequential computers of the von Neumann type. Algorithm design methodologies for RAM and sequential computers are basically the same. Complexity analysis of algorithms and algorithmic problems for RAM reflect and predict the complexity analysis of programs to solve these problems on typical sequential computers. At the same time, surprisingly, if time and space requirements for RAM are measured properly, there are mutually very efficient simulations between RAM and Turing machines.

4.2.1 Basic Model

The **memory** of a RAM (see Figure 4.15a) consists of a data memory and a program memory. The **data memory** is an infinite **random access array of registers** $R_0, R_1, R_2, \ldots$ each of which can store an arbitrary integer. The register R_0 is called the **accumulator**, and plays a special role. The **program memory** is also a random access array of registers $P_0, P_1, P_2, \ldots$ each capable of storing an instruction from the instruction set shown in Figure 4.15b. A **control unit** (also called ALU, for 'arithmetical logical unit') contains two special registers, an **address counter** AC and an **instruction counter** IC. In addition, there are **input** and **output** units.

At the beginning of a computation all data memory and control unit registers are set to 0, and a program is stored in the program memory. A **configuration** of a RAM is described by a i-tuple $(i, i_1, n_{i_1}, \ldots, i_m, n_{i_m})$, where i is the content of IC, $i_1, \ldots, i_m$ are the addresses of the registers used up to that moment during the computation, and n_{i_k} is the current content of the register R_{i_k}.

The operand of an instruction is of one of the following three types:

$=i$ – a constant i;
i – an address, referring to the register R_i,
$*i$ – an indirect address; referring to the register$R_{c(R_i)}$,

where $c(R_i)$ denotes the contents of the register R_i. (In Figure 4.15 R_{op} means i, if the operand has the form $=i$; R_{op} means R_i, if the operand is of the form i; R_{op} stands for $R_{c(R_i)}$, if the operand has the form $*i$.) A **computation** of a RAM is a sequence of computation steps. Each step leads from one configuration

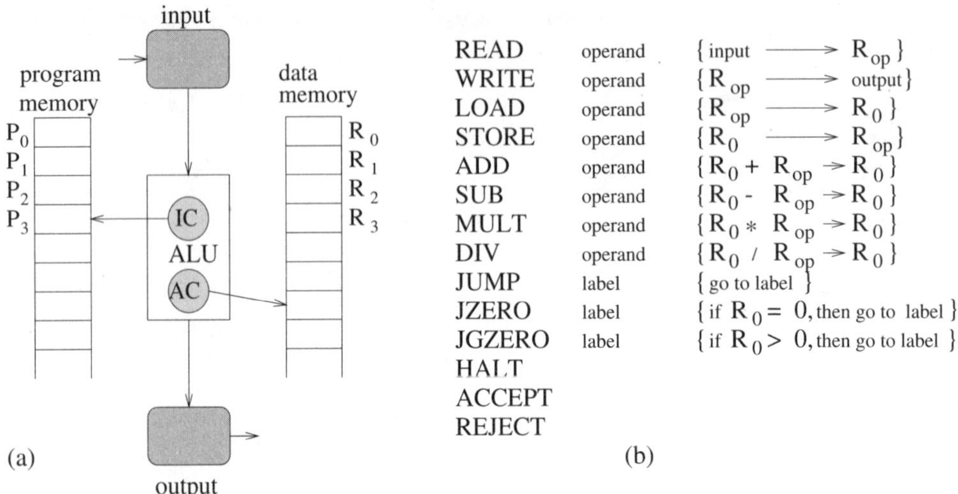

Figure 4.15 Random access machine

to another. In each computational step a RAM executes the instruction currently contained in the program register $P_{c(IC)}$. In order to perform a nonjump instruction, its operand is stored in AC, and through AC the data memory is accessed, if necessary. The READ instruction reads the next input number; the WRITE instruction writes the next output number. The memory management instructions (LOAD and STORE), arithmetical instructions and conditional jump instructions use the accumulator R_0 as one of the registers. The second register, if needed, is specified by the contents of AC. After a nonjump instruction has been performed, the content of IC is increased by 1, and the same happens if the test in a jump instruction fails. Otherwise, the label of a jump instruction explicitly defines the new contents of IC.

A computation of a function is naturally defined for a RAM. The arguments have to be provided at the input, and a convention has to be adopted to determine their number. Either their number is a constant, or the first input integer determines the total number of inputs, or there is some special number denoting the last input.[7] Language recognition requires, in addition, an encoding of symbols by integers.

Figure 4.16 depicts RAM programs to compute two functions: (a) $f(n) = 2^{2^n}$ for $n > 0$; (b) F_n – the nth Fibonacci number. In both cases n is given as the only input. Fixed symbolic addresses, like N, i, F_{i-1}, F_i, *aux* and *temp*, are used in Figure 4.16 to make programs more readable. Comments in curly brackets serve the same purpose.

The instruction set of a RAM, presented in Figure 4.15, is typical but not the only one possible. Any 'usual' microcomputer operation could be added. However, in order to get relevant complexity results in the analysis of RAM programs, sometimes only a subset of the instructions listed in Figure 4.15 is allowed – namely, those without multiplication and division. (It will soon become clear why.) Such a model is usually called a RAM$^+$. To this new model the instruction SHIFT, with the semantics $R_0 \leftarrow \lfloor R_0/2 \rfloor$, is sometimes added.

Figure 4.17 shows how a RAM$^+$ with the SHIFT operation can be used to multiply two positive integers x and y to get $z = x \cdot y$ using the ordinary school method. In comments in Figure 4.17 k

[7] For example, the number 3 can denote the end of a binary vector.

(a)

	READ	N	$\{N \leftarrow n\}$
	LOAD	$=2$	
while:	STORE	*temp*	$\{temp \leftarrow 2^{2^{n-N}}\}$
	LOAD	N	
	JGZERO	body	$\{$**while** $N > 0$ **do**$\}$
	WRITE	*temp*	
	HALT		
body:	SUB	$=1$	
	STORE	N	$\{N \leftarrow N-1\}$
	LOAD	*temp*	
	MULT	0	$\{R_0 \leftarrow temp^2\}$
	JUMP	while	

(b)

	READ	N	$\{N \leftarrow n\}$
	LOAD	$=1$	
	STORE	i	$\{i \leftarrow 1\}$
	STORE	F_{i-1}	
	STORE	F_i	
while:	SUB	N	
	JZERO	print	$\{$**while** $i < N$ **do**$\}$
	LOAD	F_i	
	STORE	*aux*	
	ADD	F_{i-1}	
	STORE	F_i	$\{F_i^{new} \leftarrow F_i + F_{i-1}\}$
	LOAD	*aux*	
	STORE	F_{i-1}	$\{F_{i-1}^{new} \leftarrow F_i\}$
	LOAD	i	
	ADD	$=1$	
	STORE	i	
	JUMP	while	
print:	WRITE	F_i	
	HALT		

Figure 4.16 RAM programs to compute (a) $f(n) = 2^{2^n}$; (b) F_n, the nth Fibonacci number.

1:	READ	0	$\{R_0 \leftarrow x\}$
2:	STORE	$x1$	$\{x1 \leftarrow x\}$
3:	READ	0	$\{R_0 \leftarrow y\}$
4:	STORE	$y1$	$\{y1 \leftarrow \lfloor y / 2^k \rfloor\}$
5:	SHIFT		
6:	STORE	$y2$	$\{y_2 \leftarrow \lfloor y / 2^{k+1} \rfloor\}$
7:	ADD	$y2$	$\{R_0 \leftarrow 2\lfloor y / 2^{k+1} \rfloor\}$
8:	SUB	$y1$	$\{R_0 \leftarrow 2\lfloor y / 2^{k+1} \rfloor - \lfloor y / 2^k \rfloor\}$
9:	JZERO	13	{if the k-th bit of y is 0}
10:	LOAD	z	{ zero at the start}
11:	ADD	$x1$	
12:	STORE	z	$\{z \leftarrow x \cdot (y \bmod 2^k)\}$
13:	LOAD	$x1$	
14:	ADD	$x1$	
15:	STORE	$x1$	
16:	LOAD	$y2$	
17:	JZERO	19	$\{\text{if } \lfloor y / 2^k = 0 \rfloor\}$
18:	JUMP	4	
19:	WRITE	z	
20:	HALT		

Figure 4.17 Integer multiplication on RAM$^+$

stands for the number of cycles performed to that point. At the beginning $k = 0$. The basic idea of the algorithm is simple: if the kth right-most bit of y is 1, then $x2^k$ is added to the resulting sum. The SHIFT operation is used to determine, using the instructions numbered 4 to 9, the kth bit.

If we use complexity measures like those for Turing machines, that is, one instruction as one time step and one used register as one space unit, the **uniform complexity measures**, then the complexity analysis of the program in Figure 4.16, which computes $f(n) = 2^{2^n}$, yields the estimations $T_u(n) = \mathcal{O}(n) = \mathcal{O}(2^{\lg n})$ for time and $S_u(n) = \mathcal{O}(1)$ for space. Both estimations are clearly unrealistic, because just to store these numbers one needs time proportional to their length $\mathcal{O}(2^n)$. One way out is to consider only the RAM$^+$ model (with or without the shift instruction). In a RAM$^+$ an instruction can increase the length of the binary representations of the numbers involved at most by one (multiplication can double it), and therefore the uniform time complexity measure is realistic. The second more general way out is to consider the **logarithmic complexity measures**. The time to perform an instruction is considered to be equal to the sum of the lengths of the binary representations of all the numbers involved in the instruction (that is, all operands as well as all addresses). The space needed for a register is then the maximum length of the binary representations of the numbers stored

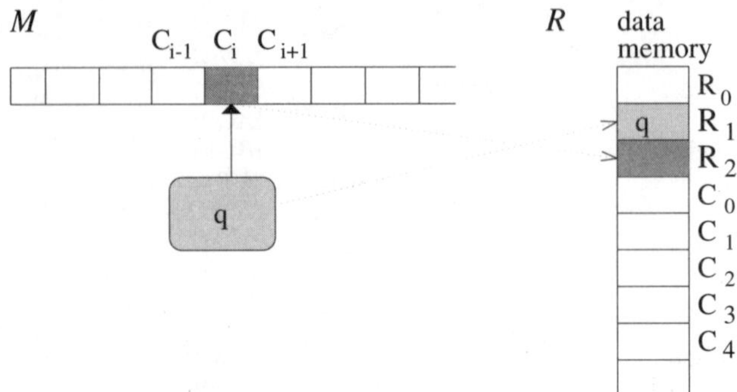

Figure 4.18 Simulation of a TM on a RAM$^+$

in that register during the program execution plus the length of the address of the register. The logarithmic space complexity of a computation is then the sum of the logarithmic space complexities of all the registers involved. With respect to these logarithmic complexity measures, the program in Figure 4.16a, for $f(n) = 2^{2^n}$, has the time complexity $T_l(n) = \Theta(2^n)$ and the space complexity $S_l(n) = \Theta(2^n)$, which corresponds to our intuition. Similarly, for the complexity of the program in Figure 4.17, to multiply two n-bit integers we get $T_u(n) = \Theta(n)$, $S_u(n) = \Theta(1)$, $T_l(n) = \Theta(n^2)$, $S_l(n) = \Theta(n)$, where the subscript u refers to the uniform and the subscript l to the logarithmic measures. In the last example, uniform and logarithmic measures differ by only a polynomial factor with respect to the length of the input. In the first example the differences are exponential.

4.2.2 Mutual Simulations of Random Access and Turing Machines

In spite of the fact that random access machines and Turing machines seem to be very different computer models, they can simulate each other efficiently.

Theorem 4.2.1 *A one-tape Turing machine $\mathcal{M}$ of time complexity $t(n)$ and space complexity $s(n)$ can be simulated by a RAM$^+$ of uniform time complexity $\mathcal{O}(t(n))$ and space complexity $\mathcal{O}(s(n))$, and with the logarithmic time complexity $\mathcal{O}(t(n)\lg t(n))$ and space complexity $\mathcal{O}(s(n))$.*

Proof: As mentioned in Section 4.1.3, we can assume without loss of generality that $\mathcal{M}$ has a one-way infinite tape. Data memory of a RAM$^+$ $\mathcal{R}$ simulating $\mathcal{M}$ is depicted in Figure 4.18. It uses the register R_1 to store the current state of $\mathcal{M}$ and the register R_2 to store the current position of the head of $\mathcal{M}$. Moreover, the contents of the jth cell of the tape of $\mathcal{M}$ will be stored in the register R_{j+2}, if $j \geq 0$.

$\mathcal{R}$ will have a special subprogram for each instruction of $\mathcal{M}$. This subprogram will simulate the instruction using the registers $R_0 - R_2$. During the simulation the instruction LOAD $*2$, with indirect addressing, is used to read the same symbol as the head of $\mathcal{M}$. After the simulation of an instruction of $\mathcal{M}$ is finished, the main program is entered, which uses registers R_1 and R_2 to determine which instruction of $\mathcal{M}$ is to be simulated as the next one. The number of operations which $\mathcal{R}$ needs to simulate one instruction of $\mathcal{M}$ is clearly constant, and the number of registers used is larger than the number of cells used by $\mathcal{M}$ by only a factor of 2. This gives the uniform complexity time and space estimations. The size of the numbers stored in registers (except in R_2) is bounded by a constant, because the alphabet of $\mathcal{M}$ is finite. This yields the $\mathcal{O}(s(n))$ bound for the logarithmic space complexity. The logarithmic factor for the logarithmic time complexity $\lg t(n)$, comes from the fact that the number representing the head position in the register R_2 may be as large as $t(n)$. □

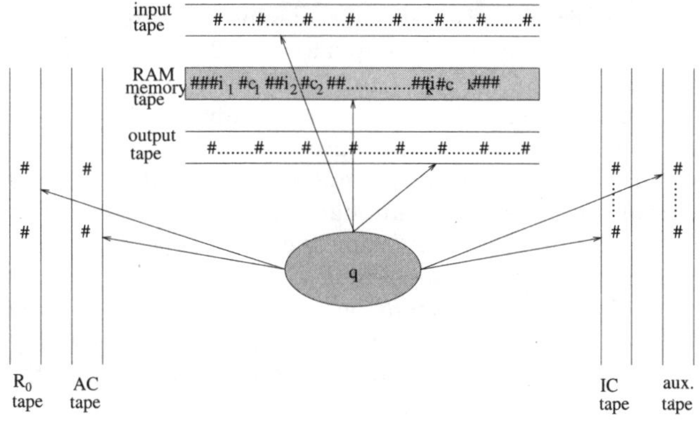

Figure 4.19 Simulation of a RAM on a TM

It is easy to see that the same result holds for a simulation of MTM on RAM$^+$, except that slightly more complicated mapping of k tapes into a sequence of memory registers of a RAM has to be used.

> **Exercise 4.2.2** *Show that the same complexity estimations as in Theorem 4.2.1 can be obtained for the simulation of k-tape MTM on RAM$^+$.*

The fact that RAM can be efficiently simulated by Turing machines is more surprising.

Theorem 4.2.3 *A RAM$^+$ of uniform time complexity $t(n)$ and logarithmic space complexity $s(n) \leq t(n)$ can be simulated by an MTM in time $\mathcal{O}(t^4(n))$ and space $\mathcal{O}(s(n))$. A RAM of logarithmic time complexity $t(n)$ and logarithmic space complexity $s(n)$ can be simulated by an MTM in time $\mathcal{O}(t^3(n))$ and space $\mathcal{O}(s(n))$.*

Proof: If a RAM$^+$ has uniform time complexity $t(n)$ and logarithmic space complexity $s(n) \leq t(n)$, then its logarithmic time complexity is $\mathcal{O}(t(n)s(n))$ or $\mathcal{O}(t^2(n))$, because each RAM$^+$ instruction can increase the length of integers stored in the memory at most by one, and the time needed by a Turing machine to perform a RAM$^+$ instruction is proportional to the length of the operands.

We show now how a RAM$^+$ $\mathcal{R}$ with logarithmic time complexity $t(n)$ and logarithmic space complexity $s(n)$ can be simulated by a 7-tape MTM $\mathcal{M}$ in time $\mathcal{O}(t^2(n))$. From this the first statement of the theorem follows.

$\mathcal{M}$ will have a general program to pre-process and post-process all RAM instructions and a special group of instructions for each RAM instruction. The first read-only input tape contains the inputs of $\mathcal{R}$, separated from one another by the marker #. Each time a RAM instruction is to be simulated, the second tape contains the addresses and contents of all registers of $\mathcal{R}$ used by $\mathcal{R}$ up to that moment in the form

$$\#\#\#i_1\#c_1\#\#i_2\#c_2\#\#i_3\#\ldots\#\#i_{k-1}\#c_{k-1}\#\#i_k\#c_k\#\#\#,$$

where $\#$ is a marker; $i_1, i_2, \ldots, i_k$ are addresses of registers used until then, stored in binary form; and c_j is the current contents of the register R_{i_j}, again in binary form. The accumulator tape contains the current contents of the register R_0. The AC tape contains the current contents of AC, and the IC tape the current value of IC. The output tape is used to write the output of $\mathcal{R}$, and the last tape is an auxiliary working tape (see Figure 4.19).

The simulation of a RAM instruction begins with the updating of AC and IC. A special subprogram of $\mathcal{M}$ is used to search the second tape for the register $\mathcal{R}$ has to work with. If the operand of the instruction has the form '$=j$', then the register is the accumulator. If the operand has the form 'j', then j is the current contents of AC, and one scan through the second tape, together with comparison of integers i_k with the number j written on the AC tape, is enough either to locate j and c_j on the second tape or to find out that the register R_j has not been used yet. In the second case, the string $\#\#j\#0$ is added at the end of the second tape just before the string $\#\#\#$. In the case of indirect addressing, '$*j$', two scans through the second tape are needed. In the first, the register address j is found, and the contents of the corresponding register, c_j, are written on the auxiliary tape. In the second the register address c_j is found in order to get c_{c_j}. (In the case j or c_j is not found as a register address, we insert on the second tape a new register with 0 as its contents.)

In the case of instructions that use only the contents of the register stored on the second tape, that is, WRITE and LOAD or an arithmetic instruction, these are copied on either the output tape or the accumulator tape or the auxiliary tape.

Simulation of a RAM instruction for changing the contents of a register R_i found on the second tape is a little bit more complicated. In this case $\mathcal{M}$ first copies the contents of the second tape after the string $\#\#i\#c_i\#$ on the auxiliary tape, then replaces $c_i\#$ with the contents of the AC tape, appends $\#$, and copies the contents of the auxiliary tape back on to the second memory tape. In the case of arithmetical instructions, the accumulator tape (with the content of R_0) and the auxiliary tape, with the second operand, are used to perform the operation. The result is then used to replace the old contents of the accumulator tape.

The key factor for the complexity analysis is that the contents of the tapes can never be larger than $\mathcal{O}(s(n))$. This immediately implies the space complexity bound. In addition, it implies that the scanning of the second tape can be done in time $\mathcal{O}(t(n))$. Simulations of an addition and a subtraction also require only time proportional to the length of the arguments. This provides a time bound $\mathcal{O}(t^2(n))$. In the case of multiplication, an algorithm similar to that described in Figure 4.17 can be used to implement a multiplication in $\mathcal{O}(t^2(n))$ time. (Actually the SHIFT instruction has been used only to locate the next bit of one of the arguments in the constant time.) This is easily implementable on a TM. A similar time bound holds for division. This yields in total a $\mathcal{O}(t^3(n))$ time estimation for the simulation of a RAM with logarithmic time complexity $t(n)$. □

Exercise 4.2.4 *Could we perform the simulation shown in the proof of Theorem 4.2.3 without a special tape for IC?*

4.2.3 Sequential Computation Thesis

Church's thesis concerns basic idealized limitations of computing. In this chapter we present two quantitative variations of Church's thesis: the **sequential computation thesis** (also called the **invariance thesis**) and the **parallel computation thesis**. Both deal with the robustness of certain quantitative aspects of computing: namely, with mutual simulations of computer models.

Turing machines and RAM are examples of computer models, or computer architectures (in a modest sense). For a deeper understanding of the merits, potentials and applicability of various

Instruction	Encoding	Instruction	Encoding	Instruction	Encoding
LOAD i	1	SUB $=i$	7	WRITE i	13
LOAD $=i$	2	MULT i	8	WRITE$=i$	14
STORE i	3	MULT $= i$	9	JUMP i	15
ADD i	4	DIV i	10	JGZERO i	16
ADD $=i$	5	DIV $=i$	11	JZERO i	17
SUB i	6	READ i	12	HALT	18

Table 4.1 Encoding of RASP instructions

computer models, the following concept of **time** (and **space**) **simulation** is the key.

Definition 4.2.5 *We say that a computer model $\mathcal{CM}'$ simulates a computer model $\mathcal{CM}$ with time (space) overhead $f(n)$, notation*

$$\mathcal{CM}' \leq \mathcal{CM} \ (time\, f(n)) \qquad or \qquad \mathcal{CM}' \leq \mathcal{CM} \ (space\, f(n))$$

if for every machine $\mathcal{M}_i \in \mathcal{CM}$ there exists a machine $\mathcal{M}_{s(i)} \in \mathcal{CM}'$ such that $\mathcal{M}_{s(i)}$ simulates $\mathcal{M}_i$; that is, for an encoding $c(x)$ of an input x of $\mathcal{M}_i$, $\mathcal{M}_{s(i)}(c(x)) = \mathcal{M}_i(x)$, and, moreover, if $t(|x|)$ is the time (space) needed by $\mathcal{M}_i$ to process x, then the time (space) needed by $\mathcal{M}_{s(i)}$ on the input $c(x)$ is bounded by $f(t(|x|))$. If, in addition, the function $s(i)$ is computable in polynomial time, then the simulation is called effective. (Another way to consider a simulation is to admit also an encoding of outputs.)

As a corollary of Theorems 4.2.1 and 4.2.3 we get

Theorem 4.2.6 *One-tape Turing machines and RAM$^+$ with uniform time complexity and logarithmic space complexity (or RAM with logarithmic time and space complexity) can simulate each other with a polynomial overhead in time and a linear overhead in space.*

We have introduced the RAM as a model of the von Neumann type of (sequential) computers. However, is it really one? Perhaps the most important contribution of von Neumann was the idea that programs and data be stored in the same memory and that programs can modify themselves (which RAM programs cannot do).

A computer model closer to the original von Neumann idea is called a RASP (**random access stored program**). A RASP is like a RAM except that RASP programs can modify themselves. The instruction set for RASP (RASP$^+$) is the same as for RAM (RAM$^+$), except that indirect addressing is not allowed. A RASP program is stored in data registers, one instruction per two registers. The first of these two registers contains the operation, encoded numerically, for example, as in Table 4.1. The second register contains either the operand or the label in the case of a jump instruction.

Exercise 4.2.7 * *Show that RAM and RASP and also RAM$^+$ and RASP$^+$ can simulate each other with linear time and space overheads, no matter whether uniform or logarithmic complexity measures are used.*

Since RAM and RASP can simulate each other with linear time and space overhead, for asymptotic complexity investigations it is of no importance which of these two models is used. However, since RAM programs cannot modify themselves they are usually more transparent, which is why RAM are nowadays used almost exclusively for the study of basic problems of the design and analysis of algorithms for sequential computers. The results concerning mutual simulations of Turing machines, RAM and RASP machines are the basis of the following thesis on which the modern ideas of **feasible computing, complexity theory** and program design theory are based.

Sequential computation thesis. There exists a standard class of computer models, which includes among others all variants of Turing machines, many variants of RAM and RASP with logarithmic time and space measures, and also RAM^+ and RASP^+, with uniform time measure and logarithmic space measure, provided only the standard arithmetical instructions of additive type are used. Machine models in this class can simulate each other with polynomial overhead in time and linear overhead in space.

Computer models satisfying the sequential computation thesis are said to form the **first machine class**. In other words, a computer model belongs to the first machine class if and only if this model and one-tape Turing machines can simulate each other within polynomial overhead in time and simultaneously with linear overhead in space. The sequential computation thesis therefore becomes a guiding rule for the determination of inherently sequential computer models that are equivalent to other such models in a reasonable sense.

The first machine class is very robust. In spite of this, it may be far from easy to see whether a computer model is in this class. For example, a RAM with uniform time and space complexity measures is not in the first machine class. Such RAM cannot be simulated by MTM with a polynomial overhead in time. Even more powerful is the RAM augmented with the operation of integer division, as we shall see later. The following exercise demonstrates the huge power of such machines.

Exercise 4.2.8* *Show that RAM with integer division can compute $n!$ in $\mathcal{O}(\lg^2 n)$ steps (or even in $\mathcal{O}(\lg n)$ steps). (Hint: use the recurrence $n! = n(n-1)!$ if n is odd and $n! = \binom{n}{n/2}((n/2)!)^2$ if n is even and the identity $(2^l+1)^{2k} = \sum_{j=0}^{2k}\binom{2k}{j}2^{lj}$, for sufficiently large l.)*

Example 4.2.9 *Another simple computer model that is a modification of RAM^+ but is not in the first machine class is the* **register machine**. *Only nonnegative integers can be stored in the registers of a register machine. A program for a register machine is a finite sequence of labelled instructions of one of the following types:*

l: PUSH α	$\{c(\alpha) \leftarrow c(\alpha)+1\}$;
l: POP α	$\{c(\alpha) \leftarrow \max\{0, c(\alpha)-1\}$;
l: TEST $\alpha : l_1$	**if** $c(\alpha) = 0$ **then go to** l_1;
l: HALT,	

where $c(\alpha)$ denotes the current content of the register α and each time a nonjumping instruction is performed or the test in a jump instruction fails, the following instruction is performed as the next one (if there is any).

Exercise 4.2.10 *Show that each one-tape Turing machine can be simulated with only linear time overhead by a Turing machine that has two pushdown tapes. On a pushdown tape the machine can read and remove only the left-most symbol and can write only at the left-most end of the tape (pushing all other symbols into the tape).*[8]

Exercise 4.2.11 *Show that each pushdown tape can be simulated by a register machine with two registers. (Hint: if* $\Gamma = \{Z_1, \ldots, Z_{k-1}\}$ *is the pushdown tape alphabet, then each word* $Z_{i_1} Z_{i_2} \ldots Z_{i_m}$ *on the pushdown tape can be represented in one register of the register machine by the integer* $i_1 + ki_2 + k^2 i_3 + \ldots + k^{m-1} i_m$. *In order to simulate a pushdown tape operation, the contents of one register are transferred, symbol by symbol or 1 by 1, to another register and during that process the needed arithmetical operation is performed.)*

Exercise 4.2.12 *Show that each one-tape TM can be simulated by a register machine with two registers. (Hint: according to the previous exercise, it is enough to show how to simulate a four-register machine by a two-register machine. The basic idea is to represent contents* i, j, k, l *of four registers by one number* $2^i 3^j 5^k 7^l$.)

Register machines are not powerful enough to simulate TM in polynomial time, but they can simulate any TM (see the exercises above).

4.2.4 Straight-line Programs

Of particular interest and importance are special RAM programs, the so-called straight-line programs. Formally, they can be defined as finite sequences of simple assignment statements

$$\begin{array}{ccc} X_1 & \leftarrow & Y_1 \odot_1 Z_1, \\ X_2 & \leftarrow & Y_2 \odot_2 Z_2, \\ \vdots & \vdots & \vdots \\ X_n & \leftarrow & Y_n \odot_n Z_n, \end{array}$$

where each X_i is a variable; Y_i and Z_i are either constants, input variables or some X_j with a $j < i$; and $\odot$ is one of the operations $+, -, \times, /$. (A variable that occurs on the right-hand side of a statement and does not occur on the left-hand side of a previous statement is called an input variable.) Figure 4.20a shows a straight-line program with four input variables.

A straight-line program can be seen as a RAM program without jump instructions, and can be depicted as a circuit, the leaves of which are labelled by the input variables, and internal nodes by the arithmetical operations – an **arithmetical circuit** (see Figure 4.20b). The number of instructions of a straight-line program or, equivalently, the number of internal nodes of the corresponding arithmetical circuit is its **size**.

Straight-line programs look very simple, but they constitute the proper framework for formulating some of the most basic and most difficult computational problems. For example, given two matrices $A = \{a_{ij}\}, B = \{b_{ij}\}$ of fixed degree n, what is the minimum number of arithmetical operations needed to compute (a) the **product** $C = A \cdot B$; (b) the **determinant**, $det(A)$, of A; (c) the **permanent**, $perm(A)$, of A, where

$$det(A) = \sum_{\sigma \in perm_n} (-1)^{i(\sigma)} a_{1\sigma(1)} \ldots a_{n\sigma(n)}, \qquad perm(A) = \sum_{\sigma \in perm_n} a_{1\sigma(1)} \ldots a_{n\sigma(n)}$$

[8] A pushdown tape is a one-way infinite tape, but its head stays on the left-most symbol of the tape. The machine can read only the left-most symbol or replace it by a string. If this string has more than one symbol, all symbols on the tape are pushed to the right to make space for a new string. If the string is empty, then all tape symbols are pushed one cell to the left.

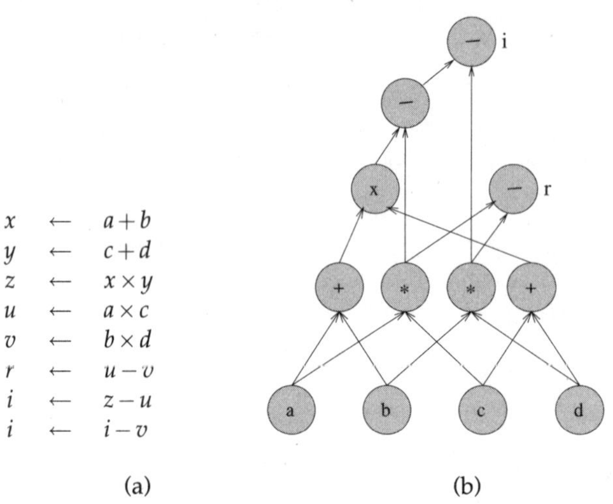

Figure 4.20 Complex number multiplication

where $perm_n$ is the set of all permutations of the set $\{1, \ldots, n\}$ and $i(\sigma)$ is the number of inversions in σ.

> **Exercise 4.2.13** *Show that the problem of computing the permanent of a* $0-1$*-matrix is equivalent to the problem of counting the number of perfect matchings of a bipartite graph.*

Let us now discuss in more detail the matrix multiplication problem. In the case $n = 2^k, k \in \mathbf{N}$, in order to multiply two matrices A and B of degree n, we can use the following divide-and-conquer method: decompose matrices A and B into four matrices of degree $n/2$, as shown in Figure 4.21a, then multiply recursively A and B, as matrices of degree 2 the elements of which are matrices of degree $n/2$. The classical 'school algorithm' for multiplying two matrices $\{a_{ij}\}$ and $\{b_{ij}\}$ of degree 2, using formulas $c_{ij} = a_{i1}b_{1j} + a_{i2}b_{2j}, 1 \leq i,j \leq 2$, requires eight multiplications and four additions (see Figure 4.21b). There exists, surprisingly, another algorithm for multiplying two matrices of degree 2, due to Strassen (see Figure 4.21c), that uses only seven multiplications (and eighteen additions/subtractions).[9]

At first sight it seems that nothing has been gained, in fact, just the opposite, because the new algorithm requires the performance of more operations than the old one. However, if this new algorithm for multiplying matrices of degree 2 is used recursively with the above divide-and-conquer method, then the following recurrence holds for the number of arithmetic operations of the resulting algorithm:

$$T(n) = 7T(\frac{n}{2}) + \Theta(n^2),$$

because $\Theta(n^2)$ operations are needed to add/subtract two matrices of degree $n/2$. By Theorem 1.6.3, $T(n) = \mathcal{O}(n^{\lg_2 7}) = \mathcal{O}(n^{2.81})$, which is asymptotically fewer than the $\Theta(n^3)$ steps required by the 'classical algorithm' (see Example 1.1.11).

[9]It has been shown that there is no algorithm for multiplying matrices of degree 2 with six multiplications only, and that any straight-line program that can multiply matrices of degree 2 with seven multiplications only has to use at least fifteen operations of addition/subtraction.

$$A = \begin{vmatrix} a_{11} & a_{12} \\ a_{21} & a_{22} \end{vmatrix} \qquad B = \begin{vmatrix} b_{11} & b_{12} \\ b_{21} & b_{22} \end{vmatrix}$$

(a)

$$\begin{array}{lll} z_1 & \leftarrow & a_{11} \times b_{11} \\ z_2 & \leftarrow & a_{12} \times b_{21} \\ c_{11} & \leftarrow & z_1 + z_2 \\ z_1 & \leftarrow & a_{11} \times b_{12} \\ z_2 & \leftarrow & a_{12} \times b_{22} \\ c_{12} & \leftarrow & z_1 + z_2 \\ z_1 & \leftarrow & a_{21} \times b_{11} \\ z_2 & \leftarrow & a_{22} \times b_{21} \\ c_{21} & \leftarrow & z_1 + z_2 \\ z_1 & \leftarrow & a_{21} \times b_{12} \\ z_2 & \leftarrow & a_{22} \times b_{22} \\ c_{22} & \leftarrow & z_1 + z_2 \end{array}$$

(b)

$$\begin{array}{lll} i & \leftarrow & a_{12} - a_{22} \\ j & \leftarrow & b_{21} + b_{22} \\ x & \leftarrow & i \times j \\ i & \leftarrow & a_{11} + a_{22} \\ j & \leftarrow & b_{11} + b_{22} \\ y & \leftarrow & i \times j \\ i & \leftarrow & a_{11} - a_{12} \\ j & \leftarrow & b_{11} + b_{12} \\ z & \leftarrow & i \times j \\ i & \leftarrow & a_{11} + a_{12} \\ u & \leftarrow & i \times b_{22} \\ i & \leftarrow & b_{12} - b_{22} \\ v & \leftarrow & a_{11} \times i \end{array} \qquad \begin{array}{lll} i & \leftarrow & b_{12} - b_{11} \\ w & \leftarrow & a_{22} \times i \\ i & \leftarrow & a_{21} + a_{22} \\ t & \leftarrow & i \times b_{11} \\ i & \leftarrow & x + y \\ j & \leftarrow & w - u \\ c_{11} & \leftarrow & i + j \\ c_{12} & \leftarrow & u + v \\ c_{21} & \leftarrow & w + t \\ i & \leftarrow & y - z \\ j & \leftarrow & v - t \\ c_{22} & \leftarrow & i + j \end{array}$$

(c)

Figure 4.21 Matrix multiplication

Strassen's algorithm for multiplying matrices of degree 2 (Figure 4.21b) and the resulting asymptotically faster algorithm for multiplying two matrices were very surprising results at the time of their discovery. They demonstrated that century-long, never challenged beliefs concerning the best possible algorithms for basic algorithmic problems can be wrong. In addition, these results initiated a rapid development of modern algorithm design and analysis theory, with enormous impact on the efficiency of computation that matches the hardware successes.[10]

Exercise 4.2.14 *A natural way to multiply two matrices of degree $n = m^k$ is to use the divide-and-conquer method in the way that the given matrices are decomposed into m^2 submatrices of degree n/m and then use this method recursively. If we find a way to multiply $m \times m$ matrices with fewer than m^3 operations, this will lead to an algorithm that is asymptotically faster than the classical one. The best current algorithm for multiplying matrices of degree 3 uses 23 multiplications. Is this sufficient to beat Strassen's algorithm? If not, how much do we need to improve the algorithm for multiplication of 3×3 matrices in order to beat Strassen's algorithm? (In 1978 Pan showed how to multiply 48×48 matrices using only 47,216 multiplications and that led to the general matrix algorithm with $\mathcal{O}(n^{2.78014})$ arithmetical operations.)*

Matrix multiplication is one of the key computational problems in scientific and engineering applications. In addition, several other practically important algorithmic problems are

[10]These results also initiated an exciting competition to find the best possible algorithm (that is, with as small a number of operations as possible) to multiply two matrices. Consequent improvements: $\mathcal{O}(n^{2.78})$, Pan in 1978; $\mathcal{O}(n^{2.779})$, Bini in 1979; $\mathcal{O}(n^{2.542})$, Schönhage in 1980; $\mathcal{O}(n^{2.522})$, Pan (1980); $\mathcal{O}(n^{2.495})$, Winograd (1981); $\mathcal{O}(n^{2.376})$, Coppersmith and Winograd (1987). (Since the best known lower bound is currently $2n^2$, there is still plenty of room for improvement.)

computationally equivalent to matrix multiplication. For many other algorithmic problems $\mathcal{P}$ an asymptotically faster algorithm for matrix multiplication immediately yields an asymptotically faster algorithm for $\mathcal{P}$. For example, matrix inversion is equivalent, with respect to the computational complexity measured by the size of the straight-line programs, to matrix multiplication. Moreover, each asymptotic upper bound for the number of operations for matrix multiplication is at the same time the asymptotic upper bound for the number of operations needed to compute determinants. The determinant of a matrix of degree n can therefore be computed within $\mathcal{O}(n^{2.376})$ arithmetical operations and also in time $\mathcal{O}(n^{2.376})$. To compute the permanent of a matrix, which looks like a problem very similar to that of computing the determinant, seems to be essentially more difficult. No polynomial time algorithm is known for computing permanents (even if the computation of a permanent can be done on a RAM with the operation of integer division in $\mathcal{O}(n^2)$ steps). A special way to compute permanents will be discussed in Chapter 9.

Observe that Strassen's algorithm works properly for any ring of matrix elements but cannot be used directly to multiply Boolean matrices, since a Boolean quasi-ring is not a ring. However, with a simple trick, Boolean matrix multiplication can be reduced to matrix multiplication over a ring.

Exercise 4.2.15 *Show that if $m(n)$ denotes the number of arithmetical operations needed to multiply two matrices of degree n, then two Boolean matrices of degree n can be multiplied using $\mathcal{O}(m(n))$ arithmetical operations. (Hint: interpret 0-1 elements of Boolean matrices as integers, multiply these integer matrices, ...)*

Exercise 4.2.16 *Show that using Boolean matrix multiplication one can decide efficiently whether a given undirected graph has a triangle.*

Another simple example, showing how misleading our common sense can sometimes be concerning computational complexity of algorithmic problems, deals with the complex number multiplication

$$(a+bi)\times(c+di) = (ac-bd)+(ad+bc)i.$$

How many multiplications of reals are needed to multiply two complex numbers? Four, as the common sense tells us? No. Figure 4.20a shows that it can be done with three multiplications only. (In the case that a,b,c,d are matrices, and we actually have multiplication of two complex matrices, this new algorithm represents a significant improvement.)

Exercise 4.2.17 *Some 'innocent' arithmetical operations have surprising power. Show, in order to demonstrate it, that multiplication of two matrices of degree n with nonnegative integers can be performed by a straight-line program with $\mathcal{O}(n^2)$ operations if integer division is allowed. (Hint: in order to multiply two matrices $A=\{a_{ij}\}$, $B=\{b_{ij}\}$ to get $C=A\cdot B$, $C=\{c_{ij}\}$, compute*

$$z = \left(\sum_{i=1}^{n}\sum_{j=1}^{n} a_{ij}\right)\left(\sum_{i=1}^{n}\sum_{j=1}^{n} b_{ij}\right)+1$$

and $A_i=\sum_{j=1}^{n} a_{ij}z^{(j-1)}$, $B_j=\sum_{i=1}^{n} b_{ij}z^{n-i+1}+1$ for $i,j=1,2,\ldots,n$, and use the operations of integer division and of modulo (which can be reduced to integer division) to compute all c_{ij} in $\mathcal{O}(n^2)$ operations.)

4.2.5 RRAM – Random Access Machines over Reals

RRAM are defined similarly to RAM, the only difference being that any real number can be an input, a constant in a register, or an operand of an instruction. Moreover, any RRAM operation is supposed to take one time unit, no matter how large the operands are or whether they are rational or irrational, and the arithmetical operations are always performed exactly.

The motivation behind the RRAM model is the desire for a computer model that will allow us to deal well with problems of numerical mathematics, scientific computing and calculus, and bring computational complexity paradigms into these areas of continuous mathematics.

At first sight it may seem that RRAM are not very different from RAM but this is misleading. We present some examples illustrating the enormous power of RRAM, as well as machines with slightly adjusted instruction sets. As we shall see, RRAM seem to go beyond even Turing machines and violate Church's thesis because they can also 'compute' functions not computable by Turing machines. But this only means that RRAM, in spite of being quite natural, are not in their full generality appropriate models for studying fundamental questions of computability, even though they seem to be quite appropriate for studying many important questions related to the efficiency and complexity of algorithmic problems of calculus and numerical mathematics.

In the following examples RRAM programs are written in an informal high-level language, in a way that makes their translation into proper RRAM programs straightforward.

Example 4.2.18 (Complement of the Cantor set) *The following RRAM program accepts those $x \in [0,1)$ that are not in the Cantor set (see Example 2.1.16).*

```
        if x < 0 or x > 1 then REJECT fi;
cycle:  x ← 3x;
        if 0 ≤ x ≤ 1 then JUMP cycle fi;
        if 2 ≤ x ≤ 3 then x ← x − 2; JUMP cycle fi;
        ACCEPT
```

Example 4.2.19 (Computation of $\lceil x \rceil$) *The following RRAM program computes $\lceil x \rceil$ for $x > 0$.*

```
if 0 ≤ x ≤ 1 then WRITE 1;
k ← 1;
while x ≥ k do k ← k × 2        {a search for an upper bound};
l ← k/2; r ← k;
while r > l+1 do if l ≤ x ≤ (r+l)/2 then r ← (r+l)/2 else l ← (r+l)/2 od      { binary search};
if l = x then WRITE l else WRITE r
```

Clearly, each cycle is performed $\mathcal{O}(\lg x)$ times, and therefore $\mathcal{O}(\lg x)$ is the total number of steps necessary to compute $\lceil x \rceil$. Interestingly enough, it is an open problem whether one can compute $\lceil x \rceil$ on an RRAM in $\mathcal{O}(1)$ steps. This may seem to be of minor interest, but actually the opposite is true. Indeed, if it were possible to compute $\lceil x \rceil$ in $\mathcal{O}(1)$ time, then we could extend the RRAM instruction repertoire by the instruction $R_0 \leftarrow \lceil R_0 \rceil$, which does not seem to be a big deal. However, we could then factor integers and test the satisfiability of Boolean expressions in a polynomial number of steps on RRAM.

Our last example shows how large the computing power of RRAM is.

Example 4.2.20 (Decidability of arbitrary sets of natural numbers) *Let $S \subset \mathbf{N}$ be any set of integers. Let us define*

$$s_S = 0.s_1s_2s_3, \ldots$$

to be a real number where each $s_i \in \{0,1\}$ and $s_i = 1$, if and only if $i \in S$. The following RRAM program with the built-in constant s_S and the ceiling operation can decide, given an $n \in \mathbf{N}^+$, whether $n \in S$:

if $\lfloor 2^n s_S \rfloor - 2\lfloor 2^{n-1} s_S \rfloor \neq 0$ **then** ACCEPT **else** REJECT

More realistic RRAM models are obtained if it is required that all inputs and constants be rational numbers. An additional useful step seems to be to restrict arithmetical operations to addition and subtraction and/or to consider a logarithmic complexity measure for rational numbers r – to be the minimum of $\lceil \lg p \rceil + \lceil \lg q \rceil$ where $r = \frac{p}{q}$ and p,q are integers.

Remark 4.2.21 Since a RAM is a single machine (a RAM program is its input), the problem of universality for RAM cannot be stated in the same way it was as for Turing machines. However, the property of self-simulation discussed in Exercise 21 comes close to it.

4.3 Boolean Circuit Families

At the lowest level of computation, a typical computer processes bits. All numbers and characters are represented by bits, and all basic operations are bit operations. Real bit computers are well modelled by Boolean circuits.

Uniformly designed families of Boolean circuits constitute another very basic computer model, very different from Turing machines and RAM. Since the structure and work of Boolean circuits are both transparent and tractable, they play an important role in theoretical studies.

Both TM and RAM are examples of **uniform** and **infinite computer models** in the sense that each particular computer can process inputs of an arbitrary size. For example, a single TM (or a RAM) program can be used to multiply matrices of an arbitrary degree. On the other hand, a single Boolean circuit computes only a single Boolean function. It can process binary strings only of a fixed size, interpreted as an assignment of Boolean values to variables. In order to make a (universal) computer model of the same power as Turing machines out of Boolean circuits, uniformly designed families of Boolean circuits have to be considered. For each integer n there must be a circuit in such a family with n inputs, and all circuits of the family must be designed in a uniform way, as described later.

4.3.1 Boolean Circuits

A Boolean circuit over a Boolean base $\mathcal{B}$ is a finite labelled directed acyclic graph (see Figure 4.22) whose nodes of in-degree 0, the **input nodes** or **leaves**, are labelled by different Boolean variables, and all other nodes, the **gates**, are labelled by Boolean functions (operators) from $\mathcal{B}$, always of the same -arity as is the in-degree of the node. The nodes of out-degree 0 are called **output nodes**. We shall consider mostly the base $\mathcal{B} = \{\text{NOT, OR, AND}\}$ ($\mathcal{B} = \{\neg, \vee, \wedge\}$) unless explicitly stated otherwise.

Each Boolean circuit C with n input nodes (labelled by variables $x_1, \ldots, x_n$) and m output nodes (labelled by variables $y_1, y_2, \ldots, y_m$), represents a Boolean function $f_C : \mathbf{B}_n \rightarrow \mathbf{B}_m$. The value of f_C for a truth assignment $T : \{x_1, \ldots, x_n\} \rightarrow \{0,1\}$ is the vector of values produced by the output nodes (gates) of C. In this computation process each input node produces the value of its variable for the given truth assignment T, and each gate produces the value of the Boolean function (operator) assigned to that node, for arguments obtained along the input edges from its predecessors. One such computation is shown in Figure 4.22.

To each Boolean expression corresponds in a natural way a Boolean circuit. Each variable corresponds to an input node, and each occurrence of an operator to a gate. See Figure 4.23b for the circuit corresponding to the Boolean expression

$$((x_1 \vee x_2) \wedge x_3 \vee \neg x_1) \wedge x_2 \vee ((x_1 \vee x_2) \wedge x_3 \vee \neg x_1) \wedge x_3. \tag{4.2}$$

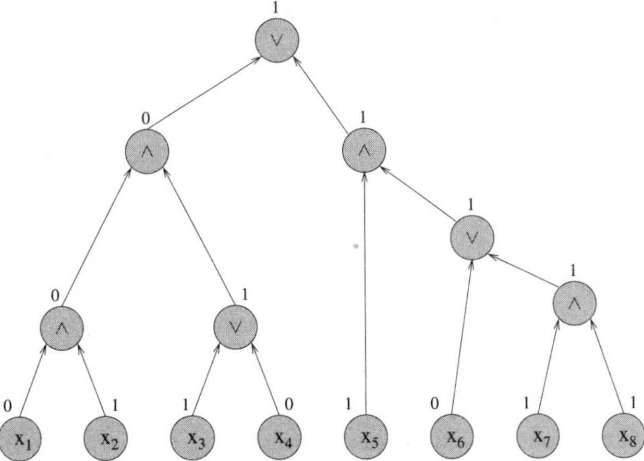

Figure 4.22 A Boolean circuit

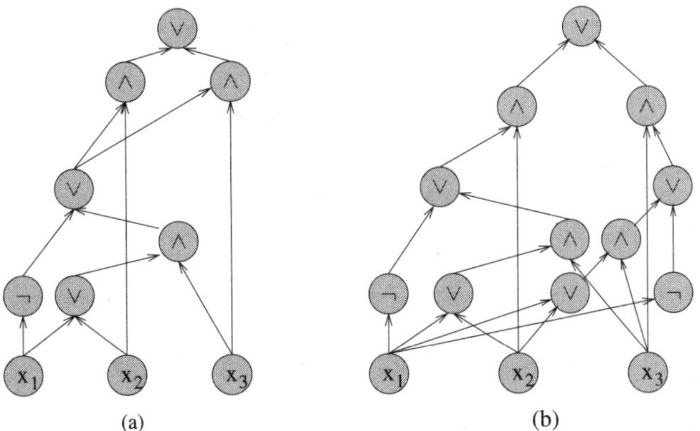

Figure 4.23 Boolean circuits

Boolean circuits often represent a more economical way of describing Boolean functions than Boolean expressions. This is due to the fact that several identical subexpressions of a Boolean expression can be represented by a single subcircuit. See the two Boolean circuits in Figure 4.23 which compute the same Boolean function: namely, the one represented by the Boolean expression (4.2).

Exercise 4.3.1 *Design a Boolean circuit over the base* $\{\vee, \wedge, \neg\}$ *to compute the Boolean function* $f \in \mathcal{B}_3^2$ *such that* $f(0, x_1, x_2) = (x_1, x_2)$ *and* $f(1, x_1, x_2) = (x_2, x_1)$.

Exercise 4.3.2* *Define in a natural way the concept of a Boolean circuit that is universal for the set of all circuits with the same number of inputs.*

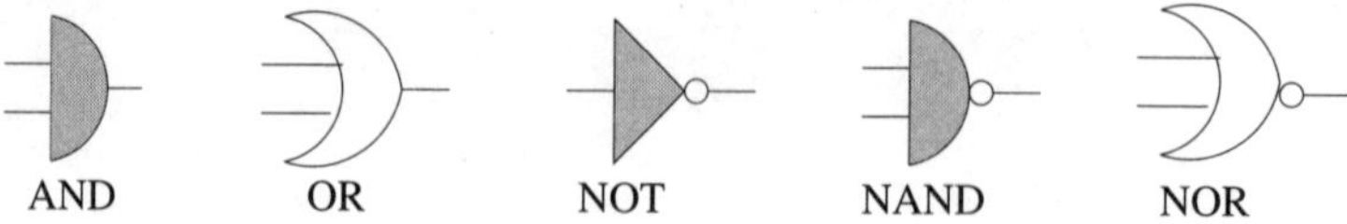

Figure 4.24 Basic gates

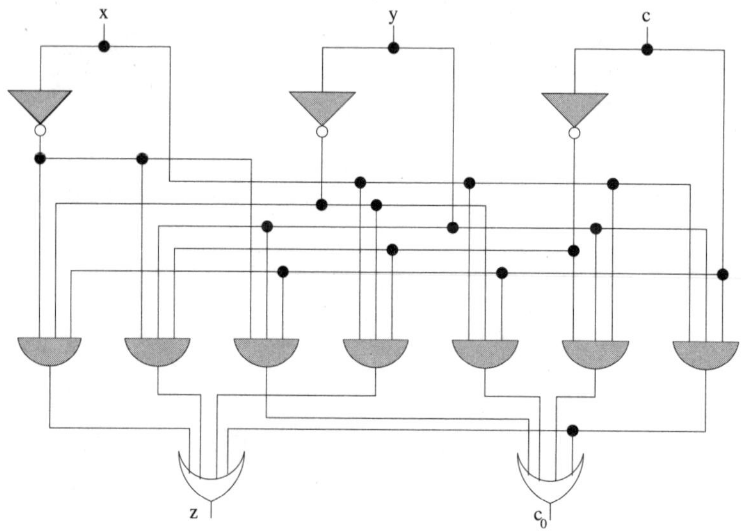

Figure 4.25 One bit adder

Exercise 4.3.3* *Design a Boolean circuit over the base* $\{\vee, \wedge, \neg\}$ *that is universal for the base* $\{\vee, \wedge, \neg\}$.

Boolean circuits are a natural abstraction from the sequential combinational circuits used to design electronic digital devices. Gates in such circuits are electronic elements each of which can have on its inputs and on the output values 0 and 1, usually represented by two different voltage levels. For the most common gates the standard notation is used (see Figure 4.24). AND and OR may have more inputs (they are easily replaced by subcircuits consisting of only the gates with two inputs). To make graphical representations for sequential circuits, another convention is usually used concerning interconnections – wires. These are not connected unless a dot is placed at a point of intersection. Figure 4.25 shows a sequential circuit for a one-bit adder. It has two bit inputs x and y, a carry input c, and two outputs z and c_0, where

$$z = \bar{x}\bar{y}c \vee \bar{x}y\bar{c} \vee x\bar{y}\bar{c} \vee xyc, \qquad c_0 = \bar{x}yc \vee x\bar{y}c \vee xy\bar{c} \vee xyc;$$

that is, z is the resulting sum bit, and c_0 is the new carry bit.

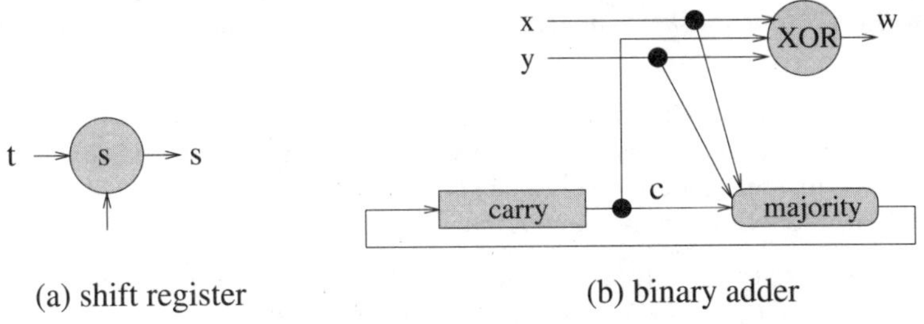

Figure 4.26 A shift register and a binary adder

Exercise 4.3.4 *Let a fixture have three switches such that flipping any of the switches turns the light on (off) when it is off (on). Design a sequential circuit that accomplishes this.*

Exercise 4.3.5 *Construct a sequential circuit that computes the product of two 3-bit integers.*

Clocked circuits versus finite state machines

The most obvious element of computation missing from Boolean circuits is repetition: timing of the work of computing elements and storage of the results between consecutive computation steps. These two functions are performed in computer circuitry using **shift registers** (also called flip-flop registers) controlled by a central clock (usually missing from diagrams). A shift register (Figure 4.26a) has two inputs (one, usually invisible, is from the clock), and at each clock pulse the bit value t on its ingoing edge becomes the new value of the register, and its old value s 'jumps' on the outgoing edge and becomes the value of the register.

A **clocked circuit** is a directed graph the vertices of which are either input nodes, Boolean gates, shift registers or output nodes, with no cycle going through Boolean gates only. Computation on a clock circuit is as follows. At the beginning initial values are written into the shift registers and on input edges, and all computations through Boolean gates propagate within one clock cycle. Then a clock pulse is sent to all shift registers, and new input values are submitted to inputs. This new input assignment is then processed, and the process continues. The response of the clock circuit to inputs depends only on those inputs and the current contents of its shift registers. If a clock circuit has n inputs, k shift registers and m outputs, and if we denote the inputs at clock cycle t by $x^t = (x^t_i, \ldots, x^t_n)$, the states of the shift register by $q^t = (q^t_1, \ldots, q^t_k)$ and the output by $y^t = (y^t_1, \ldots, y^t_m)$, then to each clock circuit two functions are associated:

$$\lambda : \{0,1\}^{k+n} \rightarrow \{0,1\}^m, \tag{4.3}$$

$$\delta : \{0,1\}^{k+n} \rightarrow \{0,1\}^k, \tag{4.4}$$

such that

$$y^t = \lambda(q_t, x_t), \tag{4.5}$$

$$q^{t+1} = \delta(q_t, x_t). \tag{4.6}$$

From the users point of view, a clock circuit is thus a Mealy machine.

Example 4.3.6 *The clock circuit shown in Figure 4.26b is the binary adder whose behaviour is described by the equations* $w^t = x^t \oplus y^t \oplus c^t$ *and* $c^{t+1} = majority(x^t, y^t, c^t)$.

The relation between clock circuits and Mealy machines also goes in the opposite direction in the following way. Both inputs and states of any Mealy machine can be encoded in binary form. Once this is done, each Mealy machine can be seen to be specified by mappings (4.3) and (4.4) and equations (4.5) and (4.6). Now the following theorem holds.

Theorem 4.3.7 *Let* $\lambda : \{0,1\}^{k+n} \rightarrow \{0,1\}^m$ *and* $\delta : \{0,1\}^{k+n} \rightarrow \{0,1\}^k$ *be any two functions. Then there is a clock circuit with input* $x^t = (x_1^t, \ldots, x_n^t)$, *states of clock registers* $q^t = (q_1^t, \ldots, q_k^t)$ *and output* $y^t = (y_1^t, \ldots, y_m^t)$, *at time* t, *whose behaviour is described by equations (4.5) and (4.6).*

Proof: The clock circuit will have k shift registers, which at time t will contain the string q^t, n input nodes with x^t as inputs, and m output nodes with outputs y^t. It contains two Boolean circuits the inputs of which are the outputs of the shift registers and the inputs of the whole circuit. One circuit computes the λ function, and its m outputs are the overall outputs of the circuit. The second Boolean circuit computes the function δ, and its outputs are the inputs of the shift registers. □

Exercise 4.3.8 *Design a clocked circuit for a memory cell (a flip-flop element).*

Any real computer is at its basic logical level a clock circuit. For example, by combining flip-flop elements with a decoder (Exercise 27), we can build a random access memory.

4.3.2 Circuit Complexity of Boolean Functions

Boolean circuits are an appropriate model for dealing in a transparent way with the three most basic computational resources: **sequential time, parallel time** and **space**. The three basic corresponding complexity measures for Boolean circuits are defined as follows:

Size(C)	the **size complexity** of C; that is, the number of gates of C.
Depth(C)	the **depth complexity** of C; that is, the maximal distance of a gate of C from an input node.
Width(C)	the **width complexity** of C is defined by $\mathrm{Width}(C) = \max_{i \leq Depth(C)} Width(C,i)$, where Width(C, i)[11] is the number of gates of the maximal distance i from an input node.

Complexity measures for circuits induce in a natural way complexity measures for Boolean functions f, relative to a chosen Boolean base $\mathcal{B}$:

$$c_{\mathcal{B}}(f) = \min\{c(C) \mid C \text{ is a Boolean circuit for } f \text{ over the base } \mathcal{B}\},$$

where c is any of the measures size, depth or width.

Between the size and depth complexity of Boolean functions the following relations hold, the first of which is easy to show:

$$Depth_{\mathcal{B}}(f) \leq Size_{\mathcal{B}}(f), \qquad Depth_{\mathcal{B}}(f) = \mathcal{O}\left(\frac{Size_{\mathcal{B}}(f)}{\lg Size_{\mathcal{B}}}\right).$$

[11] $Width(C,i)$ is sometimes defined as the number of gates of C that have depth at most i and outgoing edge into a node of depth larger than i.

Exercise 4.3.9 *Show that the choice of the base is not crucial. That is, show that if c is any of the above complexity measures and* $\mathcal{B}_1, \mathcal{B}_2$ *are arbitrary bases, then* $c_{\mathcal{B}_1}(f) = \mathcal{O}(c_{\mathcal{B}_2}(f))$.

Exercise 4.3.10 *A Boolean circuit with only* $\vee$*- and* $\wedge$*-gates is called monotone. Show that corresponding to each Boolean circuit C over the base* $\{\vee, \wedge, \neg\}$ *with variables* $x_1, \ldots, x_n$ *one can construct a monotone Boolean circuit* C' *with inputs* $x_1, \ldots, x_n, \overline{x_1}, \ldots, \overline{x_n}$ *such that* $Size(C') = \mathcal{O}(Size(C))$, *and that* C' *computes the same function as C.*

Exercise 4.3.11 *Derive the following upper bounds for the size of Boolean circuits over the base of all Boolean functions of two variables: (a)* $\mathcal{O}(n2^n)$; *(b)* $\mathcal{O}(2^n)$ *(hint:* $f(x_1, \ldots, x_n) = (x_1 \wedge f(1, x_2, \ldots, x_n)) \vee (\bar{x_1} \wedge f(0, x_2, \ldots, x_n))$*); (c)** $\mathcal{O}(\frac{2^n}{n})$; *(d)*** $(1 + o(1))\frac{2^n}{n}$.

Boolean circuits can also be seen as another representation of Boolean straight-line programs that do not use arithmetical but logical operations. Size complexity of Boolean circuits is then the same as time complexity of the corresponding Boolean straight-line programs.

Circuit complexity of Boolean functions is an area that has been much investigated with the aim of acquiring a fundamental understanding of the complexity of computation. We now present what is perhaps the most basic result concerning the size complexity of Boolean functions, and in so doing we arrive at what is perhaps the most puzzling problem in foundations of computing.

In the following lemma and theorem we consider for simplicity the base $\mathcal{B}_0 = \{\text{AND}, \text{OR}, \text{NAND}, \text{NOR}\}$, consisting of Boolean functions of two arguments. This simplifies technical details of the proofs, but has no essential effect on the main result. The problem we deal with is the size complexity of Boolean functions of n arguments.

Lemma 4.3.12 *At most* $S(b,n) = \frac{(b+n-1)^{2b}4^b b}{b!}$ *Boolean functions from* $\mathbf{B}_n$ *can be computed by Boolean circuits, over the base* $\mathcal{B}_0$*, of size b.*

Proof: Let us estimate the number of Boolean circuits of size b. For each node there are four Boolean functions to choose from (AND, OR, NAND, NOR) and $b-1+n$ possibilities for the starting node of each of the two ingoing edges of the node ($b-1$ other (Boolean) gates and n input nodes). Each circuit computes at most b different Boolean functions (because there are at most b possibilities for the choice of an output node). Finally, one must take into account that each circuit has been counted $b!$ times, for $b!$ different numberings of nodes. Altogether we get the estimation claimed in the lemma. □

Now let $b = \max\{\text{Size}_{\mathcal{B}_0}(f) \,|\, f \in \mathbf{B}_n\}$. If a Boolean function can be computed by a Boolean circuit of size k, then it can be computed by a circuit of size $k+1$, and therefore, by Lemma 4.3.12, $S(b,n) \geq |\mathbf{B}_n|$, an inequality we shall use to get an estimation for b. In doing this, we use the inequality $b! \geq cb^{b+0.5}e^{-b}$, for some constant c, which follows from Stirling's approximation of $b!$ (see page 29). Therefore,

$$\lg S(b,n) \geq \lg |\mathbf{B}_n| \Rightarrow 2b\lg(b+n-1) + 2b + \lg b - (b+\frac{1}{2})\lg b + b\lg e - \lg c \geq 2^n. \tag{4.7}$$

Since $b \geq n-1$ for sufficiently large n, the inequality 4.7 implies that

$$b\lg b + (4+\lg e)b + \frac{1}{2}\lg b. - \lg c \geq 2^n. \tag{4.8}$$

Let us now assume that $b \leq 2^n n^{-1}$. In this case we get from the above inequality a new one:

$$2^n n^{-1}(n - \lg n + 4 + \lg e) + \frac{1}{2}(n - \lg n) - \lg c \geq 2^n, \tag{4.9}$$

and the last inequality clearly does not hold for large n. Therefore,

$$b \geq 2^n n^{-1}$$

must hold for sufficiently large n.

Note that the inequalities (4.7) and (4.8) hold but (4.9) does not hold for $b \leq 2^n n^{-1}$ if on the right-hand side of all these inequalities 2^n is replaced by $2^n - 2^n n^{-1} \lg\lg n$. This implies that if we take instead of the class $\mathbf{B}_n$ only a subclass, $\mathbf{B}'_n \subset \mathbf{B}_n$, such that $\lg|\mathbf{B}'_n| \geq 2^n - 2^n n^{-1} \lg\lg n$, we again get the inequality $b \geq 2^n n^{-1}$, for $b = \max\{Size_{\mathcal{B}_0}(f) \mid f \in \mathbf{B}'_n\}$. Note too that for such an estimation it does not really matter which functions are in $\mathbf{B}'_n$; only their number is important. We can therefore take as $\mathbf{B}'_n$ those $2^{(2^n - 2^n n^{-1} \lg\lg n)}$ Boolean functions from $\mathbf{B}_n$ that have the smallest Boolean circuit size complexity. By the same considerations as above, we then get that all the remaining Boolean functions in $\mathbf{B}_n$ have a circuit size complexity of at least $2^n n^{-1}$. Therefore $2^{2^n}(1 - 2^{-2^n n^{-1} \lg\lg n})$ Boolean functions must have a circuit size complexity of at least $2^n n^{-1}$. Since $\lim_{n\to\infty} 2^{-2^n n^{-1} \lg\lg n} = 0$, we have the following theorem.

Theorem 4.3.13 (Shannon's effect) *For sufficiently large n, at least* $|\mathbf{B}_n|(1 - 2^{-2^n n^{-1} \lg\lg n})$ *out of* $|\mathbf{B}_n| = 2^{2^n}$ *Boolean functions of n variables have circuit size complexity at least* $2^n n^{-1}$. *(In other words, almost all Boolean functions in* $\mathbf{B}_n$ *have circuit size complexity at least* $2^n n^{-1}$.)

Now we have a puzzling situation. In spite of the fact that almost all Boolean functions of n variables have, for large n, exponential complexity, nobody so far has been able to find a specific family of Boolean functions $\{f_n\}_{n=1}^{\infty}, f_n \in \mathbf{B}_n$, for which we would be able to prove more than the linear asymptotic lower bound for the circuit size complexity for $f(n)$, despite the large effort of the scientific community. This has even led to the suggestion that we start to consider as an axiom that no 'explicit Boolean function' has a nonpolynomial Boolean circuit size complexity. Interestingly, this approach has so far provided results that correspond well to our intuition and can therefore be considered plausible.

An important task is to design Boolean circuits as good as possible for the key computing problems. Size and depth are the most important criteria. For example, the school algorithm for multiplying two n-bit integers can be turned into a Boolean circuit of size $\mathcal{O}(n^2)$. A better solution is due to Schönhage and Strassen: a Boolean circuit of size $\mathcal{O}(n \lg n \lg\lg n)$.

4.3.3 Mutual Simulations of Turing Machines and Families of Circuits*

A single Boolean circuit computes only one Boolean function. In order to be able to compare Turing machines and Boolean circuits as models of computers, we have to consider infinite families of Boolean circuits in $\mathcal{C} = \{C_1, C_2, \ldots\}$, where C_i is a Boolean circuit with i input nodes. We say that such a family of circuits computes a (Boolean) function $f : \{0,1\}^* \to \{0,1\}$ if $f_{C_i} = f_{\mathbf{B}_i}$; that is, the circuit C_i computes the reduction of f to the domain $\mathbf{B}_i = \{0,1\}^i$. For example, we could have a family of circuits $\mathcal{C}^{(m)} = \{C_1^{(m)}, C_2^{(m)}, \ldots\}$ such that $C_{2i^2}^{(m)}$ computes the product of two Boolean matrices of degree i.

For a family $\mathcal{C} = \{C_i\}_{i=1}^{\infty}$ of Boolean circuits, size and depth complexity bounds are defined as follows. Let $t : \mathbf{N} \to \mathbf{N}$ be a function. We say that the size complexity (depth complexity) of $\mathcal{C}$ is bounded by $t(n)$, if for all n

$$Size(C_n) \leq t(n) \qquad (Depth(C_n) \leq t(n)).$$

The concept of a Boolean circuit family, as introduced above, allows us to 'compute' nonrecursive functions. Indeed, let $f : \mathbf{N} \rightarrow \mathbf{B}$ be a nonrecursive function. Then the function $h : \mathbf{B}^* \rightarrow \mathbf{B}$ defined by

$$h(w) = \begin{cases} 0, & \text{if } f(|w|) = 0; \\ 1, & \text{if } f(|w|) = 1, \end{cases}$$

is also nonrecursive, and since $h(w)$ depends only on $|w|$, it is easy to see that h is computable by an infinite family of very simple circuits. In order to exclude such 'computations', only uniformly created families of circuits will be considered.

There are several definitions of uniformity. The following one is guided by the intuition that a circuit constructor should have no more computational power than the objects it constructs. A family of circuits $\mathcal{C} = \{C_i\}_{i=1}^{\infty}$ is called **uniform** if there is an off-line MTM $M_{\mathcal{C}}$ which for any input 1^n constructs in $\mathcal{O}(Size(C_n)\lg(C_n))$ time and $\mathcal{O}(\lg Size(C(n))$ space a description $\overline{C_n}$ of C_n in the form $\overline{C_n} = (\bar{v}_1, \ldots, \bar{v}_k)$, where $\bar{v} = (v, l(v), p(v))$ is a complete description of the node v and its neighbourhood in C_n; $l(v)$ is the variable or the Boolean operator associated with v; and $p(v)$ is the list of predecessors of v. Moreover, it is assumed that nodes are 'topologically sorted' in the sense that if v_i precedes v_j, then $i < j$. For the length $l_{\mathcal{C}}(n)$ of $\overline{C_n}$ we clearly have $l_{\mathcal{C}}(n) = \mathcal{O}(Size(C_n)\lg Size(C_n))$. (Observe that since $Size(C_n) = \mathcal{O}(2^{Depth(C_n)})$, the uniformity requirement actually demands that circuits be constructed in $\mathcal{O}(Depth(C_n))$ space.)

Our requirement of uniformity for a family of Boolean circuits therefore means that all circuits of the family must be constructed 'in the same way', using a single TM and reasonably easily: the time needed for their construction is proportional to the length of the description and the space needed is logarithmic.[12]

In the rest of this section we present several simulations of uniform families of Boolean circuits by Turing machines, and vice versa. In order to compare the computational power of these two computer models, we consider the computation of functions $f : \mathbf{B}^* \rightarrow \mathbf{B}$. In addition, for $s, d : \mathbf{N} \rightarrow \mathbf{N}$ let

- *Size*$(s(n))$ denote the family of Boolean functions $f : \mathbf{B}^* \rightarrow \mathbf{B}$ for which there is a uniform family $\mathcal{C} = \{C_n\}$ of circuits such that C_n computes $f_{\mathbf{B}_n}$ and *Size*$(C_n) \leq s(n)$.

- *Depth*$(d(n))$ denote the family of functions $f : \mathbf{B}^* \rightarrow \mathbf{B}$ for which there is a uniform family $\mathcal{C} = \{C_n\}$ of circuits such that C_n computes $f_{\mathbf{B}_n}$ and *Dept*$(C_n) \leq d(n)$.

Before going into the details of simulations, let me emphasize again that there is a one-to-one correspondence between (Boolean) functions $f : \mathbf{B}^* \rightarrow \mathbf{B}$ and languages over the alphabet $\{0,1\}$. With each such function f a language $L_f = \{w \mid w \in \mathbf{B}^*, f(w) = 1\}$ is associated, and with each language $L \subseteq \{0,1\}^*$ a function $f_L : \mathbf{B}^* \rightarrow \mathbf{B}$ is associated, with $f_L(w) = 1$ if and only if $w \in L$. The notation *Time*$(t(n))$ and *Space*$(s(n))$ used to denote the families of languages (over the alphabet $\{0,1\}$) can also be used to denote families of functions $f : \mathbf{B}^* \rightarrow \mathbf{B}$ accepted by MTM within the given time or space bounds.

We start with a series of lemmas that show polynomial relations between Turing machine and Boolean circuit complexity classes.

Lemma 4.3.14 *If* $s(n) \geq n$, *then* $Size(s(n)) \subseteq Time(s^2(n)\lg s(n))$.

[12]Notice that we assume that off-line Turing machines are used to design circuits. This implies that the space needed to write down the description of the circuit that is being constructed does not count to the overall space complexity (because this description is not stored and only written as the output). Because of this we take only $\mathcal{O}(\lg Size(n))$ bound on the space complexity of $M_{\mathcal{C}}$.

Proof: Let $f \in Size(s(n))$. We describe an MTM $\mathcal{M}_f$ which, given an input w of length n, first generates a circuit C_n that computes the function $f_{\mathbf{B}_n}$, the size of which is bounded by $s(n)$. Then $\mathcal{M}_f$ determines for all nodes v of C_n the value computed by the gate in the node v, when w is processed by C_n.

$\mathcal{M}_f$ starts by constructing, given an input w with $|w| = n$, in time $\mathcal{O}(s(n)\lg s(n))$ a description $\overline{C_n}$ of the circuit that computes $f_{\mathbf{B}_n}$, where in $\overline{C_n} = \{\bar{v}_1, \bar{v}_2, \ldots, \bar{v}_k\}$ the nodes $v_1, v_2, \ldots, v_k$ are topologically ordered. $\mathcal{M}_f$ then computes in succession $v_1^*, v_2^*, \ldots, v_k^*$, where $v_i^* = C_n(v_i, w)$, and $C_n(v_i, w)$ is the value the gate v_i outputs when the input w is processed by C_n. Since each node has at most two predecessors, $\mathcal{M}_f$ needs at most $\mathcal{O}(s(n)\lg s(n))$ time to search through $\overline{C_n}$ to find the values produced by the gates of the predecessors of the node v_i, the value of which is just being computed. Since C_n has at most $s(n)$ nodes, the overall time needed to compute the output value for the input w is $\mathcal{O}(s^2(n)\lg s(n))$.

□

Exercise 4.3.15* *If a more sophisticated divide-and-conquer algorithm is used in the previous proof to evaluate nodes of C_n, then the overall time needed can be reduced to $\mathcal{O}(s(n)\lg^2 s(n))$. Show this.*

Lemma 4.3.16 *If $d(n) \geq \lg n$, then $Depth(d(n)) \subseteq Space(d(n))$.*

Proof: Let $f \in Depth(d(n))$. First we show how to design an $\mathcal{O}(d^2(n))$-space bounded MTM $\mathcal{M}_f$ to recognize L_f.

Since $f \in Depth(d(n))$, there exists an $\mathcal{O}(d(n))$-space bounded off-line MTM $\mathcal{M}'_f$ that constructs, for an input w of length n, a description of a circuit C_n of depth at most $d(n)$, such that C_n computes f restricted to $\mathbf{B}_n$. M_f will often activate M'_f. However, and this is essential, each time $\mathcal{M}'_f$ is used, only a part of the description of C_n is stored: namely, that corresponding to the description of a single node of C_n.

$\mathcal{M}_f$ starts by activating $\mathcal{M}'_f$ and storing only the description of the output node of C_n. $\mathcal{M}_f$ then uses a depth-first search traversal through C_n to compute, gate by gate, the values produced by the gates of C_n for a given input w. Each time a new node of C_n is visited during this depth-first search, $\mathcal{M}'_f$ is activated, and only the description of the node searched for is stored. Since $Size(C_n) = \mathcal{O}(2^{d(n)})$, $\mathcal{O}(d(n))$ space is sufficient to store the description of a single node. In order to perform the whole depth-first search evaluation of the circuit C_n, the descriptions of at most $\mathcal{O}(d(n))$ nodes need to be stored simultaneously. This yields the overall space estimation $\mathcal{O}(d^2(n))$. It can be reduced to $\mathcal{O}(d(n))$ by using the following trick: to store information about which part of the tree has not yet been processed, it is not necessary to store full descriptions of the nodes on a path, but for each node only one or two of the numbers 1 and 2, specifying the successors of the node yet to be processed. This requires $\mathcal{O}(1)$ space per node. This way the overall space requirement can be reduced to $\mathcal{O}(d(n))$.

□

Let us now turn to a more complicated task: depth- and size-efficient simulations of Turing machines by families of Boolean circuits.

In order to formulate these results, new technical terms are needed. They will be used also in the following chapter.

Definition 4.3.17 *A function $f : \mathbf{N} \rightarrow \mathbf{N}$ is $t(n)$-**time-constructible** and $s(n)$-**space-constructible** if the function $f' : \{1\}^* \rightarrow \{0,1\}^*$, defined by $f'(1^n) = bin^{-1}(f(n))$, is computable by a $t(n)$-time* *bounded and $s(n)$-space bounded 2-tape TM. f is called* **time-constructible (space-constructible)** *if f is f-time-constructible (f-space-constructible). f is called* **linearly time- (space-)approximable** *if there is a function f' such that $f(n) \leq f'(n) = \mathcal{O}(f(n))$ and f' is time- (space-)constructible.*[13]

Practically all functions that one encounters during the analysis of computations are both time- and space-constructible.

Exercise 4.3.18* *Show that if functions f and g are time- (space-)constructible, then so are the functions (a) $f+g$; (b) $f\cdot g$; (c) 2^g.*

Exercise 4.3.19** *Show that the following functions are time- (space-)constructible: (a) n^2; (b) 2^n; (c) $n!$; (d) $n\lceil\lg n\rceil$.*

Lemma 4.3.20 *$Space(s(n)) \subseteq Depth(s^2(n))$, if $s(n) \geq \lg n$ and $s(n)$ is $\mathcal{O}(\lg n)$-space-constructible.*

Proof: Let $f \in Space(s(n))$ and $\mathcal{M} = \langle \Gamma, Q, q_0, \delta\rangle$ be an $s(n)$-space bounded one-tape off-line MTM computing f. $\mathcal{M}$ has at most

$$t = n|Q||\Gamma|^{s(n)}s(n) = 2^{\mathcal{O}(s(n))}$$

'partial configurations' for inputs of length n – in which the position of the head on the input tape is also taken into account. Let us assume that exactly one of them, c_t, is the terminating partial configuration, and that c_1 is the initial partial configuration. The behaviour of $\mathcal{M}$ on input w can be described by the transition matrix $A_w = \{a_{ij}\}_{i,j=1}^t$, with

$$a_{ij} = \begin{cases} 1, & \text{if } i=j \text{ or } c_i \vdash_{\mathcal{M}} c_j \text{ for the input } w; \\ 0, & \text{otherwise.} \end{cases}$$

For $k = 1, \ldots, \lceil \lg t\rceil$, we define the matrices $A^{(k)} = \{a_{ij}^k\}_{i,j=1}^t$, $k \geq 1$ by

$$A^{(1)} = A_w \odot A_w \qquad \text{and} \qquad A^{(k)} = A^{(k-1)} \odot A^{(k-1)}, \text{ if } k > 1,$$

where $\odot$ stands for the Boolean product of two matrices. Clearly, $a_{1j}^{(l)} = 1$ if and only if there is, for input w, a sequence of configurations $c_1 \vdash_{\mathcal{M}} c_{i_1} \vdash_{\mathcal{M}} \ldots \vdash_{\mathcal{M}} c_j$ of length at most 2^l, and therefore

$$\mathcal{M} \text{ accepts } w \text{ if and only if } a_{1t}^{(\lceil \lg t\rceil)} = 1.$$

A Boolean product of two matrices of the degree t can be computed by a simple Boolean circuit of size $t^2(2t-1)$ and depth $\lceil \lg 2t\rceil$. In order to compute $A^{(\lceil \lg t\rceil)}$, one only needs to connect sequentially $\lceil \lg t\rceil$ such circuits. The resulting circuit has depth $\mathcal{O}(\lg(2t)\lg t) = \mathcal{O}(s^2(n))$.

It is easy to compute elements of matrix $A^{(i)}$, and since $s(n)$ is $\lg n$-space-constructible, it is possible to determine t and the resulting circuit using only $\mathcal{O}(\lg n)$ space. Hence the lemma. □

[13]The concept of time- and space-constructible functions is often used in the following slightly different sense; f is time-constructible if there is a TM $\mathcal{M}$ computing f and such that $\mathcal{M}$ halts after exactly $f(n)$ steps for input 1^n. s is space-constructible if there is an $s(n)$ space bounded TM that writes $1^{s(n)}$ for an input 1^n (i.e. $\mathcal{M}$ marks exactly $s(n)$ cells of the tape).

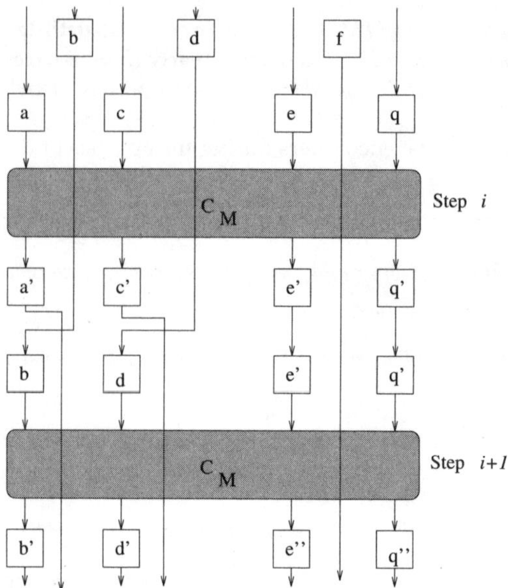

Figure 4.27 A Boolean circuit simulating an oblivious MTM

An efficient simulation of a $t(n)$-time bounded MTM $\mathcal{M}$ by a circuit family is more difficult. The source of the difficulty lies in the fact that $\mathcal{M}$ may behave differently for different inputs of the same length. In order to show that a size-efficient simulation of a Turing machine by a uniform circuit family exists, it behoves us to use a technical result (see references), showing that each MTM can be simulated efficiently by the oblivious MTM.

Definition 4.3.21 *An MTM $\mathcal{M}$ is called* **oblivious** *if the sequence of moves of the heads of $\mathcal{M}$ is the same for all inputs of the same length.*

Theorem 4.3.22 *Let $t(n)$ be $\mathcal{O}(t(n))$-time-constructible and $s(n)$ be $\mathcal{O}(s(n))$-space-constructible. Then each $t(n)$-time and $s(n)$-space bounded MTM can be simulated by an $\mathcal{O}(t(n)\lg s(n))$-time bounded and $\mathcal{O}(s(n))$-space bounded oblivious MTM.*

Equipped with the result of Theorem 4.3.22, we can handle the problem of simulation of time bounded Turing machines by uniform families of Boolean circuits.

Lemma 4.3.23 *If $t(n)$ is $\mathcal{O}(t(n))$-time- and space-constructible, then*

$$Time(t(n)) \subseteq Size(\mathcal{O}(t(n)\lg t(n)).$$

Proof: If a Boolean function $f : \mathbf{B}^* \rightarrow \mathbf{B}$ is in *Time*($t(n)$), then, by Theorem 4.3.22, there is an $\mathcal{O}(t(n)\lg t(n))$-time bounded oblivious MTM $\mathcal{M}'$ computing f.

We can encode states of $\mathcal{M}'$, and also its tape symbols, by binary words of a fixed, equal length. Then we can design a circuit of a fixed size $C_{\mathcal{M}'}$ which implements that part of the transition function of $\mathcal{M}'$ which transfers a state and the symbols read by heads to a new state and new symbols on the tape. Since $\mathcal{M}'$ is oblivious, we can now design, given a fixed n, using $t(n)\lg t(n)$ copies of the circuit

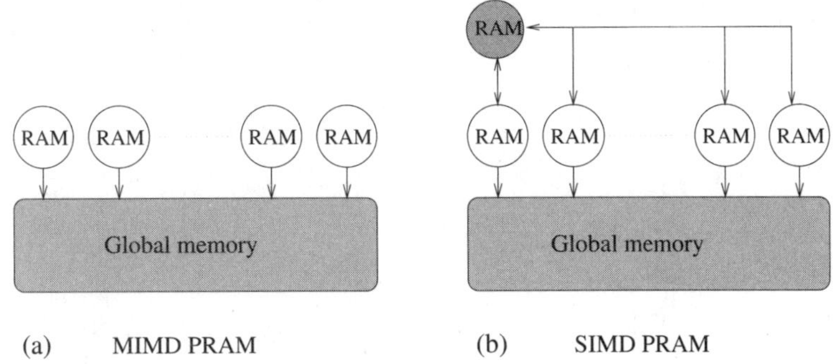

(a) MIMD PRAM (b) SIMD PRAM

Figure 4.28 MIMD and SIMD PRAM

$C_{\mathcal{M}'}$, a Boolean circuit of size $\mathcal{O}(t(n)\lg t(n))$ that computes $f_{\mathbf{B}_n}$ (see Figure 4.27). For each copy of $C'_{\mathcal{M}}$, its inputs are either the overall inputs or are connected with the outputs of some of the previous copies of $C_{\mathcal{M}'}$. The same holds for outputs. They either enter inputs of some other copies of $C_{\mathcal{M}}$ or provide total outputs. To simulate the ith step of $\mathcal{M}'$, the inputs of $C_{\mathcal{M}'}$ are connected with the last outputs of gates representing the cells the heads of $\mathcal{M}'$ are on at the end of the $(i-1)$-th step. □

As a corollary of the above series of lemmas, we get the following main result concerning the mutual simulation of Turing machines and uniform families of circuits.

Theorem 4.3.24 *The following mutual simulations of Turing machines and Boolean circuits are possible for all 'nice' bounds $t(n)$ and $s(n)$.*

$$\begin{array}{rclrcl} \mathit{Size}(s(n)) & \subseteq & \mathit{Time}(s^2(n)\lg s(n)), & \mathit{Depth}(s(n)) & \subseteq & \mathit{Space}(s(n)), \\ \mathit{Time}(t(n)) & \subseteq & \mathit{Size}(t(n)\lg t(n)), & \mathit{Space}(s(n)) & \subseteq & \mathit{Depth}(s^2(n)). \end{array}$$

Notice that for the uniform families of Boolean circuits, as a computer model, the parallel time is polynomially related to the space on Turing machines.

4.4 PRAM – Parallel RAM

Several random access machines sharing a common (shared or global) memory, **PRAM**, are from the parallel algorithm design and analysis point of view perhaps the most attractive model of parallel computing. The number of RAM processors used to solve an algorithmic problem depends usually on the size of the input.

There are several variants of PRAM. Two extremes are MIMD PRAM and SIMD PRAM. In a MIMD (multiple instruction multiple data) PRAM (see Figure 4.28a), each RAM processor may perform a different program. In a SIMD (single instruction multiple data) PRAM (see Figure 4.28b), all RAM perform the same program, and they can be seen as being controlled by a 'super-RAM'. We shall use a third, 'intermediate model' described in the sequel.

There are several reasons why such models of parallel computing are important in spite of the fact that their direct implementation can hardly be efficient with current technology.

1. PRAM programming allows us to abstract much from those levels of parallel program design that deal with concurrency, synchronization, memory organization and contention, network

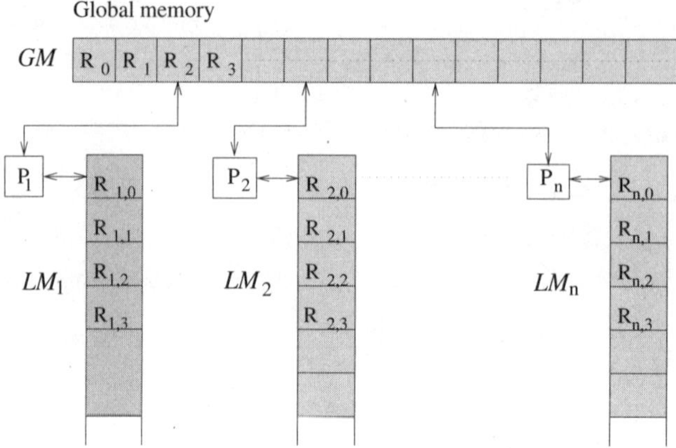

Figure 4.29 Shared (global) memory and local memories of a PRAM

topology and routing. In designing PRAM algorithms, one does not have to be concerned with how communication is accomplished, but only with what is to be communicated and where.

2. Parallel program design techniques developed for PRAM turn out to be of importance also for other models of parallel computing.

3. Theoretical results indicate that an efficient simulation of PRAM, or closely related models, on (bounded-degree) multiprocessor networks is feasible (see Section 10.5.2).

In order to be able to develop PRAM programs in a clear way and to formulate precisely complexity results, we use the following formal model of PRAM.

4.4.1 Basic Model

A PRAM consists of an infinite sequence of processors $P_1, P_2, \ldots$ (Figure 4.29). The index i of P_i serves as the **processor identifier**, and is denoted by PID. All processors are RAM enriched by the instruction LOAD PID that loads the contents of the PID register into the accumulator. A processor P_i has its local (potentially infinite) memory LM_i, consisting of a sequence of registers $R_{i,0}, R_{i,1}, R_{i,2}, \ldots,$ and P_i is the only processor with access to these registers. In addition, there is a global memory GM, consisting of a (potentially infinite) sequence of registers $R_0, R_1, R_2, \ldots$. Each of the registers of the global and also the local memories can contain an arbitrary integer. Instead of R_i we write $GM[i]$ or GM_i.

A processor P_i accesses the shared memory through the instructions READ and WRITE. The instruction 'READ j', performed by P_i, causes the transfer $R_{i,0} \leftarrow GM_j$, and the instruction 'WRITE j' causes the transfer $GM_j \leftarrow R_{i,0}$. All other instructions that P_i performs concern its local memory. Concerning inputs and outputs, the following convention will be used: in the case of n inputs $x_1, x_2, \ldots, x_n$, n is in GM_0 and x_i in GM_i, $1 \le i \le n$; in the case of m outputs $y_1, \ldots, y_m$, m is in GM_0 and y_i in GM_i, for $1 \le i \le m$. (Other input–output conventions are, naturally, possible.) In the case of language recognition, the state of P_1 – REJECT or ACCEPT – is decisive.

All processors of a PRAM perform the same program and are synchronized, and each of them performs one instruction per time step. A **computation** starts with all processors performing the first instruction of the program, and ends when the processor P_1 stops. The contents of the shared memory registers at that point are the output of the computation.

The fact that all processors perform the same program does not mean that at any moment all of them perform the same instruction with the same data. This is due to the fact that each processor can use the contents of its own PID as data. This can influence the outcomes of conditional jumps, and therefore different processors may eventually perform at the same time different instructions of the program. For example, it can happen that a processor P_i can read a register GM_j only if $j < n_0$, for some fixed n_0. As a consequence, in most naturally designed programs, at any moment only finitely many processors can perform some meaningful computation (that is, computations having an impact on outputs). In the examples we consider only such programs.

A PRAM with a potentially infinite number of processors and shared memory cells is an appropriate model for investigating the most basic question concerning the efficiency of parallel computing. Of theoretical and also practical importance is a model of PRAM with a fixed number of processors and shared memory registers. In such a case a larger input is usually assumed to be proportionally distributed through all the processors. Limitations on the amount of shared memory correspond to restricting the amount of information that can be communicated between processors.

4.4.2 Memory Conflicts

The main problems with PRAM, theoretically and practically, are conflicts, read and especially write conflicts, when more than one processor tries, concurrently, to read from the same register or to write to the same register.

Concurrent readings of a shared memory register cause no theoretical and negligible practical difficulty. In a PRAM reading, computation and writing are considered as being separated. One concurrent step of PRAM is considered to consist of a reading phase (where all readings are performed), a computational phase and, finally, a writing phase. However, concurrent writing does create conflicts and causes major problems. Several methods are used to deal with write conflicts, and according to these methods, several variants of PRAM are considered. The three most basic models are

EREW PRAM (**e**xclusive **r**ead, **e**xclusive **w**rite)

– neither concurrent reads nor concurrent writes are allowed.

CREW PRAM (**c**oncurrent **r**ead, **e**xclusive **w**rite)

– concurrent reads are allowed, but not concurrent writes.

CRCW PRAM (**c**oncurrent **r**ead, **c**oncurrent **w**rite)

– both concurrent reads and concurrent writes are allowed, but a fixed strategy is chosen to deal with concurrent writes. Such a strategy specifies what the contents of the register are after a concurrent write to the register has been executed. Different writing strategies lead to different CRCW PRAM models. Three of the most commonly investigated models of CRCW PRAM are the following ones.

CRCW^{com} **PRAM** (common PRAM)

– concurrent writes are allowed if and only if all processors that try to write to the same register try to write the same data. If this is not the case, the computation is aborted, and its results are considered as undefined.

CRCW^{arb} PRAM (arbitrary PRAM)

– if several processors try to write to the same register, then one of them is arbitrarily chosen to write.

CRCW^{pri} PRAM (priority PRAM)

– from those processors trying to write to the same register, the one with the smallest (largest) index succeeds.

Other models of CRCW PRAM are discussed in the exercises.

4.4.3 PRAM Programming

In order to describe PRAM programs in a transparent way, the following abstractions will be used.

1. Programs will be described using high-level programming language constructs that can be translated in a straightforward way into RAM instructions.
2. Direct data transports between registers of the shared memory, or between the shared and a local memory will be used. Going to the basic RAM level, these transports have to be realized through transfers via accumulators. For example, a transfer $A \leftarrow B$ in the global memory is realized through the instruction 'READ B, WRITE A'.
3. To deal with the global memory, we use freely various higher level data structures: for example, arrays $A[1:n], B[1:n]$. They may be implemented, for example, as segments $GM[1:n], GM[n+1:2n]$ of the shared memory.
4. Various indexings of processors will be used that conform to the structure of the underlying algorithm. For example, processors $P_{ij}, 1 \leq i,j \leq n$ can be considered. This stands for using processors $P_k, 1 \leq k \leq n^2$ and considering decomposition of each k as $k = (i-1)n + j, 1 \leq i,j \leq n$. To get i and j from k, a fixed-length sequence of RAM instructions can be used.

Our first example shows an extraordinary power of concurrent writing.

Example 4.4.1 (Maximum finding on a CRCW^{com} PRAM)

Input: integer n stored in GM_0; integers $x_1, \ldots, x_n$ stored in $GM[1:n]$.
Output: $\max\{x_1, \ldots, x_n\}$ stored in GM_0.
Processors: $P_{ij}, 1 \leq i,j \leq n$.
Auxiliary array: $Y[1:n]$.

Algorithm 4.4.2 *For the processor P_{ij},*

$Y[i] \leftarrow 0$;
if $GM[i] < GM[j]$ **then** $Y[i] \leftarrow 1$; $\{Y[i] = 0$ if and only if $GM[i] = \max\{GM[1], \ldots, GM[n]\}\}$
if $Y[i] = 0$, **then** $GM[0] \leftarrow GM[i]$.

If the statement '$Y[i] \leftarrow 0$' is replaced by '**if** $j = 1$ **then** $Y[i] \leftarrow 0$', then the concurrent write in the first statement can be avoided. By inserting the statement '**if** $i < j \wedge Y[i] = 0$, **then** $Y[j] \leftarrow 1$' between the second and third statements, we can achieve a situation such that after this added statement, $Y[i] = 0$ if and only if i is the smallest index such that $GM[i] = \max\{GM[i], \ldots, GM[n]\}$. Finally, by replacing the last statement with the statement '**if** $j = 1 \wedge Y[i] = 0$ **then** $GM[0] \leftarrow GM[i]$', we can also avoid concurrent writing in the last statement. Note that in all concurrent writings all processors

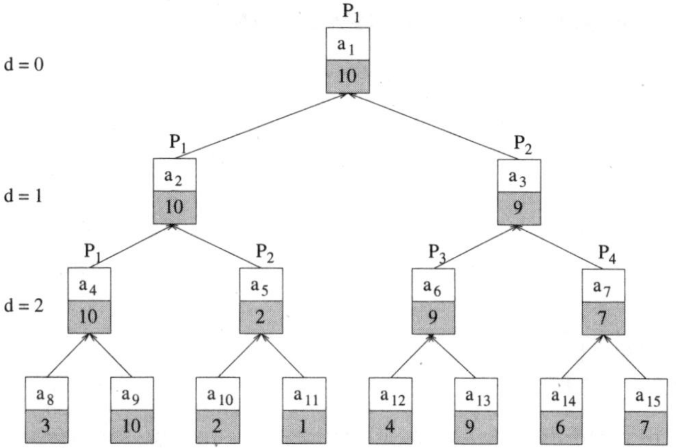

Figure 4.30 Maximum finding on a EREW PRAM

try to write the same value. The same program would therefore work correctly on models CRCW^{arb} PRAM and CRCW^{pri} PRAM.

In our second example we use another method, more global at first sight, to describe PRAM programs. Those parts of the program that can be executed with different data on different processors will be described by the concurrent constructs

$$\textbf{par}[a \leq i \leq b]P_i : S_i \qquad \text{or} \qquad \textbf{par}[a \leq i \leq b] : S_i,$$

with the semantics that the statement S_i is executed (by the processor P_i), concurrently, for all i between a and b. In addition, from now on we use freely in the descriptions of PRAM programs various arrays or sequences without referring formally to the PRAM shared memory.

Example 4.4.3 (Maximum finding on an EREW PRAM)

> **Input**: $d, n = 2^d$, numbers $a_n, \ldots, a_{2n-1}$.
> **Output**: $a_1 = \max\{a_n, \ldots, a_{2n-1}\}$.

Algorithm 4.4.4 *For a EREW PRAM,*

> **for** $d \leftarrow d-1$ **downto** 0 **do**
> **par**$[2^d \leq j \leq 2^{d+1}-1] : a_j \leftarrow \max\{a_{2j}, a_{2j+1}\}$.

The computation process described by Algorithm 4.4.4 is depicted in Figure 4.30 for $n = 8$. Note that no indication is given in the program as to which processors perform statements $a_j \leftarrow \max\{a_{2j}, a_{2j+1}\}$. At least two implementations are natural. In the first, the processor P_j performs such a statement, in which case we need n processors. In the second, only processors $P_1, \ldots, P_{n/2}$ are needed (see Figure 4.30). However, in this case it takes more time for each processor to compute the addresses of the data the processors should work with.

Exercise 4.4.5 *Design an EREW PRAM program to add n numbers in $\mathcal{O}(\lg n)$ time.*

Example 4.4.6 (Matrix multiplication on an EREW PRAM)

Input: an integer d, matrices $A[i,j]$, $B[i,j]$, $1 \le i,j \le n = 2^d$.
Output: matrix $C[i,j]$, $1 \le i,j \le n$, $C = A \cdot B$.
Processors: P_{ijl}, $1 \le i,j,l \le n$.
Auxiliary array: $D[i,j,l]$, $1 \le i,j,l \le n$.

Algorithm 4.4.7 *For processor* P_{ijl},

$D[i,j,l] \leftarrow A[i,l]B[l,j]$;
for $k \leftarrow 1$ **to** d **do**
  if $l \le \frac{n}{2^k}$ **then** $D[i,j,l] \leftarrow D[i,j,2l-1] + D[i,j,2l]$;
if $l = 1$ **then** $C[i,j] \leftarrow D[i,j,1]$.

The first statement performs, in parallel, all multiplications, and the next **for** cycle all additions. The last statement forms the output. In the case of CRCW^{com} PRAM, the last statement could be simplified to $C[i,j] \leftarrow D[i,j,1]$.

Example 4.4.8 (Boolean matrix multiplication on CRCW^{com} PRAM$^+$) *Two Boolean matrices* $A[i,j]_{ij=1}^n$, $B[i,j]_{i,j=1}^n$ *can be multiplied to get* $C = A.B$ *on a CRCW^{com} PRAM$^+$ using* n^3 *processors* $\{P_{ijk}\}_{i,j,k=1}^n$ *in* $\mathcal{O}(1)$ *steps. In the first step all* c_{ij} *can be initiated to* 0. *Then the processor* P_{ijk} *reads* a_{ik} *and* b_{kj} *and writes* 1 *in* c_{ij} *if and only if* $a_{ik} \wedge b_{kj} = 1$.

4.4.4 Efficiency of Parallelization

Intuitively, it seems to be clear that parallelization of computing, that is, the use of parallel computers, is the way to go in order to increase the performance of computers. However, theoretical considerations show and practical experience demonstrates that to harness the power of parallelism is not at all easy.

In this section we take a closer look at the problems of efficiency of parallelization, first for PRAM models, then on a more general level.

PRAM complexity measures

Three computational resources are of importance for PRAM computing: **parallel time** consumed, **number of processors** employed, and the overall **work** done by the processors. For a PRAM $\mathcal{R}$ and an input x they are defined as follows:

- $Time_{\mathcal{R}}(x)$ = the number of concurrent steps of $\mathcal{R}$ until $\mathcal{R}$ stops.
- $\mathrm{Proc}_{\mathcal{R}}(x) = \max\{i \mid i = 1$ or P_i performs a WRITE statement before $\mathcal{R}$ stops$\}$.
- $\mathrm{Work}_{\mathcal{R}}(x) = \mathrm{Proc}_{\mathcal{R}}(x) \times Time_{\mathcal{R}}(x)$.

The definition of processor complexity requires some explanations. Our intuition says that we should count only those processors whose work really influences the outputs. The above definition tries to capture this intuition in a simple way. The definition is clearly not perfect because it may happen that a processor makes computations having impact on outputs but its predecessor does not. In spite of that, this definition has turned out to be good enough to deal with not too degenerate cases.

Work complexity is also a very natural and useful measure of efficiency of PRAM programs. It can be used to set up the benchmarks one should aim for when designing PRAM programs. We say that a PRAM $\mathcal{R}$ is **optimal** for an algorithmic problem $\mathcal{P}$ if $\text{Work}_{\mathcal{R}}(n) = \Theta(t(n))$, where $t(n)$ is the asymptotically best known sequential time complexity of $\mathcal{P}$ on RAM.

The ultimate goal in designing PRAM programs is to achieve work optimality. However, this is not the end of the optimization effort. As soon as work optimality is achieved, the next aim is to keep this optimality but minimize time; the philosophy/belief behind this being that, ultimately, processors will be cheaper than time.

Trade-offs between time and number of processors are an important issue in parallel computing in general, and in PRAM computing in particular. For example, with a single RAM one needs $\Omega(n \lg n)$ time to sort n numbers, whereas with $\mathcal{O}(n^2)$ processors, sorting can be done in $\mathcal{O}(\lg n)$ time. Whereas for a RAM an algorithm is considered to be really fast if its time complexity is almost linear, $\mathcal{O}(n \lg n)$ or less, a PRAM algorithm is considered really fast if its time complexity is $\mathcal{O}(\lg n)$ or less (for example, $\mathcal{O}(\lg \lg n)$, or $\mathcal{O}(\lg^* n), \ldots$).

Example 4.4.9 *Let us analyse the computational complexity of our first three PRAM algorithms. Algorithm 4.4.2 has time complexity $\mathcal{O}(1)$ and uses $\mathcal{O}(n^2)$ processors. Its work complexity is $\mathcal{O}(n^2)$, much more than $\Theta(n)$ for the best possible sequential algorithm. Algorithm 4.4.4 needs $\Theta(\lg n)$ time and $\Theta(n)$ processors. Therefore its work complexity $\Theta(n \lg n)$ is still more than the optimal one. The matrix multiplication algorithm needs $\Theta(\lg n)$ time and $\Theta(n^3)$ processors. The product is larger than optimality suggests by a factor of at least $\Omega(n^{0.5} \lg n)$.*

Remark 4.4.10 It is important to realize why a practically unrealistic assumption, namely, that of having the quantity of processors available grow with the size of the input, does not make PRAM computation theory either wrong or irrelevant. It means only that the application of theory is indirect. It is fruitful to view the processor requirement for PRAM, or some other model of parallel computation, as a growing function of the size of the problem. This is not because the machines are (or are expected to be) so flexible, but because such a requirement allows us to focus on important intrinsic issues like parallel decomposition of the problem, and translate insights obtained into answers to various pragmatic questions like 'how big problems can be solved using a certain amount of time and a certain number of processors'. Similar arguments apply to storage as a resource.

Parallelization

One of the basic general questions concerning the advantages that parallelism can bring is the following: Given an algorithmic problem $\mathcal{A}$ and an integer k, how much can we speed up the solution of $\mathcal{A}$ using k processors?

Two measures are used to express how much parallelization helps:

$$\textit{Speed up}(\mathcal{A}) : p \rightarrow \frac{T_1(\mathcal{A})}{T_p(\mathcal{A})} \quad \text{and} \quad \text{Efficiency}(\mathcal{A}) : p \rightarrow \frac{\textit{Speedup}(\mathcal{A})}{p},$$

where $T_i(\mathcal{A})$ is the best time known for solving $\mathcal{A}$ using i processors.

Unfortunately, there are algorithmic problems $\mathcal{A}$ such that $T_1(\mathcal{A}) = T_p(\mathcal{A})$ for any p, and therefore $\text{Efficiency}(\mathcal{A})(p) = \frac{1}{p}$. In other words, parallelization does not help a bit. Exponentiation x^n is one such problem. No parallel algorithm can do asymptotically better than the sequential one presented on page 7 with respect to the number of arithmetical operations.

The goal of parallel computation is to develop algorithms that use only a reasonable quantity of processors and are very fast. The goal is fundamentally limited by the **speed-up inequality**:

$$\text{(best known sequential time)}/\text{(number of processors)} \leq \text{parallel time.}$$

This inequality implies that in order to achieve a subpolynomial time parallel algorithm, a superpolynomial number of processors must be used.

There is a simple principle that can sometimes be used to improve the performance of an almost optimal parallel algorithm by a logarithmic factor and get a fully optimal one.

Brent's scheduling principle If a parallel computation can be performed on $n = \max\{x_i \mid 1 \leq i \leq t\}$ processors in time t, where x_i is the number of operations in the ith parallel step, then on $p < n$ processors the same computation can be performed in time $t + \lceil \frac{x}{p} \rceil$, where $x = \sum_{i=1}^{t} x_i$.

Exercise 4.4.11 *Show the correctness of Brent's scheduling principle in detail.*

By taking $x = \mathcal{O}(n), t = \mathcal{O}(\lg n)$, and $p = \mathcal{O}(\frac{n}{\lg n})$, we get the following corollary from Brent's scheduling principle.

Lemma 4.4.12 *If a computation that needs sequential time $\mathcal{O}(n)$ can be performed on $\mathcal{O}(n)$ processors in $\mathcal{O}(\lg n)$ time, then the same computation can be performed on $\mathcal{O}(\frac{n}{\lg n})$ processors in time $\mathcal{O}(\lg n)$. (Such a computation is optimal because $\mathcal{O}(\lg n)\mathcal{O}(\frac{n}{\lg n}) = \mathcal{O}(n)$.)*

If Brent's scheduling principle and its corollary are applied to Algorithm 4.4.4, we get a work-optimal algorithm.

Remark 4.4.13 No general and really good method for parallelization of sequential algorithms is likely to exist. The best parallel algorithms are often designed on the basis of strikingly different ideas from those underlying the best sequential algorithms for the same problem.

4.4.5 PRAM Programming – Continuation

We present several other PRAM algorithms to demonstrate the power of PRAM and some parallel algorithm design methodologies.

Example 4.4.14 (Prefix sum) *Given a sequence of numbers $x_1, \ldots, x_n$, compute the sequence $y_1, \ldots, y_n$ of all its prefix sums; that is,*

$$y_j = \sum_{i=1}^{j} x_i.$$

This problem seems to be inherently sequential. Indeed, it seems that in order to compute y_i, one first needs to compute y_{i-1}. However, the problem has an $\mathcal{O}(\lg n)$ parallel solution.

The prefix sum problem is so important for parallel computing that algorithms for solving it were wired into some parallel computers. Its importance is due to the fact that fast parallel algorithms for many problems use a fast prefix sum algorithm as their key subalgorithm.

In order to make our first prefix sum algorithm transparent, we assume that inputs $x_1, \ldots, x_n$ are represented by $a_n, \ldots, a_{2n-1}$; we then need to compute $y_1, \ldots, y_n$, represented by $b_n, \ldots, b_{2n-1}$.

Input: $n \in N, n = 2^d, x_1, \ldots, x_n \in \mathbf{R}$.
Output: $y_1, \ldots, y_n$, with $y_j = \sum_{i=1}^{j} x_i$.

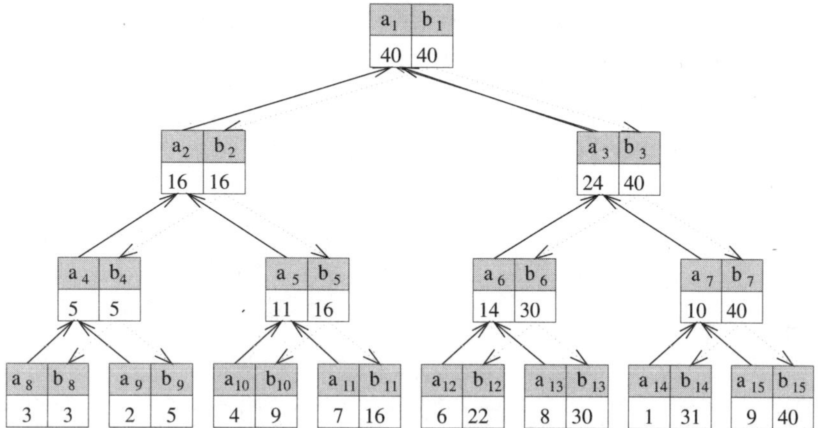

Figure 4.31 A prefix sum algorithm

Algorithm 4.4.15 (Prefix sum for EREW PRAM)

for $l \leftarrow d-1$ **downto** 0 **do** **par**$[2^l \leq j < 2^{l+1}]: a_j \leftarrow a_{2j} + a_{2j+1}$;
$b_1 \leftarrow a_1$;
for $l \leftarrow 1$ **to** $d-1$ **do**
    par$[2^l \leq j < 2^{l+1}]: b_j \leftarrow$ **if** j *is odd* **then** $b_{(j-1)/2}$ **else** $b_{j/2} - a_{j+1}$

The computation of the algorithm is depicted, for $n = 8$, in Figure 4.31. In the first phase, the leaves-to-root phase, described by the first **for** statement, all $a_i, 1 \leq i \leq n-1$, are computed. Each a_i is the sum of all a's in the leaves of the subtree with a_i in the root. In the second phase, the root-to-leaves phase, described by the second **for** statement, b's are computed, each b_i being the sum of all a's from a_1 to the right-most one in the subtree with b_i in the root. (That is why all b's along any right-most path of a subtree have the same value.) To compute new b's, each parent sends its b value to its children. The right child keeps this value, but the left child subtracts from it the current a value of its sibling.

Exercise 4.4.16 *Observe that the memory accesses are data-independent in both the above PRAM algorithms for the prefix sum. Show that these algorithms and their generalizations with any associative operation $\odot$ instead of $+$ can be represented by a circuit of depth $\mathcal{O}(\lg n)$, size $\mathcal{O}(n)$ and $\odot$-gates.*

Exercise 4.4.17 *Using the prefix sum algorithm, design an $\mathcal{O}(\lg n)$ EREW PRAM algorithm for the following variant of the knapsack problem: Given n objects $o_1, \ldots, o_n$, their weights $w_1, \ldots, w_n$, their values $v_1, \ldots, v_n$ and an integer k, find a vector $(x_1, \ldots, x_n), 0 \leq x_i \leq 1$ such that $\sum_{i=1}^{n} x_i v_i$ is maximized and $\sum_{i=1}^{n} x_i w_i \leq k$.*

Example 4.4.18 (List ranking problem) *Given a linked list of n elements $a_1, \ldots, a_n$, compute $b_1, \ldots, b_n$, where $b_i = \sum_{j=i}^{n} a_j$. (The requirement that $a_1, \ldots, a_n$ form a list means that access to a_{i+1} is only through a pointer from a_i – see Figure 4.32a.)*

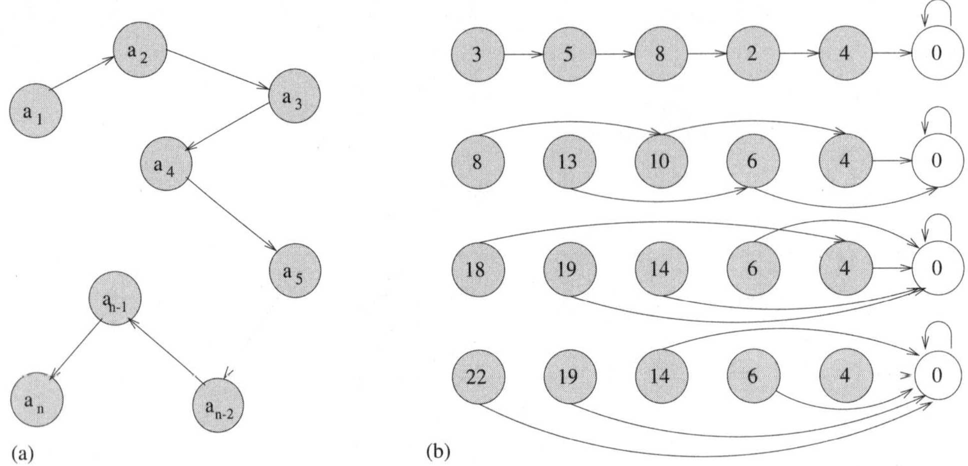

Figure 4.32 List ranking algorithm execution

Assume that the linked list is specified by the two arrays

$$\textit{contents array}:\ C[1:n] \qquad \textit{and} \qquad \textit{successor array}:\ S[1:n],$$

where $S[i]$ *is a pointer to the successor of* $a[i]$. *(That is, if* $C[i] = a_j$, *then* $C[S[i]] = a_{j+1}$.*) In the following algorithm we assume that the last element is in* $C[n]$ *and* $C[n] = 0$, $S[n] = n$.

Program 4.4.19 (Link ranking algorithm for an EREW PRAM)

do $\lceil \lg n \rceil$ times
  par$[1 \le i \le n]$: **begin** $C[i] \leftarrow C[i] + C[S[i]]; S[i] \leftarrow S[S[i]]$ **end**
par$[1 \le i \le n]$: WRITE $C[i]$

This simple program is based on the **pointer jumping method**, and its execution is illustrated, for $n = 6$, in Figure 4.32b.

The execution time is $\Theta(\lg n)$ and $\Theta(n)$ processors are needed. A work-optimal algorithm can be obtained using a more sophisticated technique.

Example 4.4.20 (Maximum finding on doubly logarithmic depth trees) *Our first CRCW PRAM algorithm for the maximum finding has work complexity* $\Theta(n^2)$, *the second algorithm, for EREW PRAM, work complexity* $\Theta(n \lg n)$. *Is there a better solution? Yes, there is. Consider a doubly logarithmic tree of processors with* $n = 2^{2^k}$ *leaves, where each internal node processor performs the constant time algorithm to find a maximum. The inductive definition of the doubly logarithmic depth trees* t_i *is given in Figure 4.33a (see also Section 2.5.3). The case* $i = 2$ *is depicted in Figure 4.33b. By induction we can show that the depth of* t_k *is* $\lg \lg n + 1$, *the ith level of* t_k *has* $2^{2^k - 2^{k-i}}$ *nodes, and each of them has* $2^{2^{k-i-1}}$ *children. The total number of operations needed to be performed on the i-th level is*

$$\underbrace{\Theta((2^{2^{k-i-1}})^2)}_{\textit{no. of operations}} \times \underbrace{\Theta(2^{2^k - 2^{k-i}})}_{\textit{no. of processors}} = \Theta(2^{2^k}) = \Theta(n).$$

The overall work complexity is therefore $\Theta(n \lg \lg n)$.

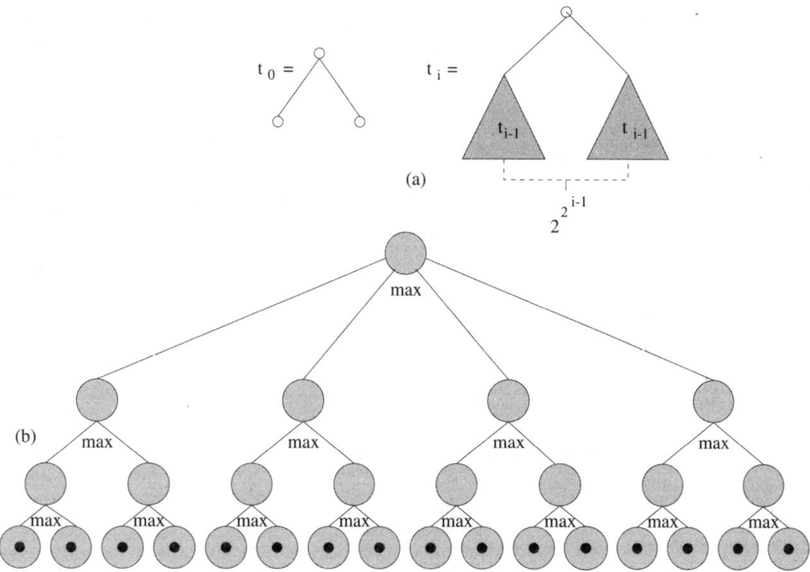

Figure 4.33 Maximum finding on a doubly logarithmic depth tree

The examples shown above, and the way they have been presented illustrate the main advantage of the PRAM model: the possibility of developing the basic ideas of the program on a 'machine-independent level' and not too much need to consider communication and synchronization problems.

Exercise 4.4.21 *Design an EREW PRAM program to sort n distinct numbers on* $\mathcal{O}(\lg n)$ *time.*

Exercise 4.4.22 (Shortest path in a graph) *Design an* $\mathcal{O}(\lg^2 n)$ *algorithm to determine the shortest path between any two nodes of an n-node complete graph whose edges are labelled by integers representing their length.*

4.4.6 Parallel Computation Thesis

Basic concepts concerning (feasible) parallel computing are very robust, and so are its main complexity classes. In addition, these classes are closely related to the complexity classes of sequential computing.

We start with a general concept of a PRAM complexity class. If Φ is a class of PRAM, and $t, p : \mathbf{N} \rightarrow \mathbf{N}$ are functions (complexity bounds), then

$$\Phi\text{-}TimeProc(t(n), p(n))$$

is the family of languages accepted by a $t(n)$-time bounded and $p(n)$-processor bounded PRAM of the family Φ. Of special importance is the class

$$PRAM\text{-}Time(t(n)) = CRCW^{+}\text{-}TimeProc(t(n), 2^{t(n)})),$$

where CRCW^{+} stands for PRAM CRCW^{pri}, all RAM of which are RAM^{+} – that is, without multiplication and division. The main advantage of CRCW^{+} is that for inputs of size $\mathcal{O}(1)$, for example, for language recognition problems, the maximal length of a register after $t(n)$ computational steps is $\mathcal{O}(t(n))$. This allows us to compare CRCW^{+} complexity classes with those of Turing machine computations.

A relation between time complexity and processor complexity of PRAM is presented in the following lemma. This lemma also shows the 'price of sequentialization'. In it Φ stands for any of the PRAM models considered so far.

Lemma 4.4.23 *Let $t,p,k : \mathbf{N} \to \mathbf{N}$, and let $k(n)$ be computable by a RAM^{+} in time $t(n)$. Then*

$$\Phi\text{-}TimeProc(t(n), p(n)) \subseteq \Phi\text{-}\ TimeProc(\mathcal{O}(k(n)t(n)), \left\lceil \frac{p(n)}{k(n)} \right\rceil).$$

Proof: Given a PRAM $\mathcal{R} \in \Phi$ of processor complexity $p(n)$, we show how to construct another PRAM $\mathcal{R}' \in \Phi$ that uses only $\lceil \frac{p(n)}{k(n)} \rceil$ processors and simulates $\mathcal{R}$ in $\mathcal{O}(k(n)t(n))$ time. For an input of length n, $\mathcal{R}'$ first computes $k(n)$, and then simulates $\mathcal{R}$ in such a way that each processor P'_i of $\mathcal{R}'$ simulates the processors $P_{(i-1)k(n)+1}, \ldots, P_{ik(n)}$ of $\mathcal{R}$. Each concurrent step of $\mathcal{R}$ is therefore simulated by $\mathcal{O}(k(n))$ steps of $\mathcal{R}'$. To do this, the local memory of P'_i is so structured that it simulates local memories of all simulated processors.

Care has to be taken that a concurrent step of $\mathcal{R}$ is simulated properly, in the sense that it does not happen that a value is overwritten before needed by some other processor in the same parallel step. Another problem concerns priority handling by CRCW^{pri} PRAM. All this can easily be taken care of if each register R of $\mathcal{R}$ is simulated by three registers of $\mathcal{R}'$: one with the old contents of R, one with new contents, and one that keeps the smallest PID of those processors of $\mathcal{R}$ that try to write into R. To read from a register, the old contents are used. To write into a register, in the case of the CRCW^{pri} PRAM model, the priority stored in one of the three corresponding registers has to be checked. This way, $\mathcal{R}'$ needs $\mathcal{O}(k(n))$ steps to simulate one step of $\mathcal{R}$. □

As a consequence we have

Theorem 4.4.24 $\bigcup_{k=1}^{\infty} CRCW^{+}\text{-}TimeProc(n^k, n^k) = \mathbf{P}$ *(polynomial time).*

Proof: For $k(n) = p(n) = t(n) = n^k$ we get from the previous lemma

$$\begin{aligned} CRCW^{+}\text{-}TimeProc(n^k, n^k) &\subseteq CRCW^{+}\text{-}TimeProc(\mathcal{O}(n^{2k}), 1) \\ &= RAM^{+}\text{-}Time(\mathcal{O}(n^{2k})) \subseteq \mathbf{P}, \end{aligned}$$

and the opposite inclusion is trivial. □

We are now in a position to look more closely at the problem of feasibility in the framework of parallel computation.

It has turned out that the following propositions are to a very large degree independent of the particular parallel computer model.

- A problem is **feasible** if it can be solved by a parallel algorithm with polynomial worst case time and processor complexity.
- A problem is **highly parallel** if it can be solved by an algorithm with worst-case polylog time complexity ($\lg^{\mathcal{O}(1)} n$) and polynomial processor complexity.
- A problem is **inherently sequential** if it is feasible but not highly parallel.

Observe that Theorem 4.4.24 implies that the class of inherently sequential problems is identical with the class of **P**-complete problems.

One of the main results that justifies the introduction of the term 'highly parallel computational problem' is now presented.

Theorem 4.4.25 *A function $f : \{0,1\}^* \rightarrow \{0,1\}^*$ can be computed by a uniform family of Boolean circuits $\{C_i\}_{i=1}^{\infty}$ with $Depth(C_n) = \lg^{\mathcal{O}(1)} n$, if and only if f can be computed by a CREW$^+$ PRAM in time $t(n) = (\lg n)^{\mathcal{O}(1)}$ and $Proc(n) = n^{\mathcal{O}(1)}$ for inputs of length n.*

The main result of this section concerns the relation between the space for TM computations and the time for PRAM computations.

Lemma 4.4.26 *$Space(s(n)) \subseteq PRAM\text{-}Time(\mathcal{O}(s(n)))$, if $s(n) \geq \lg n$ is a time-constructible function.*

Proof: Let $\mathcal{M}$ be a $s(n)$-space bounded MTM. The basic idea of the proof is the same as that for the proof of Lemma 4.3.20. The space bound $s(n)$ allows us to bound the number of possible configurations of $\mathcal{M}$ by $t(n) = 2^{\mathcal{O}(s(n))}$. For each input x of length n let us consider a $t(n) \times t(n)$ Boolean transition matrix $T_{\mathcal{M}}(x) = \{a_{ij}\}_{i,j=1}^{t}$ with $t = t(n)$ and

$$a_{ij} = 1 \Longleftrightarrow i = j \text{ or } c_i \vdash_{\mathcal{M}} c_j \qquad \text{on the input } x,$$

where c_i, c_j are configurations of $\mathcal{M}$, describing the potential behaviour of $\mathcal{M}$.

A PRAM with t^2 processors can compute all a_{ij} in one step. In order to decide whether $\mathcal{M}$ accepts x, it is enough to compute $T^t_{\mathcal{M}}(x)$ (and from the resulting matrix to read whether x is accepted). This can be done using $\lceil \lg t \rceil$ Boolean matrix multiplications. By Example 4.4.8, Boolean matrix multiplication can be done by a CRCW$^+$ PRAM in the constant time. Since $\lceil \lg t \rceil = \mathcal{O}(s(n))$, this implies the lemma.

□

Lemma 4.4.27 *If $t(n) \geq \lg n$ is time-constructible, then $PRAM\text{-}Time(t(n)) \subseteq Space(t^2(n))$.*

Proof: The basic idea of the proof is simple, but the details are technical. First observe that addresses and contents of all registers used to produce acceptance/rejection in a $t(n)$-time bounded PRAM$^+$ $\mathcal{R}$ have $\mathcal{O}(t(n))$ bits.

An MTM $\mathcal{M}$ simulating $\mathcal{R}$ first computes $t = t(n)$, where $n = |w|$, for an input w. $\mathcal{M}$ then uses recursively two procedures $state(i,\tau)$, to determine the state (the contents of the program register) of the processor P_i after the step τ, and $contents(Z,\tau)$, to determine the contents of the register Z (of the global or local memories) after the step τ, to verify that $state(1,t)$ is the address of an instruction *ACCEPT* or *REJECT*.

It is clear that by knowing $state(i,\tau-1)$ and $contents(Z,\tau-1)$ for all processors and registers used by $\mathcal{R}$ to determine $state(1,t)$, one can determine $state(i,\tau)$ and $contents$ (Z,τ) for all processors and registers needed to derive $state(1,t)$.

In order to determine $state(i,\tau)$, $\mathcal{M}$ systematically goes through all possible values of $state(i,\tau-1)$ and all possible contents of all registers used by the $(i,\tau-1)$th instruction to find the correct value of

$state(1,\tau)$. For each of these possibilities $\mathcal{M}$ verifies first whether systematically chosen values indeed produce $state(i,\tau)$ and then proceeds recursively to verify all chosen values.

In order to verify $contents(Z,\tau)$, for a Z and τ, $\mathcal{M}$ proceeds as follows: if $\tau = 0$, then $contents(Z,\tau)$ should be either an appropriate initial symbol or 0; depending on Z. In the case $\tau > 0$, $\mathcal{M}$ checks both of the following possibilities:

1. Z is not rewritten in step τ. In such a case $contents(Z,\tau) = contents(Z,\tau-1)$ and $\mathcal{M}$ proceeds by verifying $contents(Z,\tau-1)$. In addition, $\mathcal{M}$ verifies, for $1 \leq i \leq 2^t$, that P_i does not rewrite Z in step τ – this can be verified by going systematically through all possibilities for $state(i,\tau-1)$ that do not refer to an instruction rewriting Z – and verifies $state(i,\tau-1)$.

2. Z is rewritten in step τ. $\mathcal{M}$ then verifies for all $1 \leq i \leq 2^t$, whether Z has been rewritten by P_i in step τ, and then moves to verify that none of processors $P_j, j \leq i$, rewrites Z in step τ.

   These systematic searches through all possibilities and verifications need a lot of time. However, since the depth of recursion is $\mathcal{O}(t(n))$ and all registers and their addresses have at most $\mathcal{O}(t(n))$ bits, we get that the overall space requirement of $\mathcal{M}'$ is $\mathcal{O}(t^2(n))$. □

As a corollary of the last two lemmas we have the following theorem.

Theorem 4.4.28 *Turing machines with respect to space complexity and CRCW$^+$ PRAM with the respect to time complexity are polynomially related.*

As another corollary, we get

Theorem 4.4.29 $\bigcup_{k=1}^{\infty} \textit{PRAM-Time}(n^k) = \mathbf{PSPACE}$.

Observe that in principle the result stated in this last theorem is analogous to that in Theorem 4.3.24. The space on MTM and the parallel time on uniform families of Boolean circuits are polynomially related. The same results have been shown for other natural models of parallel computers and this has led to the following thesis.

Parallel computation thesis There exists a standard class of (inherently parallel) computer models, which includes among others several variants of PRAM machines and uniform families of Boolean circuits, for which the polynomial time is as powerful as the polynomial space for machines of the first machine class.

Computer models that satisfy the parallel computation thesis form the **second machine class.**

It seems intuitively clear that **PSPACE** is a much richer class than **P**. However, no proof is known, and the problem

$$\mathbf{P} = \mathbf{PSPACE}$$

is another important open question in foundations of computing.

In order to see how subtle this problem is, notice that RAM$^+$ with uniform time and space complexity measures are in the first machine class, but RAM with division and uniform time and space complexity measures are in the second machine class! (So powerful are multiplication and division!) This result also clearly demonstrates the often ignored fact that not only the overall architecture of a computer model and its instruction repertoire, but also complexity measures, form an inherent part of the model.

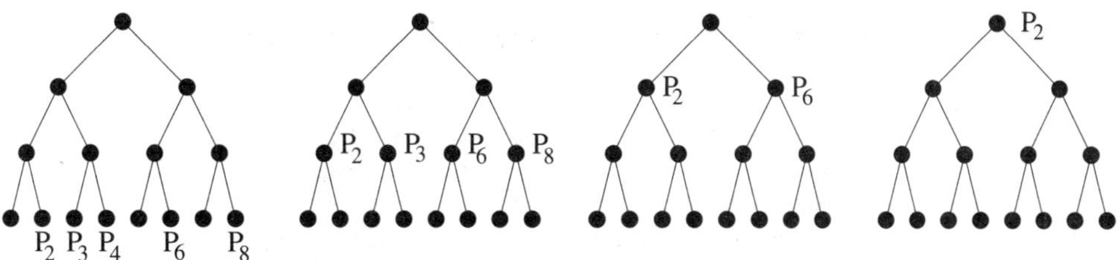

Figure 4.34 Determination of the left-most processor

Exercise 4.4.30 *Is it true that the first and second machine classes coincide if and only if* **P** = **PSPACE**?

Remark 4.4.31 Parallel compufers of the second machine class are very powerful. The source of their power lies in their capacity to activate, logically, in polynomial time an 'exponentially large hardware', for example, the large number of processors. However, if physical laws are taken into consideration, namely an upper bound on signal propagation and a lower bound on size of processors, then we can show that no matter how tight we pack n processors into a spherical body its diameter has to be $\Omega(n^{\frac{1}{3}})$. This implies that there must be processors at about the same distance and that a communication between such processors has to require $\Omega(n^{\frac{1}{3}})$ time (as discussed in more detail in Chapter 10). This in turn implies that an exponential number of processors cannot be physically activated in polynomial time. A proof that a machine model belongs to the second machine class can therefore be seen as a proof that the model is not feasible. This has naturally initiated a search for 'more realistic' models of parallel computing that would lie, with respect to their power, between two machine classes.

4.4.7 Relations between CRCW PRAM Models

There is a natural ordering between basic PRAM computer models:

$$\text{EREW PRAM} \prec \text{CREW PRAM} \prec \text{CRCW}^{com}\ \text{PRAM} \prec \text{CRCW}^{arb}\ \text{PRAM} \prec \text{CRCW}^{pri}\ \text{PRAM}$$

in the sense that each program for one of these models can be run on all 'higher' models, with respect to the ordering $\prec$. This is quite evidently true. Less easy to see is that each higher model is strictly more powerful than the previous one. In spite of that, and this seems to be even less obvious, differences between the powers of these models are actually not very big.

Theorem 4.4.32 *A step of a CRCW^{pri} PRAM $\mathcal{R}$ with p processors and m memory registers can be simulated by an EREW PRAM $\mathcal{R}'$ in $\mathcal{O}(\lg p)$ steps with p processors and mp registers.*

Proof: The ith processor P_i of $\mathcal{R}$, $1 \leq i \leq p$, will be simulated by the ith processor $\mathcal{P}_i'$ of $\mathcal{R}'$. To each register $GM_{\mathcal{R}}[j]$, $1 \leq j \leq m$, there will correspond p registers of $\mathcal{R}'$. One of them will simulate the corresponding register of $\mathcal{R}$; $p-1$ other registers will be used to resolve access conflicts for $GM_{\mathcal{R}}[j]$.

In order to perform a concurrent write to a register $GM_{\mathcal{R}}[j]$, each processor of $\mathcal{R}$ has first to find out whether it is the processor with the smallest PID wishing to write to $GM_{\mathcal{R}}[j]$. This can be done, on $\mathcal{R}'$, in parallel for $1 \leq j \leq m$, as follows. Let us imagine for a moment that if the ith processor wants to write to $GM_{\mathcal{R}}[j]$, then it is located in the ith leaf of a binary tree T_j with p leaves (see Figure 4.34a) for the case of processors P_2, P_3, P_4, P_6, P_8 wanting to write to $GM_{\mathcal{R}}[j]$. The process of determining the left-most of these processors can be carried out simultaneously for all j, by having processors 'to climb T_j trees' according to the following rules: a processor in a left-child node can always go up to the parent node; a processor in a right-child node can go up only if there is no processor in its sibling node. This way the left-most processor gets to the root and can then perform writing. Concurrent reads are performed in a similar way. The left-most processor moves to the root, reads and then starts to go down the tree to its original position. On its way down the tree, the processor distributes the data obtained to processors 'waiting for it', and they, in turn, do the same on their way to their original positions.

This 'tree climbing' can be simulated on $\mathcal{R}'$ using $p-1$ registers available for each register of $\mathcal{R}$ in time $\mathcal{O}(\lg p)$, proportional to the depth of trees. □

A CRCW^{pri} PRAM can be simulated by a CRCW^{com} PRAM without any time loss, but using a larger number of processors.

Theorem 4.4.33 *Any CRCW^{pri} PRAM with $p(n)$ processors and computation time $t(n)$ can be simulated by a CRCW^{com} PRAM with $\binom{p(n)}{2}+p(n)$ processors in time $\mathcal{O}(t(n))$.*

Proof: Let $P_1,\ldots,P_{p(n)}$ be the processors used by a CRCW^{pri} PRAM $\mathcal{R}$. A CRCW^{com} PRAM $\mathcal{R}'$ will use additional processors P_{ij}, $1\leq i<j\leq p(n), i\neq j$, and new shared memory registers $R_1,\ldots,R_{p(n)}$ initialized to 0. In order to simulate one step of $\mathcal{R}$, P_{ij} writes 1 to R_j if $i<j$, and both P_i and P_j try to write to the same memory register. A processor P_i can then determine whether it is the processor with the lowest PID wishing to write to a register by checking whether $R_i=0$. □

Finally, we present some results showing that there is a strict hierarchy between the powers of the main models of PRAM with respect to the computational power when allowing the same computational time.

Theorem 4.4.34 *(1) CREW PRAM are strictly more powerful than EREW PRAM.*
(2) To compute the function $OR(x_1,\ldots,x_n)$, a CREW PRAM needs $\Omega(\lg n)$ steps.

Theorem 4.4.35 *CRCW^{com} PRAMs are strictly more powerful than CREW PRAM.*

Proof: By Theorem 4.4.34 it is sufficient to show that a CRCW^{com} can compute $\mathrm{OR}(x_1,\ldots,x_n)$ in a constant number of steps. Indeed, GM_0 is first initialized to 0 and then, for $1,\ldots,n$, the jth processor reads x_j and writes 1 into GM_0, if and only if $x_j=1$. □

Exercise 4.4.36 *Show that a CRCW^{com} PRAM with a polynomial number of processors can add two n-bit integers in constant time.*

Exercise 4.4.37 *Show that with $n2^n$ processors a CRCW^{com} PRAM can compute any Boolean function of n variables in constant time.*

Theorem 4.4.38 *The CRCW^{pri} PRAM is a strictly more powerful model than the CRCW^{arb} PRAM, and this model is in turn strictly more powerful than the CRCW^{com} PRAM.*

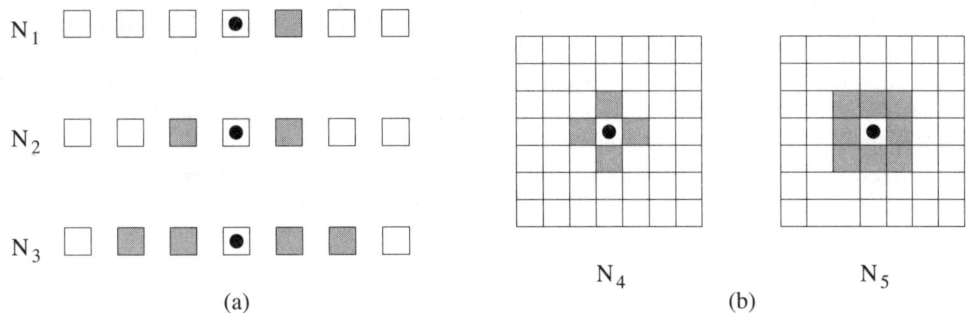

Figure 4.35 Neighbourhoods for one and two-dimensional cellular automata

4.5 Cellular Automata

One of the most intriguing scientific questions of the early 1950s was whether machines can reproduce themselves. In an attempt to find the answer, John von Neumann,[14] known today as one of the fathers of modern (sequential) computers of 'von Neumann type', in 1953 developed a cellular automata model of the biological world. This allowed him to get an affirmative answer to the above question. Since then, cellular automata have become one of the basic models of information processing, not only for the biological world but also for the world of microscopic physics (to study dynamic, complex and chaotic systems and fractal phenomena). This fundamental model of massively parallel computing is often called, paradoxically, 'non von Neumann type' computing.

Useful models of massive parallel computers have to be constructed in hardware, and should be scalable. As such, they can be based on local interactions only. This is why since the early days of modern computing a large effort has been put into trying to understand what is meaningfully achievable, in principle and in practice, by computational devices consisting of large numbers of simple, interacting processing units lacking a central executor that could provide global coordination and control. Cellular automata provide a framework to deal with these problems.

4.5.1 Basic Concepts

Informally, a d-dimensional cellular automaton $\mathcal{A}$ with a finite set of **states** Q, a finite **neighbourhood** $N \subseteq \mathbf{Z}^d$ and a **local transition function** $\delta : Q^N \rightarrow Q$ is a d-dimensional array network of identical finite automata with Q as their set of states. For each node $n \in \mathbf{Z}^d$, the neighbourhood N determines the set $\{n\} + N$ of 'neighbours' of the node n. Formally, $\mathcal{A} = \langle d, Q, N, \delta \rangle$, and elements (nodes) of $\mathbf{Z}^d$ are regarded as representing those finite automata which $\mathcal{A}$ consists of.

Figure 4.35a depicts three neighbourhoods of the dotted nodes for one-dimensional cellular automata: $N_1 = \{0,1\}$, $N_2 = \{-1,0,1\}$, $N_3 = \{-2,-1,0,1,2,\}$. Figure 4.35b illustrates two often used neighbourhoods (again for the dotted nodes) for two-dimensional cellular automata: the **von Neumann neighbourhood** $N_4 = \{(-1,0),(0,-1),(0,0),(0,1),(1,0)\}$ and the **Moore neighbourhood** $N_5 = \{(-1,-1),(-1,0),(-1,1),(0,-1),(0,0),(0,1),(1,-1),(1,0),(1,1)\}$.

[14]John von Neumann (1903–57), an American mathematician and physicist of Hungarian origin, one of the leading scientists of his period, made fundamental contributions to almost all areas of modern mathematics and its applications as well as to theoretical physics: axiomatization of set theory, functional analysis and quantum physics, mathematical logic, automata theory, probability theory, game theory, numerical mathematics, mathematical methods in economics. Von Neumann was one of the leading scientists in the development of the first very powerful electronic computer and of the first atomic bomb.

All finite automata of a cellular automaton work concurrently, synchronized and in discrete time steps. At each time moment the new state of each finite automaton is defined to be the value of the local transition function applied to its current state and to the states of all its neighbours.

In order to describe more formally the overall behaviour of a cellular automaton $\mathcal{A} = \langle d, Q, N, \delta \rangle$, we must again use the concept of configuration.

A configuration of $\mathcal{A}$ is a mapping $c \in Q^{\mathbf{Z}^d}$ which assigns to each finite automaton of $\mathcal{A}$ (that is, to each node of $\mathbf{Z}^d$) a state. The global transition function

$$G_\delta : Q^{\mathbf{Z}^d} \to Q^{\mathbf{Z}^d},$$

$$G_\delta(c)(k) = \delta(c(\{k\} + N)),$$

is used to define a **computation (behaviour)** of $\mathcal{A}$ as a sequence of configurations $c_0, c_1, c_2, \ldots$ such that $c_j = G_\delta(c_{j-1})$, for $j \geq 1$.

For example, if $d = 1$, $N = \{-1, 0, 1\}$, then for $i \in \mathbf{Z}$

$$G_\delta(c)(i) = \delta(c(i-1), c(i), c(i+1));$$

if $N = \{-k, -k+1, \ldots, -1, 0, 1, \ldots, k-1, k\}$, then for $i \in \mathbf{Z}$

$$G_\delta(c(i)) = \delta(c(i-k), c(i-k+1), \ldots, c(i+k-1), c(i+k));$$

if $d = 2$ and the von Neumann neighbourhood is considered, then for $Gj \in \mathbf{Z}$

$$G_\delta(c(i,j)) = \delta(c(i-1,j), c(i,j-1), c(i,j), c(i,j+1), c(i+1,j)).$$

It is often assumed that the set of states Q has one special state, a sleeping (or quiescent) state, such that if a finite automaton A of $\mathcal{A}$ and all its neighbours are in the sleeping state, then the next state of A is the sleeping state, too.

One of the first problems investigated in cellular automata was the question of whether there is a configuration, called the **Garden of Eden**, that cannot be obtained from another configuration by a cellular automaton step. This problem is related (as already discussed in Section 2.3.1) to the injectivity–bijectivity–reversibility problem for global transition functions.

The basic decision problem for cellular automata is the **reachability problem**: given a cellular automaton $\mathcal{A}$ with the global transition function G_δ and two configurations c and c', is there an i such that $G^i_\delta(c) = c'$?

Remark 4.5.1 Von Neumann designed a cellular automaton consisting of 29-state finite automata, and showed that there is a configuration of about 200 such finite automata that is universal (it can simulate a universal Turing machine) and a larger configuration, estimated to consist of several hundred thousand finite automata that is also self-reproducible.

Exercise 4.5.2* *Self-reproducibility in a trivial sense, without having a configuration that simulates a universal Turing machine, is easy to achieve. Consider a two-state* ($\{0,1\}$) *two-dimensional cellular automaton with neighbourhood* $N = \{(-1,0),(1,0),(0,1),(0,-1)\}$ *and transition function* $f(x,y,z,u) = (x+y+z+u) \bmod 2$, *and show that for each initial distribution of the live states (states* 1*), with only finitely many* 1 *states, there is an integer* n *such that the initial configuration reproduces itself four times after* n *steps.*

Exercise 4.5.3 *Determine the number of two-state two-dimensional cellular automata with (a) a von Neumann neighbourhood; (b) a Moore neighbourhood.*

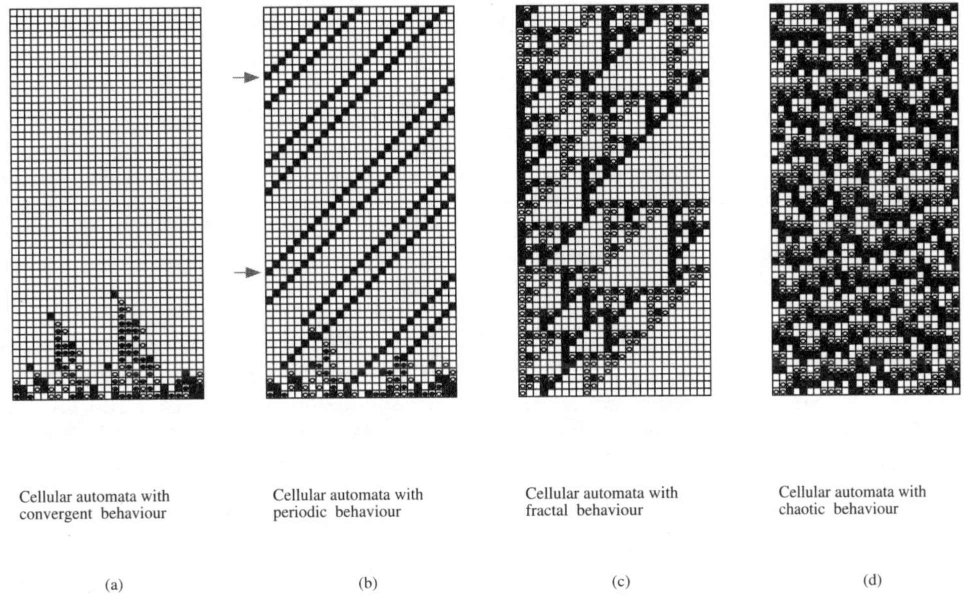

Figure 4.36 Behaviour of one-dimensional cellular automata

4.5.2 Case Studies

We will illustrate the power of cellular automata with some examples.

The behaviour of two-state one-dimensional cellular automata with neighbourhood $N = \{-1, 0, 1\}$

Even apparently very simple one-dimensional cellular automata, with only two states and a nearest neighbours neighbourhood, can exhibit very complex/chaotic behaviour.

Each such cellular automaton is uniquely defined by a mapping $\{0,1\}^N \mapsto \{0,1\}$. There are therefore 2^8 such cellular automata, each of which is uniquely specified by the following (transition) rule:

$$\begin{array}{lllllllllllll} 000 & \rightarrow & a_0 & \quad 010 & \rightarrow & a_2 & \quad 100 & \rightarrow & a_4 & \quad 110 & \rightarrow & a_6 \\ 001 & \rightarrow & a_1 & \quad 011 & \rightarrow & a_3 & \quad 101 & \rightarrow & a_5 & \quad 111 & \rightarrow & a_7, \end{array}$$

and therefore by an integer i with binary representation $bin_8^{-1}(i) = a_7a_6a_5a_4a_3a_2a_1a_0$. Such an automaton can therefore be specified by an integer $0 \leq i < 256$, and we can speak of the cellular automaton with the rule i. This terminology is often used in the literature about cellular automata.

Some of these 256 cellular automata are not very interesting, but others really are: for example, those with the numbers 18, 20, 30, 52, 54, 60, 80, 90, 102, 120, 129, 150, 184, 190 and 216. The behaviour of some of them is so complex that attempts to get a deeper and as full as possible understanding are clearly a never-ending story. Some behaviours of these one-dimensional cellular automata are shown in Figure 4.36, in which some of the **spatio-temporal evolution patterns** are depicted. The ith line shows the states of the corresponding finite automaton at time i (counting is bottom-up). Figure 4.36a depicts a convergent behaviour, Figure 4.36b a periodic behaviour, Figure 4.36c a fractal behaviour and Figure 4.36d a chaotic behaviour.

Exercise 4.5.4* *One-dimensional cellular automata can also be considered, in several ways, as language recognizers. For example, we say that a cellular automaton $\mathcal{A} = \langle 1, Q, \{-1,0,1\}, \delta\rangle$ recognizes a language $L \subseteq \Sigma^* \subset Q^*$, with respect to the set $Q_F \subset Q - \Sigma$ of final states, if $w \in L$, if and only if the automaton $\mathcal{A}$ starting with the configuration w (and all other automata in the quiescent state $\sqcup \in Q - \Sigma$) comes to a state from Q_F in the finite automaton with the first symbol of w at the beginning. Design a cellular automaton recognizing the language $\{a^n b^n c^n \,|\, n \geq 1\}$.*

LIFE game

In an attempt to develop a model of 'artificial life' in the late 1960s J. H. Conway from Cambridge, designed a two-state, two-dimensional cellular automaton with Moore neighbourhood that has become perhaps the most intensively investigated cellular automaton so far. It is called the LIFE game because one of the tasks behind was to find initial configurations that would exhibit the behaviour of 'living creatures'. The transition rule is simple.

The new state of each finite automaton is 1 if and only if one of the following conditions is satisfied:

1. Its old state was 1, and at least two and at most three of its neighbours were in the state 1.
2. Its old state was 0 and exactly three of its neighbours were in the state 1.

Figure 4.37a shows an initial configuration, called **glider**, and its four next configurations. (Black squares are used to denote the state 1; the empty squares denote the state 0.) Figure 4.37b shows a configuration that repeats itself on site after 15 steps. The configuration shown in Figure 4.37d is called Gosper's **glider gun**, because periodically, with a period of 30 steps, it fires a glider that starts to move 'south-east'. In addition, if the initial configuration from Figure 4.37b is properly positioned with respect to the way gliders move, it starts 'to eat' them. The glider gun itself can be created after 174 steps from 13 gliders properly positioned. One can also position two glider guns in such a way that the intersecting streams of gliders 'build a factory that assembles and fires a spaceship every 300 moves'. (The term 'spaceship' is used to denote a configuration that keeps moving in the plane 'throwing away some smoke'. Two of them are depicted in Figure 4.37c.) Possibilities of creating configurations with interesting behaviour for LIFE seem to be limitless. See, for example, the 'wheel' in Figure 4.37e that keeps 'rotating on site' in the sense that three internal 1s rotate.

On the more theoretical side, the power of gliders to act as 'pulses' was used to show that there is an initial configuration that can simulate a universal Turing machine! It has also been shown that LIFE has a Garden of Eden configuration.

Exercise 4.5.5 *Design a program to simulate LIFE, and use it (a)* to simulate several steps of the behaviour of the spaceships, wheel and the glider gun depicted in Figure 4.37; (b)** to determine how to position the configuration in Figure 4.37b in the way of the gliders fired from the glider gun in order to let the configuration destroy the gliders. (c)** Let us call mosaic a configuration that contains 1 in the automaton positioned in the node (i,j) if and only if $1 \leq i \leq 17$, $i \bmod 3 = 0$, $1 \leq j \leq 17$, $j \bmod 3 = 0$. The mosaic is clearly a stable configuration. We say that such a mosaic has a 'virus' if one of the automata in the middle originally in state 0 is in state 1. Find the way to position the virus in the mosaic in such a way that (1) the mosaic destroys the virus; (2) the virus destroys the mosaic.*

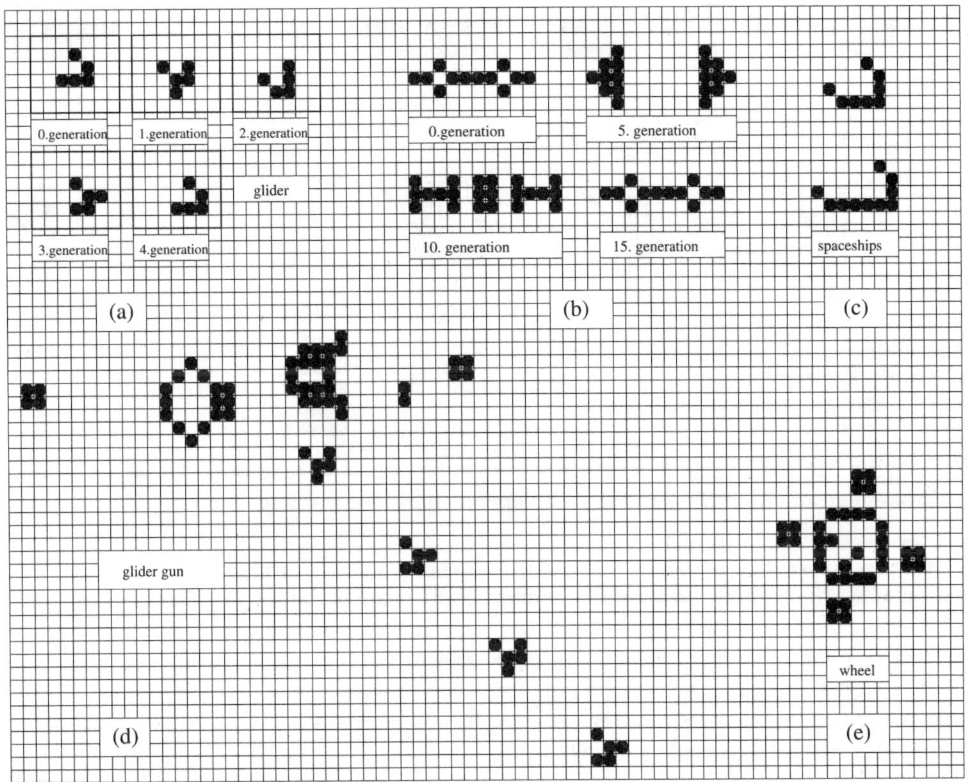

Figure 4.37 LIFE game configurations

Firing squad synchronization problem

Cellular automata are by definition infinite networks of finite automata. The full generality of the concept is needed when simulation of physical phenomena is considered. In order to deal with the computational problems, either only potential infiniteness is needed – each initial configuration has only finitely many cells with nonsleeping states – or only finite networks of finite automata are considered. Perhaps the most famous problem for the latter case is the firing squad synchronization problem (FSSP), due to J. Myhill (1957), solutions of which show a surprising synchronization power of finite automata networks.

The task is to design, if it exists, a single finite automaton, popularly called a **soldier**, with two inputs and two outputs, each new state of which depends on its old state and the two old states received at its two inputs from two neighbouring automata. The new state is then sent through its outputs to two neighbouring automata. The soldier should have among his states a **sleeping state**, a **fire** state, and a **fire when ready** state which should have the following properties.

1. If a soldier is in a sleeping state and so are its neighbours, then it remains in the sleeping state.
2. If n soldiers are connected into a row, n arbitrary, all in the sleeping state at the beginning, and the left one (usually called the general) receives the input 'fire when ready', then after a finite number of steps all the soldiers simultaneously, and each of them for the first time, come

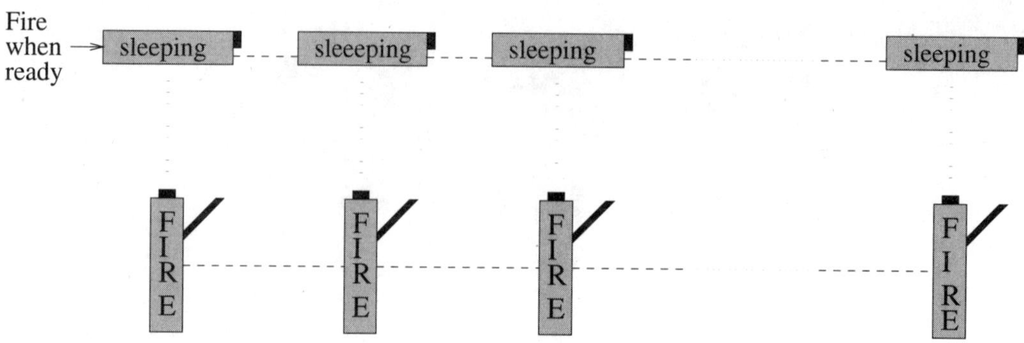

Figure 4.38 Firing squad

into the state **fire** and can therefore fire simultaneously as a squad should do (see Figure 4.38). Missing inputs of the first and last soldiers are the sleeping states.

The main point is that the soldier has to be designed as a finite automaton in such a way that the firing squad works properly no matter how many soldiers are in the squad – that is, no matter how big n is.

Four questions are of immediate interest. Has this problem a solution at all? If it does, what is the minimal time the squad needs to get synchronized? How small (simple) can the soldier be (with respect to the number of states)? Can we achieve minimality simultaneously for the time the squad needs to fire and for the size of the soldier?

It is easy to see that the minimal time needed for synchronization is $2n-2$. Indeed, this time is required so that the left-most soldier gets feedback that the general's order has reached all the soldiers.[15]

There is a simple, divide-and-conquer solution, due to Minsky, though neither time nor size is optimal, for $n = 2^k$. To describe the basic idea, we start with the situation that there is exactly one general, and he is at the left end of the array (see Figure 4.40). (Warning: in this figure not all configurations are shown, and time flows from top to bottom.)

1. Each general (♣) turns itself into a lieutenant (△), and initiates on both sides (or only on the right-hand side if it stands at the left end) a process to create a new general between itself and the next lieutenant or at the right end of the squad, whichever comes first.

2. A lieutenant goes into the firing state † if and only if both its neighbours are lieutenants.

It is easy to see that if step 1 is synchronized, which is not a problem for $n = 2^k$ if the method indicated in Exercise 4.5.6 is used, then all lieutenants simultaneously enter the firing state after $3n-1$ steps.

[15]The first minimal time solution, due to E. Goto in 1962, was estimated at that time as needing a soldier with about a million states. Currently the state-minimal solution, due to J. Mazoyer (1987), uses a 6-state soldier, described and demonstrated in Figure 4.39. It has been shown that no 4-state soldier can yield the minimal solution, and the case n=5 is open.

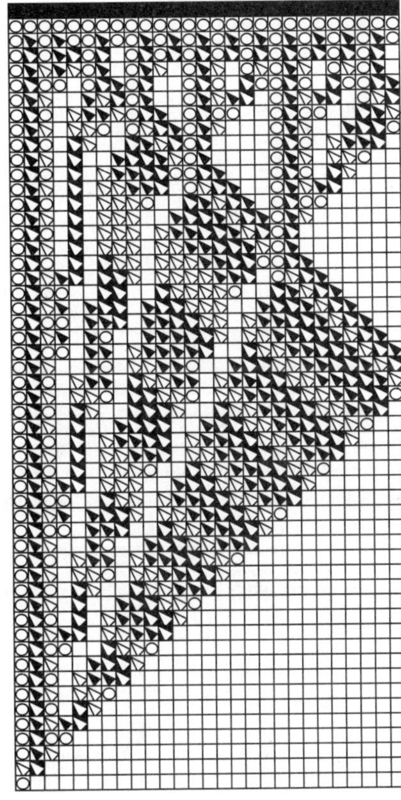

Synchronization of a line of 27 automata using Mazoyer's solution with 6 states

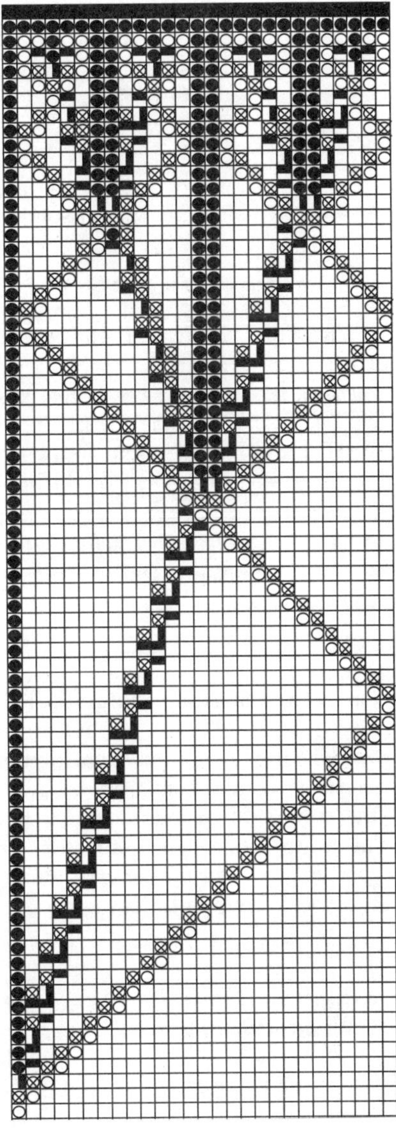

Synchronization of a line of 27 automata using Yunes' solution, a Minsky-like solution, with 7 states

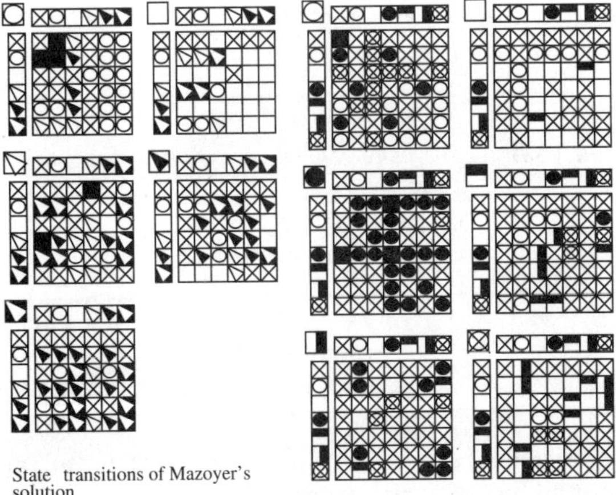

State transitions of Mazoyer's solution

State transitions of Yunes' solution

Figure 4.39 Firing squad synchronization problem solutions

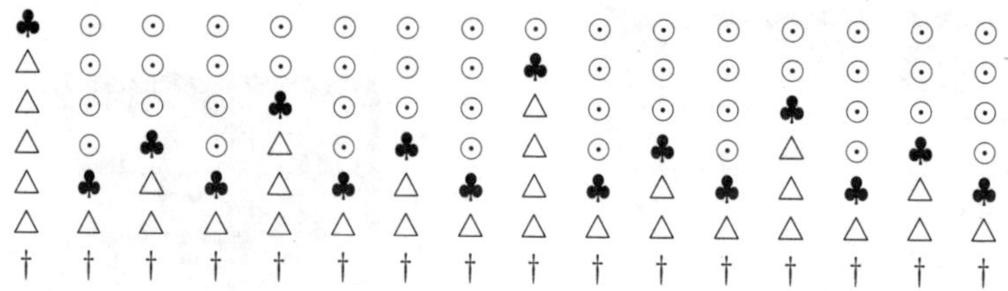

Figure 4.40 Divide-and-conquer solution of the FSSP

Exercise 4.5.6** *Design a one-dimensional cellular automaton with neighbourhood $\{-1,0,1\}$ and with states* (`left, right, sleeping, middle`} *in its set of states that is able to determine which automaton is in the middle of the row of an odd number of finite automata bounded by one in the state* `left` *and one in the state* `right`*: in other words, a cellular automaton such that when starting in the initial configuration* `left, sleeping`$^{2k-1}$, `right`*, and with all other finite automata in the* `sleeping` *state, then after a certain number of steps the automaton in the middle, between the ones in the initial states* `left` *and* `right` *comes (and for the first time) into the state* `middle` *and none of the other automata came to that state before. (Hint: the left-most automaton sends two signals to the right, each at different speed, in such a way that they meet, one of them after a reflection at the right end, in the middle.)*

The first minimal time solution of FSSP, with a small, 16-state soldier, was due to Waksman (1966). A similar 7-state soldier solution, due to J.-B. Yunes, is also described and demonstrated in Figure 4.39. Surprisingly, the firing squad synchronization problem has a solution also in the case that soldiers form a balanced tree or an arbitrary graph all nodes of which have the same degree, as well as the case that some soldiers malfunction in the sense that they only let signals go through them.

The firing squad synchronization problem solutions form the basis of solutions of various synchronization tasks for cellular automata. They also show a surprising global synchronization power of local communications.

Exercise 4.5.7 *Sketch (design) a solution of the FSSP for the more general case of one general in the squad in an arbitrary position.*

Exercise 4.5.8** *Show how to solve the FSSP for an arbitrary two-dimensional array of FA.*

4.5.3 A Normal Form

In the case of the cellular automaton LIFE, a new state of the cell depends on its old state and on the number of 1-states of its neighbours and not at all on the actual distribution of states 1 among the neighbours. Many cellular automata, especially those used in physical applications, have a similar property. They are totalistic in the following sense.

Definition 4.5.9 *A cellular automaton* $\mathcal{A} = \langle 1, Q, \{-1,0,1\}, \delta\rangle$ *is called* **totalistic** *if* $Q \subset \mathbf{N}$ *and there is a function* $\Phi : \mathbf{N} \to \mathbf{N}$ *such that*

$$\delta(x,y,z) = \Phi(x+y+z).$$

As the following theorem shows, restriction to totalistic cellular automata is not essential.

Theorem 4.5.10 *For each cellular automaton* $\mathcal{A} = \langle 1, Q, \{-1,0,1\}, \delta\rangle$, $Q \subset \mathbf{N}$, *there exists a totalistic cellular automaton* $\mathcal{A}' = \langle 1, Q', \{-1,0,1\}, \delta'\rangle$ *that has four times more states than* $\mathcal{A}$ *and simulates* $\mathcal{A}$ *without any time overhead.*

Proof: Assume that $Q = \{1, \ldots, n\}$, and denote $b = n+1$. We will use b to represent all integers and to perform all additions.

Take $Q' = \{q \cdot m \mid q \in Q, m \in \{1, 10, 100, 1000\}\}$ (that is, all states of Q' have either the form q or $q0$ or $q00$ or $q000$, where $q \in Q$ and all these numbers are in the b-nary number system). A configuration of $\mathcal{A}$

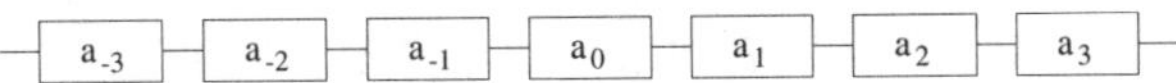

will be simulated in $\mathcal{A}'$ by the configuration

$a_{-3}000$ | $a_{-2}00$ | $a_{-1}0$ | a_0 | a_1000 | a_200 | a_30

In other words,

$$\textbf{if } n \bmod 4 = \begin{cases} 0, & \textbf{then } a_n \text{ is simulated by } a_n; \\ 1, & \textbf{then } a_n \text{ is simulated by } a_n000; \\ 2, & \textbf{then } a_n \text{ is simulated by } a_n00; \\ 3, & \textbf{then } a_n \text{ is simulated by } a_n0. \end{cases}$$

If Φ' is now defined, for $1 \le x, y, z \le b$, by

$$\begin{array}{rcl@{\qquad}rcl} \Phi'(xyz) & = & \delta(x,y,z)0 & \Phi'(xy0z) & = & \delta(z,x,y)000 \\ \Phi'(x0yz) & = & \delta(y,z,x) & \Phi'(xyz0) & = & \delta(x,y,z)00, \end{array}$$

where $xyz = xb^2 + yb + z$, and similar number representations are used for other arguments, and $\delta'(x,y,z) = \Phi'(x+y+z)$, then $\mathcal{A}'$ is totalistic, and simulates $\mathcal{A}$, step by step, in real time. □

Definition 4.5.9 and Theorem 4.5.10 can easily be extended to deal in a straightforward way with larger neighbourhoods and multi-dimensional cellular automata.

Exercise 4.5.11 *One-dimensional cellular automata with neighbourhood* $\{-1,0\}$, **one-way cellular automata**, *can also be seen as representing a normal form for one-dimensional cellular automata. Show that one-way, one-dimensional cellular automata can simulate in a natural way any other one-dimensional cellular automaton.*

Exercise 4.5.12 *Show that for every one-dimensional CA* $\mathcal{A}$ *with neighbourhood* $\{-1,0,1\}$ *and* k *states there is a one-dimensional cellular automaton* $\mathcal{A}'$ *with neighbourhood* $\{-1,0\}$ *that simulates* $\mathcal{A}$ *twice as slowly, and that* $\mathcal{A}'$ *needs at most* k^2 *states.*

4.5.4 Mutual Simulations of Turing Machines and Cellular Automata

Time as the computational complexity measure is defined for cellular automata in a natural way – as the number of steps of a computation. Space as the computational complexity measure is defined only for the case that the initial configuration has finitely many finite automata in a nonsleeping state. In this case, for one-dimensional cellular automata, the space complexity of a computation is the maximal distance during the computation between two finite automata that have ever been (during a computation) in a nonsleeping state. For multi-dimensional cellular automata the space complexity is defined analogously. On this basis we can in a natural way define $t(n)$-time and $s(n)$-space bounded computations on a cellular automaton.

Mutual simulations between Turing machines and cellular automata are in principle very easy and they show, surprisingly, that cellular automata, as the main model of massive parallelism, are in the first machine class.

Theorem 4.5.13 *(1) Each $t(n)$-time and $s(n)$-space bounded one-tape Turing machine can be simulated by a one-dimensional cellular automaton with neighbourhood $\{-1,0,1\}$ in time $t(n)$ and space $s(n)$.*

(2) Each $t(n)$-time and $s(n)$-space bounded one-dimensional cellular automaton with neighbourhood $\{-k,\ldots,0,\ldots,k\}$ and $t(n) > n$ can be simulated by a $\mathcal{O}(kt^2(n))$-time and $\mathcal{O}(s(n))$-space bounded one-tape Turing machine.

Proof: (1) Let $\mathcal{M} = \langle \Gamma, Q, q_0, \delta \rangle$ be a $t(n)$-time bounded one-tape Turing machine with a set of states Q, a tape alphabet Γ and a transition function δ. We show how to simulate $\mathcal{M}$ in time $t(n)$ on a one-dimensional cellular automaton $\mathcal{A}$ with neighbourhood $\{-1,0,1\}$ and set of states $Q' = \Gamma \cup Q \times \Gamma$. The overall simulation is based on the representation of a configuration $a_1 \ldots a_n(q, a_{n+1})a_{n+2} \ldots a_m$ of $\mathcal{M}$ by the following sequence of states of the finite automata of $\mathcal{A}$: $a_1, \ldots, a_n, (q, a_{n+1}), a_{n+2}, \ldots, a_m$. In order to simulate one transition of $\mathcal{M}$, at most two finite automata of $\mathcal{A}$ change their states. The transition function δ' of $\mathcal{A}$ is defined as follows: if $x, y, z \in \Gamma$, then

$$\delta'(x,y,z) = y;$$

if $\delta(q,x) = (q', x', \rightarrow)$, then for $y, z \in \Gamma$,

$$\delta'(y,z,(q,x)) = z, \qquad \delta'(y,(q,x),z) = x', \qquad \delta'((q,x),y,z) = (q',y).$$

Similarly, we can define the values of the transition function δ' for other cases.

(2) The simulation of a cellular automaton $\mathcal{A}$ with neighbourhood $\{-k,\ldots,k\}$ by a one-tape Turing machine $\mathcal{M}$ is straightforward once we assume that an input of $\mathcal{A}$ is written on a tape of $\mathcal{M}$ with end markers.

The simulation of one step of $\mathcal{A}$ is done by $\mathcal{M}$ in one right-to-left or left-to-right sweep. In a right-to-left sweep $\mathcal{M}$ first erases the end marker and the next $2k+1$ symbols, storing them in its finite control. Then $\mathcal{M}$ writes the end marker and, cell by cell, the new states of the finite automata of $\mathcal{A}$. After reaching the left end marker, $\mathcal{M}$ keeps writing $2k+1$ new states for automata of $\mathcal{A}$ and then the new left end marker. Once this has been done, a new left-to-right sweep can start. Since $\mathcal{A}$ can extend the number of nonsleeping finite automata in $t(n)$ steps maximally to $kt(n)+n$, $\mathcal{M}$ needs $\mathcal{O}(kt(n))$ steps to simulate one step of $\mathcal{A}$. Hence the theorem. □

Exercise 4.5.14 *Show that one can simulate Turing machines with several tapes and several heads per tape in real time on cellular automata.*

4.5.5 Reversible Cellular Automata

Let us recall the basic definition from Section 2.13.

Definition 4.5.15 *A cellular automaton $\mathcal{A} = \langle d, Q, N, \delta\rangle$ is reversible if there is another cellular automaton $\mathcal{A}' = \langle d, Q, N', \delta'\rangle$ such that for each configuration c of $\mathcal{A}$ it holds that*

$$G_\delta(c) = c_1 \qquad \text{if and only if} \qquad G_{\delta'}(c_1) = c.$$

In other words, a cellular automaton $\mathcal{A}$ is reversible if there is another cellular automaton $\mathcal{A}'$ such that for any sequence of configurations $c_1, c_2, \ldots, c_{n-1}, c_n$ of $\mathcal{A}$, where $c_i \vdash c_{i+1}$, for $1 \leq i < n$, $\mathcal{A}'$ can reverse the computation to get the sequence of configurations $c_n, c_{n-1}, \ldots, c_2, c_1$. (Note that the reverse cellular automaton $\mathcal{A}'$ may use a much smaller or larger neighbourhood than $\mathcal{A}$.)

There are two main reasons why the concept of reversibility of cellular automata is important.

1. The main physical reason why a computation needs energy is the loss of information that usually occurs during a computation, each loss of information leading to energy dissipation. (For example, a computation starting with input x and performing the statement $x \leftarrow x \times x$ causes a loss of information.) On the other hand, if a computation is reversible, then there is no loss of information and in principle such a computation can be carried out without a loss of energy.

2. Cellular automata are used to model phenomena in microscopic physics, especially in gas and fluid dynamics. Since processes in microscopic physics are in principle reversible, then so must be the cellular automata that model these microscopic processes. For this reason the problem of deciding whether a given cellular automaton is reversible is of importance for cellular automata models of microscopic physics.

The very basic problem is whether there are reversible cellular automata at all. They do exist, and the following example shows one of them. It is a cellular automaton with two states, the neighbourhood $N = \{-1, 0, 1, 2\}$ and the following transition function:

$$\begin{array}{lllllllllll}
0\underline{0}00 & \rightarrow & 0 & 0\underline{1}00 & \rightarrow & 1 & 1\underline{0}00 & \rightarrow & 0 & 1\underline{1}00 & \rightarrow & 1 \\
0\underline{0}01 & \rightarrow & 0 & 0\underline{1}01 & \rightarrow & 1 & 1\underline{0}01 & \rightarrow & 0 & 1\underline{1}01 & \rightarrow & 1 \\
0\underline{0}10 & \rightarrow & 1 & 0\underline{1}10 & \rightarrow & 0 & 1\underline{0}10 & \rightarrow & 0 & 1\underline{1}10 & \rightarrow & 1 \\
0\underline{0}11 & \rightarrow & 0 & 0\underline{1}11 & \rightarrow & 1 & 1\underline{0}11 & \rightarrow & 0 & 1\underline{1}11 & \rightarrow & 1,
\end{array}$$

where the underlined digits indicate states to be changed by the transition. It is quite easy to verify that this cellular automaton is reversible. There are only two transitions that change the state: both have neighbourhood $(0, 10)$. It is now sufficient to observe that this neighbourhood cannot be changed by any transition.

There do not seem to be many reversible cellular automata. For two-state automata with neighbourhood N where $|N| = 2$ or $|N| = 3$ there are none. For the neighbourhood $N = \{-1, 0, 1, 2\}$ there are 65,536 cellular two-state automata, but only 8 of them are reversible, and all of them are insignificant modifications of the one presented above. The following theorem, of importance for cellular automata applications, is therefore quite a surprise.

Theorem 4.5.16 *(1) Any k-dimensional CA can be simulated in real time by a $(k+1)$-dimensional reversible CA.*

(2) There is a universal cellular automaton that is reversible.

(3) It is decidable whether a one-dimensional cellular automaton is reversible, but undecidable whether a two-dimensional cellular automaton is reversible.

*	0	1	2	3
0	0	1	1	0
1	2	3	3	2
2	0	1	1	0
3	2	3	3	2

(a)

*	0	1	2	3
0	0	0	3	3
1	2	2	1	1
2	0	0	3	3
3	2	2	1	1

(b)

Figure 4.41 A cellular automaton and its reversible counterpart

Example 4.5.17 *A simple 4-state cellular automaton with neighbourhood* $\{0,1\}$ *is depicted in Figure 4.41a, and its reversible counterpart, with neighbourhood* $\{-1,0\}$ *in Figure 4.41b.*

Exercise 4.5.18 *Show that the one-dimensional cellular automaton with neighbourhood* $N=\{0,1\}$, *states* $\{0,1,\ldots,9\}$ *and transition function* $\delta(x,y)=(5x+\lceil\frac{5y}{10}\rceil) \bmod 10$ *is reversible.*

Remark 4.5.19 The concept of reversibility applies also to other models of computers, for example, to Turing machines. It is surprising that any one-tape TM can be simulated by a one-tape, two-symbol, reversible TM.

Moral: There is a surprising variety of forms in which the universality of computing can exhibit itself. A good rule of thumb in computing, as in life, is therefore to solve problems with the tools that fit best and to apply tools to the problems that fit them best.

4.6 Exercises

1. Design a Turing machine to compute the following string-to-string functions over the alphabet $\{0,1\}$, where w_i are symbols and w strings: (a) $w \mapsto w^R$; (b) $w \rightarrow ww$; (c) $w_1w_2\ldots w_n \rightarrow w_1w_1w_2w_2\ldots w_nw_n$.
2. Design a Turing machine that performs unary-to-binary conversion.
3. Design a Turing machine that generates binary representations of all positive integers separated by the marker #.
4. Design a Turing machine that for an input string x takes exactly $2^{|x|}$ steps.
5. Design a TM that generates all well-parentheticized sequences over the alphabet $\{(,)\}$, and each only once; that is, that generates an infinite string like ()$()()$(())$()()()$()(())$. . . .
6.* Show that for any Turing machine there is an equivalent two-symbol Turing machine (with symbols $\sqcup$ and 1), which can replace any blank by 1 but never rewrite 1 by the blank.
7.** Show that any computation that can be performed by a Turing machine can be simulated by a Turing machine which has two one-way infinite tapes and can neither write nor read on these tapes but only sense when the head comes to the end of the tape.

8.* Show that any TM can be simulated by a TM whose tape is always entirely empty apart from at most three 1s.

9.* Design a TM which, when started with an empty tape, writes down its own description and halts.

10. Show that a k-tape $t(n)$-time bounded TM can be simulated by a 2-tape TM in $\mathcal{O}(t(n)\lg t(n))$ time. (Hint: move tapes, not simulated heads.)

11. Show that for any function $f \in \omega(n)$ the complexity class $Time(f(n))$ is closed (a) under union; (b) under intersection; (c) under complementation.

12. Define formally the concept of Turing machines with a binary-tree-like memory.

13. Show how a TM with a tree-like memory can be simulated by a two-tape ordinary TM, and estimate the efficiency of the simulation.

14.** Find a problem that can be solved significantly more efficiently on a TM with a tree-like memory than on any TM with a finite-dimensional tape.

15. Design a RAM that computes a product of two polynomials if the coefficients of these polynomials are given.

16. Design a RAM that for a given integer n computes (a) $\lfloor \lg n \rfloor$; (b) a binary representation of n; (c) a Fibonacci representation of n.

17. Design a RASP program to compute in $\Theta(n)$ steps g_n, defined by $g_0 = -1, g_1 = 0, g_2 = 1, g_3 = 0$, $g_n = 5g_{n-1} - 4g_{n-4}$, for $n \geq 4$.

18. Consider a version of RAM with successor and predecessor operations as the only arithmetical operations. Design programs for such RAM for addition and subtraction.

19.* Show that the permanent of an $n \times n$ integer matrix $A = \{a_{ij}\}$ can be computed in $\mathcal{O}(n^2)$ arithmetical operations if integer division is allowed. (Hint: use numbers $z = (\prod_{i=1}^{n}\sum_{j=1}^{n} a_{ij})^n$, $\alpha_i = z^{n^i}, i = 1, \ldots, n, B = \sum_{i=1}^{n} n^i, T = \prod_{i=1}^{n}(\sum_{j=1}^{n} \alpha_j a_{ij})$ as well as integer division (and modulo) operations.)

20. Show how to encode by an integer $\langle p, x\rangle$ a RAM program p and a RAM input x.

21. For a RAM program p and an input x let $R(p,x)$ be the corresponding output. Show that there is a RAM program u such that $R(u, \langle p,x\rangle) = R(p,x)$, for any p and x.

22. Design a Boolean circuit over the base $\{\vee, \wedge, \neg\}$ to compute the function $f(x,y,z) =$ **if** x **then** y **else** z.

23. Design a Boolean circuit over the base $\{NOR\}$ to compute (a) $x \Rightarrow y$; (b) $x \equiv y$.

24. Design a Boolean circuit to recognize palindromes among binary strings of length (a) 8; (b) n.

25. Design a Boolean circuit, over the base $\{\vee, \wedge, \neg\}$, of depth $\mathcal{O}(\lg n)$, for the Boolean function $f_n(x_1, \ldots, x_n, y_1, \ldots, y_n) = 1 \Leftrightarrow \forall i \in \{1, \ldots, n\} : x_i \neq y_i$.

26. Design a Boolean circuit, over the base $\{\vee, \wedge, \neg\}$, of depth $\mathcal{O}(\lg n)$, for the Boolean function

$$g_n(x_{n-1}, \ldots, x_0, y_{n-1}, \ldots, y_0) = 1$$

if and only if $bin(x_{n-1} \ldots x_0) > bin(y_{n-1} \ldots y_0)$.

27. (Decoder) Show how to design a Boolean circuit over the base $\{\vee, \wedge, \neg\}$, called decoder, with n inputs and 2^n outputs such that for an input $x_1, \ldots, x_n$ there is 1 on exactly the $bin(x_1 \ldots x_n)$-th output. (This is a way in which a random access memory is addressed.)

28. k-threshold function $t_k : \{0,1\}^n \rightarrow \{0,1\}$ is the Boolean function of n arguments that has value 1 if and only if at least k of its arguments have value 1. (a) Show how to design t_k for $1 \leq k \leq n$; (2) design one Boolean circuit that computes all $t_1, \ldots, t_n$ and has as small a size as possible.

29. Design a Boolean circuit that determines whether three or more of four people have a common vote on a committee that votes yes on an issue and each committee member has a switch to vote.

30. Let $\mathcal{B}$ be a base of Boolean functions that contains the identity function, and let k be the maximal arity of functions in $\mathcal{B}$. Show that if a Boolean function f can be computed by a Boolean circuit C over the base $\mathcal{B}$, then f can be computed by a Boolean circuit C' over the base $\mathcal{B}$ such that each gate of C' has the out-degree at most 2 and $Size(C') \leq (k+1)Size(C)$.

31. Show that each Boolean function $f \in \mathbf{B}_n$ can be computed by a Boolean circuit of size $3 \cdot 2^n$. (Hint: use the disjunctive normal form for f.)

32. Show that every time-constructible function is space-constructible.

33.* Show that if s is a space-constructible function, then $2^{s(n)}$ is time-constructible.

34. (Universal Boolean circuit) Show that for each integer n there is a circuit UC_n of size $\mathcal{O}(2^n)$ with $2^n + n$ inputs such that for all binary strings p of length 2^n and any string x of length n the output of the circuit UC_n with the input px is the value of the Boolean function determined by the string p for the input x.

35. Design an EREW PRAM program to compute in $\lceil \lg n \rceil + 1$ time the Boolean function $x_1 \vee x_2 \ldots \vee x_n$.

36. Show that the following program, for an EREW PRAM, computes the function $x_1 \vee x_2 \vee \ldots \vee x_n$, where x_i is stored in the shared memory location $GM[i]$, and its computation time is strictly less than $\lceil \lg n \rceil$ steps. (F_i stands here for the ith Fibonacci number):

```
begin t ← 0; Y[i] ← 0;
    until F_{2t-1} ≤ n
        do if i + F_{2t} ≤ n then Y[i] ← (Y[i] ∨ GM[i + F_{2t}]);
           if (Y[i] = 1) ∨ (i > F_{2t+1}) then GM[i − F_{2t+1}] ← 1;
           t ← t + 1
        od
end
```

37. **(Pre-emptive scheduling)** Let m machines $M_1, \ldots, M_m$ and n jobs J_j, $1 \le j \le n$, with processing times $p_j, 1 \le j \le n$ be given. Design an EREW PRAM algorithm to construct a feasible and optimal pre-emptive scheduling of n jobs on m machines in time $\mathcal{O}(\lg n)$. (A pre-emptive schedule assigns to each job J_j a set of triples (M_i, s, t), where $1 \le i \le m$ and $0 \le s \le t$, to denote that J_j is to be processed by M_i from time s to time t. A pre-emptive schedule is *feasible* if the processing intervals for different jobs on the same machine are nonoverlapping, and the processing intervals of each job J_j on different machine are also nonoverlapping and have the total length p_j for the jth job. A pre-emptive schedule is optimal if the maximum completion time is minimal.)

38.* Show that one step of a CRCW^{pri} PRAM with p processors and m registers of shared memory can be simulated by a CRCW^{com} PRAM with p processors and m registers of shared memory in $\mathcal{O}(\lg p)$ steps.

39.** Show that one step of a CRCW^{pri} PRAM with p processors and m registers of shared memory can be simulated by a CRCW^{com} in $\mathcal{O}(\lg \lg p)$ steps using p processors and $m(p-1)$ registers of shared memory.

40. EROW (**e**xclusive **r**ead **o**wner **w**rite) PRAM is a PRAM model in which each processor has a single register of shared memory assigned to it (it 'owns this register'), and it can write only to that register. Show that any Boolean circuit of depth d and size s can be simulated by an EROW PRAM in $\mathcal{O}(d)$ steps using s processors and s shared memory 1-bit registers.

41. Show that (a) any problem in DLOGSPACE can be solved by a EROW PRAM in $\mathcal{O}(\lg n)$ steps using $n^{\mathcal{O}(1)}$ processors; (b) any problem in NLOGSPACE can be solved by a CRCW^{com} PRAM in $\mathcal{O}(\lg n)$ steps using $n^{\mathcal{O}(1)}$ processors.

42.** An **abstract** PRAM is one in which no restriction is made on the instruction set. Show that any Boolean function of n variables can be computed by an abstract EROW PRAM in $\mathcal{O}(\lg n)$ steps using $\frac{n}{\lg n}$ processors on $\frac{n}{2\lg n}$ shared memory registers, provided n input values are in n different registers of the shared memory.

43.* Very simple 'finite cellular automata' can exhibit chaotic behaviour. Demonstrate this by designing and running a program to simulate the following $n \times n$ array of two-state – 0 and 1 – finite automata with the following transition function:

$$c_{i,j}(t) = (c_{i,j}(t-1) \wedge c_{i-1,1}(t-1)) \oplus c_{i,j-1}(t-1) \oplus c_{i,j+1}(t-1)$$

that exhibit chaotic behaviour for almost any intitial configuration (provided the automata on the border of the rectangle keep getting 0 along their disconnected inputs (to the environment)).

44.* Sketch (design) a solution of the firing squad synchronization problem for the case that the squad has two generals, one at each end of the squad, and they simultaneously send the order 'fire when ready'.

45. Sketch (design) a solution of the firing squad synchronization problem for the case that the soldiers of the squad are interconnected to form a balanced binary tree all leaves of which have the same distance from the root – the general.

46. Show that one-dimensional cellular automata can recognize the language $\{a^{2^{n}} \mid n \ge 0\}$ in real time (that is, in time equal to the length of the input).

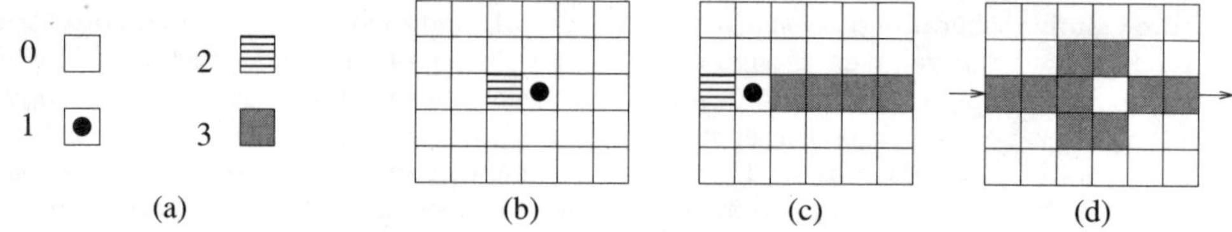

Figure 4.42 A cellular automaton to simulate computational elements

47.* Show that any one-tape Turing machine with m symbols and n states can be simulated by a one-dimensional cellular automaton with $m+2n$ states.

48.* Consider a two-dimensional cellular automaton with Moore neighbourhood and 4-state finite automata with states $\{0,1,2,3,4\}$ and the local transition function that maps the state 0 to 0, 1 to 2, 2 to 3 and 3 either to 1, if at least one and at most two neighbours are in the state 1, and to 3, otherwise. The initial configuration shown in Figure 4.42b is called 'electron' and the one in Figure 4.42c is called 'wire with an electron' because if this configuration develops the electron 'moves along the wire'. The initial configuration shown in Figure 4.42d is called 'a diode' because if the electron is attached to its input, indicated by the incoming arrow, then it moves through the diode. However, if the electron is attached to the output, it does not get through. Show that one can design initial configurations that behave like the following computational elements: (a) an *OR* gate; (b) an inverter; (c) an *AND* gate (without using inverters); (d) an *XOR* gate; (e) a one-bit memory; (f) a crossing of two wires which 'are not connected'.

49. (Universal cellular automaton) A natural way to see a universal two-dimensional cellular automaton U (for two-dimensional cellular automata with the same neighbourhood) is that for any other two-dimensional cellular automaton A with the same neighbourhood the plane of U is divided into rectangular blocks B_{ij} (of size that depends on A). With appropriate starting conditions and a fixed k, if U is run in k steps, then each block B_{ij} performs a step of simulation of one cell c_{ij} of A. Show how to construct such a universal cellular automaton. (Hint: design a cellular automaton that can simulate any Boolean circuit over the base $\{NOR\}$ in such a way that cells behave either like *NOR* gates or as horizontal or vertical wires or as crossings or turns of wires. The transition function of any given CA is then expressed by a Boolean circuit and ....)

50. (**Prime recognition by one-dimensional CA**) Design a one-dimensional CA that has in a fixed cell the state 1 in the ith step if and only if i is a prime. (Due to I. Korec this can be done with a 14-state CA and neighbourhood $\{-1,0,1\}$.)

51. (**Limit sets**) Let $G: Q^{\mathbf{Z}} \to Q^{\mathbf{Z}}$ be the global function computed by a one-way, one-dimensional cellular automaton $\mathcal{A}$ with the sleeping state. Let us define a sequence of sets of configurations $\Omega_0 = Q^{\mathbf{Z}}, \Omega_i = G(\Omega_{i-1})$, for $i > 0$. The **limit set** Ω of $\mathcal{A}$ is defined by $\Omega = \bigcap_{i=0}^{\infty} \Omega_i$. (a) Show that Ω is a nonempty set; (b) Ω is included in its pre-images, that is, $\forall c \in \Omega, \exists d \in \Omega, G(d) = c$; (c) find an example of a cellular automaton such that $\Omega_i = \Omega$ for some i; (d) find an example of a cellular automaton such that $\Omega \neq \Omega_i$ for all i.

QUESTIONS

1. What is the evidence that Church's thesis holds?
2. Can there be a universal Turing machine with one state only?
3. What are the differences, if any, between the laws of physics and theses such as Church's?
4. What modification of straight-line programs is suitable for studying computational complexity of such problems as sorting, merging, and maximum or median finding?
5. What are the relations between Church's thesis, the sequential computation thesis and the parallel computation thesis?
6. Why does Strassen's algorithm not work over the Boolean quasi-ring?
7. How many single Boolean functions of two variables form a complete base?
8. What is the relation between the length of a Boolean expression and the size of the corresponding Boolean circuit?
9. How can one naturally generalize von Neumann and Moore neighbourhoods for three-dimensional cellular automata?
10. Does the FSSP have a solution for reversible CA?

4.7 Historical and Bibliographical References

The history of Turing machines goes back to the seminal paper by Turing (1937). The basic results concerning Turing machines presented in Section 4.1 can be found in any of the numerous books on computability and computational complexity. Concerning Turing himself, an interesting biography has been written by Hedges (1983). A survey of Turing machines and their role in computing and science in general is found in Hopcroft (1984). For the broader and futuristic impacts of Turing machines see the book edited by R. Merken (1988).

The fundamental original papers of Turing, Kleene, Church, Post and others are collected in Davis (1965). For an analysis of Church's thesis see Kleene (1952) and the illuminating discussions in Rozenberg and Salomaa (1994). Basic relations between quantum theory and Church's thesis and the idea of a universal quantum Turing machine are analysed by Deutsch (1985).

The existence of a universal Turing machine with two nonterminating and one terminating state was shown by Shannon (1956). Minsky (1967) with his 4-symbol, 7-state universal Turing machine, represents the end of one period of searching for minimal universal Turing machines. See Minsky (1962) for an older history of this competition. For newer results concerning minimal universal Turing machines see Rogozhin (1996). Various approaches to the concept of universality are analysed by Priese (1979).

The busy beaver problem is due to Rado (1962); for a presentation of various results on this problem see Dewdney (1984). The concept of the off-line Turing machine and the basic results on resource-bounded Turing machines are due to Hartmanis and Stearns (1965) and Hartmanis, Lewis and Stearns (1965).

The model of the RASP machine was introduced and investigated by Shepherdson and Sturgis (1963), Elgot and Robinson (1964) and Hartmanis (1971). Cook and Reckhow (1973) introduced the RAM model as a simplification of RASP and showed basic simulations between RAM, RASP and Turing machines. A detailed analysis of the computational power of various types of RAM models is due to Schönhage (1979). Exercises 19 and 4.2.8 are due to Vyskoč (1983). Another natural modification of RAM, array-processing machines (APM), due to van Leeuwen and Wiedermann (1987), represents an extension of RAM with vectorized versions of the usual RAM instructions. APM are also in the second machine class.

A detailed presentation and analysis of various computer models and their simulations are found in van Emde Boas (1990) and Vollmar and Worsch (1995). Van Emde Boas also introduced the concepts of the first and second machine classes. Our formulation of the sequential computational thesis is from van Emde Boas (1990).

The concept of register machines, also called successor RAM or Minsky machines, is due to Minsky (1967), who also showed that each Turing machine can be simulated by a two-register machine and even by a one-register machine if multiplication and division are allowed.

For the history (and references) of the search for the fastest algorithms for matrix multiplication and related problems see Winograd (1980) and Pan (1984).

Blum, Shub and Smale (1989) initiated an investigation of RRAM and my presentation is derived from their results.

The investigation of Boolean circuit complexity goes back to Shannon (1949a), as does Theorem 4.3.13. My proof of this theorem follows Wegener (1987). His book also contains a systematic presentation of the 'older results' on the Boolean circuit complexity. See also Savage (1986). For a linear lower bound of the circuit complexity of Boolean functions see Blum (1984). Basic results concerning mutual simulations of Turing machines and uniform families of Boolean circuits are found in Schnorr (1976), Borodin (1977) and Pippenger and Fischer (1979). The first concept of uniformity for families of Boolean circuits was introduced by Borodin (1977). For references to other concepts of uniformity see, for example, Greenlaw, Hoover and Ruzzo (1995). My presentation is derived from a systematic treatment of this subject by Reischuk (1990), where one can also find a proof of the existence of oblivious TM. The assumption that no 'explicit' Boolean function has nonpolynomial-size Boolean circuit complexity was formulated and investigated by Lipton (1994).

PRAM models of parallel computing were introduced by Fortune and Wyllie (1978), CREW PRAM, Goldschlager (1982), CRCW PRAM, and Shiloach and Vishkin (1981). The basic result on the relation between parallel time on machines of the second machine class and space on machines of the first machine class is due to Goldschlager (1977). The parallel computation thesis seems to appear first in Chandra and Stockmeyer (1976), and became well known through the thesis of Goldschlager (1977). Systematic presentations of various parallel complexity classes and simulations between models of parallel and sequential computing are found in Parberry (1987) and Reischuk (1990). Basic hierarchy results between various models of PRAM were established by Cook, Dwork and Reischuk (1986). For a detailed overview of relations between various models of PRAM see Fich (1993). For fast circuits for the parallel prefix sum problem and their application to fast parallel computation of mappings computable by finite state transducers see Ladner and Fischer (1986). $\mathcal{O}(\sqrt{t(n)})$-time simulation of $t(n)$-time bounded TM on CREW PRAM is due to Dymond and Tompa (1985). For the design of parallel algorithms see, for example, Karp and Ramachandran (1990) and Ja'Ja (1992). A work-optimal algorithm for the list ranking problem is due to Cole and Vishkin (1986). Algorithm 4.4.1 is due to Kučera (1982), and the idea of using doubly logarithmic depth trees to van Emde Boas (1975). John von Neumann's decision, inspired by S. L. Ulam, to consider cellular automata as a model of the biological world within which to investigate the problem of self-reproducibility, see von Neumann (1966), started research in the area of parallelism. Since then, cellular automata have been investigated from several other points of view: as a model of the physical world, chaotic systems and dynamical systems and as a model of massive parallelism.

The original von Neumann solution of the self-reproducibility problem with 29-state FA has been improved, first by E. F. Codd (1968) who found an elegant solution with an 8-state FA. (Codd received the Turing award in 1981 for introducing an elegant, minimal and powerful model of relational data bases.) The von Neumann result was further improved by E. R. Banks (1971) who found a solution with a 4-state FA.

For an analysis of the behaviour of one-dimensional cellular automata see Wolfram (1983, 1984, 1986), Guttowitz (1990) and Garzon (1995). An exciting account of the history and achievements of Conway's LIFE game is due to Gardner (1970, 1971, 1983). The universality of the LIFE game was shown by Berlekamp, Conway and Guy (1983). Generalizations of the LIFE game to three-dimensional cellular automata were suggested by Bays (1987). The first solution to the FSSP was due to Minsky and McCarthy in time $3n$, using a divide-and-conquer method. (Minsky received the Turing award in 1969 and McCarthy in 1971, both for their contributions to artificial intelligence.) A survey of results FSSPs is due to Mazoyer (1976). The existence of the totalistic normal form for cellular automata was shown by Culik and Karhumäki (1987).

The history of reversible computation goes back to the Garden of Eden problem of Moore and received an explicit formulation in papers by Amoroso and Patt (1972), Richardson (1972) and Bennett (1973). The first claim of Theorem 4.5.16 is due to Toffoli (1977). The existence of universal reversible cellular automata was shown by Toffoli (1977) for two- and multi-dimensional cellular automata, and by Morita and Harao (1989) for one-dimensional cellular automata. The reversible cellular automata shown in Figure 4.41 and in Exercise 4.5.18 are due to Korec (1996). The fact that any one-tape TM can be simulated by a one-tape, two-symbol reversible Turing machine was shown by Morita, Shirasaki and Gono (1989). The decidability of reversibility for one-dimensional automata is due to Amoroso and Patt (1972), and the undecidability for two-dimensional cellular automata to Kari (1990). Surveys of results on reversibility and related problems of energy-less computations are due to Bennett (1988) and Toffoli and Margolus (1990). For more on cellular automata see Farmer, Toffoli and Wolfram (1984).

For critical views of models of parallel computing and approaches to a search for more realistic models see Wiedermann (1995).

5 Complexity

INTRODUCTION

Computational complexity is about quantitative laws and limitations that govern computing. It explores the space of algorithmic problems and their structure and develops techniques to reduce the search for efficient methods for the whole class of algorithmic problems to the search for efficient methods for a few key algorithmic problems. Computational complexity discovers inherent quantitative limitations to developing efficient algorithms and designs/explores methods for coping with them by the use of randomness, approximations and heuristics. Finally, computational complexity tries to understand what is feasible and what is efficient in sequential and parallel computing and, in so doing, to determine practical limitations not only of computing, but also of scientific theories and rational reasoning.

Computational complexity concepts, models, methods and results have a more general character. As such they are conceptual tools of broader importance both within and outside computing. On one hand, they provide deep insights into the power of computational models, modes and resources as well as into descriptive means. On the other, they provide guidance and frameworks that have been behind the progress achieved in the development of efficient methods and systems for practical computing.

LEARNING OBJECTIVES

The aim of the chapter is to demonstrate

1. the main computational complexity classes for deterministic, nondeterministic, randomized and parallel computing, their structure and the relations between them;

2. basic resource-bounded reductions and the concept of complete problems;

3. a variety of complete problems for such complexity classes as **NP, P** and **PSPACE** and methods for showing their completeness;

4. algorithmic problems that play a special role in complexity investigations: the graph isomorphism problem, prime recognition and the travelling salesman problem;

5. methods for overcoming the limitations that **NP**-completeness imposes (using the average case and randomized computations, approximations and heuristics) and their limitations;

6. basic relations between computational and descriptional complexity.

> To find specific candidate problems on which pure science can be expected to have the greatest impact, we have to look among the most difficult ones where no solutions are known, rather than the easier ones where several alternatives already exist. Physics has had greater influence on space travel than on violin making.
>
> *Leslie G. Valiant, 1989*

Complexity theory is about quantitative laws and limitations that govern computations. The discovery that computational problems have an intrinsic nature that obeys strong quantitative laws and that an understanding of these laws yields deep theoretical insights, and pays practical dividends in computing, is one of the main outcomes of computational theory and practice. Since the computing paradigm is universal and widespread, the quantitative laws of computational complexity apply to all information processing, from numerical simulations and computations to automatic theorem proving and formal reasoning, and from hardware to physical and biological computations.

Classification of computational problems into complexity classes with respect to the amount of computational resources needed to solve them has proved to be very fruitful. Computational complexity classes have deep structure. An understanding of them allows one to develop powerful tools for algorithm design and analysis. The concepts of resource-bounded reducibility and completeness, presented in this chapter, are among the most useful algorithm design methodologies.

The central task of complexity theory is to search for borderlines between what is and is not feasibly computable. With this task, the influence of complexity theory goes far beyond computing because the search for the limits of what is feasibly computable is the search for the limits of scientific methods, rational reasoning and the knowable.

The development of new paradigms for computing that allow satisfactory solutions to previously unsolvable problems is another of the main aims and outcomes of complexity theory.

Complexity theory has been able to discover several algorithmic problems that are important from both a theoretical and a practical point of view, and to concentrate on their in-depth study. The role of these problems can be compared with the role which some differential equations play in calculus and our ability to create mathematical models for the behaviour of nature.

The key problem of complexity theory, the **P = NP** problem, is simultaneously one of the most basic problems of current science.

As is often the case with science, the negative results of complexity theory, which show that this or that is impossible or infeasible, also have strong positive impacts on, for example, cryptography, secure communication or random number generators (see Chapters 8 and 9). In practice these are among the most useful outcomes of complexity theory.

5.1 Nondeterministic Turing Machines

We have seen in Chapter 3 that nondeterministic finite automata are of great importance for our capability to harness the concept of finite state machines, in spite of the fact that they do not constitute a realistic model of computers. This is even more true on the level of universal computers. Nondeterministic Turing machines play an almost irreplaceable role in developing and exploring the key concepts concerning computational complexity.

A one-tape **nondeterministic Turing machine** (NTM) $\mathcal{M} = \langle \Gamma, Q, q_0, \delta \rangle$ is defined formally in a similar way to a one-tape deterministic Turing machine (DTM or TM), except that instead of a transition

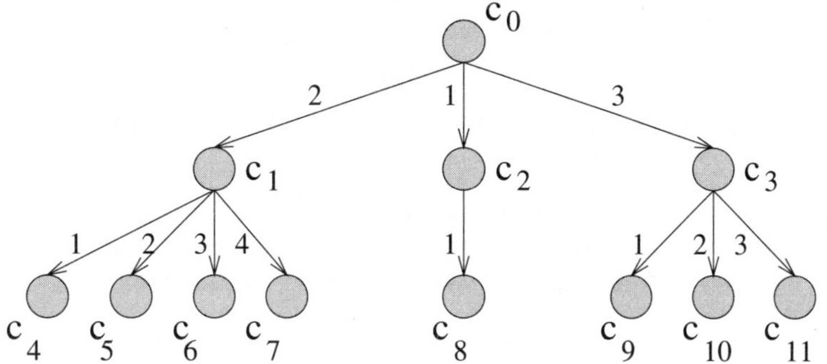

Figure 5.1 Tree of configurations

function we have a transition relation

$$\delta \subset Q \times \Gamma \times (Q \cup H) \times \Gamma \times D, \tag{5.1}$$

where $H = \{HALT, ACCEPT, REJECT\}$ and $D = \{\leftarrow, \downarrow, \rightarrow\}$. As a consequence, a configuration c of NTM $\mathcal{M}$ can have several potential next configurations, and $\mathcal{M}$ can go nondeterministically from c to one of them. We can therefore view the overall computational process of a NTM not as a sequence of configurations, but as a tree of configurations (see Figure 5.1). If we use, for each state and each tape symbol, a fixed numbering $1, 2, \ldots$ of possible transitions, then we can use this numbering to label edges of the configuration tree, as shown in Figure 5.1. Nondeterministic multi-tape TM are defined in a similar way; in what follows the notation NTM is used to denote such TM.

We say that a NTM $\mathcal{M}$ accepts an input w (in time $t(|w|)$ and space $s(|w|)$) if there is at least one path in the configuration tree, with $q_0 w$ being the configuration at the root, which ends in the accepting state (and the path has a length of at most $t(|w|)$, and none of the configurations on this path has a larger length than $s(|w|)$). This can be used to define in a natural way when a NTM computes a relation or a function within certain time and space bounds. For a NTM $\mathcal{M}$ let $L(\mathcal{M})$ be the language accepted by $\mathcal{M}$.

Exercise 5.1.1 *Show that for each NTM $\mathcal{M}$ we can design a NTM $\mathcal{M}'$ that can make at least two moves in each nonterminating configuration, and accepts the same language as $\mathcal{M}$. Moreover, $\mathcal{M}$ accepts an input w in t steps if and only if $\mathcal{M}'$ also does.*

Exercise 5.1.2 *Show that for each NTM $\mathcal{M}$ we can design a NTM $\mathcal{M}'$ that can make exactly two moves in each nonterminating configuration, accepts the same language as $\mathcal{M}$, and there is an integer k such that $\mathcal{M}$ accepts an input w in t steps if and only if $\mathcal{M}'$ accepts w in kt steps.*

Complexity classes for NTM: Denote by $Ntime(t(n))$ ($Nspace(s(n))$) the family of languages accepted by $t(n)$-time bounded ($s(n)$-space bounded) NTM, and denote

$$\mathbf{NP} = \bigcup_{k=0}^{\infty} NTime(n^k), \qquad \mathbf{NPSPACE} = \bigcup_{k=0}^{\infty} NSpace(n^k).$$

A computation of a NTM can be seen as a sequence of transition steps. Some are deterministic, there is only one possibility for the next configuration, whereas others should be seen as the result of a choice or a guess (as to how to proceed to accept the input or to solve the problem). It is exactly this guessing potential of NTM that makes them a useful tool.

Example 5.1.3 *It is easy to design a NTM that decides in $\mathcal{O}(n^2)$ time whether a Boolean formula of length n is satisfiable. Indeed, the machine first goes through the formula and replaces all variables by 0 or 1 in a consistent way – each variable is replaced by the same value over the entire formula. Each time a new variable is encountered, a nondeterministic choice is made as to whether to assign 0 or 1 to this variable. This way the machine chooses an assignment. In the next step the formula is evaluated. Both stages can be done in $\mathcal{O}(n^2)$ time. If the formula is satisfiable, then there is a sequence of correct guesses for the assignment of values to the variables and an accepting path of length $\mathcal{O}(n^2)$ in the configuration tree.*

Exercise 5.1.4 *Describe the behaviour of a NTM that accepts in polynomial time encodings of graphs with a Hamilton cycle.*

We now come to one of the main reasons for dealing with NTM. For many important algorithmic problems not known to be in **P**, it can easily be shown that they are in **NP**. Typically, they are problems for which the only known deterministic algorithms are those making an exhaustive search through all possibilities, but for each such possibility it is easy to verify whether it is correct or not. An NTM just guesses one of these possibilities, and then verifies the correctness of the guess. In addition – and this is another key point – no one has yet shown that **P** $\neq$ **NP**. It is therefore possible, though unlikely, that **P** = **NP**.

As we shall see, and as in the case of finite automata, nondeterminism does not increase essentially the power of Turing machines. It seems, however, that an NTM can be 'much faster'.

Theorem 5.1.5 *If a language L is accepted by a $t(n)$-time bounded NTM, then it is accepted by a $2^{\mathcal{O}(t(n))}$-time bounded DTM.*

Proof: We show how to simulate a $t(n)$-time bounded NTM $\mathcal{M}_{non} = \langle \Gamma, Q, q_0, \delta \rangle$ by a $2^{\mathcal{O}(t(n))}$-time DTM $\mathcal{M}_{det} = \langle \Gamma', Q', q'_0, \delta' \rangle$. Let

$$k = \max_{q \in Q, x \in \Gamma} \{\text{number of transitions for } q \text{ and } x\},$$

and denote by T_w the configuration tree of $\mathcal{M}_{non}$ for the computation with the initial configuration $q_0 w$, and assume that the edges of this tree are labelled by symbols from $\{1, \ldots, k\}$ to specify the transition used (as shown in Figure 5.1).

$\mathcal{M}_{det}$ will simply try to go through all possible computations of $\mathcal{M}_{non}$, in other words, through all possible paths in the configuration tree T_w. Some of these paths may be infinite and therefore $\mathcal{M}_{det}$ cannot use the depth-first search method to traverse the configuration tree. However, the breadth-first search will work fine. This leads to a very simple simulation method. A strict ordering of all words from $\{1, \ldots, k\}^*$ is considered. Consequently, word by word, for each $u \in \{1, \ldots, k\}^*$, the computation along the path labelled by u is simulated (if there is such a path in the configuration tree). If such a computation leads to the accepting state, then $\mathcal{M}_{det}$ accepts. Otherwise $\mathcal{M}_{det}$ goes to the simulation of the computation corresponding to the next word, in the strict ordering of words in $\{1, \ldots, k\}^*$.

This way $\mathcal{M}_{det}$ has to check at most $k^{t(n)}$ paths. Simulation of a single path takes at most $\mathcal{O}(t(n))$ time. Altogether, $\mathcal{M}_{det}$ needs $k^{t(n)}\mathcal{O}(t(n)) = 2^{\mathcal{O}(t(n))}$ time.

Let us now be more technical. The tape of M_{det} will be divided into three tracks. The first will contain only the input word, the second always a word from $\{1,\ldots,k\}^*$ representing the path to be simulated. The third track will be used to do all simulations according to the following simulation algorithm.

1. $\mathcal{M}_{det}$ starts a simulation by generating the word '1' on the second track (as the first nonempty word of the strict ordering of $\{1,\ldots,k\}^*$).
2. $\mathcal{M}_{det}$ simulates on the third track the sequence of configurations specified by the word on the second tape (in the case this word really describes a sequence of computational steps). If $\mathcal{M}_{non}$ reaches the accepting state during this simulation, M_{det} accepts; if not, $\mathcal{M}_{det}$ goes to step 3.
3. $\mathcal{M}_{det}$ changes the word on the second track to the next one in the strict ordering of the words of the set $\{1,\ldots,k\}^*$ and goes to the step 2. □

In a similar way, nondeterministic versions of other models of Turing machines can be simulated by deterministic ones, with at most an exponential increase in time. Moreover, in a similar way we can prove the following:

Exercise 5.1.6 *Show that $NTime(f(n)) \subseteq Space(f(n))$ for any time-constructible function f.*

So far, nobody has been able to come up with a polynomial time simulation of NTM by DTM. Therefore, from the time complexity point of view, nondeterminism seems to have a huge advantage for Turing machines. Interestingly, this is not so with regard to the space.

Theorem 5.1.7 (Savitch's theorem) *$NSpace(s(n)) \subseteq Space(s^2(n))$ for any space-constructible function $s(n) \geq \lg n$.*

Proof: Let $\mathcal{M}$ be a $s(n)$-space bounded NTM and $L = L(\mathcal{M})$. We describe an algorithm that accepts L and can easily be transformed into a $s^2(n)$-space bounded Turing machine accepting L.

Similarly, as in the proof of Lemma 4.3.20, we can show that there is a constant k (which depends only on size of Q and Γ) such that for any input w of size n, $\mathcal{M}$ can be in at most $k^{s(n)}$ configurations, each of which can have length at most $s(n)$. This immediately implies that if $w \in L$, then there is an accepting computation with at most $k^{s(n)} = 2^{s(n)\lg k}$ steps.

The following algorithm, one of the pearls of algorithm design, which uses the divide-and-conquer procedure *test* presented below, recognizes whether $w \in L$. The procedure test, with argument c, c' and i, simply checks whether there is a way to get from a configuration c to c' in 2^i steps.

Algorithm 5.1.8
compute $s(n)$;
for all accepting configurations c_τ such that $|c_\tau| \leq s(n)$
  do if *test*$(q_0w, c_\tau, s(n)\lg k)$ **then** accept

procedure *test*(c, c', i)
if $i = 0 \wedge [(c = c') \vee (c \vdash c')]$ **then return true**
  else for all configurations c'' with $|c''| \leq s(n)$
      do if *test*$(c, c'', i-1) \wedge$ *test*$(c'', c', i-1)$ **then return true**;
return false

With respect to space complexity analysis, each call of the procedure *test* requires $\mathcal{O}(s(n))$ space. The depth of the recursion is $\lg\lceil 2^{s(n)\lg k}\rceil = \mathcal{O}(s(n))$. The total space bound is therefore $\mathcal{O}(s^2(n))$. Moreover, $s(n)$ can be computed in $\mathcal{O}(s(n))$ space, because $s(n)$ is space-constructible. □

Corollary 5.1.9 **PSPACE = NPSPACE.**

The proof of Theorem 5.1.7 uses the reachability method to simulate space-bounded computations. With a slight modification of this method we can show the following:

Exercise 5.1.10 *NSpace*$(f(n)) \subseteq$ *Time*$(\mathcal{O}(1)^{f(n)})$ *for any time-constructible function* $f(n) \geq \lg n$.

Many results shown in Section 4.1 also hold for nondeterministic Turing machines, for example, the speed-up theorem and the compression theorem.

Nondeterministic TM also form a basis for the definition of a variety of other models of computations, for example, for randomized computations. In this, the following normal form of NTM is often of importance.

Exercise 5.1.11 (**Parallel one-tape Turing machines**) *Formally, they are specified as nondeterministic Turing machines: that is, for each state and symbol read by the head a finite number of possible transitions is given. A parallel Turing machine starts to process a given input word with the only one ordinary Turing machine active that has its head on the first symbol of the input. During the computation of the parallel Turing machine, several ordinary Turing machines can work in parallel on the same tape. At every step each currently active ordinary Turing machines reads its tape symbol and performs simultaneously all possible transitions, creating for each transition a new (ordinary) Turing machine that has the state and head position determined by that transition. In this way several (ordinary) Turing machines can simultaneously have their heads over the same cell. If several of them try to write different symbols into the same cell at the same time, the computation is interrupted.*
(a) Show that the number of distinct ordinary Turing machines that can be active on the tape of a parallel Turing machine grows only polynomially with the number of steps.
(b) Design a parallel Turing machine that can recognize palindromes in linear time.

Lemma 5.1.12 *Let a NTM $\mathcal{M}$ accept a language L within the time bound $f(n)$, where f is a time-constructible function. Then there is a NTM $\mathcal{M}'$ that accepts L in time $\mathcal{O}(f(n))$, and all its computations for inputs of size n have the same length. Moreover, we can assume that $\mathcal{M}'$ has exactly two choices to make in each nonterminating configuration.*

Proof: In order to transform $\mathcal{M}$ into a NTM $\mathcal{M}'$ that accepts the same language as $\mathcal{M}$ and for all inputs of size n has computations of the same length $\mathcal{O}(f(n))$, we proceed as follows. $\mathcal{M}'$ uses first, on an input w of size n, a TM $\mathcal{M}_f$ that in time $f(n)$ produces a 'yardstick' of length exactly $f(|w|)$ (we are here making use of the time-constructibility of f). After $\mathcal{M}_f$ finishes its job, $\mathcal{M}'$ starts to simulate $\mathcal{M}$, using the 'yardstick' to design an alarm clock. $\mathcal{M}'$ advances its pointer in the 'yardstick' each time $\mathcal{M}'$

ends its simulation of a step of $\mathcal{M}$, and halts if and only if $\mathcal{M}'$ comes to the end of the 'yardstick', that is, after exactly $f(x)$ steps. Should $\mathcal{M}$ finish sooner, $\mathcal{M}'$ keeps going, making dummy moves, until $\mathcal{M}'$ comes to the end of the yardstick, and then accepts or rejects as $\mathcal{M}$ did. For the rest of the proof we make use of the results of Exercises 5.1.1 and 5.1.2.

5.2 Complexity Classes, Hierarchies and Trade-offs

The quantity of computational resources needed to solve a problem is clearly of general importance. This is especially so for time in such real-time applications as spacecraft and plane control, surgery support systems and banking systems. It is therefore of prime practical and theoretical interest to classify computational problems with respect to the resources needed to solve them. By limiting the overall resources, the range of solvable problems gets narrower. This way we arrive at various complexity classes. In addition to the complexity classes that have been introduced already:

$$\mathbf{P} = \bigcup_{k=0}^{\infty} Time(n^k), \qquad \mathbf{NP} = \bigcup_{k=0}^{\infty} NTime(n^k),$$

$$\mathbf{PSPACE} = \bigcup_{k=0}^{\infty} Space(n^k), \qquad \mathbf{NPSPACE} = \bigcup_{k=0}^{\infty} NSpace(n^k),$$

there are four others which play a major role in complexity theory. The first two deal with logarithmic space complexity:

$$\mathbf{L} = \mathbf{LOGSPACE} = \bigcup_{k=1}^{\infty} DSpace(k \lg n), \qquad \mathbf{NL} = \mathbf{NLOGSPACE} = \bigcup_{k=1}^{\infty} NSpace(k \lg n).$$

$\mathbf{L} \subseteq \mathbf{NL} \subseteq \mathbf{P}$ are the basic inclusions between these new classes and the class **P**. The first is trivially true, whereas the second follows from Exercise 5.1.10. These inclusions imply that in order to show that a problem is solvable in polynomial time, it is enough to show that the problem can be solved using only logarithmic space. Sometimes this is easier.

The last two main complexity classes deal with exponential time bounds:

$$\mathbf{EXP} = \bigcup_{k=0}^{\infty} Time(2^{n^k}), \qquad \mathbf{NEXP} = \bigcup_{k=0}^{\infty} NTime(2^{n^k}).$$

As we shall see, all these classes represent certain limits of what can be considered as feasible in computation.

Some of the complexity classes are closed under complementation: for example, **P**, **PSPACE** and **EXP**. However, this does not seem to be true for the classes **NP** and **NEXP**. Also of importance are the classes

co-NP and **co-NEXP**,

which contain complements of languages in **NP** and **NEXP**, respectively.

With space complexity classes the situation is different, due to the following result.

Theorem 5.2.1 (Immerman–Szelepcsényi's theorem) *If* $f(n) \geq \lg n$, *then* $Nspace(f(n)) = co\text{-}NSpace(f(n))$.

Later we shall deal with other complexity classes that are so important that they also have special names. However, only some of the complexity classes have broadly accepted names and special notation. As the following deep and very technical result shows, there are infinitely many different complexity classes. In addition, the following theorem shows that even a very small increase in bounds on time and space resources provides an enlargement of complexity classes.

Theorem 5.2.2 (Hierarchy theorem) *(1) If f_1 and f_2 are time-constructible functions, then*

$$\liminf_{n\to\infty}\frac{f_1(n)\lg f_1(n)}{f_2(n)}=0 \quad\Longrightarrow\quad Time(f_1(n))\subsetneq Time(f_2(n));$$
$$\liminf_{n\to\infty}\frac{f_1(n)}{f_2(n)}=0 \quad\Longrightarrow\quad NTime(f_1(n))\subsetneq NTime(f_2(n)).$$

(2) If $f_2(n)\geq f_1(n)\geq \lg n$ are space-constructible functions, then

$$\liminf_{n\to\infty}\frac{f_1(n)}{f_2(n)}=0\Longrightarrow Space(f_1(n))\subsetneq Space(f_2(n)).$$ [1]

The following relations among the main complexity classes are a consequence of the results stated in Exercises 5.1.6 and 5.1.10 and the obvious fact that $Time(f(n))\subseteq NTime(f(n))$ and $Space(S(n))\subseteq Nspace(s(n))$ for any f:

$$\mathbf{L}\subsetneq\mathbf{NL}\subseteq\mathbf{P}\subseteq\mathbf{NP}\subseteq\mathbf{PSPACE}=\mathbf{NPSPACE}\subseteq\mathbf{EXP}\subseteq\mathbf{NEXP}. \tag{5.2}$$

It follows from Theorem 5.2.2 that $\mathbf{L}\subsetneq\mathbf{PSPACE}$, $\mathbf{P}\subsetneq\mathbf{EXP}$, $\mathbf{NP}\subsetneq\mathbf{NEXP}$. We therefore know for sure that some of the inclusions in (5.2) are proper – perhaps all of them. However, no one has been able to show which. One of the main tasks of foundations of computing is to solve this puzzle.

If f is a time-constructible function and $f(n)/\lg f(n)=\Omega(n)$, then the obvious relation $Time(f(n))\subseteq Space(f(n))$ can be strengthened to show that space is strictly more powerful than time. Indeed, it holds that

$$Time(f(n))\subseteq Space\left(\frac{f(n)}{\lg f(n)}\right).$$

It is also interesting to observe that the requirement that f is time-constructible is important in Theorem 5.2.2. Without this restriction we have the following result.

Theorem 5.2.3 (Gap theorem) *To every recursive function $\phi(n)>n$, there is a recursive function $f(n)$ such that $Time(\phi(f(n)))=Time(f(n))$.*

For example, there is a recursive function $f(n)$ such that $Time(2^{2^{f(n)}})=Time(f(n))$.

Finally, we present a result indicating that our naïve belief in the existence of the best programs is wrong. Indeed, if a language $L\in Time(t_1(n))-Time(t_2(n))$, then we say that $t_1(n)$ is the upper bound and $t_2(n)$ the lower bound on the time complexity of L on MTM. At this point it may seem that we can define the time complexity of a language (algorithmic problem) L as the time complexity of the asymptotically optimal MTM (algorithm) recognizing L. Surprisingly, this is not the way to go, because there are languages (algorithmic problems) with no best MTM (algorithms). This fact is more precisely formulated in the following weak version of the speed-up theorem.

Theorem 5.2.4 (Blum's speed-up theorem) *There exists a recursive language L such that for any MTM $\mathcal{M}$ accepting L there exists another MTM $\mathcal{M}'$ for L such that $Time_{\mathcal{M}'}(n)\leq\lg(Time_{\mathcal{M}}(n))$ for almost all n.*

[1] On the other hand, the class $Space(\mathcal{O}(1))$ is exactly the class of regular languages, and the class $Space(s(n))$ with $s(n)=o(\lg n)$ contains only regular languages.

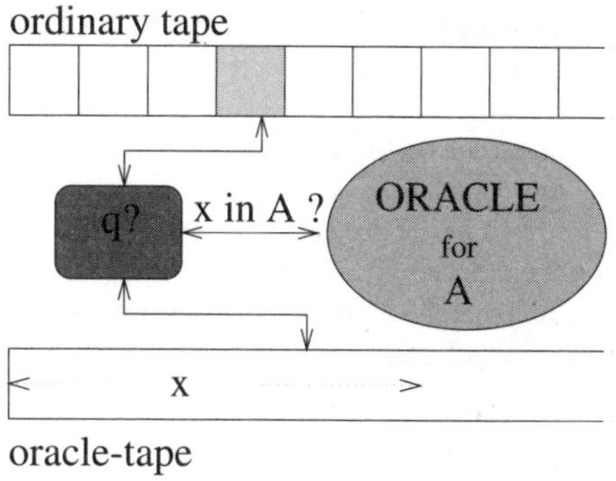

Figure 5.2 An oracle Turing machine

5.3 Reductions and Complete Problems

One of the main tasks and contributions of theory in general is to localize the key problems to which other problems can be reduced 'easily', and then to investigate in depth these key problems and reduction methods. This approach has turned out to be extraordinarily successful in the area of algorithmic problems.

The study of the so-called complete problems for the main complexity classes and algorithmic resource-bounded reductions has brought deep insights into the nature of computing and revealed surprisingly neat structures in the space of algorithmic problems and unexpected relations between algorithmic problems that seemingly have nothing in common. In this way the study of computational complexity uncovered new unifying principles for different areas of science and technology. The results of complexity theory for algorithmic reductions also represent a powerful methodology for designing algorithms for new algorithmic problems by making use of algorithms for already solved problems.

The basic tools are time- and space-bounded reductions of one algorithmic problem to another. On the most abstract level this idea is formalized through the concept of oracle Turing machines.

A (one-tape) **oracle Turing machine** $\mathcal{M}$ with oracle-tape alphabet Δ and a language $A \subseteq \Delta^*$ as **oracle** is actually a Turing machine with two tapes, an ordinary read–write tape and a special read–write **oracle-tape** (see Figure 5.2). In addition, $\mathcal{M}$ has three special states, say $q?$, q^+ and q^-, such that whenever $\mathcal{M}$ comes to the state $q?$, then the next state is either q^+ or q^-, depending on whether the content x of the oracle-tape at that moment is or is not in A. In other words, when $\mathcal{M}$ gets into the 'query' state $q?$, this can be seen as $\mathcal{M}$ asking the oracle about the membership of the word x, written on the oracle-tape, in A. In addition, and this is crucial, it is assumed that the oracle's answer is 'free' and immediate (because the oracle is supposed to be all-powerful – as oracles should be). In other words, a transition from the state $q?$ to one of the states q^+ or q^- entails one step, as for all other transitions.

Denote by $\mathcal{M}^A$ an oracle Turing machine $\mathcal{M}$ with the oracle A – the same TM can be connected with different oracles – and let $L(\mathcal{M}^A)$ denote the language accepted by such an oracle machine with the oracle A.

To see how this concept can be utilized, let us assume that there is an oracle Turing machine $\mathcal{M}^A$ that can solve in polynomial time an algorithmic problem $\mathcal{P}$. If the oracle A is then replaced by a polynomial time algorithm to decide membership for A, we get a polynomial time algorithm for accepting $L(\mathcal{M}^A)$.

Example 5.3.1 *We describe the behaviour of an oracle TM $\mathcal{M}^A$ with oracle $A = \{a^n b^n c^n \mid n \geq 1\}$ that recognizes the language $L = \{0^i 1^i 0^i 1^j 0^j 1^j 0 \mid i,j \geq 1\}$. $\mathcal{M}^A$ starts by reading the first group of 0s in the input word, and for each 0 writes the symbol a on the oracle tape, then the symbol b for each 1 in the first group of 1s and the symbol c for each 0 in the second group of 0s. After encountering the first 1 in the second group of 1s, the machine asks the oracle whether the string written on the oracle tape is in A. If not, the machine rejects the input. If yes, the machine empties the oracle tape and then proceeds by writing on it an a for each 1 in the second group of 1s, then a b for each 0 in the third group of 0s and, finally, a c for each 1 in the third group of 1s. After encountering the next 0, the machine again asks the oracle whether the content of its tape is in A. If not, the machine rejects it. If yes, $\mathcal{M}^A$ checks to see if there are any additional input symbols and if not accepts.*

> **Exercise 5.3.2** *Design in detail a simple oracle Turing machine with oracle $A = \{1^i \mid i \text{ is prime}\}$ to accept the language $L = \{a^i b^j c^k \mid i+j \text{ and } i+k \text{ are primes}\}$.*

The concept of the oracle Turing machine is the basis for our most general definition of time-bounded reducibilities.

Definition 5.3.3 *A language L_1 is* **polynomial time Turing reducible** *to the language L_2 – in short, $L_1 \leq_p^T L_2$ – if there is a polynomial time bounded oracle Turing machine $\mathcal{M}^{L_2}$ that accepts L_1.*

Very often we do not need the whole power of Turing reducibility, which puts no restriction on how often the oracle can be consulted during a computation. The following weaker concept of reducibility corresponds to the case when the oracle is consulted only once, at the very end of a reduction.

Definition 5.3.4 *A language $L_1 \subseteq \Sigma_1^*$ is* **polynomial time (many-to-one) reducible** *to the language $L_2 \subseteq \Sigma_2^*$ – in short, $L_1 \leq_p^m L_2$ – if there is a polynomial time computable function $f : \Sigma_1^* \rightarrow \Sigma_2^*$ such that, if $x \in \Sigma_1^*$, then*

$$x \in L_1 \Longleftrightarrow f(x) \in L_2. \tag{5.3}$$

A language L_1 is **logspace reducible** *to L_2 – in short, $L_1 \leq_{lg} L_2$ – if there is a logarithmic space computable (on an off-line MTM) function f such that* (5.3) *holds.*

> **Exercise 5.3.5** *The concept of polynomial time reduction was defined only for languages, but it is often used in a more general sense. Show, for example, that the problem of computing the transitive closure of a Boolean matrix is both polynomial time and logarithmic space reducible in a natural way to the problem of multiplication of two Boolean matrices.*

The following result is crucial for a broader usefulness of all three concepts of reducibility.[2]

Lemma 5.3.6 *Reducibilities $\leq_p^T$, $\leq_p^m$ and $\leq_{lg}$ are transitive.*

---

[2]It can be shown that all three of the above concepts of reducibilities are different in the sense that for any pair of them there is a pair of languages L_1 and L_2 such that L_1 is reducible to L_2 with respect to one of these reducibilities but not with respect to the second one.

Proof: Only the case of logspace reducibility is nontrivial. Let us first point out where the difficulties lie. If $x \in L_1 \Longleftrightarrow f_1(x) \in L_2$ and $y \in L_2 \Longleftrightarrow f_2(y) \in L_3$, where f_1 and f_2 are computable in logarithmic space on an off-line MTM, then clearly $x \in L_1 \Longleftrightarrow f_2(f_1(x)) \in L_3$. But is $f_2(f_1(x))$ $(\lg n)$-space computable on an off-line MTM with $n = |x|$? It may happen that to store $f_1(x)$ we need more than $(\lg n)$-space. (Notice that in order to compute $f_1(x)$ from x we are using in the first reduction an off-line MTM the output of which is not counted in the overall space estimation.) This implies that we cannot simply connect sequentially two $(\lg n)$-space bounded off-line MTM, one to compute $f_1(x)$ from x, the second to compute $f_2(f_1(x))$ from $f_1(x)$, and expect automatically to get a $(\lg n)$-space bounded MTM. The trick to use is as follows.

Let $\mathcal{M}_1$ be a $(\lg n)$-space bounded off-line Turing machine for computing f_1 and $\mathcal{M}_2$ a $(\lg n)$-space bounded off-line Turing machine for computing f_2. We design a $(\lg n)$-space bounded off-line Turing machine $\mathcal{M}$ to compute $f_2(f_1(x))$ that works as follows. $\mathcal{M}$ has a counter C that is used to store information about which bit of $f_1(x)$ the machine $\mathcal{M}_2$ needs as the next one. $\mathcal{M}$ starts by simulating $\mathcal{M}_2$ on x. Each time $\mathcal{M}_2$ needs a bit of $f_1(x)$, say the ith bit, then $\mathcal{M}$ writes the integer i into C and then simulates $\mathcal{M}_1$ on x. However, it does not produce the whole output of $\mathcal{M}_1$, only a single bit: namely, the ith bit. This way $\mathcal{M}_2$ needs at most $(\lg |f_1(x)|)$-space to write i. Since f_1 is $(\lg n)$-space computable, $|f_1(x)| \leq |x|^k$ must hold for some k. Therefore, $\lg |f_1(n)| = \mathcal{O}(\lg n)$. □

We are now ready to introduce two additional concepts concerning resource-bounded reducibilities that play a central role in complexity theory.

Definition 5.3.7 *Let $\mathcal{L}$ be a family of languages. A language L_0 is called* **hard** *for $\mathcal{L}$, with respect to a reducibility $\mathcal{R}$, if each language $L \in \mathcal{L}$ is $\mathcal{R}$-reducible to L_0. L_0 is* **complete** *for $\mathcal{L}$, with respect to a reducibility $\mathcal{R}$, if (1) L_0 is in $\mathcal{L}$; (2) L_0 is hard for $\mathcal{L}$, with respect to $\mathcal{R}$.*

For the main complexity classes the following types of completenesses are usually considered, (with respect to many-to-one time reducibilities) and the following notation is used:

NLOGSPACE-completeness	–	completeness for **NLOGSPACE** w.r.t. logspace reducib.
P-completeness	–	completeness for **P** w.r.t. logspace reducib.
NP-completeness	–	completeness for **NP** w.r.t. polynomial time reducib.
PSPACE-completeness	–	completeness for **PSPACE** w.r.t. polynom. time reducib.
NEXP-completeness	–	completeness for **NEXP** w.r.t. exponential time reducib.

Directly from Definition 5.3.7 we get

Lemma 5.3.8 *If $L_1 \leq_p^m L_2$, and $L_3 \leq_{\lg} L_4$, then it holds that:*[3]

$$\begin{aligned}
L_4 \in \mathbf{NLOGSPACE} &\implies L_3 \in \mathbf{NLOGSPACE},\\
L_2 \in \mathbf{P} &\implies L_1 \in \mathbf{P},\\
L_2 \in \mathbf{NP} &\implies L_1 \in \mathbf{NP},\\
L_2 \in \mathbf{PSPACE} &\implies L_1 \in \mathbf{PSPACE},\\
L_2 \in \mathbf{EXP} &\implies L_1 \in \mathbf{EXP}.
\end{aligned}$$

As a corollary of Lemma 5.3.8, we have the following theorem.

Theorem 5.3.9 **P = NP** *if and only if there is an* **NP**-*complete problem that is in* **P**. *Similarly,* **EXP = NEXP** *if and only if there is an* **NEXP**-*complete problem that is in* **EXP**.

[3]Two other concepts of **P**-completeness are dealt with in Section 5.10.

5.4 NP-complete Problems

The concept of **NP**-completeness is of special theoretical and practical importance. Indeed, it is one of the most important concepts in the theory and practice of computing. We therefore deal with it in detail.

Proof that a problem is **NP**-complete has three consequences. First, it implies that currently no polynomial time algorithm is known to solve the problem – only algorithms that essentially perform a complete search of exponentially many possibilities. This means that an **NP**-complete problem cannot be solved in practice for inputs of larger size. This is bad news because many practically important algorithmic problems are **NP**-complete. Second, and this is better news, **NP**-completeness of a problem implies that there is still a chance, though it is very very small, that for such a problem a polynomial time algorithm will be constructed. Third, and this is the best news, if we were to discover a polynomial time algorithm for one **NP**-complete problem, we could easily design polynomial time algorithms for all **NP**-complete problems.

There are two basic methods for proving **NP**-completeness of a language L:

Direct method. One shows first that L is in **NP**, which is generally easy, and then that each language in **NP** can be reduced to L in polynomial time. This means showing that for any polynomial time bounded NTM $\mathcal{M}$ and any input x for $\mathcal{M}$ we can, in polynomial time, construct a string $y_{\mathcal{M},x}$ such that $x \in L(\mathcal{M})$ if and only if $y_{\mathcal{M},x} \in L$.

Reduction method. One shows that $L \in$ **NP** and $L' \leq_p^m L$ for an **NP**-complete language L'. **NP**-completeness of L then follows from the transitivity of the polynomial time reducibility.

5.4.1 Direct Proofs of NP-completeness

Direct proofs of **NP**-completeness for three problems will now be described. All these problems have the property that several of their modifications have been used to show the existence of complete problems for other complexity classes as well. In addition, these problems have been used to show **NP**-completeness of other problems using the reduction method.

Bounded halting problem

In our first **NP**-completeness result we assume (see Section 4.1) that a fixed Gödel numbering $\langle\mathcal{M}\rangle$ of nondeterministic Turing machines $\mathcal{M}$ and $\langle w\rangle$ of their inputs w is given.

Theorem 5.4.1 (Time-bounded version of the halting problem) *The language*

$$L^*_{halt} = \{\langle\mathcal{M}\rangle\langle w\rangle\#^t \mid \mathcal{M} \text{ is a one-tape one-head NTM that accepts } w \text{ in at most } t \text{ steps}\}$$

is **NP**-*complete (# represents a marker).*

Proof: We design a NTM $\mathcal{M}_0$ that, for an input w', first checks whether $w' = \langle\mathcal{M}\rangle\langle w\rangle\#^t$ for some NTM $\mathcal{M}$ and input w of $\mathcal{M}$. If not, $\mathcal{M}_0$ rejects w'. If yes, $\mathcal{M}_0$ generates, nondeterministically, the string

$$\langle\mathcal{M}\rangle\langle w\rangle\#^t c_0\$c_1\$\ldots\$c_{t'},$$

where $t' \leq t$. $\mathcal{M}'$ then checks whether c_0 is the code of the initial configuration of $\mathcal{M}$ for input w, whether $c_{t'}$ is the code of a terminating configuration of $\mathcal{M}$, and whether, for all $1 \leq i \leq t'$, c_i is the code of a configuration of $\mathcal{M}$ that can be obtained from the configuration c_{i-1} by one step of $\mathcal{M}$. If all these conditions are satisfied, $\mathcal{M}'$ accepts; otherwise it rejects the input.

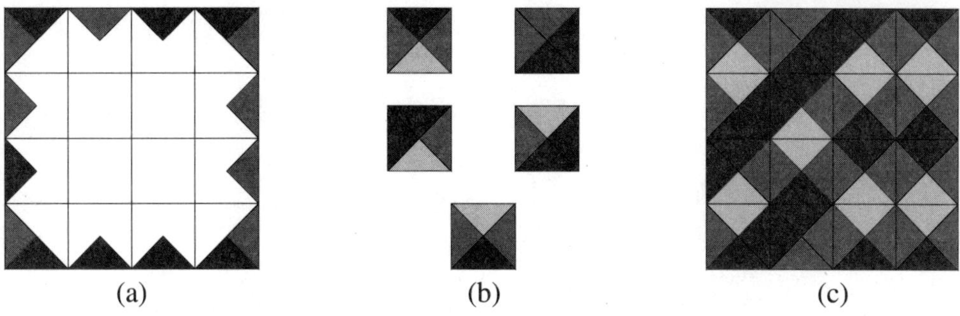

Figure 5.3 Bounded tiling

If we denote $n = |\langle\mathcal{M}\rangle\langle w\rangle\#^t|$, then $\mathcal{M}_0$ accepts L^*_{halt} in $\mathcal{O}(n^3)$ time steps, because $t \leq n$, and $\mathcal{M}_0$ needs at most $\mathcal{O}(n^2)$ time to generate a new c_i. Thus, $L^*_{halt} \in \mathbf{NP}$.

Now let $L \in \mathbf{NP}$; that is, there is a NTM $\mathcal{M}_L$ and a polynomial p_L such that $\mathcal{M}_L$ accepts L in time $p_L(n)$. Let $L \subset \Gamma^*$ and τ_L be a function defined on Γ^* such that $\tau_L(w) = \langle\mathcal{M}_L\rangle\langle w\rangle\#^{p_L(|w|)}$. Since p_L is a polynomial, $\tau_L(w)$ can be computed in polynomial time. Moreover, $w \in L$ if and only if $\tau_L(w) \in L^*_{halt}$. Thus, $L \leq_p^m L^*_{halt}$. □

Bounded tiling problem

Tiling of a plane or other geometrical objects by various types of tiles is one of the exciting, deep and applied problems discussed in more detail in Section 6.4. Here we deal with a special bounded version of the tiling problem.

We consider tiling an $n \times n$ quadratic grid G, with the outer sides of the boundary cells (1×1 squares, or unit squares) coloured from a set of colours C (see Figure 5.3a) and a finite set T of 1×1 tiles, also called Wang tiles (see Figure 5.3b), the sides of which are also coloured from C. The problem is to decide whether there is such a tiling of G, with tiles from T, that satisfies the following two conditions.

Boundary consistency condition: The colours of the outer sides of the boundary tiles match the colours of the boundary cells of G.

Adjacency condition: The colours of adjacent sides of any two neighbouring tiles are the same.

An important restriction is that neither rotation nor reflection of tiles is allowed. However, an infinite number of copies of tiles from T are available.

We show now how to associate a bounded tiling problem with a Turing machine computation. In doing so we assume that a NTM $\mathcal{M}$ has the following properties.

1. $\mathcal{M}$ uses only one-way infinite tape (see Section 4.1).

2. $\mathcal{M}$ has a unique accepting (rejecting) configuration with the empty tape and the state ACCEPT (REJECT).

3. In no state can $\mathcal{M}$ move both to the left and to the right. (In other words, there is no state q with transitions $qaq'b \leftarrow$ and $qcq''d \rightarrow$.)

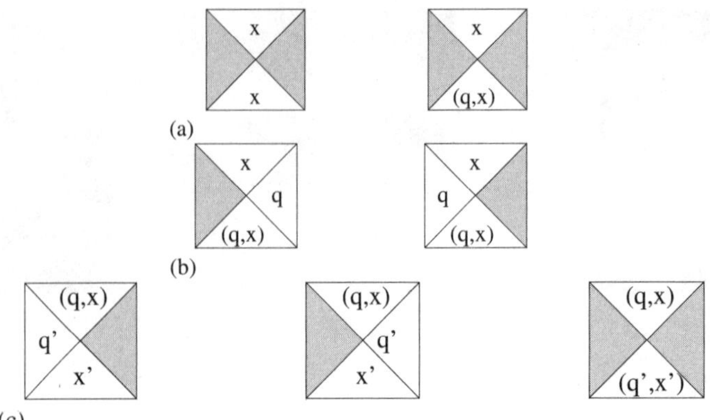

Figure 5.4 Tiles designed to simulate a TM

It is easy to show that each NTM $\mathcal{M}$ can be transformed into a NTM $\mathcal{M}'$ that satisfies these three conditions, accepts the same language as $\mathcal{M}$, and requires only a linear time overhead compared to $\mathcal{M}$.

Let $\mathcal{M} = \langle \Gamma, Q, q_0, \delta \rangle$ be a NTM satisfying the three conditions defined above. We describe a set of tiles $T_{\mathcal{M}}$ with the following properties.

1. Each configuration c of $\mathcal{M}$ can be encoded by a row of tiles from $T_{\mathcal{M}}$ that satisfies the adjacency condition. (Such a sequence of tiles can be seen as tiling a horizontal strip of height 1.)

2. Each extension of such a row tiling of a configuration c to a consistent tiling of the row below encodes a configuration obtained from c by one step of $\mathcal{M}$.

Construction: Colours $C = \Gamma \cup Q \cup (Q \times \Gamma) \cup \{\sqcup\}$. Tiles of T_M are designed as follows. For each $x \in \Gamma, q \in Q$, there are tiles as shown in Figure 5.4a, where shading stands for the symbol $\sqcup$.

The first of these tiles encodes a tape cell that contains the symbol x for the case that the head is not on that cell. The second tile encodes a cell with x in it and with the head on that cell and with the finite state control in the state q. Moreover, for each $x \in \Gamma$ and $q \in Q$ there is exactly one of the tiles shown in Figure 5.4b, depending on whether $\mathcal{M}$ moves, in the state q, only to the left or only to the right. Finally, to each of the transitions

$$(q,x,q',x',\leftarrow) \qquad (q,x,q',x',\rightarrow) \qquad (q,x,q',x',\downarrow)$$

corresponds one of the tiles shown in Figure 5.4c.

For example, the encoding of the configuration $aqbcdefgh$ and of the next three configurations obtained by the transitions

$$(q,b,q',b',\rightarrow), \qquad (q',c,q'',c',\rightarrow), \qquad (q'',d,q''',d',\downarrow),$$

has the form shown in Figure 5.5.

Theorem 5.4.2 *The bounded tiling problem (BTP) is* **NP***-complete.*

Proof: BTP is clearly in **NP** – one just guesses a tiling and verifies whether boundary consistency and adjacency conditions are satisfied.

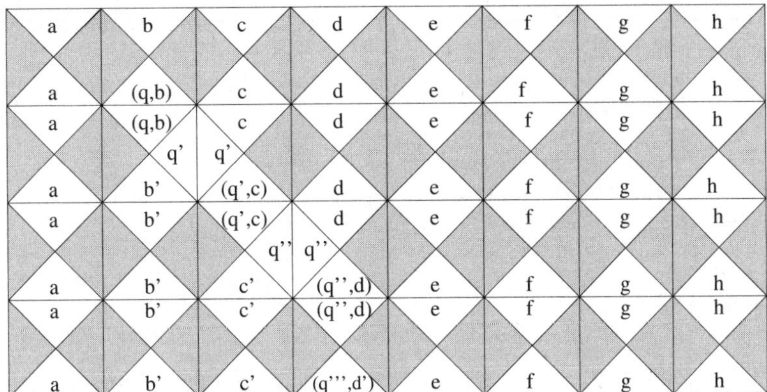

Figure 5.5 Tiling simulating a computation

Now let $L \in \mathbf{NP}$ and $\mathcal{M}$ be a NTM in the normal form defined above that accepts L in time cn^k for some constant c. Finally, let w be an input word of $\mathcal{M}$. We show how to design, in polynomial time, an instance of BTP, denoted $\text{BTP}_{\mathcal{M},w}$, such that $\mathcal{M}$ accepts w in time $c|w|^k$ if and only if $\text{BTP}_{\mathcal{M},w}$ has a solution. Once this is shown, the theorem is proved. Let $T_{\mathcal{M}}$ be the set of tiles corresponding to $\mathcal{M}$ and $G_{\mathcal{M},w}$ be the $N \times N$ grid, where $N = c|w|^k$, the sides of which are coloured as follows. In the top row there are colours determined by the word $q_0 w \sqcup^{N-|w|}$ – that is, by the initial configuration extended by blanks. The colours of the sides of the last row are determined by the encoding of the only accepting configuration. Left and right sides of $G_{\mathcal{M},w}$ are coloured by blanks (depicted in the figures by shaded areas). Clearly, $\mathcal{M}$ accepts w in time $c|w|^k$ if and only if there is a tiling of $G_{\mathcal{M},w}$ with tiles from $T_{\mathcal{M}}$. □

Satisfiability of Boolean formulas

Historically, the first known **NP**-complete problem was the satisfiability problem for Boolean formulas, due to S. A. Cook (1971). Since then, a number of variants of the satisfiability problem have turned out to play an important role in complexity theory.

Each Boolean formula $\mathcal{F}$ can be encoded in a natural way by a binary word. If $\mathcal{F}$ has length n and m variables, one needs for encoding of formula $\mathcal{F}$ $\mathcal{O}(n\lceil \lg m \rceil)$ bits. The set of all encodings of all satisfiable Boolean formulas in binary words will be denoted SAT. Formally, we show that SAT is an **NP**-complete language. Less formally, this result is stated as follows:

Theorem 5.4.3 (Cook's theorem) *The satisfiability problem for Boolean formulas is* **NP**-*complete.*

Proof: It is easy to see that SAT is in **NP**. One first checks whether a given input string is an encoding of a Boolean formula, then guesses a satisfying assignment and evaluates the formula. This can be done in polynomial time (and actually in linear time on a two-tape TM, because the set of Boolean formulas constitutes a deterministic context-free language – see Section 7.3).

Now let $L \in \mathbf{NP}$ and $\mathcal{M}$ be a one-tape NTM that accepts L in a time bounded by a polynomial p. We show how to design in polynomial time, given an input w for $\mathcal{M}$, a Boolean formula $\mathcal{F}_{\mathcal{M},w}$ that is satisfiable if and only if $\mathcal{M}$ accepts w.

Let $\mathcal{M} = \langle \Gamma, Q, q_0, \delta \rangle$, $Q = \{q_0, \ldots, q_s\}$, where $q_{s-2} = HALT$, $q_{s-1} = ACCEPT$, $q_s = REJECT$ and $\Gamma = \{\gamma_1, \ldots, \gamma_m\}$ with $\gamma_1 = \sqcup$. If $\mathcal{M}$ accepts w, then $\mathcal{M}$ makes on the input w, with $|w| = n$, at most

$p(n)$ steps, and the length of any configuration is at most $p(n)$. (We are assuming that $\mathcal{M}$ has one-way infinite tape and an idling termination.)

In order to describe $\mathcal{F}_{M,w}$ – in short, F' – we use the following variables (which are supposed to have the value 1 if the attached condition is satisfied):

$C(i,j,t)$	–	ith cell contains the symbol γ_j at time t,
$S(r,t)$	–	$\mathcal{M}$ is in state q_r at time t,
$H(i,t)$	–	the head of $\mathcal{M}$ stays on the ith cell at time t,

for $1 \le i \le p(n)$, $1 \le j \le m$, $0 \le t \le p(n)$, $0 \le r \le s$. The total number of variables is: $\mathcal{O}(p^2(n))$. The formula F' will have the form

$$F' = A \wedge B \wedge C \wedge D \wedge E \wedge F \wedge G,$$

where $A, \ldots, G$ are Boolean formulas that describe $\mathcal{M}$ and its computation on the input w. In order to shorten the descriptions of these formulas, we use the predicate

$$\bigoplus(a_1, \ldots, a_T) = (a_1 \vee a_2 \vee \cdots \vee a_T) \bigwedge_{i \neq j} (\neg a_i \vee \neg a_j)\,,$$

which has the value 1 if and only if $a_i = 1$ for exactly one i. The length of this formula is $\mathcal{O}(T^2)$.

Descriptions of subformulas are as follows:

1. $A = A_1 \wedge A_2 \wedge \cdots \wedge A_{p(n)}$,
   $A_t = \bigoplus(H(1,t), H(2,t), \ldots, H(p(n),t)), 0 \le t \le p(n)$;
   that is, $A_t = 1$ if and only if, at time t, the head of $\mathcal{M}$ stays on exactly one of the cells.

2. $B = \bigwedge_{0 \le t \le p(n),\, 0 \le i \le p(n)} B(i,t)$ with $B(i,t) = \bigoplus(C(i,1,t), \ldots, C(i,m,t))$;
   that is, $B(i,t) = 1$ if and only if the ith cell contains exactly one symbol at the time t.

3. $C = \bigwedge_{0 \le t \le p(n)} C_t$ with $C_t = \bigoplus(S(0,t), \ldots, S(s,t))$;
   that is, $C = 1$ if and only if M is in exactly one state at each moment.

4. $D = \bigwedge_{0 \le i,\, t \le p(n),\, 1 \le j \le m} [(C(i,j,t) \equiv C(i,j,t+1)) \vee H(i,t)]$;
   that is, $D = 1$ if and only if, at each moment, at most one cell changes its contents.

5. $E = \bigwedge_{0 \le i,\, t \le p(n),\, 0 \le j \le m,\, 0 \le k \le s} E_{ijkt}$ and $E_{ijkt} = \neg C(i,j,t) \vee \neg S(k,t) \vee \neg H(i,t) \vee$
   $$\bigvee_l [C(i,j_l,t+1) \wedge S(k_l,t+1) \wedge H(i+r_l,t+1)];$$

that is, $E = 1$ if and only if each next configuration is obtained from the previous one by a valid transition of $\mathcal{M}$. In the formula E_{ijkt}, l runs through all possible transitions of $\mathcal{M}$ for the case that $\mathcal{M}$ is in the state q_k and the head reads x_j. It is assumed here that an lth transition has the form $(q_k, x_j, q_{k_l}, x_{j_l}, r_l)$, where $r_l \in \{-1, 0, 1\}$, depending on the direction the head moves.

6. $F = S(0,0) \wedge H(1,0) \wedge \bigwedge_{0 \leq i \leq n} C(i, j_i, 0) \wedge \bigwedge_{n < i \leq p(n)} C(i, 1, 0)$,

   where $w = x_{j_1}, \ldots, x_{j_n}$, and $F = 1$ if and only if at time $t = 0$ $\mathcal{M}$ is in the state q_0 and the tape contains w.

7. $G = S(s-1, p(n))$;

   that is, $G = 1$ if and only if M comes finally into the accepting state.

The overall length of the Boolean formula F' is therefore $\mathcal{O}(p^3(n))$. It is now easy to verify that F' is satisfiable if and only if $\mathcal{M}$ accepts w. □

5.4.2 Reduction Method to Prove NP-completeness

The **NP**-completeness of many problems can been shown by a chain of reductions starting with the satisfiability problem.

Theorem 5.4.4 *The language* CNFF $= \{w \mid w$ *is a satisfiable Boolean formula in CNF*$\}$ *is* **NP**-*complete.*

Proof: Deciding if a formula is in the conjunctive normal form requires only polynomial time. Since SAT $\in$ **NP**, we have immediately that CNFF $\in$ **NP**. To show **NP**-completeness of CNFF, it is now enough to show that SAT $\leq_p^m$ CNFF, that is, that there is a polynomial time algorithm to reduce a Boolean formula F to a Boolean formula F' in CNF such that F is satisfiable if and only if F' is. (Observe that we do not require that formulas F and F' are equivalent.)

To design an equivalent Boolean formula in CNF we cannot use the method described in Section 2.3.2, because this method can increase the size of a formula exponentially. However, we can use the following polynomial time transformation.

Using de Morgan's laws we can shift all negations directly to the variables. In this way we get a formula with literals and conjunctions and disjunctions as the only operations. Shifting all negations can be done easily in linear time, by one pass through the formula. One has only to keep track of the depth of the subformulas with respect to negation. The resulting formula will be at most twice as long as the original one.

In order to transform the resulting Boolean formula into a conjunction of clauses, the following trick can be used. If $F = F_1 \vee F_2$ and both F_1 and F_2 are already in CNF, then we choose a new variable y that does not occur in the formulas F_1 and F_2, and replace F with the formula $F' = (F_1 \vee y) \wedge (F_2 \vee \overline{y})$. Clearly, F is satisfiable if and only if F' is. If now

$$F_i = G_1 \wedge \cdots \wedge G_k$$

with clauses G_j, $1 \leq j \leq k$, then

$$F_i \vee y \equiv (G_1 \vee y) \wedge \cdots \wedge (G_k \vee y),$$

and $G_i \vee y$ are again clauses. If we continue in this way, and the original formula is of size n, then the above construction increases its size at most by n, and the whole reduction can be performed in $\mathcal{O}(n^2)$ steps. □

Theorem 5.4.5 *The language* 3-CNFF = $\{w \mid w$ *is a Boolean formula in conjunctive normal form all clauses of which have exactly three literals (in the so-called 3-CNF form)*$\}$ *is* **NP**-*complete.*

Proof: CNFF $\in$ **NP** implies 3-CNFF $\in$ **NP**. To show CNFF $\leq_p$ 3-CNFF, we describe a polynomial time algorithm that transforms any Boolean formula in CNF into a CNF in which each clause has exactly three literals. We now show how to transform a clause $C = x_1 \vee \ldots \vee x_k$ into such a form. This is done by introducing new variables. Let us distinguish three cases:

$$\begin{array}{ll} k=1, & C \equiv (x_1 \vee y_1 \vee y_2) \wedge (x_1 \vee \neg y_1 \vee y_2) \wedge (x_1 \vee y_1 \vee \neg y_2) \wedge (x_1 \vee \neg y_1 \vee \neg y_2); \\ k=2, & C \equiv (x_1 \vee x_2 \vee y_1) \wedge (x_1 \vee x_2 \vee \neg y_1); \\ k>3, & C \equiv (x_1 \vee x_2 \vee y_1) \wedge (\neg y_1 \vee x_3 \vee y_2) \wedge (\neg y_2 \vee x_4 \vee y_3) \wedge \cdots \wedge (\neg y_{k-3} \vee x_{k-1} \vee x_k). \end{array}$$

It is clear that the resulting Boolean formula is satisfiable if and only if the original one is satisfiable and that such a transformation can be done in polynomial time. □

Exercise 5.4.6 *Let CNFF-k be the language consisting of those satisfiable Boolean formulas in CNF in which each variable occurs in at most k clauses. Show that the language CNFF-3 is* **NP**-*complete.*

Exercise 5.4.7* *Show, for example by a reduction from the* 3-CNFF *problem, that the CLIQUE problem is* **NP**-*complete. (This is the problem of deciding, given a graph G and an integer k, whether G has a clique of size k.)*

Exercise 5.4.8 *Show, for example by a reduction from the* 3-CNFF *problem, that the NODE-COLOURABILITY problem is* **NP**-*complete. (This is the problem of deciding, given a graph G and an integer k, whether G is node-colourable with k colours.)*

The **knapsack problem**, the **NP**-completeness of which we show next, is one that has played an important role in modern cryptography (see Chapter 8). It is defined as follows. Given integers $w_1, \ldots, w_n$ and c, does there exist a Boolean vector $(x_1, \ldots, x_n)$ such that

$$\sum_{j=1}^{n} x_i w_i = c\,?$$

(The story behind this: given n objects, $o_1, \ldots, o_n$, with weights $w_1, \ldots, w_n$, and a knapsack with capacity c, is there a subset of objects with total weight exactly c to be loaded into the knapsack?) In the following we assume that each knapsack problem instance, given by weights and a capacity, is encoded by a binary string. Let us denote by KNAPSACK the corresponding language of instances of solvable knapsack problems.[4]

Theorem 5.4.9 *KNAPSACK is an* **NP**-*complete problem.*

Proof: The problem is clearly in **NP**. One simply chooses a subset of weights and checks whether their sum equals the given capacity. **NP**-completeness of KNAPSACK will be proved by showing that

[4]There are several variants of the knapsack problem. The one discussed in this section is often called the SUBSET-SUM problem. Another version is discussed in Section 5.8.2.

3-CNFF $\leq_p^m$ KNAPSACK. To do this, we design an algorithm that transforms, in polynomial time, a Boolean formula F, in 3-CNFF, into an instance of the knapsack problem that is solvable if and only if the Boolean formula F is satisfiable.

Algorithm: Let $F = F_1 \wedge \ldots \wedge F_k$, where each F_i is a clause with exactly three literals from the set $\{x_1, \ldots, x_m, \neg x_1, \ldots, \neg x_m\}$. We show now how to construct the knapsack capacity c and the weights $w_1, \ldots, w_{2k+2m}$ (all in decimal – this choice of number system is of no significance because a transformation into binary form can be done in polynomial time). Let c be an integer the decimal representation of which has $(m+k)$ digits, all equal to 3:

$$c = \underbrace{3\ldots3}_{m+k},$$

(c is chosen in this special way in order to fit the whole construction) and let $w_1, \ldots, w_{2k+2m}$ be $(m+k)$-digit numbers denoted by

$$\overline{x}_1, \ldots, \overline{x}_m \qquad \neg\overline{x}_1, \ldots, \neg\overline{x}_m \qquad y_1, \ldots, y_k \qquad y'_1, \ldots, y'_k \tag{5.4}$$

and defined as follows. (The notation used in (5.4) is designed to indicate the relation of these numbers to literals $x_1, \ldots, x_m, \neg x_1, \ldots, \neg x_m$ or to the clauses $F_1, \ldots, F_k$.)

(1) For $i = 1, \ldots, m$, the ith right-most digit in $\overline{x}_i$ and also in $\neg\overline{x}_i$ is 3. For $j = 1, \ldots, k$, the $(m+j)$th right-most digit in $\overline{x}_i$ (in $\neg\overline{x}_i$) is 1 if F_j contains x_i (if F_j contains $\neg x_i$). All other digits in $\overline{x}_i$ and $\neg\overline{x}_i$ are 0.

Observe that in this way $\overline{x}_i$ contains, in its decimal representation, uniquely and easily decodable information as to which of the variables it corresponds (namely x_i) and which of the clauses x_i occurs. The same holds for $\neg\overline{x}_i$. Therefore the numbers $\overline{x}_1, \ldots, \overline{x}_m, \neg\overline{x}_1, \ldots \neg\overline{x}_m$ represent a full description of the formula F.

(2) For $j = 1, \ldots, k$, the $(m+j)$th right-most digit in y_j is 1, and all other digits are 0. Moreover, $y_i = y'_i$ for all $1 \leq i \leq k$.

Example 5.4.10 *If $F = (x_1 \vee x_2 \vee \neg x_3) \wedge (\neg x_1 \vee \neg x_2 \vee x_3)$, then $k = 2, m = 3$, c=33333 and*

$$\begin{array}{lll} \overline{x_1} = 01003 & \neg\overline{x_1} = 10003 & y_1 = 01000 = y'_1 \\ \overline{x_2} = 01030 & \neg\overline{x_2} = 10030 & y_2 = 10000 = y'_2 \ . \\ \overline{x_3} = 10300 & \neg\overline{x_3} = 01300 & \end{array}$$

Clearly, $c = \overline{x_1} + \overline{x_2} + \overline{x_3} + y_1 + y'_1 + y_2$.

We now show that the knapsack problem K_F, given by the weights $w_1, \ldots, w_{2k+2m}$ and the capacity c as described above, has a solution if and only if the formula F is satisfiable.

1. Let F be satisfiable. Fix a satisfying assignment α for F. For each $i = 1, \ldots, m$, we take $\overline{x}_i$ or $\neg\overline{x}_i$ into the solution of K_F, depending on whether x_i has the value 1 or 0 in the assignment α. The sum of all these numbers has the last m digits equal 3, and each of the first k digits of this sum is either 1, 2 or 3. By adding a proper number of y's and y''s, we get exactly c.

2. Let the knapsack problem K_F have a solution. In other words, assume that there is a subset of numbers from (5.4) that is a solution of K_F. This is possible only if, for each $i = 1, \ldots, m$, exactly one of the numbers $\overline{x}_i$ or $\neg\overline{x}_i$ is in a sum forming c. By taking exactly that one from each pair $(\overline{x_i}, \neg\overline{x_i})$, we get a satisfying assignment for F. □

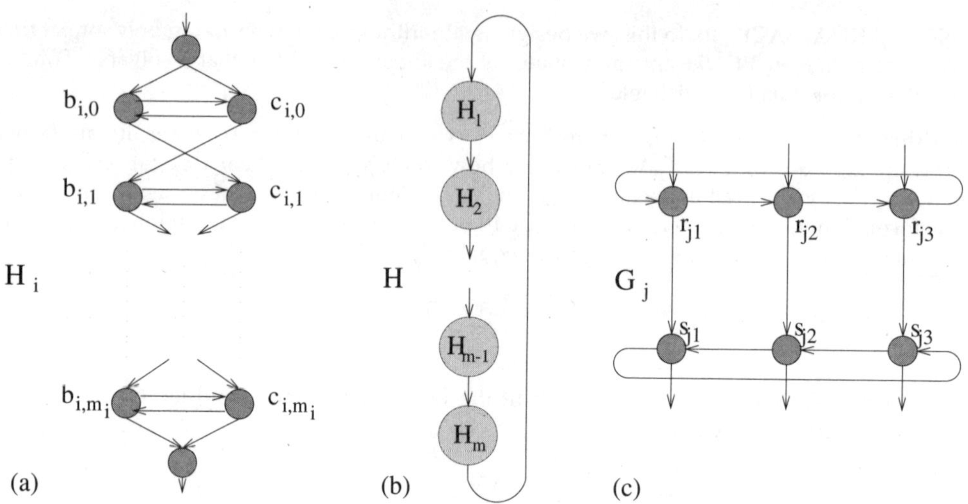

Figure 5.6 Design of a Hamiltonian graph for a satisfiable Boolean formula

The last problem, whose **NP**-completeness we now show, again by a reduction from 3-CNFF, is the Hamilton cycle problem for directed graphs – one of the basic problems concerning traversal of directed graphs. We denote by HAMILTOND the set of encodings of directed graphs that have a Hamilton cycle.

Theorem 5.4.11 *HAMILTOND is an* **NP**-*complete problem.*

Proof: It is trivial to see that HAMILTOND $\in$ **NP**, so we concentrate on showing a polynomial time reducibility of 3-CNFF to HAMILTOND.

Let a Boolean formula in 3-CNF have the form $F = F_1 \wedge \ldots \wedge F_k$, where each $F_i = y_{i1} \vee y_{i2} \vee y_{i3}$ is a clause with three literals. We show how to design in polynomial time a graph G_F such that F is satisfiable if and only if G_F has a Hamilton cycle.

Let $x_1, \ldots, x_m$ be all the variables that occur in F, and for each $1 \leq i \leq m$, let m_i be the total number of occurrences of the literals x_i and $\neg x_i$ in F. First, for each variable x_i we design a subgraph H_i, depicted in Figure 5.6a, with $2m_i + 4$ nodes, $4m_i + 6$ edges and $m_i + 3$ levels. We also design for each clause F_j a subgraph G_j, with 6 nodes, 9 internal edges, 3 ingoing and 3 outgoing edges (see Figure 5.6c). Moreover, let us connect all H_i graphs into a cycle, as indicated in Figure 5.6b, to get the graph H.

Observe that each H_i has exactly two edge-disjoint Hamilton paths. Each is uniquely determined by the edge chosen at the starting node – either to $b_{i,0}$ or to $c_{i,0}$. Observe also that in one of these two paths all edges from one level to the next are always from a b-node to a c-node, and that in the second path this is exactly in the opposite direction. The key point for our reduction is that one of the Hamilton paths through the graph H_i, say the one through $b_{i,0}$, will correspond to the assignment of 1 to the variable x_i and the second to the assignment of 0 to x_i.

As for the next step, we connect all G_j graphs with H to get a graph that encodes the whole formula F. For each clause F_j and each of its literals y_{jk}, we do the following: if $y_{jk} = x_i$, then in the subgraph H_i we introduce an edge from a c-node to the node r_{jk} and an edge from the s_{jk}-node to the corresponding b-node. If $y_{jk} = \neg x_i$, we make a similar construction, but this time a detour from a b-node to a c-node of the next level is introduced, and the corresponding nodes are connected with nodes r_{jk} and s_{jk}. It is not important which of the not-yet-used levels of H_i is taken to make these interconnections between H_i and G_j graphs. Since each H_i has exactly $m_i + 1$ levels with two nodes, the whole construction can take place. We perform this construction for all clauses and all literals in them. As a result, all input and output edges of all G_j graphs are connected with some nodes of H. The resulting graph G_F uniquely encodes F.

It remains to show that G_F has a Hamilton cycle if and only if the Boolean formula F is satisfiable. Let us first assume that F is satisfiable.

Observe that if one enters a G_j graph through a node r_{jk} in a Hamilton cycle through the graph G_F, then there is only one way to visit all nodes of G_j exactly once and to get out – through the node s_{jk}. If one leaves through any other node, then there is a node of G_j that has not yet been visited, and there is no other way to visit it on this to-be-Hamilton cycle.

If F is satisfied, then we pick up in each clause F_j one literal that takes the value 1 in the chosen assignment. If the literal corresponds to a variable x_i, this determines the way H_i should be traversed. In addition, for this single literal we make a detour from H_i to visit G_j and to take a Hamilton path through G_j. In this way we get a Hamilton cycle for G_F.

The rest of the proof, to show that the existence of a Hamilton cycle for G_F implies the existence of a satisfying assignment, is not difficult using the above arguments and is left to the reader. □

Exercise 5.4.12 *Show that the problem of deciding for a given undirected graph G whether G is Hamiltonian, the so-called HAMILTON problem, is* **NP***-complete.*

Exercise 5.4.13 *Show that the problem of deciding whether a given graph has a Hamilton path is* **NP***-complete.*

5.4.3 Analysis of NP-completeness

The concept of **NP**-completeness is one of the most important and most complex in computing. Let us analyse various aspects of it.

NP-completeness of optimization problems

The so-called decision versions of many important optimization problems, actually almost all one needs to solve in practice, are **NP**-complete in the sense discussed later. On the theoretical side, this is, for example, the problem of determining the maximum number of satisfying assignments of a Boolean formula – the MAXSAT problem. Perhaps the most important and most widely investigated optimization problem is the **travelling salesman problem** (TSP) defined as follows.

We are given n cities, denoted by $c_1, \ldots, c_n$, and a nonnegative integer distance d_{ij} between any two cities c_i and c_j (assuming $d_{ij} = d_{ji}$, for all i,j). The task is to find the shortest tour of the cities – that is, a permutation π on $\{1, \ldots, n\}$ such that $\sum_{i=1}^{n} d_{\pi(i),\pi(i+1)}$ is as small as possible (where $\pi(n+1)$ is defined to be $\pi(1)$).

Neither of these is a decision problem and therefore the concept of **NP**-completeness does not apply formally to them. In spite of this, it is common to speak of the **NP**-completeness of such problems. By this we usually understand **NP**-completeness of the decision versions of the problems, where a bound b is given, as part of the input data, and the question is to decide whether there is a solution smaller (or larger) than this bound. For example, in the case of the MAXSAT problem, the question is whether the number of satisfying assignments is larger than b. In the case of TSP the question is whether there is a tour through the graph shorter than b.

Theorem 5.4.14 *The decision version of the travelling salesman problem is* **NP**-*complete, and the travelling salesman problem is* **NP**-*hard.*

Proof: We first show how to reduce, in polynomial time, the HAMILTON problem to a bounded decision version of TSP. Let G be a graph with n nodes $c_1, \ldots, c_n$. We design a distance matrix $\{d_{ij}\}_{ij}^{n}$ and a cost limit b such that there is a Hamilton cycle in G if and only if there is a tour in G of length at most b. The distance d_{ij} is defined to be 1 if there is an edge between the nodes c_i and c_j in G; otherwise $d_{ij} = 2$, and b is defined to be n. The rest of the proof is now straightforward. □

Decision versions of hundreds or even thousands of various optimization problems have turned out to be **NP**-complete. The rationale behind viewing optimization problems in this way is that once we know a polynomial time algorithm for such a decision version of an optimization problem, then it is easy to find the optimal solution using the binary search approach.

Example 5.4.15 *Assume we have a polynomial time algorithm $\mathcal{A}$ for the bounded version of TSP. Given a graph G and a distance matrix $\{d_{ij}\}_{ij}^{n}$, we can use $\mathcal{A}$ to compute the shortest tour of G as follows. First we take a trivial upper bound on the length of such a tour, say b. Then we use $\mathcal{A}$ to decide whether G has a tour shorter than $\frac{b}{2}$. If yes, we call $\mathcal{A}$ with $\frac{b}{4}$, if not with $\frac{3b}{4}$. Continuing this binary search, we can get, with logarithmically many attempts, the shortest tour.*

Exercise 5.4.16 *Show that in the case of the TSP the task of finding the shortest tour can be reduced in polynomial time to the problem of computing the cost of the minimal tour and to the corresponding decision problem.*

Fragility of NP-completeness

There is a simple and quite good rule of thumb for finding out whether a decision problem is **NP**-complete: if checking exponentially many possibilities seems to be the only way to solve the problem and, at the same time, it is easy to verify the correctness of any to-be-solution. However, as Table 5.1 shows, this has its limits. There are pairs of algorithmic problems that look very similar but one is in **P** and the other is **NP**-complete.

Isomorphism of NP-complete problems

NP-complete problems occur in all areas of computing, mathematics, science, engineering and so on, and often at first sight one sees no relation between them. In spite of this – and this is a quite surprising and important discovery – there are no two known **NP**-complete problems that are not isomorphic in the following sense: there is a bijection, computable in polynomial time, that maps instances of one **NP**-complete problem into instances of the second one; and the inverse mapping is also computable in polynomial time. This seems to indicate that any two **NP**-complete problems are actually very similar! However, there is no proof yet that this is really true. Therefore we have only a conjecture.

Hypothesis (Berman–Hartmanis hypothesis) All **NP**-complete problems are mutually polynomial time isomorphic.

POLYNOMIAL TIME	NP-COMPLETE
EDGE COVER **Input:** Graph $G=(V,E)$, integer k. **Problem**: Is there a subset $E' \subset E$ with $\lvert E'\rvert \le k$ such that every vertex is incident with an edge in E'?	VERTEX COVER **Input:** Graph $G=(V,E)$, integer k. **Problem**: Is there a subset $V' \subset V$ with $\lvert V'\rvert \le k$ such that every edge is incident with a node in V'?
EULER CYCLE **Input:** Graph $G=(V,E)$. **Problem:** Does G have a Euler tour?	HAMILTON CYCLE **Input:** Graph $G=(V,E)$. **Problem:** Does G have a Hamilton cycle?
LINEAR DIOPHANTINE EQUATIONS **Input:** Positive integers a, b and c. **Problem**: Are there positive integers x and y such that $ax+by=c$?	QUADRATIC DIOPHANTINE EQUATIONS **Input:** Positive integers a, b and c. **Problem**: Are there positive integers x and y such that $ax^2+by=c$?
LINEAR PROGRAMMING **Input:** $k \times l$ matrix A over $\mathbf{Z}$, $b \in \mathbf{Z}^k$. **Problem**: Does there exist $y \in \mathbf{Q}^l$ such that $Ay \geq b$?	INTEGER LINEAR PROGRAMMING **Input:** $k \times l$ matrix A over $\mathbf{Z}$, $b \in \mathbf{Z}^k$. **Problem**: Does there exist $y \in \mathbf{Z}^l$ such that $Ay \geq b$?

Table 5.1 Problems in **P** and **NP**-complete problems

Currently there seems to be more doubt than belief that the hypothesis is true. The following fact also contributes to this: if the existence of good approximation algorithms for **NP**-complete problems is considered (see Section 5.8), then we can prove that there are, from the approximation point of view, essential differences among **NP**-complete problems.

NP-completeness dependence on the form of inputs

In saying that a decision problem is **NP**-complete, it is implicitly assumed that all numerical input data are given in binary (or decimal) form, and that the total number of bits needed to represent all input data is the size of the problem. This implicit assumption is sometimes essential, because an **NP**-complete problem can be in **P** if input data are given using the unary representation, or even outside **NP** if input data are given in some very compressed form!

Example 5.4.17 (Knapsack problem with input data in unary form) *We recall that*

$$KNAPSACK = \{a_1, \ldots, a_n, c \mid \exists (x_1, \ldots, x_n) \in \{0,1\}^n, \sum_{i=1}^{n} a_i x_i = c\}.$$

Now let us consider a vector $B[0,1,\ldots,c]$, defined, for $0 \le s \le c$, by

$$B[s] = \begin{cases} 1, & \textbf{if } \exists (x_1, \ldots, x_n) \in \{0,1\}^n : s = \sum_{i=1}^{n} a_i x_i; \\ 0, & \textit{otherwise.} \end{cases}$$

We can compute the vector B in $\mathcal{O}(nc)$ time using the following algorithm:

$B[0] \leftarrow 1;$
for $s \leftarrow 1$ **to** c **do** $B[s] \leftarrow 0;$
for $i \leftarrow 1$ **to** n **do for** $s \leftarrow c$ **downto** a_i **do**
    if $B[s-a_i] = 1$ **then** $B[s] \leftarrow 1$

If the input data for the KNAPSACK problem are given in unary form, their representation has a length of at least $n+c$ bits (c bits are needed to represent c, and at least one is needed for each a_i). The time complexity of the above algorithm is therefore quadratic with respect to the size of the input.

However, there are **NP**-complete problems that remain **NP**-complete even when their input data are given in unary form. Such problems are called **strongly NP-complete**.

Exercise 5.4.18 *Show that the following* **NP**-*complete problems are strongly* **NP**-*complete: (a) CLIQUE problem (see Exercise 5.4.7); (b) TSP problem (decision version).*

Example 5.4.19 *The 3-PARTITION problem is also an example that is* **NP**-*complete in the strong sense. It is the following problem: given numbers $a_i, 1 \leq i \leq 3m$, partition these numbers into m sets in such a way that the sum of the elements in each set is the same. (If $\sum_{i=1}^{3m} a_i = mb$, and it is required that, in addition, each $a_i \in (\frac{b}{4}, \frac{b}{2})$, then each partition has to have three elements – hence the name of the problem.)*

The existence of a strong dependence of the running time of some algorithms on the way inputs are presented leads to the following concept.

Definition 5.4.20 *A* **pseudo-polynomial time algorithm** *is one whose running time would be polynomial if all inputs were expressed in unary notation.*

There are also **NP**-complete problems that are no longer in **NP** if inputs are given in a very compressed form. This has been shown for various problems on regular graphs with n nodes that can be represented using $\mathcal{O}(\lg n)$ bits.

5.5 Average-case Complexity and Completeness

Most of complexity theory deals with worst-case complexity. The main reason is that worst-case complexity is much easier to deal with than average-case complexity while still providing deep insights into the nature of computing and paying large practical dividends.

However, in some cases average-case complexity of algorithms and algorithmic problems provides more adequate estimations of real computational complexity. One area where it is often insufficient for a problem to have large worst-case complexity and we need high average-case complexity is cryptography (Chapter 8). Moreover, the average-case complexity provides a different hierarchy of algorithmic problems. Indeed, there are pairs of algorithmic problems with the same worst-case complexity but with very different average-case complexity.

In addition, the existence of **NP**-complete problems for which no efficient algorithms seem to exist, with respect to worst-case complexity, led to the search for algorithms that are 'efficient' with respect to some more modest criteria. A natural approach along these lines is to consider algorithms for **NP**-complete problems which, although possibly exponential on some inputs, are fast on average with respect to a given probability distribution on inputs. This approach has turned out partially successful. Algorithms that are fast on average have been found for several **NP**-complete problems, such as Hamilton path and vertex k-colouring problems. However, some **NP**-complete problems resisted all 'average case attacks'; for example, bounded halting and tiling problems. They also seem to be hard with respect to average-case complexity.

In order to get a deeper understanding and a classification of algorithmic problems with respect to average-case complexity, several new basic concepts have to be introduced: the concept of the **average polynomial time** to study 'easiness on average' and the concepts of **feasible distributions, reductions** and the **average-case completeness**, to study 'hardness on average' of algorithmic problems.

5.5.1 Average Polynomial Time

A natural approach to measure the average efficiency of algorithms is to use expected polynomial time. An algorithm runs in **expected polynomial time** $t(n)$ over a probability distribution μ if $(\exists k \geq 0)(\forall n) \sum_{|x|=n} t(x)\mu_n(x) = \mathcal{O}(n^k)$, where $t(x)$ is the time complexity of the algorithm for input x and μ_n is the conditional probability distribution of μ on strings of length n. However, this definition is much machine dependent, as the following example shows, and therefore a more subtle approach is needed to get suitable concepts.

Example 5.5.1 *If an algorithm $\mathcal{A}$ runs in polynomial time on a $1-2^{-0.1n}$ fraction of input instances of length n, and runs in $2^{0.09n}$ time on the $2^{-0.1n}$ fraction of remaining inputs, then its expected time is bounded by a polynomial. However, as it is easy to see, the expected time for $\mathcal{A}$ will be exponential on a quadratically slower machine.*

It has turned out that in order to have an algorithm polynomial on average we need a proper balance between the fraction of hard instances and the hardness of these input instances. Actually, only a subpolynomial fraction of inputs should require superpolynomial time.

In order to motivate the definition given below let us realize that in worst-case complexity the time $t(n)$ of an algorithm is measured with respect to the length of the input – we require that $t(x) \leq |x|^k$, for some k, in the case of polynomial time computations. In the case of average-case complexity, we allow that an algorithm runs slowly on rare (less probable) inputs. In the case we have a function $r : \Sigma^* \rightarrow \mathbf{R}^+$ to measure 'rareness' of inputs from Σ^*, we may require for the average polynomial time that $t(x) \leq (|x|r(x))^k$ for some k. In such a case $t(x)^{\frac{1}{k}}|x|^{-1} \leq r(x)$ and if $\delta \leq 1$, then $\sum_x t(x)^{\delta/k}|x|^{-1}\mu(x) \leq \sum_x (t(x)^{1/k}|x|^{-1})^{\delta}\mu(x) < \sum_x r^{\delta}(x)r(x) < \infty$. This motivates the following definition.

Definition 5.5.2 *A function $f : \Sigma^* \rightarrow \mathbf{N}$ is μ-**average polynomial** (or polynomial on μ-average), with respect to the probability distribution μ, if there exists an integer k such that*

$$\sum_{x \in \Sigma^*} \mu(x)\frac{f^{\frac{1}{k}}(x)}{|x|} < \infty.$$

Note that this definition is well motivated and robust. Indeed, since the outcome is not affected by raising $f(x)$ or $|x|$ to a constant power, the definition is to a sufficient degree machine-model independent and is also not affected by polynomial reductions.

Exercise 5.5.3 *Show that a function f is μ-average polynomial if and only if there are constants $c, k > 0$ such that $\mu[f(x) > (l|x|)^k] < \frac{c}{l}$, for all $l \in \mathbf{R}^+$.*

Exercise 5.5.4* *Show that if functions f and g are μ-average polynomial, then so are functions $f+g$ and $f \cdot g$.*

In order to extend the concept of **NP**-completeness to the average-case complexity, we have to take a more general view of what a decision problem is. By that we will mean, for the rest of this section, a pair (L, μ), a **distributional decision problem**, where $L \subseteq \Sigma^*$ is a language $L = \{x \mid \mu(x) > 0\}$, and μ is a probability distribution over Σ^+.

A language L is said to be decidable in the average polynomial time with respect to a distribution μ if it can be decided by a deterministic algorithm whose time complexity is bounded from above by a μ-average polynomial function. By **AP** we denote the class of all distributional decision problems (L, μ), where L is decidable in μ-average polynomial time. Analogically, we define **ANP** to be the class of distributional decision problems (L, μ), where L is decidable in μ-average polynomial time on a nondeterministic Turing machine.

5.5.2 Reductions of Distributional Decision Problems

It has been shown that in order to introduce properly the concept of reducibility and completeness among distributional decision problems we need to put some conditions on probability distributions. A basic condition is that we consider only distributions μ such that the corresponding cumulative distribution function $\mu^*(x) = \sum_{y \preceq x} \mu(y)$ is polynomial time computable in the following sense:

Definition 5.5.5 *A function $f : \Sigma^+ \to [0,1]$ is polynomial time computable if there is a MTM which for every input $x \in \Sigma^+$ outputs a finite binary fraction y, in time polynomial in $|x|$ and k, such that $|f(x) - y| \leq 2^{-k}$.*

Observe that the requirement for μ^* to be polynomial time computable is strong, because the sum to compute $\mu^*(x)$ is taken over the exponentially many substrings smaller than x, with respect to the strict ordering.

Exercise 5.5.6 *Show that if a cumulative distribution function μ^* is computable in polynomial time, then so is μ.*

With the last result in mind we assume in the following that if we say that a distribution μ is polynomial time computable, then this means that both μ and μ^* are polynomially computable – all commonly used distributions have this property.

It is not trivial to define reductions f from one distributional problem (L_1, μ_1) to another (L_2, μ_2). A natural requirement is that **AP** should be closed under such reductions in the sense that if (L_2, μ_2) is in **AP**, then so is (L_1, μ_1). It has turned out that a suitable way to guarantee this is to require that f efficiently reduces L_1 to L_2, as in the worst-case situation, and f does not reduces 'frequent' instances of L_1 into 'rare' instances of L_2. This means that if we denote by $f(\mu_1)$ the distribution defined by $f(\mu_1)(y) = \sum_{f(x)=y} \mu_1(x)$, then the distribution $f(\mu_1)$ should be bounded from above, within a polynomial factor, by the distribution μ_2. This leads to the following definitions:

Definition 5.5.7 *(1) Let μ and ν be probability distributions on the same domain Σ^*. Then μ is dominated by ν, in short $\mu \preceq \nu$, if there exists a polynomial p such that $\mu(x) \leq p(|x|)\nu(x)$, for all $x \in \Sigma^+$.*

(2) Let μ_1 and μ_2 be distributions on strings of languages L_1 and L_2, respectively, and f be a reduction from L_1 to L_2. Then μ_1 is dominated by μ_2, with respect to f, notation $\mu_1 \preceq_f \mu_2$, if there exists a distribution μ_1' on Σ^+ such that $\mu_1 \preceq \mu_1'$ and $\mu_2(y) = f(\mu_1')(y)$, for all $y \in range(f)$.

Definition 5.5.8 *A distributional problem (L_1,μ_1) is polynomial-time reducible to (L_2,μ_2) if there is a polynomial time computable reduction f such that L_1 is many-to-one reducible to L_2 via f and $\mu_1 \preceq_f \mu_2$.*

In other words, a polynomial reduction from a distributional decision problem (L,μ), $L \subseteq \Sigma^*$, to a problem (L',μ'), is a polynomial reduction f of L to L' such that the following property holds: there exists an integer l such that, for all $x \in \Sigma^*$,

$$\mu'(x) \geq \frac{1}{|x|^l} \sum_{y \in f^{-1}(x)} \mu(y),$$

i.e., the distribution μ' should be nowhere more than polynomially smaller than the distribution induced by μ.

Exercise 5.5.9 *Show that if a distributional problem (L_1,μ_1) is polynomial time reducible to (L_2,μ_2) and $(L_2,\mu_2) \in$ **AP**, then also $(L_1,\mu_1) \in$ **AP**.*

Exercise 5.5.10* *Show that polynomial time reductions on distributional decision problems are transitive.*

5.5.3 Average-case NP-completeness

Let us denote by **DNP** the class of distributional decision problems (L,μ) such that $L \in$ **NP** and $\mu \preceq \nu$ for some polynomial time computable distribution ν. The class **DNP**, which is a proper subclass of **ANP**, seems to be the right framework to deal with average-case **NP**-completeness.

A distributional decision problem (L,μ) is said to be **average-case NP-complete** (or **DNP**-complete), if it is in **DNP** and every distributional problem in **DNP** is polynomial time reducible to it.

Several natural **NP**-complete problems have turned out to be average case **NP**-complete with respect to distributions in which each parameter of the input instances is selected uniformly and randomly, for example, the bounded halting and tiling problems (and bounded versions of the Post correspondence problem, Thue problem and the word problem for (finitely generated) groups, discussed in the next chapter).

In this context, but also in many others, it is of importance to have a good concept for a 'uniform' distribution on the set of all strings over an alphabet Σ. This is a nontrivial problem because it is impossible to select strings with equal chance from an infinite sample space. The idea formulated in the following definition has turned out to be appropriate. First choose an integer with a probability close to 'uniform' and then select uniformly a string of that length.

Definition 5.5.11 *A polynomial time computable distribution μ on Σ^+ is called* **uniform** *if there is a function $\rho : \mathbf{N} \rightarrow \mathbf{R}$ such that for all x, $\mu(x) = \rho(|x|)2^{-|x|}$, where $\sum_n \rho(n) = 1$ and there is a polynomial p such that $\rho(n) \geq \frac{1}{p(n)}$, for all but finitely many n.*

In this way it is guaranteed that about any length gets a 'fair' amount of weight to be selected. ($\sum_n \rho(n) = 1$, for example, for $\rho(n) = \frac{6}{\pi^2 n^2}$.)

The proofs of the average-case **NP**-completeness are in general more technical than for **NP**-completeness, because probability distributions are involved. As an example of such a problem we discuss the following randomized version of the bounded halting problem (RBHP) for a NTM $\mathcal{M}$:

Input: A string $w01^n$ with $n > |w|$.

Question: Is there a halting computation of $\mathcal{M}$ on $|w|$ with at most n steps.

Probability: Proportional to $n^{-3}2^{-|w|}$.

(The above probability distribution for RBHP corresponds to the following experiment: randomly choose n, then $k < n$ and, finally, a string w of length k.)

Remark 5.5.12 Let us now summarize a variety of further results that help to see merits and properties of the concepts introduced above.

1. Similarly as for **NP**-completeness, all known pairs of average-case **NP**-complete problems have been shown to be polynomially isomorphic under polynomial time reductions.

2. In order to define average-case **NP**-completeness we could also use average polynomial time reductions instead of polynomial time reductions. In addition, using average polynomial time reductions one can define completeness for the class **ANP**. All average-case **NP**-complete problems are also average polynomial time complete for **ANP**. However, there are distributional problems that are not in **DNP** but are average polynomial time complete for problems in **ANP** with polynomial time computable distributions.

3. It has been shown that there are problems not in **P** but in **AP** under any polynomial time computable distribution. However, if a problem is in **AP** under every exponential time computable distribution, then it has to be in **P**.

4. It seems unlikely that **DNP** $\subseteq$ **AP**, because this has been shown not to be true if **E** $= \bigcup_{k=1}^{\infty} Time(n^k) \neq$ **NE** $= \bigcup_{k=1}^{\infty} Ntime(n^k)$ (which is expected to be true). See also Section 5.11 for classes **E** and **NE**.

5.6 Graph Isomorphism and Prime Recognition

Two important algorithmic problems seem to have a special position in **NP**: graph isomorphism and prime recognition. All efforts to show that they are either in **P** or **NP**-complete have failed.

5.6.1 Graph Isomorphism and Nonisomorphism

As we shall see in Section 5.11.1, a proof that the graph isomorphism problem is **NP**-complete would have consequences that do not agree with our current intuition.

On the other hand, it is interesting to note that a seemingly small modification of the graph isomorphism problem, the **subgraph isomorphism problem**, is **NP**-complete. This is the problem of deciding, given two graphs G_1 and G_2, whether G_1 is isomorphic with a subgraph of G_2.

Exercise 5.6.1 *Explain how it can happen that we can prove that the subgraph isomorphism problem is* **NP**-*complete but have great difficulty in proving the same for the graph isomorphism problem?*

In addition, the graph isomorphism problem is in **P** for various important classes of graphs, for example, planar graphs.

Exercise 5.6.2 *Show that the following graph isomorphism problems are decidable in polynomial time: (a) for trees; (b) for planar graphs.*

A complementary problem, the **graph nonisomorphism problem**, is even known not to be in **NP**. This is the problem of deciding, given two graphs, whether they are nonisomorphic.

It is worth pointing out why there is such a difference between graph isomorphism and graph nonisomorphism problems. In order to show that two graphs are isomorphic, it is enough to provide and check an isomorphism. To show that two graphs are nonisomorphic, one has to prove that no isomorphism exists. This seems to be much more difficult.

We also deal with graph isomorphism and nonisomorphism problems in Chapter 9.

5.6.2 Prime Recognition

This is an algorithmic problem *par excellence* – a king of algorithmic problems. For more than two thousand years some of the best mathematicians have worked on it and the problem is still far from being solved. Moreover, a large body of knowledge in mathematics has its origin in the study of this problem.

There are several easy-to-state criteria for an integer being a prime. For example,

Wilson's test: n is a prime if and only if $(n-1)! \equiv -1 \pmod{n}$.

Lucas's test: n is a prime if and only if $\exists g \in \mathbf{Z}_n^*$ such that $g^{n-1} \equiv 1 \pmod{n}$ but $g^{(n-1)/p} \not\equiv 1 \pmod{n}$ for all prime factors p of $n-1$.

None of the known criteria for primality seems to lead to a polynomial time algorithm for primality testing. The fastest known deterministic algorithm for testing the primality of a number n has complexity $\mathcal{O}((\lg n)^{c \lg \lg \lg n})$. However, it is also far from clear that no deterministic polynomial time primality testing algorithm exists. For example, it has been shown that primality testing of an integer n can be done in the deterministic polynomial time $\mathcal{O}(\lg^5 n)$ if the generalized Riemann hypothesis holds.[5]

The following reformulation of Lucas's test provides a nondeterministic polynomial time algorithm for recognizing primes, and therefore prime recognition is in **NP**.

[5]The Riemann hypothesis says that all complex roots of the equation $\sum_{n=1}^{\infty} \frac{1}{n^z} = 0$, with the real part between 0 and 1, have as real part exactly $1/2$. This is one of the major hypotheses of number theory, and has been verified computationally for $1.5 \cdot 10^9$ roots. The generalized Riemann hypothesis makes the same claim about the roots of the equation $\sum_{n=1}^{\infty} \frac{\chi(n)}{n^y} = 0$, where $\chi(a) = \chi_n(a \bmod n)$ if $\gcd(a,n) = 1$, and 0 otherwise, and χ_n is a homomorphism of the multiplicative group Z_n^* into the multiplicative group of all complex numbers. The generalized Riemann hypothesis has also been verified for a very large number of roots.

Algorithm 5.6.3 (Nondeterministic prime recognition)

if $n = 2$ **then** accept;
if $n = 1$ or $n > 2$ is even, **then** reject;
if $n > 2$ is odd **then** choose an $1 < x < n$;
verify whether $x^{n-1} \equiv 1(\text{mod} n)$;
guess a prime factorization $p_1, \ldots, p_k$ of $n-1$;
verify that $p_1 \ldots p_k = n-1$;
for $1 \leq i \leq k$, check that p_i is prime and $x^{(n-1)/p_i} \not\equiv 1 \bmod n$;
accept, if none of the checks fails.

If $\lg n = m$, then the computation of x^{n-1} and $x^{(n-1)/p_i}$ takes time $\mathcal{O}(m^4)$. Since $p_k \leq n / 2$, one can derive in a quite straightforward way a recurrence for time complexity of the above algorithm and show that its computational complexity is $\mathcal{O}(\lg^5 n)$.

Exercise 5.6.4* *Show in detail how one can derive an $\mathcal{O}(\lg^5 n)$ time upper bound for the complexity of the above nondeterministic implementation of Lucas's test.*

Recognition of composite numbers is clearly in **NP** – one just guesses and verifies their factorization – and therefore prime recognition is in **NP** $\cap$ **co-NP**.

5.7 NP versus P

In spite of the fact that the complexity class **NP** seems to be of purely theoretical interest, because the underlying machine model is unrealistic, it actually plays a very important role in practical computing. This will be discussed in this section. In addition, we analyse the structure and basic properties of the complexity classes **NP** and **P**, as well as their mutual relation.

5.7.1 Role of NP in Computing

There is another characterization of **NP** that allows us to see better its overall role in computing. In order to show this characterization, two new concepts are needed.

Definition 5.7.1 *A binary relation $R \subset \Sigma^* \times \Sigma^*$ is called* **polynomially decidable** *if there is a deterministic Turing machine that decides the language $\{x\#y \mid (x,y) \in R\}$, with # being a marker not in Σ, in polynomial time. Moreover, a binary relation R is called* **polynomially balanced** *if there is an integer k such that $(x,y) \in R$ implies $|y| \leq |x|^k$. (In other words, the size of y is polynomially bounded by the size of x, and therefore, if $(x,y) \in R$, then y can be only polynomially larger than x.)*

Theorem 5.7.2 *A language L is in* **NP** *if and only if there is a polynomially decidable and polynomially balanced relation R such that $L = \{x \mid (x,y) \in R \text{ for some } y\}$.*

Proof: (1) If $L \in$ **NP**, then there is a NTM $\mathcal{M}$ that decides L in polynomial time n^k for some k. Let R now be the relation defined as follows: $(x,y) \in R$ if and only if y is an accepting computation for $\mathcal{M}$ and its input x. Clearly, R is polynomially balanced and decidable. Moreover, $L = \{x \mid (x,y) \in R\}$.

(2) Let a polynomially balanced and decidable relation R exist for a language L, and let k be such that $(x,y) \in R$ implies $|y| \leq |x|^k$. We show how to design a polynomial time bounded NTM $\mathcal{M}$ that decides L. For an input x, $\mathcal{M}$ first guesses a y such that $|y| \leq |x|^k$, then decides whether $(x,y) \in R$. Both tasks can be performed in polynomial time, because R is polynomially balanced and decidable. □

Note that our new characterization of **NP** from Theorem 5.7.2 does not use the concept of nondeterminism at all.

Theorem 5.7.2 throws light on the substance of the class **NP**. If a problem (language) L is in **NP**, then each 'yes' instance x of the problem ($x \in L$) has a short, of polynomial size, **certificate (witness, proof of membership)** y that x is in L. One can easily, in polynomial time, verify the correctness of a chosen certificate for x.

In the case of the satisfiability problem, a satisfying assignment is such a certificate. In that of the Hamilton cycle problem, it is a particular Hamilton cycle that is a certificate. In that of the graph isomorphism problem, it is a particular isomorphism that plays the role of a certificate. Prime recognition is an example of a problem that has a certificate, but one to show that is far from trivial.

Many important properties in **NP** are such that their negation is also in **NP**. One can demonstrate this using witnesses. For example, it is easy to give a certificate that a graph is connected, and also for the case that it is not connected. However, in many cases deep mathematical results have to be used to show the existence of a witness. For example, it is not difficult to give a witness that a graph is planar, even this is far from trivial (coordinates of nodes could have too many digits). This is based on the result of graph theory saying that if a graph is planar, then it can be drawn in the plane in such a way that each edge is a straight line segment and the coordinates of every vertex are integers whose number of digits is polynomial in the size of the graph. The existence of a certificate for nonplanarity of a graph follows from Kuratowski's theorem. To give a witness that a graph has a perfect matching is easy; one simply presents such a matching. On the other hand, the existence of a witness for the nonexistence of a perfect matching follows from Tutte's theorem.

NP is certainly the most important complexity class, containing most, though not all, of the natural problems one encounters in computing. Theorem 5.7.2 can serve as a basis for explaining why. Indeed, many computational problems require that we design objects with certain properties. Sometimes an optimal solution is required, sometimes any solution will do. These mathematical objects are often an abstraction of real objects. It is therefore only natural that they cannot be of enormous size, and that it should be easy to verify whether they have the required properties. Such objects are actually the certificates that Theorem 5.7.2 talks about.

5.7.2 Structure of NP

The study of the complexity of computational problems mostly concerns **NP**. The main task is to sort out which problems have a polynomial time solution and which do not. The concept of **NP**-completeness plays the key role here. If a problem is shown to be **NP**-complete, it is certainly among those least likely to be in **P**.

What structure does **NP** actually have? If **P** = **NP**, we get the simple picture shown in Figure 5.7a, and the whole theory of **NP**-completeness loses its merit. This, however, is very unlikely with respect to our current knowledge. If $\mathbf{P} \neq \mathbf{NP}$, we know at least two important subclasses of **NP**. They are **P** and the class of **NP**-complete problems. Is that all? Two problems discussed in the previous section indicate that it is not. Indeed, the following theorem shows that the structure of **NP** in such a case is as depicted in Figure 5.7b.

Theorem 5.7.3 *If* $\mathbf{P} \neq \mathbf{NP}$, *then (a) there is a language* $L \in \mathbf{NP} - \mathbf{P}$ *that is not* **NP**-*complete; (b) there is an infinite hierarchy of complexity classes between* **P** *and* **NP**.

5.7.3 $\mathbf{P} = \mathbf{NP}$ Problem

A proof that **P** = **NP** could clearly have a large impact on practical computing, because it would imply the existence of polynomial time algorithms for many algorithmic problems we greatly need to solve efficiently.

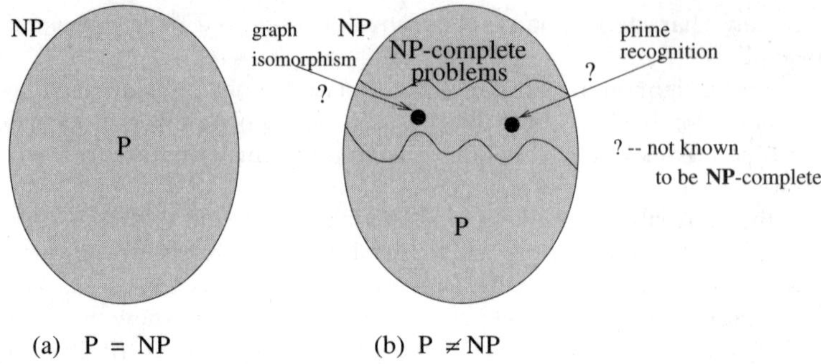

Figure 5.7 Structure of NP

> **Exercise 5.7.4** *Why is it not absolutely clear that a proof that* **P = NP** *would significantly affect practical computing? What might happen?*

A proof that $\mathbf{P} \neq \mathbf{NP}$ could also have a large impact on our understanding of the nature of computing. This is mainly due to the fact that many results of the following type are known:

P = NP if and only if . . . . . . holds.

For example,

P = NP if and only if every honest partial function computable in polynomial time has an inverse computable in polynomial time.

A function f is **honest** if and only if for every value y in the range of f there is an x in the domain of f such that $f(x) = y$ and $|x| \leq p(|y|)$ for some fixed polynomial p. The last result is sometimes interpreted as **P**≠ **NP** if and only if there is a one-way function. However, the requirement for one-way function formulated in Section 2.3.3 is stronger than that in the above result.

> **Exercise 5.7.5** *Show that if a function has an inverse computable in polynomial time, then it is honest.*

Theorem 5.7.2 also suggests another way of viewing the **P** = **NP** problem. A certificate y for a 'yes' instance x of an **NP**-complete problem can be seen as a proof for x. By Theorem 5.7.2, **NP**-complete problems have proofs that are of a reasonable size and easily verifiable. However, they may not be easy to find. **P** can be seen as the class of problems for which one can find the proof in polynomial time. The problem **P** = **NP** can therefore be seen as the problem of resolving the following puzzle: which is more difficult, to find a proof or to check a proof? The answer seems to be intuitively clear – but only until one tries to prove it.

It is natural that much current research in foundations of computing should concentrate on areas which could lead to the solution of the **P** = **NP** problem. One way that seems promising is by means of circuit complexity. By Theorem 4.3.24, for each problem in **P** there is a uniform family of polynomial size circuits. Hence, in order to show that an **NP**-complete problem is outside **P**, it would suffice to show that its circuit complexity is superpolynomial. Since almost all Boolean functions have the worst possible circuit complexity, this might not seem to be a big deal. However, currently the best lower bound for circuit complexity of an **NP**-complete problem is $3n - o(n)$.

It could also happen that the $\mathbf{P} = \mathbf{NP}$ problem is not solvable within the framework in which current logic, mathematics and computing theory are developed. It behoves us therefore also to explore this possibility. One attempt to do this is by means of **relativized complexity theory**, where relativization is understood with respect to different oracles.

5.7.4 Relativization of the $\mathbf{P} = \mathbf{NP}$ Problem*

The concept of an oracle, introduced in Section 5.3, is a formalization of an intuitive idea of computing with advice or help from an oracle or, more plainly, with subprograms.

If we fix a language A as an oracle, and consider complexity classes relativized to this oracle, we can speak of relativized complexity classes. If $\mathcal{L}$ is a complexity class, then $\mathcal{L}^A$ denotes the relativized complexity class: namely, the class of languages accepted by oracle Turing machines $\mathcal{M}^A$, where $\mathcal{M}$ is a Turing machine accepting a language from $\mathcal{L}$. If $\mathcal{A}$ is a family of languages, then $\mathcal{L}^{\mathcal{A}} = \bigcup_{A \in \mathcal{A}} \mathcal{L}^A$.

We show now that the solution of a relativized version of the $\mathbf{P} = \mathbf{NP}$ problem, namely, the $\mathbf{P}^A = \mathbf{NP}^A$ problem, depends on the choice of the oracle.

Theorem 5.7.6 *There are oracles A and B such that $\mathbf{P}^A = \mathbf{NP}^A$ and $\mathbf{P}^B \neq \mathbf{NP}^B$.*

Proof: Let A be a **PSPACE**-complete language. According to Savitch's theorem, we have

$$\mathbf{P}^A = \mathbf{P}^{\mathbf{PSPACE}} = \mathbf{PSPACE},$$

$$\mathbf{NP}^A = \mathbf{NP}^{\mathbf{PSPACE}} = \mathbf{NPSPACE} = \mathbf{PSPACE};$$

therefore $\mathbf{P}^A = \mathbf{NP}^A$.

Construction of the language B is more involved, and the diagonalization method will be used for this.

For each language B let us define a language

$$L_B = \{0^n \mid \exists w \in B, |w| = n\}.$$

Clearly, $L_B \in \mathbf{NP}^B$. In order to prove the second statement of the theorem, it is sufficient to show that there is a B such that $L_B \notin \mathbf{P}^B$. This will now be done.

Let $\mathcal{M}_1, \mathcal{M}_2, \ldots$ be an enumeration of polynomial time bounded deterministic oracle Turing machines, and let $p_1, p_2, \ldots$ be their corresponding polynomial time bounds. Such an enumeration can be obtained from an enumeration of all TM and polynomials, by putting a 'polynomial clock' to each of them, like in Lemma 5.1.12.

We design a set $B \subset \{0,1\}^*$ in phases using the following method:

Phase 0. Set $B \leftarrow \emptyset$, and $n \leftarrow 0$.
Phase $k > 0$.
1. Take m to be the smallest integer such that $2^m > p_k(m)$ and m is larger than the length of the longest string that any of the machines $\mathcal{M}_1, \ldots, \mathcal{M}_k$ asks its oracle for inputs of length at most n. (Observe that m is well defined.)
2. Set $n \leftarrow m$.
3. **if** $0^n \in L(\mathcal{M}_k^B)$

then go to the $(k+1)$th phase
else let w be a string such that $|w| = n$ and $\mathcal{M}_k$ for the input 0^n never asks
the oracle whether it contains w. (Since $2^m > p_k(m)$, such a string does exist.)
Set $B \leftarrow B \cup \{w\}$ and **go to** the $(k+1)$th phase.

We show now that the assumption $L_B \in \mathbf{P}^B$ leads to a contradiction. Let k be such that $L_B = L(\mathcal{M}_k^B)$. (Since $\mathcal{M}_1, \mathcal{M}_2, \ldots$ is an enumeration of a polynomial time bounded oracle TM, such a k must exist.) Moreover, let n_k be the integer value n receives in the kth phase. If $0^{n_k} \in L(\mathcal{M}_k^B)$, then no string of length n_k is added to B in the kth phase (and therefore $0^{n_k} \notin L_B$).

If $0^{n_k} \notin L(\mathcal{M}_k^B)$, then in the kth phase a string of length n_k is added to B. Observe also that two different phases do not mix, in the sense that they deal with different sets of strings. Thus,

$$0^{n_k} \in L_B \Leftrightarrow 0^{n_k} \notin L(\mathcal{M}_k^B) = L_B,$$

and this is a contradiction. □

Exercise 5.7.7 *Show that there are oracles A, B such that (a)* $\mathbf{NP}^A \neq \mathbf{PSPACE}^A$; *(b)* $\mathbf{P}^B \neq \textbf{co-NP}^B$.

Remark 5.7.8 There are many other results showing identity or differences between various complexity classes (not known to be either identical or different) with respect to some oracles. For example, there are oracles A, B, C and D such that (1) $\mathbf{NP}^A \neq \textbf{co-NP}^A$; (2) $\mathbf{NP}^B \neq \mathbf{PSPACE}^B$ and $\textbf{co-NP}^B \neq \mathbf{PSPACE}^B$; (3) $\mathbf{P}^C \neq \mathbf{NP}^C$ and $\mathbf{NP}^C = \textbf{co-NP}^C$; (4) $\mathbf{P}^D \neq \mathbf{NP}^D$ and $\mathbf{NP}^D = \mathbf{PSPACE}^D$. Technically, these are interesting results. But what do they actually imply? This is often discussed in the literature. The main outcome seems to be an understanding that some techniques can hardly be used to separate some complexity classes (that is, to show they are different). For example, if a technique 'relativizes' in the sense that a proof of $\mathbf{P} \neq \mathbf{NP}$ by this technique would imply $\mathbf{P}^{\mathbf{A}} \neq \mathbf{NP}^{\mathbf{A}}$, for any oracle A, then this technique cannot be used to show that $\mathbf{P} \neq \mathbf{NP}$.

5.7.5 P-completeness

The original motivation for the introduction of the concept of **P**-completeness, by S. Cook in 1972, with respect to logspace reducibility was to deal with the (still open) problem of whether everything computable in polynomial time is computable in polylogarithmic space. Other concepts of **P**-completeness will be discussed in Section 5.10.

Many problems have been shown to be **P**-complete. Some of them are a natural modification of known **NP**-complete problems.

Exercise 5.7.9 *Show, for example by a modification of the proof of* **NP**-*completeness or the bounded halting problem, that the following deterministic version of the bounded halting problem is* **P**-*complete:*

$$L_{halt}^D = \{\langle \mathcal{M} \rangle \langle w \rangle \#^t \mid \mathcal{M} \textit{ is a deterministic TM that accepts } w \textit{ in } t \textit{ steps}\}.$$

Some **P**-complete problems look surprisingly simple: for example, the **circuit value problem**, an analog of the satisfiability problem for Boolean formulas. Given a Boolean circuit C and an assignment α to its Boolean variables, decide whether C has the value 1 for the assignment α. If we take self-delimiting encodings $\langle C\rangle$ of circuits C, then we have

$$\text{CIRCUIT VALUE} = \{\langle C\rangle\alpha \,|\, C \text{ has the value 1 for the assignment } \alpha\}.$$

Theorem 5.7.10 *The CIRCUIT VALUE problem is* **P**-*complete.*

Proof: An evaluation of a circuit can clearly be made in polynomial time; therefore the problem is in **P**. It has been shown in Chapter 4, Lemma 4.3.23, that for any deterministic polynomial time bounded Turing machine that accepts a language $L \subset \Sigma^*$ and any $x \in L \subseteq \Sigma^*$, we can design in polynomial time a circuit $C_{L,x}$ such that $x \in L$ if and only if $C_{L,x}$ has the value 1 for the assignment determined by x. It is not difficult to see that this construction can actually be carried out in $O(\lg|x|)$ space. This shows **P**-completeness. □

In order to demonstrate a subtle difference between **NP**-completeness and **P**-completeness, let us mention two very important, closely related optimization problems: **rational linear programming** (RLP) and **integer linear programming** (ILP) (see Table 5.1).

The **simplex method** is a widely used method for solving the RLP problem. For many practically important inputs the method runs very fast, but its worst-case complexity is exponential. The discovery that there is a polynomial time algorithm for solving this problem, due to Khachyian (1983), was an important step in the development of efficient algorithms. By contrast, ILP seems to be an essentially more difficult problem, in spite of the fact that the set of potential solutions is smaller than that for RLP. Interestingly, these two problems have a firm place in computational complexity classes.

Theorem 5.7.11 *The rational linear programming problem is* **P**-*complete, whereas the integer linear programming problem is* **NP**-*complete.*

Exercise 5.7.12 *Show that the 3-CNFF problem can be reduced in polynomial time to the integer linear programming problem. (To show* **NP**-*completeness of ILP is a much harder task.)*

5.7.6 Structure of P

As mentioned in Section 5.2, we have the inclusions **LOGSPACE** $\subseteq$ **NLOGSPACE** $\subseteq$ **P**. It is not known which of these inclusions is proper, if any. The problem

$$\textbf{LOGSPACE} = \textbf{NLOGSPACE},$$

or, in other notation, **L** = **NL**, is another important open question in complexity theory.

For the class **NLOGSPACE** various natural complete problems are known. One of them is the 2-CNFF problem: to decide whether a Boolean formula in conjunctive normal form with two literals in each clause is satisfiable. Another **NLOGSPACE**-complete problem is the graph accessibility problem (GAP): given a directed graph G and two of its nodes, s (source) and t (sink), decide whether there is a path in G from s to t.

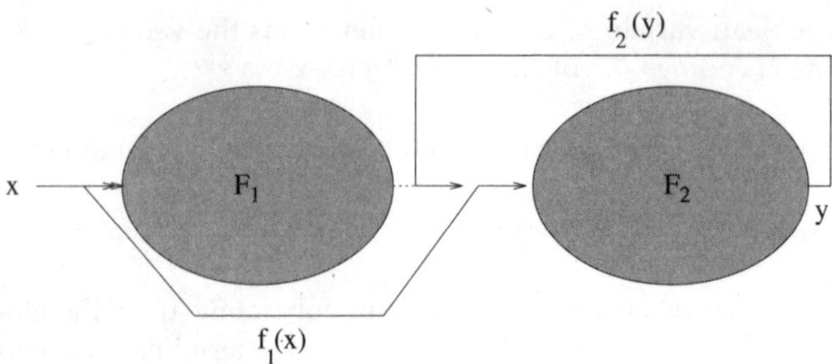

Figure 5.8 Reducibility in **FNP**

5.7.7 Functional Version of the **P** = **NP** Problem

Most complexity theory deals with decision problems – how to recognize strings in a language. However, most of computing practice deals with function problems – how to compute functions – and the search problems.

There are two reasons for this heavy concentration of complexity theory on decision problems: (1) the simplicity, elegance and power of such theory; (2) transfer to computational problems does not seem to bring much more insight; moreover, it is often quite easy.

There are two natural connections between decision and computational problems. To decide whether $x \in L$ for a language L is equivalent to computing $f_L(x)$ for the characteristic function of L. Another important relation between decision and function problems can be formulated for languages from **NP** as follows.

Definition 5.7.13 *(1) Let $L \in$ **NP** and R_L be a polynomial time-decidable and polynomially balanced relation for L – see the proof of Theorem 5.7.2. The search problem associated with L and denoted by FL is as follows: Given x, find a string y such that $R(x,y)$ holds, if such a string exists, and return 'no' if no such y exists. (2) Denote **FNP** (**FP**) the class of search problems associated with languages in **NP** (in **P**).*

We can therefore talk about such search problems as FSAT and FKNAPSACK.

Intuitively, there should be a very close relation between **P** and **FP**, between **NP** and **FNP**, and between the problems **P** = **NP** and **FP** = **FNP**. Indeed, this is true. However, in order to reveal such a close relation fully, the following subtle, and tricky at first sight, definition of the polynomial time reducibility in **FNP** is needed (see Figure 5.8).

Definition 5.7.14 *A function problem $F_1 : \Sigma_1^* \rightarrow \Sigma_1^*$ is polynomial time reducible to a function problem $F_2 : \Sigma_2^* \rightarrow \Sigma_2^*$, if there are polynomial time computable functions $f_1 : \Sigma_1^* \rightarrow \Sigma_2^*$ and $f_2 : \Sigma_2^* \rightarrow \Sigma_1^*$ such that the following conditions hold:*

1. *If F_1 is defined for some x, then F_2 is defined for $f_1(x)$.*

2. *If y is an output of F_2 for the input $f_1(x)$, then $f_2(y)$ is the correct output of F_1 for the input x.*

Observe a subtlety of this definition: from the output of F_2 for the input $f_1(x)$, we can construct, in polynomial time, the correct output of F_1.

*A function problem F is **FNP**-complete if $F \in$ **FNP**, and each problem in **FNP** can be reduced to F in polynomial time.*

It is easy to see that the SAT problem is decidable in polynomial time if and only if FSAT is computable in polynomial time. Indeed, the only nontrivial task is to show that if there is a polynomial algorithm for deciding SAT, then we can solve FSAT in polynomial time.

Let us assume that there is a polynomial time algorithm $\mathcal{A}$ to decide the SAT problem. Let F be a Boolean function of n variables $x_1, \ldots, x_n$. We can use $\mathcal{A}$ to decide whether F has a satisfying assignment. If not, we return 'no'. If 'yes', we design formulas F_0 and F_1 by fixing, in F, $x_1 = 0$ and $x_1 = 1$. We then use $\mathcal{A}$ to decide which of those two formulas has a satisfying assignment. One of them must have. Assume that it is F_0. This implies that there is a satisfying assignment for F with $x_1 = 0$. We keep doing these restrictions of F and, step by step, find values for all the variables in a satisfying assignment for F.

Remark 5.7.15 In the case of sequential computations, function problems can often be reduced with a small time overhead to decision problems. For example, the problem of computing a function $f : \mathbf{N} \to \mathbf{N}$ can be reduced to the problem of deciding, given an n and k, whether $f(n) < k$, in the case that a reasonable upper bound on $f(n)$ is easy to establish (which is often the case). Using a binary search in the interval $[0, b]$, one can then determine $f(n)$ using $\lceil \lg b \rceil$ times an algorithm for the corresponding decision problem for f and k.

Using the ideas in the proof of Theorem 5.4.3, we can easily show that FSAT is an **FNP**-complete problem. Therefore, we have the relation we expected:

Theorem 5.7.16 **P = NP** *if and only if* **FP = FNP**.

Important candidates for being in **FNP** $-$ **FP** are one-way functions in the following sense.

Definition 5.7.17 *Let $f : \Sigma^* \to \Sigma^*$. We say that f is a (weakly) one-way function if the following hold:*

1. *f is injective and for all $x \in \Sigma^*$, $|x|^{\frac{1}{k}} \leq |f(x)| \leq |x|^k$ for some $k > 0$ (that is, $f(x)$ is at most polynomially larger or smaller than x).*

2. *f is in* **FP** *but f^{-1} is not in* **FP**. *(In other words, there is no polynomial time algorithm which, given a y, either computes x such that $f(x) = y$ or returns 'no' if there is no such x.)*

Exercise 5.7.18 *Show that if f is a one-way function, then f^{-1} is in* **FNP**.

In order to determine more exactly the role of one-way functions in complexity theory, let us denote by **UP** the class of languages accepted by **unambiguous polynomial time bounded NTM**. These are polynomial time bounded NTM such that for any input there is at most one accepting computation.

Exercise 5.7.19 *Assume a one-way function $f : \Sigma^* \to \Sigma^*$. Define the language $L_f = \{(x, y) \mid$ there is a z such that $f(z) = y$ and $z \preceq x$ (in strict ordering of strings)$\}$. Show that (a) $L_f \in$* **UP**; *(b) $L_f \notin$* **P** *(for example, by showing, using a binary search, that if $L_f \in$* **P**, *then $f^{-1} \in$* **FP**); *(c)* **P** $\subseteq$ **UP** $\subseteq$ **NP**.

Theorem 5.7.20 **P** $\neq$ **UP** *if and only if there are one-way functions.*

Proof: It follows from Exercise 5.7.19 that if there is a one-way function, then **P** $\neq$ **UP**. Let us now assume that there is a language $L \in$ **UP**$-$**P**, and let $\mathcal{M}$ be an unambiguous polynomial time bounded NTM accepting L. Denote by $f_{\mathcal{M}}$ the function defined as follows:

$$f_{\mathcal{M}}(x) = \begin{cases} 1y, & \text{if } x \text{ is an accepting computation of } \mathcal{M} \text{ for } y \text{ as an input;} \\ 0y, & \text{if } x \text{ is not an accepting computation of } \mathcal{M} \text{ for } y \text{ as an input.} \end{cases}$$

Clearly, $f_{\mathcal{M}}$ is well defined, one-to-one (because of the unambiguity of $\mathcal{M}$), and computable in polynomial time. Moreover, the lengths of inputs and outputs are polynomially related. Finally, were $f_{\mathcal{M}}$ invertible in polynomial time, we would be able to recognize $L \notin$ **P** in polynomial time. □

Exercise 5.7.21 *Define the class* **FUP**, *and show that* **P** = **UP** *if and only if* **FP**=**FUP**.

5.7.8 Counting Problems – Class #P

In a decision problem we ask whether there is a solution. In a search problem we set out to find a solution. In a **counting problem** we ask how many solutions exist.

Counting problems are clearly of importance, have their own specificity and may be computationally hard even for problems in **P**.

It is common to use notation #P for a counting version of a decision problem P. For example, #SAT is the problem of determining how many satisfying assignments a given Boolean formula has. #HAMILTON PATH is the problem of determining how many Hamilton paths a given graph has.

A 'counting analog' of the class **NP** is the class **#P**, pronounced 'sharp P' (or 'number P' or 'pond P'), defined as follows.

Definition 5.7.22 *Let Q be a polynomially balanced and polynomially decidable binary relation. The counting problem associated with Q is the problem of determining, for a given x the number of y such that* $(x,y) \in Q$. *The output is required to be in binary form.* **#P** *is the class of all counting problems associated with polynomially balanced and decidable relations.*

The number of solutions of a counting problem can be exponentially large. This is the reason why in the definition of **#P** it is required that the output be in binary form.

There is another definition of the class **#P**, actually the original one, considered in the following exercise.

Exercise 5.7.23 *Show that* **#P** *is the class of functions f for which there is a NTM* $\mathcal{M}_f$ *such that* $f(x)$ *is the number of accepting computations of* $\mathcal{M}_f$ *for the input x.*

#P-completeness is defined with respect to the same reduction as **FP**-completeness. Actually, a more restricted form of reduction is often sufficient to prove **#P**-completeness. A reduction f of instances x of one counting problem $\mathcal{P}_1$ into instances of another counting problem $\mathcal{P}_2$ is called **parsimonious** if x and $f(x)$ always have the same number of solutions.

Many reductions used to prove **#P**-completeness are either parsimonious or can easily be modified to make them so. This is true, for example, for the proof of Cook's theorem. This way **#P**-completeness has been shown for counting versions of a variety of **NP**-complete problems, for example, #SAT and #HAMILTON PATH.

Of special interest are those **#P**-complete problems for which the corresponding search problem can be solved in polynomial time. Of such a type is the PERMANENT problem for Boolean matrices (which is equivalent to the problem of counting perfect matchings in bipartite graphs).

5.8 Approximability of NP-Complete Problems

From the theoretical point of view, **NP**-completeness results are beautiful and powerful. The hardest problems ('trouble-makers') have been localized and close relations between them discovered. Could we eliminate one of them, all would be eliminated.

From the practical point of view, **NP**-completeness is a disastrous phenomenon, and 'practically unacceptable'. Too many important problems are **NP**-complete. Computing practice can hardly accept such a limitation. One has to look for feasible ways to get around them, if at all possible.

There are several approaches to overcoming the limitations imposed by NP-completeness: approximation algorithms, randomized algorithms, fast average-case algorithms (with respect to 'main' probability distributions of inputs), heuristics, even exponential time algorithms that are fast for most of the inputs we encounter in applications might do, in the absence of anything better.

In this section we deal with approximation algorithms for **NP**-complete optimization problems. Perhaps the most surprising discovery in this regard is that, in spite of the isomorphism between **NP**-complete problems, they can be surprisingly different from the point of view of the design of good approximation algorithms. In addition, the existence of good approximation algorithms for some **NP**-complete problems has turned out to be deeply connected with some fundamental questions of computing.

As we shall see, the search for good approximation algorithms for **NP**-complete problems brought both good news and bad news. For some **NP**-complete problems there are approximation algorithms that are as good as we need and for others quite good approximations can be obtained. But for some **NP**-complete problems there are good reasons to believe that no good approximation algorithms exist, in a sense.

5.8.1 Performance of Approximation Algorithms

The issue is to understand how good approximation algorithms can exist for particular **NP**-complete problems. For this we need some quantitative measures for 'goodness' of approximations. We start, therefore, with some criteria.

For each instance x of an optimization problem $\mathcal{P}$ let $F_{\mathcal{P}}(x)$ be the set of feasible solutions of $\mathcal{P}$, and for each $s \in F_{\mathcal{P}}(x)$ let a $c(s) > 0$ – a cost of the solution s – be given. The optimal solution of $\mathcal{P}$ for an instance x is then defined by

$$OPT(x) = \min_{s \in F_{\mathcal{P}}(x)} c(s) \quad \text{or} \quad OPT(x) = \max_{s \in F_{\mathcal{P}}(x)} c(s),$$

depending on whether the minimal or maximal solution is required. (For example, for TSP the cost is the length of a tour.)

We say that an approximation algorithm $\mathcal{A}$, mapping each instance x of an optimization problem $\mathcal{P}$ to one of its solutions in $F_{\mathcal{P}}(x)$, has the **ratio bound** $\rho(n)$ and the **relative error bound** $\varepsilon(n)$ if

$$\max_{|x|=n}\left\{\frac{c(\mathcal{A}(x))}{c(OPT(x))},\frac{c(OPT(x))}{c(\mathcal{A}(x))}\right\}\leq\rho(n),\qquad \max_{|x|=n}\left\{\frac{|c(\mathcal{A}(x))-c(OPT(x))|}{\max\{c(OPT(x)),c(\mathcal{A}(x))\}}\right\}\leq\varepsilon(n).$$

Both definitions are chosen to correspond to our intuition and to apply simultaneously to minimization and maximization problems. Both these bounds compare an approximation solution with the optimal one, but in two different ways.

Exercise 5.8.1 *Show how one can simplify definitions of relative error bound and/or ratio bound if only maximalization (minimalization) problems are considered.*

The ratio bound is never less than 1. An optimal algorithm has the ratio bound 1. The larger the best possible ratio bound of an approximation algorithm, the worse is the algorithm. The relative error bound is never more than 1, and always between 0 and 1.

Exercise 5.8.2 *Show that (a) an algorithm $\mathcal{A}$ of a maximization problem with a relative error bound ε never produces a solution more than $(1-\varepsilon)$ times smaller than the maximum; (b) an algorithm $\mathcal{A}$ for a minimization problem with a relative error bound ε never produces a solution that would be more than $(\frac{1}{1-\varepsilon})$ times larger than the minimum.*

We shall now concentrate on two problems concerning approximation of **NP**-complete problems.

- The **constant relative error bound problem**: given an **NP**-complete optimization problem $\mathcal{P}$ with a cost of solutions c and an $\varepsilon > 0$, does there exist an approximation polynomial time algorithm for $\mathcal{P}$ with the relative error bound ε?
- **The approximation scheme problem:** does there exist for a given **NP**-complete optimization problem $\mathcal{P}$ with a cost of solutions c a polynomial time algorithm for designing, given an $\varepsilon > 0$ and an input instance x, an approximation for $\mathcal{P}$ and x with the relative error bound ε?

Let us first deal with the constant relative error bounds. We say that an algorithm $\mathcal{A}$ is an ε-approximation algorithm for an optimization problem $\mathcal{P}$ if ε is its relative error bound. The **approximation threshold** for $\mathcal{P}$ is the greatest lower bound of all $\varepsilon > 0$ such that there is a polynomial time ε-approximation algorithm for $\mathcal{P}$.

5.8.2 NP-complete Problems with a Constant Approximation Threshold

We show now that **NP**-complete optimization problems can differ very much with respect to their approximation thresholds. Note that if an optimization problem $\mathcal{P}$ has an approximation threshold 0, this means that an approximation arbitrarily close to the optimum is possible, whereas an approximation threshold of 1 means that essentially no universal approximation method is possible.

As a first example let us consider the following optimization version of the knapsack problem: Given n items with weights $w_1, \ldots, w_n$ and values $v_1, \ldots, v_n$ and a knapsack limit c, the task is to find a bit vector $(x_1, \ldots, x_n)$ such that $\sum_{i=1}^{n} x_i w_i \leq c$ and $\sum_{i=1}^{n} x_i v_i$ is as large as possible.

Exercise 5.8.3 *We get a decision version of the above knapsack problem by fixing a goal K and asking whether there is a solution vector such that $\sum_{i=1}^{n} x_i v_i \geq K$. Show that this new version of the knapsack problem is also* **NP***-complete.*

Theorem 5.8.4 *The approximation threshold for the optimization version of the KNAPSACK problem is* 0.

Proof: The basic idea of the proof is very simple. We take a modification of the algorithm in Example 5.4.17 and make out of it a polynomial time algorithm by applying it to an instance with truncated input data. The larger the truncation we make, the better the approximation we get. Details follow.

Let a knapsack instance $(w_1, \ldots, w_n, c, v_1, \ldots, v_n)$ be given, and let $V = \max\{v_1, \ldots, v_n\}$. For $1 \leq i \leq n, 1 \leq v \leq nV$ we define

$$W(i,v) = \min_{x \in \{0,1\}^i} \{\sum_{j=1}^{i} x_j w_j \mid \sum_{j=1}^{i} x_j v_j = v\}.$$

Clearly, $W(i,v)$ can be computed using the recurrences $W(0,v) = \infty$, and for all $i > 0$ and $1 \leq v \leq nV$,

$$W(i+1,v) = \min\{W(i,v), W(i, v - v_{i+1}) + w_{i+1}\}.$$

Finally, we take the largest v such that $W(n,v) \leq c$.

The time complexity of this algorithm is $\mathcal{O}(n^2 V)$. The algorithm is therefore not polynomial with respect to the size of the input. In order to make out of it a polynomial time approximation algorithm, we use the following 'truncation trick'.

Instead of the knapsack instance $(w_1, \ldots, w_n, c, v_1, \ldots, v_n)$, we take a b-approximate instance $(w_1, \ldots, w_n, c, v'_1, \ldots, v'_n)$, where $v'_i = 2^b \lfloor \frac{v_i}{2^b} \rfloor$; that is, v'_i is obtained from v_i by replacing the least significant b bits by zeros. (We show later how to choose b.)

If we now apply the above algorithm to this b-truncated instance, we get its solution in time $\mathcal{O}(\frac{n^2 V}{2^b})$, because we can ignore the last b zeros in the v_i's.

The vector $x^{(b)}$ which we obtain as the solution for this b-truncated instance may be quite different from the vector $x^{(0)}$ that provides the optimal solution. However, and this is essential, as the following inequalities show, the values that these two vectors produce cannot be too different. Indeed, it holds that

$$\sum_{i=1}^{n} x_i^{(0)} v_i \geq \sum_{i=1}^{n} x_i^{(b)} v_i \geq \sum_{i=1}^{n} x_i^{(b)} v'_i \geq \sum_{i=1}^{n} x_i^{(b)} (v_i - 2^b) \geq \sum_{i=1}^{n} x_i^{(b)} v_i - n2^b.$$

The first inequality holds because $x^{(0)}$ provides the optimal solution for the original instance; the second holds because $v_i \geq v'_i$; the third holds because $x^{(b)}$ is the optimal solution for the b-truncated instance.

We can assume without loss of generality that $w_i \leq c$ for all i. In this case V is the lower bound on the value of the optimal solution.The relative error bound for the algorithm is therefore $\varepsilon = \frac{n2^b}{V}$.

Given an $0 < \varepsilon \leq 1$, we can take $b = \lceil \lg \frac{\varepsilon V}{n} \rceil$ in order to obtain an ε-approximation algorithm for the optimization version of the knapsack problem. The time complexity of the algorithm is $\mathcal{O}(\frac{n^2 V}{2^b}) = \mathcal{O}(\frac{n^3}{\varepsilon})$; therefore we have a polynomial time algorithm. □

The second approximability problem which we will discuss is the VERTEX COVER problem. Given a graph $G = (V, E)$, we seek the smallest set of nodes C such that each edge of G coincides with at least one node of C. Let us consider the following approximation algorithm for VERTEX COVER.

Algorithm 5.8.5 (VERTEX COVER approximation algorithm)

$C \leftarrow \emptyset; E' \leftarrow E;$
while $E' \neq \emptyset$ **do** take any edge (u, v) from E';
  $C \leftarrow C \cup \{u, v\};$
  $E' \leftarrow E' - \{$ all edges in E' that are incident with one of the nodes $u, v\}$
 od.

Let C_G be a vertex cover this algorithm provides for a graph $G = (V, E)$. C_G can be seen as representing $\frac{|C_G|}{2}$ edges of G, no two of which have a common vertex. This means that if $OPT(G)$ is an optimal node covering of G, then it must have at least $\left|\frac{C_G}{2}\right|$ nodes. Thus, $|OPT(G)| \geq \frac{|C_G|}{2}$, and therefore

$$\frac{|C_G| - |OPT(G)|}{|C_G|} \leq \frac{1}{2}.$$

We have actually proved the following theorem.

Theorem 5.8.6 *The approximation threshold for the VERTEX COVER problem is* $\leq \frac{1}{2}$.

Surprisingly, the above very simple approximation algorithm is the best known approximation algorithm for the VERTEX COVER problem.

Exercise 5.8.7 *Give an example of the graph for which Algorithm 5.8.5 never produces an optimal solution.*

Exercise 5.8.8 *Design a good $\mathcal{O}(1)$ approximation algorithm for the MAX-3-CNFF problem of determining the maximum number of satisfying assignments for a Boolean formula in 3-CNF. (Hint: determine how many clauses satisfy the average assignment.)*

Theorem 5.8.12 in the next subsection shows, very unfortunately, that there are **NP**-complete problems which do not seem to have approximation algorithms with a relative error bound smaller than 1. Not only that: such a practically important optimization problem as the TSP problem has this property.

Exercise 5.8.9 *The BIN-PACKING problem is given by n integers $a_1, \ldots, a_n$ (items), a capacity c and a number b of bins. The task is to determine whether there is an assignment of integers a_i into n bins such that in no bin is the total sum of integers larger than c. This problem is* **NP**-*complete. Consider now the minimization version of the problem, which requires us to determine, given $a_1, \ldots, a_n$ and c, the minimum number of bins such that bin packing is possible. Show that the approximation threshold for the BIN-PACKING problem is at least $\frac{1}{3}$.*

Exercise 5.8.10* *The* **asymptotic approximation threshold** *for an optimization problem $\mathcal{P}$ is the smallest integer ε such that there is a δ and an approximation algorithm $\mathcal{A}$ for $\mathcal{P}$ such that for all instances x*

$$|c(\mathcal{A}(x)) - OPT(x)| \leq \varepsilon \max\{OPT(x), c(\mathcal{A}(x))\} + \delta.$$

Show that the asymptotic approximation threshold for the BIN-PACKING problem is at most $\frac{1}{2}$.

Exercise 5.8.11** *Optimization version of the SUBSET-SUM problem. Given a finite set Q of rational numbers and a bound c, compute $\max_{X \subseteq Q}\{\sum_{x \in X} x \mid \sum_{x \in X} \leq c\}$. Determine for the SUBSET SUM problem (a) the approximation threshold; (b) the asymptotic approximation threshold.*

5.8.3 Travelling Salesman Problem

This is one of the most studied **NP**-complete optimization problems. Our first result concerning its approximation is far from encouraging.

Theorem 5.8.12 *Unless* **P** = **NP**, *the approximation threshold for TSP is* 1.[6]

Proof: In order to prove the theorem, it is sufficient to show that the existence of a polynomial time approximation algorithm $\mathcal{A}$ for TSP with the relative error bound $\varepsilon < 1$ implies the existence of a polynomial time algorithm to determine whether a given graph has a Hamilton cycle (which is an **NP**-complete problem). This we show now.

Given a graph $G = (V, E)$, we first construct the following instance of TSP: let V be the set of cities, and let the distance between two cities c_i and c_j be 1 if $(i,j) \in E$, and $\frac{|V|}{1-\varepsilon}$ otherwise. To this instance of TSP we now apply the algorithm $\mathcal{A}$. If $\mathcal{A}$ returns a tour of cost $|V|$, then we know that G has a Hamilton cycle. If $\mathcal{A}$ yields a tour of greater length, then the total length of such a tour must be larger than $\frac{|V|}{1-\varepsilon}$. Since $\mathcal{A}$ is a polynomial ε-approximation algorithm, by the assumption, we know that the optimum is never less than $(1-\varepsilon)$ times the solution found by $\mathcal{A}$, and is therefore larger than $|V|$. Thus, G has no Hamilton cycle.[7] □

[6]Similar results have been shown for several other optimization **NP**-complete problems. For example, for the CLIQUE problem: given a graph G determine the maximal k such that G has a complete subgraph with k nodes.

[7]The very disappointing results of Theorems 5.4.14 and 5.8.12 do not represent the whole story concerning our ability to solve TSP. Actually TSP is an important example of a success story in the area of combinatorial optimization methods. A great effort has been made to solve well as many instances of TSP as possible. Advances in technology, theory, algorithms and data structures underlie the progress in the area of achieving an optimal solution. The largest nontrivial TSP instances solved: in 1980, 318 cities; in 1989, 2,392 cities; and in 1994, 7,397 cities (taking 3–4 years). In all cases state-of-the-art computers and methods were used.

The success story of approximations of TSP is also remarkable: with a variety of approximation algorithms tested, including those based on the ideas of simulating annealing from physics, genetic algorithms and neural networks.

It has also been shown that for several important special cases of TSP there are quite good approximation algorithms.

Let us first consider the case in which all weights are 1 or 2. Observe that in such a case each approximation algorithm is a $\frac{1}{2}$-approximation algorithm. In such a case it is even possible to prove the existence of a $\frac{1}{7}$-approximation algorithm.

Exercise 5.8.13 *Develop an 1/2-approximation algorithm for the following weighted vertex cover problem: given a graph $G = \langle V, E \rangle$ and weights of all its nodes, find a vertex cover of G with minimal sum of weights of chosen vertices. (The following method, given as a hint, represents an important technique how to design approximation algorithms: (1) Reformulate the weighted vertex cover problem in the following way, assuming $V = \{1, \ldots, n\}$ and w_i is the weight of the node i: minimize $\sum_i w_i x_i$ subject to constrains: $x_i + x_j \geq 1\, \forall (i,j) \in E; x_i \in \{0,1\}\, \forall i \in V$; (b) consider the linear program: minimize $\sum_i w_i x_i$ subject to constrains $x_i + x_j \geq 1\, \forall (i,j) \in E; 0 \leq x_i \leq 1\, \forall i \in V$, since it includes all the feasible solutions of the previous formulation. (Its optimum is a lower bound on the optimum of the weighted vertex cover problem. Moreover, its optimum can be found in polynomial time.))*

A natural generalization of the above case concerns TSP instances that satisfy the **triangle inequality**: $d(i,j) \leq d(i,k) + d(k,j)$ for any nodes i,j,k and the distance $d(x,y)$ between any two nodes x,y. It has been shown that in such a case there is a $\frac{1}{3}$-approximation algorithm.

One elegant and successful way to attack TSP is through the Held–Karp lower bound. This approach is based on an observation that if we use variable x_{ij} to represent the edge between cities c_i and c_j, $1 \leq i < j \leq n$, taking $x_{ij} = 1$ to mean that the edge (c_i, c_j) is in the optimal tour, then the TSP is equivalent to the following problem: Minimize

$$\sum_{i=1}^{n} \sum_{j=i+1}^{n} d_{ij} x_{ij}$$

subject to conditions

$$\sum_{i=k \text{ or } j=k} x_{ij} = 2,\ 1 \leq k \leq n,$$

$$\sum_{|S \cap \{i,j\}|} x_{ij} \geq 2 \text{ for all } S \subseteq \{1, \ldots, n\}$$

and $x_{ij} \in \{0,1\}$, for $1 \leq i < j \leq n$. If we relax the last condition and replace it by the condition $0 \leq x_{ij} \leq 1$, we get a RLP problem that is in **P**, solution of which provides a lower bound, the Held–Karp lower bound (HK lower bound), for the original instance of TSP. Experience shows that for a large variety of randomly generated instances of TSP the optimal tour length averages less than 0.8% over the HK bound, and for real-world instances this is almost always less than 2%. However, computation of the HK bound is also a very demanding task. In 1994, a top result was to compute the HK bound exactly for TSP instances with up to 30,000 cities and to get a good approximation of this bound for TSP instances with up to a million cities.

For a detailed presentation of current methods and results, including Held–Karp bound computations, see Johnson and McGeoch (1996) and Johnson, McGeoch and Rothberg (1996).

Exercise 5.8.14* *Show that the approximation threshold for TSP is at most $\frac{1}{2}$ for graphs satisfying the triangle inequality. (Hint: evaluate the 'goodness' of the following approximation algorithm for designing a travelling salesman tour:*

1. *Choose a node v, and design a minimum spanning tree with the root in the node v.*
2. *Label the vertices of the tree in a pre-order way and tour the graph accordingly.)*

Exercise 5.8.15* *Show that the decision version of the TSP is also* **NP**-*complete when restricted to labelled graphs satisfying the triangle inequality.*

5.8.4 Nonapproximability

The ideal case concerning approximability of a problem $\mathcal{P}$ is when there is a polynomial time algorithm $\mathcal{A}$ such that, given a problem instance x and an $\varepsilon > 0$, $\mathcal{A}$ returns a solution with the relative error bound ε. This motivation is behind the following concepts.

Definition 5.8.16 *A* **polynomial time approximation scheme** *for an optimization problem $\mathcal{P}$ is an algorithm $\mathcal{A}$ which, given an $\varepsilon > 0$ and an instance x of $\mathcal{P}$, provides a solution of $\mathcal{P}$ for x with the relative error bound ε in time bounded by a polynomial in $|x|$ (which may also depend on ε). If, in addition, this polynomial depends polynomially on $\frac{1}{\varepsilon}$ as well, then the approximation scheme is said to be a* **fully polynomial approximation scheme**.

Note that our approximation algorithm for the optimization version of the knapsack problem provides a fully polynomial approximation scheme. However, surprisingly, there is a polynomial time approximation scheme for TSP in R^2, if distances are computed accordingly to the Euclidean metric.

Another interesting optimization problem is MAXSAT, in which we are given a set of clauses and search for an assignment that satisfies the largest number of them. A decision version of this problem has a bound k, and the task is to decide whether there is an assignment that satisfies at least k of the clauses.

The decision version of the MAXSAT problem is **NP**-complete even in the case where we consider only clauses with two literals. MAXSAT is a surprisingly difficult problem with respect to approximation. The following theorem holds.

Theorem 5.8.17 *If there is a polynomial time approximation scheme for the MAXSAT problem, then* **P** = **NP**.

Similar results hold for some other **NP**-complete problems: for example, for the VERTEX-COVER and so on.

5.8.5 Complexity classes

A variety of classes of optimization problems has been introduced with respect to the degree of approximability. In addition, approximation preserving reducibilities have been introduced and basic hardness and complexity results established for them. Perhaps the most basic are the following classes.

1. **PO:** the class of optimization problems solvable in polynomial time on MTM.

2. **FPTAS:** the class of optimization problems for which fully polynomial time approximation scheme exists.

3. **PTAS:** the class of optimization problems for which a polynomial time approximation scheme exists.

4. **APX:** the class of optimization problems for which an ε-approximation algorithm exists for an $0 < \varepsilon < 1$.

5. **NPO:** the class of optimization problems whose decision version is in **NP**.

Basic inclusions between these classes are trivial:

$$\mathbf{PO} \subseteq \mathbf{FTPAS} \subseteq \mathbf{PTAS} \subseteq \mathbf{APX} \subseteq \mathbf{NPO}$$

and it can be shown for each of the above inclusions that it is proper if and only if $\mathbf{P} \neq \mathbf{NP}$.

5.9 Randomized Complexity Classes

Randomization seems to be a powerful methodology for overcoming limitations imposed by deterministic computation and for speeding-up computations. In this section we explore the power of this methodology.

5.9.1 Randomized algorithms

Before introducing the main acceptance modes and complexity classes for randomized computing, we will discuss some examples of randomized algorithms to see their advantages and methods for their analysis.

In some cases randomization is the only way to deal with the problem.

Example 5.9.1 (Symmetry breaking) *n identical processors connected in a ring have to choose one of the processors to be a 'leader', provided each of the processors knows n.*

Algorithm 5.9.2 (Election of a leader)

1. Each processor sets its local variable m to n and becomes 'active'.

2. Each active processor chooses, randomly and independently, an integer between 1 and m.

3. Those processors that choose 1 (if any) send a one-bit message around the ring.

4. After $n-1$ steps each processor knows the number l of processors that chose 1. If $l = 1$, the election ends; if $l = 0$, the election continues by repeating Step 2; if $l > 1$, then only those processors remain active that chose 1. They set their local variables m to l, and the election continues by Step 2.

The correctness of the algorithm is obvious, and one can show that its time efficiency is good and the number of bits that need to be exchanged is small.

Randomized algorithms are often very simple, and their efficiency is either comparable or better than that of deterministic ones for the same problem.

Example 5.9.3 (Randomized QUICKSORT) *To sort a sequence $S = \langle a_1, \ldots, a_n \rangle$ of n different elements we can use the following algorithm.*

Algorithm 5.9.4 (RQUICKSORT)

1. Choose randomly $1 \leq j \leq n$.
2. Partition S into sequences S_1 and S_2 of elements $a_i \leq a_j$ and $a_i > a_j$, respectively.
3. Sort recursively S_1 and S_2.

It is again clear that RQUICKSORT correctly sorts any sequence. If all input sequences are equally probable, then it can be shown that RQUICKSORT requires on average $\Theta(n \lg n)$ time.

Exercise 5.9.5 *Design a simple randomized algorithm to determine, given a sequence of n elements and $1 \leq k \leq n$, the k-th smallest element.*

Example 5.9.6 (Zero polynomial testing) *In order to decide whether a polynomial p with integer coefficients and n variables, each of degree at most k, is identically zero, we can use N times the following simple randomized algorithm: compute $p(\xi_1, \ldots, \xi_n)$, with integer values $\xi_1, \ldots, \xi_n$ chosen randomly and independently according to the uniform distribution in the interval $[0, 2kn]$. If once a value different from 0 is obtained, then p is not identically 0. If all N times the value is zero, then we can consider p to be identically zero. By Schwartz's lemma (1.9.4), the probability of error is at most 2^{-N}. (The algorithm can be used to test equality of two polynomials.)*

Such a randomized algorithm is of importance especially if p is given implicitly: for instance, as the value of the determinant of a matrix of polynomials.

Example 5.9.7 (Cuts in multigraphs) *The task is to determine the smallest set of edges of a given multigraph G whose removal disconnects G. We show that there is a simple randomized algorithm that does the job correctly, with large probability.*

The basic idea of the algorithm presented below is that an edge contraction of a multigraph does not reduce the size of its minimal cut. (By an edge contraction of a multigraph G with respect to an edge (u, v), we understand a merging of vertices u and v into one, redirecting edges to u and v to the newly created vertex and removing self-loops of the new vertex.)

Algorithm 5.9.8 (Minimal cut in a multigraph)

while there are more than two vertices in the multigraph
do an edge contraction with respect to a randomly choosen edge **od**;
Output the size of the maximal cut of the resulting two-vertex graph.

As shown in Figures 5.9a, b, c, d, e, an application of Algorithm 5.9.8 may produce the correct result (Figure 5.9e), but may not (Figure 5.9d). Let us therefore investigate how probable it is that the above algorithm makes an error.

Let G be a multigraph of n nodes, k the size of its minimal cut and C its particular minimal cut. G has to have at least $\frac{kn}{2}$ edges – otherwise G would have a vertex of degree less than k and its incidental edges would form a minimal cut of size smaller than k.

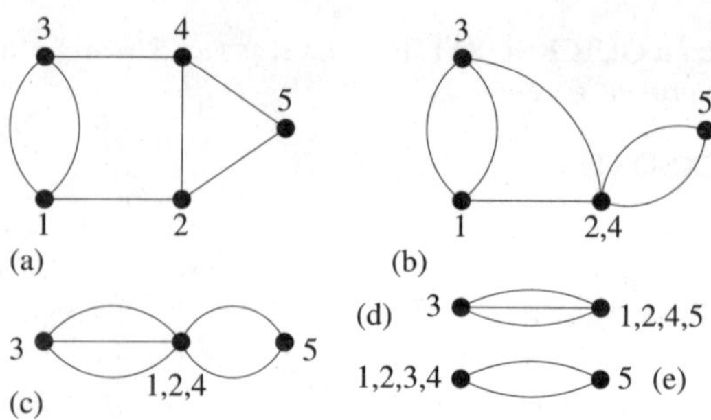

Figure 5.9 Contraction in a multigraph

We derive a lower bound on the probability that no edge of C is ever contracted during an execution of the algorithm – and therefore the edges surviving till the end are exactly those of C.

Denote by E_i the event of not choosing *an edge of C at the i-th step of the algorithm, for $1 \le i \le n-2$. The probability that the edge randomly chosen in the first step is in C is at most $k/(nk/2) = \frac{2}{n}$, and therefore $Pr(E_1) \ge 1 - \frac{2}{n}$. If E_1 occurs, then at the second contraction step there are at least $\frac{k(n-1)}{2}$ edges, and therefore the probability of picking an edge in C is at most $\frac{2}{n-1}$. Hence, $Pr(E_2|E_1) \ge 1 - \frac{2}{n-1}$. Similarly, at the i-th step, $i \ge 2$, the number of remaining vertices is $n-i+1$, the size of the minimal cut is still at least k, and therefore the multigraph has at least $\frac{k(n-i+1)}{2}$ edges remaining at this step. Thus $Pr(E_i | \bigcap_{j=1}^{i-1} E_i) \ge 1 - \frac{2}{n-i+1}$. The probability that no edge of C is ever picked during the execution of the algorithm is therefore, by a natural generalization of (1.70),*

$$Pr[\bigcap_{i=1}^{n-2} E_i] \ge \prod_{i=1}^{n-2}\left(1 - \frac{2}{n-i+1}\right) = \frac{2}{n(n-1)}.$$

The probability of discovering a particular minimal cut is therefore larger than $\frac{2}{n^2}$.

A big deal? Not so. However – and this is the point – if we repeat the above algorithm $\frac{n^2}{2}$ times, making independent random decisions each time, then the probability that a minimal cut is not found in any of the $\frac{n^2}{2}$ runs is at most

$$\left(1 - \frac{2}{n^2}\right)^{\frac{n^2}{2}} < \frac{1}{e}.$$

(Observe that by repetition of the algorithm we have reduced the probability of failure from $1 - \frac{2}{n^2}$ to a more respectable $\frac{1}{e}$. Further execution of the algorithm can make the failure probability arbitrarily small (by increasing computation time of course).

Algorithm 5.9.8 is remarkably simple compared with the known deterministic ones for the same problem.

It is nowadays clear that randomization can speed up many computations. However – and this is one of the most important questions – can randomization help also to cope with **NP**-completeness?

Satisfiability of Boolean formulas, as one of the basic **NP-complete** problems, is certainly one of the most proper choices for exploring what we can achieve with randomization in the case of the **NP**-complete problems. Surprisingly, for satisfiability too we have a very simple randomized algorithm.

Algorithm 5.9.9 (Satisfiability of Boolean formulas)

Choose randomly a truth assignment T.
while there is a truth assignment T' that differs from T in exactly
 one variable and satisfies more clauses than T
 do choose T' that satisfies the most clauses and set $T \leftarrow T'$ **od**;
return T

We show now that if a Boolean formula F in 3-CNF, with n variables, is satisfiable, then Algorithm 5.9.9 discovers, with very high probability, a satisfying assignment T' for F.

If Algorithm 5.9.9 starts with a truth assignment that agrees with T' in the values of very few variables, then it is likely that a local maximum that is not a global optimum is found. Let us therefore call a truth assignment *bad* if it agrees with T' in fewer than $(\frac{1}{2}-\theta)n$ variables, for some $\theta > 0$, and let us call all other assignments *good*. Since Algorithm 5.9.9 chooses the starting truth assignment randomly, the probability that this assignment is bad is, by Chernoff's bound in Exercise 1.9.15, with $p = \frac{1}{2}, \varepsilon = 2\theta$, at most $e^{-\theta^2 n}$. This means that our algorithm usually starts with a good truth assignment.

Consider now a good truth assignment T that agrees with a satisfying assignment T' in exactly $k \geq (\frac{1}{2}-\theta)n$ variables, and let V be a fixed variable on which T and T' disagree. Suppose we change the value of V. How many clauses do we gain, and how many do we lose? Let us denote by C_+ the set of all clauses, of three literals, on n variables, that are satisfied by T' (no matter whether they are in F or not), and that change from false to true if the value of V is flipped. Moreover, denote by C_- the set of clauses that change from true to false.

Our next task is to calculate the size of C_+ and C_-. In order to do this we can assume, without loss of generality, that T' is a uniformly true assignment (otherwise we can flip literals in F, if needed). In such a case C_+ is the set of 3-clauses that contain the variable V and two other variables that occur positively if and only if they are false in T. Hence $|C_+| = \binom{n-1}{2}$. Similarly, C_- is the set of clauses that contain the variable V negatively (that is, $\bar{V}$) and two other variables that occur positively if and only if they are false in T', excluding the case that all three variables occur negatively and two of them are among those k for which T and T' agree, because for such triples of variables T' is not satisfied. Hence, $|C_-| = \binom{n-1}{2} - \binom{k}{2}$.

Observe that by changing the value of V we do not gain anything if and only if F has at least as many clauses in C_+ as in C_-. Our next task is to determine an upper bound on the probability that this happens. In order to do this, denote $B(p,n)$ a binomial random variable the value of which gives the number of successes in n independent trials. In such a case the probability that we do not gain anything by changing the value of V is $Pr(B(p,|C_-|) \geq B'(p,|C_+|))$, where B and B' are independent binomial random variables. This probability is clearly at most

$$Pr(B(p,|C_-|) \geq m) + Pr(B'(p,|C_+|) \leq m),$$

for every m. We can now apply Chernoff's bound from Lemma 1.9.13 and Exercise 1.9.15 to get that this probability is at most

$$e^{-((m-p|C_-|)^2)/(3p|C_-|)} + e^{-((m-p|C_+|)^2)/(2p|C_+|)} \leq e^{-((m-p|C_-|)^2)/(3p|C_-|)} + e^{-((m-p|C_+|)^2)/(3p|C_+|)}. \quad (5.5)$$

If we take $m = p\sqrt{|C_-||C_+|}$, then, after elementary adjustments of the right side of the formula in (5.5) we get that the probability that by flipping V we do not gain anything is at most $2e^{-cpn^2}$, where

$$c \doteq (1-\sqrt{1-(0.5-\varepsilon)^2})^2.$$

This means that the probability that our algorithm, starting from a good truth assignment, will ever be misled by flipping a variable is at most $n2^n e^{-cpn^2}$, because there are at most $n2^{n-1}$ such possible flippings. This yields, for $p = \frac{1}{2}$, the following theorem.

Theorem 5.9.10 *If $0 < \varepsilon < \frac{1}{2}$, then there exists a constant $c \doteq (1-\sqrt{(1-(1/2-\varepsilon)^2)})^2/6$ such that for all but a fraction of at most $n2^n e^{-cn^2/2}$ of satisfiable 3-CNF Boolean formulas with n variables the probability that the greedy algorithm succeeds in discovering a truth assignment in each independent trial from a random start is at least $1-e^{-\varepsilon^2 n}$.*

Randomization is also of importance for the design of approximation algorithms.

Example 5.9.11 (MAX-CNF problem) *The task is, given a Boolean formula F, to determine a truth assignment that satisfies a maximum of clauses of F. This problem is* **NP**-*hard, but can be solved by just randomly choosing an assignment.*

Indeed, suppose that F has m clauses and that each of its variables is set randomly to 1 or 0. For $1 \le i \le m$, let Z_i be a random variable the value of which is 1 if the ith clause is satisfied, and 0, otherwise. The probability that a clause with k literals is not satisfied by a random assignment is 2^{-k}, and the probability that it is satisfied is $1-2^{-k} \ge \frac{1}{2}$. Hence $EZ_i \ge \frac{1}{2}$ for all i, and therefore the expected number of clauses satisfied by a random assignment is $\sum_{i=1}^{m} EZ_i \ge \frac{m}{2}$. Random choice of an assignment therefore yields a very simple randomized $\frac{1}{2}$-approximation algorithm.

Remark 5.9.12 An interesting problem with good but not arbitrarily good approximation algorithms is that of determining the maximum number of clauses that can be satisfied by a given Boolean formula in 3-CNF. Given a random assignment, an arbitrary clause has at least a $\frac{7}{8}$ chance of being satisfied. This implies that the average assignment satisfies at least $\frac{7}{8}$th of all clauses. Since the maximal assignment has to satisfy more clauses than the average number, we get a very good approximation by saying always, in $\mathcal{O}(1)$-time, that $\sqrt{\frac{7}{8}} = 0.935$ of clauses are satisfied. However, there is a constant $c < 1$, but very close to 1 (about 0.962) such that one can get a c-approximation only if **P** = **NP**.

In general, we talk about **randomized algorithms** if algorithms use 'coin-tossing' or various RANDOM procedures to make random decisions. The corresponding formal machine model is that of the **probabilistic Turing machine** – a Turing machine that can generate a random bit in one step or, from another point of view, has a special 'random tape' filled with new random bits each time a computation starts.

Exercise 5.9.13 *Let $t: \mathbf{N} \rightarrow \mathbf{N}$ be a space-constructible function. Show that each probabilistic $t(n)$-time bounded MTM can be simulated by a deterministic MTM in space $\mathcal{O}(t(n))$ and time $\mathcal{O}(2^{t(n)})$.*

Randomized elements of random algorithms or probabilistic Turing machines are not so easy to deal with, and the elegance and exactness used in studying deterministic computations and their models are less easily attainable. Fortunately, in order to model random steps formally and to study the power of randomization, we do not need coin-tossing or random number generators. It is enough to consider nondeterministic Turing machines that in each configuration have just two choices to make and all computations of which have the same length, and then to consider different acceptance modes. By Lemma 5.1.12, this is no essential restriction on the power of NTM; each NTM with time bounded by a polynomial can be transformed in polynomial time into one satisfying the above properties. This means that we can consider only NTM $\mathcal{M}$ such that if for some input x the length of a computation is t, then the configuration tree of $\mathcal{M}$ is a complete binary tree of depth t.

5.9.2 Models and Complexity Classes of Randomized Computing

In order to get deeper insight into the power of randomization, we need to have simple and realistic models of randomized computation in polynomial time. The following four complexity classes of randomized computations, **ZPP**, **RP**, **PP** and **BPP**, are closely related to four natural modes of randomized computing. (In the following definition only those NTM are considered that have exactly two choices to make in each nonterminating configuration and all computations of which have the same length for inputs of the same size.)

RP A language L is in RP (random **p**olynomial time) if there is a polynomial time bounded NTM $\mathcal{M}$ such that if $x \in L$, then **at least half** of all computations of $\mathcal{M}$ on x terminate in the accepting state, and if $x \notin L$, then **all** computations of $\mathcal{M}$ on x terminate in the rejecting state (*Monte Carlo acceptance* or *one-sided Monte Carlo acceptance*).

PP A language L is in PP (**p**robabilistic **p**olynomial time) if there is a polynomial time bounded NTM $\mathcal{M}$ such that $x \in L$, if and only if **more than half** of computations of $\mathcal{M}$ on x terminate in the accepting state (*acceptance by majority*).

BPP A language L is in BPP (**b**ounded error (away from $\frac{1}{2}$) **p**robabilistic **p**olynomial time) if there is a polynomial time bounded NTM $\mathcal{M}$ such that

1. If $x \in L$, then at least $\frac{3}{4}$ of the computations of $\mathcal{M}$ on x terminate in the accepting state.
2. If $x \notin L$, then at least $\frac{3}{4}$ of the computations of $\mathcal{M}$ on x terminate in the rejecting state.

(*Acceptance by clear majority* or *two-sided Monte Carlo acceptance*.)

ZPP a language L is in ZPP (**z**ero error **p**robabilistic **p**olynomial time) if $L \in$ RP$\cap$co-RP (*Las Vegas acceptance*).

Exercise 5.9.14 *Show that any constant* $0 < c < 1$ *could be substituted for* $\frac{1}{2}$ *in the definition of the class (a)* **RP**; *(b)*** **PP**.

Exercise 5.9.15 *Show that any constant* $\frac{1}{2} < c < 1$ *could be substituted for* $\frac{3}{4}$ *in the definition of the class* **BPP**.

Las Vegas algorithms, like the one for sorting in Example 5.7.4, are ideal, because an incorrect solution may be a disaster in some applications. The following exercise shows a way to derive a Las Vegas algorithm from a Monte Carlo one, provided we can verify efficiently the correctness of a to-be-solution of the problem.

Exercise 5.9.16 *Let* $\mathcal{A}$ *be a* $t(n)$ *average time bounded Monte Carlo algorithm for a problem* $\mathcal{P}$ *that produces a correct solution with probability* $\gamma(n)$. *Moreover, let the correctness of a to-be-solution to* $\mathcal{P}$ *be verifiable in time* $v(n)$. *Show how to obtain a Las Vegas algorithm for* $\mathcal{P}$ *that runs in expected time at most* $(t(n)+v(n))\,/\,\gamma(n)$. *(Hint: make a use of the mean of a geometric random variable – see Exercise 1.9.7.)*

Less formally, **RP**, **PP** and **BPP** can be defined as classes of problems for which there is a randomized algorithm A with the following properties:

RP	$x \in L \Rightarrow Pr(A(x) \text{ accepts}) \geq \frac{1}{2}$	$x \notin L \Rightarrow Pr(A(x) \text{ accepts}) = 0$
PP	$x \in L \Rightarrow Pr(A(x) \text{ accepts}) > \frac{1}{2}$	$x \notin L \Rightarrow Pr(A(x) \text{ accepts}) \leq \frac{1}{2}$
BPP	$x \in L \Rightarrow Pr(A(x) \text{ accepts}) \geq \frac{3}{4}$	$x \notin L \Rightarrow Pr(A(x) \text{ accepts}) \leq \frac{1}{4}$

ZPP, RP and **PP** fit nicely into our basic hierarchy of complexity classes.

Theorem 5.9.17 $\mathbf{P} \subseteq \mathbf{ZPP} \subseteq \mathbf{RP} \subseteq \mathbf{NP} \subseteq \mathbf{PP} \subseteq \mathbf{PSPACE}$.

Proof: Inclusions $\mathbf{P} \subseteq \mathbf{ZPP} \subseteq \mathbf{RP}$ are trivial. If $L \in \mathbf{RP}$, then there is a NTM $\mathcal{M}$ accepting L with Monte Carlo acceptance. Hence $x \in L$ if and only if $\mathcal{M}$ has at least one accepting computation for x. Thus, $L \in \mathbf{NP}$, and this proves the inclusion $\mathbf{RP} \subseteq \mathbf{NP}$.

To show $\mathbf{NP} \subseteq \mathbf{PP}$ we proceed as follows. Let $L \in \mathbf{NP}$, and let $\mathcal{M}$ be a polynomial time bounded NTM accepting L. Design a NTM $\mathcal{M}'$ such that $\mathcal{M}'$, for an input w, chooses nondeterministically and performs one of the following steps:

1. $\mathcal{M}'$ accepts.

2. $\mathcal{M}'$ simulates $\mathcal{M}$ on input w.

Using the ideas presented in the proof of Lemma 5.1.12, $\mathcal{M}'$ can be transformed into an equivalent NTM $\mathcal{M}''$ that has exactly two choices in each nonterminating configuration, all computations of which on w have the same length bounded by a polynomial, and which accepts the same language as $\mathcal{M}'$. We show that $\mathcal{M}''$ accepts L by majority, and therefore $L \in \mathbf{PP}$.

If $w \notin L$, then exactly half the computations accept w – those that start with step 1. This, however, is not enough and therefore $\mathcal{M}''$, as a probabilistic TM, does not accept w.

If $w \in L$, then there is at least one computation of $\mathcal{M}$ that accepts w. This means that more than half of all computations of $\mathcal{M}''$ accept w – all those computations that take step 1, like the first one, and at least one of those going through step 2. Hence $\mathcal{M}''$ accepts w by majority.

The last inequality $\mathbf{PP} \subseteq \mathbf{PSPACE}$ is again easy to show. Let $L \in \mathbf{PP}$, and let $\mathcal{M}$ be a NTM accepting L by majority and with time bounded by a polynomial p. In such a case no configuration of $\mathcal{M}$ is longer than $p(|w|)$ for an input w. Using the method to simulate a NTM by a DTM, as shown in the proof of Theorem 5.1.5, we easily get that $\mathcal{M}$ can be simulated in polynomial space. □

Since there is a polynomial time Las Vegas algorithm for recognizing primes (see references), prime recognition is in **ZPP** (and may be in **RP**$-$**P**).

Exercise 5.9.18 *Denote MAJSAT the problem of deciding for a given Boolean formula F whether more than half of all possible assignments to variables in F satisfy F. Show that (a) MAJSAT is in* **PP**; *(b) MAJSAT is* **PP**-*complete (with respect to polynomial time reducibility).*

Exercise 5.9.19** *Let* $0 \leq \varepsilon \leq 1$ *be a rational number. Let* $\mathbf{PP}_\varepsilon$ *be the class of languages L for which there is a NTM* $\mathcal{M}$ *such that* $x \in L$ *if and only if at least a fraction* ε *of all computations are acceptances. Show that* $\mathbf{PP}_\varepsilon = \mathbf{PP}$.

The main complexity classes of randomized computing have also been shown to be separated by oracles. For example, there are oracles A, B, C, D, E, F and G such that (a) $BPP^A \subsetneq NP^A$; (b) $NP^B \subsetneq BPP^B$; (c) $P^C \neq BPP^C$; (d) $P^D \neq RP^D$; (e) $P^E \subsetneq ZPP^E$; (f) $RP^F \neq ZPP^F$; (g) $RP^G \neq BPP^G$.

5.9.3 The Complexity Class **BPP**

Acceptance by clear majority seems to be the most important concept in randomized computation. In addition, the class **BPP** is often considered as a plausible formalization of the concept of **feasible computation**; it therefore deserves further analysis.

First of all, the number $\frac{3}{4}$, used in the definition of the class **BPP**, should not be taken as a magic number. Any number strictly larger than $\frac{1}{2}$ will do and results in the same class. Indeed, let us assume that we have a machine $\mathcal{M}$ that decides a language by a strict majority of $\frac{1}{2}+\varepsilon$. We can use this machine $2k+1$ times and accept as the outcome the majority of outcomes. By Chernoff's bound, Lemma 1.9.13, the probability of a false answer is at most $e^{-2\varepsilon^2 k}$. By taking sufficiently large k, this probability can be reduced as much as needed. For $k = \lceil \frac{\ln 2}{\varepsilon^2} \rceil$ we get a probability of error at most $\frac{1}{4}$, as desired.

Exercise 5.9.20* *Show that in the definition of the class* **BPP** ε *does not have to be a constant. It can be* $|x|^{-c}$ *for any* $c > 0$. *Show also that the bound* $\frac{3}{4}$ *can be replaced by* $1 - \frac{1}{2^{|x|}}$.

The concept of decision by clear majority seems therefore to be a robust one. A few words are also in order concerning the relation between the classes BPP and PP. BPP algorithms allow diminution, by repeated use, of the probability of error as much as is needed. This is not true for PP algorithms.

Let us now turn to another argument which shows that the class **BPP** has properties indicating that it is a reasonable extension of the class **P**.

In order to formulate the next theorem, we need to define when a language $L \subseteq \{0,1\}^*$ has polynomial size circuits. This is in the case where there is a family of Boolean circuits $C_L = \{C_i\}_{i=1}^{\infty}$ and a polynomial p such that the size of C_n is bounded by $p(n)$, C_n has n inputs, and for all $x \in \{0,1\}^*$, $x \in L$ if and only if the output of $C_{|x|}$ is 1 if its ith input is the ith symbol of x.

Theorem 5.9.21 *All languages in* **BPP** *have polynomial size Boolean circuits.*

Proof: Let $L \in$ **BPP**, and let $\mathcal{M}$ be a polynomial time bounded NTM that decides L by clear majority. We show that there is a family of circuits $\mathcal{C} = \{C_n\}_{n=1}^{\infty}$, the size of which is bounded by a polynomial, such that C_n accepts the language L restricted to $\{0,1\}^n$. The proof is elegant, but not constructive, and the resulting family of Boolean circuits is not uniform. (If certain uniformity conditions were satisfied, this would imply **P = BPP**.)

Let $\mathcal{M}$ be time bounded by a polynomial p. For each $n \in \mathbf{N}$ a circuit C_n will be designed using a set of strings $A_n = \{a_1, \ldots, a_m\}$, where $m = 12(n+1)$ and $a_i \in \{0,1\}^{p(n)}$. The idea behind this is that each string a_i represents a possible sequence of random choices of $\mathcal{M}$ during a computation, and therefore completely specifies a computation of $\mathcal{M}$ for inputs of length n.

Informally, on an input w with $|w| = n$, C_n simulates $\mathcal{M}$ with each sequence of choices from $A_{|w|}$ and then, as the outcome, takes the majority of $12(|w|+1)$ outcomes. From the proof of Lemma 4.3.23 we know how to design a circuit simulating a polynomial time computation on TM. Using those ideas, we can construct C_n with the above property and of the polynomial size with respect to n.

The task now is to show that there exists a set A_n such that C_n works correctly. This requires the following lemma.

Lemma 5.9.22 *For all $n > 0$ there is a set A_n of $12(n+1)$ binary (Boolean) strings of length $p(n)$ such that for all inputs x of length n fewer than half of the choices in A_n lead $\mathcal{M}$ to a wrong decision (either to accept $x \notin L$ or to reject $x \in L$).*

Assume now, for a moment, that Lemma 5.9.22 holds and that the set A_n has the required property. With the ideas in the proof of Lemma 4.3.23 we can design a circuit C_n with polynomially many gates that simulates $\mathcal{M}$ with each of the sequences from A_n and then takes the majority of outcomes. It follows from the property of A_n stated in Lemma 5.9.22 that C_n outputs 1 if and only if the input w is in $L \cap \{0,1\}^n$. Thus, L has a polynomial size circuit. □

Proof of Lemma 5.9.22: Let A_n be a set of $m = 12(n+1)$ Boolean strings, taken randomly and independently, of length $p(n)$. We show now that the probability (which refers to the choice of A_n) is at least $\frac{1}{2}$ that for each $x \in \{0,1\}^n$ more than half the choices in A_n lead to $\mathcal{M}$ performing a correct computation.

Since $\mathcal{M}$ decides L by a clear majority, for each $x \in \{0,1\}^n$ at most a quarter of the computations are bad (in the sense that they either accept an $x \notin L$ or reject an $x \in L$). Since Boolean strings in A_n have been taken randomly and independently, the expected number of bad computations with vectors from A_n is at most $\frac{m}{4}$. By Chernoff's bound, Lemma 1.9.13, the probability that the number of bad Boolean string choices is $\frac{m}{2}$ or more is at most $e^{-\frac{m}{12}} < \frac{1}{2^{n+1}}$. This is therefore the probability that x is wrongly accepted by $\mathcal{M}$ when simulating computations specified by A_n.

The last inequality holds for each $x \in \{0,1\}^n$. Therefore the probability that there is an x that is not correctly accepted at the given choice of A_n is at most $2^n \frac{1}{2^{n+1}} = \frac{1}{2}$. This means that most of the choices for A_n lead to correct acceptance for all $x \in \{0,1\}^n$.

This implies that there is always a choice of A_n with the required property, in spite of the fact that we have no idea how to find it. □

What does this result imply? It follows from Theorem 4.3.24 that a language L is in **P** if and only if there is a uniform family of polynomial size Boolean circuits for L. However, for no **NP**-complete problem is a family of polynomial size Boolean circuits known! **BPP** seems, therefore, to be a very small/reasonable extension of **P** (if any). Since **BPP** does not seem to contain an **NP**-complete problem, the acceptance by clear majority does not seem to help us with **NP**-completeness.

Exercise 5.9.23 *Show the inclusions* **RP** $\subseteq$ **BPP** $\subseteq$ **PP**.

Exercise 5.9.24 *Show that a language $L \subseteq \Sigma^*$ is in* **BPP** *if and only if there is a polynomially decidable and polynomially balanced (by p) relation $R \subseteq \Sigma^* \times \Sigma^*$ such that $x \in L$ ($x \notin L$) if and only if $(x,y) \in R$ ($(x,y) \notin R$) for more than $\frac{3}{4}$ of words y with $|y| \leq p(|x|)$.*

Another open question is the relation between **NP** and **BPP**. Currently, these two classes appear to be incomparable, but no proof of this fact is known. It is also not clear whether there are complete problems for classes **RP**, **BPP** and **ZPP**. (The class **PP** is known to have complete problems.)

As already mentioned, there is some evidence, but no proofs, that polynomial time randomized computing is more powerful than polynomial time deterministic computing. However, this statement is true only for computing on computers working on principles of classical physics. It has been proved by Simon (1994) that polynomial time (randomized) computing on (potential) quantum computers is more powerful than polynomial time randomized computing on classical computers. This again allows us to extend our concept of feasibility.

5.10 Parallel Complexity Classes

The most important problem concerning complexity of parallel computing seems to be to find out what can be computed in polylogarithmic time with polynomially many processors. The most interesting complexity class for parallel computing seems to be **NC**. This stands for 'Nick's class' and refers to Nicholas Pippenger, who was the first to define and explore it.

There are several equivalent definitions of **NC**. From the point of view of algorithm design and analysis, a useful and natural one is in terms of PRAM computations:

$$\mathbf{NC} = \mathit{PRAM\text{-}TimeProc}(\lg^{O(1)}(n), n^{O(1)}).$$

From a theoretical point of view, the following definition, in terms of uniform families of Boolean circuits bounded by polylogarithmic depth and polynomial size, seems to be easier to work with:

$$\mathbf{NC} = \mathit{UCIRCUIT\text{-}DepthSize}(\lg^{O(1)}(n), n^{O(1)}).$$

To get more detailed insight into the structure of the class **NC**, an appropriate question to ask is the following one: What can be computed using different amounts of parallel computation time? This leads to the following refinements of **NC**:

$$\mathbf{NC}^{\mathbf{i}} = \mathit{UCIRCUIT\text{-}DepthSize}(\lg^{i}(n), n^{O(1)}), \qquad i \geq 0.$$

In this way a possibly infinite family of complexity classes has been introduced that are related to the sequential ones in the following way:

$$\mathbf{NC}^1 \subseteq \mathbf{DLOGSPACE} \subseteq \mathbf{NLOGSPACE} \subseteq \mathbf{NC}^2 \subseteq \mathbf{NC}^3 \subseteq \ldots \subseteq \mathbf{NC} \subseteq \mathbf{P}.$$

None of these inclusions is known to be strict, and the open problem

$$\mathbf{NC}{=}\mathbf{P}$$

is considered to be a parallel analog of the **P**=**NP** problem.

From the practical point of view, it is of special interest to find out which problems are in $\mathbf{NC}^1$ and $\mathbf{NC}^2$. These classes represent problems that can be computed very fast using parallel computers. The following two lists present some of them.

$\mathbf{NC}^1$

1. Addition of two binary numbers of length m ($n = 2m$).
2. Multiplication of two binary numbers of length m ($n = 2m$).
3. Sum of m binary numbers of length m ($n = m^2$).
4. Matrix multiplication of two $m \times m$ matrices of binary numbers of length l ($n = 2m^2l$).
5. Prefix sum of m binary numbers of length l ($n = ml$).
6. Merging of two sequences of m binary numbers of length l ($n = 2ml$).
7. Regular language recognition.

NC^2

1. Division of two binary numbers of length m ($n = 2m$).[8]

2. Determinant of an $m \times m$ matrix of binary numbers of length l ($n = m^2 l$).

3. Matrix inversion of an $m \times m$ matrix of binary numbers of length l ($n = m^2 l$).

4. Sorting of m binary numbers of length l ($n = ml$).

Remark 5.10.1 In the case of parallel computing one can often reduce a function problem for $f : \mathbf{N} \mapsto \mathbf{N}$ to a decision problem with small ($\lg f(n)$) multiplicative processor overhead. One of the techniques for designing the corresponding well parallelized decision problem is for the case that a good upper bound b for $f(n)$ can be easily determined. The corresponding decision problem is one of deciding, given an n and an integer $1 \leq i \leq \lceil \lg b \rceil$, whether the ith least significant bit of $f(n)$ is 1.

Investigation of the class NC led to the introduction of two new concepts of reducibility: **NC-many-to-one reducibility**, in short $\leq^m_{NC}$, and **NC–Turing reducibility**, in short $\leq^T_{NC}$, defined analogously to many-to-one and Turing reducibility. The only difference is that reductions have to be performed in polylogarithmic time and with a polynomial number of processors. This leads naturally to two new concepts of **P**-completeness, with respect to $\leq^m_{NC}$ and $\leq^T_{NC}$ reducibilities.

Exercise 5.10.2 *Show that* $L_1 \leq_{lg} L_2 \Rightarrow L_1 \leq^m_{NC} L_2 \Rightarrow L_1 \leq^T_{NC} L_2$, *for any languages* L_1 *and* L_2.

The advantage of **P**-completeness based on **NC** reductions is that it brings important insights into the power of parallelism and a methodology to show that a problem is inherently sequential. For example, as is easy to see, the following holds.

Theorem 5.10.3 *If any* **P**-*complete problem is in* **NC**, *then* **P** = **NC**.

Theorem 5.10.3 implies that **P**-complete problems are the main candidates for inherently sequential problems. If one is able to show that a problem is **P**-complete, then it seems to be hopeless to try to design for it an algorithm working in polylogarithmic time on polynomially many processors. Similarly, if a problem withstands all effort to find a polylogarithmic parallel algorithm, then it seems best to change the strategy and try to show that the problem is **P**-complete, which is currently seen as 'evidence' that no fast parallel algorithm for solving the problem can exist. The circuit value problem, introduced in Section 5.3, is perhaps the most important **P**-complete problem for $\leq^T_{NC}$ reduction.

Exercise 5.10.4 *Argue that if an* **P**-*complete problem is in the class* $\mathbf{NC}^i, i > 1$, *then* $\mathbf{P} = \mathbf{NC}^i$.

5.11 Beyond NP

There are several important complexity classes beyond **NP**: for example, **PH, PSPACE, EXP** and **NEXP**. In spite of the fact that they seem to be much larger than **P**, there are plausible views of

[8]It is an open question whether division is in $\mathbf{NC}^1$.

polynomial time computations that coincide with them. We should therefore not rule them out as potential candidates for one of the main goals of complexity theory: to find out what is **feasible**.

PH, the polynomial hierarchy class, seems to be between **NP** and **PSPACE**, and contains a variety of naturally defined algorithmic problems. As shown in Section 4.4.6, the class **PSPACE** corresponds to polynomial time computations on second class machines. In Chapter 9 it will be shown that **PSPACE** corresponds to interactive proof systems with one prover and a polynomial number of interactions, and **NEXP** to interactive proof systems with two provers and a polynomial number of interactions. There are therefore good theoretical and also practical reasons for paying attention to these classes.

5.11.1 Between NP and PSPACE – Polynomial Hierarchy

With the help of oracles we can use **P** and **NP** to design various infinite sequences of potentially richer and richer complexity classes. Perhaps the most important is the following simplified version of the **polynomial hierarchy**

$$\Sigma_0^{\mathbf{P}} = \mathbf{P}, \qquad \Sigma_{\mathbf{k}+1}^{\mathbf{P}} = \mathbf{NP}^{\Sigma_{\mathbf{k}}^{\mathbf{P}}}, \quad k \geq 0$$

$$\Delta_0^{\mathbf{P}} = \mathbf{P}, \qquad \Delta_{\mathbf{k}+1}^{\mathbf{P}} = \mathbf{P}^{\Sigma_{\mathbf{k}}^{\mathbf{P}}}, \quad k \geq 0$$

and the **cumulative polynomial hierarchy**

$$\mathbf{PH} = \bigcup_{k=1}^{\infty} \Sigma_{\mathbf{k}}^{\mathbf{P}}.$$

In other words, $\Sigma_{\mathbf{k}+1}^{\mathbf{P}}$ ($\Delta_{\mathbf{k}+1}^{\mathbf{P}}$) is the family of languages that can be accepted by the polynomially bounded oracle NTM (DTM) with an oracle from $\Sigma_{\mathbf{k}}^{\mathbf{P}}$. The following inclusions clearly hold:

$$\mathbf{P} = \Sigma_0^{p} \subseteq \mathbf{NP} = \Sigma_1^{\mathbf{P}} \subseteq \Sigma_2^{\mathbf{P}} \subseteq \Sigma_3^{\mathbf{P}} \subseteq \ldots \subseteq \mathbf{PH} \subseteq \mathbf{PSPACE}. \qquad (5.6)$$

Exercise 5.11.1 *Show that (a)* $\Sigma_{\mathbf{k}+1}^{\mathbf{P}} = \mathbf{NP}^{\Delta_{\mathbf{k}+1}^{\mathbf{P}}}$ *for* $k \geq 0$*; (b)* $\Delta_{\mathbf{k}}^{\mathbf{P}}$ *is closed under complementation for* $k \geq 0$*; (c)* $\mathbf{P}^{\Delta_{\mathbf{k}}^{\mathbf{P}}} = \Delta_{\mathbf{k}}^{\mathbf{P}}$ *for* $k \geq 0$.

Exercise 5.11.2 *Denote* $\Pi_0^{\mathbf{P}} = \mathbf{P}$, $\Pi_{\mathbf{k}+1}^{\mathbf{P}} = \textbf{co-NP}^{\Sigma_{\mathbf{k}}^{\mathbf{P}}}$. *Show that (a)* $\Sigma_{\mathbf{k}+1}^{\mathbf{P}} = \mathbf{NP}^{\Pi_{\mathbf{k}}^{\mathbf{P}}}$ *for* $k \geq 0$*; (b)* $\Sigma_{\mathbf{k}}^{\mathbf{P}} \cup \Pi_{\mathbf{k}}^{\mathbf{P}} \subseteq \Delta_{\mathbf{k}+1}^{\mathbf{P}}$ *for* $k \geq 0$*; (c)* $\Delta_{\mathbf{k}}^{\mathbf{P}} \subseteq \Sigma_{\mathbf{k}}^{\mathbf{P}} \cap \Pi_{\mathbf{k}}^{\mathbf{P}}$ *for* $k \geq 0$*; (d) if* $\Sigma_{\mathbf{k}}^{\mathbf{P}} \subseteq \Pi_{\mathbf{k}}^{\mathbf{P}}$*, then* $\Sigma_{\mathbf{k}}^{\mathbf{P}} = \Pi_{\mathbf{k}}^{\mathbf{P}}$*; (e)* $\Sigma_{\mathbf{k}}^{\mathbf{P}} \cup \Pi_{\mathbf{k}}^{\mathbf{P}} \subseteq \Delta_{\mathbf{k}+1}^{\mathbf{P}} \subseteq \Sigma_{\mathbf{k}+1}^{\mathbf{P}} \cap \Pi_{\mathbf{k}+1}^{\mathbf{P}}$ *for* $k \geq 0$.

In spite of the fact that polynomial hierarchy classes look as if they are introduced artificially by a pure abstraction, they seem to be very reasonable complexity classes. This can be concluded from the observation that they have naturally defined complete problems.

One complete problem for $\Sigma_{\mathbf{k}}^{\mathbf{P}}, k > 0$, is the following modification of the bounded halting problem:

$$L_{\Sigma_{\mathbf{k}}^{\mathbf{P}}} = \{\langle M\rangle\langle w\rangle\#^t \,|\, M \text{ is a TM with an oracle from } \Sigma_{\mathbf{k}-1}^{\mathbf{P}} \text{ accepting } w \text{ in } t \text{ steps}\}.$$

Another complete problem for $\Sigma_{\mathbf{k}}^{\mathbf{P}}$ is the QSAT$_k$ problem. QSAT$_k$ stands for 'quantified satisfiability problem with k alternations of quantifiers', defined as follows.

Given a Boolean formula B with Boolean variables partitioned into k sets $X_1, \dots, X_k$, is it true that there is a partial assignment to the variables in X_1 such that for all partial assignments to variables in X_2 there is such a partial assignment to variables in $X_3, \dots$, that B is true by the overall assignment. An instance of QSAT_k is usually presented as

$$\exists X_1 \forall X_2 \exists X_3 \forall X_4 \dots Q X_k B,$$

where Q is either the quantifier $\exists$ if k is odd, or $\forall$ if k is even, and B is a Boolean formula.

It is an open question whether the inclusions in (5.6) are proper. Observe that if $\Sigma_{\mathrm{i}}^{\mathrm{P}} = \Sigma_{\mathrm{i+1}}^{\mathrm{P}}$ for some i, then $\Sigma_{\mathrm{i}}^{\mathrm{P}} = \Sigma_{\mathrm{k}}^{\mathrm{P}}$ for all $k \geq i$. In such a case we say that the polynomial hierarchy collapses.

It is not known whether the polynomial time hierarchy collapses. There are, however, various results of the type 'if ..., then the polynomial hierarchy collapses'. For example, the polynomial hierarchy collapses if

1. **PH** has a complete problem;
2. the graph isomorphism problem is **NP**-complete;
3. SAT has a polynomial size Boolean circuit.

In Section 5.9 we mentioned that the relation between **BPP** and **NP** = Σ_1^{P} is unclear. However, it is clear that **BPP** is not too high in the polynomial hierarchy.

Exercise 5.11.3* *Show that* **BPP** $\subseteq \Sigma_2^{\mathrm{P}}$.

PH is the first major deterministic complexity class we have considered so far that is not known to have complete problems and is very unlikely to have complete problems.

An interesting/important task in complexity theory is to determine more exactly the relation between the class **PH** and other complexity classes. For example, the **Toda theorem** says that **PH** $\subsetneq \mathbf{P}^{\mathbf{PP}}$. This result is sometimes interpreted as **PH** $\subsetneq \mathbf{P}^{\#\mathbf{P}}$ (which would mean that counting is very powerful), although we cannot directly compare the class **PH** (of decision problems) and the class **#P** (of function problems). However, the class **PP** is 'close enough' to **#P**. (Indeed, problems in **PP** can be seen as asking for the most significant bit concerning the number of accepting computations, and problems in **#P** as asking for all bits of the number of accepting computations.)

5.11.2 PSPACE-complete Problems

There is a variety of natural computational problems that are **PSPACE**-complete: for example, variants of the halting, tiling and satisfiability problems.

Theorem 5.11.4 (PSPACE-completeness of IN-PLACE-ACCEPTANCE problem) *The following problem is* **PSPACE**-*complete: given a DTM $\mathcal{M}$ and an input w, does $\mathcal{M}$ accept w without having the head ever leave w (the part of tape on which w is written)?*

Proof: Given $\mathcal{M} = \langle \Gamma, Q, q_0, \delta \rangle$ and $w \in \Gamma^*$, we simulate $\mathcal{M}$ on w and keep account of the number of steps. w is rejected if $\mathcal{M}$ rejects, or if the head of $\mathcal{M}$ attempts to leave cells in which the input w was written, or if $\mathcal{M}$ takes more than $|\Gamma|^{|w|}|Q||w|$ steps. In order to store the number of steps, $\mathcal{O}(|w|)$ bits are needed. This can be done in the space $|w|$ using a proper positional number system. Hence, the problem is in **PSPACE**.

Assume now that L can be accepted in space n^k by a machine $\mathcal{M}$. Clearly, $\mathcal{M}$ accepts an input w if and only if $\mathcal{M}$ accepts w 'in place' $w\sqcup^{n^k}$. Thus $w \in L$ if and only if $(\mathcal{M}, w\sqcup^{n^k})$ is a 'yes' instance of the IN-PLACE-ACCEPTANCE. □

PSPACE-completeness of a problem can be shown either directly or using the reduction method: for example, by reduction from the following modifications of **NP**-complete problems.

Example 5.11.5 (CORRIDOR TILING) *Given a finite set T of Wang tiles and a pair of tiled horizontal strips U and D of length n, does there exist an integer m such that it is possible to tile an $m \times n$ rectangle with U as the top row and D as the bottom row and with the left sides of the tiles of the first column and the right sides of the tiles of the last column having the same colour (m is not given)?*

Example 5.11.6 (QUANTIFIED SATISFIABILITY (QSAT)) *Given a Boolean formula B with variables $x_1, \ldots, x_n$, is the following formula valid:*

$$\exists x_1 \forall x_2 \exists x_3 \forall x_4 \ldots Qx_n B,$$

where $Q = \forall$ if n is even, and $Q = \exists$ otherwise?

A variety of game problems have been shown to be **PSPACE**-complete: for example:

Example 5.11.7 (GENERALIZED GEOGRAPHY game problem) *Given a directed graph $G = \langle V, E\rangle$ and a vertex v_0, does Player 1 have a winning strategy in the following game? Players alternate choosing new arcs from the set E. Player 1 starts by choosing an arc whose tail is v_0. Thereafter each player must choose an arc whose tail equals the head of the previous chosen arc. The first player unable to choose a new arc loses.*

Some other examples of **PSPACE**-complete problems are the word problem for context-sensitive languages, the reachability problem for cellular automata (given two configurations c_1 and c_2, is c_2 reachable from c_1?), and the existence of a winning strategy for a generalization of the game GO to arbitrarily large grids.

5.11.3 Exponential Complexity Classes

There are various ways in which exponential complexity classes can be defined. The most useful seem to be the following (see Section 5.2)

$$\mathbf{EXP} = \bigcup_{k=1}^{\infty} Time(2^{n^k}), \qquad \mathbf{NEXP} = \bigcup_{k=1}^{\infty} NTime(2^{n^k}).$$

The open problem **EXP** $=$ **NEXP** is an 'exponential version' of the **P** $=$ **NP** problem and, interestingly, these two problems are related.

Theorem 5.11.8 *If* **P** $=$ **NP**, *then* **EXP** $=$ **NEXP**.

Proof: Let $L \in$ **NEXP**, $L \subseteq \Sigma^*$ and **P** = **NP**. By definition, there is a NTM $\mathcal{M}$ that accepts L in time 2^{n^k} for some k. Consider now an 'exponentially padded' version of L

$$L' = \{wa^{2^{|w|^k} - |w|} \mid w \in L\},$$

where a is a symbol not in Σ. We show how to design a polynomial time bounded NTM $\mathcal{M}'$ that decides L'. For an input $y = wa^{2^{|w|^k}-|w|}$, $\mathcal{M}'$ first checks whether a w is followed by exactly $2^{|w|^k} - |w|$ a's, and then simulates $\mathcal{M}$ on y, treating a's as blanks. $\mathcal{M}'$ works in time $\mathcal{O}(2^{|w|^k})$ – and therefore in polynomial time with respect to the length of the input. Thus L' is in **NP** and also in **P**, due to our assumption **P** = **NP**. This implies that there is a DTM $\mathcal{M}''$ deciding L' in time ln^l for some l. We can assume, without loss of generality, that $\mathcal{M}''$ is an off-line TM that never writes on its input tape. The construction $\mathcal{M}'$ from $\mathcal{M}$ can now be reversed, and we can design a DTM $\mathcal{M}'''$ that accepts w in time $2^{|w|^{l'}}$ for some l'. $\mathcal{M}'''$ simulates, on an input w, $\mathcal{M}''$ on the input $wa^{2^{|w|^k}-|w|}$. Since $\lg(2^{|w|^k} - |w|) \doteq |w|^k$, $\mathcal{M}'''$ can easily keep track of the head of $\mathcal{M}''$ by writing down its position in binary form. □

As a corollary we get that **EXP** $\neq$ **NEXP** $\Longrightarrow$ **P** $\neq$ **NP**. This indicates that to prove **EXP** $\neq$ **NEXP** may be even harder than to prove **P** $\neq$ **NP**.

Various natural complete problems are known for the classes **EXP** and **NEXP**. Many of them are again modifications of known **NP**-complete problems. For example, the following version of the tiling problem is **EXP**-complete.

Given a finite set of tiles, a string of colours w, a number n in binary form, there is a tiling of an $n \times n$ square with a one-colour side (except for the left-most part of the top row where the string w of colours has to be)?

Many **EXP**- and **NEXP**-complete problems can be obtained from **P**- and **NP**-complete problems simply by taking 'exponentially more succinct descriptions' of their inputs (graphs, circuits, formulas).

For example, a succinct description of a graph with $n = 2^k$ nodes is a Boolean circuit C with $2k$ inputs. The graph $G_C = \langle V, E\rangle$ represented by C has $V = \{1, \ldots, n\}$ and $(i,j) \in E$ if and only if C accepts the binary representation of i and j in its inputs. Clearly, such a circuit representation of a graph is exponentially shorter than the usual one.

For example, the following problem is **NEXP**-complete: given a succinct description of a graph (in terms of a circuit), decide whether the graph has a Hamilton cycle.

Remark 5.11.9 There is also another way to define exponential complexity classes:

$$\mathbf{E} = \bigcup_{k=1}^{\infty} Time(k^n), \qquad \mathbf{NE} = \bigcup_{k=1}^{\infty} NTime(k^n).$$

Even though these classes seem to capture better our intuition as to how exponential complexity classes should look, they do not actually have such nice properties. For example, they are not closed under polynomial reductions.

The overall map of the main complexity classes is depicted in Figure 5.10.

Exercise 5.11.10 *Show that for any language $L \in$ **NEXP** there is a language $L' \in$ **NE** such that $L \leq_p^m L'$.*

Exercise 5.11.11* *Show that* **P** = **NP** *implies* **E** = **NE**.

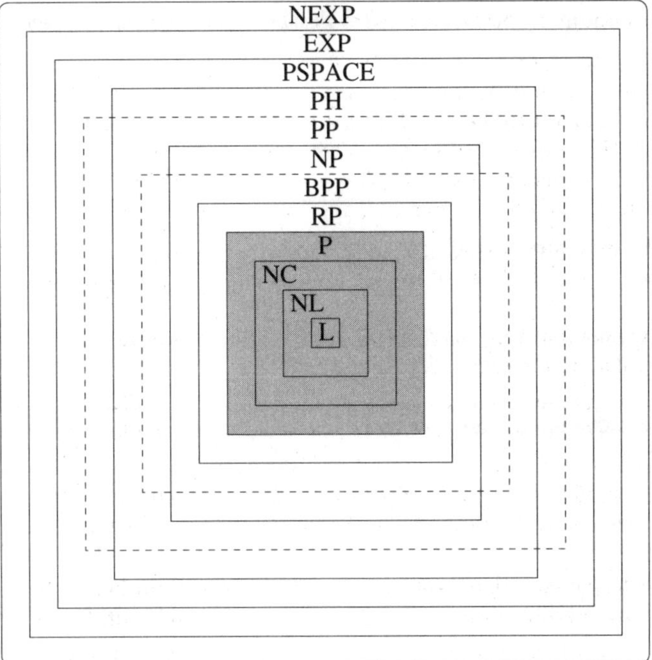

Figure 5.10 A map of complexity classes

5.11.4 Far Beyond NP – with Regular Expressions only

What is beyond **NEXP**? Two interesting classes have been defined and investigated:

$$\textbf{EXPSPACE} = \bigcup_{k=1}^{\infty} Space(2^{n^k}), \qquad \textbf{ELEMENTARY} = \bigcup_{k=1}^{\infty} Time_k(2^{2^{2^{\cdot^{\cdot^{2^n}}}}}),$$

where $Time_k$ denotes that there are k levels of exponentiation.

The name **ELEMENTARY** for such a huge class may be seen as ironical. It may be apt from the point of view of 'P-inhabitants', but is quite justified from the point of view of recursion theory considered in the next chapter. However, in spite of this, it is natural to ask whether it makes sense from a computational point of view to pay attention to such esoteric complexity classes? Does one encounter them in down-to earth computing? Unfortunately, yes.

The following theorem summarizes results which show how far we can get in the space of complexity classes with a very simple problem such as the equivalence problem for generalized regular expressions.

Theorem 5.11.12 (Stockmeyer–Meyer's theorem) *The equivalence problem for generalized regular expressions is:*

1. **co-NP**-*complete for ordinary regular expressions without iteration;*
2. **PSPACE**-*complete for ordinary regular expressions;*

3. **co-NEXP**-*complete for regular expressions with squaring but without iteration;*

4. **EXPSPACE**-*complete for regular expressions with squaring;*

5. *outside the class* **ELEMENTARY** *for regular expressions with negation.*

Exercise 5.11.13* *Show* **NP**-*completeness of the inequivalence problem for regular expressions without iteration (the star-free expressions). (Hint: use a reduction from the SAT problem.)*

Exercise 5.11.14* *Show that a regular language can be described by a star-free regular expression if and only if it is accepted by a NFA with an acyclic state diagram.*

Exercise 5.11.15 *Explain how it can happen that the last problem in Theorem 5.11.12 is computationally so hard.*

Remark 5.11.16 Two opposing streams are noticeable in computing in the search for what is **feasible**. In the pre-computing era the concept of feasibility was identified with the concept of recursive functions discussed in the next chapter. But the more powerful the computers we have and the more computation intensive the problems attacked, the more frustration grows as to what is really computable. The concept of feasibility was at first restricted to the class **ELEMENTARY** that was popular for a while, then to **P**, but nowadays there are even feelings that one should go deeper into **P**, to the class **L** or **NC**. At the same time an opposing direction is acquiring momentum: to extend the concept of feasibility beyond **P**, even into **NEXP**. This will be discussed in Chapter 9.

5.12 Computational Versus Descriptional Complexity*

The two basic classes of problems we consider in computing and its foundations can be seen as dealing with expressiveness and with computability: how to describe (efficiently) properties, algorithms, systems, objects, and how to perform (efficiently) checking of properties, execution of algorithms, design of objects.

Formal logics and theories of specification, algorithmic and database languages deal with problems of the first type. Theories of automata, computer models, algorithms and computational complexity deal with problems of the second class. These two components of computing and its foundations at first sight seem to be very different in respect to aims, methods and results. This is, surprisingly, quite misleading. There are actually deep relations between these two areas of computing. In order to recognize them we have to switch to a very abstract/theoretical level, this time to the second order logic.

Let us summarize briefly the basic concepts from logic that we need. **First order logic** is a language of formulas built up from symbols for constants, object-variables, predicates, logical connectives and quantifiers that can be applied to object-variables only. In **second order logic** there are also predicate-variables and quantifiers can be applied to such variables.

Example 5.12.1 *The following formula of the first order logic represents a property of graphs (given by the relation E), being complete:* $\forall x \forall y (xEy)$.

It can be shown that to each formula of second order logic there is an equivalent in the prenex form in which all predicate-quantifiers form a prefix of the formula. In the case where only such formulas are allowed and with only existential quantifiers applied to predicate variables, we speak about **second order existential logic**. Let us denote by **SOL (SOEL)** the class of problems/languages expressible using (existential) second order logic.

Example 5.12.2 *The following formula of the second order existential logic is satisfied by those and only those graphs (given by the relation E) that are 3-colorable:*

$$\begin{aligned} F \;\equiv\; & (\exists R)(\exists Y)(\exists B)(\forall x)[(R(x) \vee Y(x) \vee B(x)) \\ & \wedge(\forall x,y(E(x,y) \Rightarrow \neg(R(x)\wedge R(y))\wedge\neg(Y(x)\wedge Y(y))\wedge\neg(B(x)\wedge B(y))))] \end{aligned}$$

The following basic result has been the first to show that important complexity classes can be characterized in a completely different way, as classes of problems describable using certain basic tools of logic.

Theorem 5.12.3 (Fagin's theorem) NP = SOEL

There are numerous variants of this fundamental theorem putting different lights on the power of logic. One of them says that **NP** is exactly the class of all graph-theoretical properties expressible in the second order existential logic.

The second basic result shows that the complexity class of polynomial hierarchy, which could have been seen as being defined in an 'art pour art' way, is actually a very basic one.

Theorem 5.12.4 (Stockmeyer's theorem) PH = SOL

These two results naturally initiated a search to find out whether other basic computational complexity classes can be seen as being nicely defined using descriptional means only. Interestingly, this is indeed true and much can already be achieved using the first order logic. However, this time we have to consider uniform families of first order logic formulas where the concept of uniformity is analogous, as in the case of Boolean circuits, and as descriptional resources the size of formulas and the number of the distinct variables are considered.

Theorem 5.12.5 (Immermann's theorem) *If $VAR\&SIZ[v(n),s(n)]$ denotes the set of problems/languages expressible by a uniform family of first order logic formulas with $v(n)$ being their number of distinct variables and $s(n)$ being the size of formulas, then*

$$\mathbf{P} = \bigcup_{c,k=1}^{\infty} VAR\&SIZ[c,n^k],$$
$$\mathbf{PSPACE} = \bigcup_{c,k=1}^{\infty} VAR\&SIZ[c,2^{n^k}].$$

There are various other results relating computational complexity classes with those defined completely in terms of descriptional means and their resources. All these results again show how very basic are the main computational complexity classes. At the same time they show how powerful, and still far from fully explored is the very basic language of science – predicate calculus. These results also show that many problems of complexity theory (and also databases) can be formulated as problems of logic.

In order to prove the above results we would need to go into the formalism of predicate logic and to introduce a variety of concepts that is beyond the scope of this book. A use of logic to characterize important families of languages is, however, not restricted to high complexity classes. For example, logical formulas can also be used to characterize neatly regular languages and regular ω-languages.

The way logical formulas can be used to describe regular languages is simple and will now be used to demonstrate the power and weakness of logical characterizations of families of languages/problems.

Let us consider the so-called first order L_A-formulas over an arbitrary alphabet A as the usual first order logic formulas built from the logical connectives $\vee, \wedge, \neg, \Rightarrow$, quantifiers, variables, constants $0, 1$ and symbols from the set $\{<\} \cup \{R_a \mid a \in A\}$.

For each closed L_A-formula ϕ and each word $w \in A^*$ we can check whether ϕ is satisfied by w, if in ϕ:

1. variables are interpreted as having integer values from the range $[1, |w|]$;
2. relation $<$ has the usual interpretation of 'being smaller' between integers;
3. $R_a x$ is true on w if and only if the x-th letter of w is a.

With this interpretation we can associate with each L_A-formula ϕ the language $L(\phi)$ of all words from A that satisfy ϕ.

Example 5.12.6 *For the formula ϕ_1 defined by*

$$\exists x \exists y((x < y) \wedge R_a x \wedge R_a y) \wedge \forall z((x < z) \wedge (z < y) \Rightarrow R_b z)$$

we have $L(\phi_1) = A^* ab^* aA^*$.

Second order L_A-formulas are built in the same way as the first order L_A-formulas, but this time set-variables are also allowed and can be quantified. The set membership symbol $\in$ can also be used.

Example 5.12.7 *For the formula*

$$\begin{array}{rcll} \phi_2 & = & \exists X(\forall m(\forall x \neg(x < m) \Rightarrow m \in X) & \{1 \in X\} \\ & & \wedge(\forall n(\forall x \neg(n < x) \Rightarrow n \in X) & \{|w| \in X\} \\ & & \wedge(\forall x \forall y(\forall z \neg((x < z) \wedge (z < y))) & \{a \text{ position is in } X \\ & & \quad \Rightarrow (x \in X \Leftrightarrow \neg(y \in X)))) & \text{iff its successor is not}\} \\ & & \wedge \forall x(R_a x) & \{w \in A^*\} \end{array}$$

we have $L_A(\phi_2) = a(aa)^*$.

The following theorem shows how powerful are the languages of L_A-formulas.

Theorem 5.12.8 (Büchi's theorem) *(1) A language $R \subseteq A^*$ is star-free regular (i.e. expressible by an extended regular expression without iteration) if and only if $R = L_A(\phi)$ for a first order L_A-formula. (2) A language $R \subseteq A^*$ is regular if and only if $R = L_A(\phi)$ for a second order L_A-formula.*

Moral: Experience suggests that once something has been shown to be impossible, then the next step is to start a search for how to do it from a different point of view. A good rule of thumb in complexity analysis is therefore, as in life, to do your best to solve the problems you need to solve. When this turns out not to be feasible, then modify your problems.

5.13 Exercises

1. Suppose that the running time of a NTM is defined to be the length of the longest computation for a given input. Show that if **NP** is defined accordingly, then it is the same class as defined in the text.

2. Show that if a language L is recognized by a $t(n)$-time bounded TM, then L is recognized by infinitely many $t(n)$-time bounded TM.

3.* Show that 2-CNF problem is in **P**.

4. Show that the problem of deciding whether a Boolean formula in DNF is satisfiable is in **P**.

5. Show that the problem of deciding whether a Boolean formula in CNF is a tautology is in **P**.

6. Show that the problem of deciding whether a Boolean formula in DNF is a tautology is **co-NP**-complete.

7. Show that a language $L \in \mathbf{NP}$ if and only if there is a language $L_0 \in P$ (called also a witness of L), a separator \$ and a polynomial p such that $x \in L \Leftrightarrow \exists y\, |y| \leq p(|x|), x\$y \in L_0$.

8. A clause is called monotone if it consists entirely of variables (e.g. $x \vee y \vee z$) or entirely of negations of variables. Show the **NP**-completeness of the following language MONOTONE-CNFF: a set of satisfiable Boolean formulas all clauses of which are monotone.

9. Show that the following HITTING-SET problem is **NP**-complete: given a family $\mathcal{F}$ of finite sets and a $k \in \mathbf{N}$, is there a set with at most k elements intersecting every set in $\mathcal{F}$?

10. Show that the problem of colouring a graph with two colours is in **P**.

11. Show that the CIRCUIT-SAT problem is polynomially reducible to the SAT problem, where the CIRCUIT SAT problem is that of deciding whether a given Boolean circuit has a satisfying assignment.

12. Show that the DOMINATING SET problem is **NP**-complete even for bipartite graphs.

13.* Show that the VERTEX COVER problem for a graph $G = \langle V, E \rangle$ and an integer k can be solved in time $\mathcal{O}(|E| + k|V|^{k+1})$.

14.* Show **NP**-completeness of the following ANAGRAM problem: given a finite multiset $\mathcal{S}$ of strings and a string w, is there a sequence $w_1, \ldots, w_s$ of strings from $\mathcal{S}$ such that w is a permutation of the string $w_1 \ldots w_s$?

15. Show that the MAX2SAT problem is **NP**-complete. (It is the following problem: given a set of clauses, each with two literals, and an integer k, decide whether there is an assignment that satisfies at least k clauses.) (Hint: consider the clauses x, y, z, w, $\bar{x} \vee \bar{y}$, $\bar{y} \vee \bar{z}$, $\bar{z} \vee \bar{x}$, $x \vee \bar{w}$, $y \vee \bar{w}$, $z \vee \bar{w}$, and show that an assignment satisfies $x \vee y \vee z$ if and only if it satisfies seven of the above clauses.)

16. Show, for example by a reduction from the CLIQUE problem, that the VERTEX COVER problem is **NP**-complete.

17. Show, for example by a reduction from the VERTEX COVER problem, that the SET COVER problem is **NP**-complete. (It is the problem of deciding, given a family of finite sets $S_1, \ldots, S_n$ and an integer k whether there is a family of k subsets $S_{i_1}, \ldots, S_{i_k}$ such that $\bigcup_{j=1}^{k} S_{i_j} = \bigcup_{j=1}^{n} S_j$.)

18. Denote by NAE3-CNFF the problem of deciding, given a Boolean formula in 3-CNF form whether there is a satisfying assignment such that in none of the clauses do all three literals have the same truth value (NAE stands for 'not-all-equal'). (a) Show that the problem NAE3-CNFF is **NP**-complete. (b)** Use the **NP**-completeness of the NAE3-CNFF problem to show the **NP**-completeness of the 3-COLOURABILITY problem (of deciding whether a given graph is colourable with three colours).

19. Show that the INDEPENDENT SET problem is **NP**-complete, for example, by a reduction from 3-CNFF. (It is the following problem: given a graph $G = \langle V, E \rangle$ and $I \subseteq V$, I is said to be independent if for no $i, j \in I, i \neq j$, $(i, j) \in E$. Given, in addition, an integer k, decide whether G has an independent set of size at least k.)

20. Use the **NP**-completeness of the INDEPENDENT SET problem to show that (a) the CLIQUE problem is **NP**-complete; (b) the VERTEX COVER problem is **NP**-complete.

21. Show, for example by a reduction from 3-CNFF, that the TRIPARTITE MATCHING problem is **NP**-complete. (Given three sets B (boys), G (girls) and H (homes), each containing n elements, and a ternary relation $T \subseteq B \times G \times H$, find a set of n triples from T such that no two have a component in common. (That is, each boy is matched with a different girl and each couple has a home of its own.)

22. Use the **NP**-completeness of the TRIPARTITE MATCHING problem to show the **NP**-completeness of the SET COVER problem. (Hint: show this for those graphs nodes of which can be partitioned into disjoint triangles.)

23. Show the **NP**-completeness of the SET PACKING problem. (Given a family of subsets of a finite set U and an integer k, decide whether there are k pairwise disjoint sets in the family.)

24. Show that the BIN-PACKING problem is **NP**-complete (for example, by a reduction from the TRIPARTITE MATCHING problem).

25. Show, for example by a reduction from the VERTEX COVER problem, the **NP**-completeness of the DOMINATING SET problem: given a directed graph $G = \langle V, E \rangle$, and an integer k, is there a set D of k or fewer nodes such that for each $v \in V - D$ there is a $u \in D$ such that $(u, v) \in E$?

26. Show that the SUBGRAPH ISOMORPHISM problem is **NP**-complete (for example, by a reduction from the CLIQUE problem).

27. Show that (a) 3-COLOURABILITY problem is **NP**-complete; (b) the 2-COLOURABILITY problem is in **P**.

28. Show that the following Diophantine equation problem is **NP**-complete: decide whether a system of equations $Ax \leq b$ (with A being an integer matrix and b an integer vector) has an integer solution. (Hint: use a reduction from the 3-CNFF problem.)

29. Show that if f is a polynomially computable and honest function, then there is a polynomial time NTM $\mathcal{M}$ which accepts exactly the range of f and such that for an input y every accepting computation of $\mathcal{M}$ outputs a value x such that $f(x) = y$.

30.* Design a linear time algorithm for constructing an optimal vertex cover for a tree.

31. Consider the MINIMUM VERTEX COLOURING problem (to determine the chromatic number of the graph). (a) Show that unless **P** = **NP** the approximation threshold of the problem cannot be larger than $\frac{1}{4}$ (Hint: use the fact that 3-COLOURING is **NP**-complete); (b) show that the asymptotic approximation threshold (see Exercise 5.8.10) cannot be larger than $\frac{1}{4}$ (Hint: replace each node by a clique).

32. (a)* Show that the heuristic for the VERTEX COVER problem in Section 5.8.2 never produces a solution that is more than $\lg n$ times the optimum; (b) find the family of graphs for which the $\lg n$ bound can be achieved in the limit.

33. Show that the approximation threshold for the minimization version of the BIN PACKING problem is at least $\frac{1}{3}$.

34. Design an approximation algorithm for the SET COVER problem, as good as you can get it, and estimate its approximation threshold.

35. Design an $\mathcal{O}(\lg(\backslash + \Updownarrow))$-time parallel $\frac{1}{2}$-approximation algorith for MAXSAT problem for Boolean formulas in CNF with m clauses and n variables.

36.** Show that a language $L \in$ **RP** if and only if there is a language $L_0 \in P$, called also a witness language for L, and a polynomial p such that $x \in L \Leftarrow \exists y\, |y| \leq p(|x|),\, x\$y \in L_0$ and if $x \in L$, then at least half the words of length $f(|x|)$ are such that $x\$y \in L_0$.

37. Show that the following problem is in **BPP**: given polynomials $p_i(x_1, \ldots, x_n), 1 \leq i \leq m, g_j(x_1, \ldots, x_n), 1 \leq j \leq n$, decide whether $\prod_{i=1}^{m} p_i(x_1, \ldots, x_n) = \prod_{j=1}^{n} g_j(x_1, \ldots, x_n)$.

38. Show that **NP** $\subseteq$ **BPP** implies **NP** = **RP**.

39. Show that the class **PP** is closed under (a) complementation; (b) symmetric difference; (c) $\leq_p^m$ reducibility.

40. Show that the class **BPP** is closed under (a) complementation; (b) union; (c) intersection.

41. Show that the class **RP** is closed under (a) union; (b) intersection.

42. Show that the classes **RP** and **BPP** are closed under $\leq_p^m$ reducibility.

43. A **Boolean randomized circuit** is one which has, in addition to standard inputs, so-called random inputs. If these random inputs are drawn from a uniform distribution, the output of the circuit is a random variable. A random Boolean circuit with standard input $x_1, \ldots, x_n$ computes a Boolean function $f(x_1, \ldots, x_n)$ if $Pr(C(x_1, \ldots, x_n) = f(x_1, \ldots, x_n)) \geq \frac{3}{4}$ for all $x_1, \ldots, x_n$. Show that if a Boolean function can be computed by a randomized circuit of size $s(n)$, then it can be computed by a usual (deterministic) circuit of size $\mathcal{O}(ns(n))$.

44. Show that any problem in NC^k can be solved by an EROW PRAM in $\mathcal{O}(\lg n)^k$ time using $n^{\mathcal{O}(1)}$ processors.

QUESTIONS

1. Why is nondeterministic space not essentially more powerful than deterministic space?

2. How can we introduce nondeterminism into circuits?

3. The main computational complexity classes have been defined in terms of Turing machines. Could they be defined using other models of computers?
4. Can the reducibilities introduced in Section 5.3 be ordered with respect to their power?
5. Is there an essential difference between direct and indirect methods of proving **NP**-completeness?
6. Which ways of attacking the **P** = **NP** problem seem to be feasible?
7. How can the existence of complete problems contribute to the design of efficient algorithms?
8. How can the main randomized complexity classes be described informally?
9. What does it imply when a complexity class has no complete problems?
10. Why is it not easy to define complexity classes $\mathbf{NC}^i$ in terms of PRAM?

5.14 Historical and Bibliographical References

Foundations of computational complexity and a systematic investigation of time and space complexity of Turing machine computations were laid out in papers by Hartmanis and Stearns (1965) and Hartmanis, Lewis and Stearns (1965). For these contributions and further development of computational complexity Hartmanis and Stearns received the Turing award in 1993. For a personal account of the first developments in computational complexity see Hartmanis (1979).

For the earlier attempts to pose and solve computational complexity problems, of special interest is a letter from Gödel to von Neumann in 1956 (see Sipser (1992)), in which he asked for his views on the possibility of solving in linear or quadratic time, on a TM, a problem known today to be **NP**-complete. For other less formal and direct attempts to deal with computational complexity issues see Rabin (1960) and Trakhtenbrot (1964).

Observe that it is very natural that a systematic investigation of computational complexity should have started in the 1960s. The boundaries between algorithmically solvable and unsolvable problems were already quite well understood as were methods for showing unsolvability. The growing use of more and more powerful computers for more and more complex tasks and larger and larger inputs naturally brought the question of computational complexity and efficiency to the forefront of interest and importance.

There is a variety of books in which computational complexity problems are presented in detail: especially Papadimitriou (1994); Reischuk (1990); Balcázar, Díaz and Gabáro (1988); Wagner and Wechsung (1986); Papadimitriou and Steiglitz (1982); Lewis and Papadimitriou (1981). See also Cormen, Leiserson and Rivest (1990); Aho, Hopcroft and Ullman (1974); Hopcroft and Ullman (1969); Lovász (1995) and an extensive survey of complexity classes by Johnson (1990a). A less formal but very illuminating discussion of complexity problems and results is found in Harel (1987).

Theorem 5.1.7 is due to Savitch (1970). The time and space hierarchies summarized in Theorem 5.2.2 were established for deterministic computations in the above-mentioned pioneering papers by Hartmanis *et al.*, and for nondeterministic computations by Cook (1973) and Seiferas, Fischer and Meyer (1973). See also Aho, Hopcroft and Ullman (1974) for a presentation of proofs. The result that space is strictly more powerful than time, presented on page 304, is due to Hopcroft, Paul and Valiant (1975). The gap theorem is due to Trakhtenbrot (1964); see also Papadimitriou (1994). For Blum's speed-up theorem (in much stronger form) see Blum (1971).

There are many concepts of reducibility. Some have been very intensively studied already in the theory of recursive functions; see Rogers (1967). For the study of resource-bounded reductions see Ladner, Lynch and Selman (1975) and Balcázar, Díaz and Gabárro (1988).

Another key idea of computational complexity, namely, to consider class **P** as the one that is of both theoretical and practical importance and class **NP** as its natural extension for the study of computational complexity, appeared informally in several papers, especially in Cobham (1965), Edmonds (1965, 1966) and Rabin (1966). Several citations from these and other papers, including the letter from Gödel to von Neumann collected by Sipser (1992), demonstrate how an awareness emerged of the importance of class **P** and of the need to try to solve efficiently those problems that seem to be solvable only by brute force – through an exhaustive search.

The concept of **NP**-completeness, another very basic concept of computational complexity, was introduced by Cook (1971). But it was Karp (1972) who convincingly demonstrated its true wealth. (Both received Turing awards, Cook in 1982 and Karp in 1985.) See also Levin (1973). The book by Garey and Johnson (1979) containing a compendium of **NP**-complete problems, and Johnson's ongoing column on **NP**-completeness in the *Journal of Algorithms* have also contributed significantly to its broad study. A variety of **NP**-complete problems can be found in the above references and in many books on computational complexity and foundations of computing. Cook (1971) was the first precisely to formulate the **P** = **NP** problem.

NP-completeness of the satisfiability problem is due to Cook (1971). The proof presented here is due to Aho, Hopcroft and Ullman (1974). Satisfiability became the first problem to be heavily used in deriving other **NP**-completeness results. The idea of using the bounded tiling problem and other versions of tiling problems to prove **NP**-completeness and other types of completeness came from Lewis (1978). This was further developed by Lewis and Papadimitriou (1981) and especially by van Emde Boas (1982) and Savelsbergh and van Emde Boas (1984). Hartmanis–Berman hypothesis is from Hartmanis and Berman (1988).

Strong **NP**-completeness is usually defined in a more general way: a problem remains **NP**-complete even if any instance of length n is restricted to contain integers of size at most $p(n)$, where p is a fixed polynomial. For an analysis of this concept see, for example, Garey and Johnson (1988) and Papadimitriou (1994). For results on how a compressed (succinct) description of inputs can essentially change complexity of **NP**-complete problems, see Papadimitriou (1994), Galperin and Wigderson (1983), and Balcázar, Lozano and Toran (1992).

The concept of average-case completeness is due to Levin (1986). For a more detailed study of this concept see Gurevich (1991), Ben-David, Chor and Goldreich (1992), Impagliazzo (1995) and Wang (1996). Presentation here is based on Wang (1996), where one can also find references to the results mentioned in Remark 5.5.12.

Also in the RRAM framework we can define in a natural way the concept of the complexity class **P** and, using the idea of certificates, the complexity class **NP** (for computation over reals). **NP**-completeness for computations over reals was introduced by Blum, Shub and Smale (1989). There are also several fast randomized prime recognition algorithms: Rabin's algorithm (Section 8.3.4); Solovay–Strassen's algorithm (1978) (both are actually Monte Carlo algorithms for integer factorization); Rumley–Adleman's Las Vegas algorithm (see Adleman (1980)) that terminates in time $\mathcal{O}((\lg n)^{\lg \lg \lg n})$ and either provides no solution or a correct one; and a polynomial time Las Vegas algorithm due to Adleman and Hung (1984).

The concept of certificates for **NP**-complete problems and Theorem 5.7.2 are implicit in Edmonds's papers. For a rich history of the **P** = **NP** problem see Sipser (1992). For proofs and references for various statements of the type **P** = **NP** if and only if . . . see Papadimitriou (1994) and Balcázar, Díaz, and Garbárro (1988). The idea of the class **FP** goes back to Cobham (1964) and Edmonds (1965). The presentation of the subject here is based on Papadimitriou (1994). The class **UP** was introduced by Valiant (1976) and Theorem 5.7.20 is due to Grollman and Selman (1988). Theorem 5.7.6 on relativization of **P** = **NP** problems is due to Baker, Gill and Solovay (1975). A large body of results on relativization currently available, including those from Remark 5.7.8, is presented by Balcázar, Díaz and Gabárro (1988).

A compendium of **P**-complete problems and an analysis of the role that **NP**-completeness plays in seeing the limitations of parallel computing are found in Greenlaw, Hoover and Ruzzo (1993). **P**-completeness of the rational linear programming problem is due to Dobkin, Lipton and Reiss (1979); **NP**-completeness of integer linear programming is in Garey and Johnson (1979). **P**-completeness of the CIRCUIT VALUE problem is due to Ladner (1975). The connection between **P**-completeness and inherently sequential problems was first explored by Goldschlager (1977).

The class of unambiguous Turing machines was introduced by Valiant (1976). Their relation to one-way functions was established by Grollman and Selman (1988). The class **#P** was introduced by Valiant (1979), and the proof of **#P**-completeness for PERMANENT is due to him and Zankó (1991). For Toda's theorem see Toda (1989). For more on **#P**-completeness see Papadimitriou (1994).

A systematic presentation of primality testing algorithms is found in Kranakis (1986). The proof that prime recognition is in **P** provided the generalized Riemann hypothesis holds is due to Miller (1976), and that it is in **NP** is due to Pratt (1975). The fastest known deterministic algorithm for prime recognition is due to Adleman, Pomerance and Rumely (1983). For numerical verification of the Riemann hypothesis see Odlyzko (1988); for numerical verification of the generalized Riemann hypothesis see Rumely (1993).

Attempts to solve **NP**-complete problems by approximation are about as old as **NP**-completeness itself. Johnson (1974) and Garey and Johnson (1979) provided the first systematic presentation of approximation algorithms. For a more detailed presentation and analysis of some approximation problems and newer results on nonapproximability see Cormen, Leiserson and Rivest (1990); Papadimitriou (1994); Babai (1995) Ausiello, Crescenzi, and Protasi (1995) and the books by Hochbaum (ed.) (1996), Ausiello, Crescenzi, Gambosi, Kann and Marchetti-Spaccamela (1997) and Díaz, Serna, Spirakis and Torán (1997). A polynomial time approximation scheme for TSP in R^2 with Euclidean distances is due to Arora (1996). Trevisan (1996) has shown that unless $\mathbf{P} = \mathbf{NP}$ the TSP does not admit an approximation scheme when restricted to the Euclidean space of an arbitrary dimension.

The vertex cover randomized algorithm presented on page 338 is due to Gavril (1977). The TSP approximation algorithm sketched in Exercises 5.8.14 and 5.8.15 is due to Rosenkrantz, Stearns and Lewis (1977). Proofs of Theorems 5.8.6 and 5.8.12 follow Papadimitriou (1994). The first result, for the SET COVER problem, showing that approximation threshold is 1 unless $\mathbf{P} = \mathbf{NP}$ is found in Lund and Yannakakis (1993). Theorem 5.8.17 is found in Arora, Lund *et al.* (1992). For an overview of intensive experimental work on solving and approximation of TSP of large size see Johnson and McGeoch (1996), and Johnson, McGeoch and Rothberg (1996). For Held–Karp's lower bound for TSP see Held and Karp (1970).

Randomization was formally introduced by Rabin (1976) and Solovay and Strassen (1977) as a tool to get more efficient algorithms. However, the randomized algorithms on primality testing, found in Rabin (1976); Miller (1976) and Soloway with Strassen (1977), all invented in 1975, made randomization a central feature in complexity theory. The formal study of randomized complexity classes started with Gill (1977), who introduced the classes **RP**, **PP**, **ZPP** and **BPP**. For more on randomized complexity classes see Balcázar, Díaz and Gabárro (1988), Papadimitriou (1994) and Johnson (1990a). Theorem 5.9.10 is found in Kotsoupias and Papadimitriou (1992). For a detailed treatment of randomized algorithms see Montwani and Raghavan (1995).

The class **NC** was introduced by Pippenger (1979) and in detail studied by Cook (1981, 1985). For more about parallel complexity classes see Reischuk (1990) and Papadimitriou (1994). For a summary of evidences that $\mathbf{NC} \neq \mathbf{P}$ see Greenlaw, Hoover and Ruzzo (1995).

The polynomial hierarchy was introduced by Stockmeyer (1976). The proof that QSAT_k is a complete problem for Σ_k is found in Wrathall (1976) as is the result that if **PH** has a complete problem then it collapses. The collapse of the polynomial hierarchy if the graph isomorphism problem is **NP**-complete is found in Goldwasser and Sipser (1986), and for the case that SAT has a polynomial size circuit see Karp and Lipton (1980).

The first **PSPACE**-completeness results, for the quantified satisfiability and the equivalence of regular expressions, were due to Stockmeyer and Meyer (1973). Schäfer (1978) showed the **PSPACE**-completeness of some games including GENERAL GEOGRAPHY. The **PSPACE**-completeness of GO is due to Lichtenstein and Sipser (1980). Papadimitriou (1985, 1994) showed the **PSPACE**-completeness of various problems of decision making under uncertainty.

For a survey of results on exponential complexity classes and their complete problems see Papadimitriou (1994) and Johnson (1990a). Results on the completeness of various regular expression equivalence problems are due to Stockmeyer and Meyer (1973).

6 Computability

INTRODUCTION

The search for the ultimate limitations of mind and machines gave rise to a variety of concepts, methods and results of fundamental philosophical, theoretical and practical importance. This chapter deals with some of them. First, it explores basic concepts and methods concerning limitations of effective or algorithmic methods – that is, ultimate limitations of machines. We discuss which problems are algorithmically unsolvable or undecidable (and how to show that), which functions are computable and which sets are recognizable or acceptable. Second, it explores one of the main products of mind, formal systems, and shows their limitations for proving correctness of statements and the randomness of strings. Finally, a magic 'number of wisdom' is defined and analysed, which contains in a very compressed form a huge amount of knowledge.

In this search for the limitations of mind and machines, we present various concepts and methods of broader importance for both computing and outside it: for instance, Kolmogorov and Chaitin concepts of descriptional complexity.

LEARNING OBJECTIVES

The aim of the chapter is to demonstrate

1. basic concepts and relations concerning recursive and recursively enumerable sets and partial and primitive recursive functions;

2. the fundamental concept of undecidability and the main examples of undecidable problems: halting problem, tiling problems, the Thue problem, the Post correspondence problem, and Hilbert's tenth problem;

3. the fundamental concepts of Kolmogorov/Chaitin complexity, their basic properties and some applications;

4. a general concept of formal systems, and results, including Gödel's incompleteness theorem and Chaitin's theorem, showing surprising limitations of formal systems for proving correctness of theorems and randomness of strings;

5. magic 'numbers of wisdom' and their implications.

When you have eliminated the impossible, whatever remains, however improbable, must be the truth.

Arthur Conan Doyle, 1890

The search for its own limitations is one of the main characteristics of science in this century. Discovering the power and limitations of physical systems, machines, mind, knowledge and formal systems is an intellectually exciting and practically important task.

The concept of unsolvability is one of the cornerstones of modern science, computing and mathematics. Its investigation leads to questions of basic philosophical importance.

In this chapter we deal with several fundamental problems concerning unsolvability and other limitations of machines, formal systems and knowledge. Which problems are ultimately solvable by machines or within a framework of a formal system, and which are not? How can we prove that some problems are beyond the power of machines or formal systems, no matter how powerful or good they are? Where is the borderline between solvability and unsolvability?

On a more technical level these fundamental philosophical problems can be reduced to those concerning sets, functions, numbers, strings and theorems. Which sets are decidable or enumerable? Which functions are computable? Which numbers are computable? Which strings are random?Which theorems are provable?

All these problems are analysed in this chapter. We deal with basic concepts, methods and results regarding unsolvability, solvability and the boundaries between them, including the basic theorems of Gödel and Chaitin concerning the limitations of formal systems.

We shall learn several surprising methods and results. For example, we shall see that self-reference is a basic tool not only for the design of algorithms but also for determining the limitations of computing. We shall also discover that a computer-independent view of computation is possible.

The results and methods presented in this chapter demonstrate that there are simple methods, in principle, to grasp what is graspable and to show that one cannot embrace the unembraceable.

The results of this chapter imply that there are algorithmic problems that are not algorithmically solvable, correct theorems that are not provable and random strings, whose randomness cannot be proved, no matter how much humankind has in the way of computer resources and brains.

6.1 Recursive and Recursively Enumerable Sets

The concepts of recursive and recursively enumerable sets play the key role in the search for boundaries between solvability and unsolvability. To start with we describe and analyse these concepts for languages – sets of strings. We also discuss how to generalize them in order to deal with recursivness of other objects.

As defined in Section 4.1.2, a language L is recursive (recursively enumerable) if there is a TM that recognizes/decides (accepts) L. This immediately implies that each recursive language is also recursively enumerable.

Theorem 6.1.1 shows that there is an alternative way to view recursively enumerable sets – through a generation/enumeration. We say that an off-line TM $\mathcal{M}$ generates (enumerates) a language $L \subseteq \Sigma^*$, if $\mathcal{M}$, starting with the empty input tape, writes on its output tape, symbol by symbol, a word $w_L = w_1\#w_2\#w_3\#\ldots$, where $w_i \in \Sigma^*$, $\# \notin \Sigma$, $w_i \neq w_j$, for $i \neq j$, and $L = \{w_i \,|\, 1 \leq i\}$. (In short, $\mathcal{M}$ generates all words of L, none twice, and no other words.)

Theorem 6.1.1 *A language L is recursively enumerable if and only if L is generated by an off-line Turing machine.*

Proof: Let L be a recursively enumerable language and $L = L(\mathcal{M}) \subseteq \Sigma^*$ for a TM $\mathcal{M}$. We now show how to design an on-line TM $\mathcal{M}'$ generating words of L, each of them exactly once.

$\mathcal{M}'$ produces, starting with the pair $(0,0)$, all pairs $(i,j) \in \mathbf{N}^2$, one after another, with respect to the ordering $\ll$ defined as follows:

$$(i_1,j_1) \ll (i_2,j_2) \Longleftrightarrow i_1+j_1 < i_2+j_2 \vee (i_1+j_1 = i_2+j_2) \wedge (j_1 < j_2).$$

For each newly created pair (i,j), $\mathcal{M}'$ generates the ith word w_i from Σ^* (with respect to the strict ordering), and then simulates exactly j steps of $\mathcal{M}$ on w_i. If $\mathcal{M}$ accepts w_i in exactly j steps, then $\mathcal{M}'$ generates w_i by writing $w_i\#$ on its output tape. If not, $\mathcal{M}'$ does not write anything on its output tape. In both cases, as the next step, $\mathcal{M}'$ generates the next pair (i',j') with respect to the ordering $\ll$ and the whole process continues. In this way $\mathcal{M}'$ simulates, sooner or later, each terminating computation of $\mathcal{M}$, and generates all those words $\mathcal{M}$ accepts, each one exactly once.

In order to prove the opposite implication, let us assume that $L \subseteq \Sigma^*$ is a language generated by a k-tape off-line TM $\mathcal{M}$. We show how to design a TM $\mathcal{M}'$ that accepts L. $\mathcal{M}'$ will use k tapes to simulate k work tapes of $\mathcal{M}$ and two additional work tapes to simulate the input and output tapes of $\mathcal{M}$. For a given input word w, $\mathcal{M}'$ begins simulation of a computation of $\mathcal{M}$ that starts with the empty input tape. Each time $\mathcal{M}$ writes on its output tape a word of the type $\#w'\#$, with $w' \in \Sigma^*$, $\mathcal{M}'$ compares w' with w. If they agree, $\mathcal{M}'$ accepts w; otherwise, $\mathcal{M}'$ keeps simulating $\mathcal{M}$. □

Exercise 6.1.2 *Show that if an off-line TM outputs on the empty tape an infinite word* $w = w_1\#w_2\#w_3\ldots$, *where* $w_i \in \Sigma^*, \# \notin \Sigma$, *then the language* $L = \{w_i \,|\, 1 \leq i\}$ *is recursively enumerable. (The condition that each word can be generated only once is relaxed.)*

Exercise 6.1.3 *Show that the set of all TM that halt on at least two inputs is recursively enumerable.*

There is the following close relation between recursive and recursively enumerable sets.

Theorem 6.1.4 *A language* $L \subseteq \Sigma^*$ *is recursive if and only if* L *and its complement* L^c *are recursively enumerable.*

Proof: If L is a recursive language, there is a TM $\mathcal{M}$ that recognizes L. By exchanging the accepting and rejecting states in the description of $\mathcal{M}$, we get a TM that recognizes the complement L^c. Hence both L and L^c are recursive, and therefore also recursively enumerable.

On the other hand, if both L and L^c are recursively enumerable, then there are TMs $\mathcal{M}_1$ and $\mathcal{M}_2$ such that $L(\mathcal{M}_1) = L$ and $L(\mathcal{M}_2) = L^c$. From these two TMs we can design in the following way a TM $\mathcal{M}$ that recognizes L. $\mathcal{M}$ simulates, for a given input w, both $\mathcal{M}_1$ and $\mathcal{M}_2$ in parallel – that is, $\mathcal{M}$ computes, for $i = 1,2,\ldots$, the ith step of $\mathcal{M}_1$ and immediately after that the ith step of $\mathcal{M}_2$. One of these two machines has to terminate and accept. If $\mathcal{M}_1$ accepts first, then so does $\mathcal{M}$; but if $\mathcal{M}_2$ accepts first, $\mathcal{M}$ rejects w. □

Exercise 6.1.5 *Show that the family of recursive languages is closed under Boolean set operations (union, intersection and complementation).*

As one would expect, not every recursively enumerable set is recursive, and there are sets that are not even recursively enumerable. We demonstrate this by two examples.

Let us consider a fixed Gödel encoding of all TM into an alphabet Γ (see Section 4.1), and let $\mathcal{M}_1, \mathcal{M}_2, \ldots$ be an enumeration of all TM over the alphabet Γ ordered with respect to the strict ordering of their codes. Moreover, let $w_1, w_2, \ldots$ be the strict ordering of all words over Γ. We use these orderings to define two languages:

$$K = \{w_i \mid w_i \in L(\mathcal{M}_i)\}, \qquad K^c = \{w_i \mid w_i \notin L(\mathcal{M}_i)\}.$$

Theorem 6.1.6 (Post's theorem) *The language K is recursively enumerable but not recursive, and the language K^c is not recursively enumerable.*

Proof: We show first that K is recursively enumerable, but K^c is not. By Theorem 6.1.4, this implies that K is not recursive.

To show that K is recursively enumerable, we design a TM $\mathcal{M}$ that accepts K. For a given input w, $\mathcal{M}$ computes i such that $w = w_i$, then designs $\mathcal{M}_i$ and simulates $\mathcal{M}_i$ on w_i. If $\mathcal{M}_i$ accepts w_i, then so does $\mathcal{M}$.

In order to show that the language K^c is not recursively enumerable, we use the diagonalization method and consider the infinite Boolean matrix M such that $b_{i,j} = M(i,j) = 1$ if and only if $w_i \in L(\mathcal{M}_j)$. Hence the language K^c corresponds to 0's in the diagonal of M:

	$\mathcal{M}_1$	$\mathcal{M}_2$	$\mathcal{M}_3$	$\mathcal{M}_4$	$\ldots$
w_1	$b_{1,1}$	$b_{1,2}$	$b_{1,3}$	$b_{1,4}$	$\ldots$
w_2	$b_{2,1}$	$b_{2,2}$	$b_{2,3}$	$b_{2,4}$	$\ldots$
w_3	$b_{3,1}$	$b_{3,2}$	$b_{3,3}$	$b_{3,4}$	$\ldots$
w_4	$b_{4,1}$	$b_{4,2}$	$b_{4,3}$	$b_{4,4}$	$\ldots$
$\vdots$	$\vdots$	$\vdots$	$\vdots$	$\vdots$	$\vdots$

If K^c is recursively enumerable, there must exist a j_0 such that $L(\mathcal{M}_{j_0}) = K^c$. There are now two possibilities for w_{j_0}: either $w_{j_0} \in K^c$ or $w_{j_0} \notin K^c$. In both cases we derive a contradiction, as follows.

$$w_{j_0} \in K^c \Rightarrow w_{j_0} \in L(\mathcal{M}_{j_0}) \Rightarrow w_{j_0} \notin K^c,$$

$$w_{j_0} \notin K^c \Rightarrow w_{j_0} \notin L(\mathcal{M}_{j_0}) \Rightarrow w_{j_0} \in K^c.$$

This contradiction implies that our assumption – namely, that K^c is recursively enumerable – is false.

□

The concepts of recursiveness and recursive enumerability are often generalized and used to characterize sets of objects other than numbers, elements of which can be encoded in a natural way by strings. The basic idea of these generalizations is that a set is recursive (recursively enumerable) if the set of all encodings of its elements is. For example, in this sense we can speak of recursive and recursively enumerable relations, and we can also show that the set of all minimal solutions of the firing squad synchronization problem is not recursively enumerable.

Exercise 6.1.7 *Prove that a set $L \subseteq \mathbf{N}$ is recursive if and only if it can be enumerated in an increasing order by some TM.*

Exercise 6.1.8 *Show that a language L is recursively enumerable if and only if there is a recursive relation R such that $x \in L \equiv \exists y[(x,y) \in R]$.*

Remark 6.1.9 There are several other types of sets encountered quite often in the theory of computing: for example, productive, creative, immune and simple sets. Since they are easy to define, and one should have at least a basic knowledge of them, we shall introduce these concepts even though we shall not explore them.

In order to define these sets, let us observe that an effective enumeration of all TM induces an effective enumeration of all recursively enumerable sets (accepted by these TM). Therefore, once a fixed encoding and ordering of TM are adopted, we can talk about the ith recursively enumerable set S_i.

A set S is called **productive** if there is a recursive function g such that whenever $S_i \subsetneq S$, then $g(i) \in S - S_i$. A set $S \subseteq \Sigma^*$ is **creative** if S is recursively enumerable and its complement S^c is productive. (For example, the set K is creative.) A set $S \subsetneq \Sigma^*$ is **immune** if S is infinite and it has no recursively enumerable infinite subset. A set $S \subseteq \Sigma^*$ is **simple** if it is recursively enumerable and its complement is an immune set.

Exercise 6.1.10 *Show that every infinite recursively enumerable set has an infinite recursive subset.*

Exercise 6.1.11 *Show that if A and B are recursively enumerable sets, then there are recursively enumerable subsets $A' \subseteq A$ and $B' \subseteq B$ such that $A' \cap B' = \emptyset$ and $A' \cup B' = A \cup B$.*

6.2 Recursive and Primitive Recursive Functions

Two families of functions, which can be defined inductively and in a machine-independent way, play a special role in computing: primitive recursive and partial recursive functions. They are usually defined as functions from integers to integers. However, this can be generalized, for example to strings-to-string functions, as will be shown later. The most important outcome of this approach is the knowledge that all computable functions have a closed form and a method for obtaining this closed form.

6.2.1 Primitive Recursive Functions

The family of primitive recursive functions contains practically all the functions we encounter and can expect to encounter in practical computing. The basic tool for defining these functions is the operation of primitive recursion – a generalization of recurrences we considered in Chapter 1.

Definition 6.2.1 *The family of primitive recursive functions is the smallest family of integer-to-integer functions with the following properties:*

1. *It contains the following* **base functions**:

$$\begin{array}{ll} 0 & (\textbf{nullary constant}), \\ S(x) = x+1 & (\textbf{successor function}), \\ U_i^n(x_1, \ldots, x_n) = x_i & (\textbf{projection functions}), \textit{for } 1 \le i \le n. \end{array}$$

2. *It is closed under the following operations:*

- **composition**: *if* $h : \mathbf{N}^m \to \mathbf{N}, g_1 : \mathbf{N}^n \to \mathbf{N}, \ldots, g_m : \mathbf{N}^n \to \mathbf{N}$ *are primitive recursive functions, then so is the function* $f : \mathbf{N}^n \to \mathbf{N}$ *defined as follows:*

$$f(x_1, \ldots, x_n) = h(g_1(x_1, \ldots, x_n), \ldots, g_m(x_1, \ldots, x_n)).$$

- **primitive recursion**: *if* $h : \mathbf{N}^n \to \mathbf{N}, g : \mathbf{N}^{n+2} \to \mathbf{N}$ *are primitive recursive functions, then so is the function* $f : \mathbf{N}^{n+1} \to \mathbf{N}$ *defined as follows:*

$$\begin{aligned} f(0, x_1, \ldots, x_n) &= h(x_1, \ldots, x_n), \\ f(z+1, x_1, \ldots, x_n) &= g(z, f(z, x_1, \ldots, x_n), x_1, \ldots, x_n), \qquad z \geq 0. \end{aligned}$$

The following examples illustrate how to construct a primitive recursive function using the operations of composition and primitive recursion.

Example 6.2.2 *Addition:* $a(x,y) = x + y$:

$$\begin{aligned} a(0,y) &= U_1^1(y); \\ a(x+1,y) &= S(U_2^3(x, a(x,y), y). \end{aligned}$$

Example 6.2.3 *Multiplication:* $m(x,y) = x \cdot y$:

$$\begin{aligned} m(0,y) &= 0; \\ m(x+1,y) &= a(m(x,y), U_1^2(x,y)). \end{aligned}$$

Example 6.2.4 *Predecessor* $P(x) = x \dot{-} 1$:

$$\begin{aligned} P(0) &= 0; \\ P(x+1) &= U_1^1(x). \end{aligned}$$

Example 6.2.5 *Nonnegative subtraction:* $\alpha(x,y) = x \dot{-} y$:

$$\begin{aligned} \alpha(x,0) &= U_1^1(x); \\ \alpha(x,y+1) &= P(x \dot{-} y). \end{aligned}$$

Exercise 6.2.6 *Determine for Examples 6.2.2– 6.2.5 what the functions h and g are, and explain why we have used the function* $U_1^1(y)$ *in Examples 6.2.2 and 6.2.4 and the function* $U_1^2(x,y)$ *in Example 6.2.3.*

Exercise 6.2.7 *Show that the following functions are primitive recursive: (a) exponentiation; (b) factorial.*

Exercise 6.2.8 *Show that if* $f : \mathbf{N}^{n+1} \to \mathbf{N}$ *is a primitive recursive function, then so are the following functions of arguments* $x_1, \ldots, x_n$ *and* z:

$$(a) \quad \sum_{y \leq z} f(x_1, \ldots, x_n, y), \qquad (b) \quad \prod_{y \leq z} f(x_1, \ldots, x_n, y).$$

The concept of primitive recursivity can be extended to objects other than integer-to-integer functions. For example, a set of integers or a predicate on integers is called primitive recursive if its characteristic functions are primitive recursive. We can also talk about primitive recursivity of other types of functions.

Exercise 6.2.9 *Show that the following predicates are primitive recursive: (a) $x \leq y$; (b) $x = y$.*

Exercise 6.2.10 *Show that the family of primitive recursive predicates is closed under Boolean operations.*

Example 6.2.11 (Primitive recursivness of string-to-string functions) *There are two ways of generalizing the concept of primitive recursivity for string-to-string functions: an indirect one, in which a simple bijection between strings over an alphabet and integers is used, and a direct one that we now use for string-to-string functions over the alphabet $\{0,1\}$.*

Base functions: *$E(x) = \varepsilon$ (the empty string function), two successor functions $S_0(x) = x0$ and $S_1(x) = x1$, and the projection functions $U_i^n(x_1, \ldots, x_n) = x_i$, $1 \leq i \leq n$.*

Operations: *composition and the primitive recursion defined as follows:*

$$\begin{array}{rcl} f(\varepsilon, x_1, \ldots, x_n) & = & h(x_1, \ldots, x_n); \\ f(y0, x_1, \ldots, x_n) & = & g_0(y, f(y, x_1, \ldots, x_n), x_1, \ldots, x_n); \\ f(y1, x_1, \ldots, x_n) & = & g_1(y, f(y, x_1, \ldots, x_n), x_1, \ldots, x_n), \end{array}$$

where h, g_0, g_1 are primitive recursive string-to-string functions.

Exercise 6.2.12 *Show that the following string-to-string functions over the alphabet $\{0,1\}$ are primitive recursive: (a) $f(w) = ww$; (b) $f(w) = w^R$; (c) $f(x,y) = xy$.*

There is a powerful and elegant theory of computation based heavily on primitive recursive functions. This is to a large extent due to the fact that we can use primitive recursive pairing and coding functions to reduce the theory of primitive recursive functions of more variables to the theory of primitive recursive functions of one variable.

Example 6.2.13 (Pairing and de-pairing) *We describe now three primitive recursive bijections:*

$$pair : \mathbf{N} \times \mathbf{N} \rightarrow \mathbf{N} \text{ and } \pi_1, \pi_2 : \mathbf{N} \rightarrow \mathbf{N},$$

with the property

$$\pi_1(pair(x,y)) = x,\ \pi_2(pair(x,y)) = y \text{ and } pair(\pi_1(z), \pi_2(z)) = z.$$

In order to do this, let us consider the mapping of pairs of integers into integers shown in Figure 6.1.

Observe first that the i-th counterdiagonal (counting starts with 0) contains numbers corresponding to pairs (x,y) with $x + y = i$. Hence,

$$pair(x,y) = 1 + 2 + \cdots + (x+y) + y.$$

	0	1	2	3	4	5
0	0	2	5	9	14	↗
1	1	4	8	13	↗	
2	3	7	12	↗		
3	6	11	↗			
4	10	↗				
5	↗					

Figure 6.1 Pairing function – matrix representation

In order to define the 'de-pairing functions' π_1 and π_2, let us introduce an auxiliary function $cd(n)$ = 'the number of the counterdiagonal on which the n-th pair lies'. Clearly, n and $n+1$ lie on the same counterdiagonal if and only if $n+1 < pair(cd(n)+1,0)$. Therefore, we have

$$\begin{aligned} cd(0) &= 0; \\ cd(n+1) &= cd(n) + ((n+2) \dot{-} pair(cd(n)+1,0)). \end{aligned}$$

Since $\pi_2(n)$ is the position of the nth pair on the $cd\,(n)$th counterdiagonal, and $\pi_1(n)+\pi_2(n) = cd(n)$, we get

$$\pi_2(n) = n \dot{-} pair(cd(n),0), \qquad \pi_1(n) = cd(n) \dot{-} \pi_2(n).$$

Exercise 6.2.14 *Show formally, using the definition of primitive recursive functions, that the pairing and de-pairing functions* pair *π_1 and π_2 are primitive recursive.*

It is now easy to extend the pairing function introduced in Example 6.2.13 to a function that maps, in a one-to-one way, n-tuples of integers into integers, for $n > 2$. For example, we can define inductively, for any $n > 2$,

$$pair(x_1, \ldots, x_n) = pair(x_1, pair(x_2, \ldots, x_n)).$$

Moreover, we can use the de-pairing functions π_1 and π_2 to defined de-pairing functions $\pi_{n,i}, 1 \leq i \leq n$, such that $\pi_{n,i}(pair(x_1, \ldots, x_n)) = x_i$. This implies that in the study of primitive recursive functions we can restrict ourselves without loss of generality to one-argument functions.

Exercise 6.2.15 *Let* $pair(x,y,z,u) = v$. *Show how to express* x, y, z *and* u *as functions of* v, *using de-pairing functions* π_1 *and* π_2.

Exercise 6.2.16 *Let us consider the following total ordering in* $\mathbf{N} \times \mathbf{N}$: $(x,y) \prec (x',y')$ *if and only if either* $\max\{x,y\} < \max\{x',y'\}$ *or* $\max\{x,y\} = \max\{x',y'\}$ *and either* $x+y < x'+y'$ *or* $x+y = x'+y'$ *and* $x < x'$. *Denote* $pair_m(x,y)$ *the position of the pair in the ordering defined above. Show that such a pairing function is primitive recursive, as are the de-pairing functions* π_1^m, π_2^m *such that* $\pi_1^m(pair_m(x,y)) = x$ *and similarly for* π_2^m.

Remark 6.2.17 Primitive recursive functions can also be characterized syntactically in terms of programming constructs. For example, they are exactly the functions that are computable by programs written using the following statements: assignment statements, **for** statements of the form **for** N **do** S (iterate S for N times), and composed statements.

6.2.2 Partial Recursive and Recursive Functions

Partial recursive functions were introduced in Definition 4.1.2, as functions computed by Turing machines. There is also an alternative way, inductive and machine-independent, to define them, and this is now presented.

Theorem 6.2.18 *The family of partial recursive functions is the smallest family of integer-to-integer functions with the following properties:*

1. *It contains the following base functions:*

0	(nullary constant),
$S(x) = x+1$	(successor function),
$U_i^n(x_1,\ldots,x_n) = x_i$	(projection functions), $1 \leq i \leq n$.

2. *It is closed under the operations* composition, primitive recursion *and* minimalization, *defined as follows:*

   if $h : \mathbf{N}^{n+1} \rightarrow \mathbf{N}$ *is a partial recursive function, then so is the function* $f : \mathbf{N}^n \rightarrow \mathbf{N}$, *where* $f(x_1,\ldots,x_n)$ *is the smallest* $y \in \mathbf{N}$ *such that* $h(x_1,\ldots,x_n,y) = 0$ *and* $h(x_1,\ldots,x_n,z)$ *is defined for all integers* $0 \leq z \leq y$. *Otherwise,* $f(x_1,\ldots,x_n)$ *is undefined.* f *is usually written in the form*

$$f(x_1,\ldots,x_n) = \mu y\,[h(x_1,\ldots,x_n,y) = 0].$$

To prove Theorem 6.2.18 in one way is pretty easy. All functions constructed from the base functions using composition and minimization are clearly computable, and therefore, by Church's thesis, partial recursive. In a more formal way, one can design a TM for any of the base functions and show how to design for any of the operations involved (composition, primitive recursion and minimization) a Turing machine computing the resulting function under the assumption that component functions are TM computable.

To prove the theorem in the opposite direction is also in principle easy and straightforward, but this time the task is tedious. One must show that all concepts concerning Turing machine computations can be arithmetized and expressed using the base functions and operations of composition, primitive recursion and minimization – in an analogical way, as it was done in the proof of **NP**-completeness of the satisfiability problem for Boolean functions, where 'Booleanization' of Turing machine computations was used. The key role is played by the generalized pairing and de-pairing functions. For example, we can assume without loss of generality that states and tape symbols of Turing machines are integers and that moves (left, right or none) are represented by integers 0, 1 or 2. In this case each TM instruction can be represented by a 5-tuple of integers (q,a,i,b,q'), and using the pairing function $pair(q,a,i,b,q') = x$, by a single integer x. Thus $\pi_{5,1}(x) = q, \pi_{5,2}(x) = a$ and so on. This way one can express a sequence of TM instructions by one number, and show that the predicate *TM-Program*(x), which determines whether x corresponds to a valid TM program, is primitive recursive. On this basis one can express all functions and predicates specifying Turing machine computations as recursive functions and predicates. A detailed proof can be found, for example, in Smith (1994).

Remark 6.2.19 Observe that the only effective way of computing $f(x_1, \ldots, x_n)$ for a function f defined by minimalization from h is to compute first $h(x_1, \ldots, x_n, 0)$, then $h(x_1, \ldots, x_n, 1)$, ... until the desired value of y is found. Consequently, there are two ways in which f can be undefined for arguments $x_1, \ldots, x_n$: first, if there is no y such that $h(x_1, \ldots, x_n, y) = 0$; second, if $h(x_1, \ldots, x_n, y) = 0$ for some y, but $h(x_1, \ldots, x_n, z)$ is undefined for some z smaller than the smallest y for which $h(x_1, \ldots, x_n, y) = 0$.

Exercise 6.2.20* *Show that there is no primitive recursive function* $U : \mathbf{N} \times \mathbf{N} \rightarrow \mathbf{N}$ *such that for each primitive recursive function* $h : \mathbf{N} \rightarrow \mathbf{N}$ *there is an integer* i_h *for which* $U(i_h, n) = h(n)$.

It is interesting that in the process of arithmetization of Turing machine computations it is enough to use the operation of minimization only once. We can even obtain through such arithmetization the following normal form for partial recursive functions (which also represents another way of showing the existence of a universal computer).

Theorem 6.2.21 (Kleene's theorem) *There exist primitive recursive functions g and h such that for each partial recursive function f of one variable there is an integer* i_f *such that*

$$f(x) = g(\mu y\,[h(x, i_f, y) = 0]).$$

Kleene's theorem shows that the family of partial recursive functions has a universal function. However, this is not the case for primitive recursive functions (see Exercise 6.2.20).

Exercise 6.2.22* *Show that the following predicates are primitive recursive: (a)* TM-program(x) – *x is an encoding of a TM; (b)* configuration(x,t) – *x is an encoding of a configuration of the Turing machine with encoding t; (c)* comp-step(x,y,t) – *x and y are encodings of configurations of the Turing machine encoded by t, and the configuration encoded by y can be obtained from the configuration encoded as x by one step of the TM encoded by t.*

With two examples we illustrate how to use minimization.

Example 6.2.23 $\lfloor\sqrt{x}\rfloor = \mu y\{(y+1)^2 \dot{-} x \neq 0\}$.

Example 6.2.24 $\lfloor\frac{x}{y}\rfloor = \mu i\{i \leq x \wedge (x+1) \leq (i+1)y\}$.

It is the operation of minimization that has the power to create recursive functions that are not primitive recursive. On the other hand, bounded minimization, discussed in the exercises below, is a convenient tool for designing primitive recursive functions.

Exercise 6.2.25 (Bounded minimization) *Show that if $f : \mathbf{N}^{n+1} \to \mathbf{N}$ is a primitive recursive function, then so is the function $\mu z \leq y[f(x_1, \ldots, x_n, z) = 0]$, defined to be the smallest $z \leq y$ such that $f(x_1, \ldots, x_n, z) = 0$, and $y+1$ if such a z does not exist.*

Exercise 6.2.26 (Bounded minimization) *Show that if $f : \mathbf{N}^{n+1} \to \mathbf{N}$ and $b : \mathbf{N}^n \to \mathbf{N}$ are primitive recursive functions, then so is the function $\mu z \leq b(x_1, \ldots, x_n)[f(x_1, \ldots, x_n, z) = 0]$, defined to be the smallest $z \leq b(x_1, \ldots, x_n)$ such that $f(x_1, \ldots, x_n, z) = 0$, and $b(x_1, \ldots, x_n) + 1$ otherwise.*

Exercise 6.2.27 *Show that the following functions are primitive recursive: (a) the number of divisors of n; (b) the number of primes $\leq n$; (c) the n-th prime.*

One of the main sources of difficulty in dealing with partial recursive functions is due to the fact that partial functions may be undefined for an argument, and there is no effective way of knowing this beforehand. The following technique, called **dovetailing**, can be helpful in overcoming this difficulty in some cases.

Example 6.2.28 (Dovetailing) *Suppose we are given a partial recursive function $f : \mathbf{N} \to \mathbf{N}$, and we wish to find an n such that $f(n)$ is defined. We cannot do this by computing first $f(0)$, then $f(1)$ and so on, because it may happen that $f(0)$ is undefined even if $f(1)$ is defined and computation of $f(0)$ never stops. (Note too that in this case an application of the minimization operation in order to find the smallest x such that $f(x) = 0$ fails.) We can overcome this problem using the following approach.*

1. *Perform one step of the computation of $f(0)$.*

2. *For $i = 1, 2, \ldots$, until a computation terminates, perform one next step in computing $f(0)$, $f(1), \ldots, f(i-1)$, and the first step in computing $f(i)$ – that is, if $i = k$, the $(k+1)$-th step of computation of $f(0)$, the k-th step of the computation of $f(1)$, $\ldots$ and, finally, the first step of the computation of $f(k)$.*

Exercise 6.2.29 *Show that a function $f : \mathbf{N} \to \mathbf{N}$ is recursive if and only if its graph $\{(x, f(x)) \mid x \in \mathbf{N}\}$ is recursively enumerable.*

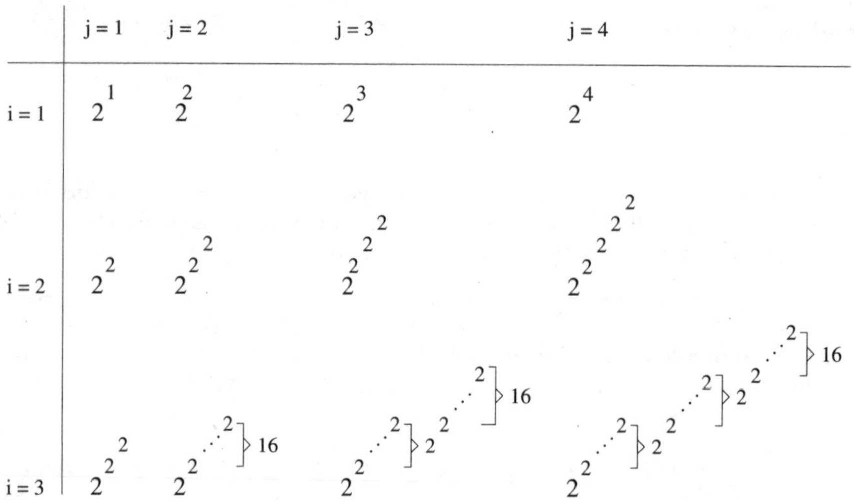

	j = 1	j = 2	j = 3	j = 4
i = 1	2^1	2^2	2^3	2^4
i = 2	2^2	2^{2^2}	$2^{2^{2^2}}$	$2^{2^{2^{2^2}}}$
i = 3	2^{2^2}	$\left.2^{2^{\cdot^{\cdot^{\cdot^{2}}}}}\right\}16$	$\left.2^{2^{\cdot^{\cdot^{\cdot^{2}}}}}\right\}\left.2^{2^{\cdot^{\cdot^{\cdot^{2}}}}}\right\}16$	$\left.2^{2^{\cdot^{\cdot^{\cdot^{2}}}}}\right\}\left.2^{2^{\cdot^{\cdot^{\cdot^{2}}}}}\right\}\left.2^{2^{\cdot^{\cdot^{\cdot^{2}}}}}\right\}16$

Figure 6.2 Ackermann function

Ackermann function

As already defined in Section 4.1, a total partial recursive function is called recursive. An example of a recursive function that is not primitive recursive is the Ackermann function, defined as follows:

$$\begin{aligned} A(1,j) &= 2^j, && \text{if } j \geq 1; \\ A(i,1) &= A(i-1,2), && \text{if } i \geq 2; \\ A(i,j) &= A(i-1,A(i,j-1)) && \text{if } i \geq 2, j \geq 2. \end{aligned}$$

Note, that the **double recursion** is used to define $A(i,j)$. This is perfectly alright, because the arguments of A on the right-hand sides of the above equations are always smaller in at least one component than those on the left. The Ackermann function is therefore computable, and by Church's thesis recursive. Surprisingly, this double recursion has the effect that the Ackermann function grows faster than any primitive recursive function, as stated in the theorem below. Figure 6.2 shows the values of the Ackermann function for several small arguments. Already $A(2,j) = 2^{2^{\cdots^{2}}}\ \{j \text{ times}\}$ is an enormously fast-growing function, and for $i > 2$, $A(i,j)$ grows even faster.

Surprisingly, this exotic function has a firm place in computing. More exactly, in the analysis of algorithms we often encounter the following 'inverse' of the Ackermann function:

$$\alpha(m,n) = \min\{i \geq 1 \mid A(i, \lfloor m / n \rfloor) > \lg n\}.$$

In contrast to the Ackermann function, its inverse grows very slowly. For all feasible m and n, we have $\alpha(m,n) \leq 4$, and therefore, from the point of view of the analysis of algorithms, $\alpha(m,n)$ is an 'almost constant function'. The following theorem summarizes the relation of the Ackermann function to primitive recursive functions.

Theorem 6.2.30 *For each primitive recursive function $f(n)$ there is an integer n_0 such that $f(n) \leq A(n,n)$, for all $n \geq n_0$.*

Exercise 6.2.31 *Show that for any fixed i the function* $f(j) = A(i,j)$ *is primitive recursive. (Even the predicate* $k = A(i,j)$ *is primitive recursive, but this is much harder to show.)*

There are also simple relations between the concepts of recursivness for sets and functions that follow easily from the previous results and are now summarized for integer functions and sets.

Theorem 6.2.32 1. *A set S is recursively enumerable if and only if S is the domain of a partial recursive function.*

2. *A set is recursively enumerable if and only if S is the range of a partial recursive function.*

3. *A set S is recursively enumerable (recursive) if and only if its characteristic function is partial recursive (recursive).*

There are also nice relations between the recursivness of a function and its graph.

Exercise 6.2.33 (Graph theorem) *Show that (a) a function is partial recursive if and only if its graph is recursively enumerable; (b) a function f is recursive if and only if its graph is a recursive set.*

The origins of recursion theory, which go back to the 1930s, pre-date the first computers. This theory actually provided the first basic understanding of what is computable and of basic computational principles. It also created an intellectual framework for the design and utilization of universal computers and for the understanding that, in principle, they can be very simple.

The idea of recursivity and recursive enumerability can be extended to real-valued functions. In order to formulate the basic concepts let us first observe that to any integer valued function $f : \mathbf{N} \rightarrow \mathbf{N}$, we can associate a rational-valued function $f' : \mathbf{N} \times \mathbf{N} \rightarrow \mathbf{Q}$ defined by $f'(x,y) = \frac{p}{q}$, where $p = \pi_1(f(pair(x,y)))$, $q = \pi_2(f(pair(x,y)))$.

Definition 6.2.34 *A real-valued function* $f' : \mathbf{N} \times \mathbf{N} \rightarrow \mathbf{R}$ *is called* **recursively enumerable** *if there is a recursive function* $g : \mathbf{N} \rightarrow \mathbf{N}$ *such that* $g'(x,k)$ *is nondecreasing in k and* $\lim_{k\rightarrow\infty} g'(x,k) = f(x)$. *A real-valued function* $f : \mathbf{N} \rightarrow \mathbf{R}$ *is called* **recursive** *if there is a recursive function* $g : \mathbf{N} \rightarrow \mathbf{N}$ *such that* $|f(x) - g'(x,k)| < \frac{1}{k}$, *for all k and x.*

The main idea behind this definition is that a recursively enumerable function can be approximated from one-side by a recursive function over integers but computing such a function we may never know how close we are to the real value. Recursive real-valued functions can be approximated to any degree of precision by recursive functions over integers.

Exercise 6.2.35 *Show that a function* $f : \mathbf{N} \rightarrow \mathbf{R}$ *is recursively enumerable if the set* $\{(x,r) \mid r < f(x), r \in Q\}$ *is recursively enumerable.*

Exercise 6.2.36 *Show the following function f is recursively enumerable but not recursive:* $f(x) = 1$ *if* $w_x \in L(\mathcal{M}_x)$ *and* $f(x) = 0$, *otherwise – for a Gödel numbering of Turing machines and words over an alphabet* Γ.

6.3 Recursive Reals

The concept of recursive functions can also be used to formalize the informal concept of a computable real number.

It is intuitively clear that such numbers as π and e are computable in the sense that given an integer n we can potentially compute the first n digits of its decimal expansion.[1]

There are various ways of defining 'recursive real numbers'. We present and discuss two of them. A real number α is called **recursive** if there are recursive functions f and g and an integer n_0 such that $||\alpha| - \frac{f(n)}{g(n)}| \leq \frac{1}{n+1}$, for $n \geq n_0$.

Exercise 6.3.1 *Show that a real number $0 \leq \alpha \leq 1$ is recursive if and only if there is a recursive function $f : \mathbf{N} \to \{0,1,\ldots,9\}$ such that $|\alpha| = \sum_{i=0}^{\infty} \frac{f(i)}{10^i}$.*

A real number α is called **limiting recursive** if there are recursive functions f, g, h and k such that the sequence $\{\alpha_n\}_{n=1}^{\infty}$, where

$$\alpha_n = \frac{f(n) - g(n)}{h(n)},$$

effectively converges to α in the sense that for each $m > 0$ there is a $k(m) \in \mathbf{N}$ such that for $n, n' > k(m)$,

$$|\alpha_n - \alpha_{n'}| \leq \frac{1}{m}.$$

It can be shown that each recursive number is limiting recursive, but not vice versa.

The set of limiting recursive numbers is clearly countable. This implies that there are real numbers that are not limiting recursive.

The number of wisdom introduced in Section 6.5.5 is an example of a limiting recursive but not a recursive real number.

6.4 Undecidable Problems

We have already seen in Section 4.1.6 that the halting problem is undecidable. This result certainly does not sound positive. But at first glance, it does not seem to be a result worth bothering with in any case. In practice, who actually needs to deal with the halting problem for Turing machines? Almost nobody. Can we not take these undecidability results merely as an intellectual curiosity that does not really affect things one way or another?

Unfortunately, such a conclusion would be very mistaken. In this section we demonstrate that there are theoretically deep and practically important reasons to be concerned with the existence of undecidable and unsolvable problems. First, such problems are much more frequent than one might expect. Second, some of the most important practical problems are undecidable. Third, boundaries between decidability and undecidability are sometimes unexpectedly sharp.

In this section we present some key undecidable problems and methods for showing undecidability.

[1] So far π has been computed to $2 \cdot 10^9$ digits.

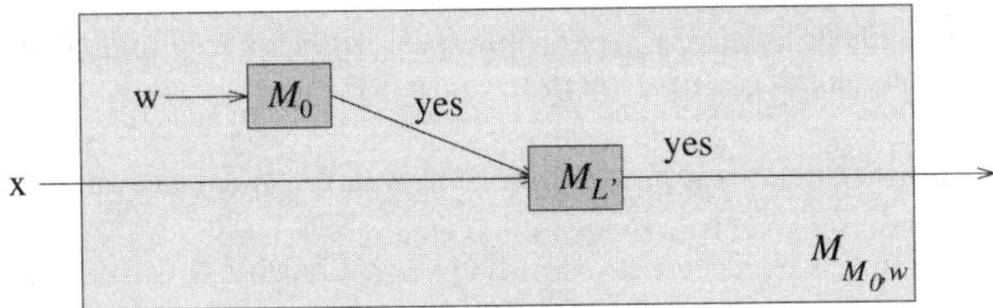

Figure 6.3 Turing machine $\mathcal{M}_{\mathcal{M}_0,w}$

6.4.1 Rice's Theorem

We start with a very general result, contra-intuitive and quite depressing, saying that on the most general level of all Turing machines nothing interesting is decidable. That is, we show first that no nontrivial property of recursively enumerable sets is decidable. This implies not only that the number of undecidable problems is surprisingly large but that at this general level there are mostly undecidable problems.

In order to show the main result, let us fix a Gödel self-delimiting encoding $\langle\mathcal{M}\rangle_\rho$ of Turing machines $\mathcal{M}$ into the alphabet $\{0,1\}$ and the corresponding encoding $\langle w\rangle_\rho$ of input words of $\mathcal{M}$. The language

$$L_u = \{\langle\mathcal{M}\rangle_\rho\langle w\rangle_\rho \,|\, \mathcal{M} \text{ accepts } w\}$$

is called the **universal language**. It follows from Theorem 4.1.23 that the language L_u is not decidable.

Definition 6.4.1 *Each family $\mathcal{S}$ of recursively enumerable languages over the alphabet $\{0,1\}$ is said to be a property of recursively enumerable languages. A property $\mathcal{S}$ is called nontrivial if $\mathcal{S} \neq \emptyset$ and $\mathcal{S}$ does not contain all recursively enumerable languages (over $\{0,1\}$).*

A nontrivial property of recursively enumerable languages is therefore characterized only by the requirement that there are recursively enumerable languages that have this property and those that do not. For example, being a regular language is such a property.

Theorem 6.4.2 (Rice's theorem) *Each nontrivial property of recursively enumerable languages is undecidable.*

Proof: We can assume without loss of generality that $\emptyset \notin \mathcal{S}$; otherwise we can take the complement of $\mathcal{S}$. Since $\mathcal{S}$ is a nontrivial property, there is a recursively enumerable language $L' \in \mathcal{S}$ (that is, one with the property $\mathcal{S}$), and let $\mathcal{M}_{L'}$ be a Turing machine that accepts L'.

Assume that the property $\mathcal{S}$ is decidable, and that therefore there is a Turing machine $\mathcal{M}_\mathcal{S}$ such that $L(\mathcal{M}_\mathcal{S}) = \{\langle\mathcal{M}\rangle_\rho, | L(\mathcal{M}) \in \mathcal{S}\}$. We now use $\mathcal{M}_{L'}$ and $\mathcal{M}_\mathcal{S}$ to show that the universal language is decidable. This contradiction proves the theorem.

We describe first an algorithm for designing, given a Turing machine $\mathcal{M}_0$ and its input w, a Turing machine $\mathcal{M}_{\mathcal{M}_0,w}$ such that $L(\mathcal{M}_{\mathcal{M}_0,w}) \in \mathcal{S}$ if and only if $\mathcal{M}_0$ accepts w (see Figure 6.3). $\mathcal{M}_{\mathcal{M}_0,w}$ first ignores its input x and simulates $\mathcal{M}_0$ on w. If $\mathcal{M}_0$ does not accept w, then $\mathcal{M}_{\mathcal{M}_0,w}$ does not accept x. On the other hand, if $\mathcal{M}_0$ accepts w, and as a result terminates, $\mathcal{M}_{\mathcal{M}_0,w}$ starts to simulate $\mathcal{M}_{L'}$ on x and accepts it if and only if $\mathcal{M}_{L'}$ accepts it. Thus, $\mathcal{M}_{\mathcal{M}_0,w}$ accepts either the empty language (not in $\mathcal{S}$) or L' (in $\mathcal{S}$), depending on whether w is not accepted by $\mathcal{M}_0$ or is. We can now use $\mathcal{M}_\mathcal{S}$ to decide whether or not $L(\mathcal{M}_{\mathcal{M}_0,w}) \in \mathcal{S}$. Since $L(\mathcal{M}_{\mathcal{M}_0,w}) \in \mathcal{S}$ if and only if $\langle\mathcal{M}_0\rangle_\rho\langle w\rangle_\rho \in L_u$, we have an algorithm to decide the universal language L_u. Hence the property $\mathcal{S}$ is undecidable. $\square$

Corollary 6.4.3 *It is undecidable whether a given recursively enumerable language is (a) empty, (b) finite, (c) regular, (d) context-free, (e) context-sensitive, (f) in* **P**, *(g) in* **NP**, ...

It is important to realize that for Rice's theorem it is crucial that all recursively enumerable languages are considered. Otherwise, decidability can result. For example, it is decidable (see Theorem 3.2.4), given a DFA $\mathcal{A}$, whether the language accepted by $\mathcal{A}$ is finite.

In the rest of this section we deal with several specific undecidable problems. Each of them plays an important role in showing the undecidability of other problems, using the reduction method discussed next.

6.4.2 Halting Problem

There are two basic ways to show the undecidability of a decision problem.

1. **Reduction to a paradox.** For example, along the lines of the Russell paradox (see Section 2.1.1) or its modification known as the **barber's paradox**: *In a small town there is a barber who shaves those and only those who do not shave themselves. Does he shave himself?* This approach is also behind the diagonalization arguments used in the proof of Theorem 6.1.6.

Example 6.4.4 (Printing problem) *The problem is to decide, given an off-line Turing machine $\mathcal{M}$ and an integer i, whether $\mathcal{M}$ outputs i when starting with the empty input tape. Consider an enumeration $\mathcal{M}_1, \mathcal{M}_2, \ldots$ of all off-line Turing machines generating sets of natural numbers, and consider the set $S = \{i \mid i$ is not in the set generated by $\mathcal{M}_i\}$. This set cannot be recursively enumerable, because otherwise there would exist a Turing machine $\mathcal{M}_S$ generating S, and therefore $\mathcal{M}_S = \mathcal{M}_{i_0}$ for some i_0. Now comes the question: is $i_0 \in S$? and we get a variant of the barber paradox.*

2. **Reduction from another problem the undecidability of which has already been shown.** In other words, to prove that a decision problem $\mathcal{P}_1$ is undecidable, it is sufficient to show that the decidability of $\mathcal{P}_1$ would imply the decidability of another decision problem, say $\mathcal{P}_2$, the undecidability of which has already been shown. All that is required is that there is an algorithmic way of transforming (with no restriction on the resources such a transformation needs), a $\mathcal{P}_2$ input into a $\mathcal{P}_1$ input in such a way that $\mathcal{P}_2$'s yes/no answer is exactly the same as $\mathcal{P}_1$'s answer to the transformed input.

Example 6.4.5 *We can use the undecidability of the printing problem to show the undecidability of the halting problem as follows. For each off-line Turing machine $\mathcal{M}$ we can easily construct a Turing machine $\mathcal{M}'$ such that $\mathcal{M}'$ halts for an input w if and only if $\mathcal{M}$ prints w. The decidability of the halting problem would therefore imply the decidability of the printing problem.*

Exercise 6.4.6 *Show that the following decision problems are undecidable. (a) Does a given Turing machine halt on the empty tape? (b) Does a given Turing machine halt for all inputs?*

The main reason for the importance of the undecidability of the halting problem is the fact that the undecidability of many decision problems can be shown by a reduction from the halting problem.

It is also worth noting that the decidability of the halting problem could have an enormous impact on mathematics and computing. To see this, let us consider again what was perhaps the most famous problem in mathematics in the last two centuries, Fermat's last theorem, which claims that there are no integers x, y, z and w such that

$$(x+1)^{w+3} + (y+1)^{w+3} = (z+1)^{w+3}. \tag{6.1}$$

Given x, y, z, w, it is easy to verify whether (6.1) holds. It is therefore simple to design a Turing machine that checks for all possible quadruples (x, y, z, w) whether (6.1) holds, and halts if such a quadruple is found. Were we to have proof that this Turing machine never halts, we would have proved Fermat's last theorem. In a similar way we can show that many important open mathematical questions can be reduced to the halting problem for some specific Turing machine.

As we saw in Chapter 5, various bounded versions of the halting problem are complete problems for important complexity classes.

Exercise 6.4.7 *Show that the decidability of the halting problem could be used to solve the famous Goldbach conjecture (1742) that each even number greater than 2 is the sum of two primes.*

Remark 6.4.8 Since the beginning of this century, a belief in the total power of formalization has been the main driving force in mathematics. One of the key problems formulated by the leading mathematician of that time, David Hilbert, was the *Entscheidungsproblem*. Is there a general mechanical procedure which could, in principle, solve all the problems of mathematics, one after another? It was the *Entscheidungsproblem* which led Turing to develop his concept of both machine and decidability, and it was through its reduction to the halting problem that he showed the undecidability of the *Entscheidungsproblem* in his seminal paper 'On computable numbers, with applications to the *Entscheidungsproblem*'. Written in 1937, this was considered by some to be the most important single paper in the modern history of computing.

Example 6.4.9 (Program verification) *The fact that program equivalence and program verification are undecidable even for very simple programming languages has very negative consequences practically. These results in effect rule out automatic program verification and reduce the hope of obtaining fully optimizing compilers capable of transforming a given program into an optimal one.*

It is readily seen that the halting problem for Turing machines can be reduced to the program verification problem. Let us sketch the idea. Given a Turing machine $\mathcal{M}$ and its input w, we can transform the pair $\langle \mathcal{M}, w \rangle$, which is the input for the halting problem, to a pair $\langle \mathcal{P}, \mathcal{M} \rangle$, as an input to the program verification problem. The algorithm (TM) $\mathcal{M}$ remains the same, and $\mathcal{P}$ is the algorithmic problem described by specifying that w is the only legal input for which $\mathcal{M}$ should terminate and that the output for this input is not of importance. $\mathcal{M}$ is now correct with respect to this simple algorithmic problem $\mathcal{P}$ if and only if $\mathcal{M}$ terminates for input w. Consequently, the verification problem is undecidable.

6.4.3 Tiling Problems

Tiling of a plane or space by tiles from various finite sets of (proto)tiles, especially of polygonal or polyhedral shapes, that is, a covering of a plane or space completely, without gaps and overlaps and with matching colours on contiguous vertices, edges or faces (if they are coloured) is an old and much investigated mathematical problem with a variety of applications. For example, it was known already to the Pythagorian school (sixth century BC) that there is only one regular polyhedron that can tile the space completely. However, there are infinitely many sets with more than one tile that

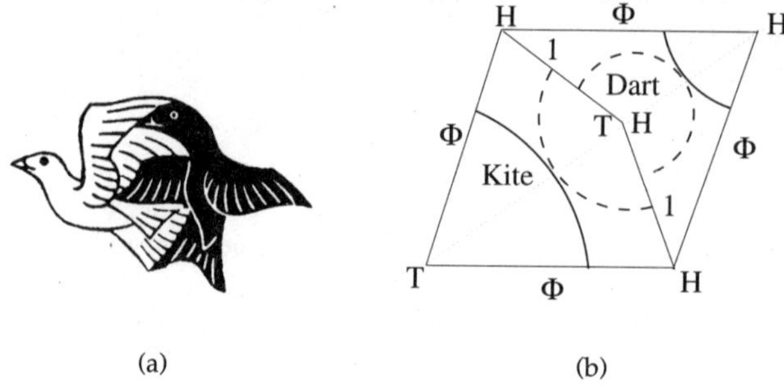

Figure 6.4 Escher's figure and Penrose's tiles

can tile a plane (space). The fact that tiling can simulate Turing machine computation and that some variants of the tiling problem are complete for the main complexity classes shows the importance of tiling for the theory of computing.

The tiling of a plane (space) is called periodic if one can outline its finite region in such a way that the whole tiling can be obtained by its translation, that is, by shifting the position of the region without rotating it. M. C. Escher became famous for his pictures obtained by periodic tilings with shapes that resemble living creatures; see Figure 6.4a for a shape (tile) consisting of a white and black bird that can be used to tile a plane periodically.

A tiling that is not periodic is called **aperiodic**. The problem of finding a (small) set of tiles that can be used to tile a plane only aperiodically (with rotation and reflection of tiles allowed) has turned out to be intriguing and to have surprising results and consequences.

Our main interest now is the following decision problem: given a set of polygon (proto)tiles with coloured edges, is there a tiling of the plane with the given set of tiles?

Of special interest for computing is the problem of tiling a plane with unit square tiles with coloured edges, called Wang tiles or dominoes, when neither rotation nor reflection of tiles is allowed. This problem is closely related to decision problems in logic. Berger (1966) showed that such a tiling problem is undecidable. His complicated proof implied that there is a set of Wang tiles which can tile the plane, but only aperiodically. Moreover, he actually exhibited a set of 20,406 tiles with such a property. This number has since been reduced, and currently the smallest set of Wang tiles with such a property, due to K. Culik, is shown in Figure 6.5.[2]

[2] Around 1975, Roger Penrose designed a set of two simple polygon tiles (see Figure 6.4b), called Kite and Darf, with coloured vertices (by colours H and T), that can tile a plane, but only aperiodically (rotation and reflection of tiles is allowed). These two tiles are derived from a rhombus with edges of length $\Phi = (1+\sqrt{5})/2$ and 1 and angles 72° and 108° by a cut shown in Figure 6.4b. (Observe that the common 'internal vertex' is coloured differently in both tiles and therefore the tiling shown in Figure 6.4b is not allowed. Note also that it is easy to change such a set of tiles with coloured vertices into polygonal tiles that are not coloured and tile the plane only aperiodically. Indeed, it is enough simply to put bumps and dents on the edges to make jigsaw pieces that fit only in the manner prescribed by the colours of the vertices.) Penrose patented his tiles in the UK, USA and Japan because of their potential for making commercial puzzles. Especially if two coloured arcs are added in the way indicated in Figure 6.4b, one can create tilings with fascinating patterns from Penrose's tiles.

Tilings of a plane with Penrose's tiles also have many surprising properties. For example, the number of different tilings of the plane is uncountable, yet, at the same time, any two tilings are alike in a special way – that every finite subtiling of any tiling of the plane is contained infinitely many times within every other tiling.

In addition, R. Ammann discovered in 1976 a set of two rhombohedra which, with suitable face-matching rules,

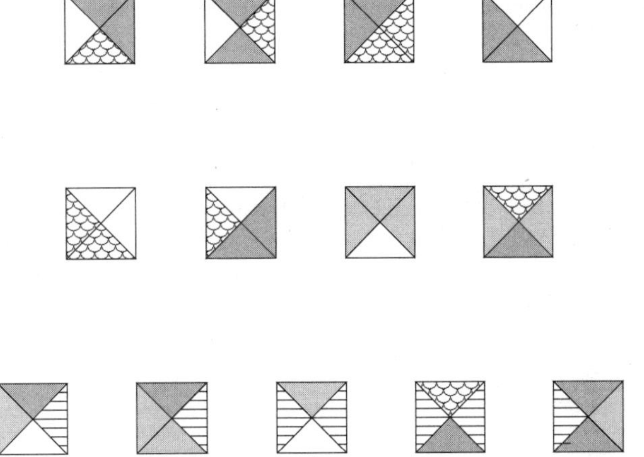

Figure 6.5 Culik's tiles

The following theorem shows the undecidability of a special variant of the tiling problem with Wang tiles.

Theorem 6.4.10 *It is undecidable, given a finite set T of Wang tiles with coloured edges which includes a tile with all edges of the same colour (say white), whether there is such a tiling of the plane that uses only finitely many, but at least one other than the completely white tile.*

Proof: We show that if such a tiling problem is decidable, then the halting problem is decidable for one-tape Turing machines that satisfy conditions 1–3 on page 309 in Section 5.4.1: that is, for Turing machines which have one-way infinite tape, a unique accepting configuration and no state in which the machine can move both left and right, and, moreover, start their computation with the empty tape.

To each such Turing machine $\mathcal{M} = \langle \Gamma, Q, q_0, \delta \rangle$ we construct a set of square tiles as follows. We take all the tiles in the proof of Theorem 5.4.1 in Section 5.4.1 and, in addition, the following sets of tiles:

1. Tiles of the forms

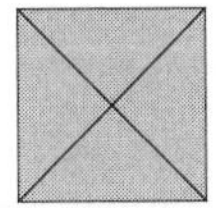

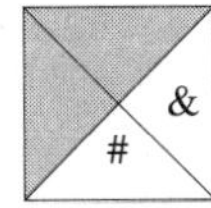

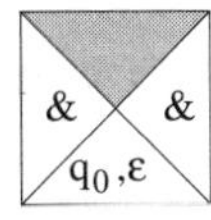

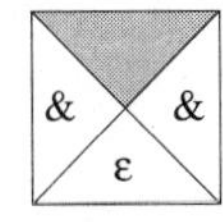

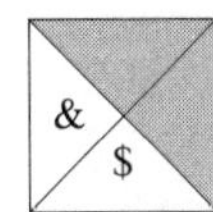

that will form the topmost row containing a non-white tile. (Observe that the second of these tiles is the only one that can be the 'top' left-most not completely white tile for a tiling with not all tiles white.) This set of tiles will be used to encode the initial configuration of $\mathcal{M}$, long enough to create space for all configurations in the computation, starting with the empty tape. Symbol & represents here a special colour not used in tiles of other sets.

can tile the space only aperiodically. This led to Penrose hypothesizing the existence of aperiodic structures in nature. This was later confirmed, first by D. Schechlman in 1984 and later by many discoveries of physicists, chemists and crystallographers.

2. A set of tiles, two for each $z \in \Gamma$, of the form

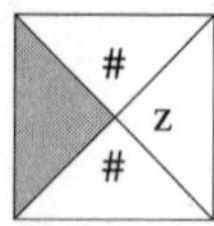

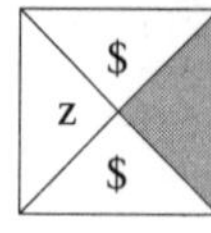

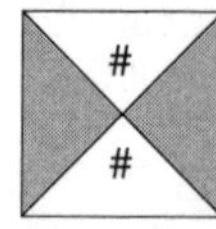

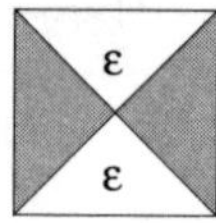

that keep the left and the right border of a computation fixed.

3. Tiles of the form

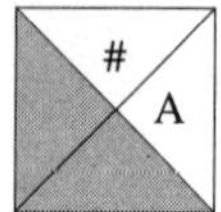

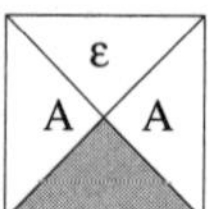

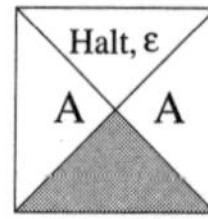

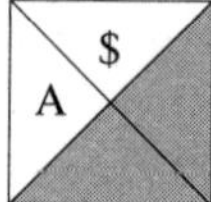

that will be used to create the last row with not all tiles white. In semantic terms, they will be used to encode the last row after a halting configuration of the Turing machine is reached. The symbol A denotes here a new colour not used in tiles of other sets.

It is now straightforward to see that there is a tiling of the plane with the set of tiles designed as above that uses only finitely many non-white tiles and at least one such tile if and only if the corresponding Turing machine halts on the empty tape – which is undecidable. □

Exercise 6.4.11 *Consider the following modification of the tiling problem with Wang tiles: the set of tiles has a 'starting tile', and the only tilings considered are ones that use this starting tile at least once. Is it true that the plane can be tiled by such a set of Wang tiles if and only if for each $n \in \mathbf{N}$, the $(2n+1) \times (2n+1)$ square board can be tiled with such a set of Wang tiles with the starting tile in the centre?*

There are many variants of the tiling problem that are undecidable, and they are of interest in themselves. In addition, the undecidability of many decision problems can be shown easily and transparently by a reduction to one of the undecidable tiling problems.

Exercise 6.4.12 *Consider the following modifications of the tiling problem (as formulated in Exercise 6.4.11).*

P1 *Tiles can be rotated through 180 degrees.*

P2 *Flipping around a vertical axis is allowed.*

P3 *Flipping around the main diagonal axis is allowed.*

Show that (a) problem P1 always has a solution; (b) problem P2 is decidable; (c)** problem P3 is undecidable.*

6.4.4 Thue Problem

The most basic decision problem in the area of rewriting, with many variations, is the word problem for Thue systems, considered in Section 7.1. This problem is often presented in the following form.

With any alphabet Σ and two lists of words over Σ

$$(E) \qquad A = (x_1, \ldots, x_n), \qquad B = (y_1, \ldots, y_n),$$

the following relation $\equiv_E$ on Σ^* is associated:

$x \equiv_E y$ if there are $u, v \in \Sigma^*$ and $1 \le i \le n$ such that either $x = ux_iv$ and $y = uy_iv$ or $x = uy_iv$ and $y = ux_iv$.

In other words, y can be obtained from x by rewriting a subword x_i of A as the corresponding y_i from B, or vice versa. In this way one can see the lists in (E) as a set of equations

$$x_i = y_i, \qquad 1 \le i \le n, \tag{6.2}$$

in the free monoid over Σ. Let $\equiv_E^*$ be the transitive and reflexive closure of the relation $\equiv_E$. The **Thue problem for semigroups,**[3] for the lists (E) is the problem of deciding, given two words $x, y \in \Sigma^*$, whether $x \equiv_E^* y$; that is, whether y can be obtained from x using equations from (6.2). In the case that the equations reflect the property that the underlying set of words is an Abelian semigroup (there is an equation $ab = ba$ for each two symbols of the underlying alphabet) or a group (there is an 'inverse' letter a^{-1} to each letter a and equations $aa^{-1} = \varepsilon$ and $a^{-1}a = \varepsilon$) or an Abelian group, we speak of a Thue problem for Abelian semigroups or groups or Abelian groups. The following theorem then holds.

Theorem 6.4.13 *The Thue problem is undecidable for semigroups and groups, and decidable for Abelian semigroups and groups.*

Example 6.4.14 *For the equations*

$$(E_1) \qquad \begin{array}{lll} EAT = AT, & LATER = LOW, & CARP = ME, \\ ATE = A, & PAN = PILLOW, & \end{array}$$

we have, as it is easy to verify,

$$LAP \equiv_{E_1}^* LEAP, \qquad MAN \equiv_{E_1}^* CATERPILLAR;$$

but

$$ARORA \equiv_{E_1}^* APPLE \tag{6.3}$$

does not hold.

There is an algorithm for deciding the word problem for (E_1). But the word problem for the equations

$$(E_2) \qquad \begin{array}{llll} \mathrm{AH = HA,} & \mathrm{AT = TA,} & \mathrm{TAI = IT,} & \mathrm{THAT = ITHT,} \\ \mathrm{OH = HO,} & \mathrm{OT = TO,} & \mathrm{HOI = IH.} & \end{array}$$

is undecidable. (This is an example of a seemingly very simple-looking specific decision problem that is undecidable.)

[3] 'Word problem' is another name used for the Thue problem.

6.4.5 Post Correspondence Problem

Reduction from the Post[4] correspondence problem (PCP) is an important method for showing the undecidability of many decision problems, especially those concerning rewritings. This will be illustrated in the next chapter. This is because PCP captures the essence of rewriting.

An **instance** of the PCP is given by the two lists

$$(u_1, \dots, u_n), \qquad (v_1, \dots, v_n) \tag{6.4}$$

of words over an alphabet Σ, the problem being to decide whether there is a sequence of integers $i_1, \dots, i_m$, where $1 \le i_k \le n$ and $1 \le k \le m$, such that

$$u_{i_1} \dots u_{i_m} = v_{i_1} \dots v_{i_m}.$$

If such a sequence $(i_1, \dots, i_m)$ exists, then it is called a **solution** of (6.4). Clearly, if an instance of the PCP has a solution, then it has infinitely many solutions.

Example 6.4.15 *For the instance of the PCP defined by the lists*

$$(a^2, b^2, ab^2) \text{ and } (a^2b, ba, b),$$

the PCP has a solution $(1,2,1,3)$. *For the instance defined by the lists*

$$(a, b^2) \text{ and } (a^2, b),$$

the PCP has no solution. (Show why.)

Exercise 6.4.16 *Determine for the following instances of the PCP whether they have a solution, and if they do, show one: (a)* (a^2b, a^2) *and* (a, ba^2)*; (b)* (a^2b, a) *and* (a, ba^2)*; (c)* (a, ba, b, ab) *and* (aaa, b, bb, ba)*; (d)* $(ab, a, c, abca)$ *and* $(ca, abac, bb, ab)$.

Exercise 6.4.17 *Show that the PCP with the list of words over a one-letter alphabet is decidable.*

The Post correspondence problem is that of deciding, given an instance of PCP, whether this instance has a solution. The following theorem can be shown by a not easy reduction from the halting problem.

Theorem 6.4.18 *The Post correspondence problem is undecidable.*

Example 6.4.19 *In order to illustrate how the PCP can be used to show the undecidability of problems concerning rewriting systems, similar to those given on page 84, let us take two rewriting systems with each instance* $u = (u_1, \dots, u_n)$ *and* $v = (v_1, \dots, v_n)$ *of the PCP over the alphabet* $\{0,1\}$: $S \to c$ *is a production in both cases and additional productions are*

$$G_1 : S \to 0^i 1 S u_i,\ 1 \le i \le n; \qquad G_2 : S \to 0^i 1 S v_i,\ 1 \le i \le n.$$

[4]Emil Post (1887–1954), an American mathematician and logician.

For the languages $L(G_1)$ and $L(G_2)$ of words over the alphabet $\{0,1\}$ generated by these two systems we have

$$\begin{aligned} L(G_1) &= \{0^{i_1}1\ldots 0^{i_k}1cu_{i_k}\ldots u_{i_1}\,|\,1\le i_j\le n, 1\le j\le k\},\\ L(G_2) &= \{0^{i_1}1\ldots 0^{i_k}1cv_{i_k}\ldots v_{i_1}\,|\,1\le i_j\le n, 1\le j\le k\},\end{aligned}$$

and therefore $L(G_1)\cap L(G_2)\neq\emptyset$ if and only if the PCP for the instance u and v has a solution.

Exercise 6.4.20 *There is another way, more compact, using morphisms, to view the Post Correspondence Problem. Let g and h be two morphisms mapping Δ^* into Σ^*. Show that the pair (g,h) can be considered as an instance of PCP that has a solution if there is a nonempty word $w\in\Delta^*$ such that $g(w)=h(w)$.*

Remark 6.4.21 The following bounded version of PCP is **NP**-complete: given an instance $(u_1,\ldots,u_n)$, $(v_1,\ldots,v_n)$ of PCP and an integer b, is there a sequence of integers $i_1,\ldots,i_m$, such that $m\le b, 1\le i_k\le n$, $1\le k\le m$ and $u_{i_1}\ldots u_{i_m}=v_{i_1}\ldots v_{i_m}$?

6.4.6 Hilbert's Tenth Problem

The decision problem known as Hilbert's tenth problem was formulated in 1900 by David Hilbert.[5] It is perhaps the most famous decision problem and can be formulated as follows: given an arbitrary polynomial $\mathcal{P}(x_1,\ldots,x_n)$ with coefficients from **Z**, decide whether the following so-called Diophantine equation

$$\mathcal{P}(x_1,\ldots,x_n)=0$$

has a solution in whole numbers.

Diophantine equations (named after Diophantus of Alexandria) represent one of the oldest areas of science, in which deeper results have been obtained already in the third century in Greece. The following examples illustrate how difficult it can be to find solutions to seemingly simple Diophantine equations.

Example 6.4.22 *(1) In the smallest nonnegative solution (x,y) of the so-called Pell equation*

$$x^2-991y^2-1=0$$

x has 30 and y 29 decimal digits.

(2) The smallest nonnegative solution, for x, of the Pell equation

$$x^2-4729494y^2-1=0,$$

[5]David Hilbert (1862–1943) was a German mathematician and logician. Of fundamental importance are his contributions to algebra, number theory, geometry and calculus (with relations to physics and functional analysis). Hilbert was perhaps the most influential mathematician of his period. A representative of formalism in logic, his school of thought produced such founders of modern computing theory as Gödel, von Neumann and Turing. For his opening talk at the World Congress of Mathematicians in 1900 in Paris, Hilbert prepared a list of 23 problems he considered to be of key importance for mathematics. His tenth problem was solved in 1970 by the Russian mathematician Y.W. Matiyasevich. (Actually it seems that Hilbert assumed that this problem was decidable and that it was only a question of time before an algorithm to decide it would be found. Anyway, the concept of undecidability was unknown at his time.) English translation of the original formulation of Hilbert's tenth problem: 'Given a Diophantine equation with any number of unknown quantities and with rational integral numerical coefficients, devise a process according to which it can be determined by a finite number of operations whether the equation is solvable in rational integers.'

which can be obtained by a reduction from the system of equations, seven linear with eight variables and two quadratic conditions, formulated by Archimedes in a letter to Eratosthenes of Cyrene in the third century, has over 206,500 digits.

(3) Factorization of an integer n is as difficult as solution of the equation $(x+2)(y+2)=n$.

There are two additional reasons for the special importance of Hilbert's tenth problem. Since this problem concerns integer arithmetic, it is a good starting point for showing that everyday considerations in mathematics can lead to undecidable problems. Second, the very difficult proof of its undecidability is actually based on a new and important characterization of recursively enumerable sets and relations, presented in the following theorem.

Theorem 6.4.23 (Matiyasevich's theorem) *A set* $S \subset \mathbf{N}^n$ *is recursively enumerable if and only if there is a polynomial* $P(a_1,\ldots,a_n,y_1,\ldots,y_m)$ *with coefficients in* $\mathbf{Z}$ *such that*

$$S=\{(x_1,\ldots,x_n)\,|\,(\exists y_1\in\mathbf{N}),\ldots,(\exists y_m\in\mathbf{N})P(x_1,\ldots,x_n,y_1,\ldots,y_m)=0\}.^6$$

Matiyasevich's theorem implies that decidability of Hilbert's tenth problem would imply decidability of the membership problem for recursively enumerable sets, but that is an undecidable problem.

As Theorem 6.4.23 says, polynomials with coefficients in **Z** have surprising power to represent all recursively enumerable sets. Some examples follow.

Example 6.4.24 *The set C of composite numbers has the following polynomial representation:*

$$x\in C\Leftrightarrow \exists y\exists z(x=(y+2)(z+2)).$$

The second example deals with primes.

Example 6.4.25 *The set of primes P has the following polynomial representation:*

$$\begin{array}{lll} x'\in P & \Leftrightarrow & \exists(a,b,c,d,e,f,g,h,i,j,k,l,m,n,o,p,q,r,s,t,u,v,w,x,y,z)\\ & & x'=(k+2)\{1-[wz+h+j-q]^2-[(gk+2g+k+1)(h+j)+h-z]^2\\ & & -[2n+p+q+z-e]^2-[16(k+1)^3(k+2)(n+1)^2+1-f^2]^2\\ & & -[e^3(e+2)(a+1)^2+1-o^2]^2-[(a^2-1)y^2+1-x^2]^2\\ & & -[16r^2y^4(a^2-1)+1-u^2]^2\\ & & -[((a+u^2(u^2-a))^2-1)(n+4dy)^2+1-(x+cu)^2]^2-[n+1+v-y]^2\\ & & -[(a^2-1)l^2+1-m^2]^2-[ai+k+1-l-i]^2\\ & & -[p+l(a-n-1)+b(2an+2a-n^2-2n-2)-m]^2\\ & & -[q+y(a-p-1)+s(2ap+2a-p^2-2p-2)-x]^2\\ & & -[z+pl(a-p)+t(2ap-p^2-1)-pm]^2\}.^7 \end{array}$$

[6]It has also been shown that in Theorem 6.4.23 it is sufficient to consider a polynomial of degree at most 4 or at most 9 variables.

[7]There is another representation of the set of all primes using due to Matiyasevich, a polynomial with only 10 variables.

Exercise 6.4.26 *Design polynomial representations for the set of integers that are not powers of 2.*

Exercise 6.4.27 *Design polynomial representations of the predicates (a) $a \leq b$; (b) $a \equiv b (\bmod n)$; (c) $a \equiv b (\bmod c)$.*

Exercise 6.4.28 *Show that the set of polynomials P with integer coefficients for which the equation $P = 0$ has a solution in natural numbers is undecidable. (Hint: you can make use of the fact that each integer is a sum of four squares of integers.)*

As another consequence of Theorem 6.4.23 we get the following result showing the existence of a universal polynomial.

Theorem 6.4.29 *There is a polynomial P_u with coefficients in **Z** such that for any recursively enumerable set S there is an integer i_S such that*

$$x \in S \Leftrightarrow (\exists y_1 \in \mathbf{N}), \ldots, (\exists y_n \in \mathbf{N})(P_u(i_S, x, y_1, \ldots, y_n) = 0).$$

Proof: Let $S_i, i = 1, 2, \ldots$ be an enumeration of all recursively enumerable sets of integers. The binary relation $\{(x,i) \mid x \in S_i\}$ is clearly recursively enumerable. This implies the existence of the universal polynomial.[8] □

For example, the last theorem implies that there is an integer i_p such that x is prime if and only if $(\exists y_1 \in \mathbf{N}), \ldots, (\exists y_n \in \mathbf{N}) P_u(i_p, x, y_1, \ldots, y_n) = 0$.

Exercise 6.4.30 *(a) Show that each Diophantine equation can be transformed into an equivalent system of Diophantine equations of the type $x = y + 2$ or $x = yz$, where x, y, z are either natural numbers or unknowns. (b) Illustrate the method on the Diophantine equation $5x^2y^2 - 6x^3z + 6xy^3 - 5xz = 0$.*

Exercise 6.4.31 *Show that in order to solve Hilbert's tenth problem positively it would be sufficient to find a method for deciding whether Diophantine equations of degree 4 have a solution.*

6.4.7 Borderlines between Decidability and Undecidability

In a few cases, quite sharp borderlines between decidability and undecidability are known. In most other cases, it is an open problem to determine such sharp borderlines. The following table summarizes the current state of the knowledge.

[8] Once the existence of a universal polynomial had been shown, the problem arose of finding such a universal polynomial with the smallest number of variables and the smallest degree. Jones (1982) gives the following pairs (# of variables, degree) for a universal polynomial: $(58,4)$, $(38,8)$, $(29,16)$, $(24,36)$, $(19,2668)$, $(13, 6.6 \cdot 10^{43})$, $(9, 1.6 \cdot 10^{45})$.

Problem	Decidable cases	Undecidable cases
halting prob. – one-dim. TM	state-symbol prod. ≤ 6	state-symbol prod. ≥ 24
halting prob. – two-dim. TM	1 instruction	8 instructions
Equiv. prob. – register mach.	7 instructions	8 instructions
Halt. prob. – register mach.	8 instructions	29 instructions
tiling of plane	1 polyomino[9]	nonperiodic for 35 tiles
Word problem for groups[10]	1 equation	3 equations
PCP	two-letter alphabet lists of length ≤ 2	two-letter alphabet list of length ≥ 7
Diophantine equations	equations of degree ≤ 2	equations of degree ≥ 4

Remark 6.4.32 Simplicity of presentation is the main reason why only decision problems are considered in this section. Each of the undecidable problems discussed here has a computational version that requires output and is not computable. For example, this property has the problem of computing, for a Turing machine $\mathcal{M}$ and an input w, the function $f(\mathcal{M},w)$, defined to be zero if $\mathcal{M}$ does not halt for w, and to be the number of steps of $\mathcal{M}$ on w, otherwise.

6.4.8 Degrees of Undecidability

It is natural to ask whether all undecidable problems are equally undecidable. The answer is no, and we approach this problem from two points of view.

First we again take a formal view of decision problems as membership problems for sets. To classify undecidable problems, several types of reductions have been used. For example, we say that a set A is (many-to-one) reducible to a set B (notation $A \leq_m B$), if there exists a recursive function f such that

$$x \in A \Leftrightarrow f(x) \in B;$$

and we say that the sets A and B belong to the same **degree of unsolvability** (with respect to the many-to-one reduction) if $A \leq_m B$ and $B \leq_m A$. It can be shown that there are infinitely many degrees of unsolvability. Some of them are comparable (that is, each problem in one class can be reduced to a problem in another class), some incomparable.

Exercise 6.4.33 *Show that if $A \leq_m B$ and B is recursive, then A is recursive too.*

Exercise 6.4.34 *Let us fix a Gödel numbering $\langle \mathcal{M} \rangle_p$ of TM $\mathcal{M}$ in the alphabet $\{0,1\}$ and the corresponding encoding $\langle w \rangle_p$ of input words of $\mathcal{M}$. Let us consider the languages*

$$\begin{aligned} K_u &= \{\langle \mathcal{M} \rangle_p \langle w \rangle_p \mid \mathcal{M} \text{ accepts } w\}, && (6.5)\\ K_d &= \{\langle \mathcal{M} \rangle_p \mid \mathcal{M} \text{ accepts } \langle \mathcal{M} \rangle_p\}, && (6.6)\\ K_p &= \{\langle \mathcal{M} \rangle_p \mid \mathcal{M} \text{ halts on at least one input}\}, && (6.7)\\ K_e &= \{\langle \mathcal{M} \rangle_p \mid \mathcal{M} \text{ halts on the empty tape}\}. && (6.8) \end{aligned}$$

Show that (a) $K_d \leq_m K_u$; (b) $K_u \leq_m K_e$; (c) $K_e \leq_m K_p$; (d) $K_p \leq_m K_d$; (e) a set L is recursively enumerable if and only if $L \leq_m K'$, where K' is any of the sets K_u, K_d, K_p and K_e.

[9] A polyomino is a polygon formed by a union of unit squares.

[10] A word problem over an alphabet Σ is said to be a word problem for groups when for any $a \in \Sigma$ there is also an equation $ab = \varepsilon$ available.

There are two natural ways of forming infinite hierarchies of more and more undecidable problems. The **jump method** is based on the concept of **Turing reducibility**: a set A is Turing-reducible to B, notation $A \leq_T B$, if there is an oracle TM with oracle B accepting A.

Definition 6.4.35 *The language*

$$K^B = \{\langle \mathcal{M} \rangle_p \,|\, \mathcal{M} \text{ is an oracle TM with oracle } B \text{ that halts on } \langle \mathcal{M} \rangle_p\}$$

is called the halting language for TM with the oracle B.

Exercise 6.4.36 *Is it true that (a) $A \leq_T B$ if and only if $A \leq_m K^B$; (b) $K^B \leq_T B$ for any languages A, B?*

Using the jump operator we can define the following infinite sequence of more and more undecidable languages:

$$K, K^K, K^{K^K}, K^{K^{K^K}}, \ldots$$

where K is any of the languages K_u, K_d, K_p, K_e defined above.

In order to introduce the second very natural hierarchy of undecidable problems, two new operators on families of languages have to be introduced. If $\mathcal{L}$ is a family of languages, then

$$\Sigma\mathcal{L} = \{L \,|\, \exists R \in \mathcal{L}, x \in L \Leftrightarrow \exists y[(x,y) \in R]\},$$

$$\Pi\mathcal{L} = \{L \,|\, \exists R \in \mathcal{L}, x \in L \Leftrightarrow \forall y[(x,y) \in R]\},$$

where (x,y) is a recursive encoding of the tuple x and y.

Definition 6.4.37 (Arithmetical hierarchy) *The families Σ_i and Π_i, $i \in \mathbf{N}$, are defined as follows:*
(a) $\Sigma_0 = \Pi_0 =$ the class of recursive languages,
(b) $\Sigma_{i+1} = \Sigma\Pi_i$ and $\Pi_{i+1} = \Pi\Sigma_i$, for $i \in \mathbf{N}$.

Note that Σ_1 is the class of recursively enumerable languages. It can be shown that the families Σ_0, $\Sigma_1 - \Sigma_0$, $\Sigma_2 - \Sigma_1$, ... and Π_0, $\Pi_1 - \Pi_0$, $\Pi_2 - \Pi_1$, ... are nonempty, and contain more and more undecidable languages.

The importance of the arithmetical hierarchy is also due to the fact that classes Σ_i and Π_i contain languages that can be defined in a very natural way, as the following exercise demonstrates.

Exercise 6.4.38 *Show, for example by induction, that*
(a) $L \in \Sigma_i$, if and only if there exists a recursive language R such that

$$x \in L \Leftrightarrow \exists y_1 \forall y_2 \exists y_3 \ldots Qy_i[(x, y_1, y_2, \ldots, y_i) \in R],$$

where $Q = \exists\,(\forall)$, if is odd (even).
(b) $L \in \Pi_i$, if and only if there exists a recursive language R such that

$$x \in L \Leftrightarrow \forall y_1 \exists y_2 \forall y_3 \ldots Qy_i[(x, y_1, y_2, \ldots, y_i) \in R],$$

where $Q = \exists\,(\forall)$, if is even (odd).

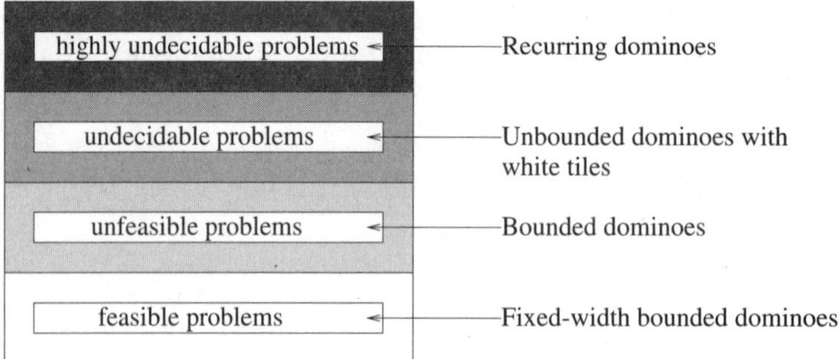

Figure 6.6 Structure of the space of algorithmic problems

It can be shown that such decision problems as the halting problem, the Post correspondence problem and the tiling problem considered in this section are of the same degree of undecidability. However, the program verification problem is 'more' undecidable, and there are even 'much more' undecidable problems. A simple example of two closely related problems that have different degrees of undecidability are that of deciding whether a given Diophantine equation has at least one solution and whether it has infinitely many solutions.

Another way to look at decision problems is through certificates (see Section 5.7.1), and thereby we come to another analogy with the **NP**-complete problems discussed in Chapter 5.

It is clear that 'yes' answers to such problems as the halting problem, PCP and Hilbert's tenth problem have finite certificates that can be verified in finite time. In the case of the tiling problem from this section it is the 'no' answer that has a finite certificate, because if the plane cannot be tiled, then there is a finite portion of it that cannot be tiled and that can be verified in finite time.

Can it happen that both 'yes' and 'no' answers to an undecidable problem have finite certificates? No, as it is easy to verify. This would imply decidability of the problem. Are there undecidable problems for which neither 'yes' nor 'no' answers have certificates? Yes, for example, the problem of deciding whether a given Turing machine halts for all inputs.

The space of algorithmic problems therefore has the structure shown in Figure 6.6. Interestingly, in each class there is an example of the domino problem. (The **Fixed-width bounded domino problem** is that of deciding, given a finite set of coloured tiles and an integer n, whether a rectangle of size $n \times c$, where c is fixed, can be tiled with tiles from T. The **Recurring domino problem** is that of deciding whether one can tile the whole plane with a given finite set of tiles in such a way that a particular tile occurs infinitely often.)

6.5 Limitations of Formal Systems

The proof of the existence of undecidable problems was historically the second of two main results that demonstrated striking limitations of formal systems and algorithmic methods. The first, which says that in each rich enough formal system there are true statements that are unprovable within the given formal system, was due to Gödel[11] in 1931. In this section we start with Gödel's result and a presentation of the simple idea underlying his ingenious proof. We then show how a more specific version of Gödel's theorem can be proved easily, using arguments with an information-theoretic flavour. The result implies that in no formal system can we prove *a theorem that contains more information than a given set of axioms*. In order to show this, two new complexity concepts are introduced: Chaitin

[11] Kurt Gödel (1886–1978), an Austrian mathematician and logician of Moravian origin.

and Kolmogorov descriptional complexity. They lead also to a new way of viewing randomness. Finally, we analyse an intriguing 'number of wisdom' that encodes very compactly the cornerstones of undecidability and can be used to show how deeply rooted randomness is, even in arithmetic.

6.5.1 Gödel's Incompleteness Theorem

The following result shows unexpected limitations of formal systems. At the time of its discovery this was a shock for scientists and caused uncertainty and depression among those who believed in the enormous power of formalization. It shook the foundations of mathematics, and thereby all science depending on mathematics.

Theorem 6.5.1 (Gödel's incompleteness theorem) *Each formal mathematical system that contains arithmetic and theorems of which form a recursively enumerable set is either inconsistent (that is, one can prove in this system a theorem and also its negation) or contains theorems which are true but cannot be proved within the system.*

Gödel's proof of Theorem 6.5.1 is tricky and difficult. Nowadays Gödel's result is considered to be almost obvious – as one that easily follows from the undecidability of the halting problem and from the existence of sets that are recursively enumerable but not recursive.

Gödel's proof is based on a variant of the Liar paradox: 'This statement is false'.[12] Gödel obtained from this the paradox he needed, namely: 'This statement is unprovable.' Indeed, if such a statement is unprovable, then it is true, and we have a true unprovable statement. If such a statement is provable, then it is false, and we have inconsistency.

The basic idea of Gödel's proof is simple, and we make a sketch of it. Let us consider a fixed formal system in which theorems (statements) are formulas of the predicate calculus, over the domain of integers, extended by basic arithmetic operations $\{+,-,\times\}$ and with variables being words of the type $x\#^i, i \geq 0$, where $x \in \{a,b,c,\ldots,z\}$, $\#$ is a special symbol, and where axioms are basic identities of the predicate calculus (for example,

$$(P \cap Q) \Rightarrow P, \quad \neg(\neg P) \Leftrightarrow P, \quad \neg\exists x(R(x)) \Leftrightarrow \forall x(\neg R(x)),$$

where capital letters denote statements), and of arithmetics (commutativity, associativity, distributivity, ...). Derivation rules are basic derivation rules of the predicate calculus such as *modus ponens* (from P and $P \Rightarrow Q$ we can deduce Q) and so on.

Such a formal system has infinitely many formulas of one variable, and they can be enumerated in many ways. Let us fix such an enumeration, and let us denote by $F_i(x)$ the ith formula. In this way $F_i(x)$ is a perfectly defined arithmetical statement with two variables.

Strings of propositions that constitute proofs in such a formal system can also be enumerated, and let P_i denote the ith proof. Consider now the following statement, perfectly well defined, which depends on the variable x:

$$\neg\exists y[P_y \text{ proves } F_x(x)], \tag{6.9}$$

which says that there is no proof of $F_x(x)$ in the formal system under consideration.

The most ingenious part of Gödel's proof shows that the predicate (6.9) can also be expressed in the formal system under consideration; that there is an integer k such that

$$F_k(x) \Leftrightarrow \neg\exists y[P_y \text{ proves } F_x(x)].$$

Details of his proof depend heavily on details of formalization, coding and enumeration of statements and proofs. However, once all this has been done, we are ready with the proof. Indeed,

[12]This is a modification of the paradox of Epimenides, the Cretan, who said: 'Cretans always lie.'

- if $F_k(k)$ is true, then $F_k(k)$ is not provable, and we have incompleteness;
- if $F_k(k)$ is false, then $F_k(k)$ is provable, and we have inconsistency.

This means that we have an example of a specific statement that is true but not provable within the formal system under consideration. Gödel's result concerns a particular formal system. A more modern approach is to show the limitations of all formal systems.

6.5.2 Kolmogorov Complexity: Unsolvability and Randomness

Data compression is an important practical problem. In the 1960s Kolmogorov and Chaitin initiated a theoretical study of compressibility in order to lay foundations for such key concepts of probability theory as the randomness of strings.[13] Their simple ideas turned out to be surprisingly powerful, and currently represent an important methodology for showing limitations and lower bounds and for establishing foundations of concepts in many areas, some outside computing (modelling, learning, statistics, physics).

How much can a given string be compressed? How much information does a given string contain? How random is a given string? All these questions are basic and closely related. They can be approached rigorously using the concepts of Kolmogorov and Chaitin complexity.

Example 6.5.2 *The string*

$$001001001001001001001001001001001001001001001001001001001001001$$

is intuitively much less random than the string

$$01101110011011001110010111100101001001000011101010001001\,10,$$

since the first string can be written as '21 times string 001*', but the second one apparently does not have a simpler description.*

The basic idea of **information complexity** of Kolmogorov and Chaitin is simple. The amount of information in a string w is the length of the shortest string p (called a program) from which w can be reconstructed (by a chosen computer C).

The above idea of information-theoretic complexity sounds natural on the one hand, but too dependent on the choice of C, on the other. Fortunately, this problem can be overcome quite satisfactorily, as we shall soon see, taking a universal computer for C.

Let us fix an alphabet Σ and consider a two-tape universal Turing machine U with the tape alphabet $\Sigma_0 = \Sigma - \{\sqcup\}$ that can simulate any one-tape TM with the tape alphabet Σ_0. The **Kolmogorov complexity** of an $x \in \Sigma_0^*$ with respect to U, notation $K_U(x)$, is the length of the shortest program p such that if U starts with ε on the first tape and p on the second tape, then it halts with x on the first tape. In other words,

$$K_U(x) = \min\{|p| \mid p \in \Sigma_0^*, U(p) = x\}$$

and $K_U(x) = \infty$ if no such p exists.

A small technical condition allows us to make the concept of Kolmogorov complexity only inessentially dependent (by an additive constant factor) on the particular choice of the universal computer. We assume that each TM can be simulated by a program that does not contain the 4-symbol

[13] Incidentally, a development of the mathematical foundations of probability was another of the famous Hilbert problems stated in 1900 at the International Congress of Mathematicians.

string DATA, and that if U gets on its second tape an input word $p\mathtt{DATA}x$, then U simulates TM p on input x. It is straightforward to show that each universal TM can be modified to meet these conditions; therefore let us assume that this is the case with the universal TM we consider.

Lemma 6.5.3 *$K_U(x) \leq |x| + c_U$, where the constant c_U depends on U only.*

Proof: Since U is universal, a one-tape TM that does nothing, but immediately halts, can be simulated by a program p_0 (not containing DATA). Hence, for the input $p_0\mathtt{DATA}x$, U writes x on the first tape and halts. Thus $c_U = |p_0| + 4$. □

The following fundamental result shows to what extent Kolmogorov complexity is independent of the choice of the universal computer. This result also justifies us in fixing an arbitrary universal computer U and writing $K(x)$ instead of $K_U(x)$.

Theorem 6.5.4 (Invariance theorem) *Let U and S be universal Turing machines over Σ_0. Then there is a constant $c_{U,S}$ such that $|K_U(x) - K_S(x)| \leq c_{U,S}$, for all $x \in \Sigma_0^*$.*

Proof: We can consider S to be simulated by a one-tape TM M in such a way that if a program p produces x on S, then M also produces x for the input p. Assume that M is simulated on U by a program p_M that does not contain DATA. Now let $x \in \Sigma^*$ be an arbitrary string and q_x be the shortest program producing x on S. Then the program $p_M\mathtt{DATA}q_x$ produces x on U, and its length is $|p_M| + |q_x| + 4 = c_{U,S}$. A similar inequality in the opposite direction can be shown analogously. □

Unfortunately, Kolmogorov complexity is not computable.

Exercise 6.5.5 *Show that $K(xx) \leq K(x) + \mathcal{O}(1)$, for $x \in \{0,1\}^*$.*

Exercise 6.5.6 *Show that for any partial recursive function $f : \Sigma^* \to \Sigma^*$ there is a constant c such that $K(f(x)) \leq K(x) + c$, for all $x \in \Sigma^*$.*

Exercise 6.5.7* *Can the Kolmogorov complexity of a string be smaller that of its substrings?*

Theorem 6.5.8 *The function $K(x)$ is not recursive.*

Proof: The reasoning is based on Berry's paradox: *Let n be the smallest positive integer that cannot be described with fewer than 99 symbols.* n is both well defined and cannot exist.

Assume that $K(x)$ is computable. Let c be an integer (to be specified later), and x_k be the kth word of Σ_0^* in the strict ordering, and y the first string such that $K(y) \geq c$. Consider the following algorithm:

begin $k \leftarrow 0$;
  while $K(x_k) < c$ **do** $k \leftarrow k+1$;
  write(x_k)
end

The above algorithm produces y such that $K(y) \geq c$. The length of the algorithm is $\lg c$ + a constant. If c is large enough, then this algorithm contains fewer than c symbols and produces x_0 – a contradiction. □

Exercise 6.5.9 *Use Theorem 6.5.8 to produce a new proof of undecidability of the halting problem. (Hint: show that given an x, we can consider in strict order all possible strings as programs, and test each of them to see whether it halts, and if yes, then simulate it, until we come to a program producing x.)*

Exercise 6.5.10* *Show that for no recursive function f is there a recursive function g such that* $K(x) \leq g(x) \leq f(K(x))$. *(That is, K cannot be approximated even in a very weak sense.)*

Exercise 6.5.11** *Show that there is no algorithm for constructing, for any integer n, a binary string x of length n such that* $K(x) > 2\lg n$.

Kolmogorov complexity allows one to deal rigorously with the concept of randomness and the degree of randomness. This is based on the intuition that a string is random if it cannot be compressed.

For finite words randomness is a matter of degree. A word w can be seen as **random** if the shortest program describing w is roughly of the same length as w: for example, if the difference $|w| - K(w)$ is small. Depending on the universal computer chosen, the additive constant can be larger or smaller. We can also say, for example, that a word is **fairly random** if $K(w) \geq |w| - 10$.

Almost all words are fairly random. This follows from this simple result:

Lemma 6.5.12 *The number of binary strings x of length n with* $K(x) \leq n - k$ *is less than* 2^{n-k+1}.

Proof: The number of binary strings of length at most $n-k$ is $1+2+\ldots+2^{n-k} < 2^{n-k+1}$. □

As a consequence, the Kolmogorov complexity of 99.9% of binary words of length n is at least $n-10$. This lemma also provides, in a sense, a 'counterexample' to Church's thesis. Indeed, let us consider the following problem: for a given n, construct a binary string of length n whose Kolmogorov complexity is greater than $\frac{n}{2}$. According to Exercise 6.5.11 this problem is unsolvable. But Lemma 6.5.12 shows that a randomly chosen string with a large probability is appropriate.

One can extend the concept of Kolmogorov complexity to all objects that can be encoded in a natural way by binary strings. For example, we define for an integer n, $K(n) = K(bin^{-1}(n))$ and for a graph G, $K(G) = K(w_G)$. On this basis one can talk about random numbers, graphs, ...

The concept of Kolmogorov complexity, capturing the degree of incompressibility, also has a variety of unexpected applications. One of them is to show limitations of various models and methods. For example, the following simple result is a useful tool to show non-regularity of languages.

Lemma 6.5.13 (KC-Regularity Lemma) *If* $L \subseteq \Sigma^*$ *is a regular language,* $x \in \Sigma^*$ *and* $L_x = \{y \mid xy \in L\}$, *then there is a constant* c_L *such that* $K(y) \leq K(m) + c_L$ *if y is the m-th string of* L_x.

Proof. A string y such that $xy \in L$ can be described by giving a DFA $\mathcal{A}$ accepting L, the state $\mathcal{A}$ is in after reading x and the order of y in L_x. Since the description of the first two items requires $\mathcal{O}(1)$ bits we have the lemma. □

Example 6.5.14 *In order to show that the language* $L = \{ww^Rx \mid x, w \in \{0,1\}^+\}$ *is not regular, take* $x = \{01\}^n$, *where* $K(n) \geq \lg n$. *The first word in* L_x *with respect to the strict order is* $y = \{01\}^n0$. *Hence* $K(y) = \Omega(\lg n)$, *contradicting the Lemma 6.5.13.*

Exercise 6.5.15 *Show that the language* $L = \{0^i 1^j \mid gcd(i,j) = 1\}$ *is not regular. (Hint: set* $x = 0^{(p-1)!}1$*, where* $p > 3$ *is a prime with sufficiently large Kolmogorov complexity.)*

6.5.3 Chaitin Complexity: Algorithmic Entropy and Information

Seemingly a minor modification of Kolmogorov complexity, independently discovered by Chaitin, leads to various concepts of fundamental importance.

In the definition of Kolmogorov complexity we have implicitly assumed that a universal computer that simulates programs over an alphabet Σ_0 actually needs to work also with the blanks in order to be able to recognize the ends of programs. Surprisingly, this fact has quite a few consequences. For example, we cannot append one program after another and expect our universal computer to simulate their serial composition unless it is denoted somehow, for example, by a delimiter, where one program ends and a second starts. Similarly, we need a way to separate programs and data. This can result, as we shall see, in adding a logarithmic factor in some considerations.

Chaitin complexity, or **self-delimiting complexity** $H_U(x)$, of a string x, with respect to a universal computer U – in short, $H(x)$ – is the length of the shortest self-delimiting program p that makes U produce x. More formally,

$$H_U(x) = \min\{|p| \mid U(p) = x, p \text{ is a self-delimiting program}\}.$$

The term 'self-delimiting' means that it is possible to recognize the end of the program by reading all its symbols and nothing else. As a consequence, the set of self-delimiting programs must be prefix-free.

Exercise 6.5.16 (Self-delimiting encodings of words (SD)) *For a binary word* w *let* $L(w)$ *be the length of* w *written in binary form with the leading* 1*, and let* $M(w)$ *be the word obtained from* w *by writing* 0 *between any two bits of* w *and* 1 *at the end. (For example,* $L(01) = 10, M(01) = 0011, L(0^{15}) = 1111, M(1111) = 10101011$*.)* $SD(w) = M(L(w))w$ *is called the self-delimiting version of* w*. (a) Show that* $|SD(w)| \leq |w| + 2\lg|w|$ *for every* w*, and show the case where the equality holds. (b) Show that if* $w = SD(w_1)SD(w_2)$*, then the decomposition of* w *into* $SD(w_1)$ *and* $SD(w_2)$ *is unique – this property is behind the adjective 'self-delimiting'.*

Exercise 6.5.17 (Kraft's inequality)* *A language* L *is* **prefix-free** *if no word of* L *is a prefix of another word in* L*. (a) Show that words in a prefix-free language can be used to encode symbols from another alphabet. (b) Show Kraft's inequality: if* $L \subseteq \Sigma^*$ *is a prefix-free language and* $|\Sigma| = p$*, then* $\sum_{w \in L} p^{-|w|} \leq 1$*.*

In addition, it has turned out to be useful to define the concept of a **conditional Chaitin complexity** of a string x, with respect to another string t and a universal computer U, as the length of the shortest program p that makes U compute x, given in addition t^*, the smallest program with respect to strict ordering, to compute t on U. Formally,

$$H(x/t) = \min\{|p| \mid U(p,t^*) = x, p \text{ is a self-delimiting program}\}.$$

$H(x/x) = \mathcal{O}(1)$,	$I(t:x) = \Omega(1)$,
$H(x) = H(x,t) + \mathcal{O}(1)$,	$I(t:x) = H(t) + H(x) - H(t,x) + \mathcal{O}(1)$,
$H(x/t) = H(x) + \mathcal{O}(1)$,	$I(x:x) = H(x) + \mathcal{O}(1)$,
$H(x,t) = H(x) + H(t/x) + \mathcal{O}(1)$,	$I(x:\varepsilon) = \mathcal{O}(1)$,
$H(x,t) = H(x) + H(t) + \mathcal{O}(1)$,	$I(\varepsilon:x) = \mathcal{O}(1)$.

Table 6.1 Properties of algorithmic entropy and information

(To illustrate the concepts of Chaitin complexity and conditional Chaitin complexity we can consider, for example, a three-tape universal Turing machine that gets, on the second tape, ε in the first case and t^* in the second case, and p on the third tape and produces x on the first tape.)

Similarly, as for Kolmogorov complexity, we can show the validity of the invariance theorem for both Chaitin and conditional Chaitin complexity and can therefore fix a universal Turing machine U and write $H(x)$ instead of $H_U(x)$.

Exercise 6.5.18 *Show the invariance theorem for (a) Chaitin complexity; (b) conditional Chaitin complexity.*

We denote briefly $H(x) = H_U(x)$, and call it the **algorithmic entropy**, or **information-theoretic complexity**, of x. Similarly, we denote $H(x/t) = H_U(x/t)$ as the **conditional Chaitin complexity** of x with respect to t. Using a pairing function on strings, that is, a bijection $\phi : \{0,1\}^* \times \{0,1\}^* \rightarrow \{0,1\}^*$, we can define how to compress a pair of strings. Let $H(x,t) = H(\phi(x,t))$ be the length of the shortest program that outputs x and t in a way that tells them apart.

The amount by which the conditional Chaitin complexity $H(x/t)$ is less than $H(x)$ can be seen as the amount of information t contains about x. This leads to the following definition of the **algorithmic information in t about x:**

$$I(t:x) = H(x) - H(x/t).$$

Remark 6.5.19 Historically, the first scientific concept of information was due to Shannon (1949). It defines the amount of information in an object as the number of bits that need to be transmitted in order *to select* the object from a previously agreed upon set of elements. On the basis of such a concept of information amount a very successful theory of data transmission has been developed. Kolmogorov/Chaitin approach considers the amount of information in an object as the number of bits needed *to describe* the object. Utilizing the concept of the universal computer it was shown that this new concept of information amount is independent from the methods used to describe the object because there is a universal description method that does not have to be the best in any case, but that is best in the sense that no other description method can provide a much better description infinitely often.

The basic properties of the algorithmic entropy, algorithmic information and the conditional Chaitin complexity are summarized in Table 6.1. These properties can be shown in a straightforward way, using the basic definitions only; therefore their proofs are left as exercises.

Exercise 6.5.20 *Show the following properties of algorithmic entropy: (a) $H(x/x) = \mathcal{O}(1)$; (b) $H(x) = H(x,t) + \mathcal{O}(1)$; (c) $H(x/t) \leq H(x) + \mathcal{O}(1)$.*

Exercise 6.5.21 *Show the following properties of algorithmic information: (a)* $I(t:\varepsilon) = \Omega(1)$*; (b)* $I(t:x) = H(t) + H(x) - H(t,x) + \mathcal{O}(1)$.

The following lemma shows that the difference between $K(x)$ and $H(x)$ is not too big, and the next exercise shows that it is essential.

Lemma 6.5.22 $K(x) \leq H(x) \leq K(x) + 2\lg_m K(x) + \mathcal{O}(1)$ *for the case of strings x over an m-element alphabet.*

Proof: It follows from Exercise 6.5.16 that each program of length n can be transformed into a self-delimiting program of length $n + \lg_m n$.[14] □

Exercise 6.5.23 *Consider Kolmogorov and Chaitin complexity of strings over an m-symbol alphabet* Σ*. Use Lemma 6.5.3 and Kraft's inequality to show that (a)* $\sum_{x\in\Sigma^*} m^{-K(x)} = \infty$*;* *(b)* $\sum_{x\in\Sigma^*} m^{-H(x)} \leq 1$.

Exercise 6.5.24 *Show, considering the function* $f(x,\varepsilon) = x$ *and the computer* $C(SD(x),\varepsilon) = x$ *that there is a constant c such that for all* $x \in \{0,1\}^*$, $H(x) \leq |x| + 2\lg(|x|) + c$.

Exercise 6.5.25 *Show that there is a constant c such that for all natural numbers n: (a)* $H(n) \leq 2\lg n + c$*; (b)* $H(n) \leq \lg n + \lg\lg n + c$.

Remark 6.5.26 On the basis of the Chaitin computer and complexity, two important probability distributions can be defined.

If $\mathcal{U}$ is a universal Chaitin computer, then the **universal a priori probability distribution** on $\{0,1\}^*$ is defined as

$$Q_{\mathcal{U}}(x) = \sum_{\mathcal{U}(p)=x} 2^{-|p|},$$

and (universal) **algorithmic probability** distribution as

$$m(x) = 2^{-H(x)}.$$

Observe that by Kraft's inequality $Q_{\mathcal{U}}(x) < 1$ for any x. It will be shown in Section 6.5.4 that $\sum_{x\in\{0,1\}^*} Q_{\mathcal{U}}(x) < 1$. Note also that the algorithmic probability is larger for regular strings and smaller for random strings. For example, if $H(x) \leq \lg|x| + 2\lg\lg|x| + c$, then $m(x) \geq \frac{1}{cn\lg^2|x|}$, and if $H(x) \geq n$, then $m(x) \leq \frac{1}{2^n}$.

Remark 6.5.27 It has been shown that under algorithmic probability distribution the expected time of any problem on strings of the same length is the same as the worst-case complexity. This implies that any complexity hierarchy results for deterministic computations, however tight, will also apply to the expected time complexity classes, for algorithmic probability distribution.

[14] A more precise relation between Kolmogorov and Chaitin complexity is: $H(x) = K(x) + K(K(x)) + \mathcal{O}(K(K(K(x))))$, $K(x) = H(x) - H(H(x)) - \mathcal{O}(H(H(H(x))))$.

Remark 6.5.28 For infinite words (strings) there is a sharp difference between randomness and nonrandomness. Indeed, it has turned out that the concept of Chaitin complexity is a proper one to define randomness of ω-words, as follows: An ω-word w is called **random** if there is a constant c such that

$$H(w_i) \geq i - c,$$

for all i, where w_i is the prefix of w of length i.

It has been shown that this concept of randomness of ω-strings is equivalent to that defined by statistical tests.

6.5.4 Limitations of Formal Systems to Prove Randomness

A general setting will now be presented in which one can introduce in a simple way such basic concepts as formal systems, computers, Kolmogorov and Chaitin complexity, and in which it can easily be shown that within each formal system it is possible to prove randomness only of finitely many strings.

The key requirement for a **formal axiomatic system** is that there is an objective criterion for deciding if a proof written in the language of the system is valid or not. In other words, there must be an algorithm for checking proofs. This leads to a very general definition of a formal axiomatic system as a recursively enumerable set.

Definition 6.5.29 *A formal system is a pair $\langle C, p_0\rangle$, where*

$$C : \{0,1\}^* \times \mathbf{N} \mapsto \{S \subseteq \{0,1\}^* \mid S \text{ is a finite set}\}$$

is a recursive mapping and $\forall p,t[C(p,t) \subseteq C(p,t+1)]$. C is called an **inference rule**, *and p an* **axiom**.

Interpretation: $C(p,t)$ is the set of theorems (statements) that one can prove from the axiom p by proofs of length $\leq t$.

In formal systems as defined above, we work with binary strings only. However, the ith string will be interpreted in the following, depending on the context, either as the ith string or the integer i or the ith statement – an encoding of a theorem.

The following notation will be used to introduce an abstract definition of a computer. If $f : \{0,1\}^* \times \{0,1\}^* \mapsto \{0,1\}^*$ is a partial function, then for each $y \in \{0,1\}^*$ the projection of f on the second component y is defined by

$$f_y(x) = f(x,y).$$

Definition 6.5.30 *A* **computer** *is a partial recursive function*

$$C : \{0,1\}^* \times \{0,1\}^* \mapsto \{0,1\}^*.$$

Moreover, if the domain of C_y is a prefix-free language for any $y \in \{0,1\}^*$, we speak about a **Chaitin computer**.

Interpretation: A computer C produces, for a program p and an input i, a set $C(p,i)$. The additional requirement for Chaitin computers is that if $C(p,i)$ is defined and p is a prefix of p', then $C(p',i)$ is not defined. In other words, no program for a successful computation of C can be a prefix to another program for a successful computation of C for the same input – which captures the idea of having only self-delimiting programs. This special requirement will later be relaxed and its importance analysed.

Also in such a general setting, there is the concept of the universal (Chaitin) computer.

Definition 6.5.31 *A (Chaitin) computer U is universal if and only if for every (Chaitin) computer C, there is a simulation constant $sim(C)$ such that whenever $C(u,v)$ is defined, then there is a program u' such that*

$$U(u',v) = C(u,v) \text{ and } |u'| \leq |u| + sim(C).$$

Theorem 6.5.32 *There exists a universal (Chaitin) computer.*

Proof: Let us take a fixed enumeration $C_1, C_2, \ldots$ of all computers.[15] The function $F : \mathbf{N} \times \{0,1\}^* \times \{0,1\}^* \mapsto \{0,1\}^*$ defined by

$$F(i,u,v) = C_i(u,v), \quad i \in \mathbf{N}, u,v \in \{0,1\}^*$$

is partial recursive, and so is the function $U : \{0,1\}^* \times \{0,1\}^* \mapsto \{0,1\}^*$ defined by

$$U(0^i 1u, v) = C_i(u,v).$$

In addition, the domain of $U(u,v)$ is prefix-free for each v in the case of a Chaitin computer, since projections of all C_i have this property. This implies that U is a universal computer with $sim(C_i) = i+1$, for each i. □

In this general setting we can define analogously the concepts of Kolmogorov and Chaitin complexity (using the concept of a Chaitin computer in the second case). The invariance theorem can also be shown analogously.

Kolmogorov complexity can be used to show the limitations of formal systems to prove randomness, as we shall now see. But first we introduce a new general concept of a generating computer.

Definition 6.5.33 *A* **generating computer** *is a pair $\langle C, h_C \rangle$ of recursive functions*

$$\begin{aligned} C : \{0,1\}^* \times \mathbf{N} &\rightarrow \{S \subseteq \{0,1\}^* \mid S \text{ is finite}\}, \\ h_C : \{0,1\}^* \times \mathbf{N} &\rightarrow \{0,1\}, \end{aligned}$$

such that $\forall p,t[C(p,t) \subseteq C(p,t+1)]$, and if $h_C(p,t') = 1$, then also $h_C(p,t'+1) = 1$ and $C(p,t') = C(p,t'+1)$.

Interpretation: p can be seen as a program and t as time. $C(p,t)$ is the set of words that C generates up to time t. If $h_C(p,t') = 1$, then C, with program p, halts at time t'.

Observe that there is a close relation between the concept of a formal system and that of a generating computer. Our abstract computer can therefore play the role of a formal system, and its program the role of an axiom.

The concept of universality can also be defined for generating computers. A generating computer U is called universal if for each other generating computer C there is a constant $sim(C)$ such that for every program p for C there is a program p' for U such that $|p'| \leq |p| + sim(C)$, $U(p')$ halts if and only if $C(p)$ does, and $U(p') = C(p)$.

Exercise 6.5.34 *Show the existence of universal generating computers.*

[15] In the following we encode a pair (i,w) of an integer and a binary string $0^i 1w$.

In the following it is assumed that there is a universal generating computer U. With respect to U we can define Kolmogorov complexity of finite sets as follows:

$$K(S) = \min\{|p| \mid U(p) = S \text{ and } U \text{ halts for } p\}.$$

If $S = \{s\}$, where s is a string, then we usually write $K(s) = K(\{s\})$.

A universal computer can therefore be seen as a universal formal system.

Let us now assume that we have a fixed natural encoding '$K(s) > n$' of statements $K(s) > n$ in the binary alphabet. (Details of the encoding will not be of importance.) The following theorem implies that in any formal system one can prove randomness of only finitely many strings.

Theorem 6.5.35 (Chaitin's theorem) *For any universal computer (formal system) U there is a constant c such that for all programs p the following holds: if for every integer n an encoding of the statement '$K(s) > n$' (as a string) is in $U(p)$ if and only if $K(s) > n$, then '$K(s) > n$' is in $U(p)$ only if $n < |p| + c$.*

Proof: Let C be a generating computer such that, for a given program p', C tries first to make the decomposition $p' = 0^k 1p$. If this is not possible, C halts, generating the empty set. Otherwise, C simulates U on p, generates $U(p)$ and searches $U(p)$ to find an encoding '$K(s) > n$' for some $n \geq |p'| + k$. If the search is successful, C halts with s as the output.

Let us now consider what happens if C gets the string $0^{sim(C)}1p$ as input. If $C(0^{sim(C)}1p) = \{s\}$, then from the definition of a universal generating computer it follows that

$$K(s) \leq |0^{sim(C)}1p| + sim(C) = |p| + 2sim(C) + 1. \tag{6.10}$$

But the fact that C halts with the output $\{s\}$ implies that

$$n \geq |p'| + k = |0^{sim(C)}1p| + sim(C) = |p| + 2sim(C) + 1,$$

and we get

$$K(s) > n > |p| + 2sim(C) + 1,$$

which contradicts the inequality (6.10). The assumption that C can find an encoding of an assertion '$K(s) > n$' leads therefore to a contradiction. Since '$K(s) > n$' if and only if $K(s) > n$, this implies that for the assertions (theorems) $K(s) > n$, $n \geq |p| + 2sim(C) + 1$ there is no proof in the formal system $\langle U, p \rangle$. □

Note that the proof is again based on Berry's paradox and its modification: Find a binary string that can be proved to be of Kolmogorov complexity greater than the number of bits in the binary version of this statement.

6.5.5 The Number of Wisdom*

We discuss now a special number that encodes very compactly the halting problem.

Definition 6.5.36 *The* **number of wisdom**, *or the* **halting probability of the universal Chaitin computer** *U, is defined by*

$$\Omega = \sum_{\substack{u \in \{0,1\}^* \\ U(u,\varepsilon) \text{ is defined}}} 2^{-|u|}.$$

The following lemma is a justification for using the term 'probability' for Ω.

Lemma 6.5.37 $0 < \Omega < 1$.

Proof: Since the domain of U_ε is a prefix-free language, Kraft's inequality (see Exercise 6.5.17), implies that $\Omega \leq 1$. Since U is a universal computer, there exists a u_1 such that $U(u_1, \varepsilon)$ converges, and a u_2 such that $U(u_2, \varepsilon)$ does not. This implies that $0 < \Omega < 1$. □

Let us now analyse Ω in order to see whether its catchy name is justified. In order to do so, let us assume that

$$\Omega = 0.b_1 b_2 b_3 \ldots$$

is the binary expansion of Ω. (As shown later, this expansion is unique.)

We first show that Ω encodes the halting problem of Turing machines very compactly, and that bits of Ω have properties that justify calling them 'magic bits'.

The domain of U_ε – that is, the set

$$dom(U_\varepsilon) = \{w \mid w \in \{0,1\}^*, U(w,\varepsilon) \text{ is defined}\}$$

is recursively enumerable. Let $g : \mathbf{N} \to dom(U_\varepsilon)$ be a bijection – a fixed enumeration of $dom(U_\varepsilon)$ (such an enumeration can be obtained, for example, by dovetailing). Denote

$$\omega_n^g = \sum_{j=1}^{n} 2^{-|g(j)|}, \text{ for } n \geq 1.$$

The sequence ω_n^g is clearly increasing, and converges to Ω. Moreover, the following lemma holds.

Lemma 6.5.38 *Whenever* $\omega_n^g > \Omega_i = 0.b_1 b_2 \ldots b_i$, *then*

$$\Omega_i < \omega_n^g < \Omega \leq \Omega_i + 2^{-i}.$$

Moreover, given any i, if we know the first i bits of Ω, *then we can decide the halting problem of any program with length* $\leq i$.

Proof: The inequality $\Omega \leq \Omega_i + 2^{-i}$ is a consequence of the inequality $2^{-i} \geq \sum_{j=i+1}^{\infty} b_j 2^{-j}$. In order to prove the second assertion of the lemma, let us assume that we know the first i bits of Ω, and therefore Ω_i. We can then compute the numbers $\omega_1^g, \omega_2^g, \ldots$ until we find an n such that $\Omega_i < \omega_n^g$. It follows from the definition of the sequence $\omega_n^g, n = 1, 2, \ldots$ that this is always possible.

Let $u \in \{0,1\}^*, |u| = i_1 \leq i$ and n be such that $\Omega_i < \omega_n^g$. We show that $U(u,\varepsilon)$ is defined if and only if u is one of the words $g(1), \ldots, g(n)$. The 'if' claim is trivially true. In order to prove the 'only if' claim, let us assume that $u = g(m)$ for an $m > n$. In this case the following inequalities lead to a contradiction:

$$\Omega > \omega_n^g + 2^{-i_1} \geq \omega_n^g + 2^{-i} > \Omega_i + 2^{-i} \geq \Omega.$$

□

It now follows from the discussion at the beginning of Section 6.4.2 that knowledge of sufficiently many bits of Ω could be used to solve the halting problems of all Turing machines up to a certain size and thereby to find an answer to many open questions of mathematics (and therefore, for example, also of the PCP of reasonable size). The question of how many bits of Ω would be needed depends on the formal system used, and also on how the universal computer is programmed. We have used programs of the type 0^i, where i represents a computer C_i. A more compact programming of U is possible: for example, using the technique of Exercise 6.5.16 to make words self-delimited. A more detailed analysis reveals that knowing 10,000 bits of Ω would be sufficient to deal with the halting problem of Turing machines looking for counter examples of practically all the famous open problems of discrete mathematics.

Ω could also be used to decide whether a well-formed formula of a formal theory is a theorem, a negation of a theorem, or independent (that is, is unprovable within the given formal system). Indeed, let us consider a formal system F with an axiom and rules of inference. For any well-formed formula α, design a Turing machine $TM(F,\alpha)$ that checks systematically all proofs of F and halts if U finds one for α. Similarly, for $\neg\alpha$. Knowing a sufficiently large portion of Ω, we could decide whether α is provable, refutable or independent. Ω therefore deserves the name 'number of wisdom' – it can help to solve many problems. Unfortunately, 'Nichts ist vollkommen' as a German proverb and the following theorem say.

Theorem 6.5.39 *If* $\Omega = 0.b_1b_2b_3\dots$, *then the* ω*-word* $b_1b_2b_3\dots$ *is random.*

Proof: We use the same notation as in the proof of Lemma 6.5.38. It was shown there that if $U(u_1,\varepsilon)$ is defined, $\omega_n^g \geq \Omega_i$, and $|u_1| \leq i$, then u_1 is one of the words $g(1),\dots,g(n)$. Therefore

$$\{U(g(j),\varepsilon)\,|\,1 \leq j \leq n \text{ and } |g(j)| \leq i\} = \{w\,|\,H(w) \leq i\}, \tag{6.11}$$

because if $H(w) \leq i$, then w has a program of length at most i.

Now let $f:\{0,1\}^* \mapsto \{0,1\}^*$ be defined as follows: if $x = x_1\dots x_t$, $x_j \in \{0,1\}$, for $1 \leq j \leq t$, and m is the smallest integer such that $\omega_m^g > \sum_{j=1}^{t} x_j 2^{-j}$, then $f(x)$ is the first word, in the strict ordering, not in the set

$$\{g(j)\,|\,1 \leq j \leq m\}.$$

Let C be the computer defined by $C(x,\varepsilon) = f(U(x,\varepsilon))$. Then for each $B_i = b_1\dots b_i$ we get

$$\begin{aligned} H(f(B_i)) &\leq H_C(f(B_i)) + sim(C) \\ &= \min\{|u|\,|\,C(u,\varepsilon) = f(B_i)\} + sim(C) \\ &= \min\{|u|\,|\,f(U(u,\varepsilon)) = f(B_i)\} + sim(C) \\ &\leq \min\{|u|\,|\,U(u,\varepsilon) = B_i\} + sim(C) \\ &= H(B_i) + sim(C). \end{aligned}$$

Since $f(B_i)$ is the smallest word not in the set $\{g(j)\,|\,1 \leq j \leq m\}$, where $\omega_m^g \geq \Omega_i$, we get from (6.11) that $H(f(B_i)) > i$, and therefore $H(B_i) \geq i - sim(C)$, which implies that B_i is random. □

It follows from Theorem 6.5.39 that we are able to determine B_i only for finitely many i in any formal system. It can also be shown that we can determine only finitely many bits of Ω.

Remarkable properties of Ω were illustrated on exponential Diophantine equations. Chaitin (1987) proved that there is a particular 'exponential' Diophantine equation

$$P(i,x_1,\dots,x_n) = Q(i,x_1,\dots,x_n), \tag{6.12}$$

where P and Q are functions built from variables and integers by the operations of addition, multiplication and exponentiation, and such that for each integer i the equation (6.12) has infinitely many solutions if and only if $b_i = 1$; that is, if and only if the ith bit of the binary expansion of Ω equals 1. This implies, in the light of the previous discussions, that in any formal system we can decide only for finitely many i whether the equation (6.12) has infinitely many solutions. This implies that randomness is already deeply rooted in elementary arithmetic.

Remark 6.5.40 The limitations of computers and formal systems that we have derived in this chapter would have extremely strong implications were it to turn out that our minds work algorithmically. This, however, seems not to be the case. Understanding the mind is currently one of the main problems of science in general.

6.5.6 Kolmogorov/Chaitin Complexity as a Methodology*

Kolmogorov/Chaitin complexity ideas have also turned out to be a powerful tool in developing scientific understanding for a variety of basic informal concepts of science in general and of computing in particular and in creating the corresponding formal concepts. Let us illustrate this on two examples.

Example 6.5.41 (Limits on energy dissipation in computing) *The ultimate limitations of miniaturization of computing devices, and therefore also of the speed of computation, are governed by the heating problems caused by energy dissipation. A reduction of energy dissipation per elementary computation step therefore determines future advances in computing power. At the same time it is known that only 'logically irreversible' operations, at which one can not deduce inputs from outputs, have to cause an energy dissipation. It is also known, see also Section 4.5, that all computations can be performed logically reversibly – at the cost of eventually filling up the memory with unneeded garbage information.*

Using Chaitin complexity we can express the ultimate limits of energy dissipation in the number of irreversibly erased bits as follows:

Let us consider an effective enumeration $\mathcal{R} = R_1, R_2, R_3, \ldots$ of reversible Turing machines. For each $R \in \mathcal{R}$ we define the **irreversibility cost function** *$E_R(x,y)$, for strings $x,y \in \Sigma^*$, of computing y from x with R by*

$$E_R(x,y) = \min\{|p| + |q| \mid R(x,p) = pairs(y,q)\},$$

where pairs is a string pairing function.

An ireversibility cost function $E_U(x,y)$ is called universal if for every $R \in \mathcal{R}$ there is a constant c_R such that for all x,y

$$E_U(x,y) \leq E_R(x,y) + c_R.$$

It can be shown that there is a reversible TM U such that the irreversibility cost function $E_U(x,y)$ is universal. Moreover, using similar arguments as for Kolmogorov/Chaitin complexity, we can show that two universal ireversibility cost functions assign the same irreversibility cost to any function computable apart from an additive constant and therefore we can define a (machine independent, apart from an additive constant) reference cost function

$$E(x,y) = E_U(x,y).$$

Using Kolmogorov/Chaitin complexity concepts and methods it has been shown that up to an additive logarithmic constant

$$E(x,y) = H(x\,/\,y) + H(y\,/\,x).$$

Example 6.5.42 (Theory formation) *One basic problem of many sciences is how to infer a theory that best fits given observational/experimental data. The Greek philosopher Epicurus (around 300 BC) proposed the* **multiple explanation principle**: if more than one theory is consistent with data, keep all such theories. *A more modern* **Occam's razor principle**, *attributed to William of Ockham (around AD 1200) says that* the simplest theory which fits data is the best. *A new, so-called* **minimal length description (MLD) principle**, *based on Kolmogorov complexity ideas, says that* the best theory to explain a set of data is the one which minimizes the sum of the length, in bits, of the description of the theory and of the length, in bits, of data when encoded with the help of the theory. *On this basis a variety of new basic scientific methodologies are being developed in various sciences.*

Exercise 6.5.43 *In order to illustrate the problem of inference, design a minimal DFA that accepts all strings from the set $\{a^i \mid i \text{ is a prime}\}$ and rejects all strings from the set $\{a^i \mid i \text{ is even}\}$.*

Moral: The search for borderlines between the possible and the impossible is one of the main aims and tools of science. The discovery of such limitations and borderlines is often the beginning of a long chain of very fruitful contributions to science. A good rule of thumb in the search for limitations in computing is, as in life, to eliminate the impossible and take whatever remains as truth.

6.6 Exercises

1. Let $A, B \subseteq \{0,1\}^*$. Which of the following claims are true? (Prove your statements.)

   (a) If A is recursively enumerable, then so is $Prefix(A)$.

   (b) If the set $\{0\}A \cup \{0\}B$ is recursive, then so are A and B.

   (c) If the set $A \cup B$ is recursive, then so are A and B.

2. Show that the following families of languages are closed under operations of iteration and shuffle: (a) recursive languages; (b) recursively enumerable languages.

3. Given a function $f : \mathbf{N} \to \mathbf{R}$, construct, using the diagonalization method, a real number that is not in the range of f.

4. Show that the following sets are not recursive: (a) $\{\langle \mathcal{M} \rangle_p \mid \mathcal{M}$ halts on an odd number of inputs$\}$; (b) $\{\langle \mathcal{M} \rangle_p \mid \mathcal{M}$ halts on all inputs$\}$.

5. Show that if $\mathcal{U}$ is a universal Turing machine for all k-tape Turing machines, then the set of inputs for which $\mathcal{U}$ halts is recursively enumerable but not recursive.

6. Let f be a recursive nondecreasing function such that $lim_{n\to\infty} f(n) = \infty$. Show that there is a primitive recursive function g such that $g(n) \leq f(n)$ for all n and $lim_{n\to\infty} g(n) = \infty$.

7.* Give an example of a partial recursive function that is not extendable to a recursive function and whose graph is recursive. (Hint: consider the running time of a universal TM.)

8. Show that if the argument functions of operations of composition and minimization are Turing machine computable, then so are the resulting functions.

9. Show that the following predicates (functions from $\mathbf{N}$ into $\{0,1\}$) are primitive recursive:

   (a) $sg(x) = 1$ if and only if $x \neq 0$; (b) $\overline{sg}(x) = 0$ if and only if $x \neq 0$; (c) $eq(x,y) = 1$ if and only if $x = y$; (d) $neq(x,y) = 1$ if and only if $x \neq y$.

10. Show that primitive recursive predicates are closed under Boolean operations.

11. Show that the following functions are primitive recursive: (a) the remainder of dividing x by y; (b) integer division; (c) $g(n) = n \dot{-} \lfloor \sqrt{n} \rfloor^2$.

12. Show that the function $f(x) =$ 'the largest integer less than or equal to $\sqrt{x}$' is primitive recursive.

13. Show, for the pairing function $pair(x,y)$ and the de-pairing functions π_1 and π_2 introduced in Section 6.2 that: (a) $pair(x,y) = \frac{(x+y)^2+x+3y}{2}$; (b) $\pi_1(x) = x \dot{-} \frac{1}{2}\lfloor\frac{\lfloor\sqrt{8x+1}\rfloor+1}{2}\rfloor \cdot \lfloor\frac{\lfloor\sqrt{8x+1}\rfloor-1}{2}\rfloor$; (c) $\pi_2 =$?.

14. Let $pair(x_1,x_2,x_3,x_4,x_5) = pair(x_1,pair(x_2,pair(x_3,pair(x_4,x_5))))$, and let us define $\pi_{5,i}(x) = x_i$ for $1 \leq i \leq 5$. Express functions $\pi_{5,i}$ using functions π_1, π_2.

15. Show that the following general pairing function $prod : \mathbf{N}^3 \to \mathbf{N}$ is primitive recursive: $prod(n,i,x) = x_i$, where $pair(x_1, \ldots, x_n) = x$.

16.* Define a primitive recursive function f as follows:

$$f(x,y) = prod(y+1, \pi_1(x)+1, \pi_2(x))$$

and a sequence $d_i, 1 \leq i$, of partial recursive functions

$$d_x(y) = \begin{cases} f(x,y)-1, & \text{if } 0 < f(x,y) \text{ and } y < \pi_1(x)+1; \\ \text{undefined}, & \text{otherwise.} \end{cases}$$

Show that the sequence of functions $d_0, d_1, \ldots$ contains all partial recursive functions with the finite domain, each exactly once. Show that if $f : \mathbf{N} \to \mathbf{N}$ is a primitive recursive, then so is the function $g(n,x) = f^{(n)}(x)$.

17. Show that the Ackermann function has the following properties for any $i,j \in \mathbf{N}$:

(a) $A(i,j+1) > A(i,j)$; (b) $A(i+1,j) > A(i,j)$.

18. There are various modifications of the Ackermann function that were introduced in Section 6.2.2: for example, the function A' defined as follows: $A'(0,j) = j+1$ for $j \geq 0$, $A'(i,0) = A'(i-1,1)$ for $i \geq 1$, and $A'(i,j) = A'(i-1, A'(i,j-1))$ for $i \geq 1, j \geq 1$. Show that $A'(i+1,j) \geq A'(i,j+1)$, for all $i,j \in \mathbf{N}$.

19.* **(Fixed-point theorem)** Let f be a recursive function that maps TM into TM. Show that there is a TM $\mathcal{M}$ such that $\mathcal{M}$ and $f(\mathcal{M})$ compute the same function.

20. Show that for every recursive function $f(n)$ there is a recursive language that is not in the complexity class $Time(f(n))$.

21. Determine for each of the following instances of the PCP whether they have a solution, and if they do, find one: (a) $A = (abb,a,bab,baba,aba)$, $B = (bbab,aa,ab,aa,a)$; (b) $A = (bb,a,bab,baba,aba)$, $B = (bab,aa,ab,aa,a)$; (c) $A = (1,10111,10)$, $B = (111,10,0)$; (d) $A = (10,011,101)$, $B = (101,11,011)$; (e) $A = (10,10,011,101)$, $B = (101,010,11,011)$; (f) $A = (10100,011,01,0001)$, $B = (1010,101,11,0010)$; (g) $A = (abba,ba,baa,aa,ab)$, $B = (baa,aba,ba,bb,a)$; (h) $A = (1,0111,10)$, $B = (111,0,0)$; (i) $A = (ab,ba,b,abb,a)$, $B = (aba,abb,ab,b,bab)$.

22. Show that the PCP is decidable for lists with (a) one element; (b) two elements.

23.* Show that the PCP with lists over a two-letter alphabet is undecidable.

24. Show that the following modification of the PCP is decidable: given two lists of words $A = (x_1, \ldots, x_n)$, $B = (y_1, \ldots, y_n)$ over the alphabet $\Sigma, |\Sigma| \geq 2$, are there $i_1, \ldots, i_k$ and $j_1, \ldots, j_l$ such that $x_{i_1} \ldots x_{i_k} = y_{j_1} \ldots, y_{j_l}$?

25. Show that the following modifications of the PCP are undecidable: (a) given two lists $(u, u_1, \ldots, u_n)$, $(v, v_1, \ldots, v_n)$, is there a sequence of integers $i_1, \ldots, i_n$, $1 \leq i_k \leq m$, $1 \leq k \leq m$, such that $uu_{i_1} \ldots u_{i_m} = vv_{i_1} \ldots v_{i_m}$? (b) given lists $(u, u_1, \ldots, u_n, u')$, $(v, v_1, \ldots, v_n v')$, is there a sequence of integers $i_1, \ldots, i_m$, $1 \leq i_k \leq n$, $1 \leq k \leq m$, such that $uu_{i_1} \ldots u_{i_m} u' = vv_{i_1} \ldots v_{i_m} v'$?

26.** An affine transformation on $\mathbf{N} \times \mathbf{N}$ is a mapping $f(x,y) = (ax + by + c, dx + ey + f)$, where a,b,c,d,e,f are fixed whole numbers. Show, for example by a reduction from the modified PCP, in Exercise 25, that it is undecidable, given a pair $(x_0, y_0) \in \mathbf{N}$ and a finite set $\mathcal{S}$ of affine transformations, whether there is a sequence $f_1, \ldots, f_k$ of affine transformations from $\mathcal{S}$ such that $f_1(f_2(\ldots f_k(x_0, y_0) \ldots)) = (x, x)$ for some x.

27. Given a set S of Wang tiles, we can assume that the colours used are numbered and that a set of tiles is represented by a word over the alphabet $\{0, 1, \#\}$ by writing in a clockwise manner the numbers of the colours of all tiles, one after another, and separating them by #. Denote by *TIL* the set of words that describe sets of tiles (with the initial tile), for which the plane can be tiled. Show that the language *TIL* is recursively enumerable.

28. Let us use quadruples (*up*, *right*, *down*, *left*) to denote the colouring of Wang tiles. Which of the following sets of Wang tiles can be used to tile the plane: (a) $(a,w,w,w), (w,w,b,c), (b,c,a,w)$; (b) $(a,w,w,w), (w,w,a,c), (b,c,b,w)$.

29. Show that the following modification of the tiling problem is also undecidable: all unit square tiles have marked corners, and a tiling is consistent if the colours of all four tiles that meet at a point are identical.

30. Show that Hilbert's tenth problem is equivalent to the problem of deciding for an arbitrary polynomial $P(x_1, \ldots, x_n)$ with integer coefficients whether the equation $P(x_1, \ldots, x_n) = 0$ has a solution in integers.

31. Show, using a result presented in this chapter, that primes have short certificates.

32. Suppose that $L = \{x \mid \exists x_1, \ldots, x_n \in \mathbf{Z}[f(x, x_1, \ldots, x_n) = 0]\}$, where f is a polynomial. Construct a polynomial g such that $L = \{g(x_1, \ldots, x_n) \mid g(x_1, \ldots, x_n) \geq 0\}$.

33. Suppose that $L = \{x \mid \exists x_1, \ldots, x_n \in \mathbf{Z}[f(x, x_1, \ldots, x_n) = 0]\}$, where f is a polynomial. Construct a polynomial g such that $L = \{x \mid \exists x_1, \ldots, x_n \in \mathbf{N}[g(x, x_1, \ldots, x_n) = 0]\}$.

34. Reduce the problem of finding rational solutions to polynomial equations to the problem of finding integer solutions to polynomial equations.

35.* Show that there is an algorithm for solving Diophantine equations over **N** if and only if there is an algorithm for solving four-degree Diophantine equations over **N**. (Hint: using the distributive law, each polynomial can be written as a sum of terms, where each term is a product of a multiset of variables; to each such multiset S associate a new variable, ...)

36. A function $f(x_1, \ldots, x_n)$ is called Diophantine if there is a Diophantine equation $D(a_1, \ldots, a_n, x_1, \ldots, x_n)$ such that

$$x = f(x_1, \ldots, x_n) \equiv \exists a_1 \ldots a_n D(a_1, \ldots, a_n, x, x_1, \ldots, x_n) = 0.$$

Show that the following functions are Diophantine: (a) gcd; (b) lcm.

37. Let A, B and C be any sets such that $A \leq_m C$ and $B \leq_m C$. Is it true that $A \oplus B \leq_m C$?

38. A recursively enumerable set S is said to be m-**complete** if and only if $S' \leq_m S$ for any recursively enumerable set S'. Show that if a recursively enumerable set S is productive and $S \leq_m S'$, then S' is also productive, and that every m-complete set is creative.

39. (Properties of the arithmetical hierarchy). Show that (a) if $A \leq_m B$ and $B \in \Sigma_i$, then $A \in \Sigma_i$; (b) if $A \leq_m B$ and $B \in \Pi_i$, then $A \in \Pi_i$; (c) $\Sigma_i \subseteq \Sigma\Sigma_i$, $\Sigma_i \subseteq \Pi\Sigma_i$, $\Pi_i \subseteq \Sigma\Pi_i$ and $\Pi_i \subseteq \Pi\Pi_i$ for $i \in \mathbf{N}$; (d) $\Sigma_i \subseteq \Pi_{i+1}$ and $\Pi_i \subseteq \Sigma_{i+1}$ for $i \in \mathbf{N}$; (e) $\Sigma_i \subseteq \Sigma_{i+1}$, $\Pi_i \subseteq \Pi_{i+1}$ for $i \in \mathbf{N}$; (f) Σ_i and Π_i are closed under union and intersection.

40. Show, for each $i \in \mathbf{N}$, that the language $\emptyset^i$, obtained by applying the jump operation to $\emptyset$ i times, is complete for the class Σ_i, in the sense that it is in Σ_i and all languages in Σ_i are m-reducible to it.

41. Show an example of a prefix-free language such that Kraft's inequality is (a) strict; (b) an equality.

42. Show that the language $S = \{SD(x) \mid x \in \{0,1\}^*\}$ is prefix-free, and that every natural number n has in S a representation with $\lg n + 2\lg\lg n$ bits.

43. Let A be a finite alphabet. Show that (a) if $S \subseteq A^*$, then the following statements are equivalent: (1) S is prefix-free, (2) $S \cap S\Sigma^+ = \emptyset$; (b) for all prefix-free languages S, T it holds that if $S\Sigma^* = T\Sigma^*$, then $S = T$.

44. Is the mapping $f : \{0,1\}^* \times \{0,1\}^* \rightarrow \{0,1\}^*$ defined by $f(x,y) = SD(x)y$ a bijection (and therefore a string pairing function)?

45. Show that $K(x,y) \leq K(x) + K(y) + \mathcal{O}(\min\{K(x), K(y)\})$.

46. (**Incompressibility Theorem**) Let $c \in \mathbf{N}^+$. Show that for each fixed string $y \in \{0,1\}^*$, every finite set $A \subseteq \{0,1\}^*$ of cardinality m has at least $n(1-2^{-c})+1$ strings x with $K(x\,/\,y) \geq \lg m - c$.

47. Show the following properties of algorithmic entropy: (a) $H(w,t) = H(w) + H(t\,/\,w) + \mathcal{O}(1)$; (b) $H(w,t) = H(w) + H(t) + \mathcal{O}(1)$.

48. Show the following properties of algorithmic information: (a) $I(w : w) = H(w) + \mathcal{O}(1)$; (b) $I(w : \varepsilon) = \mathcal{O}(1)$; (c) $I(\varepsilon : w) = \mathcal{O}(1)$.

49.* Let $CP = \{x^* \mid x \in \{0,1\}^*\}$. (That is, CP is the set of minimal programs.) Show that (a) there is a constant c such that $H(y) \geq |y| - c$ for all $y \in CP$; (b) the set CP is immune.

50.* Show that $H(x) \leq |x| + 2\lg\lg|x| + c$, for a constant c, for all $x \in \{0,1\}^*$.

51. Show that the set $I_{KC} = \{x \in \Sigma^* \mid K(x) \geq |x|\}$ is immune, and that its complement is recursively enumerable.

52. Show, using KC-regularity lemma, that the following languages are not regular: (a) $\{0^n1^m \mid m > 2n\}$; (b) $\{xcycz \mid xy = z \in \{a,b\}^*, c \notin \{a,b\}\}$.

QUESTIONS

1. How can such concepts as recursivness and recursive enumerability be transferred to sets of graphs?
2. The Ackermann function grows faster than any primitive recursive function. It would therefore seem that its inverse grows more slowly than any other nondecreasing primitive recursive function. Is it true? Justify your claim.
3. What types of problems would be solvable were the halting problem decidable?
4. Is there a set of tiles that can tile plane both periodically and aperiodically?
5. Which variants of PCP are decidable?
6. Is it more difficult to solve a system of Diophantine equations than to solve a single Diophantine equation?
7. Why is the inequality $K(x) \leq |x|$ not valid in general?
8. How is conditional Kolmogorov complexity defined?
9. How are random languages defined?
10. Is the number of wisdom unique?

6.7 Historical and Bibliographical References

Papers by Gödel (1931) and Turing (1937) which showed in an indisputable way the limitations of formal systems and algorithmic methods can be seen as marking the beginning of a new era in mathematics, computing and science in general.

Turing's model of computability based on his concept of a machine has ultimately turned out to be more inspiring than the computationally equivalent model of partial recursive functions introduced by Kleene (1936). However, it was the theory of partial recursive, recursive and primitive recursive functions that developed first, due to its elegance and more traditional mathematical framework. This theory, which has since then had a firm place in the theory of computing, was originally considered to be part of number theory and logic.

The origin of recursive function theory can be traced far back in the history of mathematics. For example, Hermann Grassmann (1809–77) in his textbook of 1861 used primitive recursive definitions for addition and multiplication. Richard Dedekind (1831–1916), known also for his saying 'Was beweisbar ist, soll in der Wissenschaft nicht ohne Beweis geglaubt werden', proved in 1881 that primitive recursion uniquely defines a function. A systematic development of recursive functions is due to Skolem (1887–1963) and Rózsa Péter (1906–77) with her book published in 1951.

The results on recursively enumerable and recursive sets are from Post (1944). The exposition of pairing and de-pairing functions is from Engeler (1973), and Exercise 16 from Smith (1994).

Nowadays there are numerous books on recursive functions, for example: Péter (1951); Malcev (1965); Davis (1958, 1965); Rogers (1967); Minsky (1967); Machtey and Young (1978); Cohen (1987); Odifredi (1989) and Smith (1994). The characterization of primitive recursive functions in terms of **for** programs is due to Meyer and Ritchie (1967).

Various concepts of computable real numbers form bases for recursive function-based approaches to calculus – see Weihrauch (1987) for a detailed exposition. The concept of limiting recursive real numbers was introduced by Korec (1986).

Undecidability is also dealt with in many books. For a systematic presentation see, for example, Davis (1965) and Rozenberg and Salomaa (1994), where philosophical and other broader aspects of undecidability and unsolvability are discussed in an illuminating way.

Theorem 6.4.2 is due to Rice (1953). The undecidability of the halting problem is due to Turing (1937). The first undecidable result on tiling is due to Berger (1966). A very thorough presentation of various tiling problems and results is found in Grünbaum and Shephard (1987). This book and Gardner (1989) contain detailed presentations of Penrose's tilings and their properties. Aperiodic tiling of a plane with 13 Wang dominoes is described by Culik (1996). For the importance of tiling for proving undecidability results see van Emde Boas (1982). The Post correspondence problem is due to Post (1946); for the proof see Hopcroft and Ullman (1969), Salomaa (1973) and Rozenberg and Salomaa (1994), where a detailed discussion of the problem can be found. The undecidability of the Thue problem was shown for semigroups by Post (1947) and Markov(1947) and for groups by Novikov (1955); the decidability of the Thue problem for Abelian semigroups is due to Malcev (1958). The Thue problem (E1) on page 389 is from Penrose (1990). The Thue problem (E2) is Penrose's modification of the problem due to G. S. Tseitin and D. Scott, see Gardner (1958). Hilbert's tenth problem (Hilbert (1935)) was solved with great effort and contributions by many authors (including J. Robinson and M. Davis). The final step was done by Matiyasevich (1971). For a history of the problem and related results see Davis (1980) and Matiyasevich (1993). For another presentation of the problem see Cohen (1978) and Rozenberg and Salomaa (1994). The first part of Example 6.4.22 is from Rozenberg and Salomaa (1994), the second from Babai (1990); for the solution of the second see Archibald (1918). For Diophantine representation see Jones, Sato, Wada and Wiens (1976). For borderlines between decidability and undecidability of the halting problem for one-dimensional, one-tape Turing machines see Rogozhin (1996); for two-dimensional Turing machines see Priese (1979b); for undecidability of the equivalence problem for register machines see Korec (1977); for undecidability of the halting problem for register machines see Korec (1996).

For a readable presentation of Gödel's incompleteness theorem see also Rozenberg and Salomaa (1994). The limitations of formal systems for proving randomness are due to Chaitin (1987a, 1987b). See Rozenberg and Salomaa (1994) for another presentation of these results, as well as results concerning the magic number of wisdom. Two concepts of descriptional complexity based on the length of the shortest description are due to Solomonoff (1960), Kolmogorov (1965) and Chaitin (1966). For a comprehensive presentation of Kolmogorov/Chaitin complexity and its relation to randomness, as well as for proofs that new concepts of randomness agree with that defined using statistical tests, see Li Ming and Vitányi (1993) and Calude (1994).There are several names and notations used for Kolmogorov and Chaitin complexities: for example, Li and Vitányi (1993) use the terms 'plain Kolmogorov complexity' ($C(x)$) and 'prefix Kolmogorov complexity' ($K(x)$). A more precise relation between these two types of complexity given on page 403 was established by R. M. Solovay.

See Li and Vitányi (1993) for properties of universal *a priori* and algorithmic distributions, Kolmogorov characterization of regular languages, various approaches to theories inference problem and limitations on energy dissipation (also Vitányi (1995)). They also discuss how the concepts of Kolmogorov/Chaitin complexities depend on the chosen Gödel numbering of Turing machines.

7 Rewriting

INTRODUCTION

Formal grammars and, more generally, rewriting systems are as indispensable for describing and recognizing complex objects, their structure and semantics, as grammars of natural languages are for allowing us to communicate with each other. The main concepts, methods and results concerning string and graph rewriting systems are presented and analysed in this chapter. In the first part the focus is on Chomsky grammars, related automata and families of languages, especially context-free grammars and languages, which are discussed in detail. Basic properties and surprising applications of parallel rewriting systems are then demonstrated. Finally, several main techniques describing how to define rewriting in graph grammars are introduced and illustrated.

The basic idea and concepts of rewriting systems are very simple, natural and general. It is therefore no wonder that a large number of different rewriting systems has been developed and investigated. However, it is often a (very) hard task to get a deeper understanding of the potentials and the power of a particular rewriting system. The basic understanding of the concepts, methods and power of basic rewriting systems is therefore of a broader importance.

LEARNING OBJECTIVES

The aim of the chapter is to demonstrate

1. the aims, principles and power of rewriting;
2. basic rewriting systems and their applications;
3. the main relations between string rewriting systems and automata;
4. the basics of context-free grammars and languages;
5. a general method for recognizing and parsing context-free languages;
6. Lindenmayer systems and their use for graphical modelling;
7. the main types of graph grammar rewritings: node rewriting as well as edge and hyperedge rewriting.

To change your language
you must change your life.

Derek Walcott, 1965

Rewriting is a technique for defining or designing/generating complex objects by successively replacing parts of a simple initial object using a set of rules. The main advantage of rewriting systems is that they also assign a structure and derivation history to the objects they generate. This can be utilized to recognize and manipulate objects and to assign a semantics to them.

String rewriting systems, usually called grammars, have their origin in mathematical logic (due to Thue (1906) and Post (1943)), especially in the theory of formal systems. Chomsky showed in 1957 how to use formal grammars to describe and study natural languages. The fact that context-free grammars turned out to be a useful tool for describing programming languages and designing compilers was another powerful stimulus for the explosion of interest by computer scientists in rewriting systems. Biological concerns lay behind the development of so-called Lindenmayer systems. Nowadays rewriting systems for more complex objects, such as terms, arrays, graphs and pictures, are also of growing interest and importance.

Rewriting systems have also turned out to be good tools for investigating the objects they generate: that is, string and graph languages. Basic rewriting systems are closely related to the basic models of automata.

7.1 String Rewriting Systems

The basic ideas of sequential string rewriting were introduced and well formalized by semi-Thue systems.[1]

Definition 7.1.1 *A* **production system** $\mathcal{S} = \langle \Sigma, P \rangle$ *over an* **alphabet** Σ *is defined by a finite set* $P \subseteq \Sigma^* \times \Sigma^*$ *of* **productions**. *A production* $(u,v) \in P$ *is usually written as* $u \underset{P}{\longrightarrow} v$ *or* $u \longrightarrow v$ *if* P *is clear from the context.*

There are many ways of using a production system to define a rewriting relation (rule), and thereby to create a rewriting system.

A production system $\mathcal{S} = \langle \Sigma, P \rangle$ is called a **semi-Thue system** if the following **rewriting relation (rule)** $\underset{P}{\Longrightarrow}$ on Σ^* is used:

$$w_1 \underset{P}{\Longrightarrow} w_2 \quad \text{if and only if} \quad w_1 = xuy, w_2 = xvy, \text{ and } (u,v) \in P.$$

A sequence of strings $w_1, w_2, \ldots, w_n$ such that $w_i \underset{P}{\Longrightarrow} w_{i+1}$ for $1 \leq i < n$ is called a **derivation**. The transitive and reflexive closure $\overset{*}{\underset{P}{\Longrightarrow}}$ of the relation $\underset{P}{\Longrightarrow}$ is called a **derivation relation**. If $w_1 \overset{*}{\underset{P}{\Longrightarrow}} w_2$, we say that the string w_2 can be derived from w_1 by a sequence of rewriting steps defined by P. A semi-Thue system $\mathcal{S} = \langle \Sigma, P \rangle$ is called a **Thue system** if the relation P is symmetric.

Example 7.1.2 $\mathcal{S}_1 = \langle \Sigma_1, P_1 \rangle$, *where* $\Sigma_1 = \{a, b, S\}$ *and*

$$P_1: \qquad S \longrightarrow aSb, \qquad S \longrightarrow ab,$$

is a semi-Thue system.

[1] Axel Thue (1863–1922), a Norwegian mathematician.

Example 7.1.3 *$\mathcal{S}_2 = \langle \Sigma_2, P_2 \rangle$, where $\Sigma_2 = \{A,C,E,I,L,M,N,O,P,R,T,W\}$ and*

$$P_2: \begin{array}{rcl rcl rcl} EAT & \longrightarrow & AT & AT & \longrightarrow & EAT & ATE & \longrightarrow & A \\ A & \longrightarrow & ATE & LATER & \longrightarrow & LOW & LOW & \longrightarrow & LATER \\ PAN & \longrightarrow & PILLOW & PILLOW & \longrightarrow & PAN & CARP & \longrightarrow & ME \\ ME & \longrightarrow & CARP & & & & & & \end{array}$$

is a Thue system.

Two basic problems for rewriting systems $\mathcal{S} = \langle \Sigma, P \rangle$ are:

- **The word problem**: given $x, y \in \Sigma^*$, is it true that $x \overset{*}{\underset{P}{\Longrightarrow}} y$?
- **The characterization problem**: for which strings $x, y \in \Sigma^*$ does the relation $x \overset{*}{\underset{P}{\Longrightarrow}} y$ hold?

For some rewriting systems the word problem is decidable, for others not.

Example 7.1.4 *For the semi-Thue system $\mathcal{S}_1$ in Example 7.1.2 we have*

$$S \overset{*}{\Longrightarrow} w \text{ if and only if } w = a^i S b^i \text{ or } w = a^i b^i \text{ for some } i \geq 1.$$

Using this result, we can easily design an algorithm to decide the word problem for $\mathcal{S}_1$.

Exercise 7.1.5* *(a) Show that the word problem is decidable for the Thue system $\mathcal{S}_2$ in Example 7.1.3. (b) Show that if $x \overset{*}{\underset{P_2}{\Longrightarrow}} y$, then both x and y have to have the same number of occurrences of symbols from the set $\{A, W, M\}$. (This implies, for example, that MEAT$\overset{*}{\not\Longrightarrow}$CARPET – see Section 6.4.4.)*

Exercise 7.1.6 *Show that there is no infinite derivation, no matter which word we start with, in the semi-Thue system with the alphabet $\{A, B\}$ and the productions $BA \longrightarrow AAAB$, $AB \longrightarrow B$, $BBB \longrightarrow AAAA$, $AA \longrightarrow A$.*

A production system $S = \langle \Sigma, P \rangle$ is called a **Post normal system** if

$$w_1 \underset{P}{\Longrightarrow} w_2 \quad \text{if and only if} \quad w_1 = uw, w_2 = wv, \text{ and } (u \longrightarrow v) \in P.$$

In other words, in a Post normal system, in each rewriting step a prefix u is removed from a given word uw and a word v is added, provided $(u \longrightarrow v)$ is a production of S.

Exercise 7.1.7 *Design a Post normal system that generates longer and longer prefixes of the Thue ω-word.*

If the left-hand sides of all productions of a Post normal system $S = \langle \Sigma, P \rangle$, have the same length, and the right-hand side of each production depends only on the first symbol of the left-hand side, we speak of a **tag system**. Observe that a tag system can be alternatively specified by a morphism $\phi : \Sigma \rightarrow \Sigma^*$ ($a \rightarrow \phi(a), a \in \Sigma$, is again called a production), an integer k, and the rewriting rule defined by

$$w_1 \Longrightarrow w_2 \quad \text{if and only if} \quad w_1 = axv, a \in \Sigma, |ax| = k, w_2 = v\phi(a).$$

In such a case we speak of a k-**tag system**.

Example 7.1.8 *In the 2-tag system with the productions*

$$a \longrightarrow b, \qquad b \longrightarrow bc, \qquad c \longrightarrow \varepsilon$$

we have, for example, the following derivation:

$$\underbrace{bb}\,b \Longrightarrow \underbrace{bb}\,c \Longrightarrow \underbrace{cb}\,c \Longrightarrow c.$$

Example 7.1.9 *A 3-tag system with productions* $0 \longrightarrow 00$ *and* $1 \longrightarrow 1101$ *was investigated by Post in 1921. The basic problem that interested Post was to find an algorithm to decide, given an initial string* $w \in \{0,1\}^*$, *whether a derivation from* w *terminates or becomes periodic after a certain number of steps. This problem seems to be still open.*

It can be shown that both semi-Thue and tag systems are as powerful as Turing machines, in that they generate exactly recursively enumerable sets.

Exercise 7.1.10* *Show that each one-tape Turing machine can be simulated by a 2-tag system.*

The basic idea of string rewriting has been extended in several interesting and important ways. For example, the idea of **parallel string rewriting** is well captured by the so-called context-independent **Lindenmayer systems** $\mathcal{S} = \langle \Sigma, P \rangle$, where $P \subseteq \Sigma \times \Sigma^*$, and the rewriting rule is defined by

$$w_1 \Longrightarrow w_2 \text{ if and only if } w_1 = u_1 \ldots u_k, w_2 = v_1 \ldots v_k, \text{ and } u_i \Longrightarrow v_i \in P, 1 \leq i \leq k.$$

In other words, $w_1 \Longrightarrow w_2$ means that w_2 is obtained from w_1 by replacing all symbols of w_1, in parallel, using the productions from P.

Example 7.1.11 *If* $\mathcal{S}_3 = \langle \Sigma_3, P_3 \rangle$, $\Sigma_3 = \{a\}$, $P_3 = \{a \longrightarrow aa\}$, *we get a derivation*

$$a \Longrightarrow aa \Longrightarrow aaaa \Longrightarrow a^8 \Longrightarrow a^{16} \Longrightarrow \ldots;$$

that is, in n *derivation steps we obtain* a^{2^n}.

We deal with Lindenmayer systems in more detail in Section 7.4.

Another natural and powerful idea is graph rewriting systems, which have an interesting theory and various applications. In Section 7.5 we look at them in more detail. Other approaches are mentioned in the historical and bibliographical references.

7.2 Chomsky Grammars and Automata

Noam Chomsky introduced three simple modifications of semi-Thue systems, crucial for both applications and theory: a specification of a **start symbol**; a partition of the alphabet into **nonterminals** (or **variables**, they correspond to the **syntactical categories** in natural languages) and **terminals**; and, finally, consideration of only those words that can be derived from the start symbol and contain only terminal symbols. This allowed him to use such rewriting systems, usually called **grammars**, to specify and study formal languages and to investigate natural languages.

7.2.1 Chomsky Grammars

Chomsky also introduced four basic types of grammars. As we shall see, all of them are closely related to the basic types of automata.

Definition 7.2.1 *A* **phrase structure grammar**, *or* **type-0 grammar**, $G = \langle V_N, V_T, S, P\rangle$ *is specified by*

- V_N *– a finite* **alphabet of nonterminals**;
- V_T *– a finite* **alphabet of terminals** *(with* $V_N \cap V_T = \emptyset$*)*;
- S *– the* **start symbol** *from* V_n;
- $P \subseteq (V_N \cup V_T)^* V_N (V_N \cup V_T)^* \times (V_N \cup V_T)^*$ *– a finite set of* **productions**.

(Observe that the left-hand side of each production must contain at least one nonterminal.)

Definition 7.2.2 *A type-0 grammar* $G = \langle V_N, V_T, S, P\rangle$ *is called*

1. *A* **context-sensitive grammar (CSG)**, *or* **type-1 grammar**, *if* $u \longrightarrow v \in P$ *implies*
   - *either* $u = \alpha A \beta$, $v = \alpha w \beta$, $A \in V_N$, $w \in (V_N \cup V_T)^+$, $\alpha, \beta \in (V_N \cup V_T)^*$,
   - *or* $u = S$, $v = \varepsilon$, *and* S *does not occur on the right-hand side of a production in* P.
2. *A* **context-free grammar (CFG)**, *or* **type-2 grammar**, *if*
   $u \longrightarrow v \in P$ *implies* $u \in V_N$.
3. *A* **regular**, *or* **type-3, grammar** *if*
   either $P \subseteq V_N \times (V_N V_T^* \cup V_T^*)$ *or* $P \subseteq V_N \times (V_T^* V_N \cup V_T^*)$.

With each Chomsky grammar a language is associated in the following way.

Definition 7.2.3 *The language generated by a Chomsky grammar* $G = \langle V_N, V_T, S, P\rangle$ *is defined by*

$$L(G) = \{w \in V_T^* \mid S \overset{*}{\underset{P}{\Longrightarrow}} w\}.$$

Moreover, when $S \overset{*}{\underset{P}{\Longrightarrow}} x \in (V_T \cup V_N)^*$, *then* x *is said to be a* **sentential form** *of* G. *The family of languages generated by the type-i Chomsky grammars will be denoted by* $\mathcal{L}_i, i = 0,1,2,3$. *On a more general level, we assign a language* $L(s)$ *to any* $s \in (V_T \cup V_N)^*$ *defined by* $L(s) = \{w \in V_T^* \mid s \overset{*}{\underset{P}{\Longrightarrow}} w\}$.

Two Chomsky grammars are said to be equivalent if they generate the same language.

Example 7.2.4 *Consider the grammar* $G = \langle\{S,L,K,W,B,C\},\{a\},S,P\rangle$, *where* P *contains productions*

(1)	S	$\longrightarrow$	LaK,	(2)	aK	$\longrightarrow$	$WCCK$,	(3)	aW	$\longrightarrow$	WCC,
(4)	LWC	$\longrightarrow$	LaB,	(5)	LWC	$\longrightarrow$	aB,	(6)	BC	$\longrightarrow$	aB,
(7)	BK	$\longrightarrow$	K,	(8)	BK	$\longrightarrow$	ε.				

An example of a derivation in G is

$$\begin{array}{lllll} S & \Longrightarrow LaK & \Longrightarrow LWCCK & \Longrightarrow LaBCK & \Longrightarrow LaaBK \\ & \Longrightarrow LaaK & \Longrightarrow LaWCCK & \Longrightarrow LWCCCCK & \Longrightarrow aBCCCK \\ & \Longrightarrow aaBCCK & \Longrightarrow aaaBCK & \Longrightarrow aaaaBK & \Longrightarrow aaaa. \end{array}$$

We now show that $L(G) = \{a^{2^i} \mid i \geq 1\}$. The production (1) generates LaK, (2) and (3) generate for each 'a' two 'C's and, in addition, using the production (3), 'W moves left'. (4) and (6) exchange a 'C' for an 'a', and with (6) 'B moves right'. (7) allows a new application of (2). A derivation leads to a terminal word if and only if the production (5) removes 'L' and (8) removes 'BK'. Observe too that $La^iK \overset{*}{\Longrightarrow} LWC^{2i}K \overset{*}{\Longrightarrow} a^{2i}$ and $LWC^{2i}K \overset{*}{\Longrightarrow} La^{2i}K$.

Exercise 7.2.5 *Which language is generated by the grammar* $G = \langle V_N, V_T, S, P\rangle$ *with* $V_N = \{S, X, Y, Z\}$, $V_T = \{a\}$ *and the productions* $S \longrightarrow YXY$, $YX \longrightarrow YZ$, $ZX \longrightarrow XXZ$, $ZY \longrightarrow XXY$, $X \longrightarrow a$, $Y \longrightarrow \varepsilon$?

Exercise 7.2.6 *Which language is generated by the grammar* $G = \langle V_N, V_T, S, P\rangle$, *with* $V_N = \{S, A, B, L, R\}$, $V_T = \{a, b\}$ *and the productions*

$$\begin{array}{llll} S \longrightarrow LR, & L \longrightarrow LaA, & L \longrightarrow LbB, & L \longrightarrow \varepsilon, \\ AR \longrightarrow Ra, & BR \longrightarrow Rb, & R \longrightarrow \varepsilon, & Xx \longrightarrow xX, \end{array}$$

where $x \in \{a, b\}$ *and* $X \in \{A, B\}$?

Remark 7.2.7 (1) Productions of a CSG of the form $uAv \longrightarrow uwv$, $A \in V_N$, $w \neq \varepsilon$, can be interpreted as follows: the nonterminal A may be replaced, in the context (u, v), by w. This is also the reason for the attribute 'context-sensitive' for such productions and those grammars all productions of which are of such a type.

(2) Productions of a CFG have the form $A \longrightarrow w$, $A \in V_N$, and one can interpret them as follows: each occurrence of the nonterminal A may be replaced by w independently of the context of A. This is the reason for the attribute 'context-free' for such productions and grammars with such productions.

(3) Each Chomsky grammar of type-i is also of type-$(i-1)$ for $i = 1, 3$. This is not, formally, true for $i = 2$, because a context-free grammar can have rules of the type $A \longrightarrow \varepsilon$, even if A is not the start symbol. However, it is possible to show that for each type-2 grammar G one can effectively construct another type-2 grammar G_1 that is already of type-1 and such that $L(G_1) = L(G)$ – see Section 7.3.2.

(4) If all productions of a regular grammar have the form

$$A \longrightarrow u \text{ or } A \longrightarrow Bu, \text{ where } A, B \in V_T, u \in V_N^*,$$

we speak of a **left-linear grammar**. Similarly, if all productions of a regular grammar are of the form

$$A \longrightarrow u \text{ or } A \longrightarrow uB, \text{ where } A, B \in V_N, u \in V_T^*,$$

we speak of a **right-linear grammar**.

In the following we demonstrate that for $i = 0, 1, 2, 3$, type-i grammars are closely related to basic models of automata.

7.2.2 Chomsky Grammars and Turing Machines

We show first that Chomsky type-0 grammars have exactly the same generating power as Turing machines.

Theorem 7.2.8 *A language is recursively enumerable if and only if it is generated by a Chomsky grammar.*

Proof: (1) Let $L = L(G)$, where $G = \langle V_N, V_T, S, P\rangle$ is a Chomsky grammar. We describe the behaviour of a two-tape nondeterministic Turing machine $\mathcal{M}_G$ that simulates derivations of G and accepts exactly L. The first tape is used to store the input word, the second to store words α generated by G. At the start of each simulation we have $\alpha = S$. $\mathcal{M}_G$ simulates one derivation step of G by the following sequence of steps:

(a) $\mathcal{M}_G$ chooses, in a nondeterministic way, a position i in α, $1 \le i \le |\alpha|$, and a production $u \longrightarrow v \in P$.

(b) If u is a prefix of $\alpha_i \ldots \alpha_{|\alpha|}$, $\mathcal{M}_G$ replaces $\alpha_i \ldots \alpha_{i+|u|-1} = u$ by v, and starts to perform step (c); otherwise $\mathcal{M}_G$ goes to step (a).

(c) $\mathcal{M}_G$ compares the contents of the two tapes. If they are identical, $\mathcal{M}_G$ accepts w; if not, it goes to step (a).

Clearly, $\mathcal{M}_G$ accepts w if and only if G generates w.

(2) Let $L = L(\mathcal{M})$ for a one-tape Turing machine $\mathcal{M} = \langle \Sigma, \Gamma, Q, q_0, \delta\rangle$. We show how to construct a Chomsky grammar $G_{\mathcal{M}} = \langle V_N, \Sigma, q_0, P\rangle$ generating L. The productions of $G_{\mathcal{M}}$ fall into three groups.

(a) The first group contains productions that generate from q_0 the set of all words of the form $\$q_0w|w\#$, where $w \in \Sigma^*$ and $\{\$, |, \#\}$ are markers not in $\Gamma \cup Q$. (It is not difficult to design such productions, see, for example, the grammar in Exercise 7.2.6 generating the language

$$\{ww \mid w \in \{a,b\}^*\}.$$

(b) Productions of the second group are used to simulate computations of $\mathcal{M}$ on the first w. For each transition $\delta(q,a) = (q', b, \rightarrow)$ of $\mathcal{M}$, $G_{\mathcal{M}}$ contains productions

$$qac \longrightarrow bq'c \text{ for all } c \in \Gamma \quad \text{and} \quad qa| \longrightarrow bq' \sqcup |.$$

(The last production is for the case that $\sqcup$, standing for the blank on the tape, is in Γ.) For each transition $\delta(q,a) = (q', b, \leftarrow)$, $G_{\mathcal{M}}$ contains productions

$$cqa \longrightarrow q'cb \text{ for each } c \in \Gamma \quad \text{and} \quad \$qa \longrightarrow \$q' \sqcup b.$$

Finally, for each transition $\delta(q,a) = (q', b, \downarrow)$ there is a production $qa \longrightarrow q'b$.

(c) Productions of the third group transform each word '$\$w_1qw_2|w\#$', $w_1, w_2 \in \Gamma^*, q = ACCEPT\}$ into the word w. (If $\mathcal{M}$ does not halt for a $w \in \Sigma^*$ or does not accept w, $G_{\mathcal{M}}$ does not generate any word from $\$q_0w|w\#$.) The generation of w from $\$w_1qw_2|w\#$ can be done, for example, by the the following productions, where $\{F, F_1, F_2\}$ are new nonterminals:

$$\begin{array}{rclcrcl}
ACCEPT & \longrightarrow & F, & & aF & \longrightarrow & Fa, a \in \Gamma, \\
\$F & \longrightarrow & F_1 & & F_1a & \longrightarrow & F_1, a \in \Gamma, \\
F_1| & \longrightarrow & F_2, & & F_2a & \longrightarrow & aF_2, a \in \Sigma, \\
F_2\# & \longrightarrow & \sqcup & & & &
\end{array}$$

□

Chomsky type-0 grammars may have many nonterminals and complicated productions. It is therefore natural to ask whether these are all necessary. The following theorem summarizes several such results, and shows that not all available means are needed, surprisingly.

Theorem 7.2.9 *(1) For every Chomsky grammar an equivalent Chomsky grammar with only two nonterminals can be constructed effectively.*

(2) Chomsky grammars with only one nonterminal generate a proper subset of recursively enumerable languages.

(3) For every Chomsky grammar an equivalent Chomsky grammar with only one noncontext-free production can be constructed.

7.2.3 Context-sensitive Grammars and Linearly Bounded Automata

The basic idea of context-sensitive grammars is both simple and beautiful and has a good linguistic motivation: a production $uAv \longrightarrow uwv$ replaces the nonterminal A by w in the context (u,v). (Indeed, in natural languages the meaning of a part of a sentence may depend on the context.)

The **monotonic Chomsky grammars** have the same generative power as the context-sensitive grammars. Their main advantage is that it is often easier to design a monotonic than a context-sensitive grammar to generate a given language.

Definition 7.2.10 *A Chomsky grammar $G = \langle V_N, V_T, S, P\rangle$ is called monotonic if, for each production $u \longrightarrow v$ in P, either $|u| \leq |v|$ or $u = S, v = \varepsilon$, and S does not occur on the right-hand side of any production. (The last condition is to allow for generation of the empty word, too.)*

Theorem 7.2.11 *A language is generated by a context-sensitive grammar if and only if it is generated by a monotonic Chomsky grammar.*

Proof: Each context-sensitive grammar is monotonic and therefore, in order to prove the theorem, let us assume that we have a monotonic grammar G. At first we transform G into an equivalent grammar that has only nonterminals on the left-hand sides of its productions. This is easy. For each terminal a we take a new nonterminal X_a, add the production $X_a \longrightarrow a$, and replace a by X_a on the left-hand sides of all productions. Now it is enough to show that to each production of a monotonic Chomsky grammar $G = \langle V_N, V_T, S, P\rangle$, with only nonterminals on its left-hand side, there is an equivalent context-sensitive Chomsky grammar. In order to do this, let us assume a fixed ordering of the productions of P, and consider an extended set of nonterminals

$$V' = \left\{ \binom{A}{k} \mid A \in V_T \cup V_N,\ 1 \leq k \leq |P| \right\} \cup V_N,$$

where $\binom{A}{i}$ denotes a pair of symbols.

The following set of context-sensitive productions corresponds to the kth production $A_1 \ldots A_n \longrightarrow B_1 \ldots B_m$, $n \leq m$:

$$\begin{array}{rcl}
A_1 \ldots A_n & \longrightarrow & \binom{A_1}{k} A_2 \ldots A_n \\
\binom{A_1}{k} A_2 \ldots A_n & \longrightarrow & \binom{A_1}{k}\binom{A_2}{k} \ldots A_n \\
\cdots\cdots & \cdots & \cdots\cdots \\
\binom{A_1}{k}\binom{A_2}{k} \ldots \binom{A_{n-1}}{k} A_n & \longrightarrow & \binom{A_1}{k} \ldots \binom{A_n}{k}\binom{B_{n+1}}{k} \ldots \binom{B_m}{k} \\
\binom{A_1}{k} \ldots \binom{A_n}{k}\binom{B_{n+1}}{k} \ldots \binom{B_m}{k} & \longrightarrow & B_1 \binom{A_2}{k} \ldots \binom{A_n}{k}\binom{B_{n+1}}{k} \ldots \binom{B_m}{k} \\
\cdots\cdots & \cdots & \cdots\cdots \\
B_1 B_2 \ldots B_{m-1} \binom{B_m}{k} & \longrightarrow & B_1 B_2 \ldots B_m.
\end{array}$$

In this way, to any two different productions of P, two different sets of context-sensitive productions correspond such that productions of these two sets contain different new nonterminals. As a consequence, if all the rules of G are replaced by the sets of context-sensitive productions designed as shown above, then we get a set of context-sensitive productions generating the same language as G. □

Example 7.2.12 *Consider the grammar G with $V_N = \{S,X,Y\}$, $V_T = \{a,b,c\}$, the start symbol S and the rules*

$$\begin{array}{llllll} (1)\ S & \longrightarrow & aSX, & (2)\ YX & \longrightarrow & bYc, & (3)\ Y \longrightarrow bc, \\ S & \longrightarrow & aY, & cX & \longrightarrow & Xc. \end{array}$$

We show now that $L(G) \subseteq \{a^n b^n c^n \mid n \geq 1\}$. Indeed, with productions (1) we derive $S \stackrel{*}{\Longrightarrow} a^n Y X^{n-1}$ for each $n > 1$. By induction we can prove that for each $1 \leq i < n$

$$YX^{n-1} \stackrel{*}{\Longrightarrow} b^i Y c^i X^{n-i-1},$$

and using the productions (3) we get that for each $n \in \mathbf{N}$

$$S \stackrel{*}{\Longrightarrow} a^n b^{n-1} Y c^{n-1} \Longrightarrow a^n b^n c^n.$$

Hence $L(G) \subseteq \{a^n b^n c^n \mid n \geq 1\}$.

Exercise 7.2.13* *Show that the grammar in Example 7.2.12 generates precisely the language $\{a^n b^n c^n \mid n \geq 1\}$.*

Exercise 7.2.14 *Design a monotonic grammar generating the languages (a) $\{w \mid w \in \{a,b\}^*, \#_a w = \#_b w\}$; (b) $\{a^n b^{2n} a^n \mid n \geq 1\}$; (c) $\{a^p \mid p \text{ is a prime}\}$.*

The following relation between context-sensitive grammars and linearly bounded automata (see Section 3.8.5) justifies the use of the attribute 'context-sensitive' for languages generated by LBA.

Theorem 7.2.15 *Context-sensitive grammars generate exactly those languages which linearly bounded automata accept.*

Proof: The proof of this theorem is similar to that of Theorem 7.2.8, and therefore we concentrate on the points where the differences lie.

Let G be a monotonic grammar. As in Theorem 7.2.8 we design a Turing machine $\mathcal{M}_G$ that simulates derivations of G. However, instead of two tapes, as in the proof of Theorem 7.2.8, $\mathcal{M}_G$ uses only one tape, but with two tracks. In addition, $\mathcal{M}_G$ checks, each time a production should be applied, whether the newly created word is longer than the input word w (stored on the first track). If this is the case, such a rewriting is not performed. Here we are making use of the fact that in a monotonic grammar a rewriting never shortens a sentential form. It is now easy to see that $\mathcal{M}_G$ can be changed in such a way that its head never gets outside the tape squares occupied by the input word, and therefore it is actually a linearly bounded automaton.

Similarly, we are able to prove that we can construct for each LBA an equivalent monotonic grammar by a modification of the proof of Theorem 7.2.8, but a special trick has to be used to ensure that the resulting grammar is monotonic.

Let $\mathcal{A} = \langle \Sigma, Q, q_0, Q_F, \spadesuit, \#, \delta \rangle$ be an LBA. The productions of the equivalent monotonic grammar fall into three groups.

Productions of the first group have the form

$$S \longrightarrow A \begin{bmatrix} x \\ x \\ \# \\ - \end{bmatrix}, \; A \longrightarrow A \begin{bmatrix} x \\ x \\ - \\ - \end{bmatrix}, \; A \longrightarrow \begin{bmatrix} x \\ x \\ \spadesuit \\ q_0 \end{bmatrix},$$

where $x \in \Sigma$, and each 4-tuple is considered to be a new nonterminal. These productions generate the following representation of 'a two track-tape', with the initial content $w = w_1 \ldots w_n, w_i \in \Sigma$:

$$\begin{bmatrix} w_1 \\ w_1 \\ \spadesuit \\ q_0 \end{bmatrix} \begin{bmatrix} w_2 \\ w_2 \\ - \\ - \end{bmatrix} \cdots \begin{bmatrix} w_n \\ w_n \\ \# \\ - \end{bmatrix}.$$

Productions of the second group, which are now easy to design, simulate $\mathcal{A}$ on the 'first track'. For each transition of $\mathcal{A}$ there is again a new set of productions.

Finally, productions of the third group transform each nonterminal word with the accepting state into the terminal word that is on the 'second track'. These productions can also be designed in a quite straightforward way. □

The family of context-sensitive languages contains practically all the languages one encounters in computing. The following theorem shows the relation between context-sensitive and recursive languages.

Theorem 7.2.16 *Each context-sensitive language is recursive. On the other hand, there are recursive languages that are not context-sensitive.*

Proof: Recursivity of context-sensitive languages follows from Theorem 3.8.27. In order to define a recursive language that is not context-sensitive, let $G_0, G_1, \ldots$ be a strict enumeration of encodings of all monotonic grammars in $\{0,1\}^*$. In addition, let $f : \{0,1\}^* \rightarrow \mathbf{N}$ be a computable bijection. (For example, $f(w) = i$ if and only if w is the ith word in the strict ordering.)

The language $L_0 = \{w \in \{0,1\}^* \,|\, w \notin L(G_{f(w)})\}$ is decidable. Indeed, for a given w one computes $f(w)$, designs $G_{f(w)}$, and tests membership of w in $L(G_{f(w)})$.

The diagonalization method will now be used to show that L_0 is not a context-sensitive language. Indeed, assuming that L_0 is context-sensitive, there must exist a monotonic grammar G_{n_0} such that $L_0 = L(G_{n_0})$.

Now let w_0 be such that $f(w_0) = n_0$. A contradiction can be derived as follows.

If $w_0 \in L_0$, then, according to the definition of L_0, $w_0 \notin L(G_{n_0})$ and therefore (by the assumption) $w_0 \notin L_0$. If $w_0 \notin L_0$, then, according to the definition of $L_0, w_0 \in L(G_{n_0})$, and therefore (again by the assumption) $w_0 \in L_0$. □

On the other hand, the following theorem shows that the difference between recursively enumerable and context-sensitive languages is actually very subtle.

Lemma 7.2.17 *If $L \subseteq \Sigma^*$ is a recursively enumerable language and $\$, \#$ are symbols not in Σ, then there is a context-sensitive language L_1 such that*

1. $L_1 \subseteq \{\#^i\$w \mid w \in L,\ i \geq 0\}$;
2. *for each* $w \in L$ *there is an* $i \geq 0$ *such that* $\#^i\$w \in L_1$.

Proof: Let $L = L(G)$, $G = \langle V_N, \Sigma, S, P\rangle$, and $\$, \#$ be symbols not in Σ. We introduce two new variables $\{S_0, Y\}$ and define three sets of productions:

$$P_1 = \{u \longrightarrow v \mid u \longrightarrow v \in P,\ |u| \leq |v|\};$$
$$P_2 = \{u \longrightarrow Y^i v \mid u \longrightarrow v \in P,\ |u| > |v|,\ i = |v| - |u|\};$$
$$P_3 = \{S_0 \longrightarrow \$S,\ \$Y \longrightarrow \#\$\} \cup \{\alpha Y \rightarrow Y\alpha,\ \alpha \in V_N \cup \Sigma\}.$$

The grammar

$$G_1 = \langle V_N \cup \{S_0, Y\},\ \Sigma \cup \{\$, \#\}, S_0, P_1 \cup P_2 \cup P_3\rangle$$

is monotonic, and the language $L(G)$ satisfies both conditions of the theorem. □

As a corollary we get the following theorem.

Theorem 7.2.18 *For each recursively enumerable language L there is a context-sensitive language* L_1 *and a homomorphism h such that* $L = h(L_1)$.

Proof: Take $h(\$) = \varepsilon$, $h(\#) = \varepsilon$ and $h(a) = a$ for all $a \in \Sigma$. □

7.2.4 Regular Grammars and Finite Automata

In order to show relations between regular grammars and finite automata, we make use of the fact that the family of regular languages is closed under the operation of reversal.

Theorem 7.2.19 *Regular grammars generate exactly those languages which finite automata accept.*

Proof: (1) Let $G = \langle V_N, V_T, S, P\rangle$ be a right-linear grammar, that is, a grammar with productions of the form

$$C \longrightarrow w \quad \text{or} \quad C \longrightarrow wB, \quad B \in V_N, w \in V_T^*.$$

We design a transition system (see Section 3.8.1), $\mathcal{A} = \langle V_N \cup \{E\}, V_T, S, \{E\}, \delta\rangle$, with a new state $E \notin V_N \cup V_T$, and with the transition relation

$$E \in \delta(C, w) \quad \text{if and only if } C \longrightarrow w \in P;$$
$$B \in \delta(C, w) \quad \text{if and only if } C \longrightarrow wB \in P.$$

By induction it is straightforward to show that $L(G) = L(\mathcal{A})$.

(2) Now let $G = \langle V_N, V_T, S, P\rangle$ be a left-linear grammar, that is, a grammar with productions of the form $C \longrightarrow w$ and $C \longrightarrow Bw$, where $C, B \in V_N$, $w \in V_T^*$. Then $G^R = \langle V_N, V_T, S, P^R\rangle$ with $P^R = \{u \longrightarrow v \mid u \longrightarrow v^R \in P\}$ is a right-linear grammar. According to (1), the language $L(G^R)$ is regular. Since $L(G) = L(G^R)^R$ and the family of regular languages is closed under reversal, the language $L(G)$ is also regular.

(3) If $\mathcal{A} = \langle Q, \Sigma, q_0, Q_F, \delta\rangle$ is a DFA, then the grammar $G = \langle Q, \Sigma, q_0, P\rangle$ with productions

$$q \longrightarrow w \in P \quad \text{if} \quad w \in \Sigma, \delta(q, w) \in Q_F;$$
$$q \longrightarrow wq_i \in P \quad \text{if} \quad w \in \Sigma, \delta(q, w) = q_i,$$
$$q_0 \longrightarrow \varepsilon \quad \text{if} \quad q_0 \in Q_F$$

is right-linear. Clearly, $q_0 \stackrel{*}{\Longrightarrow} w'q_i$, $q_i \in Q$, if and only if $\delta(q_0, w') = q_i$, and therefore $L(G) = L(\mathcal{A})$. □

Exercise 7.2.20 *Design (a) a right-linear grammar generating the language* $\{a^i b^j \mid i,j \geq 0\}$*; (b) a left-linear grammar generating the language* $L \subset \{0,1\}^*$ *consisting of words that are normal forms of the Fibonacci representations of integers. (c) Perform in detail the induction proof mentioned in part (1) of Theorem 7.2.19.*

7.3 Context-free Grammars and Languages

There are several reasons why context-free grammars are of special interest. From a practical point of view, they are closely related to the basic techniques of description of the syntax of programming languages and to translation methods. The corresponding pushdown automata are also closely related to basic methods of handling recursions. In addition, context-free grammars are of interest for describing natural languages. From the theoretical point of view, the corresponding family of context-free languages plays an important role in formal language theory – next to the family of regular languages.

7.3.1 Basic Concepts

Three rewriting (or derivation) relations are considered for context-free grammars $G = \langle V_N, V_T, S, P\rangle$.

Rewriting (derivation) relation $\underset{P}{\Longrightarrow}$:

$$w_1 \underset{P}{\Longrightarrow} w_2 \quad \text{if and only if} \quad w_1 = uAv, w_2 = uwv, A \longrightarrow w \in P.$$

Left-most rewriting (derivation) relation $\underset{P}{\Longrightarrow}_L$:

$$w_1 \underset{P}{\Longrightarrow}_L w_2 \quad \text{if and only if} \quad w_1 = uAv, w_2 = uwv, A \longrightarrow w \in P, u \in V_T^*.$$

Right-most rewriting (derivation) relation $\underset{P}{\Longrightarrow}_R$:

$$w_1 \underset{P}{\Longrightarrow}_R w_2 \quad \text{if and only if} \quad w_1 = uAv, w_2 = uwv, A \longrightarrow w \in P, v \in V_T^*.$$

A **derivation** in G is a sequence of words from $(V_N \cup V_T)^*$

$$w_1, w_2, \ldots, w_k$$

such that $w_i \underset{P}{\Longrightarrow} w_{i+1}$ for $1 \leq i < k$. If $w_i \underset{P}{\Longrightarrow}_L w_{i+1}$ ($w_i \underset{P}{\Longrightarrow}_R w_{i+1}$) always holds, we speak of a left-most (right-most) derivation. In each step of a derivation a nonterminal A is replaced by a production $A \longrightarrow u$ from P. In the case of the left-most (right-most) derivation, always the left-most (right-most) nonterminal is rewritten.

A language L is called a **context-free language (CFL)** if there is a CFG generating L.

Each derivation assigns a **derivation tree** to the string it derives (see the figures on pages 429 and 430). The internal nodes of such a tree are labelled by nonterminals, leaves by terminals or ε. If an internal node is labelled by a nonterminal A, and its children by $x_1, \ldots, x_k$, counting from the left, then $A \longrightarrow x_1 \ldots x_k$ has to be a production of the grammar.

Now we present two examples of context-free grammars. In so doing, we describe a CFG, as usual, by a list of productions, with the start symbol on the left-hand side of the first production. In addition, to describe a set of productions

$$A \longrightarrow \alpha_1, A \longrightarrow \alpha_2, \ldots, A \longrightarrow \alpha_k,$$

with the same symbol on the left-hand side, we use, as usual, the following concise description:

$$A \longrightarrow \alpha_1 \,|\, \alpha_2 \,|\, \ldots \,|\, \alpha_k.$$

Example 7.3.1 (Natural language description) *The original motivation behind introducing CFG was to describe derivations and structures of sentences of natural languages with such productions as, for example,*

⟨sentence⟩ → ⟨noun phrase⟩ ⟨verb phrase⟩,	*⟨article⟩ → The, the*
⟨noun phrase⟩ → ⟨article⟩ ⟨noun⟩,	*⟨noun⟩ → eavesdropper | message,*
⟨verb phrase⟩ → ⟨verb⟩ ⟨noun phrase⟩,	*⟨verb⟩ → decrypted,*

where the syntactical categories of the grammar (nonterminals) are denoted by words between the symbols '⟨' and '⟩' and words like 'eavesdropper' are single terminals. An example of a derivation tree:

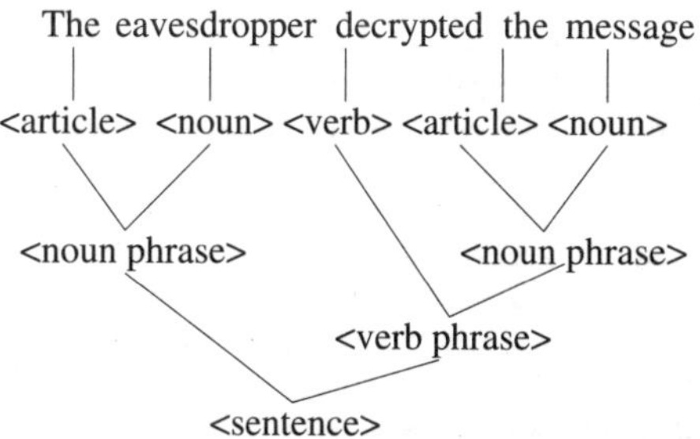

In spite of the fact that context-free grammars are not powerful enough to describe natural languages in a completely satisfactory way, they, and their various modifications, play an important role in (computational) linguistics.

The use of CFG to describe programming and other formal languages has been much more successful. With CFG one can significantly simplify descriptions of the syntax of programming languages. Moreover, CFG allowed the development of a successful theory and practice of compilation. The reason behind this is to a large extent the natural way in which many constructs of programming languages can be described by CFG.

Example 7.3.2 (Programming language description) *The basic arithmetical expressions can be described, for example, using productions of the form*

⟨expression⟩	⟶	*⟨expression⟩ ⟨ ± ⟩ ⟨expression⟩*
⟨expression⟩	⟶	*⟨expression 1⟩*
⟨expression 1⟩	⟶	*⟨expression 1⟩ ⟨mult⟩ ⟨expression 1⟩*
⟨expression 1⟩	⟶	*(⟨expression⟩)*
⟨±⟩	⟶	+ | −
⟨mult⟩	⟶	× | /
⟨expression1⟩	→	$a \,|\, b \,|\, c \,|\, \ldots \,|\, y \,|\, z$

and they can be used to derive, for example, $a\,/\,b + c$*, as in Figure 7.1.*

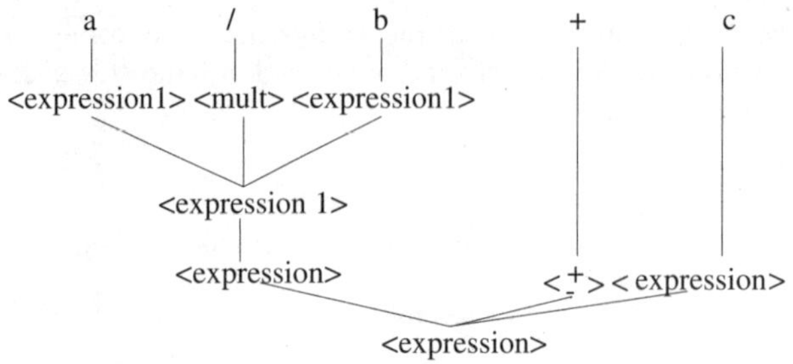

Figure 7.1 A derivation tree

Exercise 7.3.3 *Design CFG generating (a) the language of all Boolean expressions; (b) the language of Lisp expressions; (c)* $\{a^ib^{2i} \mid i,j \geq 1\}$*; (d)* $\{ww^R \mid w \in \{0,1\}$*; (e)* $\{a^ib^jc^k \mid i \neq j \text{ or } j \neq k\}$.

It can happen that a word $w \in L(G)$ has two different derivations in a CFG G, but that the corresponding derivation trees are identical. For example, for the grammar with two productions, $S \longrightarrow SS \mid ab$, we have the following two derivations of the string *abab*:

$$d_1: \qquad S \Longrightarrow SS \Longrightarrow abS \Longrightarrow abab,$$

$$d_2: \qquad S \Longrightarrow SS \Longrightarrow Sab \Longrightarrow abab,$$

both of which correspond to the derivation tree

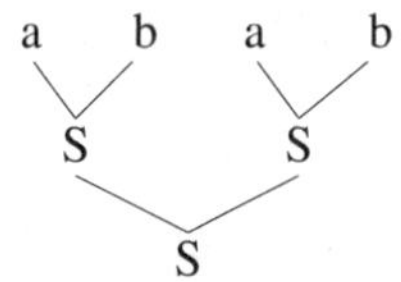

Exercise 7.3.4 *Show that there is a bijection between derivation trees and left-most derivations (right-most derivations).*

It can also happen that a word $w \in L(G)$ has two derivations in G such that the corresponding derivation trees are different. For example, in the CFG with productions $S \longrightarrow Sa \mid a \mid aa$, the word *aaa* has two derivations that correspond to the derivation trees in Figure 7.2.

A CFG G with the property that some word $w \in L(G)$ has two different derivation trees is called **ambiguous**. A context-free language is called (inherently) ambiguous if each context-free grammar for L is ambiguous. For example, the language

$$L = \{a^ib^ia^j \mid i,j \geq 1\} \cup \{a^ib^ja^j \mid i,j \geq 1\}$$

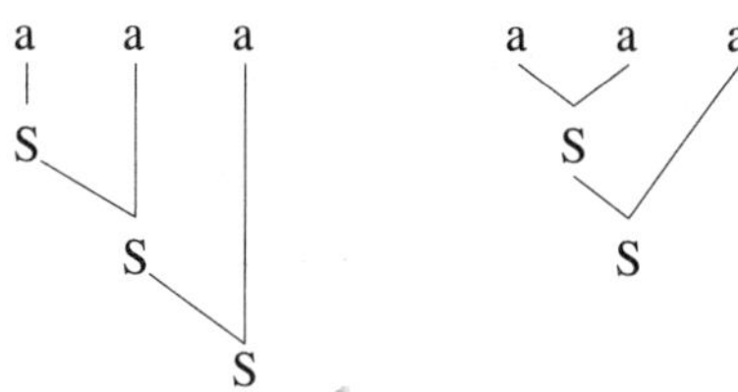

Figure 7.2 Two different derivation trees for the same string

is ambiguous. It can be shown that in each CFG for L some words of the form $a^k b^k a^k$ have two essentially different derivation trees.

Exercise 7.3.5 *Which of the following CFG is ambiguous: (a)* $S \longrightarrow a \,|\, abSb \,|\, aAb$, $A \longrightarrow bS \,|\, aAAb$; *(b)* $S \longrightarrow aSbc \,|\, c \,|\, bA$, $A \longrightarrow bA \,|\, a$; *(c)* $S \longrightarrow aS \,|\, Sa \,|\, bAb$, $A \longrightarrow aAb \,|\, acb$?

Exercise 7.3.6 *Consider a CFG G with the productions*

$$S \longrightarrow bA \,|\, aB, \; A \longrightarrow a \,|\, aS \,|\, bAA, \; B \longrightarrow b \,|\, bS \,|\, aBB.$$

Show that G is ambiguous, but L(G) is not.

Even in the case of context-free grammars it is in general not easy to show which language is generated by a given CFG, or to design a CFG generating a given language.

Example 7.3.7 *The CFG* $G = \langle V_N, V_T, S, P \rangle$ *with the productions*

$$S \longrightarrow aB \,|\, bA, \quad A \longrightarrow bAA \,|\, aS \,|\, a, \quad B \longrightarrow aBB \,|\, bS \,|\, b$$

generates the language

$$L(G) = \{w \,|\, w \in \{a,b\}^+, w \text{ contains as many } a\text{'s as } b\text{'s}\}.$$

In order to show this, it is sufficient to prove, for example by induction on the length of w, which is straightforward, the following assertions:

1. $S \stackrel{*}{\Longrightarrow} w$ *if and only if* $\#_a w = \#_b w$;
2. $A \stackrel{*}{\Longrightarrow} w$ *if and only if* $\#_a w = \#_b w + 1$;
3. $B \stackrel{*}{\Longrightarrow} w$ *if and only if* $\#_b w = \#_a w + 1$.

(In fact, it suffices to prove the first claim, but it is helpful to show the assertions 2 and 3 to get 1.)

Some languages are context-free even though one would not expect them to be. For example, the set of all satisfiable Boolean formulas is **NP**-complete (and therefore no polynomial time recognizing algorithm seems to exist for them), but, as follows from the next example, the set of all satisfiable Boolean formulas over a fixed set of variables is context-free (and, as discussed later, can be recognized in linear time).

Example 7.3.8 *Denote by $\mathcal{F}_n$ the set of Boolean formulas over the variables $x_1,\ldots,x_n$ and Boolean operations $\vee$ and $\neg$. Moreover, denote by $\mathcal{A}_n$ the set of all assignments $\alpha:\{x_1,\ldots,x_n\}\rightarrow\{0,1\}$. For $\alpha\in\mathcal{A}_n$ and $F\in\mathcal{F}_n$, let $\alpha(F)$ denote the value of F at the assignment α. The set of all tautologies over the variables $\{x_1,\ldots,x_n\}$ is defined by $\mathcal{T}_n=\{F\in\mathcal{F}_n\,|\,\forall\alpha\in\mathcal{A}_n,\alpha(F)=1\}$. We show that $\mathcal{T}_n$ is a context-free language.*

Let $G_n=\langle V_N^n,V_T^n,S_{\mathcal{A}_n},P_n\rangle$ be a CFG such that $V_N^n=\{S_A\,|\,A\subseteq\mathcal{A}_n\}$ is the set of nonterminals, one for each subset of $\mathcal{A}_n$; $V_T^n=\{x_1,\ldots,x_n\}\cup\{\vee,\neg,(,)\}$ and P_n be the set of productions

$$\begin{array}{rcllr} S_A & \longrightarrow & \neg(S_{\mathcal{A}_n-A}), & \text{if } A\in\mathcal{A}_n; & (i)\\ S_{A\vee B} & \longrightarrow & S_A\vee S_B, & \text{if } A,B\in\mathcal{A}_n; & (ii)\\ S_{\{\alpha|\alpha(x)=1\}} & \longrightarrow & x, & \text{if } x\in\{x_1,\ldots,x_n\}. & (iii)\end{array}$$

In order to show that $L(G_n)=\mathcal{T}_n$, it is sufficient to prove (which can be done in a straightforward way by induction) that if $A\in\mathcal{A}_n$, then $S_A\stackrel{*}{\Longrightarrow}F$ if and only if $A=\{\alpha\,|\,\alpha(F)=1\}$. Let $A\in\mathcal{A}_n$ and $S_A\stackrel{*}{\Longrightarrow}F$. Three cases for ϕ are possible. If $F=x\in\{x_1,\ldots,x_n\}$, then x can be derived only by rule (iii). If $S_A\Rightarrow\neg(S_B)\stackrel{*}{\Longrightarrow}F$, then $F=\neg(F')$, and, by the induction hypothesis, $B=\{\alpha\,|\,\alpha(F')=0\}$, and therefore, by (i), $S_B\stackrel{*}{\Longrightarrow}F'$ and $A=\mathcal{A}_n-B=\{\alpha\,|\,\alpha(\neg(F'))=1\}$. The last case to consider is that $S_A\Rightarrow S_B\vee S_C\stackrel{*}{\Longrightarrow}F$. Then $F=F_1\vee F_2$ and $A=B\cup C$. By (ii), $B=\{\beta\,|\,\beta(F_1)=1\}$, $C=\{\gamma\,|\,\gamma(F_2)=1\}$, and therefore $A=\{\alpha\,|\,\alpha(F_1\cup F_2)=1\}$.

In a similar way we can prove that if $A=\{\alpha\,|\,\alpha(F)=1\}$, then $S_A\stackrel{*}{\Longrightarrow}F$, and from that $L(G_n)=\mathcal{T}_n$ follows.

Exercise 7.3.9 *Show that the language of all satisfiable Boolean formulas over a fixed set of nonterminals is context-free.*

Exercise 7.3.10 *Design a CFG generating the language $\{w\in\{0,1\}^*\,|\,w$ contains three times more 1s than 0s$\}$.*

7.3.2 Normal Forms

In many cases it is desirable that a CFG should have a 'nice form'. The following three normal forms for CFG are of such a type.

Definition 7.3.11 *Let $G=\langle V_N,V_T,S,P\rangle$ be a CFG.*
G is in the **reduced normal form** *if the following conditions are satisfied:*

1. *Each nonterminal of G occurs in a derivation of G from the start symbol, and each nonterminal generates a terminal word.*
2. *No production has the form $A\longrightarrow B$, $B\in V_N$.*
3. *If $\varepsilon\notin L(G)$, then G has no production of the form $A\longrightarrow\varepsilon$ (no ε-production), and if $\varepsilon\in L(G)$, then $S\longrightarrow\varepsilon$ is the only ε-production.*

G is in the **Chomsky normal form** *if each production has either the form $A\longrightarrow BC$ or $A\longrightarrow u$, where $B,C\in V_N$, $u\in V_T^*$, or the form $S\longrightarrow\varepsilon$ (and S not occurring on the right-hand side of any other production).*

G is in the **Greibach normal form** *if each production has either the form* $A \longrightarrow a\alpha$, $a \in V_T$, $\alpha \in V_N^*$, *or the form* $S \longrightarrow \varepsilon$ *(and S not occurring on the right-hand side of any other production).*

Theorem 7.3.12 *(1) For each CFG one can construct an equivalent reduced CFG.*

(2) For each CFG one can construct an equivalent CFG in the Chomsky normal form and an equivalent CFG in the Greibach normal form.

Proof: Assertion (1) is easy to verify. For example, it is sufficient to use the results of the following exercise.

Exercise 7.3.13 *Let* $G = \langle V_N, V_T, S, P\rangle$ *be a CFG and* $n = |V_T \cup V_N|$. *(a) Consider the recurrence* $X_0 = \{A \,|\, A \in V_N, \exists (A \longrightarrow \alpha) \in P, \alpha \in V_T^*\}$ *and, for* $i > 0$, $X_i = \{A \,|\, A \in V_N, \exists (A \longrightarrow \alpha) \in P, \alpha \in (V_T \cup X_{i-1})^*\}$. *Show that* $A \in X_n$ *if and only if* $A \stackrel{*}{\Longrightarrow} w$ *for some* $w \in V_T^*$. *(b) Consider the recurrence* $Y_0 = \{S\}$ *and, for* $i > 0$, $Y_i = Y_{i-1} \cup \{A \,|\, A \in V_N,\ \exists (B \longrightarrow uAv) \in P,\ B \in Y_{i-1}\}$.
Show that $A \in Y_n$ *if and only if there are* $u', v' \in (V_T \cup V_N)^*$ *such that* $S \stackrel{*}{\Longrightarrow} u'Av'$.
(c) Consider the recurrence $Z_0 = \{A \,|\, (A \longrightarrow \varepsilon) \in P\}$ *and, for* $i > 0$ $Z_i = \{A \,|\, \exists (A \longrightarrow \alpha) \in P, \alpha \in Z_{i-1}^*\}$.
Show that $A \in Z_n$ *if and only if* $A \stackrel{*}{\Longrightarrow} \varepsilon$.

We show now how to design a CFG G' in the Chomsky normal form equivalent to a given reduced CFG $G = \langle V_N, V_T, S, P\rangle$.

For each terminal c let X_c be a new nonterminal. G' is constructed in two phases.

1. In each production $A \longrightarrow \alpha$, $|\alpha| \geq 2$, each terminal c is replaced by X_c, and all productions $X_c \longrightarrow c$, $c \in V_T$, are added into the set of productions.

2. Each production $A \longrightarrow B_1 \ldots B_m$, $m \geq 3$, is replaced by the following set of productions:

$$A \longrightarrow B_1D_1, D_1 \longrightarrow B_2D_2, \ldots, D_{m-3} \longrightarrow B_{m-2}D_{m-2}, D_{m-2} \longrightarrow B_{m-1}B_m,$$

   where $\{D_1, \ldots, D_{m-2}\}$ is, for each production, a new set of nonterminals. The resulting CFG is in the Chomsky normal form, and evidently equivalent to G.

Transformation of a CFG into the Greibach normal form is more involved (see references). □

Example 7.3.14 (Construction of a Chomsky normal form) *For a CFG with the productions* $S \longrightarrow aSbbSa \,|\, ab$, *we get, after the first step,*

$$S \longrightarrow X_aSX_bX_bSX_a \,|\, X_aX_b, \qquad X_a \longrightarrow a, \qquad X_b \longrightarrow b,$$

and after step 2,

$$S \longrightarrow X_aD_1, \quad D_1 \longrightarrow SD_2, \quad D_2, \longrightarrow X_bD_3, \quad D_3 \longrightarrow X_bD_4,$$
$$D_4 \longrightarrow SX_a, \quad X_a \longrightarrow a, \qquad X_b \longrightarrow b.$$

Exercise 7.3.15 *Design a CFG in the Chomsky normal form equivalent to the grammar in Example 7.3.7. (Observe that this grammar is already in the Greibach normal form.)*

Transformation of a CFG into a normal form not only takes time but usually leads to an increase in size. In order to specify quantitatively how big such an increase can be in the worst case, let us define the size of a CFG G as

$$\text{Size}(G) = \sum_{A \to u \in P} (|u| + 2).$$

It can be shown that for each reduced CFG G there exists an equivalent CFG G'' in the Chomsky normal form such that $\text{Size}(G') \leq 7\text{Size}(G)$ and an equivalent CFG G'' in the Greibach normal form such that $\text{Size}(G'') = \mathcal{O}(\text{Size}^3(G))$. It is not clear whether the upper bound is tight, but for some CFG G'' which are in the Greibach normal form and equivalent to G it holds that $\text{Size}(G'') \geq \text{Size}^2(G)$.

Exercise 7.3.16 *Show that for each CFG G there is a CFG G' in the Chomsky normal form such that $Size(G') \leq 7Size(G)$.*

In the case of type-0 grammars it has been possible to show that just two nonterminals are sufficient to generate all recursively enumerable languages. It is therefore natural to ask whether all the available resources of CFG – namely, potentially infinite pools of nonterminals and productions – are really necessary to generate all CFL. For example, is it not enough to consider only CFG with a fixed number of nonterminals or productions? No, as the following theorem says.

Theorem 7.3.17 *For every integer $n > 1$ there is a CFL $L_n \subseteq \{a,b\}^*$ ($L'_n \subseteq \{a,b\}^*$) such that L_n (L'_n) can be generated by a CFG with n nonterminals (productions) but not by a CFG with $n-1$ nonterminals (productions).*

7.3.3 Context-free Grammars and Pushdown Automata

Historically, pushdown automata (PDA) played an important role in the development of programming and especially compiling techniques. Nowadays they are of broader importance for computing.

Informally, a PDA is an automaton with finite control, a (potentially infinite) input tape, a potentially infinite pushdown tape, an input tape head (read-only) and a pushdown head (see Figure 7.3). The input tape head may move only to the right. The pushdown tape is a 'first-in, last-out' list. The pushdown head can read only the top-most symbol of the pushdown tape and can write only on the top of the pushdown tape. More formally:

Definition 7.3.18 *A* **(nondeterministic) pushdown automaton (PDA or NPDA)** $\mathcal{A} = \langle Q, \Sigma, \Gamma, q_0, Q_F, \gamma_0, \delta \rangle$ *has a set of* **states** Q, *with the* **initial state** q_0 *and a subset* Q_F *of* **final states**, *an* **input alphabet** Σ, *a* **pushdown alphabet** Γ, *with* $\gamma_0 \in \Gamma$ *being the* **starting pushdown symbol**, *and a* **transition function** δ *defined by*

$$\delta : Q \times (\Sigma \cup \{\varepsilon\}) \times \Gamma \to 2^{Q \times \Gamma^*}.$$

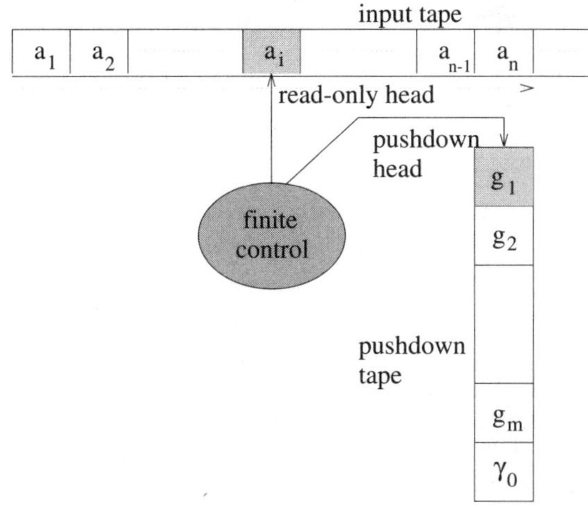

Figure 7.3 A pushdown automaton

A **configuration** of $\mathcal{A}$ is a triple (q, w, γ). We say that $\mathcal{A}$ is in a configuration (q, w, γ) if $\mathcal{A}$ is in the state q, w is the not-yet-read portion of the input tape with the head on the first symbol of w, and γ is the current contents of the pushdown tape (with the left-most symbol of γ on the top of the pushdown tape. (q_0, w, γ_0) is, for any input word w, an initial configuration.

Two types of computational steps of $\mathcal{A}$ are considered, both of which can be seen as a relation $\vdash_{\mathcal{A}} \subseteq (Q \times \Sigma^* \times \Gamma^*) \times (Q \times \Sigma^* \times \Gamma^*)$ between configurations. The Σ**-step** is defined by

$$(p, v_1 v, \gamma_1 \gamma) \vdash_{\mathcal{A}} (q, v, \bar{\gamma}\gamma) \Leftrightarrow (q, \bar{\gamma}) \in \delta(p, v_1, \gamma_1),$$

where $v_1 \in \Sigma, \gamma_1 \in \Gamma, \bar{\gamma} \in \Gamma^*$. The ε**-step** is defined by

$$(p, v, \gamma_1 \gamma) \vdash_{\mathcal{A}} (q, v, \bar{\gamma}\gamma) \Leftrightarrow (q, \bar{\gamma}) \in \delta(p, \varepsilon, \gamma_1).$$

In a Σ-step, the input head moves to the next input symbol; in an ε-step the input head does not move. In both steps the top-most pushdown symbol γ_1 is replaced by a string $\bar{\gamma} \in \Gamma^*$. If $|\bar{\gamma}| = 0$, this results in removing γ_1.

There are also two natural ways of defining an acceptance by a PDA.

Acceptance by a final state:

$$L_f(\mathcal{A}) = \{w \mid (q_0, w, \gamma_0) \vdash_{\mathcal{A}}^* (p, \varepsilon, \gamma), p \in Q_F, \gamma \in \Gamma^*\}.$$

Acceptance by the empty pushdown tape:

$$L_e(\mathcal{A}) = \{w \mid (q_0, w, \gamma_0) \vdash_{\mathcal{A}}^* (p, \varepsilon, \varepsilon), p \in Q\}.$$

However, these two acceptance modes are not essentially different.

Exercise 7.3.19 *Show that for each pushdown automaton $\mathcal{A}$ one can easily construct a pushdown automaton $\mathcal{A}'$ such that $L_e(\mathcal{A}) = L_f(\mathcal{A}')$, and vice versa.*

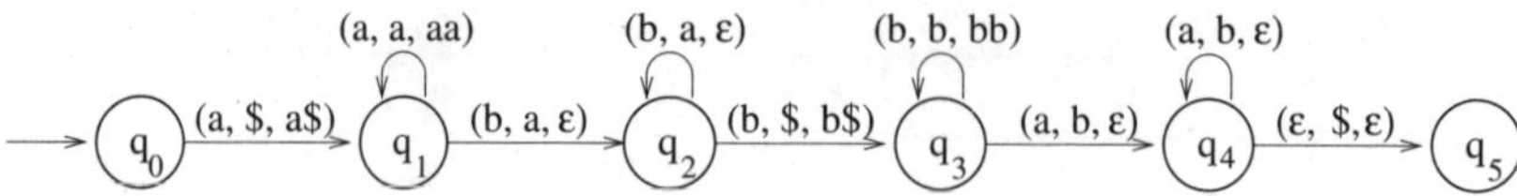

Figure 7.4 A pushdown automaton

Example 7.3.20 *PDA* $\mathcal{A}_1 = \langle\{q_1,q_2\},\{0,1,c\},\{B,0,1\},q_1,\emptyset,B,\delta\rangle$, *with the transitions*

$$\begin{array}{llllllll}
\delta(q_1,0,B) & = & (q_1,0B), & \delta(q_1,1,B) & = & (q_1,1B), & \delta(q_1,c,B) & = & (q_2,B), \\
\delta(q_1,0,0) & = & (q_1,00), & \delta(q_1,1,0) & = & (q_1,10), & \delta(q_1,c,0) & = & (q_2,0), \\
\delta(q_1,0,1) & = & (q_1,01), & \delta(q_1,1,1) & = & (q_1,11), & \delta(q_1,c,1) & = & (q_2,1), \\
\delta(q_2,0,0) & = & (q_2,\varepsilon), & \delta(q_2,1,1) & = & (q_2,\varepsilon), & \delta(q_2,\varepsilon,B) & = & (q_2,\varepsilon),
\end{array}$$

accepts, through the empty pushdown tape, the language $\{wcw^R \mid w \in \{0,1\}^*\}$. *This is easy to see. Indeed,* $\mathcal{A}_1$ *first stores* w *on the pushdown tape. After reading* c, $\mathcal{A}_1$ *goes into the state* q_2 *and starts to compare input symbols with those on the top of the pushdown tape. Each time they agree, the input head moves to the next symbol, and the top-most symbol from the pushdown tape is removed. If they do not agree once,* $\mathcal{A}$ *does not accept.*

Example 7.3.21 *PDA* $\mathcal{A}_2 = \langle\{q_1,q_2\},\{0,1\},\{B,0,1\},q_1,\emptyset,B,\delta\rangle$ *with the transitions*

$$\begin{array}{llllll}
\delta(q_1,0,B) & = & (q_1,0B), & \delta(q_1,0,0) & = & \{(q_1,00),(q_2,\varepsilon)\}, \\
\delta(q_1,1,B) & = & (q_1,1B), & \delta(q_1,1,1) & = & \{(q_1,11),(q_2,\varepsilon)\}, \\
\delta(q_1,0,1) & = & (q_1,01), & \delta(q_2,1,1) & = & (q_2,\varepsilon), \\
\delta(q_1,1,0) & = & (q_1,10), & \delta(q_2,0,0) & = & (q_2,\varepsilon), \\
\delta(q_1,\varepsilon,B) & = & (q_2,\varepsilon), & \delta(q_2,\varepsilon,B) & = & (q_2,\varepsilon),
\end{array}$$

accepts, again through the empty pushdown tape, the language $\{ww^R \mid w \in \{0,1\}^*\}$. *Indeed, the basic idea is the same as in the previous example. In the state* q_1, $\mathcal{A}_2$ *stores* w *on the pushdown tape.* $\mathcal{A}_2$ *compares, in the state* q_2, *the next input symbol with the symbol on the top of the pushdown tape, and if they agree, the input tape head makes a move and the topmost pushdown symbol is removed. However,* $\mathcal{A}_2$ *switches from state* q_1 *to* q_2 *nondeterministically only.* $\mathcal{A}_2$ *'guesses' when it is in the middle of the input word.*

Exercise 7.3.22 *Let L be the language generated by the PDA shown in Figure 7.4 through the empty pushdown tape. Determine L and design a CFG for L. (In Figure 7.4 transitions are written in the form* (a,z,z') *and mean that if the input symbol is a and z is on the top of the pushdown tape, then z is replaced by* z'.*)*

Exercise 7.3.23* *Show that to each PDA* $\mathcal{A}$ *with 2n states there is a PDA* $\mathcal{A}'$ *with n states such that* $L_e(\mathcal{A}) = L_e(\mathcal{A}')$.

Theorem 7.3.24 *To every PDA* $\mathcal{A}$ *there is a one-state PDA* $\mathcal{A}'$ *such that* $L_e(\mathcal{A}) = L_e(\mathcal{A}')$.

Now we are ready to show the basic relation between context-free grammars and pushdown automata.

Theorem 7.3.25 *A language is generated by a CFG if and only if it is accepted by a PDA.*

Proof: Let $G = \langle V_N, V_T, S, P\rangle$ be a CFG. We design a one-state PDA,

$$\mathcal{A} = \langle \{q\}, V_T, V_N \cup V_T \cup \{\gamma_0, \#\}, q, \emptyset, \gamma_0, \delta\rangle,$$

with the transition function

$$\begin{aligned} \delta(q,\varepsilon,\gamma_0) &= (q,S\#), & \delta(q,\varepsilon,A) &= \{(q,w)\,|\,A \longrightarrow w \in P\}, \\ \delta(q,a,a) &= (q,\varepsilon), & \delta(q,\varepsilon,\#) &= (q,\varepsilon), \end{aligned}$$

where $a \in V_T$. $\mathcal{A}$ first replaces the initial symbol γ_0 of the pushdown tape by the initial symbol of the grammar and a special marker. $\mathcal{A}$ then simulates the left-most derivation of G. Whenever the left-most symbol of the pushdown tape is a terminal of G, then the only way to proceed is to compare this terminal with the next input symbol. If they agree, the top pushdown symbol is removed, and the input head moves to the next symbol. If they do not agree, the computation stops. In this way, at any moment of computation, the already consumed part of the input and the contents of the pushdown tape are a sentential form of a left-most derivation. Finally, $\mathcal{A}$ empties its pushdown tape if the marker $\#$ is reached. (A more detailed proof can be given by induction.)

Now let $\mathcal{A}$ be a pushdown automaton. By Theorem 7.3.24 there is a one-state PDA $\mathcal{A}' = \langle \{q\}, \Sigma, \Gamma, q, \emptyset, z_0, \delta\rangle$, $\Sigma \cap \Gamma = \emptyset$, such that $L_e(\mathcal{A}) = L_e(\mathcal{A}')$.

Let $G = \langle \{S\} \cup \Gamma, \Sigma, S, P\rangle$ be a CFG with the following set of productions:

$$S \longrightarrow z_0, \qquad A \longrightarrow xB_1B_2\ldots B_m \;\text{ if and only if }\; (q, B_1\ldots B_m) \in \delta(q,x,A),$$

where x is a terminal symbol or $x = \varepsilon$. (If $m = 0$, then $A \longrightarrow aB_1\ldots B_m$ has the form $A \longrightarrow a$.)

A derivation in G is clearly a simulation of a computation in $\mathcal{A}'$. This derivation results in a terminal word w if the input empties the pushdown tape of $\mathcal{A}'$. □

Exercise 7.3.26 *Design a PDA accepting the languages (a)* $\{w\,|\,w \in \{a,b\}^*, |\#_a w - \#_b w| \bmod 4 = 0\}$*; (b)* $\{0^i1^j\,|\,0 \le i \le j \le 2i\}$.

Exercise 7.3.27 *Design a PDA equivalent to CFG with the productions* $S \longrightarrow BC\,|\,s$, $B \longrightarrow CS\,|\,b$, *and* $C \longrightarrow SB\,|\,c$.

7.3.4 Recognition and Parsing of Context-free Grammars

Algorithms for recognition and/or parsing of context-free grammars form important subprograms of many programs that receive their inputs in a natural or formal language form. In particular, they are key elements of most of translators and compilers. Efficient recognition and parsing of CFG is therefore an important practical task, as well as an interesting theoretical problem.

Recognition problem – for a CFG G, the problem is to decide, given a word w, whether $w \in L(G)$.

Parsing problem – for a CFG G, the problem is to construct, given a word $w \in L(G)$, a derivation tree for w.

The following general and beautiful recognition algorithm CYK (due to Cocke, Younger and Kasami), one of the pearls of algorithm design, assumes that $G = \langle V_N, V_T, S, P\rangle$ is a CFG in Chomsky normal form and $w = w_1 \ldots w_n, w_i \in V_T$, is an input word. The algorithm designs an $n \times n$ upper-triangular recognition matrix T, the elements $T_{i,j}, 1 \le i \le j \le n$, of which are subsets of V_N.

begin for $1 \le i,j \le n$ **do** $T_{i,j} \leftarrow \emptyset$;
  for $i \leftarrow 1$ **to** n **do** $T_{i,i} \leftarrow \{A \mid A \to w_i \in P\}$;
  for $d \leftarrow 1$ **to** $n-1$ **do**
    for $i \leftarrow 1$ **to** $n-d$ **do**
      begin $j \leftarrow d+i$;
        $T_{i,j} \leftarrow \{A \mid \exists k, i < k \le j$ such that
          $A \longrightarrow BC \in P, B \in T_{i,k-1}, C \in T_{k,j}\}$
      end;
  if $S \in T_{1,n}$ **then** accept **else** reject
end

In order to show the correctness of this algorithm, it is sufficient to prove by induction that

$$T_{i,j} = \{A \mid A \overset{*}{\underset{P}{\Longrightarrow}} w_i \ldots w_j\} \quad \text{if } 1 \le i \le j \le n,$$

and therefore $w \in L(G)$ if and only if $S \in T_{1,n}$.

The following table shows the values of the matrix T when the CYK algorithm is used for the CFG with the productions

$$\begin{array}{lll} (1)\ S \longrightarrow SS, & (2)\ S \longrightarrow AA, & (3)\ S \longrightarrow b, \\ (4)\ A \longrightarrow AS, & (5)\ A \longrightarrow AA, & (6)\ A \longrightarrow a, \end{array}$$

and the word 'abbaa' is recognized:

A	A	A	–	A,S
	S	S	–	S
		S	–	S
			A	A,S
				A

To design the derivation tree, we can use the matrix T. Let us assume a fixed enumeration of productions of G, and let $\pi_i, 1 \le i \le |P|$, denote the ith production. To design the derivation tree for a $w = w_1 \ldots w_n$, $w_i \in V_T$, we can use the program

if $S \in T_{1,n}$ **then** *parse*$(1,n,S)$ **else** output 'error'

and the following procedure *parse*:

procedure *parse*(i,j,A)
begin
  if $j = i$ **then** *output*(m) such that $\pi_m = A \to w_i \in P$
    else if k is the least integer such that $i < k \le j$ and there exist
      $\pi_m = A \to BC \in P$ with $B \in T_{i,k-1}$, $C \in T_{k,j}$
    then begin *output*(m);
        parse$(i,k-1,B)$; *parse*(k,j,C)
      end
end

This procedure designs in the so-called top-down manner (that is, from S to w) the left-most derivation of w. For example, for the grammar given above and $w = abbaa$, we get as the output the sequence of productions $2, 4, 6, 1, 3, 3, 5, 6, 6$ and the derivation tree.

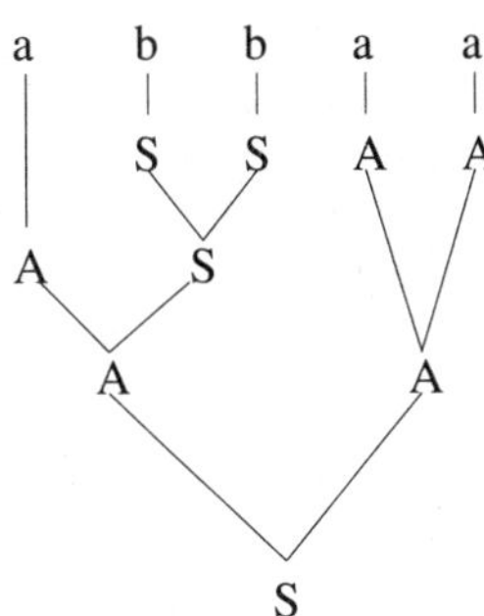

When implemented on a RAM, the time complexity is clearly $\Theta(n^3)$ for the CYK algorithm and $\Theta(n)$ for the parsing algorithm. It can be shown that both algorithms can also be implemented on Turing machines with asymptotically the same time performance. The following theorem therefore holds.

Theorem 7.3.28 *Recognition and parsing of CFG can be done in $\Theta(n^3)$ time on RAM and Turing machines.*

Exercise 7.3.29 *Design a CFG G' in the Chomsky normal form that generates the language $L(G) - \{\varepsilon\}$, where G is the grammar $S \longrightarrow aS \,|\, aSbS \,|\, \varepsilon$, and design the upper-triangular matrix that is created by the CYK algorithm when recognizing the word 'aabba'.*

Exercise 7.3.30 *Implement the CYK recognition algorithm on a multi-tape Turing machine in such a way that recognition is accomplished in $\mathcal{O}(n^3)$-time.*

Parsing algorithms are among the most often used algorithms (they are part of any text processing system), and therefore parsing algorithms with time complexity $\Theta(n^3)$ are unacceptably slow. It is important to find out whether there are faster parsing algorithms and, if so, to develop parsing algorithms for CFG that are as fast as possible.

Surprisingly, the problem of fast recognition of context-free grammars seems to be still far from being solved. Even more surprisingly, this problem has turned out to be closely related to such seemingly different problems as Boolean matrix multiplication. The following theorem holds.

Theorem 7.3.31 (Valiant's theorem) *Let $\mathcal{A}$ be a RAM algorithm for multiplying two Boolean matrices of degree n with time complexity $M(n)$ (with respect to logarithmic time complexity). Then there is an $\mathcal{O}(M(n))$-time RAM algorithm for recognizing an arbitrary context-free grammar.*

Since there is an $\mathcal{O}(n^{2.37})$ RAM algorithm for Boolean matrix multiplication (see Section 4.2.4), we have the following corollary.

Corollary 7.3.32 *There is an $\mathcal{O}(n^{2.37})$ RAM algorithm for recognizing an arbitrary CFG.*

Recognition of general CFG has also been intensively investigated with respect to other complexity measures and computational models. $\mathcal{O}(\lg^2 n)$ is the best known result for space complexity on Turing machines and also for time complexity on CRCW$^+$ PRAM (and on hypercubes, see Section 10.1, with $\mathcal{O}(n^6)$ processors).

Since parsing is used so extensively, a linear parsing algorithm is practically the only acceptable solution. This does not seem to be possible for arbitrary CFG. Therefore the way out is to consider parsing for special classes of CFG that would be rich enough for most applications.

Restrictions to unambiguous CFG or even to **linear CFG**, with productions of the form $A \longrightarrow uBv$ or $A \longrightarrow w$, where A, B are nonterminals and u, v, w are terminal words, do not seem to help. The fastest known recognition algorithms for such grammars have time complexity $\Theta(n^2)$. This has turned out practically to be a satisfactory solution – restriction to the recognition of only deterministic context-free languages leads to $\Theta(n)$ algorithms.

Definition 7.3.33 *A CFL L is a* **deterministic context-free language (DCFL)** *if $L = L_f(\mathcal{A})$ for a deterministic PDA $\mathcal{A}$. A PDA $\mathcal{A} = \langle Q, \Sigma, \Gamma, q_0, \emptyset, z, \delta \rangle$ is a* **deterministic PDA (DPDA)** *if:*

1. *$q \in Q$, $a \in \Sigma \cup \{\varepsilon\}$ and $\gamma \in \Gamma$ implies $|\delta(q, a, \gamma)| \leq 1$;*
2. *$q \in Q$, $\gamma \in \Gamma$ and $\delta(q, \varepsilon, \gamma) \neq \emptyset$, then $\delta(q, a, \gamma) = \emptyset$, for all $a \in \Sigma$.*

In other words in a DPDA in any global state at most one transition is possible. For example, the PDA in Example 7.3.20 is deterministic, but that in Example 7.3.21 is not.

Exercise 7.3.34 *Show that the following languages are DCFL: (a) $\{w \mid w \in \{a,b\}^*, \#_a w = \#_b w\}$; (b) $\{a^n b^m \mid 1 \leq n \leq 3m\}$.*

Caution: In the case of DPDA, acceptance by a final state and acceptance by an empty pushdown tape are not equivalent.

Exercise 7.3.35 *Show that every language accepted by a DPDA with respect to the empty pushdown tape can be accepted by a DPDA with respect to a final state.*

Exercise 7.3.36** *Show that the following language is acceptable by a deterministic pushdown automaton with respect to a final state but not with respect to the empty pushdown tape: $\{w \in \{a,b\}^* \mid w$ contains the same number of occurrences of a and $b\}$.*

Due to ε-moves, a DPDA may need more than $|w|$ time steps to recognize an input word w. In spite of this DCFL can be recognized in linear time.

Theorem 7.3.37 *For each DPDA $\mathcal{A}$ there is a constant $c_{\mathcal{A}}$ such that each word $w \in L_f(\mathcal{A})$ can be recognized in $c_{\mathcal{A}}|w|$ steps.*

Proof idea: From the description of $\mathcal{A}$ one can determine an upper bound $c_{\mathcal{A}}$ on the number of steps $\mathcal{A}$ can make without being in a cycle. □

There are also several well-defined subclasses of CFG that generate exactly deterministic CFL: for example, the so-called *LR*(k) grammars. They are dealt with in any book on parsing and compilation.

7.3.5 Context-free Languages

Context-free languages play an important role in formal language theory and computing, next to regular languages. We deal here with several basic questions concerning CFL: how to determine that a language is not context-free, which closure properties the family of CFL has, which decision problems are decidable (undecidable) for CFL, what the overall role of CFL is in formal language theory, and whether there are some especially important (or 'complete') context-free languages.

The most basic way to determine whether a language L is context-free is to design a CFG or a PDA for L. It is much less clear how to show that a language is not context-free (and therefore there is no sense in trying to design a CFG or a PDA for it). One way of doing this is to use the following result.

Lemma 7.3.38 (Bar-Hillel's pumping lemma) *For every CFG G one can compute an integer n_G such that for each $z \in L(G)$, $|z| > n_G$, there are words x,u,w,v,y such that*

1. $z = xuwvy, |uv| \geq 1, |uwv| \leq n_G$;
2. $xu^iwv^iy \in L(G)$ *for all* $i \geq 0$.

Example 7.3.39 *We show that the language $L = \{a^ib^ic^i \mid i \geq 1\}$ is not context-free by deriving a contradiction, using the pumping lemma, from the assumption that L is context-free.*

Proof: Assume L is context-free. Then there is a CFG G generating L. Let $n = n_G$ be an integer satisfying the conditions of the pumping lemma for G. In such a case $z = a^nb^nc^n$ can be split as $z = xuwvy$ such that the conditions of pumping lemma are fulfilled, and therefore $|uwv| \leq n$. However, then the string uwv cannot contain both an 'a' and a 'c' (any two occurrences of such symbols have to be at least $n+1$ symbols apart). Hence the word xu^2wv^2y, which should also be in L by the pumping lemma, does not contain the same number of a's, b's and c's: a contradiction. □

Exercise 7.3.40 *Show that the following languages are not context-free: (a) $L = \{ww \mid w \in \{a,b\}^*\}^c$; (b) $\{a^nb^ncb^na^n \mid n \geq 1\}$; (c) $\{a^ib^ja^ib^j \mid i,j \geq 1\}$; (d) $\{a^{n^2} \mid n \geq 1\}$; (e) $\{a^i \mid i \text{ is composite}\}$.*

Bar-Hillel's pumping lemma is an important but not universal tool for showing that a language is not context-free. For example, the language $\{a^*bc\} \cup \{a^pba^nca^n \mid p \text{ is prime}, n \geq p\}$ is not context-free, but this cannot be shown using Bar-Hillel's pumping lemma. (Show why.)

Since each CFL is clearly also context-sensitive, it follows from Example 7.3.39 that the family of context-free languages is a proper subfamily of context-sensitive languages. Similarly, it is evident that each regular language is context-free. Since the syntactical monoid of the language $L_0 = \{ww^R \mid w \in \{0,1\}^*\}$ is infinite (see Section 3.3), L_0 is an example of a context-free language that is not regular.

It can be shown that each deterministic context-free language is unambiguous, and therefore $L = \{a^ib^ja^k \mid i = j \text{ or } j = k\}$ is an example of a CFL that is not deterministic. Hence we have the hierarchy

$$L(NFA) \subsetneq L(DPDA) \subsetneq L(NPDA) \subsetneq \mathcal{L}(LBA).$$

Another method for proving that a language L is context-free is to show that it can be designed from another language, already known to be context-free, using operations under which the family of CFL is closed.

Theorem 7.3.41 *The family of CFL is closed under operations of union, concatenation, iteration, homomorphism, intersection with regular sets and difference with regular sets. It is not closed with respect to intersection, deletion and complementation.*

The family of deterministic CFL is closed under complementation, intersection with regular sets and difference with regular sets, but not with respect to union, concatenation, iteration, homomorphism and difference.

Proof: Closure of $\mathcal{L}(CFL)$ under union, concatenation, iteration and homomorphism is easy to show using CFG. Indeed, let G_1 and G_2 be two CFG with disjoint sets of nonterminals and not containing the symbol 'S', and let S_1, S_2 be their start symbols. If we take the productions from G_1 and add productions $\{S \longrightarrow SS_1 \,|\, \varepsilon\}$, we get a CFG generating, from the new start symbol S, the language $L(G_1)^*$. Moreover, if we take the productions from G_1 and G_2 and add productions $\{S \longrightarrow S_1 \,|\, S_2\}$ (or $S \longrightarrow S_1S_2$), we get a CFG generating the language $L(G_1) \cup L(G_2)$ (or $L(G_1)L(G_2)$). In order to get a CFG for the language $h(L(G_1))$, where h is a morphism, we replace, in productions of G_1, each terminal a by $h(a)$.

In order to show the closure of the family $\mathcal{L}(CFG)$ under intersection with regular languages, let us assume that L is a CFL and R a regular set. By Theorem 7.3.24, there is a one-state PDA $\mathcal{A} = \langle \{q\}, \Sigma, \Gamma, q, \emptyset, y_0, \delta_p \rangle$ which has the form shown on page 437 and $L_e(\mathcal{A}) = L$. Let $\mathcal{A}' = \langle Q, \Sigma, q_0, Q_F, \delta_f \rangle$ be a DFA accepting R. A PDA $\mathcal{A}'' = \langle Q, \Sigma, \Gamma, q_0, \emptyset, z, \delta \rangle$ with the following transition function, where q_1 is an arbitrary state from Q and $A \in \Gamma$,

$$\delta(q_0, \varepsilon, z) = \{(q_0, S\#)\}; \tag{7.1}$$

$$\delta(q_1, \varepsilon, A) = \{(q_1, w) \,|\, (q, w) \in \delta_p(q, \varepsilon, A)\}; \tag{7.2}$$

$$\delta(q_1, a, a) = \{(q_2, \varepsilon) \,|\, q_2 \in \delta_f(q_1, a)\}; \tag{7.3}$$

$$\delta(q_1, \varepsilon, \#) = \{(q_1, \varepsilon) \,|\, q_1 \in Q_F\}; \tag{7.4}$$

accepts $L \cap R$. Indeed, when ignoring states of $\mathcal{A}'$, we recover $\mathcal{A}$, and therefore $L_e(\mathcal{A}'') \subseteq L_e(\mathcal{A})$. On the other hand, each word accepted by $\mathcal{A}''$ is also in R, due to the transitions in (7.2) and (7.3). Hence $L_e(\mathcal{A}'') = L \cap R$.

Since $L - R = L \cap R^c$, we get that the family $\mathcal{L}(CFG)$ is closed also under the difference with regular languages.

For the non context-free language $L = \{a^ib^ic^i \,|\, i \geq 1\}$ we have $L = L_1 \cap L_2$, where $L = \{a^ib^ic^j \,|\, i,j \geq 1\}$, $L_2 = \{a^ib^jc^j \,|\, i,j \geq 1\}$. This implies that the family $\mathcal{L}(CFG)$ is not closed under intersection, and since $L_1 \cap L_2 = (L_1^c \cup L_2{}^c)^c$, it is not closed under complementation either. Moreover, since the language $L_3 = \{a^ib^jc^k \,|\, i,j,k \geq 1\}$ is regular and therefore context-free, and $L_4 = \{a^ib^jc^k \,|\, i \neq j \text{ or } j \neq k\}$ is also a context-free language and $L = L_3 - L_4$, we get that the family $\mathcal{L}(CFG)$ is not closed under set difference.

Proofs for closure and nonclosure properties of deterministic context-free languages are more involved and can be found in the literature (see the references). □

Concerning decision problems, the news is not good. Unfortunately, most of the basic decision problems for CFL are undecidable.

Theorem 7.3.42 *(1) The following decision problems are decidable for a CFG G: (a) Is L(G) empty? (b) Is L(G) infinite?*

(2) The following decision problems are undecidable for CFG G and G′ with the terminal alphabet Σ:

(c) Is $L(G) = \Sigma^*$*?*	*(d) Is* $L(G)$ *regular?*
(e) Is $L(G)$ *unambiguous?*	*(f) Is* $L(G)^c$ *infinite?*
(g) Is $L(G)^c$ *context-free?*	*(h) Is* $L(G) = L(G')$*?*
(i) Is $L(G) \cap L(G')$ *empty?*	*(j) Is* $L(G_1) \cap L(G_2)$ *context-free?*

Sketch of the proof: Let us consider first the assertion (1). It is easy to decide whether $L(G) = \emptyset$ for a CFG G. Indeed, if $G = \langle V_N, V_T, S, P\rangle$, we construct the following sequence of sets:

$$X_0 = V_T,\ X_{i+1} = X_i \cup \{A \mid A \longrightarrow u \in P, u \in X_i^*\}, i \geq 1.$$

Clearly, $L(G)$ is empty if and only if $S \notin X_{|V_N|}$.

We now show that the question of whether $L(G_1)$ is finite is decidable. By the pumping lemma, we can compute n such that $L(G)$ is infinite if and only if $L(G)$ contains a word longer than n. Now let $L_n(G)$ be the set of words of $L(G)$ of length $\leq n$. Since the recognition problem is decidable for CFG, $L_n(G)$ is computable. Therefore, by Theorem 7.3.41, $L(G) - L_n(G)$ is a CFL, and one can design effectively a CFG G_0 for $L(G) - L_n(G)$. Now $L(G)$ is infinite if and only if $L(G_0)$ is nonempty, which is decidable, by (a).

It was actually shown in Example 6.4.19 that it is undecidable whether the intersection of two context-free languages is empty. Let us now present a technique that can be used to show various other undecidability results for CFG.

Let $A = (u_1, \ldots, u_k)$, $B = (v_1, \ldots, v_k)$ be two lists of words over the alphabet $\Sigma = \{0,1\}$, $K = \{a_1, \ldots, a_k\}$ be a set of distinct symbols not in Σ, and $c \notin \Sigma$ be an additional new symbol.

Let

$$L_A = \{u_{i_1} \ldots u_{i_m} a_{i_m} \ldots a_{i_1} \mid 1 \leq i_s \leq k, 1 \leq s \leq m\},$$

and let L_B be a similarly defined language for the list B. The languages

$$R_{AB} = \{ycy^R \mid y \in \Sigma^* K^*\}, \qquad S_{AB} = \{ycz^R \mid y \in L_A, z \in L_B\},$$

are clearly DCFL, and therefore, by Theorem 7.3.41, their complements R^c_{AB}, S^c_{AB} are also CFL. Hence $L_{AB} = R^c_{AB} \cup S^c_{AB}$ is a CFL. It is now easy to see that

$$L_{AB} = (\Sigma \cup K \cup \{c\})^* \text{ if and only if the PCP for } A \text{ and } B \text{ has no solution.} \qquad (7.5)$$

The language L_{AB} is regular, and therefore (7.5) implies not only that the equivalence problem for CFG is undecidable, but that it is also undecidable for a CFG G and a regular language R (in particular $R = \Sigma^*$) whether $L(G) = R$.

Using the pumping lemma, we can show that the language $R_{AB} \cap S_{AB}$ is context-free if and only if it is empty. On the other hand, $R_{AB} \cap S_{AB}$ is empty if and only if the Post correspondence problem for A and B has no solution. Thus, it is undecidable whether the intersection of two CFL is a CFL.

Undecidability proofs for the remaining problems can be found in the references. □

Exercise 7.3.43 *Show that it is decidable, given a CFG G and a regular language R, whether $L(G) \subseteq R$.*

Exercise 7.3.44* *Show that the question whether a given CFG is (un)ambiguous is undecidable.*

Interestingly, several basic decision problems for CFG, such as membership, emptiness and infiniteness problems, are **P**-complete, and therefore belong to the inherently sequential problems.

Finally, we discuss the overall role played by context-free languages in formal language theory. We shall see that they can be used, together with the operations of intersection and homomorphism, to describe any recursively enumerable language. This illustrates the power of the operations of intersection and homomorphism. For example, the following theorem can be shown.

Theorem 7.3.45 *For any alphabet Σ there are two fixed DCFL, L_1^Σ and L_2^Σ, and a fixed homomorphism h^Σ such that for any recursively enumerable language $L \subseteq \Sigma^*$ there is a regular language R_L such that*

$$L = h^\Sigma(L_1^\Sigma \cup (L_2^\Sigma \cap R_L)).$$

Languages L_1^Σ and L_2^Σ seem to capture fully the essence of 'context-freeness'. It would seem, therefore, that they must be very complicated. This is not the case.

Let $\Sigma_k = \{a_1, \overline{a_1}, a_2, \overline{a_2}, \ldots, a_k, \overline{a_k}\}$ be an alphabet of k pairs of symbols. They will be used to play the role of pairs of brackets: $a_i (\overline{a_i})$ will be the ith left (right) bracket. The alphabet Σ_k is used to define the **Dyck language** D_k, $k \geq 1$. This is the language generated by the grammar

$$S \longrightarrow \varepsilon \,|\, Sa_iS\overline{a_i}, \qquad 1 \leq i \leq k.$$

Observe that if $a_1 = ($ and $\overline{a_1} =)$, then D_1 is just the set of all well-parenthesized strings.

Exercise 7.3.46 *Let D_k be the Dyck language with k parentheses. Design a homomorphism h such that $D_k = h^{-1}(D_2)$.*

The following theorem shows that Dyck languages reflect the structure of all CFL.

Theorem 7.3.47 (Chomsky–Schützenberger's theorem) *(1) For each CFL L there is an integer r, a regular language R and a homomorphism h such that*

$$L = h(D_r \cap R).$$

(2) For each CFL L there is a regular language R and two homomorphisms h_1, h_2 such that

$$L = h_2(h_1^{-1}(D_2) \cap R).$$

In addition, D_2 can be used to define 'the' context-free language, **Greibach language,**

$$\begin{aligned} L_G &= \{\varepsilon\} \cup \{x_1cy_1cz_1d \ldots x_ncy_ncz_nd \,|\, n \geq 1, y_1 \ldots y_n \in \gamma D_2, \\ &\qquad x_i, z_i \in \Sigma^*,\ 1 \leq i \leq n,\ y_i \in \{a_1, a_2, \overline{a_1}, \overline{a_2}\}^*,\ i \geq 2\}, \end{aligned}$$

where $\Sigma = \{a_1, a_2, \overline{a_1}, \overline{a_2}, \gamma, c\}$ and $d \in \Sigma$. (Note that words x_i, z_i may contain symbols 'c' and 'γ'.)

A PDA that recognizes the language L_G works as follows: it reads input, guesses the beginnings of $y_1, y_2, \ldots, y_n$, and recognizes whether $y_1, \ldots, y_n \in \gamma D_2$.

There are two reasons why L_G has a very special rôle among CFL.

Theorem 7.3.48 (Greibach's theorem) *(1) For every CFL L there is a homomorphism h such that $L = h^{-1}(L_G)$ if $\varepsilon \in L$ and $L = h^{-1}(L_G - \{\varepsilon\})$ if $\varepsilon \notin L$.*

(2) L_G is the hardest to recognize CFL. In other words, if L_G can be recognized in time $p(n)$ on a TM (or a RAM or a CA), then each CFL can be recognized in time $\mathcal{O}(p(n))$ on the same model.

This means that in order to improve the $\mathcal{O}(n^{2.37})$ upper bound for the time complexity of recognition of CFL, it is enough to find a faster recognition algorithm for a single CFL L_G – the Greibach language.

7.4 Lindenmayer Systems

Lindenmayer[2] systems, L-systems for short, were introduced to create a formal theory of plant development. Their consequent intensive investigation was mainly due to their generality and elegance and the fact that they represent the basic model of parallel context-free string rewriting systems.

7.4.1 0L-systems and Growth Functions

There is a variety of L-systems. The most basic are 0L-, D0L- and PD0L-systems.

Definition 7.4.1 *A 0L-system $G = \langle \Sigma, \omega, h\rangle$ is given by a finite* **alphabet** *Σ, an* **axiom** *(or an* **initial string***) $\omega \in \Sigma^*$, and a* **finite substitution** *$h : \Sigma \longrightarrow 2^{\Sigma^*}$ such that $h(a) = \emptyset$ for no $a \in \Sigma$. (If $u \in h(a)$, $a \in \Sigma$, then $a \longrightarrow u$ is called a* **production** *of L.) The 0L-language generated by G is defined by*

$$L(G) = \bigcup_{i\geq 0}\{h^i(\omega)\}.$$

If h is a morphism, that is, $h(a) \in \Sigma^*$ for each $a \in \Sigma$, we talk about a **D0L-system***, and if h is a nonerasing morphism, that is, $h(a) \in \Sigma^+$ for each $a \in \Sigma$, then G is said to be a* **PD0L-system**.

An 0L-system can be seen as given by an initial word and a set of context-free productions $a \longrightarrow u$, at least one for each $a \in \Sigma$. This time, however, there is no partition of symbols into nonterminals and terminals. A derivation step $w \Longrightarrow w'$ consists of rewriting each symbol of w using a production with that symbol on the left-hand side. 0L-systems can be seen as nondeterministic versions of D0L-systems; in D0L-systems there is only one production $a \longrightarrow u$ for each $a \in \Sigma$. In a PD0L-system (or a 'propagating D0L-system'), if $a \longrightarrow u$, then $|a| \leq |u|$. Each derivation in an 0L-system can be depicted, as for CFG, by a derivation tree.

Example 7.4.2 *In the D0L-system[3] with the axiom $\omega = a_r$ and productions*

$$a_r \longrightarrow a_l b_r, \qquad a_l \longrightarrow b_l a_r, \qquad b_r \longrightarrow a_r, \qquad b_l \longrightarrow a_l,$$

we have a derivation (see Figure 7.5 for the corresponding derivation tree)

$$a_r \Longrightarrow a_l b_r \Longrightarrow b_l a_r a_r \Longrightarrow a_l a_l b_r a_l b_r \Longrightarrow b_l a_r b_l a_r a_r b_l a_r a_r \Longrightarrow \ldots.$$

Exercise 7.4.3 *Show that the PD0L-system G_1 with the axiom 'a' and only one production, $a \longrightarrow aaa$, generates the language $L(G_1) = \{a^{3^n} \mid n \geq 0\}$.*

Exercise 7.4.4 *Show that the D0L-system G_2 with the axiom ab^3a and productions $P = \{a \longrightarrow ab^3a, b \longrightarrow \varepsilon\}$ generates the language $L(G_2) = \{(ab^3a)^{2^n} \mid n \geq 0\}$.*

Exercise 7.4.5 *Show that the 0L-system $G_3 = \langle\{a,b\},a,h\rangle$ with $h(a) = h(b) = S = \{aabb, abab, baab, abba, baba, bbaa\}$ generates the language $L(G) = \{a\} \cup \{a,b\}^{4^n} \cap S^*$.*

---

[2] Aristid Lindenmayer (1922–90), a Dutch biologist, introduced L-systems in 1968.

[3] This system is taken from modelling the development of a fragment of a multicellular filament such as that found in the blue-green bacteria *Anabaena catenula* and various algae. The symbols *a* and *b* represent cytological stages of the cells (their size and readiness to divide). The subscripts *r* and *l* indicate cell polarity, specifying the positions in which daughter cells of type *a* and *b* will be produced.

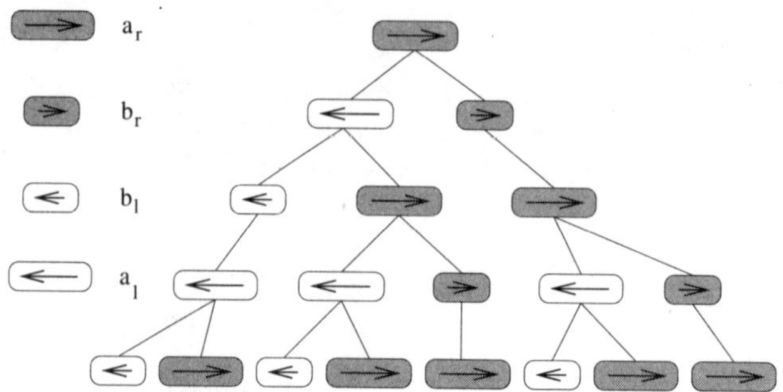

Figure 7.5 Development of a filament simulated using a D0L-system

A **derivation** in a D0L-system $G = \langle \Sigma, \omega, h \rangle$ can be seen as a sequence

$$\omega = h^0(\omega), h^1(\omega), h^2(\omega), h^3(\omega), \ldots,$$

and the function

$$f_G(n) = |h^n(\omega)|$$

is called the **growth function** of G.

With respect to the original context, growth functions capture the development of the size of the simulated biological system. On a theoretical level, growth functions represent an important tool for investigating various problems concerning languages.

Example 7.4.6 *For the PD0L-system G with axiom $\omega = a$ and morphism $h(a) = b, h(b) = ab$, we have as the only possible derivation*

$$a, b, ab, bab, abbab, bababbab, abbabbababbab, \ldots$$

and for the derivation sequence $\{h^n(\omega)\}_{n \geq 0}$, we have, for $n \geq 2$,

$$\begin{aligned} h^n(a) &= h^{n-1}(h(a)) = h^{n-1}(b) = h^{n-2}(h(b)) = h^{n-2}(ab) \\ &= h^{n-2}(a)h^{n-2}(b) = h^{n-2}(a)h^{n-1}(a), \end{aligned}$$

and therefore

$$\begin{aligned} f_G(0) &= f_G(1) = 1, \\ f_G(n) &= f_G(n-1) + f_G(n-2) \text{ for } n \geq 2. \end{aligned}$$

This implies that $f_G(n) = F_n$ – the nth Fibonacci number.

Exercise 7.4.7 *Show, for the PD0L-system with the axiom 'a' and the productions*

$$a \longrightarrow abcc, \quad b \longrightarrow bcc, \quad c \longrightarrow c,$$

for example, using the same technique as in the previous example, that $f_G(n) = f_G(n-1) + 2n + 1$, and therefore $f_G(n) = (n+1)^2$.

The growth functions of D0L-systems have a useful matrix representation. This is based on the observation that the growth function of a D0L-system does not depend on the ordering of symbol in axioms, productions and derived words.

Let $G = \langle \Sigma, \omega, h \rangle$ and $\Sigma = \{a_1, \ldots, a_k\}$. The growth matrix for G is defined by

$$M_G = \begin{vmatrix} \#_{a_1} h(a_1) & \ldots & \#_{a_k} h(a_1) \\ \ldots & & \ldots \\ \#_{a_1} h(a_k) & \ldots & \#_{a_k} h(a_k) \end{vmatrix}.$$

If $\pi_\omega = (\#_{a_1}\omega, \ldots, \#_{a_k}\omega)$ and $\eta = (1, \ldots, 1)^T$ are row and column vectors, then clearly

$$f_G(n) = \pi_\omega M_G^n \eta.$$

Theorem 7.4.8 *The growth function f_G of a D0L-system G satisfies the recurrence*

$$f_G(n) = c_1 f_G(n-1) + c_2 f_G(n-2) + \ldots + c_k f(n-k) \tag{7.6}$$

for some constants $c_1, \ldots, c_k$, and therefore each such function is a sum of exponential and polynomial functions.

Proof: It follows from linear algebra that M_G satisfies its own characteristic equation

$$M_G^k = c_1 M_G^{k-1} + c_2 M_G^{k-2} + \ldots + c_{k-1} M_G^1 + c_k M_G^0 \tag{7.7}$$

for some coefficients $c_1, \ldots, c_k$. By multiplying both sides of (7.7) by π_ω from the left and η from the right, we get (7.6). Since (7.6) is a homogeneous linear recurrence, the second result follows from the theorems in Section 1.2.3. □

There is a modification of 0L-systems, the so-called E0L-systems, in which symbols are partitioned into nonterminals and terminals.

An **E0L-system** is defined by $G = \langle \Sigma, \Delta, \omega, h \rangle$, where $G' = \langle \Sigma, \omega, h \rangle$ is an 0L-system and $\Delta \subseteq \Sigma$. The language generated by G is defined by

$$L(G) = L(G') \cap \Delta^*.$$

In other words, only strings from Δ^*, derived from the underlying 0L-system G' are taken into $L(G)$. Symbols from $\Sigma - \Delta$ (Δ) play the role of nonterminals (terminals).

Exercise 7.4.9 *Show that the E0L-system with the alphabets $\Sigma = \{S, a, b\}$, $\Delta = \{a, b\}$, the axiom SbS, and productions $S \longrightarrow S \mid a$, $a \longrightarrow aa$, $b \longrightarrow b$ generates the language $\{a^{2^i} b a^{2^j} \mid i, j \geq 0\}$.*

The family $\mathcal{L}$(E0L) of languages generated by E0L-systems has nicer properties than the family $\mathcal{L}$(0L) of languages generated by 0L-systems. For example, $\mathcal{L}$(0L) is not closed under union, concatenation, iteration or intersection with regular sets, whereas $\mathcal{L}$(E0L) is closed under all these operations. On the other hand, the equivalence problem, which is undecidable for E0L- and 0L-systems, is decidable for D0L-systems.

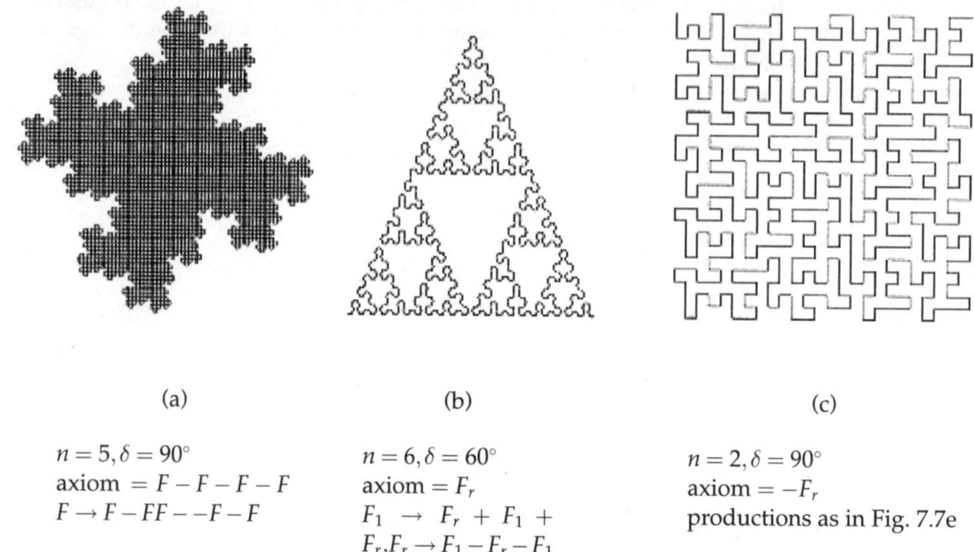

(a)

$n = 5, \delta = 90°$
axiom $= F - F - F - F$
$F \rightarrow F - FF - - F - F$

(b)

$n = 6, \delta = 60°$
axiom $= F_r$
$F_l \rightarrow F_r + F_l + F_r, F_r \rightarrow F_l - F_r - F_l$

(c)

$n = 2, \delta = 90°$
axiom $= -F_r$
productions as in Fig. 7.7e

Figure 7.6 Fractal and space-filling curves generated by the turtle interpretation of strings generated by D0L-systems

7.4.2 Graphical Modelling with L-systems

The idea of using L-systems to model plants has been questioned for a long time. L-systems did not seem to include enough details to model higher plants satisfactorily. Emphases in L-systems were on neighbourhood relations between cells, and geometrical interpretations seemed to be beyond the scope of the model. However, once various geometrical interpretations and modifications of L-systems were discovered, L-systems turned out to be a versatile tool for plant modelling.

We discuss here several approaches to graphical modelling with L-systems. They also illustrate, which is often the case, that simple modifications, twistings and interpretations of basic theoretical concepts can lead to highly complex and useful systems. For example, it has been demonstrated that there are various D0L-systems G over the alphabets $\Sigma \supseteq \{f, +, -\}$ with the following property: if the morphism $h : \Sigma \rightarrow \{F, f, +, -\}$, defined by $h(a) = F$ if $a \notin \{f, +, -\}$ and $h(a) = a$ otherwise, is applied to strings generated by G, one gets strings over the turtle alphabet $\{F, f, +, -\}$ such that their turtle interpretation (see Section 2.5.3) produces interesting fractal or space-filling curves. This is illustrated in Figure 7.6, which includes for each curve a description of the corresponding D0L-system (an axiom and productions), the number n of derivation steps and the degree δ of the angle of the turtle's turns.

No well-developed methodology is known for designing, given a family $\mathcal{C}$ of similar curves, a D0L-system that generates strings whose turtle interpretation provides exactly curves for $\mathcal{C}$. For this problem, the **inference problem,** only some intuitive techniques are available. One of them, called 'edge rewriting', specifies how an edge can be replaced by a curve, and this is then expressed by productions of a D0L-system. For example, Figures 7.7b and d show a way in which an F_l-edge (Figure 7.7a) and an F_r-edge (Figure 7.7c) can be replaced by square grid-filling curves and also the corresponding D0L-system (Figure 7.7e). The resulting curve, for the axiom 'F_l', $n = 2$ and $\delta = 90°$, is shown in Figure 7.6c.

The turtle interpretation of a string always results in a single curve. This curve may intersect itself,

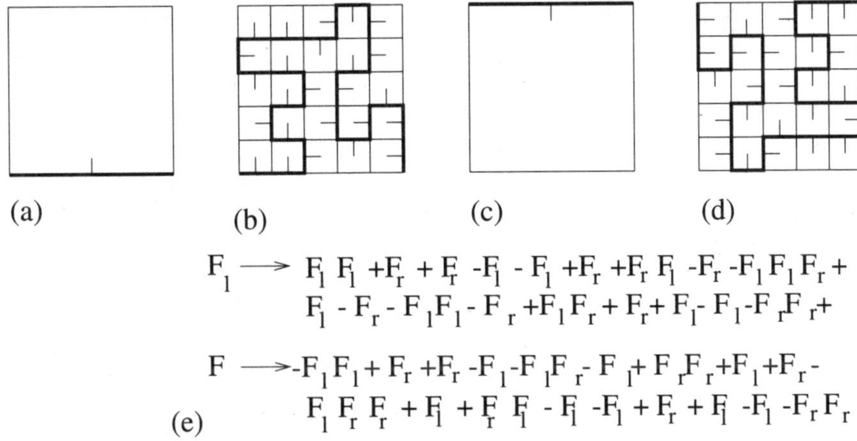

Figure 7.7 Construction of a space-filling curve on a square grid using an edge rewriting with the corresponding PD0L-system and its turtle interpretation

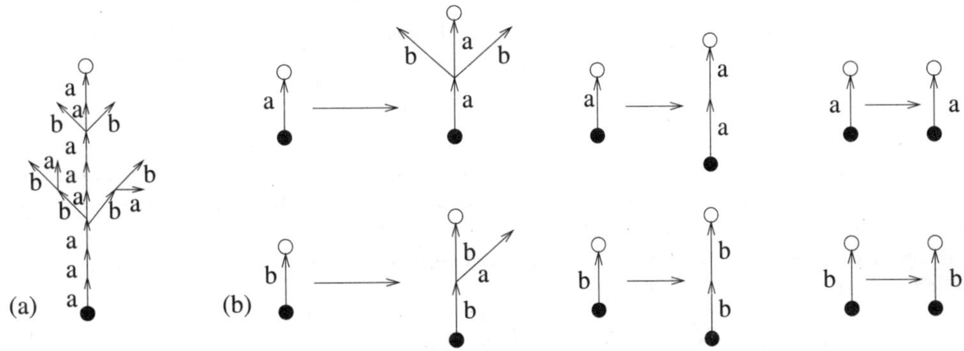

Figure 7.8 A tree 0L-system, axiom and production

have invisible lines (more precisely, interruptions caused by f-statements for turtle), and segments drawn several times, but it is always only a single curve. However, this is not the way in which plants develop in the natural world. A branching recursive structure is more characteristic. To model this, a slight modification of L-systems, so-called tree 0L-systems, and/or of string interpretations, have turned out to be more appropriate.

A **tree 0L-system** $\mathcal{T}$ is determined by three components: a set of edge labels E; an initial (axial) tree T_0, with edges labelled by labels from E (see Figure 7.8a); and a set P of tree productions (see Figure 7.8b), at least one for each edge label, in which a labelled edge is replaced by a finite, edge-labelled axial tree with a specified begin-node (denoted by a small black circle) and an end-node (denoted by a small empty circle). By an axial tree is meant here any rooted tree in which any internal node has at most three ordered successors (left, right and straight ahead – some may be missing).

An axial tree T_2 is said to be directly derived from an axial tree T_1 using a tree 0L-system $\mathcal{T}$, notation $T_1 \underset{P}{\Longrightarrow} T_2$, if T_2 is obtained from T_1 by replacing each edge of T_1 by an axial tree given by a tree production of $\mathcal{T}$ for that edge, and identifying the begin-node (end-node) of the axial tree with

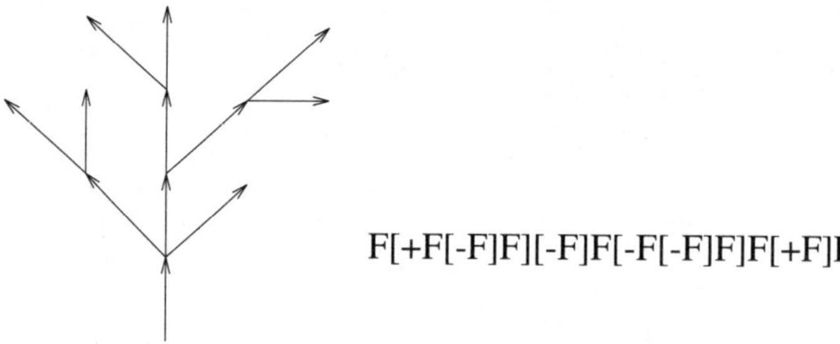

Figure 7.9 An axial tree and its bracket representation for $\delta = 45^\circ$

the starting (ending) node of the edge that is being replaced. A tree T is generated from the initial tree T_0 by a derivation (notation $T_0 \overset{*}{\underset{P}{\Longrightarrow}} T$) if there is a sequence of axial trees $T_0, T_1, \ldots, T_n$ such that $T_i \underset{P}{\Longrightarrow} T_{i+1}$ for $i = 0, 1, \ldots, n-1$, and $T = T_n$.

> **Exercise 7.4.10** *Show how the tree in Figure 7.8a can be generated using the tree 0L-system shown in Figure 7.8b for a simple tree with two nodes and the edge labelled a.*

Axial trees have a simple linear 'bracket representation' that allows one to use ordinary 0L-systems to generate them. The left bracket '[' represents the beginning of a branching and the right bracket ']' its end. Figure 7.9 shows an axial tree and its bracket representation.

In order to draw an axial tree from its bracket representation, the following interpretation of brackets is used:

[– push the current state of the turtle into the pushdown memory;

] – pop the pushdown memory, and make the turtle's state obtained this way its current state.

(In applications the current state of the turtle may contain other information in addition to the turtle's position and orientation: for example, width, length and colour of lines.)

Figure 7.10a, b, c shows several L-systems that generate bracket representations of axial trees and the corresponding trees (plants).

There are various other modifications of L-systems that can be used to generate a variety of branching structures, plants and figures: for example, stochastic and context-sensitive L-systems.

A **stochastic** 0**L-system** $G_\pi = \langle \Sigma, \omega, P, \pi \rangle$ is formed from a 0L-system $\langle \Sigma, \omega, P \rangle$ by adding a mapping $\pi : P \rightarrow (0,1]$, called a probability distribution, such that for any $a \in \Sigma$, the sum of 'probabilities' of all productions with 'a' on its left-hand side is 1. A derivation $w_1 \underset{P}{\Longrightarrow} w_2$ is called stochastic in G_π if for each occurrence of the letter a in the word w_1 the probability of applying a production $p = a \longrightarrow u$ is equal to $\pi(p)$. Using stochastic 0L-systems, various families of quite complex but similar branching structures have been derived.

Context-sensitive L-systems (IL-systems). The concept of 'context-sensitiveness' can also be applied to L-systems. Productions are of the form $uav \longrightarrow uwv$, $a \in \Sigma$, and such a production can be used to rewrite a particular occurrence of a by w only if (u, v) is the context of that occurrence of

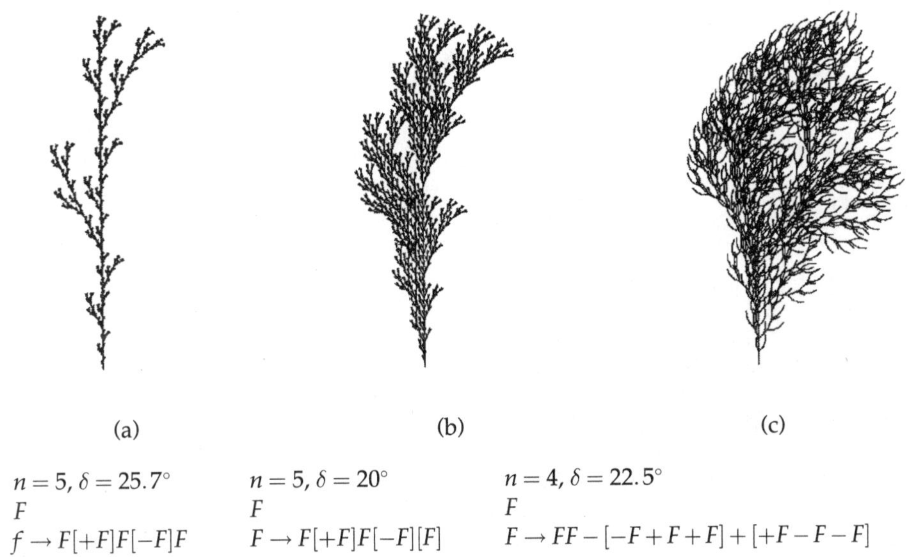

(a)
(b)
(c)
$n = 5, \delta = 25.7^\circ$
F
$f \rightarrow F[+F]F[-F]F$
$n = 5, \delta = 20^\circ$
F
$F \rightarrow F[+F]F[-F][F]$
$n = 4, \delta = 22.5^\circ$
F
$F \rightarrow FF - [-F + F + F] + [+F - F - F]$

Figure 7.10 Axial trees generated by tree L-systems

a. (It may therefore happen that a symbol cannot be replaced in a derivation step if it has no suitable context – this can be used also to handle the problem of end markers.)

It seems to be intuitively clear that IL-systems could provide richer tools for generating figures and branching structures. One can also show that they are actually necessary in the following sense. Growth functions of 0L-systems are linear combinations of polynomial and exponential functions. However, many of the growth processes observed in nature do not have growth functions of this type. On the other hand, IL-systems may exhibit growth functions not achievable by 0L-systems.

Exercise 7.4.11 *The IL-system with the axiom 'xuax' and productions*

$$\begin{array}{llllllllllll} u\underline{a}a & \longrightarrow & uua, & u\underline{a}x & \longrightarrow & udax, & a\underline{a}d & \longrightarrow & add, & x & \longrightarrow & x, \\ x\underline{a}d & \longrightarrow & xud, & u & \longrightarrow & a, & d & \longrightarrow & a, & & & \end{array}$$

has a derivation

$$\begin{array}{lllllllll} xuax & \Longrightarrow & xadax & \Longrightarrow & xuaax & \Longrightarrow & xauax & \Longrightarrow & xaadax \\ & \Longrightarrow & xadaax & \Longrightarrow & xuaaax & \Longrightarrow & xauaax & \Longrightarrow & xaauax \\ & \Longrightarrow & xaaadax & \Longrightarrow & xaadaax & \Longrightarrow & xadaaax & \Longrightarrow & xuaaaax. \end{array}$$

Show that its growth function is $\lfloor \sqrt{n} \rfloor + 4$*—not achievable by a 0L-system.*

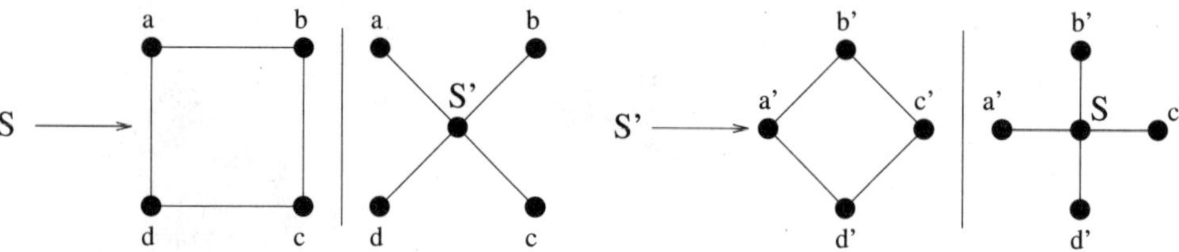

Figure 7.11 Graph grammar productions

7.5 Graph Rewriting

Graph rewriting is a method commonly employed to design larger and more complicated graphs from simpler ones. Graphs are often used to represent relational structures, which are then extended and refined. For example, this is done in software development processes, in specifications of concurrent systems, in database specifications and so on. It is therefore desirable to formalize and understand the power of various graph rewriting methods.

The basic idea of graph rewriting systems is essentially the same as that for string rewriting. A graph rewriting system is given by an initial graph G_0 (axiom), and a finite set P of rewriting productions $G_i \longrightarrow G_i'$, where G_i and G_i' are graphs. A direct rewriting relation $\underset{P}{\Longrightarrow}$ between graphs is defined analogously: $G \underset{P}{\Longrightarrow} G'$ if G' can be obtained from the (host) graph G by replacing a subgraph, say G_i (a mother graph), of G, by G_i' (a daughter graph), where $G_i \longrightarrow G_i'$ is a production of P.

To state this very natural idea more precisely and formally is far from simple. Several basic problems arise: how to specify when G_i occurs in G and how to replace G_i by G_i'. The difficulty lies in the fact that if no restriction is made, G_i' may be very different from G_i, and therefore it is far from clear how to embed G_i' in the graph obtained from G by removing G_i.

There are several general approaches to graph rewriting, but the complexity and sophistication of their basic concepts and the high computational complexity of the basic algorithms for dealing with them (for example, for parsing) make these methods hard to use. More manageable are simpler approaches based, in various ways, on an intuitive idea of 'context-free replacements'. Two of them will now be introduced.

7.5.1 Node Rewriting

The basic idea of node rewriting is that all productions are of the form $A \longrightarrow G_i'$, where A is a one-node graph. Rewriting by such a production consists of removing A and all incident edges, adding G_i', and connecting (gluing) its nodes with the rest of the graph. The problem is now how to define such a connection (gluing). The approach presented here is called 'node-label-controlled graph grammars', NLC graph grammars for short.

Definition 7.5.1 *An* **NLC graph grammar** $\mathcal{G} = \langle V_N, V_T, C, G_0, P\rangle$ *is given by a* **nonterminal alphabet** V_N, *a* **terminal alphabet** V_T, *an* **initial graph** G_0 *with nodes labelled by elements from* $V = V_N \cup V_T$, *a finite set* P *of* **productions** *of the form* $A \longrightarrow G$, *where* A *is a nonterminal (interpreted as a single-node graph with the node labelled by* A*), and* G *is a graph with nodes labelled by labels from* V. *Finally,* $C \subseteq V \times V$ *is a* **connection relation**.

Example 7.5.2 *Let* $\mathcal{G}$ *be an NLC graph grammar with* $V_T = \{a,b,c,d,a',b',c',d'\}$, $V_N = \{S,S'\}$, *the initial graph* G_0 *consisting of a single node labelled by* S, *the productions shown in Figure 7.11 and the connecting relation*

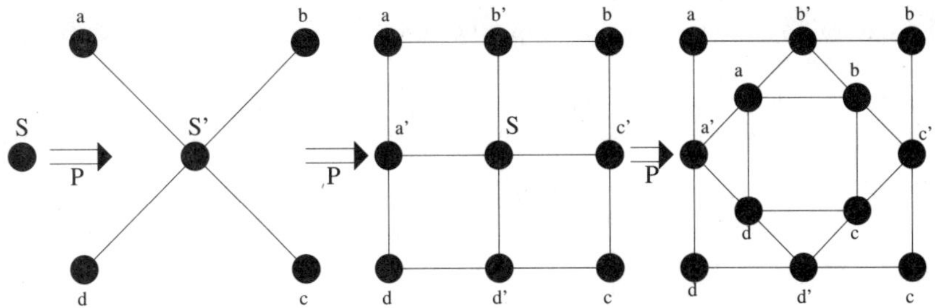

Figure 7.12 Derivation in an NLC

$$C = \{(a,a'),(a',a),(a,b'),(b',a),(b,b'),(b',b),(b,c'),(c',b),\\ (c,c'),(c',c),(c,d'),(d',c),(d,d'),(d',d),(a',d),(d,a')\}.$$

The graph rewriting relation $\underset{P}{\Longrightarrow}$ is now defined as follows. A graph G' is obtained from a graph G by a production $A \longrightarrow G_i$ if in the graph G a node $\bar{N}$ labelled by A is removed, together with all incident edges, G_i is added to the resulting graph (denote it by G'), and a node N of $G' - \{\bar{N}\}$ is connected to a node N' in G_i if and only if N is a direct neighbour of $\bar{N}$ in G and $(n,n') \in C$, where n is the label of N and n' of N'.

Example 7.5.3 *In the NLC graph grammar in Example 7.5.2 we have, for instance, the derivation shown in Figure 7.12.*

With an NLC grammar $\mathcal{G} = \langle V_N, V_T, C, G_0, P\rangle$ we can associate several sets of graphs (called 'graph languages'):

- $L_e(\mathcal{G}) = \{G \mid G_0 \overset{*}{\underset{P}{\Longrightarrow}} G\}$ – a set of all generated graphs;

- $L(\mathcal{G}) = \{G \mid G_0 \overset{*}{\underset{P}{\Longrightarrow}} G$, and all nodes of G are labelled by terminals$\}$ – a set of all generated 'terminal graphs';

- $L_u(\mathcal{G}) = \{G \mid G_0 \overset{*}{\underset{P}{\Longrightarrow}} G'$, where G is obtained from G' by removing all node labels$\}$ – a set of all generated unlabelled graphs.

In spite of their apparent simplicity, NLC graph grammars have strong generating power. For example, they can generate **PSPACE**-complete graph languages. This motivated investigation of various subclasses of NCL graph grammars: for example, **boundary NLC graph grammars**, where neither the initial graph nor graphs on the right-hand side of productions have nonterminals on two incident nodes. Graph languages generated by these grammars are in **NP**. Other approaches lead to graph grammars for which parsing can be done in low polynomial time.

Results relating to decision problems for NLC graph grammars also indicate their power. It is decidable, given an NLC graph grammar G, whether the language $L(G)$ is empty or whether it is infinite. However, many other interesting decision problems are undecidable: for example, the equivalence problem and the problem of deciding whether the language $L(G)$ contains a planar, a Hamiltonian, or a connected graph.

It is also natural to ask about the limits of NLC graph grammars and how to show that a graph language is outside their power. This can be proven using a **pumping lemma** for NLC graph grammars and languages. With such a lemma it can be shown, for example, that there is no NLC graph grammar such that $L_u(G)$ contains exactly all finite square grid graphs (such as those in the following figure).

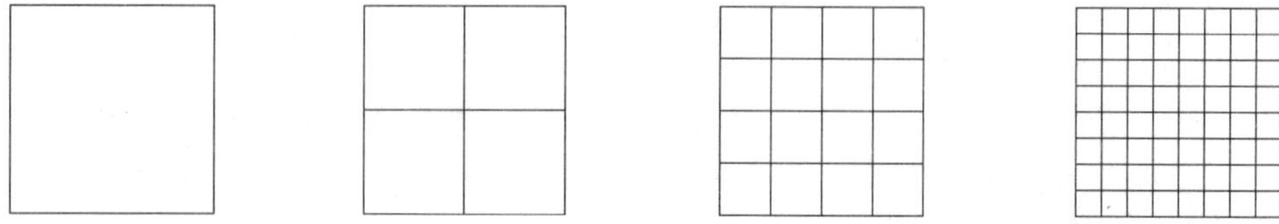

7.5.2 Edge and Hyperedge Rewriting

The second natural idea for doing a 'context-free graph rewriting' is edge rewriting. This has been generalized to hyperedge rewriting.

The intuitive idea of edge rewriting can be formalized in several ways: for example, by the **handle NLC graph grammars** (HNLC graph grammars, for short). These are defined in a similar way to NLC graph grammars, except that the left-hand sides of all productions have to be edges with both nodes labelled by nonterminals (such edges are called 'handles'). The embedding mechanism is the same as for NLC graph grammars.

Interestingly enough, this simple and natural modification of NLC graph grammars provides graph rewriting systems with maximum generative power. Indeed, it has been shown that each recursively enumerable graph language can be generated by an HNLC graph grammar.

Another approach along the same lines, presented below, is less powerful, but is often, especially for applications, more handy.

A **hyperedge** is specified by a name (label) and sequences of incoming and outgoing 'tentacles' (see Figure 7.13a). In this way a hyperedge may connect more than two nodes. The label of a hyperedge plays the role of a nonterminal in a hyperedge rewriting. A hyperedge replacement will be done within hypergraphs. Informally, hypergraphs consist of nodes and hyperedges.

Definition 7.5.4 *A* **hypergraph** $G = \langle V, E, s, t, l, \Lambda\rangle$ *is given by a set* V *of* **nodes**, *a set* E *of* **hyperedges**, *two mappings,* $s : E \longrightarrow V^*$ *and* $t : E \longrightarrow V^*$, *assigning* **a sequence of source nodes** $s(e)$ *and a* **sequence of target nodes** $t(e)$ *to each hyperedge e, and a* **labelling mapping** $l : E \rightarrow \Lambda$, *where* Λ *is a set of labels.*

A hyperedge e is called an (m,n)-**hyperedge**, *or of type* (m,n), *if* $|s(e)| = m$, $|t(e)| = n$. *A* $(1,1)$*-hyperedge is an ordinary edge.*

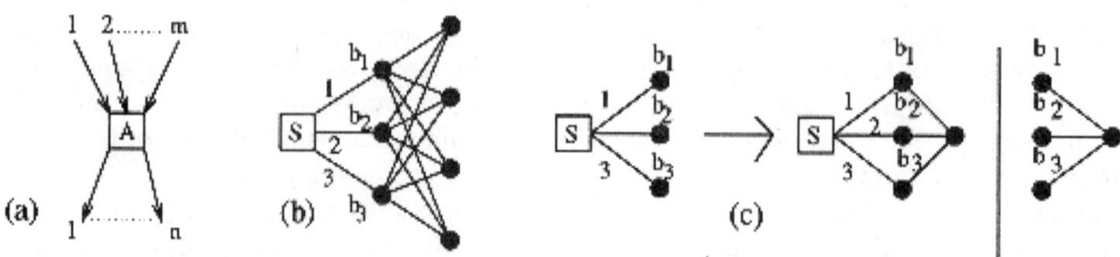

Figure 7.13 A hyperedge and hyperedge productions

A **multi-pointed hypergraph** $\mathcal{H} = \langle V, E, s, t, l, \Lambda, \texttt{begin}, \texttt{end}\rangle$ *is given by a hypergraph* $\langle V, E, s, t, l, \Lambda\rangle$ *and two strings* begin *and* end $\in V^*$. *A multi-pointed hypergraph is a* (m,n)*-hypergraph or a multigraph of type* (m,n) *if* $|\texttt{begin}| = m$, $|\texttt{end}| = n$. *The set of* **external nodes** *of* $\mathcal{H}$ *is the set of all symbols in the strings* begin *and* end.

Let $\mathcal{H}_\Lambda$ *denote the set of all multi-pointed hypergraphs with labels in* Λ.

A multi-pointed hypergraph has two sequences of external nodes represented by the strings begin and end.

Definition 7.5.5 *A* **hyperedge rewriting graph grammar** *(HR (graph) grammar in short)* $\mathcal{G} = \langle V_N, V_T, G_0, P\rangle$ *is given by a set of nonterminals* V_N, *a set of terminals* V_T, *an initial multi-pointed hypergraph* $G_0 \in \mathcal{H}_\Lambda$, $\Lambda = V_N \cup V_T$, *and a set P of productions. Each production of P has the form* $A \longrightarrow R$, *where A is a nonterminal,* $R \in \mathcal{H}_\Lambda$, *and* $type(e) = type(R)$.

Example 7.5.6 *An HR grammar is depicted in Figure 7.13. The axiom is shown in Figure 7.13b, and the productions in Figure 7.13c. (Terminal labels of* $(1,1)$*-hyperedges are not depicted.) The grammar has two productions. In both cases* begin$= b_1b_2b_3$ *and* end $= \varepsilon$, $V_N = \{A, S\}$ *and* $V_T = \{t\}$.

In order to define the rewriting relation $\underset{P}{\Longrightarrow}$ for HR grammars, one needs to describe how an (m,n)-hyperedge e is replaced by an (m,n)-hypergraph R in a hypergraph. This is done in two steps:

1. Remove the hyperedge e.
2. Add the hypergraph R, except its external nodes, and connect each tentacle of a hyperedge of R which is connected to an external node of R to the corresponding source or target node of e.

Exercise 7.5.7 *If we use, in the HR grammar shown in Figure 7.13b, c, the first production n times and then the second production once, we derive from the initial graph* G_0 *the complete bipartite graph* $K_{3,n+5}$. *Show in detail how to do this.*

Example 7.5.8 *Starting with the axiom shown in Figure 7.14a and using productions given in Figure 7.14b, c, various flow-diagram graphs can be generated.*

The graph language $L(G)$ generated by an HR grammar G is the set of graphs generated from the initial multi-pointed hypergraph that contain only $(1,1)$-hyperedges labelled by terminals.

For HR grammars there is also a pumping lemma that can be used to show for some languages that they are outside the power of HR grammars.

Concerning decision problems, the more restricted power of HR graph grammars brings greater decidability. In contrast to NLC graph grammars, it is decidable for HR graph grammars whether $L(G)$ contains a planar, Hamiltonian or connected graph.

Exercise 7.5.9 *Show that the HR graph grammar with two nonterminals* S, T *and the productions* $\{(S, T_0), (T, T_1), (T, T_2)\}$ *as depicted in Figure 7.15a, b, c generates an approximation of the Sierpiński triangle; see, for example, Figure 7.15b.*

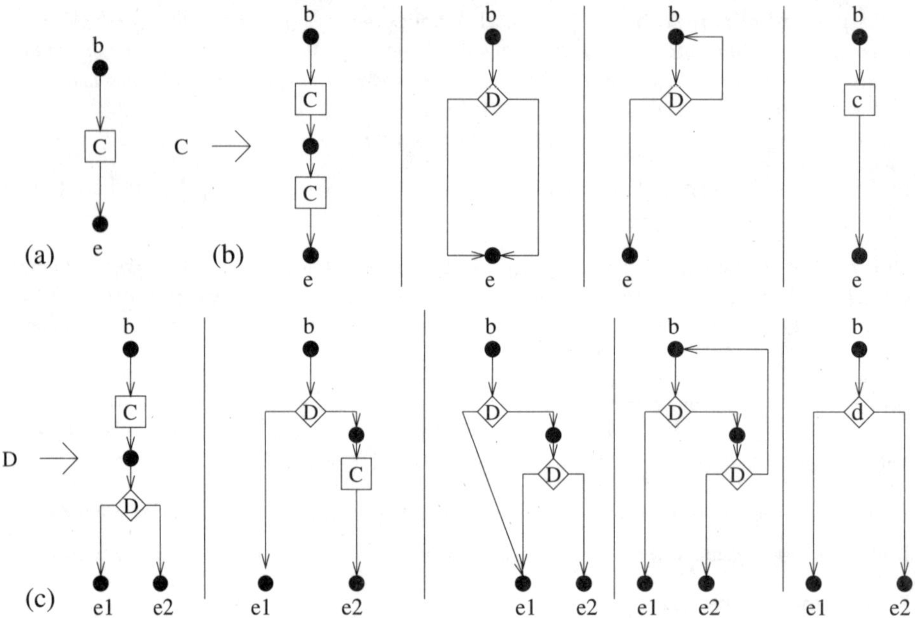

Figure 7.14 An HRG grammar to generate flowcharts

Remark 7.5.10 The idea of string rewriting, especially context-free rewriting, is simple and powerful, and allows one to achieve deeper insights and interesting results. The main motivation for considering more complex rewriting systems, such as graph rewriting systems, comes primarily from applications, and naturally leads to less elegant and more complex (but useful) systems.

Moral: Many formal languages have been developed and many rewriting systems designed and investigated. A good rule of thumb in rewriting is, as in real life, to learn as many languages as you can, and master at least one of them.

7.6 Exercises

1. Design a Post normal system that generates longer and longer prefixes of the Thue ω-word.

2.* Show that each one-tape Turing machine can be simulated by a Post normal system.

3. A group can be represented by a Thue system over an alphabet $\Sigma \cup \{a^{-1} \mid a \in \Sigma\}$ with the set P of productions that includes the productions $aa^{-1} \rightarrow \varepsilon$, $a^{-1}a \rightarrow \varepsilon$, $\varepsilon \rightarrow aa^{-1}$ and $\varepsilon \rightarrow a^{-1}a$. Show that the word problem for groups – namely, to decide, given x and y, whether $x \stackrel{*}{\Longrightarrow} y$ – is polynomial time reducible to the problem of deciding, given a z, whether $z \stackrel{*}{\Longrightarrow} \varepsilon$.

4. Design a type-0 grammar generating the language (a) $\{a^n b^{n^2} \mid n \geq 1\}$; (b) $\{a^{F_i} \mid i \geq 0\}$; (c) $\{a^{n^2} \mid n \geq 1\}$; (d) $\{a^p \mid p \text{ is a prime}\}$.

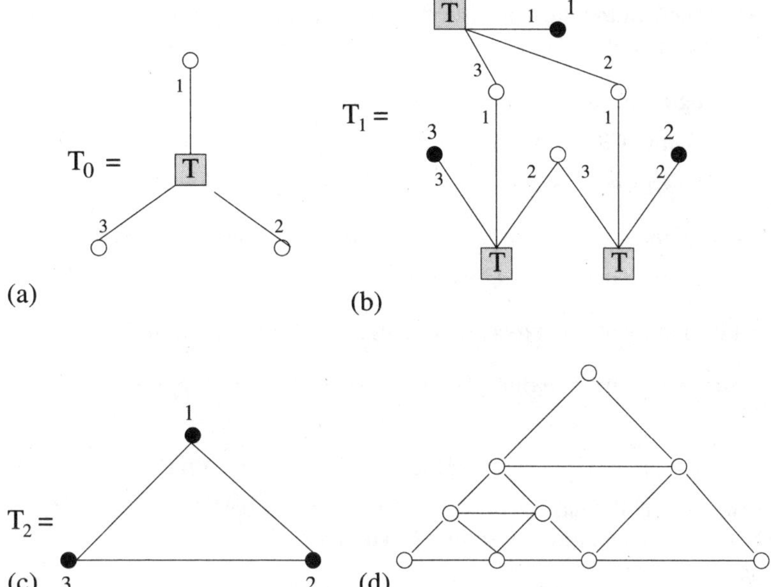

Figure 7.15 Graph grammar generating an approximation of the Sierpiński triangle

5. Describe the language generated by the Chomsky grammars (a) $S \longrightarrow aS \,|\, aSbS \,|\, \varepsilon$;
   (b) $S \longrightarrow aSAB$, $S \longrightarrow abB$, $BA \longrightarrow AB$, $bA \longrightarrow bb$, $bB \longrightarrow bc$, $cB \longrightarrow cc$;
   (c) $S \longrightarrow abc$, $S \longrightarrow aAbc$, $Ab \longrightarrow bA$, $Ac \longrightarrow Bbcc$, $bB \longrightarrow Bb$, $aB \longrightarrow aaA$, $aB \longrightarrow aa$.

6. Given two Chomsky grammars G_1 and G_2, show how to design a Chomsky grammar generating the language (a) $L(G_1) \cup L(G_2)$; (b) $L(G_1) \cap L(G_2)$; (c) $L(G_1)^*$.

7. Show that to each type-0 grammar there exists an equivalent one all rules of which have the form $A \longrightarrow \varepsilon, A \longrightarrow a, A \longrightarrow BC$, or $AB \longrightarrow CD$, where A, B, C, D are nonterminals, a is a terminal, and there is at most one ε-rule.

8. Show that each context-sensitive grammar can be transformed into a similar normal form as in the previous exercise.

9. Show that to each Chomsky grammar there is an equivalent Chomsky grammar that uses only two nonterminals.

10. Show that Chomsky grammars with one nonterminal generate a proper subset of recursively enumerable languages.

11.** (Universal Chomsky grammar) A Chomsky grammar $G_u = \langle V_T, V_N, P, \sigma \rangle$ is called universal if for every recursively enumerable language $L \subset V_T^*$ there exists a string $w_L \in (V_N \cup V_T)^*$ such that $L(w_L) = L$. Show that there exists a universal Chomsky grammar for every terminal alphabet V_T.

12. Design a CSG generating the language (a) $\{w \mid w \in \{a,b,c\}^*, w$ contains the same number of a's, b's and c's$\}$; (b) $\{0^n1^m0^n1^m \mid n,m \geq 0\}$; (c) $\{a^{n^2} \mid n \geq 0\}$; (d) $\{a^p \mid p$ is prime$\}$.

13. Determine languages generated by the grammar

    (a) $S \longrightarrow aSBC \mid aBC$, $CB \longrightarrow BC$, $aB \longrightarrow ab$, $bB \longrightarrow bb$, $bC \longrightarrow bc$, $cC \longrightarrow cc$; (b) $S \longrightarrow SaBC \mid abC$, $aB \longrightarrow Ba$, $Ba \longrightarrow aB$, $aC \longrightarrow Ca$, $Ca \longrightarrow aC$, $BC \longrightarrow CB$, $CB \longrightarrow BC$, $B \longrightarrow b$, $C \longrightarrow c$.

14. Show that the family of context-sensitive languages is closed under operations (a) union; (b) concatenation; (c) iteration; (d) reversal.

15. Show that the family of context-sensitive languages is not closed under homomorphism.

16. Show, for example, by a reduction to the PCP, that the emptiness problem for CSG is undecidable.

17. Design a regular grammar generating the language (a) $(01+101)^* + (1+00)^*01^*0$;

    (b) $((a+bc)(aa^*+ab)^*c+a)^*$; (c) $((0^*10+((01)^*100)^*+0)^*(101(10010)^*+(01)^*1(001)^*)^*)^*$. (In the last case one nonterminal should be enough!)

18. Show that there is a Chomsky grammar which has only productions of the type $A \longrightarrow wB$, $A \longrightarrow Bw$, $A \longrightarrow w$, where A and B are nonterminals and w is a terminal word that generates a nonregular language.

19. Show that an intersection of two CSL is also a CSL.

20. A nonterminal A of a CFG G is cyclic if there is in G a derivation $A \stackrel{*}{\Longrightarrow} uAv$ for some u,v with $uv \neq \varepsilon$. Let G be a CFG in the reduced normal form. Show that the language $L(G)$ is infinite if and only if G has a cyclic nonterminal.

21. Describe a method for designing for each CFG G an equivalent CFG such that all its nonterminals, with perhaps the exception of the initial symbol, generate an infinite language.

22. Design a CFG generating the language

    $L = \{a^{i_1}ba^{i_2}b\ldots a^{i_k}b \mid k \geq 2, \exists X \subset \{1,\ldots,k\}, \sum_{j \in X} i_j = \sum_{j \notin X} i_j\}$.

23. Design a CFG in the reduced normal form equivalent to the grammar

    $S \longrightarrow Ab$, $A \longrightarrow Ba \mid ab \mid B$, $B \longrightarrow bBa \mid aA \mid C$, $C \longrightarrow \varepsilon \mid Sa$.

24. Show that for every CFG G with a terminal alphabet Σ and each integer n, there is a CFG G' generating the language $L(G') = \{u \in \Sigma^* \mid |u| \leq n, u \in L(G)\}$ and such that $|v| \leq n$ for each production $A \longrightarrow v$ of G'.

25. A CFG G is **self-embedded** if there is a nonterminal A such that $A \stackrel{*}{\Longrightarrow} uAv$, where $u \neq \varepsilon \neq v$. Show that the language $L(G)$ is regular for every nonself-embedding CFG G.

26. A PDA $\mathcal{A}$ is said to be unambiguous if for each word $w \in L_f(\mathcal{A})$ there is exactly one sequence of moves by which $\mathcal{A}$ accepts w. Show that a CFL L is unambiguous if and only if there is an unambiguous PDA $\mathcal{A}$ such that $L = L_f(\mathcal{A})$.

27. Show that for every CFL L there is a PDA with two states that accepts L with respect to a final state.

28. Which of the following problems is decidable for CFG G_1 and G_2, nonterminals X and Y and a terminal a: (a) $Prefix(L(G_1)) = Prefix(L(G_2))$; (b) $L_X(G_1) = L_Y(G_1)$; (c) $|L(G_1)| = 1$; (d) $L(G_1) \subseteq a^*$; (e) $L(G_1) = a^*$?

29. Design the upper-triangular matrix which the CYK algorithm uses to recognize the string '*aababab*b' generated by a grammar with the productions $S \longrightarrow CB$, $S \longrightarrow FB$, $S \longrightarrow FA$, $A \longrightarrow a$, $B \longrightarrow FS$, $E \longrightarrow BB$, $B \longrightarrow CE$, $A \longrightarrow CS$, $B \longrightarrow b$, $C \longrightarrow a$, $F \longrightarrow b$.

30. Implement the CYK algorithm on a one-tape Turing machine in such a way that recognition is accomplished in $\mathcal{O}(n^4)$-time.

31. Design a modification of the CYK algorithm that does not require CFG to have some special form.

32. Give a proof of correctness for the CYK algorithm.

33. Show that the following context-free language is not linear: $\{a^n b^n a^m b^m \,|\, n \geq 1\}$.

34. Find another example of a CFL that is not generated by a linear CFG.

35.* Show that the language $\{a^i b^j c^k a^i \,|\, i \geq 1, j \geq k \geq 1\}$ is a DCFL that is not acceptable by a DPDA that does not make an ε-move.

36. Show that if L is a DCFL, then so is the complement of L.

37. Which of the following languages is context-free: (a) $\{a^i b^j c^k \,|\, i,j \geq 1, k > \max\{i,j\}\}$; (b) $\{ww \,|\, w \in \{0,1\}^*\}$?

38. Show that the following languages are context-free:

 (a) $L = \{w_1 c w_2 c \ldots c w_n c c w_i^R \mid 1 \leq i \leq n, w_j \in \{0,1\}^* \text{ for } 1 \leq j \leq n\}$;

 (b) $\{0^{i_1} 1^{j_1} 0^{i_2} 1^{j_2} \ldots 0^{i_n} 1^{j_n} \mid n$ is even and for n/2 pairs it holds $i_k = 2j_k\}$;

 (c) (**Goldstine language**) $\{a^{n_1} b a^{n_2} b \ldots b a^{a_p} b \mid p \geq 1, n_i \geq 0, n_j \neq j \text{ for some } 1 \leq j \leq p\}$;

 (d) the set of those words over $\{a,b\}^*$ that are not prefixes of the ω-word $x = aba^2ba^3ba^4 \ldots a^n ba^{n+1} \ldots$

39. Show that the following languages are not context-free: (a) $\{a^n b^n a^m \,|\, m \geq n \geq 1\}$; (b) $\{a^i \,|\, i \text{ is prime}\}$; (c) $\{a^i b^j c^k \,|\, 0 \leq i \leq j \leq k\}$; (d) $\{a^i b^j c^k \,|\, i \neq j, j \neq k, i \neq k\}$.

40. Show that if a language $L \subseteq \{0,1\}^*$ is regular, $c \notin \{0,1\}$, then the language $L' = \{ucu^R | u \in L\}$ is context-free.

41. Show that every CFL over a one-letter alphabet is regular.

42. Show that if L is a CFL, then the following language is context-free:

 $L_1 = \{a_1 a_3 a_5 \ldots a_{2n+1} \,|\, a_1 a_2 a_3 \ldots a_{2n} a_{2n+1} \in L\}$.

43.* Show that (a) any family of languages closed under concatenation, homomorphism, inverse homomorphism and intersection with regular sets is also closed under union; (b) any family of languages closed under iteration, homomorphism, inverse homomorphism, union and intersection with regular languages is also closed under concatenation.

44. Show that if L is a CFL, then the set $S = \{|w| \mid w \in L\}$ is an ultimately periodic set of integers (that is, there are integers n_0 and p such that if $x \in S, x > n_0$, then $(x+p) \in S$).

45. Design a PDA accepting Greibach's language.

46.* Show that the Dyck language can be accepted by a Turing machine with space complexity $\mathcal{O}(\lg n)$.

47.* Show that every context-free language is a homomorphic image of a deterministic CFL.

48. Show that the family of 0L-languages does not contain all finite languages, and that it is not closed under the operations (a) union; (b) concatenation; (c) intersection with regular languages.

49. Show that every language generated by a 0L-system is context-sensitive.

50. Determine the growth function for the following 0L-systems:

    (a) with axiom S and productions $S \longrightarrow Sbd^6, b \longrightarrow bcd^{11}, c \longrightarrow cd^6, d \longrightarrow d$;

    (b) with axiom a and productions $a \longrightarrow abcc, b \longrightarrow bcc, c \longrightarrow c$.

51. Design a 0L-system with the growth function $(n+1)^4$.

52. So-called ET0L-systems have especially nice properties. An ET0L-system is defined by $G = \langle \Sigma, \mathcal{H}, \omega, \Delta \rangle$, where $\mathcal{H}$ is a finite set of substitutions $h : \Sigma \rightarrow 2^{\Sigma^*}$ and for every $h \in \mathcal{H}$, (Σ, h, ω) is a 0L-system, and $\Delta \subseteq \Sigma$ is a terminal alphabet. The language L generated by G is defined by $L(G) = \{h_1(h_2(\ldots(h_k(\omega))\ldots)) \mid h_i \in \mathcal{H}\} \cap \Delta^*$. (In other words, an ET0L-system consists of a finite set of 0L-systems, and at each step of a derivation one of them is used. Finally, only those of the generated words go to the language that are in Δ^*.)

    (a) Show that the family of languages $\mathcal{L}(\text{ET0L})$ generated by ET0L-systems is closed under the operations (i) union, (ii) concatenation, (iii) intersection with regular languages, (iv) homomorphism and (v) inverse homomorphism. (b) Design an ET0L-system generating the language $\{a^i b^i a^i \mid i \geq 0\}$.

53. (Array rewriting) Just as we have string rewritings and string rewriting grammars, so we can consider array rewritings and array rewriting grammars. An array will now be seen as a mapping $\mathcal{A} : \mathbf{Z} \times \mathbf{Z} \rightarrow \Sigma \cup \{\#\}$ such that $\mathcal{A}(i,j) \neq \#$ only for finitely many pairs. Informally, an array rewriting production gives a rule describing how a connected subarray (pattern) can be rewritten by another one of the same geometrical shape. An extension or a shortening can be achieved by rewriting the surrounding ε's, or by replacing a symbol from the alphabet Σ by $\#$. The following 'context-free' array productions generate 'T's of 'a's from the start array S:

$$\begin{array}{c} \#\#\# \\ S \end{array} \longrightarrow \begin{array}{c} LaR \\ D \end{array}, \quad \begin{array}{c} D \\ \# \end{array} \longrightarrow \begin{array}{c} a \\ D \end{array}, \quad \begin{array}{c} D \\ \# \end{array} \longrightarrow \begin{array}{c} a \\ a \end{array},$$

$$\#L \longrightarrow La, \quad L \longrightarrow a, \quad R\# \longrightarrow aR, \quad R \longrightarrow a.$$

    Construct context-free array grammars generating (a) rectangles of 'a's; (b) squares of 'a's.

54. (Generation of strings by graph grammars) A string $a_1 \ldots a_n$ can be seen as a *string graph* with $n+1$ nodes and n edges labelled by $a_1, \ldots, a_n$, respectively, connecting the nodes. Similarly, each string graph G can be seen as representing a string G_s of labels of its edges. Show that a (context-free) HR graph grammar $\mathcal{G}$ can generate a noncontext-free string language $L \subset \{w \mid w \in \{0,1\}^*\}$ in the sense that $L = \{G_s \mid G \in L(\mathcal{G})\}$.

55. Design an HR graph grammar $\mathcal{G}$ that generates string graphs such that $\{G_s \,|\, G \in L(\mathcal{G})\} = \{a^n b^n c^n \,|\, n \geq 1\}$.

56. An NLC graph grammar $\mathcal{G} = \langle V_N, V_T, C, G_0, P\rangle$ is said to be context-free if for each $a \in V_T$ either $(\{a\} \times V_T) \cap C = \emptyset$ or $(\{a\} \times V_T) \cap C = \{a\} \times V_T$. Show that it is decidable, given a context-free NLC graph grammar $\mathcal{G}$, whether $L(\mathcal{G})$ contains a discrete graph (no two nodes of which are connected by an edge).

57.* Design a handle NLC graph grammar to generate all rings with at least three nodes. Can this be done by an NLC graph grammar?

58.* Show that if we do not use a global gluing operation in the case of handle NLC graph grammars, but for each production a special one of the same type, then this does not increase the generative power of HNLC grammars.

59. Show that for every recursively enumerable string language L there is an HNLC graph grammar $\mathcal{G}$ generating string graphs such that $L = \{G_s | G \in L(\mathcal{G})\}$. (Hint: design an HNLC graph grammar simulating a Chomsky grammar for L.)

QUESTIONS

1. Production systems, as introduced in Section 7.1, deal with the rewriting of one-dimensional strings. Can they be generalized to deal with the rewriting of two-dimensional strings? If yes, how? If not, why?

2. The equivalence of Turing machines and Chomsky grammars implies that problems stated in terms of one of these models of computation can be rephrased in terms of another model. Is this always true? If not, when is it true?

3. Can every regular language be generated by an unambiguous CFG?

4. What does the undecidability of the halting problem imply for the type-0 grammars?

5. What kind of English sentences cannot be generated by a context-free grammar?

6. How much can it cost to transform a given CFG into (a) Chomsky normal form; (b) Greibach normal form?

7. What is the difference between the two basic acceptance modes for (deterministic) pushdown automata?

8. What kind of growth functions have different types of D0L-systems?

9. How can one show that context-sensitive L-systems are more powerful than D0L-systems?

10. What is the basic idea of (a) node rewriting (b) edge rewriting, for graphs?

7.7 Historical and Bibliographical References

Two papers by Thue (1906, 1914) introducing rewriting systems, called nowadays Thue and semi-Thue systems, can be seen as the first contributions to rewriting systems and formal language theory. However, it was Noam Chomsky (1956, 1957, 1959) who presented the concept of formal grammar and basic grammar hierarchy and vigorously brought new research paradigms into linguistics. Chomsky, together with Schützenberger (1963), introduced the basic aims, tools and methods of formal language theory. The importance of context-free languages for describing the syntax of programming languages and for compiling was another stimulus to the very fast development of the area in the 1970s and 1980s. Books by Ginsburg (1966), Hopcroft and Ullman (1969) and Salomaa (1973) contributed much to that development. Nowadays there is a variety of other books available: for example, Harrison (1978) and Floyd and Beigel (1994).

Deterministic versions of semi-Thue systems, called Markov algorithms were introduced by A. A. Markov in 1951.

Post (1943) introduced systems nowadays called by his name. Example 7.1.3 is due to Penrose (1990) and credited to G. S. Tseitin and D. Scott. Basic relations between type-0 and type-3 grammars and automata are due to Chomsky (1957, 1959) and Chomsky and Schützenberger (1963). The first claim of Theorem 7.2.9 is folklore; for the second, see Exercise 10, due to Geffert, and for the third see Geffert (1991). Example 7.3.8 is due to Bertol and Reinhardt (1995). Greibach (1965) introduced the normal form that now carries her name. The formal notion of a PDA and its equivalence to a CFG are due to Chomsky (1962) and Evey (1963).

The normal form for PDA is from Maurer (1969). Kuroda (1964) has shown that NLBA and context-sensitive grammars have the same power.

Methods of transforming a given CFG into a Greibach normal form can be found in Salomaa (1973), Harrison (1978) and Floyd and Beigel (1994). The original sources for the CYK parsing algorithm are Kasami (1965) and Younger (1967). This algorithm is among those that have been often studied from various points of view (correctness and complexity). There are many books on parsing: for example, Aho and Ullman (1972) and Sippu and Soisalon-Soininen (1990). Reduction of parsing to Boolean matrix multiplication is due to Valiant (1975); see Harrison (1978) for a detailed exposition. A parsing algorithm for CFG with the space complexity $\mathcal{O}(\lg^2 n)$ on MTM is due to Lewis, Stearns and Hartmanis (1965), with $\mathcal{O}(lg^2n)$ time complexity on PRAM to Ruzzo (1980), and on hypercubes with $\mathcal{O}(n^6)$ processors to Rytter (1985). $\mathcal{O}(n^2)$ algorithm for syntactical analysis of unambiguous CFG is due to Kasami and Torii (1969). Deterministic pushdown automata and languages are dealt with in many books, especially Harrison (1978).

The pumping lemma for context-free languages presented in Section 7.3 is due to Bar-Hillel (1964). Several other pumping lemmas are discussed in detail by Harrison (1978) and Floyd and Beigel (1994). Characterization results are presented by Salomaa (1973) and Harrison (1978). For results and the corresponding references concerning closure properties, undecidability and ambiguity for context-free grammars and languages see Ginsburg (1966). For **P**-completeness results for CFG see Jones and Laaser (1976) and Greenlaw, Hoover and Ruzzo (1995). The hardest CFL is due to Greibach (1973), as is Theorem 7.3.48. Theorem 7.3.17 is due to Gruska (1969).

The concept of an L-system was introduced by Aristid Lindenmayer (1968). The formal theory of L-systems is presented in Rozenberg and Salomaa (1980), where one can also find results concerning closure and undecidability properties, as well as references to earlier work in this area. The study of growth functions was initiated by Paz and Salomaa (1973). For basic results concerning E0L-systems see Rozenberg and Salomaa (1986). The decidability of D0L-systems is due to Culik and Friš (1977).

There have been various attempts to develop graphical modelling of L-systems. The one developed by Prusinkiewicz is perhaps the most successful so far. For a detailed presentation of this approach see Prusinkiewicz and Lindenmayer (1990) which is well-illustrated, with ample references.

Section 7.4.2 is derived from this source; the examples and pictures are drawn by the system due to H. Fernau and use specifications from Prusinkiewicz and Lindenmayer. Example 7.4.2 and Figure 7.5 are also due to them.

There is a variety of modifications of L-systems other than those discussed in this chapter that have been successfully used to model plants and natural processes. Much more refined and sophisticated implementations use additional parameters and features, for example, colour, and provide interesting visual results. See Prusinkiewicz and Lindenmayer (1990) for a comprehensive treatment of the subject.

There is a large literature on graph grammars, presented especially in the proceedings of Graph Grammar Workshops (see LNCS 153, 291, 532). NLC graph grammars were introduced by Janssens and Rozenberg (1980a, 1980b) and have been intensively developed since then. These papers also deal with a pumping lemma and its applications, as well as with decidability results. For an introduction to NLC graph grammars see Rozenberg (1987), from which my presentation and examples were derived. Edge rewriting was introduced by H.-J. Kreowski (1977). The pumping lemma concerning edge rewriting is due to Kreowski (1979). Hyperedge rewriting was introduced by Habel and Kreowski (1987) and Bauderon and Courcelle (1987). The pumping lemma for HR graph grammars is due to Habel and Kreowski (1987). Decidability results are due to Habel, Kreowski and Vogler (1989). For an introduction to the subject see Habel and Kreowski (1987a), my presentation and examples are derived from it, and Habel (1990a,1990b). For recent surveys on node and hyperedge replacement grammars see Engelfriet and Rozenberg (1996) and Drewes, Habel and Kreowski (1996).

From a variety of other rewriting ideas I will mention briefly three; for some other approaches and references see Salomaa (1973, 1985). **Term rewriting**, usually credited to Evans (1951), deals with methods for transforming complex expressions/terms into simpler ones. It is an intensively developed idea with various applications, especially in the area of formal methods for software development. For a comprehensive treatment see Dershowitz and Jouannaud (1990) and Kirchner (1997). **Array grammars**, used to rewrite two-dimensional arrays (array pictures), were introduced by Milgram and Rosenfeld (1971). For an interesting presentation of various approaches and results see Wang (1989). Exercise 53 is due to R. Freund. For array grammars generating squares see Freund (1994). **Co-operating grammars** were introduced by Meersman and Rozenberg (1978). The basic idea is that several rewriting systems of the same type participate, using various rules for co-operation, in rewriting. In a rudimentary way this is true also for T0L-systems. For a survey see Paŭn (1995). For a combination of both approaches see Dassow, Freund and Paŭn (1995).

8 Cryptography

INTRODUCTION

A successful, insightful and fruitful search for the borderlines between the possible and the impossible has been highlighted since the 1930s by the development in computability theory of an understanding of what is effectively computable. Since the 1960s this has continued with the development in complexity theory of an understanding of what is efficiently computable. The work continues with the development in modern cryptography of an understanding of what can be securely communicated. Cryptography was an ancient art, became a deep science, and aims to be one of the key technologies of the information era.

Modern cryptography can be seen as an important dividend of complexity theory. The work bringing important stimuli not only for complexity theory and foundations of computing, but also for the whole of science. Cryptography is rich in deep ideas, interesting applications and contrasts. It is an area with very close relations between theory and applications.

In this chapter the main ideas of classical and modern cryptography are presented, illustrated, analysed and displayed.

LEARNING OBJECTIVES

The aim of the chapter is to demonstrate

1. the basic aims, concepts and methods of classical and modern cryptography;
2. several basic cryptosystems of secret-key cryptography;
3. the main types of cryptoanalytic attacks;
4. the main approaches and applications of public-key cryptography;
5. knapsack and RSA cryptosystems and their analysis;
6. the key concepts of trapdoor one-way functions and predicates and cryptographically strong pseudo-random generators;
7. the main approaches to randomized encryptions and their security;
8. methods of digital signatures, including the DSS system.

Secret de deux, secret de Dieu,
secret de trois, secret de tous.

French proverb

For thousands of years, **cryptography** has been the art of providing secure communication over insecure channels. **Cryptoanalysis** is the art of breaking into such communications. Until the advent of computers and the information-driven society, **cryptology**, the combined art of cryptography and cryptoanalysis, lay almost exclusively in the hands of diplomats and the military. Nowadays, cryptography is a technology without which public communications could hardly exist. It is also a science that makes deep contributions to the foundations of computing. A short modern history of cryptography would include three milestones.

During the Second World War the needs of cryptoanalysis led the development at Bletchley Park of Colossus, the first very powerful electronic computer. This was used to speed up the breaking of the ENIGMA code and contributed significantly to the success of the Allies. Postwar recognition of the potential of science and technology for society has been influenced by this achievement.

Second, the goals of cryptography were extended in order to create the efficient, secure communication and information storage without which modern society could hardly function. Public-key cryptography, digital signatures and cryptographical communication protocols have changed our views of what is possible concerning secure communications.

Finally, ideas emanating from cryptography have led to new and deep concepts such as one-way functions, zero-knowledge proofs, interactive proof systems, holographic proofs and program checking. Significant developments have taken place in understanding of the power of randomness and interactions for computing.

The first theoretical approach to cryptography, due to Shannon (1949), was based on **information theory**. This was developed by Shannon on the basis of his work in cryptography and the belief that cryptoanalysts should not have enough information to decrypt messages. The current approach is based on **complexity theory** and the belief that cryptoanalysts should not have enough time or space to decrypt messages. There are also promising attempts to develop quantum cryptography, whose security is based on the **laws of quantum physics**.

There are various peculiarities and paradoxes connected with modern cryptology. When a nation's most closely guarded secret is made public, it becomes more important. Positive results of cryptography are based on negative results of complexity theory, on the existence of unfeasible computational problems.[1] Computers, which were originally developed to help cryptoanalysts, seem now to be much more useful for cryptography. Surprisingly, cryptography that is too perfect also causes problems. Once developed to protect against 'bad forces', it can now serve actually to protect them.

There are very few areas of computing with such a close interplay between deep theory and important practice or where this relation is as complicated as in modern cryptography.

Cryptography has a unique view of what it means for an integer to be 'practically large enough'. In some cases only numbers at least 512 bits long, far exceeding the total lifetime of the universe, are considered large enough. Practical cryptography has also developed a special view of what is

[1]The idea of using unfeasible problems for the protection of communication is actually very old and goes back at least to Archimedes. He used to send lists of his recent discoveries, stated without proofs, to his colleagues in Alexandria. In order to prevent statements like 'We have discovered all that by ourselves' as a response, Archimedes occasionally inserted false statements or practically unsolvable problems among them. For example, the problem mentioned in Example 6.4.22 has a solution with more than 206,500 digits.

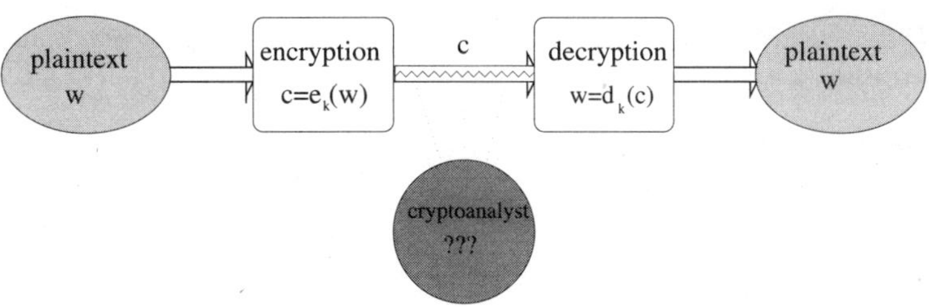

Figure 8.1 Cryptosystem

computationally unfeasible. If something can be done with a million supercomputers in a couple of weeks, then it is not considered as completely unfeasible. As a consequence, mostly only toy examples can be presented in any book on cryptology.

In this chapter we deal with two of the most basic problems of cryptography: secure encryptions and secure digital signatures. In the next chapter, more theoretical concepts developed from cryptographical considerations are discussed.

8.1 Cryptosystems and Cryptology

Cryptology can be seen as an ongoing battle, in the space of cryptosystems, between cryptography and cryptoanalysis, with no indications so far as to which side is going to win. It is also an ongoing search for proper trade-offs between security and efficiency.

Applications of cryptography are numerous, and there is no problem finding impressive examples. One can even say, without exaggeration, that an information era is impossible without cryptography. For example, it is true that electronic communications are paperless. However, we still need electronic versions of envelopes, signatures and company letterheads, and they can hardly exist meaningfully without cryptography.

8.1.1 Cryptosystems

Cryptography deals with the problem of sending an (intelligible) message (usually called a **plaintext** or **cleartext**) through an unsecure channel that may be tapped by an enemy (usually called an **eavesdropper**, **adversary**, or simply **cryptoanalyst**) to an intended receiver. In order to increase the likelihood that the message will not be learned by some unintended receiver, the sender **encrypts (enciphers)** the plaintext to produce an (unintelligible) **cryptotext (ciphertext, cryptogram)**, and sends the cryptotext through the channel. The encryption has to be done in such a way that the intended receiver is able to **decrypt** the cryptotext to obtain the plaintext. However, an eavesdropper should not be able to do so (see Figure 8.1).

Encryption and decryption always take place within a specific **cryptosystem**. Each cryptosystem has the following components:

Plaintext-space $\mathcal{P}$ – a set of words over an alphabet Σ, called plaintexts, or sentences in a natural language.

Cryptotext-space $\mathcal{C}$ – a set of words over an alphabet Δ, called cryptotexts.

Key-space $\mathcal{K}$ – a set of keys.

Each key k determines within a cryptosystem an **encryption algorithm** (function) e_k and a **decryption algorithm** (function) d_k such that for any plaintext w, $e_k(w)$ is the corresponding cryptotext and $w \in d_k(e_k(w))$. A decryption algorithm is therefore a sort of inverse of an encryption algorithm. Encryption algorithms can be probabilistic; that is, neither encryption nor decryption has to be unique. However, for practical reasons, unique decryptions are preferable.

Encryption and decryption are often specified by a general encryption algorithm e and a general decryption algorithm d such that $e_k(w) = e(k,w), d_k(c) = d(k,c)$ for any plaintext w, cryptotext c and any key k.

We start a series of examples of cryptosystems with one of the best-known classical cryptosystems.

Example 8.1.1 (CAESAR cryptosystem) *We illustrate this cryptosystem, described by Julius Caesar (100–42 BC), in a letter to Cicero, on encrypting words of the English alphabet with 26 capital letters. The key space consists of 26 integers* $0,1,\ldots,25$. *The encryption algorithm* e_k *substitutes any letter by the one occurring* k *positions ahead (cyclically) in the alphabet; the decryption algorithm* d_k *substitutes any letter by that occurring* k *position backwards (cyclically) in the alphabet. For* $k = 3$ *the substitution has the following form*

```
Old: A B C D E F G H I J K L M N O P Q R S T U V W X Y Z
New: D E F G H I J K L M N O P Q R S T U V W X Y Z A B C
```

Some encryptions:

$$e_{25}(IBM) = HAL, \quad e_{11}(KNAPSACK) = VYLADLNV, \quad e_{20}(PARIS) = JULCM.$$

The history of cryptography is about 4,000 years old if one includes cryptographic transformations in tomb inscriptions. The following cryptosystem is perhaps the oldest among so-called substitution cryptosystems.

Example 8.1.2 (POLYBIOS cryptosystem) *This is the cryptosystem described by the Greek historian Polybios (200–118 BC). It uses as keys the so-called Polybios checkerboards: for example, the one shown in Figure 8.2a with the English alphabet of 25 letters ('J' is omitted).*[2] *Each symbol is substituted by the pair of symbols representing the row and the column of the checkerboard in which the symbol is placed. For example, the plaintext 'INFORMATION' is encrypted as 'BICHBFCIDGCGAFDIBICICH'.*

The cryptosystem presented in the next example was probably never used. In spite of this, it played an important role in the history of cryptography. It initiated the development of algebraic and combinatorial methods in cryptology and attracted mathematicians to cryptography.

Example 8.1.3 (HILL cryptosystem) *In this cryptosystem, based on linear algebra and invented by L. S. Hill (1929), an integer* n *is fixed first. The plaintext and cryptotext space consists of words of length* n*: for example, over the English alphabet of 26 letters. Keys are matrices* M *of degree* n*, elements of which are integers from the set* $\Delta = \{0,1,\ldots,25\}$ *such that the inverse matrix* M^{-1} *modulo 26 exists. For a word* w *let* C_w *be the column vector of length* n *consisting of codes of* n *symbols in* w *– each symbol is replaced by its position in the alphabet.*

To encrypt a plaintext w *of length* n*, the matrix-vector product* $C_c = MC_w \bmod 26$ *is computed. In the resulting vector, the integers are decoded, replaced by the corresponding letters. To decrypt a cryptotext* c*, at*

[2]It is not by chance that the letter 'J' is omitted; it was the last letter to be introduced into the current English alphabet. The PLAYFAIR cryptosystem with keys in the form of 'Playfair squares' (see Figure 8.2b) will be discussed later.

	F	G	H	I	J
A	A	B	C	D	E
B	F	G	H	I	K
C	L	M	N	O	P
D	Q	R	S	T	U
E	V	W	X	Y	Z

(a) Polybios checkerboard

S	D	Z	I	U
H	A	F	N	G
B	M	V	Y	W
R	P	L	C	X
T	O	E	K	Q

(b) Playfair square

Figure 8.2 Classical cryptosystems

first the product $M^{-1}C_c \bmod 26$ *is computed, and then the numbers are replaced by letters. A longer plaintext first has to be broken into words of length n, and then each of them is encrypted separately .*

For an illustration, let us consider the case $n = 2$ *and*

$$M = \begin{pmatrix} 4 & 7 \\ 1 & 1 \end{pmatrix}, \qquad M^{-1} = \begin{pmatrix} 17 & 11 \\ 9 & 16 \end{pmatrix}.$$

For the plaintext $w = LONDON$ *we have* $C_{LO} = (11,14)^T, C_{ND} = (13,3)^T, C_{ON} = (14,13)^T$, *and therefore,*

$$MC_{LO} = (12,25)^T, \qquad MC_{ND} = (21,16)^T, \qquad MC_{ON} = (17,1)^T.$$

The corresponding cryptotext is then 'MZVQRB'. It is easy to check that from the cryptotext 'WWXTTX' the plaintext 'SECRET' is obtained. Indeed,

$$M^{-1}C_{WW} = \begin{pmatrix} 17 & 11 \\ 9 & 16 \end{pmatrix}\begin{pmatrix} 22 \\ 22 \end{pmatrix} = \begin{pmatrix} 18 \\ 4 \end{pmatrix} = \begin{pmatrix} S \\ E \end{pmatrix},$$

and so on.

In most practical cryptosystems, as in the HILL cryptosystem, the plaintext-space is finite and much smaller than the space of the messages that need to be encrypted. To encrypt a longer message, it must be broken into pieces and each encrypted separately. This brings additional problems, discussed later. In addition, if a message to be encrypted is not in the plaintext-space alphabet, it must first be encoded into such an alphabet. For example, if the plaintext-space is the set of all binary strings of a certain length, which is often the case, then in order to encrypt an English alphabet text, its symbols must first be replaced (encoded) by some fixed-length binary codes.

Exercise 8.1.4 *Encrypt the plaintext 'A GOOD PROOF MAKE US WISER' using (a) the CAESAR cryptosystem with* $k = 13$; *(b) the POLYBIOS cryptosystem with some checkerboard; (c) the HILL cryptosystem with some matrix.*

Sir Francis R. Bacon (1561–1626) formulated the requirements for an ideal cryptosystem. Currently we require of a **good cryptosystem** the following properties:

1. Given e_k and a plaintext w, it should be easy to compute $c = e_k(w)$.

2. Given d_k and a cryptotext c, it should be easy to compute $w = d_k(c)$.

3. A cryptotext $e_k(w)$ should be not much longer than the plaintext w.

4. It should be unfeasible to determine w from $e_k(w)$ without knowing d_k.

5. The **avalanche effect** should hold. A small change in the plaintext, or in the key, should lead to a big change in the cryptotext (for example, a change of one bit of a plaintext should result in a change of all bits of the cryptotext with a probability close to 0.5).

Item (4) is the minimum we require for a cryptosystem to be considered secure. However, as discussed later, cryptosystems with this property may not be secure enough under special circumstances.

8.1.2 Cryptoanalysis

The aim of the **cryptoanalysis** is to get as much information as possible about the plaintext or the key. It is usually assumed that it is known which cryptosystem was used, or at least a small set of the potential cryptosystems one of which was used. The main types of cryptoanalytic attacks are:

1. **Cryptotexts-only attack.** The cryptoanalysts get cryptotexts $c_1 = e_k(w_1), \ldots, c_n = e_k(w_n)$ and try to infer the key k or as many plaintexts $w_1, \ldots, w_n$ as possible.

2. **Known-plaintexts attack.** The cryptoanalysts know some pairs $(w_i, e_k(w_i)), 1 \leq i \leq n$, and try to infer k, or at least to determine w_{n+1}, for a new cryptotext $e_k(w_{n+1})$.

3. **Chosen-plaintexts attack.** The cryptoanalysts choose plaintexts $w_1, \ldots, w_n$, obtain cryptotexts $e_k(w_1), \ldots, e_k(w_n)$, and try to infer k or at least w_{n+1} for a new cryptotext $c_{n+1} = e_k(w_{n+1})$.

4. **Known-encryption-algorithm attack.** The encryption algorithm e_k is given and the cryptoanalysts try to obtain the decryption algorithm d_k before actually receiving any samples of the cryptotext.

5. **Chosen-cryptotext attack.** The cryptoanalysts know some pairs $(c_i, d_k(c_i)), 1 \leq i \leq n$, where the cryptotexts c_i have been chosen by cryptoanalysts. The task is to determine the key.

Exercise 8.1.5 *A spy group received information about the arrival of a new member. The secret police discovered the message and knew that it was encrypted using the HILL cryptosystem with a matrix of degree 2. It also learned that the code '10 3 11 21 19 5' stands for the name of the spy and '24 19 16 19 5 21' for the city, TANGER, the spy should come from. What is the name of the spy?*

One of the standard techniques for increasing the security of a cryptosystem is double encryption. The plaintext is encrypted with one key and the resulting cryptotext is encrypted with another key. In other words $e_{k_2}(e_{k_1}(w))$ is computed for the plaintext w and keys k_1, k_2. A cryptosystem is **closed under composition** if for every two encryption keys k_1, k_2, there is a single encryption key having the effect of these two keys applied consecutively. That is, $e_k(w) = e_{k_2}(e_{k_1}(w))$ for all w. Closure under composition therefore means that a consecutive application of two keys does not increase security. CAESAR is clearly composite. POLYBIOS is clearly not composite.

Exercise 8.1.6* *Show that the HILL cryptosystem is composite.*

There are two basic types of cryptosystems: **secret-key cryptosystems** and **public-key cryptosystems**. We deal with them in the next two sections.

8.2 Secret-key Cryptosystems

A cryptosystem is called a secret-key cryptosystem if some secret piece of information, the key, has to be agreed upon ahead of time between two parties that want or need to communicate through the cryptosystem. CAESAR, POLYBIOS and HILL are examples.

There are two basic types of secret-key cryptosystems: those based on **substitutions** where each letter of the plaintext is replaced by another letter or word; and those based on **transpositions** where the letters of the plaintext are permuted.

8.2.1 Mono-alphabetic Substitution Cryptosystems

Cryptosystems based on a substitution are either **mono-alphabetic** or **poly-alphabetic**. In a mono-alphabetic substitution cryptosystem the substitution rule remains unaltered during encryption, while in a poly-alphabetic substitution cryptosystem this is not the case. CAESAR and POLYBIOS are examples of mono-alphabetic cryptosystems.

A mono-alphabetic substitution cryptosystem, with letter-by-letter substitution and with the alphabet of plaintexts the same as that of cryptotexts, is uniquely specified by a permutation of letters in the alphabet. Various cryptosystems differ in the way that such a permutation is specified. The main aim is usually that the permutation should be easy to remember and use.

In the **AFFINE** cryptosystem (for English) a permutation is specified by two integers $1 \leq a, b \leq 25$, such that a and 26 are relatively prime and the xth letter of the alphabet is substituted by the $((ax+b) \bmod 26)$th letter. (The condition that a and 26 are relatively prime is necessary in order for the mapping

$$f(x) = (ax+b) \bmod 26$$

to be a permutation.)

Exercise 8.2.1 *Determine the permutation of letters of the English alphabet obtained when the AFFINE cryptosystem with $a = 3$ and $b = 5$ is used.*

Exercise 8.2.2 *For the following pairs of plaintext and cryptotext determine which cryptosystem was used:*

(a) COMPUTER - HOWEVER THE REST UNDERESTIMATES ZANINESS YOUR JUDICIOUS WISDOM;
(b) SAUNA AND LIFE - RMEMHCZZTCEZTZKKDA.

	%		%		%		%		%		%		%
E	13.04	N	7.07	H	5.28	C	2.79	G	1.99	V	0.92	Q	0.12
T	10.45	R	6.77	D	3.78	U	2.49	P	1.99	K	0.42	Z	0.08
A	8.56	S	6.27	L	3.39	M	2.49	W	1.49	X	0.17		
O	7.97	I	6.07	F	2.89	Y	1.99	B	1.39	J	0.13		

Figure 8.3 Frequency table for English letters due to A. Konheim (1981)

Exercise 8.2.3 *Decrypt the following cryptotexts which have been encrypted using one of the cryptosystems described above or some of their modifications. (Caution: not all plaintexts are in English.)*

(a) WFLEUKZFEKZFEJFWTFDGLKZEX;

(b) DANVHEYD SENHGKIIAJ VQN GNULPKCNWLDEA;

(c) DHAJAHDGAJDI AIAJ AIAJDJEH DHAJAHDGAJDI AIDJ AIBIAJDJ DHAJAHDGAJDI AIAJ DIDGCIBIDH DHAJAHDGAJDI AIAJ DICIDJDH;

(d) KLJPMYHUKV LZAL ALEAV LZ TBF MHJPS.

The decryption of a longer cryptotext obtained by a mono-alphabetic encryption from a meaningful English text is fairly easy using a frequency table for letters: for example, the one in Figure 8.3.[3]

Indeed, it is often enough to use a frequency table to determine the most frequently used letters and then to guess the rest. (One can also use the frequency tables for pairs (digrams) and triples (trigrams) that were published for various languages.) In case of an AFFINE cryptosystem a frequency table can help to determine the coefficients a and b.

Exercise 8.2.4 *On the basis of frequency analysis it has been guessed that the most common letter in a cryptotext, Z, corresponds to O and the second most frequent letter, I, corresponds to T. If you know that the AFFINE cryptosystem was used, determine its coefficients.*

Exercise 8.2.5 *Suppose the encryption is done using the AFFINE cryptosystem with* $c(x) = (ax + b) \bmod 26$. *Determine the decryption function.*

The fact that we can, with large probability, guess the rest of the plaintext, once several letters of the cryptotext have been decrypted, is based on the following result. In the case of mono-alphabetic substitution cryptosystems the expected number of potentially meaningful plaintexts for a cryptotext of length n is $2^{H(K)-nD} - 1$, where $H(K)$ is the so-called entropy of the key-space (for example, $\lg 26!$ for English), and D is a measure of the redundancy of the plaintext language in bits per letter (for example, 3.5 for English). This means that for a cryptotext of length $n > 25$, for example, only one meaningful English plaintext is expected.

Finally, let us illustrate with mono-alphabetic substitution cryptosystems the differences between the first three cryptoanalytic attacks described on page 470.

[3]The most frequently used symbols in some other languages, from Gaines (1939): French: E–15.87%, A–9.42%, I–8.41%, S–7.90%, T–7.26%, N–7.15%; German: E–18.46%, N–11.42%, I–8.02%, R–7.14%, S–7.04%; Spanish: E–13.15%, A–12.69%, O–9.49%, S–7.60%.

We have already indicated how frequency tables can be used to make cryptoanalytic attacks under the 'cryptotexts-only' condition fairly easy, though it may require some work. Mono-alphabetic substitution cryptosystems are trivial to break under the 'known-plaintext' attack as soon as the known plaintexts have used all the symbols of the alphabet. These cryptosystems are even more trivial to break in the case of the 'chosen-plaintext' attack – choose ABCDEFGHIJKLMNOPQRSTUVWXYZ as the plaintext.

Exercise 8.2.6* *Assume that the most frequent trigrams in a cryptotext obtained using the HILL cryptosystem are LME, WRI and XYC, and that they are THE, AND and THA in the plaintext. Determine the* 3×3 *matrix that was used.*

8.2.2 Poly-alphabetic Substitution Cryptosystems

The oldest idea for a poly-alphabetic cryptosystem was to divide the plaintext into blocks of two letters and then use a mapping $\phi : \Sigma \times \Sigma \rightarrow \Sigma^*$, usually described by a table. The oldest such cryptosystem is due to Giovanni Polleste Porta (1563). The cryptosystem shown in the next example, due to Charles Wheatsone (1854) and named by Baron Lyon Playfair, was first used in the Crimean War, then intensively in the field during the First World War and also in the Second World War by the Allies.

Example 8.2.7 (PLAYFAIR cryptosystem) *To illustrate the idea, we restrict ourselves again to 25 letters of the English alphabet arranged in a* 5×5 *table (Figure 8.2b) called the 'Playfair square'. To encrypt a plaintext, its letters are grouped into blocks of two, and it is assumed that no block contains two identical letters. (If this is not the case, the plaintext must be modified: for example, by introducing some trivial spelling errors.)*

The encryption of a pair of letters, X and Y, is done as follows. If X and Y are neither in the same row nor in the same column, then the smallest rectangle containing X, Y is taken, and X, Y are replaced by the pair of symbols in the remaining corners and the corresponding columns. If X and Y are in the same row (column), then they are replaced by the pair of symbols to the right (below) of them – in a cyclic way, if necessary. An illustration: using the square in Figure 8.2b, the plaintext PLAYFAIR is encrypted as LCMNNFCS.

Various poly-alphabetic cryptosystems are created as a modification of the CAESAR cryptosystem using the following scheme, illustrated again on English texts. A 26×26 table is first designed, with the first row containing all symbols of the alphabet and all columns representing CAESAR shifts, starting with the symbol of the first row. Second, for a plaintext w a key k, a word of the same length as w, is chosen. In the encryption the ith letter of the plaintext – $w(i)$ – is replaced by the letter in the $w(i)$ row and the column with $k(i)$ as the first symbol. Various such cryptosystems differ in the way the key is determined.

In **VIGENÈRE** cryptosystems, named by the French cryptographer Blaise de Vigenère (1523–96), the key k for a plaintext w is created from a keyword p as $Prefix_{|w|}\{p^{\omega}\}$. In the cryptosystem called **AUTOCLAVE**, credited to the Italian mathematician Geronimo Gardono (1501–76), the key k is created from a keyword p as $Prefix_{|w|}\{pw\}$ – in other words, the plaintext itself is used, together with the keyword p, to form the key. For example, for the keyword HAMBURG we get

Plaintext:	INJEDEMMENSCHENGESICHTESTEHTSEINEGESCHICHTE
Key in VIGENÈRE	HAMBURGHAMBURGHAMBURGHAMBURGHAMBURGHAMBURGH
Key in AUTOCLAVE:	HAMBURGINJEDEMMENSCHENGESICHTESTEHTSEINEGES
Cryptotext in VIGENÈRE:	PNVFXVSTEZTWYKUGQTCTNAEEUYYZZEUOYXKZCTJWYZL
Cryptotext in AUTOCLAVE:	PNVFXVSURWWFLQZKRKKJLGKWLMJALIAGINXKGFVGNXW

A popular way of specifying a key used to be to fix a place in a well-known book, such as the Bible, and to take the text starting at that point, of the length of the plaintext, as a key.

Exercise 8.2.8 *Encrypt the plaintext 'EVERYTHING IS POSSIBLE ONLY MIRACLES TAKE LONGER' using the key word OPTIMIST and (a) the VIGENÈRE cryptosystem; (b) the AUTOCLAVE cryptosystem.*

In the case of poly-alphabetic cryptosystems, cryptoanalysis is much more difficult. There are some techniques for guessing the size of the keyword that was used. Polish–British advances in breaking ENIGMA, which performed poly-alphabetic substitutions, belong to the most spectacular and important successes of cryptoanalysis.

In spite of their apparent simplicity, poly-alphabetic substitution cryptosystems are not to be underestimated. Moreover, they can provide perfect secrecy, as will soon be shown.

8.2.3 Transposition Cryptosystems

The basic idea is very simple and powerful: permute the plaintext. Less clear is how to specify and perform efficiently permutations.

The history of transposition encryptions and devices for them goes back to Sparta in about 475 BC.

Writing the plaintext backwards is a simple example of an encryption by a transposition. Another simple method is to choose an integer n, write the plaintext in rows with n symbols in each, and then read it by columns to get the cryptotext. This can be made more tricky by choosing a permutation of columns, or rows, or both.

Cryptotexts obtained by transpositions, called anagrams, were popular among scientists in the seventeenth century. They were also used to encrypt scientific findings. For example, Newton wrote to Leibniz:

$$a^7c^2d^2e^{14}f^2i^7l^3m^1n^8o^4q^3r^2s^4t^8v^{12}x^1,$$

which stands for 'data aequatione quodcumque fluentes quantitates involvente, fluxiones invenire et vice versa'.

Exercise 8.2.9 *Decrypt the anagrams (a) INGO DILMUR, PEINE; (b) KARL SURDORT PEINE; (c) $a^2cdef^3g^2i^2jkmn^3o^5prs^2t^2u^3z$; (d) $ro^4b^2t^3e^2$.*

Exercise 8.2.10 *Consider the following transposition cryptosystem. An integer n and a permutation π on $\{1,\ldots,n\}$ are chosen. The plaintext is divided into blocks of length n, and in each block the permutation π is applied. Show that the same effect can be obtained by a suitable HILL cryptosystem.*

Practical cryptography often combines and modifies basic encryption techniques: for example, by adding, in various ways, a garbage text to the cryptotext.

Exercise 8.2.11 *Decrypt (a) OCORMYSPOTROSTREPXIT; (b) LIASHRYNCBXOCGNSGXC.*

8.2.4 Perfect Secrecy Cryptosystems

According to Shannon[4], a cryptosystem is perfect if knowledge of the cryptotext provides no information whatsoever about the plaintext, with the possible exception of its length. It also follows from Shannon's results that perfect secrecy is possible only if the key-space is as large as the plaintext-space. This implies that the key must be at least as long as the plaintext and that the same key cannot be used more than once.

A perfect cryptosystem is the **ONE-TIME PAD** cryptosystem, invented by Gilbert S. Vernam (1917). When used to encode an English plaintext, it simply involves a poly-alphabetic substitution cryptosystem of the VIGENÈRE type, with the key a randomly chosen English alphabet word of the same length as the plaintext. Each symbol of the key specifies a CAESAR shift that is to be performed on the corresponding symbol of the plaintext.

More straightforward to implement is its original bit-version due to Vernam, who also constructed a machine and obtained a patent. In this case both plaintext and key are binary words of the same length. Encryption and decryption are both performed simply by the bitwise XOR operation.

The proof of perfect secrecy is very simple. By proper choice of the key, any plaintext of the same length could lead to the given cryptotext.

At first glance it seems that nothing has been achieved with the ONE-TIME PAD cryptosystem. The problem of secure communication of a plaintext has been transformed into the problem of secure communication of an equally long key. However, this is not altogether so.

First of all, the ONE-TIME PAD cryptosystem is indeed used when perfect secrecy is really necessary: for example, for some hot lines. Second, and perhaps most important, the ONE-TIME PAD cryptosystem provides an idea of how to design practically secure cryptosystems. The method is as follows: use a pseudo-random generator to generate, from a small random seed, a long pseudo-random word. Use this pseudo-random word as the key for the ONE-TIME PAD cryptosystem. In such a case two parties need to agree only on a much smaller random seed than the key really used. This idea actually underlies various modern cryptosystems.[5]

Exercise 8.2.12 *The following example illustrates the unbreakability of the ONE-TIME PAD cryptosystem. Consider the extended English alphabet with 27 symbols – including a space character. Given the cryptotext* `ANKYODKYUREPFJBYOJDSPLREYIUNOFDOIUERFPLVYTS`, *find*
(a) the key that yields the plaintext `COLONEL MUSTARD WITH THE CANDLESTICK IN THE HALL;`
(b) the key that yields the plaintext `MISS SCARLET WITH THE KNIFE IN THE LIBRARY;`
(c) another example of this type.

[4]Claude E. Shannon (1917–) from MIT, Cambridge, Mass., with his seminal paper 'Communication theory of secrecy systems' (1949), started the scientific era of cryptography.

[5]In addition, modern technology allows that a ONE-TIME PAD cryptosystem can be seen as fully practical. It is enough to take an optical disk, with thousands of megabytes, fill it with random bits, make a copy of it and deliver it through a secure channel. Such a source of random bits can last quite a while.

8.2.5 How to Make the Cryptoanalysts' Task Harder

Two simple but powerful methods of increasing the security of an imperfect cryptosystem are called, according to Shannon, **diffusion** and **confusion**.

The aim of diffusion is to dissipate the source language redundancy found in the plaintext by spreading it out over the cryptotext. For example, a permutation of the plaintext can rule out the possibility of using frequency tables for digrams, trigrams and so on.

Another way to achieve diffusion is to make each letter of the cryptotext depend on as many letters of the plaintext as possible. Consider, for example, the case that letters of the English alphabet are represented by integers from 0 to 25 and as a key $k = k_1, \ldots, k_s$, a sequence of such integers, is used. Let $m = m_1 \ldots m_n$ be a plaintext. Define, for $0 \leq i < s, m_{-i} = k_{s-i}$. The letters of the cryptotext are then defined by

$$c_i = (\sum_{j=0}^{s} m_{i-j}) \bmod 26$$

for each $1 \leq i \leq m$. (Observe that decryption is easy when the key is known.)

The aim of confusion is to make the relation between the cryptotext and the plaintext as complex as possible. Poly-alphabetic substitutions, as a modification of mono-alphabetic substitutions, are examples of how confusion helps. Additional examples of diffusion and confusion will be shown in Section 8.2.6.

There is also a variety of techniques for improving the security of encryption of long plaintexts when they have to be decomposed into fixed-size blocks. The basic idea is that two identical blocks should not be encrypted in the same way, because this already gives some information to cryptoanalysts. One of the techniques that can be used is to make the encryption of each block depend on the encryption of previous blocks, as has been shown above for single letters. This will be illustrated in Section 8.2.6.

8.2.6 DES Cryptosystem

A revolutionary step in secret-key cryptography was the acceptance, in 1977, by the US National Bureau of Standards of the cryptosystem DES (data encryption standard), developed by IBM. Especially revolutionary was the fact that both encryption and decryption algorithms were made public. DES became the most widely used cryptosystem of all times.

To use DES, a user first chooses a secret 56-bit long key k_{56}. This key is then preprocessed using the following algorithm.

Preprocessing. 1. A fixed, publicly known permutation π_{56} is applied to k_{56}, to get a 56-bit string $\pi_{56}(k_{56})$. The first (second) part of the resulting string is then taken to form a 28-bit block C_0 (D_0).

2. Using a fixed, publicly known sequence $s_1, \ldots, s_{16}$ of integers (each is 1 or 2), 16 pairs of blocks $(C_i, D_i), i = 1, \ldots, 16$, each of 28 bits, are created as follows: C_i (D_i) is obtained from C_{i-1} (D_{i-1}) by s_i left cyclic shifts.

3. Using a fixed, publicly known order (bits numbers: $14, 17, 11, \ldots$), 48 bits are chosen from each pair of blocks (C_i, D_i) to form a new block K_i.

The aim of this preprocessing is to make, from k_{56}, a more random sequence of bits.

Encryption. 1. A fixed, publicly known permutation π_{64} is applied to a 64-bit plaintext w to get a new plaintext $w' = \pi_{64}(w)$. (This is a diffusion step in the Shannon sense.) w' is then written in the form $w' = L_0R_0$, with each L_0 and R_0 consisting of 32 bits.

2. 16 pairs of 32-bit blocks $L_i, R_i, 1 \leq i \leq 16$, are constructed using the recurrence

$$L_i = R_{i-1}, \tag{8.1}$$
$$R_i = L_{i-1} \oplus f(R_{i-1}, K_i), \tag{8.2}$$

where f is a fixed mapping, publicly known and easy to implement both in hardware and software. (Computation of each pair of blocks actually represents one confusion step.)

3. The cryptotext is obtained as $\pi_{64}^{-1}(L_{16}R_{16})$ (another diffusion step).

Decryption. Given a cryptotext c, $\pi_{64}(c) = L_{16}R_{16}$ is first computed, then blocks L_i, R_i, $i = 15, 14, \ldots, 0$, using the recurrence

$$R_{i-1} = L_i, \tag{8.3}$$
$$L_{i-1} = R_i \oplus f(L_i, K_i), \tag{8.4}$$

and, finally, the plaintext $w = \pi_{64}^{-1}(L_0R_0)$ is obtained.

This means that the same algorithm is used for encryption and decryption. In addition, this algorithm can be implemented fast in both hardware and software. As a consequence, at the time this book went to press, DES could be used to encrypt more than 200 megabits per second using special hardware.

Because the permutations π_{56} and π_{64}, the sequence $s_1, \ldots, s_{16}$, the order to choose 48 bits out of 56, and the function f are fixed and made public, it would be perfectly possible to present them here. However, and this is the point, they have been designed so carefully, in order to make cryptoanalysis very difficult, that one hardly learns more about DES from knowing these permutations than one does from knowing that they exist and are easily available.

Since its adoption as a standard, there have been concerns about the level of security provided by DES. They fall into two categories, concerning key size and the nature of the algorithm. Various estimations have been made of how much it would cost to build special hardware to do decryption by an exhaustive search through the space of 2^{56} keys. For example, it has been estimated that a molecular computer could be built to break DES in three months. On the other hand, none of the cryptoanalytic attacks has turned out to be successful so far. It has also been demonstrated that the avalanche effect holds for DES.

There are also various techniques for increasing security when using DES. The basic idea is to use two keys and to employ the second one to encrypt the cryptotext obtained after encryption with the first key. Since the cryptosystem DES is not composite, this increases security. Another idea, which has been shown to be powerful, is to use three independent keys k_1, k_2, k_3 and to compute the cryptotext c from the plaintext w using DES three times, as follows:

$$c = DES_{k_1}(DES_{k_2}^{-1}(DES_{k_3}(w))).$$

Various ideas have also been developed as to how to increase security when encrypting long plaintexts. Let a plaintext w be divided into n 64-bit blocks $m_1, \ldots, m_n$; that is, $w = m_1 \ldots m_n$. Choose a 56-bit key k and a 64-bit block c_0. The cryptotext c_i of the block m_i can then be defined as $c_i = DES(m_i \oplus c_{i-1})$. Clearly, knowledge of k and c_0 makes decryption easy.

Exercise 8.2.13 *Show that if in DES all bits of the plaintext and of the key are replaced by their complements, then in the resulting cryptotext every bit also changes to its complement.*

8.2.7 Public Distribution of Secret Keys

The need to secure the secret key distribution ahead of transmission was an unfortunate but not impossible problem in earlier times, when only few parties needed secure communications (and time did not matter as much). This is, however, unfeasible today, when not only the number of parties that need to communicate securely has increased enormously, but also there is often a need for sudden and secure communication between two totally unacquainted parties. Diffie and Hellman (1976) solved this problem by designing a protocol for communication between two parties to achieve secure key distribution over a public channel. This has led to a new era in cryptography. Belief in the security of this protocol is based on the assumption that modular exponentiation is a one-way function (see Section 2.3.3).

Two parties, call them from now on Alice and Bob, as has become traditional in cryptography, want to agree on a secret key. First they agree on a large integer n and a g such that $1 < g < n$. They can do this over an insecure channel, or n and g may even be fixed for all users of an information system. Then Alice chooses, randomly, some large integer x and computes $X = g^x \bmod n$. Similarly, Bob chooses, again randomly, a large y and computes $Y = g^y \bmod n$. Alice and Bob then exchange X and Y, but keep x and y secret. (In other words, only Alice knows x and only Bob knows y.) Finally, Alice computes $Y^x \bmod n$, and Bob computes $X^y \bmod n$. Both these values are $g^{xy} \bmod n$ and therefore equal. This value is then the key they agree on.

Note that an eavesdropper seems to need, in order to be able to determine x from X, g and n, or y from Y, g and n, to be able to compute discrete logarithms. (However, no proof is known that such a capability is really required in order to break the system. Since modular exponentiation is believed to be a one-way function, the above problem is considered to be unfeasible. Currently the fastest known algorithms for computing discrete logarithms modulo an integer n have complexity $\mathcal{O}(2^{\sqrt{\ln n \ln\ln n}})$ in the general case and $\mathcal{O}(2^{(\lg n)^{\frac{1}{3}}(\lg\lg n)^{\frac{2}{3}}})$ if n is prime.)

Remark: Not all values of n and g are equally good. If n is a prime, then there exists a generator g such that $g^x \bmod n$ is a permutation of $\{1, \ldots, n-1\}$ and such a g is preferable.

Exercise 8.2.14 *Consider the Diffie–Hellmann key exchange system with $q = 1709$, $n = 4079$ and the secret numbers $x = 2344$ and $y = 3420$. What is the key upon which Alice and Bob agree?*

Exercise 8.2.15* *Extend the Diffie–Hellman key exchange system to (a) three users; (b) more users.*

There is also a way to have secure communication with secret-key cryptosystems without agreeing beforehand on a key – that is, with no need for a key distribution.

Let each user X have its secret encryption function e_X and a secret decryption function d_X, and assume that any two such functions, no matter of which user, are commutative. (In such a case we say that we have a **commutative cryptosystem**.) Consider the following communication protocol in which Alice wants to sent a plaintext w to Bob.

1. Alice sends $e_A(w)$ to Bob.
2. Bob sends $e_B(e_A(w))$ to Alice.
3. Alice sends $d_A(e_B(e_A(w))) = e_B(w)$ to Bob.
4. Bob decrypts $d_B(e_B(w)) = w$.

This, however, has a clear disadvantage, in that three communication rounds are needed. The idea of public-key cryptosystems discussed in the next section seems to be much better.

8.3 Public-key Cryptosystems

The key observation leading to public-key cryptography is that whoever encrypts a plaintext does not need to be able to decrypt the resulting cryptotext. Therefore, if it is not feasible from the knowledge of an encryption algorithm e_k to construct the corresponding decryption algorithm d_k, the encryption algorithm e_k can be made public! As a consequence, in such a case each user U can choose a private key k_U, make the encryption algorithm e_{k_U} public, and keep secret the decryption algorithm d_{k_U}. In such a case anybody can send messages to U, and U is the only one capable of decrypting them.

This basic idea can be illustrated by the following toy cryptosystem.

Example 8.3.1 (Telephone directory encryption) *Each user makes public which telephone directory should be used to encrypt messages for her. The general encryption algorithm is to take the directory, the key, of the intended receiver and to encrypt the plaintext by replacing each of its letters by a telephone number of a person whose name starts with that letter. To decrypt, a user is supposed to have his own reverse telephone directory, sorted by numbers; therefore the user can easily replace numbers by letters to get the plaintext. For example, using the telephone directory for Philadelphia, the plaintext CRYPTO can be encrypted using the following entries:*

Carden Frank	*3381276,*	*Roberts Victoria*	*7729094,*
Yeats John	*2890399,*	*Plummer Donald*	*7323232,*
Turne Helen	*4389705,*	*Owens Eric*	*3516765,*

as 338127677290942890399732323243897053516765.

There is also a mechanical analogy illustrating the difference between secret-key and public-key cryptography. Assume that information is sent in boxes. In a secret-key cryptosystem information is put into a box, locked with a padlock, and sent, for example by post, and the key is sent by some secure channel. In the public-key modification, anyone can get a padlock for any user U, say at the post office, put information into a box, lock it with the padlock and send it. U is the only one who has the key to open it – no key distribution is needed.

8.3.1 Trapdoor One-way Functions

The basic idea of public-key cryptosystems is simple, but do such cryptosystems exist? We know that there are strong candidates for one-way functions that can easily be computed, but to compute their inverse seems not to be feasible. This is, however, too much. Nobody, not even the sender, would be able to decrypt a cryptotext encrypted by a one-way function. Fortunately, there is a modification of the concept of one-way functions, so-called trapdoor one-way functions, that seems to be appropriate for making public-key cryptosystems.

A function $f : X \rightarrow Y$ is a **trapdoor one-way function** if f and also its inverse can be computed efficiently. Yet even a complete knowledge of the algorithm for computing f does not make it feasible to determine a polynomial time algorithm for computing its inverse. The secret needed to obtain an efficient algorithm for the inverse is known as the **trapdoor information**.

There is no proof that such functions exist, but there are several strong candidates for them.

Candidate 8.3.2 (Modular exponentiation with a fixed exponent and modulus) *It is the function $f_{n,x} : \mathbf{Z} \rightarrow \mathbf{Z}$, defined by $f_{n,x}(a) = a^x \bmod n$. As already mentioned in Chapter 1, it is known that for any fixed n and x there is an efficient algorithm for computing the inverse operation of taking the x-th root modulo* *n. However, all known algorithms for computing the x-th root modulo n require knowledge of the prime factors of n – and such a factoring is precisely the trapdoor information. A public-key cryptosystem based on this trapdoor one-way function will be discussed in Section 8.3.3.*

Candidate 8.3.3 (Modular squaring with fixed modulus) *This is another example of a trapdoor one-way function. As already mentioned in Section 1.7.3, computation of discrete square roots seems in general to be unfeasible, but easy if the decomposition of the modulus into primes is known.*

This second example has special cryptographical significance because, by Theorem 1.8.16, computation of square roots is exactly as difficult as factoring of integers.

8.3.2 Knapsack Cryptosystems

The first public-key cryptosystem, based on the knapsack problem, was developed by Ralp C. Merkle and Martin Hellmann (1978). It has been patented in ten countries and has played an important role in the history of the public-key cryptography, as did the exciting attempts to break it.

In spite of the fact that the KNAPSACK public-key cryptosystem is not much used, it has several features that make it a good illustration of how to design public-key cryptosystems, the difficulties one can encounter, and ways to overcome them.

The following simple and general idea regarding how to design a trapdoor function and a public-key cryptosystem based on it will be illustrated in this and the following sections.

1. Choose an algorithmic problem P that is provably intractable, or for which there is at least strong evidence that this is the case.

2. Find a key-space $\mathcal{K}$, a plaintext-space $\mathcal{P}$ and a general encryption algorithm e that maps $\mathcal{K} \times \mathcal{P}$ into instances of P in such a way that p is the solution of the instance $e(k,p)$ of P.

3. Using the chosen (trapdoor) data t, design and make public a specific key k_t such that knowing t it is easy to solve any instance $e(k_t,p)$ of the problem P, but without knowing t this appears to be unfeasible. (One way of doing this is to choose a key k such that anybody can easily solve any instance $e(k,p)$ of P, and then transform k, using some combination of diffusion and confusion steps (as the trapdoor information), into another key k' in such a way that whenever $e(k',p)$ is known, this can easily be transformed, using the trapdoor information, into an easily solvable instance of P.)

Now let us illustrate this idea on the KNAPSACK cryptosystem. Let K be the knapsack problem with the instances (X,s), where X is a knapsack vector and s an integer. The key-space $\mathcal{K}$ will be $\mathbf{N}^n$ for a fixed integer n – that is, the space of n-dimensional vectors.[6] The plaintext-space $\mathcal{P}$ will be the set of n-dimensional bit vectors. (This means that whenever such a cryptosystem is used, the original plaintext must be divided into blocks, and each encoded by an n-bit vector.) The encryption function e is designed to map any knapsack vector X and any plaintext p, a binary column vector, both of the same length, into the instance of the knapsack problem

$$(X, Xp),$$

where Xp is the scalar product of two vectors. Since the general knapsack problem is **NP**-complete, no polynomial time algorithm seems to exist for computing p from X and Xp; that is, for decryption.

[6]Merkle and Hellman suggested using 100-dimensional vectors.

Exercise 8.3.4 *Assume that letters of the English alphabet are encoded by binary vectors of 5 bits (space – 00000, A – 00001, B – 00010, ...) and that we use* $(1,2,3,5,8,21,34,55,89)$ *as the knapsack vector. (a) Encrypt the plaintext 'TOO HOT SUMMER'; (b) determine in how many ways one can decrypt the cryptotext* $(128,126,124,122)$.

Exercise 8.3.5 *Consider knapsack vectors* $X = (x_1, \ldots, x_n)$, *where* $x_i = P/p_i$, p_i *are distinct primes, and P is their product. Show that knapsack problems with such vectors can be solved efficiently.*

However, and this is the key to the KNAPSACK cryptosystem, any instance (X,s) of the knapsack problem can be solved in linear time (that is, one can find a $p \in \mathcal{P}$ such that $s = Xp$, if it exists, or show that it does not exist) if $X = (x_1,\ldots,x_n)$ is the **super-increasing vector**; that is, $x_i > \sum_{j=1}^{i-1} x_j$ holds for each $1 < i \leq n$. Indeed, the following algorithm does it.

Algorithm 8.3.6 (Knapsack problem with a super-increasing vector)

Input: a super-increasing knapsack vector $X = (x_1, \ldots, x_n)$ and an $s \in \mathbf{N}$.

for $i \leftarrow n$ **downto** 2 **do**
  if $s \geq 2x_i$ **then** terminate – no solution
    else if $s > x_i$ **then** $p_i \leftarrow 1; s \leftarrow s - x_i$;
      else $p_i \leftarrow 0$;
if $s = x_1$ **then** $p_1 \leftarrow 1$
  else if $s = 0$ **then** $p_1 \leftarrow 0$
    else terminate – no solution.

Example 8.3.7 *For the super-increasing vector*

$$(1,2,4,8,16,32,64,128,256,512) \tag{8.5}$$

and $s = 999$ *we get the solution* $(1,1,1,0,0,1,1,1,1,1)$. *For* $X = (1,3,5,10,20,41,94,199)$ *and* $s = 242$ *there is no solution.*

Following the general idea described above, we show how any super-increasing vector X can be transformed (using carefully chosen trapdoor information) into another vector X' in such a way that by using the trapdoor information we can easily solve any instance of the knapsack problem with X', but this does not seem to be the case without this trapdoor information.

Let $X = (x_1, \ldots, x_n)$ be a super-increasing vector. Choose an integer $m > 2x_n$ and an integer u relatively prime to m. Compute, for example, using the extended Euclid algorithm – a u^{-1} such that $uu^{-1} \equiv 1 \pmod{m}$, u and m will form the trapdoor information.

Construct now the knapsack vector $X' = (x'_1, \ldots, x'_n)$ by computing

$$x'_i = ux_i \bmod m$$

for $1 \leq i \leq n$. (Multiplication by u makes a diffusion; taking values modulo m makes a confusion and also scales the values.)

For example, taking $m = 1250, u = 41$, we get $u^{-1} = 61$, and from the super-increasing vector (8.5) we get, using the above method, the vector

$$X' = (41,82,164,328,656,62,124,248,496,992).$$

Vectors X' obtained this way usually look pretty random, and therefore it seems that to solve the knapsack problem for them can be as hard as in the general case. The following lemma guarantees that this is not so if the trapdoor information is available. This way a public-key cryptosystem can be created.

Lemma 8.3.8 *Let X, m, u, X' be defined as above; that is, X is a super-increasing vector, and for $c \in \mathbf{N}$, $c' = u^{-1}c \bmod m$. Then the knapsack problem instances (X, c') and (X', c) have at most one solution, and if one of them has a solution, then the second has the same solution.*

Proof: It follows from Algorithm 8.3.6 that if (X, c') has a solution, then it is unique. Let p' be a solution of the knapsack instance (X', c); that is, $X'p' = c$. Then

$$c' = u^{-1}c = u^{-1}X'p' = u^{-1}uXp' = Xp' \pmod{m}.$$

Since the vector X is super-increasing and $m > 2x_n$, we have

$$Xp' \bmod m = Xp',$$

and therefore,

$$c' = Xp'.$$

This means that each solution of a knapsack instance (X', c) is also a solution of the knapsack instance (X, c'). Since this knapsack instance has at most one solution, the same must hold for the instance (X', c). □

KNAPSACK cryptosystem design. A super-increasing vector X and numbers m, u are chosen, and X' is computed and made public as the key. X, u and m are kept secret as the trapdoor information.

Encryption. A plaintext w' is first divided into blocks, and each block w is encoded by a binary vector p_w of length $|X'|$. Encryption of w is then done by computing the scalar product $X'p_w$.

Decryption. $c' = u^{-1}c \bmod m$ is first computed for the cryptotext c, and then the instance (X, c') of the knapsack problem is solved using Algorithm 8.3.6.

Example 8.3.9 *Choosing $X = (1,2,4,9,18,35,75,151,302,606)$, $m = 1250$ and $u = 41$, we design the public key $X' = (41,82,164,369,738,185,575,1191,1132,1096)$.*

To encrypt an English text, we first encode its letters by 5-bit numbers: space – 00000, A – 00001, B – 00010, . . . and then divide the binary string into blocks of 10 bits. For the plaintext 'AFRIKA' we get three plaintext vectors $p_1 = (0000100110)$, $p_2 = (1001001001)$, $p_3 = (0101100001)$, which will be encrypted as

$$c_1' = X'p_1 = 3061, \qquad c_2' = X'p_2 = 2081, \qquad c_3' = X'p_3 = 2285.$$

To decrypt the cryptotext $(9133,2116,1870,3599)$, we first multiply all these numbers by $u^{-1} = 61 \bmod 1250$ to get $(693,326,320,789)$; then for all of them we have to solve the knapsack problem with the vector X, which yields the binary plaintext vector

$$(1101001001, 0110100010, 0000100010, 1011100101)$$

and, consequently, the plaintext 'ZIMBABWE'.

Exercise 8.3.10 *Take the super-increasing vector*

$$X = (103,107,211,425,863,1715,3346,6907,13807,27610)$$

and $m = 55207$, $u = 25236$. *(a) Design for* X, m *and* u *the public knapsack vector* X'. *(b) Encrypt using* X' *the plaintext 'A POET CAN SURVIVE EVERYTHING BUT A MISPRINT'; (c) Decrypt the cryptotext obtained using the vector* $X' = (80187,109,302,102943,113783,197914,178076,77610,117278,103967,124929)$.

The Merkle–Hellmann KNAPSACK cryptosystem (also called the single-iteration knapsack) was broken by Adi Shamir (1982). Naturally the question arose as to whether there are other variants of knapsack-based cryptosystems that are not breakable.

The first idea was to use several times the diffusion–confusion transformations that have produced nonsuper-increasing vectors from super-increasing. More precisely, the idea is to use an **iterated knapsack cryptosystem** – to design so-called hyper-reachable vectors and make them public keys.

Definition 8.3.11 *A knapsack vector* $X' = (x'_1, \ldots, x'_n)$ *is obtained from a knapsack vector* $X = (x_1, \ldots, x_n)$ *by* **strong modular multiplication** *if* $x'_i = u.x_i \bmod m, i = 1, \ldots, n$, *where* $m > 2\sum_{i=1}^{n} x_i$ *and u is relatively prime to m. A knapsack vector* X' *is called* **hyper-reachable** *if there is a sequence of knapsack vectors* $X = X_0, X_1, \ldots, X_k = X'$, *where* X_0 *is a super-increasing vector, and for* $i = 1, \ldots, k$, X_i *is obtained from* X_{i-1} *by strong modular multiplication.*

It has been shown that there are hyper-reachable knapsack vectors that cannot be obtained from a super-increasing vector by a single strong modular multiplication. The **multiple-iterated knapsack cryptosystem** with hyper-reachable vectors is therefore more secure. However, it is not secure enough and was broken by E. Brickell (1985).

Exercise 8.3.12* *Design an infinite sequence* $(X_i, s_i), i = 1,2, \ldots,$ *of knapsack problems such that the problem* (X_i, s_i) *has i solutions.*

Exercise 8.3.13 *A knapsack vector X is called injective if for every s there is at most one solution of the knapsack problem* (X, s). *Show that each hyper-reachable knapsack vector is injective.*

There are also variants of the knapsack cryptosystem that have not yet been broken: for example, the **dense knapsack cryptosystem**, in which two new ideas are used: dense knapsack vectors and a special arithmetic based on so-called Galois fields. The density of a knapsack vector $X = (x_1, \ldots, x_n)$ is defined as

$$d(X) = \frac{n}{\lg(\max\{x_i \mid 1 \leq i \leq n\})}.$$

The density of any super-increasing vector is always smaller than $n/(n-1)$ because the largest element has to be at least 2^{n-1}. This has actually been used to break the basic, single-iteration knapsack cryptosystem.

8.3.3 RSA Cryptosystem

The basic idea of the public-key cryptosystem of **Rivest, Shamir and Adleman** (1978), the most widely investigated one, is very simple: *it is easy to multiply two large primes p and q, but it appears not to be feasible to find p,q when only the product $n = pq$ is given and n is large.*

Design of the RSA cryptosystem. Two large primes p,q are chosen. (In Section 8.3.4 we discuss how this is done. By **large primes** are currently understood primes that have more than 512 bits.) Denote

$$n = pq, \qquad \phi(n) = (p-1)(q-1),$$

where $\phi(n)$ is Euler's totient function (see page 47). A large $d < n$ relatively prime to $\phi(n)$ is chosen, and an e is computed such that

$$ed \equiv 1 \pmod{\phi(n)}.$$

(As we shall see, this can also be done fast.) Then

$$n \text{ (modulus) and } e \text{ (encryption exponent)}$$

form the **public key**, and

$$p,q,d$$

form the **trapdoor information**.

Encryption: To get the cryptotext c, a plaintext $w \in \mathbf{N}$ is encrypted by

$$c = w^e \bmod n. \tag{8.6}$$

Decryption:

$$w = c^d \bmod n. \tag{8.7}$$

Details and correctness: A plaintext is first encoded as a word over the alphabet $\Sigma = \{0,1,\ldots,9\}$, then divided into blocks of length $i-1$, where $10^{i-1} < n < 10^i$. Each block is then taken as an integer and encrypted using the modular exponentiation (8.6).

The correctness of the decryption algorithm follows from the next theorem.

Theorem 8.3.14 *Let $c = w^e \bmod n$ be the cryptotext for the plaintext w, $ed \equiv 1 (\bmod\, \phi(n))$ and d relatively prime to $\phi(n)$. Then $w \equiv c^d (\bmod\, n)$. Hence, if the decryption is unique, $w = c^d \bmod n$.*

Proof: Let us first observe that since $ed \equiv 1(\bmod\,\phi(n))$, there exists a $j \in \mathbf{N}$ such that $ed = j\phi(n)+1$. Let us now distinguish three cases.

Case 1. Neither p nor q divides w. Hence $\gcd(n,w) = 1$, and by Euler's totient theorem,

$$c^d \equiv (w^e)^d \equiv w^{j\phi(n)+1} \equiv w \pmod{n}. \tag{8.8}$$

Case 2. Exactly one of p,q divides w – say p. This immediately implies $w^{ed} \equiv w(\bmod\, p)$. By Fermat's little theorem, $w^{q-1} \equiv 1(\bmod\, q)$, and therefore,

$$w^{q-1} \equiv 1 \pmod{q} \Rightarrow w^{\phi(n)} \equiv 1 \pmod{q} \Rightarrow w^{j\phi(n)} \equiv 1 \pmod{q} \Leftrightarrow w^{ed} \equiv w \pmod{q}; \tag{8.9}$$

and therefore, by the property (1.63) of congruences on page 45, we get $w \equiv w^{ed} \equiv c^d (\bmod\, n)$.

Case 3. Both p and q divide w. This case cannot occur, because we have assumed that $w < n$. □

Example 8.3.15 *Let us try to construct an example. Choosing* $p = 41, q = 61$, *we get* $n = 2501$, $\phi(n) = 2400$. *Taking* $e = 23$, *we get, using the extended version of Euclid's algorithm,* $d = 2087$; *the choice* $e = 29$ *yields* $d = 2069$. *Let us stick to* $e = 23, d = 2087$. *To encrypt the plaintext 'KARLSRUHE' we first represent letters by their positions in the alphabet and obtain the numerical version of the plaintext as 100017111817200704. Since* $10^3 < n < 10^4$, *the numerical plaintext is divided into blocks of three digits, and six plaintext integers are obtained:*

$$100, \quad 017, \quad 111, \quad 817, \quad 200, \quad 704.$$

To encrypt the plaintext, we need to compute

$$100^{23} \bmod 2501, \quad 17^{23} \bmod 2501, \quad 111^{23} \bmod 2501,$$

$$817^{23} \bmod 2501, \quad 200^{23} \bmod 2501, \quad 704^{23} \bmod 2501,$$

which yields the cryptotexts

$$2306, \quad 1893, \quad 621, \quad 1380, \quad 490, \quad 313.$$

To decrypt, we need to compute

$$2036^{2087} \bmod 2501 = 100, \quad 1893^{2087} \bmod 2501 = 17, \quad 621^{2087} \bmod 2501 = 111,$$

$$1380^{2087} \bmod 2051 = 817, \quad 490^{2087} \bmod 2501 = 200, \quad 313^{2087} \bmod 2051 = 704.$$

Exercise 8.3.16 *Taking small primes and large blocks can lead to a confusion. Indeed, taking* $p = 17$, $q = 23$, *we get* $n = 391$, $\phi(n) = 352$. *For* $e = 29$ *and* $d = 85$, *the plaintexts* $100, 017, 111, 817, 200, 704$ *are encrypted as* $104, 204, 314, 154, 064, 295$, *and the decryption then provides* $100, 017, 111, 035, 200, 313$. *Where is the problem?*

Exercise 8.3.17 *Consider the RSA cryptosystem with* $p = 47$, $q = 71$ *and* $e = 79$. *(a) Compute d. (b) Encrypt the plaintext 'THE TRUTH IS MORE CERTAIN THAN PROBABLE'. (c) Decrypt 3301, 1393, 2120, 1789, 1701, 2639, 895, 1150, 742, 1633, 1572, 1550, 2668, 2375, 1643, 108.*

8.3.4 Analysis of RSA

Let us first discuss several assumptions that are crucial for the design of RSA cryptosystems. The first assumption was that we can easily find large primes.

As already mentioned in Section 1.7, no deterministic polynomial time algorithm is known for deciding whether a given number n is a prime. The fastest known sequential deterministic algorithm has complexity $\mathcal{O}(n^{\mathcal{O}(1) \lg \lg n})$. There are, however, several fast randomized algorithms, both of Monte Carlo and Las Vegas type, for deciding primality. The Solovay-Strassen algorithm was presented in Section 2.6. Rabin's Monte Carlo algorithm is based on the following result from number theory.

Lemma 8.3.18 *Let* $n \in \mathbf{N}$. *Denote, for* $1 \leq x < n$, *by* $C(x)$ *the condition:*

Either $x^{n-1} \not\equiv 1 \pmod{n}$, *or there is an* $m \in \mathbf{N}$, $m = (n-1)\,/\,2^i$ *for some i, such that* $\gcd(n, x^m - 1) \neq 1$.

If $C(x)$ *holds for some* $1 \leq x < n$, *then n is not prime. If n is not prime, then* $C(x)$ *holds for at least half of x between 1 and n.*

Algorithm 8.3.19 (Rabin–Miller's algorithm, 1980)

Choose randomly integers $x_1, \ldots, x_m$ such that $1 \leq x_j < n$.
For each x_j determine whether $C(x_j)$ holds;

if $C(x_j)$ holds for some x_j
  then n is not prime
  else n is prime, with the probability of error 2^{-m}.

To find a large prime, a large pseudo-random sequence of bits is generated to represent an odd n. Using Rabin–Miller's or some other fast primality testing algorithm, it is then checked whether n is prime. If not, the primality of $n+2, n+4, \ldots$ is checked until a number is found that is prime, with very large probability.

It is not obvious that this procedure provides a prime fast enough. However, it easily follows from the prime number theorem that there are approximately

$$\frac{2^d}{\ln 2^d} - \frac{2^{d-1}}{\ln 2^{(d-1)}}$$

d-bit primes. If this is compared with the total number of odd d-bit integers, $(2^d - 2^{d-1}) / 2$, we get that the probability that a 512-bit number is prime is 0.00562, and the probability that a 1024-bit number is prime is 0.002815. This shows that the procedure described above for finding large primes is reasonably fast.

To verify that the d chosen is relatively prime to $\phi(n)$, the extended version of Euclid's algorithm can be used. This procedure provides e at the same time.

Exercise 8.3.20 *A natural question concerns how difficult it is to find, given an m, an integer that is relatively prime to m. The following results show that it is fairly easy. Denote $Pr(\gcd(m,n)=1)=P$. (a) Show that $Pr(\gcd(m,n)=d)=\frac{P}{d^2}$. (b) Use the previous result to show: $Pr(\gcd(m,n)=1)\approx 0.6$.*

The design of an RSA cryptosystem therefore seems quite simple. Unfortunately, this is not really so. For the resulting cryptosystem to be secure enough, p, q, d and e must be chosen carefully, to satisfy various conditions, among the following:

1. The difference $|p-q|$ should be neither too large nor too small. (It is advisable that their bit representations differ in length by several bits.)

2. $\gcd(p-1, q-1)$ should not be large.

3. Neither d nor e should be small.

For example, if $|p-q|$ is small, and $p > q$, then $(p+q)/2$ is only slightly larger than $\sqrt{n}$, because $(p+q)^2/4 - n = (p-q)^2/4$. In addition $(p+q)^2/4 - n$ is a square, for example, y^2. To factorize n, it is enough to test numbers $x > \sqrt{n}$ until an x is found such that $x^2 - n$ is square. In such a case $p = x+y$, $q = x-y$.

Exercise 8.3.21 *Explain why in designing an RSA cryptosystem (a)* $\gcd(p-1,q-1)$ *should be small; (b) both* $p-1$ *and* $q-1$ *should contain large prime factors.*

Exercise 8.3.22* *It is evident that d should not be too small, otherwise decryption can be done by testing all small d. In order to show that a small e can also be a security risk, let us assume that three users A, B and C use the number 3 as the encryption exponent and that they use as the modulus* n_A, n_B *and* n_C*, which are relatively prime. Assume further that they transmit the messages* $c_i = w^3 \bmod n_i$, $i = A,B,C$, $0 < w \leq \min\{n_A, n_B, n_C\}$. *Show that a cryptoanalyst can compute w using the Chinese remainder theorem.*

Exercise 8.3.23** *Show that for any choice of primes p and q we can choose* $e \notin \{1, \phi(pq)+1\}$ *in such a way that* $w^e \equiv w \bmod n$ *for all plaintexts w.*

Let us now discuss two other important questions: how hard factoring is and how important it is for the security of RSA cryptosystems.[7]

At the time this book went to press, the fastest algorithm for factoring integers ran in time $\Theta(2^{\sqrt{\ln n \ln \ln n}})$. There is no definite answer to the second question yet. This is a tricky problem, which can also be seen from the fact that knowledge of $\phi(n)$ or d is sufficient to break RSA.

Theorem 8.3.24 *(1) To factor a number n is as hard as to compute* $\phi(n)$.

(2) Any polynomial time algorithm for computing d can be converted into a polynomial time randomized algorithm for factoring n.

The first claim of Theorem 8.3.24 follows easily from the identities

$$p+q = n-\phi(n)+1, \qquad p-q = \sqrt{(p+q)^2-4n}.$$

The proof of the second statement, due to DeLaurentis (1984), is too involved to present here.

Finally, let me mention three results that indicate the strength of the security of RSA cryptosystems; how little we know about them; and how easy it is to break into them, if the utmost care is not taken in their design.

It has been shown that any algorithm which is able to determine **one bit** of the plaintext, the right-most one, can be converted into an algorithm which can determine the whole plaintext, and

[7]Factoring large numbers is another big challenge for computing theory, people and technology. In 1971, 40-digit numbers seemed to be the limit; in 1976, 80-digit numbers seemed to be the limit. In 1977, it was estimated that it would take 40 quadrillion years to factor 125-digit numbers. But in 1990, the 155-digit number $2^{2^9}+1$, the so-called 9th Fermat number, was factored, using about 1,000 computers and several hundred collaborators, by Arjen K. Lenstra, Hendrik W. Lenstra, S. Manasse and M. Pollard, into three factors – 99-digit, 49-digit and 7-digit – with 2,424,833 as the smallest. Factoring of this number was put as the challenge in one of the first papers on RSA by Gardner (1978) in *Scientific American*, and at that time this number was at the top of the list of 'most wanted to factor numbers'. In 1994 there was another spectacular cryptographical success. Using a network of about 1,600 computers, a 96-digit cryptotext, encrypted using a 129-bit modulus and the encryption exponent $e = 9007$, and set as a challenge by the RSA founders, was decrypted. See D. Atkins, M. Graff, A. K. Lenstra and P. C. Leyland (1995). The experience led to an estimation that it is possible to set up projects that would use 100,000 computers and require half a million mips years. Moreover, it became quite clear that the RSA cryptosystem with a 512-bit-long modulus is breakable by anybody willing to spend a few million dollars and wait a few months. For the factoring of a 120-digit number in 825 MIPS years see Denny, Dodson, Lenstra and Manase (1994).

that this is not of substantially larger complexity. (Actually, it is sufficient that the last bit can be determined with probability larger than $\frac{1}{2}$.)

The cryptoanalysis of any reasonable public-key cryptosystem is in both **NP** and **co-NP**, and is therefore unlikely to be **NP**-complete. (In the case of deterministic encryptions, this is trivial. To find a plaintext, one guesses it and applies the public encryption function. The same idea is used to show that the cryptoanalysis problem is in **co-NP**. It is a little bit more involved to show that this is true also for nondeterministic encryptions.)

It can also be shown that if more users employ the RSA cryptosystem with the same n, then they are able to determine in deterministic quadratic time another user's decryption exponent – without factoring n. This setting refers to the following hypothetical case: an agency would like to build up a business out of making RSA cryptosystems. Therefore, it would choose one pair p,q, send $n = pq$ to all users, and deliver to each user a unique encryption exponent and the corresponding decryption exponent.

Taking into account the simplicity, elegance, power and mystery which RSA provides, it is no wonder that already in 1993 more than ten different RSA chips were produced.

Exercise 8.3.25* (RABIN cryptosystem) *If a cryptoanalyst knows how to factor efficiently, he is able to break RSA systems. However, it is not known if the converse of this statement is true. It has been shown by Rabin (1979) that for the following cryptosystem the problem of factoring is computationally equivalent to that of breaking the cryptosystem.*

In the RABIN cryptosystem each user selects a pair p,q of distinct Blum integers, to be kept secret, and publicizes n and a $b < n$. The encryption function is $e_{n,b}(w) = w(w+b) \bmod n$. Show that the knowledge of the trapdoor information p,q is sufficient to make decryptions effectively. (In Rabin's original cryptosystem $b = 0$.)

8.4 Cryptography and Randomness*

Randomness and cryptography are closely related. The prime purpose of encryption methods is to transform a highly nonrandom plaintext into a highly random cryptotext. For example, let e_k be an encryption mapping, x_0 a plaintext, and $x_i, i = 1,2,\ldots$, be a sequence of cryptotexts constructed by encryptions $x_{i+1} = e_k(x_i)$. If e_k is cryptographically 'secure' enough, it is likely that the sequence $x_1, x_2, \ldots$ looks quite random. Encryptions can therefore produce (pseudo)-randomness.

The other aspect of the relation is more involved. It is clear that perfect randomness combined with the ONE-TIME PAD cryptosystem provides perfect cryptographical security. However, the price to be paid as a result of the need to have keys as long as the plaintext is too high. Another idea is to use, as illustrated above, a cryptosystem, or some other pseudo-random generator, to provide a long pseudo-random string from a short random seed and then to use this long sequence as the key for the ONE-TIME PAD cryptosystem. This brings us to the fundamental question: when is a pseudo-random generator good enough for cryptographical purposes? The following concept has turned out to capture this intuitive idea.

A pseudo-random generator is called **cryptographically strong** if the sequence of bits it produces from a short random seed is so good for using with the ONE-TIME PAD cryptosystem that no polynomial time algorithm allows a cryptoanalyst to learn **any** information about the plaintext from the cryptotext.

Clearly, such a pseudo-random generator would provide sufficient security in a secret-key cryptosystem if both parties agree on some short seed and never use it twice. As we shall see later, cryptographically strong pseudo-random generators could also provide perfect security for public-key cryptography. However, do they exist?

Before proceeding to a further discussion of these ideas, let me mention that the concept of a cryptographically strong pseudo-random generator is, surprisingly, one of the key concepts of foundations of computing. This follows, for example, from the fact that a cryptographically strong pseudo-random generator exists if and only if a one-way function exists, which is equivalent to $\mathbf{P} \neq \mathbf{UP}$ and implies $\mathbf{P} \neq \mathbf{NP}$.

The key to dealing with this problem, and also with the problem of randomized encryptions, is that of a (trapdoor) one-way predicate.

Definition 8.4.1 *A* **one-way predicate** *is a Boolean function $P : \{0,1\}^* \mapsto \{0,1\}$ such that*

1. *For an input $v1^k, v \in \{0,1\}$, one can choose, randomly and uniformly, in expected polynomial time, an $x \in \{0,1\}^*, |x| \leq k$, such that $P(x) = v$. (The suffix 1^k is just to render meaningful the requirement of polynomial time in the length of the input.)*

2. *For all $c > 0$ and any sufficiently large k, no polynomial time algorithm can compute $P(x)$, given $x \in \{0,1\}^*, |x| \leq k$, with a probability greater than $\frac{1}{k^c}$. (The probability is taken over the random choices made by the algorithm and x such that $|x| \leq k$.)*

A **trapdoor one-way predicate** *is a one-way predicate for which there exists, for every k, a trapdoor information t_k, the size of which is bounded by a polynomial in k, that can be used to compute, in polynomial time, $P(x)$, for all $|x| \leq k$.*

Candidate 8.4.2 *Take two large primes p, q, $n = pq$, a d relatively prime to $\phi(n)$ and e such that $ed \equiv 1 \pmod{\phi(n)}$. Define $P(x)$ to be the least significant bit of $x^d \bmod n$ for $x \in \mathbf{Z}_n^*$. To select uniformly an $x \in \mathbf{Z}_n^*$ such that $P(x) = v$, take a $y \in \mathbf{Z}_n^*$ whose least significant bit is v, and set $x = y^e \bmod n$.*

8.4.1 Cryptographically Strong Pseudo-random Generators

As is usual in cryptography, the existence of such generators has not yet been proved, but there are strong candidates for them.

It has been shown, for example, that all pseudo-random number generators that are **unpredictable to the left**, in the sense that a cryptoanalyst who knows the generator and sees the whole generated sequence except its first bit has no better way to find out this first bit than coin-tossing, are cryptographically strong. It has also been proved, that if integer factoring is intractable, then the **BBS pseudo-random generator**, introduced in Section 1.9.3, is unpredictable to the left.

To analyse the BBS pseudo-random generator in more detail, we need some basic results concerning modular squaring (see Section 1.7). Recall that computation of square roots modulo a Blum integer n is a permutation of the quadratic residues modulo n, and the problem of computing principal square roots has been proved to be computationally equivalent to that of factoring integers. In addition, it has been proved that if factoring is unfeasible, then for almost all quadratic residues x (modulo n), coin-tossing is the best possible way to estimate the least significant bit of x after seeing $x^2 \bmod n$. This fact will now be used.

Let n be a Blum integer. Choose a random quadratic residue x_0. (For example, choose a random integer x, relatively prime to n, and compute $x_0 = x^2 \bmod n$.) For $i \geq 0$ let $x_{i+1} = x_i^2 \bmod n$, and b_i be the least significant bit of x_i. For each integer i, let $BBS_{n,i}(x_0) = b_0 \ldots b_{i-1}$ be the first i bits of the pseudo-random sequence generated from the seed x_0 by the BBS pseudo-random generator.

Assume that the BBS pseudo-random generator, with a Blum integer as the modulus, is not unpredictable to the left. Let y be a quadratic residue from $\mathbf{Z}_n^*$. Compute $BBS_{n,i-1}(y)$ for some $i > 1$.

Let us now pretend that the last $(i-1)$ bits of $BBS_{n,i}(x)$ are actually the first $(i-1)$ bits of $BBS_{n,i-1}(y)$, where x is the unknown principal square root of y. Hence, if the BBS pseudo-random generator is not unpredictable to the left, then there exists a better method than coin-tossing for determining the least significant bit of x, which is, as mentioned above, impossible.

Observe too that the BBS pseudo-random generator has the nice property that one can determine, directly and efficiently, for any $i > 0$, the ith bit of the sequence of bits generated by the generator. Indeed, $x_i = x_0^{2^i} \bmod n$, and using Euler's totient theorem,

$$x_i = x_0^{2^i \bmod \phi(n)} \bmod n.$$

There is also a general method for designing cryptographically strong pseudo-random generators. This is based on the result that any pseudo-random generator is cryptographically strong that passes the **next-bit test**: if the generator generates the sequence $b_0, b_1, \ldots$ of bits, then it is not feasible to predict b_{i+1} from $b_0, \ldots, b_i$ with probability greater than $\frac{\varepsilon+1}{2}$ in polynomial time with respect to $\frac{1}{\varepsilon}$ and the size of the seed. Here, the key role is played by the following modification of the concept of a one-way predicate.

Let D be a finite set, $f : D \to D$ a permutation. Moreover, let $P : D \to \{0,1\}$ be a mapping such that it is not feasible to predict (to compute) $P(x)$ with probability larger than $\frac{1}{2}$, given x only, but it is easy to compute $P(x)$ if $f^{-1}(x)$ is given. A candidate for such a predicate is $D = \mathbf{Z}_n^*$, where n is a Blum integer, $f(x) = x^2 \bmod n$, and $P(x) = 1$ if and only if the principal square root of x modulo n is even.

To get from a seed x_0 a pseudo-random sequence of bits, the elements $x_{i+1} = f(x_i)$ are first computed for $i = 0, \ldots, n$, and then b_i are defined by $b_i = P(x_{n-i})$ for $i = 0, \ldots, n$. (Note the reverse order of the sequences – to determine b_0, we first need to know x_n.)

Suppose now that the pseudo-random generator described above does not pass the next-bit test. We sketch how we can then compute $P(x)$ from x. Since f is a permutation, there must exist x_0 such that $x = x_i$ for some i in the sequence generated from x_0. Compute $x_{i+1}, \ldots, x_n$, and determine the sequence $b_0, \ldots, b_{n-i-1}$. Suppose we can predict b_{n-i}. Since $b_{n-i} = P(x_i) = P(x)$, we get a contradiction with the assumption that the computation of $P(x)$ is not feasible if only x is known.

8.4.2 Randomized Encryptions

Public-key cryptography with deterministic encryptions solves the key distribution problem quite satisfactorily, but still has significant disadvantages. Whether its security is sufficient is questionable. For example, a cryptoanalyst who knows the public encryption function e_k and a cryptotext c can choose a plaintext w, compute $e_k(w)$, and compare it with c. In this way, some information is obtained about what is, or is not, a plaintext corresponding to c.

The purpose of randomized encryption, invented by S. Goldwasser and S. Micali (1984), is to encrypt messages, using randomized algorithms, in such a way that we can prove that no feasible computation on the cryptotext can provide any information whatsoever about the corresponding plaintext (except with a negligible probability).

As a consequence, even a cryptoanalyst familiar with the encryption procedure can no longer guess the plaintext corresponding to a given cryptotext, and cannot verify the guess by providing an encryption of the guessed plaintext.

Formally, we have again a **plaintext-space** $\mathcal{P}$, a **cryptotext-space** $\mathcal{C}$ and a **key-space** $\mathcal{K}$. In addition, there is a **random-space** $\mathcal{R}$. For any $k \in \mathcal{K}$, there is an encryption mapping $e_k : \mathcal{P} \times \mathcal{R} \to \mathcal{C}$ and a decryption mapping $d_k : \mathcal{C} \to \mathcal{P}$ such that for any plaintext p and any randomness source $r \in \mathcal{R}$ we have $d_k(e_k(p,r)) = p$. Given a k, both e_k and d_k should be easy to design and compute. However, given e_k, it should not be feasible to determine d_k without knowing k. e_k is a public key. Encryptions and decryptions are performed as in public-key cryptography. (Note that if a randomized encryption is used, then the cryptotext is not determined uniquely, but the plaintext is!)

Exercise 8.4.3 (Quadratic residue cryptosystem – QRS)** *Each user chooses primes p,q such that $n = pq$ is a Blum integer and makes public n and a $y \notin QR_n$. To encrypt a binary message $w = w_1 \ldots w_r$ for a user with the public key n, the cryptotext $c = (y^{w_1}x_1^2 \bmod n, \ldots, y^{w_r}x_r^2 \bmod n)$ is computed, where $x_1, \ldots, x_r$ is a randomly chosen sequence of elements from $\mathbf{Z}_n^*$. Show that the intended receiver can decrypt the cryptotext efficiently.*

The idea of randomized encryptions has also led to various definitions of security that have turned out to be equivalent to the following one.

Definition 8.4.4 *A* **randomized encryption cryptosystem is polynomial-time secure** *if for all $c \in N$ and sufficiently large integer s (the so-called* **security parameter***) any randomized polynomial time algorithm that takes as input s (in unary) and a public key cannot distinguish between randomized encryptions, by that key, of two given messages of length c with probability greater than $\frac{1}{2} + \frac{1}{s^c}$.*

We describe now a randomized encryption cryptosystem that has been proved to be polynomial-time secure and is also efficient. It is based on the assumption that squaring modulo a Blum integer is a trapdoor one-way function and uses the cryptographically strong BBS pseudo-random generator described in the previous section. Informally, the BBS pseudo-random generator is used to provide the key for the ONE-TIME-PAD cryptosystem. The capacity of the intended receiver to compute the principal square roots, using the trapdoor information, allows him or her to recover the pad and obtain the plaintext.

Formally, let p,q be two large Blum integers. Their product, $n = pq$, is the public key. The random-space is QR_n of all quadratic residues modulo n. The plaintext-space is the set of all binary strings – for an encryption they will not have to be divided into blocks. The cryptotext-space is the set of pairs formed by elements of QR_n and binary strings.

Encryption: Let w be a t-bit plaintext and x_0 a random quadratic residue modulo n. Compute x_t and $BBS_{n,t}(x_0)$, using the recurrence $x_{i+1} = x_i^2 \bmod n$, as shown in the previous section. The cryptotext is then the pair $\langle x_t, w \oplus BBS_{n,t}(x_0)\rangle$.

Decryption: The intended user, who knows the trapdoor information p and q, can first compute x_0 from x_t, then $BBS_{n,t}(x_0)$ and, finally, can determine w. To determine x_0, one can use a brute force method to compute, using the trapdoor information, $x_i = \sqrt{x_{i+1}} \bmod n$, for $i = t-1, \ldots, 0$, or the following, more efficient algorithm.

Algorithm 8.4.5 (Fast multiple modular square-rooting)

Compute a,b such that $ap + bq = 1$;
$x \leftarrow ((p+1)/4)^t \bmod (p-1)$;
$y \leftarrow ((q+1)/4)^t \bmod (q-1)$;
$u \leftarrow (x_t \bmod p)^x \bmod p$;
$v \leftarrow (x_t \bmod q)^y \bmod q$;
$x_0 \leftarrow (bqu + apv) \bmod n$.

There is also the following general method for making randomized encryptions, based on the concept of the trapdoor one-way predicate, that has been shown to be polynomial-time secure. Alice chooses a one-way trapdoor predicate P_A, a security parameter $s \in \mathbf{N}$, and makes public the description of P_A and s. The trapdoor information, needed to compute P_A efficiently, is kept secret. Anybody wishing to send a plaintext $p = p_1 \ldots p_s$ of s bits to Alice encrypts p as follows: for $i = 1, \ldots, s$, and $p_i \in \{0,1\}$, an x_i, $|x_i| \leq s$, is randomly chosen such that $P_A(x_i) = p_i$ (which can be done in polynomial time) and p_i is encrypted as x_i. To decrypt, Alice, who knows the trapdoor information, computes $p_i = P_A(x_i)$, for $i = 1, \ldots, s$.

Observe that such a cryptotext may be up to s times longer than the plaintext; s is here a security parameter.

8.4.3 Down to Earth and Up

In any secure randomized cryptosystem many cryptotexts have to correspond to one plaintext. **Data expansion**, as we saw at the end of the last section, is therefore unavoidable. This is certainly a drawback of randomized encryptions.

However, it has been proved that breaking the randomized encryptions described above is as hard as factoring. Such a strong statement cannot be made for the RSA cryptosystem. Moreover, randomized encryptions are usually faster than deterministic ones.

None of the public-key cryptosystems seems to be able to compete in speed with DES. (In 1994 DES was in software (hardware) about 1,000 (100) times faster than RSA.) Therefore, it seems currently best to combine both of them: to use a public-key cryptosystem to transport a key and then use this key with DES to encode messages (and change keys often). Without slowing down transmissions too much, this can significantly increase security.

Public-key cryptography does not mean an end to secret-key cryptography. One of the main applications of public-key encryptions are fast and secure key transmissions.

There is another drawback to public-key cryptography. Proofs of security of several public-key cryptosystems are based on unproved assumptions from number theory. This is not the case with quantum cryptography, based on sending photons through quantum channels, where it is impossible, in principle, to eavesdrop without a high probability of disturbing the transition in such a way as to be detectable.

8.5 Digital Signatures

The number of crucial applications of cryptography, as well as the basic concepts arising from it, have already far exceeded those related to secure encryptions. Digital signatures, with which we deal in this section, are one of the most fundamental and important inventions of modern cryptography. To make digital signatures, we can use various techniques similar to those used for encryptions, which is why we deal with them in this chapter. Other applications and fundamental concepts arising from cryptographical considerations are dealt with in the following chapter.

If Alice gets a message that claims to be from Bob, she needs to be convinced that the message really is from Bob and that nobody else, pretending to be Bob, has sent it. Moreover, for example, for legal reasons, she may need to be able to convince a third party that the message was indeed from Bob (and not from somebody else, or even that the message was not her own invention). For modern business and financial interactions these are crucial concerns.

A public-key cryptosystem, in which plaintext- and cryptotext-space are the same and each user U makes his encryption function e_U public and keeps his decryption function d_U secret, can be used for this purpose.

If Bob wants to send a plaintext w with his 'signature' to Alice, he sends her $e_A(d_B(w))$. Only Alice can get out of it w, but anybody can verify, using the public key e_B, that the message was sent by Bob. Observe also that Bob is protected against someone changing the message after he has signed it.

Note too, that a 'natural, alternative or symmetric, solution', to encode a message w as $c = d_B(e_A(w))$, is not good. An active enemy T, with his public key e_T, usually called a **tamperer**, could intercept such a message, then compute $d_T(e_B(c)) = d_T(e_A(w))$ and send it to A pretending that it is from him, without being able to decrypt the message.

Exercise 8.5.1* *Alice wants to sign a message for Bob using a secret-key cryptosystem through Trent, a trusted arbitrator, with whom both Alice and Bob share secret keys. Design a secure signature protocol to do this.*

The RSA cryptosystem can be used for digital signatures in the above way. The private key then becomes the **signing exponent**. However, not all public-key cryptosystems are equally good for this. In addition, there are some signatures-only (crypto)schemes. The crucial point is that various applications put very strong requirements on efficiency. In 1993, the National Institute of Standards and Technology proposed the following digital signature algorithm (DSA) for use in its digital signature standard (DSS).

Design of DSA

1. Global public-key components are chosen:
   - p – a random l-bit prime, $512 \leq l \leq 1024$, is chosen, and l is a multiple of 64;
   - q – a random 160-bit prime dividing $p-1$ is chosen;
   - $g = h^{(p-1)/q} \bmod p$ is computed, where h is a random integer $1 < h < p-1$ such that $g \neq 1$.
2. User's private key is chosen:
   - x – a random integer, $0 < x < q$, is chosen.
3. User's public key is computed:
   - $y = g^x \bmod p$.

Signing algorithm – w is a plaintext.[8]

- Choose a (pseudo)-random $0 < k < q$ (a user's 'per-message' secret number);
- compute $r = (g^k \bmod p) \bmod q$;
- compute $s = k^{-1}(w + xr) \bmod q$, where $kk^{-1} \equiv 1 \pmod q$.
- (r,s) is a signature.

Verification algorithm – (r,s) is a signature.

- Compute $z = s^{-1} \bmod q$;
- compute $u_1 = wz \bmod q$ and $u_2 = rz \bmod q$;

[8]In practice, one does not sign the original message w. First, a hash function h is applied to w, and then $h(w)$ is signed. A standard was also developed for hashing in 1993 by the National Institute of Standards and Technology, the so-called secure hash algorithm (SHA). This algorithm takes as an input any message that has fewer than 2^{64} bits, and transforms it into a 160-bit message digest. Observe that signing algorithm uses no key.

- compute $v = (g^{u_1} y^{u_2} \bmod p) \bmod q$.

  Test whether $v = r$. If yes, the signature is correct.

Exercise 8.5.2 *Show that the DSA signature scheme is correct, and argue that it is sufficiently secure.*

Moral: The history of cryptology is full of inventions of perfect ideas and unbreakable systems that later turned out not to be so perfect and unbreakable. A good rule of thumb in cryptology is, therefore, as in life, never to overestimate yourself, never to underestimate your opponents/enemies, and to remember that human ingenuity cannot concoct an obstacle that human ingenuity cannot resolve.

8.6 Exercises

1. Decrypt the following messages encrypted using the CAESAR cryptosystem:

   (a) EOXH MHDQV; (b) WHVW WAGOB; (c) JWUSBSFS; (d) UJQHLGYJSHZAW HJGLGUGDK.

2. Decrypt the names of the microcomputers depicted in Figure 11.1.

3. Find a meaningful English text c, as long as possible, such that there are two meaningful plaintexts w_1 and w_2 that can both be encrypted by CAESAR as c.

4. Encrypt the plaintext POPOCATEPETL using the HILL cryptosystem and the matrix

$$(a)\quad \begin{pmatrix} 11 & 2 & 19 \\ 5 & 23 & 25 \\ 20 & 7 & 1 \end{pmatrix};\quad (b)\quad \begin{pmatrix} 23 & 7 & 3 \\ 25 & 1 & 19 \\ 5 & 20 & 11 \end{pmatrix}.$$

5. Encrypt the following plaintext using the PLAYFAIR cryptosystem: 'EVEN IN CRYPTOGRAPHY SILENCE IS GOLDEN'.

6. Apply frequency analysis to decrypt the following cryptotexts encrypted using a CAESAR cryptosystem: (a) ESPNLETYESPSLE; (b) SQUIQHICUJXETMQIJEEIYCFBUJERUKIUVKB. (c) DRKYVDRKZTJTREYVCGJFCMVKYVNFICUJGIFSCVDJ;

7. Encrypt the plaintext 'ENCRYPT THE PLAINTEXT' using the AUTOCLAVE cryptosystem and the key 'SALERNO'.

8.* Find a necessary and sufficient condition for a mapping to be realized by a Playfair square. Show how this can be utilized in cryptoanalysis.

9. The cryptotext obtained using the AFFINE cryptosystem with $c(x) = (7x + 10) \bmod 26$ is LJMKG MGMXF QEXMW. Determine the plaintext.

10. Decrypt the following messages obtained using an AFFINE cryptosystem:

    (a) BIFUIMZLMJSVIZLZUUZD; (b) NXUSTUMFXUFJMCTGPOTGXWHOO.

11. Encrypt the following plaintexts using the AUTOCLAVE cryptosystem and a keyword: (a) 'THE TRUTH IS MORE CERTAIN THAN PROBABLE' with the keyword 'OPTIMIST'; (b) 'THERE IS NO ROYAL ROAD TO CRYPTOGRAPHY' with 'EUCLID'; (c) 'I CAME I SAW I CONQUER' with 'CAESAR'; (d) 'THOSE WHO KNOW HOW TO WIN ARE MUCH MORE NUMEROUS THAN THOSE WHO KNOW HOW TO MAKE A PROPER USE OF THEIR VICTORY' with 'POLYBIOS'.

12. Decrypt the following cryptotext given to the participants of EUROCRYPT '88 in Davos.

```
EXVILT   AMSYMX   EAKSSI   KIRZMS
YEKDAV   OSINAL   PVITHE   RRJMLO
OIEUSM   GPLKSM   ADAVOS   LULRVK
SIXMTA   IDAVOS
```

13. Among ten-letter English anagrams we have

    ALGORITHMS – LOGARITHMS, ANTAGONIST – STAGNATION,

    COMPRESSED – DECOMPRESS, CREATIVITY – REACTIVITY.

    Find five others that make good sense.

14. Find the binary vector $(b_1, \ldots, b_6)$, if it exists, such that $s = b_1 2 + b_2 5 + b_3 9 + b_4 19 + b_5 55 + b_6 91$, for (a) $s = 155$; (b) $s = 105$; (c) $s = 77$; (d) $s = 44$.

15.* Show that the knapsack vector $(2106, 880, 1320, 974, 2388, 1617, 1568, 2523, 48, 897)$ can be obtained from a super-increasing vector by a strong modular multiplication.

16. For each n design a super-increasing vector of length n.

17.* Show that in the set of vectors $\{(a,b,c) \mid \max\{a,b,c\} = 4\}$ there are five super-increasing vectors.

18. Determine the following numbers: (a) 7^{-1} modulo 26; (b) 13^{-1} modulo 2436; (c) 144^{-1} modulo 233.

19. Compute (a) $2^{340} \bmod 11$; (b) $2^{340} \bmod 31$; (c) $2^{340} \bmod 341$.

20. Factor the numbers: (a) 323; (b) 54,053; (c) 209,501; (d) 43,794,427;

21.* Estimate the number of possibilities for factoring n if $n = pq$ and p, q are 150-bit primes.

22. Compute the secret exponent for the RSA cryptosystem with (a) $p = 7, q = 11, e = 7$; (b) $p = 5, q = 17, e = 3$; (c) $p = 7, q = 17, e = 5$.

23. Let $p = 11$, $q = 23$. List all possibilities for encryption and decryption exponents for the RSA cryptosystem.

24. Given an RSA cryptosystem with $n = 43 \times 59$ and $e = 13$, (a) encrypt the plaintext 'CRYPTOGRAPHY'; (b) decrypt the cryptotext 0667 1947 0671.

25.** Show that for every pair of primes p, q one can choose $e \notin \{1, \phi(pq) + 1\}$ such that $w^e \equiv w \bmod n$ for all w and $n = pq$.

26.* Show that the number of blocks that are mapped into themselves with the RSA encryption is $(1 + \gcd(e-1, p-1))(1 + gcd(e-1, q-1))$.

27. Factor n if n and $\phi(n)$ are given as follows: (a) $n = 5{,}767$, $\phi(n) = 5{,}618$; (b) $n = 4{,}386{,}007$, $\phi(n) = 4{,}382{,}136$; (c) $n = 3{,}992{,}003$, $\phi(n) = 3{,}988{,}008$.

28. Consider the following modification of the RSA cryptosystem. A large prime p is known to all users. Each user chooses and keeps secret encryption and decryption exponents e and d such that $ed \equiv 1 \pmod{p-1}$. Communication goes as follows. A encrypts a plaintext w by computing $c = E_A(w) = w^{e_A} \bmod p$ and sends it to B. B responds by sending $c_1 = E_B(c)$. Finally, A sends $D_A(c_1)$ to B. Show that B is able to decrypt and analyse the security of the cryptosystem.

29. **(LUC cryptosystem and Lucas numbers)**** There is a whole family of Lucas numbers. They have certain remarkable properties, and an interesting cryptosystem is based on them. Let p,q be integers such that $d = p^2 - 4q \neq 0$, and let α and β be such that $\alpha + \beta = p$ and $\alpha\beta = q$. Clearly, $\alpha - \beta = \sqrt{d}$. For $n \geq 1$ we define Lucas numbers $V_n(p,q)$ as follows: $V_n(p,q) = \alpha^n + \beta^n$. Show that (a) $V_n(p,q) = pV_{n-1}(p,q) - qV_{n-2}(p,q)$ for $n \geq 2$; (b) $V_n(p \bmod m, q \bmod m) = V_n(p,q) \bmod m$ for all m,n; (c) $V_{nk}(p,1) = V_n(V_k(p,1),1)$ for all n,k; (d) if p,q are primes, $n = pq$, $s(n) = \mathrm{lcm}(p - (d|p), q - (d|p))$, where $(d|p)$ is the Legendre symbol, and e,d are relatively prime to $s(n)$, $ed \equiv 1 \pmod{s(n)}$, then $V_e(V_d(x,1),1) = V_d(V_e(x,1),1) = x$ for all $x < n$.

    LUC cryptosystem. Encryption: $c = V_e(w,1) \bmod n$; decryption: $V_d(c,1) \bmod n$.

30. List all quadratic residues modulo (a) 23; (b) 37.

31.* In the El Gamal cryptosystem a large prime p is chosen, as well as an $a \in \mathbf{Z}_p$ and an $x \in \mathbf{Z}_p$. p, a and $y = a^x \bmod p$ form the public key, and x forms the trapdoor information. $\mathbf{Z}_p$ is both the plaintext- and the cryptotext-space. To encrypt a plaintext w, a random k is first chosen, $K = y^k \bmod p$ is computed, and the pair $c_1 = a^k \bmod p$ and $c_2 = Kw \bmod p$ form the cryptotext. Show how one can make decryption efficient when the trapdoor information is available.

QUESTIONS

1. Why is the PLAYFAIR cryptosystem much more secure than the CAESAR cryptosystem?
2. How can one slightly modify a mono-alphabetic substitution cryptosystem in such a way that frequency counting does not help too much to make decryptions?
3. What is the maximum density of a knapsack vector of length n?
4. Why should the secret exponent d in the RSA cryptosystem have no common factors with $p-1$ and $q-1$?
5. Are the numbers π and e random?
6. Can we have one-way functions that cannot be inverted for any argument effectively?
7. Do you know some 'golden rule' for the design of public-key cryptosystems?
8. What are the main types of attacks that a cryptosystem has to be designed to detect, prevent and recover from?
9. What are the advantages and disadvantages of randomized encryptions compared with deterministic encryptions?
10. How could you formulate the properties which a good signature scheme should have?

8.7 Historical and Bibliographical References

Kahn (1967) is an interesting account of the exciting 4,000-year-old history of cryptology. There are numerous books on classical cryptology. Among the older ones see Gaines (1939). Among more recent ones see Bauer (1993) and also the introductory chapter in Salomaa (1990).

Estimations of the number of meaningful plaintexts presented in Section 8.2 are due to Hellman (1977). To guess the size of the key-word in the case of poly-alphabetic substitution cryptosystems, one can use the Kinski method; see Salomaa (1990).

For a more detailed description of DES see, for example, Salomaa (1990) and Schneier (1996). DES was developed from the encryption algorithm LUCIFER; see Feistel (1973). For a history of DES development, see Smid and Branstead (1988). The proof that the cryptosystem DES is not composite is due to Campbell and Wiener (1992). The $\theta(2^{\sqrt{\ln n \ln \ln n}})$ algorithm for computing discrete logarithms is due to Adleman (1979).

For a detailed presentation of public-key cryptography see Salomaa (1990), Brassard (1988), Schneier (1996); also the survey papers by Rivest (1990), Brickel and Odlyzko (1988) and Diffie (1988). The last describes in detail the beginnings of public-key cryptography.

The knapsack cryptosystem and its variants, including the dense knapsack, and their cryptoanalysis are presented in Salomaa (1990). Chor (1986) is the basic reference on the dense knapsack. The whole story of the knapsack cryptosystem is described in the book by O'Connor and Seberry (1987).

A detailed presentation and analysis of the RSA cryptosystem is in Salomaa (1990). Currently the fastest deterministic algorithm for primality testing is due to Adleman, Pomerance and Rumely (1983). Primality testing is discussed in detail by Kranakis (1986). The second result of Theorem 8.3.24 is due to DeLaurentis (1984). The result that any polynomial time algorithm for determining one bit of cryptotext encrypted by RSA can be transformed into a polynomial time algorithm for breaking RSA is due to Goldwasser, Micali and Tong (1982). In both cases see also Salomaa (1990) and Kranakis (1986) for a presentation of these results. For the problem of how to break RSA in case several users employ the same modulus, see Salomaa (1990). The LUC cryptosystem, discussed in Exercise 29, is due to Smith and Lennon (1993); see Stallings (1995) for a presentation.

Basic results concerning relations between randomness and cryptography, cryptographically strong pseudo-random generators and randomized encryptions are presented by Rivest (1990). The result that a cryptographically strong pseudo-random generator exists if and only if a one-way function exists is implicit in Yao (1982). The concepts of one-way predicate and polynomial-time secure randomized encryption are due to Goldwasser and Micali (1984). Rabin's randomized cryptosystem is taken from Rabin (1979), and the El Gamal cryptosystem from El Gamal (1985). Algorithm 8.4.5 is from Brassard (1988). For a general method of designing cryptographically strong pseudo-random generators, see Blum and Micali (1984). The randomized cryptosystem presented in Section 8.4 is due to Blum and Goldwasser (1985).

The development of rigorous and sufficiently adequate definitions for the basic concepts and primitives in cryptography is far from easy and perhaps a never ending story. For advances along these lines see Goldreich (1989) and Luby (1996). In the last book the problem is addressed in depth for making use of one-way functions to construct pseudo-random generators and other cryptographic primitives.

The concept of digital signature is due to Diffie and Hellmann (1976) and discussed in detail by Brassard (1988), Schneier (1996) and Mitchell, Pipper and Wild (1992). The DSS signature scheme was developed on the basis of the signature schemes of El Gamal (1985) and Schnorr (1991).

For quantum cryptography see Brassard (1988) and Bennett, Bessette, Brassard and Salvail (1992). The idea of quantum cryptography was born in the late 1960s (due to S. Wiesner). The first successful quantum exchange took place in 1989. In 1994 British Telecom announced the completion of a fully working prototype capable of implementing quantum key distribution along 10km of optical fibre.

9 Protocols

INTRODUCTION

Attempts to prove the security of cryptographic systems have given rise to a variety of important and deep concepts and methods with surprising practical and theoretical applications and implications. This chapter deals with these concepts and techniques. First, some examples of cryptographic protocols are presented that solve apparently impossible communication problems. Corresponding abstract concepts of interactive protocols and proof systems are then introduced, which give a radically new view of how to formalize one of the key concepts of modern science – evidence.

New views of interactions allow one to see, in a sense, such powerful complexity classes as **PSPACE** and **NEXP** as representing classes of problems having feasible solutions. The related concept of zero-knowledge proofs is also the basis for implementing perfect security of cryptographic protocols. One of the surprising applications of the ideas coming from the formalization of interactions is in the area of program checking, self-testing and self-correcting. A radically new approach to these problems, based on randomness, is suggested.

This chapter also explores how dramatic implications can be brought by a new paradigm, or a combination of new paradigms – this time by interactions and randomization.

LEARNING OBJECTIVES

The aim of the chapter is to demonstrate

1. several cryptographic protocols and primitives for solving apparently impossible communication problems;
2. basic concepts of interactive proof system;
3. basic complexity results, including Shamir's theorem showing the enormous computational power of interactions;
4. the concept of zero-knowledge proofs and methods for designing and analysing such proofs;
5. new approaches to one of the fundamental concepts of science – evidence;
6. a new randomized and interactive approach to program (results) checking, self-testing and self-correcting.

Faith is the substance of things hoped for,
the evidence of things not seen.

Hebrews 11:1

A variety of cryptographic primitives, operators and interactive protocols has been developed that allow two or more parties to develop trust that their communication, co-ordination/co-operation has the desired properties, despite the best efforts of adversaries or untrusted parties. This permits them to realize successfully a variety of important, though seemingly impossible, communication and co-operation tasks.

Attempts to achieve perfect secrecy, minimal disclosure of knowledge or perfect protection of co-operation in a large variety of communication and co-operation tasks have also led to the emergence of a new methodology – the so-called interactive and zero-knowledge protocols. This has initiated a new approach to one of the most fundamental concepts of science – evidence. Interactive, zero-knowledge, transparent and other new types of proofs represent radical ways of formalizing our intuitive concepts of evidence and security. New understanding has developed of the power of interactions and randomness, with applications in such seemingly remote areas as approximation algorithms and program checking and self-correcting.

9.1 Cryptographic Protocols

Cryptographic protocols are specifications regarding how parties should prepare themselves for a communication/interaction and how they should behave during the process in order to achieve their goals and be protected against adversaries. It is assumed that all the parties involved in a protocol know and follow it fully. The parties can be friends who trust each other or adversaries who do not trust each other. Cryptographic protocols often use some cryptographic primitives, but their goals usually go beyond simple security. The parties participating in a protocol may want to share some of their secrets in order to compute together some value, generate jointly random numbers, convince each other of their identity, simultaneously sign a contract or participate in secret voting. Cryptographic protocols that accomplish such tasks have radically changed our views of what mutually distrustful parties can accomplish over a network.

Protocols can be described on two levels: on an abstract level, assuming the existence of basic cryptographic operators with certain security properties (secret keys, encryptions, decryptions, one-way functions or one-way trapdoor functions, pseudo-random generators, bit commitment schemes, and so on); and on a lower level, with concentration on particular implementations of these operators. We concentrate here on the abstract level.

Randomization and interactions are two essential features of interactive protocols. In designing them, it is assumed that each party has its own private, independent source of randomness.

In order to show the potential of interactions, we present first several examples of communication problems and protocols for **two-party** and **multi-party communications**.

Example 9.1.1 *Let us consider the following simple protocol, which employs a public-key cryptosystem, for sending and acknowledging receipts of messages. (A and B stand here for strings identifying users.)*

1. *Alice sends the triple* $(A, e_B(w), B)$ *to Bob.*

2. *Bob decrypts* w *using his decryption algorithm, and acknowledges receipt of the message by sending back the triple* $(B, e_A(w), A)$.

Is the protocol in Example 9.1.1 secure, or rather, what kinds of attack must be considered in order to explore the problem of security of cryptographic protocols?

There are various types of attacks against cryptographic protocols. In a **passive attack** the attacker tries to obtain information being transmitted without altering the communication and the protocol. In an **active attack**, the attacker (**tamperer** or **man-in-the-middle**) destroys or changes information being transmitted or starts to send and receive his own messages. In the case that the attacker is one of the parties involved, we speak about a **cheater**.

For example, in the case of the protocol in Example 9.1.1 an active eavesdropper C may intercept the triple being sent in Step 1 and forward to Bob the triple $(C, e_B(w), B)$. Not realizing the danger, Bob responds, following the protocol, by sending $(B, e_C(w), C)$, so now C is able to learn w.

Exercise 9.1.2 *Consider the following communication protocol in which Alice and Bob use a public-key cryptosystem, with the encryption and decryption functions operating on integers, to send a message w.*

1. *Alice sends Bob the pair $(e_B(e_B(w)A), B)$.*
2. *Bob uses his decryption algorithm d_B to find A and w, and acknowledges receipt of the message by sending Alice the pair $(e_A(e_A(w)B), A)$.*

A and B are here strings identifying Alice and Bob. $e_B(w)A$ is the message obtained by concatenating $e_B(w)$ and A. Show how an active tamperer could intercept this protocol to learn w.

Our first problem is a variant of the identification problem.

Protocol 9.1.3 (Friend-or-foe identification) *Alice, who shares a cryptosystem and a secret key with Bob, is engaged in a communication with somebody, and wants to make sure that the person she is communicating with really is Bob. To verify this, Alice uses the following* **challenge–response** *protocol.*

1. *Alice generates a random integer r and sends r to the communicating party.*
2. *The communicating party encrypts r using the shared secret key, and returns the resulting cryptotext c.*
3. *Alice compares the cryptotext c with the one she gets by her encryption of r. If they agree, she is convinced that the other party is indeed Bob.*

This protocol seems to be more secure than asking the other party to send the shared key – an active tamperer could intercept it and later pretend to be Bob.

Example 9.1.4 (Man-in-the-middle attack) *To protect a communication against an active tamperer is one of the difficult problems of cryptography. Here is a simple way in which a tamperer, usually called Mallet (or Mallory), can simulate Bob when communicating with Alice, and Alice when communicating with Bob. His attacks work as follows.*

1. *Alice sends Bob her public key. Mallet intercepts the message and instead sends his public key to Bob.*
2. *Bob sends Alice his public key. Mallet intercepts, and sends Alice his public key.*

Now, whenever Alice sends a message to Bob, encrypted in 'Bob's' public key, Mallet intercepts it. Since the message is actually encrypted using his public key, he can decrypt it, change it, and send it to Bob using his public key. In a similar way, Mallet can intercept and change messages sent by Bob to Alice.

Exercise 9.1.5 *The* **interlock protocol** *has a good chance of fooling the man-in-the-middle attacker. Here are its first four steps.*

1. *Alice sends Bob her public key.*
2. *Bob sends Alice his public key.*
3. *Alice encrypts her message using Bob's public key, and sends half of the encrypted message to Bob.*
4. *Bob encrypts his message using Alice's public key, and sends half of the message to Alice.*

Finish the design of the protocol in such a way that Mallet cannot get the messages which Alice and Bob send to each other. Explain why.

Bit commitment problem. Two parties, located far apart, want to agree without the assistance of a trusted referee on randomly chosen bit. More precisely, Bob wants **Alice to choose a bit and be committed to it** in the following sense: Bob has no way of knowing what Alice has chosen, and Alice has no way of changing her commitment once she has made it, say after Bob announces his guess as to what Alice has chosen.

This is a very basic communication problem with many applications. For example, two parties, located far apart, want to agree on a random sequence. Popularly, this problem is called the **coin-flipping over the telephone problem**. It was formulated by Manuel Blum (1982) with the following sad story behind it. Alice and Bob have divorced. They do not trust each other any more and want to decide, communicating only by telephone, by coin-tossing, who gets the car. There are various protocols for achieving this. Two of them will now be considered.

Protocol 9.1.6 (Coin-flipping by telephone, I) *Alice sends Bob encrypted messages 'head' and 'tail'. Bob, not able to decrypt them, picks one and informs Alice of his choice. Alice then sends Bob the encryption procedure (or a key for it).*

There is a general scheme, which seems to be good enough for a protocol to solve the coin-flipping by telephone problem, based on the assumption that both Alice and Bob know a one-way function f. Alice chooses a random x and sends $f(x)$ to Bob. He guesses some '50–50 property' of x, for example, whether x is even, and informs Alice of his guess. She tells him whether the guess was correct. (Later, if necessary for some reason, she can send x to Bob.)

Is this protocol secure? Can either of them cheat? The protocol looks secure, because Bob has no way of determining x from $f(x)$. However, the situation is actually more complicated. The security of the protocol depends a lot on which of the potential one-way functions is chosen. An analysis shows the difficulties one can encounter in making communication protocols secure.

Indeed, it could happen that Alice knows two x, x_1 and x_2, such that $f(x_1) = f(x_2)$ and one of them is even and the second odd! In such a case Alice could easily cheat! Bob could also cheat were he able to find out the parity of x. (Note that the fact that he cannot determine x does not imply that he cannot determine the parity of x.)

The following secure protocol for the bit commitment problem is based on the fact that computation of square roots modulo the product of two primes is a trapdoor function.

Protocol 9.1.7 (Coin-flipping by telephone, II)

1. *Alice chooses two large primes* p,q, *sends Bob* $n = pq$, *and keeps* p,q *secret.*
2. *Bob chooses a random number* $y \in \{1,\ldots,\lfloor\frac{n}{2}\rfloor\}$, *and sends Alice* $x = y^2 \bmod n$.
3. *Alice computes four square roots* $(x_1, n-x_1, x_2, n-x_2)$ *of* x. *(Alice can compute them because she knows* p *and* q.*) Let* $x'_1 = \min\{x_1, n-x_1\}$, $x'_2 = \min\{x_2, n-x_2\}$. *Since* $y \in \{1,\ldots,\lfloor\frac{n}{2}\rfloor)$, *either* $y = x'_1$ *or* $y = x'_2$. *Alice then guesses whether* $y = x'_1$ *or* $y = x'_2$ *and tells Bob her choice (for example, by reporting the position and the value of the left-most bit in which* x'_1 *and* x'_2 *differ).*
4. *Bob tells Alice whether her guess was correct (head) or not correct (tail).*

Later, if necessary, Alice can reveal p *and* q, *and Bob can reveal* y.

Observe that Alice has no way of knowing y, so her guess is a real one. Were Bob able to cheat by changing the number y after Alice's guess, then he would have both x'_1 and x'_2; therefore he could factorize n. To avoid this, Alice tells in Step 3 only one bit, rather than the entire x'_1 or x'_2.

Exercise 9.1.8* *Consider the following protocol for the bit commitment problem. (1) Alice randomly chooses large primes* p,q, *computes* $n = pq$, *chooses* $x \in_U \mathbf{Z}_n^*$, *computes* $y = x^2 \bmod n, z = y^2 \bmod n$ *and sends Bob* n *and* z. *(2) Bob announces his guess: that is, whether* y *is even or odd. (3) Alice lets Bob know* x,y, *and Bob verifies that* $y = x^2 \bmod n, z = y^2 \bmod n$. *Is this protocol correct and secure? If not, how can one change it so that it becomes secure?*

Partial disclosure of secrets. There are k parties, $P_1,\ldots,P_k$, and they are to compute the value of a function f of k arguments. Assume that the party P_i knows only the ith argument a_i. The task is to design a protocol that allows the parties to compute together $f(a_1,\ldots,a_k)$ in such a way that at the end of the communication each party P_i knows the value $f(a_1,\ldots,a_k)$, but no party gives away any information whatsoever concerning his/her argument a_i, except for information one can learn knowing only a_i and $f(a_1,\ldots,a_k)$.

There are two popular variants of the problem. Two millionaires want to engage in a conversation that will allow them to find out who is richer (which is an understandable wish), without disclosing any information about their wealth (which is an even more understandable wish). Another variant: Alice and Bob want to find out who is older without disclosing any other information about their ages.

The following protocol, based on an arbitrary public-key cryptosystem, solves the problem. We assume, (though even this may not be very realistic) that neither Alice nor Bob is older than 100. Again we assume again that e_A is the public encryption key of Alice and d_A is her secret decryption key. Assume also that i is the age of Alice and j is that of Bob.

Protocol 9.1.9 (Age difference finding)

1. *Bob chooses a large random integer* x, *computes* $k = e_A(x)$, *and sends Alice* $s = k - j$.
2. *Alice first computes numbers*

$$y_u = d_A(s+u) \quad \textit{for} \quad 1 \leq u \leq 100,$$

then chooses a large random prime p, computes numbers

$$z_u = y_u \bmod p \quad \text{for} \quad 1 \le u \le 100, \tag{9.1}$$

and verifies that for all $u \neq v$

$$|z_u - z_v| \ge 2 \quad \text{and} \quad z_u \neq 0. \tag{9.2}$$

If this is not the case, Alice chooses a new p and repeats the computations in (9.1), and checks (9.2) again. Finally, Alice sends Bob the following sequence (the order is important!):

$$z_1, \ldots, z_i, z_{i+1} + 1, \ldots, z_{100} + 1, p. \tag{9.3}$$

3. *Bob checks whether the j-th number in this sequence, z'_j, is congruent with $x \bmod p$. If yes, he knows that $i \ge j$; otherwise he knows that $i < j$ and informs Alice.*

Correctness of the protocol: because of the condition (9.2), any two of the first 100 numbers in the sequence (9.3) are different. Moreover,

$$\begin{aligned} i \ge j \;&\Rightarrow\; z'_j = z_j \equiv y_j = d_A(k) = x \pmod p; \\ i < j \;&\Rightarrow\; z'_j = z_j + 1 \not\equiv z_j \equiv y_j = d_A(k) = x \pmod p. \end{aligned}$$

Exercise 9.1.10 *Illustrate the age difference finding protocol by considering the RSA cryptosystem with $p = 11, q = 5, e = 7, d = 23$. Assume that $i = 17, j = 20$, and the maximum age is 21 and Bob chooses $x = 39$ in Step 1.*

Example 9.1.11 *Of interest and importance also is an 'inverse' problem to that of partial disclosure of secrets – a* **secret sharing problem**. *A 'secret' $s \in \mathbf{N}$ should be 'distributed' among n parties in such a way that any t of them, for a fixed t, can determine s, but no $t-1$ of them is able to do so.*

The problem has a simple and elegant solution that is based on the well-known fact that a polynomial of degree $t-1$ is uniquely determined given its t points.

A solution of the above secret sharing problem: choose randomly a polynomial p of degree $t-1$ such that $p(0) = s$. Choose randomly n integers $a_1, \ldots, a_n$, with $a_i \neq a_j$ for $i \neq j$ and such that $a_i \neq 0$ for all i, and send to the party a_i the pair $(a_i, p(a_i))$.

There are many other interesting communication problems for two parties that have been solved by designing secure communication protocols: for example, **contract signing** (both parties sign the contract, but no party obtains the other party's signature before giving up his own) and **secret voting** (in which every voter's vote remains private and every voter can be sure that the vote-counting was correct).

Various communication primitives have also been identified and protocols for them developed. They can now be used to design protocols for other communication problems. The bit commitment problem is one of them. Any solution to the following, strange-looking communication problem was shown to be a sufficiently strong primitive to design protocols for **any** two-party communication problem.

Oblivious transfer problem. Design a protocol for sending a message from Alice to Bob in such a way that Bob receives the message with probability $\frac{1}{2}$ and garbage with probability $\frac{1}{2}$. Moreover, at the end, Bob knows whether he got a message or garbage, but Alice has no idea which of them Bob has received.

One popular interpretation is that Alice knows a secret and wants to send it to Bob in such a way that he gets it with probability $\frac{1}{2}$, and he knows whether he got it, but Alice has no idea whether he really received it. A modified version of this problem is that Alice has several secrets, and Bob wants to obtain one of them in such a way that only he knows which one he has received. (Investigate applications!)

The following protocol is based on the fact (see Theorem 1.8.16) that knowledge of two different square roots of an integer modulo n allows one to factor n.

Protocol 9.1.12 (Oblivious transfer)

1. *Alice chooses two large primes p and q and sends $n = pq$ to Bob.*
2. *Bob chooses a number x and sends $y = x^2 \bmod n$ to Alice.*
3. *Alice computes four square roots $\pm x_1, \pm x_2$ of y modulo n, and sends one of them to Bob. (Since she knows the factorization of n, she can do it. She has no idea, however, which of them is x.)*
4. *Bob checks whether the number he got is congruent with x. If yes, he has received no new information. Otherwise, Bob has two different square roots modulo n, and can therefore factor n. Alice has no way of knowing whether this is the case.*

Exercise 9.1.13* *Alice knows secrets $s_1, \ldots, s_k$ – each a sequence of bits – that are answers to important questions. Assume that Alice publicizes these questions. Bob wants to buy one of the secrets but does not want Alice to know which. Design a protocol that achieves such a secret buying of secrets and is secure against a passive adversary. (Hint: in the first step Alice sends Bob a trapdoor one-way function, but keeps the trapdoor information necessary to compute its inverse secret.)*

Exercise 9.1.14** *There is another protocol for selling secrets $s_1, \ldots, s_k$, in which a commutative cryptosystem is used and the first two steps are as follows.*

1. *Bob sends Alice random bit sequences $y_1, \ldots, y_k$ of the same length as the secrets $s_1, \ldots, s_k$.*
2. *Alice sends Bob the bit sequence $z_j = e_A(s_j \oplus y_j), j = 1, \ldots, k$.*

Finish the design of the protocol, and analyse its security.

To show the existence of powerful methods of proving security of cryptographic protocols, several new fundamental concepts concerning interactions, protocols and proofs have been developed, with impacts extending far beyond the original motivation. With these new concepts and related results we deal in the next sections.

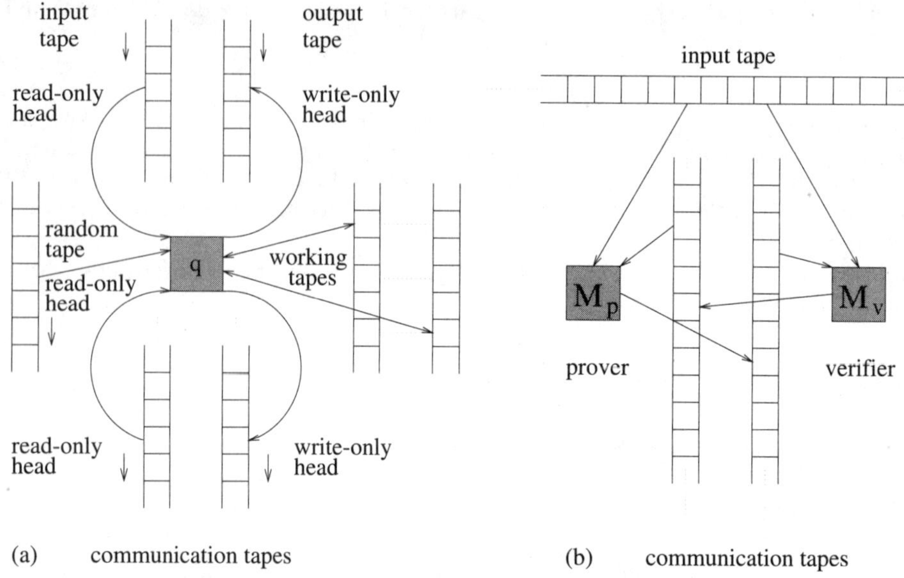

Figure 9.1 An interactive Turing machine and an interactive protocol

Exercise 9.1.15 (Poker playing by telephone) *Alice and Bob want to play a simple variant of poker, with five cards, by phone, without any third party acting as an impartial judge. Both of them have at their disposal a commutative cryptosystem for which neither decryption nor encryption functions are published. Show how Alice and Bob can play so that the following conditions are satisfied: (a) All hands (sets of five cards) are equally likely. (b) The hands of Alice and Bob are different. (c) Both players know their own hands but have no information about their opponents' hands. (d) It is possible for each player to find out eventually if the other player cheats.*

9.2 Interactive Protocols and Proofs

Very often, when new fundamental ideas are developed in computing and basic problems are investigated, Turing machines are the proper framework for setting up the corresponding formal concepts. Formalization of the ideas concerning security and evidence, motivated by cryptographic problems and solutions, is such a case.

Definition 9.2.1 *An* **interactive Turing machine** *(ITM) is a Turing machine with a one-way, read-only input tape, a one-way, read-only random tape, a one-way, read-only communication tape, a one-way, write-only communication tape, a one-way, write-only output tape and several working tapes (see Figure 9.1a).*

At the beginning of each computation of an ITM, the random tape is expected to be filled with a new random infinite sequence of bits. (Coin-tossing in an ITM is simulated by reading the next bit from its (private) random tape.) The content of the read-only (write-only) communication tape is considered to be the message which the machine receives (sends). An interactive Turing machine is a building block for the following formal model of interactions.

Definition 9.2.2 *An* **interactive protocol** *is a pair* (M_P, M_V) *of interactive Turing machines, with* M_V *being polynomial time bounded, that have a common input tape and share communication tapes as follows: the communication tape that is the read-only (write-only) tape for one of the machines is the write-only (read-only) tape for the other.* M_P *is usually called the* **prover** *or* **Peggy**, *and* M_V *the* **verifier** *or* **Vic**.

In an interactive protocol the verifier and the prover work in turns, also called **moves**. The verifier starts an interaction. At any moment of the discrete time, only one of the machines is active. When one of them is active it performs, on the contents of its accessible tapes, the usual Turing machine computations. What one of the machines writes on its write-only communication tape is considered to be the message for the other machine. The ith message of M_V (of M_P) is the message M_V (M_P) writes on its communication tape during its ith move. Any two consecutive moves, verifier $\rightarrow$ prover $\rightarrow$ verifier or prover $\rightarrow$ verifier $\rightarrow$ prover, are called a **round**. A machine terminates computation by sending no message. M_V accepts (rejects) the initial contents of the input tape when M_V ends the computation in the accepting (rejecting) state ACCEPT (REJECT). This is its output. The **history** of a computation (communication) is the sequence $h_n = (v_1, p_1, \ldots, v_n, p_n)$, where v_i (p_i) denotes the message sent from the verifier (the prover) during its ith move and $p_n = \varepsilon$.

Both M_V and M_P are probabilistic Turing machines in the sense that the way their computations proceed may depend also on the contents of their random tapes. The prover has unlimited computational power. The verifier has to work in polynomial time with respect to the length of the input. The sum of computation times during all active steps of the verifier is counted. This implies, of course, that for the prover it makes sense to write only polynomially long messages on the common communication tape. The verifier could not even read longer messages in the polynomial time.

Let $(M_P, M_V)(x)$ denote the verifier's output for an input x. For every x, $(M_P, M_V)(x)$ is a random variable on the space of all possible computations of the protocol (M_V, M_P) with respect to private random bits.

For any interactive protocol (M_P, M_V), we denote by (M_{P^*}, M_V) the interactive protocol in which the verifier M_V behaves exactly as in the original protocol, but the prover computes the function specified by M_{P^*}. This is said to be a 'cheating prover' if M_{P^*} computes differently from M_P. Similarly, we denote by (M_P, M_{V^*}) the interactive protocol in which the prover behaves exactly as in the original protocol but the (potentially cheating) verifier can behave differently. The potentially cheating prover is limited only in that the messages she sends must have polynomially bounded size with respect to the length of the input. The potentially cheating verifier is limited to randomized polynomial time computations.

9.2.1 Interactive Proof Systems

Our formal concept of an interactive protocol, expressed in terms of Turing machines, captures an intuitive idea of interactions, and forms a basis for investigating the power of interactions.

As usual, when a new concept of computation is developed, the most basic question to investigate is how powerful it is for solving decision problems. This is usually formalized in terms of language recognition. In the case of interactive protocols this leads to the following definition.

Definition 9.2.3 *The interactive protocol* (M_P, M_V) *recognizes the language* L *if for all* $x \in L$

$$Pr((M_P, M_V)(x) = ACCEPT) > \frac{2}{3};$$

and for all $x \notin L$ and all provers M_{p*}

$$Pr((M_P^*, M_V)(x) = REJECT) > \frac{2}{3}.$$

If there is an interactive protocol for a language L, we say also that L has an interactive proof system.

There are several ways of viewing such an interactive protocol.

1. The goal of any prover can be seen as to convince the verifier that $x \in L$, no matter whether this is true. The goal of the verifier is that no prover should be able to convince him that $x \in L$ if this is not true or that $x \notin L$ if this is not true. However, he is willing to tolerate a small probability of getting fooled. (However, this does not imply that if $x \in L$, then for any prover the verifier accepts with high probability.)

2. The term 'proof system' is used here in the following sense. By 'theorem' we understand a truth statement concerning specific objects: for example, that a certain x is in a certain language L or that a specific graph G_0 is 3-colourable, or that it is Hamiltonian.

   A classical formal proof of a concrete statement, for example, $x_0 \in L_0$ for a specific x_0 and L_0, is a formal reasoning showing the validity of such a theorem that can be verified (even mechanically) without doubts. An interactive proof system for a particular language L_0 can be used for any specific x to produce statistical evidence regarding whether $x \in L_0$ or not. The more times we apply the proof system to the same x, the more sure we can be whether $x \in L_0$ or not.

As an example, we show now a simple and fast interactive proof system for what is computationally a very hard problem, the graph nonisomorphism problem, which is not known to be in **NP**.

$$\begin{aligned} NONISO &= \{(G_0, G_1) \mid G_0 = \langle V, E_0\rangle \text{ and } G_1 = \langle V, E_1\rangle \\ &\quad \text{are nonisomorphic graphs; that is, } G_0 \not\cong G_1\}. \end{aligned}$$

Protocol 9.2.4 (Graph nonisomorphism) *1. The verifier, Vic, reads the input (G_0, G_1) and s bits $b_1, \ldots, b_s$ from his random tape. s is here a security parameter that guarantees, as will be shown later, a certain probability of the correctness of the outcome. Vic then designs for $1 \leq i \leq s$ a graph $H_i = \langle V, F_i\rangle$, by deriving F_i from E_{b_i} by taking a random permutation of V, and sends all H_i to the prover, Peggy. He asks her to determine for all $1 \leq i \leq s$, which of the two given graphs, G_0 and G_1 was used to design H_i. (Observe that $G_{b_i} \cong H_i$.)*

2. *Peggy also reads the input (G_0, G_1) and checks first whether these two graphs are isomorphic. (Since she has unlimited computational power, this is no problem for her.) If G_0 and G_1 are isomorphic, Peggy reads next s bits $c_i, i = 1, \ldots, s$, from her private random tape and sends them to Vic as the answer (without even looking at the inputs H_i she got from Vic – it makes no sense for her to do so, because she has no way of finding out which of the graphs G_0 or G_1 was used to design H_i). If (G_0, G_1) are not isomorphic, Peggy verifies for each $1 \leq i \leq s$ whether $H_i \cong G_0$ or $H_i \cong G_1$ and reports the results to Vic as a sequence of s bits $c_i, 1 \leq i \leq s$, where $c_i = 0$ if and only if $G_0 \cong H_i$.*

3. *Vic compares b_i and c_i for all i, $1 \leq i \leq s$. If there is an i_0 such that $b_{i_0} \neq c_{i_0}$, then Vic rejects the input (G_0, G_1), otherwise he accepts.*

The correctness proof:. If $G_0 \not\cong G_1$, then Peggy can determine whether $H_i \cong G_0$ or $H_i \cong G_1$, and therefore $b_i = c_i$ for $1 \leq i \leq n$.

If $G_0 \cong G_1$, which Peggy can find out, there is no way for Peggy to know b_i, and therefore the probability that $c_i = b_i$ is $\frac{1}{2}$. The probability that in the case $G_0 \cong G_1$ there is no i such that $b_i \neq c_i$ is 2^{-s}. □

Exercise 9.2.5* *Design an interactive proof system for the language $Q = \{(x,y) \mid y \in QNR_x\}$ in which the verifier can recognize Q using only one interaction with the prover. (Hint: for $|x| = n$, Peggy gets n random bits $b_1, \ldots, b_n$ and n random integers $z_1, \ldots, z_n$, $0 < z_i < x$, $\gcd(x, z_i) = 1, \ldots$.)*

In the following we address four basic questions about interactive protocols:

1. Which languages have interactive proofs?
2. How many interactions are needed for the prover to convince the verifier?
3. How much knowledge does the verifier get during the interaction with the prover?
4. How can we apply the idea of interactive proof systems?

9.2.2 Interactive Complexity Classes and Shamir's Theorem

Protocol 9.2.4 is very simple; it 'proves' in two rounds. The number of rounds, as we shall see, is an important complexity measure of proof systems. The following definition gives the basic concepts.

Definition 9.2.6 *(1) Let $g : \mathbf{N} \rightarrow \mathbf{N}$ be a nondecreasing function. An interactive proof system (M_P, M_V) for a language $L \subseteq \{0,1\}^*$ has a* **round complexity** *bounded by g if for every $x \in L$ the number of rounds of any computation of (M_P, M_V) on x is bounded from above by $g(|x|)$.*

(2) Denote by $IP[g(n)]$ the family of languages that have an interactive proof system with the round complexity bounded by g, and denote by

$$\mathbf{IP} = \bigcup_{i \geq 0} IP[n^i]$$

the family of languages acceptable by interactive proof systems with a polynomial number of rounds (interactions) with respect to the length of the input.

For instance, **IP[2]** is the class of languages for which there exists an interactive proof system of the following type. On an input x the verifier flips the coin, makes some computations on the basis of the outcome and sends a message to the prover. The prover, after doing whatever he does, sends a message back to the verifier – this is the first round. The verifier again flips the coin, computes and accepts or rejects the input – the second round. Observe that for languages in **NP** there are certificates verifiable in polynomial time, and therefore $\mathbf{NP} \subseteq \mathbf{IP}[2]$ – the prover sends a cerificate, and the verifier verifies it. On the other hand, clearly $\mathbf{IP}[1] = \mathbf{BPP}$.

Basic relations between these new and some old complexity classes are readily seen.

Theorem 9.2.7 *For any nondecreasing function $g : \mathbf{N} \rightarrow \mathbf{N}$, with $g(n) \geq 2$ for all n and any $1 \leq n$,*

$$\mathbf{P} \subseteq \mathbf{NP} \subseteq IP[2] \subseteq IP[g(n)] \subseteq IP[g(n+1)] \subseteq \ldots \subseteq \mathbf{IP} \subseteq \mathbf{PSPACE}.$$

The validity of all but the last inclusion is trivial. With regard to the last inclusion, it is also fairly easy. Indeed, any interactive protocol with polynomially many rounds can be simulated by a PSPACE bounded machine traversing the tree of all possible interactions. (No communication between the prover and the verifier requires more than polynomial space.)

The basic problem is now to determine how powerful are the classes $IP[k], IP[n^k]$, especially the class **IP**, and what relations hold between them and with respect to other complexity classes. Observe that the graph nonisomorphism problem, which is not known to be in **NP**, is already in IP[2]. We concentrate now on the power of the class **IP**.

Before proving the first main result of this section (Theorem 9.2.11), we present the basic idea and some examples of so-called sum protocols. These protocols can be used to make the prover compute computationally unfeasible sums and convince the verifier, by overwhelming statistical evidence, of their correctness.

The key probabilistic argument used in these protocols concerns the roots of polynomials. If $p_1(x)$ and $p_2(x)$ are two different polynomials of degree n, and α is a randomly chosen integer in the range $\{0,\ldots,N\}$, then

$$Pr(p_1(\alpha) = p_2(\alpha)) \leq \frac{n}{N}, \tag{9.4}$$

because the polynomial $p_1(x) - p_2(x)$ has at most n roots.

Example 9.2.8 (Protocol to compute a permanent) *The first problem we deal with is that of computing the permanent of a matrix $M = \{m_{i,j}\}_{i,j=1}^{n}$; that is,*

$$perm(M) = \sum_{\sigma} \prod_{i=1}^{n} m_{i,\sigma(i)},$$

where σ goes through all permutations of the set $\{1,2,\ldots,n\}$. (As already mentioned in Chapter 4, there is no polynomial time algorithm known for computing the permanent.)

In order to explain the basic idea of an interactive protocol for computing perm(M), let us first consider a 'harder problem' and assume that the verifier needs to compute permanents of two matrices A, B of degree n. The verifier asks the prover to do it, and the prover, with unlimited computational power, sends the verifier two numbers, ρ_A and ρ_B, claiming that $\rho_A = perm(A)$ and $\rho_B = perm(B)$. The basic problem now is how the verifier can be convinced that the values ρ_A and ρ_B are correct. He cannot do it by direct calculation – this is computationally unfeasible for him. The way out is for the verifier to start an interaction with the prover in such a way that the prover will be forced to make, with large probability, sooner or later, a false statement, easily checkable by the verifier, if the prover cheated in one of the values ρ_A and ρ_B. Here is the basic trick.

Consider the linear function $D(x) = (1-x)A + xB$ in the space of all matrices of degree n. $perm(D(x))$ is then clearly a polynomial, say $d(x)$, of degree n and such that $d(0) = perm(A)$ and $d(1) = perm(B)$.

Now comes the main idea. The verifier asks the prover to send him $d(x)$. The prover does so. However, if the prover cheated on ρ_A or ρ_B, he has to cheat also on the coefficients of $d(x)$ – otherwise the verifier could immediately find out that either $\rho(A) \neq d(0)$ or $\rho(B) \neq d(1)$. In order to catch out the prover, in the case of cheating, the verifier chooses a random number $\alpha \in \{0,\ldots,N\}$, where $N \geq n^3$, and asks the prover to send him $d(\alpha)$. If the prover cheated, either on ρ_A or on ρ_B, the chance of the prover sending the correct values of $d(\alpha)$ is, by (9.4), at most $\frac{n}{N}$.

In a similar way, given k matrices $A_1,\ldots,A_k$ of degree n, the verifier can design a single matrix B of degree n such that if the prover has cheated on at least one of the values $perm(A_1),\ldots,perm(A_k)$, then he will have to make, with large probability, a false statement also about $perm(B)$.

Now let A be a matrix of degree n, and $A_{1,i}, 1 \leq i \leq n$, be submatrices obtained from A by deleting the first row and the i-th column. In such a case

$$perm(A) = \sum_{i=1}^{n} a_{1,i} perm(A_{1,i}). \tag{9.5}$$

Communication in the interactive protocol now goes as follows. The verifier asks for the values perm(A), $perm(A_{1,1}), \ldots, perm(A_{1,n})$, and uses (9.5) as a first consistency check. Were the prover to cheat on perm(A), she would also have to cheat on at least one of the values $perm(A_{1,1}), \ldots, perm(A_{1,n})$. Using the idea presented above, the verifier can now choose a random number $\alpha \in \{0, \ldots, N\}$, and design a single matrix A′ of degree $n-1$ such that if the prover cheated on perm(A), she would have to cheat, with large probability, also on perm(A′). The interaction continues in an analogous way, designing matrices of smaller and smaller degree, such that were the prover to cheat on perm(A), she would also have to cheat on permanents of all these smaller matrices, until such a small matrix is designed that the verifier is capable of computing directly its permanent and so becoming convinced of the correctness (or incorrectness) of the first value sent by the prover. The probability that the prover can succeed in cheating without being caught is less than $\frac{n^2}{N}$, and therefore negligibly small if N is large enough. (Notice that in this protocol the number of rounds is not bounded by a constant; it depends on the degree of the matrix.)

Example 9.2.9 *We demonstrate now the basic ideas of the interactive protocol for the so-called #SAT problem. This is the problem of determining the number of satisfying assignments to a Boolean formula $F(x_1, \ldots, x_n)$ of n variables.*

As the first step, using the arithmetization

$$x \wedge y \rightarrow xy, \quad x \vee y \rightarrow 1-(1-x)(1-y), \quad \bar{x} \rightarrow 1-x \tag{9.6}$$

(see Section 2.3.2), a polynomial $p(x_1, \ldots, x_n)$ approximating $F(x_1, \ldots, x_n)$ can be constructed in linear time (in length of F), and the problem is thereby reduced to that of computing the sum

$$\#SAT(F) = \sum_{x_1=0}^{1} \sum_{x_2=0}^{1} \cdots \sum_{x_n=0}^{1} p(x_1, \ldots, x_n). \tag{9.7}$$

For example, if $F(x,y,z) = (x \vee y \vee z)(x \vee \bar{y} \vee z)$, then

$$p(x,y,z) = (1-(1-x)(1-y)(1-z))(1-(1-x)y(1-z)).$$

We show now the first round of the protocol that reduces computation of the expression of the type (9.7) with n sums to a computation of another expression of a similar type, but with $n-1$ sums. The overall protocol then consists of $n-1$ repetitions of such a round.

The verifier's aim is again to get from the prover the resulting sum (9.7) and to be sure that it is correct. Therefore, the verifier asks the prover not only for the resulting sum w of (9.7), but also for the polynomial

$$p_1(x_1) = \sum_{x_2=0}^{1} \cdots \sum_{x_n=0}^{1} p(x_1, \ldots, x_n).$$

The verifier first makes the consistency check, that is, whether $w = p_1(0) + p_1(1)$. He then chooses a random $r \in \{0, \ldots, N\}$, where $N \geq n^3$, and starts another round, the task of which is to get from the prover the correct value of $p_1(r)$ and evidence that the value supplied by the prover is correct. Note that the probability that the prover sends a false w but the correct $p_1(r)$ is at most $\frac{n}{N}$. After n rounds, either the verifier will catch out the prover, or he will become convinced, by the overwhelming statistical evidence, that w is the correct value.

Exercise 9.2.10 *Show why using the arithmetization (9.6) we can always transform a Boolean formula in linear time into an approximating polynomial, but that this cannot done in general in linear time if the arithmetization* $x \vee y \rightarrow x + y - xy$ *is used.*

We are now in a position to prove an important result that gives a new view of what can be seen as computationally feasible.

Theorem 9.2.11 (Shamir's theorem) IP = PSPACE.

Proof: Since **IP** $\subseteq$ **PSPACE** (see Theorem 9.2.7), in order to prove the theorem, it is sufficient to show that there exists a **PSPACE**-complete language that is in **IP**: that is, the language for which there is an interactive proof system with the number of rounds bounded by a polynomial. We show that this holds for the so-called quantified Boolean formulas satisfiability problem (see also Section 5.11.2). This is the problem of deciding whether a formula

$$\underset{x_1}{Q}\underset{x_2}{Q}\ldots\underset{x_n}{Q} F(x_1,\ldots,x_n) \tag{9.8}$$

is valid, where F is a Boolean formula, and each Q_i is either an existential or a universal bounded quantifier, bounded to the values 0 and 1.

The basic idea of the proof is simple: to use an arithmetization to reduce the decision problem (9.8) to a 'sum problem', and then to use a 'sum protocol', described above.

Unfortunately, there is a problem with this idea. A 'natural arithmetization' of the quantifiers, namely,

$$\forall x T(x) \rightarrow T(0)T(1), \qquad \exists x T(x) \rightarrow T(0) + T(1) - T(0)T(1),$$

can double, for each quantifier, the size of the corresponding polynomial. This can therefore produce formulas of an exponential size, 'unreadable' for the verifier.

Fortunately, there is a trick to get around this exponential explosion. The basic idea consists of introducing new quantifiers, notation $\underset{x}{R}$. If the quantifier$\underset{x}{R}$ is applied to a polynomial p, it reduces all powers of x, x^i,to x. This is equivalent to taking $p \bmod (x^2 - x)$. Since $0^k = 0$ and $1^k = 1$ for any integer k, such a reduction does not change the values of the polynomial on the set $\{0,1\}$. Instead of the formula (9.8), we then consider the formula

$$\underset{x_1}{Q}\underset{x_1}{R}\underset{x_2}{Q}\underset{x_1}{R}\underset{x_2}{R}\underset{x_3}{Q}\underset{x_1}{R}\underset{x_2}{R}\underset{x_3}{R}\underset{x_4}{Q}\ldots\underset{x_n}{Q}\underset{x_1}{R}\ldots\underset{x_n}{R}\, p(x_1,\ldots,x_n), \tag{9.9}$$

where $p(x_1,\ldots,x_n)$ is a polynomial approximation of F that can be obtained from F in linear time.

Note that the degree of p does not exceed the length of F, say m, and that after each group or R-quantifier is applied, the degree of each variable is down to 1. Moreover, since the arithmetization of quantifiers $\exists$ and $\forall$ can at most double the degree of each variable in the corresponding polynomials, the degree of any polynomial obtained in the arithmetization process is never more than 2 in any variable.

The protocol consists of two phases. The first phase has the number of rounds proportional to the number of quantifiers in (9.9), and in each two rounds a quantifier is removed from the formula in (9.9).

The strategy of the verifier consists of asking the prover in each round for a number or a polynomial of one variable, of degree at most 2, in such a way that were the prover to cheat once, with large probability she would have to keep on cheating, until she gets caught. To make all computations reasonable, a prime P is chosen at the very beginning, and both the prover and the verifier have to perform all computations modulo P (it will be explained later how to choose P). The first phase of the protocol starts as follows:

1. Vic asks Peggy for the value w (0 or 1) of the formula (9.9). {A stripping of the quantifier $\underset{x_1}{Q}$ begins.}
2. Peggy sends w, claiming it is correct.
3. Vic wants to be sure, and therefore asks Peggy for the polynomial equivalent of
$$\underset{x_1}{R}\underset{x_2}{Q}\underset{x_1}{R}\underset{x_2}{R}\underset{x_3}{Q}\underset{x_1}{R}\underset{x_2}{R}\underset{x_3}{R}\underset{x_4}{Q}\ldots\underset{x_n}{Q}\underset{x_1}{R}\ldots\underset{x_n}{R}\,p(x_1,\ldots,x_n).$$
{Remember, calculations are done modulo P.}
4. Peggy sends Vic a polynomial $p_1(x_1)$, claiming it is correct.
5. Vic makes a consistency check by verifying whether
   - $p(0)+p(1)-p(0)p(1)=w$ if the left-most quantifier is $\exists$;
   - $p(0)p(1)=w$ if the left-most quantifier is $\forall$.

   In order to become more sure that p_1 is correct, Vic asks Peggy for the polynomial equivalent (congruent) to
$$\underset{x_2}{Q}\underset{x_1}{R}\underset{x_2}{R}\underset{x_3}{Q}\underset{x_1}{R}\underset{x_2}{R}\underset{x_3}{R}\underset{x_4}{Q}\ldots\underset{x_n}{Q}\underset{x_1}{R}\ldots\underset{x_n}{R}\,p(x_1,\ldots,x_n).$$
6. Peggy sends a polynomial $p_2(x_1)$, claiming it is correct.
7. Vic chooses a random number α_{11} and makes a consistency check by computing the number $(p_2(x_1) \bmod (x_1^2-x_1))|_{\alpha_{11}} = p_1(\alpha_{11})$.
   In order to become more sure that p_2 is correct, Vic chooses a random α_{12} and asks Peggy for the polynomial equivalent of
$$\underset{x_1}{R}\underset{x_2}{R}\underset{x_3}{Q}\underset{x_1}{R}\underset{x_2}{R}\underset{x_3}{R}\underset{x_4}{Q}\ldots\underset{x_n}{Q}\underset{x_1}{R}\ldots\underset{x_n}{R}\,p(x_1,\ldots,x_n)|_{x_1=\alpha_{12}}.$$
8. Peggy returns a polynomial $p_3(x_2)$, claiming it is correct.
9. Vic checks as in Step 5.

⋮

The protocol continues until either a consistency check fails or all quantifiers are stripped off. Then the second phase of the protocol begins, with the aim of determining the value of p for already chosen values of variables. In each round p can be seen as being decomposed either into $p'p''$ or $1-(1-p')(1-p'')$. Vic asks Peggy for the values of the whole polynomial and its subpolynomials p' and p''.

Analysis: During the first phase, until $n+(n-1)n/2$ quantifiers are removed, the prover has to supply the verifier each time with a polynomial of degree at most 2. Since each time the chance of cheating is at most $\frac{2}{P}$, the total chance of cheating is clearly less than $\frac{2m^2}{P}$. The number of rounds in the second phase, when the polynomial itself is shrunk, is at most m, and the probability of cheating at most $\frac{m}{P}$. Therefore, the total probability that the prover could fool the verifier is at most $\frac{3m^2}{P}$. Now it is clear how large P must be in order to obtain overwhelming statistical evidence. □

Theorem 9.2.11 actually implies that there is a reasonable model of computation within which we can see the whole class **PSPACE** as consisting of problems having feasible solutions. (This is a significant change in the view of what is 'feasible'.)

9.2.3 A Brief History of Proofs

The history of the concept of proof, one of the most fundamental concepts not only of science but of the whole of civilization, is both rich and interesting. Originally developed as a key tool in the search for truth, it has since been developed as the key tool to achieve security.

There used to be a very different understanding of what a proof means. For example, in the Middle Ages proofs 'by authority' were common. For a long time even mathematicians did not overconcern themselves with putting their basic tool on a firm basis. 'Go on, the faith will come to you' used to be a response to complaints of purists about lack of exactness.[1]

Mathematicians have long been convinced that a mathematical proof, when written out in detail, can be checked unambiguously. Aristotle (384–322 BC) made attempts to formalize the rules of deduction. However, the concept of a formal proof, checkable by a machine, was developed only at the beginning of the twentieth century, by Frege (1848–1923) and Russell (1872–1970). This was a major breakthrough and proofs 'within ZF', the Zermelo–Frankel axiomatic system, became standard for 'working mathematicians'.

Some of the problems with such a concept of proof were discussed in Chapter 6. Another practical, but also theoretical, difficulty lies in the fact that some proofs are too complicated to be understood. The proof of the classification of all finite simple groups takes about 15,000 pages, and some proofs are provably unfeasible (a theorem with fewer than 700 symbols was found, any proof of which is longer than the number of particles in the universe).

The concept of interactive proof has been another breakthrough in proof history. This has motivated development of several other fundamental concepts concerning proofs and led to unexpected applications. Sections 9.3 and 9.4 deal with two of them. Two other are now briefly discussed.

Interactive proofs with multiple provers

The first idea, theoretically obvious, was to consider interactions between one polynomial time bounded verifier and several powerful provers. At first this seemed to be a pure abstraction, without any deeper motivation or applications; this has turned out to be wrong.

The formal scenario goes as follows. The verifier and all provers are probabilistic Turing machines. The verifier is again required to do all computations in polynomial time. All provers have unlimited power. The provers can agree on a strategy before an interaction starts, but during the protocol they are not allowed to communicate among themselves. In one move the verifier sends messages to all provers, but each of them can read only the message addressed to her. Similarly, in one move all provers simultaneously send messages to the verifier. Again, none of them can learn messages sent by others. The acceptance conditions for a language L are similar to those given previously: each $x \in L$ is accepted with probability greater than $\frac{2}{3}$, and each $x \notin L$ is accepted with probability at most $\frac{1}{3}$. The family of languages accepted by interactive protocols with multiple provers and a polynomial number of rounds is denote by **MIP**.

It is evident that it is meaningless to have more than polynomially many provers. Not only that: it has been shown that two provers are always sufficient. However, the second prover can significantly increase the power of interactions, as the following theorem shows.

[1]For example, Fermat stated many theorems, but proved only a few.

Theorem 9.2.12 MIP = NEXP.

The extraordinary power of two provers comes from the fact that the verifier can ask both provers questions simultaneously, and they have to answer independently, without learning the answer of the other prover. In other words, the provers are securely separated.

If we now interpret **NP** as the family of languages admitting efficient formal proof of membership (formal in the sense that a machine can verify it), then **MIP** can be seen as the class of languages admitting efficient proofs of membership by overwhelming statistical evidence. In this sense **MIP** is like a 'randomized and interactive version' of **NP**.

The result **IP = PSPACE** can also be seen as asserting, informally, that via an interactive proof one can verify in polynomial time any theorem admitting exponentially long formal proof, say in ZF, as long as the proof could (in principle) be presented on a 'polynomial-size blackboard'. The result **MIP = NEXP** asserts, similarly, that with two infinitely powerful and securely separated provers, one can verify in polynomial time any theorem admitting an exponentially long proof.

Transparent proofs and limitations of approximability

Informally, a formal proof is **transparent** or **holographic** if it can be verified, with confidence, by a small number of spot-checks. This seemingly paradoxical concept, in which randomness again plays a key role, has also turned out to be deep and powerful.

One of the main results says that every formal proof, say in ZF, can be rewritten in a transparent proof (proving the same theorem in a different proof system), without increasing the length of the proof too much.

The concept of transparent proof leads to powerful and unexpected results. If we let $PCP[f,g]$ to denote the class of languages with transparent proofs that use $\mathcal{O}(f(n))$ random bits and check $\mathcal{O}(g(n))$ bits of an n bits long proof, then the following result provides a new characterization of **NP**.

Theorem 9.2.13 (PCP-theorem) $\mathbf{NP} = PCP[\lg n, \mathcal{O}(1)]$.

This is indeed an amazing result that says that no matter how long an instance of an **NP**-problem and how long its proof, it is to look to a fixed number of (randomly) chosen bits of the proof in order to determine, with high probability, its validity. Moreover, given an ordinary proof of membership for an **NP**-language, the corresponding transparent proof can be constructed in time polynomial in the length of the original classical proof. One can even show that it is sufficient to read only 11 bits from proof of polynomial size in order to achieve the probability of error $\frac{1}{2}$.

Transparent proofs therefore have strong error-correcting properties. Basic results concerning transparent proofs heavily use methods of designing self-correcting and self-testing programs discussed in Section 9.4.

On a more practical note a surprising connection has been discovered between transparent proofs and highly practical problems of approximability of **NP**-complete problems. It has first to be shown how any sufficiently good approximation algorithm for the clique problem can be used to test whether transparent proofs exist, and hence to determine membership in **NP**-complete languages. On this basis it has been shown for the clique problem – and a variety of other **NP**-hard optimization problems, such as graph colouring – that there is a constant $\varepsilon > 0$ such that no polynomial time approximation algorithm for the clique problem for a graph with a set V of vertices can have a ratio bound less than $|V|^{\varepsilon}$ unless **P = NP**.

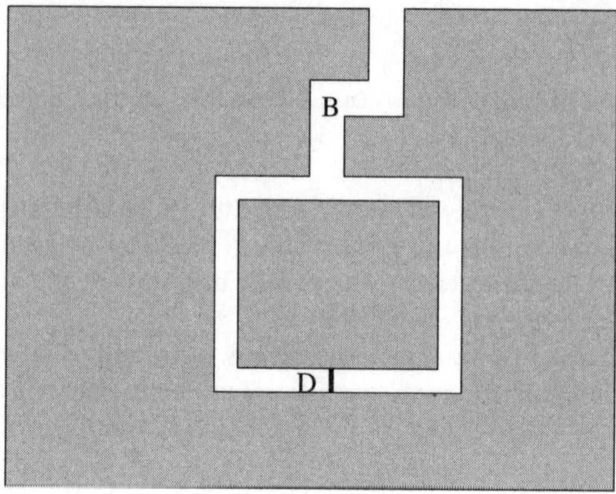

Figure 9.2 A cave with a door opening on a secret word

9.3 Zero-knowledge Proofs

A special type of interactive protocols and proof systems are zero-knowlege protocols and proofs. For cryptography they represent an elegant way of showing security of cryptographic protocols. On a more theoretical level, zero-knowledge proofs represent a fundamentally new way to formalize the concept of evidence. They allow, for example, the proof of a theorem so that no one can claim it.

Informally, a protocol is a zero-knowledge proof protocol for a theorem if one party does not learn from communication anything more than whether the theorem is true or not.

Example 9.3.1 $670,592,745 = 12,345 \times 54,321$ *is not a zero-knowledge proof of the theorem* '670,592,745 *is a composite integer', because the proof reveals not only that the theorem is true, but also additional information – two factors of* 670,592,745.

More formally, a zero-knowledge proof of a theorem T is an interactive two-party protocol with a special property. Following the protocol the prover, with unlimited power, is able to convince the verifier, who follows the same protocol, by overwhelming statistical evidence, that T is true, if this is really so, but has almost no chance of convincing a verifier who follows the protocol that the theorem T is true if this is not so. In addition – and this is essential – during their interactions the prover does not reveal to the verifier any other information, not a single bit, except for whether the theorem T is true, no matter what the verifier does. This means that for all practical purposes, whatever the verifier can do after interacting with the prover, he can do just by believing that the claim the prover makes is valid. Therefore 'zero-knowledge' is a property of the prover – her robustness against the attempts of any verifier, working in polynomial time, to extract some knowledge from an interaction with the prover.

In other words, a zero-knowledge proof is an interactive proof that provides highly convincing (but not absolutely certain) evidence that a theorem is true and that the prover knows a proof (a standard proof in a logical system that can in principle, but not necessarily in polynomial time, be checked by a machine), while providing not a single additional bit of information about the proof. In particular, the verifier who has just become convinced about the correctness of a theorem by a zero-knowledge protocol cannot turn around and prove the theorem to somebody else without proving it from scratch for himself.

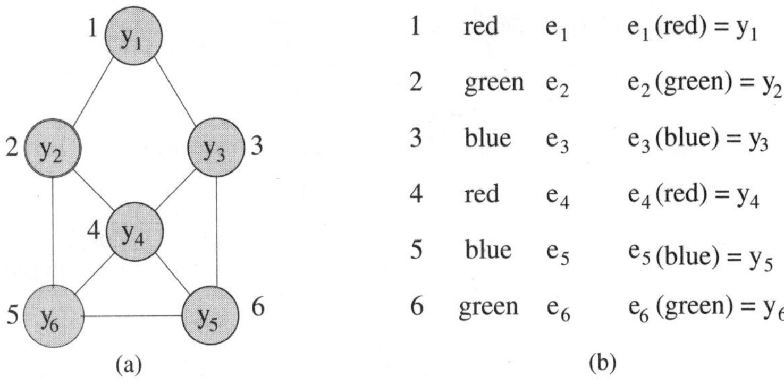

Figure 9.3 Encryption of a 3-colouring of a graph

Exercise 9.3.2 *The following problem has a simple solution that well illustrates the idea of zero-knowledge proofs. Alice knows a secret word that opens the door D in the cave in Figure 9.2. How can she convince Bob that she really knows this word, without telling it to him, when Bob is not allowed to see which path she takes going to the door and is not allowed to go into the cave beyond point B? (However, the cave is small, and Alice can always hear Bob if she is in the cave and Bob is in position B.)*

9.3.1 Examples

Using the following protocol, Peggy can convince Vic that a particular graph G, which they both know, is colourable with three colours, say red, blue and green, and that she knows such a colouring, without revealing to Vic any information whatsoever about how such a colouring of G looks.

Protocol 9.3.3 (3-colourability of graphs)
Peggy colours $G = (V, E)$ with three colours in such a way that no two neighbouring nodes are coloured by the same colour. Then Peggy engages with Vic $|E|^2$ times in the following interaction (where $v_1, \ldots, v_n$ are nodes of V):

1. *Peggy chooses a random permutation of colours (red, blue, green), correspondingly recolours the graph, and encrypts, for $i = 1, \ldots, n$, the colour c_i of the node v_i by an encryption procedure e_i – different for each i. Peggy removes colours from nodes and labels the i-th node of G with the cryptotext $y_i = e_i(c_i)$ (see Figure 9.3a). She then designs a table T_G in which, for every i, she puts the colour of the node i, the corresponding encryption procedure for that node, and the result of the encryption (see Figure 9.3b). Finally, Peggy shows Vic the graph with nodes labelled by cryptotexts (for example, the one in Figure 9.3a).*

2. *Vic chooses an edge, and sends Peggy a request to show him the colouring of the corresponding nodes.*

3. *Peggy reveals to Vic the entries in the table T_G for both nodes of the edge Vic has chosen.*

4. *Vic performs encryptions to check that the nodes really have the colours as shown.*

Vic accepts the proof if and only if all his checks agree.

The correctness proof: If G is colourable by three colours, and Peggy knows such a colouring and uses it, then all the checks Vic performs must agree. On the other hand, if this is not the case, then at each interaction there is a chance $\frac{1}{|E|}$ that Peggy gets caught. The probability that she does not get caught in $|E|^2$ interactions is $(1-1/|E|)^{|E|^2}$ – negligibly small. □

The essence of a zero-knowledge proof, as demonstrated also by Protocols 9.3.3 and 9.3.5, can be formulated as follows: the prover breaks the proof into pieces, and encrypts each piece using a new one-way function in such a way that

1. The verifier can easily verify whether each piece of the proof has been properly constructed.

2. If the verifier keeps checking randomly chosen pieces of the proof and all are correctly designed, then his confidence in the correctness of the whole proof increases; at the same time, this does not bring the verifier any additional information about the proof itself.

3. The verifier knows that each prover who knows the proof can decompose it into pieces in such a way that the verifier finds all the pieces correctly designed, but that no prover who does not know the proof is able to do this.

The key requirement, namely, that the verifier randomly picks up pieces of the proof to check, is taken care of by the prover! At each interaction the prover makes a random permutation of the proof, and uses for the encryption new one-way functions. As a result, no matter what kind of strategy the verifier chooses for picking up the pieces of the proof, his strategy is equivalent to a random choice.

Example 9.3.4 *With the following protocol, Peggy can convince Vic that the graph G they both know has a Hamilton cycle (without revealing any information about how such a cycle looks).*

Protocol 9.3.5 (Existence of Hamilton cycles)

Given a graph $G=\langle V,E\rangle$ with n nodes, say $V=\{1,2,\ldots,n\}$, each round of the protocol proceeds as follows.

Peggy chooses a random permutation π of $\{1,\ldots,n\}$, a one-way function e_i for each $i\in\{1,\ldots,n\}$, and also a one-way function $e_{i,j}$ for each pair $i,j\in\{1,\ldots,n\}$. Peggy then sends to Vic:

1. *Pairs (i,x_i), where $x_i=e_i(\pi(i))$ for $i=1,\ldots,n$ and all e_i are chosen so that all x_i are different.*

2. *Triples $(x_i,x_j,y_{i,j})$, where $y_{i,j}=e_{i,j}(b_{i,j}), i\neq j$, $b_{i,j}\in\{0,1\}$ and $b_{i,j}=1$, if and only if $(\pi(i),\pi(j))$ is an edge of G; e_{ij} are supposed to be chosen so that all y_{ij} are different.*

Vic then gets two possibilities to choose from:

1. *He can ask Peggy to demonstrate the correctness of all encryptions – that is, to reveal π and all encryption functions $e_i,e_{i,j}$. In this way Vic can become convinced that x_i and $y_{i,j}$ really represent an encryption of G.*

2. *He can ask Peggy to show a Hamilton cycle in G. Peggy can do this by revealing exactly n distinct numbers $y_{i_1,i_2},y_{i_2,i_3},\ldots,y_{i_n,i_1}$ such that $\{1,2,\ldots,n\}=\{i_1,\ldots,i_n\}$. This proves to Vic, who knows all triples $(x_i,x_j,y_{i,j})$, the existence of a Hamilton cycle in whatever graph is represented by the encryptions presented. Since the x_i are not decrypted, no information is revealed concerning the sequence of nodes defining a Hamilton cycle in G.*

Vic then chooses, randomly, one of these two offers (to show either the encryption of the graph or the Hamilton cycle), and Peggy gives the requested information.

If Peggy does not know the Hamilton cycle, then in order not to get caught, she must always make a correct guess as to which possibility Vic will choose. This means that the probability that Peggy does not get caught in k rounds, if she does not know the Hamilton cycle, is at most 2^{-k}.

Observe that the above protocol does not reveal any information whatsoever about how a Hamilton cycle for G looks. Indeed, if Vic asks for the encryption of the encoding, he gets only a random encryption of G. When asking for a Hamilton cycle, the verifier gets a random cycle of length n, with any such cycle being equally probable. This is due to the fact that Peggy is required to deal always with the same proof: that is, with the same Hamilton cycle, and π is a random permutation.

Exercise 9.3.6* *Design a zero-knowledge proof for integer factorization.*

Exercise 9.3.7* *Design a zero-knowledge proof for the knapsack problem.*

Exercise 9.3.8* *Design a zero-knowledge proof for the travelling salesman problem.*

9.3.2 Theorems with Zero-knowledge Proofs*

In order to discuss in more detail when a theorem has a zero-knowledge proof, we sketch a more formal definition of a 'zero-knowledge proof'. In doing so, the key concept is that of the **polynomial-time indistinguishability** of two **probability ensembles** $\Pi_1 = \{\pi_{1,i}\}_{i\in\mathbf{N}}$ and $\Pi_2 = \{\pi_{2,i}\}_{i\in\mathbf{N}}$ – two sequences of probability distributions on $\{0,1\}^*$, indexed by **N**, where distributions $\pi_{1,i}$ and $\pi_{2,i}$ assign nonzero probabilities only to strings of length polynomial in $|bin^{-1}(i)|$.

Let T be a probabilistic polynomial time Turing machine with output from the set $\{0,1\}$, called a **test** or a **distinguisher** here, that has two inputs, $i \in \mathbf{N}$ and $\alpha \in \{0,1\}^*$. Denote, for $j = 1,2$,

$$p_j^T(i) = \sum_{\alpha\in\{0,1\}^*} \pi_{j,i}(\alpha)Pr(T(i,\alpha) = 1);$$

that is, $p_1^T(i)$ is the probability that on inputs i and α, chosen according to the distribution $\pi_{1,i}$, the test T outputs 1. Π_1 and Π_2 are said to be **polynomial-time indistinguishable** if for all probabilistic polynomial-time tests T, all constants $c > 0$, and all sufficiently big $k \in \mathbf{N}$ (k is a 'confidence parameter'),

$$|p_1^T(i) - p_2^T(i)| < k^{-c}.$$

Informally, two probability ensembles are polynomial-time indistinguishable if they assign 'about the same probability to any efficiently recognizable set of words over $\{0,1\}^*$'.

In the following definition we use the notation $hist(M_P, M_V, x)$ for the random variable the values of which consist of the concatenated messages of the interaction of the protocol (M_P, M_V) on the input x with random bits, consumed by M_V during the interaction, attached. (Such a concatenated message is also called a **history** of communication.)

Definition 9.3.9 *The interactive protocol* (M_P, M_V) *for a language L is (computationally)* **zero-knowledge** *if, for every verifier* M_{V*}, *there exists a probabilistic polynomial-time Turing machine* M_{S*}, *called a* **simulator**, *such that the probability ensembles* $\{hist(M_P, M_{V*}, x)\}_{x\in L}$ *and* $\{M_{S*}(x)\}_{x\in L}$ *are polynomial-time indistinguishable.*

We present now two main approaches to showing that an interactive proof is a zero-knowledge proof.

1. For some interactive proofs it has been shown, on the assumption that one-way functions exist, that the histories of their protocols are polynomial-time indistinguishable from random strings.
2. Another method is to show that the verifier can actually simulate the prover. That is, the verifier can also take the prover's position in the interaction with the verifier. Any polynomial-time randomized algorithm that enables the verifier to extract some information from the interaction with the prover could be used for this process without an interaction with the prover.

Let us illustrate the last idea on the protocol proving, for a fixed graph G with n nodes, that G has a Hamilton cycle.

A verifier V first simulates the prover P. V flips coins and, according to the outcome, encrypts a random permutation of the whole graph (just as P would do), or encrypts a randomly chosen permutation of nodes. Then, acting as the prover, the verifier presents the encrypted information to the verifier, that is, to himself, and takes the position of the verifier.

V now uses his algorithm, say A, to decide whether to request a graph or a cycle. Because A has no way of knowing what V did in the guise of P, there is a 50 per cent chance that A requests exactly the option which V, in the guise of P, supplies. If not, V backs up the algorithm A to the state it was in at the beginning and restarts the entire round.

This means that in the expected two passes through each round V obtains the benefit of the algorithm A without any help from the prover. Therefore, A does not help V to do something with P in an expected polynomial time that V could not do as well without P in expected polynomial time.

The family of theorems that has a zero-knowledge proof seems to be surprisingly large. The following theorem holds.

Theorem 9.3.10 *If one-way functions exist, then every language in* **PSPACE** *has a zero-knowledge proof.*[2]

Idea of a proof: The proof of the theorem is too involved to present here, and I sketch only an idea of the proof of a weaker statement for the class **NP**. First one shows for an **NP**-complete language L_0 that it has a zero-knowledge proof system. (This we have already done – see Example 9.3.4 – on the assumption that one-way functions exist.) Second, one shows that if a language $L \in$ **NP** is in polynomial time reducible to L_0, then this reducibility can be used to transform a zero-knowledge proof for L_0 into a zero-knowledge proof for L. □

9.3.3 Analysis and Applications of Zero-knowledge Proofs*

Note first that the concept of zero-knowledge proofs brings a new view of what 'knowledge' is. Something is implicitly regarded as 'knowledge' only if there is no polynomial time computation that can produce it.

Observe also (see the next exercise) that both randomness and interaction are essential for nontriviality of the concept of zero-knowledge proofs.

Exercise 9.3.11 *Show that zero-knowledge proofs in which the verifier either tosses no coins or does not interact exist only for languages in* **BPP**.

[2]On the other hand, if one-way functions do not exist, then the class of languages having zero-knowledge proofs is identical with **BPP**.

Note too the following paradox in the concept of zero-knowledge proofs of a theorem. Such a proof can be constructed, as described above, by the verifier himself, who only believes in the correctness of the theorem, but in spite of that, such a proof does convince the verifier! The 'paradox' is resolved by noting that it is not the text of the 'conversation' that convinces the verifier, but rather the fact that the conversation is held 'on-line'.

Theorem 9.3.10 and its proofs provide a powerful tool for the design of cryptographical protocols. To see this, let us first discuss a general setting in which cryptographical protocols arise.

A cryptographical protocol can be seen as a set of interactive programs to be executed by parties who do not trust one another. Each party has a local input unknown to others that is kept secret. The protocol usually specifies actions that parties should take, depending on their local secrets and previous messages exchanged. The main problem in this context is how a party can verify that the others have really followed the protocol. Verification is difficult, because a verifier, say A, does not know the secrets of the communicating party, say B, who does not want to reveal his secret. The way out is to use zero-knowledge proofs. B can convince A that the message transmitted by B has been computed according to the protocol without revealing any secret.

Now comes the main idea as to how to design cryptographical protocols. First, design a protocol on the assumption that all parties will follow it properly. Next, transform this protocol, using already well-known, mechanical methods for making zero-knowledge proofs from 'normal proofs', into a protocol in which communication is based on zero-knowledge proofs, preserves both correctness and privacy, and works even if a minority of parties displays adversary behaviour.

There are various others surprising applications of zero-knowledge proofs.

Example 9.3.12 (User identification) *The idea of zero-knowledge proofs offers a radically new approach to the user identification problem. For each user, a theorem, the proof of which only this user knows, is stored in a directory. After login, the user starts a zero-knowledge proof of the correctness of the theorem. If the proof is convincing, his/her access is guaranteed. The important new point is that even an adversary who could follow the communication fully would not get any information allowing him/her to get access.*

The concept of a zero-knowledge proof system can be generalized in a natural way to the case of multiple provers, and the following theorem holds.

Theorem 9.3.13 *Every language in* **NEXP** *has a zero-knowledge, two-provers, interactive proof system.*

Observe that no assumption has been made here about the existence of one-way functions.

9.4 Interactive Program Validation

Program validation is one of the key problems in computing. Traditional program testing is feasible but insufficient. Not all input data can be tested and therefore, on a particular run, the user may have no guarantee that the result is correct. Program verification, while ideal in theory, is not currently, and may never be, a pragmatic approach to program reliability. It is neither feasible nor sufficient. Only programs which are not too large may be verified. Even this does not say anything about the correctness of a particular computer run, due to possible compiler or hardware failures. Interactive program (result) checking, especially interactive program self-correcting, as discussed in this section, offers an alternative approach to program validation. Program checkers may provide the bases for a debugging methodology that is more rigorous than program testing and more pragmatic than verification.

9.4.1 Interactive Result Checkers

The basic idea is to develop, given an algorithmic problem $\mathcal{P}$, a **result checker** for $\mathcal{P}$, that is capable of finding out, with large probability correctly, given any program P for $\mathcal{P}$ and any input data d for P, whether the result P produces for d is correct – in short, whether $\mathcal{P}(d) = P(d)$. To do this, the result checker may interact with P and use P to do computations for some input data other than d, if necessary. The result checker produces the answer 'PASS' if the program P is correct for all inputs, and therefore, also for d. It produces the output 'FAIL' if $\mathcal{P}(d) \neq P(d)$. (The output is not specified in the remaining cases; that is, when the program is not correct in general but $\mathcal{P}(d) = P(d)$.)

Of special interest are **simple (result) checkers** – for an algorithmic problem $\mathcal{P}$ with the best sequential time $t(n)$. They get as an input a pair (d,y) and have to return 'YES' ('NO') if $y = \mathcal{P}(d)$ (if $y \neq \mathcal{P}(d)$), in both cases with a probability (over internal randomization) close to 1. Moreover, a simple checker is required to work in time $o(t(n))$. (The last condition requires that a simple checker for $\mathcal{P}$ is essentially different and faster than any program to solve $\mathcal{P}$.)

The idea of a (simple) checker is based on the observation that for certain functions it is much easier to determine for inputs x and y whether $y = f(x)$ than to determine $f(x)$ for an input x. For example, the problem of finding a nontrivial factor p of an integer n is computationally unfeasible. But it is easy, one division suffices, to check whether p is a divisor of n. Let us now illustrate the idea of simple checkers on two examples.

Example 9.4.1 (Result checker for the generalized gcd problem) Algorithmic problem $\mathcal{P}_{GGCD}$: *Given integers m,n, compute $d = \gcd(m,n)$ and $u,v \in \mathbf{Z}$ such that $um + vn = d$.*

Program checker *$\mathcal{C}_{GGCD}$ takes a given program P to solve (supposedly) the problem $\mathcal{P}_{GGCD}$, and makes P compute, given m and n, the corresponding d,u,v. After that, it performs the following check:*

if *d does not divide m or does not divide n*
  then *$\mathcal{C}_{GGCD}$ outputs 'FAIL'*
  else if *$mu + nv \neq d$* **then** *$\mathcal{C}_{GGCD}$ outputs 'FAIL'*
        else *$\mathcal{C}_{GGCD}$ outputs 'PASS'.*

The first condition checks whether d is a divisor of both m and n, the second whether it is the largest divisor. Observe that the checker needs to perform only two divisions, two multiplications and one addition. The checker is far more efficient than any algorithm for computing $\gcd(m,n)$.

Example 9.4.2 (Freivald's checker for matrix multiplication) *If A, B and C are matrices of degree n and $AB = C$, then $A(Bv) = Cv$ for any vector v of length n. To compute AB, one needs between $\mathcal{O}(n^{2.376})$ and $\Theta(n^3)$ arithmetical operations; to compute $A(Bv)$ and Cv, $\Theta(n^2)$ operations suffice. Moreover, it can be shown that if v is a randomly chosen vector, then the probability that $AB \neq C$ once $A(Bv) = Cv$ is very small. This yields the following $\Theta(kn^2)$ simple checker for matrix multiplication.[3] Choose k random vectors $v_1, \ldots, v_k$ and compute $A(Bv_i)$ and Cv_i for $i = 1, \ldots, k$. If $A(Bv_i)$ and Cv_i once differ, then it rejects, otherwise it accepts.*

Exercise 9.4.3 *Design a simple checker for multiplication of two polynomials.*

Exercise 9.4.4 *Design a simple checker for integer multiplication. (Hint: use Exercise 1.7.12.)*

[3] Provided matrix multiplication cannot be done in $\Theta(n^2)$ time, which seems likely but has not yet been proved.

The following definition deals with the general case. Probability is here considered, as usual, over the space of all internal coin-tossings of the result checker.

Definition 9.4.5 *A result checker $C_{\mathcal{P}}$ for an algorithmic problem $\mathcal{P}$ is a probabilistic oracle Turing machine such that given any program P (supposedly) for $\mathcal{P}$, which always terminates, any particular input data x_0 for $\mathcal{P}$, and any integer k, $C_{\mathcal{P}}$ works in the expected polynomial time (with respect to $|x_0 1^k|$), and produces the following result.*

1. *If P is correct, that is, $P(x) = \mathcal{P}(x)$ for all possible inputs x, then, with probability greater than $1 - \frac{1}{2^k}$, $C_{\mathcal{P}}(P, x_0) =$ 'PASS'.*
2. *If $P(x_0) \neq \mathcal{P}(x_0)$, then $C_{\mathcal{P}}(P, x_0) =$ 'FAIL' with probability greater than $1 - \frac{1}{2^k}$.*

In Definition 9.4.5, k is a **confidence parameter** that specifies the degree of confidence in the outcome. The time needed to prepare inputs for P and to process outputs of P is included in the overall time complexity of $C_{\mathcal{P}}$, but not the time P needs to compute its results.

The program checker for the graph isomorphism problem presented in the following example is a modification of the zero-knowledge proof for the graph nonisomorphism problem in Section 9.2.1, this time, however, without an all-powerful prover.

Example 9.4.6 (Program checker for the graph isomorphism problem)

Input: a program P to determine an isomorphism of arbitrary graphs and two graphs G_0, G_1, the isomorphism of which is to be determined. The protocol for an interaction between the program checker C_{GI} and P has the following form:

begin
make P compute $P(G_0, G_1)$;
if $P(G_0, G_1) =$ *'YES'* **then**
  begin *use P (assuming that it is 'bug-free') to find out, by the method*
    described below, an isomorphism between G_0 and G_1 and to check
    whether the isomorphism obtained is correct;
    if *not correct* **then return** *'FAIL'* **else return** *'PASS'*;
  end;
if $P(G_0, G_1) =$ *'NO'* **then for** $i = 1$ **to** k **do**
  begin *get a random bit b_i;*
    generate a random permutation H_i of G_{b_i} and compute $P(G_0, H_i)$;
    if $b_i = 0$ *and* $P(G_0, H_i) =$ *'NO'*
      then return *'FAIL'*
      else if $b_i = 1$ *and* $P(G_0, H_i) =$ *'YES'* **then return** *'FAIL'*
  end
return 'PASS'
end.

In order to finish the description of the protocol, we have to demonstrate how the checker C_{GI} can use P to construct an isomorphism between G_0 and G_1 in case such an isomorphism exists. This can be done as follows. A node v from G_0 is arbitrarily chosen, and a larger clique with new nodes is attached to it – denote by G_0' the resulting graph. The same clique is then added, step by step, to various nodes of G_1, and each time this is done, P is used to check whether the resulting graph is isomorphic with G_0'. If no node of G_1 is found such that the modified graph is isomorphic with G_0', then $\mathcal{C}_{GI}$ outputs 'FAIL'. If such a node, say v', is found, then v is removed from G_0 and v' from G_1, and the same method is used to build further an isomorphism between G_0 and G_1.

It is clear that the checker always produces the result 'PASS' if the program P is totally correct. Consider the case that P sometimes produces an incorrect result. We show now that the probability that the checker produces 'PASS' if the program P is not correct is at most $\frac{1}{2^k}$. Examine two cases:

1. $P(G_0, G_1) =$ 'YES', but G_0 and G_1 are not isomorphic. Then the checker has to fail to produce an isomorphism, and therefore it has to output 'FAIL'.

2. $P(G_0, G_1) =$ 'NO', but G_0 and G_1 are isomorphic. The only way that the checker would produce 'PASS' in such a case is if P produces correct answers for all k checks $P(G_0, H_i)$. That is, P produces the answer 'YES' if H_i is a permutation of G_0 and 'NO' if H_i is a permutation of G_1. However, since b_i are random and permutations H_i of G_0 and G_1 are also random, there is the same probability that H_i is a permutation of G_0 as of G_1. Therefore, P can correctly distinguish whether H_i was designed by a permutation of G_0 or of G_1 only by chance; that is, for 1 out of 2^k possible sequences of k bits b_i.

It has been shown that there are effective result checkers for all problems in **PSPACE**. The following lemma implies that, given a result checker for a problem, one can effectively construct out of it a result checker for another problem computationally equivalent to the first. This indicates that for all practical problems there is a result checker that can be efficiently constructed.

Lemma 9.4.7 *Let $\mathcal{P}_1$ and $\mathcal{P}_2$ be two polynomial-time equivalent algorithmic problems. From any efficient result checker $\mathcal{C}_{\mathcal{P}_1}$ for $\mathcal{P}_1$ it is possible to construct an efficient result checker $\mathcal{C}_{\mathcal{P}_2}$ for $\mathcal{P}_2$.*

Proof: Let r_{12} and r_{21} be two polynomial-time computable functions such that r_{ij} maps a 'YES'-instance ('NO'-instance) of $\mathcal{P}_i$ into a 'YES'-instance ('NO'-instance) of $\mathcal{P}_j$. Let P_2 be a program for $\mathcal{P}_2$. $\mathcal{C}_{\mathcal{P}_2}(P_2, x_2)$ works as follows.

1. $\mathcal{C}_{\mathcal{P}_2}$ computes $x_1 = r_{21}(x_2)$ and designs a program P_1 for $\mathcal{P}_1$ that works thus: $P_1(x) = P_2(r_{12}(x))$.

2. $\mathcal{C}_{\mathcal{P}_2}(P_2, x_2)$ checks whether
$$P_2(x_2) = P_2(r_{12}(r_{21}(x_2))) \tag{9.10}$$
and whether
$$P_1(x_1) = \mathcal{P}(x_1) \tag{9.11}$$
(and therefore whether $P_2(x_2) = \mathcal{P}_2(x_2)$) by using $\mathcal{C}_{\mathcal{P}_1}(P_1, x_1)$.

If either of the conditions (9.10) and (9.11) fails, then $\mathcal{C}_{\mathcal{P}_2}$ returns 'NO'; otherwise it returns 'YES'.

If P_2 is correct, then both checks are satisfied, and therefore the checker reports correctly. On the other hand, if $P_2(x_2) \neq \mathcal{P}_2(x_2)$, then either the check (9.10) fails and $\mathcal{C}_{\mathcal{P}_2}$ reports correctly 'NO' or (9.10) holds and then

$$\begin{aligned}
P_1(x_1) &= P_1(r_{21}(x_2)) \\
&= P_2(r_{12}(r_{21}(x_2))), \text{ since } P_1(x) = P_2(r_{12}(x)), \\
&= P_2(x_2), \text{because (9.10) holds}, \\
&\neq \mathcal{P}_2(x_2) \text{ by assumption} \\
&= \mathcal{P}_1(r_{21}(x_2)) \\
&= \mathcal{P}_1(x_1).
\end{aligned}$$

in which case the result checker $\mathcal{C}_{\mathcal{P}_1}$ and therefore also the checker $\mathcal{C}_{\mathcal{P}_2}$ produce 'NO' correctly, with a probability of at least $1 - \frac{1}{2^k}$. □

Exercise 9.4.8 *Design an $\mathcal{O}(n)$-time result checker for sorting n integers. (Hint: use Exercise 2.3.28.)*

Although a result checker $\mathcal{C}_{\mathcal{P}}$ can be used to verify for a particular input x and program P whether $\mathcal{P}(x) = P(x)$, it does not provide a method for computing $\mathcal{P}(x)$ in the case that P is found to be faulty. From this point of view, **self-correcting/testing programs**, discussed in the next section, present an additional step forward in program validation. To simplify the presentation, we deal only with programs that compute functions.

Remark 9.4.9 Interest on the part of the scientific community in developing methods for result checking is actually very old. One of the basic tools was various formulas such as $e^x = e^{x-a}e^a$ or $\tan x = (\tan(x+a) + \tan a)/(1 - \tan(x-a)\tan a)$ that related to each other the values of a function at a given point and a few other points. Such formulas allowed both result checking and self-correcting, as discussed below. The desire to obtain such formulas was one of the main forces inspiring progress in mathematics in the eighteenth and nineteenth centuries.

Exercise 9.4.10 *Design a formula that relates values of the function $f(x) = \frac{e^x}{x}$ at points $x, x+1$ and $x+2$.*

9.4.2 Interactive Self-correcting and Self-testing Programs

Informally, a (randomized) program $\mathcal{C}_f$ is a **self-correcting program** for a function f if for any program P that, supposedly, computes f, the error probability of which is sufficiently low, and any input x, $\mathcal{C}_f$ can make use of P to compute $f(x)$ correctly.

The idea of self-correcting programs is based on the fact that for some function f we can efficiently compute $f(x)$ if we know the value of f at several other, random-looking inputs.

Example 9.4.11 *To compute the product of two matrices A and B of degree n, we choose $2k$ random matrices $R_1, R_1', R_2, R_2', \ldots, R_k, R_k'$, all of degree n, and take as the value of AB the value that occurs most often among values*

$$(A - R_i)(B - R_i') + R_i(B - R_i') + (A - R_i)R_i' + R_iR_i'. \tag{9.12}$$

Note that if a matrix multiplication algorithm P is correct and used to perform the multiplications in (9.12), then all values in (9.12) are exactly AB. If P produces correct values with high probability, then, again, most of the values from (9.12) are equal to AB.

The idea of self-correcting programs is attractive, but two basic questions arise immediately: their efficiency and correctness.

The whole idea of result checkers, as well as self-correcting and self-testing programs, requires, in order to be fully meaningful, that they are efficient in the following sense. Their **proper (incremental) running time** – that is, the time the program P, which they validate, spends whenever called by a self-testing program or a self-correcting program, is never counted – should be asymptotically smaller than the computation time of P. The **total running time** – that is, the time P spends whenever called by a self-testing program or a self-correcting program is also included – should be asymptotically of the same order as the computation time of P. This should be true for any program P computing f. It is therefore clear that self-testing and self-correcting programs for f must be **essentially different** from any program for computing f.

The problem of how to verify result checkers and self-correcting programs has no simple solution. However, it is believed and confirmed by experience that all these programs can be essentially simpler than those they must validate. Therefore, they should be easier to verify. In addition, in the case of problems where a large amount of time is spent in finding the best algorithms, for example, number operations and matrix operations, a larger effort to verify self-testing and self-correcting programs should pay off. In any case, the verification problem requires that self-testing and self-correcting programs for a function f be essentially different from any program for f.

To simplify the presentation, a uniform probability distribution is assumed on all sets of inputs of the same size, and $error(f,P)$ is used to denote the probability that $P(x) \neq f(x)$ when x is randomly chosen from inputs of the same size.

Definition 9.4.12 *(1) Let $0 \leq \varepsilon_1 \leq \varepsilon_2 \leq 1$. An $(\varepsilon_1,\varepsilon_2)$–***self-testing program** *for f is a randomized oracle program $\mathcal{T}_f$ such that for any program P for f, any integers n (the size of inputs) and k (a confidence parameter) the following holds (e denotes the base of natural logarithms).*

1. *If $error(f,P) \leq \varepsilon_1$ for inputs of size n, then $\mathcal{T}_f(P)$ outputs 'PASS' with probability at least $1 - \frac{1}{e^k}$.*
2. *If $error(f,P) \geq \varepsilon_2$, then $\mathcal{T}_f(P)$ outputs 'FAIL' with probability at least $1 - \frac{1}{e^k}$.*

*(2) Let $0 \leq \varepsilon \leq 1$. An ε-***self-correcting program** *for f is a randomized oracle program $\mathcal{C}_f$ such that for any program P for f, any integer n, any input x of size n and any integer k the following property holds: if $error(f,P) \leq \varepsilon$, then $\mathcal{C}_f(P,x) = f(x)$ with probability at least $1 - \frac{1}{e^k}$.*

The main advantage of self-correcting programs is that they can be used to transform programs correct for most of the inputs to programs correct, with high probability, on any input.

Remark 9.4.13 In discussing the incremental and total time, any dependence on the confidence parameter k has been ignored. This usually adds a multiplicative factor of the order of $\mathcal{O}(k)$.

The basic problem in designing self-testing and self-correcting programs is how to make them essentially different from programs computing f directly. One idea that has turned out to be useful is to compute f indirectly by computing f on random inputs.

Definition 9.4.14 (Random self-reducibility property) *Let $m > 1$ be an integer. A function f is called m-***random self-reducible** *if for any $x, f(x)$ can be expressed as an easily computable function F of $x, a_1, \ldots, a_m$ and $f(a_1), \ldots, f(a_m)$, where $a_1, \ldots, a_m$ are randomly chosen from inputs of the same size as x. (By 'easily computable' is understood that the total computation time of a random self-reduction – that is, of computing F from the arguments $x, a_1, \ldots, a_n$ and $f(a_1), \ldots, f(a_n)$ – is smaller than that for computing $f(x)$.)*

The first two examples are of self-correcting programs. They are easier to present and to prove correct than self-testing programs. (We use here the notation $x \in_{\mathcal{U}} A$ (see Section 2.1) to mean that X is randomly taken from A with respect to the uniform probability distribution.)

Example 9.4.15 (Self-correcting program for mod **function)** *Let $f(x) = x \bmod m$ with $x \in \mathbf{Z}_{m2^n}$ for some integer n. Assume that P is a program for computing f, for $0 \leq x \leq m2^n$, with $error(f,P) \leq \frac{1}{8}$. The inputs of the following $\frac{1}{8}$-self-correcting program are x, m, n, k and a program P for f, and $+_m$ denotes addition modulo m.*

Protocol 9.4.16 (Self-correcting program for mod **function)**

begin
  $N \leftarrow 12k$;
  for $i \leftarrow 1$ **to** N **do**
    call Random-split $(m2^n, x, x_1, x_2, e)$;
    $a_i \leftarrow P(x_1, m) +_m P(x_2, m)$;
  output the most common answer among $\{a_i \mid 1 \leq i \leq N\}$
end,

where the procedure 'Random-split', with the output parameters z_1, z_2, e, is defined as follows:

procedure *Random-split*(s, z, z_1, z_2, e)
  choose $z_1 \in_U \mathbf{Z}_s$;
  if $z_1 \leq z$ **then** $e \leftarrow 0$ **else** $e \leftarrow 1$;
  $z_2 \leftarrow es + z - z_1$.

The correctness proof: As $x_j \in_U \mathbf{Z}_{m2^n}$ for $j = 1, 2$, we get that $P(x_i, m) \neq x_i \bmod m$ with probability at most $\frac{1}{8}$. Therefore, for any $1 \leq i \leq N$, $a_i = x_1 \bmod m + x_2 \bmod m$ with probability at least $\frac{3}{4}$. The correctness of the protocol now follows from the following lemma (with $N = 12k$), a consequence of Chernoff's bound (see Section 1.9.2).

Lemma 9.4.17 *If $x_1, \ldots, x_N$ are independent 0 / 1-valued random variables such that $Pr(x_i = 1) \geq \frac{3}{4}$ for $i = 1, \ldots, N$, then*

$$Pr\left(\sum_{i=1}^{m} x_i > N / 2\right) \geq 1 - e^{-N/12}.$$

Observe that the self-correcting program presented above is essentially different from any program for computing f. Its incremental time is linear in N, and its total time is linear in time of P.

Example 9.4.18 (Self-correcting program for integer multiplication) *In this case $f(x, y) = xy$, and we assume that $x, y \in \mathbf{Z}_{2^n}$ for a fixed n. Let us also assume that there is a program P for computing f and that $error(f, P) \leq \frac{1}{16}$. The following program is a $\frac{1}{16}$-self-correcting program for f. Inputs: $n, x, y \in \mathbf{Z}_{2^n}, k$ and P.*

Protocol 9.4.19 (Self-correcting program for integer multiplication)

begin
  $N \leftarrow 12k$
  for $i \leftarrow 1$ **to** N **do**
    call Random-split$(2^n, x, x_1, x_2, c)$;
    call Random-split$(2^n, y, y_1, y_2, d)$;
    $a_i \leftarrow P(x_1, y_1) + P(x_1, y_2) + P(x_2, y_1) + P(x_2, y_2) - cy2^n - dx2^n + cd2^{2n}$;
  output the most common value from $\{a_i \mid 1 \leq i \leq N\}$
end

The correctness proof: Since $x_i, y_j, i, j = 1, 2$, are randomly chosen from $\mathbf{Z}_{2^n}$, we get, by the property of P, that $P(x_i, y_j) \neq x_k y_j$ with probability at most $\frac{1}{16}$. Therefore the probability that all four calls to

P during a pass through the cycle return the correct value is at least $\frac{3}{4}$. Since $x = x_1 + x_2 - c2^n$, and $y = y_1 + y_2 - d2^n$, we have

$$xy = x_1y_1 + x_1y_2 + x_2y_1 + x_2y_2 - cy2^n - dx2^n + cd2^{2n}.$$

Thus, if all four calls to P are correctly answered during the ith cycle, then $a_i = xy$. The correctness of the protocol follows again from Lemma 9.4.17. □

Exercise 9.4.20 *Show that we can construct a $\frac{1}{16}$-self-correcting program for modular number multiplication $f(x,y,m) = xy \bmod m$ to deal with any program P for f with error$(f,P) \leq \frac{1}{16}$.*

Example 9.4.21 (Self-correcting program for modular exponentiation) *Consider now the function $f(a,x,m) = a^x \bmod m$, where a and m are fixed and $\gcd(a,m) = 1$. Suppose that the factorization of m is known, and therefore $\phi(m)$ is known, where ϕ is Euler's totient function. Let $x \in \mathbf{Z}_{\phi(m)2^n}$. Finally, let us assume that we have a program P to compute f such that error$(f,P) \leq \frac{1}{8}$. The inputs to the following protocol are $n, x, k, a, m, \phi(m)$ and P.*

Protocol 9.4.22 (Self-correcting program for modular exponentiation)

begin
    $N \leftarrow 12k$;
    for $i \leftarrow 1$ **to** N **do**
        call Random-split$(\phi(m)2^n, x, x_1, x_2, c)$;
        $a_i \leftarrow P(a,x_1,m)P(a,x_2,m) \bmod m$;
    output the most common value among $\{a_i \mid i = 1, \ldots, N\}$
end

The correctness proof: Clearly, $P(a,x_i,m) \neq a^{x_i} \bmod m$ with probability at most $\frac{1}{8}$, and therefore the probability that a_i is computed correctly is at least $\frac{3}{4}$. As $x = x_1 + x_2 - c\phi(m)2^n$, for a $c \in \{0,1\}$ and, in addition, $\gcd(a,m) = 1$, $a^{\phi(m)} \equiv 1 \pmod{m}$, we get $a^x \equiv a^{x_1} \cdot a^{x_2} \pmod{m}$. This means that if, in the ith pass through the cycle, both calls to P are correctly answered, then $a_i = a^x \bmod m$. The correctness of the protocol now follows from Lemma 9.4.17. □

All three self-correcting programs/protocols presented above are based on a similar idea, which can be generalized as follows.

Theorem 9.4.23 *If f is a m-random self-reducible function, then there is a $(\frac{1}{4m})$-self-correcting program for f (to correct any program P for f such that error$(f,P) \leq \frac{1}{4m}$).*

Proof: Consider the following program with the inputs m, x, k and P.

Protocol 9.4.24 (Generic self-correcting program)

begin
    $N \leftarrow 12k$;
    for $i \leftarrow 1$ **to** N **do**
        randomly choose $a_1, \ldots, a_m$ of the same size as x;
        for $j \leftarrow 1$ **to** N **do** $\alpha_j \leftarrow P(a_j)$;
        $a_i \leftarrow F(x, a_1, \ldots, a_m, \alpha_1, \ldots, \alpha_m)$;
    output the most common value among $\{a_i \mid 1 \leq i \leq m\}$
end

The assumption $error(f,P) \leq \frac{1}{4m}$ implies that in the i-th cycle all values α_j are computed correctly with probability at least $\frac{3}{4}$. Moreover, due to the self-reducibility property of f, $a_i = f(x)$ also with probability at least $\frac{3}{4}$. The theorem follows, as before, from Lemma 9.4.17. □

Exercise 9.4.25 *Design a self-correcting program for integer division.*

Exercise 9.4.26 *Design a self-correcting program for polynomial multiplication.*

Exercise 9.4.27** *Construct a polynomial formula that relates values of the function $x + \sin x$ for several arguments and which can therefore be used for result checking and self-correcting programs.*

Remark 9.4.28 The concept of self-testing programs has been developed on a similar basis to result checkers and self-correcting programs.

Moral: New interactive, holographic and other proof techniques allow one to prove otherwise practically unprovable things. In spite of this, a good rule of thumb in dealing with the concept of evidence in computing is, as in life, to explore all feasible concepts of evidence but to remember that a good proof makes one wiser.

9.5 Exercises

1. Let us generalize the age difference protocol to the case that n friends want to find out who is the oldest, without disclosing any other information about their age. (a) Show how to use the age difference protocol for two persons to solve the general case. (b) Show the disadvantage of such a solution, and find a better one.

2. Alice wants to sell a computer to Bob, whom she does not trust any more. Bob wants to pay by cheque, but Alice has no way of knowing whether the cheque is valid. Alice wants Bob's cheque to clear before she hands over the computer to him. However, Bob does not trust Alice and does not want to give her a cheque without first receiving the computer. How to proceed?

3. **(Secret voting)** Design a protocol for a secret balloting system that satisfies the following conditions: (a) only legitimate voters should cast a ballot; (b) the ballot should be kept secret; (c) everybody is allowed to have only one vote; (d) any voter should be able to verify that his/her vote was taken into account in the electoral outcome.

4. Design a bit commitment protocol on the basis of discrete logarithms.

5. Design a bit commitment protocol using only the oblivious transfer protocol.

6. Design a coin-flipping protocol on the basis of the oblivious transfer protocol.

7. Construct a polynomial approximation of the following Boolean formulas:
   (a) $(x \vee y \vee \bar{z}) \wedge (v \vee \bar{x} \vee \bar{y})$; (b) $(x \vee \bar{z}) \wedge (y \vee \bar{x}) \wedge (x \vee y \vee z)$; (c) $(x \vee p) \wedge ((x \vee \bar{z}) \vee (s \wedge \bar{t}) \wedge)$.

8. Show that if F is a 3-*CNF* Boolean formula with n variables and m clauses, then there is an arithmetical formula of length at most $20m$ and degree at most $3m$ that approximates F.

9. Consider the following protocol for the **NP**-complete language $L = \{(G_0, G_1) \mid G_0$ is a subgraph of $G_1\}$:

   (1) The verifier sends G_0 and G_1 to the prover.

   (2) The prover constructs k random graphs $H_1, \ldots, H_k$ such that each H_i is a subgraph of G_1 and contains G_0 as a subgraph, and sends these graphs to the verifier.

   (3) The verifier chooses k random bits $b_1, \ldots, b_k$ and asks, for $1 \leq i \leq k$, the prover to show him either that G_0 is a subgraph of H_i (if $b_i = 0$) or that H_i is a subgraph of G_1 (if $b_i = 1$).

   (4) The prover does what the verifier asks.

   (a) Show that this protocol is an interactive protocol for the language L; (b) explain why it is not a zero-knowledge protocol for L; (c)* design a zero-knowledge protocol for L.

10. Design an interactive proof system for the following reachability problem for cellular automata. Given is a finite two-dimensional toroidal CA $\mathcal{A}$ (that is, a CA whose finite automata are connected into a toroidal interconnection structure), specified by a set of states, a neighbourhood and an integer n (the size of the array), and an initial configuration. Assume that the global mapping G of $\mathcal{A}$ is injective. This means that all computational orbits $c, G(c), G^2(c), \ldots$ form a cycle for any configuration c. The problem is to decide, given two configurations, whether they are in the same orbit.

11. Design a zero-knowledge proof for the 3-CNFF problem.

12. Design a zero-knowledge proof for the graph isomorphism problem.

13. (**Multiset equality test**) The following test plays a useful role in some result checkers. Given two arrays of elements, X and Y, and an integer k, output 'yes', if X and Y represent the same multiset and output 'no' otherwise. Show how to make this test in such a way that the probability of error is $\frac{1}{2^k}$.

14. Design a result checker for the discrete logarithm problem.

15. Design a result checker for the quadratic residue problem.

16.* Design a self-correcting program for multiplication of Boolean matrices.

QUESTIONS

1. What are the main primitives of cryptographical protocols?

2. What is the essence of the bit commitment problem? How can one implement this problem?

3. What are the potential applications of the oblivious transfer problem?

4. Is the number $\frac{2}{3}$ in Definition 9.2.3 magic, or can it be replaced by some other number without an essential impact?

5. Can the prover and the verifier of an interactive proof system be seen as having conflicting aims?
6. Why is it the case that more than two provers do not increase the power of polynomial interactions?
7. What are the basic ideas of proofs that particular interactive proofs are zero-knowledge proofs?
8. What is the main advantage of using result checkers compared with other methods of program verification?
9. In what sense must a checker be essentially different from the program to be checked?
10. What is a random self-reducibility property?

9.6 Historical and Bibliographical References

Manuel Blum (who received the Turing award for 1995) showed in his seminal paper (1982) that apparently impossible communication problems are solvable. He provided the impetus for an explosion of papers on cryptographical protocols. A systematic presentation of such protocols is found, for example, in Salomaa (1990) and Schneier (1996). For the poker playing protocol see Shamir, Rivest and Adleman (1981) and Goldwasser and Micali (1984). The age difference finding protocol is due to Yao (1982b). The notion of the oblivious transfer protocol is due to Rabin (1981), and the interlock protocol to Rivest and Shamir (1984).

The concept of an interactive proof system was developed by Goldwasser, Micali and Rackoff (1985), with applications to cryptographical protocols as the main motivation. Closely related, and more convenient for showing complexity results, is the concept of Arthur versus Merlin games due to Babai (1985). See also Babai and Moran (1988). These games are restricted cases of the Games Against Nature of Papadimitriou (1985). A systematic description of interactive proof systems is found in Balcázar, Díaz and Gabárro (1988). The graph nonisomorphism protocol in Section 9.2 is due to Goldreich, Micali and Wigderson (1986).

The protocol to compute a permanent is due to Lund, Fortnow, Karloff and Nissan (1990); that for the #SAT problem is from Beigel (1993). The **IP** = **PSPACE** result is due to Shamir (1990). See Babai (1990) for the history of efforts culminating in this result. The proof presented here follows Shen (1992).

The concept of multi-prover protocols was introduced by Benn-Or, Goldwasser, Kilian and Wigderson (1989), and the **MIP** = **NEXP** theorem is due to Babai, Fortnow and Lund (1990).

The concept of transparent proof was developed by Babai, Fortnow, Levin and Szegedy (1991). The PCP-theorem is due to Arora, Lund, Montwani, Sudan and Szegedy (1992). In this paper the relations between transparent proofs and nonapproximability of **NP**-complete problems have also been explored; the idea came up in the paper by Feige, Goldwasser, Babai, Safra and Szegedy (1991). For a more detailed exposition on transparent proofs see PhD theses by Sudan (1992) and Arora (1994), an extensive paper by Bellare, Goldreich and Sudan (1995), surveys due to Johnson (1992), Babai (1995) and a collection of papers in Hochbaum (1996). A reduction of the number of bits needed to be checked to 11 is due to Bellare, Goldreich and Sudan (1995).

The idea of zero-knowledge proofs is due to Goldwasser, Micali and Rackoff (1985), which since then has developed rapidly. See also Blum (1986), Goldreich (1988), Salomaa (1990) and Feigenbaum (1992) for surveys. Another concept of zero-knowledge proofs, which are not statistically but computationally convincing, is due to Brassard, Chaum and Crèpau (1988). Blum, Feldman and Micali (1988) showed that interaction in any zero-knowledge proof can be replaced by sharing a common, short, random string. The cave example is due to Muriel, Quisquater and Guillou (1990).

Theorem 9.3.10 is a consequence of the results of Impagliazzo and Yung (1988) and Naor (1989). Theorem 9.3.13 is due to Ben-Or, Goldwasser, Kilian and Wigderson (1988). The proof that the class of languages with zero-knowledge proofs is identical with **BPP** provided one-way functions do not exist is due to Ostrovsky and Wigderson (1993).

The first particular result checkers are due to Freivalds (1979). However, it was M. Blum (see Blum (1988), Blum and Raghavan (1989) and Blum and Kamman (1989)) who developed the general approach to result checking. Basic results on checking approximate numerical computations are due to Ar, Blum, Codenotti and Gemmell (1993). The idea of self-testing/correcting programs is due to Blum, Luby and Rubinfeld (1993), and Section 9.4 draws on their work. See also Blum and Wasserman (1994) and (1995). The last paper investigates the possibility of building result checkers and self-testing programs into microprocessors.

Vanstein (1991) has shown that for a broad class of functions (rational functions constructed from $x, e^x, \sin(ax+b)$ and $\cos(ax+b)$, using operations $+, -, \times$ and fractional exponentiation) an algebraic equation can be derived which relates to each other the values of the function at a given point and a few other points; this equation can then be used to design a result checker and a self-correcting program.

The area of interactive protocols has developed very fast. Interestingly, to a large extent this has been due to the extraordinary interaction power of e-mail, as has been well analysed by Babai (1990).

10 Networks

INTRODUCTION

Information processing and computing are in principle distributive and parallel, whether executed on computer networks, in society, or by nature. Many of the fundamental problems of computing are therefore in this area.

Distribution of tasks and co-operation are the basic engines behind the power that distributiveness and parallelism offer. Communication networks and methods for making use of them are the basic tools for harnessing this power. However, conflicting requirements on such communication networks with respect to their simplicity, regularity and efficiency, coupled with the complexity of many basic communication tasks, are the main obstacles to harnessing this potential power. A deeper understanding of basic concepts relating to networks – their characteristics, properties, algorithms, embeddings into other networks, mutual simulations and layouts – is therefore of prime importance for capturing the principles and laws of distributive and parallel computing. Fortunately, such an understanding can be achieved to a large degree on a graph-theoretic level, which is what is presented in this chapter.

LEARNING OBJECTIVES

The aim of the chapter is to demonstrate

1. basic communication networks, their characteristics and properties, and some methods to use such networks for parallel computing;
2. methods for solving basic information dissemination problems;
3. several embedding methods, especially for embeddings in hypercubes;
4. main routing methods, including randomized ones, their properties and limitations;
5. simulation universality of the main types of bounded-degree networks;
6. simulation of shared memory computers on bounded-degree network computers;
7. basic layout concepts and several layout methods and results;
8. fundamental physical limitations of layouts of highly regular but also randomly interconnected networks.

The firm, the enduring, the simple
and the modest are near to virtue.

Confucius (551–479 BC)

Co-operation between computing elements is the basic ingredient in harnessing the power of distributiveness and parallelism. Communication between processing/memory elements is the key tool for making such co-operation fruitful.

The ideal case would be to have direct, fast communication lines between all co-operating elements/memories. Thus, complete graphs would be an ideal interconnection structure. Unfortunately, with current and foreseeable technologies it is not feasible to implement such an ideal interconnection structure in the case of a large number of communicating elements. However, foreseeable technologies are likely to prefer 'nearest neighbours' interconnection structures: namely, one-, two- and three-dimensional arrays of communicating elements. A strong disadvantage of such interconnection structures is long communication paths between some processing/memory elements. There is therefore an urgent need to explore a variety of other interconnection structures for networks and relations between them.

The main difficulty in designing good interconnection graphs concerns the conflicting requirements that they should satisfy. They should be regular, so as to make it easy to design co-operating programs for computer networks on them; networks on such graphs should be able to simulate efficiently and be efficiently simulated by networks with other interconnection structures. It should be easy and fast to send messages from all processing/memory elements of the network to other processing/memory elements. Finally, networks with such interconnection structures should be reasonably easy to implement with foreseeable technologies.

In this chapter we discuss several key problems of programming, embedding, simulation and layout of communication networks. Fortunately, all these problems can be discussed on an abstract, graph-theoretic level.

The main types of networks are introduced in Section 10.1, where some of their basic properties are analysed and several techniques are demonstrated for designing algorithms to solve computational problems for such networks of processors. Basic information dissemination problems and modes are analysed in Section 10.2. Broadcasting, accumulation and gossiping are basic subproblems for many tasks if the power of distributiveness and parallelism is to be utilized. Their satisfactory solution is of key importance for effective use of particular interconnection structures. Analysis of these problems gives rise to some general techniques of communication on networks, as well as to an understanding of how difficult are even very simple communication tasks on commonly used networks, if one is looking for optimal performance.

Many problems of efficient communication between elements of networks can be further reduced to several basic routing problems: through which paths to send information from one communicating element to another, especially if many communications are to take place concurrently. A variety of routing problems and their solutions is presented and analysed in Section 10.4.

An efficient simulation of networks with one interconnection structure on networks with different interconnection structures is of great importance for the overall portability and efficiency of distributive and parallel programming. Some basic embeddings of certain networks into another are discussed in Section 10.3. Two other key problems of this type are discussed in Section 10.5: the existence of universal networks for simulation and the simulation of PRAMs on bounded-degree networks and hypercubes.

Finally, some network implementation problems, namely, layout of networks in two-dimensional grids, are discussed on graph-theoretic level in Section 10.6. Graph decomposition and separability play the key role there.

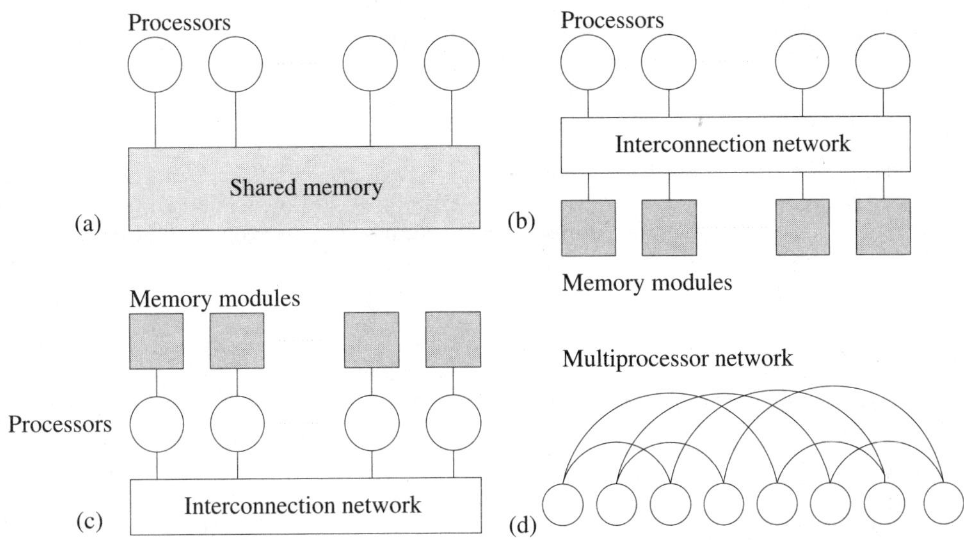

Figure 10.1 Models of parallel computing

10.1 Basic Networks

Due to its freedom from most communication problems, the PRAM (Figure 10.1a) is an easy-to-use model of parallel computing. However, the models depicted in Figures 10.1b, c, d, seem to be more realistic, where a particular communication network is used to manage communications. In the last model, Figure 10.1d, memory modules are parts of processors. In all these models the underlying interconnection network and its graph-theoretic properties play the key role.

10.1.1 Networks

There are several properties a family of graphs should have in order to be a good model of interconnection networks. Two basic ones are regularity and the existence of simple enough descriptions, for example, by means of string-identifiers of nodes, that allow one to determine easily the identifiers of neighbouring nodes from the identifier of a given node. This is of crucial importance for the communication problems discussed in Sections 10.2 and 10.4. Other requirements for good networks are discussed in Sections 10.3 and 10.6.

Clear and concise representation of strings, sets of strings and conversion operations between strings and integers is of prime importance for clear and concise description of networks and discussion of network problems. Let us therefore summarize the notation used.

For an integer n let $[n] = \{0,1,\ldots,n-1\}$ – in particular, $[2] = \{0,1\}$. $[n]^d$ is the set of all d-tuples of elements of $[n]$. A string $\bar{a} \in [n]^d$ will be denoted by $\bar{a} = (a_{d-1},\ldots,a_0)$ or $\bar{a} = a_{d-1},\ldots,a_0$, and a_0 will be called the least significant, or the right-most, symbol of $\bar{a}$. *bin* is a conversion function from binary strings to integers and $bin_d^{-1}(n), d, n \in \mathbf{N}, \lceil \lg n \rceil < d$, is the binary representation of n using exactly d bits.

To simplify descriptions of networks and reasoning about networks, we often identify nodes of networks, or of the underlying graphs, with their identifiers.

Strings $\bar{a} = (a_{d-1},\ldots,a_0)$ and $\bar{b} = (b_{d-1},\ldots,b_0)$ from $[n]^d$ and their **Hamming distance** $ham(\bar{a},\bar{b}) = \sum_{i=0}^{d-1} |a_i - b_i|$ are the fundamental elements for describing a variety of networks. The most basic ones are **arrays** and **toroids**. If $d,n \in \mathbf{N}$, then a (n,d)**-array** $A[n,d]$ is the undirected graph $G = \langle V,E \rangle$, where $V = [n]^d$, $E = \{(\bar{a},\bar{b}) \,|\, \bar{a},\bar{b} \in [n]^d,\ ham(\bar{a},\bar{b}) = 1\}$. Similarly, a (n,d)**-toroid** $T[n,d]$ is the undirected graph $G = \langle V,E \rangle$, where $V = [n]^d, E = \{(\bar{a},\bar{b}) \,|\, \bar{a},\bar{b} \in [n]^d,\ ham(\bar{a},\bar{b}) = 1$ or $\mathrm{ham}(\bar{a},\bar{b}) = n-1$ and $\bar{a},\bar{b}$ differ only in one symbol$\}$.

Example 10.1.1 *$A[n,1]$ is a* **one-dimensional array** *of n nodes (see Figure 10.2a); $T[n,1]$ is a* **ring (cycle)** *of n nodes (see Figure 10.2b) – also notation R_n will be used; $A[n,d]$ is a* **d-dimensional array** *of n^d nodes (see Figure 10.2c for $n=4, d=2$); $T[n,d]$ is a* **d-dimensional toroid** *of n^d nodes (see Figure 10.2d for $n=4, d=2$); and $A[2,d]$ is a* **d-dimensional hypercube**, *notation H_d (see Figure 10.2e for $d=3$). Another way to depict H_3 is shown in Figure 10.2j.*

The hypercube is one of the basic networks, with many natural and important properties. We shall analyse this network intensively. The following terminology will be useful. If two nodes of a hypercube H_d differ only in the ith bit from the left, then they are said to be connected by an **edge in the ith dimension**.

Exercise 10.1.2 *Show that if $\bar{a},\bar{b} \in [2]^d$, $ham(\bar{a},\bar{b}) = t$, $1 \le t \le d$, then between nodes $\bar{a}$ and $\bar{b}$ of a hypercube H_d there are (a) t node-disjoint paths of length t; (b) $d-t$ node-disjoint paths of length $t+2$.*

The following networks are closely related to the hypercube H_d: the butterfly network, B_d (see Figure 10.2f for $d=3$), the wrapped butterfly network, WB_d, and the cube-connected cycles, CCC_d (see Figure 10.2g for $d=3$).

The **butterfly network** B_d can be seen as an unfolded hypercube H_d. The ith level of edges, $1 \le i \le d$, of the butterfly network B_d can be seen as an unfolding of H_d according to the edges of the ith dimension. Formally, the butterfly network B_d is an undirected graph $B_d = \langle V_d, E_d \rangle$, where $V_d = [d+1] \times [2]^d$, and $E_d = \{((i,\bar{a}),(i+1,\bar{b})) \,|$ either $\bar{a} = \bar{b}$ or $\bar{a}$ and $\bar{b}$ differ in the $(i+1)$th left-most bit and in no other bit$\}$. For any $s \in [2]^d$, the nodes from the set $[d+1] \times \{s\}$ form a column of the butterfly. For any $j \in [d+1]$, the nodes from the set $\{j\} \times [2]^d$ form the so-called jth level (or jth **rank**) of B_d. The nodes of rank 0 (the last rank) are sometimes called the **source (target)** nodes. The **wrapped butterfly** WB_d is obtained from the butterfly B_d by identifying the first and last nodes of each column of B_d.

The **cube-connected cycles** CCC_d can be seen as being obtained from the hypercube H_d by first removing all nodes and then connecting all remaining edges incident with each node of H_d by a cycle (see Figure 10.2g). Formally, the cube-connected cycles are an undirected graph $CCC_d = \langle V_d, E_d \rangle$, where $V_d = [d] \times [2]^d$, $E_d = \{((i,\bar{a}),((i+1) \bmod d,\bar{a})) \,|\, 0 \le i < d, \bar{a} \in [2]^d\} \cup \{((i,\bar{a}),(i,\bar{b})) \,|\, \bar{a}$ and $\bar{b}$ differ in the $(i+1)$th right-most bit$, 0 \le i < d\}$. Another way to depict CCC_3 is shown in Figure 10.2k.

Exercise 10.1.3 *Show that in any butterfly network B_d there is exactly one path of length d from any node of rank zero to any node of rank d.*

Exercise 10.1.4 *Show that CCC_3 is a subgraph of WB_3. Does the same relation hold between CCC_d and WB_d for any dimension d?*

The de Bruijn graph DB_d (see Figure 10.2h for $d=3$) and the shuffle exchange graph SE_d (see

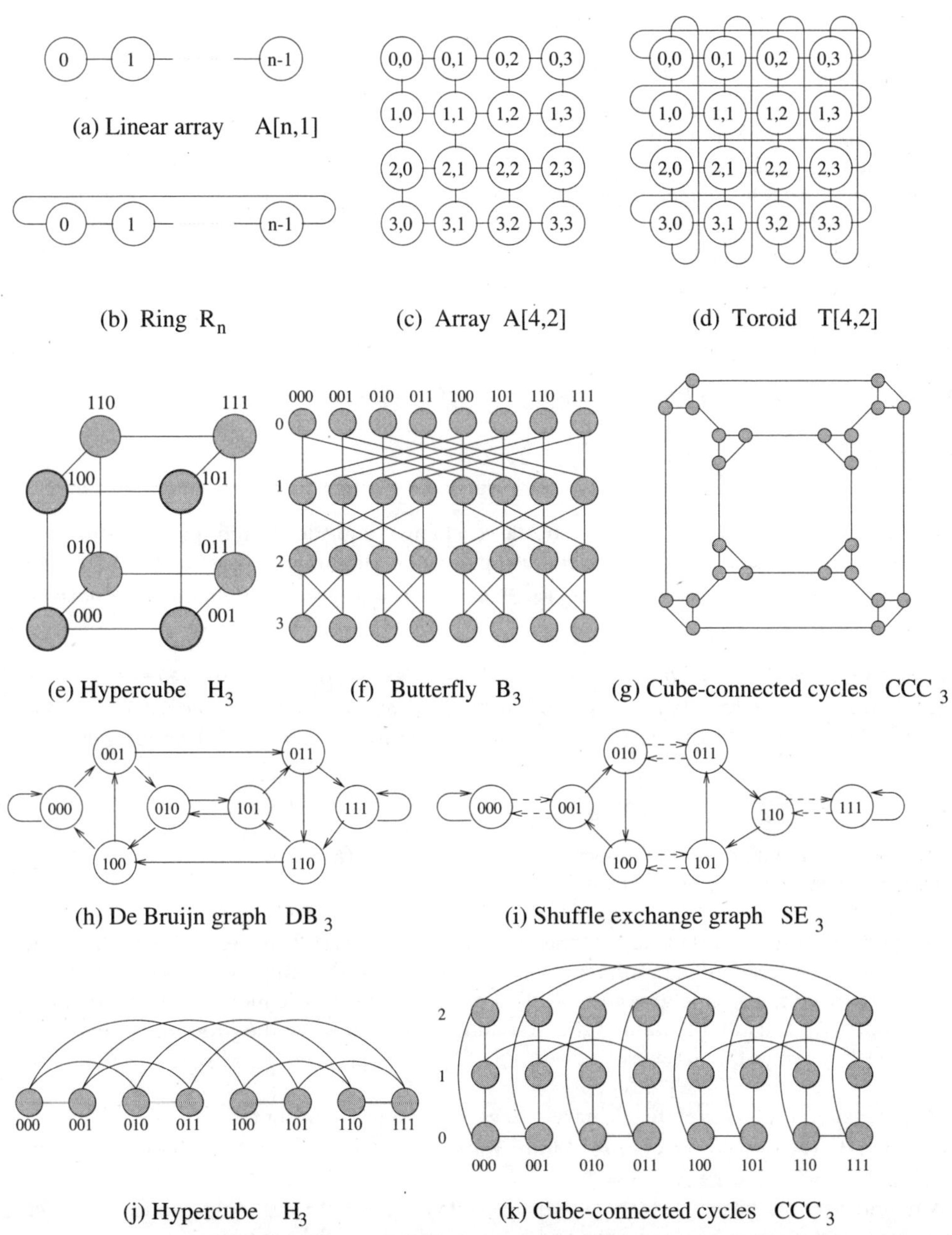
0
1
n-1
(a) Linear array A[n,1]
0
1
n-1
(b) Ring R_n
0,0
0,1
0,2
0,3
1,0
1,1
1,2
1,3
2,0
2,1
2,2
2,3
3,0
3,1
3,2
3,3
(c) Array A[4,2]
(d) Toroid T[4,2]
110
111
100
101
010
011
000
001
(e) Hypercube H_3
000 001 010 011 100 101 110 111
0
1
2
3
(f) Butterfly B_3
(g) Cube-connected cycles CCC_3
(h) De Bruijn graph DB_3
(i) Shuffle exchange graph SE_3
(j) Hypercube H_3
(k) Cube-connected cycles CCC_3

Figure 10.2 Basic networks

Figure 10.2i for $d = 3$) are also closely related to the hypercube H_d. The regularity of these graphs is better seen when they are considered as directed graphs, even though their undirected versions, UDB_d and USE_d, are also often used. The name 'perfect shuffle graphs' is also used for de Bruijn graphs.

A **de Bruijn graph** is a directed graph $DB_d = \langle V_d, E_d \rangle$, where $V_d = [2]^d$, and $E_d = \{(a_{d-1}\ldots a_0, a_{d-2}\ldots a_0 b) \,|\, a_{d-1}\ldots a_0 \in [2]^d, b \in [2]\}$.

The **shuffle exchange graph** is a directed graph $SE_d = \langle V_d, E_d \rangle$, where $V_d = [2]^d$, $E_d = \{(a_{d-1}\ldots a_0, a_{d-1}\ldots a_1\overline{a_0}) \,|\, a_{d-1}\ldots a_0 \in [2]^d\} \cup \{(a_{d-1}\ldots a_0, a_{d-2}\ldots a_0 a_{d-1}) \,|\, a_{d-1}\ldots a_0 \in [2]^d\}$ – notation $\bar{x}$ is used here to denote a negation of bits. The edges of the first set are called the **exchange edges** (depicted by dashed lines in Figure 10.2i); the edges of the second set are called the **(perfect) shuffle edges** (depicted by solid lines in Figure 10.2i).

Exercise 10.1.5 *Show that there is exactly one path of length d between any two nodes of DB_d.*

Exercise 10.1.6 *Show that USE_3 is a subgraph of UDB_3. Does the same relation hold between USE_d and UDB_d for any d?*

The neighbours of nodes in the shuffle exchange and de Bruijn graphs, and in their undirected versions, can be easily described using the following unary operations on binary strings: $EX(a_{d-1}\ldots a_0) = a_{d-1}\ldots a_1\overline{a_0}$, $PS(a_{d-1}\ldots a_0) = a_{d-2}\ldots a_0 a_{d-1}$ and $PS^{-1}(a_{d-1}\ldots a_0) = a_0 a_{d-1}\ldots a_1$, $DB(a_{d-1}\ldots a_0) = (a_{d-2}\ldots a_0\overline{a_{d-1}})$.

Example 10.1.7 *The perfect shuffle connections received their name from the following fact. Take a deck of $n = 2^d$ playing cards numbered $0, 1, \ldots, n-1$. Cut the deck exactly in half to get cards $0, 1, \ldots, \frac{n}{2} - 1$ and $\frac{n}{2}, \ldots, n-1$ in the first and second halves, respectively. Shuffle the deck perfectly. The resulting order of cards is*

$$0, \frac{n}{2}, 1, \frac{n}{2}+1, 2, \frac{n}{2}+2, \ldots, \frac{n}{2}-1, n-1.$$

Observe that the ith card moved into the position $bin(PS(bin_d^{-1}(i)))$. (Exercise 1 illustrates how the properties of shuffle exchange graphs can be used for a card trick.)

The perfect shuffle and de Bruijn connections are very powerful. To see this, let us assume that the nodes of the perfect shuffle graph represent processors and that all processors send their data, in three synchronized steps, to neighbours specified by operations PS, EX and PS^{-1} on binary identifiers of their nodes. As a result, the data in the first and second halves of the processors are exchanged – no matter how large the network. Indeed, $PS^{-1}(EX(PS(a_{d-1}\ldots a_0))) = \overline{a_{d-1}}a_{d-2}\ldots a_0$. Similarly, $PS^{-1}(DB(a_{d-1}\ldots a_0)) = \overline{a_{d-1}}a_{d-2}\ldots a_0$.

Trees, especially **complete binary trees** of depth d, notation BT_d, are another important interconnection structure. More formally, $BT_d = \langle V_d, E_d \rangle$, where $V_d = \bigcup_{i=0}^{d}[2]^i$, $E_d = \{(u, u0), (u, u1) \,|\, |u| < d\}$.

A hybrid network based on trees and arrays called a mesh of trees looks exotic, but is actually very natural, fast for parallel processing and convenient for parallel programming.

Informally, the **two-dimensional mesh of trees** of depth d, MT_d, is an $n \times n$ array, $n = 2^d$, of nodes, the so-called base nodes, that are not connected among themselves, together with binary trees above each row and column of the array; see Figure 10.3, where nodes of the basic $n \times n$ array are depicted by filled-in circles. More formally, MT_d is the graph whose nodes are pairs (u, v), where u, v are binary

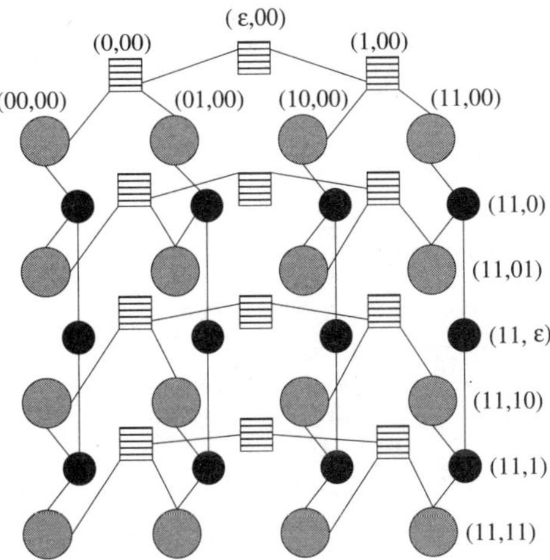

Figure 10.3 Mesh of trees, with nodes of two trees labelled

strings of length at most d, with at least one of u and v of length d, and whose node (u,v) is connected by an edge with the nodes $(u,v0)$ and $(u,v1)$ if $|v| < d$ and with $(u0,v)$ and $(u1,v)$ if $|u| < d$.

Remark 10.1.8 In this chapter the term 'network' will sometimes be used, as in the literature, in cases in which the term 'graph' would be technically sufficient because only the interconnection structure is of importance and not particularly the processors. Mostly, however, the term 'network' refers to a whole family of similar graphs. For example, the term 'hypercube network' means any network whose underlying graph is a hypercube. Similarly the term 'bounded-degree network' refers to a family of graphs for which there is a constant c such that degrees of all graphs of these networks are smaller than c.

Various modifications of networks are introduced in this section. For example, directed versions of the graphs presented above are considered, as well as their modifications where, in addition, all nodes have self-loops. For example, we can have one-directional or two-directional rings. Self-loops are used to denote that a graph models networks of processors with a memory.

10.1.2 Basic Network Characteristics

Table 10.1 summarizes the basic parameters of networks introduced in the previous section. Apart from the bisection width, most of them are easy to determine.

Let us recall (see Section 2.4) that the degree of a network is the maximum number of neighbours with which a node can be connected. The diameter of a network is the maximum distance between nodes.

Complete graphs K_n are ideal interconnection structures for multiprocessor communication. Complete bipartite graphs $K_{n,n}$ are ideal interconnection structures for communication between n processors and n memory modules. Unfortunately, these graphs have degree $n-1$ and n if they have n, respectively $2n$ nodes. The main advantage of hypercubes is that the degree is much smaller, namely $\Theta(\lg n)$ for an n-node graph. The diameter is not increased too much, again $\Theta(\lg n)$, and, in addition, regularity is preserved. The main advantage of bounded-degree networks such as complete binary

Network	number of nodes	number of edges	degree	diameter	bisection-width
Array $A[n,d], n>2$	n^d	$dn^{d-1}(n-1)$	$2d$	$d(n-1)$	n^{d-1}
Torus $T[n,d]$	n^d	dn^d	$2d$	$d\lceil\frac{n-1}{2}\rceil$	$2n^{d-1}$
Hypercube H_d	2^d	$d2^{d-1}$	d	d	2^{d-1}
Cube-conn. cycles $CCC_d, d>4$	$d2^d$	$3d2^{d-1}$	3	$\lfloor\frac{5d}{2}\rfloor-2$	2^{d-1}
Shuffle exchange SE_d	2^d	2^{d+1}	4	$2d-1$	$\Theta(\frac{2^d}{d})$
de Bruijn graph DB_d	2^d	2^{d+1}	4	d	$\Theta(\frac{2^d}{d})$
Butterfly B_d	$(d+1)2^d$	$d2^{d+1}$	4	$2d$	2^d
Wrapped butterfly WB_d	$d2^d$	$d2^{d+1}$	4	$\lfloor\frac{3d}{2}\rfloor$	2^d

Table 10.1 Characteristics of basic networks

trees, butterflies, cube-connected cycles, shuffle exchange and de Bruijn graphs is that they preserve logarithmic diameter but have very small degree.

The bisection-width[1] of a network is one of the critical factors on which the speed of computation on the network may eventually depend. It actually determines the size of the smallest bottleneck between two (almost equal) parts of the network.

For example, as is easy to see, $BW(A[n,1]) = 1, BW(A[n,2]) = n, BW(T(n,2)) = 2n, BW(H_3) = BW(CCC_3) = BW(SE_3) = BW(DB_3) = 4$.

Exercise 10.1.9 *Show for as many entries in Table 10.1 as you can that they are correct.*

We present now an elegant proof of the upper bound $BW(SE_d) = \mathcal{O}(\frac{2^d}{d})$. The proof is based on properties of a special mapping σ of nodes of $SE_d = \langle V_d, E_d\rangle$ into the complex plane.

Let $\omega_d = e^{\frac{2\pi i}{d}}$ be a dth primitive root of 1; that is, ω_d^d=1 and $\omega_d^i \neq 1$ for $1 \leq i < d$. For $\bar{a} = (a_{d-1}, \ldots, a_0) \in [2]^d$ we define

$$\sigma(\bar{a}) = a_{d-1}\omega_d^{d-1} + a_{d-2}\omega_d^{d-2} + \cdots + a_1\omega_d + a_0$$

to be a complex number, a point in the complex plane, an image of the node $\bar{a}$ (see Figure 10.4). The mapping σ has the following properties:

1. The exchange edges of SE_d are mapped into horizontal segments of length 1. Indeed,

$$\sigma(a_{d-1}\ldots a_1 1) = a_{d-1}\omega_d^{d-1} + \ldots + a_1\omega_d + 1 = \sigma(a_{d-1}\ldots a_1 0) + 1.$$

2. The shuffle edges of SE_d form cycles (called **necklaces**) with the centre at the origin of the plane. Indeed, since $\omega_d^d = 1$, we get

$$\begin{aligned}\omega_d\sigma(a_{d-1}\ldots a_0) &= a_{d-1}\omega_d^d + \ldots + a_0\omega_d = a_{d-2}\omega_d^{d-1} + \ldots + a_0\omega_d + a_{d-1}\\ &= \sigma(a_{d-2}\ldots a_0 a_{d-1}).\end{aligned}$$

[1]Remember (see Section 2.4.1) that the bisection-width $BW(G)$ of an n-node graph G is the minimum number of edges one has to remove to disconnect G into two subgraphs with $\lceil\frac{n}{2}\rceil$ and $\lfloor\frac{n}{2}\rfloor$ nodes.

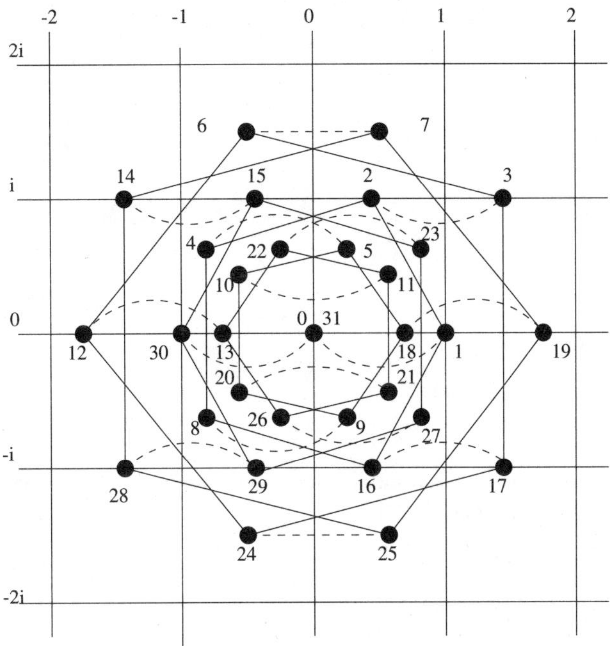

Figure 10.4 Mapping of a shuffle exchange graph into the complex plane

3. The length of necklaces is clearly at most d. Necklaces of length d are called full. Those with fewer than d nodes are called degenerate (e.g. the necklace $1010 \longrightarrow 0101 \longrightarrow 1010$ in SE_4). Degenerate necklaces are mapped by σ into the origin of the complex plane. Indeed, for any node $a_{d-1}\dots a_0$ of a degenerate necklace there is an i such that $\omega_d^i\sigma(a_{d-1}\dots a_0) = \sigma(a_{d-1}\dots a_0)$. Since $\omega_d^i \neq 0$, it follows that $\sigma(a_{d-1}\dots a_0) = 0$.

4. The number of nodes of a SE_d that are mapped by σ into the upper part of the complex plane is the same as the number of nodes that are mapped into the lower part of the plane. Indeed,

$$\sigma(a_{d-1}\dots a_0) + \sigma(\overline{a_{d-1}}\dots\overline{a_0}) = \sum_{i=0}^{d-1}(a_i + \overline{a_i})\omega_d^i = \sum_{i=0}^{d-1}\omega_d^i = 0.$$

5. At most $\mathcal{O}(\frac{2^d}{d})$ nodes are mapped into the origin. Indeed, if $\sigma(a_{d-1}\dots a_0) = 0$, then $\sigma(a_{d-1}\dots a_1\bar{a}_0)$ equals 1 or -1. Each such node has to be on a full necklace. This means that at most $2\frac{2^d}{d}$ nodes are mapped into the nodes 1 or -1. Hence, there are at most $2\frac{2^d}{d}$ nodes mapped into the origin.

6. At most $\mathcal{O}(\frac{2^d}{d})$ edges cross the real axis. Indeed, exactly two edges from each full necklace cross the real axis, and an exchange edge can 'cross' the real edge, according to the point 1, if and only if both its nodes lie on the real axis.

7. If we remove all edges that cross the real axis or lie on the real axis, and assign half of the nodes lying on the real axis to the upper plane, the other half to the lower plane, we get a 'bisection' of

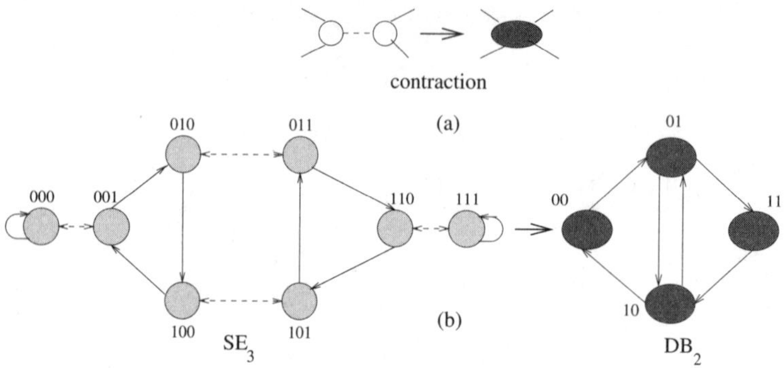

Figure 10.5 Contraction of SE_3 into DB_2

the graph into two parts; each with 2^{d-1} nodes. The number of edges that have been removed is $\mathcal{O}(\frac{2^d}{d})$, according to point six.

The relation between the shuffle exchange and de Bruijn graphs is very close. Indeed, if exchange edges of the shuffle exchange graph SE_{d+1} are contracted into single nodes, we get the de Bruijn graph DB_d. Figure 10.5a shows the contraction operation, and Figure 10.5b shows how to get DB_2 from SE_3 by contraction.

This close relation between shuffle exchange and de Bruijn graphs immediately implies that the $\Theta(\frac{2^d}{d})$ asymptotical estimation for the bisection-width also applies to de Bruijn graphs. It is an open problem to determine more exactly the bisection-widths of shuffle exchange and de Bruijn graphs.

Exercise 10.1.10 *Determine, for the two-dimensional mesh of trees of depth d, MT_d: (a) the number of nodes; (b) the number of edges; (c) the diameter; (d) the bisection-width.*

Exercise 10.1.11 (Star graphs) *These are graphs $S_n = \langle V_n, E_n \rangle$, where V_n is the set of all permutations over $\{1, \ldots, n\}$ and $E_n = \{(a,b) \,|\, a,b \in V_n, b = a \cdot t$ for some transposition $t = (1,i), 2 \leq i \leq n\}$. (a) Determine the number of nodes, edges and diameter of S_n. (b) Show that S_4 consists of four connected S_3 graphs.*

Exercise 10.1.12 (Kautz graphs) *Another family of graphs that seems to be potentially a good model for interconnection networks are Kautz graphs, $K_d = \langle V_d, E_d \rangle$, where $V_d = \{\bar{a} \,|\, \bar{a} \in [3]^d$ and no two consecutive symbols of $\bar{a}$ are the same$\}$, $E_d = \{(a_{d-1} \ldots a_0, a_{d-2} \ldots a_0 x) \,|\, a_{d-1} \ldots a_0 \in V_d, a_0 \neq x\}$. (a) Draw K_1, K_2, K_3, K_4. (b) Determine for K_d the number of nodes, number of edges, degree and diameter.*

10.1.3 Algorithms on Multiprocessor Networks

Consider the following version of the divide-and-conquer method. At the beginning one processor is assigned a problem to solve. At each successive step, each processor involved divides its problem into two subproblems, of approximately the same size, keeps one of them for itself and assigns the second to a new processor. The process stops when the decomposition is complete. The interconnection graph obtained this way after the dth step is exactly the spanning tree of the hypercube H_d (see Figure 10.6).

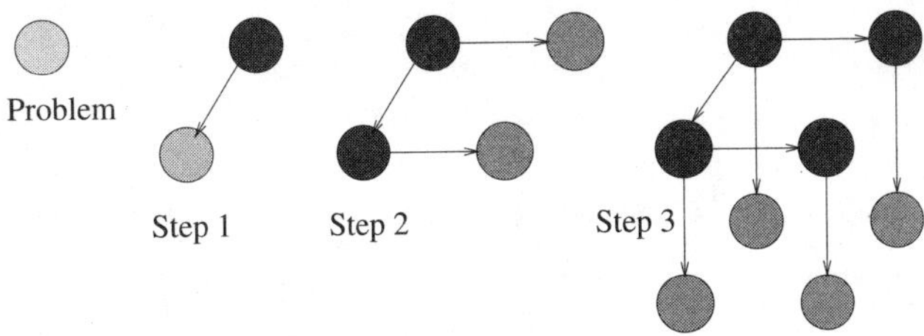

Figure 10.6 Divide-and-conquer method and a hypercube

In addition, we can say that at each step 'division is done along another dimension of the hypercube'.

This interpretation of the divide-and-conquer method shows that, from the algorithm design point of view, the hypercube interconnections naturally fit what is perhaps the most important algorithm design methodology. Moreover, it also shows how divide-and-conquer algorithms can be implemented on hypercube networks.

In the following three examples we illustrate how to solve some basic algorithmic problems on hypercube and butterfly networks. The first of these is called broadcasting – information must be sent from one node to all the others. (We deal with broadcasting in more detail in Section 10.2.)

Example 10.1.13 (Broadcasting on the hypercube H_d)[2]

Input: *Information x is in the processor $P_{0\ldots 0}$.*

Output: *Each processor contains x.*

Algorithm: **for** $i \leftarrow 1$ **to** d **do**
for $a_1 \ldots a_{i-1} \in [2]^{i-1}$ **pardo** $P_{0\ldots 0a_{i-1}\ldots a_1}$ *sends x to* $P_{\underbrace{0\ldots 01a_{i-1}\ldots a_1}_{d\ \text{symbols}}}$

Illustration:
Step 1: P_{000} sends x to P_{001} {notation $P_{000} \rightarrow_x P_{001}$},
Step 2: $P_{000} \rightarrow_x P_{010}, P_{001} \rightarrow_x P_{011}$,
Step 3: $P_{000} \rightarrow_x P_{100}, P_{001} \rightarrow_x P_{101}, P_{010} \rightarrow_x P_{110}, P_{011} \rightarrow_x P_{111}$,
⋮

Example 10.1.14 (Summation on the hypercube H_d)

Input: *Each processor $P_i, 0 \leq i < 2^d$, contains an $a_i \in \mathbf{R}$.*

Output: *The sum $\sum_{i=0}^{2^d-1} a_i$ is stored in P_0.*

Algorithm: **for** $l \leftarrow d-1$ **downto** 0
for $0 \leq i < 2^l$ **pardo** P_i: $a_i \leftarrow a_i + a_{i^{(l)}}$,

where $i^{(l)}$ is the number whose binary representation is obtained from the binary representation $bin_d^{-1}(i)$ of i by flipping the $(l+1)$th left-most bit.

[2]The convention $[2]^0 = \emptyset$ is used here.

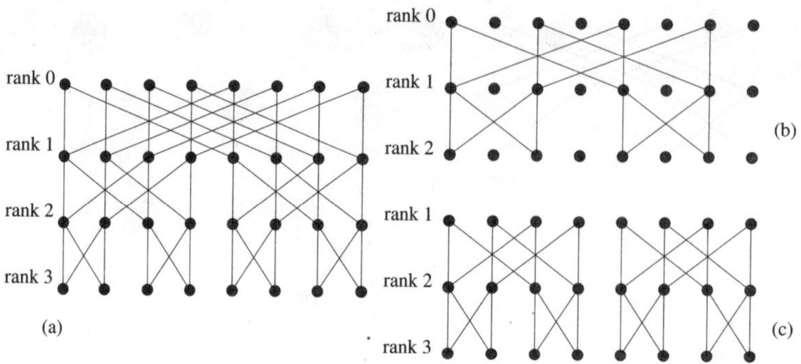

Figure 10.7 Two ways of making two butterflies out of one

For $d = 3$, the first three iterations have the form

$$
\begin{array}{llll}
a_0 \leftarrow a_0 + a_4 & a_1 \leftarrow a_1 + a_5 & a_2 \leftarrow a_2 + a_6, & a_3 \leftarrow a_3 + a_7, \\
a_0 \leftarrow a_0 + a_2, & a_1 \leftarrow a_1 + a_3, & & \\
a_0 \leftarrow a_0 + a_1. & & &
\end{array}
$$

Both algorithms belong to the class of **fully normal hypercube algorithms** (or **ascend/descend algorithms**). At each step all processors communicate along the same dimension and all dimensions are used either in ascending or descending order.

Exercise 10.1.15 *Design a (simple) algorithm for multiplying two matrices of degree $n = 2^q$ on the hypercube H_{3q} in $\mathcal{O}(\lg n)$ time.*

We show now how a butterfly network on B_d can be used to sort $n = 2^d$ numbers, stored in the processors of B_d of rank 0, one number per processor. The output, the sorted sequence, will be stored in the processors of the last rank, again one number per processor. The algorithm will be of a multiple ascend/descend type. It is based on a very straightforward observation and a merging procedure founded on a simple **merging lemma**.

Observe first that if the nodes of the highest rank of the butterfly B_d (see Figure 10.7a) are removed, we get two butterflies B_{d-1} (see Figure 10.7b). The same is true if nodes of rank zero are removed (see Figure 10.7c). This allows us to use the divide-and-conquer method for sorting on B_d as follows.

Input: A sequence of 2^d elements is stored in the nodes of rank 0 of the butterfly B_d.

Output: The sorted sequence is in the processors of the last rank.

Algorithm: *sort*(d).

Procedure: *sort*(k)
begin
  if $k = 0$ **then** done
    else copy data of processors of rank 0 into processors of rank 1;

```
        for both butterflies obtained by removing rank 0 pardo sort(k − 1);
        merge(k) {using processors of all ranks}
end
```

The procedure *merge* for merging two sequences is based on the following fact.

Lemma 10.1.16 *Let $a_1, \dots, a_n$ and $b_1, \dots, b_n$ be two sorted lists, n even. Assume that $a_1, a_3, a_5, \dots, a_{n-1}$ is merged with $b_2, b_4, \dots, b_n$ into $c_1, c_2, \dots, c_n$ and $a_2, a_4, \dots, a_n$ with $b_1, b_3, \dots, b_{n-1}$ into $d_1, \dots, d_n$. We get a fully sorted sequence by taking*

$$c_1, d_1, c_2, d_2, \dots, c_n, d_n$$

and exchanging elements of pairs $(c_i, d_i), 1 \leq i \leq n$, whenever $c_i > d_i$.

We assume that the subsequence $a_1, a_3, a_5, \dots, a_{n-1}$ of $n/2$ element is merged with the subsequence $b_2, b_4, b_6, \dots, b_n$ of $n/2$ elements into the sequence $c_1, c_2, c_3, \dots, c_n$ of n elements and the subsequence $a_2, a_4, a_6, \dots, a_n$ of $n/2$ elements is merged with the subsequence $b_1, b_3, b_5, \dots, b_{n-1}$ of $n/2$ elements into the sequence $d_1, d_2, d_3, \dots, d_n$ of n elements.

The *merge* procedure presented below assumes input data and produces output data in the processors of the last rank. It has the following form (with x_{ij} denoting the number stored in the jth processor of the rank i, and indices relate to the subbutterflies that arise at the recursion):

procedure *merge*(k)
begin
if $k = 1$ **then**
    begin $x_{0,0} \leftarrow \min\{x_{1,0}, x_{1,1}\}$, $x_{0,1} \leftarrow \max\{x_{1,0}, x_{1,1}\}$, $x_{1,0} \leftarrow x_{0,0}$, $x_{1,1} \leftarrow x_{0,1}$ **end**
    else begin
        copy-exchange $x_{k,0}, \dots, x_{k,\frac{n}{2}-1}$ into $x_{k-1,0}, \dots, x_{k-1,\frac{n}{2}-1}$;
        copy $x_{k,\frac{n}{2}}, \dots, x_{k,n-1}$ into $x_{k-1,\frac{n}{2}}, \dots, x_{k-1,n-1}$;
        for butterflies with ranks $0, \dots, k-1$ **pardo** *merge*$(k-1)$;
        for $0 \leq i \leq n$ **pardo if** i is odd **then** $x_{k,i} \leftarrow \max\{x_{k-1,i-1}, x_{k-1,i}\}$
                                else $x_{k,i} \leftarrow \min\{x_{k-1,i-1}, x_{k-1,i}\}$
        end
end,

where the procedure *copy-exchange* transfers $x_{k,i-1}$ into $x_{k-1,i}$ for odd i, and $x_{k,i+1}$ into $x_{k-1,i}$, for i even. The function of the procedures *copy-exchange* and *copy* is to transfer data from nodes of rank k to nodes of rank $k-1$ in such a way that one of the butterflies obtained by removing all nodes of rank k merges even items of the first half with odd items of the second half and the second butterfly merges the rest – exactly as Lemma 10.1.16 requires.

The correctness of the procedure *merge* follows now from Lemma 10.1.16. Parallel time complexity of the algorithm is, for $n = 2^d, \mathcal{O}(\lg^2 n)$. Indeed, the number of recursive calls of the procedure *sort* is $\mathcal{O}(\lg n)$. Each merging requires one descend and one ascend run, and this yields $\mathcal{O}(\lg n)$ time.

Exercise 10.1.17 *Design an algorithm for the butterfly B_d such that if, at the beginning of computation, the i-th node of rank 0 contains an $x_i \in \mathbf{R}$, then, after d steps, the i-th node of the final rank contains (a) $\sum_{j=0}^{2^d-1} x_j$; (b) $\sum_{j=0}^{i-1} x_j$.*

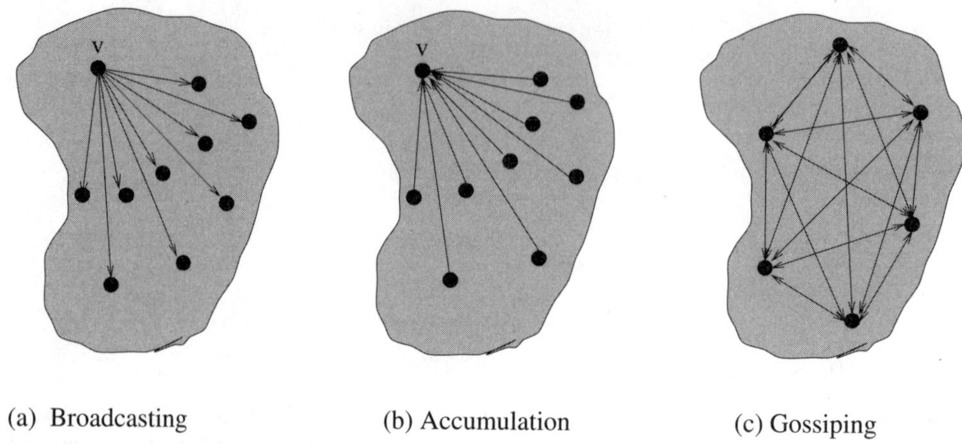

Figure 10.8 Basic information dissemination problems

One of the main advantages of the mesh of trees is that for many basic algorithmic problems one can design a simple and fast algorithm. The tree interconnections of the mesh of trees play an important role in this.

> **Exercise 10.1.18** *Design a simple $\mathcal{O}(d)$ algorithm for the two-dimensional mesh of trees of depth d for (a) sorting of 2^{2d} numbers with initially one number per each processor in a base node; (b) matrix-vector multiplication.*

10.2 Dissemination of Information in Networks

The ability of a network effectively to disseminate information is an important criterion of its suitability for parallel computing.

10.2.1 Information Dissemination Problems

In this section we first introduce three basic communication problems for networks – broadcasting, accumulation and gossiping.

Many programming strategies for networks can be reduced to these tasks, or they at least play an important role in the overall solution. We discuss two basic communication modes and present algorithms and lower bounds for these information dissemination problems for several types of communication networks. In doing so, we illustrate how difficult it is to make optimal use of the communication facilities offered by the main types of networks. We also demonstrate some techniques for managing information dissemination problems.

1. **Broadcasting problem** for a graph $G = \langle V, E \rangle$ and a node $v \in V$. Let v know a piece of information $I(v)$ which is unknown to other nodes of G. The problem is to find the best communication strategy, in the sense discussed later, such that all nodes of G get $I(v)$ (see Figure 10.8a).

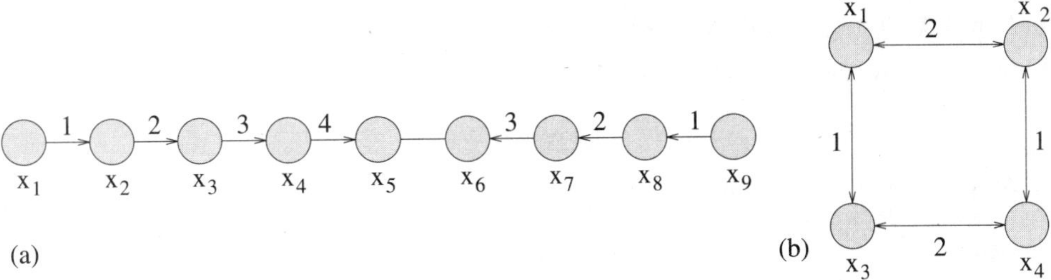

Figure 10.9 Communication algorithms

2. **Accumulation problem** for a graph $G = \langle V, E \rangle$ and a node $v \in V$. Let each node u know some information $I(u)$, and for two different nodes u, w let their informations $I(u), I(w)$ be different. The set $I(G) = \{I(u) \,|\, u \in V\}$ is called the **cumulative message** of G. The problem is to find the best communication strategy such that node v learns the cumulative message $I(G)$ (see Figure 10.8b).

3. **Gossiping problem** for a graph $G = \langle V, E \rangle$. Let each node u know information $I(u)$, and let $I(u)$ and $I(w)$ be different for different nodes u, w. The problem is to find the best communication strategy such that all nodes get the cumulative message $I(G)$ (see Figure 10.8c).

A communication strategy, or a **communication algorithm**, is a specification of a sequence of parallel communication steps (**rounds**), each of which specifies which nodes send their information and to whom or which nodes exchange information. There are two basic modes in which such communication can be carried out.

1. **Telegraph mode** (one-way communication). In each round each processor can either send or receive information, and in so doing can communicate with at most one neighbouring node. This means that a one-way communication algorithm for a graph $G = \langle V, E \rangle$ is a sequence $C_1, \ldots, C_s$, where each $C_i \subseteq C = \{(v,u),(u,v) \,|\, (u,v) \in E\}$ is such that if (x_1, y_1) and (x_2, y_2) are two different pairs from C_i, then $\{x_1, y_1\} \cap \{x_2, y_2\} = \emptyset$. (In other words, each C_i contains ordered pairs of nodes that communicate in the ith round, and no node can be in two such pairs.)

Example 10.2.1 *The following communication algorithm for a one-dimensional array*

$$\{(x_1,x_2),(x_9,x_8)\},\{(x_2,x_3),(x_8,x_7)\},\{(x_3,x_4),(x_7,x_6)\},\{(x_4,x_5)\}$$

is depicted in Figure 10.9a, where integers specify rounds.

2. **Telephone mode** (two-way communication). In each round each processor can exchange information with at most one neighbouring node. This means that a two-way communication algorithm for a graph $G = \langle V, E \rangle$ is a sequence $C_1, \ldots, C_s$ such that $C_i \subseteq E$ and such that if (x_1, y_1) and (x_2, y_2) are two different pairs from C_i, then $\{x_1, y_1\} \cap \{x_2, y_2\} = \emptyset$. (In other words, each C_i contains pairs of nodes that communicate in the ith round, and no node can be in two such pairs.)

Example 10.2.2 *A two-way gossiping algorithm* $\{(x_1,x_3),(x_2,x_4)\},\{(x_1,x_2),(x_3,x_4)\}$ *for a four-node ring is depicted in Figure 10.9b (integers specify rounds).*

Communication complexity of the basic information dissemination problems, with respect to two communication modes, is defined for graphs as follows.

Definition 10.2.3 *Let $G = \langle V,E\rangle$ be a graph, $v \in V, i = 1,2$.*

1. **Broadcasting complexity**, *$b_i(v,G)$, is the minimum number of rounds of communication algorithms for broadcasting in G from the node v in the i-way communication mode; $b_i(G) = \max\{b_i(v,G)\,|\,v \in V\}$ is the overall broadcasting complexity of the graph G.*

2. **Accumulation complexity**, *$a_i(v,G)$, is the minimum number of rounds of any communication algorithm for accumulation in G to the node v in the i-way communication mode; $a_i(G) = \max\{a_i(v,G)\,|\,v \in V\}$ is the overall accumulation complexity of the graph G.*

3. **Gossiping complexity**, *$g_i(G)$, of the graph G is the minimum number of rounds of any communication algorithm for gossiping in G in the i-way communication mode.*

For each graph G we have introduced altogether six complexity problems of information dissemination on G. However, as the following theorem says, only three of them are essentially different from the complexity point of view: one broadcasting and two gossiping problems, for both communication modes.

Theorem 10.2.4 $a_1(G) = a_2(G) = b_1(G) = b_2(G)$ *for each graph* $G = \langle V,E\rangle$.

Proof: (1) If $E_1,\ldots,E_k$ is a broadcasting algorithm in the telephone mode for the graph G and a node $v \in V$, then $E_k,\ldots,E_1$ is an accumulation algorithm for G and v, and vice versa. Therefore, $b_2(v,G) = a_2(v,G)$ for every v, and so $b_2(G) = a_2(G)$. Analogously, we can show that $b_1(G) = a_1(G)$.

(2) It is trivial that $b_2(v,G) \le b_1(v,G)$ for each $v \in V$, and therefore in order to prove the theorem, it is sufficient to show that $b_1(v,G) \le b_2(v,G)$ for each $v \in V$.

Let $E_1,\ldots,E_k$ be a broadcasting algorithm in the telephone mode for G and $v \in V$. Let $R_0 = \{v\}$ and R_i, $1 \le i \le k$, be the set of nodes that receive information $I(v)$ in the first i rounds. Then

$$V_i = R_i - \bigcup_{j=1}^{i-1} R_j$$

is the set of nodes that receive $I(v)$ exactly in the ith round. In such a case

$$E'_1,\ldots,E'_k \text{ with } E'_i = E_i \cap \{\bigcup_{s=1}^{i-1} V_s \times V_i\}$$

is a broadcasting algorithm for G and v in the telegraph mode. Hence $b_1(v,G) = b_2(v,G)$, and $b_1(G) = b_2(G)$. □

As a consequence, we can define a 'broadcasting complexity' $b(G) = b_1(G) = b_2(G)$ for any graph G.

The following theorem summarizes the basic relations between broadcasting and gossiping complexities.

Theorem 10.2.5 *For any graph G we have* $b(G) \le g_2(G) \le g_1(G) \le 2g_2(G)$.

Proof: The inequalities $b(G) \le g_2(G) \le g_1(G)$ follow directly from the definitions. In order to show $g_1(G) \le 2g_2(G)$, let $A = E_1,\ldots,E_k$ be a gossiping algorithm in the telephone mode for G. Consider any communication algorithm

$$B = E_{11}, E_{12}, E_{21}, E_{22},\ldots, E_{k1}, E_{k2},$$

where $E_i = E_{i1} \cup E_{i2}$, in the sense that for each 'exchanging edge' (u,v) in E_i one of the directed edges $\langle u,v\rangle$ or $\langle u,v\rangle$ goes to E_{i1}, the second to E_{i2}. B is then a one-way gossiping algorithm for G. □

graph	diameter	broadcasting lower bound	broadcasting upper bound	gossiping lower bound telegraph mode	gossiping upper bound telegraph mode	gossiping lower bound telephone mode	gossiping upper bound telephone mode
H_d	d	d	d	$1.44d$	$1.88d$	d	d
CCC_d	$\lfloor \frac{5d}{2} \rfloor - 2$	$\lceil \frac{5d}{2} \rceil - 2$	$\lceil \frac{5d}{2} \rceil - 1$	$\lceil \frac{5d}{2} \rceil - 2$	$\lceil \frac{7d}{2} \rceil + \left\lceil 2\sqrt{\lceil \frac{d}{2} \rceil} \right\rceil - 2$	$\lceil \frac{5d}{2} \rceil - 1$	$5\lceil \frac{d}{2} \rceil$
SE_d	$2d-1$	$2d-1$	$2d-1$	$2d-1$	$3d+3$	$2d-1$	$2d+5$
DB_d	d	$1.4404d$	$\frac{3}{2}(d+1)$	$1.31d$	$3d+3$	$1.3171d$	$2d+5$

Table 10.2 Bounds for complexity of broadcasting and gossiping

10.2.2 Broadcasting and Gossiping in Basic Networks

Table 10.2 summarizes the best known results for broadcasting and gossiping on hypercubes (H_d), cube-connected cycles (CCC_d), shuffle exchange graphs (SE_d) and de Bruijn graphs (DB_d). Some of these results will be discussed in more detail in what follows.

Broadcasting

A lower bound on broadcasting complexity is easy to derive.

Lemma 10.2.6 *If a graph G has n nodes, then $b(G) \geq \lceil \lg n \rceil$, and if it has diameter d, then $b(G) \geq d$.*

Proof: The number of informed nodes can at most double during one communication round. For the number t of necessary rounds we therefore get

$$2^t \geq n \Rightarrow t \geq \lceil \lg n \rceil .$$

The second claim of the lemma is obvious. □

Corollary 10.2.7 $b(H_d) = d$.

Proof: The inequality $b(H_d) \geq d$ follows from the previous lemma, and the inequality $b(H_d) \leq d$ from the analysis of the broadcasting algorithm in Example 10.1.13. □

Exercise 10.2.8 *Let G be a graph of degree d. Show that $b(G) \leq (d-1)diam(G)$. What kind of upper bounds does this inequality imply for broadcasting on the particular bounded-degree networks introduced in Section 10.1?*

Theorem 10.2.9 $b(SE_d) = 2d - 1$ *for* $d \geq 2$.

Proof: The lower bound follows from the fact that $2d-1$ is the diameter of SE_d. The analysis of the following algorithm shows that $2d-1$ is also an upper bound for broadcasting on SE_d. In this algorithm and its analysis the following notation is used: for any integer k and any string $w = a_k \ldots a_1 a_0 \in [2]^{k+1}$ let $w_1 = a_k$ – that is, w_1 is the first symbol of w – and $w^{(i)} = a_i a_{i-1} \ldots a_0$ for $k \geq i \geq -1$, where $w^{(-1)}$ is defined to be ε – that is, $w^{(i)}$ is the suffix of w of length $i+1$.

Algorithm 10.2.10 (Broadcasting from an arbitrary node $a_{d-1}\dots a_0$)

$w = a_{d-1}\dots a_0$ sends its message to $a_{d-1}\dots a_1\bar{a}_0$ {exchange round};
for $t \leftarrow d-1$ **downto** 1 **do**
  for all $\beta \in [2]^{d-1-t}$ **pardo**
    begin
    if $w^{(t)} \notin \{\beta_1\}^+$ **then** $w^{(t)}\beta$ sends its message to $w^{(t-1)}\beta a_t$ {shuffle round};
      $w^{(t-1)}\beta a_t$ sends its message to $w^{(t-1)}\beta\bar{a}_t$ {exchange round};
    end

The correctness of the algorithm follows from these two facts:

1. There is no conflict in any of the $2d-1$ rounds; that is, if a node is active in a round, then it is active in that round only via one edge. Indeed, there can be no conflict in the exchange rounds; in the cycle for $t = i$ each sender has the last bit a_i, and each receiver $\bar{a}_i$. Let there be a conflict in a shuffle round: that is, let there be a node that is both a sender and a receiver; that is, $w^{(t)}\beta = w^{(t-1)}\gamma a_t$ for some $\beta,\gamma \in [2]^+$. In such a case $a_t w^{(t-1)} = w^{(t-1)}\gamma_1 \Rightarrow a_t = a_{t-1} = \dots = a_0 = \gamma_1$, and therefore $w^{(t)} \in \{\gamma_1\}^+$. This contradicts our assumption that the shuffle operation is performed only if $w^{(t)} \notin \{\gamma_1\}^+$.

2. After $2r+1$ rounds, that is, after the initial round and r executions of the t-cycle, all nodes $w^{(d-r-2)}\beta, \beta \in [2]^{r+1}$ have learned $I(w)$. This can be proved by induction on $r = d-t-1$ as follows.

The assertion is clearly true after the execution of the first round. Therefore let us assume that this is true after $(r-1)$ executions of the loop for t, where $r \geq 1$; that is, all nodes $w^{(d-r-1)}\beta, \beta \in [2]^r$ have learned information $I(w)$. See now what happens after the next two rounds.

If $w^{(d-r-1)} \notin \{\beta_1\}^+$, $\beta \in [2]^r$, then all $w^{(d-r-1)}\beta$ have learned information $I(w)$ in the previous rounds, according to the induction hypothesis. In the following round $w^{(d-r-2)}\beta a_{d-r-1}$ also gets information $I(w)$.

If $w^{(d-r-1)} \in \{\beta_1\}^+$, $\beta \in [2]^r$, then $w^{(d-r-2)}\beta a_{d-r-1} = w^{(d-r-1)}\beta^{(r-2)}a_{d-r-1}$, and therefore such a node already knows information $I(w)$. In the next round $w^{(d-r-2)}\beta\bar{a}_{d-r-1}$ also gets this information, and so the induction step is proved. □

Previous results confirm that the broadcasting complexity for SE_d and also for H_d is equal to the diameter. This is not the case for de Bruijn graphs.

Theorem 10.2.11 $1.1374d \leq b(DB_d) \leq \frac{3}{2}(d+1)$ *for broadcasting on de Bruijn graphs.*

Proof: We now show the upper bound; the lower bound follows from Lemma 10.2.12. In the following algorithm any node $(a_{d-1}\dots a_0)$ sends information to nodes $(a_{d-2}\dots a_0 a_{d-1})$ and $(a_{d-2}\dots a_0\overline{a_{d-1}})$ in the following order: first to node $(a_{d-2}\dots a_0\alpha(a_{d-1}\dots a_0))$, then to node $(a_{d-2}\dots a_0\bar{\alpha}(a_{d-1}\dots a_0))$, where $\alpha(a_{d-1}\dots a_0) = (\sum_{i=0}^{d-1} a_i) \bmod 2$. Let $\bar{a} = (a_{d-1},\dots,a_0)$, $\bar{b} = (b_{d-1},\dots,b_0)$ be any two nodes. Consider the following two paths $P_i, i \in [2]$, of length $d+1$ from the node $\bar{a}$ to the node $\bar{b}$.

$$p_i : ((a_{d-1},\dots,a_0),(a_{d-2},\dots,a_0,i),(a_{d-3},\dots,a_0,i,b_{d-1}),(a_{d-4},\dots,a_0,i,b_{d-1},b_{d-2})$$
$$\dots(a_0,i,b_{d-1},\dots,b_2),(i,b_{d-1},\dots,b_1),(b_{d-1},\dots,b_1,b_0)).$$

These two paths are node-disjoint except for the first and last nodes. Let

$$v_{0,i} = (a_{d-i},\dots,a_0,0,b_{d-1},\dots,b_{d-i+2}) \quad \text{and} \quad v_{1,i} = (a_{d-i},\dots,a_0,1,b_{d-1},\dots,b_{d-i+2})$$

be the ith nodes of the paths p_0 and p_1, respectively. Since for any $i \in [d]$ the nodes $v_{0,i}$ and $v_{1,i}$ differ in one bit, we have $\alpha(v_{0,i}) \neq \alpha(v_{1,i})$. This means that the number of time steps needed to broadcast from the node $v_{0,i}$ to $v_{0,i+1}$ and from $v_{1,i}$ to $v_{1,i+1}$ is 1 in one of these two cases and 2 in the other. (One of the nodes $v_{0,i}$ and $v_{1,i}$ sends information to the next node of the path in the first round, the second in the second round.)

Let t_i denote the number of time steps to broadcast from $\bar{a}$ to $\bar{b}$ via the path p_i. Clearly

$$t_0 + t_1 = (d+1)(1+2) = 3(d+1).$$

These paths are node-disjoint, and therefore a message from $\bar{a}$ reaches $\bar{b}$ through one of these two paths in $\frac{3}{2}(d+1)$ rounds. □

Lemma 10.2.12 *If G is a graph of degree 4 with nodes, then $b(G) \geq 1.1374 \lg n$.*

Proof: Let v be an arbitrary node of G, and let $A(t)$ denote the maximum number of nodes that can be newly informed in the tth round if broadcasting starts in v. Since G has degree 4, once a node has received a piece of information, it can inform all its neighbours in the next three steps. It therefore holds that

$$A(0) = 0, A(1) = 1, A(2) = 2, A(3) = 4, A(4) = 8,$$
$$A(t) = A(t-1) + A(t-2) + A(t-3) \text{ for } t \geq 5.$$

The corresponding algebraic equation is $x^3 = x^2 + x + 1$, and its only real root is 1.8393. Hence, by the results of Section 1.2, $A(i) \approx 1.8393^i$.

For any broadcasting algorithm running in time t we therefore have

$$\sum_{i=0}^{t} A(i) \geq n,$$

and therefore

$$\sum_{i=0}^{t} A(i) \approx A(t) \approx 1.8393^t \geq n,$$

which implies $t \geq 1.1374 \lg n$. □

Exercise 10.2.13 *For a complete graph $\mathcal{K}_n$ with n nodes show that (a) $b(\mathcal{K}_n) \leq \lceil \lg n \rceil$; (b) $b(\mathcal{K}'_n) \geq \lceil \lg n \rceil$.*

Exercise 10.2.14 *Show that $b(G) \geq 1.4404 \lg n$ for each graph of degree 3 with $n > 4$ nodes.*

Exercise 10.2.15 *Denote $T_d^{(m)}$ a complete m-ary balanced tree of depth d. Let v be the root of $T_d^{(m)}$. Denote $b(v, T_d^{(m)})$ the achievable minimum, over all nodes v, of the number of rounds of a broadcasting algorithm for $T_d^{(m)}$. Show that $b(v, T_d^{(m)}) = md$.*

Using more sophisticated techniques, better lower bounds, shown in Table 10.2, can be derived for gossiping on de Bruijn graphs.

Exercise 10.2.16* *Show that* $b(CCC_d) = \lceil \frac{5d}{2} \rceil - 2$.

Exercise 10.2.17 *Find as good bounds as you can for* $b(A[n,2])$.

Gossiping

Gossiping is a much more complicated problem than broadcasting, especially in the telegraph mode.

Basic lower bounds for gossiping on a graph G with n nodes follow from Theorem 10.2.5 and Lemma 10.2.6:

$$g_1(G) \geq g_2(G) \geq b(G) \geq \lceil \lg n \rceil.$$

Graphs G such that $g_2(G) = \lceil \lg n \rceil$ are called **minimal gossip graphs**. The following lemma implies that hypercubes and any graphs for which a hypercube is a spanning graph have this property.

Lemma 10.2.18 $g_2(H_d) = d$ *for any hypercube* H_d.

Proof: By induction. The case $d = 1$ is trivially true. Let us assume that the lemma holds for some d.

The set

$$E_1 = \{((0,a_{d-1},\ldots,a_0),(1,a_{d-1},\ldots,a_0))\,|\,a_{d-1}\ldots a_0 \in [2]^d\}$$

can be seen as specifying the first round of a gossiping algorithm for the hypercube H_{d+1}. The cumulative message of H_{d+1} is the same after this round as the cumulative message in the two different subhypercubes of H_{d+1} of dimension d that can be obtained from H_{d+1} by removing edges from E_1. This means that after one round the gossiping problem for H_{d+1} is reduced to the gossiping problem for two hypercubes of dimension d. Their gossiping problem can be solved, by the induction hypothesis, in d rounds. □

Exercise 10.2.19 *Show that graphs of no bounded-degree interconnection network G can be minimal gossip graphs.*

Rings are an example of 'almost' minimal gossip graphs.

Theorem 10.2.20 $g_2(R_n) = \frac{n}{2}$ *if n is even, and* $g_2(R_n) = \lceil \frac{n}{2} \rceil + 1$ *if n is odd.*

Proof: We prove the theorem only for n even. The case n is odd is left as an exercise. Since the diameter of R_n is $\frac{n}{2}$, we get the lower bound $g_2(R_n) \geq \frac{n}{2}$ from Lemma 10.2.6. This lower bound can be reached by the following communication scheme: $E_1,\ldots,E_{n/2}$, where, for odd i, $E_i = \{(x_1,x_2),(x_3,x_4),\ldots,(x_{n-3},x_{n-2}),(x_{n-1},x_n)\}$, and, for even i, $E_i = \{(x_2,x_3),(x_4,x_5),\ldots,(x_{n-2},x_{n-1}),(x_n,x_1)\}$. Clearly, after k steps each node knows exactly $2k$ pieces of information. □

Exercise 10.2.21 *Show for a complete graph* K_n *that* $g_2(K_n) = \lceil \lg n \rceil$ *if n is even and* $g_2(K_n) = \lceil \lg n \rceil + 1$ *if n is odd.*

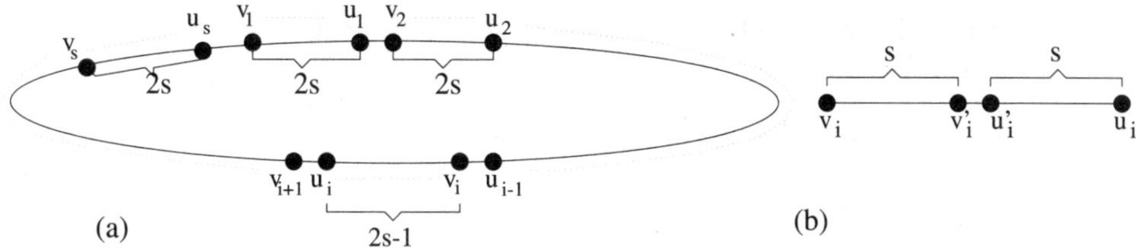

Figure 10.10 Distribution of s nodes in the ring

The case of the telegraph mode is more complicated, even for such simple networks as rings.

Theorem 10.2.22 $g_1(R_n) = \frac{n}{2} + \lceil\sqrt{2n}\rceil - 1$ *for even* $n > 3$.

Proof: We show here only the upper bound $g_1(R_n) \leq \frac{n}{2} + \lceil\sqrt{2n}\rceil - 1$ and only for the case $n = 2s^2$ and s is even. This will be enough to present the basic idea, which can then be used to prove the upper bound for all even n.

Let us divide the ring of $n = 2s^2$ nodes into s parts each with $2s$ nodes (see Figure 10.10a) with the node v_i starting and the node u_i ending the i-th part. In addition, in the ith part let u_i' be the node at distance $s-1$ from u_i, and v_i' be the node distance $s-1$ from v_i (see Figure 10.10b).

Consider now the following gossiping algorithm, consisting of two phases.

1. Each node v_i is the beginning of a communication path of length $\frac{n}{2}$ going through the node u_i. Along these paths information is accumulated in one direction. Simultaneously, each node u_i initializes a communication path of length $\frac{n}{2} - 1$ in the opposite direction, and information is accumulated in the same direction. Paths from v_i and u_{i-1} (v_1 and u_s) meet in the node $v_{((i+s/2) \bmod s+1)}$. Since there are s such paths in both directions, there may be $s-1$ 'collisions' in a node. In other words, it can happen $s-1$ times that two messages try to get through a node, one from the right and one from the left. Two rounds are needed to handle each collision. The overall number of rounds needed to perform communications along all these paths is therefore

$$\frac{n}{2} + s - 1.$$

Observe that at the end of the first phase all nodes v_i know the whole cumulative message. However, this is not true of all other nodes. The aim of the next phase is to send this cumulative message to all other nodes.

2. For each $i \in \{1, \ldots, s\}$,

- v_i sends the cumulative message to u_{i-1} (and v_1 to u_s);
- v_i sends the cumulative message to v_i' and u_i sends the cumulative message to u_i', and to all nodes on these paths.

Since the second phase needs s rounds, the overall number of rounds for this gossiping algorithm is exactly as the theorem claims. □

The above idea as to how to do gossiping on rings in two phases will now be applied to develop a gossiping scheme for the wrapped butterfly.

We show only the upper bound here. First observe that for any fixed $\alpha \in [2]^d$, all nodes of WB_d of the form $(i, \alpha), i \in [d]$ form a ring. Denote this ring by R_α. Communications along these rings play the key role in the following gossiping algorithm for WB_d.

1. Use, in all rings R_α, the first phase of the optimal algorithm for gossiping on rings to distribute the cumulative message of R_α into $s = \lfloor\sqrt{\lceil d/2\rceil}\rfloor$ 'regularly distributed' nodes $\{(v_i,\alpha)\,|\,1\leq i\leq s\}$.

2. Perform, for all $i \in \{v_j\,|\,1\leq j\leq s\}$, in parallel, the following algorithm (which distributes already accumulated messages along the butterfly edges):

for $j \leftarrow 0$ **to** $d-1$ **do**
  for $\alpha \in [2]^d$ **pardo**
    begin
      $((i+j) \bmod d, \alpha)$ sends message to $((i+j+1) \bmod d, \alpha^{((i+j) \bmod d)})$;
      $((i+j) \bmod d, \alpha)$ sends message to $((i+j+1) \bmod d, \alpha)$
    end

This means that equally distributed nodes $v_i, 0\leq i\leq l$, of all rings R_α received the cumulative message of the whole butterfly.

3. As the last step, phase 2 of the optimal gossiping algorithm for rings is used to distribute the cumulative message to all points of all rings.

The analysis of the above algorithm shows that

$$g_1(WB_d) \leq g_1(R_d) + 2d = \frac{5d}{2} + \lceil\sqrt{2d}\rceil$$

for d even, and a similar bound can be obtained for d odd.

The methods and results of this section have demonstrated that it is far from easy to design optimal algorithms even for very basic information dissemination problems and very simple networks.

Once a new type of network is suggested, those involved with broadcasting and gossiping problems are among the first to consider. Because of their fundamental importance for the design of algorithms for networks, these problems are good test sites for observing the communication qualities of networks.

Exercise 10.2.23 *Design a gossiping algorithm for the hypercube H_d for the telegraph mode with number of rounds at most 2d.*

Exercise 10.2.24 *Design, as best as you can, a gossiping algorithm in the telegraph mode for the complete graph. (It can be shown that $g_1(K_n) \leq k+1$ if n is even and k is such that $F_k \geq n/2$, where F_k is the k-th Fibonacci number. Can you beat this result?)*

Exercise 10.2.25* *Design a gossiping algorithm in the telegraph mode for the cube-connected cycles.*

10.3 Embeddings

Parallelism brings a new dimension to the problem of simulation of one computer on another. Since the existence of (very) different networks of processors is inherent in parallel computing, the task of developing efficient simulations of one network on another is the key problem for portability in parallel computing and for the efficient coexistence of different parallel architectures. In addition, the simple fact that we have more processors increases the complexity of simulation problems.

The ideal case for a simulation of networks with an interconnection graph G_1 by networks with an interconnection graph G_2 is when G_1 is a subgraph of G_2. A simulation can then be achieved with no time overhead. Less easy to deal with, but still quite good, is the case in which there is a small k

such that nodes of G_1 can be mapped by an injective mapping into nodes of G_2 in such a way that any two neighbouring nodes of G_1 are mapped into nodes of G_2 connected by a path of length at most k.

With respect to the portability of algorithms for multiprocessor networks, embedding methods can be viewed as high level descriptions of efficient methods of simulating algorithms for one type of network computer on a different type of network computer. As a consequence, a network in which others can be embedded easily and well is preferable to those without such properties.

10.3.1 Basic Concepts and Results

The basic idea of embedding is very general, simple and natural, as are the main ways of measuring the quality of embedding.

Definition 10.3.1 *Let $G = \langle V_1, E_1\rangle$ and $H = \langle V_2, E_2\rangle$ be connected graphs. An* **embedding of the 'guest graph'** *G into the* **'host graph'** *H is an injective mapping $f : V_1 \rightarrow V_2$.*

The quality of an embedding f is generally expressed using the **dilation** D_f and the **expansion** E_f defined by

$$D_f = \max_{(x,y)\in E_1} d_H(f(x),f(y)), \qquad E_f = \frac{|V_2|}{|V_1|}.$$

In other words the dilation of an embedding is the maximum distance of the images in the host graph of the adjacent nodes of the guest graph. The expansion of an embedding is the ratio of the number of nodes in the host graph to the number of nodes in the guest graph.

We shall often discuss the problem of embedding graphs from a family $\mathcal{G}_1$ of graphs into those from another graph family $\mathcal{G}_2$. In such a case a graph $G' \in \mathcal{G}_2$ will be called **optimal** for a graph $G \in \mathcal{G}_1$ if $|G| \leq |G'|$ and there is no other graph $G'' \in \mathcal{G}_2$ such that $|G| \leq |G''| < |G'|$.

A natural way to extend the above concept of embedding is to consider a mapping of edges of G into paths between the corresponding nodes of H. In such a case (embedding) **congestion** – the maximum, over all edges e of H, of the number of edges of G that are mapped into a path in H that includes e – is another important measure of embedding.

The ideal case is when all these factors are equal to 1. Observe that a graph G is embedded into a graph H with dilation factor 1 if and only if G is isomorphic with a subgraph of H.

Example 10.3.2 *Figure 10.11a shows an embedding of a ring with 16 nodes into a hypercube of 16 nodes with dilation and expansion 1. Figure 10.11b shows an embedding of a ring of 10 nodes into a hypercube of 16 nodes with dilation 1 and expansion 1.6.*

Embedding problems are inherently hard computationally even in very restricted cases. For example, the following problems are **NP**-complete:

1. Given a binary tree T, does there exist an embedding of T of dilation 1 into its optimal hypercube?

2. Given a graph (or even only a tree of depth 3) G and an integer k, does there exist an embedding of G into a complete binary tree with dilation k?

However, several important cases are easy to deal with.

Theorem 10.3.3 *The following embeddings can be achieved with dilation 1:*

1. *The cube-connected cycles CCC_d into the wrapped butterfly WB_d.*

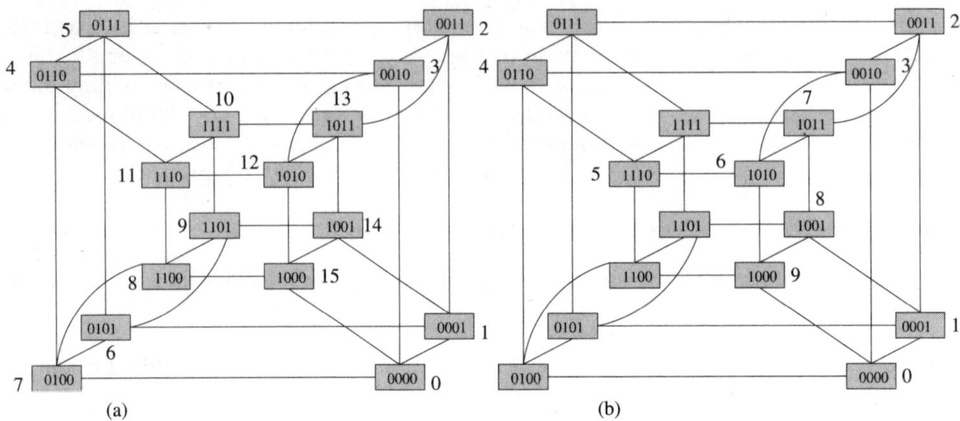

Figure 10.11 Embedding of rings into hypercube

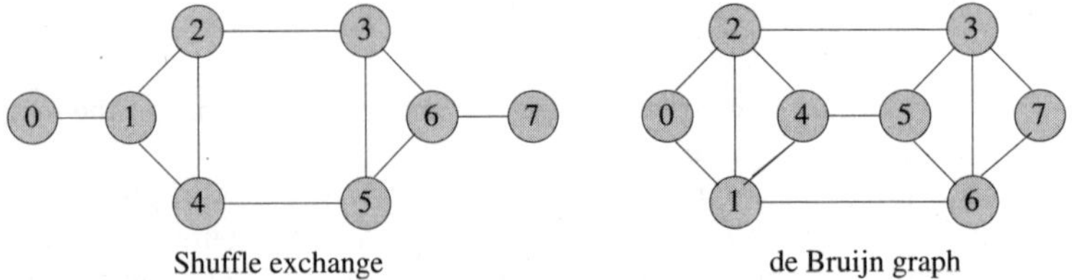

Figure 10.12 Embedding of USE_3 into UDB_3 with dilation 1

2. *The shuffle exchange graph USE_d into the de Bruijn graph UDB_d.*
3. *The complete binary tree T_d of depth d into the de Bruijn graph UDB_d.*

Proof: For a word $w \in [2]^*$ let

$$k(w) = \begin{cases} 1 & \text{if } w \text{ contains an odd number of 1s;} \\ 0 & \text{otherwise.} \end{cases}$$

1. An embedding of CCC_d in WB_d of dilation 1 is given by the mapping

$$e((i,w)) = ((i+k(w)) \bmod d, w^R).$$

   It follows directly from the definition of CCC_d and WB_d that the mapping e is a bijection, and maps any neighbouring nodes into neighbouring nodes.

2. The mapping

$$e(w) = PS^{-k(w)}(w)$$

   is a bijection, and maps neighbouring nodes of USE_d into neighbouring nodes of UDB_d for each d. The case $d = 3$ is illustrated in Figure 10.12. Proof of the general case is left as an exercise.

3. The existence of a dilation 1 embedding of a complete binary tree T_d into the de Bruijn graph UDB_d follows from the fact that in UDB_d each node $i < 2^{d-1}$ is connected by an edge with the nodes labelled by $2i+1$ and $2i$ (see Figure 10.13). □

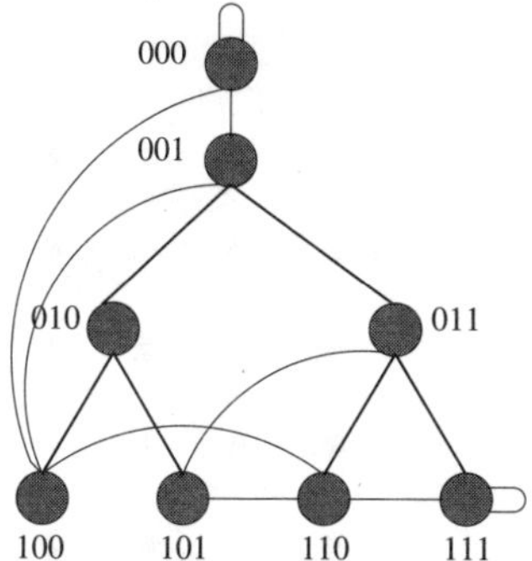

Figure 10.13 Embedding of trees in de Bruijn graphs

Relations between butterflies, cube-connected cycles, de Brujin and shuffle exchange graphs are so close that with respect to ascend/descend algorithms these networks are practically of the same quality as regards programming.

Exercise 10.3.4 *Show that ascend/descend algorithms for hypercubes can be implemented with only constant time overhead on butterflies, cube-connected cycles, perfect shuffle networks and de Bruijn networks.*

Of importance also are so-called 'many-to-one embeddings'; that is, when several nodes of a guest graph G are mapped into one node of the host graph H. This is of interest especially if G has more nodes than H. The additional key factor of such embeddings is the **load factor**, the maximum number of nodes of G mapped into one node of H; also **load balancing**, how equally nodes of G are distributed into nodes of H, the difference between the maximum and minimum number of nodes mapped into one node of H.

Example 10.3.5 (Polymorphic arrays) *One of the basic problems of many-to-one embeddings is that of embeddings of large arrays into small array-like graphs. The folding method illustrated in Figure 10.14a is simple. However, its disadvantages are unbalanced and unregular embeddings.*

There exists a universal class of simple graphs of distinct size, the **polymorphic arrays**, *that can be used to map into, regularly and with a good load balancing, rectangular arrays of any size. Polymorphic arrays P_n have $F_n \times L_n$ nodes, where F_n and L_n are Fibonacci and Lucas numbers and form diagonally connected toroids in which each node (i,j), $0 \leq i < F_n$, $0 \leq j < L_n$ has the following four incidental edges.*

$$\begin{array}{rcl} up & \Longrightarrow & ((i+1) \bmod F_n, (j+1) \bmod L_n) \\ down & \Longrightarrow & ((i-1) \bmod F_n, (j-1) \bmod L_n) \\ right & \Longrightarrow & ((i-1) \bmod F_n, (j+1) \bmod L_n) \\ left & \Longrightarrow & ((i+1) \bmod F_n, (j-1) \bmod L_n) \end{array}$$

The polymorphic array P_5 is shown in Figures 10.14b and c by depicting its 'up' and 'right' edges.

It has been shown that any rectangular two-dimensional array A can be embedded many-to-one into any polymorphic array P_n, where n is not divisible by 3, in such a way that the following properties hold:

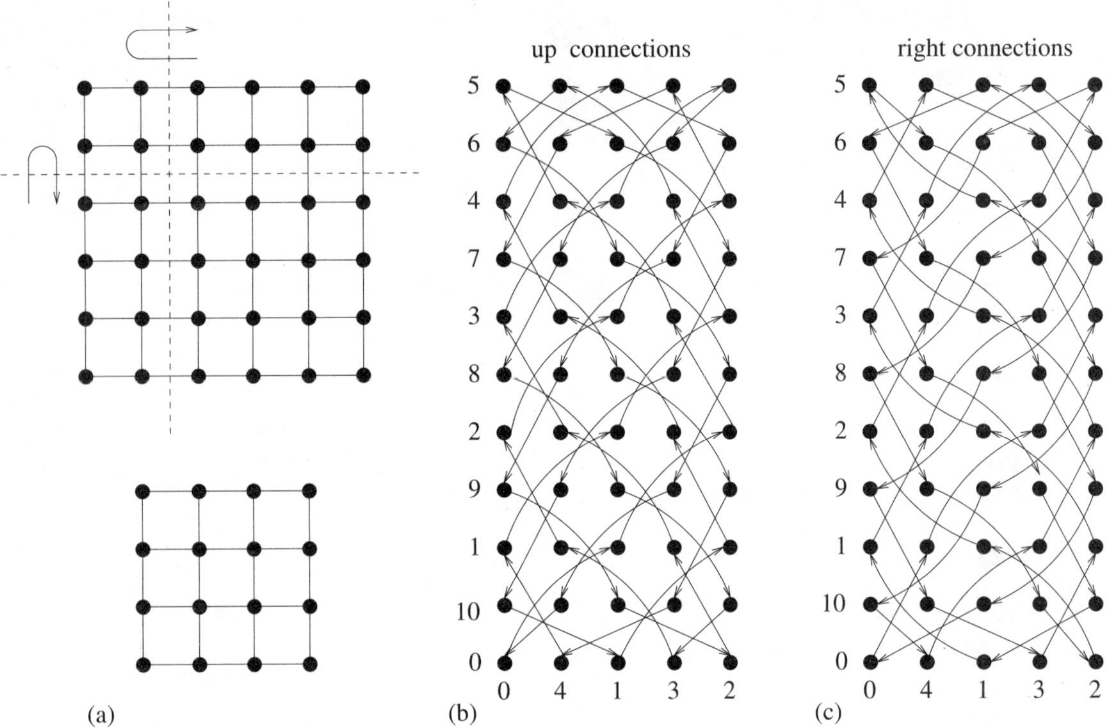

Figure 10.14 Polymorphic arrays

1. *It is sufficient to choose, arbitrarily, a mapping of any node of A into P_n; the mapping of all other nodes is uniquely determined.*

2. *If A has less than $\frac{m}{\sqrt{5}}$ nodes, $m = F_n \times L_n$, then different nodes of A are mapped into different nodes of P_n.*

3. *No matter how large A and how small P_n are, in the natural embedding of A into P_n, described in point (1), the numbers of nodes of A mapped into different nodes of P_n can differ at most by an additive factor of $\mathcal{O}(\lg m), m = F_n \times L_n$.*

10.3.2 Hypercube Embeddings

Many basic networks have elegant embeddings of dilation 1 or so into hypercubes. Hypercubes can also be embedded elegantly and efficiently into many networks. This makes the hypercube an attractive interconnection network.

Embeddings of rings and arrays

The Gray code representation of natural numbers is the basis of several embeddings of rings and arrays into hypercubes.

i	$bin_6(i)$	$G_6(i)$	i	$bin_6(i)$	$G_6(i)$	i	$bin_6(i)$	$G_6(i)$	i	$bin_6(i)$	$G_6(i)$
0	00000	000000	8	01000	001100	16	10000	011000	24	11000	010100
1	00001	000001	9	01001	001101	17	10001	011001	25	11001	010101
2	00010	000011	10	01010	001111	18	10010	011011	26	11010	010111
3	00011	000010	11	01011	001110	19	10011	011010	27	11011	010110
4	00100	000110	12	01100	001010	20	10100	011110	28	11100	010010
5	00101	000111	13	01101	001011	21	10101	011111	29	11101	010011
6	00110	000101	14	01110	001001	22	10110	011101	30	11110	010010
7	00111	000100	15	01111	001000	23	10111	011100	31	11111	010000

Table 10.3 Binary and Gray codes of integers

Let $G_n = \langle G_n(0), \ldots, G_n(2^n-1)\rangle$ denote the sequence of all n-bit binary words in the so-called Gray code ordering of binary strings, defined inductively as follows:

$$G_1 = \langle 0,1\rangle = \langle G_1(0), G_1(1)\rangle,$$

and for $n > 1$,

$$G_{n+1} = \langle 0G_n(0), \ldots, 0G_n(2^n-1), 1G_n(2^n-1), \ldots, 1G_n(0)\rangle.$$

$G_n(i)$ can be viewed as the Gray code representation of the integer i with n bits. Table 10.3 shows the binary and Gray code representations in G_6 of the first 32 integers.

The following properties of the Gray code representation of integers are straightforward to verify:

1. $G_n(i)$ and $G_n(i+1)$, $0 \leq i < 2^n - 1$, differ in exactly one bit.

2. $G_n(i)$ and $G_n(2^n - i - 1)$, $0 \leq i \leq 2^n - 1$, differ in exactly one bit.

3. If $bin_{n+1}^{-1}(i) = i_n \ldots i_0$, $i_n = 0$, $i_j \in [2]$, and $G_n(i) = g_{n-1} \ldots g_0$, then for $0 \leq j < n$

$$g_j = i_j \oplus i_{j+1} \text{ and } i_j = g_{j+1} \oplus \cdots \oplus g_{n-1}.$$

Embedding of linear arrays: A linear array $P_0, \ldots, P_{k-1}$ of $k \leq 2^d$ nodes can be embedded into the hypercube H_d by mapping the ith node of the array into $G_d(i)$. It follows from the first property of Gray codes that such an embedding has dilation 1.

Embedding of rings: A ring $P_0, \ldots, P_{k-1}$ of k nodes, $k \leq 2^d$, can be embedded by mapping the ith node of the ring into the ith node of the sequence $G_d(0 : \lceil \frac{k}{2} \rceil - 1)$, $G_d(2^d - \lfloor \frac{k}{2} \rfloor : 2^d - 1)$, where

$$G_d(i:j) = G_d(i), \ldots, G_d(j).$$

It follows from the second property of Gray codes that this embedding has dilation 1 if k is even and dilation 2 if k is odd. Observe that Figure 10.11a, b shows such embeddings for $d = 4$, $k = 16$ and $k = 10$.

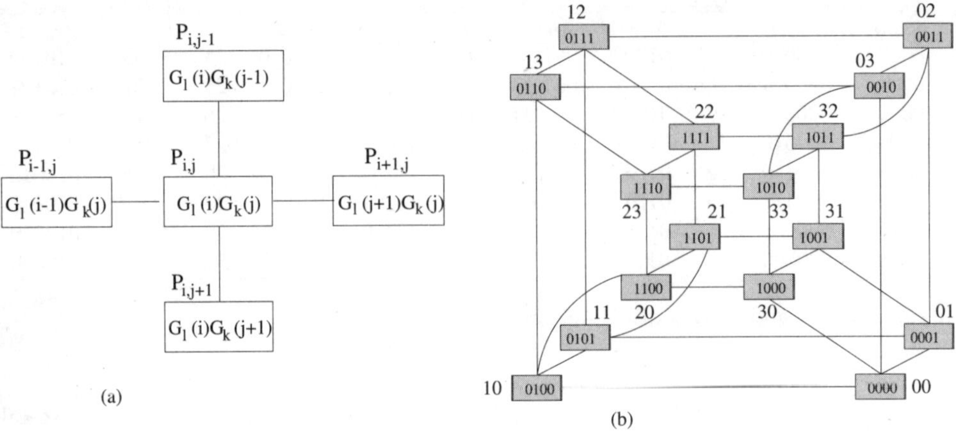

Figure 10.15 Embedding of arrays into hypercubes

Exercise 10.3.6 *Embed with dilation* 1 *(a) a* 20*-node ring in the hypercube* H_5*; (b) a* 40*-node ring into the hypercube* H_6.

Exercise 10.3.7 *Show, for example by induction, that the following graphs are Hamiltonian: (a) the wrapped butterfly; (b) the cube-connected cycles.*

Exercise 10.3.8* *Under what conditions can an n-node ring be embedded with dilation* 1 *into (a) a* $p \times q$ *array; (b) a* $p \times q$ *toroid?*

Embedding of (more-dimensional) arrays: There are special cases of arrays for which an embedding with dilation 1 exists and can easily be designed. A $2^l \times 2^k$ array can be embedded into the H_{l+k} hypercube by mapping any array node (i,j), $0 \leq i < 2^l$, $0 \leq j < 2^k$, into the hypercube node with the identifier $G_i(l)G_j(k)$. Figure 10.15a shows how neighbouring nodes of the array are mapped into neighbouring nodes of the hypercube, Figure 10.15b shows a mapping of a 4×4 array into a H_4 hypercube.

The general case is slightly more involved.

Theorem 10.3.9 *A* $n_1 \times n_2 \times \ldots \times n_k$ *array can be embedded into its optimal hypercube with dilation* 1 *if and only if*

$$\sum_{i=1}^{k} \lceil \lg n_i \rceil = \left\lceil \lg \prod_{i=1}^{k} n_i \right\rceil .$$

Example 10.3.10 *A* $3 \times 5 \times 8$ *array is not a subgraph of its optimal hypercube because*

$$\lceil \lg 3 \rceil + \lceil \lg 5 \rceil + \lceil \lg 8 \rceil \neq \lceil \lg 120 \rceil,$$

but $3 \times 6 \times 8$ *and* $4 \times 7 \times 8$ *arrays are subgraphs of their optimal hypercubes because*

$$\lceil \lg 3 \rceil + \lceil \lg 6 \rceil + \lceil \lg 8 \rceil = \lceil \lg 144 \rceil, \qquad \lceil \lg 244 \rceil = \lceil \lg 4 \rceil + \lceil \lg 7 \rceil + \lceil 8 \rceil .$$

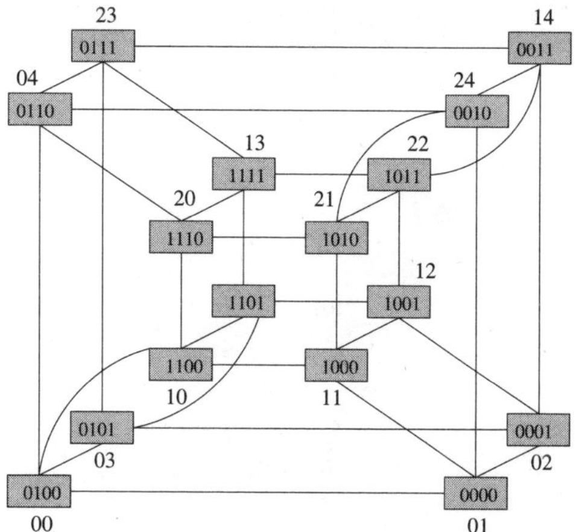

Figure 10.16 Embedding of 3×5 array in H_4

Two-dimensional arrays can in any case be embedded quite well in their optimal hypercubes. Indeed, the following theorem holds.

Theorem 10.3.11 *Each two-dimensional array can be embedded into its optimal hypercube with dilation 2. Each r-dimensional array can be embedded into its optimal hypercube with dilation $\mathcal{O}(r)$.*

Figure 10.16 shows an embedding of the 3×5 array into H_4 with dilation 2.

Exercise 10.3.12 *Embed with dilation 1: (a) an $8 \times 8 \times 8$ array into the hypercube H_9; (b) a $2 \times 3 \times 4$ array in H_5.*

Embedding of trees

Trees are among the main data structures. It is therefore important to know how they can be embedded into various networks.

Balanced binary trees can be embedded into their optimal hypercubes rather well, even though the ideal case is not achievable.

Theorem 10.3.13 *There is no embedding of dilation 1 of the complete binary tree T_d of depth d into its optimal hypercube.*

Proof: Since T_d has $2^{d+1} - 1$ nodes, H_{d+1} is its optimal hypercube. Let us assume that an embedding of T_d into H_{d+1} with dilation 1 exists; that is, T_d is a subgraph of H_{d+1}. For nodes v of H_{d+1} let us define $\phi(v) = 0$ if $bin_{d+1}^{-1}(v)$ has an even number of 1s and $\phi(v) = 1$ otherwise. Clearly, exactly half the nodes of the hypercube H_{d+1} have their ϕ-value equal to 0. In addition, if T_d is a subgraph of H_{d+1}, all nodes at the same level of T_d must have the same ϕ-value, which is different from the values of nodes at neighbouring levels. However, this implies that more than half the nodes of H_{d+1} have their ϕ-value the same as the leaves of T_d – a contradiction. □

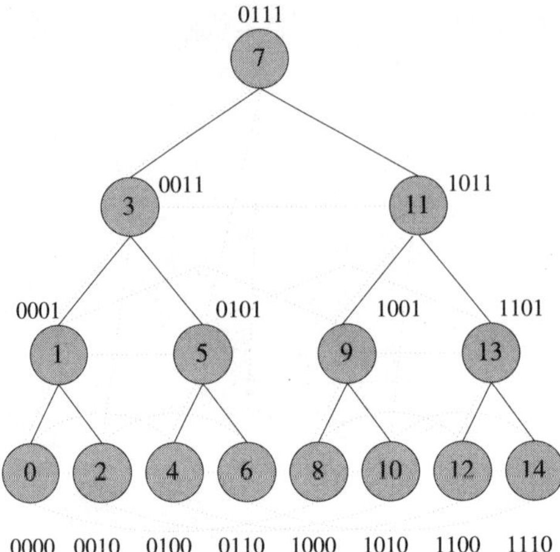

Figure 10.17 An embedding of a complete binary tree into its optimal hypercube using the in-order labelling of nodes; hypercube connections are shown by dotted lines

Theorem 10.3.14 *The complete binary tree T_d can be embedded into its optimal hypercube with dilation* 2 *by labelling its nodes with an in-order labelling.*

Proof: The case $d = 0$ is clearly true. Assume that the theorem holds for some $d \geq 0$, and label nodes of T_{d+1} using the in-order labelling. (See Figure 10.17 for the case $d = 3$.) Such a labelling assigns to nodes of the left subtree of the root of T_{d+1} labels that are obtained from those assigned by the in-order labelling applied to this subtree only by appending 0 in front. The root of T_{d+1} is assigned the label 011...1. Similarly, the in-order labelling of T_{d+1} assigns to nodes of the right subtree of the root labels obtained from those assigned by the in-order labelling of this right subtree only with an additional 1 in front. The root of the left subtree has therefore assigned as label 001...1, and the root of the right subtree has 101...1. The root of T_{d+1} and its children are therefore assigned labels that represent hypercube nodes of distance 1 and 2. According to the induction assumption, nodes of both subtrees are mapped into their optimal subhypercubes with dilation 2. □

An embedding of dilation 1 of a complete binary tree into a hypercube exists if the hypercube is next to the optimal one.

Theorem 10.3.15 *The complete binary tree T_d can be embedded into the hypercube H_{d+2} with dilation* 1.

Proof: It will actually be easier to prove a stronger claim: namely, that each **generalized tree** GT_d is a subgraph of the hypercube H_{d+2}, with $GT_d = \langle V_d, E_d \rangle$ defined as follows:

$$V_d = V'_d \cup V''_d \quad \text{and} \quad E_d = E'_d \cup E''_d,$$

where $\langle V'_d, E'_d \rangle$ is the complete binary tree T_d with $2^{d+1} - 1$ nodes and

$$V''_d = \{s_1, \ldots, s_{d+3}\}, E''_d = \{(s_i, s_{i+1}) | 1 \leq i < d+3\} \cup \{(r, s_1), (s_{d+3}, s)\},$$

where r is the root and s is the right-most leaf of the tree $\langle V'_d, E'_d \rangle$ (see Figure 10.18).

We now show by induction that generalized trees can be embedded into their optimal hypercubes with dilation 1. From this, the theorem follows.

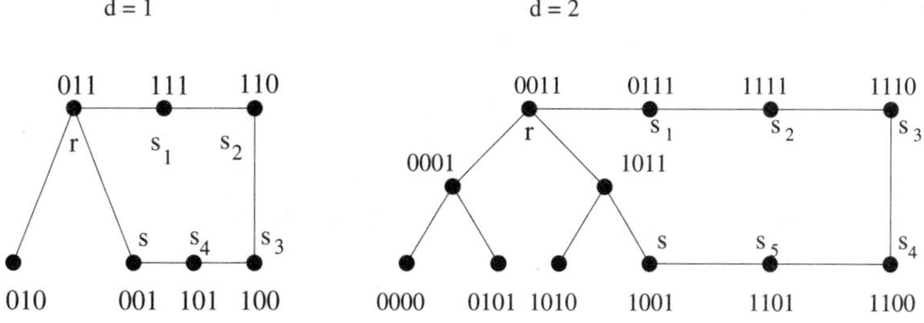

Figure 10.18 Generalized trees and their embeddings

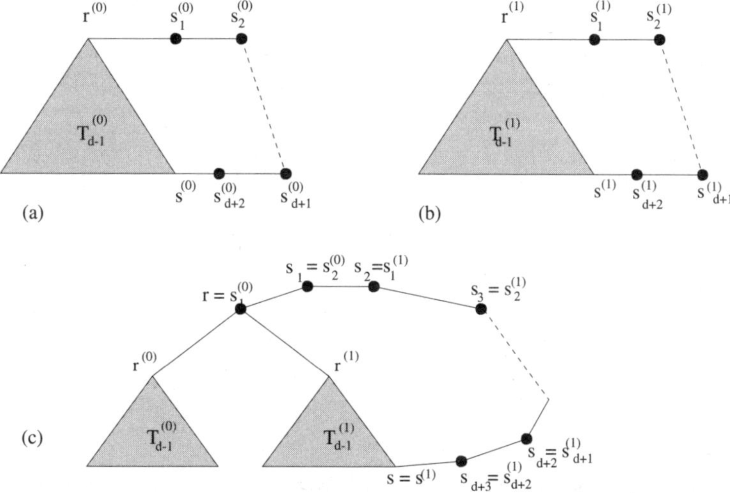

Figure 10.19 Embedding of generalized trees

The cases $d = 1$ and $d = 2$ are clearly true (see Figure 10.18). Let us now assume that the theorem holds for $d \geq 3$. Consider the hypercube H_{d+2} as being composed of two hypercubes H_{d+1}, the nodes of which are distinguished by the left-most bit; in the following (see Figure 10.19) they will be distinguished by the upper index (0) or (1).

According to the induction assumption, we can embed GT_{d-1} in H_{d+1} with dilation 1. Therefore let us embed GT_{d-1} with dilation 1 into both of these subhypercubes. It is clear that we can also do these embeddings in such a way that the node $r^{(1)}$ is a neighbour of $s_1^{(0)}$ and $s_1^{(1)}$ is a neighbour of $s_2^{(0)}$ (see Figure 10.19a, b). This is always possible, because hypercubes are edge-symmetric graphs. As a result we get an embedding of dilation 1, shown in Figure 10.19c. This means that by adding edges $(s_1^{(0)}, r^{(1)}), (s_2^{(0)}, s_1^{(1)})$ and removing nodes $s_3^{(0)}, \ldots, s_d^{(0)}$ with the corresponding edges, we get the desired embedding. □

As might be expected, embedding of arbitrary binary trees into hypercubes is a more difficult problem. It is not possible to achieve the 'optimal case' – dilation 1 and optimal expansion at the same time. The best that can be done is characterized by the following theorem.

Theorem 10.3.16 *(1) Every binary tree can be embedded into its optimal hypercube with dilation* 5.

(2) Every binary tree with n nodes can be embedded with dilation 1 *into a hypercube with* $\mathcal{O}(n \lg n)$ *nodes.*

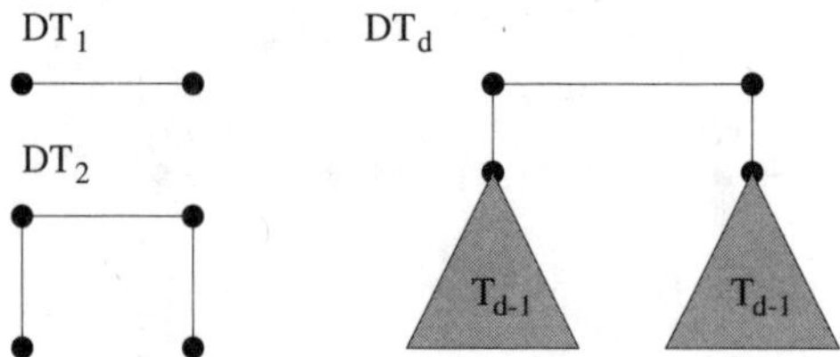

Figure 10.20 Doubly rooted binary tree

guest graph	host	dilation
k-dim. torus	k-dim. array	2
2-dim. array	hypercube	2
k-dim. array	hypercube	$2k-1$
complete binary tree	hypercube	2
compl. binary tree of depth $d+\lfloor\lg d\rfloor-1$	B_{d+3}	6
compl. bin. tree of depth d	2-dim. array	$(1+\varepsilon)\left\lceil\frac{2^{\lfloor d/2\rfloor}-1}{\lfloor d/2\rfloor}\right\rceil$
binary tree	hypercube	5
binary tree	X-tree	11
CCC_d	B_d	1
DB_d	hypercube	$2\lceil\frac{d}{5}\rceil$

Table 10.4 Embeddings

Embedding of other networks in hypercubes: What about the other networks of interest? How well can they be embedded into hypercubes?

The case of cube-connected cycles is not difficult. They can be embedded into their optimal hypercubes with dilation 2 (see Exercise 39). However, the situation is different for shuffle exchange and de Bruijn graphs. It is not yet clear whether there is a constant c such that each de Bruijn graph or shuffle exchange can be embedded into its optimal hypercube with dilation c.

Exercise 10.3.17 *A* **doubly rooted** *binary tree DT_d has 2^{d+1} nodes and is inductively defined in Figure 10.20, where T_{d-1} is a complete binary tree of depth $d-1$. Show that DT_d can be embedded into its optimal hypercube with dilation 1. (This is another way of showing that each complete binary tree can be embedded into its optimal hypercube with dilation 2.)*

Exercise 10.3.18 *Show, for the example using the previous exercise, that the mesh of trees MT_d can be embedded into its optimal hypercube H_{2d^2} with (a) dilation 2; (b)* dilation 1.*

Table 10.4 summarizes some of the best known results on embeddings in optimal host graphs. (An X-tree XT_d of depth d is obtained from the binary tree T_d by adding edges to connect all neighbouring nodes of the same level; that is, the edges of the form $(w01^k, w10^k)$, where w is an arbitrary internal node of $T_d, 0\leq k\leq d-|w|$.)

10.4 Routing

Broadcasting, accumulation and gossiping can be seen as 'one-to-all', 'all-to-one' and 'all-to-all' information dissemination problems, respectively. At the end of the dissemination, one message is delivered, either to all nodes or to a particular node. Very different, but also very basic types of communication problems, the so-called routing problems, are considered in this section. They can be seen as one-to-one communication problems. Some (source) processors send messages, each to a uniquely determined (target) processor.

There is a variety of routing problems. The most basic is the **one-packet routing problem**: how, through which path, to send a so-called packet (i,x,j) with a message x from a processor (node) P_i to a processor (node) P_j. It is naturally best to send the packet along the shortest path between P_i and P_j. All the networks considered in this chapter have the important property that one-packet routing along the shortest path can be performed by a simple **greedy routing algorithm** whereby each processor can easily decide, depending on the target, which way to send a packet it has received or wants to send.

For example, to send a packet from a node $u \in [2]^d$ to a node $v \in [2]^d$ in the hypercube H_d, the following algorithm can be used.

The **left-to-right routing on hypercubes**. The packet is first sent from u to the neighbour w of u, obtained from u by flipping in u the left-most bit different from the corresponding bit in v. Then, recursively, the same algorithm is used to send the packet from w to v.

Example 10.4.1 *In the hypercube H_6 the greedy routing takes the packet from the node $u = 010101$ to the node $v = 110011$ through the following sequence of nodes:*

$$u = \underline{0}10101 \rightarrow 110\underline{1}01 \rightarrow 1100\underline{0}1 \rightarrow 110011 = v,$$

where the underlined bits are those that determine the edge to go through in the given routing step.

In the shuffle exchange network SE_d, in order to send a packet from a processor $P_u, u = u_{d-1}\dots u_0$, to $P_v, v = v_{d-1}\dots v_0$, bits of u are rotated (which corresponds to sending a packet through a shuffle edge). After each shuffle edge routing, if necessary, the last bit is changed (which corresponds to sending a packet through an exchange edge). This can be illustrated as follows:

$$\begin{aligned}
u = {} & u_{d-1}u_{d-2}\dots u_0 \\
& \overset{PS}{\widehat{\rightarrow}}\; u_{d-2}u_{d-3}\dots u_0u_{d-1} \\
& \overset{EX?}{\widehat{\rightarrow}}\; u_{d-2}u_{d-3}\dots u_0v_{d-1} \\
& \quad \overset{PS}{\widehat{\rightarrow}}\; u_{d-3}u_{d-4}\dots u_0v_{d-1}u_{d-2} \\
& \quad \overset{EX?}{\widehat{\rightarrow}}\; u_{d-3}u_{d-4}\dots u_0v_{d-1}v_{d-2} \\
& \qquad \rightarrow \\
& \qquad \rightarrow \\
& \qquad\quad \vdots \quad \vdots \quad \vdots \\
& \qquad\qquad \rightarrow u_0v_{d-1}\dots v_1 \\
& \qquad\qquad \overset{PS}{\widehat{\rightarrow}}\; v_{d-1}\dots v_1u_0 \\
& \qquad\qquad \overset{EX?}{\widehat{\rightarrow}}\; v_{d-1}\dots v_1v_0 = v
\end{aligned}$$

Exercise 10.4.2 *Describe a greedy one-packet routing for (a) butterfly networks; (b) de Bruijn graphs; (c) mesh of trees; (d) toroids; (e) star graphs; (f) Kautz graphs.*

More difficult, but also very basic, is **the permutation routing problem**: how to design a special (permutation) network or routing protocol for a given network of processors such that all processors (senders) can simultaneously send messages to other processors (receivers) for the case in which there is a one-to-one correspondence between senders and receivers (given by a to-be-routed permutation π).

A message x from a processor P_i to a processor P_j is usually sent as a 'packet' (i,x,j). The last component of such a packet is used, by a routing protocol, to route the packet on its way from the processor P_i to the processor P_j. The first component is used when there is 'a need' for a response.

The main new problem is that of (routing) **congestion**. It may happen that several packets try to pass through a particular processor or edge. To handle such situations, processors (and edges) have buffers; naturally it is required that only small-size buffers be used for any routing. The buffer size of a network, with respect to a routing protocol, is the maximum size of the buffers needed by particular processors or edges.

A routing protocol is an algorithm which each processor executes in order to perform a routing. In one routing step each processor P performs the following operations: chooses a packet $(i,x,\pi(i))$ from its buffer, chooses a neighbourhood node P' (according to $\pi(i)$) and tries to send the packet to P', where the packet is stored in the buffer if it is not yet full. If the buffer of P' is full, the packet remains in the buffer of P.

Routing is **on-line** (**without preprocessing**) if the routing protocol does not depend on the permutation to be routed; otherwise it is **off-line** (**with preprocessing**).

The **permutation routing problem** for a graph G, and a permutation Π, is the problem of designing a permutation routing protocol for networks with G as the underlying graph such that the routing, according to Π, is done as efficiently as possible. We can therefore talk about the computational complexity of the permutation routing for a graph G and also about upper and lower bounds for this complexity.

10.4.1 Permutation Networks

A permutation network connects n source nodes P_i, $1 \leq i \leq n$, for example, processors, and n target nodes M_i, $1 \leq i \leq n$, for example, memory modules (see Figure 10.21a). Their elements are binary switches (see Figure 10.21b) that can be in one of two states: **on** or **off**. Each setting of states of switches realizes a permutation π in the following sense: for each i there is a path from P_i to $M_{\pi(i)}$, and any two such paths are edge-disjoint. Permutation networks that can realize any permutation $\pi : \{1,\ldots,n\} \rightarrow \{1,\ldots,n\}$ are called **nonblocking permutation networks** (or **permuters**).

A very simple permutation network is an $n \times n$ **crossbar switch**. At any intersection of a row and a column of an $n \times n$ grid there is a binary switch. Figure 10.22 shows a realization of the permutation $(3,5,1,6,4,2)$ on a 6×6 crossbar switch.

An $n \times n$ crossbar switch has n^2 switches. Can we do better? Is there a permutation network which can realize all permutations and has asymptotically fewer than n^2 switches?

A lower bound on the number of switches can easily be established.

Theorem 10.4.3 *Each permutation network with n inputs and n outputs has $\Omega(n \lg n)$ switches.*

Proof: A permutation network with s switches has 2^s global states. Each setting of switches (to an 'off' or an 'on' state) forms a global state. Since this network should implement any permutation of

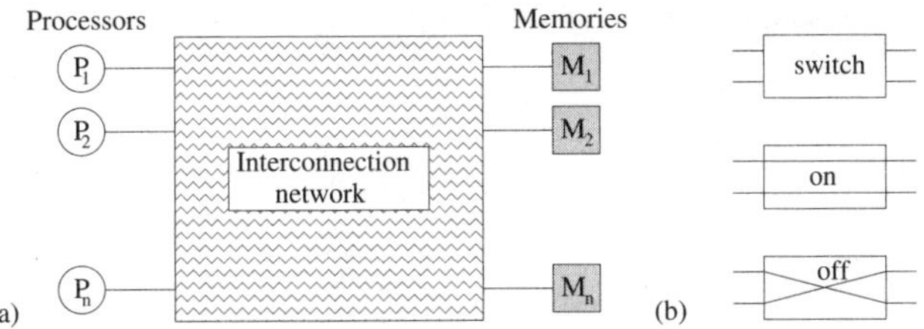

Figure 10.21 Permutation network and switches

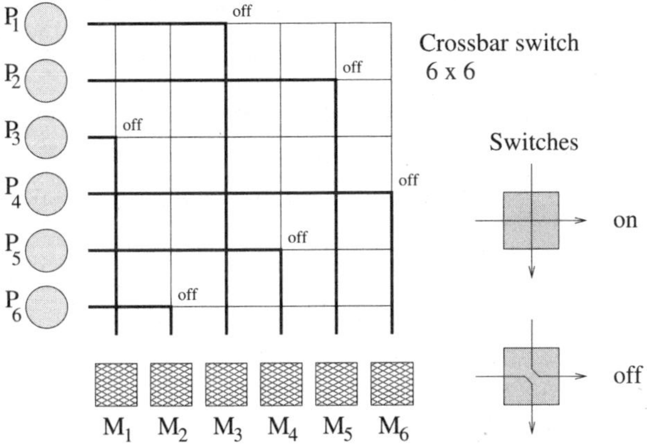

Figure 10.22 A crossbar switch and realization of a permutation on it

n elements, it must hold (using Stirling's approximation from page 29) that

$$2^s \geq n! \approx \frac{1}{\sqrt{2\pi n}} n^n e^{-(n+0.5)},$$

and therefore $s \geq n \lg n - c_1 n - c_2$, where c_1, c_2 are constants. □

We show now that this asymptotic lower bound is achievable by the **Beneš network** BE_d (also called the **Waksman network** or the **back-to-back butterfly**). This network consists for $d = 1$ of a single switch, and for $d > 1$ is recursively defined by the scheme in Figure 10.23a. The upper output of the ith switch S_i of the first column of switches is connected with the ith input of the top network BE_{d-1}. The lower output of S_i is connected with the ith input of the lower network BE_{d-1}. For outputs of BE_{d-1} networks the connections are done in the reverse way. BE_2 is shown in Figure 10.23b.

From the recursive definition of BE_d we get the following recurrence for the number $s(n)$, $n = 2^d$, of switches of the Beneš network BE_d:

$$s(2) = 1 \text{ and } s(n) = 2s\left(\frac{n}{2}\right) + n \text{ for } n > 2,$$

and therefore, using the methods of Section 1.2, we get $s(n) = n \lg n - \frac{n}{2}$.

Beneš networks have an important property.

Theorem 10.4.4 (Beneš-Slepian–Duguid's theorem) *Every Beneš network BE_d can realize any permutation of $n = 2^d$ elements.*

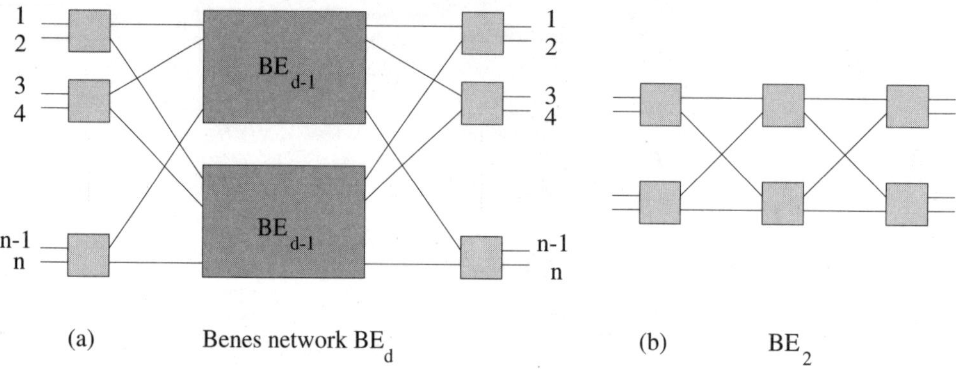

Figure 10.23 Recursive description of the Beneš networks (with $n = 2^d$) and BE_2

Proof: The proof can be performed elegantly using the following theorem from combinatorics.

Theorem 10.4.5 (Hall's theorem) *Let S be a finite set and $C = \{A_i \mid 1 \leq i \leq n\}$ a family of subsets (not necessarily disjoint) of S such that for any $1 \leq k \leq n$ the union of each subfamily of k subsets from C has at least k elements. Then there is a set of n elements $\{a_1, \ldots, a_n\}$ such that $a_i \in A_i, 1 \leq i \leq n$, and $a_i \neq a_j$ if $i \neq j$.*

We show now by induction on d that the Beneš network BE_d can realize any permutation of $n = 2^d$ inputs. The case $d = 1$ is trivially true. Let the inductive hypothesis be true for $d - 1 \geq 1$, and let $n = 2^d$ and $\pi : \{1, \ldots, n\} \rightarrow \{1, \ldots, n\}$ be a permutation.

For $1 \leq i \leq \frac{n}{2}$ let

$$A_i = \left\{ \left\lceil \frac{\pi(2i-1)}{2} \right\rceil, \left\lceil \frac{\pi(2i)}{2} \right\rceil \right\}. \tag{10.1}$$

A_i can be seen as containing the numbers of those switches in the last column, the target level, with which the ith switch of the first column, the source level, should be connected when the permutation π is realized. (Observe that each A_i contains one or two numbers.)

Let $A_{i_1}, \ldots, A_{i_k}$ be an arbitrary collection of k different sets of the type (10.1). The union $\bigcup_{j=1}^{k} A_{i_j}$ contains the numbers of all switches of the target level that should be connected by π with $2k$ inputs of the source level switches $i_1, \ldots, i_k$. Since the corresponding number of outputs is $2k$, the union $\bigcup_{j=1}^{k} A_{i_j}$ must contain at least k elements. This means that the family $C = \{A_i \mid 1 \leq i \leq \frac{n}{2}\}$ satisfies the assumptions of Hall's theorem. Therefore, there is a set of $\frac{n}{2}$ different integers $a_1, \ldots, a_{\frac{n}{2}}, a_i \in A_i$, such that a_i is the number of a switch of the target level with which the ith switch of the input level is connected when the network realizes the permutation π.

It is therefore possible to choose $\frac{n}{2}$ pairs $(i_j, \pi(i_j))$, $1 \leq j \leq \frac{n}{2}$, in such a way that i_j is the input of the jth source-level switch and $\pi(i_j)$ are from different switches of the target level. This means, by the induction hypothesis, that we can realize these $\frac{n}{2}$ connections in such a way that only switches of the upper part of the internal levels of switches are used. In this way the problem is reduced to two permutation routing problems for Beneš networks BE_{d-1}. In order to realize the remaining interconnections, we can use, again by the induction assumption, the lower subnetwork BE_{d-1}. □

Example 10.4.6 *In order to implement the permutation*

$$\pi : \begin{pmatrix} 1 & 2 & 3 & 4 & 5 & 6 & 7 & 8 \\ 8 & 7 & 6 & 5 & 4 & 3 & 2 & 1 \end{pmatrix},$$

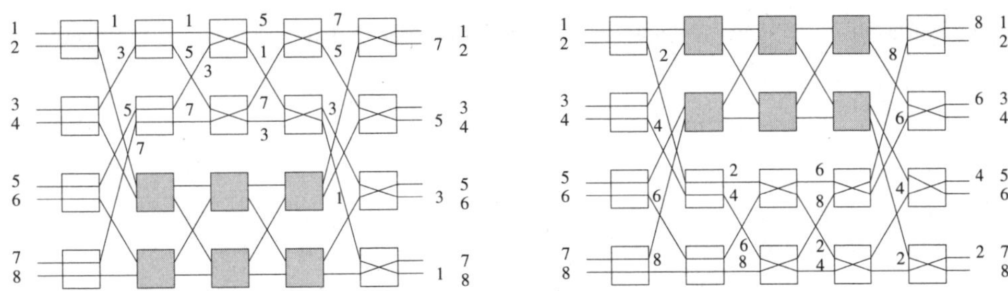

Figure 10.24 Implementation of a permutation on a Beneš network

we first use switches of the upper internal part of the network to realize the following half of the permutation

$$1 \rightarrow 8,\ 3 \rightarrow 6,\ 5 \rightarrow 4,\ 7 \rightarrow 2$$

(see Figure 10.24a), and then switches of the lower internal part of the network for the rest of the permutation (see Figure 10.24b):

$$2 \rightarrow 7,\ 4 \rightarrow 5,\ 6 \rightarrow 3,\ 8 \rightarrow 1.$$

Exercise 10.4.7 *Implement the permutations (a)* $(3,7,8,1,4,6,5,2)$*; (b)* $(8,7,6,5,4,3,2,1)$ *on the Beneš network* BE_3.

Exercise 10.4.8 (Baseline network) BN_d *consists for* $d = 1$ *of one binary switch, and for* $d > 1$ *is defined recursively in a similar way to the Beneš network, except that the last column of switches in the recursive definition in Figure 10.23 is missing. For the number* $S(n)$, $n = 2^d$, *of switches of* BN_d *we therefore have the recurrence* $S(n) = 2S(n/2) + n/2$. *(a) Show that* BN_d *cannot implement all permutations of* $n = 2^d$ *elements. (b)* Determine the upper bound on the number of permutations that* BN_d *can implement.*

10.4.2 Deterministic Permutation Routing with Preprocessing

Permutation networks, such as the Beneš network, are an example of deterministic routing with preprocessing.

It is easy to see that each Beneš network BE_d actually consists of two back-to-back connected butterfly networks B_d (with the corresponding nodes of the last ranks identified), from which comes its name 'back-to-back' butterfly. In other words, the Beneš network BE_d and the network consisting of two back-to-back connected butterflies are isomorphic as graphs. Each butterfly BE_d can be seen as an unrolling of the hypercube H_d such that edges between any two neighbouring ranks represent the edges of H_d of a fixed dimension. The previous result, namely, that Beneš networks can realize any permutation, therefore shows that one can perform permutation routing on the hypercube H_d in time $2d-1$ and with minimal buffer size 1 if preprocessing is allowed. Indeed, communications between nodes of two neighbouring columns in the Beneš network always correspond to communications between nodes of the hypercube along a fixed dimension. Hence each node of the hypercube can play the role of all nodes of the Beneš network in a fixed row. All $2d-1$ communication steps of the Beneš network can therefore be realized by a proper sequence of parallel steps on the hypercube.

This holds for other networks with logarithmic diameter that were introduced in Section 10.1. Indeed, permutation routing on the butterfly is a fully normal algorithm. Therefore (see Exercise 10.4.2) it can also run on cube-connected cycles, shuffle exchange graphs and de Bruijn graphs with only constant time overhead. In addition, preprocessing can be done in $\mathcal{O}(d^4)$ time. Consequently we have the following theorem.

Theorem 10.4.9 *Permutation routing can be done on hypercubes, butterflies, cube-connected cycles, shuffle exhange and de Bruijn graphs in $\mathcal{O}(d)$ time if ($\mathcal{O}(d^4)$-time) preprocessing is allowed.*

10.4.3 Deterministic Permutation Routing without Preprocessing

In many important cases, for example, when the PRAM is simulated on multiprocessor networks (see Section 10.5.2), the permutation is not known until the very moment when a permutation routing is to be performed. In such cases the preprocessing time must be included in the overall routing time. It is therefore important to develop permutation routing protocols that are fast and do not require preprocessing of a permutation to be routed.

Let us first recognize that a permutation routing of packets $(i, x_i, \pi(i)), 1 \leq i \leq n$, corresponds to sorting all packets according to the third key. Since sorting of 2^d elements can be done on the butterfly B_d in $\Theta(d^2)$ time (see page 545) using a multiple ascend/descend algorithm, and each such algorithm can run with only constant time overhead on the cube-connected cycles, de Bruijn and shuffle exchange graphs, we have the following result.

Theorem 10.4.10 *Permutation routing on the butterfly network B_d, hypercube H_d, cube-connected cycles CCC_d, shuffle exchange SE_d and de Bruijn graphs DB_d can be performed in time $\mathcal{O}(\lg^2 n)$ time, $n = 2^d$, without preprocessing.*

Can we do asymptotically better? The first obvious idea is to consider the so-called oblivious routing algorithms in which the way a packet $(i, x_i, \pi(i))$ travels depends only on i and $\pi(i)$, not on the whole permutation π. For example, can we route all packets using the greedy method for one packet routing?

It is intuitively clear that in such a case we may have congestion problems.

Example 10.4.11 *Let us consider the case that the greedy method is used in the hypercube H_{10} to realize the so-called bit-reversal permutation $\pi(a_9 \ldots a_0) = a_0 \ldots a_9$. In this case all 32 packets from processors $P_u, u = u_1u_2u_3u_4u_5 00000$ will try, during the first five steps, to get through the node 0000000000. To route all these packets through this node, at least 32 steps are needed – in spite of the fact that each two nodes i and $\pi(i)$ are at most 10 edges apart. This can be generalized to show that time $\Omega(\sqrt{2^d})$ is required in the worst case in order to realize the bit-reversal permutation on H_d with a greedy method.*

Whenever the greedy method is used for permutation routing, the basic question arises: Is there a strategy for solving the congestion problem that gives good routing times? In some cases the answer is yes: for example, for routing on two-dimensional arrays.

Exercise 10.4.12 *Consider an n-node linear array in which each node contains an arbitrary number of packets but from which there is at most one packet destined for each node. Show that if the edge congestion is resolved by giving priority to the packet that needs to go farthest, then the greedy algorithm routes all packets in $n-1$ steps.*

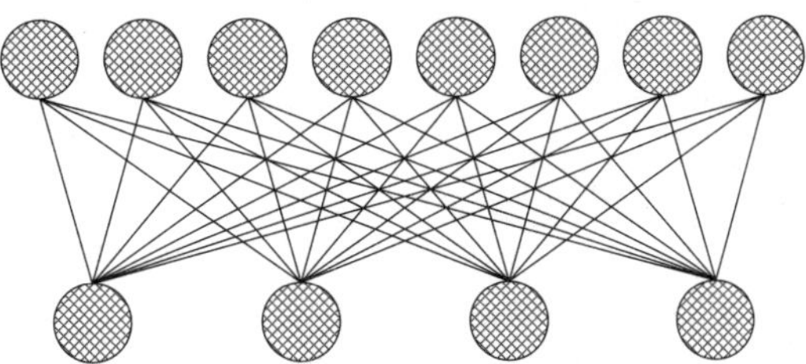

Figure 10.25 A concentrator that is both a $(\frac{1}{2},1,8,4)$- and $(\frac{1}{4},2,8,4)$-concentrator

Exercise 10.4.13* *Show that if the greedy routing is used for two-dimensional arrays – that is, at the beginning each node contains a packet and each packet is first routed to its correct column and then to its destination within that column – then the permutation routing on an $n \times n$ array can be performed in $2n-2$ steps.*

The following general result implies that oblivious routing cannot perform very well, in the worst case, on hypercubes and similar networks.

Theorem 10.4.14 (Borodin–Hopcroft's theorem) *Any oblivious permutation routing requires at least $\sqrt{\frac{n}{c}}-1$ steps in the worst case in a network with n processors and degree c.*

Oblivious permutation routing is therefore not the way to get around the $\mathcal{O}(\lg^2 n)$ upper bound for a routing without preprocessing on hypercubes. Is there some other way out? Surprisingly, yes.

We show later that the **multi-butterfly network** MB_n with n input and n output processors – with $n(\lg n+1)$ processors total – can perform any permutation routing in $\mathcal{O}(\lg n)$ time and in such a way that the buffer size of all processors is minimal (that is, 1).

Multi-butterfly networks MB_n are based on special bipartite graphs, called **concentrators**.

Definition 10.4.15 *Let $\alpha,\beta \in \mathbf{R}^+$, $m,c \in \mathbf{N}$, and let m be even. A bipartite graph $G = \langle A \dot\cup B, E\rangle$, where A and B are disjoint, is an (α,β,m,c)-**concentrator** if*

1. $|A| = m$, $|B| = \frac{m}{2}$.
2. *Degree*$(v) = c$ *if* $v \in A$ *and degree*$(v) = 2c$ *if* $v \in B$.
3. *(Expansion property) For all* $X \subseteq A$, $|X| \leq \alpha m$, *we have* $|\{v \,|\, (x,v) \in E, x \in A\}| \geq \beta|X|$.

That is, in an (α,β,m,c)-concentrator, each set X of nodes in A, up to a certain size, αm, has many neighbours in B – at least $\beta|X|$. In other words, if $\beta > 1$, then A 'expands', and β is the **expansion factor** (see Figure 10.25).

In a concentrator there are several edges through which one can get to B from a node in A. This will now be used to show that it is possible to design $\Theta(\lg n)$ permutation routing without preprocessing. In order to be able to use concentrators for permutation routing, the basic question is whether and when, given α and β, a concentrator exists. For example, the following theorem holds.

Theorem 10.4.16 *If* $\alpha \leq \frac{1}{2\beta}(4\beta e^{1+\beta})^{-\frac{1}{c-\beta-1}}$, *then there is a* (α,β,m,c)*-concentrator.*

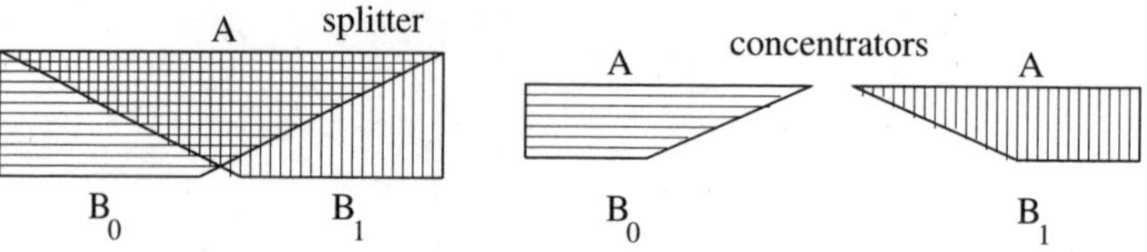

Figure 10.26 Splitter

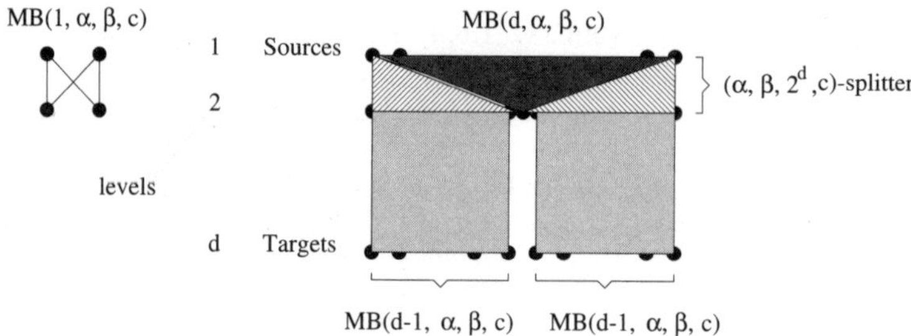

Figure 10.27 Multi-butterfly network

Observe that if α, β and c are chosen as the conditions of Theorem 10.4.16 require, then a (α, β, m, c)-concentrator exists for any m.

The basic component of a multi-butterfly network is a **splitter**, which consists of two concentrators (see Figure 10.26).

Definition 10.4.17 *An* (α, β, m, c)-**splitter** *is a bipartite graph* $\langle A \dot{\cup} (B_0 \cup B_1), E_0 \cup E_1 \rangle$, *where* $B_0 \cap B_1 = \emptyset$ *and both* $\langle A \dot{\cup} B_0, E_0 \rangle$ *and* $\langle A \dot{\cup} B_1, E_1 \rangle$ *are* (α, β, m, c)-*concentrators.*

The degree of a (α, β, m, c)-splitter is $2c$. An edge from A to B_0 is called a 0-edge, and an edge from A to B_1 is called a 1-edge.

Definition 10.4.18 *The multi-butterfly network* $MB(d, \alpha, \beta, c)$ *has* $n = 2^d(d+1)$ *nodes, degree* $4c$, *and is defined recursively in Figure 10.27. (The nodes of the first level are called sources, and the nodes of the last level targets.)*

The basic idea of routing on multi-butterfly networks is similar to the greedy strategy for hypercubes or butterflies. In order to send a packet from a source node $a_{d-1} \ldots a_0$ of level 0 to the target node $b_{d-1} \ldots b_0$ of the last level, the packet is first sent through a (b_{d-1})-edge, then through a (b_{d-2})-edge and so on. In each butterfly such a route is uniquely determined, but in a multi-butterfly there are many 0-edges and many 1-edges that can be used. (Here is the advantage of multi-butterfly networks.)

Let $L = \lceil \frac{1}{2\alpha} \rceil$, and let A_i be the set of packets with the target address j such that $j \bmod L = i$. Each of the sets A_i has approximately $\frac{n}{L}$ elements. The routing algorithm described below is such that each sub-multi-butterfly $MB(d', \alpha, \beta, c), d' < d$, will get on its source level at most $\frac{2^{d'}}{L}$ packets; the corresponding concentrator has therefore to send further at most $\frac{1}{2}\frac{2^{d'}}{L} \approx \alpha 2^{d'}$ packets. This is, however, exactly the amount that can still be expanded by the factor β according to the definition of $(\alpha, \beta, 2^d, c)$-concentrators.

The routing algorithm works in L sequential phases. In each phase packets from one of the sets $A_i, 1 \le i \le L$, are routed. Routing of one phase takes time $\mathcal{O}(\lg n)$. To route L phases, time $L \cdot \mathcal{O}(\lg n) = \mathcal{O}(\frac{\lg n}{\alpha}) = \mathcal{O}(\lg n)$ is needed. Each phase consists of several rounds. To perform one round, all processors with packets at the beginning of the round are considered as being blocked. Moreover, the edges of each splitter are divided into $2c$ matchings. (This is possible according to Hall's theorem, 2.4.20.) One round consists of the following $2c$ steps:

> **for** $j \leftarrow 1$ **to** $2c$ **do**
> Each processor that has a packet that should be sent through an s-edge ($s \in [2]$) sends it along the (only one) s-edge of the matching M_j if such an edge in M_j exists and if the edge goes to a processor that is not at that moment blocked. If a processor receives a packet, it becomes blocked.

A very technical analysis of the above routing algorithm yields the following theorem.

Theorem 10.4.19 *Let $\beta > 1$ be arbitrary and α, c be chosen in such a way that $MB(d,\alpha,\beta,c)$ exists for each d. Then an arbitrary permutation of $n = 2^d$ packets can be routed on $MB(d,\alpha,\beta,c)$ in time $\mathcal{O}(\lg n)$ using buffers of size* 1.

10.4.4 Randomized Routing*

There are several ways in which randomization can lead to probabilistically good routing algorithms. For example, randomization can be used to solve the congestion problem in the case that the greedy method is used and several packets try to pass at the same time through a node or an edge. Another way in which randomization can be used is to route in two phases: first to a randomly chosen destination, then to the real target.

In this section we consider both types of randomized routings on butterflies. The first is the so-called **randomized greedy routing**.

The greedy method for one-packet routing on a butterfly B_d takes a packet from a source node $(0, a_{d-1} \dots a_0)$ to the target node $(d, b_{d-1} \dots b_0)$ through the only possible route

$$\begin{array}{ccccc} (0,a_{d-1}\dots a_0) & \rightarrow & (1,b_{d-1}a_{d-2}\dots a_1a_0) & \rightarrow & (2,b_{d-1}b_{d-2}a_{d-3}\dots a_1a_0) \\ & \rightarrow & (3,b_{d-1}b_{d-2}b_{d-3}a_{d-4}\dots a_1a_0) & \rightarrow & \dots\dots \\ & \rightarrow & (d-1,b_{d-1}b_{d-2}\dots b_1a_0) & \rightarrow & (d,b_{d-1}\dots b_0). \end{array}$$

If this method is used to route packets from all nodes according to a given permutation, it may happen, in the worst case, as in the bit-reversal permutation on the hypercube, that $\Theta(\sqrt{2^d}) = \Theta(2^{\frac{d}{2}})$ packets have to go through the same node. However, this is clearly an extreme case. The following theorem shows that in a 'typical' situation the **congestion**, that is, the maximum number of packets that try to go simultaneously through one node, is not so big. In this theorem an average is taken over all possible permutations.

Theorem 10.4.20 *The congestion for a deterministic greedy routing on the butterfly B_d is for $(1 - \frac{1}{2^d})$ of all permutations $\pi : [2^d] \rightarrow [2^d]$ at most*

$$C = 2e + 2\lg n + \lg\lg n = \mathcal{O}(\lg n),$$

where $n = 2^d$, and e is the base of natural logarithms.

Proof: Let $\pi : [2^d] \mapsto [2^d]$ be a random permutation. Let $v = (i, \alpha)$ be a node at rank i of the butterfly B_d, and let $Pr_s(v)$ denote the probability that at least s packets go through the node v when the permutation π is routed according to the greedy method – the probability refers to the random choice of π. From the node v one can reach $2^{d-i} = \frac{n}{2^i}$ targets. This implies that if w is a source node, then

$$Pr(\text{the route starting in } w \text{ gets through } v) = \frac{\frac{n}{2^i}}{n} = \frac{1}{2^i}.$$

Since v can be reached from 2^i source nodes, there are $\binom{2^i}{s}$ ways to choose s packets in such a way that they go through the node v. The choice of targets of these packets is not important, and therefore the probability that s packets go through v is $(\frac{1}{2^i})^s$. Hence,

$$Pr_s(v) \leq \binom{2^i}{s}\left(\frac{1}{2^i}\right)^s \leq \left(\frac{2^i e}{s}\right)^s\left(\frac{1}{2^i}\right)^s = \left(\frac{e}{s}\right)^s,$$

where we have used the estimation $\binom{n}{k} \leq \frac{n^k e^k}{k^k}$ (see Exercise 23, Chapter 1).

Observe that this probability does not depend on the choice of v at all, and therefore

$$Pr(\text{there is a node } v \text{ through which at least } s \text{ packets get})$$

$$\leq \sum_{v \text{ is a node}} Pr_s(v) \leq n \lg n \left(\frac{e}{s}\right)^s,$$

because $n \lg n$ is the number of nodes of the butterfly on all ranks except the first one. Hence, for $s = 2e + 2\lg n + \lg\lg n$ we get

$$\begin{aligned} Pr(\text{there is a node } v \text{ through which at least } s \text{ packets get}) &\leq n\lg n \left(\frac{e}{s}\right)^s \\ &\leq n\lg n \left(\frac{1}{2}\right)^{2\lg n + \lg\lg n} \\ &\leq n \lg n \cdot \frac{1}{n^2 \lg n} = \frac{1}{n}. \end{aligned}$$

□

The fact that congestion is on average not so bad for the greedy routing on butterflies can be utilized in the following **randomized greedy routing** on B_d.

A $k = \Theta(\lg^2 n)$ is properly chosen, and to each packet $p_i = (i, x, \pi(i))$ a randomly chosen number $rank(p_i) \in [k]$ is assigned. These ranks are used to order packets as follows:

$$p_i \prec p_j \text{ if either } rank(p_i) < rank(p_j) \text{ or } rank(p_i) = rank(p_j) \text{ and } i < j.$$

Randomized greedy routing is now performed as follows. Each packet takes its unique route as determined by the greedy routing. If more than one packet is in the buffer of a processor, then the smallest with respect to the ordering $\prec$ is chosen to be sent in the next step.

A detailed technical analysis shows that randomized greedy routing is, surprisingly, pretty good.

Theorem 10.4.21 *Randomized greedy routing on butterflies B_d takes $\Theta(\lg n)$ steps, $n = 2^d$, with probability $(1 - \frac{1}{n})^2 \geq 1 - \frac{2}{n}$.*

Remark 10.4.22 Let us now consider a more general problem, the **p–p-routing problem**. In this problem each processor has p packets. The ith processor P_i is to send the jth packet to the destination $f(i,j)$, where $f : [n] \times [p] \rightarrow [n]$, and, for all $k \in [n]$, $|f^{-1}(k)| = p$. A slightly modified proof of Theorem 10.4.20 leads to a theorem which says that for $1 - \frac{1}{n}$ of all such functions the congestion is almost the same as it was in case of the permutation routing: namely, $\mathcal{O}(\lg n + p)$. This result will be used in Section 10.5.2.

The basic idea of the second **randomized routing algorithm** is also very simple. Let us assume that a packet has to be sent, on a butterfly, from a source node S_i to the target node $T_{\pi(i)}$, where π is a permutation. This can be done in three phases.

Algorithm 10.4.23 (Randomized routing on a butterfly)

1. The packet is sent from S_i to a randomly chosen target node T_j.
2. The packet is sent from T_j to S_j.
3. The packet is sent from S_j to $T_{\pi(i)}$.

The randomized greedy routing is used in steps (1) and (3). The routing is straightforward in step (2) – along the edges (i,j), $i = d, d-1, \ldots, 0$.

The time taken by step (1) is $\mathcal{O}(\lg n)$, with the probability at least $1 - \frac{2}{n}$, according to Theorem 10.4.21. Step (2) also requires $\mathcal{O}(\lg n)$ time. Step (3) is actually the reverse of step (1), but this time the source node is 'randomly chosen'. A detailed analysis shows that for this step we also need $\mathcal{O}(\lg n)$ time, with the probability at least $1 - \frac{1}{n}$. Therefore the following theorem holds.

Theorem 10.4.24 *The randomized routing on the butterfly B_d routes each permutation $\pi : [n] \mapsto [n]$, $n = 2^d$, in time $\mathcal{O}(\lg n)$ with probability at least $(1 - \frac{1}{n})(1 - \frac{2}{n}) \geq 1 - \frac{3}{n}$.*

Remark 10.4.25 We have discussed two randomized routing methods for butterflies only. However, these methods can be used, with small modifications, for other networks. For example, the randomized greedy routing on the hypercube H_d realizes a routing from a node A to a node B by choosing randomly a node C and sending the packet first from A to C by the greedy method, and then from C to B, again by the greedy method. The probability that the time needed is more than $8d$ is less than 0.74^d.

Exercise 10.4.26** *Consider again the permutation routing on an $n \times n$ array by the greedy method and the case that each processor sends one packet to a random target. (Hence each possible target is equally likely to be chosen, independently from the targets of other packets, it is therefore possible that more than one packet aims at a particular target.) Assume also that each processor handles a queue which stores packets that want to get through but have to wait.*
(a) Show that the size of any queue is at most the number of packets which in that node turn from a row-edge to a column-edge.
(b) Show that the probability that r or more packets turn in some particular node is at most $\binom{n}{r}(\frac{1}{n})^r$.
(c) Show, for example, using the inequality in Exercise 23, that $\binom{n}{r}(\frac{1}{n})^r \leq (\frac{e}{r})^r$.
(d) Show that the probability that any particular queue exceeds size $r = \frac{e \lg n^2}{\lg \lg n^2}$ is at most $\mathcal{O}(n^{-4})$.

10.5 Simulations

There are three main types of simulations of a network $\mathcal{N}$ on another network $\mathcal{N}'$.

Embedding: To each processor P of $\mathcal{N}$ a processor P' of $\mathcal{N}'$ is associated that simulates P.

Dynamic embedding: At each step of a discrete computation time, each processor of $\mathcal{N}$ is simulated by a processor of $\mathcal{N}'$. However, it can be dynamically changed, from step to step, which processor of $\mathcal{N}'$ simulates which processor of $\mathcal{N}$.

Multiple embedding: To each processor P of $\mathcal{N}$, several processors of $\mathcal{N}'$ are associated that simulate P.

The main network simulation problem is as follows: given two families of (uniformly defined) graphs, $\mathcal{G}_1$ and $\mathcal{G}_2$, develop a method for simulating each network with the underlying graph from $\mathcal{G}_1$ by a network with the underlying graph from $\mathcal{G}_2$. For example, how can networks on rings be simulated by networks on hypercubes?

The main network simulation problem consists actually of two subproblems. The first is on the graph-theoretical level: how to map well the nodes of graphs from $\mathcal{G}_1$ into nodes (or sets of nodes) of graphs from $\mathcal{G}_2$, in such a way that neighbouring nodes are mapped either into neighbouring nodes or at least into nodes not too far from each other. This problem has been discussed in Section 10.3. The second subproblem is to design particular processors for the network that performs simulation. In case neighbouring nodes are not mapped into neighbouring nodes, the main issue is how to realize communication by routing.

As we saw in Section 10.3, in many important cases there are good embeddings of graphs of one family in graphs of another family. This is not always so and in such cases dynamic or multiple embeddings are used.

Example 10.5.1 (Simulation of two-directional rings by one-directional rings) *There is no way to embed an n-node two-directional ring TR_n with self-loops (Figure 10.28a)*[3] *into an n-node one-directional ring OR_n also with self-loops (Figure 10.28c) in such a way that two neighbouring nodes of TR_n are always mapped into two nodes of OR_n that are only $\mathcal{O}(1)$ interconnections apart – in both communication directions. On the other hand, it is evident that each network over a modified one-way ring MR_n (Figure 10.28b) in which each node i is connected with nodes $(i+1) \bmod n$, $(i+2) \bmod n$ and itself can easily be simulated by a network over OR_n with the slowdown at most by a factor 2.*

We show now that each network over TR_n can easily be simulated by a network over MR_n using a dynamic embedding. In the ith simulation step the jth node of TR_n is simulated by the $((j+i-1) \bmod n)$th node of MR_n. This means that in this simulation processors 'travel around the ring'. This fact, together with the existence of self-loops, allows us to simulate two-directional ring communications on one-directional rings. Figures 10.28e,f show the space-time unrolling of TR_8 and MR_8 and the isomorphism of those two graphs that corresponds exactly to the dynamic embedding. (A generalization to rings with an arbitrary number of nodes is now straightforward.)

Example 10.5.2 *Figure 10.28d shows a graph consisting of two one-directional rings with opposite orientation of edges and with corresponding processors connected by undirected edges. Each network over a two-directional ring can be simulated by a network over such a graph using a multiple embedding.*

Two simulation problems are considered in this section: the existence of universal interconnection graphs and simulation of PRAMs on bounded-degree networks.

[3]Squares stand for nodes with self-loops; self-loops themselves are not explicitly depicted.

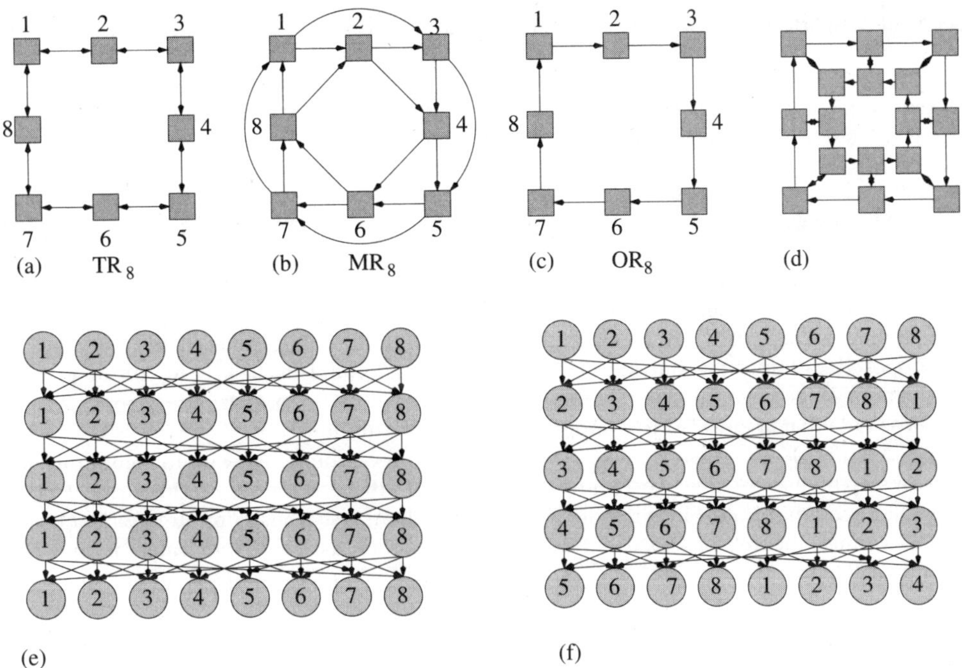

Figure 10.28 Simulation of two-directional rings on one-directional rings

10.5.1 Universal Networks

We shall see that shuffle exchange graphs and cube-connected cycles are, in a reasonable sense, universal communication structures for networks. The same can be shown for several others graphs introduced in Section 10.1: de Bruijn graphs, wrapped butterflies and hypercubes. These results again show that the graphs introduced in Section 10.1 are reasonably well chosen for modelling network–computer interconnections.

Definition 10.5.3 *A family of graphs $\mathcal{G} = \{G_1, G_2, \ldots\}$ is a family of bounded-degree graphs if there is a constant c such that degree$(G_i) \leq c$ for all $G_i \in \mathcal{G}$. A graph G_0 is k-universal, $k \in \mathbf{N}$, for a family $\mathcal{G}$ of bounded-degree graphs if each network on a graph from $\mathcal{G}$ can be simulated by a network on G_0 with the time overhead $\mathcal{O}(k)$. If $\mathcal{G}$ is the class of all graphs of degree c and n nodes, then we say that G_0 is (c,n,k)-universal. If a graph is (c,n,k)-universal for any c, then it is called (n,k)-universal.*

Example 10.5.4 *The following graph is $(2,n,1)$-universal (for the class of all graphs with n nodes and degree at most 2).*

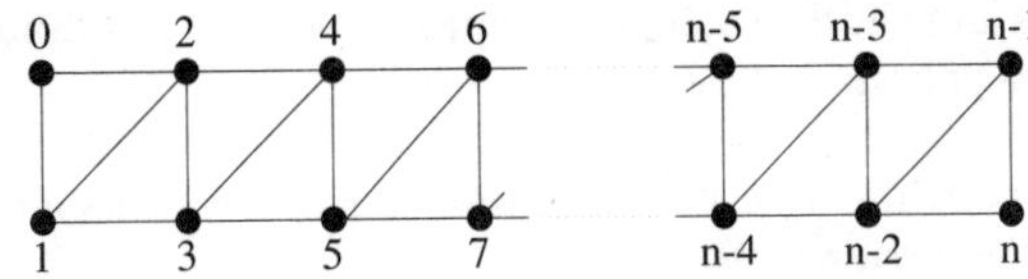

Indeed, all networks on linear arrays, rings and separate processors with up to n processors can be simulated by a network on this graph, without any time overhead.

Theorem 10.5.5 *If G_0 is a graph with n nodes on which one can route any permutation $\pi : [n] \rightarrow [n]$ in time $t(n)$, then G_0 is $(c,n,t(n))$-universal for any c (and therefore $(n,t(n))$-universal).*

Proof: Let $\mathcal{N}$ be a network with n processors $P_0, \ldots, P_{n-1}$ and degree c, and let the nodes of G_0 be numbered by integers from 0 to $n-1$, to get $N_0, \ldots, N_{n-1}$ (it does not matter how the processors of $\mathcal{N}$ and nodes of G_0 are numbered).

We describe a network $\mathcal{N}_0$ on G_0. First we describe how to initialize processors of $\mathcal{N}_0$. Note that the time taken by this initialization does not count in the overall time overhead for simulation.

The ith processor P_i of $\mathcal{N}$ will be simulated by the processor P'_i at the node N_i of $\mathcal{N}_0$. The processor P'_i is supposed to know the starting configuration K_i of P_i, and its task is to compute the next configuration. To achieve this we use the routing potential of G_0 to distribute among processors in $\mathcal{N}_0$ those data that are needed to compute the next configuration.

Since it is not clear in advance which neighbouring processors of $\mathcal{N}$ want to communicate in a particular step of discrete time, we assume the worst case – that any pair of neighbouring processors of $\mathcal{N}$ want to communicate. Since the degree of $\mathcal{N}$ is c, the worst-case assumption will not cost too much. By Vizing's theorem, 2.4.25, the underlying graph G of $\mathcal{N}$ is $(c+1)$-colourable, and we make a colouring of G with integers from $[c+1]$ as colours. To each colour $j \in [c+1]$ we define a permutation π_j by

$$\pi_j(i) = l \text{ if } (P_i, P_l) \text{ is an edge of } \mathcal{N} \text{ coloured by } j.$$

We prepare now a network $\mathcal{N}_0$ on G_0 for routing with respect to permutations $\pi_0, \ldots, \pi_c$. This preparation depends on $\mathcal{N}_0$ only, and can therefore be done before a simulation starts. The time for such preparation should not count in the overall simulation time. The simulation algorithm of one step of the network has the following form for the case that all processors only send (and do not request) data.

```
for j ← 0 to c do
    for i ← 0 to n−1 pardo
        if P_i wants to send information x_i to P_{π_j(i)}
            then P_i creates packet (i,,x_i,π_j(i)), and this packet is routed to the processor P_{π_j(i)}
    od
od
```

Observe that at this point the ith processor P'_i of $\mathcal{N}_0$ knows all the information needed to simulate one step of P_i. Simulation time is $c\mathcal{O}(t(n)) = \mathcal{O}(t(n))$. Note that this time estimate does not change if processors also need to send requests for data. This can be done using the inverse permutations $\pi_0^{-1}, \ldots, \pi_c^{-1}$. This increases the simulation time only by a constant factor. □

Corollary 10.5.6 *The graph CCC_d is $(n,\lg n)$-universal with $n = d2^d$, and the graph SE_d is also $(n,\lg n)$-universal with $n = 2^d$.*

Cube-connected cycles and shuffle exchange graphs can be used to simulate efficiently arbitrary networks, not only families of bounded-degree networks.

Definition 10.5.7 *A graph G is called a (n,k)-**simulator** if any network with n processors can be simulated by a network on G with the time overhead $\mathcal{O}(k)$.*

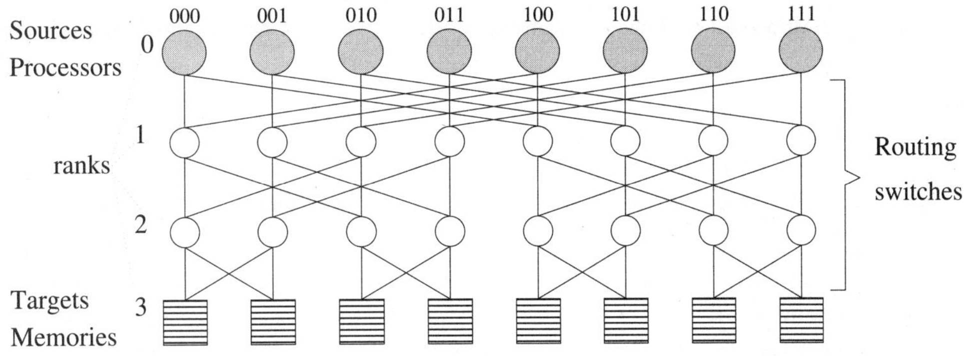

Figure 10.29 Simulation of an EREW PRAM on a butterfly network

In a similar way to how we proved Theorem 10.5.5, we can prove the following result (sorting is now used to perform routing).

Theorem 10.5.8 *If G_0 is a graph such that in a network on G one can sort n numbers in time $t(n)$, then G_0 is a $(n, t(n))$-simulator.*

Corollary 10.5.9 *The cube-connected cycles CCC_d are $(n, \lg^2 n)$-simulators with $n = d2^d$; the shuffle exchange graphs SE_d are $(n, \lg^2 n)$-simulators with $n = 2^d$.*

10.5.2 PRAM Simulations

PRAM seems to be an ideal model of parallel computers for design and analysis of parallel algorithms and therefore also for parallel programming. It has the potential to be (a basis for) a bridging model for parallel computing such as RAM is for sequential computing. For this the existence of efficient simulations of PRAM on bounded-degree networks seems to be of prime importance.

First we show how to simulate an EREW PRAM $\mathcal{P}$ with m processors and q cells of shared memory on a butterfly network B_d of size $n(\lg n + 1)$ for the case that $n = 2^d$, $m = pn$, $p \in \mathbf{N}^+$ and $q \geq n$. (Note that both the number of processors of $\mathcal{P}$ and the size of the shared memory are larger than the number of nodes of the source rank of the butterfly network.)

Let $[q]$ be the address space of the shared memory of $\mathcal{P}$. Simulation of $\mathcal{P}$ on the butterfly B_d can be done as follows.

- PRAM processors are simulated by the source-level processors of B_d. Each of these processors simulates p processors of PRAM. Denote by $P_0^{(i)}, \ldots, P_{p-1}^{(i)}$ the processors of $\mathcal{P}$ simulated by the ith processor of the source level of B_d.

- A hash function $h : [q] \rightarrow [n]$ is used to distribute cells of the shared memory of $\mathcal{P}$ among the memory modules handled by the nodes of the last rank of the butterfly.

Simulation of three phases of a PRAM step is performed as follows.

1. **Simulation of a computational phase**: Each processor of the source rank of the butterfly simulates the computational phase of all its PRAM processors on data locally available.

2. **Simulation of a reading phase:** For all $i \in [n]$ and $s \in [p]$ such that the processor $P_s^{(i)}$ wants to read from the memory $m_s^{(i)}$, the greedy routing algorithm for a p–p-routing is realized to the destination $f(i,s) = h(m_s^{(i)})$, and empty packets are sent to the corresponding target-level memory modules. On arrival, the packets are filled with the required data and sent back, again using a p–p-routing.

3. **Simulation of a writing phase:** This simulation is realized in a similar way to the reading phase – through a p–p-routing.

The overall simulation time is the sum of the time for making internal computations, for computing values of the hash functions, and for performing the p–p-routings (four times). As we have seen in Section 10.4.4, such a routing can be done fast, on average, if h is a randomly chosen function from the set $\mathcal{A} = \{g \mid g : [q] \mapsto [n]\}$. However, since h is random, a tabular format may be the only way to represent h, and therefore to choose h may require $\Theta(q)$ space and also $\Theta(q)$ time. This would mean that each source processor needs as much memory as all the shared memory. As a consequence, such preprocessing would cost too much.

The way out is to use only such hash functions that are easy to compute. The whole family of functions from which they are chosen should have good random properties. As we saw in Section 2.3.4, there are families of universal hash functions with such a property. Their existence is the key factor behind the following result, which refers to the above method of simulation of PRAM on butterflies.

Theorem 10.5.10 *There is a probabilistic simulation of an EREW PRAM with $m = np$ processors on the butterfly network $B_{\lceil \lg n \rceil}$ such that $\mathcal{O}(p \lg n + p^2)$ steps are needed on average to simulate one step of EREW PRAM. (For $p = 1$ we get time $\mathcal{O}(\lg n)$.)*

In principle, it is also easy to simulate a CRCW PRAM on a butterfly network. We sketch how this can be done for the most powerful of the PRAM models introduced in Section 4.4.1 – for CRCW^{pri} PRAM.

It is enough to show how to simulate concurrent reads (a similar idea is used to simulate concurrent writes), and the basic idea is the same as in the proof of Theorem 4.4.32.

To perform a concurrent read, all requests for reading are first sorted with respect to their targets. We saw in Section 10.1 how to sort in $\mathcal{O}(\lg^2 n)$ time on butterflies. However, when randomized methods are used, sorting can be done on the butterfly $B_d, n = 2^d$ in $\mathcal{O}(\lg n)$ time, as shown by Reif and Valiant (1983). As a result of sorting, the ith processor gets the memory request m_i.

One processor is then chosen as the **leader** from each group of processors that wants to read from the same memory location.[4] For these leaders the reading requests are implemented through one forward routing to memory modules and one backward routing. We know already that this can be done in $\mathcal{O}(\lg n)$ randomized time. After all leaders have received the required data, they must distribute them to all processors that tried to read from the same location as the leader.

The following algorithm realizes data distribution (see Figure 10.30) on the assumption that there are 2^d processors and there is a connection from any node j to any node $j + 2^i$ if $j + 2^i < n = 2^d$.

{Initially only the leaders are alive}
begin
    for $i \rightarrow 1$ **to** d **do**

[4] A processor is a leader if it is the first processor or if the memory request it gets after sorting is larger than that of its left neighbour; this can be determined in $\mathcal{O}(\lg n)$ time on a butterfly $B_d, n = 2^d$, as discussed in Section 4.3.24. Names of the leaders can then be sent to all processors with the same memory requests by a modification of the data distribution method presented above.

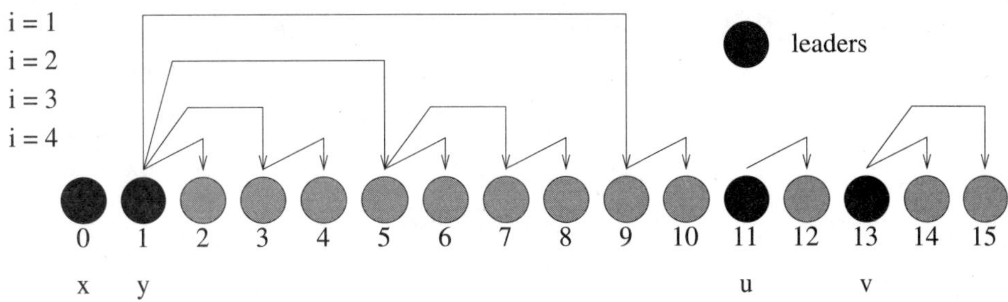

Figure 10.30 Data distribution algorithm

for $0 \le j < n$ **pardo if** node j is alive **then**
  begin pass data and the leader number from node j to node $j + 2^{d-i}$
    if the leader number of the processor in node $j + 2^{d-i}$
      agrees with that from which data is sent
    then make the node $j + 2^{d-i}$ alive and store data in that node
  end
end {It is assumed that all nodes know their leader.}

It can be shown that the above algorithm, which draws heavily on 'butterfly-like interconnections' can be implemented in time $\mathcal{O}(\lg n)$ on the butterfly network $B_d, n = 2^d$. As a consequence, simulation of one step of a CRCW^{pri} PRAM on a butterfly network can be done in randomized time $\mathcal{O}(\lg n)$.

10.6 Layouts

Of great importance are special embeddings, called layouts, of graphs in two-dimensional or, potentially, three-dimensional grids, which model layouts of integrated circuits. Layouts of nodes model processors (transistors), and layouts of edges model interconnections (wires).

The enormous number of nodes of circuits that often need to be laid out together with very strong requirements on minimality, efficiency and regularity, make layout problems difficult and complex. We can therefore present here only very basic insights, concepts, problems, methods and results and in doing so we use the simplest model of layouts.

10.6.1 Basic Model, Problems and Layouts

A layout of a graph G of degree at most 4 in a two-dimensional grid is a mapping of nodes of G into unit squares of the grid and edges of G into disjoint paths that cross squares of the grid in one of the following ways only:

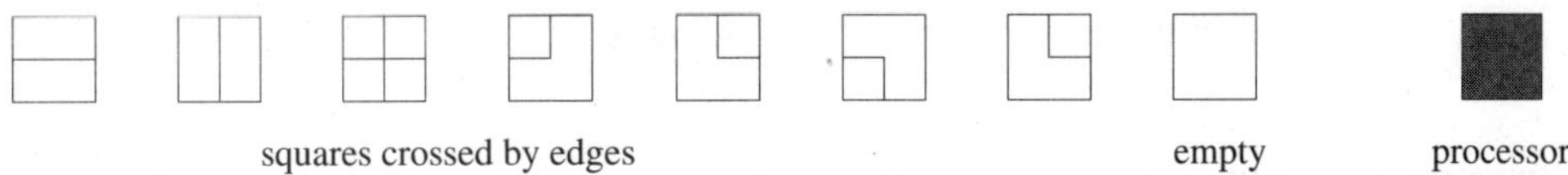

We shall be mainly concerned with layouts of graphs of degree at most 4. There are several reasons for this. Two-dimensional grids that model layout space have degree 4; the main bounded-degree networks introduced in Section 10.1 have degree at most 4; the methods of layout discussed here are easily and naturally extendable to graphs of higher degree.

Two layouts of the graph in Figure 10.31a are shown in Figure 10.31b, c; full circles denote contacts.

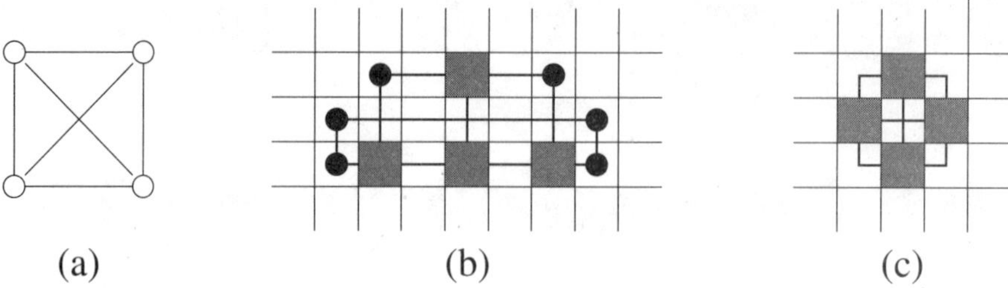

Figure 10.31 Layouts

Remark 10.6.1 We can consider this model as representing layouts with two physical layers on which to run wires – which corresponds well to main layout technologies. All vertical segments of wires run in one layer, and all horizontal segments in a second layer. This means that whenever a wire changes direction, there must be a contact. We shall not draw contacts in general; Figure 10.31b is the only case where they are depicted.

The most important complexity measure of layouts is the **area complexity**: the size of the smallest rectangle that contains all nodes and edges of the layout. For a graph G, let $area(G)$ be the size of the smallest rectangle containing a layout of G. For example, two layouts of the graph in Figure 10.31a, shown in Figure 10.31b, c, have area complexity $3 \times 7 = 21$ and $3 \times 3 = 9$, respectively. It is easy to see that 9 is also the area complexity of the graph in Figure 10.31a.

Exercise 10.6.2 *Design a layout with as small an area as possible for (a) the mesh of trees MT_2; (b) the de Bruijn graph DB_4.*

The fact that the error probability, and consequently the production cost, grows rapidly with the size of the layout is the main reason why the area complexity of layouts is of such practical importance.

Remark 10.6.3 In practice, one actually needs more layers to lay out a circuit: to run power, ground, clock, signals and so on. Our model can easily be modified to capture layouts with more layers: for example, $2k$ layers – k 'horizontal' and k 'vertical' – for an arbitrary but fixed k (see Figure 10.32a for $k = 3$). Indeed, let us represent each processor by a $k \times k$ square, and its ith vertical (horizontal) layer by the ith vertical (horizontal) edge leaving or entering a processor square. This way the area complexity is increased at most by a factor k^2. A similar technique can be used to model layouts of graphs with degree larger than 4. Indeed, if the degree of a graph G is k, it is enough to model a layout of a processor by a square of size $\lceil k/4 \rceil \times \lceil k/4 \rceil$. See Figure 10.32b for a layout of the complete graph with 6 nodes.

Two very important tasks concerning layouts are:

- to design the best layouts for the main interconnection graphs;
- to develop general layout methods.

Layouts of binary trees are well understood.

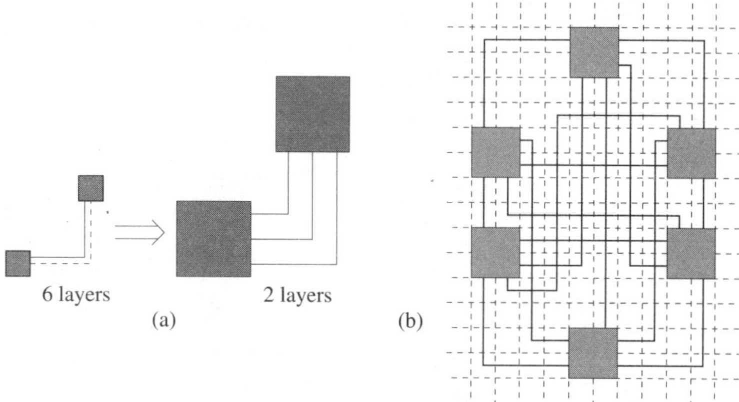

Figure 10.32 Layout of circuits with more layers or a larger degree

Example 10.6.4 *The most natural layout of the complete binary tree T_d was illustrated in the very first example in this book (Figure 1.1d). Since T_d has $n = 2^{d+1} - 1$ nodes, the area complexity of that layout is clearly $\Theta(n \lg n)$. As illustrated in Figure 1.1b, c, the so-called H-layout of complete binary trees has asymptotically the best possible area complexity – $\Theta(n)$.*

Minimal area complexity is not the only requirement which a good layout should satisfy. If a layout of a circuit is to be made, it is often highly desirable and even necessary that input nodes be on the boundaries and not inside the layout-rectangle. This is not so in the case of the *H*-layout of binary trees if all leaves are input nodes. Inputs on boundaries are more accessible; 'chips' with inputs on boundaries are easier to pack, combine, etc. Unfortunately, as the following result shows, such a requirement can asymptotically increase the area complexity of layouts.

Theorem 10.6.5 *Each layout of the complete binary tree T_d with $n = 2^d$ leaves and all leaves on the layout-rectangle boundaries has an area complexity $\Omega(n \lg n)$.*

Two lemmas will be used to prove this theorem.

Lemma 10.6.6 *Suppose that a complete binary tree T can be laid out in an area A with leaves on the boundaries of the layout-rectangle. Then there is a layout of T in area 8A with all leaves on one side of the layout-rectangle.*

Proof: By enlarging the length of each side of the layout by two length units, and therefore by at most doubling the layout area, we can ensure that no edge runs along the boundaries.

Assume now that a new layout-rectangle for T has sides h and w with $h \leq w$ and h even. We rearrange this layout as follows.

1. By extending the horizontal side of the rectangle by h, in the way shown in Figure 10.33, we can shift all nodes representing leaves – they are of degree 1 – to two horizontal boundaries of the layout-rectangle. Since $h \leq w$, this construction again at most doubles the area of the layout.

2. The next natural idea is to fold the layout around the fictive horizontal midline. This would certainly bring all leaves to one side of the layout-rectangle. However, some overlaps could occur, and therefore this idea has to be implemented with care.

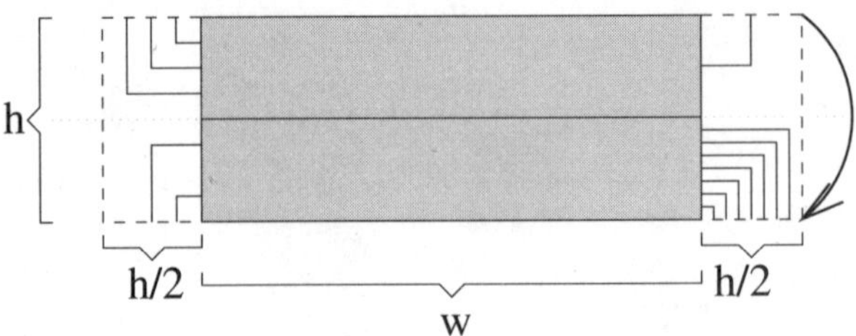

Figure 10.33 Shifting leaves of a tree to horizontal boundaries

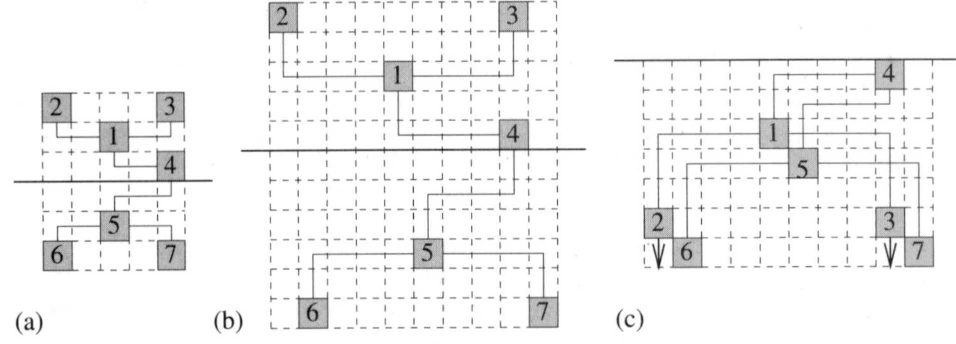

Figure 10.34 Folding of the layout-rectangle

Double both sides of the rectangle, and move all nodes and edges from the ith row and jth column above the horizontal midline to the $(2i-1)$th row and $(2j-1)$th column. Similarly, move all nodes and edges from the ith row and jth column below this midline to the $(2i)$th row and $(2j)$th column and adjust all connections (Figure 10.34b). Fold the layout-rectangle along the horizontal midline, and move all nodes representing leaves that are now not at the boundary, but next to it, to the boundary (see Figure 10.34c); this can be done because no wire runs along the boundaries.

These constructions increase the original area of the layout at most by a factor of 8. □

In order to prove Theorem 10.6.5, it is now sufficient to show that any layout of the complete binary tree with n leaves and all leaves on one side of the boundary must have an area complexity $\Omega(n \lg n)$.

The basic idea of the following proof of the lower bound for the area complexity is simple, powerful and often used. Only the length of wires – zig-zag lines connecting nodes – is estimated. Since a wire of length k occupies the area k, each asymptotic lower bound on the total length of wires provides an asymptotic lower bound of the total area occupied by both wires and processors. Interestingly, we get an asymptotically tight upper bound in this way.

For an integer d let

$$L(d) = \text{minimum of the total length of wires in any layout of } T_d,$$

$$M(d) = \text{minimum of the total length of wires in any layout of } T_d \text{ minus the sum of the length of wires on the (geometrically) longest path in the layout from the root to some leaf.}$$

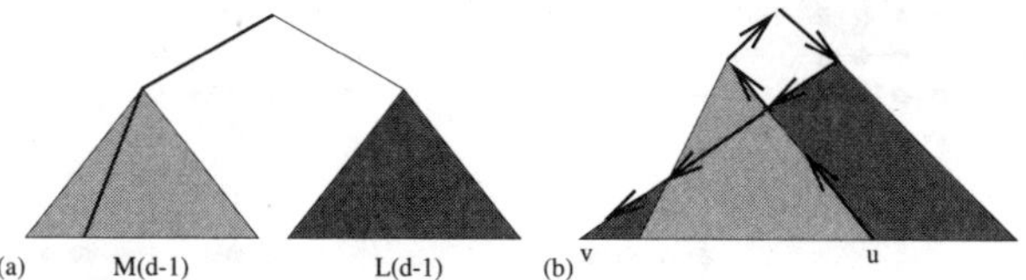

Figure 10.35 Estimations for $M(d)$ and $L(d)$

Lemma 10.6.7 *For any integer d,*

1. $M(d) \geq L(d-1) + M(d-1)$;
2. $L(d) \geq 2M(d-1) + 2^{d-1}$.

Proof: Consider a layout of T_d with $M(d)$ minimal. Since any longest path from a root to a leaf must also form a longest path from the root to a leaf in one of the subtrees of the root, we have the situation depicted in Figure 10.35a, and therefore the first claim of the lemma clearly holds.

Let us consider a layout of T_d with $L(d)$ minimal. Let v be the left-most leaf on the boundary of the layout of T_d, and let u be the right-most node in the layout, representing a leaf of the other subtree of T_d (see Figure 10.35b). Let us now remove from the layout the (bold) path between u and v. The remaining edges have a total length of at least $2M(d-1)$. The length of the bold line is at least 2^{d-1}, because of the distance between u and v. Hence the second inequality of the lemma holds. □

Proof of Theorem 10.6.5 By Lemma 10.6.6, it is sufficient to consider layouts of complete binary trees T_d with $n = 2^d$ leaves and all of them on a boundary of the layout-rectangle. In order to prove that all such layouts need $\Omega(n \lg n)$ area, it is sufficient to show that $L(d) \geq \Omega(n \lg n)$. This can be done as follows.

By Lemma 10.6.7,

$$M(d) \geq M(d-1) + 2M(d-2) + 2^{d-2}.$$

In addition, $M(0) = 0, M(1) = 1$. By induction, we now show that $M(d) \geq \frac{d2^d}{6}$. Indeed, this is clearly true for $d = 0, 1$. Induction step:

$$M(d) \geq \frac{(d-1)2^{d-1}}{6} + 2\frac{(d-2)2^{d-2}}{6} + 2^{d-2} = \frac{d2^d}{6},$$

and therefore

$$\begin{aligned} L(d) &\geq 2M(d-1) + 2^{d-1} \geq \frac{2(d-1)2^{d-1}}{6} + 2^{d-1} \\ &= 2^{d-1}\left(\frac{d-1}{3} + 1\right) \\ &= \Omega(n \lg n). \end{aligned}$$

□

Another important criterion for the quality of layouts is the minimum length of the longest wire. If a circuit is to compute in discrete time, then the length of the longest wire determines how large a unit time must be – a clock cycle. An H-layout of a complete binary tree T_d has a wire of length $\Omega(\sqrt{2^d})$. We cannot do much better, as the following result shows.

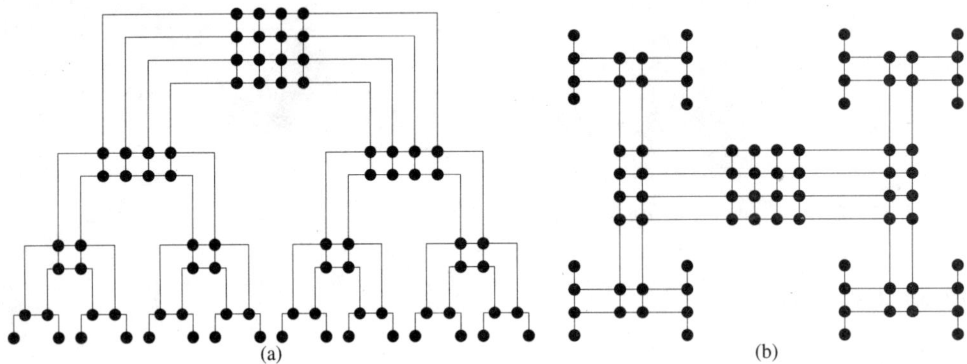

Figure 10.36 The tree of meshes TM_2 and its layout

Theorem 10.6.8 *Every layout of the complete binary tree T_d of depth d with $n = 2^d$ leaves has a wire of length $\Omega(\sqrt{n}/\lg n)$.*

Proof: Let $\mathcal{L}$ be a layout of T_d, and let l be the maximum length of its wires. Then all nodes of the tree have to be laid out in the distance $d - l$ from the root. The number of grid squares in such a circle is $\lfloor \pi d^2 l^2 \rfloor$, and such a circle should contain all $2^{d+1} - 1$ nodes of the tree. Hence,

$$\pi d^2 l^2 \geq 2^{d+1} - 1.$$

Therefore,

$$l \geq \sqrt{\frac{2^{d+1} - 1}{\pi d^2}} = \Omega(\frac{\sqrt{n}}{\lg n}).$$

□

Exercise 10.6.9* *What is the best lower bound you can get for the length of the longest wire of a layout for (a) a mesh of trees; (b) a hypercube.*

There is an interesting variation of a tree that also has nice '*H*-layouts' and, in addition, plays a role in one of the general layout techniques.

The **tree of meshes**, $TM_d, d \in N$, is obtained from a complete binary tree T_{2d} as follows: the root is replaced by an $n \times n$ array, where $n = 2^d$, its children nodes by $n \times \frac{n}{2}$ arrays, their children nodes by $\frac{n}{2} \times \frac{n}{2}$ arrays, and so on until the leaves of the tree are replaced by 1×1 arrays. In addition, the ith node of the left (right) side of an array assigned to a node is connected with the ith node of the top row of the array assigned to their children (see Figure 10.36a for TM_2).

Also, trees of meshes have *H*-layouts, as illustrated in Figure 10.36b. How large are such layouts? Let $s(n)$ denote the length of the side of the square layout of $TM_d, n = 2^d$. Clearly, $s(1) = 1$, and

$$s(n) = 2s\left(\frac{n}{2}\right) + \Theta(n);$$

therefore, by Theorem 1.6.3,

$$s(n) = \Theta(n \lg n).$$

This means that TM_d can be laid out in the area $\Theta(n^2 \lg^2 n)$ where $n = 2^d$. (Observe that such a TM_d has $2n^2 \lg n + n^2$ nodes.)

A natural and important question concerns the area required by layouts of such interconnection graphs as hypercubes, butterflies, cube-connected cycles, de Bruijn graphs and shuffle exchange graphs. Unfortunately, all of them require area $\Theta(n^2 / \lg^2 n)$, where n is the number of nodes.

There is a variety of other layout problems and most of them, even in very restricted forms, are computationally hard. For example, the following problems are **NP**-complete:

1. To determine the area complexity of a forest.

2. To determine the minimum length of the longest wire of layouts of a given graph G.

Exercise 10.6.10 *Show that each X-tree XT_d, with $2^{d+1} - 1$ nodes, can be laid out in the area $\Theta(2^d)$.*

10.6.2 General Layout Techniques

Basic general results concerning the upper bounds for layouts of graphs are easy to obtain.

Theorem 10.6.11 *(1) Each graph of degree 4 with n nodes can be laid out in the area $\mathcal{O}(n^2)$.*

(2) There are families of graphs of degree 4 such that each graph of n nodes from such a family needs $\Omega(n^2)$ area for a layout.

(3) Each n node graph can be laid out in $\mathcal{O}(n^4)$ area.

(4) There are families of graphs such that each n-node graph from such a family needs $\Omega(n^4)$ area for its layout.

Proof: We show here only upper bounds. (1) is easy to see. Indeed, all nodes are laid out in a row with a distance of two squares between them (see Figure 10.37). Clearly $\mathcal{O}(n)$ additional rows are enough to run all wires in the way indicated in Figure 10.37. The same technique can be used to lay out any graph G with n nodes in area $\mathcal{O}(n^4)$. Nodes of G are represented by $\lfloor \frac{n}{4} \rfloor \times \lfloor \frac{n}{4} \rfloor$ squares in a row each two $\frac{n}{2}$ squares apart. This takes $\mathcal{O}(n^2)$ area. Additional $\mathcal{O}(n^4)$ area is enough to wire $\mathcal{O}(n^2)$ potential edges.

It can be shown that there are graphs of degree 4 that need for their layouts $\Omega(n^2)$ area, and that complete graphs need $\Omega(n^4)$ area for their layouts. □

Several general layout techniques are based on the divide-and-conquer method. It is intuitively clear that this method is the one to try. However, there are two basic problems with applying it.

1. Is it possible, and when, to partition recursively a graph into two subgraphs of almost equal size by removing a relatively small number of edges?

2. Provided we have layouts of two subgraphs of a graph G which have been obtained by removing some edges from G, how can we then insert these edges 'back' into these two layouts of subgraphs, and how much does it cost to do so?

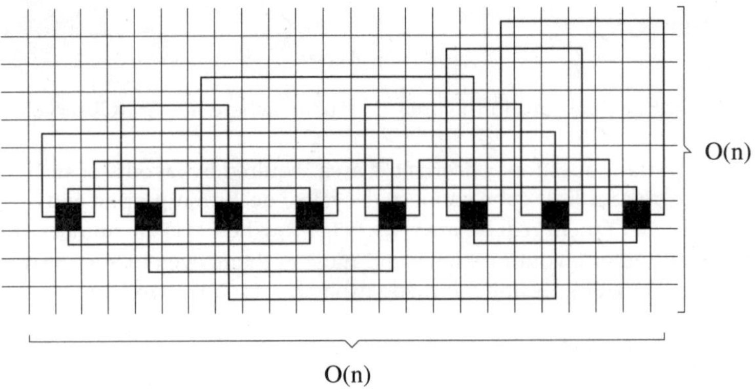

Figure 10.37 General methods to lay out graphs of degree 4

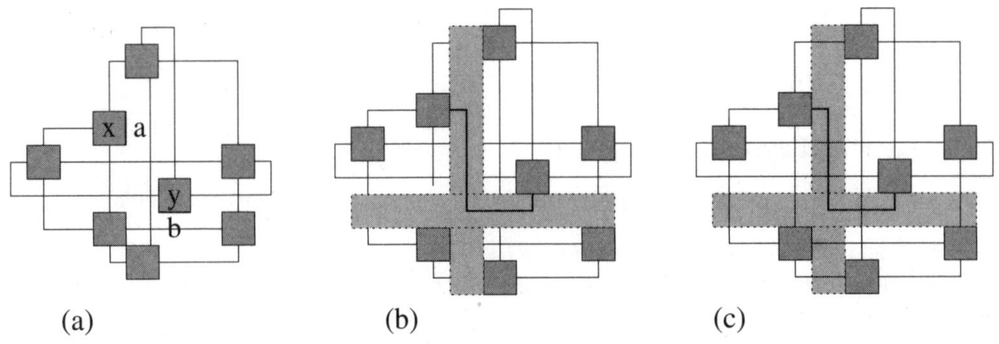

Figure 10.38 Insertion of edges in layouts: the 'corridor technique'

Let us first discuss the second problem, the easier one. Insertion of an edge in a layout can be done in a quite straightforward way by creating **corridors**. Let us assume that we want to add an edge connecting a side a of a node x with a side b of a node y (see Figure 10.38a). We create two corridors (that is, new rows or columns) next to sides a and b, and in case they are parallel also a third one perpendicular to these two. These corridors are then used to run the missing edge (see Figure 10.38b). Once this is done, we just connect all disconnected wires (see Figure 10.38c). In this way an addition of one edge to a layout-rectangle $h \times w, h \leq w$, increases its size by at most $3w$ (or by $2w + h$).

There are several approaches to the separation of graphs into two parts of almost equal size. They are usually based on deep results from graph theory. The central concept is perhaps that of a (strong) separation for a graph and a family of graphs.

Definition 10.6.12 *Let $S : \mathbf{N} \mapsto \mathbf{N}$ be a function. An n-node graph G is called $S(n)$-***separable** *if, by removing $S(n)$ edges, G can be disconnected into two subgraphs G_1 and G_2, with n_1 and n_2 nodes respectively, $n = n_1 + n_2$, in such a way that $n_1 \geq \frac{n}{3}, n_2 \geq \frac{n}{3}$, where again G_1 is $S(n_1)$-separable and G_2 is $S(n_2)$-separable. (In other words, neither of the graphs G_1 and G_2 has more than twice the number of nodes of the other one, and both are further recursively separable.)*

A family $\mathcal{G}$ of graphs is $S(n)$-separable if every n-node graph of $\mathcal{G}$ is $S(n)$-separable.

An n-node graph G is called **strongly** $S(n)$**-separable** *if, by removing* $S(n)$ *edges, G can be divided into two subgraphs* G_1 *and* G_2 *such that* G_1 *has* $\lfloor \frac{n}{2} \rfloor$ *nodes and* G_2 *has* $\lceil \frac{n}{2} \rceil$ *nodes, and both subgraphs are again* $S(\lfloor \frac{n}{2} \rfloor)$*- and* $S(\lceil \frac{n}{2} \rceil)$*-separable.*[5]

A family $\mathcal{G}$ *of graphs is called strongly* $S(n)$*-separable if every graph in that family is strongly* $S(n)$*-separable.*

Example 10.6.13 *Consider an* $\sqrt{n} \times \sqrt{n}$ *array* $\mathcal{A}_n$ *of n nodes,* $n = 2^k$. *It is clear that* $\mathcal{A}_n$ *cannot be separated by fewer than* $\sqrt{n}$ *edges, and that it can be strongly separated by removing* $\sqrt{n}$ *edges. The resulting subgraphs will have* $\frac{n}{2}$ *nodes. They can be strongly separated by removing* $\frac{\sqrt{n}}{2} \leq \sqrt{\frac{n}{2}}$ *edges. The* $\frac{\sqrt{n}}{2} \times \frac{\sqrt{n}}{2}$ *subgraphs obtained in this way can be strongly separated by removing* $\frac{\sqrt{n}}{2} = \sqrt{\frac{n}{4}}$ *edges ... Hence the family* $\mathcal{A}_n$ *is strongly* $\sqrt{n}$*-separable.*

In the following we use two results from graph theory concerning graph separability.

Theorem 10.6.14 *If a family of graphs is* $S(n)$*-separable,* $n = 3^k$, *then it is strongly* $\Gamma_S(n)$*-separable, where* Γ *is the function defined as follows:*

$$\Gamma_S(n) = S(n) + S\left(\frac{2}{3}n\right) + S\left(\frac{2^2}{3^2}n\right) \cdots = \sum_{i=0}^{\lceil \lg_{3/2} n \rceil} S\left(\left(\frac{2}{3}\right)^i n\right).$$

Example 10.6.15 *If* $S(n) = n^\alpha$, $0 < \alpha < 1$, *then*

$$\Gamma_S(n) = n^\alpha + \left(\frac{2}{3}n\right)^\alpha + \cdots \leq n^\alpha (1 + \left(\frac{2}{3}\right)^\alpha + \left(\frac{2}{3}\right)^{2\alpha} + \left(\frac{2}{3}\right)^{3\alpha} + \cdots) = n^\alpha \frac{1}{1 - (\frac{2}{3})^\alpha} = \Theta(n^\alpha).$$

If $S(n)$ *is a constant c, then* $\Gamma_c(n) = c\lceil \lg_{\frac{3}{2}} n \rceil = \Theta(\lg n)$.

The concept of separability seems to be much weaker than that of strong separability. However, Theorem 10.6.14 shows that once we have separability, we can also obtain good strong separability.

Example 10.6.16 *The family of rooted binary trees, that is, trees with one node of degree 2 and all other nodes of degree 1 (leaves) or 3 (with a parent and two children), is 1-separable. Indeed, let us take an arbitrary rooted binary tree T and let n be the number of nodes of T. If one of the subtrees has its number of nodes between* $\frac{1}{3}n$ *and* $\frac{2}{3}n$, *then removing the edge between the root of the tree and the root of the subtree will do. If not, then one of these subtrees must have more than* $\frac{2}{3}n$ *of nodes. We move to this child, and repeat the argument recursively.*

By Theorem 10.6.14 the family of rooted binary trees is strongly $\Theta(\lg n)$*-separable.*

As the following theorem shows, there is a simple recursive layout method for strongly separable graphs.

Theorem 10.6.17 *Let* $S : \mathbf{N} \rightarrow \mathbf{N}$ *be a monotonically nondecreasing function. If an n-node graph G is strongly* $S(n)$*-separable,* $n = 4^k$, *then G can be laid out in a square with the side* $\Theta(\max(\sqrt{n}, \Delta_S(n)))$, *where* Δ *is the function defined by:*

$$\Delta_S(n) = S(n) + 2S\left(\frac{n}{4}\right) + 4S\left(\frac{n}{16}\right) + \cdots = \sum_{i=0}^{\lg_4 n} 2^i S\left(\frac{n}{4^i}\right).$$

[5] Observe that the concept of strong separability is similar to that of bisection-width, though it is actually much stronger, since it requires that it can be applied recursively to subgraphs obtained after separation. Note too that from the computational point of view, it is desirable that the bisection-width of a network is as large as possible, but from the layout point of view, just the opposite is the case.

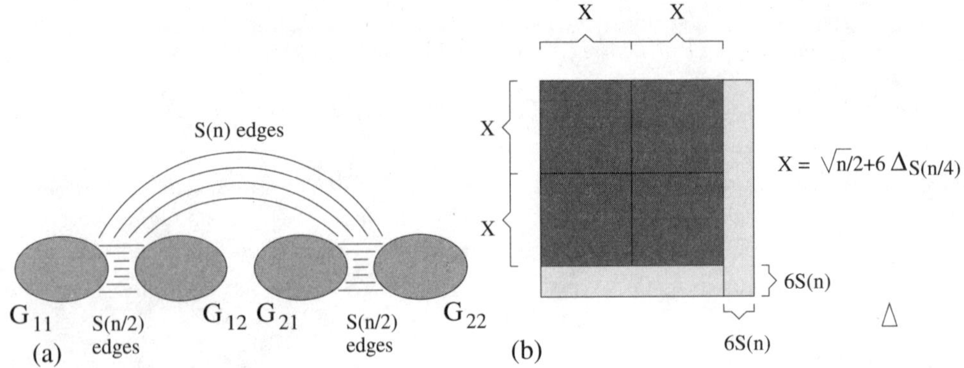

Figure 10.39 Layout of graphs using separators

Before proving the theorem, let us take a closer look at the function Δ_S.

Example 10.6.18 *If $S(n) = n^\alpha$, $n = 4^k$, then*

$$\Delta_S(n) = \sum_{i=0}^{\lg_4 n} 2^i \left(\frac{n}{4^i}\right)^\alpha = n^\alpha \sum_{i=0}^{\lg_4 n} 2^{i(1-2\alpha)},$$

and let us distinguish several cases for α.

1. $\alpha < \frac{1}{2}$. *Then $2^{1-2\alpha} > 1$, and therefore $\Delta_S(n)$ is approximately equal to the last term of the sum. Hence,*

$$\Delta_S(n) \approx \Theta(n^\alpha 2^{(\lg_4 n)(1-2\alpha)}) = \Theta(n^\alpha 2^{\frac{\lg n}{2}(1-2\alpha)}) = \Theta(n^\alpha n^{\frac{1}{2}(1-2\alpha)}) = \Theta(\sqrt{n}).$$

2. $\alpha = \frac{1}{2}$. *Then $\Delta_S(n) \sim n^{\frac{1}{2}} \lg_4 n = \Theta(\sqrt{n}\lg n)$.*
3. $\alpha > \frac{1}{2}$. *In this case $\Delta_S(n)$ is a decreasing geometric sequence, and therefore $\Delta_S(n)$ equals approximately the first term of the sum: $\Delta_S(n) = \Theta(n^\alpha)$.*

Proof of Theorem 10.6.17 We assume $n = 4^i$ and make the proof by induction on i. If n is not a power of 4, we can add isolated nodes to the graph, which does not increase the size of the set of edges that have to be deleted.

The aim is to show that G can be laid out in a square with side of length $\sqrt{n} + 6\Delta_S(n)$. The basis of induction is easy; for $i = 0$ we have a one-node graph and the theorem clearly holds.

For the induction step let $i > 1$. According to the assumption, by removing $S(n)$ edges, we get two graphs G_1, G_2, of size $\frac{n}{2}$, and by removing $S(\frac{n}{2})$ edges, we get from G_1 and G_2 graphs G_{11}, G_{12} and G_{21}, G_{22}, respectively (see Figure 10.39a). By the induction hypothesis, graphs $G_{ij}, i,j \in [2]$, can be laid out in rectangles (see Figure 10.39b), with side $\sqrt{\frac{n}{4}} + 6\Delta_S\left(\frac{n}{4}\right)$. Since S is nondecreasing, $S\left(\frac{n}{2}\right) \leq S(n)$. There are therefore at most $3S(n)$ edges that have to be added to these four layouts; they may require at most $6S(n)$ new corridors in both directions. As the total we get a layout in the square of side $2(\sqrt{\frac{n}{4}} + 6\Delta_S(\frac{n}{4})) + 6S(n)$. Since $\Delta_S(n) = S(n) + 2\Delta_S(\frac{n}{4})$, we have

$$\begin{aligned} 2\left(\sqrt{\frac{n}{4}} + 6\Delta_S(\frac{n}{4})\right) + 6S(n) &= \sqrt{n} + 6(S(n) + 2\Delta_S(\frac{n}{4})) \\ &= \sqrt{n} + 6\Delta_S(n), \end{aligned}$$

and this completes the induction step. □

Example 10.6.19 *The family of binary trees is strongly* $(\lg n)$*-separable. (See Example 10.6.18 and Exercise 41.) Since* $\lg n$ *grows more slowly than* $\sqrt{n}$*, we have (see Example 10.6.18)* $\Delta_{\lg n}(n) \leq \sqrt{n}$*. Theorem 10.6.17 therefore again implies that all binary trees can be laid out in area* $\Theta(n)$*.*

Exercise 10.6.20 *Determine* $\Delta_S(n)$ *if* $S(n)$ *is constant.*

Exercise 10.6.21 *Suppose* $S(n) = n^a \lg^b n$*. For which values of a and b is* $\Gamma_s(n) = \mathcal{O}(S(n))$*? Determine* $\Gamma_S(n)$ *in other cases.*

Exercise 10.6.22 *Show that the family of hypercubes* H_d *is strongly* 2^{d-1}*-separable.*

Let us now turn to the problem of layout of planar graphs. As we could see from Example 10.6.13, we can hardly expect to find smaller separators than $\sqrt{n}$ edges for the family of all planar graphs of n nodes. Surprisingly, a constant factor more is already sufficient. The key to this is the following result from graph theory.

Theorem 10.6.23 (Tarjan–Lipton's separator theorem) *If G is a planar graph with n nodes, then there is a set of at most* $4\lceil\sqrt{n}\rceil$ *nodes whose removal disconnects G into two parts, neither of which has more than* $\frac{2}{3}n$ *nodes.*

As a consequence we get the following theorem.

Theorem 10.6.24 *Every planar graph of degree 4 is* $\Theta(\sqrt{n})$*-separable, and therefore can be laid out in area* $\mathcal{O}(n\lg^2 n)$*.*

Proof: By Theorem 10.6.23, for any n-node planar graph G of degree 4 we can find at most $4\lceil\sqrt{n}\rceil$ nodes that separate G. Since G is of degree 4, this implies that G is $16\sqrt{n}$-separable. By Theorem 10.6.14, G is then strongly $\Theta(\sqrt{n})$-separable, and therefore, by Theorem 10.6.17 and Example 10.6.18, G can be laid out in a square with side $\mathcal{O}(\sqrt{n}\lg n)$ – hence the theorem holds. □

It is known that there are n-node planar graphs that require $\Omega(n\lg n)$ area for their layout, and even $\Omega(n^2)$ area if crossing of edges is not allowed. On the other hand, it is not known whether there are planar graphs that really require $\Omega(n\lg^2 n)$ area for their layouts.

Any technique for a layout of planar graphs can be used to make layouts of arbitrary graphs. The key concept here is that of the **crossing number** of a graph G. This is the minimum number of edge crossings needed to draw G in the plane; planar graphs have the crossing number 0.

Theorem 10.6.25 *Suppose that all planar graphs G of degree 4 and n nodes can be laid out in the area* $A(n)$*. Then every n-node graph of degree 4 and with crossing number c can be laid out in area* $\Theta(A(n+c))$ *– and therefore, by Theorem 10.6.24, in area* $\Theta((n+c)\lg^2(n+c))$*.*

Proof: Draw G in the plane with c edge crossings. At each crossing point introduce a new node. The resulting graph is planar and of degree 4, and therefore can be laid out in area $\Theta(A(n+c))$. □

An example of an interesting interconnection structure with a large crossing number is the mesh of trees.

Remark 10.6.26 Another general technique for layout of graphs is based on the concept of a 'bifurcator' for separation of graphs. It uses tree of meshes for interconnections and, again, the divide-and-conquer method. It can be shown that a large family of graphs can be separated in such a way that they can be embedded in a tree of meshes. Arrays in the nodes of the tree serve as crossbar switches to embed edges connecting nodes from two separated subgraphs.

10.7 Limitations *

For sequential computations, such as those performed by Turing machines and RAMs or on von Neumann computers, one can quite safely ignore physical aspects of the underlying computer system and deal with the design and analysis of programs in a purely logical fashion – as we have done so far. This is hardly the case in parallel and distributed computing or in various new nontraditional and nonclassical models of computers, as in quantum computing. In these areas the laws of physics have to be applied to the design and analysis of computing systems.

In this section we consider some implications which the geometry of space and the speed of light have on computation/communication networks and their performance in the case of massive parallelism. We show for regular symmetric low diameter networks, as dealt with in this chapter, and for randomly interconnected networks that length and cost of communications are prohibitively large; they grow fast with the size of networks.

We start with the following problem: let us consider a layout of a finite graph $G = \langle V, E\rangle$ in the 3-dimensional Euclidean space. Let the layout of each node have a unit volume and, for simplicity of argument, assume that it has the form of a sphere and is represented by a single point in the centre. Let the distance between the layouts of two nodes be the distance between layouts of the points representing these nodes. The length of the layout of an edge between two nodes is the distance between these two points. The question we are going to consider is how large the average length of edges has to be and how large the total length of all edges of the network should be. In doing so we assume that edges have no volume and that they can go through everything without limit and in any number. This idealized assumption implies that the reality is worse than our lower bound results will indicate.

Let us first observe that if G has n nodes and all are packed into a sphere, then the radius R of the sphere has to be at least

$$R = \left(\frac{3n}{4\pi}\right)^{\frac{1}{3}}.$$

Because of the bounded speed of light this implies that a lower bound for the maximal time needed for a communication within one computational step is $\Omega(n^{\frac{1}{3}})$ in an n-processor network on a complete graph.

10.7.1 Edge Length of Regular Low Diameter Networks

The main drawback of networks such as hypercubes is that their physical realization has to have very long communication lines.

Theorem 10.7.1 *The average Euclidean length of edges of any 3-dimensional layout of a hypercube H_d is at least $(7R)/(16d)$, where R is given as above.*

Proof: Let us consider a 3-dimensional layout of $H_d = \langle V_d, E_d \rangle$, with the layout of each node as a sphere of a unit volume, and let N be any node of H_d. Then, there are at most $\frac{2^d}{8}$ nodes of H_d within Euclidean distance $\frac{R}{2}$ of N, and layouts of at least $\frac{7 \cdot 2^d}{8}$ nodes have Euclidean distance from N more than $\frac{R}{2}$. Now let T_N be a spanning tree of H_d of depth d with N as the root. Since H_d has diameter d such a spanning tree has to exist. T_N has 2^d nodes and $2^d - 1$ paths from N to different nodes of H_d. Let P be such a path and $|P|$ the number of edges on P. Clearly, $|P| \le d$. Let us denote the Euclidean length of the path of the layout of P by $l(P)$. Since 7/8th of all nodes have Euclidean distance at least $\frac{R}{2}$ from N, for the average of $l(P)$ we get

$$(2^d - 1)^{-1} \sum_{P \in T_N} l(P) \ge \frac{7R}{16}.$$

The average Euclidean length of the layout of an edge in P is therefore bounded as follows:

$$(2^d - 1)^{-1} \sum_{P \in T_N} (|P|^{-1} \sum_{e \in P} l(e)) \ge \frac{7R}{16d}. \tag{10.2}$$

This does not yet provide a lower bound on the average Euclidean length of an edge of E_d. However, using the edge symmetry of H_d we can establish that the average length of the edge in the 3-dimensional layout of H_d is at least $\frac{7R}{16d}$.

Indeed, let us represent a node a of T_N by a d-bit string $a_{d-1} \dots a_0$ and an edge (a, b) between nodes a and b that differ in the ith bit by (a, i). In this way each edge has two representations.

Consider now the set $\mathcal{A}$ of automorphisms $\alpha_{v,j}$ of H_d consisting of a modulus two addition of a binary vector v of length d to the binary representation of a node x (which corresponds to complementing some bits of the binary representation of x), followed by a cyclic rotation over distance j. More formally, if $x = x_{d-1} \dots x_{d_0}$, $x_i \in \{0,1\}$, and $0 \le j < n$, then $\alpha_{v,j}(a) = b_{j+1} b_j \dots b_0 b_{d-1} b_{d-2} \dots b_j$, with $b_i = a_i \oplus v_i$, for all $0 \le i < d$.

Consider further the family $\mathcal{S} = \{\alpha(T_N) \mid \alpha \in \mathcal{A}\}$ of spanning trees isomorphic to T_N. By the same argument as that used to derive (10.2) we get, for each $\alpha \in \mathcal{A}$, that each path $\alpha(P)$ from the root $\alpha(N)$ to a node in $\alpha(T_N)$ has also length at least $\frac{7R}{16d}$. The same lower bound applies if we average (10.2) over all $\alpha \in \mathcal{A}$ and therefore

$$\frac{\sum_{\alpha \in \mathcal{A}} [(2^d - 1)^{-1} \sum_{P \in T_N} (|P|^{-1} \sum_{e \in P} l(\alpha(e))]}{d 2^d} \ge \frac{7R}{16d}. \tag{10.3}$$

If we now fix an edge e in T_N, then by averaging $l(\alpha(e))$ over all $\alpha \in \mathcal{A}$, we show that this average equals twice the average length of an edge layout. Indeed, for each $f \in E_d$ there are α_1 and α_2 in $\mathcal{A}$, $\alpha_1 \ne \alpha_2$, such that $\alpha_1(e) = \alpha_2(e) = f$, and $\alpha(e) \ne f$ for $\alpha \in \mathcal{A} - \{\alpha_1, \alpha_2\}$. Therefore, for each $e \in E_d$:

$$\sum_{\alpha \in \mathcal{A}} l(\alpha(e)) = 2 \sum_{f \in E_d} l(f)$$

and for any path P of H_d

$$\sum_{e \in P} \sum_{\alpha \in \mathcal{A}} l(\alpha(e)) = 2|P| \sum_{f \in E_d} l(f)). \tag{10.4}$$

By rearranging the summation order in (10.3) and substituting from Equation (10.4), we get the Theorem. □

Since H_d has $d2^{d-1}$ edges for the overall sum of layouts of all edges in a 3-dimensional layout of E_d we get

$$\sum_{e \in E_d} l(e) \geq \frac{2^d 7R}{32} \geq \left(\frac{3}{4\pi}\right)^{\frac{1}{3}} 7 \cdot 2^{4d/3-5}$$

and hence we have:

Corollary 10.7.2 *The total sum of lengths of all edges of a hypercube H_d in the 3-dimensional space is $\Omega(2^{4d/3})$ and the average length of an edge is $\Omega(d^{-1}2^{\frac{d}{3}})$.*

These results throw a different light on such outcomes of the analysis of hypercube computations as those that on a hypercube H_d we can add $n = 2^d$ numbers in $\mathcal{O}(\lg n)$ parallel steps. Indeed, since the results of calculations of any two processors have to interact somewhere, there have to be signal transition paths between each pair of processors and taking the outermost ones, the distance of a path between them has to be $\Omega(n^{\frac{1}{3}})$

The hypercube is not unique with respect to such high requirements on the length of interconnections in three- and two-dimensional layouts. It has been shown that for cube-connected cycles CCC_d the average length of an edge in a 3-dimensional layout is $\Omega(2^{d/3}d^{-2/3})$ and the length of edges is $\Omega(d^{4d/3}d^{1/3})$. Similar results hold for de Bruijn and shuffle exchange graphs. On a more general level, it can be shown that the average Euclidean length in a 3-dimensional layout of an edge-symmetric graph is $7R/(16D)$, where D is the diameter. For example, this implies that for a complete graph K_n the average edge length is $\Omega(n^{1/3})$ and the total edge length is $\Omega(n^{7/3})$. (We have quite different results for some simple interconnection structures. Indeed, for an n-node ring we have an average edge length $\Omega(n^{-2/3})$ and the total edge length $\Omega(n^{1/3})$. For a two-dimensional n-node toroid the average length of an edge is $\Omega(n^{-1/6})$ and the total wire length is $\Omega(n^{5/6})$.)

10.7.2 Edge Length of Randomly Connected Networks

Since low-diameter symmetric networks have a very high average length of edge layouts it is natural to ask whether the situation is better for much less regular networks. The extreme along these lines seem to be randomly interconnected networks. However, the average and total length of edges of layouts of random graphs is also prohibitively high, as will now be shown.

As already discussed in Section 2.4.2, an undirected graph G of n nodes can be given by a binary string w_G of length $\frac{n(n-1)}{2}$. Conversely, each binary string of such a length describes an n node undirected graph.

An undirected graph G is called **random** if the following inequality holds for conditional Kolmogorov complexity:

$$K(w_G / bin^{-1}(n)) \geq \frac{n(n-1)}{2} - cn, \tag{10.5}$$

where c is an appropriate constant ($c = 0.09$ suffices for n large enough).

Exercise 10.7.3 *Show that a fraction of at least $1 - \frac{1}{2^{cn}}$ of all graphs has conditional Kolmogorov complexity as in (10.5).*

The main result on the length of edges of random graphs presented below is based on the following lemma claiming that all nodes of random graphs have to have high degrees.

Lemma 10.7.4 *The degree d of each node of a random graph satisfies the inequality* $|d - \frac{n-1}{2}| < \frac{n}{4}$.

Proof: Let N be a node of a random graph G and let the deviation of degree of N from $\frac{n-1}{2}$ be at least k. Using Kolmogorov/Chaitin complexity reasoning, we obtain an upper bound on k as follows.

One way to describe the set of edges of G incident to N is to give an index specifying the interconnection pattern of N from the set of

$$m_k = \sum_{|d-(n-1)/2| \geq k} \binom{n-1}{d}$$

possible interconnection patterns for N.

As discussed in Section 1.6, $Pr(S_n = d) = \binom{n}{d}\frac{1}{2^n}$ for the random variable S_n that expresses the number of successes of n trials if the probability of success is $\frac{1}{2}$. If we now use another slight modification of Chernoff's bound, namely that $Pr(|S_{n-1} - \frac{n-1}{2}| \geq k) \leq 2e^{-\frac{k^2}{n-1}}$, then we get:

$$m_k \leq 2^n e^{-\frac{k^2}{n-1}}. \tag{10.6}$$

On the basis of n, m_k and N we can describe G as follows: we take the string m_G but delete from it those $n-1$ bits describing connections of N and we prefix the resulting string by

- $\lceil \lg n \rceil$ bits identifying N;
- $\lceil \lg n \rceil$ bits identifying the degree of N;
- $\lceil \lg m_k \rceil + \lceil \lg \lg m_k \rceil$ bits identifying the interconnection pattern of N in a self-delimiting form.

It is clear that one can reconstruct G from n and such a description. The total length of such a description is

$$\lg m_k + 2\lg\lg m_k + \mathcal{O}(\lg n) + \frac{n(n-1)}{2} - (n-1).$$

This has to be at least the length of the shortest binary program to construct G, i. e. $K(w_G \,/\, bin^{-1}(n))$ satisfying Equation 10.5. Hence

$$\lg m_k + 2\lg\lg m_k \geq n - 1 - \mathcal{O}(\lg n) - cn.$$

By (10.6), $\lg m_k \leq n - (\frac{k^2}{n-1})\lg e$ and therefore $k < \frac{n}{4}$ if $c = 0.09$. □

As a corollary we get:

Theorem 10.7.5 *A random graph G of n nodes has* $\Omega(n^2)$ *edges and the total length of edges of an layout of G in the 3-dimensional space is* $\Omega(n^{7/3})$ *(and* $\Omega(n^{5/2})$ *for a layout in the two-dimensional space).*

Proof: The first claim directly follows from Lemma 10.7.4 because each node of a random graph with n nodes has at least $\frac{n}{4}$ edges. Moreover, from the same lemma it follows that each node of G is incident to $\frac{n-1}{2} \pm \frac{n}{4}$ nodes and (7/8)th of these nodes are (in the 3-dimensional space) at a distance of $\Omega(n^{1/3})$. Hence the theorem for the 3-dimensional case. The argument for the two-dimensional case is similar. □

Remark 10.7.6 A more detailed analysis shows that even under a very conservative assumption that the unit length of a wire has a volume which is a constant fraction of that of components it connects, the total volume needed to layout an n node graph in the three-dimensional space is $\Omega(n^{3/2})$ for hypercubes and $\Omega(n^{3/2}\lg^{-3/2} n)$ for cube-connected cycles. The last bound is pretty good because it has been shown that every small degree graph can be laid out in the 3-dimensional space with volume $\mathcal{O}(n^{3/2})$.

Remark 10.7.7 It is well known that with modern high density technologies most of the space in any device executing computations is taken by wires. For the ratio

$$\frac{\text{volume of communication wires}}{\text{volume of computing elements}}$$

we therefore have the lower bound $\Omega(n^{1/3})$ for such networks as hypercubes and $\Omega(n^{4/3})$ for randomly connected networks.

Remark 10.7.8 From the practical point of view one of the most natural and important requirements for massive parallel computing is that networks should be scalable.

A family $\mathcal{D}$ of abstract computational devices $\{\mathcal{D}_n\}_{n\geq 1}$, where each $\mathcal{D}_n$ is capable of processing any input of size n, is called **scalable** if there is a physical realization $\mathcal{R} = \{\mathcal{R}_n\}_{n\geq 1}$ of $\mathcal{D}$ such that for every n the maximal duration of any computational step (measured in any real unit of time) on $\mathcal{R}_n$ does not depend on n.

Since for regular symmetric low-diameter networks and randomly interconnected networks, the length of interconnections rises sharply with the size of network, the only graphs scalable are symmetric high-diameter graphs like arrays. For this reason arrays of processors are often considered as the most appropriate computer architecture for really massive parallelism.

Remark 10.7.9 Under similar assumptions as above, for physical space and time consideration, it has been shown that any reasonable parallel computer of time complexity $t(n)$ can be simulated by a MTM in time $\mathcal{O}(t^{13}(n))$. This implies that if physical laws are taken into consideration, then with respect to the first machine class, only polynomial speed-up is achievable.

Moral: Communication networks are abandoned in society and nature. A good rule of thumb for dealing with networks in parallel and distributed computing is therefore, as in life, to use networks simple enough to be manageable and fast and reliable enough to be useful. It should also be remembered that modern means of communication often actually accentuate and strengthen noncommunication.

10.8 Exercises

1. (A card trick) The following card trick is based on the magician's ability to remember exactly where in the deck of cards a volunteer has inserted a chosen card, as well as on the ability to perform fast routing on shuffle exchange graph networks.

   A volunteer is asked to pick an arbitrary card from a deck of 2^d cards and to insert it back into an arbitrary position in such a way that the magician cannot see which card was chosen. The magician then performs a certain number of out-shuffle and in-shuffle operations, and as a result the chosen card appears at the top of the deck (or in the kth position where k has been announced in advance).

   Explain the trick. (An out-shuffle (in-shuffle) operation gets each card from a binary position $a_{d-1}\ldots a_0$ into the position $a_{d-2}\ldots a_0a_{d-1}(a_{d-2}\ldots a_0\overline{a_{d-1}})$.

2. Prove Lemma 10.1.16.

3. Draw nicely (a) DB_4; (b) CCC_4; (c) SE_4.

4. Show that the following graphs are Cayley graphs: (a) wrapped butterflies; (b) toroids; (c) star graphs.

5.** (Fast Fourier transform) The discrete Fourier transform of a sequence $a_0, \ldots, a_{n-1}$ is the sequence $b_0, \ldots, b_{n-1}$, where $b_j = \sum_{i=0}^{n-1} a_i \omega^{ij}$ and ω is the nth primitive root of 1. Show how to compute the discrete Fourier transform for $n = 2^d$ on the butterfly B_d in time $\Theta(\lg n)$, if we assume that the node (i,α) of B_d knows $\omega^{exp(i,\alpha)}$, where for $\alpha = w_1 \ldots w_d$, $exp(i,\alpha) = w_i w_{i-1} \ldots w_1 0 \ldots 0$.

6. (Fibonacci cube) For an integer i let i_F denote the unique Fibonacci representation of i (see Exercise 2.1.8). The Fibonacci cube of degree d, notation FC_d, is a graph $\langle V_d, E_d \rangle$, where $V_d = \{0, 1, \ldots, F_d - 1\}$ and $(i,j) \in E_d$ if and only if $ham(i_F, j_F) = 1$. (a) Draw FC_2, FC_3, FC_4, FC_5. (b) Determine for FC_d the number of edges, degree of nodes and diameter.

7. The Fibonacci cube FC_d can be decomposed in various ways into Fibonacci cubes of smaller degrees. Find such decompositions.

8. Determine the number of nodes for hypercubes and de Bruijn, star and Kautz graphs of degree and diameter $2,4,6,8,10$. (You will find that de Bruijn graphs, star graphs and Kautz graphs compare very favourably with hypercubes regarding the number of nodes that can be connected in networks of the same degree and diameter.)

9.* A set S of nodes of the de Bruijn graph DB_d forms a **necklace** if S is the set of all those nodes that can be obtained from one of them using the perfect shuffle operation repeatedly. (a) Determine the number of necklaces. (b) Show that there is a linear time algorithm for producing all necklaces.

10. Show that (a) each Euler tour for a shuffle exchange graph SE_d uniquely specifies a Hamilton cycle for DB_{d-1}; (b) each de Bruijn graph has a Hamilton cycle.

11. The problem of determining exactly the bisection-width for de Bruijn graphs and shuffle exchange graphs is still open. (a) Determine the bisection-width for SE_d and DB_d for $d = 2,3,4,5$. (b) It is possible to bisect DB_7 by removing 30 edges. Show this. Can you do better?

12. (Generalized de Bruijn and Kautz graphs) Let $m, d \in \mathbf{N}$. For generalized de Bruijn graphs $GDB(m,d) = \langle V, E \rangle, V = [m]^d$, $E = \{(a_{d-1} \ldots a_0, a_{d-2} \ldots a_0 x) \,|\, a_{d-1} \ldots a_0 \in [m]^d, x \in [m]\}$ and generalized Kautz graphs are defined as follows: $GK(m,d) = \langle V, E \rangle$, $V = \{\bar{a} \,|\, \bar{a} \in [m+1]^d$ and no two consecutive symbols of $\bar{a}$ are the same$\}$, $E = \{(a_{d-1} \ldots a_0, a_{d-2} \ldots a_0 x) \,|\, a_{d-1} \ldots a_0 \in V, a_0 \neq x\}$. Determine the number of nodes, edges, degree and diameter.

13. Show that in generalized de Bruijn graphs $GDB(m,d)$ there is exactly one path of length d between any two nodes; therefore $M(m,d)^d = I$, where $M(m,d)$ is the adjacency matrix for $GDB(m,d)$.

14.* Show that in generalized Kautz graphs $GK(m,d)$ there is exactly one path of length d or $d-1$ between any two nodes. Show that $M(m,d)^{d-1} + M(m,d)^d = I$, where $M(m,d)$ is the adjacency matrix for $GK(m,d)$.

15. Describe greedy routing methods for generalized de Bruijn and Kautz graphs.

16. (Fault tolerance) Fault tolerance of a graph is the minimum number of nodes or edges that can be removed to disconnect the graph. It is usually defined through node- and edge-connectivity. **Node-connectivity**, $k(G)$, of a graph G is the minimum number of nodes whose removal disconnects G. **Edge-connectivity**, $\lambda(G)$, is the minimum number of edges whose removal disconnects G. (a)* Show that $k(G) =$ the maximum number of node-disjoint paths $p(u,v)$ over all nodes u,v of G; (b)** $\lambda(G) =$ the maximum number of edge-disjoint paths $p(u,v)$ over all nodes u,v of G. Determine node- and edge-connectivity for the following graphs: (c) arrays; (d) toroids; (e) hypercubes; (f) cube-connected cycles; (g) de Bruijn graphs; (h) shuffle exchange graphs; (i) star graphs; (j) Kautz graphs.

17. (**Möbius graphs**) A 0-Möbius graph, notation 0-M_d is defined by 0-$M_d = \langle V,E\rangle, V = [2]^d, E = E_1 \cup E_2$, where $E_1 = \{(a_{d-1}\ldots a_0, a_{d-1}\ldots a_{i+1}\bar{a}_i a_{i-1}\ldots a_0),\ a_{i+1} = 0$ or $i = d-1\}$ $E_2 = \{(a_{d-1}\ldots a_0, a_{d-1}\ldots a_{i+1}\bar{a}_i\bar{a}_{i-1}\ldots\bar{a}_0),\ a_{i+1} = 1\}$. (a) Depict 0-$M_2$, 0-$M_3$, 0-$M_4$. (b) Show that the diameter of 0-M_d is $\lceil\frac{d+2}{2}\rceil$ (therefore smaller than for the hypercube H_d.)

18. Show that $g_2(R_n) = \lceil\frac{n}{2}+1\rceil$ for odd n.

19. Show Theorem 10.2.22 for all even n.

20. Design for star graphs (a) a greedy routing algorithm; (b) a broadcasting algorithm.

21. Show that $b(FC_d) = d-2$ for the Fibonacci cube FC_d of degree d.

22.* Define the three-dimensional mesh of trees, and show how it can be used to multiply 2 matrices of degree $n = 2^d$ in $\mathcal{O}(\lg n)$ time.

23. Design a permutation routing protocol for a one-dimensional array of n processors that works in time $\mathcal{O}(n)$ and needs buffers of maximum size three.

24. Consider the following modification of the Beneš network BE_d: each source-level node has only one input and each target-level node has only one output. Show that such a network can implement any permutation $\pi : [2]^{d-1} \mapsto [2]^{d-1}$ in such a way that no two paths have a common node.

25. Show how to simulate efficiently an ascend/descend program for the hypercube $H_d, n = 2^d, d = 2^k$, on (a) a shuffle exchange graph SE_d; (b) cube-connected cycles CCC_{d-k}; (c)* a linear array of n processors.

26. The following are often considered as permutation networks: the **Baseline network** and the **Omega network**. They are defined as follows. Baseline network: $BN_d = \langle V,E\rangle, V = \{(i,j)\,|\,0 \le i \le d, 0 \le j < 2^d\}$, $E = \{((i,a_{d-1}\ldots a_0),(i+1,a_{d-1}\ldots a_{d-i-2}0a_{d-i-1}\ldots a_0)),((i,a_{d-1}\ldots a_0),(i+1,a_{d-1}\ldots a_{d-i-2}1a_{d-i-1}\ldots a_0))\,|\,0 \le i \le d, a_{d-1}\ldots a_0 \in [2]^d\}$. Omega network: $ON_d = \langle V,E\rangle, V = \{(i,j)\,|\,0 \le i \le d, 0 \le j < 2^d\}, E = \{((i,j)(i+1,\lfloor\frac{j}{2}\rfloor),((i,j),(i+1,2^{d-1}+\lfloor\frac{j}{2}\rfloor)\,|\,0 \le i < d, 0 \le j < 2^d\}$. (a) Draw BN_4, OM_4 and B_4. (b)* Show that the baseline network, Omega network and butterfly network are isomorphic as graphs.

27. Prove the correctness of the data distribution algorithm on page 580.

28.* Show how one can implement efficiently the data distribution algorithm (page 580) on a butterfly.

29.** Show that any n-node ring or array can be embedded in any connected n-node graph with dilation 3.

30. Use the fact that each hypercube has a Hamilton cycle determined by the Gray code to depict nicely H_6. (Hint: depict nodes equally on a ring following Gray code numeration and add missing edges.)

31. Design the following embeddings: (a) a 3×10 array into a 5×6 array with dilation 2; (b) a $3 \times 2 \times 3$ array into its optimal hypercube with dilation 1.

32. Prove Theorem 10.3.9.

33. Show that the de Bruijn graph DB_d can be embedded into the shuffle exchange graph SE_d with dilation 2.

34. Show that (a) a linear array of 15 nodes can be embedded into the complete binary tree T_3 with dilation 3; (b)* any linear array can be embedded into its optimal binary tree with dilation 3.

35. Show how to embed a ring with 2^d nodes into the de Bruijn graph.

36. Embed a $5 \times 5 \times 9$ array into the hypercube H_7 with dilation 2 and load factor 2.

37. Show that an X-tree can be embedded into its optimal hypercube with dilation 2.

38. Show that if $d = 2^k$, then CCC_d can be embedded into H_{d+k} with dilation 1.

39. Show that the cube-connected cycles can be embedded into their optimal hypercubes with dilation 2.

40. Show that the hypercube H_d is a subgraph of the Fibonacci cube FC_{2d+1}, and that the Fibonacci cube FC_d is a subgraph of H_{d-2}.

41. (Separation of binary trees) Let us consider the family of all trees for which each node has degree at most 3. (a) Show that by removing one edge of a n-node tree the nodes of the tree can be separated into two sets A and B such that $|A| \leq \frac{3}{4}n, |B| \leq \frac{3}{4}n$. (b) Show that the constant $\frac{3}{4}$ is optimal by giving a small tree in which removing one edge always produces a partition such that one of the sets A, B has exactly $\frac{3}{4}n$ nodes. (c) Show that by removing $\Theta(\lg n)$ edges we can get a partition of nodes into sets A, B such that $|A| = \lceil \frac{n}{2} \rceil, B = \lfloor \frac{n}{2} \rfloor$.

42.** Show that there is an $0 < \varepsilon < 1$ such that for any undirected graph G of n nodes and any almost balanced partition π of its edges there is a set W of at least εn nodes such that each set of the partition π contains, for each node from W, at least εn edges incident with that node.

43. Show that the family of arrays is strongly $(\sqrt{n}+1)$-separable.

44. Consider layouts of complete binary trees with all leaves at the layout-rectangle boundaries. What is the minimum length of the longest edge for such layouts?

45.* Show that the crossing number for complete graphs is $\Omega(n^4)$.

46. Consider the following modification of hypercubes H_d, $d = 2^k$. Remove all edges from H_d, and replace each node by a complete binary tree with d leaves, one for each dimension of the hypercube. For a pair of trees corresponding to nodes of H_d connected by an edge of dimension i connect corresponding leaves of their trees. The resulting graph has degree 4. Show that this graph can be laid out in area $\Theta(n^2), n = 2^d$.

QUESTIONS

1. Why is the bisection-width an important characteristic of communication networks?
2. What is the difference between a mesh of trees and a tree of meshes?
3. In what lies the power of shuffle exchange interconnections?
4. Why is it the case that for many basic algorithmic problems there are simple-to-formulate algorithms for such networks as hypercube, butterfly, shuffle exchange graphs and de Bruijn graphs?
5. Which properties of splitters are utilized in making multi-butterfly networks efficient for routing?
6. How can one perform randomized routing on (a) hypercubes; (b) shuffle exchange graphs; (c) de Bruijn graphs?
7. In which cases is it proper to use dynamic or multiple embeddings?
8. What are the basic ingredients of efficient simulations of PRAMs on bounded-degree networks?
9. How many layers currently are used in integrated circuits?
10. What is the crossing number for the three-dimensional hypercube?

10.9 Historical and Bibliographical References

Communication network theory has several roots, and their offspring have merged recently. The oldest root lies in graph theory. Cayley (1889) connected graph and group theory and created grounds for a general, abstract treatment of regular graphs. In addition, graph theory in general forms an important theoretical base for communication network theory. The design of switching networks, especially in connection with the first very large-scale project in parallel and distributed communication, telephone networks, provided a significant technological impetus. Permutation and sorting network problems, well-defined, urgent and intriguing, with pioneering works by Beneš (1964, 1965) and Batcher (1968), created an important area of research.

Emerging ideas of parallel computing brought another impetus, and led to the study of hypercubes and bounded-degree regular networks; see Schwartz (1980) for a survey of earlier work. Experiences with the first designs and use of parallel computers and a search for good models of parallel computing turned attention to problems such as routing, embedding and simulation. VLSI technology brought the layout problem. The last root of modern network theory lies within computational complexity theory. Attempts to understand the power and limitations of parallel computing soon revealed communication problems as the key ones, and led to the investigation of a variety of networks – with the aim of deriving new upper and lower bounds.

The most comprehensive treatment of hypercubes and bounded-degree networks, properties, routing, simulations and embeddings, is found in Leighton (1992) and includes detailed historical and bibliographical references. Information dissemination problems are well surveyed by Hromkovič, Klasing, Monien and Peine (1995). Layout problems are systematically presented by Ullman (1984) and Lengauer (1990a, 1990b). Complexity approaches to networks are surveyed by Pippenger (1990).

Hypercubes and their properties are discussed in detail in Leighton (1992), Harary, Hayes and Wu (1988), Lakshmivarahan and Dhall (1990). The origin of the butterfly network is found in the early work on the fast Fourier transform, invented in the 1920s; see Press, Flannery, Teukolsky and Vetterling

(1986). The cube-connected cycles network was introduced by Preparata and Vuillemin (1981); shuffle exchange graphs by Stone (1971); de Bruijn graphs were reinvented by many, especially de Bruijn (1946). Kautz graphs, star graphs and Fibonacci cubes were introduced by Kautz (1968), Akers and Krishnamurthy (1986) and Hsu (1993). Meshes of trees were introduced by Muller and Preparata (1975), and trees of meshes by Leighton (1981).

The complex plane layout for the shuffle exchange graph is due to Hoey and Leiserson (1980). Full analysis of the bisection-width for the shuffle exchange graphs is found in Leighton (1992), which my presentation follows. A variety of algorithms for the hypercube and butterfly networks is presented by Akl (1989), Ranka and Sahni (1990), Lakshmivarahan and Dhall (1990) and Ja'Ja (1992).

There is a rich literature on broadcasting and gossiping. My presentation, and also Table 10.2, is an updated version from the survey by Hromkovič, Klasing, Monien and Peine (1990). This includes many bibliographical references on the subject and also to the results presented here. Some newer bounds are due to S. Perennes (1996). Another survey on this subject is by Fraigniaud and Lazard (1996).

Embeddings are covered by Leighton (1990), Monien and Sudborough (1992) and Lakhshmivarahan and Dhall (1990).

The **NP**-completeness results concerning embeddings on page 555 are due to Wagner and Corneil (1990) and Monien (1985). The first two claims in Theorem 10.3.3 are due to Greenberg, Heath and Rosenberg (1990) and Feldman and Unger (1992); the third one is folklore. Gray code embeddings are discussed in detail in Lakshmivarahan and Dhall (1990). Array embeddings are surveyed by Monien and Sudborough (1990) and Leighton (1990). Theorem 10.3.11 is due to Chan (1988, 1989). See also Chan and Chin (1988). Embeddings of complete binary trees in hypercubes were first discussed by Havel and Liebl (1973); see also Wu (1985) for Theorems 10.3.13, 10.3.14 and 10.3.15. Results on embedding of arbitrary trees into the hypercube, presented in Theorem 10.3.16, are due to Monien and Sudborough (1988) and Wagner (1987).

The concept of polymorphic arrays and the result on well balanced embedding of arbitrary arrays into polymorphic arrays are due to Fiat and Shamir (1984).

Table 10.4 is due to Ralf Klasing. The third entry in the table is due to Miller and Sudborough (1994); the fifth to Bhatt *et al.* (1988); the sixth entry to Heckmann, Klasing, Monien and Unger (1991); the seventh to Monien and Sudborough (1988); the eighth to Monien (1991); and the tenth to Heydemann, Opatrny and Sotteau (1994).

There is an extensive literature on routing. For a variety of networks for permutation routing see Beneš (1964, 1965), Leighton (1990), Lakshmivarahan and Dhall (1990) and Kruskal and Snir (1986). For routing in general and also for Exercise 10.4.26 see Leighton (1990). The result that preprocessing for a permutation routing can be done on the hypercube H_d in $\mathcal{O}(d^4)$ time is due to Nassimi and Sahni (1982). Theorem 10.4.14 is one of the improvements, due to Meyer auf der Heide (1992), of the original result $\Omega(\frac{\sqrt{n}}{c^{3/2}})$ due to Borodin and Hopcroft (1985). Theorem 10.4.16 is due to Lubotzky, Phillips and Sank (1988), and Theorem 10.4.19 to Leighton, Maggs, Ranade and Rao (1992). Valiant (1982) and Valiant and Brebner (1981) initiated research on the average-case analysis of greedy routing algorithms and randomized, two-stage routings. Further significant improvements are due to Upfal (1991), Ranade (1991) and others; see Leighton (1992) for further references.

For simulations between networks and their probabilistic analysis see Bhatt *et al.* (1988), Koch *et al.* (1989) and Meyer auf der Heide (1986). For the randomized simulation of PRAMs on hypercubes and bounded-degree networks, see Ullman (1984), Upfal and Wigderson (1987), Valiant (1990) and Karp, Luby and Meyer auf der Heide (1992). Fast implementation of the data distribution algorithm on the butterfly is due to Borodin and Hopcroft (1985). My presentation of routing and simulation owes much to Meyer auf der Heide (1992).

Layout methods and lower bound techniques are discussed in detail in Ullman (1984), Lengauer (1990a, 1990b) and Hromkovič (1996). H-tree embeddings are due to Browning (1980). Theorem 10.6.5

and $\mathcal{O}(\sqrt{n} / \lg n)$ as the upper bound are due to Brent and Kung (1980), and Theorem 10.6.8 to Paterson, Ruzzo and Snyder (1981). The **NP**-completeness results for layout problems on page 587 are due to Dolev, Leighton and Trickey (1983) and Bhatt and Cosmadakis (1982). The general layout technique, as presented in Section 10.6, is due to Valiant (1981) and Leiserson (1980, 1983). Its presentation here follows Ullman (1984), as well as the proof of Theorem 10.6.14 and further references. Theorem 10.6.23 is due to Lipton and Tarjan (1979), theorems 10.6.24 and 10.6.25 to Leighton (1981); see also Ullman (1984). For $\Theta(n^2 / \lg^2 n)$ layouts for hypercube, butterfly, cube-connected cycles, de Bruijn and shuffle exchange graphs see Ullman (1984). The method for layout of graphs based on bifurcators is due to Bhatt and Leighton (1984); see also Lengauer (1990).

For the limitations that the laws of physics impose on multiprocessor architectures, see papers by Vitányi (1994,1995); Section 10.7 is based on them.

11 Communications

INTRODUCTION

Communication is clearly of great importance for distributive, parallel and concurrent computing, and communication costs often dominate computation costs. Less obvious, but of equal importance, is that communications dominate sequential computing. Moreover, communication problems have inherent communication complexity, and the discovery of this complexity brings deep theoretical insights.

In the previous chapter we explored a variety of communication structures (graphs) *per se*, no matter what they are used to communicate. In this chapter, by contrast, we deal with communications, no matter how powerful, computationally, the communicating parties are and which way they communicate. We explore the power of various communication modes, especially deterministic and randomized ones, partitions of input data, and basic relations between communication and computational complexity.

The concepts, models, methods and results presented in this chapter allow one to understand the essence of difficulties in communication and how to handle those tasks efficiently.

LEARNING OBJECTIVES

The aim of the chapter is to demonstrate

1. the basic concepts concerning communication protocols and their complexity;
2. a variety of communication protocols presenting methods for minimizing communication needs;
3. lower bounds methods for fixed partitions and their relative power;
4. a method to determine the AT^2-complexity of VLSI circuits;
5. several types of nondeterministic and randomized protocols: Las Vegas, Monte Carlo and BPPC;
6. the relations between the power of different types of communication protocols;
7. the basic relations between communication and computational complexity.

Genuine poetry can communicate
before it is understood.

T. S. Eliot, 1929

One of the main discoveries of the modern search for the essence of difficulties in computing is that it is the inherent communication complexity of a problem, independent of a particular communication structure, that is the main contributor to the computational complexity.

This understanding first emerged in parallel and distributed computing, especially after the development of VLSI technology, where the cost of communication is the dominating factor regarding chips production and performance. The following investigations of the so-called AT^2-complexity of VLSI circuits and Boolean functions revealed clearly the central role of communication complexity. Problems with the performance and programming of networks of processors pointed to communication as the critical issue. Interactive protocols have been another area where the surprising power of communications and interactions emerged clearly, on a deep theoretical level, and with important applications.

In the PRAM model of parallel computing, communication problems are ignored and only computations are considered. Conversely, in the study of communication complexity, which is the topic of this chapter, computations are completely ignored and only communications are considered. Two communicating parties, each possessing only part of the input data, are allowed to have unlimited computational power. We are interested only in how many bits they have to exchange in order to solve a given problem (see Figure 11.1).

The idea of isolating communication from computation and studying it *per se*, which at first seems almost absurd, is actually very fruitful and gives rise to deep insights into the nature of computation and computational complexity. It has been revealed that communication complexity is closely related to computational problems which initially seem to have nothing to do with communication.

11.1 Examples and Basic Model

Given a computational problem P with its input data partitioned into two sets X and Y, the basic question is how much information two parties, A and B, both with unlimited computational power, have to exchange in order to solve P, provided that, at the beginning of a communication, party A knows only the input data from X and B only the input data from Y.

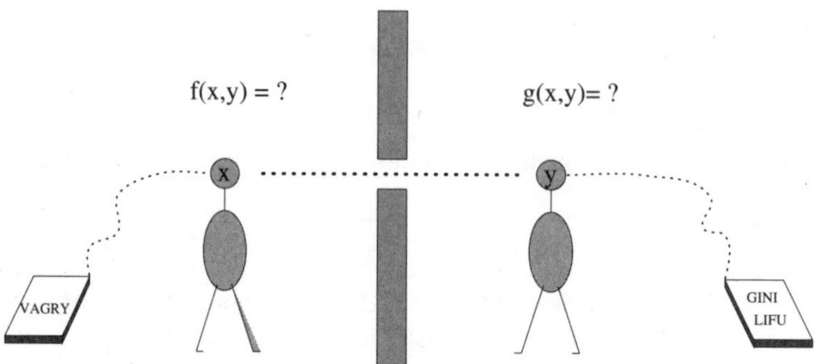

Figure 11.1 Communications between two parties to solve a problem

Example 11.1.1 *(Parity function) Let us assume that B is to compute the* **parity function** $z = (\sum_{i=1}^{n} a_i) \bmod 2$, *where* $a_i \in \{0,1\}$, *but B knows only* $n-k+1$ *bits* $a_k, \ldots, a_n$ *for some* $k > 1$, *and A knows the rest,* $a_1, \ldots, a_{k-1}$, *of the input bits. It is easy to see that it is enough for A to send B a single bit, namely* $(\sum_{j=1}^{k-1} a_j) \bmod 2$. *With this information B can determine z. Observe too that for this communication algorithm – protocol – it is of no importance how large k is. Also in the case that the input data are partitioned between A and B in some other way, it is always sufficient that A sends B a single bit (provided B knows what this one bit means). In other words, for communication during a parity function computation by two parties it is not important how the input data are partitioned between them.*

Example 11.1.2 *(Palindrome recognition) Let us again assume that party A knows a prefix* $x = a_1 \ldots a_{k-1}$ *and B knows the suffix* $y = a_k \ldots a_n$ *of a binary string* $a_1 \ldots a_n$. *This time, however, the task for B is to determine whether* $z = xy$ *is a palindrome. Intuitively, it seems clear that in the worst case it may happen that A needs to send B the whole of x, and therefore the number of bits that need to be exchanged depends on how big x is. In other words, the number of bits that need to be exchanged seems to depend very much on how the input data are partitioned between the two communicating parties. But is our intuition correct?*

Exercise 11.1.3 *Party A knows bits* $x_1, \ldots, x_n$, *B knows bits* $y_1, \ldots, y_n$. *A has to compute* $z_1 = \bigvee_{i=1}^{n}(x_i \vee y_i)$; *B has to compute* $z_2 = \bigwedge_{i=1}^{n}(x_i \wedge y_i)$. *How many bits do they have to exchange?*

Example 11.1.4 *(Addition of binary numbers) Assume that parties A and B are to compute the sum of two n-bit numbers* $x = a_n \ldots a_1$, $y = b_n \ldots b_1$, *where n is even, and each of them knows exactly half of the input bits. Assume also that B is to compute* $\frac{n}{2}$ *of the least significant bits of the sum, and A the rest. How many bits do they need to exchange?*

The answer greatly depends on how the input bits are divided between the two parties. Let us consider two possible cases.

1. If B knows $a_{\frac{n}{2}} \ldots a_1, b_{\frac{n}{2}} \ldots b_1$, *and A the rest of the input bits, then it is clearly enough if B sends A the single bit, namely 0, if*

$$bin(a_{\frac{n}{2}} \ldots a_1) + bin(b_{\frac{n}{2}} \ldots b_1) < 2^{n/2},$$

and 1 otherwise. A can then compute the remaining bits of the sum.

2. However, if A knows $a_n \ldots a_1$ *and B knows* $b_n \ldots b_1$, *then it seems to be intuitively clear that B needs to get bits* $a_{n/2} \ldots a_1$ *and A needs to get at least bits* $b_n \ldots b_{n/2}$ *and an additional bit carrying information as to whether the sum of n / 2 least significant parts of both numbers is or is not larger than* $2^{n/2}$. *Again, is our intuition correct?*

Example 11.1.5 *(*AT^2*-complexity of VLSI circuits) A VLSI circuit C is a planar layout of a Boolean network* $\mathcal{N}$ *(that is, a network all processors of which perform a Boolean operation on their inputs), of degree at most 4, together with a specification, for all input bits of* $\mathcal{N}$, *at which nodes of C they enter and when, as well as a specification of where and when one gets outputs. By a layout of* $\mathcal{N}$ *is meant a layout of the underlying graph of* $\mathcal{N}$ *into a two-dimensional grid as defined in Section 10.6, and, in addition, an assignment to nodes of C of Boolean functions that correspond to nodes of* $\mathcal{N}$. *(See, for example, Figure 11.2, in which 'id' stands for the identity function and is used just to represent input ports. Simultaneous inputs are shown on the same line.) Computation on a VLSI circuit C is done in the same way as on the network* $\mathcal{N}$, *and it is assumed that communication along an edge takes, for simplicity, one unit of time, no matter how long the edge is. The time*

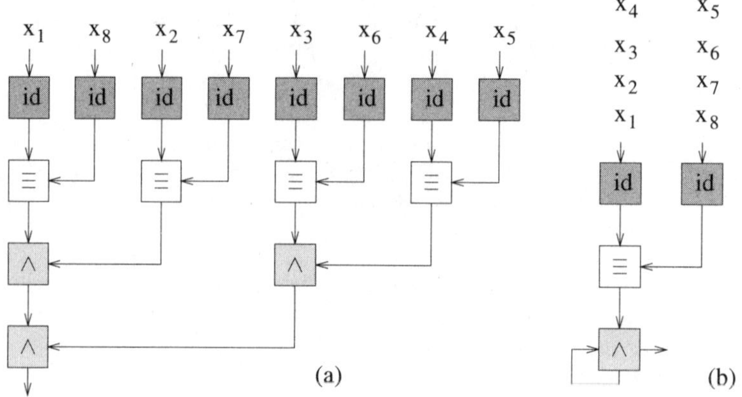

Figure 11.2 VLSI circuits

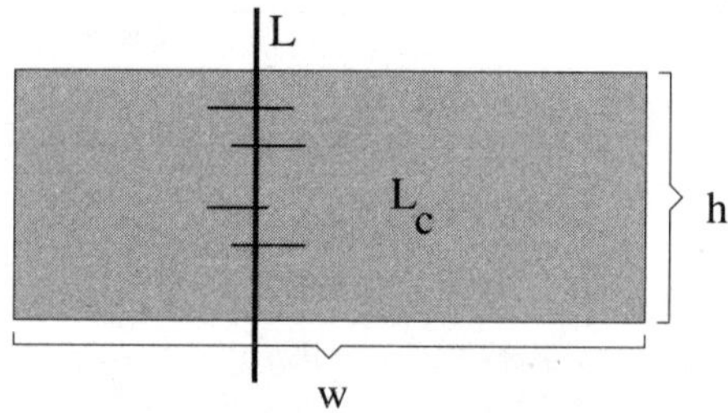

Figure 11.3 Information transfer in a VLSI circuit

of computation of a VLSI circuit is then the time needed to produce all outputs. Time-counting starts when the first input data enter the circuit.

Assume now that a VLSI circuit C_v can be laid out in a $w \times h$ rectangle, $h \leq w$. Assume also that we can cut the layout-rectangle (see Figure 11.3) by a vertical line L in such a way that it can be shown, somehow, that during a computation on this circuit, at least I bits have to be exchanged between nodes lying in two parts of the layout-rectangle separated by the line L. In other words, let I bits have to be transferred along the edges (wires) crossing L.

Since $h \leq w$, we have $h \leq \sqrt{A}$, where A is the area of the layout-rectangle. During one time unit at most h bits can cross L, and therefore we get for the computation time T of the VLSI circuit C_v the inequality $Th \geq I$. Since $h \leq \sqrt{A}$, we have the relation

$$T\sqrt{A} \geq I, \tag{11.1}$$

which yields

$$AT^2 \geq I^2. \tag{11.2}$$

The product 'area × time²' turned out to be an important complexity measure for VLSI circuits, and thereby also for Boolean functions. Observe that the two VLSI circuits depicted in Figure 11.2 compute the palindrome function of eight arguments. If generalized to the case of n inputs, their AT^2-complexity is $\Theta(n \lg^3 n)$ and $\Theta(n^2)$, respectively.

The inequality (11.2) implies that one way to prove a lower bound I^2 for AT^2-complexity of a VLSI circuit is to cut its layout into two parts in such a way that the amount of communication between these two parts is at least I.

Example 11.1.6 *The player A is given a prime x and the player B a composite number y, where* $x, y \leq 2^n$, *for some integer n. Both players again have unlimited computational power. The task is for both of them to find a prime* $p < 2n$ *such that* $x \not\equiv y (\mathrm{mod} p)$. *(The existence of such a small prime follows from the Chinese remainder theorem (see Exercise 65 in Section 1.11) and the fact that the product of all primes smaller than 2n is larger than* 2^n.*)*

Let $t(n)$ *be the minimum number of bits both players must exchange in order to solve the problem. How large is* $t(n)$*?*

It can be shown that $\Omega(\lg n) \leq t(n) \leq n + \lg n$. *The upper bound* $n + \lg n$ *can be achieved by a protocol in which A sends x to B and then B sends p to A.*

It may seem that this is a very artificial problem. Who needs to solve such a problem? Who needs to know $t(n)$*?*

Surprisingly, it is really important to know how big $t(n)$ *is. It can be shown that if* $t(n) = \Theta(\lg n)$, *then for every n there is a Boolean formula of polynomial size (in n) whose value is 1 for those and only those assignments of Boolean values to variables that represent, as binary numbers, primes. This implies that if* $t(n) = \Theta(\lg n)$, *primality could be tested by a deterministic polynomial time algorithm.*

On the other hand, if $t(n) \neq \Theta(\lg n)$, *the primality function would have no such polynomial-size formula, and this would be the first known example of such a function. This would solve a long-standing problem in the complexity of Boolean functions.*

Exercise 11.1.7* *Assume that each party knows a subtree of a commonly known tree of n nodes. Design an* $\mathcal{O}(\lg n)$*-bit protocol to determine whether these two subtrees have a common vertex.*

Example 11.1.8 *Let X and Y be two disjoint subsets of* $\{0,1\}^n$ *for a fixed n. Assume that party A gets an* $x \in X$ *and party B gets an input* $y \in Y$. *The problem is how many bits they need to exchange in order to find an index i such that the ith bits of x and y differ.*

The following simple communication requires $n + \lceil \lg n \rceil$ *bits. A sends x to B, then B computes the index i and sends it to A.*

This can be improved to a communication requiring only $n + \lg^* n$ *bits as follows.*

1. *A sends the first* $n - \lceil \lg n \rceil$ *bits of x to B.*

2. *B sends to A the bit 1 if the first* $n - \lceil \lg n \rceil$ *bits of x and y coincide. Otherwise, B sends 0 and the index of the bit in which the strings differ, and the protocol ends.*

3. *If A gets 1, then both parties continue recursively in communication, but this time only with the last* $\lceil \lg n \rceil$ *bits of x and y.*

The analysis of this recursive protocol leads to the following recursion for the number of bits that need to be exchanged:

$$C(n) = n - \lceil \lg n \rceil + \max\{1 + \lceil \lg n \rceil, 1 + C(\lceil \lg n \rceil)\},$$

which can be reduced to the inequality $C(n) - n \leq C(\lceil \lg n \rceil) - \lceil \lg n \rceil + 1$, *which has a solution* $C(n) = n + \lg^* n$.

11.1.1 Basic Model

Basic concepts concerning communication protocols and communication complexity with respect to a fixed partition of inputs, introduced informally in the previous subsection, will now be formalized. A more general case of arbitrary partitions will be dealt with in Section 11.3.

A **problem instance** is modelled by a Boolean function $f : \{0,1\}^n \rightarrow \{0,1\}^m$ (in short, $f \in \mathcal{B}_n^m$, and instead of $\mathcal{B}_n^1$ we write $\mathcal{B}_n$). An **input partition** π_{in} for $f \in \mathcal{B}_n^m$ is a partition $\pi_{in} = (A_{in}, B_{in})$ of the set $\{1,\ldots,n\}$, and an **output partition** for f is a partition $\pi_{ou} = (A_{ou}, B_{ou})$ of the set $\{1,\ldots,m\}$.

A **communication model** for f is specified by an input partition $\pi_{in} = (A_{in}, B_{in})$, an output partition $\pi_{ou} = (A_{ou}, B_{ou})$, two **output functions**

$$Output_A : \{0,1\}^{|A_{in}|} \times \{0,1\}^* \rightarrow \{0,1\}^{|A_{ou}|},$$

$$Output_B : \{0,1\}^{|B_{in}|} \times \{0,1\}^* \rightarrow \{0,1\}^{|B_{ou}|},$$

and a communication protocol.

A **communication protocol** $\mathcal{P}$ for f and partitions π_{in}, π_{ou}, is an algorithm telling two parties how to communicate in order to compute f. (We always assume that both parties know and obey the protocol.) Such a protocol is specified by two mappings

$$P_A : \{0,1\}^{|A_{in}|} \times \{0,1\}^* \rightarrow \{0,1\}^* \quad \text{and} \quad P_B : \{0,1\}^{|B_{in}|} \times \{0,1\}^* \rightarrow \{0,1\}^*$$

with the following prefix-freeness property:

1. If $z_1, z_2 \in \{0,1\}^{|A_{in}|}$, $z_1 \neq z_2$, $c \in \{0,1\}^*$, then $P_A(z_1, c)$ is not a proper prefix of $P_A(z_2, c)$.
2. If $z_1, z_2 \in \{0,1\}^{|B_{in}|}$, $z_1 \neq z_2$, $c \in \{0,1\}^*$, then $P_B(z_1, c)$ is not a proper prefix of $P_B(z_2, c)$.

Two **communicating parties**, say A and B, are involved. For an input $x \in \{0,1\}^*$, A gets all inputs x_i, $i \in A_{in}$, and is to compute all outputs $y_j, j \in A_{ou}$ – in short, $f_A(x)$. B gets all inputs $x_i, i \in B_{in}$, and is to compute all outputs $y_j, j \in B_{ou}$ – in short, $f_B(x)$.

A **communication** with respect to a protocol $\mathcal{P}$ between two parties, A and B, for an input x – x_A for A and x_B for B – designed to compute a Boolean function f is a word

$$H = m_1 m_2 \ldots m_k,$$

called the **composed message**, or **history**, of the communication, where $m_i \in \{0,1\}^*$ are **messages**, and for all $i \geq 0$

$$P_A(x_A, m_1 \ldots m_{2i}) = m_{2i+1}, \qquad P_B(x_B, m_1 \ldots m_{2i+1}) = m_{2i+2}.$$

In other words, the message one party sends to another during a communication step is determined by the initial input of the party and the composition of all the messages exchanged up to that communication step. Moreover,

$$Output_A(x_A, H) = f_A(x), \qquad Output_B(x_B, H) = f_B(x).$$

The **communication complexity** $C(\mathcal{P}, \pi_{in}, \pi_{ou}, x)$ of a protocol $\mathcal{P}$, with respect to partitions π_{in}, π_{ou}, and an input x is the length $|H|$ of the composed message.

The **communication complexity** $C(\mathcal{P}, \pi_{in}, \pi_{ou})$ of a protocol $\mathcal{P}$ for a function $f \in \mathcal{B}_n^m$, with respect to partitions (π_{in}, π_{ou}), is defined by

$$C(\mathcal{P}, \pi_{in}, \pi_{ou}) = \max\{C(\mathcal{P}, \pi_{in}, \pi_{ou}, x) \,|\, x \in \{0,1\}^n\}.$$

Finally, we define the **communication complexity** of a Boolean function f with respect to partitions (π_{in}, π_{ou}) by

$$C(f, \pi_{in}, \pi_{ou}) = \min\{C(\mathcal{P}, \pi_{in}, \pi_{ou}) \,|\, \mathcal{P} \text{ is a protocol for } f \text{ and } (\pi_{in}, \pi_{ou})\},$$

and we talk about the **communication complexity of f with respect to the fixed partition** (π_{in}, π_{ou}).

A protocol $\mathcal{P}$ is called **optimal** for a function f and a partition (π_{in}, π_{ou}) if

$$C(\mathcal{P}, \pi_{in}, \pi_{ou}) = C(f, \pi_{in}, \pi_{ou}).$$

Remark 11.1.9 All the concepts introduced above are quite natural; only the prefix-freeness condition may need some explanation. This property assures that the messages exchanged between two parties are self-delimiting and, therefore, no extra 'end of transition' is needed. It also implies that for any communication history $H = m_1 \ldots m_k$ the decomposition of H into messages $m_1, m_2, \ldots, m_k$ is unique and computable, even if one does not know the inputs x_A and x_B.

Exercise 11.1.10 *Describe formally the communication protocol presented in Example 11.1.4. (Do not forget to pay attention to the prefix-freeness property.)*

A convention regarding the output partitions will also be handy. Mostly we shall deal with the computation of functions from $\mathcal{B}_n$. In such cases, unless otherwise stated, we assume that B is to produce the result. We therefore consider, as a default, the following output partition: $\pi_{ou} = (\emptyset, \{1\})$.

There are two easy ways to show some upper bounds for communication complexity.

Theorem 11.1.11 *(1) If $f \in \mathcal{B}_n^m$, then $C(f, \pi_{in}, \pi_{ou}) \leq n$ for any partitions (π_{in}, π_{ou}).*

(2) If $f \in \mathcal{B}_n$ and $\pi_{ou} = (\emptyset, \{1\})$, then $C(f, \pi_{in}, \pi_{ou}) \leq \min\{|A_{in}|, |B_{in}| + 1\}$ for any input partition $\pi_{in} = (A_{in}, B_{in})$.

Proof: (1) A protocol that makes party A send all its inputs to B and then B to send all its inputs to A clearly has communication complexity n.

(2) Either A sends its inputs to B, that is, $|A_{in}|$ bits, or B sends its inputs to A and A computes and sends the output bit to B.

11.2 Lower Bounds

There are several methods for showing lower bounds for communication complexity of Boolean functions with respect to fixed input and output partitions. The basic underlying concept is that of the communication matrix for a Boolean function and its input partition.

Definition 11.2.1 *A* **communication matrix** *M_f for a Boolean function $f \in \mathcal{B}_n^m$ and a partition $\pi_{in} = (A_{in}, B_{in})$ is a $2^{|A_{in}|} \times 2^{|B_{in}|}$ matrix with rows labelled by values of inputs x_A from A_{in} and columns by values of inputs x_B from B_{in}, such that*

$$M_f[x_A, x_B] = f(x),$$

where x is the total input composed of x_A and x_B.

Analogously, we define matrices M_f^A and M_f^B as having the same dimensions and labelling of rows and columns as M_f, and such that $M_f^A[x_A, x_B] = f_A(x)$, $M_f^B[x_A, x_B] = f_B(x)$. (Of course, M_f^A (M_f^B) is meaningful only if $A_{ou} \neq \emptyset$ ($B_{ou} \neq \emptyset$).)

Example 11.2.2 *(Identity function) For $x,y \in \{0,1\}^n$, let*

$$IDEN_n(x,y) = \begin{cases} 1, & \text{if } x=y; \\ 0, & \text{otherwise.} \end{cases}$$

Consider now the input partition $\pi_{in} = (\{1,\ldots,n\},\{n+1,\ldots,2n\})$ and labelling of the rows and columns of M_{IDEN_n} by an arbitrary but the same labelling for rows and columns. $M_{IDEN_n} = I_{2^n}$, where I_{2^n} is the $2^n \times 2^n$ unit matrix (the matrix with 1 in the main diagonal and 0 outside it).

Example 11.2.3 *(Comparison function) For $x,y \in \{0,1\}^n$, let*

$$COMP_n(x,y) = \begin{cases} 1, & \text{if } x \preceq y; \\ 0, & \text{otherwise} \end{cases}$$

where $\preceq$ denotes the lexicographical ordering of binary strings. In the case that π_{in} is the same as in Example 11.2.2 and the labelling of rows and columns of M_{COMP_n} by strings from $\{0,1\}^n$ is in lexicographical order, the communication matrix M_{COMP_n} is the upper-triangular matrix

$$\begin{vmatrix} 1 & 1 & \cdots & 1 & 1 \\ 0 & 1 & \cdots & 1 & 1 \\ \vdots & \vdots & \cdots & \vdots & \vdots \\ 0 & 0 & \cdots & 1 & 1 \\ 0 & 0 & \cdots & 0 & 1 \end{vmatrix}$$

with 0 below the main diagonal and 1 otherwise.

Exercise 11.2.4 *Design communication matrices for Boolean functions:*
(1) $f(x_1,\ldots,x_8) = 1$, if and only if $bin(x_1\ldots x_8)$ is a prime,
(2) $f(x_1,\ldots,x_{2n}) = 1$, if and only if $x_1\ldots x_{2n}$ is a palindrome,
(3) $f(x_1,\ldots,x_n,y_1,\ldots,y_n) = \bigvee_{i=1}^{n}(x_i \wedge y_i)$,
for input partitions $(\{x_1,x_2,x_3,x_4\},\{x_5,x_6,x_7,x_8\})$ in the first case, $(\{x_1,\ldots,x_n\},\{x_{n+1},\ldots,x_{2n}\})$ in the second case and $(\{x_1,\ldots,x_n\},\{y_1,\ldots,y_n\})$ in the third case.

Exercise 11.2.5 *Show that the following communication problems cannot be solved with fewer than the trivial number of bits (n). Two parties know a subset X and Y of an n-element set. They have to decide whether (a) $X \cap Y = \emptyset$; (b) $|X \cap Y|$ is odd.*

Note that the communication matrix M_f completely describes the communication problem for computing f.

Observe too that a communication protocol actually describes a process of recursive subdivision of M_f into smaller and smaller submatrices. The process ends with all submatrices being **monochromatic**, that is, having all elements the same. Indeed, the protocol determines for each communication bit which of the parties sends it. Let us assume that the party whose inputs label the rows of the communication matrix starts a communication. In this case the protocol specifies for the first bit of communication a partition of rows of M_f into two sets, creating thereby two submatrices, and the particular bit A sends specifies only to which of these submatrices the input belongs. Similarly, for each of the next exchange bits the protocol specifies either a partition of rows of all current submatrices (if the bit is sent by A) or a partition of columns of all current submatrices (if the bit is sent by B).

The communication complexity of the problem is therefore the smallest number of such partitions of M_f and of the resulting submatrices that ends with all submatrices being monochromatic. For more about such partitions see Section 11.2.2.

11.2.1 Fooling Set Method

The basic idea is simple. If any two inputs from a set F of inputs 'require' different communications, then there must exist a communication of length $\lceil \lg |F| \rceil$. The following definition explains more precisely the phrase 'two inputs require different communications':

Definition 11.2.6 *Let $f \in \mathcal{B}_n^m$ and (π_{in}, π_{ou}) be partitions for f. Consider a set of positions in the communication matrix M_f,*

$$F = \{(u_1, v_1), \ldots, (u_k, v_k)\},$$

such that no two positions are in the same row or column. F is said to be a **fooling set** *for f with respect to (π_{in}, π_{ou}) if for every two elements $(u_i, v_i), (u_j, v_j), i \neq j$, from F, at least one of the following conditions holds (where $f_A(u,v) = M_f^A[u,v]$ and $f_B(u,v) = M_f^B[u,v]$):*

(i) $f_A(u_i, v_i) \neq f_A(u_i, v_j)$;
(ii) $f_A(u_j, v_i) \neq f_A(u_j, v_j)$;
(iii) $f_B(u_i, v_i) \neq f_B(u_j, v_i)$;
(iv) $f_B(u_i, v_j) \neq f_B(u_j, v_j)$.

Remark 11.2.7 Definition 11.2.6 captures the following reasoning: if inputs (u_i, v_i) and (u_j, v_j) yield the same (communication) history H with the given protocol, then (u_i, v_j) and (u_j, v_i) yield the history H too. But if the history is the same for (u_i, v_i), (u_j, v_j), (u_i, v_j) and (u_j, v_i), then $f_A(u_i, v_i) = f_A(u_i, v_j)$, $f_A(u_j, v_i) = f_A(u_j, v_j)$, $f_B(u_i, v_i) = f_B(u_j, v_i)$ and $f_B(u_i, v_j) = f_B(u_j, v_j)$. This is explored in more detail in the proof of the next theorem.

In the following two examples we assume that party A knows $x = x_1, \ldots, x_n$, B knows $y = y_1, \ldots, y_n$, and B produces the output.

Example 11.2.8 *For the identity function $IDEN_n$ in Example 11.2.2, with the unit matrix as the communication matrix, the set*

$$F = \{(x,x) \mid x \in \{0,1\}^n\} \tag{11.3}$$

is a fooling set. Indeed, for any pairs (x,x) and (y,y) with $x \neq y$ and $x, y \in \{0,1\}^n$, both conditions (iii) and (iv) in Definition 11.2.6 are satisfied.

Example 11.2.9 *Also for the comparison function $COMP_n$ in Example 11.2.3, the set F in (11.3) is a fooling set. Indeed, for any $(x,x), (y,y), x \neq y$, one of the inequalities (iii) and (iv) in Definition 11.2.6 is satisfied because either $x \preceq y$ or $y \preceq x$.*

The concept of a fooling set derives its importance from the following result.

Theorem 11.2.10 *Let $f \in \mathcal{B}_n^m$ and (π_{in}, π_{ou}) be its partitions. Let F be a fooling set for f and partitions (π_{in}, π_{ou}). Then*

$$C(f, \pi_{in}, \pi_{ou}) \geq \lceil \lg |F| \rceil.$$

Proof: We are done as soon as we have shown that we get two different communications for every two different inputs $(u_i,v_i),(u_j,v_j) \in F$. Indeed, this implies the existence of at least $|F|$ different communications, and so of a communication of length at least $\lceil \lg |F| \rceil$.

Assume that two different inputs

$$(u_i,v_i),(u_j,v_j) \text{ result in the same communication history } H = m_1 \ldots m_p. \tag{11.4}$$

We show that in such a case H is the communication history for the inputs (u_i,v_j) and (u_j,v_i).

According to our definition of communication, A starts a communication. Communication then goes in the following way; remember that A does not know the input of B and vice versa:

Step 1 Because of (11.4) and the prefix-freeness property, A has to send the message m_1 no matter whether it has as input u_i or u_j.

Step 2 B sees m_1, and because of (11.4) and the prefix-freeness property it has to respond with m_2, no matter whether its input is v_i or v_j.

Step 3 A sees m_1m_2, and again because of (11.4) and the prefix-freeness property it has to respond with m_3, no matter whether its input is v_i or v_j.

This continues, and in general the following steps are performed for $k \geq 1$:

Step $2k$: B sends the message m_{2k} as a function of the previous messages $m_1 \ldots m_{2k-1}$ and either of the inputs v_i or v_j. (The fact that in both cases m_{2k} is the same follows from the prefix-freeness property.)

Step $2k+1$: A sends the message m_{2k+1} as a function of the messages $m_1, \ldots, m_{2k}$ and either of the inputs u_i or u_j.

Therefore all possible combinations of inputs – $(u_i,v_i),(u_i,v_j),(u_j,v_i)$ and (u_j,v_j) – result in the same communication history and therefore in the same outputs by both parties. However, this contradicts the definition of a fooling set. □

Corollary 11.2.11 *For partitions $\pi_{in} = (\{1,\ldots,n\},\{n+1,\ldots,2n\})$ and $\pi_{ou} = (\emptyset,\{1\})$, we have*

1. $C(IDEN_n,\pi_{in},\pi_{ou}) = n$;
2. $C(COMP_n,\pi_{in},\pi_{ou}) = n$.

Proof. Upper bounds follows from Theorem 11.1.11, lower bounds from Examples 11.2.8 and 11.2.9, as well as from Theorem 11.2.10. □

Exercise 11.2.12 *Consider the function*

$$DISJ_n(x_1,\ldots,x_n,y_1,\ldots,y_n) = \begin{cases} 1, & \text{if } \sum_{i=1}^{n} x_iy_i = 0; \\ 0, & \text{otherwise,} \end{cases}$$

and the partitions $\pi_{in} = (\{1,\ldots,n\},\{n+1,\ldots,2n\})$ and $\pi_{ou} = (\emptyset,\{1\})$. (a) Design a communication matrix for f. (b) Design a fooling set for f. (c) Show that $C(DISJ_n,\pi_{in},\pi_{ou}) = n$.

11.2.2 Matrix Rank Method

This method is based on the concept of the rank of matrices, as defined in linear algebra. We show that it is enough to compute the rank of the communication matrix M_f in order to get a lower bound for the communication complexity of a Boolean function f. This method and the one in Section 11.3 can be used directly to get lower bounds for communication complexity only for functions from $\mathcal{B}_n$.

Theorem 11.2.13 *Let $f \in \mathcal{B}_n$ and (π_{in}, π_{ou}) be partitions for f. Then*

$$C(f, \pi_{in}, \pi_{ou}) \geq \lceil \lg rank(M_f) \rceil.$$

Proof: The theorem clearly holds if $rank(M_f) = 0$. Assume therefore that this is not the case, and let us analyse an arbitrary protocol for f and partitions (π_{in}, π_{ou}) in terms of the communication matrix M_f. Assume that party A starts a communication by sending a bit. For some inputs – that is, for strings by which rows of M_f are labelled – A sends 1, for others 0. On this basis we can partition rows of M_f and consider two submatrices of M_f: M_f^0 and M_f^1, the first one with rows for the inputs for which A sends 0 as the first bit. The remaining rows go to M_f^1. Since

$$rank(M_f) \leq rank(M_f^0) + rank(M_f^1),$$

one of the submatrices M_f^0 and M_f^1 must have rank at least $\frac{1}{2}rank(M_f)$. Let us assume that this holds for M_f^0. The other case can be treated similarly.

There are again two possibilities. The first is that A also sends the second bit. In this case rows of M_f^0 can again be partitioned to get submatrices M_f^{00} and M_f^{01}, with rows producing 0 or 1 as the next communication bit. In the second case, when B is to produce the next bit, we partition columns of M_f^0 to get submatrices M_f^{00} and M_f^{01}. In both cases it holds that

$$rank(M_f^0) \leq rank(M_f^{00}) + rank(M_f^{01}),$$

and one of these submatrices must have rank at least $\frac{1}{2}rank(M_f^0) \geq \frac{1}{2^2}rank(M_f)$. This process of partitioning of M_f can be continued according to the chosen protocol. After k bits have been exchanged, we get matrices $M_f^{b_1 \ldots b_k}, b_i \in \{0,1\}, 1 \leq i \leq k$, such that for at least one of them

$$rank(M_f^{b_1 \ldots b_k}) \geq \frac{1}{2^k} rank(M_f).$$

At the end of the communication either all rows of $M_f^{b_1 \ldots b_k}$ must be monochromatic[1] (when B is responsible for the output), or all columns must be monochromatic (when A is responsible for the output). In such a case the matrix $M_f^{b_1 \ldots b_k}$ has rank 1, and therefore we have

$$1 \geq \frac{1}{2^k} rank(M_f).$$

This implies that $k \geq \lceil \lg rank(M_f) \rceil$, and therefore

$$C(f, \pi_{in}, \pi_{ou}) \geq \lceil \lg rank(M_f) \rceil.$$

□

[1] A matrix is called monochromatic if all its elements are the same and an α-matrix if all its elements are α.

Example 11.2.14 *For the identity and comparison functions, $IDEN_n$ and $COMP_n$, in Examples 11.2.2 and 11.2.3, the relevant communication matrices clearly have rank 2^n. Theorem 11.2.13 in both cases, therefore, provides the optimal lower bounds $C(f, \pi_{in}, \pi_{ou}) \geq n$.*

Exercise 11.2.15 *Use the matrix rank method to show $C(\overline{IDEN}_n, \pi_{in}, \pi_{ou}) = n$ for the function $\overline{IDEN}_n$ and the partition $\pi_{in} = (\{x_1, \ldots, x_n\}, \{x_{n+1}, \ldots, x_{2n}\})$.*

Exercise 11.2.16 *Show $C(DISJ_n, \pi_{in}, \pi_{ou}) = n$ for the partition $\pi_{in} = (\{x_1, \ldots, x_n\}, \{x_{n+1}, \ldots, x_{2n}\})$ by using the matrix rank method.*

Exercise 11.2.17* *Let $f_n(x_1, \ldots, x_n, y_1, \ldots, y_n) = 1$ if and only if $\sum_{i=1}^{n} x_i = \sum_{i=1}^{n} y_i$. Show, for example using the matrix rank method, that*

$$C(f_n, \pi_{in}, \pi_{ou}) = \lceil \lg(n+1) \rceil$$

for any partition π_{in} in which both parties get the same number of input bits.

11.2.3 Tiling Method

Let us perform another analysis of the communication matrix M_f from the point of view of a protocol to compute f. Let $H = m_1 \ldots m_k$ be a communication history between parties A and B, and assume that party A starts the communication by sending m_1 as the first message. Denote by X_{m_1} the set of all inputs for A for which A sends m_1 as the first message. Party B, receiving m_1, responds with m_2, and let us denote by $Y_{m_1 m_2}$ the set of all inputs of B, for which B responds with m_2 after receiving m_1.

In this way we can associate with H, A and any $2i + 1 \leq k$ the set $X_{m_1 \ldots m_{2i+1}}$ of all those inputs of A that make A send messages $m_1, m_3, \ldots, m_{2i+1}$ provided B responds with $m_2, m_4, \ldots, m_{2i}$. Similarly, we can associate with H, B and $2i \leq k$, the set $Y_{m_1 \ldots m_{2i}}$. Therefore, we can associate with H a submatrix $M_{f,H}$ of M_f with rows from X_H and columns from $Y_{m_1 \ldots m_{k-1}}$ if k is odd and with rows from $X_{m_1 \ldots m_{k-1}}$ and columns from Y_H if n is even. Since H is the whole history of communication, either all rows or all columns of $M_{f,H}$ must be monochromatic – depending on which party, A or B, is to produce the result. This means that $M_{f,H}$ can be partitioned into two monochromatic submatrices.

To each computation, consisting of a communication and the resulting output, there corresponds a monochromatic submatrix of M_f. Clearly, for two different communications the corresponding submatrices do not overlap.

Each protocol therefore produces a partition, called a **tiling**, of M_f with a certain number, say t, of monochromatic submatrices. In order to obtain a lower bound on the length of communication H, we have only to determine how big t is.

If the protocol used is optimal, then

$$t = \text{number of communications} \leq 2^{C(f, \pi_{in}, \pi_{ou})+1}.$$

This motivates the following definition and result.

Definition 11.2.18 *Let $f \in \mathcal{B}_n$, (π_{in}, π_{ou}) be partitions for f, and M_f be the communication matrix of f. We define*

$$tiling(M_f) = \min\{k \mid \text{there is a tiling of } M_f \text{ into } k \text{ monochromatic submatrices}\}.$$

Theorem 11.2.19 *For $f \in \mathcal{B}_n$, partitions (π_{in}, π_{ou}) for f, and the communication matrix M_f, we have*

$$C(f, \pi_{in}, \pi_o) \geq \lceil \lg(tiling(M_f)) \rceil - 1.$$

Proof: Every protocol $\mathcal{P}$ for f and partitions (π_{in}, π_{ou}) unambiguously determines a tiling of M_f having the cardinality at most twice the number of different communications (histories) of $\mathcal{P}$. Thus, an optimal protocol for f with respect to partitions π_{in}, and π_{ou} yields a tiling in at most $2^{C(f,\pi_{in},\pi_{ou})+1}$ submatrices, and therefore the theorem holds. □

As we shall soon see, the tiling method provides the best estimation of the three methods for lower bounds presented above. However, this method is not easy to apply. Fortunately, good estimations can sometimes be obtained by the following modification.

Denote by $\#_1(M_f)$ ($\#_0(M_f)$) the number, or an upper bound on it, of 1s (of 0s) in M_f and by s_1 (s_0) the number of 1s (of 0s) in the largest monochromatic submatrix of M_f.

Since each tiling must have at least $\max\{\lceil \frac{\#_1(M_f)}{s_1} \rceil, \lceil \frac{\#_0(M_f)}{s_0} \rceil\}$ monochromatic submatrices, we get

$$C(f, \pi_{in}, \pi_o) \geq \max\{\lceil \lg \frac{\#_1(M_f)}{s_1} \rceil - 1, \lceil \lg \frac{\#_0(M_f)}{s_0} \rceil - 1\}.$$

Example 11.2.20 *Consider the function $MOD_{2n} \in \mathcal{B}_{2n}$, where*

$$MOD_n(x_1, \ldots, x_n, y_1, \ldots, y_n) = \bigoplus_{i=1}^{n} (x_i \wedge y_i)$$

and the partition $\pi_{in} = (\{x_1, \ldots, x_n\}, \{y_1, \ldots, y_n\})$. It can be shown that the biggest 0-submatrix of $M_{MOD_{2n}}$ has 2^n elements, and the total number of 0's is $2^{2n-1} + 2^{n-1}$. Therefore

$$C(MOD_n, \pi_{in}, \pi_{ou}) \geq \lceil \lg(\frac{2^{2n-1} + 2^{n-1}}{2^n}) \rceil = n - 1.$$

Exercise 11.2.21 *Show that $C(f_n, \pi_{in}, \pi_{ou}) \geq n$ for the function f defined by $f(x_1, \ldots, x_n, y_1, \ldots, y_n) = 1$ if and only if $\sum_{i=1}^{n} x_i y_i = 0$ and the partition $\pi_{in} = (\{x_1, \ldots, x_n\}, \{y_1, \ldots, y_n\})$, $\pi_{ou} = (\emptyset, \{1\})$ using the tiling method.*

11.2.4 Comparison of Methods for Lower Bounds

We show first that the tiling method never produces worse estimations than the other two methods.

Theorem 11.2.22 *If M_f is a communication matrix and F is a fooling set for $f \in \mathcal{B}_n$ and its partitions π_{in}, $\pi_{ou} = (\emptyset, \{1\})$, then*

1. *$|F| \leq tiling(M_f)$;*
2. *$rank(M_f) \leq tiling(M_f)$.*

Proof: (1) Assume that $F = \{(u_1, v_1), \ldots, (u_n, v_n)\}$. Since F is the fooling set and party B is responsible for the output, we get that $f(u_i, v_i) \neq f(u_j, v_i)$ or $f(u_i, v_j) \neq f(u_j, v_j)$ for all $i \neq j$.

Let $M_f^1, \ldots, M_f^s$ be a tiling of M_f into the minimum number of monochromatic matrices. It follows from the definition of the fooling set that no two elements of F lie in the same matrix M_f^l for some l. Indeed, with (u_i, v_i) and $(u_j, v_j) \in M_f^l$, (u_i, v_j) and (u_j, v_i) would also lie in M_f^l, which contradicts the definition of the fooling set. Hence $|F| \leq tiling(M_f)$.

(2) Let the tiling complexity of M_f be k. This means that $M_f = M_1 + \ldots + M_d, d \leq k$, where in each of the matrices $M_i, 1 \leq i \leq k$, all 1s can be covered by one monochromatic submatrix of M_f. Therefore $rank(M_i) = 1$ for every $1 \leq i \leq d$. Since $rank(B + C) \leq rank(B) + rank(C)$ for any matrices B, C, we get $rank(M_f) \leq d \leq tiling(M_f)$. □

Another advantage of the tiling method is that it never provides 'too bad estimations'. Indeed, the following inequality has been proved.

Theorem 11.2.23 *If $f \in \mathcal{B}_n$ and (π_{in}, π_{ou}) are the partitions for f, then*

$$\lceil \lg(tiling(M_f)) \rceil - 1 \leq C(f, \pi_{in}, \pi_{ou}) \leq (\lceil \lg(tiling(M_f)) \rceil + 1)^2.$$

This may not seem to be a big deal at first sight. However, compared with what the other two methods may provide, to be discussed soon, this is indeed not too bad.

The following theorem summarizes the best known comparisons of the rank method with the other two, and says that the rank method never provides much better estimations than the fooling set method.

Theorem 11.2.24 *Let $f : \{0,1\}^n \to \{0,1\}$, (π_{in}, π_{ou}) be partitions for f, F a fooling set for f, and M_f the communication matrix for f and its partitions. Then it holds:*

1. $\lceil \lg(tiling(M_f)) \rceil - 1 \leq rank(M_f)$;

2. $\sqrt{|F|} \leq rank(M_f)$.

The proof of the first inequality is easy. Indeed, if $rank(M) = d$ for a matrix M, then M must have at most 2^d different rows. Each group of equal rows can be covered by two monochromatic matrices, hence the first claim. The proof of the second claim is much more involved (see references).

The previous three theorems say that the tiling method provides the best estimations, which are never too bad, and that the matrix rank method seems to be the second best. In order to get a fuller picture of the relative power of these methods, it remains to answer the question of how big can the differences be between estimations provided by these methods. Unfortunately, they may be very big. Indeed, the tiling method can provide an exponentially better estimation than the matrix rank method and the fooling set method; and the matrix rank method can provide an exponentially better estimation than the fooling set method. In particular, the following have been shown:

1. There is a Boolean function $f \in \mathcal{B}_{2n}$ such that $rank(M_f) \leq n$ and $tiling(M_f) \geq 2^n$.

2. There is a Boolean function $f \in \mathcal{B}_{2n}$ such that $tiling(M_f) \geq 3n \lg n$ and $|F| \leq 2 \lg n$ for any fooling set F for f.

3. There is a Boolean function $f \in \mathcal{B}_{2n}$ such that $rank(M_f) = 2^n$ and $|F| \leq 20n$ for any fooling set F for f.

Exercise 11.2.25** *Show the existence of a Boolean function f such that there is an exponential difference between the lower bounds on communication complexity of f obtained by the matrix rank method and the tiling method.*

Exercise 11.2.26** *Show that for the function* MOD_n *there is an exponential difference between the lower bounds obtained by the fooling set and rank methods.*

11.3 Communication Complexity

As indicated in Examples 11.1.2 and 11.1.4, the ways in which inputs and outputs are partitioned may have a large impact on the communication complexity of a problem. Of principal interest is the worst case, when we have 'almost balanced' partitions of inputs and outputs.

A partition $X = A \dot{\cup} B$ of a set X into two disjoint subsets A and B is said to be an **almost balanced partition** if $\frac{1}{3}|X| \leq |A| \leq \frac{2}{3}|X|$ (and therefore also $\frac{1}{3}|X| \leq |B| \leq \frac{2}{3}|X|$). It is called a **balanced partition** if $||A| - |B|| \leq 1$.

11.3.1 Basic Concepts and Examples

We start with the main definition of communication complexity.

Definition 11.3.1 *Let* $f \in \mathcal{B}_n$ *be a Boolean function. The communication complexity of* f *with respect to an arbitrary almost balanced, or balanced, partition of inputs is defined by*

$$\begin{aligned} C_a(f) &= \min\{C(f,\pi_{in},\pi_{ou}) \mid \pi_{in} \text{ is an almost balanced partition of the inputs and} \\ &\qquad \pi_{ou} \text{ is a partition of the outputs}\}, \\ C(f) &= \min\{C(f,\pi_{in},\pi_{ou}) \mid \pi_{in} \text{ is a balanced partition of the inputs and} \\ &\qquad \pi_{ou} \text{ is a partition of the outputs}\}. \end{aligned}$$

The restriction to at least almost balanced partitions of inputs captures the most important and hardest case – two communicating parties with almost balanced amounts of input. In addition, were we to consider the communication complexity of a function as the minimum of communication complexity with respect to any nontrivial partition, that is, with respect to any partition such that each communicating party gets a nonempty portion of inputs, each Boolean function would have communication complexity equal to 1. Moreover, since we consider mainly functions from $\mathcal{B}_n$, that is, with one output bit only, it is mostly not of importance which party is charged with producing the output bit. All Boolean functions considered in Section 11.2 – that is, functions $IDEN_n, COMP_n$ and MOD_n – have communication complexity 1 with respect to some balanced partition. However, this is not always the case.

There are Boolean functions with substantially higher communication complexity. For example, this is true of the following functions:

1. $MULT_n(x,y) = bin_{2n}^{-1}(bin(x) \cdot bin(y))$, where $x,y \in \{0,1\}^n$ – multiplication of integers $bin(x)$ and $bin(y)$.

2. $SORT_n(x_1,\ldots,x_n) = (x_{\alpha(1)},\ldots,x_{\alpha(n)})$, where $x_i \in \{0,1\}^k, 1 \leq i \leq n$, $bin(x_{\alpha(i)}) \leq bin(x_{\alpha(i+1)})$, for $1 \leq i < n$ and α is a permutation on $\{1,\ldots,n\}$; k is a constant here.

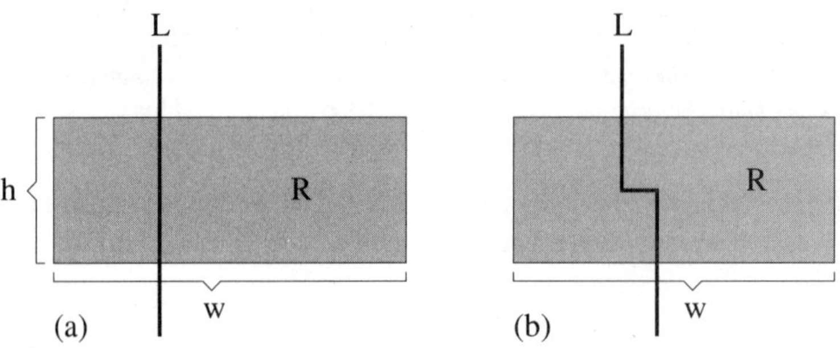

Figure 11.4 Cuts to make balanced partitions of inputs of a VLSI circuit

3. $CONN_n(x) = 1$ if and only if $x \in \{0,1\}^{n(n+1)/2}$ describes a connected oriented graph of n nodes, namely, the upper triangular part of its incidence matrix.

We now apply the concept of communication complexity with respect to an arbitrary partition of inputs to computations on VLSI circuits. The aim is to derive basic results concerning lower bounds on AT^2-complexity. Our starting point is the following claim.

Lemma 11.3.2 *Let Λ be a layout of a graph G of degree 4 into a $w \times h$ rectangle R, $h \leq w$, in the two-dimensional plane. For any selection of n nodes, $N_1, \ldots, N_n$, of G, there is a cut of R, by a vertical line of length h or a vertical-with-one-zig-zag line (see Figure 11.4a,b) of length $h+1$, which makes a balanced partition of the images of nodes $N_1, \ldots, N_n$.*

Proof: Consider the right-most vertical cut L of R along a grid line such that the left part of the rectangle R contains at most $\lfloor \frac{n}{2} \rfloor$ images of selected nodes (see Figure 11.4a). This implies that the cut along the next to the right from L vertical grid line would put more than $\lfloor \frac{n}{2} \rfloor$ nodes into the left part. Therefore there has to be a zig-zag modification of the line L (see Figure 11.4b) to satisfy the requirements of the lemma. □

We are now in a position to show our main result relating VLSI complexity and communication complexity.

Theorem 11.3.3 *(AT^2-theorem) If $f \in \mathcal{B}_n^m$ is a Boolean function, then for any VLSI circuit $\mathcal{C}$ for f such that different inputs of f enter different inputs of $\mathcal{C}$ we have*

$$Area(\mathcal{C})Time^2(\mathcal{C}) = \Omega(C^2(f)).$$

In short, $AT^2 = \Omega(C^2(f))$.

Proof: Let $\mathcal{C}$ be laid out in a $w \times h$ layout-rectangle R, $h \leq w$. By Lemma 11.3.2, there is a vertical or a vertical-with-one-zig-zag cut L of R that yields a balanced partition of input nodes of $\mathcal{C}$. A computation of $\mathcal{C}$ must lead to an exchange of at least $C(f)$ bits through L. By Example 11.1.5, this implies that $Area(\mathcal{C})Time^2(\mathcal{C}) = \Omega(C^2(f))$, hence the theorem.[2] □

Corollary 11.3.4 *$Area(\mathcal{C}) = \Omega(C^2(f))$ for every Boolean circuit $\mathcal{C}$ computing a Boolean function f.*

Proof: Each input node of a Boolean circuit $\mathcal{C}$ corresponds exactly to one input variable. Each edge of $\mathcal{C}$ transfers exactly one bit during the whole computation, because $\mathcal{A}$ has no cycle. Thus the number of edges crossing the vertical cut of Figure 11.4 must be at least $C(f)$. □

[2]Theorem 11.3.3 also holds for the case that more input can enter the circuit through the same input node.

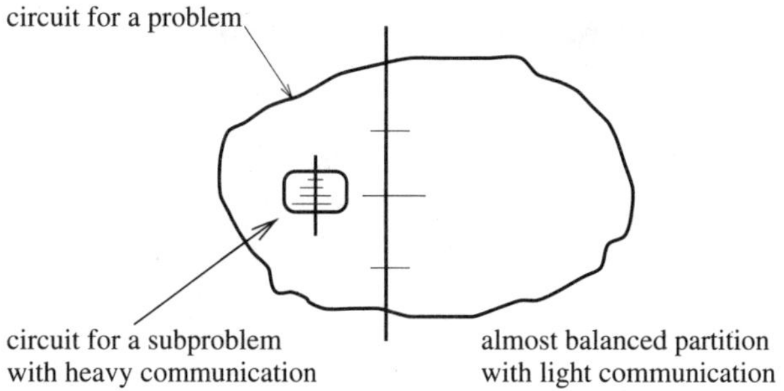

Figure 11.5 An almost balanced partition that does not partition the inputs of a communication-intensive subproblem

Exercise 11.3.5** *We can generalize in a natural way the concept of layouts and VLSI circuits to deal with three-dimensional layouts and circuits. Instead of the area complexity, we then have the volume complexity, the volume of the smallest rectangular parallelepiped containing a three-dimensional layout. Show that* $V^2T^3 = \Omega(C^3(f))$ *for any three-dimensional layout of a Boolean function* f.

Remark 11.3.6 The concept of communication complexity with respect to an arbitrary (almost) balanced partition of inputs was substantially generalized to **strong communication complexity**. The basic motivation is natural and straightforward: the strong communication complexity of a problem is defined as the maximum, taken over all subsets Z of inputs, of the minimum of communication complexity with respect to all protocols that solve the problem and all partitions that induce almost balanced partitions of inputs from Z. We may get a more realistic communication complexity of a problem this way, because it is sometimes only a subproblem, with a small proportion of input variables, solution of which requires a lot of communication. The concept of communication complexity with respect to an arbitrary almost balanced partition of inputs may not capture this situation well, because all input data of that trouble-making subproblem may go to one part of an almost balanced partition (see Figure 11.5). It has been shown that the concept of strong communication complexity is really strong: there is a language $L \subseteq \{0,1\}^*$ such that $C(F_L^n) = 0$ and its strong communication complexity is $\Omega(n)$.

Exercise 11.3.7 *(a) Define formally the concept of strong communication complexity. (b)** Construct a Boolean function for which the strong communication complexity is much larger than the communication complexity.*

Three methods were presented in Section 11.2 for how to get lower bounds for communication complexity with respect to a fixed partition of inputs and outputs. In principle, these methods can also be used to get lower bounds for communication complexity with respect to an arbitrary balanced or almost balanced partition. However, direct applications of these methods are mostly not easy.

11.3.2 Lower Bounds – an Application to VLSI Computing*

A powerful and quite general method will now be presented for using lower bounds for communication complexity for fixed partitions to obtain lower bounds for communication complexity with respect to arbitrary partitions. The starting point is the following lemma, which expresses quantitatively the intuitively clear fact that if there is a particular input for B such that different inputs for A result in many different outputs of B, then communication between A and B, for that input of B, must be heavy.

Lemma 11.3.8 *Let $f \in \mathcal{B}_n^m$ and $\pi_{in} = (A_{in}, B_{in}), \pi_{ou} = (A_{ou}, B_{ou})$, be partitions for f. If there are $y_0 \in \{0,1\}^{|B_{in}|}$ and $w \in \mathbf{N}$ such that*

$$|\{f_B(x, y_0) \,|\, x \in \{0,1\}^{|A_{in}|}\}| > 2^{w-1},$$

then $C(f, \pi_{in}, \pi_{ou}) \geq w$.

Proof: Let $\mathcal{P}$ be a protocol for computing f with respect to partitions (π_{in}, π_{ou}). Assume there are inputs (x_1, y_0) and (x_2, y_0) such that $f(x_1, y_0) \neq f(x_2, y_0)$ and for which $\mathcal{P}$ has the same communication history H. Since B gets as information for both inputs (x_1, y_0) and (x_2, y_0) only y_0 and H, it has to produce the same output in both cases. The number of communications $\mathcal{P}$ provides must therefore be at least as large as the number of different values $f_B(x, y_0)$ – that is, at least $2^{w-1} + 1$. However, in order to have such a number of different communications, at least w bits must be exchanged during some communications. □

Our next aim is to present a method that can be used to derive good lower bounds for the communication complexity of functions whose computations require a lot of communications. In other words, any algorithm to compute such functions must 'mix' the inputs in quite a complicated way to get the result. Surprisingly, this intuition can be expressed well formally by using a class of permutation groups.

Definition 11.3.9 *An n-permutation group $\mathcal{G}$ is called* **transitive of the order** *n if for all $1 \leq i, j \leq n$, there is a permutation $\pi \in \mathcal{G}$ such that $\pi(i) = j$.*

Permutation groups which are transitive of the order n have an important property: for each pair i, j, there is the same number of permutations mapping i to j.

Lemma 11.3.10 *If $\mathcal{G}$ is a transitive group of the order n, then for all $1 \leq i, j \leq n$,*

$$|\{\pi \,|\, \pi(i) = j\}| = \frac{|\mathcal{G}|}{n}.$$

Proof: For a fixed i and $1 \leq j \leq n$, let $G_j = \{\pi \,|\, \pi(i) = j\}$. $G_1, \ldots, G_n$ form a partition of the carrier of $\mathcal{G}$. Therefore, in order to prove the lemma, it is sufficient to show that $|G_1| = \ldots = |G_n|$. Let us assume, on the contrary, that for some $1 \leq r, s \leq n$, $|G_r| > |G_s|$. Since $\mathcal{G}$ is transitive there is a permutation $\pi' \in \mathcal{G}$ such that $\pi'(r) = s$. For all $\pi \in G_r$ we then have $(\pi' \circ \pi)(i) = \pi'(\pi(i)) = \pi'(r) = s$. Hence $\{\pi' \circ \pi \,|\, \pi \in G_r\} \subseteq G_s$, and therefore $|G_r| = |\{\pi' \circ \pi \,|\, \pi \in G_r\}| \leq |G_s|$ – a contradiction to the assumption $|G_r| > |G_s|$. □

A Boolean function can be used 'to compute' a permutation group in the following sense.

Definition 11.3.11 *(1) Let $f \in \mathcal{B}_{n+k}^n$ be a Boolean function and $\mathcal{G}$ a group of permutations on $\{1, \ldots, n\}$. We say that f* **computes the group** *$\mathcal{G}$ if and only if for each $\pi \in \mathcal{G}$ there exist k bits $b_{\pi,1}, \ldots, b_{\pi,k}$ such that for all $x_1, \ldots, x_n \in \{0,1\}$,*

$$f(x_1, \ldots, x_n, b_{\pi,1}, \ldots, b_{\pi,k}) = (x_{\pi(1)}, \ldots, x_{\pi(n)}).$$

(2) A function $f \in \mathcal{B}_{n+k}^m$ is **transitive of the order** *n if there is a set $X \subseteq \{1, \ldots, m\}$, $|X| = n$ and a transitive group $\mathcal{G}$ of the order n such that f_X computes $\mathcal{G}$, in the sense that if $f = (f_1, \ldots, f_m)$, $f_i : \{0,1\}^{n+k} \mapsto \{0,1\}$, $X = \{i_1, \ldots, i_n\}$, then $f_X = (f_{i_1}, \ldots, f_{i_n})$.*

The concept of a function transitive of an order looks artificial, but actually is not. Some important functions are of this type.

Example 11.3.12 *(Cyclic shift) We show that each of the following cyclic shift functions $CS_{n,k}$, $k > \lg n$, is transitive of the order n:*

$$CS_{n,k}(x_1, \ldots, x_n, w_1, \ldots, w_k) = (y_1, \ldots, y_n),$$

where $y_i = x_{1+((i-1+l) \bmod n)}$ and $l = bin(w_1 \ldots w_k)$. Informally, $CS_{n,k}$ makes l cyclic shifts of its first n arguments, where l is specified by the last k input bits.

Indeed, CS_{n+k} computes the group $\mathcal{G} = \{\pi \mid \pi(i) = 1 + ((i-1+l) \bmod n)$, for l such that $0 \le l \le n-1\}$ of cyclic permutations. $\mathcal{G}$ is transitive of order n, because for all $1 \le i,j \le n$, there is an l such that $1 + ((i-1+l) \bmod n) = j$.

Example 11.3.13 *(Sorting) Let us consider the function $SORT_{n,k}(x_1, \ldots, x_n) = (y_1, \ldots, y_n)$, where $x_1, \ldots, x_n$ are k-bit numbers and $k > \lceil \lg n \rceil + 1$, that sorts numbers $bin(x_1), \ldots, bin(x_n)$, and y_i is the ith of the sorted numbers – expressed again in binary using exactly k bits. More exactly, $SORT_{n,k}$ is a function of $n \cdot k$ binary variables that has $n \cdot k$ Boolean values. If we now take $X = \{i \cdot k \mid 1 \le i \le k\}$, then $SORT_{n,k}(x_1, \ldots, x_n)_X$ will denote the least significant bits of n sorted numbers.*

The function $SORT_{n,k}$ is transitive of the order n. This follows from the fact that $SORT_{n,k}$ computes all permutations of $\{1, \ldots, n\}$. To show this, let us decompose each x_i as follows: $x_i = u_i z_i$, $u_i \in \{0,1\}^{k-1}$, $z_i \in \{0,1\}$.

Now let π be an arbitrary permutation on $\{1, \ldots, n\}$. Denote $u_i = bin_{k-1}^{-1}(\pi^{-1}(i))$, define

$$f_X(z_1, \ldots, z_n, u_1, \ldots, u_n) = (SORT_{n,k}(x_1, \ldots, x_n))_X.$$

Then $(SORT_{n,k}(x_1, \ldots, x_n))_X$ contains n least significant bits of $y_1, \ldots, y_n$.

We now determine $f_X(z_1, \ldots, z_n, u_1, \ldots, u_n)$ as follows. Since $bin(x_i) = 2\pi^{-1}(i) + z_i$, this number is smallest if $\pi^{-1}(i) = 1$. In such a case $\pi(1) = i$ and $x_{\pi(1)}$ is the binary representation, using $k-1$ bits, of the smallest of the numbers $bin(x_1), \ldots, bin(x_n)$. Analogously, we can show that $x_{\pi(i)}$ is the binary representation of the i-th smallest number. Hence $f_X(z_1, \ldots, z_n, u_1, \ldots, u_n) = (z_{\pi^{-1}(1)}, \ldots, z_{\pi^{-1}(n)})$.

Exercise 11.3.14 *Show that the following functions are transitive: (a)** multiplication of two n-bit numbers – of the order $\lfloor \frac{n}{2} \rfloor$; (b)** multiplication of three Boolean matrices – of degree n of the order n^2.*

The main reason why we are interested in transitive functions of higher order is that they can be shown to have relatively large AT^2-complexity.

Theorem 11.3.15 *If $f \in \mathcal{B}_{n+k}^m$ is a transitive function of order n and C is a VLSI circuit that computes f such that different input bits enter different inputs of the circuit, then*

$$Area(C)Time^2(C) = \Omega(n^2).$$

Proof: According to the assumptions concerning f, there is a transitive group $\mathcal{G}$ of order n such that $f_X(x_1, \ldots, x_n, y_1, \ldots, y_k)$ computes an arbitrary permutation of $\mathcal{G}$ when fixing 'program-bits' $y_1, \ldots, y_k$ and choosing an $X \subseteq \{1, \ldots, m\}, |X| = n$, as a set of output bits. In the rest of the proof of the theorem we make essential use of the following assertion.

Claim: If π_{in} is a partition of inputs that is almost balanced on inputs $x_1, \ldots, x_n$ and π_{ou} a partition of outputs of f, then

$$C(f, \pi_{in}, \pi_{ou}) = \Omega(n).$$

Proof of the claim: Assume, without loss of generality, that B has to produce at least $\lceil \frac{n}{2} \rceil$ of outputs, and denote

$$\begin{aligned} OUT &= \{i \mid i \in X \text{ and } B \text{ must produce the } i\text{th output}\}; \\ IN &= \{i \mid i \in \{1, \ldots, n\}, A \text{ receives the input } x_i\}. \end{aligned}$$

We have $|OUT| \geq \lceil \frac{n}{2} \rceil$, $|IN| \geq \frac{n}{3}$, and therefore $|IN||OUT| \geq \frac{n^2}{6}$.

Since f computes the permutation group $\mathcal{G}$, we can define for each $\pi \in \mathcal{G}$

$$match(\pi) - \{i \mid i \in IN, \pi(i) \in OUT\}.$$

An application of Lemma 11.3.10 provides

$$\begin{aligned} \sum_{\pi \in \mathcal{G}} |match(\pi)| &= \sum_{i \in IN} \sum_{j \in OUT} \sum_{\pi \in \mathcal{G}, \pi(i) = j} 1 \\ &= \sum_{i \in IN} \sum_{j \in OUT} \frac{|\mathcal{G}|}{n} \qquad \{Lemma\ 11.3.10\} \\ &\geq \frac{n}{6} |\mathcal{G}|. \end{aligned}$$

The average value of $|match(\pi)|$ is therefore at least $\frac{n}{6}$, and this means that there is a $\pi' \in \mathcal{G}$ such that $|match(\pi')| \geq \frac{n}{6}$.

We now choose program-bits $y_1, \ldots, y_k$ in such a way that f computes π'. When computing π', party B (for some inputs from A_{in}) must be able to produce $2^{\frac{n}{6}}$ different outputs – because $|match(\pi')| \geq \frac{n}{6}$ and all possible outcomes on $|match(\pi')|$ outputs are possible. According to Lemma 11.3.8, a communication between parties A and B, which computes π', must exchange $\frac{n}{6}$ bits. This proves the claim.

Continuation of the proof of Theorem 11.3.15 Let $\mathcal{C}$ be a VLSI circuit computing f. According to Lemma 11.3.2, we can make a vertical or a vertical-with-one-zig-zag cut of the layout-rectangle that provides a balanced partition of n inputs corresponding to variables $x_1, \ldots, x_n$. We can then show, as in the proof of Theorem 11.3.3, that $Area(\mathcal{C})Time^2(\mathcal{C}) = \Omega(\bar{C}^2(f))$, where

$$\bar{C}(f) = \min\{C(f, \pi_{in}, \pi_{ou})) \mid \pi_{in} \text{ is an almost balanced partition of } x\text{-bits}\}.$$

According to the claim above, $\bar{C}(f) = \Omega(n)$, and therefore

$$Area(\mathcal{C})Time^2(\mathcal{C}) = \Omega(n^2).$$

□

Observe that Theorem 11.3.15 does not assume balanced partitions, and therefore we had to make one in order to be able to apply Lemma 11.4.

Corollary 11.3.16 *(1) $AT^2 = \Omega(n^2)$ holds for the following functions: cyclic shift (CS_n), binary number multiplication ($MULT_n$) and sorting ($SORT_n$).*

(2) $AT^2 = \Omega(n^4)$ holds for multiplication of three Boolean matrices of degree n.

How good are these lower bounds? It was shown that for any time bound T within the range $\Omega(\lg n) \leq T \leq \mathcal{O}(\sqrt{n})$ there is a VLSI circuit for sorting n $\Theta(\lg n)$-bit integers in time T such that its AT^2-complexity is $\Theta(n^2 \lg^2 n)$. Similarly, it was shown that for any time bound T such that $\Omega(\lg n) \leq T \leq \mathcal{O}(\sqrt{n})$ there is a VLSI circuit computing the product of two n-bit numbers in time T with AT^2-complexity equal to $\Theta(n^2)$.

11.4 Nondeterministic and Randomized Communications

Nondeterminism and randomization may also substantially decrease the resources needed for communications.

In order to develop an understanding of the role of nondeterminism and randomization in communications, it is again useful to consider the computation of Boolean functions $f : \{0,1\}^n \rightarrow \{0,1\}$, but this time interpreting such functions as language acceptors that accept the languages $L_f^n = \{x \,|\, x \in \{0,1\}^n, f(x) = 1\}$. The reason is that both nondeterminism and randomization may have very different impacts on recognition of a language L_f and its complement $\bar{L}_f = L_{\bar{f}}$.

11.4.1 Nondeterministic Communications

Nondeterministic protocols are defined analogously to deterministic ones. However, there are two essential differences. The first is that each party may have, at each move, a finite number of messages to choose and send. A nondeterministic protocol $\mathcal{P}$ accepts an input x if there is a communication that leads to an acceptance. The second essential difference is that in the communication complexity of a function we take into consideration only those communications that lead to an acceptance (and we do not care how many messages have to exchange other communications).

The **nondeterministic communication complexity** of a protocol $\mathcal{P}$ for a function $f \in \mathcal{B}_n$, with respect to partitions (π_{in}, π_{ou}) and an input x such that $f(x) = 1$, that is,

$$NC(\mathcal{P}, \pi_{in}, \pi_{ou}, x),$$

is the minimum number of bits of communications that lead to an acceptance of x.

The **nondeterministic communication complexity** of $\mathcal{P}$, with respect to partitions π_{in} and π_{ou}, in short $NC(\mathcal{P}, \pi_{in}, \pi_{ou})$, is defined by

$$NC(\mathcal{P}, \pi_{in}, \pi_{ou}) = \max\{NC(\mathcal{P}, \pi_{in}, \pi_{ou}, x) \,|\, f(x) = 1, x \in \{0,1\}^n\},$$

and the **nondeterministic communication complexity of f with respect to partitions** (π_{in}, π_{ou}), by

$$NC(f, \pi_{in}, \pi_{ou}) = \min\{NC(\mathcal{P}, \pi_{in}, \pi_{ou}) \,|\, \mathcal{P} \text{ is a nondeterministic protocol for } f, \pi_{in}, \pi_{ou}\}.$$

The following example shows that nondeterminism can exponentially decrease the amount of communication needed.

Example 11.4.1 *For the complement $\overline{IDEN}_n$ of the identity function $IDEN_n$, that is, for the function*

$$\overline{IDEN}_n(x_1, \ldots, x_n, y_1, \ldots, y_n) = \begin{cases} 1, & \text{if } (x_1, \ldots, x_n) \neq (y_1, \ldots, y_n); \\ 0, & \text{otherwise,} \end{cases}$$

$F = \{(x,x) \,|\, x \in \{0,1\}^n\}$ is a fooling set of 2^n elements, and therefore, by Theorem 11.2.10, $C(\overline{IDEN}_n, \pi_{in}, \pi_{ou}) \geq n$ for partitions $\pi_{in} = (\{1, \ldots, n\}, \{n+1, \ldots, 2n\}), \pi_{ou} = (\emptyset, \{1\})$.

We now show that $NC(\overline{IDEN}_n, \pi_{in}, \pi_{ou}) \leq \lceil \lg n \rceil + 1$. Indeed, consider the following nondeterministic protocol. Party A chooses one of the bits of the input and sends to B the chosen bit and its position – to describe such a position, $\lceil \lg n \rceil$ bits are sufficient. B compares this bit with the one in its input in the same position, and accepts it if these two bits are different.

On the other hand, $NC(IDEN_n, \pi_{in}, \pi_{ou}) = C(IDEN_n, \pi_{in}, \pi_{ou}) = n$, as will soon be shown. Therefore nondeterminism does not help a bit in this case. Moreover, as follows from Theorem 11.4.6, nondeterminism can never bring more than an exponential decrease of communications.

As we could see in Example 11.4.1, nondeterminism can bring an exponential gain in communications when computing Boolean functions. However – and this is both interesting and important to know – if nondeterminism brings an exponential gain in communication complexity when computing a Boolean function f, then it cannot also bring an exponential gain when computing the complement of f. It can be shown that the following lemma holds.

Lemma 11.4.2 *For any Boolean function* $f : \{0,1\}^n \to \{0,1\}$ *and any partitions* π_{in}, π_{ou},

$$C(f, \pi_{in}, \pi_{ou}) \leq (NC(f, \pi_{in}, \pi_{ou}) + 1)(NC(\bar{f}, \pi_{in}, \pi_{ou}) + 1).$$

It may happen that nondeterminism brings a decrease, though not an exponential one, in the communication complexity of both a function and its complement (see Exercise 11.4.3).

Exercise 11.4.3* *(Nondeterminism may help in computing a function and also its complement.) Consider the function* $IDEN_n^*(x_1, \ldots, x_n, y_1, \ldots, y_n)$, *where* $x_i, y_i \in \{0,1\}^n$ *and*

$$IDEN_n^*(x_1, \ldots, x_n, y_1, \ldots, y_n) = \begin{cases} 1, & \text{if there is } 1 \leq i \leq n \text{ with } x_i = y_i; \\ 0, & \text{otherwise.} \end{cases}$$

Show for $\pi_{in} = (\{x_1, \ldots, x_n\}, \{y_1, \ldots, y_n\}), \pi_{ou} = (\emptyset, \{1\})$ *that (a)* $NC(IDEN_n^*, \pi_{in}, \pi_{ou}) \leq \lceil \lg n \rceil + n$; *(b)** $NC(\overline{IDEN_n^*}, \pi_{in}, \pi_{ou}) \leq n\lceil \lg n \rceil + n$; *(c)*** $C(IDEN_n^*, \pi_{in}, \pi_{ou}) = \Theta(n^2)$.

Note that in the nondeterministic protocol of Example 11.4.1 only party A sends a message. Communication is therefore one-way. This concept of 'one-way communication' will now be generalized. The next result justifies this generalization: one-way communications are sufficient in the case of nondeterministic communications.

Definition 11.4.4 *If* $f \in \mathcal{B}_n$ *and* (π_{in}, π_{ou}) *are partitions for* f, *then the* **one-way nondeterministic communication complexity for** f *with respect to partitions* π_{in} *and* $\pi_{ou} = (\emptyset, \{1\})$ *is defined by*

$$NC_1(f, \pi_{in}, \pi_{ou}) = \min\{NC(\mathcal{P}, \pi_{in}, \pi_{ou}) \mid \mathcal{P} \text{ is a protocol for } f \text{ and only } A \text{ sends a message}\}.$$

Theorem 11.4.5 *If* $f \in \mathcal{B}_n$, *and* (π_{in}, π_{ou}) *are partitions for* f, *then*

$$NC(f, \pi_{in}, \pi_{ou}) = NC_1(f, \pi_{in}, \pi_{ou}).$$

Proof: The basic idea of the proof is very simple. For every nondeterministic protocol $\mathcal{P}$ for f, π_{in} and π_{ou}, we design a one-way nondeterministic protocol $\mathcal{P}_1$ that simulates $\mathcal{P}$ as follows. A guesses the whole communication between A and B on the basis of the input and the protocol for a two-way communication. In other words, A guesses a communication history $H = m_1 m_2 \ldots m_k$ as a communication according to $\mathcal{P}$ as follows. Depending on the input, A chooses m_1, then guesses m_2, then chooses m_3 on the assumption that the guess m_2 was correct, then guesses m_4, and so on. A then sends the whole message H to B. B checks whether guesses $m_2, m_4, \ldots$ were correct on the assumption that the choices A made were correct. If all guesses of A are correct, and it is an accepting communication, then B accepts; otherwise it rejects. Clearly, in this one-way protocol the necessary number of bits to be exchanged is the same as in the case of $\mathcal{P}$. Moreover, only one message is sent.

□

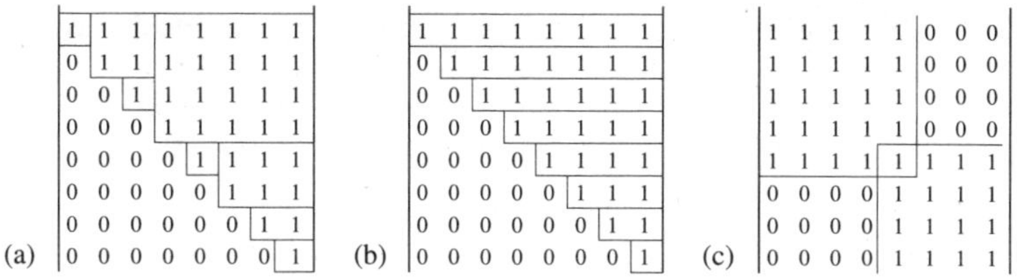

(a)

1	1	1	1	1	1	1	1
0	1	1	1	1	1	1	1
0	0	1	1	1	1	1	1
0	0	0	1	1	1	1	1
0	0	0	0	1	1	1	1
0	0	0	0	0	1	1	1
0	0	0	0	0	0	1	1
0	0	0	0	0	0	0	1

(b)

1	1	1	1	1	1	1	1
0	1	1	1	1	1	1	1
0	0	1	1	1	1	1	1
0	0	0	1	1	1	1	1
0	0	0	0	1	1	1	1
0	0	0	0	0	1	1	1
0	0	0	0	0	0	1	1
0	0	0	0	0	0	0	1

(c)

1	1	1	1	1	0	0	0
1	1	1	1	1	0	0	0
1	1	1	1	1	0	0	0
1	1	1	1	1	0	0	0
1	1	1	1	1	1	1	1
0	0	0	0	1	1	1	1
0	0	0	0	1	1	1	1
0	0	0	0	1	1	1	1

Figure 11.6 Coverings of matrices

As already mentioned, nondeterminism cannot bring more than an exponential decrease of communications.

Theorem 11.4.6 *For each $f \in \mathcal{B}_n$ and partitions (π_{in}, π_{ou}) we have*

$$C(f, \pi_{in}, \pi_{ou}) \leq 2^{NC(f,\pi_{in},\pi_{ou})}.$$

Proof: According to the previous theorem, it is enough to show that a one-way nondeterministic communication which sends only one message can be simulated by a deterministic one with at most an exponential increase in the size of communications.

If $NC_1(f, \pi_{in}, \pi_{ou}) = m$, then there is a nondeterministic one-way protocol $\mathcal{P}$ for f, π_{in} and π_{ou} such that the number of possible nondeterministic communications for all inputs is at most 2^m. Let us order lexicographically all words of length m, and let m_i denote the ith word.

The following deterministic protocol can now be used to compute f. Party A sends to B the message $H = c_1 \ldots c_{2^m}$, where $c_i = 1$ if and only if A could send m_i according to the protocol $\mathcal{P}$, and $c_i = 0$ otherwise. B accepts if and only if there is an i such that $c_i = 1$, and B would accept, according to the nondeterministic protocol, if it were to receive m_i. □

As we have seen already in Example 11.4.1, the previous upper bound is asymptotically the best possible.

The good news is that there is an exact method for determining the nondeterministic communication complexity in terms of the communication matrix M_f, which was not known to be the case for deterministic communication complexity. The key concept for this method is that of a covering of the communication matrix. The bad news is that a computation of $cover(M_f)$ is computationally a hard optimization problem.

Definition 11.4.7 *Let M be a Boolean matrix. A* **covering** *of M is a set of 1-monochromatic submatrices of M such that each 1-element of M is in at least one of these submatrices. The number of such submatrices is the size of the covering. $cover(M)$ is the minimum of the sizes of all possible coverings of M.*

Example 11.4.8 *For an $n \times n$ matrix M with 1 on and above the main diagonal and with 0 below the main diagonal, we have $cover(M) = n$. Figures 11.6a, b show two such coverings for $n = 8$. Matrix M in Figure 11.6c has $cover(M) = 2$. In this case it is essential that the submatrices which form a minimal covering can overlap.*

Theorem 11.4.9 *If $f : \{0,1\}^n \to \{0,1\}$ and (π_{in}, π_{ou}) are partitions for f, then*

$$NC(f, \pi_{in}, \pi_{ou}) = \lceil \lg(cover(M_f)) \rceil.$$

Proof: In accordance with Theorem 11.4.5, it is enough to show that $NC_1(f, \pi_{in}, \pi_{ou}) = \lceil \lg(cover(M_f)) \rceil$.

(1) Let $M_1, \ldots, M_s$ be a covering of M_f. In order to show the inequality $NC_1(f, \pi_{in}, \pi_{ou}) \leq \lceil \lg(cover(M_f)) \rceil$, it is sufficient to design a one-way nondeterministic protocol $\mathcal{P}$ for f that exchanges at most $\lceil \lg s \rceil$ bits. This property has, for example, the protocol $\mathcal{P}$, which works as follows.

For an input (x_A, x_B) such that $f(x) = 1$, A chooses an element i_0 from the set

$$\{i \mid \text{the rows labelled by } x_A \text{ belong to rows of } M_i\},$$

which must be nonempty, and sends B the binary representation of i_0. B checks whether x_B belongs to columns of M_{i_0}. If yes, B accepts; otherwise it rejects. The protocol is correct because

$$\begin{aligned} B \text{ accepts} &\Leftrightarrow \text{there is an } i \in \{1, \ldots, s\} \text{ such that } x_A \text{ is a row and } (x_B) \text{ is a column of } M_i \\ &\Leftrightarrow \text{there is an } i \text{ such that } M_i \text{ covers the entry } (x_A, x_B) \\ &\Leftrightarrow M_f(x_A, x_B) = 1 \\ &\Leftrightarrow f(x_A, x_B) = 1. \end{aligned}$$

(2) Let $\mathcal{P}$ be a one-way nondeterministic protocol for f. In order to prove the inequality $NC_1(f, \pi_{in}, \pi_{ou}) \geq \lceil \lg cover(M_f) \rceil$, it is sufficient to show that if $NC_1(\mathcal{P}, \pi_{in}, \pi_{ou}) = s$, then there is a covering of M_f with at most 2^s 1-matrices.

Let $H_1, \ldots, H_k, k \leq 2^s$ be all possible messages (or histories, in the case of one-way communications this is the same) during nondeterministic communications, according to $\mathcal{P}$ – for all possible inputs that are accepted. For $1 \leq i \leq k$, let R_i be the set of those rows of M_f and C_i the set of those columns of M_f for which communication between parties A and B produces the history H_i and B accepts. For $1 \leq i \leq k$, let us define the submatrix M_i of M_f as follows:

$$M_i = M_f[l, m]_{l \in R_i, m \in C_i}.$$

In order to finish the proof of the inequality $\geq$, it is now sufficient to show that matrices $M_i, 1 \leq i \leq k$, are 1-monochromatic and form a cover of M_f.

Indeed, if M_i covers an entry (x_A, x_B), then $x_A \in R_i$ and $x_B \in C_i$. This means that if A sends H_i to B, this message will be accepted by B, because B knows x_B. Since $\mathcal{P}$ computes f, we have $f(x_A, x_B) = 1$. Hence the matrix M_i is a 1-submatrix. On the other hand, let x_A, x_B be such that $f(x_A, x_B) = 1$. Then there is a message H_i that is sent by A and which B accepts (if its input is x_B). Thus, M_i covers $f(x_A, x_B)$.
□

Corollary 11.4.10 *$NC(IDEN_n, \pi_{in}, \pi_{ou}) = n$ for $\pi_{in} = (\{x_1, \ldots, x_n\}, \{x_{n+1}, \ldots, x_{2n}\})$.*

Indeed, the matrix M_{IDEN_n} has 1s only in the main diagonal, and therefore it is easy to see that $cover(M_{IDEN_n}) = 2^n$.

Exercise 11.4.11 *Show that $NC(\overline{IDEN}_n, \pi_{in}, \pi_{ou}) = \lceil \lg n \rceil + 1$ for $\pi_{in} = (\{x_1, \ldots, x_n\}, \{y_1, \ldots, y_n\})$, $\pi_{ou} = (\emptyset, \{1\})$.*

In order to determine the nondeterministic communication complexity of a function $f \in \mathcal{B}_n$, it is sufficient to compute $cover(M_f)$. The bad news is that this problem is **NP**-complete. The good news is that there are good approximation algorithms for it.

As an application of deterministic and nondeterministic communication complexity, we prove a lower bound result on the number of states of deterministic (nondeterministic) finite automata accepting a language of words of the same length over the alphabet $\{0, 1\}$.

Theorem 11.4.12 *Let* $L \subseteq \{0,1\}^*$, $\pi_{in} = (\{1, \ldots, \lceil \frac{n}{2} \rceil\}, \{\lceil \frac{n}{2} \rceil + 1, \ldots, n\})$ *and* $\pi_{ou} = (\emptyset, \{1\})$. *Each deterministic finite automaton for L must have at least* $2^{C(f_L, \pi_{in}, \pi_{ou})-1}$ *states, and each nondeterministic automaton for L at least* $2^{NC(f_L, \pi_{in}, \pi_{ou})-1}$ *states.*

Proof: We prove only the deterministic case; the nondeterministic case is treated analogously. Let $\mathcal{A}$ be a DFA accepting L with q states. Consider the following communication protocol to compute f_L^n: A simulates $\mathcal{A}$ on its inputs, and after the simulation is finished, A sends to B the resulting state p using $\lceil \lg q \rceil$ bits. B then finishes the simulation, starting with the state p, on its portion of the input. This one-way communication requires at most $\lceil \lg q \rceil$ bits, and therefore

$$C(f_L, \pi_{in}, \pi_{ou}) \leq \lceil \lg q \rceil < 1 + \lg q.$$

Thus $2^{C(f_L, \pi_{in}, \pi_{ou})} < 2^{1+\lg q}$, and we have

$$2^{C(f_L, \pi_{in}, \pi_{ou})-1} < q.$$

□

11.4.2 Randomized Communications

Randomized protocols behave like deterministic ones, except that the choice of messages sent at any point of the communication is determined, deterministically, as a function of their inputs, communication up to that point, and a random bit produced by a generator of random bits. In this sense these protocols are random.

In the design of protocols it is assumed that the random bits of one party are unknown to the other; this is the most difficult case for getting good upper bounds.

For lower bounds it is assumed that both parties have the same sequence of random bits; this is the most difficult case for getting good lower bounds.

As in the case of randomized algorithms, the three main types of randomized protocols are Las Vegas, Monte Carlo and BPPC. The key concept behind their definition is that of the communication tree $\mathcal{T}_{\mathcal{P}}(x)$ for a protocol $\mathcal{P}$ and an input x and its expected communication complexity. Communication trees are defined as follows.

Communications of a protocol $\mathcal{P}$ form for any input x, due to the prefix-freeness property of communications, a finite prefix-free language over the alphabet $\{0,1\}$. The corresponding labelled binary tree, with the root labelled by ε and all other nodes labelled by 0 or 1, denoted by $\mathcal{T}_{\mathcal{P}}(x)$, represents all communications, and has exactly one leaf for each communication.

The basic idea behind associating probabilities with such a communication tree is the same as with computation trees, as discussed in Section 5.1. To each node the parent of which has two children we associate the number $\frac{1}{2}$; to all other nodes the number 1. The probability of a communication represented by a leaf w – in short, $Pr(w)$ – is then the product of all numbers on the only path from the root to w (see Figure 11.7).

With each leaf w of $\mathcal{T}_{\mathcal{P}}(x)$, an output $f_x(w)$ is also associated, not shown in Figure 11.7.

The **expected length of communication of a protocol** $\mathcal{P}$ for an input x is defined by

$$E(\mathcal{P}, \pi_{in}, \pi_{ou}, x) = \sum_{w \text{ is a leaf}} Pr(w) Depth(w).$$

The **probabilistic complexity** of a protocol $\mathcal{P}$ is then defined by

$$PC(\mathcal{P}, \pi_{in}, \pi_{ou}) = \max\{E(\mathcal{P}, \pi_{in}, \pi_{ou}, x) \,|\, x \text{ is an input for } \mathcal{P}\},$$

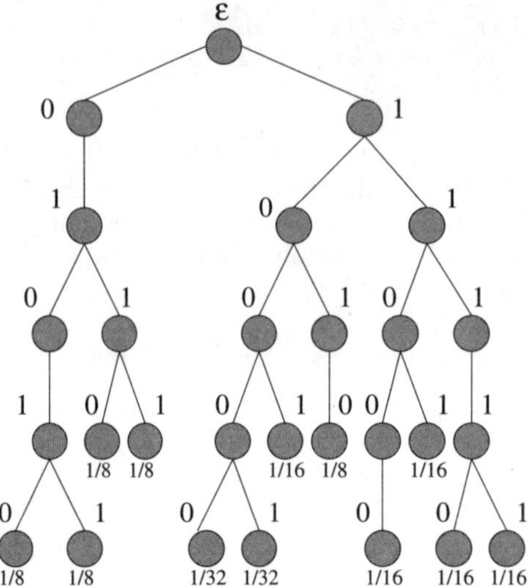

Figure 11.7 A communication tree and its probabilities

and the **error probability** for an output $y \in \{0,1\}$ and a protocol $\mathcal{P}$ by

$$error_y(\mathcal{P},\pi_{in},\pi_{ou}) = \max_{x \text{ is input} f(x)=y} \{ \sum_{\substack{w \text{ is a leaf in } \mathcal{T}_{\mathcal{P}}(x) \\ f_w(x) \neq y}} Pr(w)\},$$

where $f_w(x)$ is the output $\mathcal{P}$ produces for input x after following the communication path to w. In other words, $error_y(\mathcal{P},\pi_{in},\pi_{ou},x)$ is the sum of probabilities of all wrong computations, with y being the correct output.

Now we are in a position to define three main types of randomized protocols and randomized communication complexities.

Definition 11.4.13 *For a function $f \in \mathcal{B}_n$ and partitions (π_{in},π_{ou}),*

1. **Las Vegas communication complexity:**

$$\begin{aligned} LVC(f,\pi_{in},\pi_o) &= \min\{PC(\mathcal{P},\pi_{in},\pi_{ou}) \mid \mathcal{P} \text{ is a Las Vegas protocol for } f; \\ &\quad \text{that is, } error_0(\mathcal{P},\pi_{in},\pi_{ou}) = error_1(\mathcal{P},\pi_{in},\pi_{ou}) = 0\}. \end{aligned}$$

2. **Monte Carlo communication complexity:**

$$\begin{aligned} MCC(f,\pi_{in},\pi_{ou}) &= \min\{PC(\mathcal{P},\pi_{in},\pi_{ou}) \mid \mathcal{P} \text{ is a Monte Carlo protocol for } f; \\ &\quad \text{that is, } error_0(\mathcal{P},\pi_{in},\pi_{ou}) = 0, error_1(\mathcal{P},\pi_{in},\pi_{ou}) \leq 1/2\}. \end{aligned}$$

3. **Bounded error communication complexity** *(for $\frac{1}{2} > \varepsilon > 0$):*

$$\begin{aligned} BPPC_{\varepsilon}(\mathcal{P},\pi_{in},\pi_{ou}) &= \min\{PC(\mathcal{P},\pi_{in},\pi_{ou}) \mid \mathcal{P} \text{ is a } BPP_{\varepsilon} \text{ protocol for } f \text{ with an error at most } \varepsilon; \\ &\quad \text{that is, } error_0(\mathcal{P},\pi_{in},\pi_{ou}) \leq \varepsilon, error_1(\mathcal{P},\pi_{in},\pi_{ou}) \leq \varepsilon\}. \end{aligned}$$

Observe that Las Vegas protocols always produce correct outputs. Monte Carlo protocols have probability 0 of accepting what should not be accepted and probability at least $\frac{1}{2}$ of accepting what should be accepted. $BPPC_\varepsilon$ protocols can make an error in both cases, but its probability is not larger than ε.

The main relations between the various types of randomized communication complexity are now summarized.

Theorem 11.4.14 *Let $f \in \mathcal{B}_n$ and (π_{in}, π_{ou}) be its partitions.*

1. $NC(f,\pi_{in},\pi_{ou}) \leq MCC(f,\pi_{in},\pi_{ou}) \leq LVC(f,\pi_{in},\pi_{ou}) \leq C(f,\pi_{in},\pi_{ou})$.
2. $C(f,\pi_{in},\pi_{ou}) \leq (LVC(f,\pi_{in},\pi_{ou})+1)^2$.
3. $C(f,\pi_{in},\pi_{ou}) \leq (MCC(f,\pi_{in},\pi_{ou})+1)(MCC(\bar{f},\pi_{in},\pi_{ou})+1)$.
4. *Monte Carlo communication complexity for f can be exponentially smaller than Las Vegas communication complexity.*
5. $BPPC_{\frac{1}{4}}(f,\pi_{in},\pi_{ou}) \leq 2MCC(f,\pi_{in},\pi_{ou})$.
6. *BPPC communication complexity can be exponentially smaller than nondeterministic communication complexity.*

Proof: (1) Each deterministic protocol is also a Las Vegas protocol, and each Las Vegas protocol is also a Monte Carlo protocol. From this the last two inequalities in the first statement of the theorem follow. If $\mathcal{P}$ is a Monte Carlo protocol, then, no matter what $f(x)$ is, there is at least one communication that leads to the correct output. For a given input x, this communication can then be chosen nondeterministically. Hence, the first inequality of item (1) of the theorem holds.

(2) $C(f,\pi_{in},\pi_{ou}) \leq (NC(f,\pi_{in},\pi_{ou})+1)(NC(\bar{f},\pi_{in},\pi_{ou})+1)$ by Lemma 11.4.2, and therefore, by (1), $C(f,\pi_{in},\pi_{ou}) \leq (LVC(f,\pi_{in},\pi_{ou})+1)(LVC(\bar{f},\pi_{in},\pi_{ou})+1)$. However, as follows easily from the definition of Las Vegas communication complexity, $LVC(f,\pi_{in},\pi_{ou}) = LVC(\bar{f},\pi_{in},\pi_{ou})$, and therefore $C(f,\pi_{in},\pi_{ou}) \leq (LVC(f,\pi_{in},\pi_{ou})+1)^2$.

(3) In order to show $C(f,\pi_{in},\pi_{ou}) \leq (MCC(f,\pi_{in},\pi_{ou})+1)(MCC(\bar{f},\pi_{in},\pi_{ou})+1)$, we proceed as in point (2), applying Lemma 11.4.2, claim (1) and the inequality $NC(f,\pi_{in},\pi_{ou}) \leq MCC(f,\pi_{in},\pi_{ou})$.

(4) As we have already seen for the complement of the identity function $IDEN_n$ and partitions $\pi_{in} = (\{1,\ldots,n\},\{n+1,\ldots,2n\}), \pi_{ou} = (\emptyset,\{1\})$, we have $NC(IDEN_n,\pi_{in},\pi_{ou}) = n = C(IDEN_n,\pi_{in},\pi_{ou})$. Hence $LVC(IDEN_n,\pi_{in},\pi_{ou}) = n$ by (1), and therefore also $LVC(\overline{IDEN}_n,\pi_{in},\pi_{ou}) = n$. In order to show that $MCC(\overline{IDEN}_n,\pi_{in},\pi_{ou}) = \mathcal{O}(\lg n)$, we construct a Monte Carlo protocol for $\overline{IDEN}_n$ as follows.

- Party A chooses a random prime $p \leq n^2$, computes $m_A = bin(x_A) \bmod p$, and sends to B the binary representations of p and m_A. In order to fulfil the prefix-freeness property of communications, both binary strings are sent in a self-delimiting form (see Section 6.5.3) and therefore the whole message requires $\mathcal{O}(\lg n)$ bits.
- Party B decodes the message, gets m_A, computes $m_B = bin(x_B) \bmod p$, and accepts if and only if $m_A \neq m_B$.

Let us now analyse the correctness of the protocol. If $x_A = x_B$, then always $m_A = m_B$, and B always rejects. In other words, $error_0(\mathcal{P},\pi_{in},\pi_{ou}) = 0$.

If, on the other hand, $x_A \neq x_B$, then $\mathcal{P}$ makes an error if and only if $m_A = m_B$; that is, if p divides the difference $bin(x_A) - bin(x_B)$. Let us now count for how many p this can happen.

If $\mathcal{P}$ makes errors for primes $p_1, \ldots, p_s$, then also

$$p_1 \cdot \ldots \cdot p_s \text{ divides } (bin(x_A) - bin(x_B)).$$

Since all primes are at least 2, we have $p_1 \cdot \ldots \cdot p_s \geq 2^s$. On the other hand, $|bin(x_A) - bin(x_B)| \leq 2^n - 1$. This implies that $s \leq n-1 < n$. $\mathcal{P}$ can therefore make an error for at most n primes.

According to the formula (1.56), there are asymptotically $\mathcal{O}(\frac{n^2}{\lg n})$ primes smaller than n^2, and therefore

$$error_1(\mathcal{P}, \pi_{in}, \pi_{ou}) = \mathcal{O}\left(\frac{n}{n^2/\lg n}\right) = \mathcal{O}\left(\frac{\lg n}{n}\right).$$

(5) Each Monte Carlo protocol for a function f can have an error probability of at most $\frac{1}{2}$ for an input x such that $f(x) = 1$. For those x with $f(x) = 0$, no error is made. If a Monte Carlo protocol is used twice, and we accept an input if and only if $\mathcal{P}$ accepts at least once, we get an error probability of at most $\frac{1}{4}$. Therefore we have a $BPPC_{\frac{1}{4}}$ protocol.

(6) This claim can be shown in the same way as in the proof of (4). □

For randomized communications, Las Vegas is also a most peculiar protocol. It has no error. It is therefore quite contra-intuitive that such a randomized communication can be better than deterministic ones. We know from Theorem 11.4.14 that this improvement cannot be larger than quadratic. However, such an improvement can be obtained. The following example shows a Las Vegas protocol that obtains almost maximum improvement.

Example 11.4.15 *Consider the function $IDEN_n^*$ defined in Exercise 11.4.3; that is,*

$$IDEN_n^*(x_1, \ldots, x_n, y_1, \ldots, y_n) = 1 \text{ if and only if there is a } 1 \leq i \leq n, \text{ with } x_i = y_i,$$

where all $x_j, y_j \in \{0,1\}^n$. We know from Exercise 11.4.3 that $C(IDEN_n^*, \pi_{in}, \pi_{ou}) = \Theta(n^2)$ for $\pi_{in} = (\{x_1, \ldots, x_n\}, \{y_1, \ldots, y_n\})$ and $\pi_{ou} = (\emptyset, \{1\})$.

In order to design a Las Vegas protocol for $IDEN_n^*$, we use the Monte Carlo protocol $\mathcal{P}$ for the function $\overline{IDEN}_n$ in the proof of Theorem 11.4.14. Our Las Vegas protocol has the following form:

1. **for** $i \leftarrow 1$ **to** n **do**
   - *Check, using the above-mentioned protocol $\mathcal{P}$, whether $x_i = y_i$.*
   - *If $\mathcal{P}$ determines $x_i \neq y_i$ (this is then 100% certain), go to the next cycle, for $i+1$.*
   - *If $\mathcal{P}$ determines $x_i = y_i$ (which does not have to be 100% certain), then party A sends x_i to party B. B checks whether $x_i = y_i$. If this is true, go to step 3; otherwise go to the next iteration for $i+1$.*
2. *Produce 0 as the outcome and stop.*
3. *Produce 1 as the outcome and stop.*

It is clear that this protocol always produces the correct result. We have only to determine the average number of bits that need to be exchanged.

Denote by $E_{i,0}$ ($E_{i,1}$) the average number of bits that have to be exchanged in the i-th cycle if $x_i \neq y_i$ (if $x_i = y_i$).

It is easy to see that $E_{i,1} = \mathcal{O}(\lg n) + n$. Indeed, the Monte Carlo protocol needs $\mathcal{O}(\lg n)$ bits, and the sending of x_i requires n bits.

The proof that $E_{i,0} = \mathcal{O}(\lg n)$ is more involved. If $x_i \neq y_i$, then the Monte Carlo protocol determines this with probability at least $1 - \mathcal{O}(\frac{\lg n}{n})$ exchanging $\mathcal{O}(\lg n)$ bits. The probability that $\mathcal{P}$ does not determine it is $\mathcal{O}(\frac{\lg n}{n})$, and in such a case communication of $\mathcal{O}(n)$ bits is necessary. Thus,

$$E_{i,0} = (1 - \mathcal{O}(\frac{\lg n}{n}))\mathcal{O}(\lg n) + \mathcal{O}(\frac{\lg n}{n})\mathcal{O}(n) = \mathcal{O}(\lg n).$$

For inputs $x_1, \ldots, x_n, y_1, \ldots, y_n$ such that $IDEN_n^*(x_1, \ldots, x_n, y_1, \ldots, y_n) = 0$, we have therefore

$$E = \sum_{j=1}^{n} E_{j,0} = \mathcal{O}(n \lg n).$$

For inputs such that $IDEN_n^*(x_1, \ldots, x_n, y_1, \ldots, y_n) = 1$, there exists i for which $x_i = y_i$, and therefore

$$E = \sum_{j=1}^{i-1} E_{j,0} + E_{i,1} = \mathcal{O}((i-1)\lg n) + \mathcal{O}(n) = \mathcal{O}(n \lg n).$$

Hence $LVC(IDEN_n^*, \pi_{in}, \pi_{ou}) = \mathcal{O}(n \lg n)$.

Exercise 11.4.16* *Show that $BPPC_{\frac{3}{4}}(COMP_n, \pi_{in}, \pi_{ou}) = \mathcal{O}(\lg^2 n)$ for $\pi_{in} = (\{x_1, \ldots, x_n\}, \{y_1, \ldots, y_n\})$ and $\pi_{ou} = (\emptyset, \{1\})$.*

11.5 Communication Complexity Classes

There are two natural approaches to defining communication complexity classes: for Boolean functions and for languages.

Definition 11.5.1 *For any integers $n, m \in \mathbf{N}, m \leq n/2$, and any function $g : \mathbf{N} \mapsto \mathbf{N}$ such that $g(n) \leq n/2$ for any $n \in \mathbf{N}$, we define*

1. $COMM_n(m) = \{f \in \mathcal{B}_n \,|\, C(f) \leq m\}$;
2. $COMM_n(g(n)) = \{L \subseteq \{0,1\}^* \,|\, C(f_L^n) \leq g(n), \text{for each } n \in \mathbf{N}\}$.

In a similar way we define communication complexity classes for nondeterministic communications. They will be denoted by *NCOMM*. The following result shows that the complexity class

$$COMM_n(\mathcal{O}(1)) = \bigcup_{k=1}^{\infty} COMM_n(k)$$

of languages with constant communication complexity contains all regular languages.

Theorem 11.5.2 *For every regular language $R \subseteq \{0,1\}^*$ there exists a constant k such that $L \in COMM(k)$.*

Proof: If R is a regular language, then there exists a DFA $\mathcal{A}$ accepting R. Let $\mathcal{A}$ have s states $q_1, \ldots, q_s$. For each $n \in \mathbf{N}$ let $\mathcal{P}_n$ be the following protocol for computing f_R^n for the input partition $\pi_{in} = (\{x_1, \ldots, x_{\lfloor \frac{n}{2} \rfloor}\}, \{x_{\lfloor \frac{n}{2} \rfloor + 1}, \ldots, x_n\})$. For an input $x_1 \ldots x_n$, party A simulates $\mathcal{A}$ on the portion of the input $x_1 \ldots x_{\lfloor \frac{n}{2} \rfloor}$ and then sends the resulting state, using $\lceil \lg s \rceil$ bits, to B. Starting with this state, B simulates $\mathcal{A}$ on the rest of the input. $\square$

The fact that regular languages fit nicely, and in the expected way, into the communication complexity hierarchy may lead one to believe that the other main language families will do the same. But this is not true. There is already a context-free language that has a linear, and therefore asymptotically worst possible, communication complexity. As suggested in Exercise 19, an extreme is also possible in the other direction.

The next problem to investigate is how much we need to increase communication resources in order to get a richer complexity class. The answer is quite surprising – one bit is enough. The following theorem holds.

Theorem 11.5.3 *If* n, m *are integers,* $m \leq n/2$, $g : \mathbf{N} \rightarrow \mathbf{N}$, $g(n) \leq n/2$ *for any integer* n*, then*

1. $COMM_n(m-1) \subsetneq COMM_n(m)$;
2. $COMM_n(g(n)-1) \subsetneq COMM_n(g(n))$;
3. $COMM_n(m) - NCOMM_n(m-1) \neq \emptyset$.

A Boolean function of $2n$ variables has for a balanced partition communication complexity at most n. Are there many such communicationally difficult Boolean functions? Yes, the following theorem has been shown.

Theorem 11.5.4 $|COMM_{2n}(n-1)| = o(2^{2^{2n}})$.

Since there are $2^{2^{2n}}$ Boolean functions of $2n$ variables, this theorem says that almost all Boolean functions have the largest possible communication complexity with respect to a balanced input partition. This is actually an analogous result to the one presented in Section 4.3.2 saying that almost all Boolean functions have the worst possible size complexity.

Exercise 11.5.5 *Construct for every integer k a regular language* R_k *such that the communication complexity of* R_k *is larger than k.*

11.6 Communication versus Computational Complexity

In this section we show that communication and computational complexity are surprisingly closely related.

As we saw in Chapter 4, the most basic model of computing, which actually abstracts completely from all communications, comprises Boolean circuits. The main complexity measures for Boolean circuits, and consequently also for Boolean functions, are *Size* and *Depth*. We saw that these measures are closely related to time and space in other models of computers.

We shall see in this section that with any Boolean function f we can associate an easily defined relation R_f such that the *Depth*(f) is exactly the communication complexity of R_f. In order to show this, the concepts of a 'search communication problem' and a 'communication game' are introduced.

11.6.1 Communication Games

There are many ways to generalize the concept of communication complexity. For example, one can consider communications between more than two parties co-operating on the solution of a problem, with each party having a unique portion of the input data. Another possibility, which will now be introduced, is to consider the communication complexity of relations.

Definition 11.6.1 *A* **search communication problem** $\mathcal{S} = \langle X, Y, Z, R\rangle$ *is given by three sets* X, Y, Z, *and a relation* $R \subseteq X \times Y \times Z$. *The task is for two parties, A with an input* $x \in X$ *and B with an input* $y \in Y$, *to find, if it exists, a* $z \in Z$ *such that* $(x, y, z) \in R$.

Example 11.6.2 $X = Y = \{0,1\}^n$, *Z is a set of primes smaller than* $2n$ *and* $R = \{(x, y, p) | x \not\equiv y \pmod p)\}$ – *see Example 11.1.6.*

A **(deterministic) communication protocol** $\mathcal{P}$ for a search communication problem $\mathcal{S} = \langle X, Y, Z, R\rangle$ is an algorithm which two players follow: A, who knows an $x \in X$, and B, who knows a $y \in Y$ – with the aim of finding a $z \in Z$ such that $(x, y, z) \in R$. The **communication complexity of the protocol** $\mathcal{P}$ is defined by

$$C(\mathcal{P}, X, Y, Z, R) = \max_{(x,y)\in X\times Y} \{\text{the number of bits exchanged between the parties } A \text{ and } B \text{ for inputs } x \text{ and } y \text{ and the protocol } \mathcal{P}\},$$

and the **communication complexity of the search communication problem** $\mathcal{S} = \langle X, Y, Z, R\rangle$ by

$$C(\mathcal{S}) = \min\{C(\mathcal{P}, X, Y, Z, R) \,|\, \mathcal{P} \text{ is a protocol for } \mathcal{S}\}.$$

Definition 11.6.3 *Let* $f \in \mathcal{B}_n$ *be a Boolean function. The* **communication game for** f – *in short, game(f)* – *is the search problem* $\mathcal{S} = \langle X, Y, Z, R\rangle$ *such that*

- $X = f^{-1}(0)$, $Y = f^{-1}(1)$,
- $Z = \{1, \ldots, n\}$,
- $(x, y, i) \in R \Leftrightarrow x^{(i)} \neq y^{(i)}$,

where $w^{(i)}$ *denotes the i-th bit of w.*

In other words, the task in a communication game where party A knows an x such that $f(x) = 0$ and B knows a y such that $f(y) = 1$ is to determine, by a communication, an integer i such that x and y differ in the ith bit.

11.6.2 Complexity of Communication Games

We shall deal now with the depth complexity, *Depth(f)* of Boolean functions f, with respect to Boolean circuits over the base $\mathcal{B} = \{\vee, \wedge, \neg\}$.

In order to simplify the exposition, we consider only Boolean circuits where all internal nodes are either $\vee$-nodes or $\wedge$-nodes – thus negations are not allowed – but we allow for each variable v two input nodes, one for v itself and one for $\bar{v}$.

It is easy to see that each Boolean circuit over the base $\mathcal{B} = \{\vee, \wedge, \neg\}$ can be transformed, using de Morgan rules, into a Boolean circuit without internal nodes with negation, but with possibly two input nodes per variable and its negation, in such a way that the depth of the circuit is not increased.[3]

Surprisingly, the depth of a Boolean function f, which represents the parallel time needed to compute f, is exactly the communication complexity of the corresponding communication game.

[3]Using de Morgan rules, we just push negation to leaves. In doing so, the size of circuits can increase, but not by more than a factor of two; corresponding to each node N of the original circuit, we may now need to have two, one computing the same function as N, the other computing its complement.

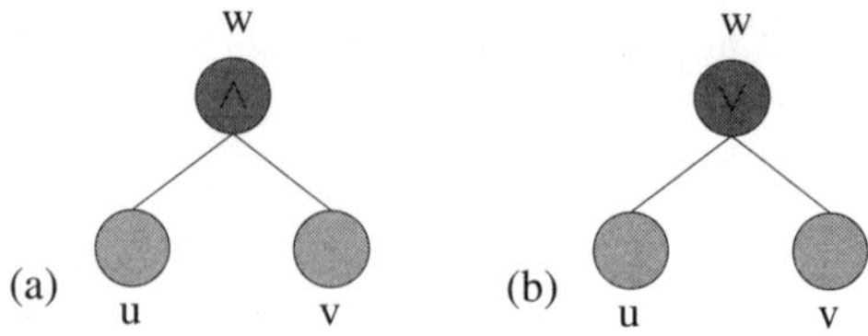

Figure 11.8 Two cases for the communication game

Theorem 11.6.4 *For any function $f \in \mathcal{B}_n$, we have*

$$C(game(f)) = Depth(f).$$

Proof: (1) First we show the inequality $C(game(f)) \leq Depth(f)$. In order to do this, let us assume that $\mathcal{C}$ is a circuit for f, over the base $\{\vee, \wedge, \neg\}$, with all negations in the inputs.

Let party A get as input an x such that $f(x) = 0$ and B a y such that $f(y) = 1$. We now describe recursively a communication protocol $\mathcal{P}$ that finds a position in which x and y differ. Actually, the protocol will do more; it will search for a path in $\mathcal{C}$, from the root to a leaf, such that all nodes on that path compute functions that produce different values for x and y. Starting with the root, A and B can design such a path as follows.

First, observe that, by definition, the root has the above property. It produces different values for x and y. Assume that such a path has already been built from the root to a node w; we show now how to make a continuation of the path by one additional node. Once this has been shown, we know how to get to a leaf. Let us consider two cases concerning w.

(a) w is a $\wedge$-node with two children u and v (Figure 11.8a). Let $f_u \in \mathcal{B}_n$ and $f_v \in \mathcal{B}_n$ be functions computed by nodes u and v, respectively. For each $z \in \{0,1\}^n$, the node w computes the function $f_w(z) = f_u(z) \wedge f_v(z)$. Since f_w has to produce different values for x and y, we can assume, without loss of generality, that $f_w(x) = 0$ (and therefore either $f_u(x) = 0$ or $f_v(x) = 0$) and $f_w(y) = 1$ (and therefore both $f_u(y) = 1$ and $f_v(y) = 1$). This means that at least one of the nodes u and v computes different values for x and y. Parties A and B, who know the circuit and the path chosen so far, can therefore choose, by exchanging one bit, one of such nodes as a continuation of the path.

(b) w is a $\vee$-node. Assume that $f_w(x) = 0$. This implies that both $f_u(x)$ and $f_v(x)$ are equal to 0, and if $f_w(x) = 0$, then at least one of $f_u(y)$ and $f_v(y)$ equals 1. Parties can again choose a node to continue the path.

Both parties can arrive, after exchanging at most $Depth(f)$ bits, at a leaf such that the values produced by that node should be different for input x and y. This is possible, however, if and only if x and y differ in the position represented by that variable. This proves our inequality.

(2) In order to finish the proof of the theorem, it is sufficient to show that $Depth(f) \leq C(game(f))$. This follows from the next lemma if we take $X = f^{-1}(0)$ and $Y = f^{-1}(1)$. □

Lemma 11.6.5 *If $X, Y \subseteq \{0,1\}^n$, $X \cap Y = \emptyset$, then there is a function $f \in \mathcal{B}_n$ such that*

- $X \subseteq f^{-1}(0), Y \subseteq f^{-1}(1)$,
- $Depth(f) \leq C(\langle X, Y, \{1, \ldots, n\}, R\rangle)$, *where* $(x, y, i) \in R$ *if and only if* $x^{(i)} \neq y^{(i)}$.

Proof: Let X, Y satisfy the assumptions of the lemma. Let $C(\langle X, Y, \{1, \ldots, n\}, R\rangle) = t$, and let $\mathcal{P}$ be a protocol that solves the search problem $\langle X, Y, \{1, \ldots, n\}, R\rangle$ with t bits. We show how to design a Boolean circuit for f, in the form of a binary tree, that has depth at most t and computes f. The proof will be constructive, by induction, and each time A (B) exchanges a bit, we add a $\wedge$-node (a $\vee$-node) to the circuit being designed.

Induction base: $t = 0$. This means that both processors can agree on an i without exchanging a single bit. There are now two possibilities:

- $x^{(i)} = 1, y^{(i)} = 0$ for all $x \in X, y \in Y$;
- $x^{(i)} = 0, y^{(i)} = 1$ for all $x \in X, y \in Y$.

In both cases the resulting circuit has a single node. In the first case this node corresponds to the ith variable u_i, in the second to $\bar{u}_i$.

Induction step: from t to $t+1$. Let party A receive an $x \in X$ and party B a $y \in Y$. Without loss of generality we can assume that A starts communication and sends bit 0 for $x \in X_0 \subseteq X$ and bit 1 for $x \in X_1 = X - X_0$. This way we decompose our search problem into two search subproblems:

$$\langle X_0, Y, \{1,\ldots,n\}, R\rangle \quad \text{and} \quad \langle X_1, Y, \{1,\ldots,n\}, R\rangle.$$

Both these search problems require at most t bits. From the induction assumption it then follows that there are two functions:

- f_0 such that $X_0 \subseteq f_0^{-1}(0), Y \subseteq f_0^{-1}(1)$ and $Depth(f_0) \leq t$,
- f_1 such that $X_1 \subseteq f_1^{-1}(0), Y \subseteq f_1^{-1}(1)$ and $Depth(f_1) \leq t$.

Since $Depth(f_0) \leq t$ and $Depth(f_1) \leq t$, there are circuits of depth at most t computing functions f_0 and f_1. Let us now connect the roots of these two circuits with a $\wedge$-node. The resulting circuit, of depth $t+1$, computes the function $f(z) = f_0(z) \wedge f_1(z)$, and it holds that

- if $z \in X_0$, then $f_0(z) = 0 \Rightarrow f(z) = 0 \Rightarrow z \in f^{-1}(0)$;
- if $z \in X_1$, then $f_1(z) = 0 \Rightarrow f(z) = 0 \Rightarrow z \in f^{-1}(0)$.

Hence $X \subseteq f^{-1}(0)$. In a similar way we can show that $f(z) = 1$ for $z \in Y$, and therefore $Y \subseteq f^{-1}(1)$. □

Exercise 11.6.6 *Define, in an analogous way, the concepts of monotone communication games for monotone Boolean functions and communication complexity for monotone communication games. Prove an analogue of the last theorem for monotone Boolean functions, computed on monotone Boolean circuits, and monotone communication games.*

Moral: Communication is an engine of progress. Radically new communication tools usually lead to new eras and new value systems. The complexity of many problems of humankind, nature and machines lies in the complexity of the underlying communication problems. At the same time, often very little needs to be communicated in order to achieve all that is required. A good rule of thumb for dealing with communication problems in computing is therefore, as in life, to find out the minimum that needs to be communicated in order to achieve all that is required and to communicate that as efficiently as possible.

11.7 Exercises

1. For a set X of n elements determine (a) the number of partitions of X; (b) the number of balanced partitions of X; (c) the number of almost balanced partitions of X.

2.* Given is an n-node graph. One party knows a complete subgraph, the other party an independent set of vertices. Design a protocol for deciding whether these two subgraphs have a vertex in common. (This can be done by exchanging $\mathcal{O}(\lg^2 n)$ bits.)

3. Consider the same problem as in Exercise 11.1.8 with $X = \{x \mid x \in \{0,1\}^*$ and the number $\#_1 x$ even$\}$, $Y = \{x \mid x \in \{0,1\}^*, \#_1 x$ is odd$\}$. Show that in this case the problem can be solved by exchanging $2\lceil \lg n \rceil$ bits.

4. Consider the problem of deciding whether an undirected graph of n nodes given by an adjacency matrix is connected. Show that for any partition π_{in} of inputs there is a protocol $\mathcal{P}$ such that $C(\mathcal{P}, \pi_{in}, \pi_{ou}) = \mathcal{O}(n \lg n)$.

5. For the function

$$f(x_1, \ldots, x_n, y_1, \ldots, y_n) = \bigwedge_{i=1}^{n} (x_i \Rightarrow y_i)$$

find an almost balanced partition π_{in} of the inputs such that the communication complexity of f with respect to π_{in} is (a) maximum; (b) minimum.

6. Let $f \in \mathcal{B}^3_{3n}$, $f(x,y,z) = (u_1, u_2, u_3)$, where $x, y, z \in \{0,1\}^n$, $u_1 = \bigwedge_{i=1}^n (x_i \equiv y_i)$, $u_2 = \bigvee_{i=1}^n (x_i \vee y_i \vee z_i)$ and $u_3 = \bigvee_{i=1}^n y_i$. Find the best possible communication protocol for computing f for the input partition $\pi_{in} = (\{x, y_1, y_2, y_3\}, \{y_4, \ldots, y_n, z\})$ and (a) $\pi_{ou} = (\{u_1\}, \{u_2, u_3\})$; (b) $\pi_{ou} = (\{u_1, u_2\}, \{u_3\})$.

7. Design, for any balanced input partition, a communication protocol for recognizing the language

$$L = \{w \mid w \in \{0,1\}^*, \#_1(w) = \#_0(w)\},$$

with communication complexity $\lceil \lg(n+1) \rceil$ for input words of length $2n$.

8. Find the fooling set for the function $f \in \mathcal{B}^2_n$, n even, where $f(x_1, \ldots, x_n, y_1, \ldots, y_n) = (z_1, z_2)$,

$$z_1 = \bigoplus_{i=1}^{n} (x_i \wedge y_i), \quad z_2 = \bigwedge_{i=1}^{n/2} (x_i \equiv x_{i+n/2}),$$

and π_{in}, π_{ou} are partitions with $\pi_{in} = (\{x_1, \ldots, x_{\frac{n}{2}}, y_{\frac{n}{2}+1}, \ldots, y_n\}, \{x_{\frac{n}{2}+1}, \ldots, x_n, y_1, \ldots, y_{\frac{n}{2}}\})$, $\pi_{ou} = (\{z_1\}, \{z_2\})$, and show that $C(f, \pi_{in}, \pi_{ou}) \geq n+1$.

9. Consider the Boolean function $f(x_1, \ldots, x_{2n}) = (y_1, \ldots, y_n)$, where

$$y_i = f_i(x_1, \ldots, x_{2n}) = \bigwedge_{j=1}^{n} (x_j \equiv x_{(n+i+j-1) \bmod n)}.$$

Show that (a) $C(f_i) \leq 1$ for each $1 \leq i \leq n$; (b) for each balanced partition π_{in} of $\{x_1, \ldots, x_{2n}\}$ there exists a $1 \leq j \leq n$ such that $C(f_j, \pi_{in}, \pi_{ou}) \geq \frac{n}{4}$.

10. Show that for the function $f_k \in \mathcal{B}_n, f_k(x_1, \ldots, x_{2n}) = 1$ if and only if the sequence $x_1, \ldots, x_{2n}$ has exactly k 1's, and for the partition $\pi_{in} = (\{1, \ldots, n\}, \{n+1, \ldots, 2n\})$, we have $C(f, \pi_{in}, \pi_{ou}) \geq \lceil \lg k \rceil$.

11. Show $C(MULT_n, \pi_{in}, \pi_{ou}) = \Omega(n)$ for the multiplication function defined by $MULT_n(x,y,z) = 1$, where $x, y \in \{0,1\}^n$ and $z \in \{0,1\}^{2n}$, if and only if $bin(x) \cdot bin(y) = bin(z)$, and for partitions $\pi_{in} = (\{x,y\}, \{z\}), \pi_{ou} = (\emptyset, \{1\})$.

12. Design some Boolean functions for which the matrix rank method provides optimal lower bounds.

13. (Tiling complexity) The concept of a communication matrix of a communication problem and its tiling complexity gave rise to the following definition of a characteristic matrix of a language $L \subset \Sigma^*$ and its tiling complexity. It is the infinite Boolean matrix M_L with rows and columns labelled by strings from Σ^* and such that $M_L[x,y] = 1$ if and only if $xy \in L$. For any $n \in N$, let M_L^n be the submatrix of M_L whose rows and columns are labelled by strings from $\Sigma^{\leq n}$, and let $T(M_L^n)$ be the minimum number of 1-submatrices of M_L^n that cover all 1-entries of M_L^n. Tiling complexity t_L of L is the mapping $t_L(n) = T(M_L^n)$. (a) Design M_L^3 for the language of binary palindromes of length at most 8. (b)* Show that a language L is regular if and only if $t_L(n) = \mathcal{O}(1)$.

14. Show the lower bound $\Omega(n)$ for the communication complexity of the problem of determining whether a given undirected graph with n nodes is connected. (Hint: you can use Exercise 11.2.5.)

15. Show that the communication complexity equals n for the problem of determining whether $X \cup Y = Z$, where Z is an n-element set, provided party A knows X and Z and party B knows Y and Z.

16.* Find a language $L \subseteq \{0,1\}^*$ such that $C(f_L^n) = \Omega(n)$ and $C_a(f_L^n) \leq 1$.

17.** Show that the function $MULT(x,y) = z$, where $x, y \in \{0,1\}^{2n}, z \in \{0,1\}^{4n}, bin(z) = bin(x) \cdot bin(y)$, is transitive of the order n.

18. Show that the communication complexity classes $COMM_{2n}(m)$ and $COMM(g(n))$ are closed under complementation for any $n, m \in \mathbf{N}$, and any function $g : \mathbf{N} \mapsto \mathbf{N}, g(n) \leq \frac{n}{2}$.

19. Show that the class $COMM(0)$ contains a language that is not recursively enumerable.

20. Show Lemma 11.4.2.

21. Let $f \in \mathcal{B}_{n(n-1)/2}$ be such that $f(x_1, \ldots, x_{n(n-1)/2}) = 1$ if and only if the graph $G(x_1, \ldots, x_{n(n-1)/2})$ contains a triangle. Show that $NC(f, \pi_{in}, \pi_{ou}) = \mathcal{O}(\lg n)$, if $\pi_{in} = (\{x_1, \ldots, x_{\lfloor n(n-1)/4 \rfloor}\}, \{x_{\lceil n(n-1)/4 \rceil + 1}, \ldots, x_{n(n-1/2}\}), \pi_{ou} = (\emptyset, \{1\})$.

22.* A nondeterministic protocol is called unambiguous if it has exactly one communication leading to acceptance for each input it accepts. For a Boolean function $f \in \mathcal{B}_n$ and partitions (π_{in}, π_{ou}) of its inputs, define $UNC(f, \pi_{in}, \pi_{ou}) = \min\{NC(\mathcal{P}, \pi_{in}, \pi_{ou}) \,|\, \mathcal{P}$ computes f and is unambiguous$\}$. Show that (a) $C(f, \pi_{in}, \pi_{ou}) \leq (UNC(f, \pi_{in}, \pi_{ou}) + 1)(UNC(f, \pi_{in}, \pi_{ou}) + 2)$;
(b) $C(f, \pi_{in}, \pi_{ou}) \leq (UNC(f, \pi_{in}, \pi_{ou}) + 1)^2$; (c) $\lceil \lg(rank M_f) \rceil \leq UNC(f, \pi_{in}, \pi_{ou}) + 1)^2$.

23.** Find a Boolean function $f : \{0,1\}^n \mapsto \{0,1\}$ such that the inequality $\lceil \lg rank(M_f) \rceil \leq NC(f, \pi_{in}, \pi_o)$ does not hold.

24. Let $COMP_n(x_1,\dots,x_n,y_1,\dots,y_n) = 1$ if and only if $bin(x_1\dots x_n) \leq bin(y_1\dots y_n)$ (see Example 11.2.3), $\pi_{in} = (\{x_1,\dots,x_n\},\{x_{n+1},\dots,x_{2n}\})$ and $\pi_{ou} = (\emptyset,\{1\})$. Show that (a) $NC(COMP_n,\pi_{in},\pi_{ou}) = n$; (b) $NC(\overline{COMP}_n,\pi_{in},\pi_{ou}) = n$.

25. Consider the language $STAR = \{w \in \{0,1\}^* \mid |w| = \binom{m}{2}$ for some $m \geq 2, m \in \mathbf{N}$ and $G(w)$ is a graph containing at least one star – a node adjacent to all other nodes of $G(w)\}$. Let $X = \{x_{ij} \mid i < j, i,j \in \{1,\dots,m\}\}$ be the set of input variables of the function f^n_{STAR} for $n = \binom{m}{2}$, and let π_{in} be a balanced partition of X. Show that $NC_1(f^n_{STAR}) \leq \lg n + 1$.

26. Let $f_1,f_2 \in \mathcal{B}_n$, and π_{in} be a balanced partition of $\{x_1,\dots,x_n\}$. Show that if $NC(f_1,\pi_{in},\pi_{ou}) \leq m \leq \frac{n}{2}$, $NC(f_2,\pi_{in},\pi_{ou}) \leq m$, then $NC(f_1 \vee f_2,\pi_{in},\pi_{ou}) \leq m+1$.

27.* Show that there are languages $L_1,L_2 \subseteq \{0,1\}^*$ such that $NC(f^n_{L_1}) \leq 1$, $NC(f^n_{L_2}) \leq 1$ and $NC(f^n_{L_1\cup L_2}) = \Omega(n)$.

28. Let $f_1,f_2 \in \mathcal{B}_n$, and let π_{in} be a balanced partition of $\{x_1,\dots,x_n\}$. Show that

$$NC(f_1 \wedge f_2,\pi_{in},\pi_{ou}) \leq NC(f_1,\pi_{in},\pi_{ou}) + NC(f_2,\pi_{in},\pi_{ou}) + 1.$$

29.** Let $f: \{0,1\}^* \mapsto \{0,1\}$ and f_n be a restriction of f to the set $\{0,1\}^n$. For each $n \in \mathbf{N}$ let $\pi^n_{in} = (\{x_1,\dots,x_{\lceil \frac{n}{2}\rceil}\},\{x_{\lceil \frac{n}{2}\rceil+1},\dots,x_n\})$ be the input partition for f_n. Let $\pi^n_{ou} = (\emptyset,\{1\})$. Show that if $\mathcal{M}$ is an NTM that recognizes the language corresponding to $f(n)$ in time $t(n)$, then $t(n) = \Omega(NC(f_n,\pi^n_{in},\pi^n_{ou}))$.

30.** For a Boolean matrix M denote by $\rho(M)$ the largest t such that M has a $t\times t$ submatrix whose rows and columns can be rearranged to get the unit matrix. Moreover, each Boolean matrix M can be considered as a communication matrix for the function $f_M(i,j) = 1$ if $1 \leq i \leq n$, $1 \leq j \leq n$, and $M(i,j) = 1$, and for the partition of the first arguments to one party and second arguments to second party. On this basis we can define the communication complexity and the nondeterministic communication complexity of an arbitrary Boolean matrix M as $C(M) = C(f_M)$ and $NC(M) = NC(f_M)$. Show that (a) $\rho(M) \leq rank(M)$; (b) $\lg\rho(M) \leq NC(M)$; (c) $C(M) \leq \lg\rho(M)(NC(\bar{M})+1)$.

31. Define Las Vegas communication complexity classes, and show that they are closed under complementation.

32.* (Choice of probabilities for Monte Carlo and BPPC protocols) Let $k \in \mathbf{N}$. Show that if $\mathcal{P}$ is a Monte Carlo ($BPP_{1/4}$) protocol that computes a Boolean function f with respect to partitions (π_{in},π_{ou}) exchanging at most s bits, then there is a Monte Carlo ($BPPC_{2^{-k}}$) protocol, that computes f with respect to the same partitions with an error probability of at most 2^{-k}, and exchanges at most ks bits. (Hint: in the case of $BPPC$ protocols use Chernoff's bound from Example 76 in Chapter 1.)

33.** (Randomization does not always help.) Show that randomization does not help for the problem of determining whether a given undirected graph is bipartite.

34.** (An analogy between communication and computational complexity) Let $\mathcal{C}$ be a set of 0–1 quadratic matrices (communication matrices). Define $\mathcal{C} \in \mathbf{P}^{comm}$ if the communication complexity of any $n\times n$ matrix $M \subseteq \mathcal{C}$ is not greater than a polynomial in $\lg\lg n$ (and therefore its communication complexity is exponentially smaller than a trivial lower bound). Similarly, let us define $\mathcal{C} \in \mathbf{NP}^{comm}$ if the nondeterministic communication complexity of every matrix $M \in \mathcal{C}$ is polynomial in $\lg\lg n$. We say that $\mathcal{C} \in$ co-NP^{comm} if the complement of every matrix in $\mathcal{C}$ is in $\mathbf{NP}^{comm}$. Show that (a) P$^{comm} \neq$ NP^{comm}; (b) $\mathbf{P}^{comm} = \mathbf{NP}^{comm} \cap$ **co–NP**^{comm}.

QUESTIONS

1. How can communication protocols and communication complexity for communications between three parties be defined?
2. A party A knows an n-bit integer x and a party B knows an n-bit integer y. How many bits must they exchange in order to compute $x \cdot y$?
3. Why is it the most difficult case for lower (upper) bounds in randomized communications when random bits of one party are known (unknown) by the other party?
4. How can you explain informally the fooling set method for proving lower bounds?
5. Is there some magic in the numbers $\frac{1}{3}$ and $\frac{2}{3}$ used in the definition of almost balanced partitions, or can they be replaced by some other numbers without an essential impact on the results?
6. Can we define nondeterministic communication complexity in terms of certificates, as in the case of computational complexity?
7. What is the difference between tiling and covering communication matrices?
8. What is the basic difference between the main randomized protocols?
9. Does a communication game for a function f always have a solution? Why?
10. For what communication problems does strong communication complexity provide more realistic results than ordinary communication complexity?

11.8 Historical and Bibliographical References

The idea of considering communication complexity as a method for proving lower bounds came up in various papers on distributed and parallel computing, especially in theoretical approaches to complexity in VLSI computing. The most influential were Thompson's paper (1979) and his PhD thesis (1980), papers by Lipton and Sedgewick (1981) and Yao (1979, 1981) and Ullman's book (1984). There is nowadays much literature on this subject, well overviewed by Lengauer (1990a) and Hromkovič (1997) .

A formal definition of protocols and communication complexity, deterministic and nondeterministic, was introduced by Papadimitriou and Sipser (1982, 1984). Randomized communications were introduced by Yao (bounded-error protocols, Monte Carlo and BPPC, 1979, 1981, 1983); Mehlhorn and Schmidt (Las Vegas, 1982); Paturi and Simon (unbounded error protocols, 1986). The concept of multi-party protocols was introduced by Chandra, Furst and Lipton (1983). The concept of communication games is due to Karchmer and Wigderson (1988), from which Theorem 11.6.4 also comes.

A systematic presentation of communication complexity concepts, methods and results can be found in the survey paper by Orlitsky and El Gamal (1988), lecture notes by Schnitger and Schmetzer (1994) and the book by Hromkovič (1997). The last two of these much influenced the presentation in this chapter, and likewise most of the exercises.

The concept of a communication matrix and the tiling method are due to Yao (1981); the matrix rank method is due to Mehlhorn and Schmidt (1982). The fooling set concept and method were developed by various authors and explicitly formulated by Aho, Ullman and Yannakakis (1983), where several basic relations between methods for proving lower bounds at fixed partition were also established, including, essentially, Theorems 11.2.19 and 11.2.22. The exponential gap between the fooling set and the tiling method, mentioned on page 616, is due to Dietzfelbinger, Hromkovič and Schnitger (1994), as is the result showing that the fooling set method can be much weaker than the matrix rank method – both gaps are shown in an existential way – and that the fooling set method cannot be much better than the rank method. The exponential gap between the rank method and the fooling set method was established by Aho, Ullman and Yannakakis (1983). The Exercise 13 is due to Condon, Hellerstein, Potte and Widgerson (1994).

The application of communication complexity to proving bounds on AT^2-complexity of circuits presented in Section 11.3.3, which follows Schnitger and Schmetzer (1994), is due to Vuillemin (1980). The trade-offs mentioned on page 623 between area and time complexity for sorting and integer multiplication are due to Bilardi and Preparata (1985) and Mehlhorn and Preparata (1983), respectively.

The lower bounds method for nondeterministic communications in Section 11.4.1 is due to Aho, Ullman and Yannakakis (1983), where Lemma 11.4.2 is also shown. An exponential gap between deterministic and nondeterministic communication complexity was established by Papadimitriou and Sipser (1982). Relations between various types of randomized protocols are summarized in Hromkovič (1997), as well as by Schnitger and Schmetzer (1994). An exponential gap between communication complexity and Monte Carlo complexity and between nondeterministic communication complexity and BPPC complexity is shown by Ja'Ja, Prassana, Kamar and Simon (1984). Another approach to randomized communications (see, for example, Hromkovič (1997)), is to consider BPPC communication (probability of the correct result is at least $\frac{1}{2}$), one-sided Monte Carlo communication (probability of error in the case of acceptance is $\varepsilon > 0$) and two-sided Monte Carlo communication (similar to BPPC, but the probability of the correct answer is at least $\frac{1}{2} + \varepsilon$ with $\varepsilon > 0$).

The study of communication complexity classes was initiated by Papadimitriou and Sipser (1982, 1984), and the basic hierarchy results in Section 11.5 are due to them. The result that $m + 1$ bits deterministically communicated can be more powerful than the m bits used by nondeterministic protocols is due to Ďuriš, Galil and Schnitger (1984). The claim that almost all Boolean functions have the worst possible communication complexity is due to Papadimitriou and Sipser (1982, 1984). Strong communication complexity was introduced by Papadimitriou and Sipser (1982) and was worked out by Hromkovič (1997) with an example showing that strong communication complexity can be exponentially higher than ordinary communication complexity. Hromkovič's book is the most comprehensive source of historical and bibliographical references for communication complexity and its applications.

Bibliography

Leonard M. Adleman. A subexponential algorithm for the discrete logarithm problem with applications to cryptography. In *Proceedings of 20th IEEE FOCS*, pages 55–60, 1979.

Leonard M. Adleman. On distinguishing prime numbers from composite numbers. In *Proceedings of 21st IEEE FOCS*, pages 387–406, 1980.

Leonard M. Adleman. Algorithmic number theory—the complexity contribution. In *Proceedings of 35th IEEE FOCS*, pages 88–113, 1994.

Leonard M. Adleman and Ming-Deh Hung. Recognizing primes in random polynomial time. In *Proceedings of 19th ACM STOC*, pages 462–466, 1987.

Leonard M. Adleman, Kenneth L. Manders, and Gary L. Miller. On taking roots in finite fields. In *Proceedings of 18th IEEE FOCS*, pages 175–178, 1977.

Leonard M. Adleman, Carl Pomerance, and Robert S. Rumely. On distinguishing prime numbers from composite numbers. *Annals of Mathematics*, 117:173–206, 1983.

Alfred A. Aho, John E. Hopcroft, and Jeffery D. Ullman. *The design and analysis of computer algorithms*. Addison-Wesley, Reading, Mass., 1974.

Alfred A. Aho, John E. Hopcroft, and Jeffery D. Ullman. *Data structures and algorithms*. Addison-Wesley, Reading, Mass., 1983.

Alfred A. Aho and Jeffery D. Ullman. *The theory of parsing, translation and compiling, I, II*. Prentice Hall, Englewood Cliffs, 1972.

Alfred A. Aho, Jeffery D. Ullman, and Mihalis Yannakakis. On notions of information transfer in VLSI circuits. In *Proceedings of 15th ACM STOC*, pages 133–139, 1983.

Martin Aigner. *Diskrete Mathematik*. Vieweg Studium, Wiesbaden, 1993.

Sheldon B. Akers and Balakrishnan Krishnamurthy. A group-theoretical model for symmetric interconnection networks. In S. K. Hwang, M. Jacobs, and E. E. Swartzlander, editors, *Proceedings of International Conference on Parallel Processing*, pages 216–223. IEEE Computer Press, 1986. see also IEEE Transactions on Computers, C-38, 1989, 555-566.

Selim G. Akl. *The design and analysis of parallel algorithms*. Prentice-Hall, Englewood Cliffs, 1989.

Serafino Amoroso and Yale N. Patt. Decision procedures for surjectivity and injectivity of parallel maps for tessellation structures. *Journal of Computer and System Sciences*, 6:448–464, 1972.

Kenneth Appel and Wolfgang Haken. Every planar graph is four colorable. Part 1. Discharging, Part 2. Reducibilities. *Illinois Journal of Mathematics*, 21:429–567, 1971.

Sigal Ar, Manuel Blum, Bruno Codenotti, and Peter Gemmell. Checking approximate computations over reals. In *Proceedings of 25th ACM STOC*, pages 786–795, 1993.

Raymond A. Archibald. The cattle problem. *American Mathematical Monthly*, 25:411–414, 1918.

Andre Arnold and Irene Guessarian. *Mathematics for Computer Science*. Prentice Hall, London, 1996.

Sanjeev Arora. *Probabilistic checking of proofs and hardness of approximation problems*. PhD thesis, CS Division, UC Berkeley, 1994. Available also as Tech. Rep. CS-TR-476-94, Princeton University.

Sanjeev Arora. Polynomial time approximation schemes for Euclidean TSP and other geometric problems. In *Proceedings of 37th IEEE FOCS*, 1996.

Sanjeev Arora, Carsten Lund, Rajeev Montwani, Madhu Sudan, and Mario Szegedy. Proof verification and hardness of approximation problems. In *Proceedings of 33rd IEEE FOCS*, pages 2–11, 1992.

Derek Atkins, Michael Graff, Arjen K. Lenstra, and Paul C. Leyland. The magic words are squeamish ossifrage. In J. Pieprzyk and R. Safani-Naini, editors, *Proceedings of ASIACRYPT'94*, pages 263–277. LNCS 917, Springer-Verlag, Berlin, New York, 1995.

Georgio Ausiello, Pierluigi Crescenzi, and Marco Protasi. Approximate solution of NP approximation problems. *Theoretical Computer Science*, 150:1–55, 1995.

Giorgio Ausiello, Pierluigi Crescenzi, Giorgio Gambosi, Viggo Kann, and Alberto Marchetti-Spaccamela. *Approximate solution of hard optimization problems, with a compendium of NP optimization problems*. 1997 to appear.

László Babai. Trading groups theory for randomness. In *Proceedings of 17th ACM STOC*, pages 421–429, 1985.

László Babai. E-mail and unexpected power of interactions. In *Proceedings of 5th IEEE Symposium on Structure in Complexity Theory*, pages 30–44, 1990.

László Babai. Transparent proofs and limits to approximation. In S. D. Chatterji, editor, *Proceedings of the First European Congress of Mathematicians*, pages 31–91. Birkhäuser, Boston, 1995.

László Babai, Lance Fortnow, Leonid A. Levin, and Mario Szegedy. Checking computations in polylogarithmic time. In *Proceedings of 23rd ACM STOC*, pages 21–31, 1991.

László Babai, Lance Fortnow, and Carsten Lund. Nondeterministic exponential time has two-prover interactive protocol. In *Proceedings of 31st IEEE FOCS*, pages 16–25, 1990.

László Babai and Shlomo Moran. Arthur-Merlin games: a randomized proof system and a hierarchy of complexity classes. *Journal of Computer and System Sciences*, 36:254–276, 1988.

Christian Bailly. *Automata - Golden age, 1848-1914*. P. Wilson Publisher, London, 1982. (With Sharon Bailey).

Theodore P. Baker, Joseph Gill, and Robert Solovay. Relativization of the P = NP question. *SIAM Journal of Computing*, 4:431–442, 1975.

José L. Balcázar, Josep Díaz, and Joaquim Gabárro. *Structural complexity I and II*. Springer-Verlag, Berlin, New York, 1988. Second edition of the first volume in 1994 within Texts in Theoretical Computer Science, Springer-Verlag.

José L. Balcázar, Antoni Lozano, and Jacobo Toran. The complexity of algorithmic problems in succinct instances. In R. Baeza-Yates and V. Menber, editors, *Computer Science*, pages 351–377. Plenum Press, New York, 1992.

Edwin R. Banks. Information processing and transmission in cellular automata. TR-81, Project MAC, MIT, 1971.

Yehoshu Bar-Hillel. *Language and Information*. Addison Wesley, Reading, Mass., 1964.

Bruce H. Barnes. A two-way automaton with fewer states than any equivalent one-way automaton. *IEEE Transactions on Computers*, TC-20:474–475, 1971.

Kenneth E. Batcher. Sorting networks and their applications. In *Proceedings of the AFIPS Spring Joint Computing Conference, V 32*, pages 307–314. Thomson Book Company, Washington, 1968.

Michel Bauderon and Bruno Courcelle. Graph expressions and graph rewriting. *Mathematical Systems Theory*, 20:83–127, 1987.

Friedrich L. Bauer. *Kryptologie*. Springer-Lehrbuch, 1993. English version: Decoded secrets, to appear in 1996.

Carter Bays. Candidates for the game of LIFE in three dimensions. *Complex Systems*, 1(3):373–380, 1987.

Richard Beigel. Interactive proof systems. Technical Report YALEU/DCS/TR-947, Department of Computer Science, Yale University, 1993.

Mihir Bellare, Oded Goldreich, and Madhu Sudan. Free bits, PCPs and non-approximability—towards tight results. In *Proceedings of 36th FOCS*, pages 422–431, 1995. Full version, available from ECCC, Electronic Colloqium on Computational Complexity, via WWW using http:/www.eccc.uni-trier.de/eccc/.

Shai Ben-David, Benny Z. Chor, Oded Goldreich, and Michael Luby. On the theory of average case complexity. *Journal of Computer and Systems Sciences*, 44:193–219, 1992.

Michael Ben-Or, Shaffi Goldwasser, Joe Kilian, and Avi Wigderson. Multiprover interactive proof systems: how to remove intractability assumption. In *Proceedings of 20th ACM STOC*, pages 86–97, 1988.

Václav Beneš. Permutation groups, complexes and rearangeable graphs: multistage connecting networks. *Bell System Technical Journal*, 43:1619–1640, 1964.

Václav Beneš. *Mathematical theory of connecting networks and telephone traffic*. Academic Press, New York, 1965.

Charles H. Bennett. Logical reversibility of computation. *IBM Journal of Research and Development*, 6:525–532, 1973.

Charles H. Bennett. Notes on the history of reversible computations. *IBM Journal of Research and Development*, 32(1):16–23, 1988.

Charles H. Bennett, François Bessette, Gilles Brassard, and Louis Salvail. Experimental quantum cryptography. *Journal of Cryptology*, 5:3–28, 1992.

Jon L. Bentley, Dorothea Haken, and James B. Saxe. A general method for solving divide and conquer recurrences. *SIGACT News*, 12(3):36–44, 1980.

Roger L. Berger. The undecidability of the domino problem. *Memoires of American Mathematical Society*, 66, 1966.

Elwyn R. Berlekamp. Factoring polynomials over large finite fields. *Mathematics of Computation*, 24:713–735, 1970.

Elwyn R. Berlekamp, John H. Conway, and Richard K. Guy. *Winnings ways for your mathematical plays, V2*. Academic Press, New York, 1982.

Jean Berstel. Fibonacci words—a survey. In G. Rozenberg and A. Salomaa, editors, *BOOK of L*, pages 13–28. Springer-Verlag, Berlin, New York, 1985.

Michael Bertol and Klaus Reinhardt. The tautologies over a finite set are context-free. *Bulletin of EATCS*, 57:196–197, Oct. 1995.

Sandeep N. Bhatt, Fan R. K. Chung, Jia-Wei Hong, F. Thomson Leighton, and Arnold L. Rosenberg. Optimal simulations by butterfly networks. In *Proceedings of 20th ACM STOC*, pages 192–204, 1988.

Sandeep N. Bhatt and Staros Cosmadakis. The complexity of minimazing wire lengths in VLSI layouts. Technical report, MIT, Cambridge, 1982.

Sandeep N. Bhatt and F. Thomson Leighton. A framework for solving VLSI graph layout problems. *Journal of Computer and System Sciences*, 28:300–343, 1984.

Gianfranco Bilardi and Franco P. Preparata. A minimum area VLSI network for $\mathcal{O}(\lg n)$-time sorting. *Transactions on Computing*, 34(4):336–343, 1985.

Patrick Billingsley. *Probability and measure*. Wiley, New York, 1986.

Lenore Blum, Manuel Blum, and Mike Shub. A simple unpredictable pseudo-random number generator. *SIAM Journal of Computing*, 15(2):364–383, 1986.

Lenore Blum, Mike Shub, and Steve Smale. On a theory of computation and complexity over the real numbers: NP-completeness recursive functions and universal machines. *Bulletin of the AMS*, 21(1):1–46, 1989.

Manuel Blum. On effective procedures for speeding up algorithms. *Journal of the ACM*, 18(2):290–305, 1971.

Manuel Blum. Coin flipping by telephone. A protocol for solving impossible problems. In *Proceedings of the 24th IEEE Computer Society Conference (CompCon)*, pages 133–137, 1982.

Manuel Blum. How to prove a theorem that nobody can claim it. In M. Gleason, editor, *Proceedings of the International Congress of Mathematicians*, pages 1444–1451, Berkeley, 1986. American Mathematical Society, Providence.

Manuel Blum. Designing programs to check their work. Technical Report TR-88-009, International Computer Science Institute, Berkeley, 1988.

Manuel Blum, Paul Feldman, and Silvio Micali. Non-interactive zero-knowledge and its applications. In *Proceedings of 20th ACM STOC*, pages 103–131, 1988.

Manuel Blum and Shaffi Goldwasser. An efficient probabilistic public-key encryption scheme that hides all partial information. In D. Chaum, G. R. Blakley, editors, *Proceedings of CRYPTO'84*, pages 289–299. LNCS 196, Springer-Verlag, Berlin, New York, 1985.

Manuel Blum and Sampath Kamman. Designing programs that check their work. In *Proceedings of 21st ACM STOC*, pages 86–97, 1989.

Manuel Blum, Michael Luby, and Ronett Rubinfeld. Self-testing/correcting with applications to numerical programs. *Journal of Computer and System Sciences*, 47:549–595, 1993.

Manuel Blum and Silvio Micali. How to generate cryptographically strong sequence of pseudo-random bits. *SIAM Journal of Computing*, 13(4):850–864, 1984.

Manuel Blum and Prabhakar Raghavan. Program correctness: can one test for it ?. In G. X. Ritter, editor, *Information Proceedings'89*, pages 127–134. Elsevier, 1989.

Manuel Blum and Hal Wasserman. Program result-checking: a theory of testing meets a test of theory. In *Proceedings of 35th FOCS*, pages 382–392, 1994.

Manuel Blum and Hal Wasserman. Software-reliability via run-time result checking. In *Proceedings of the 8th International Conference, Software Quality Week*, San Francisco, 1995.

Norbert Blum. A Boolean function requiring $3n$ network size. *Theoretical Computer Science*, 28:337–345, 1984.

J. Adrean Bondy and Uppaluri S. R. Murty. *Graph theory with applications*. Elsevier, North Holland, New York, 1976.

Alan Borodin. On relating time and space to size and depth. *SIAM Journal of Computing*, 6:733–744, 1977.

Alan Borodin and John E. Hopcroft. Routing, merging and sorting on parallel models of computation. *Journal of Computer and System Sciences*, 30:130–145, 1985.

Gilles Brassard. *Modern Cryptology*. LNCS 325, Springer-Verlag, Berlin, New York, 1988.

Gilles Brassard and Paul Brattey. *Algorithmics: theory and practice*. Prentice-Hall, Englewood Cliffs, 1988.

Gilles Brassard, David Chaum, and Claude Crépau. Minimum disclosure proofs of knowledge. *Journal of Computer and System Sciences*, 37:156–189, 1988.

Wilfried Brauer. *Automatentheorie*. Teubner, Stuttgart, 1984.

Wilfried Brauer. On minimizing finite automata. *Bulletin of EATCS*, 35:113–116, 1988.

Richard P. Brent and H. T. Kung. On the area of binary-tree layouts. *Information Processing Letters*, 11(1):46–48, 1980.

Ernest F. Brickell. Breaking iterated knapsack. In D. Chaum, G. R. Blakley, editors, *Proceedings of CRYPTO'84*, pages 342–358. LNCS 196, Springer-Verlag, 1985.

Ernest F. Brickell and Andrew M. Odlyzko. Cryptoanalysis: a survey of recent results. *Proceedings of the IEEE*, 76(5):560–577, 1988.

Sally A. Browning. *The tree machine: a highly concurrent computing environment*. PhD thesis, Department of Computer Science, California Institute of Technology, Pasadena, 1980.

John A. Brzozowski. Cannonical regular expressions and minimal state graphs for definite events. In *Mathematical Theory of Automata, V 12 of the MRI Symposia Series*, pages 529–561. Polytechnic Press of the Polytechnic Institute of Brooklyn, 1962.

John A. Brzozowski. Derivatives of regular expressions. *Journal of the ACM*, 11:481–494, 1964.

Rais G. Bucharaev. Some equivalences in the theory of probabilistic automata (in Russsian). *Notes of Kazan State University*, 124(2):45–65, 1964.

Rais G. Bucharaev. *Theorie der stochastischen Automaten*. Teubner, Stuttgart, 1995.

J. Richard Büchi. On a decision method in restricted second order arithmetic. In E. Nagel, P. Suppes, and A. Tarski, editors, *Proceedings of International Congress on Logic, Methodology and Philosophy of Science*, pages 66–92, Standford, 1960. Standford University Press.

Arthur W. Burks. *Essays on cellular automata*. University of Illinois Press, 1970.

Cristian Calude. *Information and randomness: an algorithmic perspective*. Springer-Verlag, Berlin, New York, 1994.

Keith W. Campbell and Michael J. Wiener. Proof that DES is not a group. In E. F. Brickell, editor, *Proceedings of CRYPTO'92*, pages 518–526. LNCS 740, Springer-Verlag, Berlin, New York, 1992.

Jack W. Carlyre. Reduced forms for stochastic sequential machines. *Journal of Mathematical Analysis and Applications*, 7(3):167–175, 1963.

J. Lawrence Carter and Mark N. Wegman. Universal classes of hash functions. *Journal of Computer and System Sciences*, 18:143–154, 1979.

Arthur Cayley. The theory of groups. *American Journal of Mathematics*, 1:50–52, 174–176, 1878.

Gregory J. Chaitin. On the length of programs for computing finite binary sequences. *Journal of the ACM*, 13:547–569, 1966.

Gregory J. Chaitin. *Algorithmic Information Theory*. Cambridge University Press, 1987a.

Gregory J. Chaitin. *Information, randomness and incompleteness*. World Scientific Publisher, Singapore, 1987b.

Mee-Yee Chan. Dilation 2 embeddings of grids into hypercube. Technical report, University of Texas, Computer Science Program, 1988.

Mee-Yee Chan. Embedding of d-dimensional grids into optimal hypercubes. In *Proceedings of the 1989 ACM Symposium on Parallel Algorithms and Architectures*, pages 52–57, 1989.

Mee-Yee Chan and Francis Y. L. Chin. On embedding rectangular grids in hypercubes. *IEEE Transactions on Computers*, 37:1285–1288, 1988.

Ashok K. Chandra, Merrick L. Furst, and Richard J. Lipton. Multiparty protocols. In *Proceedings of 15th ACM STOC*, pages 94–99, 1983.

Ashok K. Chandra and Larry J. Stockmeyer. Alternation. In *Proceedings of 17th IEEE FOCS*, pages 98–108, 1976.

Shiva Chaudhuri and Devdatt Dubhashi. (Probabilistic) reccurrence relations revisited. In R. Baeza-Yates, E. Goles, and P. Poblete, editors, *Proceedings of LATIN'95*, pages 207–219. LNCS 911, Springer-Verlag, 1995.

Noam Chomsky. Three models for the description of languages. *IRE Transactions of Information Theory*, IT-2:113–124, 1956.

Noam Chomsky. *Syntactic structures*. Gravenhage, Mouton, 1957.

Noam Chomsky. On certain formal properties of grammars. *Information and Control*, 2:137–167, 1959.

Noam Chomsky. Context-free grammars and pushdown storage. Research Laboratory Electron, Quarterly Progress Report 65, MIT, 1962.

Noam Chomsky and Marcel P. Schützenberger. The algebraic theory of context-free languages. In P. Braffort and D. Hischberg, editors, *Computer Programming and Formal Systems*, pages 118–161. North Holland, Amsterdam, 1963.

Benny Z. Chor. *Two issues in public key cryptography*. MIT Press, Cambridge, 1986.

Alonzo Church. The calculi of lambda-conversion. *Annals of Mathematical Studies*, 6:77, 1941.

Alan Cobham. The intrinsic computational complexity of functions. In Y. Bar-Hillel, editor, *Proceedings of the 1964 Congress on Logic, Mathematics and the Methodology of Science*, pages 24–30. North-Holland, Amsterdam, 1965.

Edgard F. Codd. *Cellular automata*. Academic Press, New York, 1988.

Daniel E. Cohen. *Computability and logic*. Ellis Horwood Limited, Chichester, 1987.

Richard Cole and Uzi Vishkin. Deterministic coin-tossing with applications to optimal parallel list ranking. *Information and Control*, 70:32–53, 1986.

Anne Condon, Lisa Hellerstein, Samuel Potte, and Avi Wigderson. On the power of finite automata with both nondeterministic and probabilistic states. In *Proceedings of 26th ACM STOC*, pages 667–685, 1994.

Stephen Cook, Cynthia Dwork, and Karl R. Reischuk. Upper and lower bounds for parallel random access machines with simultaneous writes. *SIAM Journal of Computing*, 15:87–97, 1986.

Stephen A. Cook. The complexity of theorem proving procedures. In *Proceedings of 3rd IEEE FOCS*, pages 151–158, 1971.

Stephen A. Cook. A hierarchy for nondeterministic time complexity. *Journal of Computer and System Sciences*, 7:343–353, 1973a.

Stephen A. Cook. An observation on time-storage trade off. In *Proceedings of 5th ACM STOC*, pages 29–33, 1973b.

Stephen A. Cook. Towards a complete theory of synchronous parallel computations. *L'enseignement Mathématique, Serie II*, 27:99–124, 1981.

Stephen A. Cook. A taxanomy of problems with fast parallel algorithms. *Information and Control*, 64:2–22, 1985.

Stephen A. Cook and Robert A. Reckhow. Time bounded random access machines. *Journal of Computer and System Sciences*, 7:354–375, 1973.

Don Coppersmith and Shmuel Winograd. Matrix multiplication via arithmetic progressions. In *Proceedings of 19th ACM STOC*, pages 1–6, 1987.

Thomas H. Cormen, Charles Leiserson, and Ronald L. Rivest. *Introduction to algorithms*. The MIT Press — McGraw Hill, Cambridge, New York, 1990.

Karel Culik II. An aperiodic set of 13 Wang tiles. *Discrete Applied Mathematics*, 160:245–251, 1996.

Karel Culik II and Simant Dube. Rational and affine expressions for image description. *Discrete Applied Mathematics*, 41:85–120, 1993.

Karel Culik II and Ivan Friš. The decidability of the equivalence problem for D0L systems. *Information and Control*, 35:20–39, 1977.

Karel Culik II and Ivan Friš. Weighted finite transducers in image processing. *Discrete Applied Mathematics*, 58:223–237, 1995.

Karel Culik II and Juhani Karhumäki. On totalistic systolic networks. *Information Processing Letters*, 26:231–236, 1987.

Karel Culik II and Juhani Karhumäki. Finite automata computing real functions. *SIAM Journal of Computing*, 23:789–814, 1994.

Karel Culik II and Jarrko Kari. Image compression using weighted finite automata. *Computers and Graphics*, 17:305–313, 1993.

Karel Culik II and Jarrko Kari. Image-data compression using edge-optimizing algorithm for WFA inference. *Journal of Information Processing and Management*, 30:829–838, 1994.

Karel Culik II and Jarrko Kari. Finite state transformation of images. In F. Gécseg Z. Fülope, editors, *Proceedings of ICALP'95*, pages 51–62. LNCS 944, Springer-Verlag, Berlin, New York, 1995.

Karel Culik II and Peter Rajčáni. Iterative weighted finite transducers. *Acta Informatica*, 32:681–703, 1995.

Karel Culik II, Arto Salomaa, and Derick Wood. Systolic tree acceptors. *RAIRO Informatique Théorique et Applications*, 18:53–69, 1984.

Jürgen Dassow, Rudolf Freund, and Gheorgh Paŭn. Cooperating array grammars. *International Journal of Pattern Recognition and Artificial Intelligence*, 9(6):1–25, 1995.

Martin Davis. *Computability and Undecidability*. McGraw Hill, New York, 1958.

Martin Davis. *The undecidable*. Raven Press, Hewlet, NY, 1965.

Martin Davis. Hilbert's tenth problem. *American Mathematical Monthly*, 80:233–269, 1980.

Nicolas G. de Bruijn. A combinatorial problem. In *Proceedings of the Section of Science, Appl. Mathematical Science, Koninklijke*, pages 758–764. Nederlandse Academie van Wetenshapen, Amsterdam, 1946.

John M. DeLaurentis. A further weakness in the common modulus protocol for the RSA cryptoalgorithm. *Cryptologia*, 8:253–259, 1984.

Thomas Denny, Bruce A. Dodson, Arjen K. Lenstra, and Mark S. Manasse. On the factorization of RSA-120. In D. R. Stinson, editor, *Advances in Cryptology—CRYPTO-93*, pages 166–174. LNCS 773, Springer-Verlag, Berlin, New York, 1994.

Denis Derencourt, Juhani Karhumäki, Michel Latteaux, and Alen Terlutte. On continuous functions computed by finite automata. *RAIRO Informatique Théorique et Applications*, 28(3-4):387–403, 1994.

Denis Derencourt, Juhani Karhumäki, Michel Latteaux, and Alen Terlutte. On computational power of weighted finite automata. *Fundamenta Informatica*, 25:285–294, 1996.

Nachum Dershowitz and Jean Pierre Jouannaud. Rewrite systems. In J. van Leeuwen, editor, *Handbook of Theoretical Computer Science, V B, Formal Models and Semantics*, pages 243–320. Elsevier, Amsterdam, 1990.

David Deutsch. Quantum theory, the Church-Turing principle and the universal quantum computer. *Proceedings of Royal Society (London)*, A-400:97–117, 1985.

A. K. Dewdney. A computer trap for busy beaver, the hardest working Turing machine. *Scientific American*, 251:16–23, August 1984.

Josep Díaz, Maria Serna, Paul Spirakis, and Jacobo Torán. *Paradigms for fast parallel approximability*. Cambridge University Press, 1997.

Martin Dietzfelbinger, Juraj Hromkovič, and Georg Schnitger. A comparison of two lower bound methods for communication complexity. In I. Prívara, B. Rovan, and P. Ružička, editors, *Proceedings of MFCS'94*, pages 326–335. LNCS 841, Springer-Verlag, Berlin, New York, 1994.

Whitfield Diffie. The first ten years of public-key cryptography. *Proceedings of the IEEE*, 76:560–577, 1988.

Whitfield Diffie and Martin E. Hellman. New directions in cryptography. *IEEE Transactions on Information Theory*, IT-22:644–656, 1976.

David P. Dobkin, Richard J. Lipton, and Steven Reiss. Linear programming is log-space hard for P. *Information Processing Letters*, 8:96–97, 1979.

Danny Dolev, F. Thomson Leighton, and Howard Trickey. Planar embeddings of planar graphs. Technical report, MIT LCS, 1983.

Frank Drewes, Annegret Habel, and Hans-Jörg Kreowski. Hyperedge replacement graph grammars. In G. Rozenberg, editor, *Handbook of Graph Rewriting, Vol. I: Foundations*, pages 95–182. World Scientific, Singapore, 1996.

Pavol Ďuriš, Zvi Galil, and Georg Schnitger. Lower bounds on communication complexity. In *Proceedings of 16th ACM STOC*, pages 81–91, 1984.

Patrick W. Dymond and Martin Tompa. Speedups of deterministic machines by synchronous parallel machines. *Journal of Computer and System Sciences*, 30(2):144–161, 1985.

Freeman Dyson. Time without end: physics and biology in an open universe. *Reviews of Modern Physics*, 52(3):447–460, 1979.

John Edmonds. Paths, trees and flowers. *Canadian Journal of Mathematics*, 17(3):449–467, 1965.

John Edmonds. Systems of distinct representatives and linear algebra and optimum branching. *Journal of Research, National Burreau of Standards*, Part B, 17B(4):233–245, 1966.

Ömer Eğecioğlu. An introduction to formal language theory. Lecture notes, Dept. of Computer Science, University of California, Santa Barbara, 1995.

Hartmut Ehrig and Bernd Mahr. *Fundamentals of algebraic specifications, I.* Springer-Verlag, Berlin, New York, 1985.

Samuel Eilenberg. *Automata, languages and machines.* Academic Press, New York, London, 1974.

Taher ElGamal. A public-key cryptosystem and a signature scheme based on discrete logarithms. *IEEE Transactions on Information Theory*, IT-31(4):469–472, 1985.

Calvin C. Elgot and Abraham Robinson. Random access stored program machines. *Journal of the ACM*, 5(3):232–245, 1964.

Erwin Engeler. *Introduction to the theory of computation.* Academic Press, New York, London, 1973.

Joost Engelfriet and Grzegorz Rozenberg. Node replacement graph grammars. In G. Rozenberg, editor, *Handbook of Graph Rewriting, Vol. I: Foundations*, pages 1–94. World Scientific, 1996.

Trevor Evans. On multiplicative systems defined by generators and relations. In *Proceedings of the Cambridge Philosophical Society*, pages 637–649, Cambridge, 1951.

Robert J. Evey. The theory and applications of pushdown store machines. PhD thesis and research report, Mathematical Linguistic and Automatic Translation Language Project, NSF-10, Harward University, May 1963.

Doyne Farmer, Tommaso Toffoli, and Stephen Wolfram (Eds.). Cellular automata, Proceedings of an interdisciplinary workshop. *Physica D*, 10(1, 2), 1984.

Uriel Feige, Shaffi Goldwasser, László Babai, Shmuel Safra, and Mario Szegedy. Approximating clique is almost NP-complete. In *Proceedings of 32nd IEEE FOCS*, pages 2–12, 1991.

Joan Feigenbaum. Overview of interactive proof systems and zero-knowledge. In G. J. Simmons, editor, *The science of information integrity*, pages 424–438. Piscatoway, N. J. IEEE Press, 1992.

Horst Feistel. Cryptology and computer privacy. *Scientific American*, 228(5):15–23, 1973.

Rainer Feldman and Walter Unger. The cube-connected cycles. *Parallel Processing Letters*, 2(1):13–19, 1992.

William Feller. *An introduction to probability theory.* Wiley, New York, 1964.

Amos Fiat and Adi Shamir. Polymorphic arrays: a novel VLSI layout for systolic computers. In *Proceedings of the 16th ACM STOC*, pages 37–45, 1984.

Faith E. Fich. The complexity of computation on parallel random access machines. In *Synthesis of parallel algorithms (J. H. Reif, editor)*. Morgen Kaufmann, San Mateo, Ca., 1993.

Robert Floyd and Richard Beigel. *The language of machines.* Computer Science Press, New York, 1994.

Steven Fortune and James Wyllie. Parallelism in RAMs. In *Proceedings of 10th ACM STOC*, pages 114–118, 1978.

Pierre Fraigniaud and Emmanuel Lazard. Methods and problems of communication in usual networks. *Discrete Applied Mathematics*, 53(79-133), 1994.

Rūsiņš Freivalds. Fast probabilistic algorithms. In J. Bečvař, editor, *Proceedings of MFCS'79*, pages 57–68. LNCS 74, Springer-Verlag, 1979.

Rudolf Freund. Control mechanisms on context-free array grammars. In G. Păun, editor, *Mathematical Aspects of Natural and Formal Languages*, pages 97–137. World Scientific Series in Computer Science, Singapore, V 43, 1994.

Helen F. Gaines. *Cryptoanalysis*. Dover, New York, 1939.

David Gale and Frank M. Stewart. Infinite games with perfect information. In H. W. Kuhn and A. W. Tucker, editors, *Contributions to the theory of games*, pages 1950–59, Princeton, N.J., 1953. Princeton University Press.

Hana Galperin and Avi Wigderson. Succinct representation of graphs. *Information and Control*, 56:183–198, 1983.

Martin Gardner. *Logic machines and diagrams*. McGraw-Hill, New York, 1958.

Martin Gardner. A new kind of cipher that would take milions years to break. *Scientific American*, 237(8):120–124, August 1977.

Martin Gardner. *Wheels, life and other mathematical amusements*. W. H. Freeman and Company, San Francisco, 1983.

Martin Gardner. *Penrose tiles to trapdoor functions*. W. H. Freeman and Company, San Francisco, 1989.

Michael R. Garey and David S. Johnson. Strong NP-completeness results: motivation, examples, and implications. *Journal of the ACM*, 25:499–508, 1978.

Michael R. Garey and David S. Johnson. *Computers and intractability: a guide to the theory of NP-completeness*. W. H. Freeman and Company, San Francisco, 1979.

Max Garzon. *Analysis of modeĺs of massive parallelism: cellular automata and neural networks*. Springer-Verlag, Berlin, New York, 1995.

Fănică Gavril. Algorithms for minimum coloring, maximum clique, minimum covering by cliques, and maximum independent set of a choral graph. *SIAM Journal of computing*, 1(2):180–187, 1977.

T. D. Gedeon. The Reve's puzzle: an iterative solution produced by transformation. *The Computer Journal*, 35(2):186–187, 1992.

Viliam Geffert. Normal forms for phrase-structure grammars. *RAIRO Informatique Théorique et Applications*, 25(5):473–496, 1991.

Murray Gesternhaber. The 152-nd proof of the law of quadratic reciprocity. *American Mathematical Monthly*, 70:397–398, 1963.

John Gill. Computational complexity of probabilistic Turing machines. *SIAM Journal of Computing*, 6:675–695, 1977.

Seymour Ginsburg. *The mathematical theory of context-free languages*. McGraw Hill, New York, London, 1966.

Seymour Ginsburg and Gene F. Rose. Operations that preserve definability in languages. *Journal of the ACM*, 10:175–195, 1963.

Seymour Ginsburg and Gene F. Rose. A characterization of machine independent mappings. *Canadian Journal of Mathematics*, 18:381–388, 1966.

Kurt Gödel. Über formal unentscheidbare Sätze der Principia Mathematica und verwandter Systeme I. *Monatshefte für Mathematik und Physik*, 38:173–178, 1931. English translation in: Davis (1965), pages 4-38.

Oded Goldreich. Randomness, interactive proofs, and zero-knowledge. A survey. In R. Merken, editor, *The Universal Turing Machine: A half century survey*, pages 377–405, Hamburg, 1988. Kammer & Univerzagt.

Oded Goldreich. Foundations of cryptography. Technical report, Computer Science Department, Technion, Haifa, 1989.

Oded Goldreich and Leonid A. Levin. A hard-core predicate for all one-way functions. In *Proceedings of 21st ACM STOC*, pages 327–377, 1989.

Oded Goldreich, Silvio Micali, and Avi Wigderson. Proofs that yield nothing but their validity and a methodology for protocol design. In *Proceedings of the 27th IEEE FOCS*, pages 174–187, 1986.

Leslie M. Goldschlager. *Synchronous parallel computations*. PhD thesis, University of Toronto, Computer Science Department, 1977.

Leslie M. Goldschlager. A unified approach to models of synchronous parallel machines. In *Proceedings of 10th ACM STOC*, pages 89–94, 1978.

Leslie M. Goldschlager. A universal interconnection pattern for parallel computers. *Journal of the ACM*, 29:1073–1086, 1982.

Shaffi Goldwasser and Silvio Micali. Probabilistic encryption. *Journal of Computer and System Sciences*, 28(2):270–299, 1984.

Shaffi Goldwasser, Silvio Micali, and Charles Rackoff. The knowledge complexity of interactive proofs. In *Proceedings of 17th ACM STOC*, pages 291–305, 1985.

Shaffi Goldwasser, Silvio Micali, and Charles Rackoff. The knowledge complexity of interactive proof systems. *SIAM Journal of Computing*, 18(1):186–208, 1989.

Shaffi Goldwasser, Silvio Micali, and Po Tong. Why and how to establish a private code on a public network. In *Proceedings of 23rd IEEE FOCS*, pages 134–144, 1982.

Shaffi Goldwasser and Michael Sipser. Private coins versus public coins in interactive proof systems. In *Proceedings of 18th ACM STOC*, pages 59–68, 1986.

Gaston H. Gonnet. *Handbook of algorithms and data structures*. Addison-Wesley, Reading, Mass., 1984.

David Gorenstein. The enormous theorem. *Scientific American*, 253(6):104–115, 1985.

Joseph A. Gougen, James W. Thatcher, Eric W. Wagner, and Jesse G. Wright. Initial algebra semantics and continuous algebras. *Journal of the ACM*, 24:68–95, 1977.

Ronald L. Graham, Donald E. Knuth, and Oren Patashnik. *Concrete mathematics*. Addison-Wesley, Reading, Mass., 1989.

David S. Greenberg, Lenwood Heath, and Arnold L. Rosenberg. Optimal embeddings of butterfly-like graphs in the hypercube. *Mathematical Systems Theory*, 23(1):61–67, 1990.

Daniel H. Greene and Donald E. Knuth. *Mathematics for the analysis of algorithms*. Bikhäuser, Boston, 1981.

Raymond Greenlaw, H. James Hoover, and Walter L. Ruzzo. *Limits to parallel computing*. Oxford University Press, New York, Oxford, 1993.

Sheila A. Greibach. A new normal form theorem for context-free phrase-structure grammars. *Journal of the ACM*, 12(1):47–52, 1965.

Sheila A. Greibach. The hardest context-free language. *SIAM Journal of Computing*, 2:304–310, 1973.

Joachim Grollman and Alan L. Selman. Complexity measures for public-key cryptosystems. *SIAM Journal of Computing*, 17(2):309–335, 1988.

Branko Grünbaum and G. C. Shephard. *Tilings and patterns*. W. H. Freeman and Company, San Francisco, 1987.

Jozef Gruska. Some classification of context-free languages. *Information and Control*, 14:152–171, 1969.

Jozef Gruska, Margherita Napoli, and Dominico Parente. State complexity of BSTA languages. In B. Pehrson and I. Simon, editors, *Information Processing'94, Technology and Foundations, IFIP Transductions*, pages 247–252. North-Holland, 1994.

Yuri Gurevich. Average case completeness. *Journal of Computer and System Sciences*, 42:346–398, 1991.

Howard Gutowitz. *Cellular automata: theory and experiments*. North-Holland, Amsterdam, 1990.

Annegret Habel. Graph grammars, transformational and algebraic aspects. *Journal of Information Processing and Cybernetics, EIK*, 28:241–277, 1990.

Annegret Habel. *Hypercube replacement: grammars and languages*. LNCS 643, Springer-Verlag, Berlin, New York, 1990a.

Annegret Habel and Hans-Jörg Kreowski. Some structural aspects of hypergraph languages generated by hyperedge replacement. In F. J. Brandenburg, G. Vidal-Naquet, and M. Wirsing, editors, *Proceedings of STACS'87*, pages 207–219. LNCS 247, Springer-Verlag, Berlin, New York, 1987.

Annegret Habel and Hans-Jörg Kreowski. May we introduce to you hyperedge replacement? In H. Ehrig, M. Nagl, G. Rozenberg, and A. Rosenfeld, editors, *Proceedings of the Graph Grammars Workshop*, pages 15–26. LNCS 291, Springer-Verlag, Berlin, New York, 1987a.

Annegret Habel, Hans-Jörg Kreowski, and Walter Vogler. Metatheorems for decision problems on hyperedge replacement graph languages. *Acta Informatica*, 26:657–677, 1989.

Torben Hagerup and Christine Rüb. A guided tour of Chernoff bounds. *Information Processing Letters*, 33:305–308, 1989.

Frank Harary, Patrick J. Hayes, and H. Jr Wu. A survey of the theory of hypercube graphs. *Computers and Mathematics with Applications*, 15(4):277–289, 1988.

Godfrey H. Hardy. Properties of logarithmico-exponential functions. *Proceedings of London Mathematical Society*, 10:54–90, 1911.

Godfrey H. Hardy. Orders of infinity, the "infinitetärcalcül of Paul du Bois-Rymond, v. 12. In *Cambridge Tracks in Mathematics and Mathematical Physics*. Cambridge University Press, 1924.

David Harel. *Algorithmics*. Addison-Wesley, Wokingam, Reading, Mass, 1987.

Michael A. Harrison. *Introduction to formal language theory*. Addison-Wesley, Reading, Mass., 1978.

Juris Hartmanis. Computational complexity of random access stored program machines. *Mathematical Systems Theory*, 5(3):232–245, 1971.

Juris Hartmanis. Observations about the development of theoretical computer science. In *Proceedings of 20th IEEE FOCS*, pages 224–233, 1979.

Juris Hartmanis and Leonard Berman. On isomorphism and density of NP and other complete problems. *Journal of Computer System Sciences*, 16:418–422, 1978.

Juris Hartmanis, Philip M. Lewis, and Richard E. Stearns. Hierarchies of memory limited computations. In *Proceedings of 6th IEEE Symposium on Switching Circuit Theory and Logic Design*, pages 179–190, 1965.

Juris Hartmanis and Richard E. Stearns. On the computational complexity of algorithms. *Transactions of the ACM*, 117:285–306, 1965.

Ivan Havel and Petr Liebl. Embedding the polytonic tree into the n-cube. *Časopis pro pěstovaní matematiky*, 98:307–314, 1973.

Ralf Heckmann, Ralf Klasing, Burkhard Monien, and Walter Unger. Optimal embedding of complete binary trees into lines and grids. In R. Berghammer and G. Schmidt, editors, *Proceedings of 17th Workshop on Graph-Theoretic Concepts in Computer Science*, pages 25–35. LNCS 570, Springer-Verlag, Berlin, New York, 1991.

Andrew Hedges. *Alan Turing: The Enigma*. Burnett Books Ltd., London, 1983.

Michael Held and Richard M. Karp. The traveling salesman problem and minimum spanning trees. *Operational Research*, 18:1138–1162, 1970.

Martin E. Hellman. Extension of the Shannon theory approach to cryptography. *Transactions on Information Theory*, IT-23(3):289–295, 1977.

Marie-Claude Heydemann, Jaroslav Opatrny, and Dominique Sotteau. Embeddings of hypercubes and grids into de Bruijn graphs. *Journal of Parallel and Distributed Computing*, 23:104–111, 1991.

David Hilbert. Mathematische Probleme. Vortrag gehalten auf dem Internationalen Mathematiker-Kongres zu Paris 1900. In *Gesammelte Abhandlungen*, pages 290–329. Springer, Berlin, 1935. Reprinted by Chelsa, Bronx, 1965. English translation in Bulletin of the American Mathematical Society, V8, 437-478, 1902.

Lester S. Hill. Cryptography in an algebraic alphabet. *American Mathematical Monthly*, 36:306–312, 1929.

Dorit S. Hochbaum. Approximation algorithms for set covering and vertex cover problems. *SIAM Journal of Computing*, 11:555–556, 1982.

Dorit S. Hochbaum, editor. *Approximation algorithms for NP-hard problems*. PWS Publishing, 1997.

Dan Hoey and Charles E. Leiserson. A layout for the shuffle exchange network. In *Proceedings of the 1980 IEEE International Conference on Parallel Processing*, pages 329–336. IEEE Computer Society, Los Alamitos, 1980.

Micha Hofri. *Analysis of algorithms*. Oxford University Press, 1995.

Ian Holyer. The NP-completeness of edge-coloring. *SIAM Journal of Computing*, 10:718–720, 1981.

John E. Hopcroft. An $n \lg n$ algorithm for minimizing states in a finite automaton. In Z. Kohavi and A. Paz, editors, *Theory of Machines and Computations*, pages 189–196. Academic Press, New York, 1971.

John E. Hopcroft. Turing machines. *Scientific American*, 250:86–98, May 1984.

John E. Hopcroft, Wolfgang J. Paul, and Leslie G. Valiant. On time versus space and related problems. In *Proceedings of 16th IEEE FOCS*, pages 57–64, 1975.

John E. Hopcroft and Jeffery D. Ullman. *Formal languages and their relation to automata*. Addison-Wesley, Reading, Mass., 1969.

Juraj Hromkovič. *Communication complexity and parallel computing*. Springer-Verlag, Berlin, New York, 1997.

Juraj Hromkovič, Ralf Klasing, Burkhard Monien, and Regine Peine. Dissemination of information in interconnection networks (broadcasting and gossiping). In F. Hsu and D-Z. Du, editors, *Combinatorial network theory*, pages 125–212. Kluger Academic Publisher, 1995.

Wen-Jing Hsu. Fibonacci cubes—a new interconnection topology. *IEEE Transactions on Parallel and Distributed Systems*, 4(1):3–12, 1993.

David A. Huffman. The synthesis of sequential switching circuits. *Journal of the Franklin Institute*, 257(3-4):275–303, 1954.

Neil Immerman. Nondeterministic space is closed under complementation. *SIAM Journal of Computing*, 17:935–938, 1988.

Russel Impagliazzo. A personal view of average-case complexity. In *Proceedings of 10th IEEE Structure in Complexity Theory*, pages 134–147, 1995.

Russel Impagliazzo and Moti Yung. Direct minimum-knowledge computations. In *Proceedings CRYPTO'87*, pages 40–51. LNCS 293, Springer-Verlag, Berlin, New York, 1988.

Kenneth E. Iverson. *A programming language*. Wiley, New York, 1962.

Joseph Ja'Ja. *An Introduction to Parallel Algorithms*. Addison-Wesley, Reading, Mass., 1992.

Joseph Ja'Ja, V. K. Prassana Kamar, and Janos Simon. Information transfer under different sets of protocols. *SIAM Journal of Computing*, 13:840–849, 1984.

Dirk Janssens and Grzegorz Rozenberg. On the structure of node label controlled graph languages. *Information Sciences*, 20:191–216, 1980.

Dirk Janssens and Grzegorz Rozenberg. Restrictions, extensions and variations on NLC grammars. *Information Sciences*, 20:217–249, 1980a.

David S. Johnson. Approximation algorithms for combinatorial problems. *Journal of Computer and System Sciences*, 9:256–278, 1974.

David S. Johnson. The NP-completeness column: An on-going guide. *Journal of Algorithms*, 4:393–405, 1981.

David S. Johnson. A catalog of complexity classes. In J. van Leeuwen, editor, *Handbook of Theoretical Computer Science, Volume A, Algorithms and Complexity*, pages 68–161. Elsevier, Amsterdam, 1990.

David S. Johnson. The NP-completeness column: an ongoing guide. *Journal of Algorithms*, 13:502–524, 1992.

David S. Johnson and Lyle McGeoch. The traveling salesman problem: a case study in local optimization. In H. L. Aarts and J. K. Lenstra, editors, *Local search in combinatorial optimization*. Wiley, Chichester, 1996.

David S. Johnson, Lyle A McGeoch, and Ed E. Rothberg. Asymptotic experimental analysis for the Held-Karp traveling salesman bound. In *Proceedings of the 7th Annual ACM-SIAM Symposium on Discrete Algorithms*, pages 341–350, 1996.

James P. Jones. Universal Diophantine equation. *Journal of Symbolic Logic*, 47:549–571, 1982.

James P. Jones, Daihachiro Sato, Hideo Wada, and Douglas Wiens. Diophantine representation of the set of prime numbers. *The American Mathematical Monthy*, 83(6):449–464, 1976.

Neil D. Jones and William T. Laaser. Complete problems for deterministic polynomial time. *Theoretical Computer Science*, 33(1):105–117, 1976.

David Kahn. *The codebreaker: the story of secret writing*. Macmillan, New York, 1967.

Mauricio Karchmer and Avi Wigderson. Monotone circuits for connectivity require super-logarithmic depth. In *Proceedings of 20th ACM STOC*, pages 539–550, 1988.

Jarrko Kari. Reversibility of 2D cellular automata is undecidable. *Physica D*, 45:379–385, 1990.

Richard M. Karp. Reducibility among combinatorial problems. In R. E. Miller, J. W. Thatcher, editors, *Complexity of computer computations*, pages 85–103. Plenum Press, New York, 1972.

Richard M. Karp. An introduction to randomized algorithms. *Discrete Applied Mathematics*, 34:165–201, 1991a.

Richard M. Karp. Probabilistic recurrence relations. In *Proceedings of 23rd ACM STOC*, pages 190–197. ACM Press, 1991b.

Richard M. Karp and Richard J. Lipton. Some connections between nonuniform and uniform complexity classes. In *Proceedings of 12th ACM STOC*, pages 303–309, 1980.

Richard M. Karp, Michael Luby, and Friedhelm Meyer auf der Heide. Efficient PRAM simulations in a distributed memory machine. In *Proceedings of 24th ACM STOC*, pages 318–326, 1992.

Richard M. Karp and Vijaya Ramachandran. Parallel algorithms for stored memory machines. In J. van Leeuwen, editor, *Handbook of Theoretical Computer Science, Volume A, Algorithms and Complexity*, pages 867–941. Elsevier, Amsterdam, 1990.

Tadao Kasami. An efficient recognition and syntax-analysis for context-free languages. Research Report AFCRL-65-758, Air Force Cambridge Research Laboratory, Bedford, Mass, 1965.

Tadao Kasami and Koji Torii. A syntax analysis procedure for unambiguous context-free grammars. *Journal of the ACM*, 16, 1969.

William H. Kautz. Bounds on directed (d,k)-graphs. In *Theory of cellular logic networks and machines*, pages 20–28. SRI project 7258, AFCRL 69-0668 Final report, 1968.

Leonid G. Khachyian. A polynomial time algorithm for linear programming (in Russian). *DAN SSSR*, 244:1093–1097, 1979.

Hélène Kirchner. Term rewriting. In *Algebraic Foundations of Systems Specifications*, 1997. In preparation.

Stephen C. Kleene. General recursive functions of natural numbers. *Mathematische Annalen*, 112:727–742, 1936.

Stephen C. Kleene. *An introduction to metamathematics*. D. van Nostrad, Princeton, 1952.

Stephen C. Kleene. Representation of events in nerve nets and finite automata. In C. E. Shannon and J. McCarthy, editors, *Automata studies*, Princeton, 1956. Princeton Press.

Donald E. Knuth. *The art of computer programming I: Fundamental algorithms*. Addison Wesley, Reading, Mass., 1968.

Donald E. Knuth. *The art of computer programming II: Seminumeral algorithms*. Addison Wesley, Reading, Mass., 1969.

Donald E. Knuth. *The art of computer programming III: Sorting and searching*. Addison Wesley, Reading, Mass., 1973.

Donald E. Knuth, James H. Morris, and Vaughan R. Pratt. Fast pattern matching in strings. *SIAM Journal of Computing*, 6:323–350, 1977.

Richard Koch, F. Thomson Leighton, Bruce M. Maggs, Satish Rao, and Arnold L. Rosenberg. Work-preserving emulations of fixed-connection networks. In *Proceedings of 21st ACM STOC*, pages 227–240, 1989.

Andrei N. Kolmogorov. Three approaches to the quantitative definition of information (in Russian). *Problems Information Transmission*, 1(1):1–7, 1965.

Alan G. Konheim. *Cryptography: a primer*. Wiley, New York, 1981.

Ivan Korec. Decidability (undecidability) of equivalence of Minsky machines with components of at most seven (eight) components. In J. Gruska, editor, *Proceedings of MFCS'77*, pages 324–332. LNCS 53, Springer-Verlag, 1977.

Ivan Korec. Small universal Turing machines. *Theoretical Computer Science*, 168:267–301, 1996.

Elias Kotsoupias and Christos H. Papadimitriou. On the greedy algorithm for satisfiability. *Information Processing Letter*, 43:53–55, 1992.

Dexter C. Kozen. *The design and analysis of algorithms*. Springer-Verlag, Berlin, New York, 1991.

Evangelos Kranakis. *Primality and Cryptography*. Teubner-Wiley, Stuttgart, 1986.

Hans-Jörg Kreowski. *Manipulationen von Graphmanipulationen*. PhD thesis, Computer Science Department, Technische Universität Berlin, 1977.

Hans-Jörg Kreowski. A pumping lemma for context-free graph languages. In J. Bečvař, editor, *Proceedings of MFCS'79*. 270-283, LNCS 74, Springer-Verlag, 1979.

Clyde P. Kruskal and Mare Snir. A unified theory of interconnection networks. *Theoretical Computer Science*, 48:75–94, 1986.

Ludvig Kučera. Parallel computation and conflicts in memory access. *Information Processing Letters*, 14:93–96, 1982.

Shige-Yuki Kuroda. Classes of languages and linear bounded automata. *Information and Control*, 7:207–223, 1964.

Richard E. Ladner. The circuit value problem is lg-space complete for P. *SIGACT News*, 7(1):18–20, 1975.

Richard E. Ladner and Michael J. Fischer. Parallel prefix computation. *Journal of the ACM*, 27(4):831–838, 1986.

Richard E. Ladner, Nancy A. Lynch, and Alan L. Selman. A comparison of polynomial time reducibilities. *Theoretical Computer Science*, 1:103–124, 1975.

Jeffery C. Lagarias. The $3x+1$ problem and its generalizations. *American Mathematical Monthly*, 92:3–23, 1985.

Jeffery C. Lagarias, Victor S. Miller, and Andrew M. Odlyzko. Computing $\pi(x)$: The Meissel-Lehmer method. *Mathematics and Computations*, 44:537–560, 1985.

S. Lakshmivarahan and Sudarshan Dhall. *Analysis and design of parallel algorithms*. McGraw Hill, New York, 1990.

Edmund Landau. *Verteilung der Primzalen*, volume I. Chelsa, New York, 1953. Original edition in 1909 by Teubner, Leipzig.

Peter S. Landweber. Three theorems on phrase-structure grammars of type 1. *Information and Control*, 6:131–136, 1963.

Derrick H. Lehmer. Mathematical methods in large-scale computing. In *Proceedings of 2nd Symposium on Large-Scale Digital Calculating Machinery*, pages 141–146. Harward University Press, Cambridge, 1951.

F. Thomson Leighton. New lower bound techniques for VLSI. In *Proceedings of 22nd IEEE FOCS*, pages 1–12, 1981.

F. Thomson Leighton. *Introduction to parallel algorithms and architectures*. Morgan Kaufman, San Mateo, California, 1992.

F. Thomson Leighton, Bruce M. Maggs, Abhiram G. Ranade, and Satish B. Rao. Randomized routing and sorting in fixed connection network. *Journal of Algorithms*, 17(1):157–205, 1992.

Charles E. Leiserson. Area efficient graph algorithms (for VLSI). In *Proceedings of 21th IEEE FOCS*, pages 270–281, 1980.

Charles E. Leiserson. *Area efficient VLSI computation*. MIT Press, Cambridge, Mass., 1983.

Thomas Lengauer. *Combinatorial Algorithms for Integrated Circuit Layout*. Wiley-Teubner, Stuttgart, Chichester, 1990a.

Thomas Lengauer. VLSI theory. In J. van Leeuwen, editor, *Handbook of Theoretical Computer Science, Volome A, Algorithms and Complexity*, pages 835–868. Elsevier, Amsterdam, 1990b.

Arjen K. Lenstra, Hendrik W. Lenstra, Mark. S. Manasse, and John M. Pollard. The factorization of the ninth Fermat number. *Mathematics and Computation*, 61:319–349, 1993.

Leonid A. Levin. Universal sequential search problems (in Russian). *Problems Information Transmission*, 9:265–266, 1973.

Leonid A. Levin. Average-case complete problems. *SIAM Journal of Computing*, 15:285–286, 1986. (Preliminary version appeared in Proceedings of 16th ACM STOC, page 465, 1984).

Harry R. Lewis. Complexity of solvable cases of the decision problems for predicate calculus. In *Proceedings of 19th IEEE FOCS*, pages 35–47, 1978.

Harry R. Lewis and Christos H. Papadimitriou. *Elements of theory of computation*. Prentice Hall, Englewood Cliffs, 1981.

Philip M. Lewis, Richard E. Stearns, and Juris Hartmanis. Memory bounds for recognition of context-free and context-sensitive languages. In *Proceedings of 6th IEEE, Annual Symposium on Switching Circuits Theory and Logic Design*, pages 191–202, 1965.

Ming Li and Paul Vitányi. *An introduction to Kolmogorov complexity and its applications*. Springer-Verlag, New York, Berlin, 1993.

David Lichtenstein and Michael Sipser. GO is polynomial space hard. *Journal of the ACM*, 27:393–401, 1980.

Shen Lin and Tibor Rado. Computer studies of Turing machine problems. *Journal of the ACM*, 12(2):196–212, 1965.

Aristid Lindenmayer. Mathematical models for cellular automata in development, I and II. *Journal of Theoretical Biology*, 18:280–315, 1968.

Richard J. Lipton. Some consequences of our failure to prove non-linear lower bounds on explicit functions. In *Proceedings of 35th IEEE FOCS*, pages 79–87, 1994.

Richard J. Lipton and Robert Sedgewick. Lower bounds for VLSI. In *Proceedings of 13th ACM STOC*, pages 300–307, 1981.

Richard J. Lipton and Robert E. Tarjan. A planar graph separator. *SIAM Journal of Applied Mathematics*, 36(2):177–189, 1979.

László Lovász. Computational complexity. Lecture notes, Dept. of Computer Science, Princeton University, 1995.

Alexander Lubotzky, Robert G. Phillips, and P. Sank. Ramanuyan graphs. *Combinatorica*, 8:261–277, 1988.

Michael Luby. *Pseudorandomness and cryptographic applications*. Princeton University Press, 1996.

Édouard Lucas. *Récréations mathématiques*, volume 4. Gauthier-Villas, Paris, 1891-1894.

George S. Luecker. Some techniques for solving recurrences. *Computing Surveys*, 12(4):419–436, 1980.

Carsten Lund, Lance Fortnow, Howard Karloff, and Noam Nissan. Algebraic methods for interactive proof systems. In *Proceedings of 31th IEEE FOCS*, pages 2–10, 1990.

Carsten Lund and Mihalis Yannakakis. On the hardness of approximating minimalization problems. In *Proceedings of 25th ACM STOC*, pages 286–295, 1993.

Oleg B. Lupanov. Comparison of finite sources of two types (in Russian). *Problems of Cybernetics*, 9:321–326, 1963.

Saunders Mac Lane and Garrett Birkhoff. *Algebra*. The Macmillan Company, New York, 1967.

Michael Machtey and Paul Young. *An introduction to the general theory of algorithms*. North Holland, New York, 1978.

Anatolij I. Malcev. On homomorphisms of finite groups (in Russian). *Ivanov. Gos. Ped. Inst. Uchen. Zap.*, 18:49–60, 1958.

Anatolij I. Malcev. *Algorithms and recursive functions (in Russian)*. Nauka, Moskva, 1965.

Andrei A. Markov. The impossibility of certain algorithms in the theory of associative systems (in Russian). *DAN*, 55 and 58:587–590 and 353–356, 1947.

Heiner Marxen. Attacking the busy beaver 5. *Bulletin of EATCS*, 40:247–251, 1990.

Yuri V. Matiyasevich. Diofantine representation of enumerable predicates (in Russian). *Izvestija Akademii Nauk, seria Matematichnaja*, 35:3–30, 1971.

Yuri V. Matiyasevich. *Hilbert's Tenth Problem*. The MIT Press, Cambridge, Massachussets, London, 1993.

Hermann A. Maurer. *Theoretische Grundlagen der Programmier-Sprachen-Theorie der Syntax*. BI Hochschul-Taschenbücher Band 484, Bibl. Institut Mannheim, 1969.

Hermann A. Maurer, Grzegorz Rozenberg, and Emo Welzl. Using string languages to describe picture languages. *Information and Control*, 54:155–185, 1982.

Jacques Mazoyer. A six-state minimum time solution to the firing squad synchronization problem. *Theoretical Computer Science*, 50(2):183–240, 1987.

Jacques Mazoyer. An overview of the firing squad problem. In C. Choffrut, editor, *Automata networks*, pages 82–93. LNCS 316, Springer-Verlag, Berlin, New York, 1988.

Warren McCulloch and Walter Pitts. A logical calculus of the ideas immanent in nervous activities. *Bulletin Mathematical Biophysics*, 5:115–133, 1943.

Robert McNaughton. Testing and generating infinite sequences by a finite automaton. *Information and Control*, 9:521–530, 1966.

Gregory H. Mealy. Methods for synthetizing sequential circuits. *Bell System Techn. Journal*, 34:1045–1079, 1955.

Robert Meersman and Grzegorz Rozenberg. Cooperating grammar systems. In J. Winkowski, editor, *Proceedings MFCS'78*, pages 364–374. LNCS 78, Springer-Verlag, 1978.

Kurt Mehlhorn. *Data structures and algorithms I- III*. Springer-Verlag, Berlin, New York, 1984.

Kurt Mehlhorn and Franco P. Preparata. Area-time optimal VLSI integer multiplier with minimum computation time. *Information and Control*, 58:137–156, 1983.

Kurt Mehlhorn and Erik M. Schmidt. Las Vegas is better than determinism in VLSI and distributed computing. In *Proceedings of 14th ACM STOC*, pages 330–337, 1982.

Ralf Merken, editor. *The universal Turing machine: a half century survey*. Kammer & Univerzagt, Hamburg, 1988.

Ralp C. Merkle and Martin E. Hellman. Hiding information and signatures in trapdoor knapsack. *IEEE Transactions on Information Theory*, 24(5):525–530, 1978.

Albert R. Meyer and Michael J. Fischer. Economy of description by automata, grammars and formal systems. In *Proceedings of 12th IEEE FOCS*, pages 188–191, 1971.

Friedhelm Meyer auf der Heide. Efficient simulations among several models of parallel computers. *Journal of Computing*, 15:106–119, 1986.

Friedhelm Meyer auf der Heide. Kommunikation in parallelen Rechnenmodellen. Lecture Notes, Fachbereich Informatik, Universität-GH Paderborn, 1992.

David L. Milgram and Azriel Rosenfeld. Array automata and array languages. In *Information Proceedings'71*, pages 69–74. North-Holland, 1971.

Gary L. Miller. Riemann's hypothesis and tests for primality. *Journal for Computer and System Sciences*, 13:300–317, 1976.

Zevi Miller and Hal I. Sudborough. Compressing grids into small hypercubes. *Networks*, 24(6):327–358, 1994.

Marvin L. Minsky. Size and structure of universal Turing machines using a tag system. In *Recursive function theory, Symposia in Pure Mathematics, V 5*. American Mathematical Society, 1962.

Marvin L. Minsky. *Computation: finite and infinite machines*. Prentice-Hall, Englewood Cliffs, 1967.

Chris J. Mitchell, Fred Pipper, and P. Wild. Digital signatures in contemporary cryptography. In G. J. Sinnars, editor, *The science of information integrity*, pages 327–377. Piscatoway, N.J, IEEE Press, 1992.

Burkhard Monien. Two-way multihead automata over a one-letter alphabet. *RAIRO Informatique Théorique et Application*, 14:68–82, 1980.

Burkhard Monien. The problem of embedding trees into binary trees is NP-complete. In L. Budach, editor, *Proceedings of FCT'85*, pages 300–309. LNCS 199, Springer-Verlag, Berlin, New York, 1985.

Burkhard Monien. Simulating binary trees on X-trees. In *Proceedings of 3rd Annual ACM Symposium on Parallel Algorithms and Architectures*, pages 147–158. ACM, New York, 1991.

Burkhard Monien and Hal I. Sudborough. Simulating binary trees on hypercube. In J. Reif, editor, *Proceedings of Aegean Workshop on Computing: VLSI Algorithms and Architectures-AWOC-88*, pages 170–180. LNCS 319, Springer-Verlag, New York, Berlin, 1988.

Burkhard Monien and Hal I. Sudborough. Embedding one interconnection network in another. *Computing Supplement 7*, 7:257–282, 1990.

Rajeev Montwani and Prabhakar Raghavan. *Randomized algorithms*. Cambridge University Press, 1995.

Edward F. Moore. Gedanken experiments on sequential machines. In C. E. Shannon and J. Mc Carthy, editors, *Automata Studies*, pages 129–153, Princeton, 1956. Princeton University Press.

Edward F. Moore. Machine models of self-reproduction. In C. E. Shannon and J. Mc. Carthy, editors, *Proceedings of Symposia in Applied Mathematics, V 14*, pages 17–33, 1962.

Kenichi Morita and Masateru Harao. Computation universality of one-dimensional reversible (injective) cellular automata. *Transactions of IEICE*, E 72(3):213–231, 1989.

Kenichi Morita, Akihiko Shirasaki, and Yoshifumi Gono. A 1-tape 2-symbol reversible Turing machine. *Transactions of the IEICE*, E 72(3):223–228, 1989.

David E. Muller. Infinite sequences and finite machines. In *Proceedings of 4th IEEE Symposium on Switching Theory and Logical Design*, pages 3–10, 1963.

David E. Muller and Franco P. Preparata. Bound to complexities of networks for sorting and switching. *Journal of the ACM*, 22(2):195–201, 1975.

Myriam Muriel, Jean-Jacques Quisquater, and Louis C. Guillou. How to explain zero-knowledge protocols to your children. In G. Brassard, editor, *Proceedings of CRYPTO'89*, pages 628–631. LNCS 435, Springer-Verlag, Berlin, New York, 1990.

John Myhill. Finite automata and the representation of events. WADD Tech. Report, 57-624, Wright Patterson Air Force Base, 1957.

John Myhill. Linear bounded automata. WADD Tech. Report, 60-165, Wright Patterson Air Force Base, 1960.

John Myhill. The converse to Moore's Garden-of-Eden theorem. *Proceedings of American Mathematical Society*, 14:685–686, 1963.

Moni Naor. Bit commitment using pseudo-randomness. In G. Brassard, editor, *Proceedings of CRYPTO'89*, pages 128–136. LNCS 435, Springer-Verlag, Berlin, New York, 1990.

David Nassimi and Sartaj Sahni. Parallel algorithms to set up the Beneš permutation network. *IEEE Transactions on Computers*, 31:148–154, 1982.

Anil Nerode. Linear automaton transformations. *Proceedings of American Mathematical Society*, 9:541–544, 1958.

Petr S. Novikov. Algorithmic unsolvability of word problem for groups (in Russian). *Transactions of Steklov Mathematical Institute*, 44, 1955. Translation: Amer. Math. Soc. Trans. 9, 1229, 1958.

Luke J. O'Conner and Jennifer Seberry. *The cryptographic significance of the knapsack problem*. Aegan Park Press, Ca., 1987.

Piorgiorgio Odifredi. *Classical recursion theory*. North-Holland, Amsterdam, 1989.

Andrew M. Odlyzko. The 10^{20}-th zero of the Riemann zeta function and its 175 milions of its neighbours. Preprint, IBM, 1988. To be published in a revised form with a different title.

Alon Orlitsky and Taher El Gamal. *Complexity in Information Theory, Eds. Y. Abu Mostafa*, chapter Communication complexity. Springer-Verlag, Berlin, New York1988.

Rafail Ostrovsky and Avi Wigderson. One-way functions are essential for non-trivial zero-knowledge. In *Proceedings of 2nd Israel Symposium on Theory of Computing and Systems*, pages 3–17. IEEE, Los Alamitos, 1993.

Victor Ya. Pan. *How to multiply matrices fast*. LNCS 179, Springer-Verlag, Berlin, New York, 1984.

Christos H. Papadimitriou. Games against nature. *Journal of Computer and System Sciences*, 31:288–301, 1985.

Christos H. Papadimitriou. *Computational Complexity*. Addison-Wesley, Reading, Mass., 1994.

Christos H. Papadimitriou and Michael Sipser. Communication complexity. In *Proceedings of 14th ACM STOC*, pages 196–200, 1982.

Christos H. Papadimitriou and Michael Sipser. Communication complexity. *Journal of Computer and System Sciences*, 28:260–269, 1984.

Christos H. Papadimitriou and Kenneth Steiglitz. *Combinatorial optimization, algorithms and complexity*. Prentice-Hall, Englewood Cliffs, 1982.

Ian Parbery. *Circuit complexity and neural networks*. The MIT Press, Cambridge, Mass., 1994. 270 p.

Michael S. Paterson, Walter L. Ruzzo, and Larry Snyder. Bounds in minimax edge length for complete binary trees. In *Proceedings of 13th ACM STOC*, pages 293–299, 1981.

Ramamohan Paturi and Janos Simon. Probabilistic communication complexity. *Journal of Computer and System Sciences*, 33:106–123, 1986.

Gheorgh Paŭn. Grammar systems. In F. Gécseg, Z. Fülöp, editors, *Proceedings of ICALP'95*, pages 429–443. LNCS 944, Springer-Verlag, Berlin, New York, 1995.

Azaria Paz. *Introduction to probabilistic automata*. Academic Press, New York, 1971.

Azaria Paz and Arto Salomaa. Integral sequential word functions and growth equivalence of Lindenmayer systems. *Information and Control*, 23:313–343, 1973.

Heintz-Otto Peitgen, Hartmut Jürgens, and Dietmar Saupe. *Chaos and fractals*. Springer-Verlag, New York, 1992.

Roger Penrose. *The emperor's new mind*. Oxford University Press, Oxford, 1990.

Stéphane Perennes. Broadcasting and gossiping on de Bruijn, shuffle-exchange and similar networks. Technical report, UNSA, CARS-URA, Valbaine-France, 1995.

Dominique Perrin. Finite automata. In J. van Leeuwen, editor, *Handbook of Theoretical Computer Science, Volume B, Formal Models and Semantics*, pages 1–58. Elsevier, Amsterdam, 1990.

Rózsa Péter. *Recursive Funktionen*. Akadémiai Kiadó, Budapest, 1951. English translation: Recursive Functions, Academic Press, New York, London, 1967.

Nicholas Pippenger. On simultaneous resource bounds. In *Proceedings of 20th IEEE FOCS*, pages 307–311, 1979.

Nicholas Pippenger. Communication networks. In J. van Leeuwen, editor, *Handbook of Theoretical Computer Science, Volume A, Algorithms and Complexity*, pages 805–833. Elsevier, Amsterdam, 1990.

Nicholas Pippenger and Michal Fischer. Relations among complexity measures. *Journal of the ACM*, 26:361–381, 1979.

Joan B. Plumstead. Inferring a sequence generator by a linear congruence. In *Proceedings of 23rd IEEE FOCS*, pages 153–159, 1982.

Stephen C. Pohlig and Martin E. Hellman. An improved algorithm for computing logarithms over $GF(p)$ and its cryptographic significance. *IEEE Transactions on Information Theory*, IT-24:106–110, 1978.

Emil L. Post. Formal reductions of the general combinatorial decision problems. *American Journal of Mathematics*, 65:197–215, 1943.

Emil L. Post. Recursively enumerable sets of positive integers and their decision problems. *Bulletin of the American Mathematical Society*, 50:284–316, 1944.

Emil L. Post. A variant of recursively unsolvable problems. *Bulletin of the American Mathematical Society*, 52:264–268, 1946.

Vaughan R. Pratt. Every prime has a succinct certificate. *SIAM Journal of Computing*, 4:214–220, 1975.

Franco P. Preparata and Jean-Etienne Vuillemin. The cube-connected cycles: a versatile network for parallel computation. *Communications of the ACM*, 24(5):300–309, 1981.

William H. Press, Brian P. Flannery, Saul A. Teukolsky, and William T. Vetterling. *Numerical recipes: the art of scientific computing*. Cambridge University Press, 1986.

Lutz Priese. Towards a precise characterization of the complexity of universal and nonuniversal Turing machines. *SIAM Journal of Computing*, 8(4):508–523, 1979a.

Lutz Priese. Über eine minimale universelle Turing Machine. In K. Weihrauch, editor, *Proceedings of 4th GI Conference on TCS*, pages 244–259. LNCS 67, Springer-Verlag, Berlin, New York, 1979b.

Przemyslaw Prusinkiewicz and Aristid Lindenmayer. *The algorithmic beauty of plants*. Springer-Verlag, Berlin, New York, 1990.

Paul W. Purdom and Cynthia A. Brown. *The analysis of algorithms*. Holt, Rinehart and Winston, New York, 1985.

Michael O. Rabin. Degree of difficulties of computing a function and a partial ordering of recursive sets. Tech. Rep. 2, Hebrew University, Jerusalem, 1960.

Michael O. Rabin. Probabilistic automata. *Information and Control*, 6(3):230–244, 1963.

Michael O. Rabin. Mathematical theory of automata. In *Proceedings of Symposium in Applied Mathematics, V 19*, pages 153–175. American Mathematical Society, 1966.

Michael O. Rabin. Decidability of second order theories and automata on infinite trees. *Transactions of American Mathematical Society*, 141:1–35, 1969.

Michael O. Rabin. Probabilistic algorithms. In J. F. Traub, editor, *Algorithms and Complexity: Recent Results and New Directions*, pages 21–36, New York, 1976. Academic Press.

Michael O. Rabin. Digital signatures and public key functions as intractable as factorization. Technical Report TR 212, MIT Laboratory for Computer Science, January 1979.

Michael O. Rabin. Probabilistic algorithm for primality testing. *Journal of Number Theory*, 12:128–138, 1980.

Michael O. Rabin. How to exchange secrets by oblivious transfer. Technical Report TR-81, Aiken Computation Laboratory, Harward University, 1981.

Michael O. Rabin and Dana Scott. Finite automata and their decision problems. *IBM Journal Research and Development*, 3(2):115–125, 1959.

Tibor Rado. On noncomputable functions. *Bell System Technical Journal*, 41:877–884, 1962.

Peter Rajčani. *Application of weighted finite automata and transducers to image processing*. PhD thesis, Department of Computer Science, University of Southern Carolina, 1995.

Abhiram G. Ranade. How to simulate shared memory. *Journal of Computer and System Sciences*, 42:307–326, 1991.

Sanjay Ranka and Sartaj Sahni. *Hypercube Algorithms*. Springer-Verlag, Berlin, New York, 1990.

John H. Reif and Leslie G. Valiant. A logarithmic time sort for linear size networks. In *Proceedings of 15th ACM STOC*, pages 10–16, 1983.

Karl R. Reischuk. *Einführung in die Komplexitätstheorie*. Teubner, Sttutgart, 1990.

Paulo Ribenboim. *The new book of prime number records*. Springer-Verlag, Berlin, New York, 1996.

Henry G. Rice. Classes of recursively enumerable sets and their decision problems. *Transaction of the American Mathematical Society*, 74:358–366, 1953.

Daniel Richardson. Tesselation with local transformations. *Journal of Computer and System Sciences*, 6:373–385, 1972.

Ronald L. Rivest. Cryptography. In J. van Leeuwen, editor, *Handbook of Theoretical Computer Science, Volume A, Algorithms and Complexity*, pages 718–755. Elsevier, Amsterdam, 1990.

Ronald L. Rivest and Adi Shamir. How to expose an eavesdropper. *Communication of the ACM*, 27(4):393–395, 1984.

Ronald L. Rivest, Adi Shamir, and Leonard A. Adleman. A method for obtaining digital signatures and public-key cryptosystems. *Communications of the ACM*, 21(2):120–126, Febr. 1978.

Hartley Rogers. *Theory of recursive functions and effective computability*. McGraw-Hill, New York, 1967.

Yurii Rogozhin. On the notion of universality and small universal Turing machines. *Theoretical Computer Science*, 168:215–240, 1996.

Keneth H. Rosen. *Discrete mathematics and its applications*. McGraw-Hill, New York, 1981.

Arnold L. Rosenberg. On multi-head finite automata. *IBM Journal of Research and Development*, 10:388–394, 1966.

Daniel J. Rosenkrantz, Richard E. Stearns, and Philip M. Lewis. An analysis of several heuristics for the traveling salesman problem. *SIAM Journal of Computing*, 6:563–581, 1977.

J. Barkley Rosser and Lowell Schoenfeld. Approximate formulas for some functions of prime numbers. *Illinois Journal of Mathematics*, 6:64–94, 1962.

Grzegorz Rozenberg. An introduction to the NLC way of rewriting systems. In H. Ehrig, M. Nagl, G. Rozenberg, and A. Rosenfeld, editors, *Proceedings of 3rd Graph Grammars Workshop*, pages 55–66. LNCS 291, Springer-Verlag, Berlin, New York, 1987.

Grzegorz Rozenberg and Arto Salomaa. *The mathematical theory of L systems*. Academic Press, New York, London, 1980.

Grzegorz Rozenberg and Arto Salomaa. *Cornerstones of undecidability*. Prentice-Hall, Englewood Cliffs, 1994.

Grzegorz Rozenberg and Emo Welzl. Boundary NLC graph grammars—basic definitions, normal forms and complexity. *Information and Control*, 69:136–167, 1986.

Walter L. Ruzzo. Tree-size bounded alteration. *Journal of Computer and System Sciences*, 21(2):218–235, 1980.

Wojciech Rytter. On the recognition of context-free languages. In A. Skowron, editor, *Proceedings of Computation Theory*, pages 318–325. LNCS 208, Springer-Verlag, Berlin, New York, 1984.

Arto Salomaa. *Theory of Automata*. Oxford, Pergammon Press, 1969.

Arto Salomaa. *Formal languages*. Academic Press, New York, London, 1973.

Arto Salomaa. *Computation and Automata*. Cambridge University Press, 1985.

Arto Salomaa. *Public-key cryptography*. Springer-Verlag, Berlin, New York, 1990.

John E. Savage. *The complexity of computing*. John Wiley, New York, London, 1986.

Matieu W.P. Savelsbergh and Peter van Emde Boas. Bounded tiling, an alternative to satisfiability. In G. Wechsung, editor, *Proceedings of 2nd Frege Conference*, pages 354–363. Mathematische Forschung 20, Academie Verlag, Berlin, 1984.

Walter J. Savitch. Relationship between nondeterministic and deterministic tape classes. *Journal of Computer and System Sciences*, 4:177–192, 1970.

Thomas J. Schäfer. Complexity of some two person perfect information games. *Journal of Computer and System Sciences*, 16:185–225, 1978.

Bruce Schneier. *Applied cryptography, Second Edition*. Wiley, New York, Chichester, 1996.

Georg Schnitger and Christine Schmetzer. Kommunikationstheorie. Lecture Notes, Fachbereich Informatik, Universität-GH Paderborn, 1994.

Claus-Peter Schnorr. The network complexity and the Turing machine complexity of finite functions. *Acta Informatica*, 7:95–107, 1976.

Claus-Peter Schnorr. Efficient signatures for smart cards. *Journal of Cryptology*, 4(3):161–174, 1991.

Arnold Schönhage. On the power of random access machines. In H. A. Maurer, editor, *Proceedings of ICALP'79*, pages 520–529. LNCS 71, Springer-Verlag, Berlin, New York, 1979.

Arnold Schönhage and Volker Strassen. Schnelle Multiplikationen grosser Zahlen. *Computing*, 7:281–292, 1971.

Amir Schorr. Physical parallel devices are not much faster than sequential ones. *Information Processing Letters*, 17:103–106, 1983.

Jacob T. Schwartz. Ultracomputers. *ACM Transactions on Programming Languages and Systems*, 2(4):484–521, 1980.

Robert Sedgewick and Philippe Flayolet. *An introduction to the analysis of algorithms*. Addison-Wesley, Reading, Mass., 1996.

Joel I. Seiferas, Michael J. Fischer, and Albert R. Meyer. Refinment of nondeterministic time and space hierarchies. In *Proceedings of 14th IEEE FOCS*, pages 130–137, 1973.

Adi Shamir. Factoring numbers in $\mathcal{O}(\lg n)$ arithmetical steps. *Information Processing Letters*, 8(1):28–31, 1979.

Adi Shamir. A polynomial time algorithm for breaking the basic Merkle-Hellman cryptosystem. In *Proceedings of 23rd IEEE FOCS*, pages 145–152, 1982.

Adi Shamir. IP = PSPACE. *Journal of the ACM*, 39:869–877, 1992. Preliminary version in Proceedings of 31th IEEE FOCS, 1990, 11-15.

Adi Shamir, Ronald L. Rivest, and Leonard M. Adleman. Mental poker. In D. A. Klarner, editor, *The mathematical gardner*, pages 37–43. Wadsworth International, Belmont, 1981.

Claude E. Shannon. Communication theory of secrecy systems. *Bell System Technical Journal*, 28:656–715, 1949.

Claude E. Shannon. The synthesis of two terminals switching circuits. *Bell Systems Technical Journal*, 28:59–98, 1949a.

Claude E. Shannon. A universal Turing machine with two internal states. In *Automata Studies, Annals of Mathematical Studies 34*, Princeton, 1956.

Alexander Shen. IP = PSPACE. Simplified proof. *Journal of the ACM*, 34(4):878–880, 1992.

John C. Shepherdson. The reduction of two-way automata to one-way. *IBM Journal of Research*, 3:198–200, 1959.

John C. Shepherdson and Howard E. Sturgis. Computability of recursive functions. *Journal of the ACM*, 10(2):217–255, 1963.

Yossi Shiloach and Uzi Vishkin. Finding the maximum, merging and sorting in parallel computation models. *Journal of Algorithms*, 4:88–102, 1981.

Peter W. Shor. Algorithms for quantum computation; discrete logarithms and factoring. In *Proceedings of 35th IEEE FOCS*, pages 116–123, 1994.

Daniel R. Simon. On the power of quantum computation. In *Proceedings of 35th IEEE FOCS*, pages 116–123, 1994.

Seppo Sippu and Eljas Soisalon-Soininen. *Parsing theory, I, II*. Springer-Verlag, Berlin, New York, 1990.

Michael Sipser. The history and status of the P versus NP problem. In *Proceedings of 24th ACM STOC*, pages 603–618, 1992.

Miles E. Smid and Dennis K. Branstead. The data encryption standards: past and future. *Proceedings of IEEE*, 76(5):550–559, 1988.

Carl H. Smith. *A recursive introduction to the theory of computation*. Springer-Verlag, Berlin, New York, 1994.

P. Smith and M. J. J. Lennon. LUC—a new public-key system. In E. G. Dougall, editor, *Proceedings of IFIP TC11 Ninth International Conference on Information Security, IFIP Transactions, A-37*, pages 103–112. Elsevier, Amsterdam, 1993.

Ray J. Solomonoff. A preliminary report on a general theory of inductive inference. Tech. Rep. ZTB-138, Zator Company, Cambridge, November 1960.

Robert M. Solovay and Volker Strassen. A fast Monte Carlo test for primality. *SIAM Journal of Computing*, 6:84–85, 1977.

Siang W. Song. *On a high performance VLSI solution to database problems*. PhD thesis, Department of Computer Science, Carnegie-Mellon University, Pittsburg, 1981.

William Stallings. *Network and internetwork security*. Prentice Hall, Englewood Cliffs, 1995.

Peter H. Starke. Theorie der stochastischen Automaten I, II. *Journal of Information processing and Cybernetics, EIK*, 1:5–32, 71–98, 1965.

Peter H. Starke. *Abstrakte Automaten*. VEB Deutscher Verlag der Wissenschaften, Berlin, 1969. English translation, "Abstract Automata" published by North-Holland, Amsterdam in 1972.

Larry J. Stockmeyer. The polynomial time hierarchy. *Theoretical Computer Science*, 3:1–22, 1976.

Larry J. Stockmeyer and Albert R. Meyer. Word problems requiring exponential time. In *Proceedings of 5th ACM STOC*, pages 1–9, 1973.

Harold S. Stone. Parallel processing with the perfect shuffle. *IEEE Transactions on Computers*, C-20(2):153–161, 1971.

Volker Strassen. Gaussian elimination is not optimal. *Numerische Mathematik*, 3:354–356, 1969.

Madhu Sudan. *Efficient checking of polynomials and proofs and the hardness of approximation problems*. PhD thesis, CS Division, UC Berkeley, 1992. Available as "ACM Distinguished Theses, LNCS 1001, Springer-Verlag".

Róbert Szelepcsényi. The method of forcing for nondeterministic automata . *Bulletin of EATCS*, 33:96–100, 1987.

Wolfgand Thomas. Finite state strategies in regular infinite games. In P. S. Thiagarajan, editor, *Proceedings of Foundations of Software Technology and Theoretical Computer Science*, pages 149–158. LNCS 880, Springer-Verlag, 1994.

Wolfgang Thomas. Automata on infinite objects. In J. van Leeuwen, editor, *Handbook of Theoretical Computer Science, Volume B, Formal Models and Semantics*, pages 133–186. Elsevier, Amsterdam, 1990.

Clark D. Thompson. Area-time complexity for VLSI. In *Proceedings of 11th ACM STOC*, pages 81–88, 1979.

Clark D. Thompson. *A complexity theory for VLSI*. PhD thesis, Computer Science Department, Carnegie-Mellon University, 1980. CMU-CS-80-140.

Axel Thue. Über unendliche Zeichenreihen. *Skrifter utgit av Videnskapsselskapet i Kristiania I*, (1-22), 1906.

Axel Thue. Probleme über Veränderungen von Zeichenreihen nach gegebenen Regeln. *Skrifter utgit av Videnskapsselskapet i Kristiania I*, 10:34p, 1914.

Seinosuke Toda. On the computational power of PP and $\oplus$P. In *Proceedings of 30th IEEE FOCS*, pages 514–519, 1989.

Tommaso Toffoli. Computation and construction universality of reversible cellular automata. *Journal of Computer and System Sciences*, 15:213–231, 1977.

Tommaso Toffoli and Norman Margolus. *Cellular automata machines*. The MIT Press, Cambridge, Mass., 1987.

Tommaso Toffoli and Norman Margolus. Invertible cellular automata, a review. *Physica D*, 45:229–253, 1990.

Boris A. Trakhtenbrot. Turing computations with logarithmic delays (in Russian). *Algebra and Logic*, 3(4):38–48, 1964.

Boris A. Trakhtenbrot and Jan Barzdin. *Finite automata: behaviour and synthesis*. Fundamental Studies in Computer Science. North-Holland, Amsterdam, 1973.

Luca Trevisan. On the approximability of the multidimensional Euclidean TSP. Tech. report SI/RR/96/15, University of Roma 1, 1996.

Alan M. Turing. On computable numbers, with applications to the Entscheidungsproblem. *Proceedings of the London Mathematical Society*, 42:230–265, 1936.

Jeffery D. Ullman. *Computational aspects of VLSI*. Computer Science Press, Rockville, Mass., 1984.

Eli Upfal. Efficient schemes for parallel communication. In *Proceedings of the 10th ACM-SIGACT Symposium on Principles of Distributed Computing*, pages 55–59. ACM, New York, 1991.

Eli Upfal and Avi Wigderson. How to share memory in a distributed system. *Journal of the ACM*, 34:116–127, 1987.

Leslie G. Valiant. General context-free recognition in less than cubic time. *Journal of Computer and System Sciences*, 10:308–315, 1975.

Leslie G. Valiant. Relative complexity of checking and evaluating. *Information Processing Letters*, 5:20–23, 1976.

Leslie G. Valiant. The complexity of computing the permanet. *Theoretical Computer Science*, 8:189–201, 1979.

Leslie G. Valiant. Universality considerations in VLSI circuits. *IEEE Transactions on VLSI Circuits*, C-30(2):135–140, 1981.

Leslie G. Valiant. A scheme for fast parallel communications. *SIAM Journal of Computing*, 11(2):350–361, May 1982.

Leslie G. Valiant. General purpose parallel architecture. In J. van Leeuwen, editor, *Handbook of Theoretical Computer Science, Volume A, Algorithms and Complexity*, pages 945–971. Elsevier, Amsterdam, 1990.

Leslie G. Valiant and Gorden J. Brebner. Universal schemes for parallel simulations. In *Proceedings of 13th ACM STOC*, pages 263–277, 1981.

Bartel L. van der Wärden. *Erwachsende Wissenschaft*. Birkhäuser, Basel, 1966.

Peter van Emde Boas. Preserving order in a forest in less than logarithmic time. In *Proceedings of 16th IEEE FOCS*, pages 75–84, 1975.

Peter van Emde Boas. Dominoes are forever. In *Proceedings of 1st GTI Workshop Paderborn*, pages 75–95. UH Paderborn, Reihe Theoretische Informatik, Bericht N. 13, Oct. 11-15 1982.

Jan van Leeuwen and Juraj Wiedermann. Array processing machines: an abstract model. *BIT*, 27:25–43, 1987.

Paul Vitányi. Multiprocessor architectures and physical law. In *Proceedings of the 3rd Workshop on Physics and Computation*, pages 24–29. IEEE Computer Society Press, 1994.

Paul Vitányi. Physics and the new computation. In P. Hajek and J. Wiedermann, editors, *Proceedings of MFCS'95*, pages 106–128. LNCS 969, Springer-Verlag, Berlin, New York, 1995.

Roland Vollmar. *Algorithmen in Zellularautomaten*. Teubner, Stuttgart, 1979.

Roland Vollmar and Thomas Worsch. *Modelle der Parallelverarbeitung*. Teubner, Stuttgart, 1995.

John von Neumann. The general and logical theory of automata. In *Cerebral Mechanisms in Behaviour—The Nixon Symposium*, pages 1–41, Pasadena, 1951. (Also in: John von Neumann, Collected Works, Pergamon, Oxford, 1963, 288-328.)

John von Neumann. *Theory of self-reproducing automata*. University of Illinois Press, Urbana, 1966. Edited and completed by A. W. Burks.

Jean-Etienne Vuillemin. A combinatorial limit to the power of VLSI circuits. In *Proceedings of 12th ACM STOC*, pages 294–300, 1980.

Jozef Vyskoč. A note on the power of integer division. *Information Processing Letters*, 17:71–72, 1983.

Alan Wagner. Embedding arbitrary trees in the hypercube. *Journal of Parallel and Distributed Computing*, 7:503–520, 1987.

Alan Wagner and Dereck G. Corneil. Embedding trees in a hypercube is NP-complete. *SIAM Journal on Computing*, 19(3):570–590, 1990.

Klaus Wagner and Gerd Wechsung. *Computational Complexity*. VEB Deutscher Verlag der Wissenschaften, Berlin, 1986.

Abraham Waksman. An optimum solution to the firing squad problem. *Information and Control*, 9:66–78, 1966.

Jie Wang. Average-case computational complexity theory. In L. Hemaspandra and A. Selman, editors, *Complexity theory retrospectives II*, page 34. Springer-Verlag, Berlin, New York, 1996.

Patrick S.-P. Wang, editor. *Array grammars, patterns and recognizers*. World Scientific Publisher Series in Computer Science, Singapore, V 18, 1989.

Stephen Warshall. A theorem on Boolean matrices. *Journal of the ACM*, 9(1):11–12, 1962.

Ingo Wegener. *The complexity of Boolean functions*. Teubner-Wiley, Stuttgart, Chichester, 1987.

Klaus Weihrauch. *Computability*. Springer-Verlag, Berlin, 1987.

Bruno Weimann, K. Casper, and W. Fenzl. Untersuchungen über haltende Programme für Turing Machinen mit 2 Zeichen and bis zu 5 Befehlen. In *2-Jahrestagung, Lecture Notes in Economics and Mathematical Systems, V78*, pages 77–81. Springer-Verlag, Berlin, 1973.

Juraj Wiedermann. Parallel Turing machines. Tech. Rep. RUU-CS-84-11, Dept. of Computer Science, Utrecht University, 1984.

Juraj Wiedermann. Quo vaditas, parallel machine models. In J. van Leeuwen, editor, *Computer science today*, pages 101–114. LNCS 1000, Springer-Verlag, 1995.

Shmuel Winograd. *Arithmetic complexity of computation*. SIAM, Philadelphia, 1980.

Stephen Wolfram. Statistical mechanics of cellular automata. *Revue of Modern Physics*, 55:601–644, 1983.

Stephen Wolfram. Universality and complexity in cellular automata. *Physica D*, 10:1–35, 1984.

Stephen Wolfram. *Theory and applications of cellular automata*. World Scientific Press, Singapore, 1986.

Celia Wrathall. Complete sets for polynomial time hierarchy. *Theoretical Computer Science*, 3:23–34, 1976.

A. Wu. Embedding of tree networks into hypercubes. *Journal of Parallel and Distributed Computing*, 2(3):3–12, 1985.

Andrew C. Yao. Some complexity questions related to distributed computing. In *Proceedings of 11th ACM STOC*, pages 209–213, 1979.

Andrew C. Yao. The entropic limitations on VLSI computations. In *Proceedings of 13th ACM STOC*, pages 308–311, 1981.

Andrew C. Yao. Protocols for secure computations. In *Proceedings of the 23rd ACM FOCS*, pages 160–164, 1982a.

Andrew C. Yao. Theory and applications of trapdoor functions. In *Proceedings of 23rd IEEE FOCS*, pages 80–91, 1982b.

Andrew C. Yao. Lower bounds by probabilistic arguments. In *Proceedings of 25th IEEE FOCS*, pages 420–428, 1983.

Andrew C. Yao and Ronald L. Rivest. $k+1$ heads are better than k heads. *Journal of the ACM*, 25:337–340, 1978.

Daniel H. Younger. Recognition and parsing of context-free languages in time n^3. *Information and Control*, 10(189-208), 1967.

Jean-Baptiste Yunes. Seven-state solutions to the firing squad problem. *Theoretical Computer Science*, 127:313–332, 1994.

Don Zagier. The first 50 million prime numbers. *Mathematical Intelligencer*, 0:7–19, 1977.

Viktoria Zankó. #P-completeness via many–one reductions. *International Journal on Foundations of Computer Science*, 2:77–82, 1991.

Index